CONSTITUTIONAL LAW

UNDERGRADUATE EDITION

Second Edition, Volume 2

GREGORY E. MAGGS
JUDGE
U.S. COURT OF APPEALS FOR THE ARMED FORCES

PETER J. SMITH
ARTHUR SELWYN MILLER RESEARCH PROFESSOR OF LAW
GEORGE WASHINGTON UNIVERSITY LAW SCHOOL

WEST
ACADEMIC
PUBLISHING

© 2019 LEG, Inc. d/b/a West Academic
© 2021 LEG, Inc. d/b/a West Academic
    444 Cedar Street, Suite 700
    St. Paul, MN 55101
    1-877-888-1330

West, West Academic Publishing, and West Academic are trademarks of West Publishing Corporation, used under license.

Printed in the United States of America

ISBN: 978-1-63659-329-6

Preface

The meaning of the Constitution is far too important a subject to leave solely to lawyers and those who want to become lawyers. All adults should know about the powers that the Constitution grants to the federal government and rights that it gives to individuals. Many widely debated issues, such as health insurance, same-sex marriage, free speech on campus, and so forth, require some understanding of the Constitution. College and graduate school are ideal places to study these subjects in depth, whether a student is focusing on history, political science, or some other subject. Accordingly, this book is specifically designed for use by non-law students in undergraduate or graduate constitutional law courses.

Non-law students, however, face a disadvantage in tackling a course on constitutional law because studying the subject requires them to understand Supreme Court cases, which are often technically complicated. Law students do not have the same difficulty; they generally excel at reading cases because they receive thorough instruction on how to do it and practice the skill in all of their courses. Some textbooks for non-law students attempt to deal with this issue by summarizing Supreme Court decisions, and thus eliminating the need to read them. This book takes a different approach because the authors believe that non-law students can read Supreme Court cases if they are given some initial instruction on the subject and the cases are appropriately edited. The book contains over one hundred explanatory text boxes that clarify legal terms in cases.

We have selected the principal cases very carefully, and we have tried to avoid the problem created by the aggressive editing in many books, which present excerpts so brief that the students in effect read only *about* what the Supreme Court has decided. Supreme Court opinions should be presented as more than a series of conclusory assertions that have been stitched together by a space-sensitive editor. We have tried to edit the principal cases to ensure that they are short enough to read, but rich enough to give the students a clear sense of the Court's reasoning. We have also chosen not to create the illusion of breadth that characterizes many books in the field. Rather than provide summaries of dozens of decisions in each area that we take up, we focus on fuller excerpts of the principal cases, which are designed to be illustrative. Our book is self-consciously a casebook, and does not aspire to be a treatise.

Rather than follow the principal cases with pages and pages of notes and questions—an ineffective approach that students universally resent—we include multiple sidebars in the excerpts of each principal case to focus the students' attention on important questions at the very moment when they are reading the relevant portions of the opinion. Among other things, the sidebars focus attention on particularly salient passages of the opinions; draw connections between the discussion in the case and other topics that the students have explored (or will explore) in the book; supply food for thought; and direct the students to secondary materials to enrich their studies. After each case, we provide brief points for discussion, to focus the students' attention on the central themes in the case. Each chapter also contains hypothetical problems—often drawn from real cases—to encourage the students to apply the doctrine that they have learned, and ends with an "executive summary" of the material, to identify the main themes and doctrines covered in the chapter.

Throughout the book we include "Point-Counterpoints," in which we provide arguments for and against central questions raised by the materials in the book. To be sure, throughout the book—in the points for discussion and in short excerpts from scholarly articles by leading experts in the field—we present a diversity of views on every subject. But the Point-Counterpoint discussions are presented in our own voices and reflect our genuine points of disagreement on the many disputed questions raised in the book. We think that the students will find these discussions rich and stimulating.

Although we have attempted to provide fuller excerpts of the principal cases than is perhaps common in casebooks in the field, we of course nevertheless have had to do substantial editing. We have used three asterisks to indicate that text has been omitted within a paragraph, although we have often omitted entire paragraphs without providing a similar indication. We have omitted most footnotes from the cases; when we have included them, we have used the original numbering from the cases. Footnotes that we have inserted in the cases, on the other hand, are indicated by an asterisk and conclude with the notation "—Eds." We have also omitted many of the citations, but we have attempted to preserve the most important ones.

This book is based on the fifth edition of *Constitutional Law: A Contemporary Approach*, a textbook that we wrote for law students. Many people helped us with the law school edition. At the risk of inadvertently leaving some out, we wish to acknowledge Brad Clark, Tom Colby, Ronald Collins, Elizabeth Joh, William Kelley, Chip Lupu, Alan Morrison, Jeff Powell, Michael Rappaport, David Stras, and Robert Tuttle for their helpful comments.

Gregory Maggs dedicates his contributions to the book to his patient family and to the many generations of law students at the George Washington University who have contributed to his understanding of constitutional law. Peter Smith dedicates his contributions to the book to Eileen Smith, the memory of David Smith, and to Laurie, Jonah, and Sarah, whose highly refined sense of justice has consistently challenged his own.

We hope that reading this book is as enjoyable for you as writing it was for us.

Gregory E. Maggs

Peter J. Smith

June 2021
Washington, DC

Table of Contents

PART IV. THE FIRST AMENDMENT

Table of Cases

CONSTITUTIONAL LAW

UNDERGRADUATE EDITION

Second Edition, Volume 2

CHAPTER 1

Introduction and Background

A. EARLY HISTORY

As we saw in Volume 1, Anti-Federalist opponents of ratification of the Constitution were concerned that the federal government would become too powerful and pose a threat to individual liberties. To be sure, the Constitution as originally proposed did contain a few express limitations on federal authority. The most prominent among them were in Article I, § 9, which includes the Suspension Clause, which prohibits the suspension of habeas corpus except in cases of rebellion or invasion, and the prohibitions on bills of attainder and *ex post facto* laws.

> **FYI**
>
> An *ex post facto* law is a criminal law that purports to apply to conduct that occurred before the law's enactment. We considered bills of attainder in Volume 1.

But the Constitution as originally proposed did not contain a more comprehensive group of provisions expressly guaranteeing individual liberties, such as a right to free speech and the freedom of the press. The omission of this guarantee—indeed, the absence of a complete Bill of Rights—was very controversial. At the Constitutional Convention, George Mason of Virginia and Elbridge Gerry of Massachusetts refused to sign the document for this reason. 2 *The Records of the Federal Convention of 1787* 646–47, 649 (Max Farrand, ed. 1911).

The Federalists initially responded to this objection during the ratification debates by asserting that a Bill of Rights was neither necessary nor a good idea. Speaking at the Pennsylvania ratifying convention on December 4, 1787, James Wilson, a former delegate to the Constitutional Convention, argued that the omission of a Bill of Rights was not a problem and, indeed, was a virtue. He explained:

> [A] bill of rights is by no means a necessary measure. In a government possessed of enumerated powers, such a measure would be not only

unnecessary, but preposterous and dangerous. * * * A bill of rights annexed to a constitution is an enumeration of the powers reserved. If we attempt an enumeration, every thing that is not enumerated is presumed to be given. The consequence is, that an imperfect enumeration would throw all implied power into the scale of the government, and the rights of the people would be rendered incomplete. On the other hand, an imperfect enumeration of the powers of government reserves all implied power to the people; and by that means the constitution becomes incomplete. But of the two, it is much safer to run the risk on the side of the constitution; for an omission in the enumeration of the powers of government is neither so dangerous nor important.

2 *Elliot's Debates* 436 (1836). In other words, Federalists argued that the Constitution protects individual rights indirectly by limiting the powers of the federal government, and that the addition of a separate bill of rights might have suggested that the federal government's powers really were not truly limited. James Madison subsequently repeated these same arguments in The Federalist No. 84, which appeared in print on May 28, 1788. He addressed the omission of a Bill of Rights, stating: "I go further, and affirm that bills of rights, in the sense and to the extent in which they are contended for, are not only unnecessary in the proposed Constitution, but would even be dangerous. They would contain various exceptions to powers not granted; and, on this very account, would afford a colorable pretext to claim more than were granted."

The Federalists' arguments against a Bill of Rights have an important and easily recognized flaw. Although the federal government has only limited powers, Congress could still use some of these powers to impair the freedom of speech, freedom of the press, or other personal rights. For example, in the absence of any guarantee of rights, Congress could restrict the interstate distribution of newspapers using its plenary power to regulate interstate commerce. Or Congress could use its powers of taxation to make newspapers expensive and drive their publishers out of business. The same was true of other precious freedoms, such as the right to hold property and the right to fair process when accused of a crime.

The Federalists' arguments, it turned out, were not entirely convincing. Although the states, of course, did ratify the Constitution, five of them passed resolutions specifically urging the adoption of a Bill of Rights. See 2 Francis Newton Thorpe, *The Constitutional History of the United States* 198 (1902). James Madison took these resolutions seriously when he became a member of the House of Representatives. On June 8, 1789, Madison reversed his prior position from the ratification period and proposed a group of amendments to the Constitution that he specifically called the "Bill of

> **FYI**
>
> Although some states promptly ratified the second of the twelve amendments approved by the first Congress, not enough states ratified it until 1992, more than 200 years later. It is now the Twenty-Seventh Amendment to the Constitution. It says: "No law, varying the compensation for the services of the Senators and Representatives, shall take effect, until an election of Representatives shall have intervened." The states have never ratified the first of the twelve amendments approved by the first Congress, which concerned the number of Representatives in the House.

Rights." 1 Annals of Congress 451–453. Congress debated, redrafted, and ultimately approved twelve of Madison's proposals and sent them to the states for ratification. By the end of 1791, the states had ratified numbers 3 through 12; they became the first ten Amendments to the Constitution, colloquially called the "Bill of Rights." The provisions of those amendments—and of several others, most prominently the Fourteenth Amendment—will be the focus of the remainder of this book.

> **Make the Connection**
>
> In *McCulloch v. Maryland*, U.S. *Term Limits v. Thornton*, and the cases concerning the Dormant Commerce Clause Doctrine, which we considered in Volume 1, we saw that the Court has sometimes found implied limits on the authority of the states to act.

The original Constitution also did not contain many express limits on the authority of the states (as opposed to the federal government). In Volume 1, we considered Article IV, § 2, cl. 1, which provides that the "Citizens of each State shall be entitled to all Privileges and Immunities of Citizens in the several States." As we saw, that provision has been interpreted to impose some modest limits on the states' ability to treat non-residents worse than their own residents. Perhaps more important—particularly in the first several decades of the Republic—Article I, § 10, cl. 1 prohibits the states from passing "any Bill of Attainder, *ex post facto* Law, or Law impairing the Obligation of Contracts." We will consider the last clause in this provision—the "Contract Clause"—in Chapter 12. But even though this provision was one of only a few express limitations on state authority, the Court in the early years interpreted its protections narrowly.

In *Calder v. Bull*, 3 U.S. 386 (1798), for example, the Supreme Court addressed a 1795 "law or resolution" of the Connecticut legislature that set aside a state court's 1793 ruling in a dispute over the interpretation of a will. The law directed the state court to conduct a new hearing on the matter, which it promptly did. On rehearing, the state court directed the party who had prevailed in the original judgment to forfeit the property that was the subject of the will. He sought review in the Supreme Court, contending that the Connecticut legislature's action amounted to an *ex post facto* law. The Court declined to grant relief to the plaintiff in error. In his opinion, Justice Chase explained (among other things) that *ex post facto* laws had been historically understood as retroactive criminal laws (as opposed to laws regulating property or contract). More important for present purposes, Justice Chase asserted in dicta that the Court had authority to invalidate such criminal laws because they were "manifestly unjust and oppressive." In Justice Chase's view, limits on state authority derived from natural law—the idea that certain principles that are inherent in nature and self-evidently true govern our rights, wholly aside from positive law. (This conception of rights had found voice, among other places, in the Declaration of Independence.) In a separate opinion, Justice Iredell rejected the natural-law approach, declaring that "some speculative jurists have held, that a legislative act against natural justice must, in itself, be void; but I cannot think that, under such a government, any Court of Justice would possess a power to declare it so." In Justice Iredell's view, the Court is empowered to invalidate a law only when there is some positive constitutional restraint.

> **Make the Connection**
>
> As we turn to the Constitution's protections for individual rights, consider the extent to which the Court has—explicitly or implicitly—adopted Justice Chase's natural-law view or instead Justice Iredell's skepticism towards that view.

Twelve years later, the Court for the first time invalidated a state law. In 1795, the Georgia legislature passed a law that authorized the Governor to sell land in the western portion of the state to individual buyers; in return, the individual buyers who anticipated purchasing the land agreed to give members of the legislature an interest in the land. Peck purchased a tract of land shortly after it was sold by Georgia under the act, and in 1803 he conveyed it to Fletcher. At the time, neither party had knowledge of the graft that had tainted the original conveyance of the land. When the scandal broke, the Georgia legislature repealed the 1795 law and asserted ownership of any land conveyed under it. Fletcher brought suit against Peck for breach of covenant, claiming that Peck did not have clear title to the land in 1803. (A "covenant" was a formal kind of contract that involved putting a promise into writing, signing the writing, sealing the writing in wax, and then delivering it to the promisee. "Clear title" to land means complete ownership of the land free of claims of anyone else.)

In an opinion for a unanimous Court in *Fletcher v. Peck*, 10 U.S. 87 (1810), Chief Justice Marshall concluded that the rescinding legislation was invalid, on three grounds. First, he concluded that the 1795 Act was essentially a contract between the Georgia legislature and the purchasers of the land. Although "one legislature is competent to repeal any act which a former legislature was competent to pass," the Contract Clause limits the states' authority to impair the obligations of contracts. Second, he concluded that the law rescinding the original Act had "the effect of an *ex post facto* law," because it applied to transactions that had already taken place. Third, he suggested that, even aside from the provisions of Article I, § 10, the rescinding legislation was inconsistent with natural law. According to the Court, "Georgia was restrained, either by general principles which are common to our free institutions, or by the particular provisions of the constitution of the United States, from passing a law whereby the estate of the plaintiff in the premises so purchased could be constitutionally and legally impaired and rendered null and void."

POINTS FOR DISCUSSION

a. Natural Law

Marcus Tullius Cicero, a Roman philosopher, gave the following classical description of natural law:

> [Natural law is a body of standards that are] universal, unchangeable, eternal, whose commands urge us to duty, and whose prohibitions restrain us from evil. * * * This law cannot be contradicted by any other law, and is not liable either to derogation or abrogation. Neither the senate nor the people can give us any dispensation for not obeying this universal law of justice. It needs no other expositor and interpreter than our own conscience. It is not one thing at Rome, and another at Athens; one thing to-day, and another to-morrow; but in all times and nations this universal law must for ever reign, eternal and imperishable.

The Treatises of M.T. Cicero on the Nature of the Gods 360 (Thomas Francklin, trans. 1853). In other words, on this view there are universal "law-like standards" for right and wrong that never change, regardless of what statutes may say at any particular time and place. See Brian Bix, *Jurisprudence: Theory and Context* 63–64 (2d ed. 1999). These law-like standards constitute "natural law." Adherents to natural-law theory might conclude, for example, that murder is wrong, regardless of whether it is outlawed by any particular statute, and that murder will always be wrong. Are there rights—such as a right to be free from cruel and unusual punishment—to which all people are entitled *regardless* of what a particular statute or constitution might say?

Food for Thought

Even if natural law exists, does it follow that courts in the United States can or should use natural law to protect individual rights? Consider the view of Robert H. Bork, a leading critic of judges who stray from the original meaning of the Constitution: "I am far from denying that there is a natural law, but I do deny that we have given judges the authority to enforce it and that judges have greater access to that law than do the rest of us. Judges, like the rest of us, are apt to confuse their strongly held beliefs with the order of nature." Robert H. Bork, *The Tempting of America* 66 (1990). Do you agree?

Natural law is a profoundly important philosophical idea. Many prominent philosophers and political theorists—including John Locke, on whose work many of the Framers relied in the movement for independence and in crafting the Constitution—relied heavily on natural-law theories. But even assuming that there are principles of justice that inhere in nature, how do we—and, more important for our purposes, judges—find them? In his criticism of natural-law theories, Justice Iredell asserted: "The ideas of natural justice are regulated by no fixed standard: the ablest and the purest men have differed upon the subject; and all that the court could properly say, in such an event, would be, that the legislature (possessed of an equal right of opinion) had passed an act which, in the opinion of the judges, was inconsistent with abstract principles of natural justice." Do you agree that when judges rely on natural law, they effectively rely only on their own personal intuitions about right and wrong?

b. Positive Law

Justice Iredell did not believe that there were no limits on the ability of legislatures to act, but in his view those limits inhered only in positive law—law, that is, such as the Constitution, which had been affirmatively enacted through defined law-making processes. Reliance on positive law in theory limits judges to applying the judgments of authorized law-makers, rather than making the law themselves. As we will see in Chapters 2 and 5, however, a positive-law approach in the first half of the nineteenth century would presumably have required courts to recognize and uphold, at least in some circumstances, the institution of slavery. Reliance on natural law might, by contrast, have permitted courts to reject slavery. Does this suggest that the positive-law approach is flawed? Or merely that the original decision at the Constitutional Convention not to insist on the abolition of slavery was flawed? In this regard, keep in mind that many proponents of slavery in the years leading up to the Civil War themselves relied on conceptions of natural law to *defend* the institution.

In practice, as we will see, the competing approaches tend to blur. When, for example, the Court interprets the First Amendment to prohibit the criminalization of flag burning or the Due Process Clause to prohibit laws banning abortion—subjects we will consider in Chapters 8 and 2, respectively—is it relying on natural law or positive law? The constitutional text, after all, is often quite vague and indeterminate. As a result, the process of interpretation of positive law sometimes resembles a natural-law approach. As you read the materials in the remainder of the book, consider whether it is always possible to identify whether a judge is pursuing one approach or the other.

Although there was debate in the early years over the extent to which natural-law principles applied, there was general agreement that the Constitution's limitations on state action had force, as well. However broadly the Court interpreted Article I, § 10's limitations on state authority, however, their application was still likely to be quite limited. The Bill of Rights, on the other hand, contained protections for individual rights with an apparently much wider sweep. But did the provisions of the first eight amendments—including the First Amendment's protections for speech and religious exercise and the Fourth, Fifth, Sixth, and Eighth Amendments' protections for criminal defendants—apply to the states, in addition to the federal government? The Court addressed that question in the case that follows.

BARRON V. BALTIMORE
32 U.S. (7 Pet.) 243 (1833)

[Barron sued the City of Baltimore claiming that the City had destroyed the value of his wharf, which was on the Baltimore harbor, when it diverted streams while conducting street maintenance. He asserted that the work had left the water at his wharf too shallow to be used by most vessels. He claimed that the City's actions (which were authorized under state law) deprived him of

> **Make the Connection**
>
> Can a city project that does not actually transfer title of property to the city amount to a "taking" of property within the meaning of the Fifth Amendment? We will consider this question—and "regulatory takings"—in Chapter 12.

his property without just compensation, in violation of the Fifth Amendment, which he argued "ought to be construed as to restrain the legislative power of a state, as well as that of the United States."]

MARSHALL, CH. J. delivered the opinion of the court.

The question thus presented is, we think, of great importance, but not of much difficulty. The constitution was ordained and established by the people of the United States for themselves, for their own government, and not for the government of the individual states. Each state established a constitution for itself, and in that constitution, provided such limitations and restrictions on the powers of its particular government, as its judgment dictated. The people of the United States framed such a government for the United States as they supposed best adapted to their situation and best calculated to promote their interests. The powers they conferred on this government were to be exercised by itself; and the limitations on power, if expressed in general terms, are naturally, and, we think, necessarily, applicable to the government created by the instrument. They are limitations of power granted in the instrument itself; not of distinct governments, framed by different persons and for different purposes.

> **FYI**
>
> In this case, one of the City of Baltimore's attorneys was Roger Brooke Taney. Taney later became the Chief Justice of the United States. He is remembered for his notorious opinion in *Dred Scott v. Sandford*, 60 U.S. (19 How.) 393 (1857), included in Chapter 5, which held that persons of African descent can never be citizens of the United States. As we will see, the Fourteenth Amendment negated what Taney considered two of his greatest achievements, overruling *Dred Scott* by making all persons born in the United States citizens and implicitly overruling *Barron v. Baltimore* by making most of the Bill of Rights applicable to the states.

If these propositions be correct, the fifth amendment must be understood as restraining the power of the general government, not as applicable to the states. [But the] counsel for the plaintiff in error insists, that the constitution was intended to secure the people of the several states against the undue exercise of power by their respective state governments; as well as against that which might be attempted by their general government. [In] support of this argument he relies on the inhibitions contained in the tenth section of the first article. We think, that section affords a strong, if not a conclusive, argument in support of the opinion already indicated by the court. The preceding section contains restrictions which are obviously intended for the exclusive purpose of restraining the exercise of power by the departments of the general government. * * * The ninth section having enumerated, in the nature of a bill of rights, the limitations intended to be imposed on the powers of the general government, the tenth proceeds to enumerate those which were to operate on the state legislatures. These restrictions are brought together in the same section, and are by express words applied to the states.

If the original constitution, in the ninth and tenth sections of the first article, draws this plain and marked line of discrimination between the limitations it imposes on the powers of the general government, and on those of the state; if, in every inhibition intended to act on state power, words are employed, which directly express that intent; some strong reason must be assigned for departing from this safe and judicious course, in framing the amendments, before that departure can be assumed. We search in vain for that reason. * * * Had the framers of these amendments intended them to be limitations on the powers of the state governments, they would have imitated the framers of the original constitution, and have expressed that intention.

But it is universally understood, it is a part of the history of the day, that the great revolution which established the constitution of the United States, was not effected without immense opposition. Serious fears were extensively entertained, that those powers which the patriot statesmen [deemed essential to union] might be exercised in a manner dangerous to liberty. In almost every convention by which the constitution was adopted, amendments to guard against the abuse of power were recommended. These amendments demanded security against the apprehended encroachments of the general government—not against those of the local governments. In compliance with a sentiment thus generally expressed, to quiet fears thus extensively entertained, amendments were proposed by the required majority in congress, and adopted by the states. These amendments contain no expression indicating an intention to apply them to the state governments. This court cannot so apply them. * * * We are, therefore, of opinion, that there is no repugnancy between the several acts of the general assembly of Maryland and the constitution of the United States.

POINTS FOR DISCUSSION

a. Text and Original Meaning

Chief Justice Marshall concluded that the provisions of the Bill of Rights restrained the federal government, but not the states. He relied principally on text and the original meaning. Is his reasoning persuasive? Are there other indications in the ten amendments of the original meaning? The First Amendment states that "*Congress* shall make no law respecting an establishment of religion, or prohibiting the free exercise thereof * * *" (emphasis added). Does this support Marshall's argument? Or does it instead suggest that the Framers knew how to limit a provision to the federal government when they wanted to, and that other provisions of the Bill of Rights— including the Takings Clause, which is phrased in the passive voice—therefore do not apply only to the federal government?

b. State Authority

The consequence of the Court's decision in *Barron* was that the Constitution imposed very few limits on the states' authority. To be sure, the states could adopt similar limitations in their own Constitutions, and indeed many did. But *Barron* also meant that states would, if they chose, be free to act as censors (in tension with the idea of free speech) and deny criminal defendants many of the protections that the Bill of Rights afforded to persons accused of federal crimes. Is it troubling that states could act oppressively, particularly towards unpopular individuals, even while, as a matter of constitutional principle, the federal government could not? If so, should the Court have decided *Barron* differently?

c. Natural Law

Does natural law prohibit the government from depriving a person of property without compensation? If so, does *Barron* implicitly reject the proposition that courts are to enforce natural-law rights?

———————

In the years after *Barron*, federal constitutional challenges to state legislation had to rely on the limitations deriving from Article I, § 10, Article IV, the Dormant Commerce Clause Doctrine, and constitutional structure. In the five years after the end of the Civil War, however, Congress passed and the states ratified the Thirteenth, Fourteenth, and Fifteenth Amendments to the Constitution, which imposed new limits on the powers of the states. Together, these provisions are known as the "Reconstruction Amendments." We will consider two of those— the Thirteenth Amendment, which abolished slavery and involuntary servitude, and the Fifteenth Amendment, which ensured that the right to vote would "not be denied or abridged by the United States or by any State on account of race, color, or previous condition of servitude"—only briefly, principally in Chapter 7. The Fourteenth Amendment will be a central focus of the next few chapters.

As we will see, the Fourteenth Amendment contains several profoundly important provisions. It makes all persons born or naturalized in the United States citizens both of the United States and the state in which they reside, thus overruling one of the holdings of the *Dred Scott* case, which we will consider in Chapter 5. In addition, it prohibits the states from abridging the privileges or immunities of citizens of the United States; it bars the states from depriving any person of life, liberty, or property without due process of law; and it prevents the states from denying equal protection of the laws to persons within their boundaries. And it confers on Congress the power to enforce its provisions by "appropriate legislation."

These provisions clearly were significant limitations on state authority. But just how sweeping were they? In Chapter 4, we will begin our consideration of the reach of the Equal Protection Clause. But what about the other provisions in

Section 1 of the Fourteenth Amendment? Were the protections afforded by the Due Process Clause identical to those that the Fifth Amendment provides against federal action? Did the Privileges or Immunities Clause provide a different set of protections than those in the similarly (but not identically) worded provision in Article IV? Most important, did the protections afforded—either by one of the clauses, or by all of them working in tandem—to individual rights against state action parallel those afforded against federal action by the Bill of Rights?

The case that follows was the Court's first meaningful opportunity to address some of those questions.

B. PRIVILEGES OR IMMUNITIES

SLAUGHTER-HOUSE CASES

83 U.S. 36 (1873)

MR. JUSTICE MILLER delivered the opinion of the Court.

[In 1869, the Louisiana legislature passed a statute permitting the slaughtering of animals in New Orleans only in a slaughter-house owned by a corporation chartered by the statute. The statute required the corporation to permit independent butchers to slaughter their animals at its slaughter-house at a cost fixed by statute, but it also ordered all other slaughter-houses to close. The slaughter-house would be large enough to accommodate all butchers and to allow 500 animals to be slaughtered each day. Butchers aggrieved by the statutory monopoly brought suit challenging the constitutionality of the statute. Louisiana's Supreme Court upheld the law.]

It is not, and cannot be successfully controverted, that it is both the right and the duty of the legislative body—the supreme power of the State or municipality—to prescribe and determine the localities where the business of slaughtering for a great city may be conducted. To do this effectively it is indispensable that all persons who slaughter animals for food shall do it in those places and nowhere else.

The statute under consideration defines these localities and forbids slaughtering in any other. It does not, as has been asserted, prevent the butcher from doing his own slaughtering. On the contrary, the Slaughter-House Company is required, under a heavy penalty, to permit any person who wishes to do so, to slaughter in their houses; and they are bound to make ample provision for the convenience of all the slaughtering for the entire city. The butcher then is still permitted to slaughter, to prepare, and to sell his own meats; but he is required to slaughter at a specified place and to pay a reasonable compensation for the use of the accommodations furnished him at that place.

The wisdom of the monopoly granted by the legislature may be open to question, but it is difficult to see a justification for the assertion that the butchers are deprived of the right to labor in their occupation, or the people of their daily service in preparing food, or how this statute, with the duties and guards imposed upon the company, can be said to destroy the business of the butcher, or seriously interfere with its pursuit.

[Plaintiffs contend that the statute violates the Thirteenth Amendment and the Privileges or Immunities, Equal Protection, and Due Process Clauses of the Fourteenth Amendment.] This court is thus called upon for the first time to give construction to these articles. The most cursory glance at these articles discloses a unity of purpose, when taken in connection with the history of the times, which cannot fail to have an important bearing on any question of doubt concerning their true meaning. * * * [U]ndoubtedly the overshadowing and efficient cause [of the Civil War] was African slavery. * * * [O]n the most casual examination of the language of [the Reconstruction] amendments, no one can fail to be impressed with the one pervading purpose found in them all, lying at the foundation of each, and without which none of them would have been even suggested; we mean the freedom of the slave race, the security and firm establishment of that freedom, and the protection of the newly-made freeman and citizen from the oppressions of those who had formerly exercised unlimited dominion over him.

We do not say that no one else but the negro can share in this protection. * * * Undoubtedly while negro slavery alone was in the mind of the Congress which proposed the thirteenth article, it forbids any other kind of slavery, now or hereafter. * * * And so if other rights are assailed by the States which properly and necessarily fall within the protection of these articles, that protection will apply, though the party interested may not be of African descent. But what we do say, and what we wish to be understood is, that in any fair and just construction of any section or phrase of these amendments, it is necessary to look to the purpose which we have said was the pervading spirit of them all, the evil which they were designed to remedy, and the process of continued addition to the Constitution, until that purpose was supposed to be accomplished, as far as constitutional law can accomplish it.

The first section of the fourteenth article, to which our attention [is] specially invited, opens with a definition of citizenship—not only citizenship of the United States, but citizenship of the States. No such definition was previously found in the Constitution, nor had any attempt been made to define it by act of Congress. * * * [It] had been held by this court, in [the] *Dred Scott v. Sandford,* 60 U.S. 393 (1868) case, only a few

> **Make the Connection**
>
> We will discuss the *Dred Scott* decision in Chapter 2, when we consider "substantive due process," and in Chapter 5, when we consider discrimination on the basis of race.

years before the outbreak of the civil war, that a man of African descent, whether a slave or not, was not and could not be a citizen of a State or of the United States. [T]he first clause of the first section overturns the *Dred Scott* decision by making *all persons* born within the United States and subject to its jurisdiction citizens of the United States. That its main purpose was to establish the citizenship of the negro can admit of no doubt.

[T]he distinction between citizenship of the United States and citizenship of a State is clearly recognized and established. Not only may a man be a citizen of the United States without being a citizen of a State, but an important element is necessary to convert the former into the latter. He must reside within the State to make him a citizen of it, but it is only necessary that he should be born or naturalized in the United States to be a citizen of the Union. It is quite clear, then, that there is a citizenship of the United States, and a citizenship of a State, which are distinct from each other, and which depend upon different characteristics or circumstances in the individual.

We think this distinction and its explicit recognition in this amendment of great weight in this argument, because the next paragraph of this same section, which is the one mainly relied on by the plaintiffs in error, speaks only of privileges and immunities of citizens of the United States, and does not speak of those of citizens of the several States. * * * The language is, "No State shall make or enforce any law which shall abridge the privileges or immunities of citizens of *the United States.*" It is a little remarkable, if this clause was intended as a protection to the citizen of a State against the legislative power of his own State, that the word citizen of the State should be left out when it is so carefully used, and used in contradistinction to citizens of the United States, in the very sentence which precedes it. It is too clear for argument that the change in phraseology was adopted understandingly and with a purpose.

Take Note

The Court here misquotes the language of Article IV. Can you see how? Does the Court's language change the meaning of the provision?

Of the privileges and immunities of the citizen of the United States, and of the privileges and immunities of the citizen of the State, and what they respectively are, we will presently consider; but we wish to state here that it is only the former which are placed by this clause under the protection of the Federal Constitution, and that the latter, whatever they may be, are not intended to have any additional protection by this paragraph of the amendment. [Article IV, § 2 provides:] "The citizens of each State shall be entitled to all the privileges and immunities of citizens of the several States." Fortunately we are not without judicial construction of this clause of the Constitution. The first and the leading case on the subject is that of *Corfield v. Coryell,* [6 Fed. Case 546 (C.C.E.Dist. Pa. 1823),] decided by Mr. Justice Washington in the Circuit Court for the District of Pennsylvania in 1823. "The inquiry," he says, "is, what are the privileges and immunities of

FYI

Until 1891, Justices of the Supreme Court were required to "ride circuit," which meant that they sat as judges on the courts of appeals for a significant part of each year. Justice Washington was riding circuit when he issued the opinion in *Corfield*. His opinion in this case was therefore not the opinion of the Supreme Court.

citizens of the several States? We feel no hesitation in confining these expressions to those privileges and immunities which are *fundamental;* which belong of right to the citizens of all free governments, and which have at all times been enjoyed by citizens of the several States which compose this Union, from the time of their becoming free, independent, and sovereign. What these fundamental principles are, it would be more tedious than difficult to enumerate. They may all, however, be comprehended under the following general heads: protection by the government, with the right to acquire and possess property of every kind, and to pursue and obtain happiness and safety, subject, nevertheless, to such restraints as the government may prescribe for the general good of the whole."

The description, when taken to include others not named, but which are of the same general character, embraces nearly every civil right for the establishment and protection of which organized government is instituted. They are, in the language of Judge Washington, those rights which [are] fundamental. Throughout his opinion, they are spoken of as rights belonging to the individual as a citizen of a State. They are so spoken of in the constitutional provision which he was construing. And they have always been held to be the class of rights which the State governments were created to establish and secure.

The constitutional provision there alluded to did not create those rights, which it called privileges and immunities of citizens of the States. * * * Nor did it profess to control the power of the State governments over the rights of its own citizens. Its sole purpose was to declare to the several States, that whatever those rights, as you grant or establish them to your own citizens, or as you limit or qualify, or impose restrictions on their exercise, the same,

> **Food for Thought**
>
> If the Privileges and Immunities Clause of Article IV requires states only to treat non-residents the same as residents, what does it mean to say that it applies only to "fundamental rights"? If the rights are truly fundamental, can a state really deprive both its residents and non-residents of them?

neither more nor less, shall be the measure of the rights of citizens of other States within your jurisdiction.

It would be the vainest show of learning to attempt to prove by citations of authority, that up to the adoption of the recent amendments, no claim or pretence was set up that those rights depended on the Federal government for their existence or protection, beyond the very few express limitations which the Federal Constitution imposed upon the States—such, for instance, as the prohibition against ex post facto laws, bills of attainder, and laws impairing the obligation of contracts. But with the exception of these and a few other restrictions, the entire domain of the privileges and immunities of citizens of the States, as above defined, lay within the constitutional and legislative power of the States, and without that of the Federal government. Was it the purpose of the fourteenth amendment, by the simple declaration that no State should make or enforce any law which shall abridge the privileges and immunities of *citizens of the United States*, to transfer the security and protection of all the civil rights which we have mentioned, from the States to the Federal government? And where it is declared that Congress shall have the power to enforce that article, was it intended to bring within the power of Congress the entire domain of civil rights heretofore belonging exclusively to the States?

All this and more must follow, if the proposition of the plaintiffs in error be sound. For not only are these rights subject to the control of Congress whenever in its discretion any of them are supposed to be abridged by State legislation, but that body may also pass laws in advance, limiting and restricting the exercise of legislative power by the States, in their most ordinary and usual functions, as in its judgment it may think proper on all such subjects. And still further, such a construction followed by the reversal of the judgments of the Supreme Court of Louisiana in these cases, would constitute this court a perpetual censor upon all legislation of the States, on the civil rights of their own citizens, with authority to nullify such as it did not approve as consistent with those rights, as they existed at the time of the adoption of this amendment. The argument we admit is not always the most conclusive which is drawn from the consequences urged against the adoption of a particular construction of an instrument. But when, as in the case before us, these consequences are so serious, so far-reaching and pervading, so great a departure from the structure and spirit of our institutions; when the effect is to fetter and degrade the State governments by subjecting them to the control of Congress, in the exercise of powers heretofore universally conceded to them of the most ordinary and fundamental character; when in fact it radically changes the whole theory of the relations of the State and Federal governments to each

> **Take Note**
>
> Section 5 of the Fourteenth Amendment gives Congress the power to enforce the Amendment's substantive provisions, including the Privileges or Immunities Clause in Section 1. Wasn't this authority conferred precisely to protect civil rights from state encroachment? In this sense, didn't the Reconstruction Amendments "radically change[ ] the whole theory of the relations" between the state and federal governments?

other and of both these governments to the people; the argument has a force that is irresistible, in the absence of language which expresses such a purpose too clearly to admit of doubt. We are convinced that no such results were intended by the Congress which proposed these amendments, nor by the legislatures of the States which ratified them.

[Thus,] we may hold ourselves excused from defining the privileges and immunities of citizens of the United States which no State can abridge, until some case involving those privileges may make it necessary to do so. But lest it should be said that no such privileges and immunities are to be found if those we have been considering are excluded, we venture to suggest some which [owe] their existence to the Federal government, its National character, its Constitution, or its laws. One of these is well described in the case of *Crandall v. Nevada,* 73 U.S. 35 (1867). It is said to be the right of the citizen of this great country, protected by implied guarantees of its Constitution, "to come to the seat of government to assert any claim he may have upon that government, to transact any business he may have with it, to seek its protection, to share its offices, to engage in administering its functions. He has the right of free access to its seaports, through which all operations of foreign commerce are conducted, to the subtreasuries, land offices, and courts of justice in the several States." Another privilege of a citizen of the United States is to demand the care and protection of the Federal government over his life, liberty, and property when on the high seas or within the jurisdiction of a foreign government. * * * The right to peaceably assemble and petition for redress of grievances, the privilege of the writ of *habeas corpus*, are rights of the citizen guaranteed by the Federal Constitution. [One] of these privileges is conferred by the very article under consideration. It is that a citizen of the United States can, of his own volition, become a citizen of any State of the Union by a *bona fide* residence therein, with the same rights as other citizens of that State.

But it is useless to pursue this branch of the inquiry, since we are of opinion that the rights claimed by these plaintiffs in error, if they have any existence, are not privileges and immunities of citizens of the United States within the meaning of the clause of the fourteenth amendment under consideration.

[The Court also concluded that the challenged statute did not violate the Due Process or Equal Protection Clauses of the Fourteenth Amendment.]

MR. JUSTICE FIELD, [joined by CHIEF JUSTICE CHASE, JUSTICE SWAYNE, and JUSTICE BRADLEY,] dissenting:

The question presented is * * * nothing less than the question whether the recent amendments to the Federal Constitution protect the citizens of the United States against the deprivation of their common rights by State legislation. In my judgment the fourteenth amendment does afford such protection, and was so intended by the Congress which framed and the States which adopted it.

The amendment was adopted to obviate objections which had been raised and pressed with great force to the validity of the Civil Rights Act [of 1866], and to place the common rights of American citizens under the protection of the National government. * * * The amendment does not attempt to confer any new privileges or immunities upon citizens, or to enumerate or define those already existing. It assumes that there are such privileges and immunities which belong of right to citizens as such, and ordains that they shall not be abridged by State legislation. If this inhibition has no reference to privileges and immunities of this character, but only refers, as held by the majority of the court in their opinion, to such privileges and immunities as were before its adoption specially designated in the Constitution or necessarily implied as belonging to citizens of the United States, it was a vain and idle enactment, which accomplished nothing, and most unnecessarily excited Congress and the people on its passage. With privileges and immunities thus designated or implied no State could ever have interfered by its laws, and no new constitutional provision was required to inhibit such interference. * * * But if the amendment refers to the natural and inalienable rights which belong to all citizens, the inhibition has a profound significance and consequence.

What, then, are the privileges and immunities which are secured against abridgment by State legislation? * * * The terms, privileges and immunities, are not new in the amendment; they were in the Constitution before the amendment was adopted. They are found in the second section of the fourth article; * * * [the] privileges and immunities designated are those *which of right belong to the citizens of all free governments.* [*Corfield v. Coryell.*] * * * What [Article IV] did for the protection of the citizens of one State against hostile and discriminating legislation of other States, the fourteenth amendment does for the protection of every citizen of the United States against hostile and discriminating legislation against him in favor of others, whether they reside in the same or in different States. If under the fourth article of the Constitution equality of privileges and immunities is secured between citizens of different States, under the fourteenth amendment the same equality is secured between citizens of the United States.

All monopolies in any known trade or manufacture are an invasion of these privileges, for they encroach upon the liberty of citizens to acquire property and pursue happiness * * *. [F]reedom of pursuit has been always recognized as the common right of [Louisiana's] citizens. But were this otherwise, the fourteenth amendment secures the like protection to all citizens in that State against any abridgment of their common rights, as in other States. That amendment was intended to give practical effect to the declaration of 1776 of inalienable rights, rights which are the gift of the Creator, which the law does not confer, but only recognizes.

This equality of right, with exemption from all disparaging and partial enactments, in the lawful pursuits of life, throughout the whole country, is the distinguishing privilege of citizens of the United States. To them, everywhere, all pursuits, all professions, all avocations are open without other restrictions than such as are imposed equally upon all others of the same age, sex, and condition.

> **Make the Connection**
>
> In Justice Field's view, the Privileges or Immunities Clause requires equal treatment for persons who are similarly situated. If this view is correct, then in what way is that clause different from the Equal Protection Clause? We will consider the Equal Protection Clause in Chapters 4 and 5, and the relationship between Equal Protection and fundamental rights in Chapter 6.

The State may prescribe such regulations for every pursuit and calling of life as will promote the public health, secure the good order and advance the general prosperity of society, but when once prescribed, the pursuit or calling must be free to be followed by every citizen who is within the conditions designated, and will conform to the regulations. This is the fundamental idea upon which our institutions rest, and unless adhered to in the legislation of the country our government will be a republic only in name. The fourteenth amendment, in my judgment, makes it essential to the validity of the legislation of every State that this equality of right should be respected.

[I]t is to me a matter of profound regret that [the challenged Act's] validity is recognized by a majority of this court, for by it the right of free labor, one of the most sacred and imprescriptible rights of man, is violated. As stated by the Supreme Court of Connecticut [in *Norwich Gaslight Co. v. The Norwich City Gas Co.*, 25 Conn. 19 (1856),] grants of exclusive privileges, such as is made by the act in question, are opposed to the whole theory of free government, and it requires no aid from any bill of rights to render them void. That only is a free government, in the American sense of the term, under which the inalienable right of every citizen to pursue his happiness is unrestrained, except by just, equal, and impartial laws.

MR. JUSTICE BRADLEY, dissenting:

[T]here are certain fundamental rights which [the state] cannot infringe. * * * I speak now of the rights of citizens of any free government. * * * In this free country, the people of which inherited certain [rights] and privileges from their ancestors, citizenship means something. It has certain privileges and immunities attached to it which the government, whether restricted by express or implied limitations, cannot take away or impair. [And] these privileges and immunities attach as well to citizenship of the United States as to citizenship of the States.

The people of this country brought with them to its shores the rights of Englishmen; the rights which had been wrested from English sovereigns at various periods of the nation's history. * * * A violation of one of the fundamental principles of [the unwritten English] constitution in the Colonies, namely, the principle that recognizes the property of the people as their own, and which, therefore, regards all taxes for the support of government as gifts of the people through their representatives, and regards taxation without representation as subversive of free government, was the origin of our own revolution. * * * [T]he Declaration of Independence, which was the first political act of the American people in their independent sovereign capacity, [identified fundamental rights that] belong to the citizens of every free government.

But we are not bound to resort to implication, or to the constitutional history of England, to find an authoritative declaration of some of the most important privileges and immunities of citizens of the United States. It is in the Constitution itself. * * * But even if the Constitution were silent, the fundamental privileges and immunities of citizens, as such, would be no less real and no less inviolable than they now are. It was not necessary to say in words that the citizens of the

United States should have and exercise all the privileges of citizens; [t]heir very citizenship conferred these privileges, if they did not possess them before.

[Even admitting that] formerly the States were not prohibited from infringing any of the fundamental privileges and immunities of citizens of the United States, except in a few specified cases, that cannot be said now, since the adoption of the fourteenth amendment. In my judgment, it was the intention of the people of this country in adopting that amendment to provide National security against violation by the States of the fundamental rights of the citizen. * * * If my views are correct with regard to what are the privileges and immunities of citizens, it follows conclusively that any law which establishes a sheer monopoly, depriving a large class of citizens of the privilege of pursuing a lawful employment, does abridge the privileges of those citizens.

MR. JUSTICE SWAYNE, dissenting:

By the Constitution, as it stood before the war, ample protection was given against oppression by the Union, but little was given against wrong and oppression by the States. That want was intended to be supplied by this amendment. Against the former this court has been called upon more than once to interpose. Authority of the same amplitude was intended to be conferred as to the latter. But this arm of our jurisdiction is, in these cases, stricken down by the judgment just given. Nowhere, than in this court, ought the will of the nation, as thus expressed, to be more liberally construed or more cordially executed. This determination of the majority seems to me to lie far in the other direction.

POINTS FOR DISCUSSION

a. History, Context, and Federalism

The Court asserted that the Privileges or Immunities Clause should not be interpreted to "transfer the security and protection" of civil rights from the states to the federal government. But didn't the experience of slavery and the secession crisis that led to the Civil War suggest that the states might be inappropriate guardians of such rights? Is that history relevant in interpreting the Privileges or Immunities Clause—or, for that matter, the other provisions in the Reconstruction Amendments? Did the Reconstruction Amendments fundamentally change the original understanding of federalism?

b. What's Left?

Even before the ratification of the Fourteenth Amendment, states presumably were prohibited from depriving United States citizens of the various rights that come with national citizenship. (In this regard, recall *McCulloch v. Maryland* and U.S. *Term*

Limits v. Thornton, which we considered in Volume 1.) If this is true, then what, in the Court's view, did the Privileges or Immunities Clause add to the Constitution? Does Section 5 of the Fourteenth Amendment offer a hint for one possible answer?

c. History and Original Meaning

The principal author of the Fourteenth Amendment was Representative John Bingham. In a speech before the House of Representatives voted on the proposed amendment, Representative Bingham stated that the amendment was designed "to arm the Congress of the United States, by the consent of the people of the United States, with the power to enforce the bill of rights as it stands in the Constitution today." He also stated that it was intended to protect "by national law the privileges and immunities of all citizens of the Republic *and the inborn rights* of every person within its jurisdiction

Rep. John Bingham (1815–1900)
Library of Congress

whenever the same shall be abridged or denied by the unconstitutional acts of any State." 39th Cong. Globe 1088–90 (1866) (emphasis added). Similarly, Senator Jacob Howard, the principal sponsor of the amendment in the Senate, explained in a floor speech that the proposed amendment was designed to protect "the personal rights guarantied and secured by the first eight amendments of the Constitution" and all of the fundamental rights described by Justice Washington in *Corfield v. Coryell,* which interpreted the phrase "privileges and immunities" in Article IV to refer to all fundamental natural-law rights. He then declared, "The great object of the first section of this amendment is, therefore, to restrain the power of the States and compel them at all times to respect these great fundamental guarantees." 39th Cong. Globe 2765–66 (1866). What is the relevance of this history to the question presented in the *Slaughter-House Cases?* What does it suggest about the Court's interpretation of the Privileges or Immunities Clause?

d. Another View of the Privileges or Immunities Clause

The traditional view of the Privileges or Immunities Clause is that the clause protects substantive rights but, under the interpretation advanced in the *Slaughter-House Cases,* the rights protected are only those rights already protected by federal law. The Clause, as interpreted, thus accomplishes very little. Professor John Harrison has challenged this entire view in a very influential article, arguing that the Clause instead promotes a specific kind of equality instead of protecting substantive rights. He explains his argument as follows:

A *substantive* protection either prescribes or forbids a certain content of state law. An *equality-based* protection, by contrast, says nothing about the substance of the state's law; it instead requires that the law, whatever it is, be the same for all citizens. I argue that the Privileges or Immunities Clause is, with respect to everyday rights of state law, the latter kind of protection. The main point of the clause is to require that every state give the same privileges and immunities of state citizenship—the same positive law rights of property, contract, and so forth—to all of its citizens.

John Harrison, *Reconstructing the Privileges or Immunities Clause*, 101 Yale L.J. 1385 (1992). Harrison relies not only on the legislative history of the Privileges or Immunities Clause, but also on a careful examination of its text. What words in the Fourteenth Amendment support Harrison's view? On this view, what does the Equal Protection Clause add to the Fourteenth Amendment?

e. The Privileges or Immunities Clause in the Modern Era

The Court did not strike down any state laws under the Privileges or Immunities Clause in the century and a quarter after the Court's decision in the *Slaughter-House Cases*. In 1999, however, the Court held, in *Saenz v. Roe*, 526 U.S. 489 (1999), that a California law that limited the maximum welfare benefits available to residents who had been in the state for less than twelve months to the amount they would have received in their prior state of residence was invalid under the Clause. Justice Stevens, in his opinion for the Court, declared that the Privileges or Immunities Clause protects "the right of the newly arrived citizen to the same privileges and immunities enjoyed by other citizens of the same State," a right protected "not only by the new arrival's status as a state citizen, but also by her status as a citizen of the United States." Justice Stevens noted that the opinion in the *Slaughter-House Cases* explained that one of the privileges conferred by the Clause "is that a citizen of the United States can, of his own volition, become a citizen of any State of the Union by a *bona fide* residence therein, with the same rights as other citizens of that State." Because "[n]either the duration of respondents' California residence, nor the identity of their prior States of residence, [had] any relevance to their need for benefits," and because those factors did not "bear any relationship to the State's interest in making an equitable allocation of the funds to be distributed among its needy citizens," the Court invalidated the statute.

Was the Court's decision in *Saenz* merely an application of the *Slaughter-House* view of the meaning of the Privileges or Immunities Clause? Or did it signal a willingness to expand the reach of the Clause? The Court has not invalidated any other state laws under the Privileges or Immunities Clause since the decision in *Saenz*, but, as we will see in the next section, at least one Justice has urged the Court to revisit the *Slaughter-House* Court's interpretation of the Clause.

C. INCORPORATION

One possible interpretation of the Privileges or Immunities Clause would have been that it effectively applied to the states the protections for individual rights that the first eight Amendments afford against federal action. Indeed, there is substantial historical evidence that those who drafted and proposed the provision—particularly Congressman John Bingham, the Fourteenth Amendment's principal author—believed that it would "incorporate" the protections of the Bill of Rights, see, e.g., Richard L. Aynes, *On Misreading John Bingham and the Fourteenth Amendment*, 103 Yale L.J. 57 (1993), although the question is controversial, see Charles Fairman, *Does the Fourteenth Amendment Incorporate the Bill of Rights?*, 2 Stan. L. Rev. 5 (1949). Incorporation through the Privileges or Immunities Clause of the protections of the Bill of Rights would also help to minimize the difficulties of interpretation that would ensue if the Court were forced to define—without reference to the Bill of Rights—the privileges and immunities of national citizenship. But the Court has never accepted the view that the Privileges or Immunities Clause serves this function.

The Court has, however, looked to the Due Process Clause of the Fourteenth Amendment to play this role. The Due Process Clause prevents the states from denying any person "life, liberty, or property" without due process of law. At a minimum, the Due Process Clause seems to require the states to provide appropriate process before they can deprive a person of an important interest. But the Clause does not specify what process is due; it merely speaks tautologically, requiring us to look elsewhere to determine what process it requires. It has always seemed clear that it would violate the Due Process Clause for a state to seek to imprison a person for life without first giving notice of the charges and a trial at which the person has an opportunity to contest the charges. But what other rights does the Clause guarantee?

The Constitution, of course, includes a list of rights, many of them procedural in nature, in the Bill of Rights. Accordingly, one possibility is that the process that is due when a state seeks to deprive a person of life, liberty, or property is the list of procedural rights mentioned in the first eight amendments: the right to be free from warrantless searches, the right to counsel, the right to a jury trial, and so forth. On this view, the Due Process Clause of the Fourteenth Amendment "incorporates" the procedural rights mentioned in the Bill of Rights, thereby imposing limits on actions by states and state officials. This view is appealing, but it still has some difficulties. It is not entirely obvious, at the margins, which rights are "procedural" in nature; for example, is the right to be free from cruel and unusual punishment, protected by the Eighth Amendment, a "procedural" right, or is it instead a substantive protection of liberty? In addition, if this view is correct, what should we make of the fact that the Fifth Amendment, which protects several specific procedural rights, also includes a Due Process Clause, suggesting that the term "due process of law" has some content *independent* of the other specific rights mentioned in the Bill of Rights?

To complicate matters further, the term "due process" has a deep historical pedigree—dating to English laws designed to implement Magna Carta's mandate that government action comply with the "law of the land"—that arguably embraced substantive, as well as procedural, rights. See, e.g., Frederick M. Gedicks, *An Originalist Defense of Substantive Due Process: Magna Carta, Higher-Law Constitutionalism, and the Fifth Amendment*, 58 Emory L.J. 585 (2009). In addition, as noted above, there is substantial evidence that the framers of the Fourteenth Amendment thought that it would incorporate *all* of the rights mentioned in the Bill of Rights—not just procedural rights, such as the right to a trial by jury, but substantive rights, such as the right to free speech, as well. And if the Privileges or Immunities Clause does not protect those rights, then perhaps the Due Process Clause does.

Indeed, although this approach was not without controversy, see, e.g., Raoul Berger, *Government by Judiciary: The Transformation of the Fourteenth Amendment* 221–44 (2d ed. 1997), the Court at the end of the nineteenth century began to hold that the Due Process Clause of the Fourteenth Amendment protects individuals against some state actions that would, if engaged in by the federal government, violate provisions in the Bill of Rights. In *Chicago, Burlington & Quincy R.R. Co. v. Chicago*, 166 U.S. 226 (1897), for example, the Court held that the Due Process Clause prohibited a state from taking private property for public use without just compensation, a form of protection (we saw in *Barron*) that is guaranteed against federal action by the Fifth Amendment. And in *Twining v. New Jersey*, 211 U.S. 78, 99 (1908), the Court stated that "it is possible that some of the personal rights safeguarded by the first eight Amendments against national action may also be safeguarded against state action, because a denial of them would be a denial of due process of law." But the Court also explicitly held during that era that some rights protected against federal action in the Bill of Rights did not apply to state action. See, e.g., *Hurtado v. California*, 110 U.S. 516 (1884) (grand jury indictment requirement); *Minneapolis & St. Louis R.R. Co. v. Bombolis*, 241 U.S. 211 (1916) (right to a jury trial in a civil case).

In the middle of the twentieth century, the Court began a more systematic effort to define the scope of the rights protected by the Due Process Clause. In *Palko v. Connecticut*, 302 U.S. 319 (1937), for example, the Court concluded that a state law that permitted a state to appeal a judgment of acquittal of a criminal defendant—and thus permitted the state, after prevailing on appeal, to re-try the defendant for the same crime—did not violate the Due Process Clause of the Fourteenth Amendment, even though the Fifth Amendment provides that no person shall be "subject for the same offense to be twice put in jeopardy of life or limb." The Court reasoned that the mere inclusion of a right in the Bill of Rights does not require the conclusion that it is protected against state interference by the Due Process Clause. Instead, the Court declared that the Due Process Clause protects only those rights that are "implicit in the concept of ordered liberty," essential to "a fair and enlightened system of justice," or (as it said in another case) "so rooted in the traditions and conscience of our people as to be ranked as fundamental." On this view, some of the rights identified in the first eight amendments to the Constitution are protected against state interference by the Due Process Clause of the Fourteenth Amendment, but only because they are "implicit in the concept of ordered liberty," and not simply because they are enumerated in the Bill of Rights.

How does a Court go about deciding whether a right mentioned in the Bill of Rights—or, for that matter, a right not specifically enumerated in the Bill of Rights—is "implicit in the concept of ordered liberty" or "fundamental"? This question divided the Court in the middle of the twentieth century. Would it make more sense simply to conclude that the Due Process Clause "incorporates" all of the rights mentioned in the first eight amendments and thus applies them against state action? The dueling opinions in the case that follows addressed these questions. As the notes after the case make clear, however, the majority's approach in *Adamson*—and the Court's specific holding in the case—is no longer the law.

ADAMSON V. CALIFORNIA

332 U.S. 46 (1947)

MR. JUSTICE REED delivered the opinion of the Court.

> **FYI**
>
> Legislation in California, like legislation in many states, distinguishes "first degree" murder from "second degree" murder, with the former involving killing by more egregious methods or in more egregious circumstances. The current California statute says: "All murder which is perpetrated by means of a destructive device or explosive, a weapon of mass destruction, knowing use of ammunition designed primarily to penetrate metal or armor, poison, lying in wait, torture, or by any other kind of willful, deliberate, and premeditated killing, or which is committed in the perpetration of, or attempt to perpetrate, arson, rape, carjacking, robbery, burglary, mayhem, kidnapping, train wrecking, or . . . any murder which is perpetrated by means of discharging a firearm from a motor vehicle, intentionally at another person outside of the vehicle with the intent to inflict death, is murder of the first degree. All other kinds of murders are of the second degree." Cal. Penal Code § 189.

The appellant [was] convicted [by] a jury in a Superior Court of the State of California of murder in the first degree [and sentenced to death.] * * * The provisions of California law which were challenged in the state proceedings as invalid under the Fourteenth Amendment [permit] the failure of a defendant to explain or to deny evidence against him to be commented upon by court and by counsel and to be considered by court and jury. The defendant did not testify. [The prosecutor urged the jury to infer that the defendant was guilty because he failed to deny evidence offered against him. The court instructed the jury that this inference was permissible under California law.]

We shall assume, but without any intention thereby of ruling upon the issue, that state permission by law to the court, counsel and jury to comment upon and consider the failure of defendant [to testify] would infringe defendant's privilege against self-incrimination under the Fifth Amendment if this were a trial in a court of the United States under a similar law. Such an assumption does not determine appellant's rights under the Fourteenth Amendment. * * *

[Appellant] contends that [the] privilege against self-incrimination, * * * to its full scope under the Fifth Amendment, inheres in the right to a fair trial. A right to a fair trial is a right admittedly protected by the due process clause of the Fourteenth Amendment. * * * The due process clause of the Fourteenth Amendment,

> **FYI**
>
> The Fifth Amendment provides that no person "shall be compelled in any criminal case to be a witness against himself." Putting aside the question whether the Fourteenth Amendment makes the privilege against self-incrimination applicable to state action, why was California law arguably in conflict with the privilege? How would an approach like California's affect a defendant's decision whether to testify in his own defense?

[handwritten marginalia: "criminals want to use Protect didn't constitution to Protect"]

however, does not draw all the rights of the federal Bill of Rights under its protection. That contention was made and rejected in *Palko v. Connecticut,* 302 U.S. 319, 323 [(1937)]. *Palko* held that such provisions of the Bill of Rights as were "implicit in the concept of ordered liberty" became secure from state interference by the clause. But it held nothing more.

> **Food for Thought**
>
> If the privilege against self-incrimination is not essential for a fair trial, why does the Fifth Amendment create such a privilege for federal criminal cases? Is there a coherent justification for the conclusion that the same practice that is considered unfair, as a matter of constitutional law, in federal cases is not unfair in state cases?

For a state to require testimony from an accused is not necessarily a breach of a state's obligation to give a fair trial. * * * California has prescribed a method for advising the jury in the search for truth. However sound may be the legislative conclusion that an accused should not be compelled in any criminal case to be a witness against himself, we see no reason why comment should not be made upon his silence. * * * The purpose of due process is not to protect an accused against a proper conviction but against an unfair conviction. When evidence is before a jury that threatens conviction, it does not seem unfair to require him to choose between leaving the adverse evidence unexplained and subjecting himself to impeachment through disclosure of former crimes. Indeed, this is a dilemma with which any defendant may be faced.

MR. JUSTICE FRANKFURTER [concurring].

For historical reasons a limited immunity from the common duty to testify was written into the Federal Bill of Rights, and I am prepared to agree that, as part of that immunity, comment on the failure of an accused to take the witness stand is forbidden in federal prosecutions. * * * But to suggest that such a limitation can be drawn out of "due process" in its protection of ultimate decency in a civilized society is to suggest that the Due Process Clause fastened fetters of unreason upon the States.

Between the incorporation of the Fourteenth Amendment into the Constitution and the beginning of the present membership of the Court—a period of 70 years—the scope of that Amendment was passed upon by 43 judges. Of all these judges, only one, who may respectfully be called an eccentric exception, ever indicated the belief that the Fourteenth Amendment was a shorthand summary of the first eight Amendments theretofore limiting only the Federal Government, and that due process incorporated those eight Amendments as restrictions upon the powers of the States. [The rest of those judges were] mindful of the relation of our federal system to a progressively democratic society and therefore duly regardful of the scope of authority that was left to the States even after the Civil War. And so they did not find that the Fourteenth Amendment, concerned as it was with matters fundamental to the pursuit of justice, fastened upon the States procedural arrangements which, in the language of Mr. Justice Cardozo, only those who are "narrow or provincial" would deem essential to "a fair and enlightened system of justice." *Palko v. Connecticut,* 302 U.S. 319, 325 (1937). To suggest that it is inconsistent with a truly free society to begin prosecutions without an indictment, to try petty civil cases without the paraphernalia of a common law jury, to take into consideration that one who has full opportunity to make a defense remains silent is, in de Tocqueville's phrase, to confound the familiar with the necessary.

The short answer to the suggestion that the [due process clause] was a way of saying that every State must thereafter initiate prosecutions through indictment by a grand jury, must have a trial by a jury of 12 in criminal cases, and must have trial by such a jury in common law suits where the amount in controversy exceeds $20, is that it is a strange way of saying it. * * * Those reading the English language with the meaning which it ordinarily conveys, those conversant with the political and legal history of the concept of due process, those sensitive to the relations of the States to the central government as well as the relation of some of the provisions of the Bill of Rights to the process of justice, would hardly recognize the Fourteenth Amendment as a cover for the various explicit provisions of the first eight Amendments. * * * The notion that the Fourteenth Amendment was a covert way of imposing upon the States all the rules which it seemed important to Eighteenth Century statesmen to write into the Federal Amendments, was rejected by judges who were themselves witnesses of the process by which the Fourteenth Amendment became part of the Constitution.

Remarks of a particular proponent of the Amendment, no matter how influential, are not to be deemed part of the Amendment. What was submitted for ratification was his proposal, not his speech. Thus, at the time of the ratification of the Fourteenth Amendment the constitutions of nearly half of the ratifying States did not have the rigorous requirements of the Fifth Amendment for instituting criminal proceedings through a grand jury. It could hardly have occurred to these States that by ratifying the Amendment they uprooted their established methods for prosecuting crime and fastened upon themselves a new prosecutorial system. * * * As judges charged with the delicate task of subjecting the government of a continent to the Rule of Law we must be particularly mindful that it is "a constitution we are expounding," so that it should not be imprisoned in what are merely legal forms even though they have the sanction of the Eighteenth Century.

It may not be amiss to restate the pervasive function of the Fourteenth Amendment in exacting from the States observance of basic liberties. The Amendment neither comprehends the specific provisions by which the founders deemed it appropriate to restrict the federal government nor is it confined to them. The Due Process Clause of the Fourteenth Amendment has an independent potency, precisely as does the Due Process Clause of the Fifth Amendment in relation to the Federal Government. It ought not to require argument to reject the notion that due process of law meant one thing in the Fifth Amendment and another in the Fourteenth. The Fifth Amendment specifically [precludes] deprivation of "life, liberty, or property, without due process of law." Are Madison and his contemporaries in the framing of the Bill of Rights to be charged with writing into it a meaningless clause? To consider "due process of law" as merely a shorthand statement of other specific clauses in the same amendment is to attribute to the authors and proponents of this Amendment ignorance of, or indifference to, a historic conception which was one of the great instruments in the arsenal of constitutional freedom which the Bill of Rights was to protect and strengthen.

A construction which gives to due process no independent function but turns it into a summary of the specific provisions of the Bill of Rights would [tear] up by the roots much of the fabric of law in the several States, and would deprive the States of opportunity for reforms in legal process designed for extending the area of freedom. It would assume that no other abuses would reveal themselves in the course of time than those which had become manifest in 1791. Such a view not only disregards the historic meaning of "due process." It leads inevitably to a warped construction of specific provisions of the Bill of Rights to bring within their scope conduct clearly condemned by due process but not easily fitting into the pigeon-holes of the specific provisions. It seems pretty late in the day to suggest that a phrase so laden with historic meaning should be given an improvised content consisting of some but not all of the provisions of the first eight Amendments, selected on an undefined basis, with improvisation of content for the provisions so selected.

And so, [the] issue is not whether an infraction of one of the specific provisions of the first eight Amendments is disclosed by the record. The relevant question is whether the criminal proceedings which resulted in conviction deprived the accused of the due process of law. Judicial review of that guaranty of the Fourteenth Amendment inescapably imposes upon this Court an exercise of judgment upon the whole course of the proceedings in order to ascertain whether they offend those canons of decency and fairness which express the notions of justice of English-speaking peoples even toward those charged with the most heinous offenses. These standards of justice are not authoritatively formulated anywhere as though they were prescriptions in a pharmacopoeia. But neither does the application of the Due Process Clause imply that judges are wholly at large. The judicial judgment in applying the Due Process Clause must move within the limits of accepted notions of justice and is not to be based upon the idiosyncrasies of a merely personal judgment. * * * An important safeguard against such merely individual judgment is an alert deference to the judgment of the State court under review.

> **FYI**
>
> Justice Black attached a lengthy appendix to his dissenting opinion containing, among other things, transcripts of the congressional debates concerning the Fourteenth Amendment. Justice Black relied in particular on statements in support of the proposed Fourteenth Amendment by Congressman Bingham, to whom Justice Black referred as "the Madison of the first section of the Fourteenth Amendment." For a sampling of the scholarly debate over the original meaning of the Fourteenth Amendment, compare William Crosskey, *Charles Fairman, "Legislative History," and the Constitutional Limitations on State Authority*, 22 U. Chi. L. Rev. 1 (1954), with Charles Fairman, *Does the Fourteenth Amendment Incorporate the Bill of Rights? The Original Understanding*, 2 Stan. L. Rev. 5 (1949) (disagreeing with Justice Black). For additional information about the drafting of the Fourteenth Amendment, see Gregory E. Maggs, *A Critical Guide to Using the Legislative History of the Fourteenth Amendment to Determine the Amendment's Original Meaning*, 49 Conn. L. Rev. 1069 (2017).

MR. JUSTICE BLACK, [with whom MR. JUSTICE DOUGLAS joins,] dissenting.

[The Court asserts] a constitutional theory [that] this Court is endowed by the Constitution with boundless power under "natural law" periodically to expand and contract constitutional standards to conform to the Court's conception of what at a particular time constitutes "civilized decency" and "fundamental principles of liberty and justice." * * * I think that [the] "natural law" theory of the Constitution upon which it relies [degrades] the constitutional safeguards of the Bill of Rights and simultaneously appropriate for this Court a broad power which we are not authorized by the Constitution to exercise.

My study of the historical events that culminated in the Fourteenth Amendment, and the expressions of those who sponsored and favored, as well as those who opposed its submission and passage, persuades me that one of the chief objects that the provisions of the Amendment's first section, separately, and as a whole, were intended to accomplish was to make the Bill of Rights applicable to the states. With full knowledge of the import of the *Barron* decision, the framers and backers of the

Fourteenth Amendment proclaimed its purpose to be to overturn the constitutional rule that case had announced.

I cannot consider the Bill of Rights to be an outworn 18th Century "strait jacket." Its provisions may be thought outdated abstractions by some. And it is true that they were designed to meet ancient evils. But they are the same kind of human evils that have emerged from century to century wherever excessive power is sought by the few at the expense of the many. In my judgment the people of no nation can lose their liberty so long as a Bill of Rights like ours survives and its basic purposes are conscientiously interpreted, enforced and respected so as to afford continuous protection against old, as well as new, devices and practices which might thwart those purposes. I fear to see the consequences of the Court's practice of substituting its own concepts of decency and fundamental justice for the language of the Bill of Rights as its point of departure in interpreting and enforcing that Bill of Rights. * * * I would follow what I believe was the original purpose of the Fourteenth Amendment—to extend to all the people of the nation the complete protection of the Bill of Rights. To hold that this Court can determine what, if any, provisions of the Bill of Rights will be enforced, and if so to what degree, is to frustrate the great design of a written Constitution.

It is an illusory apprehension that literal application of some or all of the provisions of the Bill of Rights to the States would unwisely increase the sum total of the powers of this Court to invalidate state legislation. The Federal Government has not been harmfully burdened by the requirement that enforcement of federal laws affecting civil liberty conform literally to the Bill of Rights. Who would advocate its repeal? It must be conceded, of course, that the natural-law-due-process formula, which the Court today reaffirms, has been interpreted to limit substantially this Court's power to prevent state violations of the individual civil liberties guaranteed by the Bill of Rights. But this formula also has been used in the past and can be used in the future, to license this Court, in considering regulatory legislation, to roam at large in the broad expanses of policy and morals and to trespass, all too freely, on the legislative domain of the States as well as the Federal Government.

[Judicial review], of course, involves interpretation, and since words can have many meanings, interpretation obviously may result in contraction or extension of the original purpose of a constitutional provision thereby affecting policy. But to pass upon the constitutionality of statutes by looking to the particular standards enumerated in the Bill of Rights and other parts of the Constitution is one thing; to invalidate statutes because of application of "natural law" deemed to be above and undefined by the Constitution is another. "In the one instance, courts proceeding within clearly marked constitutional boundaries seek to execute policies written into the Constitution; in the other they roam at will in the limitless area of their own beliefs as to reasonableness and actually select policies, a responsibility which the Constitution entrusts to the legislative representatives of the people."

MR. JUSTICE MURPHY, with whom MR. JUSTICE RUTLEDGE concurs, dissenting.

While in substantial agreement with the views of Mr. Justice BLACK, I have one reservation and one addition to make. I agree that the specific guarantees of the Bill of Rights should be carried over intact into the first section of the Fourteenth Amendment. But I am not prepared to say that the latter is entirely and necessarily limited by the Bill of Rights. Occasions may arise where a proceeding falls so far short of conforming to fundamental standards of procedure as to warrant constitutional condemnation in terms of a lack of due process despite the absence of a specific provision in the Bill of Rights. That point, however, need not be pursued here inasmuch as the Fifth Amendment is explicit in its provision that no person shall be compelled in any criminal case to be a witness against himself. * * * Accordingly, I would reverse the judgment below.

POINTS FOR DISCUSSION

a.   Selective or Total Incorporation?

In *Adamson*, the principal competing positions were advanced by Justices Frankfurter and Black. Justice Frankfurter concluded that the Due Process Clause of the Fourteenth Amendment affords rights that are "implicit in the concept of ordered liberty." Under this view, some of the same rights that the Bill of Rights provides against the federal government might apply against the states, but only because their recognition is essential to the notion of fundamental fairness embodied by the Due Process Clause. Justice Black, in contrast, believed that the Due Process Clause incorporated all of the protections of the first eight amendments—nothing more, and nothing less. This approach is generally known as "total incorporation."

In the years after *Adamson*, the Court continued, at least as a formal matter, to interpret the Due Process Clause by asking which rights were "implicit in the concept of ordered liberty." But increasingly, the Court—particularly the Warren Court in the 1960s—looked to the first eight amendments to give content to that standard. What resulted was an approach that came to be known as "selective incorporation." Under this approach, the Court continued formally to ask whether a right is necessary to ensure fundamental fairness in determining whether the right is protected by the Due Process Clause. But building on Justice Black's approach, the Court treated the mere inclusion of a right in the Bill of Rights as strongly indicative of the right's fundamental status. In addition, once the court concluded that a right mentioned in the Bill of Rights applied to the States, it held that the right applied in exactly the same way, with all of the same limits, that it applies to the federal government. In addition, once the Court concluded that a right mentioned in the Bill of Rights applied to the states, it held that the right applied in exactly the same way, with the same set of limits, that it applies to the federal government. Selective incorporation thus was a compromise between Justice Frankfurter's fundamental fairness approach and Justice Black's total incorporation approach. In practice, the approach lead to the incorporation of most of the provisions of the Bill of Rights, for which Justice Black had advocated, but it also (to Justice Black's dismay) left open the possibility that the Due Process Clause does not protect every right mentioned in the Bill of Rights— and, perhaps more important, the possibility that the Due Process Clause also protects some rights that are *not* mentioned in the Bill of Rights.

We will return shortly to the question whether the Due Process Clause protects "unenumerated rights"—that is, rights not explicitly mentioned in the Bill of Rights or elsewhere in the Constitution. But for present purposes, it is enough to note that, in a series of decisions beginning a half-century before *Adamson* and continuing for several decades after the decision, the Court decided that the Due Process Clause incorporates virtually every provision in the first eight amendments. The Court has held, for example, that the Due Process Clause incorporates all of the substantive rights in the First Amendment, see e.g., *Everson v. Board of Education*, 330 U.S. 1 (1947) (establishment); *Cantwell v. Connecticut*, 310 U.S. 296 (1940) (free exercise); *Gitlow v. New York*, 268 U.S. 652 (1925) (speech); the Fourth Amendment, see, e.g., *Wolf v. Colorado*,

> **Make the Connection**
>
> In Chapter 2, we will begin our consideration of the doctrine of "substantive due process," which holds that the Due Process Clause protects some substantive rights that cannot be abridged by government action regardless of the process that the government provides. When we do, keep in mind the debate over incorporation, and consider whether the process of incorporation itself is a form of "substantive due process."

338 U.S. 25 (1949) (warrant requirement); the Fifth Amendment, see, e.g., *Benton v. Maryland*, 395 U.S. 784 (1969) (double jeopardy); *Chicago, Burlington & Quincy R.R. Co. v. Chicago*, 166 U.S. 226 (1897) (takings); most of the substantive rights in the Sixth Amendment, see, e.g., *Gideon v. Wainwright*, 372 U.S. 335 (1963) (counsel); *Irvin v. Dowd*, 366 U.S. 717 (1961) (impartial jury); and the Eighth Amendment, see, e.g., *Robinson v. California*, 370 U.S. 660 (1962) (cruel and unusual punishment); *Timbs v. Indiana*, 139 S.Ct. 682 (2019) (excessive fines).

There are only two provisions in the first eight amendments that the Court has expressly determined are not incorporated, and those decisions, discussed above, predated the era of selective incorporation. See *Hurtado v. California*, 110 U.S. 516

(1884) (right to a grand jury indictment); *Minneapolis & St. Louis R.R. Co. v. Bombolis*, 241 U.S. 211 (1916) (right to a jury trial in civil cases). In addition, the Court has never decided whether the Third Amendment right not to have soldiers quartered in a home is incorporated.

b.   Incorporation of the Privilege Against Self-Incrimination

Once the Warren Court had begun more aggressively to find that the Due Process Clause incorporated protections in the first eight amendments, it was only a matter of time before it reconsidered whether the Fourteenth Amendment incorporated the privilege against self-incrimination. In *Malloy v. Hogan*, 378 U.S. 1 (1964), the Court held that it did, and one year later, in *Griffin v. California*, 380 U.S. 609 (1965), the Court overruled the specific holding in *Adamson* and declared unconstitutional California's law permitting comment on the defendant's failure to testify. We will consider the privilege against self-incrimination in Chapter 14.

c.   Incorporation and the Judicial Role

Both Justices Frankfurter and Black claimed that their approaches were more consistent with the judicial role. Justice Frankfurter asserted that because total incorporation would impose more limits on state action (by expanding the number of individual rights that trump state action), that approach would empower judges to limit the ability of the democratic process to operate effectively in the states. Justice Black, by contrast, asserted that Justice Frankfurter's approach would give judges virtually standardless discretion to decide what rights are "implicit in the concept of ordered liberty." Which approach do you think is more consistent with the judicial role?

As we saw in Volume 1, the Court in *District of Columbia v. Heller*, 554 U.S. 570 (2008), held for the first time that the Second Amendment protects an individual right to keep and bear arms unconnected with service in a state-regulated militia. Does the Fourteenth Amendment also limit the authority of the states to interfere with the right to keep and bear arms? The case that follows addresses that question.

McDonald v. City of Chicago
561 U.S. 742 (2010)

JUSTICE ALITO announced the judgment of the Court and delivered the opinion of the Court [except as stated in footnote 1].

[The City of Chicago and the Village of Oak Park, a Chicago suburb, have ordinances that ban or effectively ban private possession of handguns. Petitioners sought declarations that the bans violate the Second and Fourteenth Amendments. The Court of Appeals rejected those claims, relying on three cases—*United States v. Cruikshank*, 92 U.S. 542 (1876), *Presser v. Illinois*, 116 U.S. 252 (1886), and *Miller v. Texas*, 153 U.S. 535 (1894)—that the Court decided shortly after its decision in the *Slaughter-House Cases* and that held that the Second Amendment does not apply to the states, of its own force or through the Privileges or Immunities Clause of the Fourteenth Amendment. Petitioners urged the Court to overrule those decisions and to hold that the right to keep and bear arms is one of the "privileges or immunities of citizens of the United States."]

We see no need to reconsider that interpretation [of the Privileges or Immunities Clause] here.* For many decades, the question of the rights protected by the Fourteenth Amendment against state infringement has been analyzed under the Due Process Clause [and] not under the Privileges or Immunities Clause. We therefore decline to disturb the *Slaughter-House* holding. At the same time, however, this Court's decisions in *Cruikshank*, *Presser*, and *Miller* do not preclude us from considering whether the Due Process Clause of the Fourteenth Amendment makes the Second Amendment right binding on the States. [Those cases] all preceded the era in which the Court began the process of "selective incorporation" under the Due Process Clause, and we have never previously addressed the question whether the right to keep and bear arms applies to the States under that theory.

In the late 19th century, the Court began to consider whether the Due Process Clause prohibits the States from infringing rights set out in the Bill of Rights. Five features of the approach taken during the ensuing era should be noted. First, the Court viewed the due process question as entirely separate from the question whether a right was a privilege or immunity of national citizenship. *Twining v. New Jersey*, 211 U.S. 78, 99 (1908). Second, the Court explained that [w]hile it was "possible that some of the personal rights safeguarded by the first eight Amendments against National action [might] also be safeguarded against state action," [this] was "not because those rights are enumerated in the first eight Amendments." [*Id.*]. The Court used different formulations in describing the boundaries of due process. * * * In *Snyder v. Massachusetts*, 291 U.S. 97, 105 (1934), the Court spoke of rights that are "so rooted in the traditions and conscience of our people as to be ranked as fundamental." And in *Palko v. Connecticut*, 302 U.S. 319 (1937), the Court famously said that due process protects those rights that are "the very essence of a scheme of ordered liberty" and essential to "a fair and enlightened system of justice."

---

*   Justice Thomas did not join this paragraph of the Court's opinion.—*Eds.*

Third, in some cases decided during this era the Court "can be seen as having asked, when inquiring into whether some particular procedural safeguard was required of a State, if a civilized system could be imagined that would not accord the particular protection." *Duncan v. Louisiana,* 391 U.S. 145, 149, *n.* 14 (1968). * * * Fourth, the Court during this era was not hesitant to hold that a right set out in the Bill of Rights failed to meet the test for inclusion within the protection of the Due Process Clause. The Court found that some such rights qualified, see, *e.g., Gitlow v. New York,* 268 U.S. 652, 666 (1925) (freedom of speech and press), [but that] others did not, see, *e.g., Hurtado v. California,* 110 U.S. 516 (1884) (grand jury indictment requirement). Finally, even when a right set out in the Bill of Rights was held to fall within the conception of due process, the protection or remedies afforded against state infringement sometimes differed from the protection or remedies provided against abridgment by the Federal Government.

An alternative theory regarding the relationship between the Bill of Rights and § 1 of the Fourteenth Amendment was championed by Justice Black. This theory held that § 1 of the Fourteenth Amendment totally incorporated all of the provisions of the Bill of Rights. See, *e.g., Adamson v. California,* 332 U.S. 46, 71–72 (1947) (Black, J., dissenting). As Justice Black noted, the chief congressional proponents of the Fourteenth Amendment espoused the view that the Amendment made the Bill of Rights applicable to the States and, in so doing, overruled this Court's decision in *Barron.*

While Justice Black's ["total incorporation"] theory was never adopted, the Court eventually moved in that direction by initiating what has been called a process of "selective incorporation," *i.e.,* the Court began to hold that the Due Process Clause fully incorporates particular rights contained in the first eight Amendments. The decisions during this time [in the 1960s] abandoned three of the previously noted characteristics of the earlier period. The Court made it clear that the governing standard is not whether *any* "civilized system [can] be imagined that would not accord the particular protection." *Duncan.* Instead, the Court inquired whether a particular Bill of Rights guarantee is fundamental to *our* scheme of ordered liberty and system of justice. The Court also shed any reluctance to hold that rights guaranteed by the Bill of Rights met the requirements for protection under the Due Process Clause. The Court eventually incorporated almost all of the provisions of the Bill of Rights. Only a handful of the Bill of Rights protections remain unincorporated.

Finally, [the Court] decisively held that incorporated Bill of Rights protections "are all to be enforced against the States under the Fourteenth Amendment according to the same standards that protect those personal rights against federal encroachment." *Malloy v. Hogan,* 378 U.S. 1, 10 (1964). * * * Employing this approach, the Court overruled earlier decisions in which it had held that particular Bill of Rights guarantees or remedies did not apply to the States. See, *e.g., Mapp v. Ohio,* 367 U.S. 643 (1961) (exclusionary rule).

With this framework in mind, we now turn directly to the question whether the Second Amendment right to keep and bear arms is incorporated in the concept of due process. In answering that question, [we] must decide whether the right to keep and bear arms is fundamental to our scheme of ordered liberty, or as we have said in a related context, whether this right is "deeply rooted in this Nation's history and tradition," *Washington v. Glucksberg,* 521 U.S. 702, 721 (1997).

> **Make the Connection**
>
> We consider *Glucksberg,* which involved the right to physician-assisted suicide, in Chapter 2. We considered the Court's decision in *Heller* in Volume 1.

Our decision in *Heller* points unmistakably to the answer. Self-defense is a basic right, recognized by many legal systems from ancient times to the present day, and in *Heller,* we held that individual self-defense is "the *central component*" of the Second Amendment right. Explaining that "the need for defense of self, family, and property is most acute" in the home, we found that this right applies to handguns because they are "the most preferred firearm in the nation to 'keep' and use for protection of one's home and family."

Heller makes it clear that this right is "deeply rooted in this Nation's history and tradition." *Heller* explored the right's origins, noting that the 1689 English Bill of Rights explicitly protected a right to keep arms for self-defense, and that by 1765, Blackstone was able to assert that the right to keep and bear arms was "one of the fundamental rights of Englishmen." Blackstone's assessment was shared by the American colonists. * * * The right to keep and bear arms was considered no less fundamental by those who drafted and ratified the Bill of Rights. * * * Antifederalists and Federalists alike agreed that the right to bear arms was fundamental to the newly formed system of government. But those who were fearful that the new Federal Government would infringe traditional rights such as the right to keep and bear arms insisted on the adoption of the Bill of Rights as a condition for ratification of the Constitution. This is surely powerful evidence that the right was regarded as fundamental in the sense relevant here. This understanding persisted in the years

> **Food for Thought**
>
> Under the Court's historical argument, isn't every provision in the Bill of Rights necessarily "fundamental in the sense relevant here"? If so, wouldn't the Court's reasoning support the "total incorporation" theory?

immediately following the ratification of the Bill of Rights. In addition to the four States that had adopted Second Amendment analogues before ratification, nine more States adopted state constitutional provisions protecting an individual right to keep and bear arms between 1789 and 1820.

By the 1850's, the perceived threat that had prompted the inclusion of the Second Amendment in the Bill of Rights—the fear that the National Government would disarm the universal militia—had largely faded as a popular concern, but the right to keep and bear arms was highly valued for purposes of self-defense. Abolitionist authors wrote in support of the right. * * * After the Civil War, many of the over 180,000 African Americans who served in the Union Army returned to the States of the old Confederacy, where systematic efforts were made to disarm them and other blacks. * * * Congress concluded that legislative action was necessary. Its efforts to safeguard the right to keep and bear arms demonstrate that the right was still recognized to be fundamental.

The most explicit evidence of Congress' aim appears in § 14 of the Freedmen's Bureau Act of 1866, [which] explicitly guaranteed that "all the citizens," black and white, would have "the constitutional right to bear arms." [The Civil Rights Act of 1866] protected the same rights as enumerated in the Freedmen's Bureau bill. * * * Congress, however, ultimately deemed these legislative remedies insufficient. Southern resistance, Presidential vetoes, and this Court's pre-Civil-War precedent persuaded Congress that a constitutional amendment was necessary to provide full protection for the rights of blacks. Today, it is generally accepted that the Fourteenth Amendment was understood to provide a constitutional basis for protecting the rights set out in the Civil Rights Act of 1866. [In addition, a] clear majority of [state constitutions in 1868] recognized the right to keep and bear arms as being among the foundational rights necessary to our system of Government. In sum, it is clear that the Framers and ratifiers of the Fourteenth Amendment counted the right to keep and bear arms among those fundamental rights necessary to our system of ordered liberty.

Municipal respondents' main argument is nothing less than a plea to disregard 50 years of incorporation precedent and return (presumably for this case only) to a bygone era. * * * According to municipal respondents, if it is possible to imagine *any* civilized legal system that does not recognize a particular right, then the Due Process Clause does not make that right binding on the States. Therefore, the municipal respondents continue, because such countries as England, Canada, Australia, Japan, Denmark, Finland, Luxembourg, and New Zealand either ban or severely limit handgun ownership, it must follow that no right to possess such weapons is protected by the Fourteenth Amendment.

This line of argument is, of course, inconsistent with the long-established standard we apply in incorporation cases. And the present-day implications of municipal respondents' argument are stunning. * * * [For

> **Make the Connection**
>
> We consider the Court's cases construing the Establishment Clause in Chapter 11.

example,] several of the countries that municipal respondents recognize as civilized have established state churches. If we were to adopt municipal respondents' theory, all of this Court's Establishment Clause precedents involving actions taken by state and local governments would go by the boards.

Municipal respondents maintain that the Second Amendment differs from all of the other provisions of the Bill of Rights because it concerns the right to possess a deadly implement and thus has implications for public safety. * * * The right to keep and bear arms, however, is not the only constitutional right that has controversial public safety implications. All of the constitutional provisions that impose restrictions on law enforcement and on the prosecution of crimes fall into the same category. * * * Unless we turn back the clock or adopt a special incorporation test applicable only to the Second Amendment, municipal respondents' argument must be rejected. * * * [We] hold that the Due Process Clause of the Fourteenth Amendment incorporates the Second Amendment right recognized in *Heller*.

JUSTICE SCALIA, concurring.

I join the Court's opinion. Despite my misgivings about Substantive Due Process as an original matter, I have acquiesced in the Court's incorporation of certain guarantees in the Bill of Rights "because it is both long established and narrowly limited." *Albright v. Oliver*, 510 U.S. 266, 275 (1994) (SCALIA, J., concurring). * * * I write separately only to respond to some aspects of Justice STEVENS' dissent.

Justice STEVENS begins with the odd assertion that "firearms have a fundamentally ambivalent relationship to liberty," since sometimes they are used to cause (or sometimes accidentally produce) injury to others. * * * Justice STEVENS supplies neither a standard for how severe the impairment on others' liberty must be for a right to be disqualified, nor (of course) any method of measuring the severity.

Justice STEVENS next suggests that the Second Amendment right is not fundamental because * * * owning a handgun is not "critical to leading a life of autonomy, dignity, or political equality." Who says? Deciding what is essential to an enlightened, liberty-filled life is an inherently political, moral judgment—the antithesis of an objective approach that reaches conclusions by applying neutral rules to verifiable evidence.

Justice STEVENS' final reason for rejecting incorporation of the Second Amendment [is that the] States' "right to experiment" with solutions to the problem of gun violence [is] at its apex here because "the best solution is far from clear." That is true of most serious social problems * * *. The implication of Justice STEVENS' call for abstention is that if We The Court conclude that They The People's answers to a problem are silly, we are free to "interven[e]," but if we too are uncertain of the right answer, or merely think the States may be on to something, we can loosen the leash. * * * I would not—and no judge should—presume to have that sort of omniscience, which seems to me far more "arrogant" than confining courts' focus to our own national heritage.

JUSTICE THOMAS, concurring in part and concurring in the judgment.

I agree with [the plurality's] description of the right [to keep and bear arms as "fundamental."] But I cannot agree that it is enforceable against the States through a clause that speaks only to "process." Instead, the right to keep and bear arms is a privilege of American citizenship that applies to the States through the Fourteenth Amendment's Privileges or Immunities Clause.

On its face, [the Clause] appears to grant the persons just made United States citizens [by the first Clause of the Fourteenth Amendment] a certain collection of rights—*i.e.*, privileges or immunities—attributable to that status. [But as] a consequence of this Court's marginalization of the Clause [in *Slaughter-House*], litigants seeking federal protection of fundamental rights turned to the remainder of § 1 in search of an alternative fount of such rights. They found one in a most curious place—that section's command that every State guarantee "due process" to any person before depriving him of "life, liberty, or property." [T]he Court has determined that the Due Process Clause [not only incorporates "fundamental" rights mentioned in the Bill of Rights but also] applies rights against the States that are not mentioned in the Constitution at all * * *. See, *e.g.*, *Lochner v. New York,* 198 U.S. 45 (1905); *Roe v. Wade,* 410 U.S. 113 (1973).

All of this is a legal fiction. The notion that a constitutional provision that guarantees only "process" before a person is deprived of life, liberty, or property could define the substance of those rights strains credulity for even the most casual user of words. Moreover, this fiction is a particularly dangerous one. The one theme that links the Court's substantive due process precedents together is their lack of a guiding principle to distinguish "fundamental" rights that warrant protection from nonfundamental rights that do not. * * * I cannot accept a theory of constitutional interpretation that rests on such tenuous footing. * * * I believe the original meaning of the Fourteenth Amendment offers a superior alternative, and that a return to that meaning would allow this Court to enforce the rights the Fourteenth Amendment is designed to protect with greater clarity and predictability than the substantive due process framework has so far managed.

The evidence overwhelmingly demonstrates that the privileges and immunities of [U.S. citizens protected by Section 1 of the Fourteenth Amendment] included individual rights enumerated in the Constitution, including the right to keep and bear arms. [Several nineteenth-century] treaties through which the United States acquired territory from other sovereigns * * * promised inhabitants of the newly acquired territories that they would enjoy all of the "rights," "privileges," and "immunities" of United States citizens, [and] identif[ied] liberties enumerated in the Constitution as [such] privileges and immunities * * *.

Statements made by Members of Congress leading up to, and during, the debates on the Fourteenth Amendment point in the same direction. * * * Representative John Bingham, the principal draftsman of § 1 [of the Fourteenth Amendment], emphasized [on the floor of the House] that § 1 was designed "to arm the Congress of the United States, by the consent of the people of the United States, with the power to enforce the bill of rights as it stands in the Constitution today." 39th Cong. Globe 1088 (1866). * * * [While Bingham's original draft of § 1 was tabled for several months,] he delivered a second well-publicized speech, again arguing that a constitutional amendment was required to give Congress the power to enforce the Bill of Rights against the States.

By the time the debates on the Fourteenth Amendment resumed, Bingham had amended his draft of § 1 to include the text of the Privileges or Immunities Clause that was ultimately adopted. Senator Jacob Howard introduced the new draft on the floor of the Senate * * *. [Howard explained that the protected rights] included "the privileges and immunities spoken of" in Article IV, § 2 [as described in *Corfield v. Coryell* and] *"the personal rights guaranteed and secured by the first eight amendments of the Constitution."* [39 Cong. Globe 2765–66] (emphasis added). [T]hese

> **FYI**
>
> In *Corfield*, Justice Washington concluded that the Privileges and Immunities Clause of Article IV protected rights "which are, in their nature, fundamental." We briefly considered *Corfield* along with the *Slaughter-House* Cases earlier in this chapter.

well-circulated speeches indicate that § 1 was understood to enforce constitutionally declared rights against the States, and they provide no suggestion that any language in the section other than the Privileges or Immunities Clause would accomplish that task. * * *

[The] ratifying public understood the Privileges or Immunities Clause to protect constitutionally enumerated rights, including the right to keep and bear arms. * * * In the contentious years leading up to the Civil War, those who sought to retain the institution of slavery found that to do so, it was necessary to eliminate more and more of the basic liberties of slaves, free blacks, and white abolitionists. * * * The overarching goal of pro-slavery forces was to repress the spread of abolitionist thought and the concomitant risk of a slave rebellion. * * * The fear [of] rebellions led Southern legislatures to take particularly vicious aim at the rights of free blacks and slaves to speak or to keep and bear arms for their defense. * * * After the Civil War, Southern anxiety about an uprising among the newly freed slaves peaked, [which led Southern states to prohibit blacks from possessing firearms and forcibly to disarm them].

The publicly circulated Report of the Joint Committee on Reconstruction extensively detailed these abuses, and statements by citizens indicate that they looked to the Committee to provide a federal solution to this problem, see, *e.g.*, 39th Cong. Globe 337 (remarks of Rep. Sumner) (introducing "a memorial from the colored citizens of the State of South Carolina" asking for, *inter alia*, "constitutional protection in keeping arms, in holding public assemblies, and in complete liberty of speech and of the press"). * * * "Notwithstanding the provision in the Constitution of the United States, that the right to keep and bear arms shall not be abridged," [Frederick] Douglass explained that "the black man has never had the right either to keep or bear arms." Absent a constitutional amendment to enforce that right against the States, he insisted that "the work of the Abolitionists [wa]s not finished." This history confirms what the text of the Privileges or Immunities Clause most naturally suggests: Consistent with its command that "[n]o State shall . . . abridge" the rights of United States citizens, the Clause establishes a minimum baseline of federal rights, and the constitutional right to keep and bear arms plainly was among them.

My conclusion is contrary to this Court's precedents, which hold that the Second Amendment right to keep and bear arms is not a privilege of United States citizenship. * * * I reject [the *Slaughter-House* Court's] understanding [of the Privileges or Immunities Clause]. There was no reason to interpret the Privileges or Immunities Clause as putting the Court to the extreme choice of interpreting the "privileges and immunities" of federal citizenship to mean either all those rights listed in *Corfield*, or almost no rights at all. * * * The better view, in light of the States and Federal Government's shared history of recognizing certain inalienable rights in their citizens, is that the privileges and immunities of state and federal citizenship overlap. * * * [In addition,] *Cruikshank* is not a precedent entitled to any respect. * * * *Cruikshank*'s holding that blacks could look only to state governments for protection of their right to keep and bear arms enabled private forces, often with the assistance of local governments, to subjugate the newly freed slaves and their descendants through a wave of private violence designed to drive blacks from the voting booth and force them into peonage, an effective return to slavery.

In my view, the record makes plain that the Framers of the Privileges or Immunities Clause and the ratifying-era public understood—just as the Framers of the Second Amendment did—that the right to keep and bear arms was essential to the preservation of liberty. The record makes equally plain that they deemed this right necessary to include in the minimum baseline of federal rights that the Privileges or Immunities Clause established in the wake of the War over slavery.

JUSTICE STEVENS, dissenting.

[T]he term "incorporation," like the term "unenumerated rights," is something of a misnomer. Whether an asserted substantive due process interest is explicitly named in one of the first eight Amendments to the Constitution or is not mentioned, the underlying inquiry is the same: We must ask whether the interest is "comprised within the term liberty." *Whitney v. California,* 274 U.S. 357, 373 (1927) (Brandeis, J., concurring). * * * This Court's "selective incorporation" doctrine is not simply "related" to substantive due process; it is a subset thereof.

The question in this case [is] whether the particular right asserted by petitioners applies to the States because of the Fourteenth Amendment itself, standing on its own bottom. And to answer that question, we need to determine, first, the nature of the right that has been asserted and, second, whether that right is an aspect of Fourteenth Amendment "liberty." [T]he liberty interest petitioners have asserted is the "right to possess a functional, personal firearm, including a handgun, within the home." Complaint ¶ 34, App. 23. * * * I would not foreclose the possibility that a particular plaintiff—say, an elderly widow who lives in a dangerous neighborhood and does not have the strength to operate a long gun— may have a cognizable liberty interest in possessing a handgun. But I cannot accept petitioners' broader submission.

First, firearms have a fundamentally ambivalent relationship to liberty. Just as they can help homeowners defend their families and property from intruders, they can help thugs and insurrectionists murder innocent victims. * * * Hence, in evaluating an asserted right to be free from particular gun-control regulations, liberty is on both sides of the equation. * * * Second, the right to possess a firearm of one's choosing is different in kind from the liberty interests we have recognized under the Due Process Clause. [I]t does not appear to be the case that the ability to own a handgun, or any particular type of firearm, is critical to leading a life of autonomy, dignity, or political equality.

Third, the experience of other advanced democracies, including those that share our British heritage, undercuts the notion that an expansive right to keep and bear arms is intrinsic to ordered liberty. Many of these countries place restrictions on the possession, use, and carriage of firearms far more onerous than the restrictions found in this Nation. * * * While the "American perspective" must always be our focus, it is silly—indeed, arrogant—to think we have nothing to learn about liberty from the billions of people beyond our borders.

Fourth, the Second Amendment differs in kind from the Amendments that surround it * * *. Notwithstanding the *Heller* Court's efforts to write the Second Amendment's preamble out of the Constitution, the Amendment still serves the structural function of protecting the States from encroachment by an overreaching Federal Government. * * * The Second Amendment * * * is directed at preserving the autonomy of the sovereign States, and its logic therefore "resists" incorporation by a federal court *against* the States.

Fifth, [the] States have a long and unbroken history of regulating firearms. * * * This history of intrusive regulation is not surprising given that the very text of the Second Amendment calls out for regulation, and the ability to respond to the social ills associated with dangerous weapons goes to the very core of the States' police powers. * * * Finally, even apart from the States' long history of firearms regulation and its location at the core of their police powers, this is a quintessential area in which federalism ought to be allowed to flourish without this Court's meddling. * * * Across the Nation, States and localities vary significantly in the patterns and problems of gun violence they face, as well as in the traditions and cultures of lawful gun use they claim. The city of Chicago, for example, faces a pressing challenge in combating criminal street gangs. Most rural areas do not. The city of Chicago has a high population density, which increases the potential for a gunman to inflict mass terror and casualties. Most rural areas do not. The city of Chicago offers little in the way of hunting opportunities. Residents of rural communities are, one presumes, much

> **Definition**
>
> The "state police power" is the "power of a state to enforce laws for the health, welfare, morals, and safety of its citizens, if enacted so that the means are reasonably calculated to protect those legitimate state interests." *Black's Law Dictionary* (10th ed. 2014).

more likely to stock the dinner table with game they have personally felled. * * * Given that relevant background conditions diverge so much across jurisdictions, the Court ought to pay particular heed to state and local legislatures' "right to experiment." *New State Ice Co. v. Liebmann,* 285 U.S. 262, 311 (1932) (Brandeis, J., dissenting). * * * I respectfully dissent.

JUSTICE BREYER, with whom JUSTICE GINSBURG and JUSTICE SOTOMAYOR join, dissenting.

Two years ago, in *Heller,* the Court rejected the pre-existing judicial consensus that the Second Amendment was primarily concerned with the need to maintain a "well regulated Militia." * * * The Court based its conclusions almost exclusively upon its reading of history. But the relevant history in *Heller* was far from clear. * * * [And since] *Heller,* historians, scholars, and judges have continued to express the view that the Court's historical account was flawed. * * * At the least, where *Heller*'s historical foundations are so uncertain, why extend its applicability?

In my view, taking *Heller* as a given, the Fourteenth Amendment does not incorporate the Second Amendment right to keep and bear arms for purposes of private self-defense. * * * The majority here, like that in *Heller,* relies almost exclusively upon history to make the necessary showing. But to do so for incorporation purposes is both wrong and dangerous. [O]ur society has historically made mistakes—for example, when considering certain 18th- and 19th-century property rights to be fundamental. And in the incorporation context, as elsewhere, history often is unclear about the answers. Accordingly, this Court, in considering an incorporation question, has never stated that the historical status of a right is the only relevant consideration. Rather, the Court has either explicitly or implicitly made clear in its opinions that the right in question has remained fundamental over time.

[T]here is no popular consensus that the private self-defense right described in *Heller* is fundamental. [E]very State regulates firearms extensively, and public opinion is sharply divided on the appropriate level of regulation. * * * One side believes the right essential to protect the lives of those attacked in the home; the other side believes it essential to regulate the right in order to protect the lives of others attacked with guns. It seems unlikely that definitive evidence will develop one way or the other. And the appropriate level of firearm regulation has thus long been, and continues to be, a hotly contested matter of political debate.

Moreover, there is no reason here to believe that incorporation of the private self-defense right will further any other or broader constitutional objective. * * * Unlike the First Amendment's rights of free speech, free press, assembly, and petition, the private self-defense right does not comprise a necessary part of the democratic process that the Constitution seeks to establish. Unlike the First Amendment's religious protections, the Fourth Amendment's protection against unreasonable searches and seizures, the Fifth and Sixth Amendments' insistence upon fair criminal procedure, and the Eighth Amendment's protection against cruel and unusual punishments, the private self-defense right does not significantly seek to protect individuals who might otherwise suffer unfair or inhumane treatment at the hands of a majority. Unlike the protections offered by many of these same Amendments, it does not involve matters as to which judges possess a comparative expertise, by virtue of their close familiarity with the justice system and its operation. And, unlike the Fifth Amendment's insistence on just compensation, it does not involve a matter where a majority might unfairly seize for itself property belonging to a minority.

Finally, incorporation of the right *will* work a significant disruption in the constitutional allocation of decisionmaking authority, thereby interfering with the Constitution's ability to further its objectives. *First*, on any reasonable accounting, the incorporation of the right recognized in *Heller* would amount to a significant incursion on a traditional and important area of state concern, altering the constitutional relationship between the States and the Federal Government. * * * *Second*, determining the constitutionality of a particular state gun law requires finding answers to complex empirically based questions of a kind that legislatures are better able than courts to make. * * * Government regulation of the right to bear arms normally embodies a judgment that the regulation will help save lives. The determination whether a gun regulation is constitutional would thus almost always require the weighing of the constitutional right to bear arms against the "primary concern of every government—a concern for the safety and indeed the lives of its citizens." * * * *Third*, the ability of States to reflect local preferences and conditions—both key virtues of federalism—here has particular importance. * * * States and local communities have historically differed about the need for gun regulation as well as about its proper level.

I can find much in the historical record that shows that some Americans in some places at certain times thought it important to keep and bear arms for private self-defense. [But the historical] record is insufficient to say that the right to bear arms for private self-defense, as explicated by *Heller*, is fundamental in the sense relevant to the incorporation inquiry. * * * States and localities have consistently enacted firearms regulations, including regulations similar to those at issue here, throughout our Nation's history. Courts have repeatedly upheld such regulations. * * * [N]othing in 18th-, 19th-, 20th-, or 21st-century history shows a consensus that the right to private armed self-defense, as described in *Heller*, is "deeply rooted in this Nation's history or tradition" or is otherwise "fundamental." * * * With respect, I dissent.

POINTS FOR DISCUSSION

a. The Second Amendment

In *Heller*, the Court concluded that the Second Amendment protects an individual right to keep and bear arms for self-defense. The dissenting Justices disagreed, reasoning that the Amendment was designed to protect the states from federal over-reaching. If the dissenters had prevailed, then there likely would not have been any argument about whether the Amendment's protections were incorporated by the Fourteenth Amendment, because it would make no sense to apply a structural protection for the states as a limit on state action. (Similarly, it would make no sense to incorporate the Tenth Amendment, which "reserve[s]" powers to the states.) How much of the debate between the majority and the dissenting Justices in *McDonald* was over the proper approach to incorporation, and how much was over whether *Heller* was correctly decided?

b. Due Process

As we have seen, the Court has held that the Due Process Clause incorporates most of the provisions in the Bill of Rights, including provisions that are addressed to substance rather than procedure. For example, the Court has held that the Due Process Clause incorporates the First Amendment right to free speech, which protects speech even if the government provides fair procedures before an act of censorship. See *Gitlow v. New York*, 268 U.S. 652, 666 (1925). Accordingly, the Court in *McDonald* cited not only "incorporation" precedents, but also "substantive due process" precedents, and Justice Stevens explicitly stated that the case was about substantive due process. Keep this in mind when we consider fundamental rights and the doctrine of substantive due process in Chapter 2.

c. Privileges or Immunities

The petitioners urged the Court to conclude that the Privileges or Immunities Clause "protects all of the rights set out in the Bill of Rights, as well as some others," but the Court noted that the petitioners were "unable to identify the Clause's full scope." Justice Thomas agreed with the petitioners that the incorporation doctrine should be anchored in the Privileges or Immunities Clause, rather than the Due Process Clause. He relied in significant part on the views of the Fourteenth Amendment's chief congressional sponsors. But Representative Bingham and Senator Howard declared not only that the Fourteenth Amendment would apply the Bill of Rights to the states, but also that it would protect *unenumerated* fundamental rights from state infringement. Representative Bingham declared that it would protect the "inborn rights" of all citizens, 39th Cong. Globe 2542 (1866), and Senator Howard argued that it would protect the (unenumerated) rights that Justice Washington declared fundamental in *Corfield v. Coryell.*

Would the logical consequence of Justice Thomas's approach be, as the petitioners argued, that the Fourteenth Amendment protects some unenumerated fundamental rights—including, perhaps, the right to an abortion and other rights that, as we will see in Chapter 2, the Court has declared are fundamental? In a portion of his opinion that has been omitted here, Justice Thomas stated, "Because this case does not involve an unenumerated right, it is not necessary to resolve the question whether the [Privileges or Immunities] Clause protects such rights." He declared, however, that the "mere fact that the Clause does not expressly list the rights it protects does not render it incapable of principled judicial application. * * * To be sure, interpreting the Privileges or Immunities Clause may produce hard questions. But [I] believe those questions are more worthy of this Court's attention—and far more likely to yield discernable answers—than the substantive due process questions the Court has for years created on its own, with neither textual nor historical support." As we turn to the materials in the chapters that follow, consider the implications of Justice Thomas's view.

Executive Summary of This Chapter

Some early decisions of the Supreme Court invalidating state laws were based in part on theories of natural law, which hold that there are principles inherent in the natural order that limit the power of governments to act. *Calder v. Bull* (1798); *Fletcher v. Peck* (1810). This approach contrasts with the view that the only limits on governmental power derive from positive law, such as the Constitution and other laws affirmatively enacted through defined law-making processes. Other early decisions upheld governmental actions without considering whether they violated natural law. *Barron v. Baltimore* (1833).

Before the ratification of the Fourteenth Amendment, the Court held that the provisions in the Bill of Rights protecting individual liberty applied only to actions by the federal government, not by the states. *Barron v. Baltimore* (1833). However, the Court eventually held, in a series of cases, that the Due Process Clause of the Fourteenth Amendment effectively incorporated most of the provisions in the Bill of Rights, thus imposing their limits on the states, as well. *Wolf v. Colorado* (1949). This is known as the incorporation doctrine.

The Court has held that the Privileges or Immunities Clause of the Fourteenth Amendment limits the states from abridging only the privileges or immunities of national citizenship, not of state citizenship. *Slaughter-House Cases*

(1873). This view was long thought to render the Privileges or Immunities Clause largely superfluous. More recently, however, the Court has held that the Clause prohibits a state from distinguishing among its citizens, for purposes of eligibility for welfare benefits, on the basis of how long they have been citizens. *Saenz v. Roe* (1999).

POINT-COUNTERPOINT

Is it too late to question the incorporation doctrine?

POINT: GREGORY E. MAGGS

The "incorporation doctrine" says that the Due Process Clause of the Fourteenth Amendment protects many of the rights in the first eight Amendments from state interference. We have seen arguments for and against this doctrine. Without rehashing the dispute, let's suppose a majority of the Supreme Court has considered the matter and has concluded that the incorporation doctrine is an incorrect interpretation of the Fourteenth Amendment. Is it too late now for the Court to abolish the doctrine, given decades of precedent holding that the Fourteenth Amendment forbids states to abridge the freedom of speech, to conduct unreasonable searches and seizures, to deny a right of counsel in criminal cases, and so forth?

The answer, in my view, draws on the familiar distinction between matters of principle and practical considerations. While the Court might disagree with the incorporation doctrine as a matter of principle, it still might decide that practical considerations preclude completely overruling the doctrine. Put simply, even if the doctrine is wrong, reversing course after all these years might work hardships on people who have come to rely on it. This notion that practical considerations may limit principles runs throughout our nation's history. The Declaration of Independence itself cautions that "all experience hath shewn that mankind are more disposed to suffer, while evils are sufferable than to right themselves by abolishing the forms to which they are accustomed."

But even if practical considerations would dissuade the Court from entirely abandoning the incorporation doctrine, the Court still would have room to question it. Most importantly, the Court could decide not to extend the doctrine further. For example, the Court has not yet held that the Fourteenth Amendment incorporates the right to a grand jury indictment or the right to a jury trial in civil cases. Although the logic of the doctrine may dictate including these rights, Justices who disagree with the doctrine could decline to extend it so far without unsettling any expectations.

In addition, even without overruling the whole doctrine, the Court might decide to keep or overrule parts of the doctrine based on practical considerations. For instance, the Justices might conclude that the incorporation of the Free Exercise Clause should not be overruled because many people have relied on it; they have built places of worship, attended seminaries, and so forth. On the other hand, the Court might perceive that people have relied less on the Establishment Clause, and thus be more inclined to reject cases incorporating it.

But what the Court should not do is decide whether to overrule incorporation doctrine precedents based on substantive views about the rights at issue. For example, while the Justices might decide to preserve the right to counsel to avoid upsetting settled expectations, they should not decide to preserve this right merely because they consider it especially important and beneficial. That would be a question of policy, not practicality, and questions of policy are for others to decide.

COUNTERPOINT: PETER J. SMITH

Imagine that the legislature in the state in which you live enacts a statute that makes it a crime to question the divinity of Jesus Christ. The statute authorizes the police to search the home and private papers, without first obtaining a warrant, of any person who might possibly hold such beliefs. The statute also provides that a person convicted of violating the statute, after a trial with all of the procedural rights that we ordinarily expect criminal defendants to receive, shall be publicly flogged and then drawn and quartered. Imagine further that the statute is consistent with the state's constitution. Would the statute be constitutional? As we will see in later chapters, it seems clearly inconsistent with the Establishment, Free Exercise, and Speech clauses of the First Amendment; the Fourth Amendment's warrant requirement; and (probably) the Eighth Amendment's prohibition on cruel and unusual punishment. But in light of the Court's decision in *Barron v. Baltimore*, those provisions apply only to federal action. And the statute affords a defendant a fair trial before being deprived of life and liberty, in seeming compliance with the literal terms of the Due Process Clause of the Fourteenth Amendment. If not for the incorporation doctrine, therefore, the statute apparently would not violate the United States Constitution—a result that most people would find untenable. It is too late in the day, in other words, for abandonment of the incorporation doctrine.

This is not to say, however, that the incorporation doctrine is unassailable. The Due Process Clause of the Fourteenth Amendment, which seems on its face to promise only fair process, not substantive liberty, was an awkward textual anchor for the doctrine. And the process of selective incorporation is subject to criticism for lacking a clear standard for deciding which provisions in the Bill of Rights should apply to the states. But that does not mean that incorporation was misguided or illegitimate. There is ample historical evidence that the Framers of the Fourteenth Amendment intended the *Privileges or Immunities Clause* to incorporate at least the protections of the Bill of Rights; indeed, that clause, which seems to confer substantive liberties, is a natural vehicle for the incorporation of rights against the states. And the general terms of that clause also make clear by implication that the Framers were comfortable with the prospect that other actors—presumably the courts—would engage in a process of identifying and defining rights that are immune from state infringement.

As matters stand, however, the Court has chosen to base the incorporation of rights against the states on the Due Process Clause. And widespread acceptance of that choice tends to undermine the frequently expressed assertion that the doctrine of "substantive due process" is indefensible. As we will see in Chapter 2, the Court has interpreted the Due Process Clause to protect substantive liberties, wholly aside from the procedures that the state provides before depriving a person of them. If the Fourteenth Amendment is properly read to incorporate the protections for substantive liberty found in the Bill of Rights—such as the right to free speech—then the assertion that the Due Process Clause has nothing to do with "substance" falters. (We will return to this theme in the Point-Counterpoint after Chapter 2.) Incorporation, in other words, not only was defensible, but also strengthens the argument that the Due Process Clause protects substantive liberty, as well.

PART I

Due Process

Introduction

There are two Due Process Clauses in the Constitution. The Fifth Amendment, which (we saw in Chapter 1) applies to the federal government, provides that no person shall be "deprived of life, liberty, or property, without due process of law," and the Fourteenth Amendment provides that no State shall "deprive any person of life, liberty, or property, without due process of law."

As you can see, the Due Process Clauses are as vague as they are majestic. They do not provide concrete definitions of "liberty" and "property," and they promise, somewhat tautologically, only that persons will not be denied the process that is due. But these constitutional provisions have a deep historical pedigree. Magna Carta, a charter that English nobility forced King John to sign in 1215 to guarantee certain rights to his subjects, originally provided protections against arbitrary imprisonment and seizure, and subsequent versions of the charter referred to due process explicitly: "No man of what state or condition he be, shall be put out of

> **Go Online**
>
> You can view Magna Carta at the website of the National Archives at http://www.archives.gov/exhibits/featured-documents/magna-carta/.

his lands or tenements nor taken, nor disinherited, nor put to death, without he be brought to answer by due process of law." At a minimum, this concept means that the government cannot arbitrarily imprison a person or seize his property without first providing notice and an opportunity to be heard. In the next two chapters, we consider what else the concept means.

Substantive Due Process

The Due Process Clauses in the United States Constitution are the source of a dizzying array of constitutional doctrines. For example, the Court has tethered the constitutional requirements of notice before judgment and personal jurisdiction to the Due Process Clauses. And we saw in Chapter 1 how the Court has held that most of the protections in the Bill of Rights have been "incorporated" against state action by virtue of the Due Process Clause of the Fourteenth Amendment.

Notice that the Due Process Clauses refer to "liberty" and "property." Are the Clauses properly read to create and define rights inhering in those concepts? Or do they simply protect those concepts, elsewhere defined, from deprivation without adequate procedural protections, such as notice and an opportunity to be heard? In this part, we will focus on two principal doctrines that respond to these questions. "Procedural due process," which we will consider in Chapter 3, refers to the government's obligation to provide adequate procedural protections before depriving a person of some important interest. There is little doubt that, if nothing else, the Clauses impose this obligation, although (as we will see) there is much debate about when that obligation is triggered and what procedural protections actually are "due" when it is. The (somewhat oxymoronically named) doctrine of "substantive due process," which we will consider in this chapter, concerns the extent to which the "liberty" mentioned in the Due Process Clauses is protected from government deprivation, wholly aside from the fairness of the procedures that the government provides before the deprivation.

Although you might not have realized it at the time, we have already seen examples of both of these due process doctrines. Recall that the Court has held that the Due Process Clause of the Fourteenth Amendment "incorporates" most of the protections of the Bill of Rights. Some of those protections—such as the privilege against self-incrimination or the right to a trial by jury in a criminal case—seem quite clearly to be "procedural" in nature. When the Court held that those provisions of the Fifth and Sixth Amendments apply against the states through the force of the Due Process Clause, it effectively defined the process that is "due" when the state seeks to imprison or otherwise punish a person.

But other rights that the Court has held are incorporated through the Due Process Clause of the Fourteenth Amendment seem more like substantive forms of liberty than elaborations of the process that is due when the government seeks to deprive a person of liberty. As we will see in Chapters 8–11, for example, the First Amendment's rights of free speech and free exercise of religion cannot be abridged (except under rare circumstances) by state actors, because those protections have been incorporated through the Due Process Clause. But those rights now exist against state action wholly aside from the fairness of the procedure that the state supplies before it seeks to abridge them. (The state cannot, for example, imprison you solely because it disagrees with your political views, even if it provides you with a fair trial to show what views you actually hold.) These incorporation decisions effectively defined the "liberty" mentioned in the Due Process Clause, and in that sense were a form of "substantive due process." In this chapter, we consider just how far that doctrine extends.

As we saw in Chapter 1, the doctrine of incorporation was very controversial, at least for a time in the middle of the twentieth century. But even assuming that the Court was correct to conclude that the Due Process Clause applies the *explicit* protections for substantive liberty in the Bill of Rights—including the rights to free speech and free exercise of religion in the First Amendment—to state action, it does not necessarily follow that the Due Process Clause of the Fourteenth Amendment also protects forms of liberty that are *not* expressly enumerated in the constitutional text. Whether it does will be the focus of this chapter.

A. SUBSTANTIVE DUE PROCESS AND ECONOMIC LIBERTY

In Chapter 12, we will see that the Constitution provides some explicit protections for economic liberty. The Contract Clause limits the authority of states to "impair[ ] the Obligation of Contracts," and the Takings Clause imposes some constraints on the authority of the federal government (and, the Court has held, through incorporation the authority of the states) to take private property. Does the reference in the Due Process Clauses to "liberty" and "property" suggest broader protections for economic liberty?

The doctrine of substantive due process—and, in particular, the theory that the Due Process Clauses protect economic rights—is generally thought to have originated in the Court's infamous decision in *Dred Scott v. Sandford*, 60 U.S. 393 (1857). See David P. Currie, *The Constitution in the Supreme Court: Article IV and Federal Powers, 1836–64*, 1983 Duke L.J. 695, 735–36, and nn. 255–64. In that case, the Court considered the claim of a slave that he became free upon residing in the free state of Illinois and the free territory of Wisconsin, where he had been sent by his owner. In the course of its decision, the Court held that the Missouri Compromise, which abolished slavery in some of the territories, was unconstitutional. One part of its reasoning (the importance of which scholars debate) was the following:

> **Make the Connection**
> We will consider the Court's decision in *Dred Scott*, and in particular its role in the Constitution's evolution in its treatment of racial discrimination, in Chapter 5.

> [T]he rights of property are united with the rights of person, and placed on the same ground by the fifth amendment to the Constitution, which provides that no person shall be deprived of life, liberty, and property, without due process of law. And an act of Congress which deprives a citizen of the United States of his liberty or property, merely because he came himself or brought his property into a particular Territory of the United States, and who had committed no offence against the laws, could hardly be dignified with the name of due process of law.

Does this genesis of the doctrine of substantive due process taint it by association? Or are there good reasons to read the Due Process Clauses to protect (and define) a class of liberty and property that cannot be deprived even after a fair proceeding?

LOCHNER V. NEW YORK
198 U.S. 45 (1905)

MR. JUSTICE PECKHAM delivered the opinion of the Court.

[The New York Legislature enacted a law providing: "No employee shall be required or permitted to work in a biscuit, bread, or cake bakery or confectionery establishment more than sixty hours in any one week, or more than ten hours in any one day, unless for the purpose of making a shorter work day on the last day of the week; nor more hours in any one week than will make an average of ten hours per day for the number of days during such week in which such employee

FYI

One of Lochner's attorneys was Henry Weismann. Weismann was a former union official who played a leading role in getting New York to enact the 10-hour workday limit. He was thus arguing that the law that he had formerly supported was unconstitutional. For additional interesting facts about this case, including Weismann's early career as a terrorist bomber and the suggestion that the 10-hour workday law was largely supported by German-American bakers who wanted to drive Jewish bakers out of business, see David E. Bernstein, *The Story of Lochner v. New York: Impediment to the Growth of the Regulatory State*, in Constitutional Law Stories 325 (Michael C. Dorf ed., 2004).

shall work." Lochner was convicted of permitting an employee to work more than sixty hours during one week of work. He defended on the ground that the statute violated the Due Process Clause of the Fourteenth Amendment.]

The statute necessarily interferes with the right of contract between the employer and employees, concerning the number of hours in which the latter may labor in the bakery of the employer. The general right to make a contract in relation to his business is part of the liberty of the individual protected by the 14th Amendment of the Federal Constitution. *Allgeyer v. Louisiana*, 165 U. S. 578 (1897) * * * The right to purchase or to sell labor is part of the liberty protected by this amendment, unless there are circumstances which exclude the right. There are, however, certain powers, existing in the sovereignty of each state in the Union, somewhat vaguely termed police powers, the exact description and limitation of which have not been attempted by the courts. Those powers, broadly stated, and without, at present, any attempt at a more specific limitation, relate to the safety, health, morals, and general welfare of the public.

It must, of course, be conceded that there is a limit to the valid exercise of the police power by the state. [Otherwise] the 14th Amendment would have no efficacy and the legislatures of the states would have unbounded power, and it would be enough to say that any piece of legislation was enacted to conserve the morals, the health, or the safety of the people * * *. [In] every case that comes before this court, therefore, where legislation of this character is concerned, and where the protection of the Federal Constitution is sought, the question necessarily arises: Is this a fair, reasonable, and appropriate exercise of the police power of the state, or is it an unreasonable, unnecessary, and arbitrary interference with the right of the individual to his personal liberty, or to enter into those contracts in relation to labor which may seem to him appropriate or necessary for the support of himself and his family? Of course the liberty of contract relating to labor includes both parties to it. The one has as much right to purchase as the other to sell labor.

This is not a question of substituting the judgment of the court for that of the legislature. If the act be within the power of the state it is valid, although the judgment of the court might be totally opposed to the enactment of such a law. But the question would still remain: Is it within the police power of the state? and that question must be answered by the court.

The question whether this act is valid as a labor law, pure and simple, may be dismissed in a few words. There is no reasonable ground for interfering with the liberty of person or the right of free contract, by determining the hours of labor, in the occupation of a baker. There is no contention that bakers as a class are not equal in intelligence and capacity to men in other trades or manual occupations, or that they are not able to assert their rights and care for themselves without the protecting arm of the state, interfering with their independence of judgment and of action. * * * Viewed in the light of a purely labor law, with no reference whatever to the question of health, we think that a law like the one before us involves neither the safety, the morals, nor the welfare, of the public, and that the interest of the public is not in the slightest degree affected by such an act. The law must be upheld, if at all, as a law pertaining to the

> **Food for Thought**
>
> Do you agree with the Court that it is not substituting its judgment for that of the legislature? Does the Court defer at all to the legislature's judgments at issue here?

health of the individual engaged in the occupation of a baker. It does not affect any other portion of the public than those who are engaged in that occupation. Clean and wholesome bread does not depend upon whether the baker works but ten hours per day or only sixty hours a week. * * * The mere assertion that the subject relates, though but in a remote degree, to the public health, does not necessarily render the enactment valid. The act must have a more direct relation, as a means to an end, and the end itself must be appropriate and legitimate, before an act can be held to be valid which interferes with the general right of an individual to be free in his person and in his power to contract in relation to his own labor.

There is, in our judgment, no reasonable foundation for holding this to be necessary or appropriate as a health law to safeguard [the] health of the individuals who are following the trade of a baker. * * * To the common understanding the trade of a baker has never been regarded as an unhealthy one. * * * Some occupations are more healthy than others, but we think there are none which might not come under the power of the legislature to supervise and control the hours of working therein, if the mere fact that the occupation is not absolutely and perfectly healthy is to confer that right upon the legislative department of the government. * * * There must be more than the mere fact of the possible existence of some small amount of unhealthiness to warrant legislative interference with liberty. It is unfortunately true that labor, even in any department, may possibly carry with it the seeds of unhealthiness. But are we all, on that account, at the mercy of legislative majorities? A printer, a tinsmith, a locksmith, a carpenter, a cabinetmaker, a dry goods clerk, a bank's, a lawyer's, or a physician's clerk, or a clerk in almost any kind of business, would all come under the power of the legislature, on this assumption. No trade, no occupation, no mode of earning one's living, could escape this all-pervading power, and the acts of the legislature in limiting the hours of labor in all employments would be valid, although such limitation might seriously cripple the ability of the laborer to support himself and his family.

It is also urged, pursuing the same line of argument, that it is to the interest of the state that its population should be strong and robust, and therefore any legislation which may be said to tend to make people healthy must be valid as health laws, enacted under the police power. * * * Scarcely any law but might find shelter under such assumptions, and conduct, properly so called, as well as contract, would come under the restrictive sway of the legislature. Not only the hours of employees, but the hours of employers, could be regulated, and doctors, lawyers, scientists, all professional men, as well as athletes and artisans, could be forbidden to fatigue their brains and bodies by prolonged hours of exercise, lest the fighting strength of the state be impaired. We mention these extreme cases because the contention is extreme. * * * Statutes of the nature of that under review, limiting the hours in which grown and intelligent men may labor to earn their living, are mere meddlesome interferences with the rights of the individual, and they are not saved from condemnation by the claim that they are passed in the exercise of the police power and upon the subject of the health of the individual whose rights are interfered with, unless there be some fair ground, reasonable in and of itself, to say that there is material danger to the public health, or to the health of the employees, if the hours of labor are not curtailed.

This interference on the part of the legislatures of the several states with the ordinary trades and occupations of the people seems to be on the increase. * * * It is impossible for us to shut our eyes to the fact that many of the laws of this character, while passed under what is claimed to be the police power for the purpose of protecting the public health or welfare, are, in reality, passed from other motives. * * * It seems to us that the real object and purpose [of the challenged law] were simply to regulate the hours of labor between the master and his employees (all being men, *Sui juris*), in a private business, not dangerous in any degree to morals, or in any real and substantial degree to the health of the employees. Under such circumstances the freedom of master and

Definition

"*Sui juris*" means "[o]f full age and capacity." *Black's Law Dictionary* (10th ed. 2014).

employee to contract with each other in relation to their employment, and in defining the same, cannot be prohibited or interfered with, without violating the Federal Constitution. *Reversed.*

**Justice Oliver Wendell Holmes Jr.
(1841–1935)**
Library of Congress

MR. JUSTICE HOLMES dissenting.

This case is decided upon an economic theory which a large part of the country does not entertain. If it were a question whether I agreed with that theory, I should desire to study it further and long before making up my mind. But I do not conceive that to be my duty, because I strongly believe that my agreement or disagreement has nothing to do with the right of a majority to embody their opinions in law. It is settled by various decisions of this court that state constitutions and state laws may regulate life in many ways which we as legislators might think as injudicious, or if you like as tyrannical, as this, and which, equally with this, interfere with the liberty to contract. Sunday laws and usury laws are ancient examples. A more modern one is the prohibition of lotteries. The liberty of the citizen to do as he likes so long as he does not interfere with the liberty of others to do the same, which has been a shibboleth for some well-known writers, is interfered with by school laws, by the Post Office, by every state or municipal institution which takes his money for purposes thought desirable, whether he likes it or not. The 14th Amendment does not enact Mr. Herbert Spencer's Social Statics. [A] Constitution is not intended to embody a particular economic theory, whether of paternalism and the organic relation of the citizen to the state or of *laissez faire*. It is made for people of fundamentally differing views, and the accident of our finding certain opinions natural and familiar, or novel, and

FYI

Herbert Spencer was a British biologist, philosopher, and libertarian who argued that evolutionary theory provided a guiding principle for human society. He coined the term "survival of the fittest."

even shocking, ought not to conclude our judgment upon the question whether statutes embodying them conflict with the Constitution of the United States.

General propositions do not decide concrete cases. The decision will depend on a judgment or intuition more subtle than any articulate major premise. But I think that the proposition just stated, if it is accepted, will carry us far toward the end. Every opinion tends to become a law. I think that the word "liberty," in the 14th Amendment, is perverted when it is held to prevent the natural outcome of a dominant opinion, unless it can be said that a rational and fair man necessarily would admit that the statute proposed would infringe fundamental principles as they have been understood by the traditions of our people and our law. It does not need research to show that no such sweeping condemnation can be passed upon the statute before us. A reasonable man might think it a proper measure on the score of health. Men whom I certainly could not pronounce unreasonable would uphold it as a first installment of a general regulation of the hours of work. Whether in the latter aspect it would be open to the charge of inequality I think it unnecessary to discuss.

MR. JUSTICE HARLAN (with whom MR. JUSTICE WHITE and MR. JUSTICE DAY concurred) dissenting.

I take it to be firmly established that what is called the liberty of contract may, within certain limits, be subjected to regulations designed and calculated to promote the general welfare, or to guard the public health, the public morals, or the public safety. Granting, then, that there is a liberty of contract which cannot be violated even under the sanction of direct legislative enactment, but assuming [that] such liberty of contract is subject to such regulations as the state may reasonably prescribe for the common good and the well-being of society, what are the conditions under which the judiciary may declare such regulations to be in excess of legislative authority and void? [A] legislative enactment, Federal or state, is never to be disregarded or held invalid unless it be, beyond question, plainly and palpably in excess of legislative power. * * * If there be doubt as to the validity of the statute, that doubt must therefore be resolved in favor of its validity, and the courts must keep their hands off, leaving the legislature to meet the responsibility for unwise legislation.

It is plain that this statute was enacted in order to protect the physical well-being of those who work in bakery and confectionery establishments. It may be that the statute had its origin, in part, in the belief that employers and employees in such establishments were not upon an equal footing, and that the necessities of the latter often compelled them to submit to such exactions as unduly taxed their strength. Be this as it may, the statute must be taken as expressing the belief of the people of New York that, as a general rule, and in the case of the average man, labor in excess of sixty hours during a week in such establishments may endanger the health of those who thus labor. Whether or not this be wise legislation it is not the province of the court to inquire. [I]n determining the question of power to interfere with liberty of contract, the court may inquire whether the means devised by the state are germane to an end which may be lawfully accomplished and have a real or substantial relation to the protection of health, as involved in the daily work of the persons, male and female, engaged in bakery and confectionery establishments. But when this inquiry is entered upon I find it impossible, in view of common experience, to say that there is here no real or substantial relation between the means employed by the state and the end sought to be accomplished by its legislation.

[Justice Harlan cited research that demonstrated that bakers were often sleep deprived because of the long hours that they worked; suffered from bronchial problems because they constantly inhaled flour; were susceptible to disease because of exposure to extremes of heat and cold; and had shorter average life expectancies.] There are many reasons of a weighty, substantial character, based upon the experience of mankind, in support of the theory that, all things considered, more than ten hours' steady work each day, from week to week, in a bakery or confectionery establishment, may endanger the health and shorten the lives of the workmen, thereby diminishing their physical and mental capacity to serve the state and to provide for those dependent upon them. If such reasons exist that ought to be the end of this case, for the state is not amenable to the judiciary, in respect of its legislative enactments, unless such enactments are plainly, palpably, beyond all question, inconsistent with the Constitution of the United States.

POINTS FOR DISCUSSION

a. Substantive Due Process

The Court's approach in *Lochner* is referred to as substantive due process because it effectively concluded that there is a substantive component to the "liberty" protected by the Due Process Clause that cannot be deprived regardless of the adequacy of the process provided. Critics have chided the Court for ascribing substantive content to that term. Was that Justice Holmes's criticism? If the critics are correct, then is the Fourteenth Amendment's reference to "liberty" and "property" surplusage? Or do they refer to property and liberty established by state and federal common-law and statutory law? Without defining those terms, how does the Court even know if the Clause's protections are triggered?

b. Level of Scrutiny

What level of scrutiny did the Court apply to the challenged statute? Did it hold that a state categorically cannot regulate the number of hours that an employee can work, or instead that a state can do so only under certain circumstances? If the latter, then what might justify such state regulation? Contrast the Court's approach with Justice Harlan's approach. In his view, a state regulation must have a legitimate objective and be germane to that objective. Even assuming that the Court's test is too searching, why should a statute that fails Justice Harlan's test violate the Due Process Clause? His proposed test, after all, does not turn on the procedure followed in enacting the law. Should the Due Process Clause impose any limits on state legislative or regulatory, as opposed to judicial, action?

c. Judicial Role

We saw in Volume 1 that any time the Court invalidates a democratically enacted statute, it is presumptively acting in a counter-majoritarian fashion. Assuming (as most have) that the Court's approach in *Lochner* was problematic, is the problem that the Court was acting in such a fashion? That it was acting in that fashion in order to protect an unenumerated right? Or that the right that the Court chose to protect did not warrant constitutional protection?

In the three decades after *Lochner*, the Court invalidated dozens of laws and regulations on the ground that they violated economic rights protected by the Due Process Clauses. See Michael J. Phillips, *The Lochner Court, Myth and Reality: Substantive Due Process from the 1890s to the 1930s* 55 (2000). Most of the invalidated regulation was progressive-era legislation, at the state and federal level, that protected workers or fixed prices. In *Adair v. United States*, 208 U.S. 161 (1908), for example, the Court struck down a federal law that protected the right of employees to organize unions, and in *Coppage v. Kansas*, 236 U.S. 1 (1915), the Court invalidated a similar state law. To be sure, the Court also upheld many such regulations during this period. But there remained significant support on the Court for *Lochner*'s general approach; indeed, even in the cases that upheld state regulation, the reasoning did not always indicate a repudiation of *Lochner*'s approach. In *Muller v. Oregon*, 208 U.S. 412 (1908), for example, the Court upheld an Oregon law that limited the number of hours per day that women could work in factories and laundries. But the Court's rationale in that case—that "inherent differences between the two sexes" justified the regulation notwithstanding the decision in *Lochner*—was based less on a relaxation of the scrutiny given to regulation of the workplace than it was on a paternalistic view of women.

And not even that rationale always prevailed. In *Adkins v. Children's Hospital*, 261 U.S. 525 (1923), the Court struck down a law enacted by Congress providing for minimum wages for women and children in the District of Columbia. Justice Sutherland, writing for the majority of the Court, declared that the law impermissibly interfered with the "freedom of contract included within the guaranties of the due process clause of the Fifth Amendment." The Court stated that it was "no longer open to question" that "the right to contract about one's affairs is a part of the liberty of the individual protected by this clause." The Court continued: "Within this liberty are contracts of employment of labor. In making such contracts, generally speaking, the parties have an equal right to obtain from each other the best terms they can as the result of private bargaining." The law was inconsistent with this principle: "The law takes account of the necessities of only one party to the contract. It ignores the necessities of the employer by compelling him to pay not less than a certain sum, not only whether the employee is capable of earning it, but irrespective of the ability of his business to sustain the burden, generously leaving him, of course, the privilege of abandoning his business as an alternative for going on at a loss." Although the freedom of contract was "subject to a great variety of restraints," it was, the Court declared, "the general rule and restraint the exception, and the exercise of legislative authority to abridge it can be justified only by the existence of exceptional circumstances." Because the amount of the wage was unrelated to the employee's health, no such circumstances existed to justify the law. Chief Justice Taft and Justices Holmes and Sanford dissented.

In the 1930s, with the country facing the Great Depression, both the federal government and the states began more aggressively to regulate the market. Pressure built on the Court to change course. In *Nebbia v. New York*, 291 U.S. 502 (1934), the Court upheld an order issued by the New York Milk Control Board setting minimum and maximum retail prices for milk. The Board issued the order after the price of milk declined rapidly, creating the risk that farmers would not seek to produce it. In his opinion for the Court, Justice Roberts, who had usually been in the *Lochner* majority, declared that "a regulation valid for one sort of business, or in given circumstances, may be invalid for another sort, or for the same business under other circumstances, because the reasonableness of each regulation depends upon the relevant facts." But the test he proposed sounded more generous than the approach of the *Lochner* Court: "So

Make the Connection

In Volume 1, we considered how the Court changed course in its view of the scope of Congress's power to regulate pursuant to the Commerce Clause. The change that we considered there occurred simultaneously with the change that we take up here.

far as the requirement of due process is concerned, * * * a state is free to adopt whatever economic policy may reasonably be deemed to promote public welfare, and to enforce that policy by legislation adapted to its purpose. * * * If the laws passed are seen to have a reasonable relation to a proper legislative purpose, and are neither arbitrary nor discriminatory, the requirements of due process are satisfied."

Three years later, the Court explicitly repudiated the *Lochner* approach.

WEST COAST HOTEL CO. V. PARRISH
300 U.S. 379 (1937)

MR. CHIEF JUSTICE HUGHES delivered the opinion of the Court.

[A Washington statute required the payment of minimum wages to women and minors. Respondent, an employee of West Coast Hotel, brought suit to recover the difference between the wages she received and those required under state law. West Coast Hotel defended on the ground that the statute violated the Fourteenth Amendment, as interpreted in *Adkins*. The state Supreme Court upheld the statute.]

We are of the opinion that this ruling of the state court demands on our part a re-examination of the *Adkins* Case. The importance of the question, in which many states having similar laws are concerned, the close division by which the decision in the *Adkins* Case was reached, and the economic conditions which have supervened, and in the light of which the reasonableness of the exercise of the protective power of the state must be considered, make it not only appropriate, but we think imperative, that in deciding the present case the subject should receive fresh consideration.

In each case the violation alleged by those attacking minimum wage regulation for women is deprivation of freedom of contract. What is this freedom? The Constitution does not speak of freedom of contract. It speaks of liberty and prohibits the deprivation of liberty without due process of law. In prohibiting that deprivation, the Constitution does not recognize an absolute and uncontrollable liberty. Liberty in each of its phases has its history and connotation. But the liberty safeguarded is liberty in a social organization which requires the protection of law against the evils which menace the health, safety, morals, and welfare of the people. Liberty under the Constitution is thus necessarily subject to the restraints of due process, and regulation which is reasonable in relation to its subject and is adopted in the interests of the community is due process. This essential limitation of liberty in general governs freedom of contract in particular.

The minimum wage to be paid under the Washington statute is fixed after full consideration by representatives of employers, employees, and the public. It may be assumed that the minimum wage is fixed in consideration of the services that are performed in the particular occupations under normal conditions. Provision is made for special licenses at less wages in the case of women who are incapable of full service. The statement of Mr. Justice Holmes in the *Adkins* Case is pertinent: "This statute does not compel anybody to pay anything. It simply forbids employment at rates below those fixed as the minimum requirement of health and right living. It is safe to assume that women will not be employed at even the lowest wages allowed unless they earn them, or unless the employer's business can sustain the burden." 261 U.S. at 570. We think that the views thus expressed are sound and that the decision in the *Adkins* Case was a departure from the true application of the principles governing the regulation by the state of the relation of employer and employed. Those principles have been reenforced by our subsequent decisions. See *Nebbia v. New York*, 291 U.S. 502 (1934).

What can be closer to the public interest than the health of women and their protection from unscrupulous and overreaching employers? And if the protection of women is a legitimate end of the exercise of state power, how can it be said that the requirement of the payment of a minimum wage fairly fixed in order to meet the very necessities of existence is not an admissible means to that end? The Legislature of the state was clearly entitled to consider the situation of women in employment, the fact that they are in the class receiving the least pay, that their bargaining power is relatively weak, and that they are the ready victims of those who would take advantage of their necessitous circumstances. The Legislature was entitled to adopt measures to reduce the evils of the "sweating system," the exploiting of workers at wages so low as to be insufficient to meet the bare cost of living, thus making their very helplessness the occasion of a most injurious competition. The adoption of similar requirements by many states evidences a deepseated conviction both as to the presence of the evil and as to the means adapted to check it. Legislative response to that conviction cannot be regarded as arbitrary or capricious and that is all we have to decide. Even if the wisdom of the policy be regarded as debatable and its effects uncertain, still the Legislature is entitled to its judgment.

> **Make the Connection**
>
> The statute at issue here applied to women but not to men. Should the Court have found that the statute violated the Equal Protection Clause, on the ground that it discriminated against men or reflected a paternalistic view of women? We will consider such questions, and sex discrimination more generally, in Chapter 5.

There is an additional and compelling consideration which recent economic experience has brought into a strong light. The exploitation of a class of workers who are in an unequal position with respect to bargaining power and are thus relatively defenseless against the denial of a living wage is not only detrimental to their health and well being, but casts a direct burden for their support upon the community. What these workers lose in wages the taxpayers are called upon to pay. The bare cost of living must be met. We may take judicial notice of the unparalleled demands for relief which arose during the recent period of depression and still continue to an alarming extent despite the degree of economic recovery which has been achieved. * * * The community is not bound to provide what is in effect a subsidy for unconscionable employers.

Our conclusion is that the case of *Adkins* should be, and it is, overruled. The judgment of the Supreme Court of the state of Washington is affirmed.

MR. JUSTICE SUTHERLAND [joined by MR. JUSTICE VAN DEVANTER, MR. JUSTICE MCREYNOLDS, and MR. JUSTICE BUTLER, dissenting].

It is urged that the question involved should now receive fresh consideration, among other reasons, because of "the economic conditions which have supervened"; but the meaning of the Constitution does not change with the ebb and flow of economic events. We frequently are told in more general words that the Constitution must be construed in the light of the present. If by that it is meant that the Constitution is made up of living words that apply to every new condition which they include, the statement is quite true. But to say [that] the words of the Constitution mean today what they did not mean when written—that is, that they do not apply to a situation now to which they would have applied then—is to rob that instrument of the essential element which continues it in force as the people have made it until they, and not their official agents, have made it otherwise. * * * The judicial function is that of interpretation; it does not include the power of amendment under the guise of interpretation. * * * If the Constitution, intelligently and reasonably construed in the light of these principles, stands in the way of desirable legislation, the blame must rest upon that instrument, and not upon the court for enforcing it according to its terms. The remedy in that situation—and the only true remedy—is to amend the Constitution.

POINTS FOR DISCUSSION

a. The Basis of the Decision

Did the Court depart from *Adkins* because that case simply interpreted the Constitution incorrectly? Or because circumstances had changed sufficiently—with the onset of the Great Depression—that the government's interest in regulating was suddenly substantially more compelling? If the latter, would the Court have overruled *Adkins*, or merely distinguished it?

b.   Level of Scrutiny

Is the holding in *West Coast Hotel* that the liberty protected by the Due Process Clause does not embrace a freedom to contract? Or that the government may abridge that constitutionally protected freedom as long as the regulation reasonably relates to some legitimate governmental interest?

c.   Parallel Developments

At the same time that the Court was deciding finally to depart from *Lochner*'s approach, the Court was beginning to recognize broad congressional power to regulate pursuant to the Commerce Clause. Recall from Volume 1 that in *Jones & Laughlin Steel* and *Darby* the Court effectively applied the rational-basis test— essentially the same test that the Court applied in *West Coast Hotel*—to determine whether a statute fell within Congress's power to regulate pursuant to that clause. Recall as well that in early 1937 President Roosevelt announced his "Court-packing plan," which would have added a new seat on the Court for every Justice over age 70 who stayed on the bench, until the Court included fifteen members. If adopted, the plan would have enabled Roosevelt to dilute the votes of the members of the Court who were most committed to the *Lochner* line of cases (and to a narrow view of federal power). By the time of his proposal, the Court had already issued its decision in *West Coast Hotel*, and two months after Roosevelt announced the proposal it issued its decision in *Jones & Laughlin Steel*.

The Court's decision in *West Coast Hotel* signaled that the Court would no longer searchingly review ordinary social and economic regulation. But did that mean that such regulation would not be subject to any scrutiny under the Due Process Clause at all? In *United States v. Carolene Products Co.*, 304 U.S. 144 (1938), the Court upheld a federal statute that prohibited the shipment in interstate commerce of skim milk mixed with some fat or oil other than milk fat. The Court rejected the defendant's argument that the statute violated the Due Process Clause of the Fifth Amendment, reasoning that "regulatory legislation affecting ordinary commercial transactions is not to be pronounced unconstitutional unless in the light of the facts made known or generally assumed it is of such a character as to preclude the assumption that it rests upon some rational basis within the knowledge and experience of the legislators." This approach came to be known as "rational-basis review." As we will see shortly, rational-basis review is a very deferential form of judicial scrutiny.

The Court noted, however, that such a deferential approach might not always be appropriate. In footnote 4 of the opinion—perhaps the most famous footnote in Supreme Court history—Justice Stone stated:

> There may be narrower scope for operation of the presumption of constitutionality when legislation appears on its face to be within a specific prohibition of the Constitution, such as those of the first ten Amendments, which are deemed equally specific when held to be embraced within the Fourteenth. It is unnecessary to consider now whether legislation which restricts those political processes which can ordinarily be expected to bring about repeal of undesirable legislation, is to be subjected to more exacting judicial scrutiny under the general prohibitions of the Fourteenth Amendment than are most other types of legislation. [The Court cited cases concerning "restrictions upon the right to vote," "restraints upon the dissemination of information," "interferences with political organizations," and "prohibition of peaceable assembly."] Nor need we enquire whether similar considerations enter into the review of statutes directed at particular religious, *Pierce v. Society of Sisters*, 268 U.S. 510 (1925), or national, *Meyer v. Nebraska*, 262 U.S. 390 (1923), or racial minorities; whether prejudice against discrete and insular minorities may be a special condition, which tends seriously to curtail the operation of those political processes ordinarily to be relied upon to protect minorities, and which may call for a correspondingly more searching judicial inquiry. Compare *McCulloch v. Maryland*, 4 Wheat. 316, 428 (1803).

Footnote 4 suggested that heightened judicial scrutiny might be warranted when regulation "restricts those political processes which can ordinarily be expected to bring about repeal of undesirable legislation." This has come be known as the "political process" rationale for heightened judicial scrutiny of regulation. Why might judicial intervention be more justified in such cases? Does the footnote 4 approach properly respond to the defects of the Court's approach in the *Lochner* era? Does it correctly identify those cases that call for more aggressive judicial intervention?

If nothing else, the Court made clear in subsequent cases that judicial scrutiny under the Due Process Clause would be quite deferential when ordinary social and economic regulation is at issue. Consider the case that follows.

WILLIAMSON V. LEE OPTICAL OF OKLAHOMA, INC.
348 U.S. 483 (1955)

MR. JUSTICE DOUGLAS delivered the opinion of the Court.

[An Oklahoma statute prohibited any person not licensed as an optometrist or ophthalmologist from fitting, duplicating, or replacing lenses without a written prescription from a licensed ophthalmologist or optometrist. After an optician challenged the provision, the District Court held that the ban on fitting without a prescription was not "reasonably and rationally related to the health and welfare of the people," and that the ban on duplication without a prescription was "neither reasonably necessary nor reasonably related to the end sought to be achieved."]

In practical effect, [the challenged statute] means that no optician can fit old glasses into new frames or supply a lens * * *. The Oklahoma law may exact a needless, wasteful requirement in many cases. But it is for the legislature, not the courts, to balance the advantages and disadvantages of the new requirement. It appears that in many cases the optician can easily supply the new frames or new lenses without reference to the old written prescription. It also appears that many written prescriptions contain no directive data in regard to fitting spectacles to the face. But in some cases the directions contained in the prescription are essential, if the glasses are to be fitted so as to correct the particular defects of vision or alleviate the eye condition. The legislature might have concluded that the frequency of occasions when a prescription is necessary was sufficient to justify this regulation of the fitting of eyeglasses. Likewise, when it is necessary to duplicate a lens, a written prescription may or may not be necessary. But the legislature might have concluded that one was needed often enough to require one in every case. Or the legislature may have concluded that eye examinations were so critical, not only for correction of vision but also for detection of latent ailments or diseases, that every change in frames and every duplication of a lens should be accompanied by a prescription from a medical expert. To be sure, the present law does not require a new examination of the eyes every time the frames are changed or the lenses duplicated. * * * But the law need not be in every respect logically consistent with its aims to be constitutional. It is enough that there is an evil at hand for correction, and that it

> **Take Note**
>
> The Court offers a series of possible justifications for the law. Are they the ones that actually motivated the Oklahoma legislature? Does the Court require that the legislature even have thought of them? Can you think of any other reasons—including, perhaps, less admirable ones—why the legislature might have enacted the requirements in question?

might be thought that the particular legislative measure was a rational way to correct it.

The day is gone when this Court uses the Due Process Clause of the Fourteenth Amendment to strike down state laws, regulatory of business and industrial conditions, because they may be unwise, improvident, or out of harmony with a particular school of thought. [Reversed in relevant part.]

POINTS FOR DISCUSSION

a.   Rational-Basis Review

> **Make the Connection**
>
> In this chapter and in Chapters 5 and 6, we will see some cases in which the Court applies (or at least purports to apply) rational-basis review and yet invalidates a challenged regulation. When you read those cases—including *Romer v. Evans* and *Cleburne v. Cleburne Living Center*—consider whether the Court is adhering to the form of rational-basis review that the Court applied in *Williamson*.

The Court in *Williamson* applied what has come to be known as "rational-basis review" to the challenged statute. Over the years, the Court has articulated the standard in various ways; but the "general rule is that legislation is presumed to be valid and will be sustained" if the regulation is "rationally related to a legitimate state interest." *City of Cleburne v. Cleburne Living Center*, 473 U.S. 432, 440 (1985). This is a highly deferential form of review, and it virtually always results in a conclusion that the challenged regulation is valid. The Court has stated, for example, that "[w]e have returned to the original constitutional proposition that courts do not substitute their social and economic beliefs for the judgment of legislative bodies, who are elected to pass laws," regardless of whether the laws are "wise or unwise." *Ferguson v. Skrupa*, 372 US. 726, 730–32 (1963).

Should the Court have any role to play in reviewing regulation for rationality? Why does such a requirement flow from the Due Process Clause? Conversely, is rational-basis review unduly deferential to legislative action? Does the Court's approach in *Williamson* amount effectively to judicial abdication?

b.   "Legitimate Governmental Interest"

Notice that the Court in *Williamson* several times referred to what the legislature "*might have*concluded." Under rational-basis review, a court generally will not seek to determine the legislature's *actual* objective in enacting the challenged statute, but instead will judge it in light of *possible* objectives that the legislature might have sought to accomplish. See, e.g., *U.S. Railroad Retirement Board v. Fritz*, 449 U.S. 166 (1980). Indeed, courts will accept governmental interests that may well not have been on the minds of any of the legislators but that the government can articulate *post hoc* for the purposes of litigation. See, e.g., *Schweiker v. Wilson*, 450 U.S. 221 (1981).

Suppose that there had been strong evidence that the legislature had enacted the statute at issue in *Williamson* in order to create a monopoly for optometrists and ophthalmologists, after lobbyists for those professions showered the legislators with campaign contributions. Would it still be relevant that the statute arguably advances other legitimate governmental interests? Should the Court at least have inquired in *Williamson* whether the actual legislative objective was legitimate?

c.   "Reasonably Related"

Even assuming that the statute at issue in *Williamson* was designed to serve the interests that the Court identified, it was not a particularly effective measure to accomplish those ends, as it was both under- and over-inclusive. It was under-inclusive because, to the extent that the statute was designed to promote frequent eye exams, it did not actually require optometrists and ophthalmologists to conduct such exams when they fitted, duplicated, or replaced lenses. And it was over-inclusive because, to the extent that the statute was designed to ensure proper medical guidance to opticians, the prescription requirement applied even when the optician was merely duplicating an existing pair of lenses, which presumably had been prepared on the basis of a prescription. Yet the Court stated that "the law need not be in every respect logically consistent with its aims to be constitutional." Under this approach, is it possible to imagine a state regulation that would fail this prong of the rational-basis test?

Perspective and Analysis

For the last seventy years, most commentators have criticized *Lochner* and the use of substantive due process to protect economic rights. Professor Richard Epstein, however, has argued for a return to *Lochner*'s approach:

> *Lochner* may well have given *too much* scope to the police power * * *. [The police power] does not sanction wholesale interference with financial arrangements, such as is mandated by a minimum-wage law. These statutes can impose heavy burdens upon both employer and employee for the benefit of parties who are strangers to the relationship—organized labor, for example, whose members are in competition with nonunion workers. To uphold minimum-wage legislation may be to invite, in the name of the police power, the very rent-seeking that any theory of limited government is designed to avoid.

> **Richard A. Epstein, *Toward a Revitalization of the Contract Clause*, 51 U. Chi. L. Rev. 703, 713–15, 734 (1984).**

There are indications that judicial protection for economic rights is once again becoming more popular. See Thomas B. Colby & Peter J. Smith, *The Return of Lochner*, 100 Cornell L. Rev. 527 (2015). But it remains a minority view. Are "economic" rights any different from other forms of liberty that we have come to prize? The following section takes up that question.

B. SUBSTANTIVE DUE PROCESS AND FUNDAMENTAL RIGHTS

Notwithstanding the support of a few hearty commentators, *Lochner* has been subject to broad condemnation. But what exactly was wrong with the decision and the approach that it embodied? Is it that any judicial protection of rights not enumerated in the Constitution is tantamount to impermissible judicial legislation that reflects the judges' individual policy preferences rather than constitutional law as actually embodied in the Constitution's text? Or is the problem with *Lochner* not that it involved judicial protection for unenumerated rights, but rather that "the Court chose the wrong values to enforce, wrong in the sense that complete laissez-faire capitalism was neither required by the historical understanding of 'liberty,' nor did it meaningfully enhance the freedom of the vast majority of Americans in the industrialized age"? Laurence H. Tribe & Michael C. Dorf, *On Reading the Constitution* 65–67 (1991). Or is the problem simply that most modern commentators have different values? Consider what the cases that follow suggest about the defect (if any) of *Lochner*.

1. Prelude

Lochner and the cases that we considered earlier in this chapter concerned economic liberties, such as the freedom to contract. During the *Lochner* era, the Court also decided several cases that found protection in the Due Process Clauses for other forms of liberty, as well. In *Meyer v. Nebraska*, 262 U. S. 390 (1923), for example, the Court overturned the conviction of a parochial school teacher for violating a law prohibiting teaching in any language other than English. The Court stated that the liberty protected by the due process clause "denotes not merely freedom from bodily restraint but also the right of the individual to contract, to engage in any of the common occupations of life, to acquire useful knowledge, to marry, establish a home and bring up children, to worship God according to the dictates of his own conscience, and generally to enjoy those privileges long recognized at common law as essential to the orderly pursuit of happiness by free men." The Court held that the state had shown no justification for interference with "the calling of modern language teachers, with the opportunities of pupils to acquire knowledge, and with the power of parents to control the education of their own." The following case, also decided during the *Lochner* era, elaborated on this view of the Due Process Clause.

PIERCE V. SOCIETY OF THE SISTERS
268 U.S. 510 (1925)

MR. JUSTICE MCREYNOLDS delivered the opinion of the Court.

[Two private schools in Oregon—one a parochial school and the other an independent school—challenged an Oregon law that required children between 8 and 16 years old to attend public school.]

The inevitable practical result of enforcing the act under consideration would be destruction of appellees' primary schools, and perhaps all other private primary schools for normal children within the state of Oregon. Appellees are engaged in a kind of undertaking not inherently harmful, but long regarded as useful and meritorious. Certainly there is nothing in the present records to indicate that they have failed to discharge their obligations to patrons, students, or the state. And there are no peculiar circumstances or present emergencies which demand extraordinary measures relative to primary education.

> **Food for Thought**
> The plaintiffs in *Pierce* were private schools that were affected by the challenged law. But according to the Court, the "right" invaded by the statute belonged to the parents of the children that the schools hoped to enroll. Should the Court have concluded that these plaintiffs lacked standing to assert the rights of others? Or did the Court conclude that the schools have a protected right, as well?

Under the doctrine of *Meyer v. Nebraska*, 262 U. S. 390 (1923), we think it entirely plain that the Act of 1922 unreasonably interferes with the liberty of parents and guardians to direct the upbringing and education of children under their control. As often heretofore pointed out, rights guaranteed by the Constitution may not be abridged by legislation which has no reasonable relation to some purpose within the competency of the state. The fundamental theory of liberty upon which all governments in this Union repose excludes any general power of the state to standardize its children by forcing them to accept instruction from public teachers only. The child is not the mere creature of the state; those who nurture him and direct his destiny have the right, coupled with the high duty, to recognize and prepare him for additional obligations.

Generally, it is entirely true, as urged by counsel, that no person in any business has such an interest in possible customers as to enable him to restrain exercise of proper power of the state upon the ground that he will be deprived of patronage. But the injunctions here sought are not against the exercise of any proper power. Appellees asked protection against arbitrary, unreasonable, and unlawful interference with their patrons and the consequent destruction of their business and property. Their interest is clear and immediate. * * *

POINTS FOR DISCUSSION

a.   Level of Scrutiny

The Court appeared to hold that the Act had no reasonable relation to any legitimate state interest. What do you think the state's purpose was in enacting the statute? Is that purpose obviously illegitimate? If not, how could the statute fail the test that the Court proposed? Is the Court's real point that there are some rights that are simply beyond the competency of the state to regulate, regardless of how "reasonable" the regulation is? Or is it instead that it would take a much more compelling state interest to justify the abridgement of those rights?

b.   Fundamental Right

What is the "fundamental theory of liberty" to which the Court referred? Where does it come from? Would this theory of liberty permit the state to require all children to receive schooling, regardless of the setting in which they receive it? If so, why is it problematic to require that all children be educated in public schools?

c.   *Lochner* Redux?

Justice McReynolds wrote the opinion in *Pierce* (and *Meyer*) during the *Lochner* era. (Indeed, we saw earlier in this chapter, in his dissent in *Nebbia* and his position in *West Coast Hotel*, that Justice McReynolds was deeply committed to the *Lochner* line of cases.) Is there a difference between concluding that the Due Process Clause protects economic liberties such as the freedom to contract, on the one hand, and other forms of personal liberty, such as the right to make choices about child-rearing, on the other? If *Lochner* is indefensible, then is *Pierce* necessarily indefensible, too?

Recall that the Court effectively overruled *Lochner* in 1937 in *West Coast Hotel*. In so doing, did the Court also completely repudiate the view that the Due Process Clause protects some substantive definition of liberty wholly aside from the fairness of the process that precedes its deprivation?

In the case that follows, the Court relied on the Equal Protection Clause to invalidate a state law providing for the forced sterilization of felons convicted for the third time of crimes involving "moral turpitude." The Court had previously upheld a statute providing that "the health of the patient and the welfare of society may be promoted in certain cases by the sterilization of mental defectives" held in state institutions. In *Buck v. Bell*, 274 U.S. 200 (1927), Justice Holmes, writing for the Court, rejected the argument that forced sterilization can never be justified:

> We have seen more than once that the public welfare may call upon the best citizens for their lives. It would be strange if it could not call upon those who already sap the strength of the State for these lesser sacrifices, often not felt to be such by those concerned, in order to prevent our being swamped with incompetence. It is better for all the world, if instead of waiting to execute degenerate offspring for crime, or to let them starve for their imbecility, society can prevent those who are manifestly unfit from continuing their kind. * * * Three generations of imbeciles are enough.

Justice Holmes rejected the petitioner's equal protection claim as the "usual last resort of constitutional arguments." We will consider the Equal Protection Clause, which generally speaking prohibits some forms of government classification, in Chapters 4–6. For the time being, consider whether the Court's conclusion in the case that follows is really about the government's general obligation to treat similarly situated persons the same, or is instead about individual liberty that cannot be abridged even when done even-handedly.

SKINNER V. OKLAHOMA

316 U.S. 535 (1942)

MR. JUSTICE DOUGLAS delivered the opinion of the Court.

This case touches a sensitive and important area of human rights. Oklahoma deprives certain individuals of a right which is basic to the perpetuation of a race—the right to have offspring. [The Oklahoma Habitual Criminal Sterilization Act] defines an "habitual criminal" as a person who, having been convicted two or more times for crimes "amounting to felonies involving moral turpitude," is thereafter convicted of such a felony in Oklahoma and is sentenced to a term of imprisonment in an Oklahoma penal institution. Machinery is provided for the institution by the Attorney General of a proceeding against such a person in the Oklahoma courts for a judgment that such person shall be rendered sexually sterile. * * * If [after notice and an opportunity to be heard] the court or jury finds that the defendant is an "habitual criminal" and that he "may be rendered sexually sterile without detriment to his or her general health," then the court "shall render judgment to the effect that said defendant be rendered sexually sterile." [The Act also] provides that "offenses arising out of the violation of the prohibitory laws, revenue acts, embezzlement, or political offenses, shall not come or be considered within the terms of this Act."

[Between 1926 and 1934, petitioner was convicted once of stealing chickens and twice of robbery with fire arms. In 1936, the Attorney General instituted proceedings against him, and the Oklahoma Supreme Court ultimately affirmed a judgment directing that the petitioner be sterilized.]

Several objections to the constitutionality of the Act have been pressed upon us. It is urged that the Act cannot be sustained as an exercise of the police power in view of the state of scientific authorities respecting inheritability of criminal traits. It is argued that due process is lacking because under this Act, unlike the act upheld in *Buck v. Bell*, 274 U.S. 200 (1927), the defendant is given no opportunity to be heard on the issue as to whether he is the probable potential parent of socially undesirable offspring. It is also suggested that the Act is penal in character and that the sterilization provided for is cruel and unusual punishment and violative of the Fourteenth Amendment. We pass those points without intimating an opinion on them, for there is a feature of the Act which clearly condemns it. That is its failure to meet the requirements of the equal protection clause of the Fourteenth Amendment.

We do not stop to point out all of the inequalities in this Act. A few examples will suffice. * * * A clerk who appropriates over $20 from his employer's till and a stranger who steals the same amount are [both] guilty of felonies. If the latter repeats his act and is convicted three times, he may be sterilized. But the clerk is not subject to the pains and penalties of the Act no matter how large his embezzlements nor how frequent his convictions. * * * Whether a particular act is larceny by fraud or embezzlement [turns] not on the intrinsic quality of the act but on when the felonious intent arose.

[If] we had here only a question as to a State's classification of crimes, such as embezzlement or larceny, no substantial federal question would be raised. * * * For a State is not constrained in the exercise of its police power to ignore experience which marks a class of offenders or a family of offenses for special treatment. Nor is it prevented by the equal protection clause from confining "its restrictions to those classes of cases where the need is deemed to be clearest." *Miller v. Wilson*, 236 U.S. 373, 384 (1915). * * *

But [w]e are dealing here with legislation which involves one of the basic civil rights of man. Marriage and procreation are fundamental to the very existence and survival of the race. The power to sterilize, if exercised, may have subtle, far reaching and devastating effects. In evil or reckless hands it can cause races or types which are inimical to the dominant group to wither and disappear. There is no redemption for the individual whom the law touches. Any experiment which the State conducts is to his irreparable injury. He is forever deprived of a basic liberty. We mention these matters not to reexamine the scope of the police power of the States. We advert to them merely in emphasis of our view that strict scrutiny of the classification which a State makes in a sterilization law is essential, lest unwittingly or otherwise invidious discriminations are made against groups or types of individuals in violation of the constitutional guaranty of just and equal laws.

> **Food for Thought**
>
> If the Constitution protects a "basic liberty" to reproduce, then why is the Equal Protection Clause relevant? Could the state avoid the defect that the Court finds here by providing for sterilization as a punishment for *all* crimes? If not, then what does that suggest about the Court's equal protection argument?

When the law lays an unequal hand on those who have committed intrinsically the same quality of offense and sterilizes one and not the other, it has made as invidious a discrimination as if it had selected a particular race or nationality for oppressive treatment. Sterilization of those who have thrice committed grand larceny with immunity for those who are embezzlers is a clear, pointed, unmistakable discrimination. Oklahoma makes no attempt to say that he who commits larceny by trespass or trick or fraud has biologically inheritable traits which he who commits embezzlement lacks. * * * We have not the slightest basis for inferring that [Oklahoma's line between larceny by fraud and embezzlement] has any significance in eugenics nor that the inheritability of criminal traits follows the neat legal distinctions which the law has marked between those two offenses.

* * * The equal protection clause would indeed be a formula of empty words if such conspicuously artificial lines could be drawn. * * * If such a classification were permitted, [a common-law distinction] could readily become a rule of human genetics. Reversed.

MR. CHIEF JUSTICE STONE concurring.

I concur in the result, but I am not persuaded that we are aided in reaching it by recourse to the equal protection clause. If Oklahoma may resort generally to the sterilization of criminals on the assumption that their propensities are transmissible to future generations by inheritance, I seriously doubt that the equal protection clause requires it to apply the measure to all criminals in the first instance, or to none.

* * * I think the real question we have to consider is not one of equal protection, but whether the wholesale condemnation of a class to such an invasion of personal liberty, without opportunity to any individual to show that his is not the type of case which would justify resort to it, satisfies the demands of due process.

Although petitioner here was given a hearing to ascertain whether sterilization would be detrimental to his health, he was given none to discover whether his criminal tendencies are of an inheritable type. Undoubtedly a state may, after appropriate inquiry, constitutionally interfere with the personal liberty of the individual to prevent the transmission by inheritance of his socially injurious tendencies. *Buck v. Bell*, 274 U.S. 200 (1927). But until now we have not been called upon to say that it may do so without giving him a hearing and opportunity to challenge the existence as to him of the only facts which could justify so drastic a measure.

MR. JUSTICE JACKSON, concurring.

There are limits to the extent to which a legislatively represented majority may conduct biological experiments at the expense of the dignity and personality and natural powers of a minority—even those who have been guilty of what the majority define as crimes. But this Act falls down before reaching this problem, which I mention only to avoid the implication that such a question may not exist because not discussed. On it I would also reserve judgment.

POINTS FOR DISCUSSION

a. Historical Context

This case was decided in 1942, when the United States was beginning to learn about the extent of the atrocities that were being committed by the Nazis in Germany in the name of "eugenics" and the "science" of racial purity and superiority. Until this point, however, eugenics—that is, the "science" of improving the hereditary qualities of a race or breed by controlling reproduction—was not the subject of universal disapproval, and in fact had the support of prominent figures such as Woodrow Wilson. The Court made no reference in its opinion to events abroad. But would it have been appropriate for the Court to consider the Nazi example in construing the Constitution in 1942?

b. Other Possible Bases for the Decision

The Court appeared to indicate that it is not the enforced sterilization of criminals *per se* that is unconstitutional, but rather the different treatment accorded to persons convicted of similar crimes. Should the Court have concluded—as the petitioner argued—that sterilization is a cruel and unusual punishment in violation of the Eighth Amendment? Or that it violates a protected liberty interest in reproduction? Was the Court's decision really based on the Equal Protection Clause?

c. Precedent

The Court in *Skinner* did not purport to overrule *Buck*. Instead, it stated:

"In *Buck v. Bell*, the Virginia statute was upheld though it applied only to feebleminded persons in institutions of the State. But it was pointed out that "so far as the operations enable those who otherwise must be kept confined to be returned to the world, and thus open the asylum to others, the equality aimed at will be more nearly reached." 274 U.S. at 208. Here there is no such saving feature. Embezzlers are forever free. Those who steal or take in other ways are not."

Is this a sensible ground for distinguishing *Buck*? Are Chief Justice Stone's grounds for distinguishing *Buck* any more convincing?

d. Procedural v. Substantive Due Process

Chief Justice Stone reasoned that the Oklahoma statute failed to accord adequate procedural protection to persons subject to the penalty of sterilization. We discuss arguments of this kind—usually called, somewhat redundantly, "procedural due process" arguments—in Chapter 3. Justice Jackson suggested that the statute might have been constitutionally problematic even if more process had been afforded, and wholly aside from any classifications that the statute created. There are hints of this view in the Court's opinion, as well. Putting aside for a moment the equal protection rationale, which view is a more defensible basis for the decision?

2.   Contraception and Abortion

Skinner at least suggested that, notwithstanding the repudiation of *Lochner*, the Court might continue to interpret the Due Process Clauses to protect some substantive spheres of liberty. In the cases that follow, the Court considered claims of personal autonomy in intimate relationships.

GRISWOLD V. CONNECTICUT
381 U.S. 479 (1965)

MR. JUSTICE DOUGLAS delivered the opinion of the Court.

Appellant Griswold is Executive Director of the Planned Parenthood League of Connecticut. Appellant Buxton is a licensed physician and a professor at the Yale Medical School who served as Medical Director for the League at its Center in New Haven. * * * They gave information, instruction, and medical advice to *married persons* as to the means of preventing conception. * * * [They were convicted and fined $100 as accessories to the violation of § 53–32 of the General Statutes of Connecticut, which provided: "Any person who uses any drug, medicinal article or instrument for the purpose of preventing conception shall be fined not less than fifty dollars or imprisoned not less than sixty days nor more than one year or be both fined and imprisoned." (An accessory is someone "who aids or contributes in the commission or concealment of a crime." *Black's Law Dictionary* (10th ed. 2014).) The state appellate courts affirmed the convictions notwithstanding appellants' claim that the statute as applied violated the Fourteenth Amendment.]

[W]e are met with a wide range of questions that implicate the Due Process Clause of the Fourteenth Amendment. Overtones of some arguments suggest that *Lochner v. New York* should be our guide. But we decline that invitation as we did in *West Coast Hotel Co. v. Parrish*. We do not sit as a super-legislature to determine the wisdom, need, and propriety of laws that touch economic problems, business affairs, or social conditions. This law, however, operates directly on an intimate relation of husband and wife and their physician's role in one aspect of that relation.

The association of people is not mentioned in the Constitution nor in the Bill of Rights. The right to educate a child in a school of the parents' choice—whether public or private or parochial—is also not mentioned. Nor is the right to study any particular subject or any foreign language. Yet [b]y *Pierce v. Society of Sisters*, the

[handwritten margin note: Doesn't want to read a right into the Const.]

right to educate one's children as one chooses is made applicable to the States by the force of the First and Fourteenth Amendments. By *Meyer v. State of Nebraska*, the same dignity is given the right to study the German language in a private school. In other words, the State may not, consistently with the spirit of the First Amendment, contract the spectrum of available knowledge. The right of freedom of speech and press includes not only the right to utter or to print, but the right to distribute, the right to receive, the right to read and freedom of inquiry, freedom of thought, and freedom to teach. * * * Without those peripheral rights the specific rights would be less secure. And so we reaffirm the principle of the *Pierce* and the *Meyer* cases.

> **Take Note**
>
> Do you agree that in *Pierce* and *Meyer* the Court relied on the First Amendment as incorporated by the Fourteenth Amendment? If it did, is that a more defensible basis for those decisions than the more general claim that the "liberty" protected by the Due Process Clause includes the right to raise children or study foreign languages?

The foregoing cases suggest that specific guarantees in the Bill of Rights have penumbras, formed by emanations from those guarantees that help give them life and substance. Various guarantees create zones of privacy. The right of association contained in the penumbra of the First Amendment is one, as we have seen. The Third Amendment in its prohibition against the quartering of soldiers "in any house" in time of peace without the consent of the owner is another facet of that privacy. The Fourth Amendment explicitly affirms the "right of the people to be secure in their persons, houses, papers, and effects, against unreasonable searches and seizures." The Fifth Amendment in its Self-Incrimination Clause enables the citizen to create a zone of privacy which government may not force him to surrender to his detriment. The Ninth Amendment provides: "The enumeration in the Constitution, of certain rights, shall not be construed to deny or disparage others retained by the people." * * * We have had many controversies over these penumbral rights of "privacy and repose." See, *e.g.*, *Skinner v. Oklahoma*, 316 U.S. 535, 541 (1942). These cases bear witness that the right of privacy which presses for recognition here is a legitimate one.

The present case, then, concerns a relationship lying within the zone of privacy created by several fundamental constitutional guarantees. And it concerns a law which, in forbidding the use of contraceptives rather than regulating their manufacture or sale, seeks to achieve its goals by means having a maximum destructive impact upon that relationship. Such a law cannot stand in light of the familiar principle, so often applied by this Court, that a "governmental purpose to control or prevent activities constitutionally subject to state regulation may not be achieved by means which sweep unnecessarily broadly and thereby invade the area of protected freedoms." *NAACP v. Alabama*, 377 U.S. 288, 307 (1964). Would we allow the police to search the sacred precincts of marital bedrooms for telltale signs of the use of contraceptives? The very idea is repulsive to the notions of privacy surrounding the marriage relationship.

We deal with a right of privacy older than the Bill of Rights—older than our political parties, older than our school system. Marriage is a coming together for better or for worse, hopefully enduring, and intimate to the degree of being sacred. It is an association that promotes a way of life, not causes; a harmony in living, not political faiths; a bilateral loyalty, not commercial or social projects. Yet it is an association for as noble a purpose as any involved in our prior decisions. [Reversed.]

MR. JUSTICE GOLDBERG, whom THE CHIEF JUSTICE and MR. JUSTICE BRENNAN join, concurring.

I agree with the Court that Connecticut's birth-control law unconstitutionally intrudes upon the right of marital privacy, and I join in its opinion and judgment. Although I have not accepted the view that "due process" as used in the Fourteenth Amendment includes all of the first eight Amendments * * *, I do agree that the concept of liberty protects those personal rights that are fundamental, and is not confined to the specific terms of the Bill of Rights. My conclusion that the concept of liberty is not so restricted and that it embraces the right of marital privacy though that right is not mentioned explicitly in the Constitution is supported both by numerous decisions of this Court, referred to in the Court's opinion, and by the language and history of the Ninth Amendment. * * * This Court, in a series of decisions, has held that the Fourteenth Amendment absorbs and applies to the States those specifics of the first eight amendments which express fundamental personal rights. The language and history of the Ninth Amendment reveal that the Framers of the Constitution believed that there are additional fundamental rights, protected from governmental infringement, which exist alongside those fundamental rights specifically mentioned in the first eight constitutional amendments.

The Ninth Amendment reads, "The enumeration in the Constitution, of certain rights, shall not be construed to deny or disparage others retained by the people." The Amendment is almost entirely the work of James Madison. It was introduced in Congress by him and passed the House and Senate with little or no debate and virtually no change in language. It was proffered to quiet expressed fears that a bill of specifically enumerated rights could not be sufficiently broad to cover all essential rights and that the specific mention of certain rights would be interpreted as a denial that others were protected. In presenting the proposed Amendment, Madison said:

> "It has been objected also against a bill of rights, that, by enumerating particular exceptions to the grant of power, it would disparage those rights which were not placed in that enumeration; and it might follow by implication, that those rights which were not singled out, were intended to be assigned into the hands of the General Government, and were consequently insecure. This is one of the most plausible arguments I have ever heard urged against the admission of a bill of rights into this system; but, I conceive, that it may be guarded against. I have attempted it, as gentlemen may see by turning to the last clause of [the proposed Ninth Amendment]." I Annals of Congress 439 (Gales and Seaton ed. 1834).

While this Court has had little occasion to interpret the Ninth Amendment, "it cannot be presumed that any clause in the constitution is intended to be without effect." *Marbury v. Madison*, 1 Cranch 137, 174 (1803). * * * To hold that a right so basic and fundamental and so deep-rooted in our society as the right of privacy in marriage may be infringed because that right is not guaranteed in so many words by the first eight amendments to the Constitution is to ignore the Ninth Amendment and to give it no effect whatsoever.

[I] do not mean to imply that the Ninth Amendment is applied against the States by the Fourteenth. Nor do I mean to state that the Ninth Amendment constitutes an independent source of rights protected from infringement by either the States or the Federal Government. Rather, [the] Ninth Amendment simply shows the intent of the Constitution's authors that other fundamental personal rights should not be denied such protection or disparaged in any other way simply because they are not specifically listed in the first eight constitutional amendments.

In determining which rights are fundamental, judges are not left at large to decide cases in light of their personal and private notions. Rather, they must look to the "traditions and collective conscience of our people" to determine whether a principle is "so rooted there as to be ranked as fundamental."

> **Food for Thought**
>
> Does Justice Goldberg's opinion provide any real guidance in determining what rights should be deemed fundamental? Is it helpful to refer to "the traditions and collective conscience of our people" and "fundamental principles of liberty and justice"? Is the Court the most sensible institution to give content to such broad concepts?

Snyder v. Massachusetts, 291 U.S. 97, 105 (1934). The inquiry is whether a right involved is of such a character that it cannot be denied without violating those "fundamental principles of liberty and justice which lie at the base of all our civil and political institutions." *Powell v. State of Alabama*, 287 U.S. 45, 67 (1932).

Make the Connection

The level of scrutiny of the Connecticut law that Justice Goldberg urges here is known as "strict scrutiny," which generally requires the state to demonstrate that the challenged law or policy serves a compelling governmental interest and is narrowly tailored to advance that interest. We will consider strict scrutiny again when we discuss the Equal Protection Clause in Chapters 4–6.

I agree fully with the Court that, applying these tests, the right of privacy is a fundamental personal right, emanating "from the totality of the constitutional scheme under which we live." * * * [W]here fundamental personal liberties are involved, * * * "the State may prevail only upon showing a subordinating interest which is compelling," [and by showing that the] law is "necessary, and not merely rationally related to, the accomplishment of a permissible state policy." Although the Connecticut birth-control law obviously encroaches upon a fundamental personal liberty, the State [has not met this standard.]

MR. JUSTICE HARLAN, concurring in the judgment.

I fully agree with the judgment of reversal, but find myself unable to join the Court's opinion. The reason is that it seems to me to evince an approach to this case very much like that taken by my Brothers BLACK and STEWART in dissent, namely: the Due Process Clause of the Fourteenth Amendment does not touch this Connecticut statute unless the enactment is found to violate some right assured by the letter or penumbra of the Bill of Rights.

In my view, the proper constitutional inquiry in this case is whether this Connecticut statute infringes the Due Process Clause of the Fourteenth Amendment because the enactment violates basic values "implicit in the concept of ordered liberty," *Palko v. Connecticut*, 302 U.S. 319, 325 (1937). For reasons stated at length in my dissenting opinion in *Poe v. Ullman*, 367 US. 497 (1961), I believe that it does. While the relevant inquiry may be aided by resort to one or more of the provisions of the Bill of Rights, it is not dependent on them or any of their radiations. The Due Process Clause of the Fourteenth Amendment stands, in my opinion, on its own bottom.

[Justices Black and Stewart rest on] the thesis that by limiting the content of the Due Process Clause of the Fourteenth Amendment to the protection of rights which can be found elsewhere in the Constitution, in this instance in

---

FYI

We provide excerpts from Justice Harlan's dissenting opinion in *Poe v. Ullman* in the Points for Discussion after the case.

[handwritten margin note:] 14th amendment + Due Process

the Bill of Rights, judges will thus be confined to "interpretation" of specific constitutional provisions, and will thereby be restrained from introducing their own notions of constitutional right and wrong into the "vague contours of the Due Process Clause." *Rochin v. People of State of California*, 342 U.S. 165, 170 (1952). While I could not more heartily agree that judicial "self restraint" is an indispensable ingredient of sound constitutional adjudication, I do submit that the formula suggested for achieving it is more hollow than real. "Specific" provisions of the Constitution, no less than "due process," lend themselves as readily to "personal" interpretations by judges whose constitutional outlook is simply to keep the Constitution in supposed "tune with the times." Judicial self-restraint * * * will be achieved in this area, as in other constitutional areas, only by continual insistence upon respect for the teachings of history, solid recognition of the basic values that underlie our society, and wise appreciation of the great roles that the doctrines of federalism and separation of powers have played in establishing and preserving American freedoms.

MR. JUSTICE WHITE, concurring in the judgment.

An examination of the justification offered [for the statute] cannot be avoided by saying that the Connecticut anti-use statute invades a protected area of privacy and association or that it demeans the marriage relationship. [S]uch statutes, if reasonably necessary for the effectuation of a legitimate and substantial state interest, and not arbitrary or capricious in application, are not invalid under the Due Process Clause.

The State claims but one justification for its anti-use statute. * * * The statute is said to serve the State's policy against all forms of promiscuous or illicit sexual relationships, be they premarital or extramarital, concededly a permissible and legitimate legislative goal. * * * I wholly fail to see how the ban on the use of contraceptives by married couples in any way reinforces the State's ban on illicit sexual relationships. * * * Perhaps the theory is that the flat ban on use

> **Take Note**
>
> What level of scrutiny does Justice White apply to this law? Under that level of scrutiny, does Justice White accord sufficient deference to the legislature's judgment?

prevents married people from possessing contraceptives and without the ready availability of such devices for use in the marital relationship, there will be no or less temptation to use them in extramarital ones. * * * At most the broad ban is of marginal utility to the declared objective. A statute limiting its prohibition on use to persons engaging in the prohibited relationship would serve the end posited by Connecticut in the same way, and with the same effectiveness, or ineffectiveness, as the broad anti-use statute under attack in this case. I find nothing in this record justifying the sweeping scope of this statute, with its telling effect on the freedoms of married persons, and therefore conclude that it deprives such persons of liberty without due process of law.

MR. JUSTICE BLACK, with whom MR. JUSTICE STEWART joins, dissenting.

There is no single one of the graphic and eloquent strictures and criticisms fired at the policy of this Connecticut law either by the Court's opinion or by those of my concurring Brethren to which I cannot subscribe—except their conclusion that the evil qualities they see in the law make it unconstitutional. * * * The Court talks about a constitutional "right of privacy" as though there is some constitutional provision or provisions forbidding any law ever to be passed which might abridge the "privacy" of individuals. But there is not. There are, of course, guarantees in certain specific constitutional provisions which are designed in part to protect privacy at certain times and places with respect to certain activities. Such, for example, is the Fourth Amendment's guarantee against "unreasonable searches and seizures." But I think it belittles that Amendment to talk about it as though it protects nothing but "privacy." * * * "Privacy" is a broad, abstract and ambiguous concept which can easily be shrunken in meaning but which can also, on the other hand, easily be interpreted as a constitutional ban against many things other than searches and seizures. * * * I like my privacy as well as the next one, but I am nevertheless compelled to admit that government has a right to invade it unless prohibited by some specific constitutional provision.

The due process argument which my Brothers HARLAN and WHITE adopt here is based, as their opinions indicate, on the premise that this Court is vested with power to invalidate all state laws that it considers to be arbitrary, capricious, unreasonable, or oppressive, or this Court's belief that a particular state law under scrutiny has no "rational or justifying" purpose, or is offensive to a "sense of fairness and justice." If these formulas based on "natural justice," or others which mean the same thing, are to prevail, they require judges to determine what is or is not constitutional on the basis of their own appraisal of what laws are unwise or unnecessary. The power to make such decisions is of course that of a legislative body.

The Ninth Amendment was * * * passed, not to broaden the powers of this Court or any other department of "the General Government," but, as every student of history knows, to assure the people that the Constitution in all its provisions was intended to limit the Federal Government to the powers granted expressly or by necessary implication. * * * This fact is perhaps responsible for the peculiar phenomenon

> **Food for Thought**
>
> If, as Justice Black concludes, the Constitution does not prohibit a state from *banning* the use of contraceptives, must it also necessarily be read to permit the state, if it chooses, to *require* birth control? If so, is that prospect problematic? If a statute requiring birth control would violate the Constitution, then why doesn't the statute at issue here violate it, as well?

that for a period of a century and a half no serious suggestion was ever made that the Ninth Amendment, enacted to protect state powers against federal invasion, could be used as a weapon of federal power to prevent state legislatures from passing laws they consider appropriate to govern local affairs. So far as I am concerned, Connecticut's law as applied here is not forbidden by any provision of the Federal Constitution as that Constitution was written, and I would therefore affirm.

MR. JUSTICE STEWART, whom MR. JUSTICE BLACK joins, dissenting.

I think this is an uncommonly silly law. As a practical matter, the law is obviously unenforceable, except in the oblique context of the present case. As a

> **FYI**
>
> Before the controversy in *Griswold* reached the Court, the Court twice declined to review challenges to Connecticut's law brought by doctors who had not been prosecuted. The appellants in *Griswold* opened their clinic with the hope of testing the constitutionality of the ban on the use of contraceptives, which they were able to do once they were prosecuted.

philosophical matter, I believe the use of contraceptives in the relationship of marriage should be left to personal and private choice, based upon each individual's moral, ethical, and religious beliefs. As a matter of social policy, I think professional counsel about methods of birth control should be available to all, so that each individual's choice can be meaningfully made. But we are not asked in this case to say whether we think this law is unwise, or even asinine. We are asked to hold that it violates the United States Constitution. And that I cannot do.

In the course of its opinion the Court refers to no less than six Amendments to the Constitution: the First, the Third, the Fourth, the Fifth, the Ninth, and the Fourteenth. But the Court does not say which of these Amendments, if any, it thinks is infringed by this Connecticut law. * * * There is no claim that this law,

[handwritten margin note: No statement of privacy anywhere in Const.]

duly enacted by the Connecticut Legislature, is unconstitutionally vague. There is no claim that the appellants were denied any of the elements of procedural due process at their trial, so as to make their convictions constitutionally invalid. And, as the Court says, the day has long passed since the Due Process Clause was regarded as a proper instrument for determining "the wisdom, need, and propriety" of state laws.

As to the First, Third, Fourth, and Fifth Amendments, I can find nothing in any of them to invalidate this Connecticut law, even assuming that all those Amendments are fully applicable against the States. * * * The Ninth Amendment, like its companion the Tenth, which this Court held "states but a truism that all is retained which has not been surrendered," *United States v. Darby*, 312 U.S. 100, 124 (1941), was framed by James Madison and adopted by the States simply to make clear that the adoption of the Bill of Rights did not alter the plan that the *Federal* Government was to be a government of express and limited powers, and that all rights and powers not delegated to it were retained by the people and the individual States. * * * If, as I should surely hope, the law before us does not reflect the standards of the people of Connecticut, the people of Connecticut can freely exercise their true Ninth and Tenth Amendment rights to persuade their elected representatives to repeal it. That is the constitutional way to take this law off the books.

POINTS FOR DISCUSSION

a.   "Penumbras": Justice Douglas's View

According to Justice Douglas, what is the constitutional source of the right that is protected in *Griswold*? According to his theory, is the right "enumerated" or "unenumerated"? How far do the penumbras of the rights that are enumerated in the Constitution extend?

b.   Due Process: Justice Harlan's View

Even though the Constitution contains some provisions that protect privacy, is it an over-generalization to conclude from these provisions that the Constitution protects privacy as a general matter? In his concurrence in *Griswold*, Justice Harlan referred to his dissent in *Poe v. Ullman*, 367 U.S. 497 (1961), which involved a challenge to the same Connecticut statute at issue in *Griswold*. The Court in that case declined to reach the merits, concluding that, because there was no showing that the statute would actually be enforced against the plaintiffs, the case was not justiciable. Justice Harlan disagreed and accordingly reached the merits. He stated:

Due process has not been reduced to any formula; its content cannot be determined by reference to any code. The best that can be said is that through the course of this Court's decisions it has represented the balance which our Nation, built upon postulates of respect for the liberty of the individual, has struck between that liberty and the demands of organized society. If the supplying of content to this Constitutional concept has of necessity been a rational process, it certainly has not been one where judges have felt free to roam where unguided speculation might take them. The balance of which I speak is the balance struck by this country, having regard to what history teaches are the traditions from which it developed as well as the traditions from which it broke. That tradition is a living thing. A decision of this Court which radically departs from it could not long survive, while a decision which builds on what has survived is likely to be sound. No formula could serve as a substitute, in this area, for judgment and restraint. This "liberty" is [a] rational continuum which, broadly speaking, includes a freedom from all substantial arbitrary impositions and purposeless restraints, and which also recognizes, what a reasonable and sensitive judgment must, that certain interests require particularly careful scrutiny of the state needs asserted to justify their abridgment.

I think the sweep of the Court's decisions, under both the Fourth and Fourteenth Amendments, amply shows that the Constitution protects the privacy of the home against all unreasonable intrusion of whatever character. * * * [I]t is difficult to imagine what is more private or more intimate than a husband and wife's marital relations. [T]he intimacy of husband and wife is necessarily an essential and accepted feature of the institution of marriage, an institution which the State not only must allow, but which always and in every age it has fostered and protected. It is one thing when the State exerts its power either to forbid extra-marital sexuality altogether, or to say who may marry, but it is quite another when, having acknowledged a marriage and the intimacies inherent in it, it undertakes to regulate by means of the criminal law the details of that intimacy.

Since, as it appears to me, the statute marks an abridgment of important fundamental liberties protected by the Fourteenth Amendment, it will not do to urge in justification of that abridgment simply that the statute is rationally related to the effectuation of a proper state purpose. A closer scrutiny and stronger justification than that are required. * * * [C]onclusive, in my view, is the utter novelty of this enactment. Although the Federal Government and many States have at one time or other had on their books statutes forbidding or regulating the distribution of contraceptives, none, so far as I can find, has made the *use* of contraceptives a crime. Indeed, a diligent search has revealed that no nation, including several which quite evidently share Connecticut's moral policy, has seen fit to effectuate that policy by the means presented here.

In Justice Harlan's view, the Due Process Clause protects liberty as defined by the nation's traditions, which he describes as "living." Does he mean by this that the meaning of "liberty" changes from generation to generation? Is it possible that the liberty that he found in *Poe* (and *Griswold*) will not be constitutionally protected in the future?

c.   Due Process and the Role of the Ninth Amendment: Justice Goldberg's View

The Ninth Amendment states: "The enumeration in the Constitution of certain rights shall not be construed to deny or disparage others retained by the people." Justices Goldberg and Black disagreed on the meaning of this Amendment. Justice Black asserted that the Amendment was never intended to create judicially enforceable rights. Did Justice Goldberg suggest that the Ninth Amendment itself creates enforceable rights? If not, what did he think it adds to the analysis? And if the Ninth Amendment does not itself create rights, where do they come from? Are they created by the limitation on federal powers?

Justice Stewart compared the Ninth Amendment to the Tenth Amendment, which we considered in Volume 1, and he concluded that it was merely designed to confirm the enumeration. Is this a plausible reading of the Ninth Amendment's text? Conversely, for Justice Goldberg's view to be plausible, must he conclude that the Ninth Amendment applies to the states through the Fourteenth Amendment?

d.   Scrutiny

The Court's analysis did not end once it had concluded that the law in question interfered with a constitutionally protected right. Instead, the Court appeared to consider (even if only briefly) whether the law could have been crafted in a way that would have advanced the government's interests without interfering as much with the right in question. The Court stated that the government cannot achieve its otherwise legitimate goals "by means which sweep unnecessarily broadly * * *."

As we will see, when confronted with a claim that a law interferes with a fundamental right, the Court considers both whether the government has a sufficiently important justification for the interference and whether the government could have achieved its goals without interfering with the right. The Court in *Griswold*, however, did not elaborate on the level of scrutiny that it applied; for example, it did not identify the interests that the state asserted were advanced by the statute, and it did not explain whether the state could have accomplished its goals in another way. But in cases involving interference with a constitutionally protected right, the Court generally engages in such an inquiry. Was there an argument that Connecticut had a sufficiently strong interest to justify the law at issue in *Griswold*? What was Connecticut's interest in prohibiting contraceptive use? Could it have advanced that interest without prohibiting married couples from using contraceptives?

e. Contraception and Marriage

Griswold specifically addressed the rights of married persons to be free from governmental interference with their decisions regarding contraception. Indeed, Justices Douglas, Harlan, and White relied explicitly on the marital relationship in identifying the right at issue. In *Eisenstadt v. Baird*, 405 U.S. 438 (1972), decided seven years later, the Court invalidated a statute that permitted the distribution of contraceptives only to married—and thus not to unmarried—persons. Although the Court relied on the Equal Protection, rather than the Due Process, Clause, it suggested that the right at issue in *Griswold* did not exist solely by virtue of marriage:

> If under *Griswold* the distribution of contraceptives to married persons cannot be prohibited, a ban on distribution to unmarried persons would be equally impermissible. It is true that in *Griswold* the right of privacy in question inhered in the marital relationship. Yet the marital couple is not an independent entity with a mind and heart of its own, but an association of two individuals each with a separate intellectual and emotional makeup. If the right of privacy means anything, it is the right of the *individual*, married or single, to be free from unwarranted governmental intrusion into matters so fundamentally affecting a person as the decision whether to bear or beget a child.

Does the Court's decision in *Eisenstadt* suggest that *Griswold* was about more than simply *marital* privacy? Or was *Eisenstadt* an impermissible extension of *Griswold*?

ROE V. WADE

410 U.S. 113 (1973)

MR. JUSTICE BLACKMUN delivered the opinion of the Court.

[Texas law makes] it a crime to "procure an abortion," as therein defined, or to attempt one, except with respect to "an abortion procured or attempted by medical advice for the purpose of saving the life of the mother." Similar statutes are in existence in a majority of the States. [A woman alleging that she wished to terminate her pregnancy by an abortion performed by a licensed physician, and that she could not afford to travel to another jurisdiction in order to secure a legal abortion under safe conditions, filed suit to challenge the law. A separate action was instituted by a married couple who alleged that the woman suffered from a condition that made pregnancy dangerous to her health, that their physician had counseled them not to use birth control, and that they would wish to seek an abortion if she became pregnant. The Court first engaged in a lengthy discussion of the history of legal treatment of abortion, observing that it "perhaps is not generally appreciated that the restrictive criminal abortion laws in effect in a majority of States today are of relatively recent vintage. Those laws [derive] from statutory changes effected, for the most part, in the latter half of the 19th century." The Court then proceeded to the "main thrust" of the plaintiffs' argument.]

> **Take Note**
>
> This paragraph and the one that follows are among the most controversial in the history of the Court. What are the two steps in the Court's reasoning? Can the questions whether there is a general right of privacy and whether it is broad enough to embrace a right to have an abortion be decided so simply?

The Constitution does not explicitly mention any right of privacy. In a line of decisions, however, [the] Court has recognized that a right of personal privacy, or a guarantee of certain areas or zones of privacy, does exist under the Constitution. In varying contexts, the Court or individual Justices have, indeed, found at least the roots of that right in the First Amendment, *Stanley v. Georgia*, 394 U.S. 557, 564 (1969); in the Fourth and Fifth Amendments, *Terry v. Ohio*, 392 U.S. 1, 8–9 (1968); in the penumbras of the Bill of Rights, *Griswold v. Connecticut*, 381 U.S. 479, 484–485 (1965); in the Ninth Amendment, *id.* at 486; or in the concept of liberty guaranteed by the first section of the Fourteenth Amendment, see *Meyer v. Nebraska*, 262 U.S. 390, 399 (1923). These decisions make it clear that only personal rights that can be deemed "fundamental" or "implicit in the concept of ordered liberty," *Palko v. Connecticut*, 302 U.S. 319, 325 (1937), are included in this guarantee of personal privacy. They also make it clear that the right has some extension to activities relating to marriage, *Loving v. Virginia*, 388 U.S. 1, 12 (1967); procreation, *Skinner v. Oklahoma*, 316 U.S. 535, 541–542 (1942); contraception, *Eisenstadt v. Baird*, 405 U.S. 438, 453–454 (1972); family relationships, *Prince v. Massachusetts*, 321 U.S. 158, 166 (1944); and child rearing and education, *Pierce v. Society of Sisters*, 268 U.S. 510, 535 (1925).

This right of privacy, whether it be founded in the Fourteenth Amendment's concept of personal liberty and restrictions upon state action, as we feel it is, or, as the District Court determined, in the Ninth Amendment's reservation of rights to the people, is broad enough to encompass a woman's decision whether or not to terminate her pregnancy. The detriment that the State would impose upon the pregnant woman by denying this choice altogether is apparent. Specific and direct harm medically diagnosable even in early pregnancy may be involved. Maternity, or additional offspring, may force upon the woman a distressful life and future. Psychological harm may be imminent. Mental and physical health may be taxed by child care. There is also the distress, for all concerned, associated with the unwanted child, and there is the problem of bringing a child into a family already unable, psychologically and otherwise, to care for it. In other cases, as in this one, the additional difficulties and continuing stigma of unwed motherhood may be involved. All these are factors the woman and her responsible physician necessarily will consider in consultation.

We, therefore, conclude that the right of personal privacy includes the abortion decision, but that this right is not unqualified and must be considered against important state interests in regulation. * * * Where certain "fundamental rights" are involved, the Court has held that regulation limiting these rights may be justified only by a "compelling state interest," *Kramer v. Union Free School District*, 395 U.S. 621, 627 (1969), and that legislative enactments must be narrowly drawn to express only the legitimate state interests at stake. *Griswold*, 381 U.S., at 485.

Definition

"Amicus curiae" (Latin for "a friend of the court") is "[s]omeone who is not a party to a lawsuit but who petitions the court or is requested by the court to file a brief in the action because that person has a strong interest in the subject matter." *Black's Law Dictionary* (10th ed. 2014). Judicial opinions often shorten amicus curiae to amicus. The plural of amicus is "amici."

The appellee and certain amici argue that the fetus is a "person" within the language and meaning of the Fourteenth Amendment. * * * If this suggestion of personhood is established, the appellant's case, of course, collapses, for the fetus' right to life would then be guaranteed specifically by the Amendment. * * * The Constitution does not define "person" in so many words. Section 1 of the Fourteenth Amendment contains three references to "person." * * * "Person" is [also] used in other places in the Constitution [b]ut in nearly all these instances, the use of the word is such that it has application only postnatally. All this * * * persuades us that the word "person," as used in the Fourteenth Amendment, does not include the unborn.

Food for Thought

If the Court had accepted Texas's argument that the fetus is a "person" entitled to protection under the Fourteenth Amendment, would the provision in Texas law permitting abortions for the purpose of saving the life of the mother have been constitutional?

> **Take Note**
>
> Is the Court exercising judicial restraint in declining to decide when life begins? Or is the Court, in rejecting the theory advanced by Texas, effectively making just such a decision—or at least ruling out one possible view?

Texas [also] urges that, apart from the Fourteenth Amendment, life begins at conception and is present throughout pregnancy, and that, therefore, the State has a compelling interest in protecting that life from and after conception. When those trained in the respective disciplines of medicine, philosophy, and theology are unable to arrive at any consensus, the judiciary, at this point in the development of man's knowledge, is not in a position to speculate as to the answer. * * *

[However, the] State does have an important and legitimate interest in preserving and protecting the health of the pregnant woman, whether she be a resident of the State or a non-resident who seeks medical consultation and treatment there, and [it] has still another important and legitimate interest in protecting the potentiality of human life. These interests are separate and distinct. Each grows in substantiality as the woman approaches term and, at a point during pregnancy, each becomes "compelling."

With respect to the State's important and legitimate interest in the health of the mother, the "compelling" point, in the light of present medical knowledge, is at approximately the end of the first trimester. This is so because of the now-established medical fact [that] until the end of the first trimester mortality in abortion may be less than mortality in normal childbirth. It follows that, from and after this point, a State may regulate the abortion procedure to the extent that the regulation reasonably relates to the preservation and protection of maternal health. * * * This means, on the other hand, that, for the period of pregnancy prior to this "compelling" point, the attending physician, in consultation with his patient, is free to determine, without regulation by the State, that, in his medical judgment, the patient's pregnancy should be terminated. If that decision is reached, the judgment may be effectuated by an abortion free of interference by the State.

With respect to the State's important and legitimate interest in potential life, the "compelling" point is at viability. This is so because the fetus then presumably has the capability of meaningful life outside the mother's womb. State regulation protective of fetal life after viability thus has both logical and biological justifications. If the State is interested in protecting fetal life after viability, it may go so far as to proscribe abortion during that period, except when it is necessary to preserve the life or health of the mother.

Measured against these standards, [the Texas law] sweeps too broadly. The statute makes no distinction between abortions performed early in pregnancy and those performed later, and it limits to a single reason, "saving" the mother's life, the legal justification for the procedure. The statute, therefore, cannot survive the constitutional attack made upon it here.

To summarize and to repeat: * * * (a) For the stage prior to approximately the end of the first trimester, the abortion decision and its

> **Food for Thought**
>
> The Court rests its constitutional analysis in significant part on biological and medical realities. Does this mean that the scope of a woman's right to an abortion—and, conversely, the state's power to regulate abortion—will evolve over time as scientific understanding develops and medical technology advances? For example, what if techniques are invented to keep a fetus viable at any age? As a related point, does the Court explain why the life of a *viable* fetus must be subordinate to the *life or health* of the mother?

effectuation must be left to the medical judgment of the pregnant woman's attending physician. (b) For the stage subsequent to approximately the end of the first trimester, the State, in promoting its interest in the health of the mother, may, if it chooses, regulate the abortion procedure in ways that are reasonably related to maternal health. (c) For the stage subsequent to viability, the State in promoting its interest in the potentiality of human life may, if it chooses, regulate, and even proscribe, abortion except where it is necessary, in appropriate medical judgment, for the preservation of the life or health of the mother.

[Our] decision vindicates the right of the physician to administer medical treatment according to his professional judgment up to the points where important state interests provide compelling justifications for intervention. Up to those points, the abortion decision in all its aspects is inherently, and primarily, a medical decision, and basic responsibility for it must rest with the physician.

Take Note

What level of scrutiny does the Court apply in invalidating the Texas law? It refers to state interests that are "legitimate," important," and "compelling." Which of these does it require before the state can regulate the right to an abortion? And must any such regulation satisfy a "means" test, as well?

MR. JUSTICE STEWART, concurring.

In 1963, this Court, in *Ferguson v. Skrupa*, 372 U.S. 726 (1963), purported to sound the death knell for the doctrine of substantive due process * * *. Barely two years later, in *Griswold*, the Court held a Connecticut birth control law unconstitutional. In view of what had been so recently said in *Skrupa*, the Court's opinion in *Griswold* understandably did its best to avoid reliance on the Due Process Clause of the Fourteenth Amendment as the ground for decision. Yet, the Connecticut law did not violate any provision of the Bill of Rights, nor any other specific provision of the Constitution. So it was clear to me then, and it is equally clear to me now, that the *Griswold* decision can be rationally understood only as a holding that the Connecticut statute substantively invaded the "liberty" that is protected by the Due Process Clause of the Fourteenth Amendment. As so understood, *Griswold* stands as one in a long line of pre-*Skrupa* cases decided under the doctrine of substantive due process, and I now accept it as such.

The Constitution nowhere mentions a specific right of personal choice in matters of marriage and family life, but the "liberty" protected by the Due Process Clause of the Fourteenth Amendment covers more than those freedoms explicitly named in the Bill of Rights. * * * Several decisions of this Court

Take Note

Justice Stewart dissented in *Griswold*. Did he change his mind about the meaning of the Due Process Clause? Or did he just feel compelled to follow precedent? If the latter, is it an act consistent with the judicial role, or instead one in tension with it?

make clear that freedom of personal choice in matters of marriage and family life is one of the liberties protected by the Due Process Clause of the Fourteenth Amendment. * * * As recently as last Term, in *Eisenstadt v. Baird*, 405 U.S. 438 (1972), we recognized "the right of the individual, married or single, to be free from unwarranted governmental intrusion into matters so fundamentally affecting a person as the decision whether to bear or beget a child." That right necessarily includes the right of a woman to decide whether or not to terminate her pregnancy.

MR. JUSTICE REHNQUIST, dissenting.

I have difficulty in concluding, as the Court does, that the right of "privacy" is involved in this case. * * * A transaction resulting in an [abortion] is not "private" in the ordinary usage of that word. * * * If the Court means by the term "privacy" no more than that the claim of a person to be free from unwanted state regulation of consensual transactions may be a form of "liberty" protected by the Fourteenth Amendment, there is no doubt that similar claims have been upheld in our earlier decisions on the basis of that liberty. I agree with [Justice STEWART that "liberty"] embraces more than the rights found in the Bill of Rights. But that liberty is not guaranteed absolutely against deprivation, only against deprivation without due process of law. The test traditionally applied in the area of social and economic legislation is whether or not a law such as that challenged has a rational relation to a valid state objective. *Williamson v. Lee Optical Co.*, 348 U.S. 483, 491 (1955). [T]he Court's sweeping invalidation of any restrictions on abortion during the first trimester is impossible to justify under that standard, and the conscious weighing of competing factors that the Court's opinion apparently substitutes for the established test is far more appropriate to a legislative judgment than to a judicial one.

As in *Lochner* and similar cases applying substantive due process standards to economic and social welfare legislation, the adoption of the compelling state interest standard will inevitably require this Court to examine the legislative policies and pass on the wisdom of these policies in the very process of deciding whether a particular state interest put forward may or may not be "compelling." The decision here to break pregnancy into three distinct terms and to outline the permissible restrictions the State may impose in each one, for example, partakes more of judicial legislation than it does of a determination of the intent of the drafters of the Fourteenth Amendment.

The fact that a majority of the States reflecting, after all the majority sentiment in those States, have had restrictions on abortions for at least a century is a strong indication, it seems to me, that the asserted right to an abortion is not "so rooted in the traditions and conscience of our people as to be ranked as fundamental," *Snyder v. Massachusetts*, 291 U.S. 97, 105 (1934). Even today, when society's views on abortion are changing, the very existence of the debate is evidence that the "right" to an abortion is not so universally accepted as the appellant would have us believe.

To reach its result, the Court necessarily has had to find within the scope of the Fourteenth Amendment a right that was apparently completely unknown to the drafters of the Amendment. * * * By the time of the adoption of the Fourteenth Amendment in 1868, there were at least 36 laws enacted by state or territorial legislatures limiting abortion. * * * The only conclusion possible from this history is that the drafters did not intend to have the Fourteenth Amendment withdraw from the States the power to legislate with respect to this matter. * * *

MR. JUSTICE WHITE, with whom MR. JUSTICE REHNQUIST joins, dissenting.

The Court apparently values the convenience of the pregnant woman more than the continued existence and development of the life or potential life that she carries. Whether or not I might agree with that marshaling of values, I can in no event join the Court's judgment because I find no constitutional warrant for imposing such an order of priorities on the people and legislatures of the States. In a sensitive area such as this, involving as it does issues over which reasonable men may easily and heatedly differ, I cannot accept the Court's exercise of its clear power of choice by interposing a constitutional barrier to state efforts to protect human life and by investing

women and doctors with the constitutionally protected right to exterminate it. This issue, for the most part, should be left with the people and to the political processes the people have devised to govern their affairs.

[JUSTICE DOUGLAS's concurring opinion is omitted.]

POINTS FOR DISCUSSION

a.   Due Process

In his opinion for the Court, Justice Blackmun declared that the right of privacy is "founded in the Fourteenth Amendment's concept of personal liberty"—that is, that the right is one protected by substantive due process. What does this mean for the "penumbras" approach that Justice Douglas advanced for the Court in *Griswold*? In fact, Justice Douglas issued a concurring opinion in *Roe* (and in a companion case) that asserted that the right at issue was "peripheral" to other rights specified in the Constitution. No other member of the Court joined his opinion.

b.   The Trimester Framework

The Court determined that the right of a woman to choose an abortion depends on timing. Under *Roe*, in the first trimester of pregnancy, the state cannot ban abortion. In roughly the third trimester—the stage subsequent to "viability"—the state can prohibit abortion except where necessary to preserve the life or health of the mother. The Court also stated that in the second trimester, the state can regulate abortion "in ways that are reasonably related to maternal health." Where did this framework come from? Is it a sensible interpretation of the Due Process Clause? Is it the best interpretation?

c.   Constitutional Interpretation or Judicial Legislation?

A familiar refrain in cases involving substantive due process claims is that the Court is engaging in so-called "judicial legislation." Concerns about "judicial activism" and the separation of powers are obviously not unique to Due Process Clause cases; recall, for instance, Justice Scalia's criticisms of the Dormant Commerce Clause Doctrine, which we considered in Volume 1. Nor is reliance on the implications from broad constitutional text unusual; consider the Court's decisions in *New York v. United States* and *Printz v. United States*, which we considered in Volume 1 and which concluded that "structural" postulates prohibit Congress from compelling the states to enact or administer federal regulatory programs.

Are *Griswold* and *Roe* any more problematic than the countless other instances in which the Court has interpreted vague constitutional provisions to be rights-creating? If so, why?

d.   Scrutiny

What level of scrutiny did the Court apply to Texas's ban on abortion? Notice that the Court described Texas's "important and legitimate interest" in protecting the health of the mother and in "potential life"; it concluded that the interest in the mother's health became "compelling" "at approximately the end of the first trimester," and that the interest in potential life became "compelling" at the point of viability.

In cases that followed Roe, the Court made clear that strict scrutiny applied state laws that interfere with the right to an abortion. See, e.g., *City of Akron v. Akron Center for Reproductive Health, Inc.*, 462 U.S. 416 (1983) ("[R]estrictive state regulation of the right to choose abortion, as with other fundamental rights subject to searching judicial examination, must be supported by a compelling state interest."). Strict scrutiny requires the government to demonstrate that the law is narrowly tailored to advance a compelling government interest. As we will see in Chapter 5, the Court applies strict scrutiny to laws that classify on the basis of race, alienage, or national origin; "[s]imilar oversight by the courts is due when state laws impinge on personal rights protected by the Constitution." *City of Cleburne v. Cleburne Living Center*, 473 U.S. 432 (1985). Should the states have to justify regulation of the right to an abortion under such a searching standard?

e.   History and Debate

In a section of the opinion omitted here, the Court engaged in a lengthy discussion of the history of abortion, including philosophical, medical, and legal issues debated in the West over the last 2000 years. Why did the Court believe that this discussion was necessary to the constitutional analysis?

The debate over abortion obviously did not end with the Court's decision in *Roe*, as some of the Justices apparently believed that it would. Does the continuing debate tend to justify the Court's decision, or instead undermine it?

The Court's decision in *Roe* was not the last word on the subject. In the two decades after the decision, the Court decided many cases concerning the right to an abortion. But the Court continued to be divided; some members of the Court asserted that *Roe* should be overruled. See *Thornburgh v. American College of Obstetricians and Gynecologists*, 476 U.S. 747, 797 (1986) (White, J., dissenting). After several appointments to the Court by President Reagan, who had pledged to appoint Justices who would overrule *Roe*, many people believed that the Court was poised to do just that. And indeed, some of those Justices explicitly wrote in favor of overruling *Roe*. See *Webster v. Reproductive Health Services*, 492 U.S. 490 (1989) (Scalia, J., concurring in part and concurring in the judgment).

The Court, however, declined to do so in the case that follows. In it, the Court reviewed a Pennsylvania statute that limited the right to an abortion in several ways, including requiring a 24-hour waiting period before a woman could obtain an abortion; requiring spousal consent before a woman could obtain an abortion; requiring parental consent for minors who sought abortions; and requiring abortion clinics to report information to the state about abortions performed. (The statute also prohibited "sex-selection" abortions, but the petitioners did not challenge that section. Why do you suppose they did not?)

PLANNED PARENTHOOD OF SOUTHEASTERN PENN. V. CASEY
505 U.S. 833 (1992)

JUSTICE O'CONNOR, JUSTICE KENNEDY, and JUSTICE SOUTER announced the judgment of the Court and delivered the opinion of the Court with respect to Parts I, II, III, V-A, V-C, and VI, an opinion with respect to Part V-E, in which Justice STEVENS joins, and an opinion with respect to Parts IV, V-B, and V-D.

Undue Burden Analysis

I

Liberty finds no refuge in a jurisprudence of doubt. Yet 19 years after our holding that the Constitution protects a woman's right to terminate her pregnancy in its early stages, that definition of liberty is still questioned. Joining the respondents as amicus curiae, the United States, as it has done in five other cases in the last decade, again asks us to overrule *Roe*. * * * After considering the fundamental constitutional questions resolved by *Roe*, principles of institutional integrity, and the rule of *stare decisis*, we are led to conclude this: the essential holding of *Roe v. Wade* should be retained and once again reaffirmed.

II

Constitutional protection of the woman's decision to terminate her pregnancy derives from the Due Process Clause of the Fourteenth Amendment. Although a literal reading of the Clause might suggest that it governs only the procedures by which a State may deprive persons of liberty, for at least 105 years, since *Mugler v. Kansas*, 123 U.S. 623, 660–661 (1887), the Clause has been understood to contain a substantive component as well, one "barring certain government actions regardless of the fairness of the procedures used to implement them." *Daniels v. Williams*, 474 U.S. 327, 331 (1986). As Justice Brandeis (joined by Justice Holmes) observed, "[d]espite arguments to the contrary which had seemed to me persuasive, it is settled that the due process clause of the Fourteenth Amendment applies to matters of substantive law as well as to matters of procedure. Thus all fundamental rights comprised within the term liberty are protected by the Federal Constitution from invasion by the States." *Whitney v. California*, 274 U.S. 357, 373 (1927) (concurring opinion).

It is tempting, as a means of curbing the discretion of federal judges, to suppose that liberty encompasses no more than those rights already guaranteed to the individual against federal interference by the express provisions of the first eight Amendments to the Constitution. But of course this Court has never accepted that view. * * * It is a promise of the Constitution that there is a realm of personal liberty which the government may not enter. We have vindicated this principle before. Marriage is mentioned nowhere in the Bill of Rights and interracial marriage was illegal in most States in the 19th century, but the Court was no doubt correct in finding it to be an aspect of liberty protected against state interference by the substantive component of the Due Process Clause in *Loving v.*

Make the Connection

We will consider the Court's decision in *Loving* later in this chapter, and again in Chapter 5, when we discuss the Equal Protection Clause.

Virginia, 388 U.S. 1, 12 (1967). * * * Neither the Bill of Rights nor the specific practices of States at the time of the adoption of the Fourteenth Amendment marks the outer limits of the substantive sphere of liberty which the Fourteenth Amendment protects. See U.S. Const., Amdt. 9. * * * It is settled now, as it was when the Court heard arguments in *Roe v. Wade*, that the Constitution places limits on a State's right to interfere with a person's most basic decisions about family and parenthood, see *Eisenstadt, Loving, Griswold, Skinner, Pierce, Meyer*, as well as bodily integrity, see, *e.g., Washington v. Harper*, 494 U.S. 210, 221–222 (1990).

The inescapable fact is that adjudication of substantive due process claims may call upon the Court in interpreting the Constitution to exercise that same capacity which by tradition courts always have exercised: reasoned judgment. Its boundaries are not susceptible of expression as a simple rule. That does not mean we are free to invalidate state policy choices with which we disagree; yet neither does it permit us to shrink from the duties of our office.

Men and women of good conscience can disagree, and we suppose some always shall disagree, about the profound moral and spiritual implications of terminating a pregnancy, even in its earliest stage. Some of us as individuals find abortion offensive to our most basic principles of morality, but that cannot control our decision. Our obligation is to define the liberty of all, not to mandate our own moral code. The underlying constitutional issue is whether the State can resolve these philosophic questions in such a definitive way that a woman lacks all choice in the matter, except perhaps in those rare circumstances in which the pregnancy is itself a danger to her own life or health, or is the result of rape or incest.

Our law affords constitutional protection to personal decisions relating to marriage, procreation, contraception, family relationships, child rearing, and education. * * * These matters, involving the most intimate and personal choices a person may make in a lifetime, choices central to personal dignity and autonomy, are central to the liberty protected by the Fourteenth Amendment. At the heart of liberty is the right to define one's own concept of existence, of meaning, of the universe, and of the mystery of human life. Beliefs about these matters could not define the attributes of personhood were they formed under compulsion of the State.

> **Food for Thought**
>
> What does the penultimate sentence of this paragraph mean? What authority might support this conception of liberty?

[T]hough the abortion decision may originate within the zone of conscience and belief, it is more than a philosophic exercise. Abortion [is] an act fraught with consequences for others: for the woman who must live with the implications of her decision; for the persons who perform and assist in the procedure; for the spouse, family, and society which must confront the knowledge that these procedures exist, procedures some deem nothing short of an act of violence against innocent human life; and, depending on one's beliefs, for the life or potential life that is aborted. Though abortion is conduct, it does not follow that the State is entitled to proscribe it in all instances. That is because the liberty of the woman is at stake in a sense unique to the human condition and so unique to the law. The mother who carries a child to full term is subject to anxieties, to physical constraints, to pain that only she must bear.

> **Food for Thought**
>
> The Court seems to suggest here that the Constitution protects a conception of liberty that is largely at odds with the vision that has been "dominant" in "our history and culture." Even assuming, as the Court states, that the Constitution protects unenumerated "fundamental rights," how can the Court define those rights to be largely in conflict with widely held views about the limits on personal liberty? Is the Court's approach consistent with Justice Harlan's approach in *Griswold* and *Poe*?

That these sacrifices have from the beginning of the human race been endured by woman with a pride that ennobles her in the eyes of others and gives to the infant a bond of love cannot alone be grounds for the State to insist she make the sacrifice. Her suffering is too intimate and personal for the State to insist, without more, upon its own vision of the woman's role, however dominant that vision has been in the course of our history and our culture. The destiny of the woman must be shaped to a large extent on her own conception of her spiritual imperatives and her place in society.

While we appreciate the weight of the arguments [that] *Roe* should be overruled, the reservations any of us may have in reaffirming the central holding of *Roe* are outweighed by the explication of individual liberty we have given combined with the force of *stare decisis*. We turn now to that doctrine.

III

The obligation to follow precedent begins with necessity, and a contrary necessity marks its outer limit. [N]o judicial system could do society's work if it eyed each issue afresh in every case that raised it. Indeed, the very concept of the rule of law underlying our own Constitution requires such continuity over time that a respect for precedent is, by definition, indispensable. At the other extreme, a different necessity would make itself felt if a prior judicial ruling should come to be seen so clearly as error that its enforcement was for that very reason doomed.

Even when the decision to overrule a prior case is not, as in the rare, latter instance, virtually foreordained, it is common wisdom that the rule of *stare decisis* is not an "inexorable command," and certainly it is not such in every constitutional case. * * * While [*Roe*] has engendered disapproval, it has not been unworkable. An entire generation has come of age free to assume *Roe*'s concept of liberty in defining the capacity of women to act in society, and to make reproductive decisions; no erosion of principle going to liberty or personal autonomy has left *Roe*'s central holding a doctrinal remnant; *Roe* portends no developments at odds with other precedent for the analysis of personal liberty; and no changes of fact have rendered viability more or less appropriate as the point at which the balance of interests tips. Within the bounds of normal *stare decisis* analysis, then, and subject to the considerations on which it customarily turns, the stronger argument is for affirming *Roe*'s central holding, with whatever degree of personal reluctance any of us may have, not for overruling it.

let decision stand

In a less significant case, *stare decisis* analysis could, and would, stop at the point we have reached. But the sustained and widespread debate *Roe* has provoked calls for some comparison between that case and others of comparable dimension that have responded to national controversies and taken on the impress of the controversies addressed. Only two such decisional lines from the past century present themselves for examination, and in each instance the result reached by the Court accorded with the principles we apply today.

The first example is that line of cases identified with *Lochner v. New York*, 198 U.S. 45 (1905). [By 1937, it] seemed unmistakable to most people [that] the interpretation of contractual freedom protected in [*Lochner* and its progeny] rested on fundamentally false factual assumptions about the capacity of a relatively unregulated market to satisfy minimal levels of human welfare. * * * The facts upon which the earlier case had premised a constitutional resolution of social controversy had proven to be untrue, and history's demonstration of their untruth not only justified but required the new choice of constitutional principle that *West Coast Hotel Co. v. Parrish*, 300 U.S. 379 (1937), announced.

The second comparison that 20th century history invites is with the cases employing the separate-but-equal rule for applying the Fourteenth Amendment's equal protection guarantee. They began with *Plessy v. Ferguson*, 163 U.S. 537 (1896), holding that legislatively mandated racial segregation in public transportation works no denial of equal protection, rejecting the argument that racial separation enforced by the legal machinery of American society treats the black race as inferior. * * * But [by 1954, when the Court decided *Brown v. Board of Education*, 347 U.S. 483 (1954), it was clear] that legally sanctioned segregation had just such an effect, to the point that racially separate public educational facilities were deemed inherently unequal.

> **Make the Connection**
>
> We will consider *Plessy* and *Brown* in Chapter 5.

> **Food for Thought**
>
> Was it really only the understanding of markets and the facts of economic life that changed in the three decades before 1937, or the understanding of the effects of segregation that changed in the half century before 1954, that explain the Court's decisions in *West Coast Hotel* and *Brown*? Don't social and moral shifts that made the old decisions unpalatable help to explain those decisions? Or even a change in the composition of the Court itself? How might a different view of these cases have affected the application of *stare decisis* to *Roe*?

West Coast Hotel and *Brown* each rested on facts, or an understanding of facts, changed from those which furnished the claimed justifications for the earlier constitutional resolutions. * * * In constitutional adjudication as elsewhere in life, changed circumstances may impose new obligations, and the thoughtful part of the Nation could accept each decision to overrule a prior case as a response to the Court's constitutional duty. Because the cases before us present no such occasion it could be seen as no such response. Because neither the factual underpinnings of *Roe*'s central holding nor our understanding of it has changed * * *, the Court could not pretend to be reexamining the prior law with any justification beyond a present doctrinal disposition to come out differently from the Court of 1973. To overrule prior law for no other reason than that would run counter to the view repeated in our cases, that a decision to overrule should rest on some special reason over and above the belief that a prior case was wrongly decided.

[O]verruling *Roe*'s central holding [would also] seriously weaken the Court's capacity to exercise the judicial power and to function as the Supreme Court of a Nation dedicated to the rule of law. * * * As Americans of each succeeding generation are rightly told, the Court cannot buy support for its decisions by spending money and, except to a minor degree, it cannot independently coerce obedience to its decrees. The Court's power lies, rather, in its legitimacy, [which] depends on making legally principled decisions under circumstances in which their principled character is sufficiently plausible to be accepted by the Nation.

Where, in the performance of its judicial duties, the Court decides a case in such a way as to resolve the sort of intensely divisive controversy reflected in *Roe* and those rare, comparable cases, its decision has a dimension that the resolution of the normal case does not carry. It is the dimension present whenever the Court's interpretation of the Constitution calls the contending sides of a national controversy to end their national division by accepting a common mandate rooted in the Constitution. The Court is not asked to do this very often, having thus addressed the Nation only twice in our lifetime, in the decisions of *Brown* and *Roe*. But when the Court does act in this way, its decision requires an equally rare precedential force to counter the inevitable efforts to overturn it and to thwart its implementation. Some of those efforts may be mere unprincipled emotional reactions; others may proceed from principles worthy of profound respect. But whatever the premises of opposition may be, only the most convincing justification under accepted standards of precedent could suffice to demonstrate that a later decision overruling the first was anything but a surrender to political pressure, and an unjustified repudiation of the principle on which the Court staked its authority in the first instance. So to overrule under fire in the absence of the most compelling reason to reexamine a watershed decision would subvert the Court's legitimacy beyond any serious question. * * * It is therefore imperative to adhere to the essence of *Roe*'s original decision, and we do so today.

> **Take Note**
>
> Is the Court suggesting here that it should use a heightened standard for departing from *stare decisis* whenever one of its previous decisions has proved controversial? Doesn't this approach simply entrench the very decisions about which a national dialogue is most likely to take place, and most likely to reveal the values that the Nation holds to be "fundamental"?

IV

From what we have said so far it follows that it is a constitutional liberty of the woman to have some freedom to terminate her pregnancy. We conclude that the basic decision in *Roe* was based on a constitutional analysis which we cannot now repudiate. The woman's liberty is not so unlimited, however, that from the outset the State cannot show its concern for the life of the unborn, and at a later point in fetal development the State's interest in life has sufficient force so that the right of the woman to terminate the pregnancy can be restricted.

We conclude the line should be drawn at viability, so that before that time the woman has a right to choose to terminate her pregnancy. * * * Any judicial act of line-drawing may seem somewhat arbitrary, but *Roe* was a reasoned statement, elaborated with great care. [In addition,] the concept of viability, as we noted in *Roe*, is the time at which there is a realistic possibility of maintaining and nourishing a life outside the womb, so that the independent existence of the second life can in reason and all fairness be the object of state protection that now overrides the rights of the woman. * * * The woman's right to terminate her pregnancy before viability is the most central principle of *Roe*. It is a rule of law and a component of liberty we cannot renounce.

Yet it must be remembered that *Roe* speaks with clarity in establishing not only the woman's liberty but also the State's "important and legitimate interest in potential life." * * * A logical reading of the central holding in *Roe* itself, and a necessary reconciliation of the liberty of the woman and the interest of the State in promoting prenatal life, require, in our view, that we abandon the trimester framework as a rigid prohibition on all previability regulation aimed at the protection of fetal life. The trimester framework * * * misconceives the nature of the pregnant woman's interest [and] in practice it undervalues the State's interest in potential life, as recognized in *Roe*. * * * Not all burdens on the right to decide whether to terminate a pregnancy will be undue. In our view, the undue burden standard is the appropriate means of reconciling the State's interest with the woman's constitutionally protected liberty.

A finding of an undue burden is a shorthand for the conclusion that a state regulation has the purpose or effect of placing a substantial obstacle in the path of a woman seeking an abortion of a nonviable fetus. A statute with this purpose is invalid because the means chosen by the State to further the interest in potential life must be calculated to inform the woman's free choice, not hinder it. And a statute which, while furthering the interest in potential life or some other valid state interest, has the effect of placing a substantial obstacle in the path of a woman's choice cannot be considered a permissible means of serving its legitimate ends.

We give this summary: [T]hroughout pregnancy the State may take measures to ensure that the woman's choice is informed, and measures designed to advance this interest will not be invalidated as long as their purpose is to persuade the woman to choose childbirth over abortion. These measures must not be an undue burden on the right. As with any medical procedure, the State may enact regulations to further the health or safety of a woman seeking an abortion. Unnecessary health regulations that have the purpose or effect of presenting a substantial obstacle to a woman seeking an abortion impose an undue burden on the right. Regardless of whether exceptions are made for particular circumstances, a State may not prohibit any woman from making the ultimate decision to terminate her pregnancy before viability. [And] "subsequent to viability, the State in promoting its interest in the potentiality of human life may, if it chooses, regulate, and even proscribe, abortion except where it is necessary, in appropriate medical judgment, for the preservation of the life or health of the mother." *Roe.*

These principles control our assessment of the Pennsylvania statute [at issue in this case], and we now turn to the issue of the validity of its challenged provisions.

V

[Section V.A is omitted.]

B

Except in a medical emergency, the statute requires that at least 24 hours before performing an abortion a physician inform the woman of the nature of the procedure, the health risks of the abortion and of childbirth, and the "probable gestational age of the unborn child." * * * In attempting to ensure that a woman apprehend the full consequences of her decision, the State furthers the legitimate purpose of reducing the risk that a woman may elect an abortion, only to discover later, with devastating psychological consequences, that her decision was not fully informed. * * * [R]equiring that the woman be informed of the availability of information relating to fetal development and the assistance available should she decide to carry the pregnancy to full term is a reasonable measure to ensure an informed choice, one which might cause the woman to choose childbirth over abortion.

Whether the mandatory 24-hour waiting period is nonetheless invalid because in practice it is a substantial obstacle to a woman's choice to terminate her pregnancy is a closer question. The findings of fact by the District Court indicate that because of the distances many women must travel to reach an abortion provider, the practical effect will often be a delay of much more than a day because the waiting period requires that a woman seeking an abortion make at least two visits to the doctor. As a result, the District Court found that for those women who have the fewest financial resources, those who must travel long distances, and those who have difficulty explaining their whereabouts to husbands, employers, or others, the 24-hour waiting period will be "particularly burdensome." 744 F. Supp. 1323, 1352 (E.D. Pa. 1990).

These findings are troubling in some respects, but they do not demonstrate that the waiting period constitutes an undue burden. We do not doubt that, as the District Court held, the waiting period has the effect of "increasing the cost and risk of delay of abortions." * * * Yet, as we have stated, under the undue burden standard a State is permitted to enact persuasive measures which favor childbirth over abortion, even if those measures do not further a health interest. * * * A particular burden is not of necessity a substantial obstacle. Whether a burden falls on a particular group is a distinct inquiry from whether it is a substantial obstacle even as to the women in that group. And the District Court did not conclude that the waiting period is such an obstacle even for the women who are most burdened by it. Hence, on the record before us, and in the context of this facial challenge, we are not convinced that the 24-hour waiting period constitutes an undue burden.

C

Pennsylvania's abortion law provides, except in cases of medical emergency, that no physician shall perform an abortion on a married woman without receiving a signed statement from the woman that she has notified her spouse that she is about to undergo an abortion. The woman has the option of providing an alternative signed statement certifying that her husband is not the man who impregnated her; that her husband could not be located; that the pregnancy is the result of spousal sexual assault which she has reported; or that the woman believes that notifying her husband will cause him or someone else to inflict bodily injury upon her.

> **Food for Thought**
>
> What weight, if any, should the Court accord the father's interest in the choice whether to carry a pregnancy to term? Is that right constitutionally protected? What would be the consequences of recognizing such a right?

A physician who performs an abortion on a married woman without receiving the appropriate signed statement will have his or her license revoked, and is liable to the husband for damages.

The District Court [made] detailed findings of fact regarding the effect of this statute [including that mere] "notification of pregnancy is frequently a flashpoint for battering and violence within the family." These findings are supported by studies of domestic violence. * * * In well-functioning marriages, spouses discuss important intimate decisions such as whether to bear a child. But there are millions of women in this country who are the victims of regular physical and psychological abuse at the hands of their husbands. Should these women become pregnant, they may have very good reasons for not wishing to inform their husbands of their decision to obtain an abortion. * * * The spousal notification requirement is thus likely to prevent a significant number of women from obtaining an abortion.

We recognize that a husband has a "deep and proper concern and interest [in] his wife's pregnancy and in the growth and development of the fetus she is carrying." [But it] is an inescapable biological fact that state regulation with respect to the child a woman is carrying will have a far greater impact on the mother's liberty than on the father's. * * * For the great many women who are victims of abuse inflicted by their husbands, or whose children are the victims of such abuse, a spousal notice requirement enables the husband to wield an effective veto over his wife's decision. [The] women most affected by this law—those who most reasonably fear the consequences of notifying their husbands that they are pregnant—are in the gravest danger.

The husband's interest in the life of the child his wife is carrying does not permit the State to empower him with this troubling degree of authority over his wife. * * * A State may not give to a man the kind of dominion over his wife that parents exercise over their children. [The spousal notification requirement] embodies a view of marriage consonant with the common-law status of married women but repugnant to our present understanding of marriage and of the nature of the rights secured by the Constitution. Women do not lose their constitutionally protected liberty when they marry. [The spousal notification provision is invalid.]

D

We next consider the parental consent provision. Except in a medical emergency, an unemancipated young woman under 18 may not obtain an abortion unless she and one of her parents (or guardian) provides informed consent * * *. Our cases establish, and we reaffirm today, that a State may require a minor seeking an abortion to obtain the consent of a parent or guardian, provided that there is an adequate judicial bypass procedure. *Ohio v. Akron Center for Reproductive Health*, 497 U.S., 502, 510–519 (1990).

> **FYI**
>
> A "judicial bypass procedure" permits a minor to seek judicial, rather than parental, consent for an abortion, for example when the pregnant minor's father is also the father of the fetus.

E

Under the recordkeeping and reporting requirements of the statute, every facility which performs abortions is required to file a report [including, for each abortion performed, the identity of the physician; the woman's age; the number of prior pregnancies and prior abortions she has had; gestational age; and similar information.] The collection of information with respect to actual patients is a vital element of medical research, and so it cannot be said that the requirements serve no purpose other than to make abortions more difficult. Nor do we find that the requirements impose a substantial obstacle to a woman's choice. At most they might increase the cost of some abortions by a slight amount. While at some point increased cost could become a substantial obstacle, there is no such showing on the record before us.

VI

Our Constitution is a covenant running from the first generation of Americans to us and then to future generations. * * * Each generation must learn anew that the Constitution's written terms embody ideas and aspirations that must survive more ages than one. We accept our responsibility not to retreat from interpreting the full meaning of the covenant in light of all of our precedents. We invoke it once again to define the freedom guaranteed by the Constitution's own promise, the promise of liberty.

JUSTICE STEVENS, concurring in part and dissenting in part.

[Justice Stevens would have concluded that the 24-hour waiting period required by the Pennsylvania statute was unconstitutional.] While there are well-established and consistently maintained reasons for the Commonwealth to view with skepticism the ability of minors to make decisions, none of those reasons applies to an adult woman's decision-making ability. * * * Part of the constitutional liberty to choose is the equal dignity to which each of us is entitled. A woman who decides to terminate her pregnancy is entitled to the same respect as a woman who decides to carry the fetus to term. The mandatory waiting period denies women that equal respect.

JUSTICE BLACKMUN, concurring in part, concurring in the judgment in part, and dissenting in part.

Three years ago, [four] Members of this Court appeared poised to [overrule *Roe*]. All that remained between the promise of *Roe* and the darkness [was] a single, flickering flame. * * * But now, just when so many expected the darkness to fall, the flame has grown bright. I do not underestimate the significance of today's joint opinion. Yet I remain steadfast in my belief that the right to reproductive choice is entitled to the full protection afforded by this Court [in *Roe*]. And I fear for the darkness as four Justices anxiously await the single vote necessary to extinguish the light.

[C]ompelled continuation of a pregnancy infringes upon a woman's right to bodily integrity by imposing substantial physical intrusions and significant risks of physical harm. [In addition,] when the State restricts a woman's right to terminate her pregnancy, it deprives a woman of the right to make her own decision about reproduction and family planning—critical life choices that this Court long has deemed central to the right to privacy. A State's restrictions on a woman's right to terminate her pregnancy also implicate constitutional guarantees of gender equality. * * * By restricting the right to terminate pregnancies, the State conscripts women's bodies into its service, forcing women to continue their pregnancies, suffer the pains of childbirth, and in most instances, provide years of maternal care. [The] assumption [that] women can simply be forced to accept the "natural" status and incidents of motherhood [appears] to rest upon a conception of women's role that has triggered the protection of the Equal Protection Clause.

Strict scrutiny of state limitations on reproductive choice still offers the most secure protection of the woman's right to make her own reproductive decisions, free from state coercion. [T]he *Roe* framework is far more administrable, and far less manipulable, than the "undue burden" standard adopted by the joint opinion. [Applying strict scrutiny, Justice Blackmun would have concluded that the provisions requiring content-based counseling, a 24-hour delay, informed parental consent, and reporting of abortion-related information were unconstitutional.]

> **FYI**
>
> Justice Blackmun retired in 1994, two years after the decision in *Casey*. To fill his seat, President Clinton appointed Justice Breyer, who has generally followed the approach of the plurality in *Casey*.

In one sense, the Court's approach is worlds apart from that of THE CHIEF JUSTICE and Justice SCALIA. And yet, in another sense, the distance between the two approaches is short—the distance is but a single vote. I am 83 years old. I cannot remain on this Court forever, and when I do step down, the confirmation process for my successor well may focus on the issue before us today. That, I regret, may be exactly where the choice between the two worlds will be made.

CHIEF JUSTICE REHNQUIST, with whom JUSTICE WHITE, JUSTICE SCALIA, and JUSTICE THOMAS join, concurring in the judgment in part and dissenting in part.

In our view, authentic principles of *stare decisis* do not require that any portion of the reasoning in *Roe* be kept intact. [Erroneous] decisions in such constitutional cases are uniquely durable, because correction through legislative action, save for constitutional amendment, is impossible. It is therefore our duty to reconsider constitutional interpretations that "depar[t] from a proper understanding" of the Constitution. [S]urely there is no requirement, in considering whether to depart from *stare decisis* in a constitutional case, that a decision be more wrong now than it was at the time it was rendered.

[The] joint opinion [argues that *Roe*] is exempt from reconsideration under established principles of *stare decisis* in constitutional cases [because the Court must] take special care not to be perceived as "surrendering to political pressure" and continued opposition. This is a truly novel principle, one which is contrary to both the Court's historical practice and to the Court's traditional willingness to tolerate criticism of its opinions. Under this principle, when the Court has ruled on a divisive issue, it is apparently prevented from overruling that decision for the sole reason that it was incorrect, unless opposition to the original decision has died away. * * *

The end result of the joint opinion's paeans of praise for legitimacy is the enunciation of a brand new standard for evaluating state regulation of a woman's right to abortion—the "undue burden" standard. * * * Despite the efforts of the joint opinion, the undue burden standard presents nothing more workable than the trimester framework which it discards today. Under the guise of the Constitution, this Court will still impart its own preferences on the States in the form of a complex abortion code.

[W]e think that the correct analysis is [as follows:] A woman's interest in having an abortion is a form of liberty protected by the Due Process Clause, but States may regulate abortion procedures in ways rationally related to a legitimate state interest. * * * [Under this approach, the dissent would have concluded that all of the provisions in the Pennsylvania statute are constitutional.]

JUSTICE SCALIA, with whom THE CHIEF JUSTICE, JUSTICE WHITE, and JUSTICE THOMAS join, concurring in the judgment in part and dissenting in part.

The States may, if they wish, permit abortion on demand, but the Constitution does not require them to do so. The permissibility of abortion, and the limitations upon it, are to be resolved like most important questions in our democracy: by citizens trying to persuade one another and then voting. [The issue in this case is] not whether the power of a woman to abort her unborn child is a "liberty" in the absolute sense; or even whether it is a liberty of great importance to many women. Of course it is both. The issue is whether it is a liberty protected by the Constitution of the United States. I am sure it is not. I reach that conclusion not because of anything so exalted as my views concerning the "concept of existence, of meaning, of the universe, and of the mystery of human life." Rather, I reach it [because] of two simple facts: (1) the Constitution says absolutely nothing about it, and (2) the longstanding traditions of American society have permitted it to be legally proscribed.

Beyond that brief summary of the essence of my position, I will not swell the United States Reports with repetition of what I have said before; and applying the rational basis test, I would uphold the Pennsylvania statute in its entirety. I must, however, respond to a few of the more outrageous arguments in today's opinion, which it is beyond human nature to leave unanswered.

[The joint opinion insists that the Court will apply "reasoned judgment."] The emptiness of the "reasoned judgment" that produced *Roe* is displayed in plain view by the fact that, after more than 19 years of effort by some of the brightest (and most determined) legal minds in the country, after more than 10 cases upholding abortion rights in this Court, and after dozens upon dozens of amicus briefs submitted in these and other cases, the best the Court can do to explain how it is that the word "liberty" must be thought to include the right to destroy human fetuses is to rattle off a collection of adjectives that simply decorate a value judgment and conceal a political choice.

[The joint opinion states,] "Liberty finds no refuge in a jurisprudence of doubt." One might have feared to encounter this august and sonorous phrase in an opinion defending the real *Roe v. Wade*, rather than the revised version fabricated today by the authors of the joint opinion. The shortcomings of *Roe* did not include lack of clarity: Virtually all regulation of abortion before the third trimester was invalid. But to come across this phrase in the joint opinion—which calls upon federal district judges to apply an "undue burden" standard as doubtful in application as it is unprincipled in origin—is really more than one should have to bear. * * * Reason finds no refuge in this jurisprudence of confusion.

The Court's reliance upon *stare decisis* can best be described as contrived. It insists upon the necessity of adhering not to all of *Roe*, but only to what it calls the "central holding." It seems to me that *stare decisis* ought to be applied even to the doctrine of *stare decisis*, and I confess never to have heard of this new, keep-what-you-want-and-throw-away-the-rest version. * * *

The Court's description of the place of *Roe* in the social history of the United States is unrecognizable. Not only did *Roe* not, as the Court suggests, resolve the deeply divisive issue of abortion; it did more than anything else to nourish it, by elevating it to the national level where it is infinitely more difficult to resolve. * * * *Roe* fanned into life an issue that has inflamed our national politics in general, and has obscured with its smoke the selection of Justices to this Court in particular, ever since. And by keeping us in the abortion-umpiring business, it is the perpetuation of that disruption, rather than of any Pax Roeana, that the Court's new majority decrees.

I cannot agree with, indeed I am appalled by, the Court's suggestion that the decision whether to stand by an erroneous constitutional decision must be strongly influenced—against overruling, no less—by the substantial and continuing public opposition the decision has generated. * * * But whether it would "subvert the Court's legitimacy" or not, the notion that we would decide a case differently from the way we otherwise would have in order to show that we can stand firm against public disapproval is frightening. * * * In truth, I am as distressed as the Court is [about] the "political pressure" directed to the Court: the marches, the mail, the protests aimed at inducing us to change our opinions. * * * The Court would profit, I think, from giving less attention to the fact of this distressing phenomenon, and more attention to the cause of it. That cause permeates today's opinion: a new mode of constitutional adjudication that relies not upon text and traditional practice to determine the law, but upon what the Court calls "reasoned judgment," which turns out to be nothing but philosophical predilection and moral intuition.

> **FYI**
>
> The unedited joint opinion takes up 58 pages in the U.S. Reports, and the entire document, including concurring and dissenting opinions, takes up 169 pages.

There is a poignant aspect to today's opinion. Its length, and what might be called its epic tone, suggest that its authors believe they are bringing to an end a troublesome era in the history of our Nation and of our Court.

There comes vividly to mind a portrait by Emanuel Leutze that hangs in the Harvard Law School: Roger Brooke Taney, painted in 1859, the 82d year of his life, the 24th of his Chief Justiceship, the second after his opinion in *Dred Scott*. * * * There seems to be on his face, and in his deep-set eyes, an expression of profound sadness and disillusionment. * * * I expect that two years earlier he, too, had thought himself "call[ing] the contending sides of national controversy to end their national division by accepting a common mandate rooted in the Constitution." It is no more realistic for us in this litigation, than it was for him in that, to think that an issue of the sort they both involved—an issue involving life and death, freedom and subjugation—can be "speedily and finally settled" by the Supreme Court. [B]y foreclosing all democratic outlet for the deep passions this issue arouses, by banishing the issue from the political forum that gives all participants, even the losers, the satisfaction of a fair hearing and an honest fight, by continuing the imposition of a rigid national rule instead of allowing for regional differences, the Court merely prolongs and intensifies the anguish. We should get out of this area, where we have no right to be, and where we do neither ourselves nor the country any good by remaining.

POINTS FOR DISCUSSION

a.   The Role of *Stare Decisis*

Why does *stare decisis* play such a prominent role in the decision in *Casey*? In a portion of his dissent omitted here, Chief Justice Rehnquist stated that the joint opinion followed *Roe* even though it could not "bring itself to say that *Roe* was correct as an original matter." Is his characterization of the joint opinion correct? If so, does that undermine the plurality's approach? Would *stare decisis* have any force if it applied only to cases that were correctly decided?

The various opinions differed in their approaches to interpreting the Constitution. Does the force of *stare decisis* vary depending upon the interpretive methodology that the Court employs? For an originalist, can *stare decisis* vindicate a decision that is otherwise inconsistent with the original meaning? For a non-originalist, can *stare decisis* freeze constitutional meaning, ensuring that the Constitution does not "evolve"?

b.   When Can a State Regulate Abortions?

After *Casey*, what types of restrictions can a state impose on the right to an abortion? Look carefully at the votes for each section of the joint opinion. Section IV, which announces the undue burden standard and the rejection of *Roe*'s trimester framework, attracted the votes of only three Justices. Is the undue burden standard now the governing standard? In decisions that do not command five votes for any one approach, generally only the most narrow ground for decision is entitled to binding force. What was the most narrow ground for the Court's conclusions for each challenged provision of the statute?

In assigning binding force to the various opinions in *Casey*, is it relevant that some of the Justices are no longer on the Court? (Since the decision, Chief Justice Rehnquist and Justices Blackmun and White have passed away, and Justices O'Connor, Stevens, and Souter retired.) If so, how?

c.   "Undue Burden"

What exactly is an "undue burden"? Is Justice Scalia correct in suggesting that it is an empty standard that invites judges to impose their own views of public policy and morality? Does the plurality's application of the standard provide any guidance about its content, and about how it should be applied in the future? If so, does it rebut Justice Scalia's criticism or validate it?

d. Abortion and Sex Equality

Justice Stevens asserted in his separate opinion that the 24-hour waiting period was unconstitutional because it denied women equal "dignity" and "respect." Similarly, the plurality concluded that the spousal notification provision was invalid for this reason. Justice Blackmun went further, asserting that, as a general matter, restrictions on the right to an abortion presume that "women can simply be forced to accept the 'natural' status and incidents of motherhood," a "conception of women's role that has triggered the protection of the Equal Protection Clause."

If nothing else, it seems difficult to dispute that the most immediate burdens of laws restricting access to (or prohibiting) abortions fall on women, who have to carry a fetus to term. (The most immediate benefits are, of course, to the fetus.) Should laws regulating abortion be viewed as a form of sex discrimination subject to heightened scrutiny under the Equal Protection Clause? On this point, consider the argument that then-Judge Ginsburg advanced seven years before the decision in *Casey*:

> **Make the Connection**
> We will consider sex discrimination in Chapter 5.

> "The conflict, however, is not simply one between a fetus' interests and a woman's interests, narrowly conceived, nor is the overriding issue state versus private control of a woman's body for a span of nine months. Also in the balance is a woman's autonomous charge of her full life's course— as Professor Karst put it, her ability to stand in relation to man, society, and the state as an independent, self-sustaining, equal citizen."

Ruth Bader Ginsburg, *Some Thought on Autonomy and Equality in Relation to* Roe v. Wade, 63 N.C. L. Rev. 375, 383 (1985) (citing Kenneth L. Karst, *Foreword: Equal Citizenship Under the Fourteenth Amendment*, 91 Harv. L. Rev. 1, 57–59 (1977)). Do you agree that the availability of abortion enhances women's autonomy?

Casey, like *Roe* before it, did not succeed in ending political controversy over the subject of abortion, and states continued to seek to impose limits on abortion. In *Stenberg v. Carhart*, 530 U.S. 914 (2000), the Court, in a 5–4 decision, invalidated a Nebraska law that banned one form of "dilation and evacuation" abortions (often called "partial-birth abortions" by opponents of the procedure) without providing an exception in cases where necessary to preserve the mother's health. Justice Breyer, who wrote for the Court, accepted the District Court's finding that medical evidence demonstrated that the procedure was sometimes necessary to protect the health of the mother. Justice Breyer also noted that the law's definition of the banned procedure was sufficiently imprecise that it might be invoked to prosecute doctors who performed other procedures. Applying *Casey*'s undue burden standard, the Court invalidated the statute. Justices Stevens and Ginsburg wrote separately to express their support for the central holding of *Roe*. Justice O'Connor wrote separately to suggest that a more carefully drawn statute might survive scrutiny under the undue burden standard. And Justice Kennedy, who had been one of the authors of the joint opinion in *Casey*, dissented, as did Chief Justice Rehnquist and Justices Scalia and Thomas.

Not long after the Court's decision in *Stenberg*, Congress enacted a law banning the same procedure that was banned by the Nebraska statute at issue in *Stenberg*. The Court considered that statute in the case that follows.

GONZALES V. CARHART
550 U.S. 124 (2007)

JUSTICE KENNEDY delivered the opinion of the Court.

These cases require us to consider the validity of the Partial-Birth Abortion Ban Act of 2003 (Act), 18 U.S.C. § 1531. * * * The surgical procedure referred to as "dilation and evacuation" or "D & E" is the usual abortion method in [the second] trimester. * * * The abortion procedure that was the impetus for the numerous bans on "partial-birth abortion," including the Act, is a variation of this standard D & E. [For] discussion purposes this D & E variation will be referred to as intact D & E. The main difference between the two procedures is that in intact D & E a doctor extracts the fetus intact or largely intact with only a few passes [of the forceps]. * * * In an intact D & E procedure the doctor extracts the fetus in a way conducive to pulling out its entire body, instead of ripping it apart. [Intact D & E often involves the evacuation of the fetus's skull contents before the removal of the fetus from the patient.]

[The statute made it a crime for any physician knowingly to perform the banned procedure and "thereby [to kill] a human fetus," and provided that a person convicted under the statute could be fined or imprisoned for up to two years. The ban did "not apply to a partial-birth abortion that is necessary to save the life of a mother," but did not include an exception to protect the health of the mother. Physicians and abortion advocacy groups filed separate suits challenging the constitutionality of the statute on its face. The district courts held that the statute was unconstitutional, and the Court of Appeals affirmed.]

In 2003, after this Court's decision in *Stenberg*, Congress passed the Act at issue here. The Act responded to *Stenberg* in two ways. First, Congress made factual findings. * * * Congress found, among other things, that "[a] moral, medical, and ethical consensus exists that the practice of performing a partial-birth abortion [is] a gruesome and inhumane procedure that is never medically necessary and should be prohibited." Second, and more relevant here, the Act's language differs from that of the Nebraska statute struck down in *Stenberg*.

The principles set forth in the joint opinion in *Planned Parenthood of Southeastern Pa. v. Casey*, 505 U.S. 833 (1992), did not find support from all those who join the instant opinion. Whatever one's views concerning the *Casey* joint opinion, it is evident a premise central to its conclusion—that the government has a legitimate and substantial interest in preserving and promoting fetal life—would be repudiated were the Court now to affirm the judgments of the Courts of Appeals. * * * We now apply [*Casey*'s] standard to the cases at bar.

The Act punishes "knowingly perform[ing]" a "partial-birth abortion." § 1531(a). It defines the unlawful abortion in explicit terms. First, the person performing the abortion must "vaginally delive[r] a living fetus." § 1531(b)(1)(A). * * * Second, the Act's definition of partial-birth abortion requires the fetus to be delivered "until, in the case of a head-first presentation, the entire fetal head is outside the body of the mother, or, in the case of breech presentation, any part of the fetal trunk past the navel is outside the body of the mother." § 1531(b)(1)(A). * * * Third, to fall within the Act, a doctor must perform an "overt act, other than completion of delivery, that kills the partially delivered living fetus." § 1531(b)(1)(B). * * * Fourth, the Act contains scienter requirements concerning all the actions involved in the prohibited abortion.

A review of the statutory text discloses the limits of its reach. The Act prohibits intact D & E [and] does not prohibit the D & E procedure in which the fetus is removed in parts. * * * [In contrast, the] statute in *Stenberg* prohibited "deliberately and intentionally delivering into the vagina a living unborn child, or a substantial portion thereof, for the purpose of performing a procedure that the person performing such procedure knows will kill the unborn child and does kill the unborn child." The Court concluded that this statute encompassed D & E because "D & E will often involve a physician pulling a 'substantial portion' of a still living fetus, say, an arm or leg, into the vagina prior to the death of the fetus." 530 U.S. at 939. Congress, it is apparent, responded to these concerns * * *.

Under the principles accepted as controlling here, the Act, as we have interpreted it, would be unconstitutional "if its purpose or effect is to place a substantial obstacle in the path of a woman seeking an abortion before the fetus attains viability." *Casey*, 505 U.S. at 878. * * * The question is whether the Act, measured by its text in this facial attack, imposes a substantial obstacle to late-term, but previability, abortions. The Act does not on its face impose a substantial obstacle, and we reject this [facial] challenge to its validity.

The Act proscribes a method of abortion in which a fetus is killed just inches before completion of the birth process. [Congress made findings that assert that the] Act expresses respect for the dignity of human life [and that Congress was concerned] with the effects on the medical community and on its reputation caused by the practice of partial-birth abortion. [See Congressional Findings (14), in notes following 18 U.S.C. § 1531.] There can be no doubt the government "has an interest in protecting the integrity and ethics of the medical profession."

Casey reaffirmed these governmental objectives. The government may use its voice and its regulatory authority to show its profound respect for the life within the woman. * * * [*Casey*'s] premise, that the State, from the inception of the pregnancy, maintains its own regulatory interest in protecting the life of the fetus that may become a child, cannot be set at naught by interpreting *Casey*'s requirement of a health exception so it becomes tantamount to allowing a doctor to choose the abortion method he or she might prefer. Where it has a rational basis to act, and it does not impose an undue burden, the State may use its regulatory power to bar certain procedures and substitute others, all in furtherance of its legitimate interests in regulating the medical profession in order to promote respect for life, including life of the unborn.

The Act's ban on abortions that involve partial delivery of a living fetus furthers the Government's objectives. No one would dispute that, for many, D & E is a procedure itself laden with the power to devalue human life. Congress could nonetheless conclude that the type of abortion proscribed by the Act requires specific regulation because it implicates additional ethical and moral concerns that justify a special prohibition. Congress determined that the abortion methods it proscribed had a "disturbing similarity to the killing of a newborn infant," and thus it was concerned with "draw[ing] a bright line that clearly distinguishes abortion and infanticide." The Court has in the past confirmed the validity of drawing boundaries to prevent certain practices that extinguish life and are close to actions that are condemned. *Washington v. Glucksberg*, 521 U.S. 702 (1997).

> **Make the Connection**
>
> We will consider the Court's decision in *Glucksberg*, which involved physician-assisted suicide, later in this chapter.

Respect for human life finds an ultimate expression in the bond of love the mother has for her child. The Act recognizes this reality as well. Whether to have an abortion requires a difficult and painful moral decision. While we find no reliable data to measure the phenomenon, it seems unexceptionable to conclude some women come to regret their choice to abort the infant life they once created and sustained. Severe depression and loss of esteem can follow. In a decision so fraught with emotional consequence some doctors may prefer not to disclose precise details of the means that will be used, confining themselves to the required statement of risks the procedure entails. * * * It is, however, precisely this lack of information concerning the way in which the fetus will be killed that is of legitimate concern to the State. The State has an interest in ensuring so grave a choice is well informed. It is self-evident that a mother who comes to regret her choice to abort must struggle with grief more anguished and sorrow more profound when she learns, only after the event, what she once did not know: that she allowed a doctor to pierce the skull and vacuum the fast-developing brain of her unborn child, a child assuming the human form. * * * In sum, we reject the contention that the congressional purpose of the Act was "to place a substantial obstacle in the path of a woman seeking an abortion."

[The] prohibition in the Act would be unconstitutional, under precedents we here assume to be controlling, if it "subject[ed] [women] to significant health risks." * * * There is documented medical disagreement whether the Act's prohibition would ever impose significant health risks on women. * * * The question becomes whether the Act can stand when this medical uncertainty persists.

> **Take Note**
>
> This is not the first time in this opinion that Justice Kennedy referred to precedent that the Court "assume[s]" to be controlling. Why does he use such an unusual verbal formulation?

The Court's precedents instruct that the Act can survive this facial attack. The Court has given state and federal legislatures wide discretion to pass legislation in areas where there is medical and scientific uncertainty. * * * The law need not give abortion doctors unfettered choice in the course of their medical practice, nor should it elevate their status above other physicians in the medical community. Medical uncertainty does not foreclose the exercise of legislative power in the abortion context any more than it does in other contexts. The medical uncertainty over whether the Act's prohibition creates significant health risks provides a sufficient basis to conclude in this facial attack that the Act does not impose an undue burden.

> **Take Note**
>
> A litigant making a "facial challenge" to the constitutionality of a statute argues that no set of circumstances exists under which the Act would be valid. *United States v. Salerno*, 481 U.S. 739, 745 (1987). In contrast, a litigant making an "as applied challenge" argues that "the law has in fact been (or is sufficiently likely to be) unconstitutionally applied to him." *McCullen v. Coakley*, 573 U.S. 464, 484 n.4 (2014).

[An as-applied challenge] is the proper manner to protect the health of the woman if it can be shown that in discrete and well-defined instances a particular condition has or is likely to occur in which the procedure prohibited by the Act must be used. In an as-applied challenge the nature of the medical risk can be better quantified and balanced than in a facial attack.

JUSTICE THOMAS, with whom JUSTICE SCALIA joins, concurring.

Make the Connection

Although the Court and Justice Thomas did not address the question, was the Act a valid exercise of Congress's power under the Commerce Clause? Is the connection between interstate commerce and abortion practices less attenuated than the relationship between interstate commerce and violence against women, which was at issue in *United States v. Morrison*? (We considered *Morrison* in Volume 1.) Why do you suppose the respondents here chose not to attack the Act on these grounds?

I join the Court's opinion because it accurately applies current jurisprudence, including *Planned Parenthood of Southeastern Pa. v. Casey*, 505 U.S. 833 (1992). I write separately to reiterate my view that the Court's abortion jurisprudence, including *Casey* and *Roe v. Wade*, 410 U.S. 113 (1973), has no basis in the Constitution. I also note that whether the Act constitutes a permissible exercise of Congress' power under the Commerce Clause is not before the Court. The parties did not raise or brief that issue; it is outside the question presented; and the lower courts did not address it.

JUSTICE GINSBURG, with whom JUSTICE STEVENS, JUSTICE SOUTER, and JUSTICE BREYER join, dissenting.

Today's decision is alarming. It refuses to take *Casey* and *Stenberg* seriously. It tolerates, indeed applauds, federal intervention to ban nationwide a procedure found necessary and proper in certain cases by the American College of Obstetricians and Gynecologists (ACOG). It blurs the line, firmly drawn in *Casey*, between previability and postviability abortions. And, for the first time since *Roe*, the Court blesses a prohibition with no exception safeguarding a woman's health.

In *Stenberg*, we expressly held that a statute banning intact D & E was unconstitutional in part because it lacked a health exception. 530 U.S. at 930, 937. * * * In 2003, a few years after our ruling in *Stenberg*, Congress passed the Partial-Birth Abortion Ban Act—without an exception for women's health.[4] The congressional findings on which the Partial-Birth Abortion Ban Act rests do not withstand inspection, as the lower courts have determined and this Court is obliged to concede. Many of the Act's recitations are incorrect. * * * Congress

---

[4]   The Act's sponsors left no doubt that their intention was to nullify our ruling in *Stenberg*. See, e.g., 149 Cong. Rec. 5731 (2003) (statement of Sen. Santorum) ("Why are we here? We are here because the Supreme Court defended the indefensible. We have responded to the Supreme Court."). See also 148 Cong. Rec. 14273 (2002) (statement of Rep. Linder) (rejecting proposition that Congress has "no right to legislate a ban on this horrible practice because the Supreme Court says [it] cannot").

claimed there was a medical consensus that the banned procedure is never necessary. But the evidence "very clearly demonstrate[d] the opposite." *Planned Parenthood Fed. of Am. v. Ashcroft*, 320 F.Supp.2d 957, 1025 [(N.D. CA 2004)]. Similarly, Congress found that "[t]here is no credible medical evidence that partial-birth abortions are safe or are safer than other abortion procedures." But the congressional record includes letters from numerous individual physicians stating that pregnant women's health would be jeopardized under the Act, as well as statements from nine professional associations.

In contrast to Congress, the District Courts made findings after full trials at which all parties had the opportunity to present their best evidence. * * * Based on thoroughgoing review of the trial evidence and the congressional record, each of the District Courts to consider the issue rejected Congress' findings as unreasonable and not supported by the evidence. * * * The District Courts' findings merit this Court's respect.

Today's ruling, the Court declares, advances [the] Government's "legitimate and substantial interest in preserving and promoting fetal life." But the Act scarcely furthers that interest: The law saves not a single fetus from destruction, for it targets only a *method* of performing abortion. * * * Ultimately, the Court admits that "moral concerns" are at work, concerns that could yield prohibitions on any abortion. Notably,

> **Take Note**
>
> The Court deferred substantially to Congress's factual findings, whereas Justice Ginsburg asserted that the Court should defer to the trial courts' fact finding. Who is better suited to make findings about the nature of the banned procedure and the likely health effects of the ban?

the concerns expressed are untethered to any ground genuinely serving the Government's interest in preserving life. [T]he Court invokes an antiabortion shibboleth for which it concededly has no reliable evidence: Women who have abortions come to regret their choices, and consequently suffer from "[s]evere depression and loss of esteem." * * * The solution the Court approves [is] not to require doctors to inform women, accurately and adequately, of the different procedures and their attendant risks. Instead, the Court deprives women of the right to make an autonomous choice, even at the expense of their safety. * * * This way of thinking reflects ancient notions about women's place in the family and under the Constitution—ideas that have long since been discredited.

The Court's hostility to the right *Roe* and *Casey* secured is not concealed. Throughout, the opinion refers to obstetrician-gynecologists and surgeons who perform abortions not by the titles of their medical specialties, but by the pejorative label "abortion doctor." A fetus is described as an "unborn child," and

> **Take Note**
>
> Justice Ginsburg suggested here that the Court chose loaded language used by opponents of abortion. Is it possible for the Court to choose "neutral" language to describe matters that are the subject of such intense debate?

as a "baby." * * * And, most troubling, *Casey*'s principles, confirming the continuing vitality of "the essential holding of *Roe*," are merely "assume[d]" for the moment, rather than "retained" or "reaffirmed," *Casey*, 505 U.S. at 846.

The Court's allowance only of an "as-applied challenge in a discrete case" jeopardizes women's health and places doctors in an untenable position. Even if courts were able to carve-out exceptions through piecemeal litigation for "discrete and well-defined instances," women whose circumstances have not been anticipated by prior litigation could well be left unprotected. In treating those women, physicians would risk criminal prosecution, conviction, and imprisonment if they exercise their best judgment as to the safest medical procedure for their patients. The Court is thus gravely mistaken to conclude that narrow as-applied challenges are "the proper manner to protect the health of the woman."

[T]he Act, and the Court's defense of it, cannot be understood as anything other than an effort to chip away at a right declared again and again by this Court—and with increasing comprehension of its centrality to women's lives.

POINTS FOR DISCUSSION

a. Federal Action and the Due Process Clause

The Court in *Roe* and *Casey* concluded that the right to an abortion derives from the Due Process Clause of the Fourteenth Amendment, which limits state action. *Carhart*, however, concerned the constitutionality of a *federal* statute. The Court did not specifically identify the provision of the Constitution on which the respondents' challenge was based. The Court of Appeals, however, declared that "the Due Process Clause of the Fifth Amendment is textually identical to the Due Process Clause of the Fourteenth Amendment, and both proscribe virtually identical governmental conduct." Should the Court interpret the Fifth Amendment's Due Process Clause to protect the same rights that it has held are protected by the Fourteenth Amendment's Due Process Clause?

b. Undue Burden

What does Justice Kennedy's approach in *Carhart* signal about the meaning of the undue burden test? Can Congress (or a state) ban any single procedure—without providing an exception for the health of the mother—as long as it leaves available some other procedure? What if there are government-imposed limits on the availability of that other procedure, as well?

c.   The Future of the Right to an Abortion

The Court declared that Congress has a "legitimate and substantial interest in preserving and promoting fetal life" and a legitimate interest in "promot[ing] respect for life, including life of the unborn." The Court also noted, however, that the banned abortion procedure was challenged as imposing an undue burden on *pre*-viability abortions. Under *Roe* and *Casey*, does the government have a substantial (or compelling) interest in protecting actual fetal life *before* the point of viability? If not, then does *Carhart* signal that the Court now believes that the government can act to protect fetal life before viability? If so, what does that suggest about the enduring viability of *Roe* and *Casey*?

The Court also reasoned that the government has a legitimate interest in seeking to protect women from the psychological effects of the decision to have an abortion. Is there a logical stopping point for the implications of this concern? Wouldn't it justify bans on all forms of abortion, at all stages of pregnancy? Does the decision in *Carhart* signal that the Court is poised to overrule *Roe* and *Casey*? Or simply that the particular procedure at issue raised unique concerns?

WHOLE WOMAN'S HEALTH V. HELLERSTEDT
136 S.Ct. 2292 (2016)

JUSTICE BREYER delivered the opinion of the court.

We must here decide whether two provisions of Texas' House Bill 2 violate the Federal Constitution * * *. The first provision, which we shall call the "*admitting-privileges requirement*," says that "[a] physician performing or inducing an abortion . . . must, on the date the abortion is performed or induced, have active admitting privileges at a hospital that . . . is located not further than 30 miles from the location at which the abortion is performed or induced." Tex. Health & Safety Code Ann. § 171.0031(a). * * * The second provision, which we shall call the "*surgical-center requirement*," says that "the minimum standards for an abortion facility must be equivalent to the minimum standards adopted under [the Texas Health and Safety Code section] for ambulatory surgical centers." Tex. Health & Safety Code Ann. § 245.010(a).

[Petitioners, a group of abortion providers, challenged these provisions in federal district court. After a four-day bench trial, the district court invalidated both provisions. The court found that, whereas there were more than 40 licensed abortion facilities in Texas prior to the enactment of H.B. 2, the number "dropped by almost half leading up to and in the wake of enforcement of the admitting-privileges requirement that went into effect in late-October 2013." The court also found that, if the surgical-center provision were allowed to take effect, "only seven facilities and a potential eighth will exist in Texas." 46 F.Supp.3d 673, 681 (W.D.Tex.2014). The court found that "this would result in each facility serving between 7,500 and 10,000 patients per year," and that the number of women living far from a clinic would increase substantially. The court further found that the "cost of coming into compliance" with the surgical-center requirement "for existing clinics is significant," "undisputedly approach[ing] 1 million dollars," and "most likely exceed[ing] 1.5 million dollars," with "[s]ome . . . clinics" unable to "comply due to physical size limitations of their sites." The court of appeals reversed the district court's holding that both provisions are unconstitutional, but it upheld in part the district court's conclusion that the requirements are unconstitutional as applied to one facility.]

We begin with the standard, as described in *Planned Parenthood of Southeastern Pa. v. Casey*, 505 U.S. 833, 878 (1992). We recognize that the "State has a legitimate interest in seeing to it that abortion, like any other medical procedure, is performed under circumstances that insure maximum safety for the patient." *Roe v. Wade*, 410 U.S. 113, 150 (1973). But, we added, "a statute which, while furthering [a] valid state interest, has the effect of placing a substantial obstacle in the path of a woman's choice cannot be considered a permissible means of serving its legitimate ends." *Casey*, 505 U.S., at 877 (plurality opinion). Moreover, "[u]nnecessary health regulations that have the purpose or effect of presenting a substantial obstacle to a woman seeking an abortion impose an undue burden on the right." *Id.*, at 878.

The Court of Appeals wrote that a state law is "constitutional if: (1) it does not have the purpose or effect of placing a substantial obstacle in the path of a woman seeking an abortion of a nonviable fetus; and (2) it is reasonably related to (or designed to further) a legitimate state interest." 790 F.3d, at 572. The Court of Appeals went on to hold that "the district court erred by substituting its own judgment for that of the legislature" when it conducted its "undue burden inquiry," in part because "medical uncertainty underlying a statute is for resolution by legislatures, not the courts." *Id.*, at 587 (citing *Gonzales v. Carhart*, 550 U.S. 124, 163 (2007)).

The Court of Appeals' articulation of the relevant standard is incorrect. The first part of the Court of Appeals' test may be read to imply that a district court should not consider the existence or nonexistence of medical benefits when considering whether a regulation of abortion constitutes an undue burden. The rule announced in *Casey*, however, requires that courts consider the burdens a law imposes on abortion access together with the benefits those laws confer. See 505 U.S., at 887–898 (opinion of the Court) (performing this balancing with respect to a spousal notification provision); *id.*, at 899–901 (joint opinion of O'CONNOR, KENNEDY, and SOUTER, JJ.) (same balancing with respect to a parental notification provision). And the second part of the test is wrong to equate the judicial review applicable to the regulation of a constitutionally protected personal liberty with the less strict review applicable where, for example, economic legislation is at issue. See, *e.g.*, *Williamson v. Lee Optical of Okla., Inc.*, 348 U.S. 483, 491 (1955). The Court of Appeals' approach simply does not match the standard that this Court laid out in *Casey*, which asks courts to consider whether any burden imposed on abortion access is "undue."

The statement that legislatures, and not courts, must resolve questions of medical uncertainty is also inconsistent with this Court's case law. Instead, the Court, when determining the constitutionality of laws regulating abortion procedures, has placed considerable weight upon evidence and argument presented in judicial proceedings.

[W]e first consider the admitting-privileges requirement. * * * We conclude that there is adequate legal and factual support for the District Court's conclusion [that the requirement imposed an undue burden on a woman's right to have an abortion]. The purpose of the admitting-privileges requirement is to help ensure that women have easy access to a hospital should complications arise during an abortion procedure. But the District Court found that it brought about no such health-related benefit. The court found that "[t]he great weight of evidence demonstrates that, before the act's passage, abortion in Texas was extremely safe with particularly low rates of serious complications and virtually no deaths occurring on account of the procedure." 46 F.Supp.3d, at 684. Thus, there was no significant health-related problem that the new law helped to cure. [In reaching this conclusion, the district court relied on multiple peer-reviewed studies and expert testimony about abortion complications.] We have found nothing in Texas' record evidence that shows that, compared to prior law (which required [admitting privileges *or*] a "working arrangement" with a doctor with admitting privileges), the new law advanced Texas' legitimate interest in protecting women's health.

At the same time, the record evidence indicates that the admitting-privileges requirement places a "substantial obstacle in the path of a woman's choice." *Casey*, 505 U.S., at 877 (plurality opinion). The District Court found, as of the time the admitting-privileges requirement began to be enforced, the number of facilities providing abortions dropped in half, from about 40 to about 20. Eight abortion clinics closed in the months leading up to the requirement's effective date. Eleven more closed on the day the admitting-privileges requirement took effect.

Other evidence helps to explain why the new requirement led to the closure of clinics. We read that other evidence in light of a brief filed in this Court by the Society of Hospital Medicine. That brief describes the undisputed general fact that "hospitals often condition admitting privileges on reaching a certain number of admissions per year." Returning to the District Court record, we note that, in direct testimony, the president of Nova Health Systems, implicitly relying on this general fact, pointed out that it would be difficult for doctors regularly performing abortions at the El Paso clinic to obtain admitting privileges at nearby hospitals because "[d]uring the past 10 years, over 17,000 abortion procedures were performed at the El Paso clinic [and n]ot a single one of those patients had to be transferred to a hospital for emergency treatment, much less admitted to the hospital." App. 730. In a word, doctors would be unable to maintain admitting privileges or obtain those privileges for the future, because the fact that abortions are so safe meant that providers were unlikely to have any patients to admit.

In our view, the record contains sufficient evidence that the admitting-privileges requirement led to the closure of half of Texas' clinics, or thereabouts. Those closures meant fewer doctors, longer waiting times, and increased crowding. Record evidence also supports the finding that after the admitting-privileges provision went into effect, the "number of women of reproductive age living in a county . . . more than 150 miles from a provider increased from approximately 86,000 to 400,000 . . . and the number of women living in a county more than 200 miles from a provider from approximately 10,000 to 290,000." 46 F.Supp.3d, at 681. We recognize that increased driving distances do not always constitute an "undue burden." See *Casey,* 505 U.S., at 885–887. But here, those increases are but one additional burden, which, when taken together with others that the closings brought about, and when viewed in light of the virtual absence of any health benefit, lead us to conclude that the record adequately supports the District Court's "undue burden" conclusion.

[T]he dissent suggests that one benefit of H.B. 2's requirements would be that they might "force unsafe facilities to shut down." To support that assertion, the dissent points to the Kermit Gosnell scandal. Gosnell, a physician in Pennsylvania, was convicted of first-degree murder and manslaughter. He "staffed his facility with unlicensed and indifferent workers, and then let them practice medicine unsupervised" and had "[d]irty facilities; unsanitary instruments; an absence of functioning monitoring and resuscitation equipment; the use of cheap, but dangerous, drugs; illegal procedures; and inadequate emergency access for when things inevitably went wrong." Report of Grand Jury in No. 0009901–2008 (1st Jud. Dist. Pa., Jan. 14, 2011). Gosnell's behavior was terribly wrong. But there is no reason to believe that an extra layer of regulation would have affected that behavior. Determined wrongdoers, already ignoring existing statutes and safety measures, are unlikely to be convinced to adopt safe practices by a new overlay of regulations. Regardless, Gosnell's deplorable crimes could escape detection only because his facility went uninspected for more than 15 years. Pre-existing Texas law already contained numerous detailed regulations covering abortion facilities, including a requirement that facilities be inspected at least annually. The record contains nothing to suggest that H.B. 2 would be more effective than pre-existing Texas law at deterring wrongdoers like Gosnell from criminal behavior.

The second challenged provision of Texas' new law sets forth the surgical-center requirement. Prior to enactment of the new requirement, Texas law required abortion facilities to meet a host of health and safety requirements. Under those pre-existing laws, facilities were subject to annual reporting and recordkeeping requirements; a quality assurance program; personnel policies and staffing requirements; physical and environmental requirements; infection control standards; disclosure requirements; patient-rights standards; and medical- and clinical-services standards, including anesthesia standards. These requirements are policed by random and announced inspections, at least annually, as well as administrative penalties, injunctions, civil penalties, and criminal penalties for certain violations.

H.B. 2 added the requirement that an "abortion facility" meet the "minimum standards . . . for ambulatory surgical centers" under Texas law. The surgical-center regulations include, among other things, detailed specifications relating to the size of the nursing staff, building dimensions, and other building requirements. [For example, facilities] must include a full surgical suite with an operating room that has "a clear floor area of at least 240 square feet" in which "[t]he minimum clear dimension between built-in cabinets, counters, and shelves shall be 14 feet." § 135.52(d)(15)(A). There must be a preoperative patient holding room and a postoperative recovery suite. The former "shall be provided and arranged in a one-way traffic pattern so that patients entering from outside the surgical suite can change, gown, and move directly into the restricted corridor of the surgical suite," § 135.52(d)(10)(A), and the latter "shall be arranged to provide a one-way traffic pattern from the restricted surgical corridor to the postoperative recovery suite, and then to the extended observation rooms or discharge," § 135.52(d)(9)(A). Surgical centers must meet numerous other spatial requirements, see generally § 135.52, including specific corridor widths,

§ 135.52(e)(1)(B)(iii). * * * Dozens of other sections list additional requirements that apply to surgical centers. See generally §§ 135.1–135.56.

The record makes clear that the surgical-center requirement provides no benefit when complications arise in the context of an abortion produced through medication. That is because, in such a case, complications would almost always arise only after the patient has left the facility. The record also contains evidence indicating that abortions taking place in an abortion facility are safe—indeed, safer than numerous procedures that take place outside hospitals and to which Texas does not apply its surgical-center requirements. The total number of deaths in Texas from abortions was five in the period from 2001 to 2012, or about one every two years (that is to say, one out of about 120,000 to 144,000 abortions). Nationwide, childbirth is 14 times more likely than abortion to result in death, but Texas law allows a midwife to oversee childbirth in the patient's own home. Colonoscopy, a procedure that typically takes place outside a hospital (or surgical center) setting, has a mortality rate 10 times higher than an abortion. Medical treatment after an incomplete miscarriage often involves a procedure identical to that involved in a nonmedical abortion, but it often takes place outside a hospital or surgical center.

> **Food for Thought**
>
> What is the relevance of the mortality statistics regarding childbirths and colonoscopies? Is the Court suggesting that the undue burden standard prohibits a state from regulating abortion to a higher safety standard than it regulates other medical procedures? If Texas were to impose the same surgical-center requirements for childbirths and colonoscopies, would H.B. 2 be constitutional? Or is the Court suggesting that the legislature's purpose was something other than the desire to protect women's health?

And Texas partly or wholly grandfathers (or waives in whole or in part the surgical-center requirement for) about two-thirds of the facilities to which the surgical-center standards apply. But it neither grandfathers nor provides waivers for any of the facilities that perform abortions. 46 F.Supp.3d, at 680–681. These facts indicate that the surgical-center provision imposes "a requirement that simply is not based on differences" between abortion and other surgical procedures "that are reasonably related to" preserving women's health, the asserted "purpos[e] of the Act in which it is found." *Doe v. Bolton,* 410 U.S. 179, 194 (1973) (quoting *Morey v. Doud,* 354 U.S. 457, 465 (1957)).

Moreover, many surgical-center requirements are inappropriate as applied to surgical abortions. Requiring scrub facilities; maintaining a one-way traffic pattern through the facility; having ceiling, wall, and floor finishes; separating soiled utility and sterilization rooms; and regulating air pressure, filtration, and humidity control can help reduce infection where doctors conduct procedures that penetrate the skin. But abortions typically involve either the administration of medicines or procedures performed through the natural opening of the birth canal, which is itself not sterile. * * * Further, since the few instances in which serious complications do arise following an abortion almost always require hospitalization, not treatment at a surgical center, surgical-center standards will not help in those instances either.

The upshot is that this record evidence, along with the absence of any evidence to the contrary, provides ample support for the District Court's conclusion that "[m]any of the building standards mandated by the act and its implementing rules have such a tangential relationship to patient safety in the context of abortion as to be nearly arbitrary." 46 F.Supp.3d, at 684.

At the same time, the record provides adequate evidentiary support for the District Court's conclusion that the surgical-center requirement places a substantial obstacle in the path of women seeking an abortion. The parties stipulated that the requirement would further reduce the number of abortion facilities available to seven or eight facilities, located in Houston, Austin, San Antonio, and Dallas/Fort Worth. In the District Court's view, the proposition that these "seven or eight providers could meet the demand of the entire State stretches credulity." 46 F.Supp.3d, at 682. We take this statement as a finding that these few facilities could not "meet" that "demand."

Texas suggests that the seven or eight remaining clinics could expand sufficiently to provide abortions for the 60,000 to 72,000 Texas women who sought them each year. * * * [I]n the face of no threat to women's health, Texas seeks to force women to travel long distances to get abortions in crammed-to-capacity superfacilities. Patients seeking these services are less likely to get the kind of individualized attention, serious conversation, and emotional support that doctors at less taxed facilities may have offered. * * * Surgical centers attempting to accommodate sudden, vastly increased demand may find that quality of care declines.

We agree with the District Court that the surgical-center requirement, like the admitting-privileges requirement, provides few, if any, health benefits for women, poses a substantial obstacle to women seeking abortions, and constitutes an "undue burden" on their constitutional right to do so. * * * For these reasons the judgment of the Court of Appeals is reversed, and the case is remanded for further proceedings consistent with this opinion.

[JUSTICE GINSBURG's concurring opinion is omitted.]

JUSTICE THOMAS, dissenting.

* * * I remain fundamentally opposed to the Court's abortion jurisprudence. Even taking *Casey* as the baseline, however, the majority radically rewrites the undue-burden test in three ways. First, today's decision requires courts to "consider the burdens a law imposes on abortion access together with the benefits those laws confer." Second, today's opinion tells the courts that, when the law's justifications are medically uncertain, they need not defer to the legislature, and must instead assess medical justifications for abortion restrictions by scrutinizing the record themselves. Finally, even if a law imposes no "substantial obstacle" to women's access to abortions, the law now must have more than a "reasonabl[e] relat[ion] to . . . a legitimate state interest." These precepts are nowhere to be found in *Casey* or its successors, and transform the undue-burden test to something much more akin to strict scrutiny. * * * I respectfully dissent.

JUSTICE ALITO, with whom THE CHIEF JUSTICE and JUSTICE THOMAS join, dissenting.

Under our cases, petitioners must show that the admitting privileges and [ambulatory surgical center ("ASC")] requirements impose an "undue burden" on women seeking abortions. *Gonzales v. Carhart*, 550 U.S. 124, 146 (2007). And in order to obtain the sweeping relief they seek—facial invalidation of those provisions—they must show, at a minimum, that these provisions have an unconstitutional impact on at least a "large fraction" of Texas women of reproductive age. *Id.,* at 167–168. Such a situation could result if the clinics able to comply with the new requirements either lacked the requisite overall capacity or were located too far away to serve a "large fraction" of the women in question.

> **Food for Thought**
>
> What other kinds of evidence might the petitioners have provided regarding the actual capacity of the facilities?

Petitioners did not make that showing. Instead of offering direct evidence, they relied on two crude inferences. First, they pointed to the number of abortion clinics that closed after the enactment of H.B. 2, and asked that it be inferred that all these closures resulted from the two challenged provisions. * * * Second, they pointed to the number of abortions performed annually at ASCs before H.B. 2 took effect and, because this figure is well below the total number of abortions performed each year in the State, they asked that it be inferred that ASC-compliant clinics could not meet the demands of women in the State. Petitioners failed to provide any evidence of the actual capacity of the facilities that would be available to perform abortions in compliance with the new law * * *.

I do not dispute the fact that H.B. 2 caused the closure of some clinics. Indeed, it seems clear that H.B. 2 was intended to force unsafe facilities to shut down. The law was one of many enacted by States in the wake of the Kermit Gosnell scandal * * *. [The] Philadelphia grand jury that investigated the case recommended that the Commonwealth adopt a law requiring abortion clinics to comply with the same regulations as ASCs. [I]f there were any similarly unsafe facilities in Texas, H.B. 2 was clearly intended to put them out of business.

While there can be no doubt that H.B. 2 caused some clinics to cease operation, the absence of proof regarding the reasons for particular closures is a problem because some clinics have or may have closed for [reasons] other than the two H.B. 2 requirements at issue here. * * * In 2011, Texas passed a law preventing family planning grants to providers that perform abortions and their affiliates. [P]etitioners' expert admitted that some clinics closed "as a result of the defunding." [In addition, there has been a] nationwide decline in abortion demand. [Furthermore,] the retirement of a physician who performs abortions can cause the closing of a clinic or a reduction in the number of abortions that a clinic can perform. * * * To the extent that clinics closed (or experienced a reduction in capacity) for any reason unrelated to the challenged provisions of H.B. 2, the corresponding burden on abortion access may not be factored into the access analysis. Because there was ample reason to believe that some closures were caused by these other factors, the District Court's failure to ascertain the reasons for clinic closures means that, on the record before us, there is no way to tell which closures actually count. Petitioners—who, as plaintiffs, bore the burden of proof—cannot simply point to temporal correlation and call it causation.

POINTS FOR DISCUSSION

a. Undue Burden

The Court in *Whole Woman's Health* stated that *Casey*'s undue burden test "requires that courts consider the burdens a law imposes on abortion access together with the benefits those laws confer." Under this test, a regulation that limits the availability of abortion is more likely to be invalidated if it does not meaningfully advance the state's interest. In this case, for example, the Court concluded that the law did not produce any genuine benefits for the health of women seeking abortions, and thus that the benefits of the regulation did not justify the substantial burdens that it imposed on the right to obtain an abortion.

Justice Thomas, in contrast, asserted (in a part of his dissent that has been omitted here) that "the majority's free-form balancing test is contrary to *Casey*." In his view, the Court in *Casey* "did not weigh [the challenged provisions'] benefits and burdens," but instead simply considered whether those provisions presented a substantial number of women from obtaining abortions. On this view, on which the court of appeals also relied, the only relevant question is whether the challenged regulation has the purpose or effect of imposing a substantial obstacle in the path of women seeking abortions. If not, then it does not matter whether the regulation's burdens outweigh its benefits.

Which view do you find most convincing? Which approach did the Court in *Casey* actually follow? Which view did the Court in *Gonzalez v. Carhart* follow? If the undue burden test requires the court to weigh the burdens of the regulation against its benefits, then is the "substantial obstacle" inquiry beside the point? On the other hand, doesn't the inquiry whether a burden is "undue" by definition require a balancing of the regulation's costs and benefits?

b.   Purpose or Effect

The plurality in *Casey* stated that a "finding of an undue burden is a shorthand for the conclusion that a state regulation has the *purpose or effect* of placing a substantial obstacle in the path of a woman seeking an abortion of a nonviable fetus." The Court in *Whole Woman's Health*, however, focused only on whether the regulations at issue had such an effect. Was there an argument that the purpose of the Texas legislature in enacting the regulations was to make abortion substantially less-readily available? If so, why didn't the Court focus on the purpose prong of the undue burden test?

c.   Deference

The Court in *Gonzalez v. Carhart* declared that the "medical uncertainty over whether the Act's criminal prohibition creates significant health risks provides a sufficient basis to conclude in this facial attack that the Act does not impose an undue burden." In *Whole Woman's Health*, in contrast, the Court chided the court of appeals for its assertion that "legislatures, and not courts, must resolve questions of medical uncertainty," and it held that the challenged provisions were unconstitutional on their face. Is it possible to reconcile the two decisions? After *Whole Woman's Health*, when if ever is it appropriate to defer to a state's assertion that a particular regulation of abortion is designed to advance the interest in women's health?

d.   Subsequent Developments

In *June Medical Services v. Russo*, 140 S.Ct. 2103 (2020), the Court invalidated a Louisiana statute was "almost word-for-word identical to Texas' admitting-privileges law." See La. Rev. Stat. Ann. § 40:1061.10(A)(2)(a) (West 2020). In an opinion for a plurality, Justice Breyer concluded that the district court's findings that the law would pose a substantial obstacle to women seeking an abortion without any corresponding health-related benefits had "ample evidentiary support" in the record.

Chief Justice Roberts provided the fifth vote for the view that the law was unconstitutional. He stated:

I joined the dissent in *Whole Woman's Health* and continue to believe that the case was wrongly decided. The question today however is not whether *Whole Woman's Health* was right or wrong, but whether to adhere to it in deciding the present case. * * * The legal doctrine of *stare decisis* requires us, absent special circumstances, to treat like cases alike. The Louisiana law imposes a burden on access to abortion just as severe as that imposed by the Texas law, for the same reasons. Therefore Louisiana's law cannot stand under our precedents. * * *

He disagreed, however, with the plurality's (and the *Whole Woman's Health* majority's) understanding of the undue burden test. He explained:

> In this context, courts applying a balancing test [that weighs "the law's asserted benefits against the burdens it imposes on abortion access"] would be asked in essence to weigh the State's interests in "protecting the potentiality of human life" and the health of the woman, on the one hand, against the woman's liberty interest in defining her "own concept of existence, of meaning, of the universe, and of the mystery of human life" on the other. *Casey*, 505 U.S. at 851. There is no plausible sense in which anyone, let alone this Court, could objectively assign weight to such imponderable values and no meaningful way to compare them if there were. Attempting to do so would be like "judging whether a particular line is longer than a particular rock is heavy," *Bendix Autolite Corp. v. Midwesco Enterprises, Inc.*, 486 U.S. 888, 897 (1988) (Scalia, J., concurring in judgment). Pretending that we could pull that off would require us to act as legislators, not judges, and would result in nothing other than an "unanalyzed exercise of judicial will" in the guise of a "neutral utilitarian calculus." *New Jersey v. T. L. O.*, 469 U.S. 325, 369 (1985) (Brennan, J., concurring in part and dissenting in part).
>
> Nothing about *Casey* suggested that a weighing of costs and benefits of an abortion regulation was a job for the courts. On the contrary, we have explained that the "traditional rule" that "state and federal legislatures [have] wide discretion to pass legislation in areas where there is medical and scientific uncertainty" is "consistent with *Casey*." *Gonzales v. Carhart*, 550 U.S. 124, 163 (2007). *Casey* instead focuses on the existence of a substantial obstacle, the sort of inquiry familiar to judges across a variety of contexts. * * *

In his view, "*Casey*'s requirement of finding a substantial obstacle before invalidating an abortion regulation is [a] sufficient basis for the decision, as it was in *Whole Woman's Health*."

What does the undue burden test entail after the Court's decision in *June Medical Services*?

3.   Marriage and Family

We began this section on fundamental rights by considering the Court's decision in *Pierce*, which held that the Due Process Clause protects the right of parents to direct the education and upbringing of their children. *Pierce*, then, concerned the parent-child relationship, which of course is an important part of the family relationship. Similarly, the Court in *Griswold* considered another aspect of the family relationship. Recall that in *Griswold*, the Justices who voted to invalidate Connecticut's ban on contraceptives all invoked the marriage relationship in giving content to the protected right. Justice Douglas referred to the "privacy surrounding the marriage relationship"; Justice Goldberg found a right of "marital privacy"; Justice White focused on the "freedom of married persons"; and Justice Harlan (in his separate opinion in *Poe*) was concerned with "intimacy" in the "institution of marriage."

To be sure, the Court made clear shortly after its decision in *Griswold* that its view of the liberty protected by the Due Process Clause extended to intimate relationships outside of marriage, as well. But clearly the Court has long viewed family relationships as particularly deserving of protection under the Due Process Clause. Just how far does this constitutional protection for marital or family relationships extend?

LOVING V. VIRGINIA
388 U.S. 1 (1967)

MR. CHIEF JUSTICE WARREN delivered the opinion of the Court.

Make the Connection

The portion of *Loving v. Virginia* excerpted here concerns substantive due process. Another portion of the case, excerpted in Chapter 5, concerns equal protection.

This case presents a constitutional question never addressed by this Court: whether a statutory scheme adopted by the State of Virginia to prevent marriages between persons solely on the basis of racial classifications violates the Equal Protection and Due Process Clauses of the Fourteenth Amendment. For reasons which seem to us to reflect the central meaning of those constitutional commands, we conclude that these statutes cannot stand consistently with the Fourteenth Amendment.

In June 1958, two residents of Virginia, Mildred Jeter, a Negro woman, and Richard Loving, a white man, were married in the District of Columbia pursuant to its laws. Shortly after their marriage, the Lovings returned to Virginia and established their marital abode in Caroline County. [In October 1958, a grand jury in the Circuit Court of Caroline County] issued an indictment charging the Lovings with violating Virginia's ban on interracial marriages. [After the Lovings pleaded guilty, the trial judge suspended their one-year sentence] on the condition that the Lovings leave the State and not return to Virginia together for 25 years. [Five years later they challenged Virginia's anti-miscegenation statute, but the Supreme Court of Appeals of Virginia held that it was constitutional.]

In upholding the constitutionality of these provisions in the decision below, the Supreme Court of Appeals of Virginia referred to its 1955 decision in *Naim v. Naim*, 197 Va. 80, as stating the reasons supporting

> **FYI**
>
> At the time *Loving* was decided, Virginia was one of 16 states that had statutes prohibiting interracial marriages. The Virginia statute prohibited marriages between a "white person and a colored person."

the validity of these laws. In *Naim*, the state court concluded that the State's legitimate purposes were "to preserve the racial integrity of its citizens," and to prevent "the corruption of blood," "a mongrel breed of citizens," and "the obliteration of racial pride," obviously an endorsement of the doctrine of White Supremacy. The court also reasoned that marriage has traditionally been subject to state regulation without federal intervention, and, consequently, the regulation of marriage should be left to exclusive state control by the Tenth Amendment.

[The Court first held that the Virginia law violated the Equal Protection Clause. We will consider that portion of the Court's opinion in Chapter 5.]

These statutes also deprive the Lovings of liberty without due process of law in violation of the Due Process Clause of the Fourteenth Amendment. The freedom to marry has long been recognized as one of the vital personal rights essential to the orderly pursuit of happiness by free men.

Marriage is one of the "basic civil rights of man," fundamental to our very existence and survival. *Skinner v. Oklahoma*, 316 U.S. 535, 541 (1942). To deny this fundamental freedom on so unsupportable a basis as the racial classifications embodied in these statutes, classifications so directly subversive of the principle of equality at the heart of the Fourteenth Amendment, is surely to deprive all the State's citizens of liberty without due process of law. The Fourteenth Amendment requires that the freedom of choice to marry not be restricted by invidious racial discriminations. Under our Constitution, the freedom to marry or not marry, a person of another race resides with the individual and cannot be infringed by the State. These convictions must be reversed.

POINTS FOR DISCUSSION

a.   Due Process and Equal Protection

What was the basis for the Court's conclusion in the portion of the opinion excerpted here? As we will see in Chapter 5, the state presumptively violates the Equal Protection clause when it classifies on the basis of race, even when no constitutionally protected "right" is at issue; for example, it would violate the Equal Protection Clause to make driver's licenses available only to people who are white, even though there is no constitutional right to a driver's license. But the Court in *Loving* also stated that to deny the "fundamental freedom" to marry on the basis of an invidious racial classification "deprive[s] *all* the State's citizens of liberty without due process of law."

What is the scope of this right to marry? State-law restrictions on the right to marry, after all, are commonplace; virtually every state prohibits marriages between siblings, marriages involving a person younger than a certain age, and marriages to more than one person simultaneously. These prohibitions are plainly different from the one at issue in *Loving*, which involved an invidious racial classification, but they suggest that the "right" to marry is far from absolute. Just how far does the right extend?

b.   Level of Scrutiny

What level of scrutiny did the Court apply to the Virginia statute? The Court stated that "the freedom to marry [a] person of another race [cannot] be infringed by the State," but did it mean that *no* state interest, no matter how compelling, could justify an infringement on the general freedom to marry? Was the Court applying strict scrutiny? Did it conclude that Virginia's interest in upholding the statute was illegitimate, and thus that the law was invalid? If so, does that mean that a state need advance only a legitimate—as opposed to a compelling—interest to justify regulation of marriage (absent invidious racial discrimination)? Should the Court apply strict scrutiny to all limitations on the right to marry?

c.   Subsequent Developments

The Court addressed some of these questions in subsequent cases. In *Zablocki v. Redhail*, 434 U.S. 374 (1978), the Court reviewed a Wisconsin statute that required a court's permission for a person who was already under an obligation to pay child support to obtain a marriage license. In order to be granted permission to marry, the individual had to show that he or she was paying the support and that the child was not likely in the future to be put in public charge. The Court invalidated the statute, relying in part on *Loving* and earlier Due Process cases. The Court observed that "[a]lthough *Loving* arose in the context of racial discrimination, prior and subsequent decisions of this Court confirm that the right to marry is of fundamental importance for all individuals." The Court acknowledged that "reasonable regulations that do not significantly interfere with decisions to enter into the marital relationship may legitimately be imposed," but concluded that more searching scrutiny was warranted for regulations, such as the one at issue, that "interfere directly and substantially with the right to marry." Although the Court assumed that the State's interests in counseling parents and providing for children were sufficiently important, the Court held that the ends employed by the State were not necessary to advancing those interests.

Are the rights protected in *Loving* and *Zablocki* uniquely related to the institution of marriage? Recall the Court's decision in *Pierce*, which involved parental rights. What protection does the Due Process Clause provide for other familial arrangements?

In *Moore v. City of East Cleveland*, 431 U.S. 494 (1977), the Court held that a city ordinance that used a narrow definition of family to dictate who could live together under one roof was unconstitutional as applied to a grandmother who shared a home with two grandsons who were not siblings. The Court rejected the city's argument that the Constitution's protections for family relationships extend only to nuclear families, concluding that regulations that "intrude on choices concerning family living arrangements" warrant heightened review. In a dissent, Justice Stewart asserted that equating the interests of a group of people who wish to live together with "the fundamental decisions to marry and to bear and raise children is to extend the limited substantive contours of the Due Process Clause beyond recognition."

The Court has also had occasion to revisit the Constitution's protection for parents' child-rearing decisions, an issue that the Court had long ago addressed in *Pierce*. In *Troxel v. Granville*, 530 U.S. 57 (2000), the Court reiterated that parents have a "fundamental" right "to make decisions concerning the care, custody, and control of their children." The Court held that a Washington statute that allowed the court to give visitation rights to anyone if it was found to be in the best interests of the child was unconstitutional as applied to the petitioner, a mother who sought to limit the extent to which her children's paternal grandparents could visit her children after their father died.

But surely the Constitution's protection for parental rights is not absolute; a parent does not have a right, for example, cavalierly and unnecessarily to subject his child to the risk of serious and imminent injury. How exactly does the Court define the scope of parental rights? Consider the case that follows.

MICHAEL H. V. GERALD D.
491 U.S. 110 (1989)

JUSTICE SCALIA announced the judgment of the Court and delivered an opinion, in which THE CHIEF JUSTICE joins, and in all but footnote 6 of which JUSTICE O'CONNOR and JUSTICE KENNEDY join.

> **Take Note**
>
> Justice Scalia's opinion is only for a plurality of the Court.

Under California law, a child born to a married woman living with her husband is presumed to be a child of the marriage. Cal.Evid.Code Ann. § 621 (West Supp.1989). The presumption of legitimacy may be rebutted only by the husband or wife, and then only in limited circumstances. *Ibid.* The instant appeal presents the claim that this presumption infringes upon the due process rights of a man who wishes to establish his paternity of a child born to the wife of another man, and the claim that it infringes upon the constitutional right of the child to maintain a relationship with her natural father.

[The petitioner claimed that he was the father of a child, Victoria D., who was in the care of the respondent and respondent's wife, Carole D. Petitioner specifically claimed that he had had an adulterous liaison with Carole D., and that he was Victoria D.'s biological father. A blood test established a 98% probability that the petitioner was the biological father. California law permitted the presumption of paternity to be rebutted by blood tests, but only if a motion for such tests was made within two years of the date of the child's birth, either by the husband or, if the natural father has filed an affidavit acknowledging paternity, by the wife. Cal.Evid.Code Ann. §§ 621(c) and (d). Because this had not occurred, the California courts, applying the statutory presumption, rejected the petitioner's claim for paternity and visitation. On appeal, the petitioner asserted (among other things) that the trial court's application of the presumption violated his rights under the Due Process Clause of the Fourteenth Amendment.]

The California statute that is the subject of this litigation is, in substance, more than a century old. California Code of Civ.Proc. § 1962(5), enacted in 1872, provided that "[t]he issue of a wife cohabiting with her husband, who is not impotent, is indisputably presumed to be legitimate." * * * In 1980, the legislature [amended] the statute to provide the husband an opportunity to introduce blood-test evidence in rebuttal of the presumption, 1980 Cal.Stats., ch. 1310, p. 4433;

and in 1981 amended it to provide the mother such an opportunity, 1981 Cal.Stats., ch. 1180, p. 4761. * * *

At the outset, it is necessary to clarify what [Michael] sought and what he was denied. California law, like nature itself, makes no provision for dual fatherhood. Michael was seeking to be declared *the* father of Victoria. The immediate benefit he evidently sought to obtain from that status was visitation rights. But if Michael were successful in being declared the father, other rights would follow—most importantly, the right to be considered as the parent who should have custody, a status which "embrace[s] the sum of parental rights with respect to the rearing of a child" * * *. All parental rights, including visitation, were automatically denied by denying Michael status as the father. * * *

Michael raises two related challenges to the constitutionality of § 621. First, he asserts that requirements of procedural due process prevent the State from terminating his liberty interest in his relationship with his child without affording him an opportunity to demonstrate his paternity in an evidentiary hearing. We believe this claim derives from a fundamental misconception of the nature of

> **Make the Connection**
>
> We consider the so-called doctrine of "procedural due process"—the idea that the government cannot deprive a person of an important interest without first giving adequate notice and an opportunity to be heard—in Chapter 3.

the California statute. While § 621 is phrased in terms of a presumption, that rule of evidence is the implementation of a substantive rule of law. California declares it to be, except in limited circumstances, *irrelevant* for paternity purposes whether a child conceived during, and born into, an existing marriage was begotten by someone other than the husband and had a prior relationship with him. * * * Of course the conclusive presumption not only expresses the State's substantive policy but also furthers it, excluding inquiries into the child's paternity that would be destructive of family integrity and privacy. * * * We therefore reject Michael's procedural due process challenge and proceed to his substantive claim.

Michael contends as a matter of substantive due process that, because he has established a parental relationship with Victoria, protection of Gerald's and Carole's marital union is an insufficient state interest to support termination of that relationship. This argument is, of course, predicated on the assertion that Michael has a constitutionally protected liberty interest in his relationship with Victoria.

It is an established part of our constitutional jurisprudence that the term "liberty" in the Due Process Clause extends beyond freedom from physical restraint. See, *e.g., Pierce v. Society of Sisters,* 268 U.S. 510 (1925); *Meyer v. Nebraska,*

262 U.S. 390 (1923). * * * In an attempt to limit and guide interpretation of the Clause, we have insisted not merely that the interest denominated as a "liberty" be "fundamental" (a concept that, in isolation, is hard to objectify), but also that it be an interest traditionally protected by our society. As we have put it, the Due Process Clause affords only those protections "so rooted in the traditions and conscience of our people as to be ranked as fundamental." *Snyder v. Massachusetts,* 291 U.S. 97, 105 (1934) (Cardozo, J.). Our cases reflect "continual insistence upon respect for the teachings of history [and] solid recognition of the basic values that underlie our society. . . ." *Griswold v. Connecticut,* 381 U.S. 479, 501 (1965) (Harlan, J., concurring in judgment).

This insistence that the asserted liberty interest be rooted in history and tradition is evident, as elsewhere, in our cases according constitutional protection to certain parental rights. * * * As Justice Powell stated for the plurality in *Moore v. East Cleveland,* 431 U.S. 494, 503 (1977): "Our decisions establish that the Constitution protects the sanctity of the family precisely because the institution of the family is deeply rooted in this Nation's history and tradition."

Thus, the legal issue in the present case reduces to whether the relationship between persons in the situation of Michael and Victoria has been treated as a protected family unit under the historic practices of our society, or whether on any other basis it has been accorded special protection. We think it impossible to find that it has. In fact, quite to the contrary, our traditions have protected the marital family (Gerald, Carole, and the child they acknowledge to be theirs) against the sort of claim Michael asserts.

The presumption of legitimacy was a fundamental principle of the common law. Traditionally, that presumption could be rebutted only by proof that a husband was incapable of procreation or had had no access to his wife during the relevant period. * * * The primary policy rationale underlying the common law's severe restrictions on rebuttal of the presumption appears to have been an aversion to declaring children illegitimate, thereby depriving them of rights of inheritance and succession, and likely making them wards of the state. A secondary policy concern was the interest in promoting the "peace and tranquillity of States and families," J. Schouler, Law of the Domestic Relations § 225, p. 304 (3d ed. 1882), a goal that is obviously impaired by facilitating suits against husband and wife asserting that their children are illegitimate. * * *

We have found nothing in the older sources, nor in the older cases, addressing specifically the power of the natural father to assert parental rights over a child born into a woman's existing marriage with another man. Since it is Michael's burden to establish that such a power (at least where the natural father has established a relationship with the child) is so deeply embedded within our traditions as to be a fundamental right, the lack of evidence alone might defeat his case. But the evidence shows that even in modern times—when [the] rigid protection of the marital family has in other respects been relaxed—the ability of a person in Michael's position to claim paternity has not been generally acknowledged. * * *

Moreover, even if it were clear that one in Michael's position generally possesses, and has generally always possessed, standing to challenge the marital child's legitimacy, that would still not establish Michael's case. As noted earlier, what is at issue here is not entitlement to a state pronouncement that Victoria was begotten by Michael. It is no conceivable denial of constitutional right for a State to decline to declare facts unless some legal consequence hinges upon the requested declaration. What Michael asserts here is a right to have himself declared the natural father *and thereby to obtain parental prerogatives.* What he must establish, therefore, is not that our society has traditionally allowed a natural father in his circumstances to establish paternity, but that it has traditionally accorded such a father parental rights, or at least has not traditionally denied them. Even if the law in all States had always been that the entire world could challenge the marital presumption and obtain a declaration as to who was the natural father, that would not advance Michael's claim. Thus, it is ultimately irrelevant, even for purposes of determining *current* social attitudes towards the alleged substantive right Michael asserts, that the present law in a number of States appears to allow the natural father—including the natural father who has not established a relationship with the child—the theoretical power to rebut the marital presumption, see Note, Rebutting the Marital Presumption: A Developed Relationship Test, 88 Colum.L.Rev. 369, 373 (1988). What counts is whether the States in fact award substantive parental rights to the natural father of a child conceived within, and born into, an extant marital union that wishes to embrace the child. We are not aware of a single case, old or new, that has done so. This is not the stuff of which fundamental rights qualifying as liberty interests are made.[6]

> **Take Note**
>
> In footnote 6, Justice Scalia explains his approach to determining whether the asserted right is fundamental, and he criticizes the approach that Justice Brennan offers in dissent. Why does Justice Scalia define the right at issue the way that he does? Why does only one other Justice join the footnote?

---

[6] Justice BRENNAN criticizes our methodology in using historical traditions specifically relating to the rights of an adulterous natural father, rather than inquiring more generally "whether parenthood is an interest that historically has received our attention and protection." * * * We do not understand why, having rejected our focus upon the societal tradition regarding the natural father's rights vis-à-vis a child whose mother is

We do not accept Justice BRENNAN's criticism that this result "squashes" the liberty that consists of "the freedom not to conform." It seems to us that reflects the erroneous view that there is only one side to this controversy—that one disposition can expand a "liberty" of sorts without contracting an equivalent "liberty" on the other side. Such a happy choice is rarely available. Here, to *provide* protection to an adulterous natural father is to *deny* protection to a marital father, and vice versa. If Michael has a "freedom not to conform" (whatever that means), Gerald must equivalently have a "freedom to conform." One of them will pay a price for asserting that "freedom"—Michael by being unable to act as father of the child he has adulterously begotten, or Gerald by being unable to preserve the integrity of the traditional family unit he and Victoria have established. Our disposition does not choose between these two "freedoms," but leaves that to the people of California. Justice BRENNAN's approach chooses one of them as the constitutional imperative, on no apparent basis except that the unconventional is to be preferred. [Affirmed.]

JUSTICE O'CONNOR, with whom JUSTICE KENNEDY joins, concurring in part.

I concur in all but footnote 6 of Justice SCALIA's opinion. This footnote sketches a mode of historical analysis to be used when identifying liberty interests

---

married to another man, Justice BRENNAN would choose to focus instead upon "parenthood." Why should the relevant category not be even more general—perhaps "family relationships"; or "personal relationships"; or even "emotional attachments in general"? Though the dissent has no basis for the level of generality it would select, we do: We refer to the most specific level at which a relevant tradition protecting, or denying protection to, the asserted right can be identified. If, for example, there were no societal tradition, either way, regarding the rights of the natural father of a child adulterously conceived, we would have to consult, and (if possible) reason from, the traditions regarding natural fathers in general. But there is such a more specific tradition, and it unqualifiedly denies protection to such a parent.

One would think that Justice BRENNAN would appreciate the value of consulting the most specific tradition available, since he acknowledges that "[e]ven if we can agree . . . that 'family' and 'parenthood' are part of the good life, it is absurd to assume that we can agree on the content of those terms and destructive to pretend that we do." Because such general traditions provide such imprecise guidance, they permit judges to dictate rather than discern the society's views. The need, if arbitrary decisionmaking is to be avoided, to adopt the most specific tradition as the point of reference—or at least to announce, as Justice BRENNAN declines to do, some other criterion for selecting among the innumerable relevant traditions that could be consulted—is well enough exemplified by the fact that in the present case Justice BRENNAN's opinion and Justice O'CONNOR's opinion, which disapproves this footnote, *both* appeal to tradition, but on the basis of the tradition they select reach opposite results. Although assuredly having the virtue (if it be that) of leaving judges free to decide as they think best when the unanticipated occurs, a rule of law that binds neither by text nor by any particular, identifiable tradition is no rule of law at all.

Finally, we may note that this analysis is not inconsistent with the result in cases such as *Griswold v. Connecticut,* 381 U.S. 479 (1965), or *Eisenstadt v. Baird,* 405 U.S. 438 (1972). None of those cases acknowledged a longstanding and still extant societal tradition withholding the very right pronounced to be the subject of a liberty interest and then rejected it. Justice BRENNAN must do so here. In this case, the existence of such a tradition, continuing to the present day, refutes any possible contention that the alleged right is "so rooted in the traditions and conscience of our people as to be ranked as fundamental," *Snyder v. Massachusetts,* 291 U.S. 97, 105 (1934), or "implicit in the concept of ordered liberty," *Palko v. Connecticut,* 302 U.S. 319, 325 (1937).

protected by the Due Process Clause of the Fourteenth Amendment that may be somewhat inconsistent with our past decisions in this area. See *Griswold v. Connecticut,* 381 U.S. 479 (1965); *Eisenstadt v. Baird,* 405 U.S. 438 (1972). On occasion the Court has characterized relevant traditions protecting asserted rights at levels of generality that might not be "the most specific level" available. See *Loving v. Virginia,* 388 U.S. 1, 12 (1967); *Turner v. Safley,* 482 U.S. 78, 94 (1987). I would not foreclose the unanticipated by the prior imposition of a single mode of historical analysis. *Poe v. Ullman,* 367 U.S. 497, 542, 544 (1961) (Harlan, J., dissenting).

JUSTICE STEVENS, concurring in the judgment.

As I understand this case, it raises two different questions about the validity of California's statutory scheme. First, is § 621 unconstitutional because it prevents Michael and Victoria from obtaining a judicial determination that he is her biological father—even if no legal rights would be affected by that determination? Second, does the California statute deny appellants a fair opportunity to prove that Victoria's best interests would be served by granting Michael visitation rights?

On the first issue I agree with Justice SCALIA that the Federal Constitution imposes no obligation upon a State to "declare facts unless some legal consequence hinges upon the requested declaration." * * * On the second issue I do not agree with Justice SCALIA's analysis. He seems to reject the possibility that a natural father might ever have a constitutionally protected interest in his relationship with a child whose mother was married to, and cohabiting with, another man at the time of the child's conception and birth. * * * I therefore would not foreclose the possibility that a constitutionally protected relationship between a natural father and his child might exist in a case like this. Indeed, I am willing to assume for the purpose of deciding this case that Michael's relationship with Victoria is strong enough to give him a constitutional right to try to convince a trial judge that Victoria's best interest would be served by granting him visitation rights. I am satisfied, however, that the California statute, as applied in this case, gave him that opportunity.

Section 4601 of the California Civil Code Annotated (West Supp.1989) provides: "[R]easonable visitation rights [shall be awarded] to a parent unless it is shown that the visitation would be detrimental to the best interests of the child. In the discretion of the court, reasonable visitation rights may be granted *to any other person having an interest in the welfare of the child.*" (Emphasis added.) The presumption established by § 621 denied Michael the benefit of the first sentence of § 4601 because, as a matter of law, he is not a "parent." It does not, however, prevent him from proving that he is an "other person having an interest in the welfare of the child." On its face, therefore, the statute plainly gave the trial judge the authority to grant Michael "reasonable visitation rights." * * *

JUSTICE BRENNAN, with whom JUSTICE MARSHALL and JUSTICE BLACKMUN join, dissenting.

Once we recognized that the "liberty" protected by the Due Process Clause of the Fourteenth Amendment encompasses more than freedom from bodily restraint, today's plurality opinion emphasizes, the concept was cut loose from one natural limitation on its meaning. This innovation paved the way, so the plurality hints, for judges to substitute their own preferences for those of elected officials. Dissatisfied with this supposedly unbridled and uncertain state of affairs, the plurality casts about for another limitation on the concept of liberty.

It finds this limitation in "tradition." Apparently oblivious to the fact that this concept can be as malleable and as elusive as "liberty" itself, the plurality pretends that tradition places a discernible border around the Constitution. The pretense is seductive; it would be comforting to believe that a search for "tradition" involves nothing more idiosyncratic or complicated than poring through dusty volumes on American history. * * * [But because] reasonable people can disagree about the content of particular traditions, and because they can disagree even about which traditions are relevant to the definition of "liberty," the plurality has not found the objective boundary that it seeks.

Even if we could agree, moreover, on the content and significance of particular traditions, we still would be forced to identify the point at which a tradition becomes firm enough to be relevant to our definition of liberty and the moment at which it becomes too obsolete to be relevant any longer. The plurality supplies no objective means by which we might make these determinations. * * *

It is ironic that an approach so utterly dependent on tradition is so indifferent to our precedents. * * * Throughout our decisionmaking in this important area runs the theme that certain interests and practices—freedom from physical restraint, marriage, childbearing, childrearing, and others—form the core of our definition of "liberty." Our solicitude for these interests is partly the result of the fact that the Due Process Clause would seem an empty promise if it did not protect them, and partly the result of the historical and traditional importance of these interests in our society. In deciding cases arising under the Due Process Clause, therefore, we have considered whether the concrete limitation under consideration impermissibly impinges upon one of these more generalized interests.

Today's plurality, however, does not ask whether parenthood is an interest that historically has received our attention and protection; the answer to that question is too clear for dispute. Instead, the plurality asks whether the specific variety of parenthood under consideration—a natural father's relationship with a child whose mother is married to another man—has enjoyed such protection.

> **Food for Thought**
>
> Can you articulate the level of generality at which Justice Brennan would have identified the right at issue in this case? How does Justice Brennan decide the appropriate level of generality for identifying the right?

If we had looked to tradition with such specificity in past cases, many a decision would have reached a different result. Surely the use of contraceptives by unmarried couples, *Eisenstadt v. Baird,* 405 U.S. 438 (1972), or even by married couples, *Griswold v. Connecticut,* 381 U.S. 479 (1965), * * * were not "interest[s] traditionally protected by our society" at the time of their consideration by this Court. If we had asked, therefore, in *Eisenstadt* [or] *Griswold* * * * whether the specific interest under consideration had been traditionally protected, the answer would have been a resounding "no." That we did not ask this question in those cases highlights the novelty of the interpretive method that the plurality opinion employs today.

The plurality's interpretive method is more than novel; it is misguided. It ignores the good reasons for limiting the role of "tradition" in interpreting the Constitution's deliberately capacious language. In the plurality's constitutional universe, we may not take notice of the fact that the original reasons for the conclusive presumption of paternity are out of place in a world in which blood tests can prove virtually beyond a shadow of a doubt who sired a particular child and in which the fact of illegitimacy no longer plays the burdensome and stigmatizing role it once did. * * *

In construing the Fourteenth Amendment to offer shelter only to those interests specifically protected by historical practice, moreover, the plurality ignores the kind of society in which our Constitution exists. We are not an assimilative, homogeneous society, but a facilitative, pluralistic one, in which we must be willing to abide someone else's unfamiliar or even repellent practice because the same tolerant impulse protects our own idiosyncracies. Even if we can agree, therefore, that "family" and "parenthood" are part of the good life, it is absurd to assume that we can agree on the content of those terms and destructive to pretend that we do. In a community such as ours, "liberty" must include the freedom not to conform. The plurality today squashes this freedom by requiring specific approval from history before protecting anything in the name of liberty.

The document that the plurality construes today is unfamiliar to me. It is not the living charter that I have taken to be our Constitution; it is instead a stagnant, archaic, hidebound document steeped in the prejudices and superstitions of a time long past. *This* Constitution does not recognize that times change, does not see that sometimes a practice or rule outlives its foundations. I cannot accept an interpretive method that does such violence to the charter that I am bound by oath to uphold.

The plurality's reworking of our interpretive approach is all the more troubling because it is unnecessary. This is not a case in which we face a "new" kind of interest, one that requires us to consider for the first time whether the Constitution protects it. On the contrary, we confront an interest—that of a parent and child in their relationship with each other—that was among the first that this Court acknowledged in its cases defining the "liberty" protected by the Constitution, see, *e.g., Meyer v. Nebraska,* 262 U.S. 390, 399 (1923); *Skinner v. Oklahoma,* 316 U.S. 535, 541 (1942); *Prince v. Massachusetts,* 321 U.S. 158, 166 (1944), and I think I am safe in saying that no one doubts the wisdom or validity of those decisions. Where the interest under consideration is a parent-child relationship, we need not ask, over and over again, whether that interest is one that society traditionally protects.

Thus, to describe the issue in this case as whether the relationship existing between Michael and Victoria "has been treated as a protected family unit under the historic practices of our society, or whether on any other basis it has been accorded special protection" is to reinvent the wheel. The better approach—indeed, the one commanded by our prior cases and by common sense—is to ask whether the specific parent-child relationship under consideration is close enough to the interests that we already have protected to be deemed an aspect of "liberty" as well. On the facts before us, therefore, the question is not what "level of generality" should be used to describe the relationship between Michael and Victoria, but whether the relationship under consideration is sufficiently substantial to qualify as a liberty interest under our prior cases.

Because the plurality decides that Michael and Victoria have no liberty interest in their relationship with each other, it need consider neither the effect of § 621 on their relationship nor the State's interest in bringing about that effect. It is obvious, however, that the effect of § 621 is to terminate the relationship between Michael and Victoria before affording any hearing whatsoever on the issue whether Michael is Victoria's father. This refusal to hold a hearing is properly analyzed under our procedural due process cases, which instruct us to consider the State's interest in curtailing the procedures accompanying the termination of a constitutionally protected interest. California's interest, minute in comparison with a father's interest in his relationship with his child, cannot justify its refusal to hear Michael out on his claim that he is Victoria's father.

[JUSTICE WHITE's dissenting opinion has been omitted.]

POINTS FOR DISCUSSION

a. Defining "Family"

In each of the cases above—*Moore*, *Troxel*, and *Michael H.*—the Court was required to define the "family" and the familial relationships that are protected by the Fourteenth Amendment. Is the plurality's approach in *Michael H.* consistent with the Court's approach in *Moore*? If not, which is more convincing? What are the implications of the two approaches for other questions about the scope of protection for familial rights? What are the implications for the judicial role?

b. Competing Rights

Even assuming that the Court can neatly define the scope of familial rights, how should the Court rule when a case involves *competing* claims of right? For example, although the Court in *Troxel* based its analysis on a consideration of the *mother's* rights, in his dissent Justice Stevens asserted that the *children's* rights were entitled to consideration, as well. (Indeed, one could have argued that the *grandparents* also had some interest.) Is the substantive protection afforded by the Due Process Clause the same for children as it is for adults? Do children have different or attenuated rights? The Court in *Michael H.* declined to take up a related issue—"whether a child has a liberty interest, symmetrical with that of her parent, in maintaining her filial relationship." How would you resolve these questions based on the cases discussed so far in this chapter?

c. History and the Level of Generality Reprised

In *Michael H.*, Justices Scalia and Brennan debated the appropriate level of generality at which to identify fundamental rights. Justice Scalia reprised the debate, this time with Justice Stevens, in *McDonald v. City of Chicago*, 561 U.S. 742 (2010), which we considered in Chapter 1. In Justice Stevens's view, "the liberty safeguarded by the Fourteenth Amendment is not merely preservative in nature but rather is a 'dynamic concept.' Its dynamism provides a central means through which the Framers enabled the Constitution to 'endure for ages to come,' *McCulloch v. Maryland*, 4 Wheat. 316, 415 (1819)." He asserted that the "judge who would outsource the interpretation of 'liberty' to historical sentiment has turned his back on a task the Constitution assigned to him and drained the document of its intended vitality."

Justice Stevens offered several reasons for rejecting a "rigid historical test" for identifying rights protected by the Due Process Clause. First, he asserted that such an approach "would effect a major break from our case law," because "our substantive due process doctrine has never evaluated substantive rights in purely, or even predominantly, historical terms." Second and "[m]ore fundamentally," he asserted:

> [A] rigid historical methodology is unfaithful to * * * the expansive principle Americans laid down when they ratified the Fourteenth Amendment and to the level of generality they chose when they crafted its language; it promises an objectivity it cannot deliver and masks the value judgments that pervade any analysis of what customs, defined in what manner, are sufficiently "rooted"; it countenances the most revolting injustices in the name of continuity, for we must never forget that not only slavery but also the subjugation of women and other rank forms of discrimination are part of our history; and it effaces this Court's distinctive role in saying what the law is, leaving the development and safekeeping of liberty to majoritarian political processes. It is judicial abdication in the guise of judicial modesty. * * *

> Although Justice Scalia aspires to an "objective," "neutral" method of substantive due process analysis, his actual method is nothing of the sort. * * * [H]istory is not an objective science, and [its] use can therefore "point in any direction the judges favor." * * * [A] limitless number of subjective judgments may be smuggled into his historical analysis. Worse, they may be buried in the analysis. * * * Justice Scalia's method invites not only bad history, but also bad constitutional law. * * * The fact that we have a written Constitution does not consign this Nation to a static legal existence. [I]t is not fidelity to the Constitution to ignore its use of deliberately capacious language, in an effort to transform foundational legal commitments into narrow rules of decision.

Justice Stevens also rejected Justice Scalia's charge that his "dynamic" approach was a "license for unbridled judicial lawmaking." He acknowledged that his approach requires judges to "exercise judgment," because when "answering a constitutional question to which the text provides no clear answer, there is always some amount of discretion." But he asserted that there are several "constraints on the decisional process." First, he stated that "liberty" is "capable of being refined and delimited" by the "central values" of "[s]elf-determination, bodily integrity, freedom of conscience, intimate relationships, political equality, dignity and respect." Second, he stressed "respect for the democratic process": "If a particular liberty interest is already being given careful consideration in, and subjected to ongoing calibration by, the States, judicial enforcement may not be appropriate." Third, the Court can apply "both the doctrine of *stare decisis*—adhering to precedents, respecting reliance interests, prizing stability and order in the law—and the common-law method—taking cases and controversies as they present themselves, proceeding slowly and incrementally, building on what came before."

Justice Scalia responded by asserting that Justice Stevens's approach is "subjective," and that his claim that courts should "update" the Due Process Clause "basically means picking the rights we want to protect and discarding those we do not." In Justice Scalia's view, "[d]eciding what is essential to an enlightened, liberty-filled life is an inherently political, moral judgment—the antithesis of an objective approach that reaches conclusions by applying neutral rules to verifiable evidence." He acknowledged that "[h]istorical analysis can be difficult" and "sometimes requires * * * making nuanced judgments about which evidence to consult and how to interpret it." But he asserted that "the question to be decided is not whether the historically focused method is a *perfect means* of restraining aristocratic judicial Constitution-writing; but whether it is the *best means available* in an imperfect world." In his view, it clearly is, because it is less subjective and more compatible with democracy:

> It is less subjective because it depends upon a body of evidence susceptible of reasoned analysis rather than a variety of vague ethico-political First Principles whose combined conclusion can be found to point in any direction the judges favor. * * * Moreover, the methodological differences that divide historians, and the varying interpretive assumptions they bring to their work, are nothing compared to the differences among the American people (though perhaps not among graduates of prestigious law schools) with regard to the moral judgments Justice Stevens would have courts pronounce. * * * And the Court's approach intrudes less upon the democratic process because the rights it acknowledges are those established by a constitutional history formed by democratic decisions; and the rights it fails to acknowledge are left to be democratically adopted or rejected by the people, with the assurance that their decision is not subject to judicial revision. Justice Stevens's approach, on the other hand, deprives the people of that power, since whatever the Constitution and laws may say, the list of protected rights will be whatever courts wish it to be.

Whose view do you find most convincing?

4. Sexuality

In *Eisenstadt v. Baird*, which we considered in our discussion of *Griswold*, the Court held that the state cannot prohibit the use of contraceptives by unmarried persons. If the Due Process Clause protects a right of intimate relations between unmarried persons, then how far does that right extend?

In *Bowers v. Hardwick*, 478 U.S. 186 (1986), the Court, in a 5–4 decision, upheld a Georgia statute that criminalized "sodomy"—defined as acts of oral or anal sex—as applied to the respondent's homosexual conduct. The Court began by declaring that "[t]he issue presented is whether the Federal Constitution confers a fundamental right upon homosexuals to engage in sodomy." Looking to historic prohibitions and the contemporaneous prevalence of anti-sodomy laws throughout the fifty states, the Court concluded that "homosexual sodomy" cannot be considered a fundamental right under the Due Process Clause. It distinguished *Griswold* and its progeny by noting that "no connection between family, marriage, or procreation [and] homosexual activity [has] been demonstrated." After concluding that the right to engage in "homosexual sodomy" is not fundamental, the Court applied rational-basis review to the statute. It rejected respondent's argument that the state's interest in advancing morality was an insufficient basis for the statute, stating that law in general "is constantly based on notions of morality, and if all laws representing essentially moral choices are to be invalidated under the Due Process Clause, courts will be very busy indeed." Chief Justice Burger concurred, stating that "proscriptions against sodomy have very 'ancient roots.' Decisions of individuals relating to homosexual conduct have been subject to state intervention throughout the history of Western civilization. Condemnation of those practices is firmly rooted in Judeo-Christian moral and ethical standards. * * * To hold that the act of homosexual sodomy is somehow protected as a fundamental right would be to cast aside millennia of moral teaching."

Justice Blackmun, joined by Justices Brennan, Marshall, and Stevens, dissented. He declared: "[T]his case is about 'the most comprehensive of rights and the right most valued by civilized men,' namely, 'the right to be let alone.' *Olmstead v. United States*, 277 U.S. 438, 478 (1928) (Brandeis, J., dissenting). * * * The Court claims that its decision today merely refuses to recognize a fundamental right to engage in homosexual sodomy; what the Court really has refused to recognize is the fundamental interest all individuals have in controlling the nature of their intimate associations with others."

The Court revisited the holding in *Bowers* in the case that follows.

LAWRENCE V. TEXAS

539 U.S. 558 (2003)

JUSTICE KENNEDY delivered the opinion of the Court.

Liberty protects the person from unwarranted government intrusions into a dwelling or other private places. In our tradition the State is not omnipresent in the home. And there are other spheres of our lives and existence, outside the home, where the State should not be a dominant presence. Freedom extends beyond spatial bounds. Liberty presumes an autonomy of self that includes freedom of thought, belief, expression, and certain intimate conduct. The instant case involves liberty of the person both in its spatial and in its more transcendent dimensions.

The question before the Court is the validity of a Texas statute making it a crime for two persons of the same sex to engage in certain intimate sexual conduct. In Houston, Texas, officers of the Harris County Police Department were dispatched to a private residence in response to a reported weapons disturbance. They entered an apartment where one of the petitioners, John Geddes Lawrence, resided. * * * The officers observed Lawrence and another man, Tyron Garner, engaging in a sexual act. The two petitioners were arrested, held in custody overnight, and charged and convicted before a Justice of the Peace. [The statute under which they were convicted prohibited "deviate sexual intercourse"—which the statute defined as oral or anal sex—"with another individual of the same sex."] The petitioners were adults at the time of the alleged offense. Their conduct was in private and consensual.

We conclude the case should be resolved by determining whether the petitioners were free as adults to engage in the private conduct in the exercise of their liberty under the Due Process Clause of the Fourteenth Amendment to the Constitution. For this inquiry we deem it necessary to reconsider the Court's holding in *Bowers*. [The Court's statement of the issue in *Bowers*] discloses the Court's own failure to appreciate the extent of the liberty at stake. To say that the issue in *Bowers* was simply the right to engage in certain sexual conduct demeans the claim the individual put forward, just as it would demean a married couple were it to be said marriage is simply about the right to have sexual intercourse. The laws involved in *Bowers* and here are, to be sure, statutes that purport to do no more than prohibit a particular sexual act. Their penalties and purposes, though, have more far-reaching consequences, touching upon the most private human conduct, sexual behavior, and in the most private of places, the home. The statutes do seek to control a personal relationship that, whether or not entitled to formal recognition in the law, is within the liberty of persons to choose without being punished as criminals.

This, as a general rule, should counsel against attempts by the State, or a court, to define the meaning of the relationship or to set its boundaries absent injury to a person or abuse of an institution the law protects. It suffices for us to acknowledge that adults may choose to enter upon this relationship in the confines of their homes and their own private lives and still retain their dignity as free persons. When sexuality finds overt expression in intimate conduct with another person, the conduct can be but one element in a personal bond that is more enduring. The liberty protected by the Constitution allows homosexual persons the right to make this choice.

> **Food for Thought**
>
> Is the Court here articulating a libertarian vision of the Constitution? Recall that Justice Holmes criticized the Court in *Lochner* for concluding in effect that the Constitution "enact[s] Mr. Herbert Spencer's Social Statics." Does the Court here effectively conclude that the Constitution enacts John Stuart Mill's "On Liberty," which enunciated the "harm principle"—that is, the principle that "the only purpose for which power can be rightfully exercised over any member of a civilized community, against his will, is to prevent harm to others"?

Having misapprehended the claim of liberty there presented to it, and thus stating the claim to be whether there is a fundamental right to engage in consensual sodomy, the *Bowers* Court said: "Proscriptions against that conduct have ancient roots." *Id.* at 192. * * * At the outset it should be noted that there is no longstanding history in this country of laws directed at homosexual conduct as a distinct matter. * * * It was not until the 1970's that any State singled out same-sex relations for criminal prosecution, and only nine States have done so. [T]he historical grounds relied upon in *Bowers* are more complex than the majority opinion and the concurring opinion by Chief Justice Burger indicate. Their historical premises are not without doubt and, at the very least, are overstated.

It must be acknowledged, of course, that the Court in *Bowers* was making the broader point that for centuries there have been powerful voices to condemn homosexual conduct as immoral. The condemnation has been shaped by religious beliefs, conceptions of right and acceptable behavior, and respect for the traditional family. For many persons these are not trivial concerns but profound and deep convictions accepted as ethical and moral principles to which they aspire and which thus determine the course of their lives. These considerations do not answer the question before us, however. The issue is whether the majority may use the power of the State to enforce these views on the whole society through operation of the criminal law. "Our obligation is to define the liberty of all, not to mandate our own moral code." *Planned Parenthood of Southeastern Pa. v. Casey*, 505 U.S. 833, 850 (1992).

[W]e think that our laws and traditions in the past half century are of most relevance here. These references show an emerging awareness that liberty gives substantial protection to adult persons in deciding how to conduct their private lives in matters pertaining to sex. * * * This emerging recognition should have been apparent when *Bowers* was decided.

The sweeping references by Chief Justice Burger [in his concurring opinion in *Bowers*] to the history of Western civilization and to Judeo-Christian moral and ethical standards did not take account of other authorities pointing in an opposite direction. A committee advising the British Parliament recommended in 1957 repeal of laws punishing homosexual conduct [and] Parliament enacted the substance of those recommendations 10 years later. Of even more importance, almost five years before *Bowers* was decided the European Court of Human Rights * * * held that the laws

> **Food for Thought**
>
> With which view of the Due Process Clause is the Court's emphasis on an "emerging awareness" consistent? With Justice Harlan's focus on "living" traditions? With Justice Scalia's focus on historical tradition at the highest level of specificity? At what point does an "emerging awareness" of a particular conception of liberty achieve the status of liberty protected by the Due Process Clause? Is there a way for the Court to recognize changing values and yet not be controlled by the whims of public opinion?

proscribing [consensual homosexual conduct] were invalid under the European Convention on Human Rights. *Dudgeon v. United Kingdom*, 45 Eur. Ct. H.R. (1981). Authoritative in all countries that are members of the Council of Europe (21 nations then, 45 nations now), the decision is at odds with the premise in *Bowers* that the claim put forward was insubstantial in our Western civilization.

Two principal cases decided after *Bowers* cast its holding into even more doubt. In *Planned Parenthood of Southeastern Pa. v. Casey*, 505 U.S. 833 (1992), [we] confirmed that our laws and tradition afford constitutional protection to personal decisions relating to marriage, procreation, contraception, family relationships, child rearing, and education. In explaining the respect the Constitution demands for the autonomy of the person in making these choices, we stated[:] "At the heart of liberty is the right to define one's own concept of existence, of meaning, of the universe, and of the mystery of human life. Beliefs about these matters could not define the attributes of personhood were they formed under compulsion of the State." Persons in a homosexual relationship may seek autonomy for these purposes, just as heterosexual persons do. The decision in *Bowers* would deny them this right.

The second post-*Bowers* case of principal relevance is *Romer v. Evans*, 517 U.S. 620 (1996). There the Court struck down class-based legislation directed at

Make the Connection

We will consider *Romer*, and discrimination on the basis of sexual orientation, in Chapter 5.

homosexuals as a violation of the Equal Protection Clause. * * * As an alternative argument in this case, counsel for the petitioners and some amici contend that *Romer* provides the basis for declaring the Texas statute invalid under the Equal Protection Clause. That is a tenable argument, but we conclude the instant case requires us to address whether *Bowers* itself has continuing validity. Were we to hold the statute invalid under the Equal Protection Clause some might question whether a prohibition would be valid if drawn differently, say, to prohibit the conduct both between same-sex and different-sex participants.

Equality of treatment and the due process right to demand respect for conduct protected by the substantive guarantee of liberty are linked in important respects, and a decision on the latter point advances both interests. If protected conduct is made criminal and the law which does so remains unexamined for its substantive validity, its stigma might remain even if it were not enforceable as drawn for equal protection reasons. When homosexual conduct is made criminal by the law of the State, that declaration in and of itself is an invitation to subject homosexual persons to discrimination both in the public and in the private spheres. The central holding of *Bowers* has been brought in question by this case, and it should be addressed. Its continuance as precedent demeans the lives of homosexual persons.

The foundations of *Bowers* have sustained serious erosion from our recent decisions in *Casey* and *Romer*. When our precedent has been thus weakened, criticism from other sources is of greater significance. In the United States criticism of *Bowers* has been substantial and continuing, disapproving of its reasoning in all respects, not just as to its historical assumptions. The courts of five different States have declined to follow it in interpreting provisions in their own state constitutions parallel to the Due Process Clause of the Fourteenth Amendment. To the extent *Bowers* relied on values we share with a wider civilization, it should be noted that the reasoning and holding in *Bowers* have been rejected elsewhere. The European Court of Human Rights has [not followed] *Bowers* * * *. The right the petitioners seek in this case has been accepted as an integral part of human freedom in many other countries. There has been no showing that in this country the governmental interest in circumscribing personal choice is somehow more legitimate or urgent.

The doctrine of *stare decisis* is essential to the respect accorded to the judgments of the Court and to the stability of the law. It is not, however, an inexorable command. [T]here has been no individual or societal reliance on *Bowers* of the sort that could counsel against overturning its holding once there are compelling reasons to do so. *Bowers* itself causes uncertainty, for the precedents before

> **Make the Connection**
>
> Justice Kennedy was one of the authors of the joint opinion in *Casey*, which included an extended discussion of the role of *stare decisis* in constitutional adjudication. Is his approach here consistent with the plurality's approach in *Casey*?

and after its issuance contradict its central holding. * * * *Bowers* was not correct when it was decided, and it is not correct today. * * * *Bowers v. Hardwick* should be and now is overruled.

The present case does not involve minors. It does not involve persons who might be injured or coerced or who are situated in relationships where consent might not easily be refused. It does not involve public conduct or prostitution. It does not involve whether the government must give formal recognition to any relationship that homosexual persons seek to enter. The case does involve two adults who, with full and mutual consent from each other, engaged in sexual practices common to a homosexual lifestyle. The petitioners are entitled to respect for their private lives. The State cannot demean their existence or control their destiny by making their private sexual conduct a crime. Their right to liberty under the Due Process Clause gives them the full right to engage in their conduct without intervention of the government. * * * The Texas statute furthers no legitimate state interest which can justify its intrusion into the personal and private life of the individual.

JUSTICE O'CONNOR, concurring in the judgment.

The Court today overrules *Bowers v. Hardwick*, 478 U.S. 186 (1986). I joined *Bowers*, and do not join the Court in overruling it. Nevertheless, I agree with the Court that Texas' statute banning same-sex sodomy is unconstitutional. Rather than relying on the substantive component of the Fourteenth Amendment's Due Process Clause, as the Court does, I base my conclusion on the Fourteenth Amendment's Equal Protection Clause.

The statute at issue here makes sodomy a crime only if a person "engages in deviate sexual intercourse with another individual of the same sex." Tex. Penal Code Ann. § 21.06(a) (2003). Sodomy between opposite-sex partners, however, is not a crime in Texas. That is, Texas treats the same conduct differently based solely on the participants. * * * The Texas statute makes homosexuals unequal in the eyes of the law by making particular conduct—and only that conduct—subject to criminal sanction.

Texas attempts to justify its law, and the effects of the law, by arguing that the statute satisfies rational basis review because it furthers the legitimate governmental interest of the promotion of morality. * * * This case raises a different issue than *Bowers*: whether, under the Equal Protection Clause, moral disapproval is a legitimate state interest to justify by itself a statute that bans homosexual sodomy, but not heterosexual sodomy. It is not. Moral disapproval of this group, like a bare desire to harm the group, is an interest that is insufficient to satisfy rational basis review under the Equal Protection Clause. Indeed, we have never held that moral disapproval, without any other asserted state interest, is a sufficient rationale under the Equal Protection Clause to justify a law that discriminates among groups of persons.

> **Food for Thought**
>
> The Georgia statute upheld in *Bowers* on its face applied both to heterosexual and homosexual conduct. Is it relevant that the Georgia statute was, in practice, enforced only against homosexual conduct? If so, does it undermine Justice O'Connor's reasoning here? Or the Court's decision in *Bowers*?

Moral disapproval of a group cannot be a legitimate governmental interest under the Equal Protection Clause because legal classifications must not be "drawn for the purpose of disadvantaging the group burdened by the law." * * * Whether a sodomy law that is neutral both in effect and application would violate the substantive component of the Due Process Clause is an issue that need not be decided today. I am confident, however, that so long as the Equal Protection Clause requires a sodomy law to apply equally to the private consensual conduct of homosexuals and heterosexuals alike, such a law would not long stand in our democratic society.

A law branding one class of persons as criminal based solely on the State's moral disapproval of that class and the conduct associated with that class runs contrary to the values of the Constitution and the Equal Protection Clause, under any standard of review. I therefore concur in the Court's judgment that Texas' sodomy law banning "deviate sexual intercourse" between consenting adults of the same sex, but not between consenting adults of different sexes, is unconstitutional.

JUSTICE SCALIA, with whom THE CHIEF JUSTICE and JUSTICE THOMAS join, dissenting.

[In *Casey*,] when *stare decisis* meant preservation of judicially invented abortion rights, the widespread criticism of *Roe* was strong reason to reaffirm it. * * * Today, however, the widespread opposition to *Bowers*, a decision resolving an issue as "intensely divisive" as the issue in *Roe*, is offered as a reason in favor of overruling it. * * * [The Court today has] exposed *Casey's* extraordinary deference to precedent for the result-oriented expedient that it is.

Having decided that it need not adhere to *stare decisis*, the Court still must establish that *Bowers* was wrongly decided and that the Texas statute, as applied to petitioners, is unconstitutional. * * * We have held repeatedly, in cases the Court today does not overrule, that only fundamental rights qualify for [so-called] "heightened scrutiny" protection—that is, rights which are "deeply rooted in this Nation's history and tradition." *Washington v. Glucksberg*, 521 U.S. 702, 721 (1997). All other liberty interests may be abridged or abrogated pursuant to a validly enacted state law if that law is rationally related to a legitimate state interest.

[A]n "emerging awareness" is by definition not "deeply rooted in this Nation's history and tradition[s]." Constitutional entitlements do not spring into existence because some States choose to lessen or eliminate criminal sanctions on certain behavior. Much less do they spring into existence, as the Court seems to believe, because foreign nations decriminalize conduct. * * * The Court's discussion of these foreign views (ignoring, of course, the many countries that have retained criminal prohibitions on sodomy) is therefore meaningless dicta. Dangerous dicta, however, since "this Court should not impose foreign moods, fads, or fashions on Americans." *Foster v. Florida*, 537 U.S. 990, n. (2002) (THOMAS, J., concurring in denial of certiorari).

I turn now to the ground on which the Court squarely rests its holding: the contention that there is no rational basis for the law here under attack. The Texas statute undeniably seeks to further the belief of its citizens that certain forms of sexual behavior are "immoral and unacceptable"—the same interest furthered by criminal laws against fornication, bigamy, adultery, adult incest, bestiality, and obscenity. *Bowers* held that this was a legitimate state interest. The Court today reaches the opposite conclusion. * * * This effectively decrees the end of all morals legislation. If, as the Court asserts, the promotion of majoritarian sexual morality is not even a legitimate state interest, none of the above-mentioned laws can survive rational-basis review.

Today's opinion is the product of a Court, which is the product of a law-profession culture, that has largely signed on to the so-called homosexual agenda, by which I mean the agenda promoted by some homosexual activists directed at eliminating the moral opprobrium that has traditionally attached to homosexual conduct. * * * Many Americans do not want persons who openly engage in homosexual conduct as partners in their business, as scoutmasters for their children, as teachers in their children's schools, or as boarders in their home. They

> **Take Note**
>
> Justice Scalia defends the authority of the states to promote "majoritarian sexual morality." Couldn't the statute invalidated in *Loving*—which prohibited interracial marriage—have been defended on the same ground? (Indeed, wasn't it?) If the state can legislate majoritarian sexual morality to prohibit the conduct at issue here, then does that mean that the Court decided the substantive due process issue in *Loving* incorrectly, as well? If not, why are the two cases different?

view this as protecting themselves and their families from a lifestyle that they believe to be immoral and destructive. * * * Let me be clear that I have nothing against homosexuals, or any other group, promoting their agenda through normal democratic means. [But] persuading one's fellow citizens is one thing, and imposing one's views in absence of democratic majority will is something else. * * * What Texas has chosen to do is well within the range of traditional democratic action, and its hand should not be stayed through the invention of a brand-new "constitutional right" by a Court that is impatient of democratic change. It is indeed true that "later generations can see that laws once thought necessary and proper in fact serve only to oppress," and when that happens, later generations can repeal those laws. But it is the premise of our system that those judgments are to be made by the people, and not imposed by a governing caste that knows best.

[JUSTICE THOMAS's dissenting opinion is omitted.]

POINTS FOR DISCUSSION

a.   Stating the Issue

The outcome in *Lawrence* turned in part on how the Court chose to frame the issue. Did the case involve the broad question whether government can interfere in personal relationships occurring within the home? Or did it instead involve the narrower question whether the state can prohibit "deviate" sexual acts? Framing it the first way practically guarantees that the case will fall into the sphere of liberty at issue in Griswold and Casey. Defining it the second way, by contrast, poses a more significant obstacle to petitioners' claim, particularly if the constitutional protection turns on whether the case involves a fundamental right that is deeply rooted in the Nation's history. Which is the more appropriate way to conceptualize the issue?

b.   Level of Scrutiny

To what level of scrutiny did the Court subject the Texas statute? Was it heightened scrutiny, on the theory that the statute interferes with a fundamental right? The Court stated that the Texas statute furthered "no legitimate state interest." Does that suggest that the Court was applying rational-basis review? (Justice Scalia thought so.) Does it matter for purposes of this case?

c. Morality as a State Interest

What does it mean to say—as Justice O'Connor (and perhaps the Court) did—that moral disapproval alone is not a legitimate state interest under either the Equal Protection or Due Process Clause? If, for instance, a state passes a law against murder, must it seek a reason for the law outside of the moral disapproval most people feel towards this act of violence? Or is the point that we can conceive of other valid state interests served by the criminalization of murder?

Consider the perspective offered by Justice Blackmun in his dissent in Bowers: "Petitioner and the Court fail to see the difference between laws that protect public sensibilities and those that enforce private morality." Is this a valid distinction? Is the line between these types of laws clear? If people disagree as fundamentally about what is publicly acceptable as they do about what is privately acceptable, then does it make sense to allow the majority to dictate public sensibilities but not private sensibilities?

d. Reliance on Foreign Law

The Court cited a decision of the European Court of Human Rights and noted the approach that other countries have taken to the issue that confronted the Court. Did the Court treat these decisions as authoritative sources of meaning of the United States Constitution? As persuasive authority? Is such reliance problematic? If so, why?

Robert Delahunty and John Yoo have criticized the practice, reasoning that:

"Non-ornamental use of foreign decisions undermines the separation of powers and violates the constitutional rules against delegation of federal authority to bodies outside the control of the national government. * * * Relying on decisions that interpret a wholly different document [from our Constitution] runs counter to the notion that judicial review derives from the Court's duty to enforce the Constitution. * * * Foreign and international laws, other than treaties ratified by the United States, are not enumerated among the three kinds of law that can be 'the supreme Law of the Land.' Therefore, they should not be treated as outcome-determinative in constitutional adjudication." Robert J. Delahanty & John Yoo, *Against Foreign Law*, 29 Harv. J.L. & Publ. Pol'y 291, 295–97, 313 (2005).

Vicki Jackson, in contrast, has defended the practice:

"Foreign or international examples, both negative and positive, can [inform] the court's determination of appropriate measures to protect U.S. constitutional rights. * * * Foreign practice and decisions can also be helpful in evaluating the justification for government action. * * * Foreign law can also help illustrate the possible consequences of different interpretive choices. * * * Many of our constitutional rights and values—liberty, equal protection of the law, due process, freedom of expression—reflect not only specific decisions made in the United States, but also widely shared commitments of many Western democracies." Vicki Jackson, "Yes Please, I'd Love to Talk With You," Legal Affairs (July/August 2004).

Which view do you find more persuasive?

e. Equal Protection v. Due Process

The Court in *Lawrence* declined to rely on the Equal Protection Clause, reasoning that such a basis for decision would have suggested that the state could ban private sexual conduct as long as the ban applied equally to heterosexual and homosexual conduct. Is it a realistic fear—given the "emerging awareness" that the Constitution protects intimate sexual conduct—that states would have responded to such a decision by banning an entire class of sexual activity? Why couldn't the Court, as it had done in *Loving*, invalidate the statute under *both* the Due Process and Equal Protection Clauses?

Was the Court's reluctance to rely on the Equal Protection Clause more because of the Court's unwillingness to conclude that gays and lesbians are entitled to heightened judicial protection under the Clause? Keep this question in mind as you read the next case, and when we take up the subject of Equal Protection—and specifically whether the Clause protects gays and lesbians from discrimination—in Chapter 5.

————————

Near the end of its opinion in *Lawrence*, the Court stated that the case did "not involve whether the government must give formal recognition to any relationship that homosexual persons seek to enter." In addition, in a portion of Justice O'Connor's separate opinion that has been omitted here, she asserted:

> That this law as applied to private, consensual conduct is unconstitutional under the Equal Protection Clause does not mean that other laws distinguishing between heterosexuals and homosexuals would similarly fail under rational basis review. * * * Unlike the moral disapproval of same-sex relations—the asserted state interest in this case—other reasons exist to promote the institution of marriage beyond mere moral disapproval of an excluded group.

Justice Scalia responded:

> Today's opinion dismantles the structure of constitutional law that has permitted a distinction to be made between heterosexual and

homosexual unions, insofar as formal recognition in marriage is concerned. If moral disapprobation of homosexual conduct is "no legitimate state interest" for purposes of proscribing that conduct * * *, what justification could there possibly be for denying the benefits of marriage to homosexual couples exercising "[t]he liberty protected by the Constitution"?

Shortly after the Court's decision in *Lawrence*, the Massachusetts Supreme Judicial Court held that a ban on same-sex marriages violates the state's constitution. *Goodridge v. Department of Public Health*, 798 N.E.2d 941 (Mass. 2003). The Court cited *Lawrence* and echoed the Court's language, but it based its decision on state constitutional law. Does *Lawrence* compel the conclusion that prohibitions on same-sex marriages violate the United States Constitution, as well?

A complete answer to the question whether the Constitution protects a right of same-sex couples to marry requires consideration of not only the Court's cases interpreting the Due Process Clause, but also the Court's cases interpreting the Equal Protection Clause. After all, if a state licenses marriages between opposite-sex couples but refuses to do so for same-sex couples, the state effectively discriminates against same-sex couples. As we will see in Chapter 5, the Equal Protection Clause is implicated when the state discriminates against a class of persons. But whether such differential treatment actually violates the Clause generally depends on the basis for the state's discrimination. When the state treats ophthalmologists better than opticians, for example, and thus "discriminates" against opticians, a reviewing court will ask only whether the distinction is rationally related to a legitimate government interest. Cf. *Williamson v. Lee Optical*, 348 U.S. 483 (1955). In contrast, when a law discriminates on the basis of race, the state can justify the distinction only if it can demonstrate that it is narrowly tailored to advance a compelling government interest.

As we will see in Chapter 5, however, the Court has not squarely addressed whether discrimination on the basis of sexual orientation triggers rational-basis review, strict scrutiny, or instead something in between. In *Romer v. Evans*, 517 U.S. 620 (1996), the Court invalidated an amendment to the Colorado constitution that prohibited the state and its localities from providing protection to gays and lesbians from discrimination on the basis of sexual orientation. But the Court did not make clear whether discrimination on that basis triggers heightened scrutiny. And in *United States v. Windsor*, 570 U.S. 744 (2013), the Court invalidated a provision of the federal Defense of Marriage Act that defined marriage for the purpose of federal law as a union between a man and a woman. But the Court again did not clearly choose a level of scrutiny for laws that discriminate on the basis of sexual orientation.

In 2015, after the courts of appeals had divided on the question whether state bans on same-sex marriage are constitutional, the Court agreed to decide the issue.

The Court's opinion follows, though we will revisit it in Chapter 5, when we consider the Equal Protection Clause.

OBERGEFELL V. HODGES

576 U.S. 644 (2015)

JUSTICE KENNEDY delivered the opinion of the Court.

The Constitution promises liberty to all within its reach, a liberty that includes certain specific rights that allow persons, within a lawful realm, to define and express their identity. The petitioners in these cases seek to find that liberty by marrying someone of the same sex and having their marriages deemed lawful on the same terms and conditions as marriages between persons of the opposite sex.

These cases come from Michigan, Kentucky, Ohio, and Tennessee, States that define marriage as a union between one man and one woman. See, *e.g.,* Mich. Const., Art. I, § 25; Ky. Const. § 233A; Ohio Rev.Code Ann. § 3101.01 (Lexis 2008); Tenn. Const., Art. XI, § 18. The petitioners are 14 same-sex couples and two men whose same-sex partners are deceased. The respondents are state officials responsible for enforcing the laws in question. The petitioners claim the respondents violate the Fourteenth Amendment by denying them the right to marry or to have their marriages, lawfully performed in another State, given full recognition.

Before addressing the principles and precedents that govern these cases, it is appropriate to note the history of the subject now before the Court. From their beginning to their most recent page, the annals of human history reveal the transcendent importance of marriage. The lifelong union of a man and a woman always has promised nobility and dignity to all persons, without regard to their station in life. Marriage is sacred to those who live by their religions and offers unique fulfillment to those who find meaning in the secular realm. Its dynamic allows two people to find a life that could not be found alone, for a marriage becomes greater than just the two persons. Rising from the most basic human needs, marriage is essential to our most profound hopes and aspirations.

The centrality of marriage to the human condition makes it unsurprising that the institution has existed for millennia and across civilizations. * * * The ancient origins of marriage confirm its centrality, but it has not stood in isolation from developments in law and society. The history of marriage is one of both continuity and change. That institution—even as confined to opposite-sex relations—has evolved over time. For example, marriage was once viewed as an arrangement by the couple's parents based on political, religious, and financial concerns; but by the time of the Nation's founding it was understood to be a voluntary contract between a man and a woman. See N. Cott, Public Vows: A History of Marriage and the Nation 9–17 (2000); S. Coontz, Marriage, A History 15–16 (2005). As the role and status of women changed, the institution further evolved. Under the centuries-old doctrine of coverture, a married man and woman were treated by the State as a single, male-dominated legal entity. See 1 W. Blackstone, Commentaries on the Laws of England 430 (1765). As women gained legal, political, and property rights, and as society began to understand that women have their own equal dignity, the law of coverture was abandoned. These and other developments in the institution of marriage over the past centuries were not mere superficial changes. Rather, they worked deep transformations in its structure, affecting aspects of marriage long viewed by many as essential. These new insights have strengthened, not weakened, the institution of marriage. Indeed, changed understandings of marriage are characteristic of a Nation where new dimensions of freedom become apparent to new generations, often through perspectives that begin in pleas or protests and then are considered in the political sphere and the judicial process.

This dynamic can be seen in the Nation's experiences with the rights of gays and lesbians. Until the mid-20th century, same-sex intimacy long had been condemned as immoral by the state itself in most Western nations, a belief often embodied in the criminal law. * * * Even when a greater awareness of the humanity and integrity of homosexual persons came in the period after World War II, the argument that gays and lesbians had a just claim to dignity was in conflict with both law and widespread social conventions. Same-sex intimacy remained a crime in many States. Gays and lesbians were prohibited from most government employment, barred from military service, excluded under immigration laws, targeted by police, and burdened in their rights to associate. For much of the 20th century, moreover, homosexuality was treated as an illness. * * * Only in more recent years have psychiatrists and others recognized that sexual orientation is both a normal expression of human sexuality and immutable. See Brief for American Psychological Association et al. as *Amici Curiae* 7–17.

In the late 20th century, following substantial cultural and political developments, same-sex couples began to lead more open and public lives and to establish families. This development was followed by a quite extensive discussion of the issue in both governmental and private sectors and by a shift in public attitudes toward greater tolerance. As a result, questions about the rights of gays and lesbians soon reached the courts, where the issue could be discussed in the formal discourse of the law.

[The Court described its decisions in *Bowers v. Hardwick,* 478 U.S. 186 (1986), *Romer v. Evans,* 517 U.S. 620 (1996), *Lawrence v. Texas,* 539 U.S. 558, 575 (2003), and *United States v. Windsor,* 133 S. Ct. 2675 (2013), as well as the decisions addressing same-sex marriage in Hawaii, *Massachusetts,* and the United States Courts of Appeals.] After years of litigation, legislation, referenda, and the discussions that attended these public acts, the States are now divided on the issue of same-sex marriage.

* * * The fundamental liberties protected by [the Due Process] Clause include most of the rights enumerated in the Bill of Rights. See *Duncan v. Louisiana,* 391 U.S. 145, 147–149 (1968). In addition these liberties extend to certain personal choices central to individual dignity and autonomy, including intimate choices that define personal identity and beliefs. See, *e.g., Eisenstadt v. Baird,* 405 U.S. 438, 453 (1972); *Griswold v. Connecticut,* 381 U.S. 479, 484–486 (1965).

The identification and protection of fundamental rights is an enduring part of the judicial duty to interpret the Constitution. That responsibility, however, "has not been reduced to any formula." *Poe v. Ullman,* 367 U.S. 497, 542 (1961) (Harlan, J., dissenting). Rather, it requires courts to exercise reasoned judgment in identifying interests of the person so fundamental that the State must accord them its respect. That process is guided by many of the same considerations relevant to analysis of other constitutional provisions that set forth broad principles rather than specific requirements. History and tradition guide and discipline this inquiry but do not set its outer boundaries. That method respects our history and learns from it without allowing the past alone to rule the present.

Applying these established tenets, the Court has long held the right to marry is * * * fundamental under the Due Process Clause. It cannot be denied that this Court's cases describing the right to marry presumed a relationship involving opposite-sex partners. The Court, like many institutions, has made assumptions defined by the world and time of which it is a part. This was evident in *Baker v. Nelson,* 409 U.S. 810 (1972), a one-line summary decision issued in 1972, holding the exclusion of same-sex couples from marriage did not present a substantial federal question.

Still, [in] defining the right to marry [this Court's] cases have identified essential attributes of that right based in history, tradition, and other constitutional liberties inherent in this intimate bond. And in assessing whether the force and rationale of its cases apply to same-sex couples, the Court must respect the basic reasons why the right to marry has been long protected.

This analysis compels the conclusion that same-sex couples may exercise the right to marry. The four principles and traditions to be discussed demonstrate that the reasons marriage is fundamental under the Constitution apply with equal force to same-sex couples. A first premise of the Court's relevant precedents is that the right to personal choice regarding marriage is inherent in the concept of individual autonomy. This abiding connection between marriage and liberty is why *Loving v. Virginia*, 388 U.S. 1 (1967), invalidated interracial marriage bans under the Due Process Clause. Like choices concerning contraception, family relationships, procreation, and childrearing, all of which are protected by the Constitution, decisions concerning marriage are among the most intimate that an individual can make. See *Lawrence, supra,* at 574. Indeed, the Court has noted it would be contradictory "to recognize a right of privacy with respect to other matters of family life and not with respect to the decision to enter the relationship that is the foundation of the family in our society." *Zablocki v. Redhail*, 434 U.S. 374, 386 (1978). The nature of marriage is that, through its enduring bond, two persons together can find other freedoms, such as expression, intimacy, and spirituality. This is true for all persons, whatever their sexual orientation. There is dignity in the bond between two men or two women who seek to marry and in their autonomy to make such profound choices.

A second principle in this Court's jurisprudence is that the right to marry is fundamental because it supports a two-person union unlike any other in its importance to the committed individuals. This point was central to Griswold, which held the Constitution protects the right of married couples to use contraception. * * * Marriage responds to the universal fear that a lonely person might call out only to find no one there. It offers the hope of companionship and understanding and assurance that while both still live there will be someone to care for the other.

As this Court held in *Lawrence,* same-sex couples have the same right as opposite-sex couples to enjoy intimate association. * * * But while *Lawrence* confirmed a dimension of freedom that allows individuals to engage in intimate association without criminal liability, it does not follow that freedom stops there. Outlaw to outcast may be a step forward, but it does not achieve the full promise of liberty.

A third basis for protecting the right to marry is that it safeguards children and families and thus draws meaning from related rights of childrearing, procreation, and education. See *Pierce v. Society of Sisters*, 268 U.S. 510 (1925); *Meyer*, 262 U.S., at 399. The Court has recognized these connections by describing the varied rights as a unified whole: "[T]he right to 'marry, establish a home and bring

up children' is a central part of the liberty protected by the Due Process Clause."
Zablocki, 434 U.S., at 384 (quoting *Meyer*, supra, at 399). * * * By giving recognition
and legal structure to their parents' relationship, marriage allows children "to
understand the integrity and closeness of their own family and its concord with
other families in their community and in their daily lives." *Windsor*. Marriage also
affords the permanency and stability important to children's best interests.

As all parties agree, many same-sex couples provide loving and nurturing
homes to their children, whether biological or adopted. And hundreds of
thousands of children are presently being raised by such couples. Most States have
allowed gays and lesbians to adopt, either as individuals or as couples, and many
adopted and foster children have same-sex parents. This provides powerful
confirmation from the law itself that gays and lesbians can create loving,
supportive families.

Excluding same-sex couples from marriage thus conflicts with a central
premise of the right to marry. Without the recognition, stability, and predictability
marriage offers, their children suffer the stigma of knowing their families are
somehow lesser. They also suffer the significant material costs of being raised by
unmarried parents, relegated through no fault of their own to a more difficult and
uncertain family life. The marriage laws at issue here thus harm and humiliate the
children of same-sex couples. That is not to say the right to marry is less
meaningful for those who do not or cannot have children. * * * In light of
precedent protecting the right of a married couple not to procreate, it cannot be
said the Court or the States have conditioned the right to marry on the capacity
or commitment to procreate. The constitutional marriage right has many aspects,
of which childbearing is only one.

Fourth and finally, this Court's cases and the Nation's traditions make clear
that marriage is a keystone of our social order. * * * For that reason, just as a
couple vows to support each other, so does society pledge to support the couple,
offering symbolic recognition and material benefits to protect and nourish the
union. Indeed, while the States are in general free to vary the benefits they confer
on all married couples, they have throughout our history made marriage the basis
for an expanding list of governmental rights, benefits, and responsibilities. These
aspects of marital status include: taxation; inheritance and property rights; rules of
intestate succession; spousal privilege in the law of evidence; hospital access;
medical decisionmaking authority; adoption rights; the rights and benefits of
survivors; [and] child custody, support, and visitation rules. * * * The States have
contributed to the fundamental character of the marriage right by placing that
institution at the center of so many facets of the legal and social order.

There is no difference between same- and opposite-sex couples with respect to this principle. Yet by virtue of their exclusion from that institution, same-sex couples are denied the constellation of benefits that the States have linked to marriage. This harm results in more than just material burdens. * * * As the State itself makes marriage all the more precious by the significance it attaches to it, exclusion from that status has the effect of teaching that gays and lesbians are unequal in important respects. It demeans gays and lesbians for the State to lock them out of a central institution of the Nation's society. Same-sex couples, too, may aspire to the transcendent purposes of marriage and seek fulfillment in its highest meaning.

The limitation of marriage to opposite-sex couples may long have seemed natural and just, but its inconsistency with the central meaning of the fundamental right to marry is now manifest. With that knowledge must come the recognition that laws excluding same-sex couples from the marriage right impose stigma and injury of the kind prohibited by our basic charter.

Objecting that this does not reflect an appropriate framing of the issue, the respondents refer to *Washington v. Glucksberg*, 521 U.S. 702, 721 (1997), which called for a "careful description" of fundamental rights. They assert the petitioners do not seek to exercise the right to marry but rather a new and nonexistent "right to same-sex marriage." *Glucksberg* did insist that liberty under the Due Process Clause must be defined in a most

> **Food for Thought**
>
> Earlier in this chapter, we considered the various approaches to defining the level of generality at which the Court should define fundamental rights under the Due Process Clause. Which approach does the Court follow here? Is that approach consistent with other cases? Is it sensible and defensible?

circumscribed manner, with central reference to specific historical practices. Yet while that approach may have been appropriate for the asserted right there involved (physician-assisted suicide), it is inconsistent with the approach this Court has used in discussing other fundamental rights, including marriage and intimacy. *Loving* did not ask about a "right to interracial marriage"; *Turner* did not ask about a "right of inmates to marry"; and *Zablocki* did not ask about a "right of fathers with unpaid child support duties to marry." Rather, each case inquired about the right to marry in its comprehensive sense, asking if there was a sufficient justification for excluding the relevant class from the right.

That principle applies here. If rights were defined by who exercised them in the past, then received practices could serve as their own continued justification and new groups could not invoke rights once denied. This Court has rejected that approach, both with respect to the right to marry and the rights of gays and lesbians. See *Loving*, 388 U.S., at 12; *Lawrence*, 539 U.S., at 566–567.

The right to marry is fundamental as a matter of history and tradition, but rights come not from ancient sources alone. They rise, too, from a better informed understanding of how constitutional imperatives define a liberty that remains urgent in our own era. Many who deem same-sex marriage to be wrong reach that conclusion based on decent and honorable religious or philosophical premises, and neither they nor their beliefs are disparaged here. But when that sincere, personal opposition becomes enacted law and public policy, the necessary consequence is to put the imprimatur of the State itself on an exclusion that soon demeans or stigmatizes those whose own liberty is then denied. Under the Constitution, same-sex couples seek in marriage the same legal treatment as opposite-sex couples, and it would disparage their choices and diminish their personhood to deny them this right.

The right of same-sex couples to marry that is part of the liberty promised by the Fourteenth Amendment is derived, too, from that Amendment's guarantee of the equal protection of the laws. The Due Process Clause and the Equal Protection Clause are connected in a profound way, though they set forth independent principles. Rights implicit in liberty and rights secured by equal protection may rest on different precepts and are not always co-extensive, yet in some instances each may be instructive as to the meaning and reach of the other. In any particular case one Clause may be thought to capture the essence of the right in a more accurate and comprehensive way, even as the two Clauses may converge in the identification and definition of the right. This interrelation of the two principles furthers our understanding of what freedom is and must become.

The Court's cases touching upon the right to marry reflect this dynamic. In *Loving* the Court invalidated a prohibition on interracial marriage under both the Equal Protection Clause and the Due Process Clause. * * * The reasons why marriage is a fundamental right became more clear and compelling from a full awareness and understanding of the hurt that resulted from laws barring interracial unions.

This dynamic also applies to same-sex marriage. It is now clear that the challenged laws burden the liberty of same-sex couples, and it must be further acknowledged that they abridge central precepts of equality. Here the marriage laws enforced by the respondents are in essence unequal: same-sex couples are denied all the benefits afforded to opposite-sex couples and are barred from exercising a fundamental right. Especially against a long history of disapproval of their relationships, this denial to same-sex couples of the right to marry works a grave and continuing harm. The imposition of this disability on gays and lesbians serves to disrespect and subordinate them. And the Equal Protection Clause, like the Due Process Clause, prohibits this unjustified infringement of the fundamental right to marry. See, *e.g., Zablocki, supra,* at 383–388; *Skinner,* 316 U.S., at 541.

These considerations lead to the conclusion that the right to marry is a fundamental right inherent in the liberty of the person, and under the Due Process and Equal Protection Clauses of the Fourteenth Amendment couples of the same-sex may not be deprived of that right and that liberty. The Court now holds that same-sex couples may exercise the fundamental right to marry. No longer may this liberty be denied to them. *Baker v. Nelson* must be and now is overruled, and the State laws challenged by Petitioners in these cases are now held invalid to the extent they exclude same-sex couples from civil marriage on the same terms and conditions as opposite-sex couples.

There may be an initial inclination in these cases to proceed with caution— to await further legislation, litigation, and debate. The respondents warn there has been insufficient democratic discourse before deciding an issue so basic as the definition of marriage. * * * Yet there has been far more deliberation than this argument acknowledges. There have been referenda, legislative debates, and grassroots campaigns, as well as countless studies, papers, books, and other popular and scholarly writings. There has been extensive litigation in state and federal courts. * * * [The] dynamic of our constitutional system is that individuals need not await legislative action before asserting a fundamental right. * * * It is of no moment whether advocates of same-sex marriage now enjoy or lack momentum in the democratic process. The issue before the Court here is the legal question whether the Constitution protects the right of same-sex couples to marry.

The respondents also argue allowing same-sex couples to wed will harm marriage as an institution by leading to fewer opposite-sex marriages. This may occur, the respondents contend, because licensing same-sex marriage severs the connection between natural procreation and marriage. That argument, however, rests on a counterintuitive view of opposite-sex couple's decisionmaking processes regarding marriage and parenthood. Decisions about whether to marry and raise children are based on many personal, romantic, and practical considerations; and it is unrealistic to conclude that an opposite-sex couple would choose not to marry simply because same-sex couples may do so. * * * Indeed, with respect to this asserted basis for excluding same-sex couples from the right to marry, it is appropriate to observe these cases involve only the rights of two consenting adults whose marriages would pose no risk of harm to themselves or third parties.

Finally, it must be emphasized that religions, and those who adhere to religious doctrines, may continue to advocate with utmost, sincere conviction that, by divine precepts, same-sex marriage should not be condoned. * * * The same is true of those who oppose same-sex marriage for other reasons. * * * The Constitution, however, does not permit the State to bar same-sex couples from marriage on the same terms as accorded to couples of the opposite sex.

It follows that the Court also must hold—and it now does hold—that there is no lawful basis for a State to refuse to recognize a lawful same-sex marriage performed in another State on the ground of its same-sex character.

No union is more profound than marriage, for it embodies the highest ideals of love, fidelity, devotion, sacrifice, and family. In forming a marital union, two people become something greater than once they were. As some of the petitioners in these cases demonstrate, marriage embodies a love that may endure even past death. It would misunderstand these men and women to say they disrespect the idea of marriage. Their plea is that they do respect it, respect it so deeply that they seek to find its fulfillment for themselves. Their hope is not to be condemned to live in loneliness, excluded from one of civilization's oldest institutions. They ask for equal dignity in the eyes of the law. The Constitution grants them that right.

CHIEF JUSTICE ROBERTS, with whom JUSTICE SCALIA and JUSTICE THOMAS join, dissenting.

The majority's decision is an act of will, not legal judgment. The right it announces has no basis in the Constitution or this Court's precedent. The majority expressly disclaims judicial "caution" and omits even a pretense of humility, openly relying on its desire to remake society according to its own "new insight" into the "nature of injustice." As a result, the Court invalidates the marriage laws of more than half the States and orders the transformation of a social institution that has formed the basis of human society for millennia, for the Kalahari Bushmen and the Han Chinese, the Carthaginians and the Aztecs. Just who do we think we are?

Understand well what this dissent is about: It is not about whether, in my judgment, the institution of marriage should be changed to include same-sex couples. It is instead about whether, in our democratic republic, that decision should rest with the people acting through their elected representatives, or with five lawyers who happen to hold commissions authorizing them to resolve legal disputes according to law. The Constitution leaves no doubt about the answer.

As the majority acknowledges, marriage "has existed for millennia and across civilizations." For all those millennia, across all those civilizations, "marriage" referred to only one relationship: the union of a man and a woman. * * * This universal definition of marriage as the union of a man and a woman is no historical coincidence. Marriage [arose] in the nature of things to meet a vital need: ensuring that children are conceived by a mother and father committed to raising them in the stable conditions of a lifelong relationship. * * * This singular understanding of marriage has prevailed in the United States throughout our history. * * * There is no dispute that every State at the founding—and every State throughout our history until a dozen years ago—defined marriage in the traditional, biologically rooted way.

As the majority notes, some aspects of marriage have changed over time. * * * [These developments] did not, however, work any transformation in the core structure of marriage as the union between a man and a woman. If you had asked a person on the street how marriage was defined, no one would ever have said, "Marriage is the union of a man and a woman, where the woman is subject to coverture." The majority may be right that the "history of marriage is one of both continuity and change," but the core meaning of marriage has endured.

The majority purports to identify four "principles and traditions" in this Court's due process precedents that support a fundamental right for same-sex couples to marry. In reality, however, the majority's approach has no basis in principle or tradition, except for the unprincipled tradition of judicial policymaking that characterized discredited decisions such as *Lochner v. New York*, 198 U.S. 45 (1905). Stripped of its shiny rhetorical gloss, the majority's argument is that the Due Process Clause gives same-sex couples a fundamental right to marry because it will be good for them and for society. If I were a legislator, I would certainly consider that view as a matter of social policy. But as a judge, I find the majority's position indefensible as a matter of constitutional law.

Allowing unelected federal judges to select which unenumerated rights rank as "fundamental"—and to strike down state laws on the basis of that determination—raises obvious concerns about the judicial role. * * * The need for restraint in administering the strong medicine of substantive due process is a lesson this Court has learned the hard way. The Court first applied substantive due process to strike down a statute in *Dred Scott v. Sandford*, 19 How. 393 (1857). * * * *Dred Scott*'s holding was overruled on the battlefields of the Civil War and by constitutional amendment after Appomattox, but its approach to the Due Process Clause reappeared. * * * By empowering judges to elevate their own policy judgments to the status of constitutionally protected "liberty," the *Lochner* line of cases left "no alternative to regarding the court as a . . . legislative chamber." L. Hand, The Bill of Rights 42 (1958).

Eventually, the Court recognized its error and vowed not to repeat it. * * * [But the majority's] aggressive application of substantive due process breaks sharply with decades of precedent and returns the Court to the unprincipled approach of *Lochner*. The majority's driving themes are that marriage is desirable and petitioners desire it. * * * As a matter of constitutional law, however, the sincerity of petitioners' wishes is not relevant.

When the majority turns to the law, it relies primarily on precedents discussing the fundamental "right to marry." *Turner v. Safley*, 482 U.S. 78, 95 (1987); *Zablocki v. Redhail*, 434 U.S. 374, 383 (1978); *Loving v. Virginia*, 388 U.S. 1, 12 (1967). These cases do not hold, of course, that anyone who wants to get married has a constitutional right to do so. They instead require a State to justify barriers to marriage as that institution has always been understood. * * * None of the laws at issue in those cases purported to change the core definition of marriage as the union of a man and a woman. * * * [T]he "right to marry" cases stand for the important but limited proposition that particular restrictions on access to marriage *as traditionally defined* violate due process. These precedents say nothing at all about a right to make a State change its definition of marriage, which is the right petitioners actually seek here. * * *

Neither *Lawrence* nor any other precedent in the privacy line of cases supports the right that petitioners assert here. Unlike criminal laws banning contraceptives and sodomy, the marriage laws at issue here involve no government intrusion. They create no crime and impose no punishment. Same-sex couples remain free to live together, to engage in intimate conduct, and to raise their families as they see fit. * * * [T]he privacy cases provide no support for the majority's position, because petitioners do not seek privacy. Quite the opposite, they seek public recognition of their relationships, along with corresponding government benefits. * * * [A]lthough the right to privacy recognized by our precedents certainly plays a role in protecting the intimate conduct of same-sex couples, it provides no affirmative right to redefine marriage and no basis for striking down the laws at issue here.

The truth is that today's decision rests on nothing more than the majority's own conviction that same-sex couples should be allowed to marry because they want to, and that "it would disparage their choices and diminish their personhood to deny them this right." Whatever force that belief may have as a matter of moral philosophy, it has no more basis in the Constitution than did the naked policy preferences adopted in *Lochner*.

In addition to their due process argument, petitioners contend that the Equal Protection Clause requires their States to license and recognize same-sex marriages. The majority does not seriously engage with this claim. Its discussion is, quite frankly, difficult to follow. * * * Absent from this portion of the opinion [is] anything resembling our usual framework for deciding equal protection cases. * * * In any event, the marriage laws at issue here do not violate the Equal Protection Clause, because distinguishing between opposite-sex and same-sex couples is rationally related to the States' "legitimate state interest" in "preserving the traditional institution of marriage." *Lawrence,* 539 U.S., at 585 (O'Connor, J., concurring in judgment).

When decisions are reached through democratic means, some people will inevitably be disappointed with the results. But those whose views do not prevail at least know that they have had their say, and accordingly are—in the tradition of our political culture—reconciled to the result of a fair and honest debate. * * * But today the Court puts a stop to all that. By deciding this question under the Constitution, the Court removes it from the realm of democratic decision. There will be consequences to shutting down the political process on an issue of such profound public significance. Closing debate tends to close minds. People denied a voice are less likely to accept the ruling of a court on an issue that does not seem to be the sort of thing courts usually decide. * * * Indeed, however heartened the proponents of same-sex marriage might be on this day, it is worth acknowledging what they have lost, and lost forever: the opportunity to win the true acceptance that comes from persuading their fellow citizens of the justice of their cause. And they lose this just when the winds of change were freshening at their backs.

Perhaps the most discouraging aspect of today's decision is the extent to which the majority feels compelled to sully those on the other side of the debate. * * * By the majority's account, Americans who did nothing more than follow the understanding of marriage that has existed for our entire history—in particular, the tens of millions of people who voted to reaffirm their States' enduring definition of marriage—have acted to "lock . . . out," "disparage," "disrespect and subordinate," and inflict "[d]ignitary wounds" upon their gay and lesbian neighbors. * * * It is one thing for the majority to conclude that the Constitution protects a right to same-sex marriage; it is something else to portray everyone who does not share the majority's "better informed understanding" as bigoted.

In the face of all this, a much different view of the Court's role is possible. That view is more modest and restrained. It is more skeptical that the legal abilities of judges also reflect insight into moral and philosophical issues. It is more sensitive to the fact that judges are unelected and unaccountable, and that the legitimacy of their power depends on confining it to the exercise of legal judgment. It is more attuned to the lessons of history, and what it has meant for the country and Court when Justices have exceeded their proper bounds. And it is less pretentious than to suppose that while people around the world have viewed an institution in a particular way for thousands of years, the present generation and the present Court are the ones chosen to burst the bonds of that history and tradition.

If you are among the many Americans—of whatever sexual orientation—who favor expanding same-sex marriage, by all means celebrate today's decision. Celebrate the achievement of a desired goal. Celebrate the opportunity for a new expression of commitment to a partner. Celebrate the availability of new benefits. But do not celebrate the Constitution. It had nothing to do with it.

JUSTICE SCALIA, with whom JUSTICE THOMAS joins, dissenting.

Until the courts put a stop to it, public debate over same-sex marriage displayed American democracy at its best. Individuals on both sides of the issue passionately, but respectfully, attempted to persuade their fellow citizens to accept their views. Americans considered the arguments and put the question to a vote. * * * That is exactly how our system of government is supposed to work.

The Constitution places some constraints on self-rule—constraints adopted *by the People themselves* when they ratified the Constitution and its Amendments. * * * These cases ask us to decide whether the Fourteenth Amendment contains a limitation that requires the States to license and recognize marriages between two people of the same sex. Does it remove *that* issue from the political process? Of course not. * * * When the Fourteenth Amendment was ratified in 1868, every State limited marriage to one man and one woman, and no one doubted the constitutionality of doing so. That resolves these cases. When it comes to determining the meaning of a vague constitutional provision—such as "due process of law" or "equal protection of the laws"—it is unquestionable that the People who ratified that provision did not understand it to prohibit a practice that remained both universal and uncontroversial in the years after ratification. We have no basis for striking down a practice that is not expressly prohibited by the Fourteenth Amendment's text, and that bears the endorsement of a long tradition of open, widespread, and unchallenged use dating back to the Amendment's ratification. Since there is no doubt whatever that the People never decided to prohibit the limitation of marriage to opposite-sex couples, the public debate over same-sex marriage must be allowed to continue.

But the Court ends this debate, in an opinion lacking even a thin veneer of law. Buried beneath the mummeries and straining-to-be-memorable passages of the opinion is a candid and startling assertion: No matter *what* it was the People ratified, the Fourteenth Amendment protects those rights that the Judiciary, in its "reasoned judgment," thinks the Fourteenth Amendment ought to protect. * * * [R]ather than focusing on *the People's* understanding of "liberty"—at the time of ratification or even today—the majority focuses on four "principles and traditions" that, *in the majority's view*, prohibit States from defining marriage as an institution consisting of one man and one woman.

This is a naked judicial claim to legislative—indeed, *super*-legislative—power; a claim fundamentally at odds with our system of government. Except as limited by a constitutional prohibition agreed to by the People, the States are free to adopt whatever laws they like, even those that offend the esteemed Justices' "reasoned judgment." A system of government that makes the People subordinate to a committee of nine unelected lawyers does not deserve to be called a democracy.

JUSTICE THOMAS, with whom JUSTICE SCALIA joins, dissenting.

The majority's decision today will require States to issue marriage licenses to same-sex couples and to recognize same-sex marriages entered in other States largely based on a constitutional provision guaranteeing "due process" before a person is deprived of his "life, liberty, or property." * * * Even if the doctrine of substantive due process were somehow defensible—it is not—petitioners still would not have a claim. * * * As used in the Due Process Clauses, "liberty" most likely refers to "the power of locomotion, of changing situation, or removing one's person to whatsoever place one's own inclination may direct; without imprisonment or restraint, unless by due course of law." 1 W. Blackstone, Commentaries on the Laws of England 130 (1769) (Blackstone). That definition is drawn from the historical roots of the Clauses and is consistent with our Constitution's text and structure.

The Framers drew heavily upon Blackstone's formulation, adopting provisions in early State Constitutions that replicated Magna Carta's language, but were modified to refer specifically to "life, liberty, or property." * * * When read in light of the history of that formulation, it is hard to see how the "liberty" protected by the [Due Process] Clause could be interpreted to include anything broader than freedom from physical restraint. * * *

Even assuming that the "liberty" in those Clauses encompasses something more than freedom from physical restraint, it would not include the types of rights claimed by the majority. In the American legal tradition, liberty has long been understood as individual freedom *from* governmental action, not as a right *to* a particular governmental entitlement. * * * Whether we define "liberty" as locomotion or freedom from governmental action more broadly, petitioners have in no way been deprived of it. Petitioners cannot claim * * * that the States have restricted their ability to go about their daily lives as they would be able to absent governmental restrictions. * * * Instead, the States have refused to grant them governmental entitlements. * * * But receiving governmental recognition and benefits has nothing to do with any understanding of "liberty" that the Framers would have recognized.

> **Food for Thought**
>
> Justice Thomas asserts here that the Constitution protects "negative" rights—that is, the right not to have the government do something to you—but does not generally protect "positive" rights—that is, the right to have the government do something for you. This is why the Court has interpreted our Constitution not to protect, for example, a right to education or health care. (We consider these cases in Chapter 6.) On Justice Thomas's view, does the Constitution protect a right of opposite-sex couples to marry? Could a state announce that it would no longer grant marriage licenses at all, to gay or straight couples?

Perhaps recognizing that these cases do not actually involve liberty as it has been understood, the majority goes to great lengths to assert that its decision will advance the "dignity" of same-sex couples. The flaw in that reasoning, of course, is that the Constitution contains no "dignity" Clause, and even if it did, the government would be incapable of bestowing dignity. Human dignity has long been understood in this country to be innate. * * * The corollary of that principle is that human dignity cannot be taken away by the government. Slaves did not lose their dignity (any more than they lost their humanity) because the government allowed them to be enslaved. Those held in internment camps did not lose their dignity because the government confined them. And those denied governmental benefits certainly do not lose their dignity because the government denies them those benefits. The government cannot bestow dignity, and it cannot take it away.

The majority's musings are thus deeply misguided, but at least those musings can have no effect on the dignity of the persons the majority demeans. * * * Its rejection of laws preserving the traditional definition of marriage can have no effect on the dignity of the people who voted for them. Its invalidation of those laws can have no effect on the dignity of the people who continue to adhere to the traditional definition of marriage. And its disdain for the understandings of liberty and dignity upon which this Nation was founded can have no effect on the dignity of Americans who continue to believe in them.

JUSTICE ALITO, with whom JUSTICE SCALIA and JUSTICE THOMAS join, dissenting.

* * * Although the Court expresses the point in loftier terms, its argument is that the fundamental purpose of marriage is to promote the well-being of those who choose to marry. Marriage provides emotional fulfillment and the promise of support in times of need. And by benefiting persons who choose to wed, marriage indirectly benefits society because persons who live in stable, fulfilling, and supportive relationships make better citizens. * * * This understanding of the States' reasons for recognizing marriage enables the majority to argue that same-sex marriage serves the States' objectives in the same way as opposite-sex marriage.

This understanding of marriage, which focuses almost entirely on the happiness of persons who choose to marry, is shared by many people today, but it is not the traditional one. For millennia, marriage was inextricably linked to the one thing that only an opposite-sex couple can do: procreate. [T]he States defending their adherence to the traditional understanding of marriage have explained [that they] formalize and promote marriage, unlike other fulfilling human relationships, in order to encourage potentially procreative conduct to take place within a lasting unit that has long been thought to provide the best atmosphere for raising children. They thus argue that there are reasonable secular grounds for restricting marriage to opposite-sex couples.

[handwritten margin note: religious implication]

While, for many, the attributes of marriage in 21st-century America have changed, those States that do not want to recognize same-sex marriage have not yet given up on the traditional understanding. They worry that by officially abandoning the older understanding, they may contribute to marriage's further decay. It is far beyond the outer reaches of this Court's authority to say that a State may not adhere to the understanding of marriage that has long prevailed, not just in this country and others with similar cultural roots, but also in a great variety of countries and cultures all around the globe.

The system of federalism established by our Constitution provides a way for people with different beliefs to live together in a single nation. If the issue of same-sex marriage had been left to the people of the States, it is likely that some States would recognize same-sex marriage and others would not. It is also possible that some States would tie recognition to protection for conscience rights. The majority today makes that impossible. By imposing its own views on the entire country, the majority facilitates the marginalization of the many Americans who have traditional ideas. Recalling the harsh treatment of gays and lesbians in the past, some may think that turnabout is fair play. But if that sentiment prevails, the Nation will experience bitter and lasting wounds.

POINTS FOR DISCUSSION

a.   Same-Sex Marriage and the Due Process Clause

In order to decide whether the right of the petitioners to marry was fundamental, and thus entitled to meaningful judicial protection under the Due Process Clause, the Court first had to define the precise right at issue. The Court appears to have defined the right protected by the Due Process Clause as the right of two consenting adults to marry, and accordingly concluded that the right embraced the petitioners' claims. Chief Justice Roberts, by contrast, asserted that the right was properly defined as the right of a man and a woman to marry. If the level of generality at which the majority defined the right was correct, then what other marital arrangements can claim constitutional protection? In a portion of his dissent that was omitted above, Chief Justice Roberts asserted:

> One immediate question invited by the majority's position is whether States may retain the definition of marriage as a union of two people. Although the majority randomly inserts the adjective "two" in various places, it offers no reason at all why the two-person element of the core definition of marriage may be preserved while the man-woman element may not. Indeed, from the standpoint of history and tradition, a leap from opposite-sex marriage to same-sex marriage is much greater than one from a two-person union to plural unions, which have deep roots in some cultures around the world. If the majority is willing to take the big leap, it is hard to see how it can say no to the shorter one.

Is there any limiting principle in the Court's opinion that makes the case of same-sex marriage different from the case of plural marriage? If not, is there nevertheless a principle that the Court could invoke in the future?

Conversely, if the level of generality at which the dissenters defined the right was correct, then is it clear that the Court's decision in *Loving* was correct? After all, the common practice in most states from before the framing until at least the middle of the twentieth century—and certainly at the time of the ratification of the Fourteenth Amendment—was to limit marriage not only to opposite-sex couples, but also to opposite-sex couples of the same race. If Chief Justice Roberts was correct that the right protected by the Due Process Clause is the right to "marriage *as traditionally defined*," then wasn't the Court's Due Process conclusion in *Loving* wrong? And if the Court was correct in *Loving* to conclude that the constitutionally protected right was something slightly more abstract—that is, the right of a man and a woman, regardless of race, to marry—then was the level of generality at which the majority defined the right in *Obergefell* obviously too abstract?

b.   Same-Sex Marriage and Popular Democracy

The dissenters in *Obergefell* asserted that the Court's decision short-circuited the democratic process, because the voters in the various states—many of whom were in the process of debating and addressing the issue of same-sex marriage—now cannot resolve the issue by denying marriage licenses to same-sex couples. The majority responded that it is the Court's responsibility to protect fundamental rights. Does the view expressed by the dissenting Justices necessarily presume that the Constitution does not protect unenumerated rights, and thus that it leaves the matter to the people to decide? Or can the dissenting opinions (or at least some of them) be read to acknowledge that the Constitution protects some unenumerated rights, but nevertheless to suggest that, absent more time and political debate, the right at issue in this case has not yet achieved fundamental status? In other words, is the debate about popular democracy—or, in Justice Alito's dissent, federalism—really just another way of framing the debate over whether same-sex couples have a fundamental right to marry?

c.   Same-Sex Marriage and the Equal Protection Clause

The Court concluded that the state laws at issue not only violated the Due Process Clause, but also violated the Equal Protection Clause because "same-sex couples are denied all the benefits afforded to opposite-sex couples and are barred from exercising a fundamental right." We will return in Chapter 5 to the role that the Equal Protection Clause played (or could have played) in the Court's approach to this issue.

d.   Same-Sex Marriage and Religious Liberty

In a section of his dissent that was omitted above, Chief Justice Roberts contended:

> Hard questions arise when people of faith exercise religion in ways that may be seen to conflict with the new right to same-sex marriage—when, for example, a religious college provides married student housing only to opposite-sex married couples, or a religious adoption agency declines to place children with same-sex married couples. Indeed, the Solicitor General candidly acknowledged that the tax exemptions of some religious institutions would be in question if they opposed same-sex marriage. There is little doubt that these and similar questions will soon be before this Court. Unfortunately, people of faith can take no comfort in the treatment they receive from the majority today.

Assuming the Court was correct to conclude that the Constitution protects a right of gay couples to enter same-sex marriages, should individuals motivated by sincerely held religious beliefs be permitted to discriminate against same-sex couples who seek to exercise the right? We will consider the extent to which the Free Exercise Clause of the First Amendment protects conduct motivated by religious belief in Chapter 11.

5. Life

In referring to "*life*, liberty, [and] property," do the Due Process Clauses protect a minimum level of personal safety, security, or quality of life? Consider the case that follows.

DeShaney v. Winnebago County Dept. of Social Services
489 U.S. 189 (1989)

CHIEF JUSTICE REHNQUIST delivered the opinion of the Court.

The facts of this case are undeniably tragic. [Notwithstanding indications of child abuse by his father, state officials declined to remove Joshua DeShaney from his father's custody.] In March 1984, [the father] beat 4-year-old Joshua so severely that he fell into a life-threatening coma. Emergency brain surgery revealed a series of hemorrhages caused by traumatic injuries to the head inflicted over a long period of time. Joshua did not die, but he suffered brain damage so severe that he is expected to spend the rest of his life confined to an institution for the profoundly retarded. [His father] was subsequently tried and convicted of child abuse. Joshua and his mother brought this action under 42 U.S.C. § 1983 [against] respondents Winnebago County, DSS, and various individual employees of DSS [alleging] that respondents had deprived Joshua of his liberty without due process of law [by] failing to intervene to protect him against a risk of violence at his father's hands of which they knew or should have known. The District Court granted summary judgment for respondents [and the Court of Appeals affirmed.]

[N]othing in the language of the Due Process Clause itself requires the State to protect the life, liberty, and property of its citizens against invasion by private actors. The Clause is phrased as a limitation on the State's power to act, not as a guarantee of certain minimal levels of safety and security. It forbids the State itself to deprive individuals of life, liberty, or property without "due process of law," but its language cannot fairly be extended to impose an affirmative obligation on the State to ensure that those interests do not come to harm through other means. Nor does history support such an expansive reading of the constitutional text. Like its counterpart in the Fifth Amendment, the Due Process Clause

> **Food for Thought**
>
> The majority notes that history reveals a purpose to limit the State's power to deprive individuals of life, liberty, and property. Today, however, many people rely on government services—including social security, welfare, and health care—to ensure "minimal levels of safety and security." Is increased reliance on the state and changed expectations an argument for reading the Due Process Clause more broadly than in the past? Or is it instead a reason not to expand the protections of the Clause, for fear of effectively making the State the insurer of everyone's well-being?

of the Fourteenth Amendment was intended to prevent government "from abusing [its] power, or employing it as an instrument of oppression." Its purpose was to protect the people from the State, not to ensure that the State protected them from each other. The Framers were content to leave the extent of governmental obligation in the latter area to the democratic political processes. Consistent with these principles, our cases have recognized that the Due Process Clauses generally confer no affirmative right to governmental aid, even where such aid may be necessary to secure life, liberty, or property interests of which the government itself may not deprive the individual. * * * If the Due Process Clause does not require the State to provide its citizens with particular protective services, it follows that the State cannot be held liable under the Clause for injuries that could have been averted had it chosen to provide them. As a general matter, then, we conclude that a State's failure to protect an individual against private violence simply does not constitute a violation of the Due Process Clause.

> **Food for Thought**
>
> If the state is not required to provide a particular service, does it necessarily follow that, once it decides to provide it, the state has no obligation to avoid harms that flow from its provision of the service? Does the greater power always include the lesser power?

Petitioners contend, however, that even if the Due Process Clause imposes no affirmative obligation on the State to provide the general public with adequate protective services, such a duty may arise out of certain "special relationships" created or assumed by the State with respect to particular individuals. Petitioners argue that such a "special relationship" existed here because the State knew that Joshua faced a special danger of abuse at his father's hands, and specifically proclaimed, by word and by deed, its intention to protect him against that danger. Having actually undertaken to protect Joshua from this danger— which petitioners concede the State played no part in creating—the State acquired an affirmative "duty," enforceable through the Due Process Clause, to do so in a reasonably competent fashion. Its failure to discharge that duty, so the argument goes, was an abuse of governmental power that so "shocks the conscience" as to constitute a substantive due process violation.

> **Food for Thought**
>
> How convincing is the Court's distinction here, given that Joshua is a child? Did Joshua actually have more freedom to act on his own behalf in his father's house than he would have in a state institution? Assuming that the Court is correct that ordinarily an affirmative duty to protect under the Due Process Clause arises only when the State limits an individual's freedom, should a different rule apply when the person at issue is a child who the state knows is the victim of abuse?

We reject this argument. It is true that in certain limited circumstances the Constitution imposes upon the State affirmative duties of care and protection with respect to particular individuals. In *Estelle v. Gamble*, 429 U.S. 97 (1976), we recognized that the Eighth Amendment's prohibition against cruel and unusual punishment, made applicable to the States through the Fourteenth Amendment's Due Process Clause, requires the State to provide adequate medical care to incarcerated prisoners. * * * In *Youngberg v. Romeo*, 457 U.S. 307 (1982), we extended this analysis beyond the Eighth Amendment setting holding that the substantive component of the Fourteenth Amendment's Due Process Clause requires the State to provide involuntarily committed mental patients with such services as are necessary to ensure their "reasonable safety" from themselves and others. * * * The rationale for this principle is simple enough: when the State by the affirmative exercise of its power so restrains an individual's liberty that it renders him unable to care for himself, and at the same time fails to provide for his basic human needs—e.g., food, clothing, shelter, medical care, and reasonable safety—it transgresses the substantive limits on state action set by the Eighth Amendment and the Due Process Clause. The affirmative duty to protect arises not from the State's knowledge of the individual's predicament or from its expressions of intent to help him, but from the limitation which it has imposed on his freedom to act on his own behalf. In the substantive due process analysis, it is the State's affirmative act of restraining the individual's freedom to act on his own behalf—through incarceration, institutionalization, or other similar restraint of personal liberty— which is the "deprivation of liberty" triggering the protections of the Due Process

Clause, not its failure to act to protect his liberty interests against harms inflicted by other means.

Petitioners concede that the harms Joshua suffered occurred not while he was in the State's custody, but while he was in the custody of his natural father, who was in no sense a state actor. While the State may have been aware of the dangers that Joshua faced in the free world, it played no part in their creation, nor did it do anything to render him any more vulnerable to them.

Judges and lawyers, like other humans, are moved by natural sympathy in a case like this to find a way for Joshua and his mother to receive adequate compensation for the grievous harm inflicted upon them. But before yielding to that impulse, it is well to remember once again that the harm was inflicted not by the State of Wisconsin, but by Joshua's father. The most that can be said of the state functionaries in this case is that they stood by and did nothing when suspicious circumstances dictated a more active role for them. In defense of them it must also be said that had they moved too soon to take custody of the son away from the father, they would likely have been met with charges of improperly intruding into the parent-child relationship, charges based on the same Due Process Clause that forms the basis for the present charge of failure to provide adequate protection.

The people of Wisconsin may well prefer a system of liability which would place upon the State and its officials the responsibility for failure to act in situations such as the present one. They may create such a system, if they do not have it already, by changing the tort law of the State in accordance with the regular lawmaking process. But they should not have it thrust upon them by this Court's expansion of the Due Process Clause of the Fourteenth Amendment.

JUSTICE BRENNAN, with whom JUSTICE MARSHALL and JUSTICE BLACKMUN join, dissenting.

In a constitutional setting that distinguishes sharply between action and inaction, one's characterization of the misconduct alleged [may] effectively decide the case. Thus, by leading off with a discussion (and rejection) of the idea that the Constitution imposes on the States an affirmative duty to take basic care of their citizens, the Court foreshadows—perhaps even preordains—its conclusion that no duty existed even on the specific facts before us. This initial discussion establishes the baseline from which the Court assesses the DeShaneys' claim * * *. The Court's baseline is the absence of positive rights in the Constitution and a concomitant suspicion of any claim that seems to depend on such rights. From this perspective, the DeShaneys' claim is first and foremost about inaction (the failure, here, of respondents to take steps to protect Joshua), and only tangentially about action (the establishment of a state program specifically designed to help children like Joshua). * * * I would begin from the opposite direction. I would focus first on the action that Wisconsin has taken with respect to Joshua and children like him, rather than on the actions that the State failed to take.

Wisconsin has established a child-welfare system specifically designed to help children like Joshua. Wisconsin law invites—indeed, directs—citizens and other governmental entities to depend on local departments of social services such as respondent to protect children from abuse. The specific facts before us bear out this view of Wisconsin's system of protecting children. Each time someone voiced a suspicion that Joshua was being abused, that information was relayed to the Department for investigation and possible action. Even more telling than these examples is the Department's control over the decision whether to take steps to protect a particular child from suspected abuse. While many different people contributed information and advice to this decision, it was up to the people at DSS to make the ultimate decision whether to disturb the family's current arrangements.

In these circumstances, a private citizen, or even a person working in a government agency other than DSS, would doubtless feel that her job was done as soon as she had reported her suspicions of child abuse to DSS. Through its child-welfare program, in other words, the State of Wisconsin has relieved ordinary citizens and governmental bodies other than the Department of any sense of obligation to do anything more than report their suspicions of child abuse to DSS. If DSS ignores or dismisses these suspicions, no one will step in to fill the gap. Wisconsin's child-protection program thus effectively confined Joshua DeShaney within the walls of Randy DeShaney's violent home until such time as DSS took action to remove him. * * * Through its child-protection program, the State actively intervened in Joshua's life and, by virtue of this intervention, acquired ever more certain knowledge that Joshua was in grave danger. These circumstances, in my view, plant this case solidly within the tradition of cases like *Youngberg* and *Estelle*.

I would allow Joshua and his mother the opportunity to show that respondents' failure to help him arose, not out of the sound exercise of professional judgment that we recognized in *Youngberg* as sufficient to preclude liability, but from the kind of arbitrariness that we have in the past condemned.

JUSTICE BLACKMUN, dissenting.

Like the antebellum judges who denied relief to fugitive slaves, the Court today claims that its decision, however harsh, is compelled by existing legal doctrine. On the contrary, the question presented by this case is an open one, and our Fourteenth Amendment precedents may be read more broadly or narrowly depending upon how one chooses to read them. Faced with the choice, I would adopt a "sympathetic" reading, one which comports with dictates of fundamental justice and recognizes that compassion need not be exiled from the province of judging.

Poor Joshua! Victim of repeated attacks by an irresponsible, bullying, cowardly, and intemperate father, and abandoned by respondents who placed him in a dangerous predicament and who knew or learned what was going on, and yet did essentially nothing except, as the Court revealingly observes, "dutifully recorded these incidents in [their] files." It is a sad commentary upon American life, and constitutional principles, [that] this child, Joshua DeShaney, now is assigned to live out the remainder of his life profoundly retarded. Joshua and his mother, as petitioners here, deserve—but now are denied by this Court—the opportunity to have the facts of their case considered in the light of the constitutional protection that 42 U.S.C. § 1983 is meant to provide.

POINTS FOR DISCUSSION

a.   The Nature of Liberty

What was the Court's theory of the form of liberty protected by the Due Process Clause? Consider Judge Posner's theory, which he offered in *Bowers v. DeVito*, 686 F.2d 616 (7th Cir. 1982). The case involved a tort suit by the administrator of the estate of a woman who was murdered by a man who had previously been committed to a state facility after being found not guilty of murder in a different case by reason of insanity. The plaintiff sued, among others, the state-employed physicians who had approved the release of the man before he committed the murder in question. The court affirmed the district court's grant of summary judgment. Judge Posner explained:

> There is a constitutional right not to be murdered by a state officer, for the state violates the Fourteenth Amendment when its officer, acting under color of state law, deprives a person of life without due process of law. But there is no constitutional right to be protected by the state against being murdered by criminals or madmen. * * * The Constitution is a charter of negative liberties; it tells the state to let people alone; it does not require the federal government or the state to provide services, even so elementary a service as maintaining law and order.

Judge Posner acknowledged that "the line between action and inaction" is not always clear. But he declared that "the defendants in this case did not place Miss Bowers in a place or position of danger; they simply failed adequately to protect her, as a member of the public, from a dangerous man." Do you agree that the Constitution is a "charter of negative liberties"? Why was Judge Posner so certain that it is? Did the Court in *DeShaney* share this view?

b.   A Slippery Slope?

Justice Blackmun asserted in dissent that the question presented was an open one. Assuming for a moment that the Due Process Clause could plausibly have been read either to permit or to preclude the petitioners' claims, which view of the Clause's protection makes more sense? What would have been the impact of Justice Brennan's and Blackmun's view on federal, state, and local governments? Would it have opened the door to suits against policemen, judges, and many other officials alleging that they provided inadequate protection for life and liberty? If so, such suits could be very costly for public servants and might affect their judgment while on the job, not to mention their willingness to take the job in the first place. Are these considerations relevant when the Court interprets the Constitution? Do you think that the Court implicitly considered them in *DeShaney*?

c.   Judicial Oversight of the Provision of Government Services

Justice Brennan asserted that the petitioners should have had an opportunity to demonstrate that Joshua's injuries were the result not of professional judgment, but of arbitrary action by the government agency. Are the courts competent to draw such distinctions? What if, in its discretion, DSS had chosen not to give Joshua's case high priority because the agency had limited resources and was busy dealing with several even more pressing cases of child abuse? And if the constitutional defect is that the state failed to protect Joshua after affirmatively assuming an obligation to do so, why does it matter whether the failure to protect was because of what turned out ultimately to be a faulty prediction or instead was because of neglect or arbitrariness?

Yet is the Court's approach preferable? The Court asserted that the remedy for someone like Joshua lies with the democratic process—presumably, to change the law to require action from the state, or to permit suits for damages when it fails to provide adequate protection. Even if this approach might prevent some abuse, is this a satisfying resolution for the DeShaneys?

d.   Equal Protection

In a footnote in its opinion, the Court stated, "The State may not, of course, selectively deny its protective services to certain disfavored minorities without violating the Equal Protection Clause." Under this view, if the state had failed to protect Joshua because of, say, his race, he would have had a valid claim under the

Equal Protection Clause. Yet even in such a case, it would still be the state's "inaction" that gave rise to the claim. Is this view consistent with the Court's insistence that the government has no affirmative obligation to act to protect its citizens? Or would the unconstitutional decision represent a form of "action" after all?

e. Substantive Due Process or Procedural Due Process?

The Court in *DeShaney* held that the substantive component of the Due Process Clause does not require the state to protect the well being of its citizens against the acts of other private citizens. In a portion of the opinion omitted here, the Court "decline[d] to consider" whether the state's child-protection statutes gave Joshua an "entitlement" to receive protective services of which he could not be deprived without adequate procedural protections. As we will see in Chapter 3, the Due Process Clause (not surprisingly) has a procedural component, which generally requires the state to give notice and some kind of hearing when it seeks to deprive a person of a "protected" liberty or property interest.

In *Town of Castle Rock v. Gonzales*, 545 U.S. 748 (2005), the Court confronted a claim that the town had violated the Due Process Clause when its police officers did not respond to the plaintiff's repeated reports over several hours that her estranged husband was violating the

> **Make the Connection**
>
> We will consider the definition of "liberty" and "property" for purposes of the procedural due process doctrine in Chapter 3.

terms of a restraining order by kidnapping their children, whom he subsequently murdered. The respondent argued that the failure to respond had deprived her of a property interest because she had a legitimate expectation, based on the terms of the restraining order, that the police would respond to her calls. The Court rejected her claim, reasoning that because a "benefit is not a protected property or liberty entitlement if government officials may grant it or deny it in their discretion," respondent did not enjoy a protected property interest in favorable police action.

6. Death

The Court in *Casey* and *Lawrence* stated that "[a]t the heart of liberty is the right to define one's own concept of existence, of meaning, of the universe, and of the mystery of human life." Does this definition of liberty embrace a right to define the circumstances under which a person may end his or her life?

CRUZAN V. DIRECTOR, MISSOURI DEP'T OF HEALTH
497 U.S. 261 (1990)

CHIEF JUSTICE REHNQUIST delivered the opinion of the Court.

Petitioner Nancy Beth Cruzan was rendered incompetent as a result of severe injuries sustained during an automobile accident. Lester and Joyce Cruzan, Nancy's parents and co-guardians, sought a court order directing the withdrawal of their daughter's artificial feeding and hydration equipment after it became apparent that she had virtually no chance of recovering her cognitive faculties. The Supreme Court of Missouri held that because there was no clear and convincing evidence of Nancy's desire to have life-sustaining treatment withdrawn under such circumstances, her parents lacked authority to effectuate such a request. We [affirm].

[T]he common-law doctrine of informed consent is viewed as generally encompassing the right of a competent individual to refuse medical treatment. This is the first case in which we have been squarely presented with the issue whether the United States Constitution grants what is in common parlance referred to as a "right to die." * * * The principle that a competent person has a constitutionally protected liberty interest in refusing unwanted medical treatment may be inferred from our prior decisions. In *Jacobson v. Massachusetts*, 197 U.S. 11, 24–30 (1905), for instance, the Court balanced an individual's liberty interest in declining an unwanted smallpox vaccine against the State's interest in preventing disease. * * * Just this Term, in the course of holding that a State's procedures for administering antipsychotic medication to prisoners were sufficient to satisfy due process concerns, we recognized that prisoners possess "a significant liberty interest in avoiding the unwanted administration of antipsychotic drugs under the Due Process Clause of the Fourteenth Amendment." *Washington v. Harper*, 494 U.S. 210, 221–222 (1990). * * * Petitioners insist that under the general holdings of our cases, the forced administration of life-sustaining medical treatment, and even of artificially delivered food and water essential to life, would implicate a competent person's liberty interest. Although we think the logic of the cases discussed above would embrace such a liberty interest, the dramatic consequences involved in refusal of such treatment would inform the inquiry as to whether the deprivation of that interest is constitutionally permissible. But for purposes of this case, we assume that the United States Constitution would grant a competent person a constitutionally protected right to refuse lifesaving hydration and nutrition.

Missouri has in effect recognized that under certain circumstances a surrogate may act for the patient in electing to have hydration and nutrition withdrawn in such a way as to cause death, but it has established a procedural safeguard to assure that the action of the surrogate conforms as best it may to the wishes expressed by the patient while competent. Missouri requires that evidence of the incompetent's wishes as to the withdrawal of treatment be proved by clear and convincing evidence. The question, then, is whether the United States Constitution forbids the establishment of this procedural requirement by the State. We hold that it does not.

Whether or not Missouri's clear and convincing evidence requirement comports with the United States Constitution depends in part on what interests the State may properly seek to protect in this situation. Missouri relies on its interest in the protection and preservation of human life, and there can be no gainsaying this interest. As a general matter, the States—indeed, all civilized nations—demonstrate their commitment to life by treating homicide as a serious crime. Moreover, the majority of States in this country have laws imposing criminal penalties on one who assists another to commit suicide. We do not think a State is required to remain neutral in the face of an informed and voluntary decision by a physically able adult to starve to death.

> **Take Note**
>
> Missouri law did not prohibit a person who is dependent upon life support from withdrawing that support, or even from indicating in advance—for example, in a "living will"—her desire to do so should she become dependent upon life support. It only required clear proof of a person's wishes to withdraw life support. Can a state prohibit a person who *has* clearly expressed her intent—either contemporaneously or in a living will—not to be maintained by life support from withdrawing such support?

But in the context presented here, a State has more particular interests at stake. The choice between life and death is a deeply personal decision of obvious

> **Make the Connection**
>
> Is the Court's analysis of the parents' interests consistent with the Court's decisions, discussed earlier in this chapter, about the Constitution's protections for family relationships? Does the protection afforded to choices by parents about child rearing vary depending upon the age of the child? Regardless, is there a difference for these purposes between a decision about how to raise a child and the decision at issue here?

and overwhelming finality. We believe Missouri may legitimately seek to safeguard the personal element of this choice through the imposition of heightened evidentiary requirements. It cannot be disputed that the Due Process Clause protects an interest in life as well as an interest in refusing life-sustaining medical treatment. Not all incompetent patients will have loved ones available to serve as surrogate decisionmakers. And even where family members are present, "[t]here will, of course, be some unfortunate situations in which family members will not act to protect a patient." A State is entitled to guard against potential abuses in such situations.

In our view, Missouri has permissibly sought to advance these interests through the adoption of a "clear and convincing" standard of proof to govern such proceedings. * * * The more stringent the burden of proof a party must bear, the more that party bears the risk of an erroneous decision. We believe that Missouri may permissibly place an increased risk of an erroneous decision on those seeking to terminate an incompetent individual's life-sustaining treatment.

The Supreme Court of Missouri held that in this case the testimony adduced at trial did not amount to clear and convincing proof of the patient's desire to have hydration and nutrition withdrawn. In so doing, it reversed a decision of the Missouri trial court which had found that the evidence "suggest [ed]" Nancy Cruzan would not have desired to continue such measures. * * * The testimony adduced at trial consisted primarily of Nancy Cruzan's statements made to a housemate about a year before her accident that she would not want to live should she face life as a "vegetable," and other observations to the same effect. The observations did not deal in terms with withdrawal of medical treatment or of hydration and nutrition. We cannot say that the Supreme Court of Missouri committed constitutional error in reaching the conclusion that it did.

Petitioners alternatively contend that Missouri must accept the "substituted judgment" of close family members even in the absence of substantial proof that their views reflect the views of the patient. * * * No doubt is engendered by anything in this record but that Nancy Cruzan's mother and father are loving and caring parents. [But] we do not think the Due Process Clause requires the State to repose judgment on these matters with anyone but the patient herself. [T]here is no automatic assurance that the view of close family members will necessarily be the same as the patient's would have been had she been confronted with the prospect of her situation while competent.

JUSTICE O'CONNOR, concurring.

> **Take Note**
> Is Justice O'Connor's point here that if a national consensus emerges from the "laboratory," it will become a rule of constitutional dimension? If so, is that a sensible approach to this issue?

Today's decision, holding only that the Constitution permits a State to require clear and convincing evidence of Nancy Cruzan's desire to have artificial hydration and nutrition withdrawn, does not preclude a future determination that the Constitution requires the States to implement the decisions of a patient's duly appointed surrogate. Nor does it prevent States from developing other approaches for protecting an incompetent individual's liberty interest in refusing medical treatment. [N]o national consensus has yet emerged on the best solution for this difficult and sensitive problem. Today we decide only that one State's practice does not violate the Constitution; the more challenging task of crafting appropriate procedures for safeguarding incompetents' liberty interests is entrusted to the "laboratory" of the States, in the first instance.

JUSTICE SCALIA, concurring.

The various opinions in this case portray quite clearly the difficult, indeed agonizing, questions that are presented by the constantly increasing power of science to keep the human body alive for longer than any reasonable person would want to inhabit it. The States have begun to grapple with these problems through legislation.

I would have preferred that we announce, clearly and promptly, that the federal courts have no business in this field; that American law has always accorded the State the power to prevent, by force if necessary, suicide—including suicide by refusing to take appropriate measures necessary to preserve one's life; that the point at which life becomes "worthless," and the point at which the means necessary to preserve it become "extraordinary" or "inappropriate," are neither set forth in the Constitution nor known to the nine Justices of this Court any better than they are known to nine people picked at random from the Kansas City telephone directory; and hence, that even when it is demonstrated by clear and convincing evidence that a patient no longer wishes certain measures to be taken to preserve his or her life, it is up to the citizens of Missouri to decide, through their elected representatives, whether that wish will be honored. * * * To determine that [a deprivation of liberty without due process of law] would not occur if Nancy Cruzan were forced to take nourishment against her will, it is unnecessary to reopen the historically recurrent debate over whether "due process" includes substantive restrictions. It is at least true that no "substantive due process" claim can be maintained unless the claimant demonstrates that the State has deprived him of a right historically and traditionally protected against state interference. *Michael H. v. Gerald D.*, 491 U.S. 110, 122 (1989); *Bowers v. Hardwick*, 478 U.S. 186, 192 (1986). That cannot possibly be established here. At common law in England, a suicide [was] criminally liable. * * * Case law at the time of the adoption of the Fourteenth Amendment generally held that assisting suicide was a criminal offense.

It seems to me [that] Justice BRENNAN's position ultimately rests upon the proposition that it is none of the State's business if a person wants to commit suicide. Justice STEVENS is explicit on the point * * *. This is a view that some societies have held, and that our States are free to adopt if they wish. But it is not a view imposed by our constitutional traditions, in which the power of the State to prohibit suicide is unquestionable.

Are there, then, no reasonable and humane limits that ought not to be exceeded in requiring an individual to preserve his own life? There obviously are, but they are not set forth in the Due Process Clause. What assures us that those limits will not be exceeded is the same constitutional guarantee that is the source of most of our protection—what protects us, for example, from being assessed a tax of 100% of our income above the subsistence level, from being forbidden to drive cars, or from being required to send our children to school for 10 hours a day, none of which horribles are categorically prohibited by the Constitution. Our salvation is the Equal Protection Clause, which requires the democratic majority to accept for themselves and their loved ones what they impose on you and me. This Court need not, and has no authority to, inject itself into every field of human activity where irrationality and oppression may theoretically occur, and if it tries to do so it will destroy itself.

Make the Connection

In citing the Equal Protection Clause, is Justice Scalia suggesting that the infirm or terminally ill—or perhaps the elderly, who are more likely to become infirm or terminally ill—do not need protection from majoritarian politics because we all recognize the possibility that we might one day be old or ill? Keep this view in mind when we consider, in Chapter 5, the groups accorded special protection under the Equal Protection Clause. As we will see in that chapter, the Court has held that the Equal Protection Clause does not afford any special protection from legislation that classifies on the basis of age.

JUSTICE BRENNAN, with whom JUSTICE MARSHALL and JUSTICE BLACKMUN join, dissenting.

The right to be free from medical attention without consent, to determine what shall be done with one's own body, is deeply rooted in this Nation's traditions, as the majority acknowledges. This right has long been "firmly entrenched in American tort law" and is securely grounded in the earliest common law. Anglo-American law starts with the premise of thorough-going self determination. It follows that each man is considered to be master of his own body, and he may, if he be of sound mind, expressly prohibit the performance of lifesaving surgery, or other medical treatment. * * * Thus, freedom from unwanted medical attention is unquestionably among those principles "so rooted in the traditions and conscience of our people as to be ranked as fundamental." *Snyder v. Massachusetts*, 291 U.S. 97, 105 (1934).

The only state interest asserted here is a general interest in the preservation of life. But the State has no legitimate general interest in someone's life, completely abstracted from the interest of the person living that life, that could outweigh the person's choice to avoid medical treatment. * * * [T]he State's general interest in life must accede to Nancy Cruzan's particularized and intense interest in self-determination in her choice of medical treatment.

This is not to say that the State has no legitimate interests to assert here. As the majority recognizes, Missouri has [an] interest in providing Nancy Cruzan, now incompetent, with as accurate as possible a determination of how she would exercise her rights under these circumstances. [But] until Nancy's wishes have been determined, the

> **Food for Thought**
>
> Does Chief Justice Rehnquist disagree with Justice Brennan that there is a fundamental right to reject medical care, or does he differ only in his view of the weight that should be accorded to the state's interests in limiting this right?

only state interest that may be asserted is an interest in safe-guarding the accuracy of that determination. * * * Missouri may constitutionally impose only those procedural requirements that serve to enhance the accuracy of a determination of Nancy Cruzan's wishes or are at least consistent with an accurate determination. The Missouri "safeguard" that the Court upholds today does not meet that standard. The determination needed in this context is whether the incompetent person would choose to live in a persistent vegetative state on life support or to avoid this medical treatment. Missouri's rule of decision imposes a markedly asymmetrical evidentiary burden. Only evidence of specific statements of treatment choice made by the patient when competent is admissible to support a finding that the patient, now in a persistent vegetative state, would wish to avoid further medical treatment. Moreover, this evidence must be clear and convincing. No proof is required to support a finding that the incompetent person would wish to continue treatment. * * * Too few people execute living wills or equivalently formal directives for such an evidentiary rule to ensure adequately that the wishes of incompetent persons will be honored. While it might be a wise social policy to encourage people to furnish such instructions, no general conclusion about a patient's choice can be drawn from the absence of formalities.

JUSTICE STEVENS, dissenting.

Choices about death touch the core of liberty. * * * Our ethical tradition has long regarded an appreciation of mortality as essential to understanding life's significance. It may, in fact, be impossible to live for anything without being prepared to die for something.

Missouri asserts that its policy is related to a state interest in the protection of life. In my view, however, it is an effort to define life, rather than to protect it, that is the heart of Missouri's policy. Missouri insists, without regard to Nancy Cruzan's own interests, upon equating her life with the biological persistence of her bodily functions. * * * But for patients like Nancy Cruzan, who have no consciousness and no chance of recovery, there is a serious question as to whether the mere persistence of their bodies is "life" as that word is commonly understood, or as it is used in both the Constitution and the Declaration of Independence. The State's unflagging determination to perpetuate Nancy Cruzan's physical existence is comprehensible only as an effort to define life's meaning, not as an attempt to preserve its sanctity.

In my view, [the] best interests of the individual, especially when buttressed by the interests of all related third parties, must prevail over any general state policy that simply ignores those interests. Indeed, the only apparent secular basis for the State's interest in life is the policy's persuasive impact upon people other than Nancy and her family. * * * However commendable may be the State's interest in human life, it cannot pursue that interest by appropriating Nancy Cruzan's life as a symbol for its own purposes.

POINTS FOR DISCUSSION

a. The Right to Die

What exactly is embraced by the "right to die"? Consider these possibilities: (1) The right to refuse medical treatment; (2) The right to refuse life support; (3) The right to withdraw life support once connected; (4) The right of a person who is terminally ill but who does not require life support to the assistance of a physician in ending his or her life; (5) The right of a terminally ill person who is not on life support to commit suicide; (6) The right of a healthy person to physician assistance in committing suicide; (7) The right of a healthy person to commit suicide.

Did the Court in *Cruzan* find that any of these actions is constitutionally protected? Is it possible that some are protected and that others are not? If so, is it because the state has a greater interest in regulating some than in regulating others, or instead because there simply is no liberty interest at all in some of these actions?

b. Competing Evidence and Competing Claims of Familial Rights

Nancy Cruzan's parents argued that their daughter wished to refuse medical treatment, and no one apparently contested this view. But what if her parents' evidence had been contradicted by evidence presented by her husband, who argued that she in fact wished to continue medical treatment and be kept alive? Are there any constitutional limits on the way that the state may referee these competing claims?

What if the patient had left a living will expressing her wishes that she not be maintained on life support, but her husband nevertheless wanted her to remain on life support? Are there any circumstances under which the wishes of a family member can trump the wishes of a terminally ill person?

c. Defining Life

Recall that the Court grappled in *Roe* with the general question of how to define life, and with the specific question of when life begins. In his dissent in *Cruzan*, Justice Stevens asserted that the state effectively (and impermissibly) sought to define life in erecting an obstacle to the termination of life support for a patient with "no consciousness and no chance of recovery." How (if at all) does Justice Stevens define "life"? Is his point that each individual gets to define his or her own life, and therefore the circumstances under which it should end? If so, is Justice Stevens in effect asserting (as Justice Scalia suggested that he was) that there is a constitutional right to commit suicide?

d. Meaning of the Opinion

A key sentence in the Court's opinion is: "[For] the purposes of this case, we assume that the United States Constitution would grant a competent person a constitutionally protected right to refuse lifesaving hydration and nutrition." The meaning of this sentence was disputed when the opinion came out, and remains so today.

One possibility is that the Court meant: "We *hold* that a competent person has the right to refuse lifesaving measures." Many commentators initially read the Court's decision in this way. See, e.g., Linda Greenhouse, *Justices Find a Right to Die, but the Majority See Need for Clear Proof of Intent*, N.Y. Times, Jun. 26, 1990, at A1 ("Eight members of the Supreme Court, venturing for the first time into the sensitive 'right to die' issue, said in a ruling today that a person whose wishes are clearly known has a constitutional right to the discontinuance of life-sustaining treatment."). Under this interpretation, the Court decided both the substantive due process question of whether a right exists and the procedural due process question of whether the state could require clear and convincing evidence of an intent to exercise this right.

But another possibility is that the Court meant: "We *merely assume, without deciding*, that there is a constitutionally protected right to refuse lifesaving measures." See, e.g., John E. Nowak & Ronald Rotunda, *Constitutional Law* 920 (6th ed. 2000) ("The majority opinion * * * assumed for the purposes of the case (but did not decide) that the 'liberty' protected by the due process clauses * * * included a right of mentally competent individuals to refuse live saving or life sustaining medical treatment. Even assuming that such a right existed, the majority found that the state could limit the ability to refuse such treatment * * *."). Under this interpretation, the Court did not decide the substantive due process question, but concluded that no procedural due process violation occurred even if the substantive right did exist.

In reading the opinion, which meaning appears more likely? Did the Court give reasons for its conclusion that the Constitution protects a right to refuse lifesaving measures? Could the Court decide whether the procedural requirement for invoking the right was constitutional on the assumption that the right exists without actually determining whether the right exists? Which approach would have been more likely to gather eight votes? The Supreme Court has never clarified this ambiguity, as a careful reading of the following case will show.

WASHINGTON V. GLUCKSBERG
521 U.S. 702 (1997)

CHIEF JUSTICE REHNQUIST delivered the opinion of the Court.

The question presented in this case is whether Washington's prohibition against "caus[ing]" or "aid[ing]" a suicide offends the Fourteenth Amendment to the United States Constitution. We hold that it does not.

[W]e "ha[ve] always been reluctant to expand the concept of substantive due process because guideposts for responsible decisionmaking in this unchartered area are scarce and open-ended." *Collins v. Harker Heights,* 503 U.S. 115, 125 (1992). By extending constitutional protection to an asserted right or liberty interest, we, to a great extent, place the matter outside the arena of public debate and legislative action. We must therefore "exercise the utmost care whenever we are asked to break new ground in this field," lest the liberty protected by the Due Process Clause be subtly transformed into the policy preferences of the Members of this Court.

> **Food for Thought**
>
> Another provision of the statute challenged in this case addressed the circumstances that were at issue in *Cruzan*, by specifically providing that "withholding or withdrawal of life-sustaining treatment" at a patient's direction does not constitute suicide. Is this a clear or defensible line to draw? Is it constitutionally problematic to permit patients who are on life support to "pull the plug," but prohibit patients who are terminally ill but not on life support from ending their lives? If so, why?

Our established method of substantive-due-process analysis has two primary features: First, we have regularly observed that the Due Process Clause specially protects those fundamental rights and liberties which are, objectively, "deeply rooted in this Nation's history and tradition," and "implicit in the concept of ordered liberty," such that "neither liberty nor justice would exist if they were sacrificed," *Palko v.*

Connecticut, 302 U.S. 319, 325, 326 (1937). Second, we have required in substantive-due-process cases a "careful description" of the asserted fundamental liberty interest. Our Nation's history, legal traditions, and practices thus provide the crucial "guideposts for responsible decisionmaking" that direct and restrain our exposition of the Due Process Clause. * * * This approach tends to rein in the subjective elements that are necessarily present in due-process judicial review. In addition, by establishing a threshold requirement—that a challenged state action implicate a fundamental right—before requiring more than a reasonable relation to a legitimate state interest to justify the action, it avoids the need for complex balancing of competing interests in every case.

Turning to the claim at issue here, the [respondents, doctors and terminally ill patients to whom they provide care,] assert a "liberty to choose how to die" and a right to "control of one's final days," and describe the asserted liberty as "the right to choose a humane, dignified death" and "the liberty to shape death." * * * The Washington statute at issue in this case prohibits "aid[ing] another person to attempt suicide," and, thus, the question before us is whether the "liberty" specially protected by the Due Process Clause includes a right to commit suicide which itself includes a right to assistance in doing so.

[We] are confronted with a consistent and almost universal tradition that has long rejected the asserted right, and continues explicitly to reject it today, even for terminally ill, mentally competent adults. To hold for respondents, we would have to reverse centuries of legal doctrine and practice, and strike down the considered policy choice of almost every State. Respondents contend, however, that the liberty interest they assert is consistent with this Court's substantive-due-process line of cases, if not with this Nation's history and practice. Pointing to *Casey* and *Cruzan*, respondents read our jurisprudence in this area as reflecting a general tradition of "self-sovereignty," and as teaching that the "liberty" protected by the Due Process Clause includes "basic and intimate exercises of personal autonomy." * * * The right assumed in *Cruzan*, however, was not simply deduced from abstract concepts of personal autonomy. Given the common-law rule that forced medication was a battery, and the long legal tradition protecting the decision to refuse unwanted medical treatment, our assumption was entirely consistent with this Nation's history and constitutional traditions. The decision to commit suicide with the assistance of another may be just as personal and profound as the decision to refuse unwanted medical treatment, but it has never enjoyed similar legal protection. Indeed, the two acts are widely and reasonably regarded as quite distinct.

[Respondents also rely on *Casey*.] The Court's opinion in *Casey* described, in a general way and in light of our prior cases, those personal activities and decisions that this Court has identified as so deeply rooted in our history and traditions, or so fundamental to our concept of constitutionally ordered liberty, that they are protected by the Fourteenth Amendment. * * * That many of the rights and liberties protected by the Due Process Clause sound in personal autonomy does not warrant the sweeping conclusion that any and all important, intimate, and personal decisions are so protected, and *Casey* did not suggest otherwise.

The history of the law's treatment of assisted suicide in this country has been and continues to be one of the rejection of nearly all efforts to permit it. That being the case, our decisions lead us to conclude that the asserted "right" to assistance in committing suicide is not a fundamental liberty interest protected by the Due Process Clause. The Constitution also requires, however, that Washington's assisted-suicide ban be rationally related to legitimate government interests. This requirement is unquestionably met here. * * * Washington has an "unqualified interest in the preservation of human life." The State's prohibition on assisted suicide, like all homicide laws, both reflects and advances its commitment to this interest. * * * Relatedly, all admit that suicide is a serious public-health problem, especially among persons in otherwise vulnerable groups. The State has an interest in preventing suicide, and in studying, identifying, and treating its causes.

The State also has an interest in protecting the integrity and ethics of the medical profession. [The] American Medical Association, like many other medical and physicians' groups, has concluded that "[p]hysician-assisted suicide is fundamentally incompatible with the physician's role as healer." And physician-assisted suicide could, it is argued, undermine the trust that is essential to the doctor-patient relationship by blurring the time-honored line between healing and harming. Next, the State has an interest in protecting vulnerable groups—including the poor, the elderly, and disabled persons—from abuse, neglect, and mistakes. * * * The State's assisted-suicide ban reflects and reinforces its policy that the lives of terminally ill, disabled, and elderly people must be no less valued than the lives of the young and healthy, and that a seriously disabled person's suicidal impulses should be interpreted and treated the same way as anyone else's. Finally, the State may fear that permitting assisted suicide will start it down the path to voluntary and perhaps even involuntary euthanasia.

We need not weigh exactly the relative strengths of these various interests. They are unquestionably important and legitimate, and Washington's ban on assisted suicide is at least reasonably related to their promotion and protection.

We therefore hold that [Washington's prohibition on assisted suicide] does not violate the Fourteenth Amendment, either on its face or "as applied to competent, terminally ill adults who wish to hasten their deaths by obtaining medication prescribed by their doctors." * * * Throughout the Nation, Americans are engaged in an earnest and profound debate about the morality, legality, and practicality of physician-assisted suicide. Our holding permits this debate to continue, as it should in a democratic society.

JUSTICE SOUTER, concurring in the judgment.

I conclude that the statute's application to the doctors has not been shown to be unconstitutional, but I write separately to give my reasons for analyzing the substantive due process claims as I do. * * * My understanding of unenumerated rights [avoids] the absolutist failing of many older cases without embracing the opposite pole of equating reasonableness with past practice described at a very specific level. That understanding begins with a concept of "ordered liberty," comprising a continuum of rights to be free from "arbitrary impositions and purposeless restraints." [Justice Souter then quoted from Justice Harlan's dissent, excerpted earlier in this chapter, in *Poe v. Ullman*, 367 U.S. 497 (1961).] This approach calls for a court to assess the relative "weights" or dignities of the contending interests, and to this extent the judicial method is familiar to the common law.

> **Definition**
>
> "Common law" is the "body of law derived from judicial decisions, rather than from statutes or constitutions." *Black's Law Dictionary* (10th ed. 2014). Much of the law of contracts, torts, and property is common law.

Common-law method is subject, however, to two important constraints in the hands of a court engaged in substantive due process review. First, such a court is bound to confine the values that it recognizes to those truly deserving constitutional stature, either to those expressed in constitutional text, or those exemplified by "the traditions from which [the Nation] developed" or revealed by contrast with "the traditions from which it broke."

The second constraint, again, simply reflects the fact that constitutional review, not judicial lawmaking, is a court's business here. * * * It is no justification for judicial intervention merely to identify a reasonable resolution of contending values that differs from the terms of the legislation under review. It is only when the legislation's justifying principle, critically valued, is so far from being

> **Food for Thought**
>
> Justice Souter's approach clearly embraces the idea that constitutional protections can evolve to embrace new rights. How different is this approach from Chief Justice Rehnquist's approach? Does Chief Justice Rehnquist's opinion leave any room for a "living tradition" that would establish new fundamental rights over time?

commensurate with the individual interest as to be arbitrarily or pointlessly applied that the statute must give way.

Just as results in substantive due process cases are tied to the selections of statements of the competing interests, the acceptability of the results is a function of the good reasons for the selections made. It is here that the value of common-law method becomes apparent, for the usual thinking of the common law is suspicious of the all-or-nothing analysis that tends to produce legal petrification instead of an evolving boundary between the domains of old principles. Common-law method tends to pay respect instead to detail, seeking to understand old principles afresh by new examples and new counterexamples.

In my judgment, the importance of the individual interest here, as within that class of "certain interests" demanding careful scrutiny of the State's contrary claim, cannot be gainsaid. Whether that interest might in some circumstances, or at some time, be seen as "fundamental" to the degree entitled to prevail is not, however, a conclusion that I need draw here, for I am satisfied that the State's interests [are] sufficiently serious to defeat the present claim that its law is arbitrary or purposeless. [It] is enough to say that our examination of legislative reasonableness should consider the fact that the Legislature of the State of Washington is no more obviously at fault than this Court is in being uncertain about what would happen if respondents prevailed today. We therefore have a clear question about which institution, a legislature or a court, is relatively more competent to deal with an emerging issue as to which facts currently unknown could be dispositive. The answer has to be [that] the legislative process is to be preferred.

JUSTICE O'CONNOR, concurring.

I join the Court's opinions because I agree that there is no generalized right to "commit suicide." But respondents urge us to address the narrower question whether a mentally competent person who is experiencing great suffering has a constitutionally cognizable interest in controlling the circumstances of his or her imminent death. I see no need to reach that question in the context of the facial challenges to the [Washington] laws at issue here. The parties and amici agree that [a] patient who is suffering from a terminal illness and who is experiencing great pain has no legal barriers to obtaining medication, from qualified physicians, to alleviate that suffering, even to the point of causing unconsciousness and hastening death. In this light, even assuming that we would recognize such an interest, I agree that the State's interests in protecting those who are not truly competent or facing imminent death, or those whose decisions to hasten death would not truly be voluntary, are sufficiently weighty to justify a prohibition against physician-assisted suicide.

JUSTICE STEVENS, concurring in the [judgment].

Today, the Court decides that Washington's statute prohibiting assisted suicide is not invalid "on its face," that is to say, in all or most cases in which it might be applied. That holding, however, does not foreclose the possibility that some applications of the statute might well be invalid. * * * A State, like Washington, that has authorized the death penalty, and thereby has concluded that the sanctity of human life does not require that it always be preserved, must acknowledge that there are situations in which an interest in hastening death is legitimate. Indeed, not only is that interest sometimes legitimate, I am also convinced that there are times when it is entitled to constitutional protection. * * * In my judgment, [it] is clear that the so-called "unqualified interest in the preservation of human life," *Cruzan*, 497 U.S., at 282, is not itself sufficient to outweigh the interest in liberty that may justify the only possible means of preserving a dying patient's dignity and alleviating her intolerable suffering.

JUSTICE BREYER, concurring in the [judgment].

I do not agree [with] the Court's formulation of [respondents'] claimed "liberty" interest [as] a "right to commit suicide with another's assistance." [I] would not reject the respondents' claim without considering a different formulation, for which our legal tradition may provide greater support. That formulation would use words roughly like a "right to die with dignity." But irrespective of the exact words used, at its core would lie personal control over the manner of death, professional medical assistance, and the avoidance of unnecessary and severe physical suffering * * *. I do not believe, however, that this Court need or now should decide whether or a not such a right is "fundamental." That is because, in my view, the avoidance of severe physical pain (connected with death) would have to constitute an essential part of any successful claim and because, as Justice O'CONNOR points out, the laws before us do not force a dying person to undergo that kind of pain.

POINTS FOR DISCUSSION

a.   Physician-Assisted Suicide and Federalism

As the Court predicted, the decision in this case allowed the debate over physician-assisted suicide to continue in the States. To date, only Oregon has adopted a law that allows this practice. In 2006, the United States Attorney General announced that physicians assisting patients to commit suicide pursuant to Oregon's Death with Dignity Act faced the loss of their federal licenses to prescribe drugs under the Controlled Substances Act. After doctors filed suit to enjoin the Attorney General from taking action, the Court rejected the Attorney General's view of the Controlled Substances Act while avoiding any implication that there is a "right" to physician-assisted suicide. *Gonzales v. Oregon*, 546 U.S. 243 (2006). Was the Attorney General's approach consistent with the Court's call for state experimentation on the question of the propriety of physician-assisted suicide? If not, is there some other justification for federal intervention?

b.   Competing Approaches

Although Chief Justice Rehnquist and Justice Souter agreed on the outcome in the case, they disagreed on the reasoning. Justice Souter employed a "common-law" approach that he believed to be superior because of its focus on the relative importance of the contending interests—governmental and individual—at stake. By contrast, Chief Justice Rehnquist believed that his approach—which defines the liberty interest narrowly and focuses on tradition—was superior *precisely because* it "avoids the need for complex balancing of interests in every case."

What are the advantages and disadvantages of Justice Souter's more ad hoc, flexible approach? What are the advantages and disadvantages of Chief Justice Rehnquist's approach? Looking back at the substantive due process cases that we have considered in this chapter, has one approach typically prevailed over the other? If so, why do you think that is?

c.   Reconciling *Glucksberg* with *Lawrence*

The Court in *Glucksberg* stated that a right falls within the substantive reach of the Due Process Clause only if, after it has been "carefully described," it is "deeply rooted in the Nation's history and tradition." Is this approach consistent with the approach of the Court only six years later in *Lawrence v. Texas*, which we considered earlier in this chapter? For an argument that it is not, see Yale Kamisar, *Foreword: Can* Glucksberg *Survive* Lawrence? *Another Look at the End of Life and Personal Autonomy*, 106 Mich. L. Rev. 1453 (2008).

d.   Facial v. As-Applied Challenges

The Court treated respondents' claim as a facial challenge to the Washington statute. Justices O'Connor, Stevens, and Breyer indicated that they might be open to a properly argued as-applied challenge. Does that mean that, in their view, the right to assistance in committing suicide *is* a fundamental liberty interest under the Due Process Clause? Can you articulate what sort of as-applied challenge these Justices might have found convincing? Are there individual interests that might trump a state's ban on assisted suicide in some circumstances? What are they?

e.   "Death with Dignity"

Justices Breyer, O'Connor, and Stevens all suggested that terminally ill people in severe pain might have a constitutional right to choose the manner of their death— to "die with dignity." But there is no suggestion in their opinions that people who are not terminally ill—including people in physical pain or those suffering from emotional and mental afflictions—enjoy a similar right. What justifies such a distinction? Are there historical justifications for this view, perhaps in the Nation's common-law traditions? Or are the Justices effectively applying the balancing test advocated by Justice Souter and weighing the interests of the patients against the interests of the State?

Executive Summary of This Chapter

Under the doctrine of **substantive due process**, the Court has held that the Due Process Clauses protect forms of liberty that the government cannot impair even after providing procedural protections. Although the Court held in the late nineteenth and early-twentieth centuries that the Due Process Clauses protect a **freedom to contract**, *Lochner v. New York* (1905); *Adkins v. Children's Hospital* (1923), the Court has since held that government regulation of social and economic matters is generally subject only to review for rationality, *West Coast Hotel Co. v. Parrish* (1936); *Williamson v. Lee Optical Co.* (1955).

Although the Court has abandoned the cases holding that economic liberty is entitled to heightened protection under the Due Process Clauses, the Court has held that the Clauses do protect **fundamental rights** regardless of the level of procedure that accompanies governmental efforts to impair them.

The Supreme Court has held that the Due Process Clauses protect various personal decisions concerning **intimate relationships, sex,** and **reproduction**. In particular, the government cannot prohibit the **use of contraceptives** by married couples, *Griswold v. Connecticut* (1965), or by unmarried couples, *Eisenstadt v. Baird* (1972). The government also cannot make it a crime to engage in **private, consensual sexual conduct,** including homosexual sex. *Lawrence v. Texas* (2003).

The Due Process Clauses also protect a woman's right to choose to have an **abortion,** at least under certain circumstances. *Roe v. Wade* (1973). The government may not prohibit a woman from choosing to terminate a pregnancy before viability, and the government may not impose an **undue burden** on that right. *Planned Parenthood of Southeastern Pennsylvania v. Casey* (1992). The government may, however, regulate or prohibit abortions after the time of viability, except where necessary to preserve the life or health of the mother. *Id.* The government may also prohibit certain abortion procedures, such as "intact D & E," to advance its interest in protecting the life of the fetus, as long as in doing so it does not impose an undue burden on the right to an abortion. *Gonzales v. Carhart* (2007).

The government also cannot use **sterilization** as a punishment for crime, at least when persons who commit similar crimes are exempt from that punishment. *Skinner v. Oklahoma* (1942).

The Supreme Court has held that the Due Process Clauses protect certain rights relating to marriage and family. **Marriage** is a fundamental right protected by the Due Process Clauses. *Loving v. Virginia* (1967). The state cannot limit the right to persons who choose to marry persons of the same race, *id.,* and cannot condition the right on a court's permission for persons who are under the obligation to pay child support, *Zablocki v. Redhail* (1978). The state also cannot limit the right to marry to opposite-sex couples, as the Fourteenth Amendment protects the right of same-sex couples to marry. *Obergefell v. Hodges* (2015).

The Due Process Clauses also protect the "liberty of parents and guardians to direct the upbringing and education of children under their control." *Pierce v. Society of the Sisters* (1925); *Meyer v. Nebraska* (1923). This right embraces parental decisions about who can visit their children, *Troxel v. Granville* (2000), but does not limit the power of a state to establish a virtually unrebuttable presumption that a child born to a married woman is a child of the marriage, *Michael H. v. Gerald D.* (1989).

The Due Process Clauses do not impose an affirmative obligation on the government to guarantee a minimum level of personal security or safety. *DeShaney v. Winnebago County Dept. of Social Services* (1989). Nor do they prevent the government from insisting on clear evidence of an incompetent person's desire to have life-sustaining treatment withdrawn, *Cruzan v. Director, Missouri Dept. of Health* (1990), or from prohibiting persons (including doctors) from assisting others to commit suicide, *Washington v. Glucksberg* (1997).

POINT-COUNTERPOINT

Does the Constitution protect unenumerated rights?

POINT: PETER J. SMITH

The argument that the Constitution does not protect unenumerated rights has an appealing simplicity: the Framers would not have bothered to spell out some rights if others were entitled to the same judicial protection; and even if they thought that there were undefined rights that are entitled to protection, they would not have left it to unelected judges—and their largely unconstrained discretion—to decide what they are. But several uncontroversial propositions, when viewed together, suggest that the matter is substantially more complex.

First, there is general agreement that some rights that are not expressly defined in the Constitution's text nevertheless are properly implied from the enumeration of other rights. As we will see in Chapter 11, for example, there is little dispute that the First Amendment's explicit protections—for speech, religion, and so forth—also imply the existence of a "freedom of association," even though the Amendment nowhere mentions such a right. See, e.g., *Scales v. United States*, 367 U.S. 203, 229 (1961).

Second, most of the Constitution's express rights-granting provisions—such as the Due Process and Privileges or Immunities Clauses—are framed at very high levels of generality. As a result, the ordinary process of interpretation inevitably will lead to the identification of rights—such as the right, derived from the Due Process Clause, to insist that the government prove an allegation of criminal conduct beyond a reasonable doubt, *In re Winship*, 397 U.S. 358 (1970)—that are not explicitly mentioned in the constitutional text.

Once one accepts that expressly defined rights imply the existence of other rights, and that broadly defined rights necessarily entail the existence of specific (but not specifically defined) rights, one has essentially accepted the proposition that there are rights that the Constitution protects but that are not expressly enumerated in the document's text. Moreover, if such rights exist, they must be judicially enforceable, or it would be misleading to refer to them as "rights."

There are other reasons to conclude that the Constitution protects unenumerated rights. First, the Constitution's text in several places seems to presuppose that such rights exist. The Ninth Amendment makes the point explicitly, and the Privilege or Immunities Clause of the Fourteenth Amendment plainly protects something, even though it does not specifically enumerate what it is. Second, in other contexts, proponents of the view that the Constitution does not protect unenumerated rights see no problem with implying, from constitutional structure or general "postulates" that underlie the text, limits on the government's authority. In federalism cases such as *Printz v. United States*, 521 U.S. 898 (1997), and *Alden v. Maine*, 527 U.S. 706 (1999), for example, the Justices who are most skeptical of claims of unenumerated rights have nevertheless discovered unenumerated "immunities" that the states enjoy from federal regulation. If the Constitution is properly interpreted to protect these unenumerated states' rights, then it becomes more difficult to suggest that it does not also protect some unenumerated individual rights.

To be sure, concluding that the Constitution protects unenumerated rights does not tell us much about *which* rights it actually protects, and how to define them. There will always be disagreements at the margins about such questions of definition. But once we accept that there are rights that are not explicitly defined in the constitutional text but that nevertheless are entitled to judicial protection, the question simply becomes one of judgment. And that, of course, is what we ordinarily expect judges to exercise.

COUNTERPOINT: GREGORY E. MAGGS

The Constitution does not secure unenumerated rights just because they may exist according to natural law or some political theory. Although the Supreme Court has decided otherwise, its decisions are incorrect as an originalist matter.

True, the Founders believed in natural-law rights. The Declaration of Independence, for instance, prominently appeals to the "Laws of Nature" in specifying how England had violated the rights of American colonists. But acknowledging that the Founders recognized natural law is different from concluding that the Constitution makes unenumerated rights judicially enforceable.

The text of the Constitution itself indicates that unenumerated natural-law rights are not protected. In Article I, §§ 9 & 10, the Constitution lists specific rights, including rights to be free from ex post facto laws, bills of attainder, suspensions of habeas corpus, and state impairments of contracts. The inclusion of these rights objectively indicates that similar rights, which are not enumerated, are not secured. Why list any rights if they are protected without enumeration based on a natural-law theory?

Additional support for this conclusion comes from a debate at the Constitutional Convention about whether to enumerate rights. Some delegates thought including an express prohibition against ex post facto laws was unnecessary because ex post facto laws are naturally void. But delegate Hugh Williamson disagreed, arguing: "Such a prohibitory clause is in the Constitution of N. Carolina, and tho it has been violated, it has done good there & may do good here, because the Judges can take hold of it." 2 The Records of the Federal Convention of 1787 at 376 (Max Farrand ed. 1911). Given that Williamson's view prevailed, a majority of the Convention presumably agreed that judges would enforce enumerated rights, but not unenumerated natural-law rights.

Subsequent events also confirm this was the original understanding. A major objection to ratification of the Constitution was the lack of enumerated rights. Opponents believed that only a listing of rights would guarantee their protection. The First Congress addressed their concern with the Bill of Rights, which would have been unnecessary if courts could enforce unenumerated rights. Why expressly provide for freedom of speech, protection against cruel and unusual punishment, and so forth if courts could enforce any natural-law rights? Also significant is that early court decisions did not enforce unenumerated natural-law rights.

Although the Constitution does not secure unenumerated rights based on natural-law, it does protect one limited kind of unenumerated rights: those arising because the federal government has limited powers. For example, in *United States v. Lopez*, 514 U.S. 549 (1995), the Supreme Court held that Congress lacks power to ban guns in school zones. This means that the defendant in the case had a correlative, although unenumerated, right against the federal government to possess a gun at school. The specific enumeration of other rights in the Constitution should not be construed to deny or disparage rights of this kind retained by the people because of our federal structure. See U.S. Const. amend. 9.

CHAPTER 3

Procedural Due Process

The Due Process Clauses in the Fifth and Fourteenth Amendments provide that persons are entitled to due process of law when the government seeks to deprive them of "life, liberty, or property." We saw in the last chapter how the Court has struggled to define the liberty substantively protected by the Due Process Clauses. But whatever one's views about the Court's substantive due process doctrine, there is little doubt that the clauses provide *procedural* protections in at least some cases involving the deprivation of important interests. However, the Clauses themselves do not provide very much guidance about when exactly those protections are triggered, and what consequences flow when they are. What follows is a brief overview of the principal issues in cases involving procedural due process claims.

POINT FOR DISCUSSION

Procedural due process was a major concern at the time of the American Revolution. In the Declaration of Independence, the Second Continental Congress famously listed the American grievances against the Crown. Several of their complaints concerned unfair trials and biased tribunals. How should this history and context influence our understanding of the Fifth and Fourteenth Amendments?

CLEVELAND BOARD OF EDUCATION V. LOUDERMILL
470 U.S. 532 (1985)

JUSTICE WHITE delivered the opinion of the Court.

In these cases we consider what pretermination process must be accorded a public employee who can be discharged only for cause. In 1979 the Cleveland Board of Education * * * hired respondent James Loudermill as a security guard. On his job application, Loudermill stated that he had never been convicted of a felony. Eleven months later, as part of a routine examination of his employment records, the Board discovered that in fact Loudermill had been convicted of grand larceny in 1968. By letter dated November 3, 1980, the Board's Business Manager informed Loudermill that he had been dismissed because of his dishonesty in filling out the employment application. Loudermill was not afforded an opportunity to respond to the charge of dishonesty or to challenge his dismissal. On November 13, the Board adopted a resolution officially approving the discharge.

[Under Ohio law, Loudermill could be terminated only for cause. Pursuant to state law, he sought administrative review of his discharge. After a hearing before a referee, at which Loudermill argued that he had thought that his 1968 larceny conviction was for a misdemeanor rather than a felony, and oral arguments before the Cleveland Civil Service Commission, the Commission upheld the dismissal. Loudermill filed suit in federal court alleging that the applicable provision of Ohio law was unconstitutional on its face because it did not provide an employee an opportunity to respond to charges against him prior to removal. The Court consolidated Loudermill's case with another case presenting similar facts.]

Respondents' federal constitutional claim depends on their having had a property right in continued employment. If they did, the State could not deprive them of this property without due process. Property interests are not created by the Constitution, "they are created and their dimensions are defined by existing rules or understandings that stem from an independent source such as state law." *Board of Regents v. Roth,* 408 U.S. 564, 576–578 (1972). The Ohio statute plainly creates such an interest. Respondents were "classified civil service employees," Ohio Rev. Code Ann. § 124.11 (1984), entitled to retain their positions "during good behavior and efficient service," who could not be dismissed "except [for] misfeasance, malfeasance, or nonfeasance in office," § 124.34. The statute plainly supports the conclusion, reached by both lower courts, that respondents possessed property rights in continued employment.

[Petitioner] argues, however, that the property right is defined by, and conditioned on, the legislature's choice of procedures for its deprivation. The Board stresses that in addition to specifying the grounds for termination, the statute sets out procedures by which termination may take place. According to petitioner, "[t]o require additional procedures would in effect expand the scope of the property interest itself." [This] "bitter with the sweet" approach misconceives the constitutional guarantee. [T]he Due Process Clause provides that certain substantive rights—life, liberty, and property—cannot be deprived except pursuant to constitutionally adequate procedures. The categories of substance and procedure are distinct. Were the rule otherwise, the Clause would be reduced to a mere tautology. "Property" cannot be defined by the procedures provided for its deprivation any more than can life or liberty. The right to due process "is conferred, not by legislative grace, but by constitutional guarantee. While the legislature may elect not to confer a property interest in [public] employment, it may not constitutionally authorize the deprivation of such an interest, once conferred, without appropriate procedural safeguards." *Arnett v. Kennedy,* 416 U.S. 134, 167 (1974) (POWELL, J., concurring in part and concurring in result in part). * * * In short, once it is determined that the Due Process Clause applies, "the question remains what process is due." *Morrissey v. Brewer,* 408 U.S. 471, 481 (1972). The answer to that question is not to be found in the Ohio statute.

An essential principle of due process is that a deprivation of life, liberty, or property "be preceded by notice and opportunity for hearing appropriate to the nature of the case." *Mullane v. Central Hanover Bank & Trust Co.,* 339 U.S. 306, 313 (1950). We have described "the root requirement" of the Due Process Clause as being "that an individual be given an opportunity for a hearing *before* he is deprived of any significant property interest." *Boddie v. Connecticut,* 401 U.S. 371, 379 (1971). This principle requires "some kind of a hearing" prior to the discharge of an employee who has a constitutionally protected property interest in his employment.

The need for some form of pretermination hearing [is] evident from a balancing of the competing interests at stake. These are the private interests in retaining employment, the governmental interest in the expeditious removal of unsatisfactory employees and the avoidance of administrative burdens, and the risk of an erroneous termination. See *Mathews v. Eldridge,* 424 U.S. 319, 335 (1976).

First, the significance of the private interest in retaining employment cannot be gainsaid. We have frequently recognized the severity of depriving a person of the means of livelihood. While a fired worker may find employment elsewhere, doing so will take some time and is likely to be burdened by the questionable circumstances under which

> **Take Note**
>
> The Court notes that pre-termination hearings are useful in these circumstances because the decision whether to terminate often turns on disputed factual questions and often involves the discretion of the decision-maker. Loudermill did not dispute at his termination hearings that he had been convicted for grand larceny. Is there any "fact" that the Commission might have found at a pre-termination hearing that would have affected its decision whether to terminate? (Was Loudermill terminated because he was an ex-felon?) And why might a pre-termination hearing for Loudermill have made it more likely that the employer would exercise its discretion not to terminate him?

he left his previous job. * * * Second, some opportunity for the employee to present his side of the case is recurringly of obvious value in reaching an accurate decision. Dismissals for cause will often involve factual disputes. Even where the facts are clear, the appropriateness or necessity of the discharge may not be; in such cases, the only meaningful opportunity to invoke the discretion of the decisionmaker is likely to be before the termination takes effect.

The cases before us illustrate these considerations. [G]iven the Commission's ruling we cannot say that [Loudermill's] discharge was mistaken. Nonetheless, in light of the referee's recommendation, neither can we say that a fully informed decisionmaker might not have exercised its discretion and decided not to dismiss him, notwithstanding its authority to do so. In any event, the termination involved arguable issues, and the right to a hearing does not depend on a demonstration of certain success.

The governmental interest in immediate termination does not outweigh these interests. [A]ffording the employee an opportunity to respond prior to termination would impose neither a significant administrative burden nor intolerable delays. Furthermore, the employer shares the employee's interest in avoiding disruption and erroneous decisions; and until the matter is settled, the employer would continue to receive the benefit of the employee's labors. It is preferable to keep a qualified employee on than to train a new one. A governmental employer also has an interest in keeping citizens usefully employed rather than taking the possibly erroneous and counterproductive step of forcing its employees onto the welfare rolls. Finally, in those situations where the employer perceives a significant hazard in keeping the employee on the job, it can avoid the problem by suspending with pay.

Food for Thought

Does the Court adequately state the government's interest in avoiding a pre-termination hearing in this case? What other costs might requiring a hearing impose on the government?

The foregoing considerations indicate that the pretermination "hearing," though necessary, need not be elaborate. We have pointed out that "[t]he formality and procedural requisites for the hearing can vary, depending upon the importance of the interests involved and the nature of the subsequent proceedings." *Boddie v. Connecticut,* 401 U.S., at 378. In general, "something less" than a full evidentiary hearing is sufficient prior to adverse administrative action. *Mathews v. Eldridge,* 424 U.S., at 343. Under state law, respondents were later entitled to a full administrative hearing and judicial review. The only question is what steps were required before the termination took effect.

In only one case, *Goldberg v. Kelly*, 397 U.S. 254 (1970), has the Court required a full adversarial evidentiary hearing prior to adverse governmental action. [T]hat case presented significantly different considerations than are present in the context of public employment. Here, the pretermination hearing need not definitively resolve the propriety of the discharge. It should be an initial check against mistaken decisions—essentially, a determination of whether there are reasonable grounds to believe that the charges against the employee are true and support the proposed action.

> **FYI**
>
> In *Goldberg*, the Court held that a welfare beneficiary was entitled to a trial-type hearing before the termination of benefits. In what way does that context present "significantly different considerations than are present in the context of public employment"?

> **Take Note**
>
> Does the Court hold that Loudermill is entitled to appear *in person* at a hearing before his employment is terminated? Is there a substantial difference between the right to appear in person at a hearing, on the one hand, and the right simply to present evidence and argument *in writing* before the decision-maker acts, on the other? If so, why doesn't the Court make clear what type of hearing Loudermill is entitled to receive?

The essential requirements of due process, and all that respondents seek or the Court of Appeals required, are notice and an opportunity to respond. The opportunity to present reasons, either in person or in writing, why proposed action should not be taken is a fundamental due process requirement. The tenured public employee is entitled to oral or written notice of the charges against him, an explanation of the employer's evidence, and an opportunity to present his side of the story. * * * To require more than this prior to termination would intrude to an unwarranted extent on the government's interest in quickly removing an unsatisfactory employee.

Our holding rests in part on the provisions in Ohio law for a full post-termination hearing. * * * We conclude that all the process that is due is provided by a preterMination opportunity to respond, coupled with post-termination administrative procedures as provided by the Ohio statute.

JUSTICE MARSHALL, concurring in part and concurring in the judgment.

I write separately * * * to reaffirm my belief that public employees who may be discharged only for cause are entitled, under the Due Process Clause of the Fourteenth Amendment, to more than respondents sought in this case. I continue to believe that *before the decision is made to terminate an employee's wages,* the employee is entitled to an opportunity to test the strength of the evidence "by confronting and cross-examining adverse witnesses and by presenting witnesses on his own behalf, whenever there are substantial disputes in testimonial evidence," *Arnett v. Kennedy,* 416 U.S. 134, 214 (1974) (MARSHALL, J., dissenting).

[T]he disruption caused by a loss of wages may be so devastating to an employee that, whenever there are substantial disputes about the evidence, additional pre-deprivation procedures are necessary to minimize the risk of an erroneous termination. * * * By limiting the procedures due prior to termination of wages, the Court accepts an impermissibly high risk that a wrongfully discharged employee will be subjected to this often lengthy wait for vindication, and to the attendant and often traumatic disruptions to his personal and economic life. Considerable amounts of time may pass between the termination of wages and the decision in a post-termination evidentiary hearing * * *. During this period the employee is left in limbo, deprived of his livelihood and of wages on which he may well depend for basic sustenance. In that time, his ability to secure another job might be hindered, either because of the nature of the charges against him, or because of the prospect that he will return to his prior public employment if permitted. * * * Absent an interim source of wages, the employee might be unable to meet his basic, fixed costs, such as food, rent or mortgage payments. * * * Given that so very much is at stake, I am unable to accept the Court's narrow view of the process due to a public employee before his wages are terminated, and before he begins the long wait for a public agency to issue a final decision in his case.

[JUSTICE BRENNAN's separate opinion concurring in part and dissenting in part has been omitted.]

JUSTICE REHNQUIST, dissenting.

[I]n one legislative breath Ohio has conferred upon civil service employees such as respondents in these cases a limited form of tenure during good behavior, and prescribed the procedures by which that tenure may be terminated. * * * We stated in *Board of Regents v. Roth,* 408 U.S. 564, 577 (1972): "Property interests, of course, are not created by the Constitution. Rather, they are created and their dimensions are defined by existing rules or understandings that stem from an independent source such as state law—rules or understandings that secure certain benefits and that support claims of entitlement to those benefits." We ought to recognize the totality of the State's definition of the property right in question, and not merely seize upon one of several paragraphs in a unitary statute to proclaim that in that paragraph the State has inexorably conferred upon a civil service employee something which it is powerless under the United States Constitution to qualify in the next paragraph of the statute. This practice ignores our duty under *Roth* to rely on state law as the source of property interests for purposes of applying the Due Process Clause of the Fourteenth Amendment. While it does not impose a federal definition of property, the Court departs from the full breadth of the holding in *Roth* by its selective choice from among the sentences the Ohio Legislature chooses to use in establishing and qualifying a right.

Having concluded by this somewhat tortured reasoning that Ohio has created a property right in the respondents in these cases, the Court naturally proceeds to inquire what process is "due" before the respondents may be divested of that right. This customary "balancing" inquiry conducted by the Court in these cases reaches a result that is quite unobjectionable, but it seems to me that it is devoid of any principles which will either instruct or endure. The balance is simply an ad hoc weighing which depends to a great extent upon how the Court subjectively views the underlying interests at stake. The results in previous cases and in these cases have been quite unpredictable. * * * Every different set of facts will present a new issue on what process was due and when. One way to avoid this subjective and varying interpretation of the Due Process Clause in cases such as these is to hold that one who avails himself of government entitlements accepts the grant of tenure along with its inherent limitations.

POINTS FOR DISCUSSION

a.   "Life, Liberty, or Property"

The Due Process Clauses require some process (that which is "due") only when the government deprives a person of "life, liberty, or property." The Court in *Loudermill* concluded that Mr. Loudermill, a public employee who could be fired only for cause, had a property interest in continued employment. How did the Court define "property"—or, for that matter, the companion terms "life" and "liberty"?

It seems clear that when a state takes a person's land in order to build a highway, it deprives him or her of property. Similarly, it seems plain that sending a person to prison as punishment for a crime involves the deprivation of liberty, and that sentencing a person to death as punishment for a crime involves the deprivation not only of liberty but also of life. In these instances, the Due Process Clauses require the government to accord some process to the person subject to the deprivation—in the case of the taking, a hearing to determine (at a minimum) the fair market value of the land, and in the case of criminal punishment, a hearing with the full protections of a criminal trial.

But the Due Process Clauses do not define the terms "life, liberty, [and] property." One can conceive of countless interests that people value—including their jobs, their reputations, and their government-provided benefits, such as health care or pension support. Does the "life, liberty, or property" protected by the Due Process Clauses embrace these important interests, as well, thus requiring some kind of hearing when the government takes action that impairs them?

For much of the twentieth century, the Court typically concluded that life, liberty, or property was at issue only when the government sought to deprive a person of a "right," rather than a "privilege." As (then state-court) Justice Holmes explained in a famous case involving a claim by a police officer that he was entitled to a hearing before he was fired for engaging in political activities, "The petitioner may have a constitutional right to talk politics, but he has no constitutional right to be a policeman." *McAuliffe v. New Bedford*, 29 N.E. 517 (Mass. 1892). Of course, on this view, the courts were still called upon to identify "rights"; but the approach typically freed the government from the obligation of providing a hearing whenever it sought to deprive a person of something to which, according to the courts, he was not entitled as a matter of right.

Two developments in the middle of the twentieth century led the Court to reconsider this approach. First, the Court developed the "unconstitutional conditions doctrine," which (at least sometimes) prevents the government from granting a privilege—that is, something to which a person is not entitled as a matter of constitutional right—only on the condition that the person forfeit a constitutional right. For example, the Court held that the government cannot condition the availability of unemployment compensation benefits on a person's willingness to work on the Sabbath, in violation of his genuinely held religious beliefs. *Sherbert v. Verner*, 374 U.S. 398 (1963). Second, the government increasingly provided important benefits, such as health care, welfare, disability insurance, and retirement security, to many citizens as a matter of statutory entitlement, and many citizens relied on these benefits much as they relied on traditional sources of property. See Charles A. Reich, *The New Property*, 73 Yale L.J. 733 (1964). These developments stood in at least some tension with the right-privilege distinction.

> **Make the Connection**
>
> We will consider the Court's decision in *Sherbert v. Verner*, and the free exercise of religion, in Chapter 11.

In 1970, the Court held in *Goldberg v. Kelly*, 397 U.S. 254 (1970), that the government was required to provide an evidentiary hearing before terminating a welfare recipient's benefits. The Court held that "the extent to which procedural due process must be afforded to the recipient is influenced by the extent to which he may be condemned to suffer grievous loss, and depends upon whether the recipient's interest in avoiding that loss outweighs the governmental interest in summary adjudication." Because terminating benefits to welfare recipients threatened to leave them without any source of sustenance, the Court held that the Due Process Clause required a hearing, at which the recipients could attempt to demonstrate that they remained eligible for benefits, before the government could terminate their benefits. In *Goldberg*, the government did not dispute that welfare benefits are a form of property, and the Court thus had little occasion to define specifically the interests protected by the Clauses. The Court did, however, cite Professor Reich's view of the "new property," explaining that it "may be realistic today to regard welfare entitlements as more like 'property' than a 'gratuity,' " and that "[m]uch of the existing wealth in this country takes the form of rights that do not fall within traditional common-law concepts of property." 397 U.S. at 262 n.8.

Two years later, the Court addressed the question directly, in two cases that it decided on the same day. In *Board of Regents v. Roth*, 408 U.S. 564 (1972), a professor at a public university sued when he was fired after a fixed, one-year term of teaching. Under state law, a professor was guaranteed tenure after four years of teaching, and a non-tenured professor was granted an opportunity to review a termination decision only if he was dismissed during the academic year. Using the balancing test set out in *Goldberg*, the lower courts concluded that the professor's interest in continued employment outweighed the university's interest in dismissing him without a hearing. Declaring that it was necessary to look at "the nature of the interest at stake" before looking at the "weights" of the interests, however, the Supreme Court held that the state did not deprive the respondent of a protected property interest. The Court stated: "Property interests, of course, are not created by the Constitution. Rather they are created and their dimensions are defined by existing rules or understandings that stem from an independent source such as state law—rules or understandings that secure certain benefits and that support claims of entitlement to those benefits." The Court explained that "[t]o have a property interest in a benefit, a person clearly must have more than an abstract need or desire for it. He must have more than a unilateral expectation of it. He must, instead, have a legitimate claim of entitlement to it." Because the professor's contract did not include any provision for employment for the next year and no state statute or university rule guaranteed him continued employment, the Court concluded that he did not have a property interest in continued employment and, accordingly, that the Due Process Clause did not entitle him to a pre-termination hearing.

By contrast, in *Perry v. Sindermann*, 408 U.S. 593 (1972), a companion case to *Roth*, the Court held that a professor at a different public university had a property interest in his job that required the university to accord him a hearing prior to termination. Although the professor did not have formal tenure, he had been employed by the state college system for ten years under a series of one-year contracts. The Court held that this arrangement, coupled with the university's official employment policies, created a legitimate expectation of renewal tantamount to tenure, and accordingly that the university could not terminate respondent without providing notice and a hearing.

The Court elaborated on the "legitimate expectation" test in *Town of Castle Rock v. Gonzales*, 545 U.S. 748 (2005). In that case, the respondent, who sued for damages under 42 U.S.C. § 1983, claimed that Castle Rock violated the Due Process Clause when its police officers did not respond to her repeated reports that her estranged husband was violating the terms of a restraining order to protect their children. The husband subsequently kidnapped and murdered the children. Although a statement on the back of the restraining order informed law enforcement officials that they "shall use every reasonable means to enforce this restraining order," the Supreme Court found that this language, even when coupled with state domestic violence statutes, did not render the enforcement of restraining orders mandatory. Because a "benefit is not a protected property * * * entitlement if government officials may grant it or deny it in their discretion," the Court held that the respondent did not enjoy a protected property interest in the hope that the police would arrest someone.

Property interests accordingly are created and defined by positive law, and not by the courts. (Indeed, it is this fact that led to the argument, rejected in *Loudermill*, that a person is not entitled to a hearing if the state, in creating a property interest, identifies the procedural rights that flow from the interest's termination.) In deciding whether a person has a protected property interest, therefore, a court must look to state or federal law—statutory or otherwise—to determine whether the person has some legally protected entitlement to the interest.

Food for Thought

Why has the Court concluded that the Constitution defines protected liberty interests, but leaves the definition of protected property interests to "independent sources," such as legislatively enacted or judicially developed state law?

But the Court in *Roth* made clear that some *liberty* interests, unlike property interests, are defined by the Constitution, subject of course to the Court's interpretation. Accordingly, the government may have to accord notice and an opportunity to be heard when it deprives a person of any liberty interest protected in the Bill of Rights or any unenumerated interest that the Court has held is protected by the Constitution. Following this approach, the Court has concluded that the government must provide a hearing when it seeks, among other things, to institutionalize a person, *O'Connor v. Donaldson*, 422 U.S. 563 (1975), terminate a person's parental rights, *Santosky v. Kramer*, 455 U.S. 745 (1982), or discipline school children, *Ingraham v. Wright*, 430 U.S. 651 (1977) (corporal punishment); *Goss v. Lopez*, 419 U.S. 565 (1975) (suspension).

In light of this background, can you articulate why Loudermill had a protected interest in "continued employment"? Did Loudermill have both property and liberty interests in his job?

b. "Due Process of Law"

If there is a deprivation of a protected interest, then to what process is the person entitled? The Due Process Clauses, of course, are notoriously vague, circularly requiring only that the government provide the process that is "due." In some cases, immediate government action, without any pre-action hearing, will be justified by some threat to public health or safety. See, e.g., *North American Cold Storage Co. v. Chicago*, 211 U.S. 306 (1908) (holding that government can seize and destroy rancid food without a pre-seizure hearing). But what about cases that do not involve such exigent circumstances? Is there one set of requirements that is always triggered by a deprivation, regardless of the nature of the deprivation or the particular protected interests at stake? After all, the Due Process Clauses are implicated by a large range of actions; must the government accord a full-blown trial-type hearing before it can fire an employee? Terminate welfare benefits? Suspend a child from school? The individuals subjected to these actions obviously would like to have ample opportunity to demonstrate why the government should not take the action after all. But requiring a judicial-type proceeding before the government can take countless actions could effectively slow government to a crawl—or lead the government not to create any entitlements in the first place.

There is no perfect formula to capture the Court's holdings in this area. In *Goldberg v. Kelly*, the Court stated, after balancing the interests of the welfare recipients with those of the government in the prompt termination of welfare benefits, that the hearing to which welfare recipients were entitled before the termination of their benefits did not have to "take the form of a judicial or quasi-judicial trial." But it nevertheless required notice, an opportunity for the recipient to be heard in person, an impartial decision-maker limited to a decision based on evidence in the record, and the right to cross-examine adverse witnesses and to use a lawyer.

Six years later, however, in *Mathews v. Eldridge*, 424 U.S. 319 (1976), the Court concluded that recipients of disability benefits were not entitled to such a hearing before the termination of their benefits, when a post-termination hearing was available. The Court explained that "due process generally requires consideration of three distinct factors: First, the private interest that will be affected by the official action; second, the risk of an erroneous deprivation of such interest through the procedures used, and the probable value, if any, of additional or substitute procedural safeguards; and finally, the Government's interest, including the function involved and the fiscal and administrative burdens that the additional or substitute procedural requirement would entail." The Court concluded that the government interest outweighed the individual interest because requiring a full evidentiary hearing prior to termination would substantially increase the cost of the program, and because eligibility for disability benefits was not based on financial need. Can *Goldberg* and *Mathews* be reconciled? Which case was *Loudermill* more like?

In his dissent in *Loudermill*, then-Justice Rehnquist lamented that the Court's decisions in this area lack a principled pattern. In light of the cases described above, do you agree with his criticism?

Executive Summary of This Chapter

The Due Process Clauses ordinarily require **notice** and an **opportunity to be heard** when the government seeks to deprive a person of "life, liberty, or property." *Cleveland Board of Education v. Loudermill* (1985).

The procedural protections of the Clauses are triggered when the government deprives a person of a protected interest. The Constitution defines some liberty interests, which can include liberties accorded explicit protection (for example, in the Bill of Rights) and fundamental rights that the Court has concluded are implicit in the constitutional scheme. *Board of Regents v. Roth* (1972).

Property interests, on the other hand, are defined by independent sources of law, such as state common law or state or federal statutory law. Such independent sources of law create property interests when they create a **legitimate claim of entitlement** to continued possession. *Board of Regents v. Roth* (1972); *Perry v. Sindermann* (1972). A person does not have a legitimate claim of entitlement to a government benefit if the government may grant or deny it in its discretion. *Town of Castle Rock v. Gonzales* (2005).

Although the independent source of authority determines whether a person has a legitimate claim of entitlement, that source of law cannot define the procedures that must accompany a deprivation of the property interest. *Cleveland Board of Education v. Loudermill* (1985).

If there has been a deprivation of a protected interest, the Due Process Clauses typically require notice and some kind of hearing. In deciding exactly what process must be provided, particularly before the deprivation takes place, the Court applies a **balancing test** that considers three factors: (1) the private interest; (2) the risk of an erroneous deprivation and the probable value, if any, of additional or substitute procedural safeguards; and (3) the government's interest. *Mathews v. Eldridge* (1976).

PART II

Equal Protection

Inscribed on the façade of the Supreme Court's majestic building in Washington, D.C., is the phrase, "Equal Justice Under Law." Americans have come to accept that this basic concept is essential to a just, democratic society. Yet the Constitution that was ratified in 1789—and the Bill of Rights, ratified in 1791—did not include any provision explicitly guaranteeing equal treatment under the laws other than the Privileges and Immunities Clause in Article IV. That provision, however, limits only certain kinds of discrimination by states against citizens of other states. It was not until 1868—after the nation had fought a bloody Civil War largely over the institution of slavery—that a general provision requiring some form of equal treatment under law became part of the Constitution.* The Fourteenth Amendment provides, in relevant part, that "No State shall [deny] to any person within its jurisdiction the equal protection of the laws." In the next two chapters, we consider the meaning and application of this important provision.

---

* As we will see in Chapter 4, the Supreme Court subsequently ruled that the Due Process Clause of the Fifth Amendment includes an equal protection principle. See *Bolling v. Sharpe*, 347 U.S. 497 (1954). But the Court did not interpret the Fifth Amendment this way before ratification of the Fourteenth Amendment.

Introduction and Framework

A. DISTINCTIONS AND CLASSIFICATIONS

If equal treatment under the law is of exceeding importance, then so is the practical fact that government often must draw distinctions in order to govern sensibly, effectively, and fairly. Surely, for example, a public school teacher can award an "A" to a student who turns in an exceptional academic performance and a "C" to a student who has done mediocre work, even though those decisions distinguish between the students on the basis of their demonstrated academic ability. Similarly, although there might be debate over the wisdom of particular tax and social welfare policies, almost all would now agree that the government has power to impose a higher marginal tax rate on the wealthy than it imposes on the poor, or to award welfare benefits to the poor and not to the wealthy. But see *Knowlton v. Moore*, 178 U.S. 41, 110 (1900) (Brewer, J., dissenting from the Court's conclusion that a "progressive rate of tax can be validly imposed").

Indeed, one can find government distinctions and classifications wherever one turns. A city that wants to limit the number of sidewalk vendors on its streets might choose to grant licenses to operate sidewalk stands only to vendors who have already been engaged in business for a certain period of time. See *New Orleans v. Dukes*, 427 U.S. 297 (1976). The same city might decide to hire as police officers only those applicants who can, among other things, demonstrate competency with a firearm. And, to take an example familiar to virtually all students, the state can deny driver's licenses to all persons younger than, say, 16 years old, regardless of their demonstrated driving ability.

There would be serious (and fairly obvious) costs if the Equal Protection Clause prohibited these distinctions, even though each can be said to "discriminate" on some ground—in the examples above, on the basis respectively of academic ability, wealth, time in business, technical competence, and age. It is perhaps for this reason that Justice Oliver Wendell Holmes, one of our most famous jurists, ridiculed claims based on the Equal Protection Clause as "the last resort of constitutional arguments." *Buck v. Bell*, 274 U.S. 200, 208 (1927).

Yet the Clause must ban at least some forms of government discrimination. We have come to see, for example, that discrimination on the basis of race is dangerous and morally problematic; we can intuitively understand the difference between a rule denying driver's licenses to people younger than 16 years old and a rule denying licenses to persons because of the color of their skin. Indeed, as we will see in the first part of Chapter 5, classifications on the basis of race (other than affirmative action programs and remedial measures for past discrimination) are virtually always inconsistent with the Equal Protection Clause.

But outside of the context of race, whether a classification is presumptively problematic is sometimes a considerably more difficult question. May the government distinguish among persons on the basis of gender? National origin? Citizenship status? Sexual orientation? These questions have provoked serious debate and often divided the Court. At bottom, the question for our consideration is: if some government classifications are unobjectionable under the Equal Protection Clause and others are deeply problematic, then how do we distinguish between the defensible ones and the suspect ones?

One possibility would be to conclude that because the problem of racial discrimination was the principal motivation for the ratification of the Fourteenth Amendment, the Equal Protection Clause prohibits only classifications based on race. But the Clause does not, at least on its face, apply only to unequal treatment on the basis of race. And the Court has never accepted the view that the Clause is silent on all forms of discrimination other than racial discrimination.

Instead, the Court, at least in theory, subjects all challenged government classifications to some form of judicial review. In any case challenging a government classification, the Court assesses its constitutionality by considering the nature of the classification, the government's interest in the challenged regulation, and the relationship between the government's interest and the classification. But the "level of scrutiny" that the Court applies—the extent to which the Court insists on particularly weighty

> **Make the Connection**
>
> We considered rational-basis review (and various forms of heightened scrutiny) in Chapter 2 when we considered the Court's cases concerning substantive due process and "fundamental rights."

interests, accords deference to the government's judgment, and tolerates imperfect means to accomplish those ends—depends upon the basis for the classification. Under "strict scrutiny," the Court's most searching form of review, a law will be upheld only if it is "narrowly tailored" to advance a "compelling" government interest. Under "intermediate scrutiny," the Court will uphold a law only if it is "substantially related" to an "important" government interest. Finally, under the "rational-basis test" (also called "rationality review"), a law will be upheld if it is "rationally related" to a "legitimate" government interest. Unlike strict and intermediate scrutiny, rational-basis review is highly deferential.

But how does the Court know which level of scrutiny to apply to any given classification? The answer inheres in part in history, in part in contestable notions about the normative validity of certain bases of discrimination, and in part on political theory. Perhaps the Court's most famous attempt to identify when heightened scrutiny is warranted for a particular classification came in the famous footnote 4 of the Court's decision in *United States v. Carolene Products Co.*, 304 U.S. 144 (1938), which we considered in Chapter 2. In that case, the Court applied rational-basis review to a federal law that regulated the sale of milk. After declaring that ordinary regulatory legislation is entitled to a presumption of constitutionality, the Court stated in footnote 4:

> It is unnecessary to consider now whether legislation which restricts those political processes which can ordinarily be expected to bring about repeal of undesirable legislation, is to be subjected to more exacting judicial scrutiny under the general prohibitions of the Fourteenth Amendment than are most other types of legislation. Nor need we enquire whether similar considerations enter into the review of statutes directed at particular religious, or national, or racial minorities; whether prejudice against discrete and insular minorities may be a special condition, which tends seriously to curtail the operation of those political processes ordinarily to be relied upon to protect minorities, and which may call for a correspondingly more searching judicial inquiry.

The Court's suggestion—that judicial intervention might be warranted, among other times, to protect "discrete and insular minorities" from the political process—has informed the Court as it has sought, over the last half-century, to determine which government classifications are problematic. But note that the Court's approach in *Carolene Products* leaves many questions—including, significantly, who constitutes a "discrete and insular minority" not adequately protected by the political process—unanswered.

Perspective and Analysis

Professor John Hart Ely argued that the *Carolene Products* footnote suggested a "representation-reinforcement approach" to judicial review, including review under the Equal Protection Clause. Under that approach,

Courts would intervene to invalidate actions by the elected branches only under certain circumstances:

> Our government cannot fairly be said to be "malfunctioning" simply because it sometimes generates outcomes with which we disagree, however strongly * * *. Malfunction occurs when the *process* is undeserving of trust, when (1) the ins are choking off the channels of political change to ensure that they will stay in and the outs will stay out, or (2) though no one is actually denied a voice or a vote, representatives beholden to an effective majority are systematically disadvantaging some minority out of simple hostility or a prejudiced refusal to recognize commonalities of interest, and thereby denying that minority the protection afforded other groups by a representative system.

John Hart Ely, *Democracy and Distrust* 103 (1980).

As we will see in Chapter 5, the Court has translated the *Carolene Products* approach into a sprawling body of doctrine. The Court applies "strict scrutiny" to classifications based on race and national origin, and "intermediate scrutiny" to classifications based on gender and the marital status of one's parents. Most other classifications are reviewed only for rationality. But various Justices have, over the years, contested an approach to review under the Equal Protection Clause that rigidly defines three "tiers" of scrutiny. They have instead suggested that judicial review should—and, in fact, does, as a matter of practice—vary along a sliding scale depending upon the concerns raised by the particular basis for classification and the importance of the government interests advanced by the classification. As we explore the doctrine in the next two chapters, consider the extent to which the Court has in practice, even if not in rhetoric, followed just such an approach.

B. TO WHOM DOES THE OBLIGATION OF EQUAL PROTECTION APPLY?

The Equal Protection Clause provides specifically that "[n]o *State*" shall deny any person equal protection of the laws. Does that mean that the federal government is free to discriminate on bases on which the states are forbidden to discriminate?

BOLLING V. SHARPE

347 U.S. 497 (1954)

MR. CHIEF JUSTICE WARREN delivered the opinion of the Court.

[Petitioners, African-American school children, were refused admission to segregated public schools in the District of Columbia. They filed suit against the school board, alleging that such segregation deprived them of due process of law under the Fifth Amendment.]

> **FYI**
>
> At oral argument, the Justices became concerned that this case was moot because members of the D.C. School Board, apparently embarrassed by the segregation policy, had made public statements that they supported the plaintiffs and desegregation. But no mention of the mootness issue appeared in the decision.

We have this day held that the Equal Protection Clause of the Fourteenth Amendment prohibits the states from maintaining racially segregated public schools. * * * The Fifth Amendment, which is applicable in the District of Columbia, does not contain an equal protection clause as does the Fourteenth Amendment which applies only to the states. But the concepts of equal protection and due process, both stemming from our American ideal of fairness, are not mutually exclusive. The "equal protection of the laws" is

> **Make the Connection**
>
> The Court decided *Bolling* on the same day that it decided *Brown v. Board of Education*, which addressed the constitutionality of segregation in education in the states. We will consider *Brown* in Chapter 5.

a more explicit safeguard of prohibited unfairness than "due process of law," and, therefore, we do not imply that the two are always interchangeable phrases. But, as this Court has recognized, discrimination may be so unjustifiable as to be violative of due process.

Classifications based solely upon race must be scrutinized with particular care, since they are contrary to our traditions and hence constitutionally suspect. [*Korematsu v. United States*, 323 U.S. 214, 216 (1944); *Hirabayashi v.*

> **Make the Connection**
>
> We will consider the Court's decision in *Korematsu* in Chapter 5.

United States, 320 U.S. 81, 100 (1943).] As long ago as 1896, this Court declared the principle "that the constitution of the United States, in its present form, forbids, so far as civil and political rights are concerned, discrimination by the general government, or by the states, against any citizen because of his race." [*Gibson v. Mississippi*, 162 U.S. 565, 591 (1896).] And in *Buchanan v. Warley*, 245 U.S. 60 (1917), the Court held that a statute which limited the right of a property owner to convey his property to a person of another race was, as an unreasonable discrimination, a denial of due process of law.

Although the Court has not assumed to define "liberty" with any great precision, that term is not confined to mere freedom from bodily restraint. Liberty under law extends to the full range of conduct which the individual is free to pursue, and it cannot be restricted except for a proper governmental objective. Segregation in public education is not reasonably related to any proper governmental objective, and thus it imposes on Negro children of the District of Columbia a burden that constitutes an arbitrary deprivation of their liberty in violation of the Due Process Clause.

In view of our decision that the Constitution prohibits the states from maintaining racially segregated public schools, it would be unthinkable that the same Constitution would impose a lesser duty on the Federal Government. We hold that racial segregation in the public schools of the District of Columbia is a denial of the due process of law guaranteed by the Fifth Amendment to the Constitution.

POINTS FOR DISCUSSION

a.   Interpretation and Reverse Incorporation

In addition to the Equal Protection Clause, there is a Due Process Clause in the Fourteenth Amendment. If the concept of due process prohibits the government from discriminating on the basis of race (or any other ground that is "not reasonably related to any proper governmental objective"), then isn't the Equal Protection Clause redundant?

If nothing else, it seems clear that the Due Process Clause of the Fifth Amendment was not originally understood to prohibit racial discrimination. After all, the institution of slavery co-existed for over 60 years with the Due Process Clause, and the Court in the *Dred Scott* decision (which we will consider in Chapter 5) even concluded that a slave owner's interest in his slaves was *protected* by that Clause. By what process of interpretation, then, does the Court reach the conclusion that the Due Process Clause of the Fifth Amendment includes an equal protection component generally and prohibits racial discrimination specifically?

The Court's approach in *Bolling* is often considered an instance of "reverse incorporation." Just as the Court has held, as we saw in Chapter 1, that the Due Process Clause of the Fourteenth Amendment "incorporated" (most of) the protections of the Bill of Rights, the Court in *Bolling* effectively held that, presumably upon the ratification of the Fourteenth Amendment, the Due Process Clause of the

Fifth Amendment incorporated the rights afforded by the Equal Protection Clause. Such an approach could hypothetically be justified on originalist grounds—if, for example, the ratifiers of the Fourteenth Amendment also understood that it would modify the reach of the Fifth Amendment. The originalist case, however, is a difficult one to advance, because there appears to have been no such understanding of the Fourteenth Amendment after its ratification. See, e.g., *La Belle Iron Works v. United States*, 256 U.S. 377, 392 (1921) (rejecting an equality-based challenge to federal action on the ground that "[t]he Fifth Amendment has no equal protection clause"). The Court in *Bolling* (and, we will see shortly, *Brown*) does not seem to have relied on an originalist approach, insisting instead that it would be "unthinkable" for the Constitution to permit the federal government to discriminate on the basis of race while forbidding the states from doing so. Is rejection of the "unthinkable" a generalizable basis for interpreting the Constitution?

Bolling was not the first case in which the Court suggested that there is an equal protection component to the Due Process Clause of the Fifth Amendment. In *Korematsu*, which the Court cited in *Bolling* and which we will consider in Chapter 5, the Court upheld the criminal conviction of an American citizen of Japanese ancestry for remaining in a city in California after a military commander has ordered persons of Japanese ancestry to be excluded from the city during World War II. The Court stated, however, that "all legal restrictions which curtail the civil rights of a single racial group are immediately suspect"—including, presumably, restrictions, such as those at issue in the case, imposed by the federal government. The Court in *Korematsu*, however, did not specify what provision of the Constitution imposed limits on the federal government's ability to discriminate on the basis of race.

b.   "Liberty" and Due Process

The Court declared in *Bolling* that liberty "cannot be restricted except for a proper governmental objective," and it concluded that segregation in the D.C. schools constituted "an arbitrary deprivation" of the school children's "liberty in violation of the Due Process Clause." Did the Court in *Bolling* rely on a theory of substantive due process, which we considered in Chapter 2? If, as some Justices have contended, the doctrine of substantive due process is illegitimate, does that mean that the Court's decision in *Bolling* necessarily was illegitimate, as well?

c.   The Fifth Amendment v. the Fourteenth Amendment

Are there any differences between the protection against discrimination provided by the Equal Protection Clause of the Fourteenth Amendment and the Due Process Clause of the Fifth Amendment? In *Bolling*, the Court stated that it was not "imply[ing] that [due process and equal protection] are always interchangeable phrases." In *Buckley v. Valeo*, 424 U.S. 1 (1976), however, the Supreme Court expressly declared that "[e]qual protection analysis in the Fifth Amendment area is the same as that under the Fourteenth Amendment." Would there be any justification for applying different standards to actions by the federal and state governments that discriminate on the basis of race?

This question has considerable history. In *Metro Broadcasting, Inc. v. F.C.C.*, 497 U.S. 547 (1990), the Supreme Court held that it owed deference to Congress, as a co-equal branch of government, in assessing the constitutionality of federal race-based affirmative action policies and would not subject them to strict scrutiny. Instead, the Court held that "benign race-conscious measures mandated by Congress—even if those measures are not 'remedial' in the sense of being designed to compensate victims of past governmental or societal discrimination—are constitutionally permissible to the extent that they serve important governmental objectives within the power of Congress and are substantially related to achievement of those objectives." *Id.* at 564–565. But just five years later, in *Adarand Constructors, Inc. v. Peña*, 515 U.S. 200, 227 (1995), the Supreme Court overruled *Metro Broadcasting*, holding that

> **Make the Connection**
>
> We will consider the Court's decision in *Adarand*, and the constitutionality of affirmative action programs, in Chapter 5.

"all racial classifications, imposed by whatever federal, state, or local governmental actor, must be analyzed by a reviewing court under strict scrutiny." What might be the hazards of deferring to Congress when Congress classifies on the basis of race?

C. RATIONALITY REVIEW

As noted above, government classifications on bases that are not suspect are generally reviewed solely for rationality. Under this level of scrutiny, the Court asks whether the classification is rationally related to a legitimate government interest. As we saw in Chapter 2 when we considered the Court's review under the Due Process Clauses of social and economic regulation, this is a highly deferential form of review. Indeed, it is virtually always possible to articulate some legitimate interest served by a challenged government regulation. Otherwise, why would Congress or a state legislature enact the law?

But the simple fact that the government has not classified on some suspect basis, such as race or gender, does not mean that all government classifications are therefore fair or sensible. Just how aggressively should the courts review government classifications to avoid unfairness or arbitrariness?

RAILWAY EXPRESS AGENCY V.
PEOPLE OF STATE OF NEW YORK
336 U.S. 106 (1949)

MR. JUSTICE DOUGLAS delivered the opinion of the Court.

[The Traffic Regulations of the City of New York prohibited the operation of "advertising vehicles"—vehicles that essentially served as moving billboards—but permitted the use of "business notices upon business delivery vehicles, so long as such vehicles [were] engaged in the usual business or regular work of the owner and not used merely or mainly for advertising." Appellant operated 1,900 trucks in New York City and sold the space on the exterior sides of these trucks for advertising for the most part unconnected with its own business. It was convicted and fined, and it appealed to challenge the constitutionality of the regulation.]

The Court of Special Sessions concluded that advertising on vehicles using the streets of New York City constitutes a distraction to vehicle drivers and to pedestrians alike and therefore affects the safety of the public in the use of the streets. [But it] is pointed out that the regulation draws the line between advertisements of products sold by the owner of the truck and general advertisements. It is argued that unequal treatment on the basis of such a distinction is not justified by the aim and purpose of the regulation. It is said, for example, that one of appellant's trucks carrying the advertisement of a commercial house would not cause any greater distraction of pedestrians and vehicle drivers than if the commercial house carried the same advertisement on its own truck. Yet the regulation allows the latter to do what the former is forbidden from doing. It is therefore contended that the classification which the regulation makes has no relation to the traffic problem since a violation turns not on what kind of advertisements are carried on trucks but on whose trucks they are carried.

That, however, is a superficial way of analyzing the problem * * *. The local authorities may well have concluded that those who advertised their own wares on their trucks do not present the same traffic problem in view of the nature or extent of the advertising which they use. It would take a degree of omniscience which we lack to say that such is not the case. If that judgment is correct, the advertising displays that are exempt have less incidence on traffic than those of appellants.

We cannot say that that judgment is not an allowable one. Yet if it is, the classification has relation to the purpose for which it is made and does not contain the kind of discrimination against which the Equal Protection Clause affords protection. [T]he fact that New York City sees fit to eliminate from traffic this

Take Note

What level of scrutiny does the Court apply under the Equal Protection Clause? Is there a rational basis for believing that the challenged regulation furthers the government's interest in preventing distractions to motorists? How important can that interest be to the government when it permits advertisements on the side of other types of vehicles?

kind of distraction but does not touch what may be even greater ones in a different category, such as the vivid displays on Times Square, is immaterial. It is no requirement of equal protection that all evils of the same genus be eradicated or none at all.

MR. JUSTICE JACKSON, concurring.

The burden should rest heavily upon one who would persuade us to use the due process clause to strike down a substantive law or ordinance. Even its provident use against municipal regulations frequently disables all government—state, municipal and federal—from dealing with the conduct in question because the requirement of due process is also applicable to State and Federal Governments. Invalidation of a statute or an ordinance on due process grounds leaves ungoverned and ungovernable conduct which many people find objectionable.

Invocation of the equal protection clause, on the other hand, does not disable any governmental body from dealing with the subject at hand. It merely means that the prohibition or regulation must have a broader impact. I regard it as a salutary doctrine that cities, states and the Federal Government must exercise their powers so as not to discriminate between their inhabitants except upon some reasonable differentiation fairly related to the object of regulation. This equality is not merely abstract justice. The framers of the Constitution knew, and we should not forget today, that there is no more effective practical guaranty against arbitrary and unreasonable government than to require that the principles of law which officials would impose upon a minority must be imposed generally. Conversely, nothing opens the door to arbitrary action so effectively as to allow those officials to pick and choose only a few to whom they will apply legislation and thus to escape the political retribution that might be visited upon them if larger numbers were affected. Courts can take no better measure to assure that laws will be just than to require that laws be equal in operation.

In this case, if the City of New York should assume that display of any advertising on vehicles tends and intends to distract the attention of persons using the highways and to increase the dangers of its traffic, I should think it fully within its constitutional powers to forbid it all. * * * Instead of such general regulation of advertising, however, the City seeks to reduce the hazard only by saying that while some may, others may not exhibit such appeals. The same display, for example, advertising cigarettes, which this appellant is forbidden to carry on its trucks, may be carried on the trucks of a cigarette dealer and might on the trucks of this appellant if it dealt in cigarettes. And almost an identical advertisement, certainly one of equal size, shape, color and appearance, may be carried by this appellant if it proclaims its own offer to transport cigarettes. But it may not be carried so long as the message is not its own but a cigarette dealer's offer to sell the same cigarettes.

The question in my mind comes to this. Where individuals contribute to an evil or danger in the same way and to the same degree, may those who do so for hire be prohibited, while those who do so for their own commercial ends but not for hire be allowed to continue? I think the answer has to be that the hireling may be put in a class by himself and may be dealt with differently than those who

> **Take Note**
>
> What is the difference between advertising to serve one's "own commercial ends" and doing so for hire? Why would a city tolerate one while forbidding the other? Aren't both done to serve the self-interest of the operator of the vehicle?

act on their own. But this is not merely because such a discrimination will enable the lawmaker to diminish the evil. That might be done by many classifications, which I should think wholly unsustainable. It is rather because there is a real difference between doing in self-interest and doing for hire, so that it is one thing to tolerate action from those who act on their own and it is another thing to permit the same action to be promoted for a price.

POINTS FOR DISCUSSION

a. Under-Inclusiveness in Regulation

The challenged regulation in *Railway Express* distinguished between trucks whose sole purpose was to advertise and trucks that engaged in some business in addition to advertising. Of course, if the point of the regulation was, as the government argued, to promote traffic safety by eliminating distractions on the road, then the regulation was far from a comprehensive effort to achieve that end; there would still be many trucks on the road with advertising on the side, and thus there would still be many distractions.

To the extent that there was a problem with the regulation, therefore, it was not with the legitimacy of the government's interest in enacting the regulation—there is plainly a valid interest in promoting traffic safety—but was instead with the extent to which the government's chosen means advanced that interest. The regulation at issue was "under-inclusive," in that it failed to impose the same prohibition on others who were similarly situated, and thus failed completely to address the problem of distractions on the roads. *Railway Express* demonstrates that, at least when the Court is applying rational-basis review, under-inclusiveness does not mean that the regulation is not rationally related to the government's interest.

In what way was the distinction that the challenged regulation created "rational"? Should it have been enough that the regulation would remove at least some distractions from the road? Why shouldn't a court insist that the legislature treat all similarly situated parties the same? In thinking about this question, consider the implications of an approach that would have invalidated the regulation. If the city sought to promote traffic safety by eliminating distractions, would it also be required to eliminate signs on stores along the streets? To ban talking on a cell phone while driving? If not, who should draw lines of this sort—legislatures or courts?

b. Legitimate Government Interests

The Court in *Railway Express* treated as legitimate the government's assertion that the regulation was adopted for the purpose of ensuring traffic safety. Suppose that the appellant had offered evidence that the City had adopted the challenged regulation after large campaign contributions to City Council members by owners of conventional, street-side billboards, who did not want to be forced to compete with advertising vehicles. Would the government's assertion that the regulation promotes traffic safety still have qualified as a legitimate interest for purposes of rationality review?

As we saw in Chapter 2 when we considered the Court's decision in *Williamson v. Lee Optical Co.*, 348 U.S. 483 (1955), the answer is generally yes. The Court has repeatedly made clear that a challenged regulation will be upheld under the rational-basis test as long as the government can identify some plausible legitimate interest served by the regulation, even if it was not the "actual" purpose of the regulation and was instead devised by government lawyers defending the regulation in court. See, e.g., *United States Railroad Retirement Bd. v. Fritz*, 449 U.S. 166, 179 (1980) ("It is, of course, 'constitutionally irrelevant whether this reasoning in fact underlay the legislative decision,' because this Court has never insisted that a legislative body articulate its reasons for enacting a statute." (quoting *Flemming v. Nestor*, 363 U.S. 603, 612 (1960)).

Given that the Court will accept any conceivable legitimate interest offered, even if it was not the real purpose of the regulation, isn't rational-basis review in practice no meaningful review at all, and thus an abdication of the judicial role? On the other hand, how would a court determine the "actual" purpose of a regulation? And if the legislature can simply reenact the identical regulation and expressly assert a legitimate purpose, would it make any sense to permit courts to invalidate regulations because the "real" purpose was problematic?

NEW YORK CITY TRANSIT AUTHORITY V. BEAZER

440 U.S. 568 (1979)

MR. JUSTICE STEVENS delivered the opinion of the Court.

[The New York City Transit Authority ("TA") employs about 47,000 persons, many of them in positions potentially posing a danger to themselves or the general public. TA enforced a general policy against employing persons who use narcotic drugs. This included persons receiving methadone maintenance treatment for heroin addiction. Two former employees of TA who were dismissed while receiving methadone treatment and two others who were refused employment while receiving methadone treatment filed a class action challenging the policy. The District Court held that TA's blanket exclusion from employment of all persons undergoing methadone treatment violated the Equal Protection Clause of the Fourteenth Amendment, and the Court of Appeals affirmed.]

The Equal Protection Clause of the Fourteenth Amendment [announces] a fundamental principle: the State must govern impartially. General rules that apply evenhandedly to all persons within the jurisdiction unquestionably comply with this principle. Only when a governmental unit adopts a rule that has a special impact on less than all the persons subject to its jurisdiction does the question whether this principle is violated arise.

[The District Court upheld] rules requiring special supervision of methadone users to detect evidence of drug abuse, and excluding them from high-risk employment. [But] the District Court [concluded] that employment in nonsensitive jobs could not be denied to methadone users who had progressed satisfactorily with their treatment for one year, and who, when examined individually, satisfied TA's employment criteria.

[A]ny special rule short of total exclusion that TA might adopt is likely to be less precise—and will assuredly be more costly than the one that it currently enforces. If eligibility is marked at any intermediate point—whether after one year of treatment or later—the classification will inevitably discriminate between employees or applicants equally or almost equally apt to achieve full recovery. Even the District Court's opinion did not rigidly specify one year as a constitutionally mandated measure of the period of treatment that guarantees full recovery from drug addiction. The uncertainties associated with the rehabilitation of heroin addicts precluded it from identifying any bright line marking the point at which the risk of regression ends. [The District Court found that methadone is an effective cure for the physical aspects of heroin addiction, and that the risk of reversion to drug or alcohol abuse declines dramatically after the first few months of treatment, but that 20 to 30 percent of patients on methadone still revert to drug use.] By contrast, the "no drugs" policy now enforced by TA is supported by the legitimate inference that as long as a treatment program (or other drug use) continues, a degree of uncertainty persists. Accordingly, an employment policy that postpones eligibility until the treatment program has been completed, rather than accepting an intermediate point on an uncertain line, is rational. It is neither unprincipled nor invidious in the sense that it implies disrespect for the excluded subclass.

At its simplest, the District Court's conclusion was that TA's rule is broader than necessary to exclude those methadone users who are not actually qualified to work for TA. We may assume not only that this conclusion is correct but also that it is probably unwise for a large employer like TA to rely on a general rule instead of individualized consideration of every job applicant. But these assumptions concern matters of personnel policy that do not implicate the principle safeguarded by the Equal Protection Clause. As the District Court recognized, the special classification created by TA's rule serves the general objectives of safety and efficiency. Moreover, the exclusionary line challenged by respondents "is not one which is directed 'against' any individual or category of persons, but rather it represents a policy choice made by that branch of Government vested with the power to make such choices." Because it does not circumscribe a class of persons characterized by some unpopular trait or affiliation, it does not create or reflect any special likelihood of bias on the part of the ruling majority. Under these circumstances, it is of no constitutional significance that the degree of rationality is not as great with respect to certain ill-defined subparts of the classification as it is with respect to the classification as a whole.

Food for Thought

Is it clear that the challenged rule—which burdens current and former drug users—does not single out a class of persons "characterized by some unpopular trait or affiliation"? Would a rule that accords different treatment to alcoholics create a classification based on an unpopular trait? What consequences would flow from a conclusion that a classification did distinguish on such a basis?

No matter how unwise it may be for TA to refuse employment to individual car cleaners, track repairmen, or bus drivers simply because they are receiving methadone treatment, the Constitution does not authorize a federal court to interfere in that policy decision. [*Reversed.*]

MR. JUSTICE WHITE, with whom MR. JUSTICE MARSHALL joins, dissenting.

The question before us is the rationality of placing successfully maintained or recently cured persons in the same category as those just attempting to escape heroin addiction or who have failed to escape it, rather than in with the general population. The asserted justification for the challenged classification is the objective of a capable and reliable work force, and thus the characteristic in question is employability. "Employability," in this regard, does not mean that any particular applicant, much less every member of a given group of applicants, will turn out to be a model worker. Nor does it mean that no such applicant will ever become or be discovered to be a malingerer, thief, alcoholic, or even heroin addict. All employers take such risks. Employability, as the District Court used it in reference to successfully maintained methadone users, means only that the employer is no more likely to find a member of that group to be an unsatisfactory employee than he would an employee chosen from the general population.

Petitioners had every opportunity, but presented nothing to negative the employability of successfully maintained methadone users as distinguished from those who were unsuccessful. * * * That 20% to 30% are unsuccessful after one year in a methadone program tells us nothing about the employability of the successful group, and it is the latter category of applicants that the District Court and the Court of Appeals held to be unconstitutionally burdened by the blanket rule disqualifying them from employment.

The District Court and the Court of Appeals were therefore fully justified in finding that petitioners could not reasonably have concluded that the protected group is less employable than the general population and that excluding it "[has] no rational relation to the demands of the jobs to be performed." * * * Justification of the blanket exclusion is not furthered by the statement that "any special rule short of total exclusion is likely to be less precise" than the current rule. If the rule were narrowed as the District Court ordered, it would operate more precisely in at least one respect, for many employable persons would no longer be excluded.

> **Take Note**
>
> Justice White compares TA's policy to the hypothetical policy that the District Court held would have satisfied scrutiny under the Equal Protection Clause. Is it clear that the District Court's proposal would have been equally effective at furthering the TA's interests in safety and efficiency? If not, how would a Court decide when a policy impermissibly burdens some class of persons? If there is at least some danger in employing successfully maintained methadone users—that is, the danger that they might regress to heroin addiction—then what weight should the Court give to that danger in the analysis?

Finally, even were the District Court wrong, and even were successfully maintained persons marginally less employable than the average applicant, the blanket exclusion of only these people, when but a few are actually unemployable and when many other groups have varying numbers of unemployable members, is arbitrary and unconstitutional. Many persons now suffer from or may again suffer from some handicap related to employability. But petitioners have singled out respondents—unlike ex-offenders, former alcoholics and mental patients, diabetics, epileptics, and those currently using tranquilizers, for example—for sacrifice to this at best ethereal and likely nonexistent risk of increased unemployability. Such an arbitrary assignment of burdens among classes that are similarly situated with respect to the proffered objectives is the type of invidious choice forbidden by the Equal Protection Clause.

POINTS FOR DISCUSSION

a. Over-Inclusiveness in Regulation

Unlike the regulation at issue in *Railway Express*, the regulation at issue in *Beazer* was challenged as *over*-inclusive. The problem was not that it failed to impose on one class of actors a burden that it imposed on others who were similarly situated, but instead that it imposed the burden on others who (at least arguably) were *not* similarly situated. The plaintiffs in *Beazer* argued that even if the government can refuse to employ drug users in certain jobs, because of the risk that their employment would pose to the public welfare, it could not refuse to hire persons undergoing methadone maintenance treatment for at least one year, because members of that class generally do not revert to illicit drug use. An over-inclusive regulation, in other words, regulates more people than necessary to accomplish the government's purpose.

Are over-inclusive regulations more problematic than under-inclusive ones? As the class of persons to whom a regulatory burden applies grows, do the protections of the political process increase or decrease?

b. The Point of Rationality Review

What is the objective of rationality review? Is it to "smoke out" classifications that were motivated by animus or prejudice against unpopular and thus politically powerless groups, as the Court implied? If so, how does the Court determine the "real" motivation for the regulation? Is the objective instead to prevent arbitrary regulation, as Justice White suggested? If so, should the Court defer to the legislature's judgment about the rationality of the regulation?

> **Make the Connection**
> We considered the Court's decision in *District of Columbia v. Heller*, 554 U.S. 570 (2008), in Volume 1.

Consider the view that Justice Scalia expressed for the Court in holding that the District of Columbia's ban on handguns violated the Second Amendment:

[R]ational-basis scrutiny is a mode of analysis we have used when evaluating laws under constitutional commands that are themselves prohibitions on irrational laws. In those cases, "rational basis" is not just the standard of scrutiny, but the very substance of the constitutional guarantee.

To which constitutional provisions was Justice Scalia referring?

c.   Burden of Persuasion

Justice White stated in his dissent that the government "presented nothing to negative the employability of successfully maintained methadone users as distinguished from those who were unsuccessful." In his view, in other words, the government bore the burden of demonstrating that its classification was valid. But the Court traditionally has placed the burden on those challenging government regulation that is subject to rationality review to demonstrate that it is not rationally related to some legitimate government interest. Who should bear the burden of persuasion in equal protection cases?

————————————

In the two chapters that follow, we will consider how the Court has addressed government classifications on a variety of bases. Some of the cases—such as those concerning discrimination on the basis of race and gender—will involve the application of heightened forms of scrutiny. Others—such as those concerning discrimination on the basis of age and wealth—involve the application of rational-basis review. As you read the cases—particularly those in the latter category—consider whether the Court has strictly adhered to the approach based on "tiers" of scrutiny, and whether the Court always applies rational-basis review in the same way that it did in the cases that we have just considered.

Executive Summary of This Chapter

The Equal Protection Clause of the Fourteenth Amendment imposes some limits on the ability of the states to engage in certain forms of discrimination. The Court has held that the Due Process Clause of the Fifth Amendment, which applies to the federal government, includes an equal protection component. *Bolling v. Sharpe* (1954). The same standards apply to evaluate state and federal action under the equal protection principle. *Buckley v. Valeo* (1976); *Adarand Constructors, Inc. v. Peña* (1995).

The Court generally reviews Equal Protection challenges to government classifications by considering the nature of the classification, the government's interest in the challenged regulation, and the relationship between the government's interest and the classification. The extent to which the Court insists on particularly weighty interests, accords deference to the government's judgment, and tolerates imperfect means to accomplish the government's ends depends upon which **level of scrutiny** the Court applies.

Under **strict scrutiny**, a law will be upheld only if it is "narrowly tailored" to advance a "compelling" government interest. *Adarand v. Peña* (1995). Under **intermediate scrutiny**, the Court will uphold a law only if it is "substantially related" to an "important" government interest. *United States v. Virginia* (1996). Under the **rational-basis test** (or **rationality review**), a law will be upheld if it is "rationally related" to a "legitimate" government interest. *New York City Transit Authority v. Beazer* (1979).

In deciding whether to apply a level of scrutiny more searching than rational-basis review, the Court sometimes considers whether the group disadvantaged by the challenged regulation is (1) a "discrete and insular" minority that is (2) the victim of societal prejudice and (3) unable to achieve adequate protection through the ordinary operation of the political process. *United States v. Carolene Products Co.* (1938).

Rational-basis review is highly deferential. When the Court applies rational-basis review, the fact that the challenged regulation is **under-inclusive**—that is, fails fully to address all manifestations of the problem that it is designed to remedy—generally will not be a sufficient basis for invalidation of the regulation. *Railway Express Agency v. New York* (1949). Similarly, the fact that a regulation is **over-inclusive**—that is, regulates more people than is arguably necessary to achieve its goal—is not generally a basis for invalidation under the rational-basis test. *New York City Transit Authority v. Beazer* (1979).

POINT-COUNTERPOINT

Was *Bolling v. Sharpe* correctly decided?

POINT: GREGORY E. MAGGS

Our Constitution contains many great features. It establishes a democratic federal government in which powers are checked and balanced. It guarantees that all of the states will have a republican form of government. It bans slavery. It protects the freedom of speech and freedom of the press. The list could go on and on.

But any fair assessment of the Constitution must acknowledge that our Constitution also contains serious flaws. It does not require Congress to create any lower federal courts. It does not say whether states can secede from the Union. While the Constitution spells out how the federal government can enter treaties, it does not specify how the government can extricate itself from them. The Seventh Amendment guarantees a right to a jury trial in any civil case in which the value in controversy exceeds $20 without any provision to adjust this figure for inflation.

Very high among the list of flaws is the following defect: The Constitution contains no provision requiring the federal government to treat all persons equally. Although the Fourteenth Amendment has an Equal Protection Clause, by its own terms, this clause applies only to the states. Nothing comparable limits the federal government. But as a matter of policy, surely the federal government should not have the power to discriminate on the basis of race or otherwise deny the equal protection of laws.

This serious defect in the Constitution could have been remedied in two ways: legitimately or illegitimately. A legitimate way of addressing the problem would have been to use the procedures specified in Article V to amend the Constitution to add a federal Equal Protection Clause. Amendments have cured other defects in the Constitution: they have guaranteed a freedom of religion, they have banned slavery, they have given women the right to vote, and so forth. A properly adopted amendment similarly could have imposed an equal protection requirement on the federal government.

The Supreme Court, however, chose to remedy the problem in an illegitimate manner. The Court simply declared by fiat that the federal government must provide equal protection. This action was wrong because nothing in the Constitution gives the Supreme Court the power to amend the Constitution to remedy the document's shortcomings. Although the Court in *Bolling* relied on precedent applying equal protection principles to the federal government through the Due Process clause, and its outcome may be justified on that ground, neither *Bolling* nor the precedent it followed is consistent with the imperfect text of the Constitution.

Some people might argue that ending racial discrimination is so important that any process to achieve that goal is warranted. In other words, in truly extreme cases, the ends can justify the means, however illegitimate the means otherwise might be. Maybe you could think of an outrageous hypothetical in which nearly everyone would concede this point. But requiring the federal government to provide Equal Protection is not controversial. The Constitution could have been amended to achieve the same result.

———————————

COUNTERPOINT: PETER J. SMITH

It is difficult to dispute that the Constitution as originally understood did not prohibit the federal government from discriminating on the basis of race; indeed, the original document expressly *precluded* Congress from banning the slave trade—a practice that actively institutionalized racial inequality—for 20 years. The original Constitution was indeed, as Professor Maggs notes, imperfect.

Was the Court's decision in *Bolling* an illegitimate attempt to remedy that serious imperfection? I believe that it was not, for three related reasons. First, the original document has been formally amended in ways that bear directly on the federal government's authority to discriminate on the basis of race. The Thirteenth Amendment applies to more than simply action by the states; it provides, categorically, that "[n]either slavery nor involuntary servitude * * * *shall exist* within the United States * * *." This language presumably would prevent Congress from enacting legislation mandating better protections for white workers than for African-American workers, and thereby replicating a system functionally equivalent to slavery. If this is true, then it is not a big leap to conclude that Congress is constrained, as a more general matter, from exercising its authority in a way that subordinates persons solely based on an arbitrary classification, such as race or national origin. And although the Fourteenth Amendment's provisions apply by their terms only to the states, their response to slavery and institutionalized discrimination can be read to embody a deeper constitutional anti-discrimination principle.

Second, even if we assume that the Reconstruction Amendments, standing alone, do not impose an equal protection principle on the federal government, it oversimplifies the nature of constitutional change—and threatens serious damage to the Constitution itself—to maintain that the only remedy for constitutional defects—including a defect so profound that it would permit our nation's government to discriminate on the basis of race—is to rely on the amendment process to cure constitutional imperfections. In practice, the amendment process is often as imperfect as the document it is designed to improve.

To see why, ask whether you think an amendment imposing the equal protection principle on the federal government would have been ratified by three-quarters of the states in 1954, when the Court decided *Bolling*. If you can think of 13 states (out of the 48 that were states at the time) that would not have ratified—because, for example, they were aggressively seeking to *preserve* segregation and institutionalized white supremacy—then you have your answer. (If you are wondering why the southern states ratified the Reconstruction Amendments, it was because they were forced to as a condition of reentry to the Union.) Then ask yourself whether you would consider our Constitution legitimate if the federal government were permitted to discriminate on the basis of race (or gender or other suspect grounds). Would you be comfortable living under a Constitution that, to take a timely example, permitted the federal government, in the name of national security, to prevent all persons of Arab descent from flying on planes or riding on trains and buses or attending sporting events?

Third, if the Court's decision in *Bolling* was wrong—because it failed properly to implement the original meaning of the Constitution, and because that meaning had never been changed pursuant to the formal amendment process—then the Court's decision in *Brown v. Board of Education of Topeka*, 347 U.S. 483 (1954), decided the same day, was almost certainly wrong, too. After all, virtually all commentators who have examined the question have concluded that the Framers of the Fourteenth Amendment did not understand it to prohibit segregated schools, and the Court in *Brown* very openly eschewed the original meaning in deciding whether segregation was constitutional.

Yet *Bolling* and *Brown* were a central reason why so many people today continue to find our Constitution a legitimate charter. I do not agree with Professor Maggs that the Court's decision in *Bolling* was wrong; but even if it was, it was a small price to pay to maintain a Constitution that we can continue to respect and admire—and, ultimately, follow.

CHAPTER 5

Status-Based Classifications

We saw in Chapter 4 how government regularly classifies on all sorts of bases, and how usually those classifications are defensible. Surely, for example, a state must be permitted to deny driver's licenses to children, or to accord different tax treatment to rich and poor people. The Court reviews such classifications solely for rationality, a highly deferential standard that largely leaves the question of line-drawing to legislative (or at least non-judicial) action.

But some classifications are more problematic. The context in which the Fourteenth Amendment was ratified, for example, makes clear—if nothing else—that classifications based on race are suspect, and accordingly must be subjected to more searching scrutiny. Classifications based on race are suspect not merely because of history; race is an immutable characteristic, and (to borrow the *Carolene Products* framework that we considered in Chapter 4) members of racial minorities historically have been the victims of societal prejudice and lacked significant electoral power. And race is rarely, if ever, a relevant characteristic for government decision-making. (Whether it is ever relevant will be the focus of our consideration of affirmative action programs later in this chapter.) We begin this chapter with a consideration of the constitutionality of government classifications on the basis of race.

Race plainly is not the only immutable characteristic that is arguably irrelevant to government decision-making. Are government decisions based on gender similarly suspect? What about decisions based on age, sexual orientation, disability, or other status-based characteristics? After our consideration of race-based classifications, we turn to these classifications. As you read the materials in this chapter, pay close attention to (1) the process by which the Court identifies classifications that trigger heightened judicial scrutiny and (2) the variety of forms of scrutiny that the Court applies to such classifications.

A. CLASSIFICATIONS BASED ON RACE AND NATIONAL ORIGIN

1.   Historical Perspective: Pre-Reconstruction

As we saw in Volume 1, slavery was a thorny issue at the Constitutional Convention. Several delegates from Northern states wanted the Constitution to prohibit it, but the Southern states sought to preserve the institution. The resulting compromise acknowledged, sometimes circumspectly and awkwardly, the institution of slavery, and in fact effectively preserved it for at least 20 years. Article I, § 2, cl. 3 treated slaves as three-fifths of a person for purposes of apportionment of Congress; Article I, § 9, cl. 1 prohibited Congress from ending the slave trade before 1808, and Article V prohibited the amendment of that provision before 1808; and Article IV, § 2, cl. 3 provided for the return of fugitive slaves. There was, of course, no equal protection clause in the original Constitution.

Laws permitting slavery—and protecting the rights of slaveholders— obviously classified, in the most invidious way, on the basis of race. It was therefore a stretch to argue that the Constitution as originally ratified and understood prohibited laws discriminating on the basis of race. The case that follows addressed the constitutional status of slaves and slavery before the Civil War. It is perhaps the Court's most infamous decision, and by most accounts it helped to precipitate the Civil War.

DRED SCOTT V. SANDFORD
60 U.S. 393 (1857)

MR. CHIEF JUSTICE TANEY delivered the opinion of the Court.

[Dred Scott, a slave owned by Dr. John Emerson, was taken from the slave state of Missouri to the free state of Illinois and later to the free territory of Wisconsin. In 1838, after Emerson married, he summoned Scott back to Missouri. Upon Emerson's death, Scott filed a diversity suit in federal court in Missouri against John Sandford, a citizen of New York and the administrator of Emerson's estate, for assault and imprisonment. Scott claimed that his residence in Illinois and later the Wisconsin territory made him a free person. In response, Sandford moved to dismiss on the ground that the court lacked jurisdiction. Sandford asserted that Scott was not a citizen, and therefore that there was no diversity of citizenship. The Supreme Court could not address the merits of Scott's claim if it did not have jurisdiction.]

The question is simply this: Can a negro, whose ancestors were imported into this country, and sold as slaves, become a member of the political community formed and brought into existence by the Constitution of the United States, and as such become entitled to all the rights, and privileges, and immunities, guarantied by that instrument to the citizen? * * * We think they are not, and that they are not included, and were not intended to be included, under the word "citizens" in the Constitution, and can therefore claim none of the rights and privileges which that instrument provides for and secures to citizens of the

Dred Scott (c. 1799–1858)
Library of Congress

United States. On the contrary, they were at that time considered as a subordinate and inferior class of beings, who had been subjugated by the dominant race, and, whether emancipated or not, yet remained subject to their authority, and had no rights or privileges but such as those who held the power and the Government might choose to grant them. * * * [N]o State can, by any act or law of its own, passed since the adoption of the Constitution, introduce a new member into the political community created by the Constitution of the United States. It cannot make him a member of this community by making him a member of its own.

[Because the Court concluded that Scott was not a "citizen" of the United States—regardless of whether he was ever a citizen of Missouri, under Missouri state laws—it held that the court lacked diversity jurisdiction. Notwithstanding the Court's conclusion that it lacked subject-matter jurisdiction over Scott's suit, it turned to the question whether Scott had become free by residing in the territories. In this inquiry, the Court addressed the constitutionality of the Missouri Compromise, which Congress had enacted in 1820 to abolish slavery in territories north of the 36° 30' latitude line, except within the boundaries of what became the state of Missouri.]

[T]he difficulty which meets us at the threshold of this part of the inquiry is, whether Congress was authorized to pass this law under any of the powers granted to it by the Constitution; for if the authority is not given by that instrument, it is the duty of this court to declare it void and inoperative, and incapable of conferring freedom upon any one who is held as a slave. * * *

Make the Connection

Many commentators regard this passage as the birth of "substantive due process," which we considered in Chapter 2. Regardless of what one thinks of modern substantive due process doctrine, does this genesis—a conclusion that Congress lacks authority to regulate slavery because slaves are "property" of which a person cannot be deprived merely by transporting the slaves into a territory—render the doctrine problematic?

[T]he rights of property are united with the rights of person, and placed on the same ground by the fifth amendment to the Constitution, which provides that no person shall be deprived of life, liberty, and property, without due process of law. And an act of Congress which deprives a citizen of the United States of his liberty or property, merely because he came himself or brought his property into a particular Territory of the United States, and who had committed no offence against the laws, could hardly be dignified with the name of due process of law.

[T]he right of property in a slave is distinctly and expressly affirmed in the Constitution. The right to traffic in it, like an ordinary article of merchandise and property, was guarantied to the citizens of the United States, in every State that might desire it, for twenty years. And the Government in express terms is pledged to protect it in all future time, if the slave escapes from his owner.

This is done in plain words—too plain to be misunderstood. And no word can be found in the Constitution which gives Congress a greater power over slave property, or which entitles property of that kind to less protection than property of any other description. The only power conferred is the power coupled with the duty of guarding and protecting the owner in his rights. Upon these considerations, it is the opinion of the court that the [Missouri Compromise] is not warranted by the Constitution, and is therefore void; and that neither Dred Scott himself, nor any of his family, were made free by being carried into [a free territory]; even if they had been carried there by the owner, with the intention of becoming a permanent resident.

FYI

The Court here is referring to Article I, § 9, cl. 1, which protected the slave trade until 1808, and Article IV, § 2, cl. 3, which provides that "No Person held to Service or Labour in one State, under the Laws thereof, escaping into another, shall, in Consequence of any Law or Regulation therein, be discharged from such Service or Labour, but shall be delivered up on Claim of the Party to whom such Service or Labour may be due." After the Civil War, the latter provision was superseded by the Thirteenth Amendment, which prohibits slavery.

[Scott also contends] that he is made free by being taken to [the] State of Illinois, independently of his residence in the territory of the United States; and being so made free, he was not again reduced to a state of slavery by being brought back to Missouri. * * * As Scott was a slave when taken into the State of Illinois by his owner, and was there held as such, and brought back in that character, his *status*, as free or slave, depended on the laws of Missouri, and not of Illinois.

[Before he had filed his federal suit, Scott had sued for freedom in Missouri state court, relying on the established principle of Missouri state law that once a slave became free by virtue of residence in a free state, he would remain free upon his return to Missouri. When his suit reached the Missouri Supreme Court in 1852, however, the Court reversed long-standing precedent, abandoned the principle of "once a free man, always a free man," and held that Scott was not a free man.]

Upon the whole, therefore, it is the judgment of this court, that it appears by the record before us that the plaintiff in error is not a citizen of Missouri, in the sense in which that word is used in the Constitution; and that the Circuit Court of the United States, for that reason, had no jurisdiction in the case, and could give no judgment in it. Its judgment for the defendant must, consequently, be reversed, and a mandate issued, directing the suit to be dismissed for want of jurisdiction.

[JUSTICE CURTIS and JUSTICE MCLEAN dissented.]

POINTS FOR DISCUSSION

a.   Judicial Review and Judicial Restraint

The *Dred Scott* case was only the second time that the Court declared a federal statute unconstitutional. (The first, of course, was *Marbury*.) The Court's conclusion that the Missouri Compromise exceeded Congress's power was particularly striking in light of the Court's prior holding that it lacked subject-matter jurisdiction over the case.

Many accounts of the decision suggest that the Court initially planned to decide the case on the ground that the Missouri Supreme Court should have the final word on the content of Missouri law—specifically, on whether, under Missouri law, a slave who had lived in a free state remained a slave in Missouri. Pressure from President-elect James Buchanan and the sense that the political branches were unable to resolve the impasse over slavery, however, led the Court to attempt to put the question beyond the realm of ordinary politics. Is such a motivation ever a legitimate basis for a particular constitutional interpretation? If so, was it a legitimate basis in *Dred Scott*?

b.   The Constitution and Slavery

As noted above, the Constitution acknowledged (and, at least for a time, explicitly preserved) the institution of slavery. Did the Constitution's recognition of slavery effectively compel the Court to conclude as it did in *Dred Scott*? Or did the Court have room—or even a moral obligation—to conclude otherwise?

c.   State Law and Slavery

The Court's decision in *Dred Scott* left Scott's fate to Missouri law, which the Missouri Supreme Court had construed a few years before, in what was widely viewed as a partisan, aggressively pro-slavery decision, to retain as slaves even those who had lived in free states and territories. In that case—*Scott v. Emerson*, 15 Mo. 576 (1852)—the Court declared:

> As to the consequences of slavery, they are much more hurtful to the master than the slave. There is no comparison between the slave in the United States and the cruel, uncivilized negro in Africa. When the condition of our slaves is contrasted with the state of their miserable race in Africa; when their civilization, intelligence and instruction in religious truths are considered, and the means now employed to restore them to the country from which they have been torn, bearing with them the blessings of civilized life, we are almost persuaded, that the introduction of slavery amongst us was, in the providence of God, who makes the evil passions of men subservient to His own glory, a means of placing that unhappy race within the pale of civilized nations.

Was the United States Supreme Court in 1857 truly bound to interpret the Constitution to indulge this sort of reasoning?

2.   Facial Discrimination Against Minorities

After the Civil War, Congress proposed, and the states ratified, the Thirteenth, Fourteenth, and Fifteenth Amendments. The Thirteenth Amendment outlawed slavery, and the first sentence of the Fourteenth Amendment, which provides that "All persons born or naturalized in the United States, and subject to the jurisdiction thereof, are citizens of the United States and the State wherein they reside," overruled *Dred Scott*.

The Equal Protection Clause of the Fourteenth Amendment—unlike Section 1 of the Fifteenth Amendment—does not refer explicitly to race; instead, it extends its protection to "any person" within the jurisdiction of the state. But whatever the scope of its application to classifications other than those based on race, there is little doubt that it imposes severe limits on the power of states to discriminate on the basis of race.

In this section, we consider state action that discriminates on its face against racial minorities. A state law or regulation discriminates on its face against racial minorities when the very terms of the provision treat members of one or more minority races differently from members of other races. Can such state action ever be justified?

STRAUDER V. WEST VIRGINIA
100 U.S. 303 (1879)

MR. JUSTICE STRONG delivered the opinion of the court.

The plaintiff in error, a colored man, was indicted for murder in the Circuit Court of Ohio County, in West Virginia, on the 20th of October, 1874, and upon trial was convicted and sentenced. [The grand and petit juries were constituted pursuant to a state law that provided: "All white male persons who are twenty-one years of age and who are citizens of this State shall be liable to serve as jurors, except as herein provided." The defendant challenged his conviction on the ground that blacks were excluded from jury service.]

It is to be observed that the [question] is not whether a colored man, when an indictment has been preferred against him, has a right to a grand or a petit jury composed in whole or in part of persons of his own race or color, but it is whether, in the composition or selection of jurors by whom he is to be indicted or tried, all persons of his race or color may be excluded by law, solely because of their race or color, so that by no possibility can any colored man sit upon the jury.

[The Fourteenth Amendment] is one of a series of constitutional provisions having a common purpose; namely, securing to a race

> **Take Note**
>
> A grand jury (which typically has around 20 jurors) is convened before criminal charges are brought against a suspect. The role of the grand jury is to determine whether there is sufficient evidence for charging a person with a crime. The petit jury (which typically has 12 jurors) is convened to hear a criminal trial. The role of the petit jury is to determine whether the government has proved any criminal charges beyond a reasonable doubt.

recently emancipated, a race that through many generations had been held in slavery, all the civil rights that the superior race enjoy. * * * The words of the amendment, it is true, are prohibitory, but they contain a necessary implication of a positive immunity, or right, most valuable to the colored race—the right to exemption from unfriendly legislation against them distinctively as colored, exemption from legal discriminations, implying inferiority in civil society, lessening the security of their enjoyment of the rights which others enjoy, and discriminations which are steps towards reducing them to the condition of a subject race.

That the West Virginia statute respecting juries—the statute that controlled the selection of the grand and petit jury in the case of the plaintiff in error—is such a discrimination ought not to be doubted. Nor would it be if the persons excluded by it were white men. If in those States where the colored people constitute a majority of the entire population a law should be enacted excluding all white men from jury service, thus denying to them the privilege of participating equally with the blacks in the administration of justice, we apprehend no one would be heard to claim that it would not be a denial to white men of the equal protection of the laws. Nor if a law should be passed excluding all naturalized Celtic Irishmen, would there by any doubt of its inconsistency with the spirit of the amendment. The very fact that colored people are singled out and expressly denied by a statute all right to participate in the administration of the law, as jurors, because of their color, though they are citizens, and may be in other respects fully qualified, is practically a brand upon them, affixed by the law, an assertion of their inferiority, and a stimulant to that race prejudice which is an impediment to securing to individuals of the race that equal justice which the law aims to secure to all others.

Make the Connection

When the Court decided *Strauder*, it had not yet held that (most of) the protections of the Bill of Rights were incorporated by the Fourteenth Amendment. Accordingly, the Court did not rely on the Sixth Amendment right to trial by jury. We considered the doctrine of incorporation in Chapter 1.

The right to a trial by jury is guaranteed to every citizen of West Virginia by the Constitution of that State, and the constitution of juries is a very essential part of the protection such a mode of trial is intended to secure. It is well known that prejudices often exist against particular classes in the community, which sway the judgment of jurors, and which, therefore, operate in some cases to deny to persons of those classes the full enjoyment of that protection which others enjoy. * * * The framers of the constitutional amendment must have known full well the existence of such prejudice and its likelihood to continue against the manumitted slaves and their race, and that knowledge was doubtless a motive that led to the amendment.

In view of these considerations, it is hard to see why the statute of West Virginia should not be regarded as discriminating against a colored man when he is put upon trial for an alleged criminal offence against the State. It is not easy to comprehend how it can be said that while every white man is entitled to a trial by a jury selected from persons of his own race or color, or, rather, selected without discrimination against his color, and a negro is not, the latter is equally protected by the law with the former. Is not protection of life and liberty against race or color prejudice, a right, a legal right, under the constitutional amendment? And how can it be maintained that compelling a colored man to submit to a trial for his life by a jury drawn from a panel from which the State has expressly excluded every man of his race, because of color alone, however well qualified in other respects, is not a denial to him of equal legal protection?

We do not say that within the limits from which it is not excluded by the amendment a State may not prescribe the qualifications of

> **Take Note**
>
> Under the Court's reasoning, it seems clear that the exclusion of black people from jury service violates the Equal Protection rights of those who are excluded. But the Court's holding is that the *defendant*'s rights under the Clause also are violated by such exclusion. What leap must the Court make to reach that conclusion? Does the Court adequately explain that leap here?

its jurors, and in so doing make discriminations. It may confine the selection to males, to freeholders, to citizens, to persons within certain ages, or to persons having educational qualifications. We do not believe the Fourteenth Amendment was ever intended to prohibit this. * * * Its aim was against discrimination because of race or color. As we have said more than once, its design was to protect an emancipated race, and to strike down all possible legal discriminations against those who belong to it.

[T]he statute of West Virginia, discriminating in the selection of jurors, as it does, against negroes because of their color, amounts to a denial of the equal protection of the laws to a colored man when he is put upon trial for an alleged offence against the State * * *. The judgment of the Supreme Court of West Virginia will be reversed, and the case remitted with instructions to reverse the judgment of the Circuit Court.

[JUSTICE FIELD's dissent, which was joined by JUSTICE CLIFFORD, is omitted.]

POINTS FOR DISCUSSION

a. Equal Protection and Juries

The law at issue in *Strauder* discriminated on its face, categorically excluding non-whites from jury service. The Court held that a state may not categorically exclude persons from jury service solely because of their race. Jury selection, however, is a complicated process that usually involves the parties to the litigation, as well. Most states permit attorneys for the parties, in both civil and criminal cases, to exclude up to a certain number of prospective jurors without having to give a reason. Laws authorizing these "peremptory challenges" do not classify on the basis of race, but they certainly could be used (by attorneys for the government or for private parties) intentionally to exclude jurors because of their race unless some restrictions are placed on their use.

The Court has held that the use of peremptory challenges purposefully to exclude jurors of a particular race violates the Constitution. *Batson v. Kentucky*, 476 U.S. 79 (1986). The Court has held, moreover, that the prohibition applies not simply to peremptory challenges by prosecutors acting for the state, but also to the discriminatory use of challenges by criminal defendants, see *Georgia v. McCollum*, 505 U.S. 42 (1992), and civil litigants, see *Edmonson v. Leesville Concrete Co., Inc.*, 500 U.S. 614 (1991). The Court has also held that the Equal Protection Clause prohibits the use of peremptory challenges purposefully to exclude women from juries. See *J.E.B. v. Alabama ex rel. T.B.*, 511 U.S. 127 (1994).

b. Original Intent and Expected Application

The Court in *Strauder* declared that the "aim" of the Fourteenth Amendment "was to protect an emancipated race, and to strike down all possible legal discriminations against those who belong to it." But the Court also suggested that the Equal Protection Clause forbids *all* discrimination on the basis of race, regardless of which race is the victim of discrimination. Does the second conclusion necessarily follow from the first? If it does, then why was it so clear to the Court that the Equal Protection Clause does not protect against discrimination on the basis of gender? As we will see later in this chapter, that view did not endure.

In Chapter 4, we saw that the Court has extended the equal protection principle to action by the federal government. The case that follows was the first case to do so, although it ultimately upheld the challenged federal action. The case arose as a challenge to the federal government's policy during World War II of internment of persons of Japanese descent, including American citizens.

KOREMATSU V. UNITED STATES
323 U.S. 214 (1944)

MR. JUSTICE BLACK delivered the opinion of the Court.

The petitioner, an American citizen of Japanese descent, was convicted in a federal district court for remaining in San Leandro, California, a "Military Area," contrary to Civilian Exclusion Order No. 34 of the Commanding General of the Western Command, U.S. Army, which directed that after May 9, 1942, all persons of Japanese ancestry should be excluded from that area. No question was raised as to petitioner's loyalty to the United States.

It should be noted, to begin with, that all legal restrictions which curtail the civil rights of a single racial group are immediately suspect. That is not to say that all such restrictions are unconstitutional. It is to say that courts must subject them to the most rigid scrutiny. Pressing public necessity may sometimes justify the existence of such restrictions; racial antagonism never can.

[W]e are unable to conclude that it was beyond the war power of Congress and the Executive to exclude those of Japanese ancestry from the West Coast war area at the time they did. [E]xclusion from a threatened area [has] a definite and close relationship to the prevention of espionage and sabotage. The military authorities, charged with the primary responsibility of defending our shores, concluded that curfew provided inadequate protection and ordered exclusion. They did so * * * in accordance with Congressional authority to the military to say who should, and who should not, remain in the threatened areas.

> **FYI**
>
> The transcript of the record in this case reveals many interesting facts. Fred Korematsu, 23 years old and living with his parents in Oakland, California, had no connection with Japan other than his lineage. When the War broke out, he tried to enlist in the Army but was rejected because of ulcers. He then went to work in the shipyards as a welder but the welders' union objected to him because of his race and he lost his job. When ordered to evacuate Oakland, he did not want to leave because he would have to part from his girlfriend (who was not of Japanese ancestry). He assumed the name Clyde Sarah and paid a plastic surgeon to make his face look less Japanese, but he was caught and charged with violating an evacuation order authorized by a recently enacted federal law. (The case did not directly raise any issue regarding internment.) In the trial court, his attorney argued—more than ten years before the Supreme Court adopted this reverse incorporation theory in *Bolling v. Sharpe*, 347 U.S. 497 (1954)—that the discriminatory evacuation order "operates to deny [him] the equal protection of the laws in violation of the Fifth Amendment of the U.S. Constitution."

> **Take Note**
>
> Justice Black prided himself on being a strict constitutional textualist. Yet he did not cite a constitutional provision to support the assertion that "*all* legal restrictions" discriminating on the basis of race, including those imposed by the federal government, are suspect. What constitutional provision renders federal decisions that discriminate on the basis of race suspect?

Like curfew, exclusion of those of Japanese origin was deemed necessary because of the presence of an unascertained number of disloyal members of the group, most of whom we have no doubt were loyal to this country. It was because we could not reject the finding of the military authorities that it was impossible to bring about an immediate segregation of the

FYI

Military officials promulgated the Order at issue here pursuant to authority delegated by the President in Executive Order 9066, which sought to prevent "espionage" and "sabotage" by authorizing military commanders to designate "military areas" from which "any or all persons" could be excluded. In addition to issuing Exclusion Order No. 34, which prohibited individuals of Japanese descent from *entering* the area, the Commanding General issued Proclamation No. 4, which prohibited the same individuals from *leaving* the area. To avoid violating these contradictory orders, persons of Japanese descent were forced to report to "Assembly Centers." Some detainees were eventually released but not allowed to return to the prohibited zones; others were shipped to "Relocation Centers," also known as internment camps.

disloyal from the loyal that we sustained [in *Hirabayashi v. United States*, 320 U.S. 81 (1943),] the validity of the curfew order as applying to the whole group. In the instant case, temporary exclusion of the entire group was rested by the military on the same ground. The judgment that exclusion of the whole group was for the same reason a military imperative answers the contention that the exclusion was in the nature of group punishment based on antagonism to those of Japanese origin. That there were members of the group who retained loyalties to Japan has been confirmed by investigations made subsequent to the exclusion. Approximately five thousand American citizens of Japanese ancestry refused to swear unqualified allegiance to the United States and to renounce allegiance to the Japanese Emperor, and several thousand evacuees requested repatriation to Japan.

[W]e are not unmindful of the hardships imposed by [the order] upon a large group of American citizens. But hardships are part of war, and war is an aggregation of hardships. All citizens alike, both in and out of uniform, feel the impact of war in greater or lesser measure. Citizenship has its responsibilities as well as its privileges, and in time of war the burden is always heavier. Compulsory exclusion of large groups of citizens from their homes, except under circumstances of direst emergency and peril, is inconsistent with our basic governmental institutions. But when under conditions of modern warfare our shores are threatened by hostile forces, the power to protect must be commensurate with the threatened danger.

We are [being] asked to pass at this time upon the whole subsequent detention program in both assembly and relocation centers * * *. Since the petitioner has not been convicted of failing to report or to remain in an assembly or

Take Note

The Court assessed the constitutionality only of the exclusion order, but declined to review the detention order. Given the Court's reasoning in upholding the exclusion order, is there reason to think that the Court would have reached a different conclusion with respect to the detention order, if confronted with it?

relocation center, we cannot in this case determine the validity of those separate provisions of the order. * * *

Some of the members of the Court are of the view that evacuation and detention in an Assembly Center were inseparable. * * * It is said that we are dealing here with the case of imprisonment of a citizen in a concentration camp solely because of his ancestry, without evidence or inquiry concerning his loyalty and good disposition towards the United States. Our task would be simple, our duty clear, were this a case involving the imprisonment of a loyal citizen in a concentration camp because of racial prejudice. Regardless of the true nature of the assembly and relocation centers—and we deem it unjustifiable to call them concentration camps with all the ugly connotations that term implies—we are dealing specifically with nothing but an exclusion order. Korematsu was not excluded from the Military Area because of hostility to him or his race. He was excluded because we are at war with the Japanese Empire, because the properly constituted military authorities feared an invasion of our West Coast and felt constrained to take proper security measures, because they decided that the military urgency of the situation demanded that all citizens of Japanese ancestry be segregated from the West Coast temporarily, and finally, because Congress, reposing its confidence in this time of war in our military leaders—as inevitably it must—determined that they should have the power to do just this. There was evidence of disloyalty on the part of some, the military authorities considered that the need for action was great, and time was short. We cannot—by availing ourselves of the calm perspective of hindsight—now say that at that time these actions were unjustified.

MR. JUSTICE FRANKFURTER, concurring.

[T]he validity of action under the war power must be judged wholly in the context of war. That action is not to be stigmatized as lawless because like action in times of peace would be lawless. To talk about a military order that expresses an allowable judgment of war needs by those entrusted with the duty of conducting war as "an unconstitutional order" is to suffuse a part of the Constitution with an atmosphere of unconstitutionality. * * * If a military order such as that under review does not transcend the means appropriate for conducting war, such action by the military is as constitutional as would be any authorized action by the Interstate Commerce Commission within the limits of the constitutional power to regulate commerce. * * * To find that the Constitution does not forbid the military measures now complained of does not carry with it approval of that which Congress and the Executive did. That is their business, not ours.

MR. JUSTICE MURPHY, dissenting.

This exclusion of "all persons of Japanese ancestry, both alien and non-alien," from the Pacific Coast area on a plea of military necessity in the absence of martial law * * * goes over "the very brink of constitutional power" and falls into the ugly abyss of racism.

In dealing with matters relating to the prosecution and progress of a war, we must accord great respect and consideration to the judgments of the military authorities who are on the scene and who have full knowledge of the military facts. * * * At the same time, however, it is essential that there be definite limits to military discretion, especially where martial law has not been declared. Individuals must not be left impoverished of their constitutional rights on a plea of military necessity that has neither substance nor support.

The judicial test of whether the Government, on a plea of military necessity, can validly deprive an individual of any of his constitutional rights is whether the deprivation is reasonably related to a public danger that is so "immediate, imminent, and impending" as not to admit of delay and not to permit the intervention of ordinary constitutional processes to alleviate the danger. [The challenged order] clearly does not meet that test.

It must be conceded that the military and naval situation in the spring of 1942 was such as to generate a very real fear of invasion of the Pacific Coast, accompanied by fears of sabotage and espionage in that area. * * * But the exclusion, either temporarily or permanently, of all persons with Japanese blood in their veins has no such reasonable relation. And that relation is lacking because the exclusion order necessarily must rely for its reasonableness upon the assumption that all persons of Japanese ancestry may have a dangerous tendency to commit sabotage and espionage and to aid our Japanese enemy in other ways. It is difficult to believe that reason, logic or experience could be marshalled in support of such an assumption.

That this forced exclusion was the result in good measure of this erroneous assumption of racial guilt rather than bona fide military necessity is evidenced by the Commanding General's Final Report on the evacuation from the Pacific Coast area[, which] refers to all individuals of Japanese descent as "subversive," as belonging to "an enemy race" whose "racial strains are undiluted," and as constituting "over 112,000 potential enemies * * * at large today" along the Pacific Coast. In support of this blanket condemnation of all persons of Japanese descent, however, no reliable evidence is cited to show that such individuals were generally disloyal, or had generally so conducted themselves in this area as to constitute a special menace to defense installations or war industries, or had otherwise by their behavior furnished reasonable ground for their exclusion as a group.

The main reasons relied upon by those responsible for the forced evacuation, therefore, [appear] to be largely an accumulation of much of the misinformation, half-truths and insinuations that for years have been directed against Japanese Americans by people with racial and economic prejudices * * *. A military judgment based upon such racial and sociological considerations is not entitled to the great weight ordinarily given the judgments based upon strictly military considerations.

No one denies, of course, that there were some disloyal persons of Japanese descent on the Pacific Coast who did all in their power to aid their ancestral land. Similar disloyal activities have been engaged in by many persons of German, Italian and even more pioneer stock in our country. But to infer that examples of individual disloyalty prove group disloyalty and justify discriminatory action against the entire group is to deny that under our system of law individual guilt is the sole basis for deprivation of rights. * * * To give constitutional sanction to that inference in this case, however well-intentioned may have been the military command on the Pacific Coast, is to adopt one of the cruelest of the rationales used by our enemies to destroy the dignity of the individual and to encourage and open the door to discriminatory actions against other minority groups in the passions of tomorrow.

FYI

At the time that the orders in question were issued, the United States was also at war with Nazi Germany, whose treatment of minority groups was well known. Is Justice Murphy's implicit comparison of the United States' internment policy to Nazi policy fair?

I dissent, therefore, from this legalization of racism. * * * All residents of this nation are kin in some way by blood or culture to a foreign land. Yet they are primarily and necessarily a part of the new and distinct civilization of the United States. They must accordingly be treated at all times as the heirs of the American experiment and as entitled to all the rights and freedoms guaranteed by the Constitution.

MR. JUSTICE JACKSON, dissenting.

Korematsu was born on our soil, of parents born in Japan. The Constitution makes him a citizen of the United States by nativity and a citizen of California by residence. No claim is made that he is not loyal to this country. There is no suggestion that apart from the matter involved here he is not law-abiding and well disposed. Korematsu, however, has been convicted of an act not commonly a crime. It consists merely of being present in the state whereof he is a citizen, near the place where he was born, and where all his life he has lived.

A citizen's presence in the locality [was] made a crime only if his parents were of Japanese birth. Had Korematsu been one of four—the others being, say, a German alien enemy, an Italian alien enemy, and a citizen of American-born ancestors, convicted of treason but out on parole—only Korematsu's presence would have violated the order. The difference between their innocence and his crime would result, not from anything he did, said, or thought, different than they, but only in that he was born of different racial stock.

Now, if any fundamental assumption underlies our system, it is that guilt is personal and not inheritable. Even if all of one's antecedents had been convicted of treason, the Constitution forbids its penalties to be visited upon him, for it provides that "no Attainder of Treason shall work Corruption of Blood, or Forfeiture except during the Life of the Person attained." Article III, § 3, cl. 2. But here is an attempt to make an otherwise innocent act a crime merely because this prisoner is the son of parents as to whom he had no choice, and belongs to a race from which there is no way to resign. If Congress in peace-time legislation should enact such a criminal law, I should suppose this Court would refuse to enforce it.

It would be impracticable and dangerous idealism to expect or insist that each specific military command in an area of probable operations will conform to conventional tests of constitutionality. When an area is so beset that it must be put under military control at all, the paramount consideration is that its measures be successful, rather than legal. * * * But if we cannot confine military expedients by the Constitution, neither would I distort the Constitution to approve all that the military may deem expedient. [I] cannot say, from any evidence before me, that the orders of General DeWitt were not reasonably expedient military precautions, nor could I say that they were. But even if they were permissible military procedures, I deny that it follows that they are constitutional. If, as the Court holds, it does follow, then we may as well say that any military order will be constitutional and have done with it.

Much is said of the danger to liberty from the Army program for deporting and detaining these citizens of Japanese extraction. But a judicial construction of the due process clause that will sustain this order is a far more subtle blow to liberty than the promulgation of the order itself. A military order, however unconstitutional, is not apt to last longer than the military emergency. Even during that period a succeeding commander may revoke it all. But once a judicial opinion rationalizes such an order to show that it conforms to the Constitution, or rather rationalizes the Constitution to show that the Constitution sanctions such an order, the Court for all time has validated the principle of racial discrimination in criminal procedure and of transplanting American citizens. The principle then lies about like a loaded weapon ready for the hand of any authority that can bring forward a plausible claim of an urgent need. Every repetition imbeds that principle more deeply in our law and thinking and expands it to new purposes. * * * A military commander may overstep the bounds of constitutionality, and it is an incident. But if we review and approve, that passing incident becomes the doctrine of the Constitution. There it has a generative power of its own, and all that it creates will be in its own image. Nothing better illustrates this danger than does the Court's opinion in this case.

I should hold that a civil court cannot be made to enforce an order which violates constitutional limitations even if it is a reasonable exercise of military authority. The courts can exercise only the judicial power, can apply only law, and must abide by the Constitution, or they cease to be civil courts and become instruments of military policy.

Of course the existence of a military power resting on force, so vagrant, so centralized, so necessarily heedless of the individual, is an inherent threat to liberty. But I would not lead people to rely on this Court for a review that seems to me wholly delusive. The military reasonableness of these orders can only be determined by military superiors. If the people ever let command of the war power fall into irresponsible and unscrupulous hands, the courts wield no power equal to its restraint. The chief restraint upon those who command the physical forces of the country, in the future as in the past, must be their responsibility to the political judgments of their contemporaries and to the moral judgments of history.

My duties as a justice as I see them do not require me to make a military judgment as to whether General DeWitt's evacuation and detention program was a reasonable military necessity. I do not suggest that the courts should have attempted to interfere with the Army in carrying out its task. But I do not think they may be asked to execute a military expedient that has no place in law under the Constitution. I would reverse the judgment and discharge the prisoner.

Take Note

Justice Jackson suggests that the Court should not "interfere" with the military in the execution of its responsibilities, but he also asserts that the Court should have reversed Korematsu's conviction. Are these positions reconcilable?

[JUSTICE ROBERTS's dissenting opinion has been omitted.]

POINTS FOR DISCUSSION

a. Understanding the Opinion

The Court stated that government discrimination on the basis of race or national origin is subject to "rigid" scrutiny. Since *Korematsu*, the Court has made clear that this level of scrutiny—now known as "strict scrutiny"—requires the government to demonstrate that the classification advances a "compelling" interest and is "narrowly tailored" to achieve the desired end—that is, could not be achieved through any less discriminatory means. Yet even assuming that the classification here advanced a compelling interest in preventing espionage and sabotage, was it narrowly tailored to achieve that end? Notice that it was both over-inclusive—in that all persons of Japanese descent were forced to relocate even though perhaps only a few were (or might have been) disloyal—and under-inclusive—because individuals not of Japanese descent who nevertheless might pose a danger (including persons of German and Italian descent) were not subject to the same harsh treatment. As Justice Murphy pointed out in his dissent, loyalty hearings and investigations could have been conducted for those of Japanese descent in the same manner as was done for those of German and Italian descent. *Korematsu* is the only case decided since the ratification of the Fourteenth Amendment in which the Court applied strict scrutiny but upheld a racial classification that facially burdened racial minorities.

Accordingly, perhaps *Korematsu* is instead best understood as an example of the Court's deference to military decisions in times of war. Does the Court have a role to play in reviewing such decisions, particularly while the war is still in progress? If so, how much deference should the Court afford military decisions during times of war? If the Court does have a role to play, but the decision at issue in *Korematsu* was within the military's discretion, is it possible to conceive of a military war-time decision that the Court would second-guess?

b. Politics, the Military, and the Court

Justice Frankfurter, who agreed with the outcome of the case, stated: "To find that the Constitution does not forbid the military measures now complained of does not carry with it approval of that which Congress and the Executive did. That is their business, not ours." Do you agree?

c. Aftermath

In 1976, President Gerald Ford formally rescinded Executive Order No. 9066. Twelve years later, President Ronald Reagan signed the Civil Liberties Act of 1988. The Act's purpose, among other things, was to "(1) acknowledge the fundamental injustice of the evacuation, relocation, and internment of United States citizens and permanent resident aliens of Japanese ancestry during World War II;" and "(2) apologize on behalf of the people of the United States for the evacuation, relocation, and internment of [Japanese Americans]." The act also provided for reparations of $20,000 for each surviving detainee. What do these actions suggest about the validity of the Court's decision in *Korematsu*?

d. Alternatives to the Military Order

Assume, hypothetically, that everything that the military authorities believed and feared was in fact true: (1) the Japanese were preparing to attack the West Coast; (2) thousands of West Coast residents of Japanese ancestry were not loyal to the United States; and (3) among these thousands might be spies who were helping Japan. Recall also that in 1941, Japan had won devastating victories against the United States at Pearl Harbor and in the Philippines, and that the United States believed that Japan had benefited from the assistance of spies. How else could the United States have addressed the situation?

e. *Korematsu* and the Law

Justice Jackson warned that the Court's decision would lie about "like a loaded weapon ready for the hand of any authority that can bring forward a plausible claim of an urgent need." But the Court's decision has been roundly criticized for many years. Is it still good law?

In *Trump v. Hawaii*, 138 S.Ct. 2392 (2018), the Court upheld an Executive Order designed to prevent the entry of persons from a list of countries. Although the order did not by its terms apply only to Muslims, the plaintiffs relied on the context surrounding the order's issuance to argue that it was designed to exclude Muslims from the United States. The Court upheld the order, concluding that it did not violate the Establishment Clause of the First Amendment, which (among other things) prohibits government actions designed to disadvantage persons on the basis of religion.

In dissent, Justice Sotomayor compared the Court's decision to the decision in *Korematsu*. The Court responded:

> Whatever rhetorical advantage the dissent may see in doing so, *Korematsu* has nothing to do with this case. The forcible relocation of U.S. citizens to concentration camps, solely and explicitly on the basis of race, is objectively unlawful and outside the scope of Presidential authority. But it is wholly inapt to liken that morally repugnant order to a facially neutral policy denying certain foreign nationals the privilege of admission. The entry suspension is an act that is well within executive authority and could have been taken by any other President—the only question is evaluating the actions of this particular President in promulgating an otherwise valid Proclamation.

The dissent's reference to *Korematsu*, however, affords this Court the opportunity to make express what is already obvious: *Korematsu* was gravely wrong the day it was decided, has been overruled in the court of history, and—to be clear—"has no place in law under the Constitution." 323 U.S., at 248 (Jackson, J., dissenting).

Was it "obvious" to you that *Korematsu* was not good law? What did the Court mean when it said that it was "overruled in the court of history"? Was *Korematsu* wrong because it stated incorrect legal standards or because it applied correct standards incorrectly? See *Bolling v. Sharpe*, 347 U.S. 497, 498 & n.3 (1954) (citing *Korematsu* and little else for the proposition that "[c]lassifications based solely upon race must be scrutinized with particular care, since they are contrary to our traditions and hence constitutionally suspect.")

3. Discriminatory Purpose and Effect

The provisions at issue in *Strauder* and *Korematsu* were facially discriminatory—that is, by their very terms they classified (and imposed burdens) on the basis of race. The Louisiana law at issue in *Strauder* excluded blacks (and other non-whites) from jury service, and the order at issue in *Korematsu* applied only to persons of Japanese descent. As *Korematsu* suggests, such facially discriminatory government actions are subject to strict scrutiny.

That is not to say, however, that laws that are facially *neutral*—that is, laws that by their terms do not classify on the basis of race—can never give rise to Equal Protection problems. Indeed, if the only constitutional requirement were that a law be neutral on its face, then legislatures could achieve discriminatory ends simply by enacting statutes that are certain to have a discriminatory effect but that do not mention race on their face at all.

Consider the case of *Gomillion v. Lightfoot*, 364 U.S. 339 (1960), which addressed a challenge to an Alabama law that redefined the boundaries of the City of Tuskegee. The statute would have altered the shape of the City from "a square to an uncouth twenty-eight-sided figure" and would

CHART SHOWING TUSKEGEE, ALABAMA, BEFORE AND AFTER ACT 140

(The entire area of the square comprised the City prior to Act 140. The irregular black-bordered figure within the square represents the post-enactment city.)

Gomillion v. Lightfoot, 364 U.S. 339, 348 (1960) (appendix to the opinion of the court)

have resulted in the removal from the city of all but four or five of its 400 African-American voters while not removing a single white voter or resident. The Court concluded that the complaint, which recited these facts, "amply allege[d] a claim of racial discrimination," even though the statute was race-neutral on its face, because the conclusion "would be irresistible, tantamount for all practical purposes to a mathematical demonstration, that the legislation [was] solely concerned with segregating white and colored voters by fencing Negro citizens out of town so as to deprive them of their pre-existing municipal vote." In other words, because the statute had a racially discriminatory purpose, it was presumptively unconstitutional under the Equal Protection Clause, even though it was race neutral on its face. The Court has since made clear that laws and regulations that are race-neutral on their face but that were motivated by a discriminatory purpose are subject to strict scrutiny and presumptively unconstitutional.

It is easier to state the rule, however, than to apply it. How does a Court decide whether a law was motivated by a discriminatory purpose? Consider *Hunter v. Underwood*, 471 U.S. 222 (1985), in which the Court invalidated a provision of the Alabama Constitution that disenfranchised all persons convicted of crimes involving "moral turpitude." The plaintiffs argued that the provision had been adopted in 1901 to disenfranchise blacks, and the Court agreed. The Court noted that the provision had disenfranchised about ten times as many blacks as whites; that at the Alabama Constitutional Convention in 1901 a "zeal for white supremacy ran rampant"; and that the crimes that qualified under the provision—including vagrancy, adultery, and wife beating—"were thought [at the time of the Convention] to be more commonly committed by blacks."

In *Hunter*, the Court did not find it difficult to ascertain the state's purpose in adopting the challenged provision. As the Court noted, the "delegates to the all-white [1901 state constitutional] convention were not secretive about their purpose." Indeed, "John B. Knox, president of the convention, stated in his opening address: 'And what is it that we want to do? Why it is within the limits imposed by the Federal Constitution, to establish white supremacy in this State.' "

In most cases, however, we can expect it to be more difficult to prove that a facially neutral law or policy was adopted for discriminatory reasons. Benign, non-discriminatory purposes can be articulated for almost any law; the legislators who voted for the law may have had widely varying motives; and in most cases, even legislators motivated by discriminatory animus are unlikely to have openly declared their actual purpose. How does a Court assess the purpose of a law when there is not a "smoking gun" as there was in *Hunter*?

Consider *Village of Arlington Heights v. Metropolitan Housing Development Corp.*, 429 U.S. 252 (1977), which addressed a decision by a predominantly white Chicago suburb to deny a request from a non-profit developer, who hoped to build townhouse units that would be accessible to low-and moderate-income tenants, to rezone property from single-family to multiple-family use. The respondents claimed that the town had denied the application for rezoning because it did not want a racially integrated housing development in the town. The Court concluded that the respondents failed to demonstrate discriminatory purpose.

The Court began by acknowledging that "[r]arely can it be said that a legislature or administrative body operating under a broad mandate made a decision motivated solely by a single concern, or even that a particular purpose was the 'dominant' or 'primary' one." The Court then made clear that a person challenging government action under the Equal Protection Clause is not required to prove that "the challenged action rested solely on racially discriminatory purposes." Instead, the Court declared, "[w]hen there is a proof that a discriminatory purpose has been a motivating factor in the decision, this judicial deference is no longer justified." The Court then explained:

> Determining whether invidious discriminatory purpose was a motivating factor demands a sensitive inquiry into such circumstantial and direct evidence of intent as may be available. The impact of the official action—whether it "bears more heavily on one race than another"—may provide an important starting point. Sometimes a clear pattern, unexplainable on grounds other than race, emerges from the effect of the state action even when the governing legislation appears neutral on its face. The evidentiary inquiry is then relatively easy. But such cases are rare. Absent a pattern as stark as that in *Gomillion* or *Yick Wo*, impact alone is not determinative, and the Court must look to other evidence.

> The historical background of the decision is one evidentiary source, particularly if it reveals a series of official actions taken for invidious purposes. The specific sequence of events leading up the challenged decision also may shed some light on the decisionmaker's purposes. * * * Departures from the normal procedural sequence also might afford evidence that improper purposes are playing a role. Substantive departures too may be relevant, particularly if the factors usually considered important by the decisionmaker strongly favor a decision contrary to the one reached. The legislative or administrative history

may be highly relevant, especially where there are contemporary statements by members of the decisionmaking body, minutes of its meetings, or reports.

The Court went on to say that even if the plaintiff offered evidence that the government was motivated at least in part by a discriminatory purpose, the plaintiff would not automatically prevail: "Such proof would [have] shifted to the Village the burden of establishing that the same decision would have resulted even had the impermissible purpose not been considered. If this were established, the complaining party in a case of this kind no longer fairly could attribute the injury complained of to improper consideration of a discriminatory purpose." This inquiry was unnecessary, however, because the Court concluded that the respondents had failed to demonstrate that a discriminatory purpose was a motivating factor in the decision.

Village of Arlington Heights essentially involved a challenge to a denial of an application for a permit. If the criteria for granting such a permit are neutral, is it possible for the denial of a permit ever to violate the Equal Protection Clause? Consider the case that follows.

YICK WO V. HOPKINS
118 U.S. 356 (1886)

MR. JUSTICE MATTHEWS delivered the opinion of the court.

[In 1880, San Francisco passed an ordinance requiring persons operating laundries in buildings not constructed either of brick or stone to petition for a permit from the Board of Supervisors. Of the 320 laundries in San Francisco when the ordinance was enacted, 310 were constructed of wood and 240 were owned and operated by persons of Chinese descent. The plaintiff in error, a Chinese immigrant who had been engaged in the laundry business for 22 years, and 200 other laundry operators of Chinese descent petitioned the Board for permission to continue operating their businesses in their wooden buildings. Their

> **FYI**
> The courts in this case mistakenly believed that the plaintiff in error's name was Yick Wo. In fact, his name was Lee Yick. Yick Wo was the name of Lee Yick's laundry business. See Gerald F. Uelman, *A Lawyer's Walking Tour of San Francisco*, 68 ABA J. 958 (1982).

petitions were denied; yet all but one of the 81 petitions of laundry operators not of Chinese descent were granted. After he was fined and imprisoned for continuing to operate his laundry without a permit, Lee Yick sought a writ of *habeas corpus* in state court.]

[The provisions of the Fourteenth Amendment] are universal in their application, to all persons within the territorial jurisdiction, without regard to any differences of race, of color, or of nationality; and the equal protection of the laws is a pledge of the protection of equal laws. * * * In the present cases, we are not obliged to reason from the probable to the actual, and pass upon the validity of the ordinances complained of, as tried merely by the opportunities which their terms afford, of unequal and unjust discrimination in their administration; for the cases present the ordinances in actual operation, and the facts shown establish an administration directed so exclusively against a particular class of persons as to warrant and require the conclusion that, whatever may have been the intent of the ordinances as adopted, they are applied by the public authorities charged with their administration, and thus representing the state itself, with a mind so unequal and oppressive as to amount to a practical denial by the state of that equal protection of the laws which is secured to the petitioners, as to all other persons, by the broad and benign provisions of the fourteenth amendment to the constitution of the United States. Though the law itself be fair on its face, and impartial in appearance, yet, if it is applied and administered by public authority with an evil eye and an unequal hand, so as practically to make unjust and illegal discriminations between persons in similar circumstances, material to their rights, the denial of equal justice is still within the prohibition of the constitution.

The present cases, as shown by the facts disclosed in the record, are within this class. It appears that both petitioners have complied with every requisite deemed by the law, or by the public officers charged with its administration, necessary for the protection of neighboring property from fire, or as a precaution

> **Take Note**
>
> The Court holds that even though the San Francisco ordinance was facially neutral, the Board violated the Equal Protection Clause by administering it in a racially discriminatory manner. Was there an argument that the ordinance was motivated by a purpose to burden laundry owners of Chinese descent, and thus was invalid on its face? Is it possible for an ordinance that is race neutral on its face to violate the Equal Protection Clause's prohibition on racially discriminatory regulation, without any showing of discriminatory application?

against injury to the public health. No reason whatever, except the will of the supervisors, is assigned why they should not be permitted to carry on, in the accustomed manner, their harmless and useful occupation, on which they depend for a livelihood; and while this consent of the supervisors is withheld from them, and from 200 others who have also petitioned, all of whom happen to be Chinese subjects, 80 others, not Chinese subjects, are permitted to carry on the same business under similar conditions. * * * No reason for [this discrimination] is shown, and the conclusion cannot be resisted that no reason for it exists except hostility to the race and nationality to which the petitioners belong, and which, in the eye of the law, is not justified. The discrimination is therefore illegal, and the public administration which enforces it is a denial of the equal protection of the laws, and a violation of the fourteenth amendment of the constitution. The imprisonment of the petitioners is therefore illegal, and they must be discharged.

POINTS FOR DISCUSSION

a. Facially Neutral Laws and Discriminatory Application

Yick Wo stands for an uncontroversial proposition: discriminatory application of an otherwise facially neutral law triggers heightened scrutiny under the Equal Protection Clause. Indeed, this must be the case if the Equal Protection Clause is to have any serious force. There is little difference in practice, after all, between a statute expressly forbidding people of Chinese descent to receive permits and a statute that purportedly makes all applicants eligible but that is administered purposefully to deny permits to all applicants of Chinese descent.

But how does one demonstrate a case of discriminatory application? Are numbers or statistics enough? In *Yick Wo*, permits had been denied to all applicants of Chinese descent but granted to all but one of the white applicants (who, incidentally, was a woman). What if half of the applicants of Chinese descent had been granted permits, whereas all but one of the white applicants had received permits? What if two-thirds of the applicants of Chinese descent had received permits, and virtually all white applicants had?

b. Discretion

The discretion conferred on the Board of Supervisors was quite broad. The California Supreme Court had concluded that the ordinance vested the Board with discretion to grant or withhold permits "with a view to the protection of the public against the dangers of fire." (The permit requirement applied only to buildings made of wood.) But the United States Supreme Court observed, in a portion of the opinion omitted above, that the ordinance "seem[s] intended to confer, and actually to confer, not a discretion to be exercised upon a consideration of the circumstances of each case, but a naked and arbitrary power to give or withhold consent, not only as to places, but as to persons * * *."

On this view, the ordinance conferred authority that was so unbridled as to raise a serious risk of arbitrary application. Putting aside the Equal Protection Clause's limitation on discriminatory exercises of discretionary authority, is there an independent constitutional defect to standardless delegations of authority at the state and local level? Might such delegations violate the Due Process Clause of the

Fourteenth Amendment? Or might they violate the Equal Protection Clause, even absent a showing of a pattern of discriminatory application, on the theory that they facilitate discrimination?

c. Scrutiny

The Court states that "no reason" is shown for the apparently discriminatory exercise of the permitting authority. What sort of reason would have justified the discrimination? Does the Court have in mind a reason that would demonstrate that the applicants' races in fact were not a basis for the determinations, or instead a reason that is so substantial that it would justify the Board's discrimination against applicants of Chinese descent?

Yick Wo confirms, among other things, that government action can be suspect even absent a law or regulation that is facially discriminatory, as long as the action was motivated by a discriminatory purpose. What is the constitutional status of laws that were *not* motivated by any discriminatory *purpose*, but that nevertheless have a demonstrable discriminatory *effect* or *impact*—that is, laws that disproportionately burden members of a particular racial group? The case that follows addresses that question.

WASHINGTON V. DAVIS
426 U.S. 229 (1976)

MR. JUSTICE WHITE delivered the opinion of the Court.

[Respondents alleged that a qualifying test administered to applicants for positions as police officers in the District of Columbia Metropolitan Police Department violated the Fifth Amendment because it excluded a disproportionately high number of African-American applicants.] [T]o be accepted by the Department and to enter an intensive 17-week training program, the police recruit was required to satisfy certain physical and character standards, to be a high school graduate or its equivalent, and to receive a grade of at least 40 out of 80 on "Test 21," which [was] "designed to test verbal ability, vocabulary, reading and comprehension."

[Respondents did not claim that the Police Department designed or administered Test 21 with any racially discriminatory purpose or intent. The Court of Appeals] declare[d] that lack of discriminatory intent in designing and administering Test 21 was irrelevant; the critical fact was rather that a far greater proportion of blacks—four times as many—failed the test than did whites. This disproportionate impact, standing alone and without regard to whether it indicated a discriminatory purpose, was held sufficient to establish a constitutional violation, absent proof by petitioners that the test was an adequate measure of job performance in addition to being an indicator of probable success in the training program, a burden which the court ruled petitioners had failed to discharge. * * * But our cases have not embraced the proposition that a law or other official act, without regard to whether it reflects a racially discriminatory purpose, is unconstitutional [s]olely because it has a racially disproportionate impact.

This is not to say that the necessary discriminatory racial purpose must be express or appear on the face of the statute, or that a law's disproportionate impact is irrelevant in cases involving Constitution-based claims of racial discrimination. A statute, otherwise neutral on its face, must not be applied so as invidiously to discriminate on the basis of race. *Yick Wo v. Hopkins*, 118 U.S. 356 (1886). * * * Necessarily, an invidious discriminatory purpose may often be inferred from the totality of the relevant facts, including the fact, if it is true, that the law bears more heavily on one race than another. * * * Nevertheless, we have not held that a law, neutral on its face and serving ends otherwise within the power of government to pursue, is invalid under the Equal Protection Clause simply because it may affect a greater proportion of one race than of another. Disproportionate impact is not irrelevant, but it is not the sole touchstone of an invidious racial discrimination forbidden by the Constitution. Standing alone, it does not trigger the rule that racial classifications are to be subjected to the strictest scrutiny and are justifiable only by the weightiest of considerations.

As an initial matter, we have difficulty understanding how a law establishing a racially neutral qualification for employment is nevertheless racially discriminatory and denies "any person . . . equal protection of the laws" simply because a greater proportion of Negroes fail to qualify than members of other racial or ethnic groups. Had respondents, along with all others who had failed Test 21, whether white or black, brought an action claiming that the test denied each of them equal protection of the laws as compared with those who had passed with high enough scores to qualify them as police recruits, it is most unlikely that their challenge would have been sustained. Test 21, which is administered generally to prospective Government employees, concededly seeks to ascertain whether those who take it have acquired a particular level of verbal skill; and it is untenable that the Constitution prevents the Government from seeking modestly to upgrade the communicative abilities of its employees rather than to be satisfied with some lower level of competence, particularly where the job requires special ability to communicate orally and in writing. Respondents, as Negroes, could no more successfully claim that the test denied them equal protection than could white applicants who also failed. The conclusion would not be different in the face of proof that more Negroes than whites had been disqualified by Test 21. That other Negroes also failed to score well would, alone, not demonstrate that respondents individually were being denied equal protection of the laws by the application of an otherwise valid qualifying test being administered to prospective police recruits.

Nor on the facts of the case before us would the disproportionate impact of Test 21 warrant the conclusion that it is a purposeful device to discriminate against Negroes and hence an infringement of the constitutional rights of respondents as well as other black applicants. As we have said, the test is neutral on its face and rationally may be said to serve a purpose the Government is constitutionally empowered to pursue. * * * A rule that a statute designed to serve neutral ends is nevertheless invalid, absent compelling justification, if in practice it benefits or burdens one race more than another would be far-reaching and would raise serious questions about, and perhaps invalidate, a whole range of tax, welfare, public service, regulatory, and licensing statutes that may be more burdensome to the poor and to the average black than to the more affluent white. * * * The judgment of the Court of Appeals accordingly is reversed.

> **Take Note**
>
> The Court concludes that the qualifying test was not designed with a discriminatory purpose, and thus declines to subject it to strict scrutiny. What is the appropriate level of scrutiny for a neutral policy that is not motivated by a discriminatory purpose?

MR. JUSTICE STEVENS, concurring.

[T]he burden of proving a prima facie case [of discriminatory purpose] may well involve differing evidentiary considerations. * * * Frequently the most probative evidence of intent will be objective evidence of what actually happened rather than evidence describing the subjective state of mind of the actor. For normally the actor is presumed to have intended the natural consequences of his deeds. This is particularly true in the case of governmental action which is frequently the product of compromise, of collective decisionmaking, and of mixed motivation. It is unrealistic, on the one hand, to require the victim of alleged discrimination to uncover the actual subjective intent of the decisionmaker or, conversely, to invalidate otherwise legitimate action simply because an improper motive affected the deliberation of a participant in the decisional process.

My point in making this observation is to suggest that the line between discriminatory purpose and discriminatory impact is not nearly as bright, and perhaps not quite as critical, as the reader of the Court's opinion might assume. I agree, of course, that a constitutional issue does not arise every time some disproportionate impact is shown. On the other hand, when the disproportion is as dramatic as in *Yick Wo v. Hopkins*, 118 U.S. 356 (1886), it really does not matter whether the standard is phrased in terms of purpose or effect. Therefore, although I accept the statement of the general rule in the Court's opinion, I am not yet prepared to indicate how that standard should be applied in the many cases which have formulated the governing standard in different language.

[JUSTICE BRENNAN and JUSTICE MARSHALL dissented from the Court's resolution of the respondents' claims under Title VII of the Civil Rights Act of 1964. They did not reach the constitutional issue.]

POINTS FOR DISCUSSION

a. Constitutional Law and Statutory Law

In *Davis*, the Court held that a facially neutral law's discriminatory effect is not alone sufficient to establish an equal protection violation. Instead, a plaintiff must also demonstrate that the law was motivated by a discriminatory purpose. In a portion of the opinion that has been omitted here, the Court addressed respondents' claims that the qualifying test violated Title VII of the Civil Rights Act of 1964. Although the Court did not find a violation of that statute, the Court has held that some employment practices that have a disproportionate and negative effect on protected minorities violate Title VII. Accordingly, although "discriminatory impact" claims against government actors are not, without more, *constitutionally* cognizable, they are sometimes cognizable under federal *statutory* law. See, e.g., *Griggs v. Duke Power Co.*, 401 U.S. 424 (1971).

> **Make the Connection**
>
> Section 5 of the Fourteenth Amendment gives Congress power to "enforce, by appropriate legislation," the substantive provisions of the Amendment. If facially neutral laws and practices that were not motivated by a discriminatory purpose do not violate Section 1 of the Fourteenth Amendment, then is Congress properly "enforc[ing]" the Fourteenth Amendment when it makes state and local actors liable for adopting such practices? We will consider Congress's authority to enforce the Reconstruction Amendments in Chapter 7.

b. Requiring Discriminatory Purpose

Consider the difficulty of proving discriminatory purpose. When the challenged policy was enacted legislatively, the problems are significant. We have already seen ways in which considering legislative history is fraught. If nothing else, as Justice Stevens observed, it is unrealistic to expect potential plaintiffs to be able to gauge the "subjective state of mind" of multiple legislative actors. When executive or administrative action is challenged, plaintiffs might be able to avoid the multiple-actor problem, but the other obstacles remain.

In light of these problems of proof, is the Court's rejection in *Davis* of discriminatory effect claims satisfying? The answer may rest on one's view about the form of equality protected by the Equal Protection Clause. Does the Equal Protection clause require the government to treat individuals equally, or does it instead require the government to ensure equal results from its actions? In any event, what if the Police Department's use of the test—and the Court's view of the test's neutrality—in fact itself reflects unconscious racial prejudice?

c. Proving Discriminatory Purpose

As we noted at the beginning of this section, the Court has held that, once a person challenging a government action demonstrates that racial discrimination was a "motivating factor" in the decision, the burden shifts to the government to prove that the "same decision would have resulted even had the impermissible purpose not been considered." *Village of Arlington Heights v. Metropolitan Housing Development Corp.*, 429 U.S. 252 (1977). If the government successfully makes that showing, then the reviewing court will conclude that the decision, for purposes of the Equal Protection Clause, was not motivated by a discriminatory purpose. That finding, in turn, means that heightened scrutiny will not apply, because the Court held in *Washington v. Davis* a discriminatory effect without a discriminatory purpose is not sufficient to trigger heightened scrutiny.

Does it make sense to validate government decisions motivated in part by a racially discriminatory purpose when the decision likely would have been the same absent the discriminatory animus? Or should the Court conclude that such government decisions are so tainted that they are constitutionally impermissible?

d. Justifying Policies with a Discriminatory Impact

Even if the discriminatory impact of the verbal skills test at issue in *Davis* did not render it subject to strict scrutiny, should the Police Department have been required to justify or explain the need for the test? What was the correlation between the test and good police work? Would it make sense to subject policies with a disparate racial impact to a level of scrutiny more searching than rational-basis review, even if not as searching as strict scrutiny?

e. Discriminatory Purpose and Discriminatory Effect

In *Davis*, the Court considered whether proof of discriminatory purpose was required in a case in which proof of discriminatory effect existed. Does that mean that proof of discriminatory purpose is sufficient, by itself, to establish an Equal Protection violation? In *Palmer v. Thompson*, 403 U.S. 217 (1971), the Court considered a decision by the City Council of Jackson, Mississippi, to close its swimming pools after a District Court ordered integration of the City's public recreational facilities. The plaintiffs contended that the decision was designed to prevent the pools from becoming integrated. The Court rejected the challenge. Justice Black, in a 5–4 opinion for the Court, stated that "no case in this Court has held that a legislative act may violate equal protection solely because of the motivations of the men who voted for it." He explained:

> [I]t is extremely difficult for a court to ascertain the motivation, or collection of different motivations, that lie behind a legislative enactment. Here, for example, petitioners have argued that the Jackson pools were closed because of ideological opposition to racial integration in swimming pools. Some evidence in the record appears to support this argument. On the other hand the courts below found that the pools were closed because the city council felt they could not be operated safely and economically on an integrated basis. There is substantial evidence in the record to support this conclusion. It is difficult or impossible for any court to determine the "sole" or "dominant" motivation behind the choices of a group of legislators. Furthermore, there is an element of futility in a judicial attempt to invalidate a law because of the bad motives of its supporters. If the law is struck down for this reason, rather than because of its facial content or effect, it would presumably be valid as soon as the legislature or relevant governing body repassed it for different reasons.
>
> It is true there is language in some of our cases interpreting the [Fourteenth Amendment] which may suggest that the motive or purpose behind a law is relevant to its constitutionality. But the focus in those cases was on the actual effect of the enactments, not upon the motivation which led the States to behave as they did. * * * Here the record indicates only that Jackson once ran segregated public swimming pools and that no public pools are now maintained by the city. Moreover, there is no evidence in this record to show that the city is now covertly aiding the maintenance and operation of pools which are private in name only. It shows no state action affecting blacks differently from whites.

Justice White, who later wrote the Court's opinion in *Davis*, dissented, asserting that the decision to close the pools was "an expression of official policy that Negroes are unfit to associate with whites." Do *Davis* and *Palmer*, when viewed together, suggest that a facially neutral policy triggers strict scrutiny only when there is proof of *both* a discriminatory purpose *and* a discriminatory effect? If so, do you agree that there was no discriminatory effect in *Palmer*?

Problem

A statistical study that examined 2,000 murder cases in Georgia in the 1970s found that defendants charged with killing white persons received the death penalty in 11% of cases, whereas defendants charged with killing black persons received the death penalty in only 1% of cases. In addition, the study found that the death penalty was assessed in 22% of cases involving black defendants and white victims; 8% of cases involving white defendants and white victims; and 1% of cases involving black defendants and black victims. Finally, the study found that prosecutors sought the death penalty in 70% of the cases involving black defendants and white victims, but only 32% of the cases involving white defendants and white victims and 15% of the cases involving black defendants and black victims. A black man sentenced to death in Georgia for killing a white police officer challenges his sentence, arguing that the death penalty was administered in a racially discriminatory manner. How should the Court rule? (These facts are drawn from *McCleskey v. Kemp*, 481 U.S. 279 (1987).)

4.   Race-Specific but Facially Symmetrical Laws

The cases that we have seen so far in this chapter have involved challenges to laws that treated one class of persons defined by race differently than they treated others. What is the constitutional status of laws that are race-conscious but that purport to impose symmetrical obligations or burdens on persons of different races? Does a law that classifies on the basis of race but that treats members of different races the "same" violate the Equal Protection Clause? Perhaps the most well-known manifestations of this type of law are those laws that required "separate but equal" facilities for whites and blacks. In the following now-infamous case, *Plessy v. Ferguson*, the Court upheld such a law.

PLESSY V. FERGUSON
163 U.S. 537 (1896)

MR. JUSTICE BROWN delivered the opinion of the Court.

This case turns upon the constitutionality of an act of the general assembly of the state of Louisiana, passed in 1890, providing for separate railway carriages for the white and colored races. The first section of the statute enacts "that all railway companies carrying passengers in their coaches in this state, shall provide equal but separate accommodations for the white, and colored races, by providing two or more passenger coaches for each passenger train, or by dividing the passenger coaches by a partition so as to secure separate accommodations * * *. No person or persons shall be permitted to occupy seats in coaches, other than the ones assigned to them, on account of the race they belong to."

The petition for the writ of prohibition averred that petitioner was seven-eighths Caucasian and one-eighth African blood; that * * * he took possession of a vacant seat in a coach where passengers of the white race were accommodated, and was ordered by the conductor to vacate said coach, and take a seat in another, assigned to persons of the colored race, and, having refused to comply with such demand, he was forcibly ejected, with the aid of a police officer, and imprisoned in the parish jail to answer a charge of having violated the above act.

The object of the [fourteenth] amendment was undoubtedly to enforce the absolute equality of the two races before the law, but, in the nature of things, it could not have been intended to abolish distinctions based upon color, or to enforce social, as distinguished from political, equality, or a commingling of the two races upon terms unsatisfactory to either. Laws permitting, and even requiring, their separation, in places where they are liable to be brought into contact, do not necessarily imply the inferiority of either race to the other, and have been generally, if not universally, recognized as within the competency of the state legislatures in the exercise of their police power. The most common instance of this is connected with the establishment of separate schools for white and colored children, which have been held to be a valid exercise of the legislative power even by courts of states where the political rights of the colored race have been longest and most earnestly enforced.

So far, then, as a conflict with the fourteenth amendment is concerned, the case reduces itself to the question whether the statute of Louisiana is a reasonable regulation, and with respect to this there must necessarily be a large discretion on the part of the legislature. [I]t is at liberty to act with reference to the established usages, customs, and traditions of the people, and with a view to the promotion of their comfort, and the preservation of the public peace and good order. Gauged by this standard, we cannot say that a law which authorizes or even requires the

> **Take Note**
>
> What level of scrutiny does the Court employ in evaluating the constitutionality of the Louisiana statute? If the test is mere reasonableness, did the Equal Protection Clause add anything to the Fourteenth Amendment, which also includes a Due Process Clause? And even assuming that standard, are you convinced that the end of preserving the "public peace and good order" is permissibly advanced by this law?

rational test

separation of the two races in public conveyances is unreasonable, or more obnoxious to the fourteenth amendment than the acts of congress requiring separate schools for colored children in the District of Columbia, the constitutionality of which does not seem to have been questioned, or the corresponding acts of state legislatures.

Food for Thought

The Court suggests here that government action cannot succeed when it challenges entrenched individual views. The same argument certainly could have been advanced in *Brown*, which follows, or in response to the Civil Rights Act of 1964, which we considered in Volume 1. As you read about *Brown* and its long aftermath, consider what it suggests about the validity of the Court's assertion here.

We consider the underlying fallacy of the plaintiff's argument to consist in the assumption that the enforced separation of the two races stamps the colored race with a badge of inferiority. If this be so, it is not by reason of anything found in the act, but solely because the colored race chooses to put that construction upon it. The argument necessarily assumes that if, as has been more than once the case, and is not unlikely to be so again, the colored race should become the dominant power in the state legislature, and should enact a law in precisely similar terms, it would thereby relegate the white race to an inferior position. We imagine that the white race, at least, would not acquiesce in this assumption. The argument also assumes that social prejudices may be overcome by legislation, and that equal rights cannot be secured to the negro except by an enforced commingling of the two races. We cannot accept this proposition. If the two races are to meet upon terms of social equality, it must be the result of natural affinities, a mutual appreciation of each other's merits, and a voluntary consent of individuals. * * * Legislation is powerless to eradicate racial instincts, or to abolish distinctions based upon physical differences. * * * If the civil and political rights of both races be equal, one cannot be inferior to the other civilly or politically. If one race be inferior to the other socially, the constitution of the United States cannot put them upon the same plane.

MR. JUSTICE HARLAN dissenting.

It was said in argument that the statute of Louisiana does not discriminate against either race, but prescribes a rule applicable alike to white and colored citizens. But this argument does not meet the difficulty. Every one knows that the statute in question had its origin in the purpose, not so much to exclude white persons from railroad cars occupied by blacks, as to exclude colored people from coaches occupied by or assigned to white persons. * * * The thing to accomplish was, under the guise of giving equal accommodation for whites and blacks, to compel the latter to keep to themselves while traveling in railroad passenger coaches. No one would be so wanting in candor as to assert the contrary. * * * If a white man and a black man choose to occupy the same public conveyance on a public highway, it is their right to do so; and no government, proceeding alone on grounds of race, can prevent it without infringing the personal liberty of each.

Make the Connection

Justice John Marshall Harlan (1833–1911) dissented not only in *Plessy*, but also in the *Civil Rights Cases*, 109 U.S. 3 (1883), which we consider in Volume 1. Harlan had been a colonel in the Union Army during the Civil War and a politician before joining the Supreme Court in 1877. While on the Court, Harlan taught constitutional law at the George Washington University for over two decades. His grandson, John Marshall Harlan II, was a Supreme Court Justice from 1955–1971.

Justice John Marshall Harlan (1833–1911)
Library of Congress

The white race deems itself to be the dominant race in this country. And so it is, in prestige, in achievements, in education, in wealth, and in power. So, I doubt not, it will continue to be for all time, if it remains true to its great heritage, and holds fast to the principles of constitutional liberty. But in view of the constitution, in the eye of the law, there is in this country no superior, dominant, ruling class of citizens. There is no caste here. Our constitution is color-blind, and neither knows nor tolerates classes among citizens. In respect of civil rights, all citizens are equal before the law. The humblest is the peer of the most powerful. The law regards man as man, and takes no account of his surroundings or of his color when his civil rights as guaranteed by the supreme law of the land are involved. It is therefore to be regretted that this high tribunal, the final expositor of the fundamental law of the land, has reached the conclusion that it is competent for a state to regulate the enjoyment by citizens of their civil rights solely upon the basis of race. In my opinion, the judgment this day rendered will, in time, prove to be quite as pernicious as the decision made by this tribunal in the *Dred Scott* Case.

> **Food for Thought**
>
> Justice Harlan asserted that the Constitution is "color-blind." Yet the Thirteenth, Fourteenth, and Fifteenth Amendments give Congress the power to enforce their substantive provisions with "appropriate" legislation. Does Justice Harlan's view mean that Congress would have been prohibited, even in the years immediately after the amendments were ratified, from mandating affirmative action for black citizens who had suffered from slavery and institutionalized racism? Does it mean that Congress is prohibited from doing so today? We will take up these questions later in this chapter and in Chapter 7.

POINTS FOR DISCUSSION

a. Separate but Equal

The Court suggested in *Plessy* that because the law was consistent with a formal notion of equality—in that on its face it imposed symmetrical burdens on people of different races—it was consistent with the Equal Protection Clause. The Court eventually repudiated this view. But even if the Court was correct that symmetrical laws are virtually by definition consistent with the Equal Protection Clause, was this law *designed* to apply—or did it *in fact* apply—equally to people of different races? Mr. Plessy, for example, was "seven-eighths Caucasian and one-eighth African blood." What does his assignment to the coach reserved for the "colored races" suggest about the operation of the statute?

b. Justice Harlan's Dissent

Justice Harlan was the lone dissenter in *Plessy*, but his opinion is regularly hailed today as visionary. He advanced a "color-blind" theory of the Equal Protection

Clause, which holds that race is never an appropriate basis for government decision-making. We will consider this view in more detail shortly, when we turn to the constitutionality of public affirmative action programs. But it is important to note that Justice Harlan's regularly revered dissent was not as pure an endorsement of the color-blind Constitution as many choose to remember.

In a portion of the opinion that was omitted above, Justice Harlan stated that "[t]here is a race so different from our own that we do not permit those belonging to it to become citizens of the United States. * * * I allude to the Chinese race." He then appeared to rely on the fact that the statute apparently permitted persons of Chinese descent to sit in the coaches reserved for whites, even though it did not permit blacks to do so, as a further ground for objecting to the statute. This was not the only time that Justice Harlan expressed this view. He joined Justice Fuller's dissent in *United States v. Wong Kim Ark*, 169 U.S. 649 (1898), an opinion that asserted that persons of Chinese descent but born in the United States did not become citizens notwithstanding the first clause of the Fourteenth Amendment. See *id.* at 731 (Fuller, J., joined by Harlan, J., dissenting) (noting the danger of "the presence within our territory of large numbers of Chinese laborers, of a distinct race and religion, remaining strangers in the land, residing apart by themselves, tenaciously adhering to the customs and usages of their own country, unfamiliar with our institutions, and apparently incapable of assimilating with our people," and arguing that "[i]t is not to be admitted that the children of persons so situated become citizens by accident of birth"). See generally Gabriel J. Chin, *The Plessy Myth: Justice Harlan and the Chinese Cases*, 82 Iowa L. Rev. 151 (1996).

Do Justice Harlan's views about persons of Chinese descent suggest a defect in the theory of the color-blind Constitution? Or only in the consistency with which Justice Harlan followed it?

BROWN V. BOARD OF EDUCATION OF TOPEKA
347 U.S. 483 (1954)

MR. CHIEF JUSTICE WARREN delivered the opinion of the Court.

These cases come to us from the States of Kansas, South Carolina, Virginia, and Delaware. [In] each of the cases, minors of the Negro race, through their legal representatives, seek the aid of the courts in obtaining admission to the public schools of their community on a nonsegregated basis. In each instance, they have been denied admission to schools attended by white children under laws requiring or permitting segregation according to race. * * * In [all the cases but one], a three-judge federal district court denied relief to the plaintiffs on the so-called "separate but equal" doctrine announced by this Court in *Plessy v. Ferguson*, 163 U.S. 537 (1896).

The plaintiffs contend that segregated public schools are not "equal" and cannot be made "equal," and that hence they are deprived of the equal protection of the laws. Because of the obvious importance of the question presented, the Court took jurisdiction. Argument was heard in the 1952 Term, and reargument was heard this Term on certain questions propounded by the Court. Reargument was largely devoted to the circumstances surrounding the adoption of the Fourteenth Amendment in 1868. It covered exhaustively consideration of the Amendment in Congress, ratification by the states, then existing practices in racial segregation, and the views of proponents and opponents of the Amendment. This discussion and our own investigation convince us that, although these sources cast some light, it is not enough to resolve the problem with which we are faced. At best, they are inconclusive. The most avid proponents of the post-War Amendments undoubtedly intended them to remove all legal distinctions among "all persons born or naturalized in the United States." Their opponents, just as certainly, were antagonistic to both the letter and the spirit of the Amendments and wished them to have the most limited effect. What others in Congress and the state legislatures had in mind cannot be determined with any degree of certainty.

An additional reason for the inconclusive nature of the Amendment's history, with respect to segregated schools, is the status of public education at that time. In the South, the movement toward free common schools, supported by general taxation, had not yet taken hold. Education of white children was largely in the hands of private groups. Education of Negroes was almost nonexistent, and practically all of the race were illiterate. In fact, any education of Negroes was forbidden by law in some states. Today, in contrast, many Negroes have achieved outstanding success in the arts and sciences as well as in the business and professional world. It is true that public school education at the time of the Amendment had advanced further in the North, but the effect of the Amendment on Northern States was generally ignored in the congressional debates. Even in the North, the conditions of public education did not approximate those existing today. The curriculum was usually rudimentary; ungraded schools were common in rural areas; the school term was but three months a year in many states; and compulsory school attendance was virtually unknown. As a consequence, it is not surprising that there should be so little in the history of the Fourteenth Amendment relating to its intended effect on public education.

In [recent cases involving challenges to segregated public education], all on the graduate school level, inequality was found in that specific benefits enjoyed by white students were denied to Negro students of the same educational qualifications. In none of these cases was it necessary to re-examine the doctrine [of "separate but equal"] to grant relief to the Negro plaintiff. * * * Here, [there] are findings below that the Negro and white schools involved have been equalized, or are being equalized, with respect to buildings, curricula, qualifications and salaries of teachers, and other "tangible" factors. Our decision, therefore, cannot turn on merely a comparison of these tangible factors in the Negro and white schools involved in each of the cases. We must look instead to the effect of segregation itself on public education.

In approaching this problem, we cannot turn the clock back to 1868 when the Amendment was adopted, or even to 1896 when *Plessy v. Ferguson* was written. We must consider public education in the light of its full development and its present place in American life throughout the Nation. Only in this way can it be determined if segregation in public schools deprives these plaintiffs of the equal protection of the laws.

Today, education is perhaps the most important function of state and local governments. Compulsory school attendance laws and the great expenditures for education both demonstrate our recognition of the importance of education to our democratic society. It is required in the performance of our most basic public responsibilities, even service in the armed forces. It is the very foundation of good citizenship. Today it is a principal instrument in awakening the child to cultural values, in preparing him for later professional training, and in helping him to adjust normally to his environment. In these days, it is doubtful that any child may reasonably be expected to succeed in life if he is denied the opportunity of an education. Such an opportunity, where the state has undertaken to provide it, is a right which must be made available to all on equal terms.

We come then to the question presented: Does segregation of children in public schools solely on the basis of race, even though the physical facilities and other "tangible" factors may be equal, deprive the children of the minority group of equal educational opportunities? We believe that it does.

In *Sweatt v. Painter*, 339 U.S. 629 (1950), in finding that a segregated law school for Negroes could not provide them equal educational opportunities, this Court relied in large part on "those qualities which are incapable of objective measurement but which make for greatness in a law school." In *McLaurin v. Oklahoma State Regents*, 339 U.S. 637 (1950), the Court, in requiring that a Negro admitted to a white graduate school be treated like all other students, again resorted to intangible considerations: "his ability to study, to engage in discussions and exchange views with other students, and, in general, to learn his profession." Such considerations apply with added force to children in grade and high schools.

To separate them from others of similar age and qualifications solely because of their race generates a feeling of inferiority as to their status in the community that may affect their hearts and minds in a way unlikely ever to be undone. The effect of this separation on their educational opportunities was well stated by a finding in the Kansas case by a court which nevertheless felt compelled to rule against the Negro plaintiffs: "Segregation of white and colored children in public schools has a detrimental effect upon the colored children. The impact is greater when it has the sanction of the law; for the policy of separating the races is usually interpreted as denoting the inferiority of the negro group. A sense of inferiority affects the motivation of a child to learn. Segregation with the sanction of law, therefore, has a tendency to [retard] the educational and mental development of Negro children and to deprive them of some of the benefits they would receive in a racial[ly] integrated school system." Whatever may have been the extent of psychological knowledge at the time of *Plessy v. Ferguson*, this finding is amply supported by modern authority.[11] Any language in *Plessy v. Ferguson* contrary to this finding is rejected.

We conclude that in the field of public education the doctrine of "separate but equal" has no place. Separate educational facilities are inherently unequal. Therefore, we hold that the plaintiffs and others similarly situated for whom the actions have been brought are, by reason of the segregation complained of, deprived of the equal protection of the laws guaranteed by the Fourteenth Amendment. * * * In order that we may have the full assistance of the parties in formulating decrees, the cases will be restored to the docket, and the parties are requested to present further argument on [the appropriate remedy].

POINTS FOR DISCUSSION

a.   Public Education and Beyond

Did the Court in *Brown* expressly overrule *Plessy v. Ferguson*? Did it at least do so to the extent that *Plessy* was read to permit segregation in public education? In this regard, note that the Court suggested that the school context presented unique concerns. Shortly after the decision in *Brown*, the Court concluded, in a series of cases decided with terse, per curiam orders, that segregation in other public facilities—

---

[11]   K. B. Clark, Effect of Prejudice and Discrimination on Personality Development (Midcentury White House Conference on Children and Youth, 1950); Witmer and Kotinsky, Personality in the Making (1952), c. VI; Deutscher and Chein, The Psychological Effects of Enforced Segregation: A Survey of Social Science Opinion, 26 J. Psychol. 259 (1948); Chein, What are the Psychological Effects of Segregation Under Conditions of Equal Facilities?, 3 Int. J. Opinion and Attitude Res. 229 (1949); Brameld, Educational Costs, in Discrimination and National Welfare (MacIver, ed., 1949), 44–48; Frazier, The Negro in the United States (1949), 674–681. And see generally Myrdal, An American Dilemma (1944).

including municipal parks, *New Orleans City Park Improvement Ass'n v. Detiege*, 358 U.S. 54 (1958), buses, *Gayle v. Browder*, 352 U.S. 903 (1956), and golf courses, *Holmes v. City of Atlanta*, 350 U.S. 879 (1955)—was unconstitutional, as well.

b. Segregation and the Federal Government

We began our consideration of Equal Protection (in Chapter 4) with the Court's decision in *Bolling v. Sharpe*, which concluded that there is an equal protection component of the Due Process Clause of the Fifth Amendment that imposes limits on the federal government in much the same way that the Equal Protection Clause of the Fourteenth Amendment limits the states. The Court decided *Bolling* on the same day that it decided *Brown*.

c. The Fourteenth Amendment and the Original Meaning

The Supreme Court originally heard arguments in *Brown* in the October 1952 term, but the Court requested briefing and further argument on the original meaning of the Fourteenth Amendment. In its opinion, the Court determined that the original meaning was "inconclusive," and then appeared explicitly to eschew an originalist approach, declaring that "[i]n approaching this problem, we cannot turn the clock back to 1868 when the Amendment was adopted."

Others, however, have endeavored to discern the original meaning of the Fourteenth Amendment with respect to the question of segregated schools. Most commentators have concluded that the Fourteenth Amendment was not originally understood to prohibit segregated public schools. These scholars have generally noted that segregation in public schools was widespread, even in most parts of the North, immediately before the ratification of the Fourteenth Amendment, see Michael J. Klarman, Brown, *Originalism, and Constitutional Theory: A Response to Professor McConnell*, 81 Va. L. Rev. 1881 (1995), and that Republicans in Congress repeatedly reassured northern voters that the Amendment would have only a small impact on their states' laws, see Earl M. Maltz, *Originalism and the Segregation Decisions—A Response to Professor McConnell*, 13 Const. Comment. 223 (1996). In addition, these commentators have noted that, contemporaneously with the ratification of the Amendment, the same Republican members of Congress who supported the Amendment provided for segregated schools in the District of Columbia. See Raoul Berger, *Government By Judiciary* 117–34 (1977). See generally Alexander Bickel, *The Original Understanding and the Segregation Decision*, 69 Harv. L. Rev. 1 (1955).

Some, however, have argued that *Brown* was in fact consistent with the original meaning. Michael McConnell, for example, has relied on statements of members of Congress during debates over proposals to abolish segregation in public schools. These efforts did not succeed, but did ultimately culminate in the enactment of the Civil Rights Act of 1875, which prohibited some forms of public discrimination, though it did not require integrated schools. Michael W. McConnell, *Originalism and the Desegregation Decisions*, 81 Va. L. Rev. 947 (1995); see also Michael W. McConnell, *Segregation and the Original Understanding: A Reply to Professor Maltz*, 13 Const. Comment. 233 (1996). Robert Bork, a former judge, Supreme Court nominee, and legal scholar, has also argued that *Brown* was consistent with the original understanding. Consider his argument below.

Perspective and Analysis

"The ratifiers [of the Fourteenth Amendment] probably assumed that segregation was consistent with equality but they were not addressing segregation. The text itself demonstrates that the equality under law was the primary goal. By 1954, when *Brown* came up for decision, it had been apparent for some time that segregation rarely if ever produced equality. * * * Since equality and segregation were mutually inconsistent, though the ratifiers did not understand that, both could not be honored."

Robert Bork, *The Tempting of America: The Political Seduction of the Law* 82 (1990).

Is Judge Bork's argument—which presumes that the Equal Protection Clause can today prohibit conduct that its ratifiers believed it would permit—consistent with your understanding of what originalism entails?

What does it mean for originalism if the Court's decision in *Brown* in fact was inconsistent with the original meaning? Does it make originalism more difficult to defend, or perhaps even illegitimate? Or does it instead reveal that the Constitution that we actually have is more difficult to defend or even illegitimate?

d.   The Court's Rationale

Although they might strike us as odious, it is not self-evident that race-conscious laws that treat people of different races the same violate the Equal Protection Clause. What was the basis of the decision in *Brown* that the doctrine of separate but equal violated the Clause? The Court was surprisingly cryptic about it.

Was the principal justification for the Court's decision the recognition that segregation, which on its face applied equally to blacks and whites, in fact was designed to *subordinate* blacks? Even if this seemed, given the historical context, the obvious objective of segregated schools in many parts of the country *in 1954*, how should the Court determine *today* which race-conscious policies are designed to subordinate? (On this theory, is affirmative action constitutionally problematic?)

Was the justification for the Court's decision the sociological evidence presented in footnote 11, which (in the Court's view) demonstrated that racial segregation of children "generates a feeling of inferiority as to [minority children's] status in the community that may affect their hearts and minds in a way unlikely ever to be undone"? Under this view, segregation was problematic because it stigmatized black children, effectively treating them as inferior. If this was the basis of the Court's decision, what would be the constitutional status of separate schools if powerful sociological evidence emerges that single-race schools—for example, all-black-male schools in urban settings—in fact advance self-esteem and increase student performance?

Was the basis of the decision the fact that segregation was the product of a distorted political system in which blacks were largely excluded, or in which they at least lacked effective electoral strength? If so, would this mean that segregation would be constitutionally permissible as long as it is a product of a political system in which all groups are fairly represented?

Was the basis of the decision the instrumental view that integration in education produces good social results, because it teaches people to get along with others who are different than they are? (Recall that the Court emphasized the "importance of education to our democratic society.") If so, is this an appropriate way to interpret the Constitution?

Was the Court's decision based on the color-blind theory of the Constitution? This, after all, had been the basis of Justice Harlan's dissent in *Plessy*. But did the Court ever explicitly endorse this view in the opinion in *Brown*?

Or was the theory simply that by 1954 common experience had shown that separate facilities were invariably unequal facilities and that a condition of "separate but equal" was all but impossible? Subject only to a few possible exceptions, the reality was that schools that the government provided for white children were always in better condition than the corresponding schools that the government provided for black children, that white restrooms were invariably better equipped than black restrooms, and so forth. In this context, did it make any sense to tell states that they could segregate, so long as they treated races equally?

As we explore the cases that follow—particularly the cases on affirmative action—consider the implications of these various views of *Brown*'s rationale.

e.   ***Brown*'s Implementation**

The Court concluded its opinion by requesting briefing on remedies for the constitutional defects of the policies in the school districts at issue, remedies that likely would soon apply to countless other districts around the country. This was quite a delicate task, as it became clear almost immediately that *Brown* would face fierce resistance in some quarters.

One year after the decision in *Brown*, the Court announced the remedy. In *Brown v. Board of Education*, 349 U.S. 294 (1955) ("*Brown II*"), the Court acknowledged that "[f]ull implementation of [*Brown*] may require solution of varied local school problems." Accordingly, the Court declared that "[s]chool authorities have the primary responsibility for elucidating, assessing, and solving these problems," but emphasized that the courts that heard the initial challenges would "have to consider whether the action of school authorities constitutes good faith implementation of the governing constitutional principles." The Court instructed the lower courts to rely on equitable principles, which are "characterized by a practical flexibility in shaping its remedies and by a facility for adjusting and reconciling public and private needs." The Court stated that courts could "properly take into account the public interest in the elimination of [obstacles to integration] in a systematic and effective manner," but emphasized that "the vitality of these constitutional principles cannot be allowed to yield simply because of disagreement with them." The Court then ordered the school districts to make a "prompt and reasonable start toward full compliance" with *Brown*. The Court acknowledged the complexity of the task, but directed the lower courts to issue decrees "as are necessary and proper to admit to public schools on a racially nondiscriminatory basis with all deliberate speed the parties to these cases."

Make the Connection

Judicially supervised desegregation efforts often met massive resistance, particularly in the South. We considered the implications of such resistance in Volume 1, when we discussed the Court's decision in *Cooper v. Aaron*.

The process of desegregation was a slow one. Some school districts did not adopt aggressive reforms to eliminate segregated schools, such as those that implemented "freedom of choice plans," which did not consolidate the formerly separate schools but permitted students to choose which school to attend. The Court held in *Green v. County School Board*, 391 U.S. 430 (1968), that such an approach failed to comply with *Brown II* in a district in which no white children had chosen to attend the schools formerly reserved for blacks and almost all of the district's black students remained in an all-black school. Other school districts eliminated *de jure* segregation—that is, segregation by law or official policy—but nevertheless retained schools that were segregated in fact, because school assignments were done by place of residence, and most neighborhoods remained segregated. The Court has made clear that "the Constitution is not violated by racial imbalance in the schools, without more," *Milliken v. Bradley*, 433 U.S. 267, 280, n. 14 (1977), but often it is difficult to tell whether the cause of segregation is official policy or instead simply *de facto* residential segregation.

In *Swann v. Charlotte-Mecklenburg Board of Education*, 402 U.S. 1 (1971), the Court unanimously affirmed a district court order requiring a large, urban school system in the South to redraw its district lines and bus elementary school students to schools not in their immediate neighborhoods in order to achieve a "unitary"—that is, formally de-segregated—school district. The Court accepted, at least in school systems with a history of *de jure* segregation, "a presumption against schools that are substantially disproportionate in their racial composition," and it declared that courts had the authority to use "frank—and sometimes drastic—gerrymandering of school districts and attendance zones" and to use busing plans.

The Court has, however, imposed some limits on district court discretion in overseeing the process of desegregation. Inter-district remedies—that is, remedies that apply both to districts that were segregated *de jure* and surrounding districts, such as a city and its suburban areas—are inappropriate "absent an inter-district violation." *Milliken v. Bradley*, 418 U.S. 717 (1974). District courts generally cannot order a district to raise taxes to finance a desegregation plan. *Missouri v. Jenkins*, 495 U.S. 33 (1990).

We will return to this line of cases later in this chapter, when we consider the Court's decision in *Parents Involved in Community Schools v. Seattle School Dist. No. 1*. In your view, has the promise of *Brown* yet been fulfilled?

LOVING V. VIRGINIA
388 U.S. 1 (1967)

MR. CHIEF JUSTICE WARREN delivered the opinion of the Court.

[This case involved a challenge to a Virginia law that prohibited marriages between a "white person and a colored person." More detailed facts are recited in Chapter 2, where we considered the part of the opinion in which the Court relied on the Due Process Clause.]

In upholding the constitutionality of these provisions in the decision below, the Supreme Court of Appeals of Virginia [relied on its earlier decisions holding that] the State's legitimate purposes were "to preserve the racial integrity of its citizens," and to prevent "the corruption of blood," "a mongrel breed of citizens," and "the obliteration of racial pride," obviously an endorsement of the doctrine of White Supremacy.

[T]he State argues that the meaning of the Equal Protection Clause, as illuminated by the statements of the Framers, is only that state penal laws containing an interracial element as part of the definition of the offense must apply equally to whites and Negroes in the sense that members of each race are punished to the same degree. Thus, the State contends that, because its miscegenation statutes punish equally both the white and the Negro participants in an interracial marriage, these statutes, despite their reliance on racial classifications do not constitute an invidious discrimination based upon race. The second argument advanced by the State assumes the validity of its equal application theory. The argument is that, if the Equal Protection Clause does not outlaw miscegenation statutes because of their reliance on racial classifications, the question of constitutionality would thus become whether there was any rational basis for a State to treat interracial marriages differently from other marriages. On this question, the State argues, the scientific evidence is substantially in doubt and, consequently, this Court should defer to the wisdom of the state legislature in adopting its policy of discouraging interracial marriages.

Because we reject the notion that the mere "equal application" of a statute containing racial classifications is enough to remove the classifications from the Fourteenth Amendment's proscription of all invidious racial discriminations, we do not accept the State's contention that these statutes should be upheld if there is any possible basis for concluding that they serve a rational purpose. * * * [W]e deal [here] with statutes containing racial classifications, and the fact of equal application does not immunize the statute from the very heavy burden of justification which the Fourteenth Amendment has traditionally required of state statutes drawn according to race.

The State argues that statements in the Thirty-ninth Congress about the time of the passage of the Fourteenth Amendment indicate that the Framers did not intend the Amendment to make unconstitutional state miscegenation laws. Many of the statements alluded to by the State concern the debates over the Freedmen's Bureau Bill, which President Johnson vetoed, and the Civil Rights Act of 1866, 14 Stat. 27, enacted over his veto. While these statements have some relevance to the intention of Congress in submitting the Fourteenth Amendment, it must be understood that they pertained to the passage of specific statutes and not to the broader, organic purpose of a constitutional amendment. As for the various statements directly concerning the Fourteenth Amendment, we have said in connection with a related problem, that although these historical sources "cast some light" they are not sufficient to resolve the problem; "at best, they are inconclusive." *Brown v. Board of Education of Topeka*, 347 U.S. 483, 489 (1954). See also *Strauder v. State of West Virginia*, 100 U.S. 303, 310 (1880).

> **Food for Thought**
>
> Is the Court's point here that the original meaning of the Fourteenth Amendment governs, but that the meaning is elusive with respect to this question? Or that the original meaning of the Amendment simply does not govern here?

[T]he Equal Protection Clause requires the consideration of whether the classifications drawn by any statute constitute an arbitrary and invidious discrimination. The clear and central purpose of the Fourteenth Amendment was to eliminate all official state sources of invidious racial discrimination in the States. *Slaughter-House Cases*, 16 Wall. 36, 71 (1873); *Strauder v. State of West Virginia*, 100 U.S. 303, 307–308 (1880); *Ex parte Virginia*, 100 U.S. 339, 344–345 (1880); *Shelley v. Kraemer*, 334 U.S. 1 (1948); *Burton v. Wilmington Parking Authority*, 365 U.S. 715 (1961). There can be no question but that Virginia's miscegenation statutes rest solely upon distinctions drawn according to race. The statutes proscribe generally accepted conduct if engaged in by members of different races. Over the years, this Court has consistently repudiated "[d]istinctions between citizens solely because of their ancestry" as being "odious to a free people whose institutions are founded upon the doctrine of equality." *Hirabayashi v. United States*, 320 U.S. 81, 100 (1943). At the very least, the Equal Protection Clause demands that racial classifications, especially suspect in criminal statutes, be subjected to the "most rigid scrutiny," *Korematsu v. United States*, 323 U.S. 214, 216 (1944), and, if they are ever to be upheld, they must be shown to be necessary to the accomplishment of some permissible state objective, independent of the racial discrimination which it was the object of the Fourteenth Amendment to eliminate.

There is patently no legitimate overriding purpose independent of invidious racial discrimination which justifies this classification. The fact that Virginia prohibits only interracial marriages involving white persons demonstrates that the racial classifications must stand on their own justification, as measures designed to maintain White Supremacy.[11] We have consistently denied the constitutionality of measures which restrict the rights of citizens on account of race. There can be no doubt that restricting the freedom to marry solely because of racial classifications violates the central meaning of the Equal Protection Clause.

MR. JUSTICE STEWART, concurring.

I have previously expressed the belief that "it is simply not possible for a state law to be valid under our Constitution which makes the criminality of an act depend upon the race of the actor." *McLaughlin v. State of Florida*, 379 U.S. 184, 198

---

[11] Appellants point out that the State's concern in these statutes, as expressed in the words of the 1924 Act's title, "An Act to Preserve Racial Integrity," extends only to the integrity of the white race. While Virginia prohibits whites from marrying any nonwhite (subject to the exception for the descendants of Pocahontas), Negroes, Orientals, and any other racial class may intermarry without statutory interference. Appellants contend that this distinction renders Virginia's miscegenation statutes arbitrary and unreasonable even assuming the constitutional validity of an official purpose to preserve "racial integrity." We need not reach this contention because we find the racial classifications in these statutes repugnant to the Fourteenth Amendment, even assuming an even-handed state purpose to protect the "integrity" of all races.

(1964) (concurring opinion). Because I adhere to that belief, I concur in the judgment of the Court.

POINTS FOR DISCUSSION

a.   Theory of Equality

Why exactly did Virginia's ban on inter-racial marriages violate the Equal Protection Clause? Notice that the statute prevented white people from marrying black people, just as it prevented black people from marrying white people. If the Equal Protection Clause requires equality of treatment, rather than equality of result—which seemed to be the view of the Court in *Davis*, above—then why aren't laws that impose equal burdens on persons of different races constitutional? Does *Brown* provide the answer?

Was the problem with the statute at issue in *Loving* that it did not in fact impose such equal burdens? Consider footnote 11 to the Court's opinion, which seems to make clear that the statute in fact did not apply equally to persons of different races. Why didn't the Court simply rely on this ground to invalidate the statute? If it had, would it have in effect been suggesting that a more carefully drawn, but still race-conscious, statute that prohibited all inter-racial marriages would be permissible?

Is the point that all regulation that consciously distinguishes on the basis of race is constitutionally suspect, even if the law does not "burden" one race any more than it burdens any other race? Or was the Court's theory instead that the statute was so clearly designed to advance the cause of "white supremacy" that its purpose was therefore to *discriminate* on the basis of race? Or instead was the theory simply that, under the Equal Protection Clause, it is not enough for the government to treat *races* equally, but instead the government must also treat *persons* equally? If the law says that a white person may marry a white person but that a black person may not marry a white person, is the black person being treated equally? What view does the text of the Equal Protection Clause support?

b.   Marriage and Race

In *Palmore v. Sidoti*, 466 U.S. 429 (1984), the Court held that a state court violated the Equal Protection Clause when it denied custody of a child to the mother because the mother, who was white, had married an African-American man. The state court had reasoned that the child would face stigmatization at school because she lived in a "racially mixed household." The Supreme Court acknowledged that it "would ignore reality to suggest that racial and ethnic prejudices do not exist or that all manifestations of those prejudices have been eliminated." But even if "[p]rivate biases [are] outside the reach of the law, [the] law cannot, directly or indirectly, give them effect." The Court concluded that the "effects of racial prejudice, however real, cannot justify a racial classification removing an infant child from the custody of its natural mother found to be an appropriate person to have such custody."

c.   Are   Race-Conscious   but   Facially   Symmetrical   Policies   Ever Constitutional?

In *Johnson v. California*, 543 U.S. 499 (2005), the Court considered an unwritten policy that the California Department of Corrections (CDC) followed of assigning new inmates who had been transferred from another correctional facility to double cells, for a period of up to 60 days, based on the inmates' race. The CDC admitted that the chances of an inmate being assigned a cellmate of another race during this 60-day period were "pretty close to zero percent." At the end of the 60-day period, inmates were assigned to cells without consideration of race. The state defended the policy on the ground that it was necessary to prevent violence caused by racial gangs; the state argued that the 60-day period of segregation enabled prison officials to determine whether new inmates posed a danger to others. The state argued that the policy should not be subject to strict scrutiny because it "neither benefit[ed] nor burden[ed] one group or individual more than any other group or individual," and thus did not have a discriminatory effect on persons of any particular race. The Court disagreed, holding that the policy was subject to strict scrutiny, although the Court did not decide whether the policy survived that level of scrutiny. Does the Court's decision in *Johnson* mean that race-conscious policies that are not motivated by a discriminatory purpose and that do not have a racially discriminatory effect are nevertheless always suspect?

5.   Affirmative Action

The Court in *Loving* stated that the Equal Protection Clause forbids all "*invidious* racial discriminations" (emphasis added). Are there laws or government policies that classify on the basis of race but that are not invidious? This question has had significant salience for at least the last several decades for the debate over race-based affirmative action. Affirmative action programs typically seek to give preference, in school admissions, hiring, or similar decisions, to members of certain disadvantaged or historically under-represented minority groups. Are such programs unconstitutional because they distribute benefits and burdens on the basis of race? Or is there a fundamental difference between policies that seek to exclude and those that seek to include—or, as Justice Stevens once put it, between "a 'No Trespassing' sign and a welcome mat"? *Adarand Constructors, Inc. v. Peña*, 515 U.S. 200, 245 (1995) (Stevens, J., dissenting). If the answer to these questions comes from the Court's decision in *Brown*—which, after all, many view as the paradigmatic statement of the Equal Protection Clause's commitment to racial equality—then which of the rationales that we discussed above for *Brown* should provide that answer?

———————————

In 1978, the Court held in *Regents of the University of California v. Bakke*, 438 U.S. 265 (1978), that a university may constitutionally consider race as one factor in its admissions process. The medical school at the University of California at Davis reserved 16 out of the 100 slots in each incoming class for disadvantaged members of certain minority groups. Allan Bakke, a white male, sued the university after he was rejected twice for admission, even though minorities with lower scores had been granted admission. The Court issued a fractured opinion. Justice Stevens, joined by Chief Justice Burger and Justices Stewart and Rehnquist, asserted that the set-aside system violated Title VI of the Civil Rights Act of 1964, which prohibits discrimination on the basis of race by institutions receiving federal funds; because of this conclusion, they did not reach the constitutional question. They would have affirmed an injunction preventing the University from considering race in admissions. Justice Brennan, joined by Justices White, Marshall, and Blackmun, found no statutory violation and urged the application of intermediate scrutiny for racial classifications that benefit minorities; under this standard, the four Justices would have upheld the affirmative action program. Finally, Justice Powell, who wrote only for himself but cast the deciding vote, concluded that strict scrutiny should apply, and that under that standard a quota system is unconstitutional. But he also declared that a public university may permissibly consider race as one factor in admissions in order to achieve a diverse student body. Justice Powell stated:

> Petitioner urges us to [hold] that discrimination against members of the white "majority" cannot be suspect if its purpose can be characterized as "benign." [But] the difficulties entailed in varying the level of judicial review according to a perceived "preferred" status of a particular racial or ethnic minority are intractable. [T]he white "majority" itself is composed of various minority groups, most of which can lay claim to a history of prior discrimination at the hands of the State and private individuals. * * * Moreover, there are serious problems of justice connected with the idea of preference itself. First, it may not always be clear that a so-called preference is in fact benign. * * * Second, preferential programs may only reinforce common stereotypes holding that certain groups are unable to achieve success without special protection based on a factor having no relationship to individual worth. Third, there is a measure of inequity in forcing innocent persons in

respondent's position to bear the burdens of redressing grievances not of their making. * * * When [classifications] touch upon an individual's race or ethnic background, he is entitled to a judicial determination that the burden he is asked to bear on that basis is precisely tailored to serve a compelling governmental interest.

The State certainly has a legitimate and substantial interest in ameliorating, or eliminating where feasible, the disabling effects of identified discrimination. [But the goal of redressing] specific instances of racial discrimination [is] far more focused than the remedying of the effects of "societal discrimination," an amorphous concept of injury that may be ageless in its reach into the past. We have never approved a classification that aids persons perceived as members of relatively victimized groups at the expense of other innocent individuals in the absence of judicial, legislative, or administrative findings of constitutional or statutory violations. * * * Without such findings of constitutional or statutory violations, it cannot be said that the government has any greater interest in helping one individual than in refraining from harming another.

[The attainment of a diverse student body] clearly is a constitutionally permissible goal for an institution of higher education. * * * As the interest of diversity is compelling in the context of a university's admissions program, the question remains whether the program's racial classification is necessary to promote this interest. * * * [P]etitioner's argument that [the set-aside program] is the only effective means of serving the interest of diversity is seriously flawed. * * * The diversity that furthers a compelling state interest encompasses a far broader array of qualifications and characteristics of which racial or ethnic origin is but a single though important element. Petitioner's special admissions program, focused *solely* on ethnic diversity, would hinder rather than further attainment of genuine diversity.

The experience of other university admissions programs, which take race into account in achieving [educational diversity], demonstrates that the assignment of a fixed number of places to a minority group is not a necessary means toward that end. [Justice Powell cited Harvard College's policy, under which the race of an otherwise qualified applicant] "may tip the balance in his favor just as geographic origin or a life spent on a farm may tip the balance in other candidates' cases." In such an admissions program, race or ethnic background may be deemed a "plus" in a particular applicant's file, yet it does not insulate the individual from comparison with all other candidates for the available seats. * * * This kind of program treats each applicant as an individual in the admissions process. * * * [Whereas a] facial intent to discriminate [is] evident in petitioner's preference program, [no] such facial infirmity exists in an admissions program where race or ethnic background is simply one element—to be weighed fairly against other elements—in the selection process. * * * And a court would not assume that a university, professing to employ a facially nondiscriminatory admissions policy, would operate it as a cover for the functional equivalent of a quota system.

Justice Powell's views were particularly important because he provided the fifth vote to invalidate the petitioner's admissions policy and the fifth vote for the view that universities can use race as a factor in the admissions process (and thus for dissolving the injunction precluding the University from considering race in admissions decisions).

In the years after *Bakke*, the Court continued to struggle with the constitutional status of affirmative action programs, unable to produce a majority for any one approach. The Court finally found five votes for one approach in the case that follows.

CITY OF RICHMOND V. J. A. CROSON CO.
488 U.S. 469 (1989)

JUSTICE O'CONNOR announced the judgment of the Court and delivered the opinion of the Court with respect to Parts I, III-B, and IV, an opinion with respect to Part II, in which THE CHIEF JUSTICE and JUSTICE WHITE join, and an opinion with respect to Parts III-A and V, in which THE CHIEF JUSTICE, JUSTICE WHITE, and JUSTICE KENNEDY join.

I

On April 11, 1983, the Richmond City Council adopted the Minority Business Utilization Plan (the Plan). The Plan required prime contractors to whom the city awarded construction contracts to subcontract at least 30% of the dollar amount of the contract to one or more Minority Business Enterprises (MBE's). * * * The Plan defined an MBE as "[a] business at least fifty-one (51) percent of which is owned and controlled [by] minority group members," [who in turn were] defined as "[c]itizens of the United States who are Blacks, Spanish-speaking, Orientals, Indians, Eskimos, or Aleuts." * * * The Plan authorized the Director of the Department of General Services [to] "allow waivers in those individual situations where a contractor can prove to the satisfaction of the director that the requirements herein cannot be achieved."

Proponents of the set-aside provision relied on a study which indicated that, while the general population of Richmond was 50% black, only 0.67% of the city's prime construction contracts had been awarded to minority businesses in the 5-year period from 1978 to 1983. * * * There was no direct evidence of race discrimination on the part of the city in letting contracts or any evidence that the city's prime contractors had discriminated against minority-owned subcontractors.

[Respondent Croson, a mechanical plumbing and heating contractor, submitted a bid to install plumbing fixtures at the city jail. Although the city initially accepted Croson's bid, the company was unable to find MBE subcontractors that would work on the job for a price that respondent considered appropriate.] The city denied both Croson's request for a waiver and its suggestion that the contract price be raised. The city informed Croson that it had decided to rebid the project. [Croson filed suit arguing that the Richmond ordinance was unconstitutional.]

II

In [*Fullilove v. Klutznick,* 448 U.S. 448 (1980)], we upheld [a] minority set-aside [that Congress had created for certain contracts with the federal government]. The principal opinion in *Fullilove* [did] not employ "strict scrutiny" or any other traditional standard of equal

> **Make the Connection**
>
> We will consider the scope of Congress's power to enforce the Fourteenth Amendment in Chapter 7.

protection review. [Instead, relying on Congress's remedial powers under Section 5 of the Fourteenth Amendment, the principal opinion concluded that the limited use of racial and ethnic criteria was a permissible means for Congress to carry out its objectives.]

That Congress may identify and redress the effects of society-wide discrimination does not mean that, *a fortiori,* the States and their political subdivisions are free to decide that such remedies are appropriate. Section 1 of the Fourteenth Amendment is an explicit *constraint* on state power, and the States must undertake any remedial efforts in accordance with that provision. [T]he Framers of the Fourteenth Amendment [desired] to place clear limits on the States' use of race as a criterion for legislative action, and to have the federal courts enforce those limitations.

III

A

The Richmond Plan denies certain citizens the opportunity to compete for a fixed percentage of public contracts based solely upon their race. To whatever racial group these citizens belong, their "personal rights" to be treated with equal dignity and respect are implicated by a rigid rule erecting race as the sole criterion in an aspect of public decisionmaking. Absent searching judicial inquiry into the justification for such race-based measures, there is simply no way of determining what classifications are "benign" or "remedial" and what classifications are in fact motivated by illegitimate notions of racial inferiority or simple racial politics. * * * Classifications based on race carry a danger of stigmatic harm. Unless they are strictly reserved for remedial settings, they may in fact promote notions of racial inferiority and lead to a politics of racial hostility. [T]he standard of review under the Equal Protection Clause is not dependent on the race of those burdened or benefited by a particular classification.

In this case, blacks constitute approximately 50% of the population of the city of Richmond. Five of the nine seats on the city council are held by blacks. The concern that a political majority will more easily act to the disadvantage of a minority based on unwarranted assumptions or incomplete facts would seem to militate for, not against, the application of heightened judicial scrutiny in this case.

B

While there is no doubt that the sorry history of both private and public discrimination in this country has contributed to a lack of opportunities for black entrepreneurs, this observation, standing alone, cannot justify a rigid racial quota in the awarding of public contracts in Richmond, Virginia. [An] amorphous claim that there has been past discrimination in a particular industry cannot justify the use of an unyielding racial quota. * * * While the States and their subdivisions may take remedial action when they possess evidence that their own spending practices are exacerbating a pattern of prior discrimination, they must identify that discrimination, public or private, with some specificity before they may use race-conscious relief.

[None] of the evidence presented by the city points to any identified discrimination in the Richmond construction industry. We, therefore, hold that the city has failed to demonstrate a compelling interest in apportioning public contracting opportunities on the basis of race. To accept Richmond's claim that past societal discrimination alone can serve as the basis for rigid racial preferences would be to open the door to competing claims for "remedial relief" for every disadvantaged group. The dream of a Nation of equal citizens in a society where race is irrelevant to personal opportunity and achievement would be lost in a mosaic of shifting preferences based on inherently unmeasurable claims of past wrongs. * * * We think such a result would be contrary to both the letter and spirit of a constitutional provision whose central command is equality.

IV

[I]t is almost impossible to assess whether the Richmond Plan is narrowly tailored to remedy prior discrimination since it is not linked to identified discrimination in any way. We limit ourselves to two observations in this regard. First, there does not appear to have been any consideration of the use of race-neutral means [such as a program of city financing for small firms] to increase minority business participation in city contracting. Second, the 30% quota cannot be said to be narrowly tailored to any goal, except perhaps outright racial balancing. It rests upon the "completely unrealistic" assumption that minorities will choose a particular trade in lockstep proportion to their representation in the local population. * * * Under Richmond's scheme, a successful black, Hispanic, or Oriental entrepreneur from anywhere in the country enjoys an absolute preference over other citizens based solely on their race. We think it obvious that such a program is not narrowly tailored to remedy the effects of prior discrimination.

V

Nothing we say today precludes a state or local entity from taking action to rectify the effects of identified discrimination within its jurisdiction. If the city of Richmond had evidence before it that nonminority contractors were systematically excluding minority businesses from subcontracting opportunities it could take action to end the discriminatory exclusion. Where there is a significant statistical disparity between the number of qualified minority contractors willing and able to perform a particular service and the number of such contractors actually engaged by the locality or the locality's prime contractors, an inference of discriminatory exclusion could arise. Under such circumstances, the city could act to dismantle the closed business system by taking appropriate measures against those who discriminate on the basis of race or other illegitimate criteria. In the extreme case, some form of narrowly tailored racial preference might be necessary to break down patterns of deliberate exclusion.

JUSTICE STEVENS, concurring in part and concurring in the judgment.

I [do] not agree with the premise that seems to underlie today's decision, [that] a governmental decision that rests on a racial classification is never permissible except as a remedy for a past wrong. [I]nstead of engaging in a debate over the proper standard of review to apply in affirmative-action litigation, I believe it is more constructive to try to identify the characteristics of the advantaged and disadvantaged classes that may justify their disparate treatment. In this case that approach convinces me that, instead of carefully identifying the characteristics of the two classes of contractors that are respectively favored and disfavored by its ordinance, the Richmond City Council has merely engaged in the type of stereotypical analysis that is a hallmark of violations of the Equal Protection Clause. Whether we look at the class of persons benefited by the ordinance or at the disadvantaged class, the same conclusion emerges.

JUSTICE SCALIA, concurring in the judgment.

I do not agree [with] Justice O'CONNOR's dictum suggesting that, despite the Fourteenth Amendment, state and local governments may in some circumstances discriminate on the basis of race in order (in a broad sense) "to ameliorate the effects of past discrimination." * * * It is plainly true that in our society blacks have suffered discrimination immeasurably greater than any directed at other racial groups. But those who believe that racial preferences can help to "even the score" display, and reinforce, a manner of thinking by race that was the source of the injustice and that will, if it endures within our society, be the source of more injustice still. * * * Racial preferences appear to "even the score" (in some small degree) only if one embraces the proposition that our society is appropriately viewed as divided into races, making it right that an injustice rendered in the past to a black man should be compensated for by discriminating against a white. Nothing is worth that embrace.

[JUSTICE KENNEDY's opinion concurring in part and concurring in the judgment is omitted.]

JUSTICE MARSHALL, with whom JUSTICE BRENNAN and JUSTICE BLACKMUN join, dissenting.

It is a welcome symbol of racial progress when the former capital of the Confederacy acts forthrightly to confront the effects of racial discrimination in its midst. * * * Richmond has two powerful interests in setting aside a portion of public contracting funds for minority-owned enterprises. The first is the city's interest in eradicating the effects of past racial discrimination. [The second] interest is the prospective one of preventing the city's own spending decisions from reinforcing and perpetuating the exclusionary effects of past discrimination. * * * The more government bestows its rewards on those persons or businesses that were positioned to thrive during a period of private racial discrimination, the tighter the deadhand grip of prior discrimination becomes on the present and future.

In my judgment, Richmond's set-aside plan [is] substantially related to the interests it seeks to serve in remedying past discrimination and in ensuring that municipal contract procurement does not perpetuate that discrimination. [The plan] is limited to five years in duration, [contains] a waiver provision freeing from its subcontracting requirements those nonminority firms that demonstrate that they cannot comply with its provisions[, and affects only] 3% of overall Richmond area contracting.

A profound difference separates governmental actions that themselves are racist, and governmental actions that seek to remedy the effects of prior racism or to prevent neutral governmental activity from perpetuating the effects of such racism. * * * Racial classifications "drawn on the presumption that one race is inferior to another or because they put the weight of government behind racial hatred and separatism" warrant the strictest judicial scrutiny because of the very irrelevance of these rationales. By contrast, racial classifications drawn for the purpose of remedying the effects of discrimination that itself was race based have a highly pertinent basis: the tragic and indelible fact that discrimination against blacks and other racial minorities in this Nation has pervaded our Nation's history and continues to scar our society.

In concluding that remedial classifications warrant no different standard of review under the Constitution than the most brutal and repugnant forms of state-sponsored racism, a majority of this Court signals that it regards racial discrimination as largely a phenomenon of the past, and that government bodies need no longer preoccupy themselves with rectifying racial injustice. I, however, do not believe this Nation is anywhere close to eradicating racial discrimination or its vestiges. In constitutionalizing its wishful thinking, the majority today does a grave disservice not only to those victims of past and present racial discrimination in this Nation whom government has sought to assist, but also to this Court's long tradition of approaching issues of race with the utmost sensitivity.

[JUSTICE BLACKMUN's dissenting opinion is omitted.]

POINTS FOR DISCUSSION

a. Individuals v. Groups

Does the Equal Protection Clause protect only individuals, or does it instead pay attention to group rights? Justices O'Connor and Scalia suggested in *Croson* that its protections from discrimination on the basis of race are solely individualistic. It follows from this view that the government cannot deny a person a benefit solely on the basis of the person's race, regardless of the status of the group that benefits from the denial. Justice Marshall, in contrast, appeared to assert that the Clause's protections can be group-based as well as individualistic, and thus that policies that seek to protect disadvantaged racial groups are permissible. Which view do you find more compelling?

b.   Affirmative Action and the Federal Government

After *Croson*, it appeared that state and federal efforts to use affirmative action in their public contracting programs might be subject to different levels of judicial scrutiny. In *Adarand Constructors, Inc. v. Peña*, 515 U.S. 200 (1995), however, the Court held, in a 5–4 decision, that "federal racial classifications, like those of a State, must serve a compelling governmental interest, and must be narrowly tailored to further that interest." Although the Court, under that standard, invalidated a set-aside program in federal contracting, it sought to "dispel the notion that strict scrutiny is 'strict in theory, but fatal in fact.' The unhappy persistence of both the practice and the lingering effects of racial discrimination against minority groups in this country is an unfortunate reality, and government is not disqualified from acting in response to it."

Justice Scalia concurred in part, asserting that "government can never have a 'compelling interest' in discriminating on the basis of race in order to 'make up' for past racial discrimination in the opposite direction." He declared that "under our Constitution, there can be no such thing as either a creditor or a debtor race. That concept is alien to the Constitution's focus upon the individual * * *. In the eyes of government, we are just one race here. It is American."

Justice Thomas also concurred in part, writing separately to "express [his] disagreement with the premise underlying Justice Stevens' and Justice Ginsburg's dissents: that there is a racial paternalism exception to the principle of equal protection." In Justice Thomas's view, there is a "moral [and] constitutional equivalence between laws designed to subjugate a race and those that distribute benefits on the basis of race in order to foster some current notion of equality." He asserted that "[s]o-called 'benign' discrimination * * * stamp[s] minorities with a badge of inferiority and may cause them to develop dependencies or to adopt an attitude that they are 'entitled' to preferences." To Justice Thomas, both affirmative action and "discrimination inspired by malicious prejudice" are "racial discrimination, plain and simple."

Justice Stevens dissented, asserting that "[t]here is no moral or constitutional equivalence between a policy that is designed to perpetuate a caste system and one that seeks to eradicate racial subordination. Invidious discrimination is an engine of oppression, subjugating a disfavored group to enhance or maintain the power of the majority." In contrast, he asserted, "[r]emedial race-based preferences reflect the opposite impulse: a desire to foster equality in society. No sensible conception of the Government's constitutional obligation to 'govern impartially' should ignore this distinction." Justice Ginsburg also dissented, contending that "[b]ias both conscious and unconscious, reflecting traditional and unexamined habits of thought, keeps up barriers that must come down if equal opportunity and nondiscrimination are ever genuinely to become this country's law and practice." She asserted that given the history of racial discrimination and its practical consequences, "Congress surely can conclude that a carefully designed affirmative action program may help to realize, finally, the 'equal protection of the laws' the Fourteenth Amendment has promised since 1868."

After *Adarand*, all government-sponsored affirmative action programs are subject to strict scrutiny. Are there any such programs that can survive that level of scrutiny? Note that *Croson* and *Adarand* both involved affirmative action programs in public contracting. Are there stronger constitutional arguments for affirmative action in the context of education? Recall that five Justices concluded in *Bakke* that there were. Did the view expressed by five Justices in *Bakke* that universities may take race into account in admissions decisions survive *Croson* and *Adarand*? Consider the two cases that follow, which the Court decided on the same day.

GRUTTER V. BOLLINGER

539 U.S. 306 (2003)

JUSTICE O'CONNOR delivered the opinion of the Court.

This case requires us to decide whether the use of race as a factor in student admissions by the University of Michigan Law School is unlawful. * * * The hallmark of [the Law School's admissions] policy is its focus on academic ability coupled with a flexible assessment of applicants' talents, experiences, and potential "to contribute to the learning of those around them." * * * In reviewing an applicant's file, admissions officials must consider the applicant's undergraduate grade point average (GPA) and Law School Admission Test (LSAT) score because they are important (if imperfect) predictors of academic success in law school. [In addition, so-called] "soft variables" such as "the enthusiasm of recommenders, the quality of the undergraduate institution, the quality of the applicant's essay, and the areas and difficulty of undergraduate course selection" are all brought to bear in assessing an "applicant's likely contributions to the intellectual and social life of the institution."

The policy aspires to "achieve that diversity which has the potential to enrich everyone's education and thus make a law school class stronger than the sum of its parts." The policy does not restrict the types of diversity contributions eligible for "substantial weight" in the admissions process * * *. The policy does, however, reaffirm the Law School's longstanding commitment [to] "racial and ethnic diversity with special reference to the inclusion of students from groups which have been historically discriminated against, like African-Americans, Hispanics and Native Americans, who without this commitment might not be represented in our student body in meaningful numbers." * * *

Petitioner Barbara Grutter is a white Michigan resident who applied to the Law School in 1996 with a 3.8 GPA and 161 LSAT score. The Law School initially placed petitioner on a waiting list, but subsequently rejected her application. [She filed suit contending, among other things, that the admissions policy was inconsistent with the Equal Protection Clause.]

We have held that all racial classifications imposed by government "must be analyzed by a reviewing court under strict scrutiny." *Adarand Constructors, Inc. v. Peña,* 515 U.S. 200 (1995). * * * Not every decision influenced by race is equally objectionable, and strict scrutiny is designed to provide a framework for carefully examining the importance and the sincerity of the reasons advanced by the governmental decisionmaker for the use of race in that particular context.

Take Note

The Court defers to the school's judgment that diversity is important and beneficial. Is this deference consistent with the Court's ordinary approach in cases involving strict scrutiny?

[W]e have never held that the only governmental use of race that can survive strict scrutiny is remedying past discrimination. Nor, since *Bakke,* have we directly addressed the use of race in the context of public higher education. Today, we hold that the Law School has a compelling interest in attaining a diverse student body. The Law School's educational judgment that such diversity is essential to its educational mission is one to which we defer. * * * We have long recognized that, given the important purpose of public education and the expansive freedoms of speech and thought associated with the university environment, universities occupy a special niche in our constitutional tradition.

As part of its goal of "assembling a class that is both exceptionally academically qualified and broadly diverse," the Law School seeks to "enroll a 'critical mass' of minority students." The Law School's interest is not simply "to assure within its student body some specified percentage of a particular group merely because of its race or ethnic origin." *Bakke,* 438 U.S., at 307 (opinion of

Powell, J.). That would amount to outright racial balancing, which is patently unconstitutional. Rather, the Law School's concept of critical mass is defined by reference to the educational benefits that diversity is designed to produce.

These benefits are substantial. As the District Court emphasized, the Law School's admissions policy promotes "cross-racial understanding," helps to break down racial stereotypes, and "enables [students] to better understand persons of different races." These benefits are "important and laudable," because "classroom discussion is livelier, more spirited, and simply more enlightening and interesting" when the students have "the greatest possible variety of backgrounds."

The Law School's claim of a compelling interest is further bolstered by its *amici,* who point to the educational benefits that flow from student body diversity. [N]umerous studies show that student body diversity promotes learning outcomes, and "better prepares students for an increasingly diverse workforce and society, and better prepares them as professionals." * * * These benefits are not theoretical but real, as major American businesses have made clear that the skills needed in today's increasingly global marketplace can only be developed through exposure to widely diverse people, cultures, ideas, and viewpoints. * * * What is more, high-ranking retired officers and civilian leaders of the United States military assert that, "[b]ased on [their] decades of experience," a "highly qualified, racially diverse officer corps [is] essential to the military's ability to fulfill its principal mission to provide national security."

Effective participation by members of all racial and ethnic groups in the civic life of our Nation is essential if the dream of one Nation, indivisible, is to be realized. Moreover, universities, and in particular, law schools, represent the training ground for a large number of our Nation's leaders. [In] order to cultivate a set of leaders with legitimacy in the eyes of the citizenry, it is necessary that the path to leadership be visibly open to talented and qualified individuals of every race and ethnicity.

We [also] find that the Law School's admissions program bears the hallmarks of a narrowly tailored plan. As Justice Powell made clear in *Bakke,* * * * universities cannot establish quotas for members of certain racial groups or put members of those groups on separate admissions tracks. * * * Universities can, however, consider race or ethnicity more flexibly as a "plus" factor in the context of individualized consideration of each and every applicant.

The Law School's goal of attaining a critical mass of underrepresented minority students does not transform its program into a quota. * * * "[S]ome attention to numbers," without more, does not transform a flexible admissions system into a rigid quota. [B]etween 1993 and 1998, the number of African-American, Latino, and Native-American students in each class at the Law School varied from 13.5 to 20.1 percent, a range inconsistent with a quota.

Take Note

What does it mean to say that the Law School seeks a "critical mass" of minority students? Doesn't it have to mean that there is some threshold below which the number of students cannot drop? If so, why isn't it tantamount to a quota?

That a race-conscious admissions program does not operate as a quota does not, by itself, satisfy the requirement of individualized consideration. When using race as a "plus" factor in university admissions, a university's admissions program must remain flexible enough to ensure that each applicant is evaluated as an individual and not in a way that makes an applicant's race or ethnicity the defining feature of his or her application. Here, the Law School engages in a highly individualized, holistic review of each applicant's file, giving serious consideration to all the ways an applicant might contribute to a diverse educational environment. * * * There is no policy, either *de jure* or *de facto,* of automatic acceptance or rejection based on any single "soft" variable. Unlike the program at issue in *Gratz v. Bollinger,* 539 U.S. 244 (2003), [which is discussed below], the Law School awards no mechanical, predetermined diversity "bonuses" based on race or ethnicity. [And the] Law School does not [limit] in any way the broad range of qualities and experiences that may be considered valuable contributions to student body diversity.

Petitioner and the United States argue that the Law School's plan is not narrowly tailored because race-neutral means exist to obtain the educational benefits of student body diversity that the Law School seeks. We disagree. Narrow tailoring does not require exhaustion of every conceivable race-neutral alternative. Nor does it require a university to choose between maintaining a reputation for excellence or fulfilling a commitment to provide educational opportunities to members of all racial groups. Narrow tailoring does, however, require serious, good faith consideration of workable race-neutral alternatives that will achieve the diversity the university seeks.

[T]he Law School sufficiently considered workable race-neutral alternatives. The District Court took the Law School to task for failing to consider race-neutral alternatives such as "using a lottery system" or "decreasing the emphasis for all applicants on undergraduate GPA and LSAT scores." But these alternatives would require a dramatic sacrifice of diversity, the academic quality of all admitted students, or both. * * * So too with the suggestion that the Law School simply lower admissions standards for all students, a drastic remedy that would require the Law School to become a much different institution and sacrifice a vital component of its educational mission. The United States advocates "percentage plans," recently adopted by public undergraduate institutions in Texas, Florida, and California, to guarantee admission to all students above a certain class-rank threshold in every high school in the State. The United States does not, however, explain how such plans could work for graduate and professional schools. Moreover, even assuming such plans are race-neutral, they may preclude the university from conducting the individualized assessments necessary to assemble a student body that is not just racially diverse, but diverse along all the qualities valued by the university. We are satisfied that the Law School adequately considered race-neutral alternatives currently capable of producing a critical mass without forcing the Law School to abandon the academic selectivity that is the cornerstone of its educational mission.

We are mindful, however, that "[a] core purpose of the Fourteenth Amendment was to do away with all governmentally imposed discrimination based on race." *Palmore v. Sidoti,* 466 U.S. 429, 432 (1984). Accordingly, race-conscious admissions policies must be limited in time. This requirement reflects that racial classifications, however compelling their goals, are potentially so dangerous that they may be employed no more broadly than the interest demands. Enshrining a permanent justification for racial preferences would offend this fundamental equal protection principle. * * * It has been 25 years since Justice Powell first approved the use of race to further an interest in student body diversity in the context of public higher education. Since that time, the number of minority applicants with high grades and test scores has indeed increased. We expect that 25 years from now, the use of racial preferences will no longer be necessary to further the interest approved today.

> **Food for Thought**
>
> Is the Court suggesting here that the Constitution will mean something different in 25 years? Or does it mean that circumstances will have changed sufficiently in 25 years such that affirmative action will no longer survive strict scrutiny? If the latter, how does the Court know? Is it realistic to believe that affirmative action in education will end in the year 2028?

[JUSTICE GINSBURG's concurring opinion and JUSTICE SCALIA's opinion concurring in part and dissenting in part are omitted.]

JUSTICE THOMAS, with whom JUSTICE SCALIA joins [in relevant part], concurring in part and dissenting in part.

I believe blacks can achieve in every avenue of American life without the meddling of university administrators. * * * No one would argue that a university could set up a lower general admissions standard and then impose heightened requirements only on black applicants. Similarly, a university may not maintain a high admissions standard and grant exemptions to favored races. The Law School, of its own choosing, and for its own purposes, maintains an exclusionary admissions system that it knows produces racially disproportionate results. Racial discrimination is not a permissible solution to the self-inflicted wounds of this elitist admissions policy.[4]

A majority of the Court has validated only two circumstances where "pressing public necessity" or a "compelling state interest" can possibly justify racial discrimination by state actors. First, the lesson of *Korematsu* is that national security constitutes a "pressing public necessity," though the government's use of race to advance that objective must be narrowly tailored. Second, the Court has recognized as a compelling state interest a government's effort to remedy past discrimination for which it is responsible. *Richmond v. J.A. Croson Co.*, 488 U.S. 469, 504 (1989). * * * Where the Court has accepted only national security, and rejected even the best interests of a child, [see *Palmore v. Sidoti*, 466 U.S. 429 (1984),] as a justification for racial discrimination, I conclude that only those measures the State must take to provide a bulwark against anarchy, or to prevent violence, will constitute a "pressing public necessity."

Unlike the majority, I seek to define with precision the interest being asserted by the Law School before determining whether that interest is so compelling as to justify racial discrimination. * * * The proffered interest that the majority vindicates today [is] not simply "diversity." Instead the Court upholds the use of racial discrimination as a tool to advance the Law School's interest in offering a marginally superior education while maintaining an elite institution. * * * While legal education at a public university may be good policy or otherwise laudable, it is obviously not a pressing public necessity * * *. Michigan [thus] has no compelling interest in having a law school at all, much less an *elite* one. Still, even assuming that a State may, under appropriate circumstances, demonstrate a cognizable interest in having an elite law school, Michigan has failed to do so here.

The only cognizable state interests vindicated by operating a public law school [are] the education of that State's citizens and the training of that State's

<hr>

[4] The Law School believes both that the educational benefits of a racially engineered student body are large and that adjusting its overall admissions standards to achieve the same racial mix would require it to sacrifice its elite status. If the Law School is correct that the educational benefits of "diversity" are so great, then achieving them by altering admissions standards should not compromise its elite status. The Law School's reluctance to do this suggests that the educational benefits it alleges are not significant or do not exist at all.

lawyers. * * * The Law School today, however, does precious little training of those attorneys who will serve the citizens of Michigan. [Less] than 16% of the Law School's graduating class elects to stay in Michigan after law school. * * * It does not take a social scientist to conclude that it is precisely the Law School's status as an elite institution that causes it to be a waystation for the rest of the country's lawyers, rather than a training ground for those who will remain in Michigan. The Law School's decision to be an elite institution does little to advance the welfare of the people of Michigan or any cognizable interest of the State of Michigan.

With the adoption of different admissions methods, such as accepting all students who meet minimum qualifications, the Law School could achieve its vision of the racially aesthetic student body without the use of racial discrimination. [Indeed,] the Court ignores the fact that other top law schools have succeeded in meeting their aesthetic demands without racial discrimination. * * * The sky has not fallen at Boalt Hall at the University of California, Berkeley, for example. Prior to [an amendment to the state Constitution that] bars the State from "grant[ing] preferential treatment [on] the basis of race [in] the operation of [public] education," Boalt Hall enrolled 20 blacks and 28 Hispanics in its first-year class for 1996. In 2002, without deploying express racial discrimination in admissions, Boalt's entering class enrolled 14 blacks and 36 Hispanics.

I must contest the notion that the Law School's discrimination benefits those admitted as a result of it. * * * The Law School tantalizes unprepared students with the promise of a University of Michigan degree and all of the opportunities that it offers. These overmatched students take the bait, only to find that they cannot succeed in the cauldron of competition. Indeed, to cover the tracks of [supporters of affirmative action], this cruel farce of racial discrimination must continue—in selection for the Michigan Law Review and in hiring at law firms and for judicial clerkships—until

> **Take Note**
>
> The *Michigan Law Review* is a student-edited journal. Traditionally, the best students were selected to be editors. A judicial clerkship is typically a one or two-year position working for a state or federal judge. Clerkships are considered prestigious, and selection of clerks is very competitive.

the "beneficiaries" are no longer tolerated. While these students may graduate with law degrees, there is no evidence that they have received a qualitatively better legal education (or become better lawyers) than if they had gone to a less "elite" law school for which they were better prepared.

It is uncontested that each year, the Law School admits a handful of blacks who would be admitted in the absence of racial discrimination. Who can differentiate between those who belong and those who do not? The majority of blacks are admitted to the Law School because of discrimination, and because of this policy all are tarred as undeserving. This problem of stigma does not depend on determinacy as to whether those stigmatized are actually the "beneficiaries" of racial discrimination. When blacks take positions in the highest places of government, industry, or academia, it is an open question today whether their skin color played a part in their advancement. The question itself is the stigma— because either racial discrimination did play a role, in which case the person may be deemed "otherwise unqualified," or it did not, in which case asking the question itself unfairly marks those blacks who would succeed without discrimination.

CHIEF JUSTICE REHNQUIST, with whom JUSTICE SCALIA, JUSTICE KENNEDY, and JUSTICE THOMAS join, dissenting.

In practice, the Law School's program bears little or no relation to its asserted goal of achieving "critical mass." * * * From 1995 through 2000, the Law School admitted between 1,130 and 1,310 students. Of those, between 13 and 19 were Native American, between 91 and 108 were African-American, and between 47 and 56 were Hispanic. * * * [T]he correlation between the percentage of the Law School's pool of applicants who are members of the three minority groups and the percentage of the admitted applicants who are members of these same groups is far too precise to be dismissed as merely the result of the school paying "some attention to [the] numbers."

The Law School has offered no explanation for its actual admissions practices and, unexplained, we are bound to conclude that the Law School has managed its admissions program, not to achieve a "critical mass," but to extend offers of admission to members of selected minority groups in proportion to their statistical representation in the applicant pool. But this is precisely the type of racial balancing that the Court itself calls "patently unconstitutional."

[JUSTICE KENNEDY's dissenting opinion is omitted.]

GRATZ V. BOLLINGER
539 U.S. 244 (2003)

CHIEF JUSTICE REHNQUIST delivered the opinion of the Court.

[Petitioners Jennifer Gratz and Patrick Hamacher were white students who were denied admission to the University of Michigan's College of Literature, Science, and the Arts (LSA). They filed suit to challenge the University's admission policies, pursuant to which the Office of Undergraduate Admissions used a "selection index" to award points to each applicant. The maximum score was 150 points, and all students with 100 points or more were admitted. Points were awarded based on high school grade point average, standardized test scores, academic

> **Make the Connection**
>
> Even if LSA did not have an affirmative action policy, there is no guarantee that the plaintiffs would have been admitted, as there may have been many other white students with stronger qualifications who were also denied admission under the policy. Should the Court have concluded that the plaintiffs lacked standing? We considered standing—and this question in particular—in Volume 1.

quality of an applicant's high school, strength or weakness of high school curriculum, in-state residency, alumni relationship, personal essay, and personal achievement or leadership. In addition, African-American, Hispanic, and Native-American applicants were awarded 20 points for their membership in under-represented racial or ethnic minority groups. During the period in question, the University admitted virtually every qualified applicant from these groups.]

We find that the University's policy [is] not narrowly tailored to achieve the interest in educational diversity that respondents claim justifies their program. * * * The current LSA policy does not provide [individualized] consideration. The LSA's policy automatically distributes 20 points to every single applicant from an "underrepresented minority" group, as defined by the University. The only consideration that accompanies this distribution of points is a factual review of an application to determine whether an individual is a member of one of these minority groups. Moreover, unlike Justice Powell's example, where the race of a "particular black applicant" could be considered without being decisive, see *Bakke,* 438 U.S., at 317, the LSA's automatic distribution of 20 points has the effect of making "the factor of [race] decisive" for virtually every minimally qualified underrepresented minority applicant. * * * Instead of considering how the differing backgrounds, experiences, and characteristics of students A, B, and C might benefit the University, admissions counselors reviewing LSA applications would simply award both A and B 20 points because their applications indicate that they are African-American, and student C, [whose "extraordinary artistic talent" rivaled that of Monet or Picasso,] would receive [only] up to 5 points for his "extraordinary talent" [under LSA's system].

We conclude, therefore, that because the University's use of race in its current freshman admissions policy is not narrowly tailored to achieve respondents' asserted compelling interest in diversity, the admissions policy violates the Equal Protection Clause of the Fourteenth Amendment.

JUSTICE O'CONNOR, concurring.

Unlike the law school admissions policy the Court upholds today in [*Grutter*,] the procedures employed by the University of Michigan [do] not provide for a meaningful individualized review of applicants. [T]he Office of Undergraduate Admissions relies on the selection index to assign *every* underrepresented minority applicant the same, *automatic* 20-point bonus without consideration of the particular background, experiences, or qualities of each individual applicant. And this mechanized selection index score, by and large, automatically determines the admissions decision for each applicant. * * * Although the Office of Undergraduate Admissions does assign 20 points to some "soft" variables other than race, the points available for other diversity contributions, such as leadership and service, personal achievement, and geographic diversity, are capped at much lower levels. Even the most outstanding national high school leader could never receive more than five points for his or her accomplishments * * *. [T]he selection index, by setting up automatic, predetermined point allocations for the soft variables, ensures that the diversity contributions of applicants cannot be individually assessed. * * * As a result, I join the Court's opinion reversing the decision of the District Court.

[JUSTICE BREYER concurred in the judgment, joined JUSTICE O'CONNOR's opinion "except insofar as it joins that of the Court," and joined Part I of JUSTICE GINSBURG's dissenting opinion. JUSTICE THOMAS's concurring opinion is omitted.]

JUSTICE SOUTER, with whom JUSTICE GINSBURG joins [in relevant part], dissenting.

The record does not describe a system with a quota like the one struck down in *Bakke*, which "insulate[d]" all nonminority candidates from competition from certain seats. *Bakke, supra*, at 317 (opinion of Powell, J.). * * * The plan here, in contrast, lets all applicants compete for all places and values an applicant's offering for any place not only on grounds of race, but on grades, test scores, strength of high school, quality of course of study, residence, alumni relationships, leadership, personal character, socioeconomic disadvantage, athletic ability, and quality of a personal essay. [To be sure,] membership in an underrepresented minority is given a weight of 20 points on the 150-point scale. On the face of things, however, this assignment of specific points does not set race apart from all other weighted considerations. Nonminority students may receive 20 points for athletic ability, socioeconomic disadvantage, attendance at a socioeconomically disadvantaged or predominantly minority high school, or at the Provost's discretion; they may also receive 10 points for being residents of Michigan, 6 for residence in an underrepresented Michigan county, 5 for leadership and service, and so on.

The very nature of a college's permissible practice of awarding value to racial diversity means that race must be considered in a way that increases some applicants' chances for admission. Since college admission is not left entirely to inarticulate intuition, it is hard to see what is inappropriate in assigning some stated value to a relevant characteristic, whether it be reasoning ability, writing style, running speed, or minority race. * * * Nor is it possible to say that the 20 points convert race into a decisive factor comparable to reserving minority places as in *Bakke*. Of course we can conceive of a point system in which the "plus" factor given to minority applicants would be so extreme as to guarantee every minority applicant a higher rank than every nonminority applicant in the university's admissions system. But petitioners do not have a convincing argument that the freshman admissions system operates this way. * * * It suffices for me [that] there are no *Bakke*-like set-asides and that consideration of an applicant's whole spectrum of ability is no more ruled out by giving 20 points for race than by giving the same points for athletic ability or socioeconomic disadvantage.

> **Food for Thought**
>
> Do you agree with Justice Souter that the challenged policy is meaningfully different from the set-aside program invalidated in *Bakke*? At what point in his view would the "plus" factor approach become tantamount to a quota? Do you agree that it is "hard to see what is inappropriate" about giving someone 20 points solely because of his race, regardless of any other information about the person?

[I]t seems especially unfair to treat the candor of the admissions plan as an Achilles' heel. In contrast to the college's forthrightness in saying just what plus factor it gives for membership in an underrepresented minority, it is worth considering the character of one alternative thrown up as preferable, because supposedly not based on race. Drawing on admissions systems used at public universities in California, Florida, and Texas, the United States contends that Michigan could get student diversity in satisfaction of its compelling interest by guaranteeing admission to a fixed percentage of the top students from each high school in Michigan. While there is nothing unconstitutional about such a practice,

it nonetheless suffers from [the] disadvantage of deliberate obfuscation. The "percentage plans" are just as race conscious as the point scheme (and fairly so), but they get their racially diverse results without saying directly what they are doing or why they are doing it. In contrast, Michigan states its purpose directly and, if this were a doubtful case for me, I would be tempted to give Michigan an extra point of its own for its frankness. Equal protection cannot become an exercise in which the winners are the ones who hide the ball.

JUSTICE GINSBURG, with whom JUSTICE SOUTER joins, dissenting.

[T]he Court once again maintains that the same standard of review controls judicial inspection of all official race classifications. This insistence on "consistency" would be fitting were our Nation free of the vestiges of rank discrimination long reinforced by law. But we are not far distant from an overtly discriminatory past, and the effects of centuries of law-sanctioned inequality remain painfully evident in our communities and schools. In the wake "of a system of racial caste only recently ended," *Adarand Constructors, Inc. v. Peña*, 515 U.S. 200, 273 (1995) (GINSBURG, J., dissenting), large disparities endure. Unemployment, poverty, and access to health care vary disproportionately by race. Neighborhoods and schools remain racially divided. African-American and Hispanic children are all too often educated in poverty-stricken and underperforming institutions. Adult African-Americans and Hispanics generally earn less than whites with equivalent levels of education. Equally credentialed job applicants receive different receptions depending on their race. Irrational prejudice is still encountered in real estate markets and consumer transactions. "Bias both conscious and unconscious, reflecting traditional and unexamined habits of thought, keeps up barriers that must come down if equal opportunity and nondiscrimination are ever genuinely to become this country's law and practice." *Id.,* at 274.

In implementing [the instructions of the Equal Protection Clause], as I see it, government decisionmakers may properly distinguish between policies of exclusion and inclusion. Actions designed to burden groups long denied full citizenship stature are not sensibly ranked with measures taken to hasten the day when entrenched discrimination and its aftereffects have been extirpated. * * * Our jurisprudence ranks race a "suspect" category, "not because [race] is inevitably an impermissible classification, but because it is one which usually, to our national shame, has been drawn for the purpose of maintaining racial inequality." *Norwalk Core v. Norwalk Redevelopment Agency*, 395 F.2d 920, 931–932 (C.A.2 1968). But where race is considered "for the purpose of achieving equality," no automatic proscription is in order.

Like other top-ranking institutions, the College has many more applicants for admission than it can accommodate in an entering class. Every applicant admitted under the current plan, petitioners do not here dispute, is qualified to attend the College. The racial and ethnic groups to which the College accords special consideration [historically] have been relegated to inferior status by law and social practice; their members continue to experience class-based discrimination to this day. There is no suggestion that the College adopted its current policy in order to limit or decrease enrollment by any particular racial or ethnic group, and no seats are reserved on the basis of race. * * * The stain of generations of racial oppression is still visible in our society, and the determination to hasten its removal remains vital.

[JUSTICE STEVENS dissented on the ground that petitioners lacked standing.]

POINTS FOR DISCUSSION

a. When Is Affirmative Action Permissible?

The Court in *Grutter* upheld a policy that gave some non-numerical advantage to minorities in order to achieve a "critical mass," but in *Gratz* invalidated a policy that awarded actual points on a numerical scale. Accordingly, an institution of higher education may sometimes constitutionally prefer minority applicants in order to advance the interest in diversity. Are you convinced that there is a meaningful difference between the types of admissions policies at issue in the two cases?

b. "Critical Mass"

How did the Law School (and the Court) define "critical mass"? If the admitted class would not have a critical mass of minority students absent an affirmative action program, then wouldn't the Law School's policy effectively operate to make the race of some admitted minority students dispositive? If so, how is that approach different in practice from the College's policy?

c. The Point of Affirmative Action

Isn't the whole point of affirmative action to give preference on the basis of race? After all, affirmative action would not be perceived as necessary in university admissions if race-neutral admissions policies could yield an optimally diverse class. Yet, as Justice Souter suggested, the import of the Court's decisions in *Grutter* and *Gratz* seems to be that affirmative action is permissible in higher education only when the school makes it seem as if race really doesn't matter. Is the Court's real point that a university is permitted to engage in race-based decision-making as long as it does not do so in a way that is too obvious?

d.   Strict Scrutiny

The Court in *Grutter* concluded that the law school's affirmative action policy survived strict scrutiny, because it was narrowly tailored to advance the compelling interest in attaining a diverse student body. Is this consistent with your understanding of strict scrutiny? In *Korematsu*, the case that first articulated the principle that racial classifications trigger searching review, the Court declared that only "pressing public necessity" can justify racial classifications. Is the desire to attain a diverse student body at an institution of higher learning such an interest? The Court in *Grutter* also concluded that "[n]arrow tailoring does not require exhaustion of every conceivable race-neutral alternative." But does—or should—it require the state at least to adopt obvious race-neutral alternatives that would do roughly as good a job at achieving the state's interest as the challenged race-conscious policy?

e.   Original Meaning of the Fourteenth Amendment

In March 1865, shortly before General Lee's surrender marked the end of the Civil War, Congress enacted the Freedmen's Bureau Act, 13 Stat. 507 (1865). Among other things, Congress charged the Bureau with providing relief and educational services to the freed slaves. Three years later, the Fourteenth Amendment was ratified. What does this suggest about the original understanding of race-conscious government policies designed to help disadvantaged minorities? See Eric Schnapper, *Affirmative Action and the Legislative History of the Fourteenth Amendment*, 71 Va. L. Rev. 753 (1985) (noting that around the time of ratification of the Fourteenth Amendment, Congress enacted a series of programs "whose benefits were expressly limited to blacks" and arguing that this history "strongly suggests that the framers of the amendment could not have intended it generally to prohibit affirmative action for blacks or other disadvantaged groups"). Is the Freedmen's Bureau Act arguably irrelevant in determining the original meaning of the Fourteenth Amendment, because it was enacted by Congress and the Fourteenth Amendment by its terms applies only to state governments? Is the Act irrelevant in determining the meaning of the Fourteenth Amendment, because its enactment predated the passage of the Amendment?

In any event, was Justice O'Connor's approach in *Grutter* originalist? Was Justice Thomas's? Does the "color-blind" vision of the Equal Protection Clause find support in the historical materials that we generally consult in determining the original meaning?

f.   An Expiration Date on Affirmative Action?

Justice O'Connor suggested that affirmative action programs would no longer be constitutional in 25 years. Can constitutional rules have an expiration date? Or is the point that affirmative action will not be narrowly tailored in 25 years because of changes between now and then? What if nothing changes in those 25 years? Is the 25-year limit binding as a matter of *stare decisis*?

g. The Aftermath of the Decisions

After the Court's decisions in *Grutter* and *Gratz*, Michigan voters approved an amendment to the state constitution to prohibit the use of race-based preferences in admissions at state universities. Advocates of affirmative action filed suit challenging the constitutionality of the amendment. After a district court upheld its constitutionality, the United States Court of Appeals for the Sixth Circuit held that it was unconstitutional, relying on *Washington v. Seattle School Dist. No. 1*, 458 U.S. 457 (1982), which invalidated a voter initiative overturning a school board decision to authorize busing to desegregate schools. The Court, in *Schuette v. BAMN*, 572 U.S. 291 (2014), reversed the Court of Appeals in a 6–2 decision and upheld the amendment to the state constitution. Justice Kennedy, writing for himself and two other Justices, reasoned that the decision challenged in *Seattle* "was designed to be used, or was likely to be used, to encourage infliction of injury by reason of race." The Michigan case, in contrast, was "not about how the debate about racial preferences should be resolved," but rather was "about who may resolve it." Justice Kennedy concluded that there "is no authority in the Constitution of the United States or in this Court's precedents for the Judiciary to set aside Michigan laws that commit this policy determination to the voters." Justice Scalia, joined by Justice Thomas, concurred in the judgment, but would have overruled *Seattle* and related cases. Justices Sotomayor and Ginsburg dissented.

h. The Future of Affirmative Action Litigation

In his dissent in *Grutter*, Justice Scalia made the following prediction:

[Today's] split double header seems perversely designed to prolong the controversy and the litigation. Some future lawsuits will presumably focus on whether the discriminatory scheme in question contains enough evaluation of the applicant "as an individual," and sufficiently avoids "separate admissions tracks" * * *. Some will focus on whether a university has [so] zealously pursued its "critical mass" as to make it an unconstitutional *de facto* quota system * * *. Other lawsuits may focus on whether, in the particular setting at issue, any educational benefits flow from racial diversity. Still other suits may challenge the bona fides of the institution's expressed commitment to the educational benefits of diversity that immunize the discriminatory scheme in *Grutter*. (Tempting targets, one would suppose, will be those universities that talk the talk of multiculturalism and racial diversity in the courts but walk the walk of tribalism and racial segregation on their campuses—through minority-only student organizations, separate minority housing opportunities, separate minority student centers, even separate minority-only graduation ceremonies.) And still other suits may claim that the institution's racial preferences have gone below or above the mystical *Grutter*-approved "critical mass." Finally, litigation can be expected on behalf of minority groups intentionally short changed in the institution's composition of its generic minority "critical mass."

Do you agree that such suits are likely to follow? Who is likely to resolve them? If they reach the Supreme Court, how is it likely to decide them?

———————

In answering the last question, consider the litigation over the University of Texas's affirmative action policies. The Court described the evolution of those policies as follows:

In recent years the University has used three different programs to evaluate candidates for admission. The first is the program it used for some years before 1997, when the University considered two factors: a numerical score reflecting an applicant's test scores and academic performance in high school (Academic Index or AI), and the applicant's race. In 1996, this system was held unconstitutional by the United States Court of Appeals for the Fifth Circuit. It ruled the University's consideration of race violated the Equal Protection Clause because it did not further any compelling government interest. *Hopwood v. Texas*, 78 F.3d 932, 955 (5th Cir. 1996).

[In response, the] University stopped considering race in admissions and substituted instead a new holistic metric of a candidate's potential contribution to the University, to be used in conjunction with the Academic Index. This "Personal Achievement Index" (PAI) measures a student's leadership and work experience, awards, extracurricular activities, community service, and other special circumstances that give insight into a student's background. These included growing up in a single-parent home, speaking a language other than English at home, significant family responsibilities assumed by the applicant, and the general socioeconomic condition of the student's family. Seeking to address the decline in minority enrollment after *Hopwood*, the University also expanded its outreach programs.

The Texas State Legislature also responded to the *Hopwood* decision. It enacted a measure known as the Top Ten Percent Law, codified at Tex. Educ.Code Ann. § 51.803 (West 2009). [T]he Top Ten

Percent Law grants automatic admission to any public state college, including the University, to all students in the top 10% of their class at high schools in Texas that comply with certain standards.

The University's revised admissions process, coupled with the operation of the Top Ten Percent Law, resulted in a more racially diverse environment at the University. Before the admissions program at issue in this case, in the last year under the post-*Hopwood* AI/PAI system that did not consider race, the entering class was 4.5% African-American and 16.9% Hispanic. This is in contrast with the 1996 pre-*Hopwood* and Top Ten Percent regime, when race was explicitly considered, and the University's entering freshman class was 4.1% African-American and 14.5% Hispanic.

Following this Court's decisions in *Grutter* and *Gratz*, the University adopted a third admissions program, [in] which the University reverted to explicit consideration of race. * * * The University's plan to resume race-conscious admissions was given formal expression in June 2004 in an internal document entitled Proposal to Consider Race and Ethnicity in Admissions. The Proposal relied in substantial part on a study of a subset of undergraduate classes containing between 5 and 24 students. It showed that few of these classes had significant enrollment by members of racial minorities. In addition the Proposal relied on what it called "anecdotal" reports from students regarding their "interaction in the classroom." The Proposal concluded that the University lacked a "critical mass" of minority students and that to remedy the deficiency it was necessary to give explicit consideration to race in the undergraduate admissions program.

To implement the Proposal the University included a student's race as a component of the PAI score, beginning with applicants in the fall of 2004. * * * Race is not assigned an explicit numerical value, but it is undisputed that race is a meaningful factor. Once applications have been scored, they are plotted on a grid with the Academic Index on the x-axis and the Personal Achievement Index on the y-axis. On that grid students are assigned to so-called cells based on their individual scores. All students in the cells falling above a certain line are admitted. All students below the line are not. * * *

Fisher v. University of Texas at Austin, 570 U.S. 297 (2013) ("*Fisher I*").

In 2008, Abigail Fisher applied for admission to the University of Texas's freshman class. The University denied her application. She then sued the University, claiming that its admission policies discriminated against her and other white applicants because of their race in violation of the Equal Protection Clause. The District Court granted summary judgment to the University, concluding that *Grutter* required courts to give substantial deference to the University, both in the definition of the compelling interest in diversity's benefits and in deciding whether its specific plan was narrowly tailored to achieve its stated goal. The Court of Appeals affirmed. 631 F.3d 213, 217–218 (5th Cir. 2011).

The Supreme Court reversed in *Fisher I*. The Court, in an opinion by Justice Kennedy, began by stating, "We take [*Grutter, Gratz,* and *Regents of Univ. of Cal. v. Bakke*, 438 U.S. 265 (1978)] as given for purposes of deciding this case." The Court then held that the lower courts "were correct in finding that *Grutter* calls for deference to the University's conclusion, based on its experience and expertise, that a diverse student body would serve its educational goals." But the Court then explained that "[o]nce the University has established that its goal of diversity is consistent with strict scrutiny," it "must prove that the means chosen [to] attain diversity are narrowly tailored to that goal." The Court continued:

> On this point, the University receives no deference. * * * True, a court can take account of a university's experience and expertise in adopting or rejecting certain admissions processes. But, as the Court said in *Grutter*, it remains at all times the University's obligation to demonstrate, and the Judiciary's obligation to determine, that admissions processes "ensure that each applicant is evaluated as an individual and not in a way that makes an applicant's race or ethnicity the defining feature of his or her application."
>
> Narrow tailoring also requires that the reviewing court verify that it is "necessary" for a university to use race to achieve the educational benefits of diversity. *Bakke, supra*, at 305. This involves a careful judicial inquiry into whether a university could achieve sufficient diversity without using racial classifications. Although "[n]arrow tailoring does not require exhaustion of every conceivable race-neutral alternative," strict scrutiny does require a court to examine with care, and not defer to, a university's "serious, good faith consideration of workable race-neutral alternatives." See *Grutter*, 539 U.S., at 339–340 (emphasis added). Consideration by the university is of course necessary, but it is not sufficient to satisfy strict scrutiny: The reviewing court must ultimately be satisfied that no workable race-neutral alternatives would produce

the educational benefits of diversity. If "a nonracial approach . . . could promote the substantial interest about as well and at tolerable administrative expense," *Wygant v. Jackson Bd. of Ed.*, 476 U.S. 267, 280, n. 6 (1986), then the university may not consider race. [S]trict scrutiny imposes on the university the ultimate burden of demonstrating, before turning to racial classifications, that available, workable race-neutral alternatives do not suffice. * * * Strict scrutiny does not permit a court to accept a school's assertion that its admissions process uses race in a permissible way without a court giving close analysis to the evidence of how the process works in practice. The higher education dynamic does not change the narrow tailoring analysis of strict scrutiny applicable in other contexts.

Because the District Court and the Court of Appeals had impermissibly deferred to the University's judgment that its admissions plan was narrowly tailored to achieve a compelling interest in diversity, the Court reversed and remanded. (Justice Thomas concurred, but made clear that he would overrule *Grutter*.) On remand, the Court of Appeals concluded that the University of Texas had met its burden of demonstrating that the challenged affirmative action plan was narrowly tailored. Fisher again sought certiorari, and the Court agreed to hear the case again.

FISHER V. UNIVERSITY OF TEXAS AT AUSTIN ("FISHER II")
136 S.Ct. 2198 (2016)

JUSTICE KENNEDY delivered the opinion of the court, in which JUSTICES GINSBURG, BREYER, and SOTOMAYOR, joined.

In seeking to reverse the judgment of the Court of Appeals, petitioner makes four arguments. First, she argues that the University has not articulated its compelling interest with sufficient clarity. According to petitioner, the University must set forth more precisely the level of minority enrollment that would constitute a "critical mass." Without a clearer sense of what the University's ultimate goal is, petitioner argues, a reviewing court cannot assess whether the University's admissions program is narrowly tailored to that goal.

As this Court's cases have made clear, however, the compelling interest that justifies consideration of race in college admissions is not an interest in enrolling a certain number of minority students. Rather, a university may institute a race-conscious admissions program as a means of obtaining "the educational benefits that flow from student body diversity." *Fisher I*. As this Court has said, enrolling a diverse student body "promotes cross-racial understanding, helps to break down racial stereotypes, and enables students to better understand persons of different races." Equally important, "student body diversity promotes learning outcomes, and better prepares students for an increasingly diverse workforce and society."

Increasing minority enrollment may be instrumental to these educational benefits, but it is not, as petitioner seems to suggest, a goal that can or should be reduced to pure numbers. Indeed, since the University is prohibited from seeking a particular number or quota of minority students, it cannot be faulted for failing to specify the particular level of minority enrollment at which it believes the educational benefits of diversity will be obtained. On the other hand, asserting an interest in the educational benefits of diversity writ large is insufficient. A university's goals cannot be elusory or amorphous—they must be sufficiently measurable to permit judicial scrutiny of the policies adopted to reach them.

The record reveals that in first setting forth its current admissions policy, the University articulated concrete and precise goals. On the first page of its 2004 [Proposal], the University identifies the educational values it seeks to realize through its admissions process: the destruction of stereotypes, the "promot[ion of] cross-racial understanding," the preparation of a student body "for an increasingly diverse workforce and society," and the "cultivat[ion of] a set of leaders with legitimacy in the eyes of the citizenry." Later in the proposal, the University explains that it strives to provide an "academic environment" that offers a "robust exchange of ideas, exposure to differing cultures, preparation for the challenges of an increasingly diverse workforce, and acquisition of competencies required of future leaders." All of these objectives, as a general matter, mirror the "compelling interest" this Court has approved in its prior cases.

Second, petitioner argues that the University has no need to consider race because it had already "achieved critical mass" [under a prior admissions policy] using the Top Ten Percent Plan and race-neutral holistic review. Petitioner is correct that a university bears a heavy burden in showing that it had not obtained the educational benefits of diversity before it turned to a race-conscious plan. The record reveals, however, that, at the time of petitioner's application, the University could not be faulted on this score. Before changing its policy the University conducted "months of study and deliberation, including retreats, interviews, [and] review of data," and concluded that "[t]he use of race-neutral policies and programs ha[d] not been successful in achieving" sufficient racial diversity at the

University. At no stage in this litigation has petitioner challenged the University's good faith in conducting its studies * * *.

Third, petitioner argues that considering race was not necessary because such consideration has had only a " 'minimal impact' in advancing the [University's] compelling interest." Again, the record does not support this assertion. In 2003 [before race was taken into account], 11 percent of the Texas residents enrolled through holistic review were Hispanic and 3.5 percent were African-American. In 2007, by contrast, 16.9 percent of the Texas holistic-review freshmen were Hispanic and 6.8 percent were African-American. Those increases—of 54 percent and 94 percent, respectively—show that consideration of race has had a meaningful, if still limited, effect on the diversity of the University's freshman class.

> **Food for Thought**
>
> The Court defers to the University's conclusion that race-neutral admissions policies did not achieve sufficient racial diversity. How would a university decide how much diversity is sufficient and how much is not? Does any university in the United States have sufficient racial diversity? If not, does that mean all universities may adopt race conscious admissions policies?

In any event, it is not a failure of narrow tailoring for the impact of racial consideration to be minor. The fact that race consciousness played a role in only a small portion of admissions decisions should be a hallmark of narrow tailoring, not evidence of unconstitutionality.

Petitioner's final argument is that "there are numerous other available race-neutral means of achieving" the University's compelling interest. A review of the record reveals, however, that, at the time of petitioner's application, none of her proposed alternatives was a workable means for the University to attain the benefits of diversity it sought. For example, petitioner suggests that the University could intensify its outreach efforts to African-American and Hispanic applicants. But the University submitted extensive evidence of the many ways in which it already had intensified its outreach efforts to those students. The University has created three new scholarship programs, opened new regional admissions centers, increased its recruitment budget by half-a-million dollars, and organized over 1,000 recruitment events. Perhaps more significantly, * * * the University spent seven years attempting to achieve its compelling interest using race-neutral holistic review. None of these efforts succeeded, and petitioner fails to offer any meaningful way in which the University could have improved upon them at the time of her application.

Petitioner also suggests altering the weight given to academic and socioeconomic factors in the University's admissions calculus. This proposal ignores the fact that the University tried, and failed, to increase diversity through enhanced consideration of socioeconomic and other factors. And it further ignores this Court's precedent making clear that the Equal Protection Clause does not force universities to choose between a diverse student body and a reputation for academic excellence.

Petitioner's final suggestion is to uncap the Top Ten Percent Plan, and admit more—if not all—the University's students through a percentage plan. * * * Even if, as a matter of raw numbers, minority enrollment would increase under such a regime, petitioner would be hard-pressed to find convincing support for the proposition that college admissions would be improved if they were a function of class rank alone. That approach would sacrifice all other aspects of diversity in pursuit of enrolling a higher number of minority students. A system that selected every student through class rank alone would exclude the star athlete or musician whose grades suffered because of daily practices and training. It would exclude a talented young biologist who struggled to maintain above-average grades in humanities classes. And it would exclude a student whose freshman-year grades were poor because of a family crisis but who got herself back on track in her last three years of school, only to find herself just outside of the top decile of her class.

These are but examples of the general problem. Class rank is a single metric, and like any single metric, it will capture certain types of people and miss others. This does not imply that students admitted through holistic review are necessarily more capable or more desirable than those admitted through the Top Ten Percent Plan. It merely reflects the fact that privileging one characteristic above all others does not lead to a diverse student body. Indeed, to compel universities to admit students based on class rank alone is in deep tension with the goal of educational diversity as this Court's cases have defined it. At its center, the Top Ten Percent Plan is a blunt instrument that may well compromise the University's own definition of the diversity it seeks.

In short, none of petitioner's suggested alternatives—nor other proposals considered or discussed in the course of this litigation—have been shown to be "available" and "workable" means through which the University could have met its educational goals, as it understood and defined them in 2008. *Fisher I*, 570 U.S. at 312. The University has thus met its burden of showing that the admissions policy it used at the time it rejected petitioner's application was narrowly tailored.

The Court's affirmance of the University's admissions policy today does not necessarily mean the University may rely on that same policy without refinement. It is the University's ongoing obligation to engage in constant deliberation and continued reflection regarding its admissions policies. [Affirmed.]

JUSTICE ALITO, with whom THE CHIEF JUSTICE and JUSTICE THOMAS join, dissenting.

UT's race-conscious admissions program cannot satisfy strict scrutiny. UT says that the program furthers its interest in the educational benefits of diversity, but it has failed to define that interest with any clarity or to demonstrate that its program is narrowly tailored to achieve that or any other particular interest. By accepting UT's rationales as sufficient to meet its burden, the majority licenses UT's perverse assumptions about different groups of minority students—the precise assumptions strict scrutiny is supposed to stamp out.

It is important to understand what is and what is not at stake in this case. *What is not at stake* is whether UT or any other university may adopt an admissions plan that results in a student body with a broad representation of students from all racial and ethnic groups. UT previously had a race-neutral plan that it claimed had "effectively compensated for the loss of affirmative action," and UT could have taken other steps that would have increased the diversity of its admitted students without taking race or ethnic background into account.

What is at stake is whether university administrators may justify systematic racial discrimination simply by asserting that such discrimination is necessary to achieve "the educational benefits of diversity," without explaining—much less proving—why the discrimination is needed or how the discriminatory plan is well crafted to serve its objectives. Even though UT has never provided any coherent explanation for its asserted need to discriminate on the basis of race, and even though UT's position relies on a series of unsupported and noxious racial

> **Food for Thought**
>
> Is what the dissent seeks realistic in an area in which so much depends on the judgment of educators? How can a university prove that racial discrimination is necessary to achieve educational benefits?

assumptions, the majority concludes that UT has met its heavy burden. This conclusion is remarkable—and remarkably wrong.

POINTS FOR DISCUSSION

a. Applying *Grutter*

The Court in *Fisher I* concluded that strict scrutiny of race-based affirmative action programs requires "a careful judicial inquiry into whether a university could achieve sufficient diversity without using racial classifications," and that the reviewing court "must ultimately be satisfied that no workable race-neutral alternatives would produce the educational benefits of diversity." Is it clear that the Court applied such a test in *Grutter*? After all, there was evidence that facially race-neutral alternatives, such as top-ten plans, could have produced comparably diverse admitted classes. If not, does that mean that the Court in *Fisher I* signaled its desire to apply a more traditional form of strict scrutiny to race-conscious affirmative action programs? If so, did the Court apply such scrutiny in *Fisher II*?

b.   Narrow Tailoring and Critical Masses

Using facially race-neutral admissions policies between 1996 and 2004, the University of Texas succeeded in enrolling classes that were as racially diverse as the classes it had enrolled under its prior, race-conscious policies. In light of that fact, can the 2004 admissions plan at issue in the *Fisher* cases satisfy the requirement that there be "no workable race-neutral alternatives" that would produce the educational benefits of diversity? The University contended that its prior approaches were inadequate because small courses often did not enroll a critical mass of minority students. At what level of granularity should the courts define a "critical mass" for purposes of assessing whether a race-conscious affirmative action plan is justified by the absence of "workable" race-neutral alternatives? After *Fisher II*, what is the minimum evidence that a university needs to present to justify a race conscious admissions policy?

Grutter, *Gratz*, and *Fisher* all addressed the constitutionality of race-conscious student-selection policies at universities. Since the desegregation decisions, which we considered earlier in this chapter, many public school districts have also considered race in assigning students to high schools, in order more fully to integrate their schools. What is the constitutional status of such policies? The case that follows addresses that question.

PARENTS INVOLVED IN COMMUNITY SCHOOLS V. SEATTLE SCHOOL DIST. NO. 1
551 U.S. 701 (2007)

CHIEF JUSTICE ROBERTS announced the judgment of the Court, and delivered the opinion of the Court with respect to Parts I, II, III-A, and III-C, and an opinion with respect to Parts III-B and IV, in which JUSTICES SCALIA, THOMAS, and ALITO join.

The school districts in these cases voluntarily adopted student assignment plans that rely upon race to determine which public schools certain children may attend. The Seattle school district classifies children as white or nonwhite; the Jefferson County school district as black or "other." In Seattle, this racial classification is used to allocate slots in oversubscribed high schools. In Jefferson

County, [which embraces Louisville, Kentucky,] it is used to make certain elementary school assignments and to rule on transfer requests. In each case, the school district relies upon an individual student's race in assigning that student to a particular school, so that the racial balance at the school falls within a predetermined range based on the racial composition of the school district as a whole. Parents of students denied assignment to particular schools under these plans solely because of their race brought suit, contending that allocating children to different public schools on the basis of race violated the Fourteenth Amendment guarantee of equal protection.

[There are ten high schools in the Seattle School District, where white students constitute 41 percent of enrolled students and non-white students 59 percent. Incoming students rank the schools according to their preferences. If too many choose the same school, the District uses a series of "tiebreakers" to determine who will get to attend. If the school's racial composition deviates by more than 10% from the district's overall balance between white and non-white students, the race of the students who seek to attend is the second tiebreaker. In Jefferson County, where 34 percent of the students are black, the plan requires all non-magnet schools to maintain a black enrollment between 15 and 50 percent.]

III

A

It is well established that when the government distributes burdens or benefits on the basis of individual racial classifications, that action is reviewed under strict scrutiny. *Grutter v. Bollinger,* 539 U.S. 306, 326 (2003). [Our] prior cases, in evaluating the use of racial classifications in the school context, have recognized two interests that qualify as compelling. The first is the compelling interest of remedying the effects of past intentional discrimination. Yet the Seattle public schools have not shown that they were ever segregated by law, and were not subject to court-ordered desegregation decrees. The Jefferson County public schools were previously segregated by law and were subject to a desegregation decree entered in 1975. [But once] Jefferson County achieved unitary status, it had remedied the constitutional wrong that allowed race-based assignments. Any continued use of race must be justified on some other basis.

> **Definition**
>
> A school district achieved "unitary status" by eliminating *de jure* segregation and its vestiges, in compliance with the mandate of *Brown* and *Brown II.*

The second government interest we have recognized as compelling for purposes of strict scrutiny is the interest in diversity in higher education upheld in

Grutter, 539 U.S., at 328. The specific interest found compelling in *Grutter* was student body diversity "in the context of higher education." * * * The entire gist of the analysis in *Grutter* was that the admissions program at issue there focused on each applicant as an individual, and not simply as a member of a particular racial group. In the present cases, by contrast, race is not considered as part of a broader effort to achieve "exposure to widely diverse people, cultures, ideas, and viewpoints"; race, for some students, is determinative standing alone. The districts argue that other factors, such as student preferences, affect assignment decisions under their plans, but under each plan when race comes into play, it is decisive by itself. It is not simply one factor weighed with others in reaching a decision, as in *Grutter*; it is *the* factor. * * * Even when it comes to race, the plans here employ only a limited notion of diversity, viewing race exclusively in white/nonwhite terms in Seattle and black/"other" terms in Jefferson County.

B

Each school district argues that educational and broader socialization benefits flow from a racially diverse learning environment * * *. The parties and their *amici* dispute whether racial diversity in schools in fact has a marked impact on test scores and other objective yardsticks or achieves intangible socialization benefits. The debate is not one we need to resolve, however, because it is clear that the racial classifications employed by the districts are not narrowly tailored to the goal of achieving the educational and social benefits asserted to flow from racial diversity. In design and operation, the plans are directed only to racial balance, pure and simple, an objective this Court has repeatedly condemned as illegitimate.

The plans are tied to each district's specific racial demographics, rather than to any pedagogic concept of the level of diversity needed to obtain the asserted educational benefits. [But the] districts offer no evidence that the level of racial diversity necessary to achieve the asserted educational benefits happens to coincide with the racial demographics of the respective school districts * * *. This working backward to achieve a particular type of racial balance, rather than working forward from some demonstration of the level of diversity that provides the purported benefits, is a fatal flaw under our existing precedent. * * * Accepting racial balancing as a compelling state interest would justify the imposition of racial proportionality throughout American society, contrary to our repeated recognition that "[a]t the heart of the Constitution's guarantee of equal protection lies the simple command that the Government must treat citizens as individuals, not as simply components of a racial, religious, sexual or national class." * * *

Racial balancing is not transformed from "patently unconstitutional" to a compelling state interest simply by relabeling it "racial diversity."

C

[The] minimal effect these classifications have on student assignments [suggests] that other means would be effective. Seattle's racial tiebreaker results, in the end, only in shifting a small number of students between schools. * * * Similarly, Jefferson County's use of racial classifications has only a minimal effect on the assignment of students. * * * Jefferson County estimates that the racial guidelines account for only 3 percent of assignments. [While] we do not suggest that *greater* use of race would be preferable, the minimal impact of the districts' racial classifications on school enrollment casts doubt on the necessity of using racial classifications. [The] districts have also failed to show that they considered methods other than explicit racial classifications to achieve their stated goals.

> **Food for Thought**
>
> Can you think of any race-neutral approaches that the school districts could take to achieve their goals? If so, do you think that they would be effective?

IV

In *Brown v. Board of Education*, 347 U.S. 483 (1954), [it] was not the inequality of the facilities but the fact of legally separating children on the basis of race on which the Court relied to find a constitutional [violation]. * * * The parties and their *amici* debate which side is more faithful to the heritage of *Brown*, but the position of the plaintiffs in *Brown* was spelled out in their brief and could not have been clearer: "[T]he Fourteenth Amendment prevents states from according differential treatment to American children on the basis of their color or race." What do the racial classifications at issue here do, if not accord differential treatment on the basis of race? As counsel who appeared before this Court for the plaintiffs in *Brown* put it: "We have one fundamental contention which we will seek to develop in the course of this argument, and that contention is that no State has any authority under the equal-protection clause of the Fourteenth Amendment to use race as a factor in affording educational opportunities among its citizens." There is no ambiguity in that statement. And it was that position that prevailed in this Court * * *.

Before *Brown*, schoolchildren were told where they could and could not go to school based on the color of their skin. The school districts in these cases have not carried the heavy burden of demonstrating that we should allow this once again—even for very different reasons. For schools that never segregated on the basis of race, such as Seattle, or that have removed the vestiges of past segregation, such as Jefferson County, the way "to achieve a system of determining admission to the public schools on a nonracial basis," *Brown II,* 349 U.S., at 300–301, is to stop assigning students on a racial basis. The way to stop discrimination on the basis of race is to stop discriminating on the basis of race.

JUSTICE THOMAS, concurring.

Racial imbalance is not segregation. Although presently observed racial imbalance might result from past *de jure* segregation, racial imbalance can also result from any number of innocent private decisions, including voluntary housing choices. Because racial imbalance is not inevitably linked to unconstitutional segregation, it is not unconstitutional in and of itself. * * * Although there is arguably a danger of racial imbalance in schools in Seattle and Louisville, there is no danger of resegregation.

Remediation of past *de jure* segregation is a one-time process involving the redress of a discrete legal injury inflicted by an identified entity. At some point, the discrete injury will be remedied, and the school district will be declared unitary. Unlike *de jure* segregation, there is no ultimate remedy for racial imbalance. Individual schools will fall in and out of balance in the natural course, and the appropriate balance itself will shift with a school district's changing demographics. Thus, racial balancing will have to take place on an indefinite basis—a continuous process with no identifiable culpable party and no discernable end point.

Most of the dissent's criticisms of today's result can be traced to its rejection of the color-blind Constitution. The dissent attempts to marginalize the notion of a color-blind Constitution by consigning it to me and Members of today's plurality. But I am quite comfortable in the company I keep. My view of the Constitution is Justice Harlan's view in *Plessy:* "Our Constitution is color-blind, and neither knows nor tolerates classes among citizens." *Plessy v. Ferguson,* 163 U.S. 537, 559 (1896) (dissenting opinion). And my view was the rallying cry for the lawyers who litigated *Brown.* See, *e.g.,* Brief for Appellants in *Brown v. Board of Education* ("That the Constitution is color blind is our dedicated belief"). * * * What was wrong in 1954 cannot be right today.

JUSTICE KENNEDY, concurring in part and concurring in the judgment.

[P]arts of the opinion by the Chief Justice imply an all-too-unyielding insistence that race cannot be a factor in instances when, in my view, it may be taken into account. * * * To the extent the plurality opinion suggests the Constitution mandates that state and local school authorities must accept the status quo of racial isolation in schools, it is, in my view, profoundly mistaken. * * * The statement by Justice Harlan that "[o]ur Constitution is color-blind" was most certainly justified in the context of his dissent in *Plessy*. [A]s an aspiration, Justice Harlan's axiom must command our assent. In the real world, it is regrettable to say, it cannot be a universal constitutional principle.

> **Take Note**
>
> Justice Kennedy joined only part of Chief Justice Roberts's opinion. He was the fifth vote for those parts. As you read his opinion, consider what it suggests about the precedential effect of the Chief Justice's opinion.

In the administration of public schools by the state and local authorities it is permissible to consider the racial makeup of schools and to adopt general policies to encourage a diverse student body, one aspect of which is its racial composition. If school authorities are concerned that the student-body compositions of certain schools interfere with the objective of offering an equal educational opportunity to all of their students, they are free to devise race-conscious measures to address the problem in a general way and without treating each student in different fashion solely on the basis of a systematic, individual typing by race.

School boards may pursue the goal of bringing together students of diverse backgrounds and races through other means, including strategic site selection of new schools; drawing attendance zones with general recognition of the demographics of neighborhoods; allocating resources for special programs; recruiting students and faculty in a targeted fashion; and tracking enrollments, performance, and other statistics by race. These mechanisms are race conscious but do not lead to different treatment based on a classification that tells each student he or she is to be defined by race, so it is unlikely any of them would demand strict scrutiny to be found permissible. * * * Assigning to each student a personal designation according to a crude system of individual racial classifications is quite a different matter; and the legal analysis changes accordingly.

[I] agree that in the context of these plans, the small number of assignments affected suggests that the schools could have achieved their stated ends through different means. These include the facially race-neutral means set forth above or, if necessary, a more nuanced, individual evaluation of school needs and student characteristics that might include race as a component.

[The dissent raises the following question:] If it is legitimate for school authorities to work to avoid racial isolation in their schools, must they do so only by indirection and general policies? * * * Why may the authorities not recognize the problem in candid fashion and solve it altogether through resort to direct assignments based on student racial classifications? So, the argument proceeds, if race is the problem, then perhaps race is the solution.

The argument ignores the dangers presented by individual classifications, dangers that are not as pressing when the same ends are achieved by more indirect means. When the government classifies an individual by race, it must first define what it means to be of a race. Who exactly is white and who is nonwhite? To be forced to live under a state-mandated racial label is inconsistent with the dignity of individuals in our society. And it is a label that an individual is powerless to change. Governmental classifications that command people to march in different directions based on racial typologies can cause a new divisiveness. The practice can lead to corrosive discourse, where race serves not as an element of our diverse heritage but instead as a bargaining chip in the political process. On the other hand race-conscious measures that do not rely on differential treatment based on individual classifications present these problems to a lesser degree.

This Nation has a moral and ethical obligation to fulfill its historic commitment to creating an integrated society that ensures equal opportunity for all of its children. A compelling interest exists in avoiding racial isolation, an interest that a school district, in its discretion and expertise, may choose to pursue. Likewise, a district may consider it a compelling interest to achieve a diverse student population. Race may be one component of that diversity, but other demographic factors, plus special talents and needs, should also be considered. What the government is not permitted to do, absent a showing of necessity not made here, is to classify every student on the basis of race and to assign each of them to schools based on that classification. Crude measures of this sort threaten to reduce children to racial chits valued and traded according to one school's supply and another's demand. * * * The decision today should not prevent school districts from continuing the important work of bringing together students of different racial, ethnic, and economic backgrounds.

JUSTICE STEVENS, dissenting.

There is a cruel irony in the Chief Justice's reliance on our decision in *Brown v. Board of Education,* 349 U.S. 294 (1955). The first sentence in the concluding paragraph of his opinion states: "Before *Brown,* schoolchildren were told where they could and could not go to school based on the color of their skin." * * * The Chief Justice fails to note that it was only black schoolchildren who were so ordered; indeed, the history books do not tell stories of white children struggling to attend black schools. In this and other ways, the Chief Justice rewrites the history of one of this Court's most important decisions.

The Chief Justice rejects the conclusion that the racial classifications at issue here should be viewed differently than others, because they do not impose burdens on one race alone and do not stigmatize or exclude. The only justification for refusing to acknowledge the obvious importance of that difference is the citation of a few recent opinions—none of which even approached unanimity—grandly proclaiming that all racial classifications must be analyzed under "strict scrutiny." [This approach] obscures *Brown*'s clear message. Perhaps the best example is provided by our approval of the decision of the Supreme Judicial Court of Massachusetts in 1967 upholding a state statute mandating racial integration in that State's school system [through the allocation of students based on race]. See *School Comm. of Boston v. Board of Education,* 352 Mass. 693 (1967). Invoking our mandatory appellate jurisdiction, the Boston plaintiffs prosecuted an appeal in this Court. Our ruling on the merits simply stated that the appeal was "dismissed for want of a substantial federal question." *School Comm. of Boston v. Board of Education,* 389 U.S. 572 (1968) *(per curiam).* That decision not only expressed our appraisal of the merits of the appeal, but it constitutes a precedent that the Court overrules today.

The Court has changed significantly since it decided *School Comm. of Boston* in 1968. It was then more faithful to *Brown* and more respectful of our precedent than it is today. It is my firm conviction that no Member of the Court that I joined in 1975 would have agreed with today's decision.

JUSTICE BREYER, with whom JUSTICE STEVENS, JUSTICE SOUTER, and JUSTICE GINSBURG join, dissenting.

A longstanding and unbroken line of legal authority tells us that the Equal Protection Clause permits local school boards to use race-conscious criteria to achieve positive race-related goals, even when the Constitution does not compel it. Because of its importance, I shall

Make the Connection

We considered the line of cases to which Justice Breyer refers earlier in this chapter, after our discussion of *Brown*.

repeat what this Court said about the matter in *Swann v. Charlotte-Mecklenburg Bd. of Ed.,* 402 U.S. 1, 16 (1971). Chief Justice Burger, on behalf of a unanimous Court in a case of exceptional importance, wrote:

"School authorities are traditionally charged with broad power to formulate and implement educational policy and might well conclude, for example, that in order to prepare students to live in a pluralistic society each school should have a prescribed ratio of Negro to white students reflecting the proportion for the district as a whole. To do this as an educational policy is within the broad discretionary powers of school authorities."

The statement was not a technical holding in the case. But the Court set forth in *Swann* a basic principle of constitutional law—a principle of law that has found "wide acceptance in the legal culture." Thus, in *North Carolina Bd. of Ed. v. Swann,* 402 U.S. 43, 45 (1971), this Court [restated] the point. "[S]chool authorities," the Court said, "have wide discretion in formulating school policy, and [as] a matter of educational policy school authorities may well conclude that some kind of racial balance in the schools is desirable quite apart from any constitutional requirements." Then-Justice Rehnquist echoed this view in *Bustop, Inc. v. Los Angeles Bd. of Ed.,* 439 U.S. 1380, 1383 (1978)[:] "While I have the gravest doubts that [a state supreme court] was *required* by the United States Constitution to take the [race-conscious student assignment] action that it has taken in this case, I have very little doubt that it was *permitted* by that Constitution to take such action."

These statements nowhere suggest that this freedom is limited to school districts where court-ordered desegregation measures are also in effect. Indeed, in *McDaniel v. Barresi,* 402 U.S. 39, 40, n. 1 (1971), a case decided the same day as *Swann,* a group of parents challenged a race-conscious student assignment plan that the Clarke County School Board had *voluntarily* adopted as a remedy without a court order * * *. The plan required that each elementary school in the district maintain 20% to 40% enrollment of African-American students, corresponding to the racial composition of the district. This Court upheld the plan, rejecting the parents' argument that "a person may not be *included* or *excluded* solely because he is a Negro or because he is white."

Swann is predicated upon a well-established legal view of the Fourteenth Amendment. That view understands the basic objective of those who wrote the Equal Protection Clause as forbidding practices that lead to racial exclusion. * * * There is reason to believe that those who drafted an Amendment with this basic purpose in mind would have understood the legal and practical difference between the use of race-conscious criteria in defiance of that purpose, namely to keep the races apart, and the use of race-conscious criteria to further that purpose, namely to bring the races together. * * * Sometimes Members of this Court have disagreed about the degree of leniency that the Clause affords to programs designed to include. But I can find no case in which this Court has followed Justice THOMAS' "colorblind" approach. And I have found no case that otherwise repudiated this constitutional asymmetry between that which seeks to *exclude* and that which seeks to *include* members of minority races. [N]o case—not *Adarand, Gratz, Grutter,* or any other—has ever held that the test of "strict scrutiny" means that all racial classifications—no matter whether they seek to include or exclude—must in practice be treated the same.

This context is *not* a context that involves the use of race to decide who will receive goods or services that are normally distributed on the basis of merit and which are in short supply. It is not one in which race-conscious limits stigmatize or exclude; the limits at issue do not pit the races against each other or otherwise significantly exacerbate racial tensions. They do not impose burdens unfairly upon members of one race alone but instead seek benefits for members of all races alike. The context here is one of racial limits that seek, not to keep the races apart, but to bring them together.

I believe that the law requires application here of a standard of review that is not "strict" in the traditional sense of that word * * *. Nonetheless, [I conclude] that the plans before us pass both parts of the [conventional] strict scrutiny test. [T]he interest at stake possesses three essential elements. First, there is a historical and remedial element: an interest in setting right the consequences of prior conditions of segregation. * * * Second, there is an educational element: an interest in overcoming the adverse educational effects produced by and associated with highly segregated schools. * * * Third, there is a democratic element: an interest in producing an educational environment that reflects the "pluralistic society" in which our children will live. [It] is an interest in teaching children to engage in the kind of cooperation among Americans of all races that is necessary to make a land of three hundred million people one Nation. * * * If an educational interest that combines these three elements is not "compelling," what is?

Several factors, taken together, [lead] me to conclude that the boards' use of race-conscious criteria in these plans passes even the strictest "tailoring" test. First, the race-conscious criteria at issue only help set the outer bounds of *broad* ranges. They constitute but one part of plans that depend primarily upon other, nonracial elements. [In] fact, the defining feature of both plans is greater emphasis upon student choice. In Seattle, for example, in more than 80% of all cases, that choice alone determines which high schools Seattle's ninth graders will attend. * * * Second, [the] plans before us are *more narrowly tailored* than the race-conscious admission plans that this Court approved in *Grutter*. Here, race becomes a factor only in a fraction of students' non-merit-based assignments—not in large numbers of students' merit-based applications. Moreover, [d]isappointed students are not rejected from a State's flagship graduate program; they simply attend a different one of the district's many public schools, which in aspiration and in fact are substantially equal. * * * Third, [each] plan is the product of a process that has sought to enhance student choice, while diminishing the need for mandatory busing.

Nor could the school districts have accomplished their desired aims (*e.g.*, avoiding forced busing, countering white flight, maintaining racial diversity) by other means. Nothing in the extensive history of desegregation efforts over the past 50 years gives the districts, or this Court, any reason to believe that another method is possible to accomplish these goals. The wide variety of different integration plans that school districts use throughout the Nation suggests that the problem of racial segregation in schools, including *de facto* segregation, is difficult to solve. The fact that many such plans have used explicitly racial criteria suggests that such criteria have an important, sometimes necessary, role to play.

The lesson of history [is] not that efforts to continue racial segregation are constitutionally indistinguishable from efforts to achieve racial integration. Indeed, it is a cruel distortion of history to compare Topeka, Kansas, in the 1950's to Louisville and Seattle in the modern day—to equate the plight of Linda Brown (who was ordered to attend a Jim Crow school) to the circumstances of Joshua McDonald (whose request to transfer to a school closer to home was initially declined). * * * The last half-century has witnessed great strides toward racial equality, but we have not yet realized the promise of *Brown*. To invalidate the plans under review is to threaten the promise of *Brown*. The plurality's position, I fear, would break that promise. This is a decision that the Court and the Nation will come to regret.

POINTS FOR DISCUSSION

a. The Use of Race in School Assignments

After the Court's decision in *Parents Involved*, is there any use of race in the assignment of students to schools that can survive scrutiny? Notice that Justice Kennedy declined to join some sections of Chief Justice Roberts's opinion and suggested a greater willingness to permit race-conscious decision-making in this context. Is a narrowly drawn plan whose purpose is to avoid "racial isolation" and achieve "a diverse student population" constitutional?

Both Chief Justice Roberts and Justice Kennedy relied, in concluding that the plans were unconstitutional, in part on the availability of race-neutral means to achieve racial balance in schools. Suppose that a school district gives preference in school assignments to students from certain zip codes in which most of the district's minority population is concentrated, with the avowed purpose of achieving greater racial balance in schools. Such an approach would be race-neutral on its face, as it would apply equally to white students from the neighborhoods in question, but geography would be used quite intentionally as a proxy for race. Would such an approach survive scrutiny under the Court's approach? If so, why is it meaningfully different from the Seattle and Louisville plans?

b. The Role of Racial Identity

The various opinions disputed the utility and value of achieving "racial balance" in public schools. But even assuming that it is a desirable aim, the question of *when* a student population should be considered "racially balanced" is a difficult one. Seattle measured racial balance according to a binary "white/nonwhite" standard, and Jefferson County used a "black/other" standard. Such approaches are potentially problematic for at least two reasons. First, they appear to identify a significant percentage of the population only in contradistinction to one, perhaps arbitrarily defined, group. Second, they ignore the considerably more complex and rich set of racial and ethnic backgrounds that characterize the American population, particularly in the urban areas most likely to adopt plans such as those at issue in the case. Are such definitions of racial balance themselves problematic under the Fourteenth Amendment? Would an approach to racial balancing that explicitly considers other racial and ethnic groups avoid the problems of the challenged plans, or would it suffer from the same—or even a worse—defect as the plans at issue in *Parents Involved*?

c. Formal Strict Scrutiny v. Contextualized Strict Scrutiny

Traditionally, formal strict scrutiny is characterized as being "strict in theory, and fatal in fact." Gerald Gunther, *Foreword: In Search of Evolving Doctrine on a Changing Court: A Model for a Newer Equal Protection*, 86 Harv. L. Rev. 1, 8 (1972). But in *Grutter*, Justice O'Connor declared that "[c]ontext matters when reviewing race-based governmental action under the Equal Protection Clause," leading some commentators to believe that the Court was articulating a new, contextualized approach to strict scrutiny that examined historical circumstance and social conditions. The Ninth Circuit had applied this approach in upholding Seattle's student-assignment plan, and Justice Breyer would have applied it, as well. Is such an approach "strict scrutiny" in the conventional sense at all? If not, then to what types of classifications does it apply?

d. Competing Views of *Brown*

The competing opinions offer dramatically different views of the meaning of *Brown v. Board of Education*. To Chief Justice Roberts and Justice Thomas, *Brown* was, at its core, about the constitutional status of government actions that deviate from the color-blind ideal. To Justice Breyer, by contrast, *Brown* was about the status of government policies predicated on racial subordination or exclusion. Whose view is more faithful to the Court's decision in *Brown*? Whose view is more faithful to the original meaning of the Fourteenth Amendment? Is this a policy issue that the Justices should decide for themselves without reference to either the original meaning or precedent?

6. Race and Redistricting

As we will see in more detail in Chapter 7, there is a disturbing history of official attempts to deny the franchise to racial minorities. The Fifteenth Amendment sought to end these practices, but subtle forms of racial

> **Definition**
>
> A gerrymander is when legislative district lines are drawn to benefit a particular group. The term is derived from Elbridge Gerry, a founding father and the governor of Massachusetts, who was accused of manipulating district lines to benefit his political party.

discrimination in voting persisted. Some states—particularly in the South—imposed various obstacles to the right to vote, including poll taxes and discriminatorily administered literacy tests. In addition, some states engaged in racial gerrymandering to dilute the strength of minority voters at the polls. See, e.g., *Gomillion v. Lightfoot*, 364 U.S. 339 (1960); *Rogers v. Lodge,* 458 U.S. 613 (1982).

Congress enacted the Voting Rights Act of 1965, codified as amended at 42 U.S.C. § 1973 *et seq.*, to prevent voting practices that burden disadvantaged minorities. Since that time, some state legislatures have sought to increase the voting power of minorities, particularly African Americans. The following case concerns the constitutionality of one means to that end.

SHAW V. RENO
509 U.S. 630 (1993)

JUSTICE O'CONNOR delivered the opinion of the Court.

As a result of the 1990 census, North Carolina became entitled to a 12th seat in the United States House of Representatives. The General Assembly enacted a reapportionment plan that included one majority-black congressional district. After the Attorney General of the United States objected to the plan pursuant to

§ 5 of the Voting Rights Act of 1965 the General Assembly passed new legislation creating a second majority-black district. Appellants allege that the revised plan, which contains district boundary lines of dramatically irregular shape, constitutes an unconstitutional racial gerrymander.

[W]hat appellants object to is redistricting legislation that is so extremely irregular on its face that it rationally can be viewed only as an effort to segregate the races for purposes of voting, without regard for traditional districting principles and without sufficiently compelling justification. * * * Appellants contend that redistricting legislation that is so bizarre on its face that it is "unexplainable on grounds other than race" demands the same close scrutiny that we give other state laws that classify citizens by race. Our voting rights precedents support that conclusion.

A reapportionment plan that includes in one district individuals who belong to the same race, but who are otherwise widely separated by geographical and political boundaries, and who may have little in common with one another but the color of their skin, bears an uncomfortable resemblance to political apartheid. It reinforces the perception that members of the same racial group—regardless of their age, education, economic status, or the community in which they live—think alike, share the same political interests, and will prefer the same candidates at the polls. We have rejected such perceptions elsewhere as impermissible racial stereotypes. [Furthermore, when] a district obviously is created solely to effectuate the perceived common interests of one racial group, elected officials are more likely to believe that their primary obligation is to represent only the members of that group, rather than their constituency as a whole. This is altogether antithetical to our system of representative democracy.

For these reasons, we conclude that a plaintiff challenging a reapportionment statute under the Equal Protection Clause may state a claim by alleging that the legislation, though race-neutral on its face, rationally cannot be understood as anything other than an effort to separate voters into different districts on the basis of race, and that the separation lacks sufficient justification. * * * We hold [that], on the facts of this case, appellants have stated a claim sufficient to defeat the state appellees' motion to dismiss.

Justice STEVENS argues that racial gerrymandering poses no constitutional difficulties when district lines are drawn to favor the minority, rather than the majority. We have made clear, however, that equal protection analysis "is not dependent on the race of those burdened or benefited by a particular classification." *City of Richmond v. J.A. Croson Co.*, 488 U.S. 469, 494 (1989) (plurality opinion). Indeed, racial classifications receive close scrutiny even when they may be said to burden or benefit the races equally. [The] very reason that the Equal Protection Clause demands strict scrutiny of all racial classifications is because without it, a court cannot determine whether or not the discrimination truly is "benign."

[A]ppellees assert that the deliberate creation of majority-minority districts is the most precise way—indeed the only effective way—to overcome the effects of racially polarized voting. This question [need] not be decided at this stage of the litigation. * * * Today we hold only that appellants have stated a claim under the Equal Protection Clause by alleging that the North Carolina General Assembly adopted a reapportionment scheme so irrational on its face that it can be understood only as an effort to segregate voters into separate voting districts because of their race, and that the separation lacks sufficient justification. If the allegation of racial gerrymandering remains uncontradicted, the District Court further must determine whether the North Carolina plan is narrowly tailored to further a compelling governmental interest.

FYI

On remand, the district court held that the redistricting plan was narrowly tailored to serve the state's compelling interest in complying with the requirements of the Voting Rights Act. The Supreme Court reversed that decision, holding that the redistricting plan violated the Equal Protection Clause. See *Shaw v. Hunt*, 517 U.S. 899 (1996).

JUSTICE WHITE, with whom JUSTICE BLACKMUN and JUSTICE STEVENS join, dissenting.

[T]he issue is whether the classification based on race discriminates against *anyone* by denying equal access to the political process. [I]t strains credulity to suggest that North Carolina's purpose in creating a second majority-minority district was to discriminate against members of the majority group by "impair[ing] or burden[ing their] opportunity [to] participate in the political process." The State has made no mystery of its intent, which was to respond to the Attorney General's objections by improving the minority group's prospects of electing a candidate of its choice. I doubt that this constitutes a discriminatory purpose as defined in the Court's equal protection cases—*i.e.,* an intent to aggravate "the unequal distribution of electoral power." But even assuming that it does, there is no question that appellants have not alleged the requisite discriminatory effects. Whites constitute roughly 76% of the total population and 79% of the voting age population in North Carolina. Yet, under the State's plan, they still constitute a voting majority in 10 (or 83%) of the 12 congressional districts. Though they might be dissatisfied at the prospect of casting a vote for a losing candidate—a lot shared by many, including a disproportionate number of minority voters—surely they cannot complain of discriminatory treatment. [The redistricting plan involves] an attempt to *equalize* treatment, and to provide minority voters with an effective voice in the political process. The Equal Protection Clause of the Constitution, surely, does not stand in the way.

JUSTICE BLACKMUN, dissenting.

It is particularly ironic that the case in which today's majority chooses to abandon settled law and to recognize for the first time this "analytically distinct" constitutional claim is a challenge by white voters to the plan under which North Carolina has sent black representatives to Congress for the first time since Reconstruction.

JUSTICE STEVENS, dissenting.

[This case gives] rise to three constitutional questions: Does the Constitution impose a requirement of contiguity or compactness on how the States may draw their electoral districts? Does the Equal Protection Clause prevent a State from drawing district boundaries for the purpose of facilitating the election of a member of an identifiable group of voters? And, finally, if the answer to the second question is generally "No," should it be different when the favored group is defined by race?

The first question is easy. There is no independent constitutional requirement of compactness or contiguity, and the Court's opinion (despite its many references to the shape of District 12) does not suggest otherwise. * * * As for the second question, I believe that the Equal Protection Clause is violated when the State creates [uncouth] district boundaries [for] the sole purpose of making it more difficult for members of a minority group to win an election. The duty to govern impartially is abused when a group with power over the electoral process defines electoral boundaries solely to enhance its own political strength at the expense of any weaker group. That duty, however, is not violated when the majority acts to facilitate the election of a member of a group that lacks such

Make the Connection

We will consider the constitutionality of "political gerrymanders"—that is, efforts to draw district lines for partisan purposes—in Chapter 6.

power because it remains underrepresented in the state legislature—whether that group is defined by political affiliation, by common economic interests, or by religious, ethnic, or racial characteristics. The difference between constitutional and unconstitutional gerrymanders has nothing to do with whether they are based on assumptions about the groups they affect, but whether their purpose is to enhance the power of the group in control of the districting process at the expense of any minority group, and thereby to strengthen the unequal distribution of electoral power. [Finally, if] it is permissible to draw boundaries to provide adequate representation for rural voters, for union members, for Hasidic Jews, for Polish Americans, or for Republicans, it necessarily follows that it is permissible to do the same thing for members of the very minority group whose history in the United States gave birth to the Equal Protection Clause. A contrary conclusion could only be described as perverse.

JUSTICE SOUTER, dissenting.

Unlike other contexts in which we have addressed the State's conscious use of race, electoral districting calls for decisions that nearly always require some consideration of race for legitimate reasons where there is a racially mixed population. As long as members of racial groups have the commonality of interest implicit in our ability to talk about concepts like "minority voting strength," and "dilution of minority votes," [which are important in cases interpreting the Voting Rights Act,] and as long as racial bloc voting takes place, legislators will have to take race into account in order to avoid dilution of minority voting strength in the districting plans they adopt. One need look no further than the Voting Rights Act to understand that this may be required, and we have held that race may constitutionally be taken into account in order to comply with that Act. *United Jewish Organizations of Williamsburgh, Inc. v. Carey,* 430 U.S. 144, 161–162 (1977).

A second distinction between districting and most other governmental decisions in which race has figured is that those other decisions using racial criteria characteristically occur in circumstances in which the use of race to the advantage of one person is necessarily at the obvious expense of a member of a different race. * * * In districting, by contrast, the mere placement of an individual in one district instead of another denies no one a right or benefit provided to others. All citizens may register, vote, and be represented. In whatever district, the individual voter has a right to vote in each election, and the election will result in the voter's representation. * * * It is true, of course, that one's vote may be more or less effective depending on the interests of the other individuals who are in one's district, and our cases recognize the reality that members of the same race often have shared interests. "Dilution" thus refers to the effects of districting decisions not on an individual's political power viewed in isolation, but on the political power of a group. * * * Under our cases there is in general a requirement that in order to obtain relief under the Fourteenth Amendment, the purpose and effect of the districting must be to devalue the effectiveness of a voter compared to what, as a group member, he would otherwise be able to enjoy.

POINTS FOR DISCUSSION

a. Subsequent Developments

The Court in *Shaw* held that "bizarre" shapes for districts can demonstrate a prima facie case of racial gerrymandering. Several years after *Shaw*, the Court held that strict scrutiny is also warranted if the plaintiffs can demonstrate that race was a "predominant" factor in the drawing of district lines. *Bush v. Vera*, 517 U.S. 952 (1996); *Miller v. Johnson*, 515 U.S. 900 (1995). What kind of evidence is relevant to a determination that race was the "predominant" factor in districting?

The Court has also held, however, that government may use race as a factor in districting if the predominant factor in districting is political. *Easley v. Cromartie*, 532 U.S. 234 (2001). In *Cromartie*, the Court concluded that the legislature had considered race because African-American voters had voted overwhelmingly for Democrats, and thus that the legislative objective had been the permissible one of creating seats that were safe for candidates of one party. Is this a convincing distinction? We will consider the constitutionality of gerrymandering for political reasons in Chapter 6.

b. "Benign" and "Invidious" Uses of Race

Is there a meaningful difference between a redistricting plan that seeks to dilute the votes of blacks—by ensuring that no district has a very high concentration of black voters—and one that seeks to ensure that there are some districts in which blacks constitute a majority, or at least a strong plurality? Are some uses of race benign? If so, how can a court tell the benign uses from the invidious ones?

c. Individual or Group Rights?

As noted above, the affirmative action cases reveal that the Justices disagree about whether the Fourteenth Amendment protects individual or instead group rights. Regardless of whether it protects individual rights generally, is the context of voting sufficiently different that it could be said to protect group rights in that context? After all, doesn't it take a group of voters to elect a candidate? And wasn't the assumption of the legislators who unconstitutionally drew district lines in the 1960s to dilute the votes of African Americans, see, e.g., *Gomillion v. Lightfoot*, 364 U.S. 339 (1960), that blocs of voters act collectively in exercising the franchise?

d.   Racial and Partisan Gerrymandering

The classic form of gerrymandering is the drawing of legislative district lines to benefit one political party over another. (Even in a state with an equal number of Democrats and Republicans and ten legislative seats, for example, a legislature could end up with nine Republican representatives by loading one district with Democrats and giving a slight majority to Republican voters in the other nine.) As this example suggests, and as we will see in Chapter 6 (and as we briefly noted in Volume 1 when we considered *Baker v. Carr*, the political question doctrine case), part of the problem with gerrymandering is that it entrenches in power particular groups, even if they do not have clear majority voting power. There accordingly is not an easy political (as opposed to judicial) remedy for political gerrymandering. The same is true of gerrymandering plans that disadvantage voters who belong to racial minority groups. Is there a political remedy for racial gerrymandering plans that *benefit* members of minority groups?

B. SEX CLASSIFICATIONS

In *Strauder v. West Virginia*, which the Court decided in the nineteenth century and which we considered earlier in this chapter, the Court declared that a state may "prescribe the qualifications of its jurors, and in so doing make discriminations." Among other things, the Court stated, a state "may confine the selection to males." The Court did "not believe the Fourteenth Amendment was ever intended to prohibit this," because its "aim was against discrimination because of race or color."

For the first hundred years after the ratification of the Fourteenth Amendment, the Court adhered to this view that the Equal Protection Clause does not prevent discrimination on the basis of sex. Is it clear, either from the text of the Clause or from the history of its ratification, that it prevents only discrimination on the basis of race? As we will see in this section, the Court's view of the scope of the Equal Protection Clause's application has changed over time.

1.   The Early View

Take Note

Bradwell was argued (and decided) as a Privileges or Immunities case, rather than as an Equal Protection case. Why do you suppose that was?

The Court first addressed the Fourteenth Amendment's application to sex discrimination in *Bradwell v. People of the State of Illinois*, 83 U.S. 130 (1872). Myra Bradwell sought a license to practice law in Illinois, but was refused based on the reasoning that as a married woman, she would not be bound by the contracts normally formed between attorney and client (a common-law rule no longer in existence). Mrs. Bradwell filed suit, claiming that she was entitled to the license under the Privileges or Immunities Clause of the Fourteenth Amendment. The Court rejected her claim, concluding that a right to practice law is not among the privileges protected by the Clause.

In his concurring opinion, Justice Bradley addressed the permissibility of sex discrimination in natural-law terms. He stated:

> [The] civil law, as well as nature herself, has always recognized a wide difference in the respective spheres and destinies of man and woman. Man is, or should be, woman's protector and defender. The natural and proper timidity and delicacy which belongs to the female sex evidently unfits it for many of the occupations of civil life. The constitution of the family organization, which is founded in the divine ordinance, as well as in the nature of things, indicates the domestic sphere as that which properly belongs to the domain and functions of womanhood. The harmony, not to say identity, of interest and views which belong, or should belong, to the family institution is repugnant to the idea of a woman adopting a distinct and independent career from that of her husband. * * * The paramount destiny and mission of woman are to fulfill the noble and benign offices of wife and mother. This is the law of the Creator. [I]n view of the peculiar characteristics, destiny, and mission of woman, it is within the province of the legislature to ordain what offices, positions, and callings shall be filled and discharged by men * * *.

Women gradually gained political, social, and legal rights in the years after *Bradwell*, but these gains were largely the product of legislative action or constitutional amendment. (The Nineteenth Amendment, for example, prohibited discrimination on the basis of sex in the grant of the franchise.) Courts, however, continued to hold that laws discriminating on the basis of sex were consistent with the Constitution. Indeed, the Court in the early twentieth century was more likely, at least before the adoption of the Nineteenth Amendment, to uphold laws that interfered with contractual relationships when they protected women, rather than all workers. Compare *Lochner v. New York*, 198 U.S. 45 (1905) (striking down a law limiting the number of hours a baker could work), with *Muller v. Oregon*, 208 U.S. 412 (1908) (upholding a law limiting the number of hours women could work in factories). The Court in *Muller* relied explicitly on women's "physical structure" and maternal obligations, which "place [them] at a disadvantage in the struggle for subsistence."

2. Heightened Scrutiny

Matters changed in the latter part of the twentieth century. In October 1971, the House of Representatives approved the Equal Rights Amendment, which provided, "Equality of rights under the law shall not be denied or abridged by the United States or by any State on account of sex." Before the Senate voted, the Court decided *Reed v. Reed*, 404 U.S. 71 (1971), which raised a challenge to a law that required courts, in deciding whom to appoint as administrators of estates of persons who died intestate, to prefer males to equally qualified females. The Court purported to apply rational-basis review, stating the question presented as "whether a difference in the sex of competing applicants for letters of administration bears a rational relationship to a state objective that is sought to be advanced by the operation" of the statute. But the Court nevertheless invalidated the statute. The Court noted that "the objective of reducing the workload on probate courts by eliminating one class of contests is not without some legitimacy." But the Court concluded that this interest was insufficient to justify the discrimination: "To give a mandatory preference to members of either sex over members of the other, merely to accomplish the elimination of hearings on the merits, is to make the very kind of arbitrary legislative choice forbidden by the Equal Protection Clause of the Fourteenth Amendment; and whatever may be said as to the positive values of avoiding intrafamily controversy, the choice in this context may not lawfully be mandated solely on the basis of sex."

Reed ushered in a new era of Equal Protection challenges to state discrimination on the basis of sex. In *Frontiero v. Richardson*, 411 U.S. 677 (1973), the Court considered a challenge to a federal law permitting men in the armed services automatically to claim their wives as dependents (and thus receive a greater allowance for housing and medical benefits), while permitting women in the service to receive such benefits only by proving that their husbands were dependent upon them for more than half of their support. Justice Brennan, writing for himself and three others, declared that classifications based on sex "are inherently suspect, and therefore must be subjected to strict judicial scrutiny." He reasoned that a "long and unfortunate history of sex discrimination," which traditionally was "rationalized by an attitude of 'romantic paternalism,'" "in practical effect [put] women, not on a pedestal, but in a cage." Justice Brennan contended that women continued to face pervasive discrimination, and that sex, "like race and national origin, is an immutable characteristic determined solely by birth." But there were not five votes for this view. Justice Stewart concurred in the judgment, stating his belief that the law was unconstitutional under the form of scrutiny applied in *Reed*. Justices Powell, Burger, and Blackmun also concurred in the judgment, asserting that the Court should not apply strict scrutiny before the nation decided finally on whether to ratify the Equal Rights Amendment. Justice Rehnquist was alone in dissent.

When the Court decided *Frontiero*, the Senate had already joined the House in passing the Equal Rights Amendment by the requisite majority, and 25 states had already ratified it. After the initial flurry of ratifications, however, the Amendment ran into political opposition. In 1976, when the Court decided the case that follows, the Amendment still had not achieved ratification in the requisite 38 states. (Indeed, in the end, only 35 states ratified the Equal Rights Amendment, and some of those later rescinded their ratification.)

CRAIG V. BOREN
429 U.S. 190 (1976)

MR. JUSTICE BRENNAN delivered the opinion of the Court.

[Oklahoma law] prohibits the sale of "nonintoxicating" 3.2% beer to males under the age of 21 and to females under the age of 18. The question to be decided is whether such a gender-based differential constitutes a denial to males 18–20 years of age of the equal protection of the laws in violation of the Fourteenth Amendment.

To withstand constitutional challenge, previous cases establish that classifications by gender must serve important governmental objectives and must be substantially related to achievement of those objectives. Thus, in *Reed v. Reed*, 404 U.S. 71 (1971), the objectives of "reducing the workload on probate courts" and "avoiding intrafamily controversy" were deemed of insufficient importance to sustain use of an overt gender criterion in the appointment of administrators of intestate decedents' estates. Decisions following *Reed* similarly have rejected administrative ease and convenience as sufficiently important objectives to justify gender-based classifications. See, e. g., *Frontiero v. Richardson*, 411 U.S. 677, 690 (1973).

Reed has also provided the underpinning for decisions that have invalidated statutes employing gender as an inaccurate proxy for other, more germane bases of classification. Hence, "archaic and overbroad" generalizations concerning the financial position of servicewomen, *Frontiero*, and working women, *Weinberger v. Wiesenfeld*, 420 U.S. 636, 643 (1975), could not justify use of a gender line in determining eligibility for certain governmental entitlements. Similarly, increasingly outdated misconceptions concerning the role of females in the home rather than in the "marketplace and world of ideas" were rejected as loose-fitting characterizations incapable of supporting state statutory schemes that were premised upon their accuracy. *Stanton v. Stanton*, 421 U.S. 7 (1975). In light of the weak congruence between gender and the characteristic or trait that gender purported to represent, it was necessary that the legislatures choose either to realign their substantive laws in a gender-neutral fashion, or to adopt procedures for identifying those instances where the sex-centered generalization actually comported with fact.

In this case, too, "*Reed*, we feel is controlling." *Stanton*. * * * We accept for purposes of discussion the District Court's identification of the objective underlying [the challenged statutes] as the enhancement of traffic safety. Clearly, the protection of public health and safety represents an important function of state and local governments. However, appellees' statistics in our view cannot support the conclusion that the gender-based distinction closely serves to achieve that objective * * *. Even were this statistical evidence accepted as accurate, it nevertheless offers only a weak answer to the equal protection question presented here. The most focused and relevant of the statistical surveys, arrests of 18–20-year-olds for alcohol-related driving offenses, exemplifies the ultimate unpersuasiveness of this evidentiary record. Viewed in terms of the correlation between sex and the actual activity that Oklahoma seeks to regulate—driving while under the influence of alcohol—the statistics broadly establish that .18% of females and 2% of males in that age group were arrested for that offense. While such a disparity is not trivial in a statistical sense, it hardly can form the basis for employment of a gender line as a classifying device. Certainly if maleness is to serve as a proxy for drinking and driving, a correlation of 2% must be considered an unduly tenuous "fit." * * * Moreover, the statistics exhibit a variety of other shortcomings that seriously impugn their value to equal protection analysis. Setting aside the obvious methodological problems,[14] the surveys do not adequately justify the salient features of Oklahoma's gender-based traffic-safety law. None purports to measure the use and dangerousness of 3.2% beer as opposed to alcohol generally, a detail that is of particular importance since, in light of its low alcohol level, Oklahoma apparently considers the 3.2% beverage to be "nonintoxicating."

[This analysis] illustrates that proving broad sociological propositions by statistics is a dubious business, and one that inevitably is in tension with the

---

[14] The very social stereotypes that find reflection in age-differential laws are likely substantially to distort the accuracy of these comparative statistics. Hence "reckless" young men who drink and drive are transformed into arrest statistics, whereas their female counterparts are chivalrously escorted home. Moreover, the Oklahoma surveys, gathered under a regime where the age-differential law in question has been in effect, are lacking in controls necessary for appraisal of the actual effectiveness of the male 3.2% beer prohibition.

normative philosophy that underlies the Equal Protection Clause. Suffice to say that the showing offered by the appellees does not satisfy us that sex represents a legitimate, accurate proxy for the regulation of drinking and driving. In fact, when it is further recognized that Oklahoma's statute prohibits only the selling of 3.2% beer to young males and not their drinking the beverage once acquired (even after purchase by their 18–20-year-old female companions), the relationship between gender and traffic safety becomes far too tenuous to satisfy *Reed*'s requirement that the gender-based difference be substantially related to achievement of the statutory objective. We hold, therefore, that under *Reed*, Oklahoma's 3.2% beer statute invidiously discriminates against males 18–20 years of age.

MR. JUSTICE POWELL, concurring.

[I] find it unnecessary, in deciding this case, to read [*Reed*] as broadly as some of the Court's language may imply. * * * I view this as a relatively easy case. * * * It seems to me that the statistics offered by appellees and relied upon by the District Court do tend generally to support the view that young men drive more, possibly are inclined to drink more, and for various reasons are involved in more accidents than young women. Even so, I am not persuaded that these facts and the inferences fairly drawn from them justify this classification based on a three-year age differential between the sexes, and especially one that it so easily circumvented as to be virtually meaningless. Putting it differently, this gender-based classification does not bear a fair and substantial relation to the object of the legislation.

MR. JUSTICE STEVENS, concurring.

There is only one Equal Protection Clause. It requires every State to govern impartially. It does not direct the courts to apply one standard of review in some cases and a different standard in other cases. * * * I am inclined to believe that what has become known as the two-tiered analysis of equal protection claims does not describe a completely logical method of deciding cases, but rather is a method the Court has employed to explain decisions that actually apply a single standard in a reasonably consistent fashion.

In this case, the classification * * * is objectionable because it is based on an accident of birth, because it is a mere remnant of the now almost universally rejected tradition of discriminating against males in this age bracket, and because, to the extent it reflects any physical difference between males and females, it is actually perverse. The question then is whether the traffic safety justification put forward by the State is sufficient to make an otherwise offensive classification acceptable. The classification is not totally irrational. For the evidence does indicate that there are more males than females in this age bracket who drive and also more who drink. Nevertheless, [it] is difficult to believe that the statute was actually intended to cope with the problem of traffic safety, since it has only a minimal effect on access to a not very intoxicating beverage and does not prohibit its consumption. Moreover, [the] legislation imposes a restraint on 100% of the males in the class allegedly because about 2% of them have probably violated one or more laws relating to the consumption of alcoholic beverages. It is unlikely that this law will have a significant deterrent effect either on that 2% or on the law-abiding 98%. But even assuming some such slight benefit, it does not seem to me that an insult to all of the young men of the State can be justified by visiting the sins of the 2% on the 98%.

MR. JUSTICE STEWART, concurring in the judgment.

The disparity created by these Oklahoma statutes amounts to total irrationality. For the statistics upon which the State now relies, whatever their other shortcomings, wholly fail to prove or even suggest that 3.2% beer is somehow more deleterious when it comes into the hands of a male aged 18–20 than of a female of like age. The disparate statutory treatment of the sexes here, without even a colorably valid justification or explanation, thus amounts to invidious discrimination. See *Reed*.

MR. JUSTICE REHNQUIST, dissenting.

Most obviously unavailable to support any kind of special scrutiny in this case is a history or pattern of past discrimination, such as was relied on by the plurality in *Frontiero* to support its invocation of strict scrutiny. There is no suggestion in the Court's opinion that males in this age group are in any way peculiarly disadvantaged, subject to systematic discriminatory treatment, or otherwise in need of special solicitude from the courts. * * * [T]he Court's reliance on our previous sex-discrimination cases [thus] is ill-founded.

The Court's [proposed level of scrutiny] apparently comes out of thin air. The Equal Protection Clause contains no such language, and none of our previous cases adopt that standard. I would think we have had enough difficulty with the two standards of review which our cases have recognized [so] as to counsel weightily against the insertion of still another "standard" between those two. How is this Court to divine what objectives are important? How is it to determine whether a particular law is "substantially" related to the achievement of such objective, rather than related in some other way to its achievement? Both of the phrases used are so diaphanous and elastic as to invite subjective judicial preferences or prejudices relating to particular types of legislation, masquerading as judgments whether such legislation is directed at "important" objectives or, whether the relationship to those objectives is "substantial" enough.

The Oklahoma Legislature could have believed that 18–20-year-old males drive substantially more, and tend more often to be intoxicated than their female counterparts; that they prefer beer and admit to drinking and driving at a higher rate than females; and that they suffer traffic injuries out of proportion to the part they make up of the population. Under the appropriate rational-basis test for equal protection, it is neither irrational nor arbitrary to bar them from making purchases of 3.2% beer * * *.

[JUSTICE BLACKMUN's concurring opinion and CHIEF JUSTICE BURGER's dissenting opinion are omitted.]

POINTS FOR DISCUSSION

a. Heightened Scrutiny

Where did the form of scrutiny that the Court announced in *Craig* come from? Justice Brennan stated that "previous cases establish[ed]" this form of intermediate scrutiny for sex classifications. Is that an accurate statement of the law? If not, is the level of scrutiny that the Court announced otherwise defensible?

b. Sex Discrimination and the Original Meaning

Are there legitimate reasons to treat race and sex classifications differently? Considering the history of the Fourteenth Amendment and the Civil War, can you make an argument that race classifications should be more suspect? Conversely, can you make an originalist argument that sex discrimination is constitutionally suspect? (Consider former-Judge Bork's view of *Brown* and the original meaning, which we considered earlier in this chapter.) Does the ratification of the Nineteenth Amendment affect the argument?

c. Constitutional Interpretation and Constitutional Amendment

Do you think that the Equal Rights Amendment, which was pending ratification when the Court decided *Reed*, *Frontiero*, and *Craig*, influenced the Court's interpretation in those cases of the Equal Protection Clause? If so, does this put the cart before the horse? Was Congress's adoption (and many states' ratification) of the proposed Amendment relevant to the meaning of the Equal Protection Clause? Did the proposed Amendment's ultimate failure demonstrate that the Court was wrong in these cases? Or did the Amendment fail in part because the Court offered the protection that the Amendment otherwise would have conferred?

United States v. Virginia

518 U.S. 515 (1996)

Justice Ginsburg delivered the opinion of the Court.

Founded in 1839, VMI is today the sole single-sex school among Virginia's 15 public institutions of higher learning. VMI's distinctive mission is to produce "citizen-soldiers," men prepared for leadership in civilian life and in military service. VMI pursues this mission through pervasive training of a kind not available anywhere else in Virginia. Assigning prime place to character development, VMI uses an "adversative method" modeled on English public schools and once characteristic of military instruction. VMI constantly endeavors to instill physical and mental discipline in its cadets and impart to them a strong moral code. The school's graduates leave VMI with heightened comprehension of their capacity to deal with duress and stress, and a large sense of accomplishment for completing the hazardous course. VMI has notably succeeded in its mission to produce leaders; among its alumni are military generals, Members of Congress, and business executives. * * * Nevertheless, Virginia has elected to preserve exclusively for men the advantages and opportunities a VMI education affords.

Since [*Reed v. Reed*, 404 U.S. 71 (1971),] the Court has repeatedly recognized that neither federal nor state government acts compatibly with the equal protection principle when a law or official policy denies to women, simply because they are women, full citizenship stature—equal opportunity to aspire, achieve, participate in and contribute to society based on their individual talents and capacities. * * * Without equating gender classifications, for all purposes, to classifications based on race or national origin, the Court, in post-*Reed* decisions, has carefully inspected official action that closes a door or denies opportunity to women (or to men). To summarize the Court's current directions for cases of official classification based on gender: Focusing on the differential treatment or denial of opportunity for which relief is sought, the reviewing court must determine whether the proffered justification is "exceedingly persuasive." The burden of justification is demanding and it rests entirely on the State. The State must show "at least that the [challenged] classification serves 'important governmental objectives and that the discriminatory means employed' are 'substantially related to the achievement of those objectives.' " The justification must be genuine, not hypothesized or invented post hoc in response to litigation. And it must not rely on overbroad generalizations about the different talents, capacities, or preferences of males and females.

Virginia [asserts] two justifications in defense of VMI's exclusion of women. First, the Commonwealth contends, "single-sex education provides important educational benefits," and the option of single-sex education contributes to "diversity in educational approaches." Second, the Commonwealth argues, "the unique VMI method of character development and leadership training," the school's adversative approach, would have to be modified were VMI to admit women. We consider these two justifications in turn.

Single-sex education affords pedagogical benefits to at least some students, Virginia emphasizes, and that reality is uncontested in this litigation. Similarly, it is not disputed that diversity among public educational institutions can serve the public good. But Virginia has not shown that VMI was established, or has been maintained, with a view to diversifying, by its categorical exclusion of women, educational opportunities within the Commonwealth. In cases of this genre, our precedent instructs that "benign" justifications proffered in defense of categorical exclusions will not be accepted automatically; a tenable justification must describe actual state purposes, not rationalizations for actions in fact differently grounded.

Neither recent nor distant history bears out Virginia's alleged pursuit of diversity through single-sex educational options. In 1839, when the Commonwealth established VMI, [higher education] was considered dangerous for women. In admitting no women, VMI followed the lead of the Commonwealth's flagship school, the University of Virginia, founded in 1819. * * * Virginia eventually [in the late-nineteenth and early-twentieth centuries] provided for several women's seminaries and colleges. * * * By the mid-1970's, all four schools had become coeducational. * * * Debate concerning women's admission as undergraduates at the main university continued well past the [twentieth] century's midpoint. * * * Ultimately, in 1970, "the most prestigious institution of higher education in Virginia," the University of Virginia, introduced coeducation and, in 1972, began to admit women on an equal basis with men.

Virginia describes the current absence of public single-sex higher education for women as "an historical anomaly." But the historical record indicates action more deliberate than anomalous: First, protection of women against higher education; next, schools for women far from equal in resources and stature to schools for men; finally, conversion of the separate schools to coeducation. * * * In sum, we find no persuasive evidence in this record that VMI's male-only admission policy "is in furtherance of a state policy of diversity." * * * A purpose genuinely to advance an array of educational options [is] not served by VMI's historic and constant plan—a plan to "affor[d] a unique educational benefit only to males." However "liberally" this plan serves the Commonwealth's sons, it makes no provision whatever for her daughters. That is not *equal* protection.

Virginia next argues that VMI's adversative method of training provides educational benefits that cannot be made available, unmodified, to women. Alterations to accommodate women would necessarily be "radical," so "drastic," Virginia asserts, as to transform, indeed "destroy," VMI's program. [It] is uncontested that women's admission would require accommodations, primarily in arranging housing assignments and physical training programs for female cadets. It is also undisputed, however, that "the VMI methodology could be used to educate women." 852 F.Supp., at 481. The District Court even allowed that some women may prefer it to the methodology a women's college might pursue. * * * The parties, furthermore, agree that "some women can meet the physical standards [VMI] now impose[s] on men." 976 F.2d, at 896. * * * In support of its initial judgment for Virginia, a judgment rejecting all equal protection objections presented by the United States, the District Court made "findings" on "gender-based developmental differences." These "findings" restate the opinions of Virginia's expert witnesses, opinions about typically male or typically female "tendencies." For example, "[m]ales tend to need an atmosphere of adversativeness," while "[f]emales tend to thrive in a cooperative atmosphere." [One expert maintained that] educational experiences must be designed "around the rule," [and] not "around the exception."

State actors controlling gates to opportunity, we have instructed, may not exclude qualified individuals based on "fixed notions concerning the roles and abilities of males and females." It may be assumed, for purposes of this decision, that most women would not choose VMI's adversative method. * * * The issue, however, is not whether "women—or men—should be forced to attend VMI"; rather, the question is whether the Commonwealth can constitutionally deny to women who have the will and capacity, the training and attendant opportunities that VMI uniquely affords. The notion that admission of women would downgrade VMI's stature, destroy the adversative system and, with it, even the school, is a judgment hardly proved, a prediction hardly different from other "self-fulfilling prophecies" once routinely used to deny rights or opportunities. * * * Women's successful entry into the federal military academies, and their participation in the Nation's military forces, indicate that Virginia's fears for the future of VMI may not be solidly grounded. The Commonwealth's justification for excluding all women from "citizen-soldier" training for which some are qualified, in any event, cannot rank as "exceedingly persuasive," as we have explained and applied that standard.

A proper remedy for an unconstitutional exclusion, we have explained, aims to "eliminate [so far as possible] the discriminatory effects of the past" and to "bar like discrimination in the future." [In the second phase of this litigation, Virginia proposed maintaining VMI's exclusionary policy and creating Virginia Women's Institute for Leadership (VWIL) as a separate program for women. VWIL is] different in kind from VMI and unequal in tangible and intangible facilities. * * * VWIL affords women no opportunity to experience the rigorous military training for which VMI is famed. Instead, the VWIL program "deemphasize[s]" military education, and uses a "cooperative method" of education "which reinforces self-esteem." * * * Virginia maintains that these methodological differences are "justified pedagogically," based on "important differences between men and women in learning and developmental needs," "psychological and sociological differences" Virginia describes as "real" and "not stereotypes." The Task Force charged with developing the leadership program for women * * * "determined that [VMI's adversative method] would be wholly inappropriate for educating and training most women." As earlier stated, generalizations about "the way women are," estimates of what is appropriate for most women, no longer justify denying opportunity to women whose talent and capacity place them outside the average description.

In myriad respects other than military training, VWIL does not qualify as VMI's equal. VWIL's student body, faculty, course offerings, and facilities hardly match VMI's. Nor can the VWIL graduate anticipate the benefits associated with VMI's 157-year history, the school's prestige, and its influential alumni network. * * * Virginia, in sum, while maintaining VMI for men only, has failed to provide any "comparable single-gender women's institution." Instead, the Commonwealth has created a VWIL program fairly appraised as a "pale shadow" of VMI in terms of the range of curricular choices and faculty stature, funding, prestige, alumni support and influence.

A prime part of the history of our Constitution [is] the story of the extension of constitutional rights and protections to people once ignored or excluded. VMI's story continued as our comprehension of "We the People" expanded. There is no reason to believe that the admission of women capable of all the activities required of VMI cadets would destroy the Institute rather than enhance its capacity to serve the "more perfect Union."

CHIEF JUSTICE REHNQUIST, concurring in the judgment.

The Court defines the constitutional violation in these cases as "the categorical exclusion of women from an extraordinary educational opportunity afforded to men." [I] would not define the violation in this way; it is not the "exclusion of women" that violates the Equal Protection Clause, but the maintenance of an all-men school without providing any—much less a comparable—institution for women.

Accordingly, the remedy should not necessarily require either the admission of women to VMI or the creation of a VMI clone for women. An adequate remedy in my opinion might be a demonstration by Virginia that its interest in educating men in a single-sex environment is matched by its interest in educating women in a single-sex institution. To demonstrate such, the Commonwealth does not need to create two institutions with the same number of faculty Ph.D.'s, similar SAT scores, or comparable athletic fields. * * * It would be a sufficient remedy, I think, if the two institutions offered the same quality of education and were of the same overall caliber.

In the end, the women's institution Virginia proposes, VWIL, fails as a remedy, because it is distinctly inferior to the existing men's institution and will continue to be for the foreseeable future. * * * I therefore ultimately agree with the Court that Virginia has not provided an adequate remedy.

JUSTICE SCALIA, dissenting.

I have no problem with a system of abstract tests such as rational basis, intermediate, and strict scrutiny (though I think we can do better than applying strict scrutiny and intermediate scrutiny whenever we feel like it). * * * But in my view the function of this Court is to preserve our society's values regarding (among other things) equal protection, not to revise them; to prevent backsliding from the degree of restriction the Constitution imposed upon democratic government, not to prescribe, on our own authority, progressively higher degrees. * * * For that reason it is my view that, whatever abstract tests we may choose to devise, they cannot supersede—and indeed ought to be crafted so as to reflect—those constant and unbroken national traditions that embody the people's understanding of ambiguous constitutional texts. The all-male constitution of VMI comes squarely within such a governing tradition. * * * Today, however, change is forced upon Virginia, and reversion to single-sex education is prohibited nationwide, not by democratic processes but by order of this Court. [This] is not the interpretation of a Constitution, but the creation of one.

To reject the Court's disposition today, however, it is not necessary to accept my view that the Court's made-up tests cannot displace longstanding national traditions as the primary determinant of what the Constitution means. It is only necessary to apply honestly the test the Court has been applying to sex-based classifications for the past two decades. * * * Only the amorphous "exceedingly persuasive justification" phrase, and not the standard elaboration of intermediate scrutiny, can be made to yield this conclusion that VMI's single-sex composition is unconstitutional because there exist several women (or, one would have to conclude under the Court's reasoning, a single woman) willing and able to undertake VMI's program. Intermediate scrutiny has never required a least-restrictive-means analysis, but only a "substantial relation" between the classification and the state interests that it serves.

The Court's [application of a more searching level of scrutiny is] particularly out of place because it is perfectly clear that, if the question of the applicable standard of review for sex-based classifications were to be regarded as an appropriate subject for reconsideration, the stronger argument would be not for elevating the standard to strict scrutiny, but for reducing it to rational-basis review. * * * It is hard to consider women a "discrete and insular minorit[y]" unable to employ the "political processes ordinarily to be relied upon" when they constitute a majority of the electorate. And the suggestion that they are incapable of exerting that political power smacks of the same paternalism that the Court so roundly condemns. Moreover, a long list of legislation proves the proposition false.

It is beyond question that Virginia has an important state interest in providing effective college education for its citizens. That single-sex instruction is an approach substantially related to that interest should be evident enough from the long and continuing history in this country of men's and women's colleges. * * *

Under the constitutional principles announced and applied today, single-sex public education is unconstitutional. By going through the motions of applying a balancing test—asking whether the State has adduced an "exceedingly persuasive justification" for its sex-based classification—the Court creates the illusion that government officials in some future case will have a clear shot at justifying some sort of single-sex public education. [R]egardless of whether the Court's rationale leaves some small amount of room for lawyers to argue, it ensures that single-sex public education is functionally dead.

POINTS FOR DISCUSSION

a.   Level of Scrutiny

In his dissent, Justice Scalia suggested that the Court applied a different level of scrutiny than the intermediate scrutiny that the Court had applied in sex classification cases since *Craig v. Boren*. Do you agree that the Court's approach here was different? If so, in what way?

b.   Separate but Equal?

The Court rejected the creation of VWIL as a remedy for sex discrimination at VMI, concluding that VWIL was a "pale shadow" of VMI. Chief Justice Rehnquist agreed, but suggested that the creation of an all-female institution that "offered the same quality of education and [was] of the same overall caliber" would eliminate the constitutional defect. Justice Scalia, in contrast, predicted that no public single-sex school would be able to survive the majority's decision. Given the Court's view— expressed here and in the affirmative action cases, which we considered earlier in this chapter—about the importance of diversity in education, should equal, single-sex, parallel schools be a constitutionally acceptable approach to education? If so, how would the Court determine whether the parallel schools were in fact equal?

c.   Sex Discrimination and the *Carolene Products* Test

Justice Scalia suggested in his dissent that, putting aside *stare decisis*, discrimination on the basis of sex should be subject only to rational-basis review, because women are in no meaningful sense a "minority" in need of judicial protection. Would this view have been correct in 1976, when the Court decided *Craig v. Boren*? Even if not, can't we today rely on the political process to protect women from discrimination?

Problem

The City of Milwaukee, Wisconsin, relying on studies showing that girls tend to tune out in co-educational math and science classes, creates an all-girls Math and Science Academy and an all-boys magnet high school. The same faculty teach (on a rotating schedule) at both schools, which have comparable, state-of-the-art facilities. A boy who wishes to attend the Math and Science Academy sues, arguing that his exclusion on the basis of gender violates the Equal Protection Clause. How should the court rule? Would it matter if the all-boys school was a "Math and Science Academy," too?

3. Sex Differences and Stereotypes

In *United States v. Virginia*, the state defended the exclusion of women from VMI in part by pointing to differences between men and women. The Court rejected these arguments, noting that the state "may not exclude qualified individuals based on 'fixed notions concerning the roles and abilities of males and females.' " Are differences between men and women ever an acceptable basis for different treatment by the government? Consider the cases that follow.

ORR V. ORR
440 U.S. 268 (1979)

MR. JUSTICE BRENNAN delivered the opinion of the Court.

[Mr. Orr, the appellant, challenged an Alabama divorce decree directing him to pay alimony to his ex-wife.] The question presented is the constitutionality of Alabama alimony statutes which provide that husbands, but not wives, may be required to pay alimony upon divorce.

The fact that the classification expressly discriminates against men rather than women does not protect it from scrutiny. *Craig v. Boren*, 429 U.S. 190 (1976). "To withstand scrutiny" under the Equal Protection Clause, "classifications by gender must serve important governmental objectives and must be substantially related to achievement of those objectives." *Califano v. Webster*, 430 U.S. 313, 316–317 (1977). We shall, therefore, examine the three governmental objectives that might arguably be served by Alabama's statutory scheme.

Appellant views the Alabama alimony statutes as effectively announcing the State's preference for an allocation of family responsibilities under which the wife plays a dependent role, and as seeking for their objective the reinforcement of that model among the State's citizens. We agree, as he urges, that prior cases settle that this purpose cannot sustain the statutes. *Stanton v. Stanton*, 421 U.S. 7, 10 (1975), held that the "old notio[n]" that "generally it is the man's primary responsibility to provide a home and its essentials," can no longer justify a statute that discriminates on the basis of gender. "No longer is the female destined solely for the home and the rearing of the family, and only the male for the marketplace and the world of ideas." If the statute is to survive constitutional attack, therefore, it must be validated on some other basis.

The opinion of the Alabama Court of Civil Appeals suggests other purposes that the statute may serve. Its opinion states that the Alabama statutes were "designed" for "the wife of a broken marriage who needs financial assistance." This may be read as asserting either of two legislative objectives. One is a legislative purpose to provide help for needy spouses, using sex as a proxy for need. The other is a goal of compensating women for past discrimination during marriage, which assertedly has left them unprepared to fend for themselves in the working world following divorce. We concede, of course, that assisting needy spouses is a legitimate and important governmental objective. We have also recognized "[r]eduction of the disparity in economic condition between men and women caused by the long history of discrimination against women [as] an important governmental objective." It only remains, therefore, to determine whether the classification at issue here is "substantially related to achievement of those objectives."

[E]ven if sex were a reliable proxy for need, and even if the institution of marriage did discriminate against women, these factors still would "not adequately justify the salient features of" Alabama's statutory scheme. Under the statute, individualized hearings at which the parties' relative financial circumstances are considered already occur. There is no reason, therefore, to use sex as a proxy for need. Needy males could be helped along with needy females with little if any additional burden on the State. In such circumstances, not even an administrative-convenience rationale exists to justify operating by generalization or proxy. Similarly, since individualized hearings can determine which women were in fact discriminated against vis-à-vis their husbands, as well as which family units defied the stereotype and left the husband dependent on the wife, Alabama's alleged compensatory purpose may be effectuated without placing burdens solely on husbands. Progress toward fulfilling such a purpose would not be hampered, and it would cost the State nothing more, if it were to treat men and women equally by making alimony burdens independent of sex.

> **FYI**
>
> On remand, the Alabama Court of Civil Appeals held that alimony could be awarded to husbands as well as to wives, curing the Equal Protection violation. But the court proceeded to order Mr. Orr to pay alimony to his wife. Was this result consistent with the Supreme Court's decision?

Legislative classifications which distribute benefits and burdens on the basis of gender carry the inherent risk of reinforcing the stereotypes about the "proper place" of women and their need for special protection. Thus, even statutes purportedly designed to compensate for and ameliorate the effects of past discrimination must be carefully tailored. Where, as here, the State's compensatory and ameliorative purposes are as well served by a gender-neutral classification as one that gender classifies and therefore carries with it the baggage of sexual stereotypes, the State cannot be permitted to classify on the basis of sex. [Reversed.]

[JUSTICE BLACKMUN's concurring opinion is omitted.]

POINTS FOR DISCUSSION

a. Discrimination Against Men

The Court subjected the Alabama statute, which disadvantaged men, to the same level of scrutiny to which it subjects statutes that disadvantage women. In light of the reasons that the Court applies heightened scrutiny to sex classifications, do you agree that statutes that impose a heavier burden on men should be subjected to the same level of scrutiny? If in fact men enjoy disproportionate political power and historically women have been the victims of discrimination, then does it make sense to provide judicial protection to men who are burdened by legislative action? Or is the Court's point that statutes such as the one at issue in *Orr* in fact represent the institutionalization of invidious sex stereotypes, and thus in effect perpetuate discrimination against *women*?

b. The Relevance of Past Discrimination

The Court in *Orr* did not identify the circumstances under which a sex classification that is asserted to compensate for past discrimination can survive intermediate scrutiny. Several years earlier, however, in *Weinberger v. Wiesenfeld*, 420 U.S. 636 (1975), the Court invalidated a provision of the Social Security Act that provided for the payment of additional insurance benefits to women upon the death of their husbands, but did not provide comparable benefits to a man whose wife had died. Although the Court recognized that the government has a legitimate interest in helping women to overcome economic disadvantages, it noted that a "mere recitation of a benign, compensatory purpose is not an automatic shield which protects against any inquiry into the actual purposes underlying a statutory scheme." The Court concluded that Congress's purpose in enacting the provision was not to compensate women for past economic discrimination, but rather to provide a single mother with the choice to stay home with a child. Because widowers were deprived of this choice, the provision appeared driven by the assumption that women, but not men, should be (or at least more typically were) stay-at-home parents.

By contrast, in *Califano v. Webster*, 430 U.S. 313 (1977), the Court upheld a provision of the Social Security Act that allowed women to exclude from their computation of their average monthly wage three more lower-earning years than a similarly situated male wage earner. As with the provision at issue in *Weinberger*, the net effect was to provide higher benefits to women than to men. The Court distinguished *Weinberger* by noting that the clear purpose of the favorable treatment for women in the provision at issue was the "permissible one of redressing our society's longstanding disparate treatment of women," and that the provision "operated directly to compensate women for past economic discrimination." In the Court's view, the different treatment of the sexes was based upon real, calculable economic differences, rather than on mere gender stereotypes.

But since then, the Court has been skeptical of government arguments that sex classifications are warranted to provide a remedy for past discrimination against women. In *Mississippi Univ. for Women v. Hogan*, 458 U.S. 718 (1982), the Court, in an opinion by Justice O'Connor, declared unconstitutional the public university's policy of excluding men from its School of Nursing. The University had been founded as an all-women's school in 1884, and the School of Nursing had been established in 1971. Mississippi argued that continuing to deny men admission to the school served a compensatory purpose for past discrimination against women. But the Court, noting that women earn more than 90% of the nursing degrees in Mississippi and nationwide, concluded that "[r]ather than compensate for discriminatory barriers faced by women, MUW's policy of excluding males from admission to the School of Nursing tends to perpetuate the stereotyped view of nursing as an exclusively women's job."

To be sure, some classifications on the basis of sex are based solely upon stereotypes that have historically disadvantaged women. But there are, of course, also real and important physiological differences between men and women. In *United States v. Virginia*, 518 U.S. 515 (1996), for example, Justice Ginsburg explained:

> The heightened review standard our precedent establishes does not make sex a proscribed classification. Supposed "inherent differences" are no longer accepted as a ground for race or national origin classifications. Physical differences between men and women, however, are enduring. * * * "Inherent differences" between men and women, we have come to appreciate, remain cause for celebration, but not for denigration of the members of either sex or for artificial constraints on an individual's opportunity.

But, as it turns out, it is no easy task to identify the circumstances under which the government may take physiological differences between men and women into account. The next case is illustrative of the challenge.

MICHAEL M. v. SUPERIOR COURT OF SONOMA COUNTY

450 U.S. 464 (1981)

JUSTICE REHNQUIST announced the judgment of the Court and delivered an opinion, in which THE CHIEF JUSTICE, JUSTICE STEWART, and JUSTICE POWELL joined.

The question presented in this case is whether California's "statutory rape" law [violates] the Equal Protection Clause of the Fourteenth Amendment. Section 261.5 [of the California Penal Code] defines unlawful sexual intercourse as "an act of sexual intercourse accomplished with a female not the wife of the perpetrator, where the female is under the age of 18 years." The statute thus makes men alone

> **Take Note**
>
> Justice Rehnquist wrote only for a plurality; Justice Blackmun, whose separate reasoning follows, provided the fifth vote to affirm the court below. After you have read both opinions, consider the extent to which Justice Rehnquist's reasoning has binding force.

criminally liable for the act of sexual intercourse. [Petitioner, a 17-year-old male, was prosecuted for having sex with a 16-year-old female.]

Underlying [our] decisions is the principle that a legislature may not "make overbroad generalizations based on sex which are entirely unrelated to any differences between men and women or which demean the ability or social status of the affected class." But because the Equal Protection Clause does not "demand that a statute necessarily apply equally to all persons" or require "things which are different in fact [to] be treated in law as though they were the same," this Court has consistently upheld statutes where the gender classification is not invidious, but rather realistically reflects the fact that the sexes are not similarly situated in certain circumstances. As the Court has stated, a legislature may "provide for the special problems of women." *Weinberger v. Wiesenfeld*, 420 U.S. 636, 653 (1975).

Applying those principles to this case, the fact that the California Legislature criminalized the act of illicit sexual intercourse with a minor female is a sure indication of its intent or purpose to discourage that conduct. Precisely why the legislature desired that result is of course somewhat less clear. This Court has long recognized that "[i]nquiries into congressional motives or purposes are a hazardous matter," and the search for the "actual" or "primary" purpose of a statute is likely to be elusive. Here, for example, the individual legislators may have voted for the statute for a variety of reasons. Some legislators may have been concerned about preventing teenage pregnancies, others about protecting young females from physical injury or from the loss of "chastity," and still others about promoting various religious and moral attitudes towards premarital sex.

The justification for the statute offered by the State, and accepted by the Supreme Court of California, is that the legislature sought to prevent illegitimate teenage pregnancies. That finding, of course, is entitled to great deference. And although our cases establish that the State's asserted reason for the enactment of a statute may be rejected, if it "could not have been a goal of the legislation," this is not such a case. We are satisfied not only that the prevention of illegitimate pregnancy is at least one of the "purposes" of the statute, but also that the State has a strong interest in preventing such pregnancy. At the risk of stating the obvious, teenage pregnancies, which have increased dramatically over the last two decades, have significant social, medical, and economic consequences for both the mother and her child, and the State. Of particular concern to the State is that approximately half of all teenage pregnancies end in abortion. And of those children who are born, their illegitimacy makes them likely candidates to become wards of the State.

> **Take Note**
>
> If the "true" purpose of the statute was to protect the virtue and chastity of young women, then that purpose likely would not be sufficient under heightened scrutiny, as it arguably rests on archaic stereotypes about women. The Court concludes, however, that because there is at least one legitimate motive for the statute, it is irrelevant that other motives were impermissible. Is this consistent with the Court's approach in other cases involving sex classifications? What about the likelihood that the sex classification will itself perpetuate stereotypes?

We need not be medical doctors to discern that young men and young women are not similarly situated with respect to the problems and the risks of sexual intercourse. Only women may become pregnant, and they suffer disproportionately the profound physical, emotional and psychological consequences of sexual activity. The statute at issue here protects women from sexual intercourse at an age when those consequences are particularly severe.

The question thus boils down to whether a State may attack the problem of sexual intercourse and teenage pregnancy directly by prohibiting a male from having sexual intercourse with a minor female. * * * We hold that such a statute is sufficiently related to the State's objectives to pass constitutional muster. Because virtually all of the significant harmful and inescapably identifiable consequences of teenage pregnancy fall on the young female, a legislature acts well within its authority when it elects to punish only the participant who, by nature, suffers few of the consequences of his conduct. It is hardly unreasonable for a legislature acting to protect minor females to exclude them from punishment. Moreover, the risk of pregnancy itself constitutes a substantial deterrence to young females. No similar natural sanctions deter males. A criminal sanction imposed solely on males thus serves to roughly "equalize" the deterrents on the sexes.

We are unable to accept petitioner's contention that the statute is impermissibly underinclusive and must, in order to pass judicial scrutiny, be broadened so as to hold the female as criminally liable as the male. It is argued that this statute is not necessary to deter teenage pregnancy because a gender-neutral statute, where both male and female would be subject to prosecution, would serve that goal equally well. The relevant inquiry, however, is not whether the statute is drawn as precisely as it might have been * * *. In any event, we cannot say that a gender-neutral statute would be as effective as the statute California has chosen to enact. The State persuasively contends that a gender-neutral statute would frustrate its interest in effective enforcement. Its view is that a female is surely less likely to report violations of the statute if she herself would be subject to criminal prosecution. In an area already fraught with prosecutorial difficulties, we decline to hold that the Equal Protection Clause requires a legislature to enact a statute so broad that it may well be incapable of enforcement.

JUSTICE STEWART, concurring.

The Constitution is violated when government, state or federal, invidiously classifies similarly situated people on the basis of the immutable characteristics with which they were born. Thus, detrimental racial classifications by government always violate the Constitution, for the simple reason that, so far as the Constitution is concerned, people of different races are always similarly situated. By contrast, while detrimental gender classifications by government often violate the Constitution, they do not always do so, for the reason that there are differences between males and females that the Constitution necessarily recognizes. [I]n certain narrow circumstances men and women are not similarly situated; in these circumstances a gender classification based on clear differences between the sexes is not invidious, and a legislative classification realistically based upon those differences is not unconstitutional.

Young women and men are not similarly situated with respect to the problems and risk associated with intercourse and pregnancy, and the statute is realistically related to the legitimate state purpose of reducing those problems and risks. In short, the Equal Protection Clause does not mean that the physiological differences between men and women must be disregarded. While those differences must never be permitted to become a pretext for invidious discrimination, no such discrimination is presented by this case. The Constitution surely does not require a State to pretend that demonstrable differences between men and women do not really exist.

JUSTICE BLACKMUN, concurring in the judgment.

It is gratifying that the plurality recognizes that "teenage pregnancies * * * have significant social, medical, and economic consequences for both the mother and her child, and the State." There have been times when I have wondered whether the Court was capable of this perception, particularly when it has struggled with the different but not unrelated problems that attend abortion issues. * * * [I think the California statutory rape law] is a sufficiently reasoned and constitutional effort to control the problem at its inception.

JUSTICE BRENNAN, with whom JUSTICES WHITE and MARSHALL join, dissenting.

[T]he plurality opinion and Justices STEWART and BLACKMUN [place] too much emphasis on the desirability of achieving the State's asserted statutory goal—prevention of teenage pregnancy—and not enough emphasis on the fundamental question of whether the sex-based discrimination in the California statute is substantially related to the achievement of that goal. [E]ven assuming that prevention of teenage pregnancy is an important governmental objective and that it is in fact an objective of § 261.5, California still has the burden of proving that there are fewer teenage pregnancies under its gender-based statutory rape law than there would be if the law were gender neutral. To meet this burden, the State must show that because its statutory rape law punishes only males, and not females, it more effectively deters minor females from having sexual intercourse.

The State has not produced such evidence in this case. Moreover, there are at least two serious flaws in the State's assertion that law enforcement problems created by a gender-neutral statutory rape law would make such a statute less effective than a gender-based statute in deterring sexual activity. First, [t]here are now at least 37 States that have enacted gender-neutral statutory rape laws, [and] the laws of Arizona, Florida, and Illinois permit prosecution of both minor females and minor males for engaging in mutual sexual conduct. California has introduced no evidence that those States have been handicapped by the enforcement problems the plurality finds so persuasive. * * * [Second, common sense] suggests that a gender-neutral statutory rape law is potentially a *greater* deterrent of sexual activity than a gender-based law, for the simple reason that a gender-neutral law subjects both men and women to criminal sanctions and thus arguably has a deterrent effect on twice as many potential violators. Even if fewer persons were prosecuted under the gender-neutral law, as the State suggests, it would still be true that twice as many persons would be *subject* to arrest. The State's failure to prove that a gender-neutral law would be a less effective deterrent than a gender-based law, like the State's failure to prove that a gender-neutral law would be difficult to enforce, should have led this Court to invalidate § 261.5.

Until very recently, no California court or commentator had suggested that the purpose of California's statutory rape law was to protect young women from the risk of pregnancy. Indeed, the historical development of § 261.5 demonstrates that the law was initially enacted on the premise that young women, in contrast to young men, were to be deemed legally incapable of consenting to an act of sexual intercourse. Because their chastity was considered particularly precious, those young women were felt to be uniquely in need of the State's protection. In contrast, young men were assumed to be capable of making such decisions for themselves; the law therefore did not offer them any special protection.

It is perhaps because the gender classification in California's statutory rape law was initially designed to further these outmoded sexual stereotypes, rather than to reduce the incidence of teenage pregnancies, that the State has been unable to demonstrate a substantial relationship between the classification and its newly asserted goal. * * * I would hold that § 261.5 violates the Equal Protection Clause of the Fourteenth Amendment.

JUSTICE STEVENS, dissenting.

The question in this case is whether the difference between males and females justifies this statutory discrimination based entirely on sex. But the plurality surely cannot believe that the risk of pregnancy confronted by the female—any more than the risk of venereal disease confronted by males as well as females—has provided an effective deterrent to voluntary female participation in the risk-creating conduct. Yet the plurality's decision seems to rest on the assumption that the California Legislature acted on the basis of that rather fanciful notion.

The fact that the California Legislature has decided to apply its prohibition only to the male may reflect a legislative judgment that in the typical case the male is actually the more guilty party. Any such judgment must, in turn, assume that the decision to engage in the risk-creating conduct is always—or at least typically—a male decision. If that assumption is valid, the statutory classification should also be valid. But what is the support for the assumption? * * * I think it is supported to some extent by traditional attitudes toward male-female relationships. But the possibility that such a habitual attitude may reflect nothing more than an irrational prejudice makes it an insufficient justification for discriminatory treatment that is otherwise blatantly unfair. For, as I read this statute, it requires that one, and only one, of two equally guilty wrongdoers be stigmatized by a criminal conviction.

POINTS FOR DISCUSSION

a.   Identifying Stereotypes

The plurality in *Michael M.* concluded that the statute at issue was designed to prevent teen pregnancy; because the capacity to become pregnant is an uncontested physical difference between men and women, the plurality concluded that the statute permissibly treated men and women differently. Both Justices Brennan and Stevens, by contrast, concluded that the statute reflected archaic and invidious stereotypes about gender roles. Assuming that laws motivated by gender stereotypes should be invalidated, how does the Court know when a law is based on such stereotypes? Even putting aside the problem of identifying legislative motive, how does the Court determine that a particular view is an invidious stereotype, rather than a reflection of real differences?

b.   Pregnancy and Sex Discrimination

There was little doubt that the statute at issue in *Michael M.* classified on the basis of sex; under the statute, if a male and female under the age of 18 had sexual intercourse, only the male was criminally liable. The plurality's conclusion that the statute survived scrutiny was based in significant part on the state's interest in reducing the incidence of teen pregnancy, and in particular on the fact that "[o]nly women may become pregnant." Does that mean that classifications based on pregnancy themselves are always sex classifications subject to heightened scrutiny under the Equal Protection Clause?

In *Geduldig v. Aiello*, 417 U.S. 484 (1974), the Court considered a challenge to California's disability insurance system. Under the system, the state paid benefits to persons in private employment who were temporarily unavailable to work because of disability. The system did not pay benefits, however, for certain disabilities that are attributable to pregnancy. The appellees claimed that the exclusion of pregnancy-related disabilities violated the Equal Protection Clause. The Court upheld the exclusion under rational-basis review. In a footnote, the Court rejected the assertion that the exclusion of pregnancy-related disabilities constituted sex discrimination. The Court reasoned:

> The California insurance program does not exclude anyone from benefit eligibility because of gender but merely removes one physical condition— pregnancy—from the list of compensable disabilities. While it is true that only women can become pregnant it does not follow that every legislative classification concerning pregnancy is a sex-based classification * * *. The lack of identity between the excluded disability and gender as such under this insurance program becomes clear upon the most cursory analysis. The program divides potential recipients into two groups—pregnant women

and nonpregnant persons. While the first group is exclusively female, the second includes members of both sexes. The fiscal and actuarial benefits of the program thus accrue to members of both sexes.

Justice Brennan, joined by Justices Douglas and Marshall, dissented. He asserted that "by singling out for less favorable treatment a gender-linked disability peculiar to women, the State has created a double standard for disability compensation: a limitation is imposed upon the disabilities for which women workers may recover, while men receive full compensation for all disabilities suffered, including those that affect only or primarily their sex, such as prostatectomies, circumcision, hemophilia, and gout. In effect, one set of rules is applied to females and another to males. Such dissimilar treatment of men and women, on the basis of physical characteristics inextricably linked to one sex, inevitably constitutes sex discrimination." Which view do you find more persuasive?

c.   Further Developments

Note that Justice Rehnquist wrote only for a plurality in *Michael M.* Since that decision, the Court has continued to struggle with classifications that purport to turn on differences between men and women. In *Nguyen v. INS*, 533 U.S. 53 (2001), for example, the Court upheld a statute that made it more difficult for a child born abroad out of wedlock to one United States parent to claim citizenship if the citizen parent was the father rather than the mother. The Court explained that the "distinction embodied in the statutory scheme here at issue is not marked by misconception and prejudice, nor does it show disrespect for either class. The difference between men and women in relation to the birth process is a real one." The Court concluded that Congress was justified in concluding that because a mother, unlike a father, must be present at the birth of the child, and because mothers are thus more likely to develop a relationship with the child, maternity—and thus citizenship—should be easier to demonstrate.

Justice O'Connor dissented, asserting that the law was based on a stereotypical view of women as more likely to establish and maintain a meaningful relationship with their children. In her view, a stereotype does not need to be disrespectful or devoid of empirical support in order to be an unconstitutional basis for a sex classification. Rather, she asserted that the Equal Protection Clause forbids any classification that "relies upon the simplistic outdated assumption that gender could be used as a proxy for other, more germane bases of classification." Which approach do you find more persuasive?

4. Purpose and Effect

PERSONNEL ADMINISTRATOR OF MASSACHUSETTS V. FEENEY
442 U.S. 256 (1979)

MR. JUSTICE STEWART delivered the opinion of the Court.

This case presents a challenge to the constitutionality of the Massachusetts veterans' preference statute, Mass. Gen. Laws Ann., ch. 31, § 23, on the ground that it discriminates against women in violation of the Equal Protection Clause of the Fourteenth Amendment. Under ch. 31, § 23, all veterans who qualify for state civil service positions must be considered for appointment ahead of any qualifying nonveterans. The preference operates overwhelmingly to the advantage of males. [Ms. Feeney received the second highest score on a civil service examination for a job with the Board of Dental Examiners, and the third highest on a test for an Administrative Assistant position with a mental health center, but male veterans who had scored lower on the examinations received the positions.]

The [Massachusetts] veterans' preference statute [has long] defined the term "veterans" in gender-neutral language. * * * Women who have served in official United States military units during wartime, then, have always been entitled to the benefit of the preference. [At the time, of the litigation, 98% of veterans in Massachusetts were male. Although 54% of the men appointed to civil service positions were veterans, only 1.8% of the women were.]

[As] was made clear in *Washington v. Davis*, 426 U.S. 229 (1976), and *Arlington Heights v. Metropolitan Housing Dev. Corp.*, 429 U.S. 252 (1977), even if a neutral law has a disproportionately adverse effect upon a racial minority, it is unconstitutional under the Equal Protection Clause only if that impact can be traced to a discriminatory purpose. * * * Those principles apply with equal force to a case involving alleged gender discrimination.

The appellee has conceded that ch. 31, § 23, is neutral on its face. [Nor is the classification a covert form of gender discrimination.] Veteran status is not uniquely male. Although few women benefit from the preference, the *nonveteran* class is not substantially all female. To the contrary, significant numbers of nonveterans are men, and all nonveterans—male as well as female—are placed at a disadvantage. Too many men are affected by ch. 31, § 23, to permit the inference that the statute is but a pretext for preferring men over women.

The dispositive question, then, is whether the appellee has shown that a gender-based discriminatory purpose has, at least in some measure, shaped the Massachusetts veterans' preference legislation. * * * "Discriminatory purpose" [implies] more than intent as volition or intent as awareness of consequences. It implies that the decisionmaker, in this case a state legislature, selected or reaffirmed a particular course of action at least in part "because of," not merely "in spite of," its adverse effects upon an identifiable group. Yet, nothing in the record

> **Take Note**
>
> The Court concludes that the classification does not reflect a discriminatory purpose because it disadvantages many men, as well. If the class of persons benefited were *exclusively* male, would it matter that the disadvantaged class includes men as well as women? If the police force excluded all women from consideration, would the fact that many male applicants are also denied positions mean that there is no discrimination? If not, why is this case different?

demonstrates that this preference for veterans was originally devised or subsequently re-enacted because it would accomplish the collateral goal of keeping women in a stereotypic and predefined place in the Massachusetts Civil Service.

> **Food for Thought**
>
> In the Court's view, who bears the burden of persuasion on the question of the state's purpose? Must the person challenging the law demonstrate that the state had a discriminatory purpose? Or should the showing that the law has a substantial disparate impact on women shift the burden to the state to demonstrate that it was enacted for *non*-discriminatory purposes?

Veterans' hiring preferences represent an awkward—and, many argue, unfair—exception to the widely shared view that merit and merit alone should prevail in the employment policies of government. * * * But the Fourteenth Amendment "cannot be made a refuge from ill-advised [laws]." The appellee [has] simply failed to demonstrate that the law in any way reflects a purpose to discriminate on the basis of sex.

MR. JUSTICE STEVENS, with whom MR. JUSTICE WHITE joins, concurring.

[F]or me the answer is largely provided by the fact that the number of males disadvantaged by Massachusetts' veterans' preference (1,867,000) is sufficiently large—and sufficiently close to the number of disadvantaged females (2,954,000)—to refute the claim that the rule was intended to benefit males as a class over females as a class.

MR. JUSTICE MARSHALL, with whom MR. JUSTICE BRENNAN joins, dissenting.

That a legislature seeks to advantage one group does not, as a matter of logic or of common sense, exclude the possibility that it also intends to disadvantage another. * * * Absent an omniscience not commonly attributed to the judiciary, it will often be impossible to ascertain the sole or even dominant purpose of a given statute. * * * Moreover, since reliable evidence of subjective intentions is seldom obtainable, resort to inference based on objective factors is generally unavoidable. To discern the purposes underlying facially neutral policies, this Court has therefore considered the degree, inevitability, and foreseeability of any disproportionate impact as well as the alternatives reasonably available.

Where the foreseeable impact of a facially neutral policy is so disproportionate, the burden should rest on the State to establish that sex-based considerations played no part in the choice of the particular legislative scheme. * * * Clearly, that burden was not sustained here. The legislative history of the statute reflects the Commonwealth's patent appreciation of the impact the preference system would have on women, and an equally evident desire to mitigate that impact only with respect to certain traditionally female occupations. Until 1971, the statute and implementing civil service regulations exempted from operation of the preference any job requisitions "especially calling for women." In practice, this exemption, coupled with the absolute preference for veterans, has created a gender-based civil service hierarchy, with women occupying low-grade clerical and secretarial jobs and men holding more responsible and remunerative positions. * * * Such a statutory scheme both reflects and perpetuates precisely the kind of archaic assumptions about women's roles which we have previously held invalid.

> **Food for Thought**
>
> Justice Marshall suggests that the state could have accomplished its (non-discriminatory) objective here—to recognize and reward veterans for their military service—through means that would not disproportionately affect women. Can you think of any such alternatives?

To survive challenge under the Equal Protection Clause, statutes reflecting gender-based discrimination must be substantially related to the achievement of important governmental objectives. * * * In its present unqualified form, the veterans' preference statute precludes all but a small fraction of Massachusetts women from obtaining any civil service position also of interest to men. Given the range of alternatives available, this degree of preference is not constitutionally permissible.

POINTS FOR DISCUSSION

a.   Purpose v. Effects

Recall that in *Washington v. Davis*, which we considered earlier in this chapter, the Court held that a facially neutral law that has a discriminatory effect on members of a racial minority does not violate the Equal Protection Clause absent a finding of discriminatory purpose. Does Justice Marshall quarrel with that conclusion here, in the context of sex discrimination? That is, does Justice Marshall suggest here that even absent a discriminatory purpose, discriminatory effects can be sufficient to invalidate an otherwise neutral classification? Or does he simply conclude that the statute is invalid because the effects are sufficient evidence of a discriminatory purpose? Assuming that *Davis*'s approach makes sense in the context of racial discrimination, does it make sense to apply that approach in the context of sex discrimination?

b. Ascertaining Discriminatory Purpose

If nothing else, the majority and the dissent appeared to agree that a law reflecting a purpose to discriminate against women must be subjected to heightened scrutiny. In what ways do they differ over the appropriate method for demonstrating such a purpose? When should a court infer a discriminatory purpose from the mere existence of disparate effects? And when, if ever, should indications of "subjective" legislative intent—such as the statements by one or two lawmakers that reflect discriminatory animus—be relevant?

c. Women and the Military

Is the real question in *Feeney* whether the one-time prohibition on women's serving in the military—and the present limits on the capacities in which women may serve—is itself an unconstitutional form of sex discrimination? Two years after the decision in *Feeney*, the Court held in *Rostker v. Goldberg*, 453 U.S. 57 (1981), that the Military Selective Service Act, which authorized the President to require the registration of males but not females, did not violate the Equal Protection component of the Due Process Clause of the Fifth Amendment. The Court emphasized the deference that the Court has applied to congressional judgments in matters of "national defense and military affairs" and the government's "important" interest in "raising and supporting armies." The Court reasoned that the "purpose of registration was to prepare for a draft of combat troops." Because "women are excluded from combat," Congress permissibly concluded that "they would not be needed in the event of a draft, and therefore decided not to register them." Do you agree with this decision? Does its validity turn on whether the exclusion of women from combat roles itself constitutes invidious discrimination?

If women can constitutionally be excluded from the draft (and, under Department of Defense policy in effect when the Court decided *Rostker*, from combat roles), can there really be any constitutional objection to the classification at issue in *Feeney*? Or is there a difference between the exclusion of women from many forms of military service, on the one hand, and the conferral of benefits on a basis that largely reflects that exclusion, on the other? Conversely, should statutes like the one at issue in *Feeney* be relevant to the determination whether women can constitutionally be excluded from military service in the first place? In 2013, the Secretary of Defense announced that he would end the official prohibition on women's serving in combat.

C. OTHER CLASSIFICATIONS

So far, we have seen that a wide range of bases for government classifications receive only rational-basis review. We have also seen that classifications based on race or national origin are subject to strict scrutiny, and that classifications based on sex are subject to intermediate scrutiny. And as we will see in Chapters 8–11, the Constitution explicitly defines some other bases for classifications. The First Amendment, which protects both the "freedom of speech" and the "free exercise" of religion, clearly limits the government's authority to discriminate on the basis of a person's views or religious beliefs. (Indeed, sometimes the Court has even articulated these limits as inhering in the Equal Protection Clause. See, e.g., *Police Department of Chicago v. Mosley*, 408 U.S. 92 (1972).)

Are there other bases for classification that are subject to heightened scrutiny? Recall the Court's suggestion in *Carolene Products*, which we considered in Chapter 4, that "discrete and insular minorities" that face prejudice and have difficulty obtaining protection from ordinary political processes might be entitled to heightened judicial protection. Is this the proper test for identifying groups subject to heightened protection under the Equal Protection Clause? Either way, what other groups, if any, are deserving of such heightened judicial protection? The materials that follow address that question.

1. Alienage

GRAHAM V. RICHARDSON
403 U.S. 365 (1971)

MR. JUSTICE BLACKMUN delivered the opinion of the Court.

[Carmen Richardson was a lawfully admitted resident alien who had lived in Arizona for thirteen years. She was denied benefits under Arizona's disability insurance program because she was not a citizen and had not resided in Arizona for fifteen years. Elsie Leger was a lawfully admitted resident alien living and paying taxes in the state of Pennsylvania. After illness forced her to give up her employment, she applied for public assistance but was denied because she was not a citizen. Ms. Richardson and Mrs. Leger filed separate suits claiming that the denials violated the Equal Protection Clause.]

It has long been settled, and it is not disputed here, that the term "person" in [the Equal Protection Clause] encompasses lawfully admitted resident aliens as well as citizens of the United States and entitles both citizens and aliens to the equal protection of the laws of the State in which they reside. *Yick Wo v. Hopkins*, 118 U.S. 356, 369 (1886). Nor is it disputed that the Arizona and Pennsylvania statutes in question create two classes of needy persons, indistinguishable except with respect to whether they are or are not citizens of this country. Otherwise qualified United States citizens living in Arizona are entitled to federally funded categorical assistance benefits without regard to length of national residency, but aliens must have lived in this country for 15 years in order to qualify for aid. United States citizens living in Pennsylvania [may] be eligible for state-supported general assistance, but resident aliens as a class are precluded from that assistance.

Under traditional equal protection principles, a State retains broad discretion to classify as long as its classification has a reasonable basis. This is so in "the area of economics and social welfare." *Dandridge v. Williams*, 397 U.S. 471, 485 (1970). But the Court's decisions have established that classifications based on alienage, like those based on nationality or race, are inherently suspect and subject to close judicial scrutiny. Aliens as a class are a prime example of a "discrete and insular"

> **Food for Thought**
>
> Is discrimination on the basis of citizenship status tantamount to discrimination on the basis of national origin, which the Court subjects to strict scrutiny? If not, why is it different? Is alienage status immutable?

minority (see *United States v. Carolene Products Co.*, 304 U.S. 144, 152–153 (1938)) for whom such heightened judicial solicitude is appropriate.

> **FYI**
>
> In *Crane v. New York*, 239 U.S. 195 (1915), the Court upheld a state statute prohibiting the employment of aliens on public works projects, reasoning that state employment is a privilege, not a right, that can be limited to citizens. In the early twentieth century, the Court also upheld state laws limiting the rights of aliens to own land and to exploit state natural resources. The Court refers to these holdings as the "special public-interest doctrine."

Arizona and Pennsylvania seek to justify their restrictions on the eligibility of aliens for public assistance solely on the basis of a State's "special public interest" in favoring its own citizens over aliens in the distribution of limited resources such as welfare benefits. It is true that this Court on occasion has upheld state statutes that treat citizens and noncitizens differently, the ground for distinction having been that such laws were necessary to protect special interests of the State or its citizens. * * *

Whatever may be the contemporary vitality of the special public-interest doctrine, we conclude that a State's desire to preserve limited welfare benefits for its own citizens is inadequate to justify Pennsylvania's making noncitizens ineligible for public assistance, and Arizona's restricting benefits to citizens and longtime resident aliens. First, [this] Court now has rejected the concept that constitutional rights turn upon whether a governmental benefit is characterized as a "right" or as a "privilege." *Sherbert v. Verner*, 374 U.S. 398 (1963).

Second, as the Court recognized in *Shapiro v. Thompson*, 394 U.S. 618, 633 (1969), "[a] State has a valid interest in preserving the fiscal integrity of its programs. It may legitimately attempt to limit its expenditures, whether for public assistance, public education, or any other program. But a State may not accomplish such a purpose by invidious distinctions between classes of its citizens." Since an alien as well as a citizen is a "person" for equal protection purposes, a concern for fiscal integrity is no more compelling a justification for the questioned classification in these cases than it was in *Shapiro*.

We agree with the three-judge court in the Pennsylvania case that the "justification of limiting expenses is particularly inappropriate and unreasonable when the discriminated class consists of aliens. Aliens like citizens pay taxes and may be called into the armed forces." * * * There can be no "special public interest" in tax revenues to which aliens have contributed on an equal basis with the residents of the State. Accordingly, we hold that a state statute that denies welfare benefits to resident aliens and one that denies them to aliens who have not resided in the United States for a specified number of years violates the Equal Protection Clause.

POINTS FOR DISCUSSION

a. Level of Scrutiny

What level of scrutiny did the Court apply to the state statutes? The Court compared classifications based on citizenship status to those based on nationality and race, and declared that they are "inherently suspect and subject to close judicial scrutiny." But the Court did not make clear whether the state interest justifying the classification must be "compelling," and the Court did not discuss the required relationship between the state interest and the classification.

Two years later, in *Sugarman v. Dougall*, 413 U.S. 634 (1973), the Court applied strict scrutiny to invalidate a New York law that excluded non-citizens from permanent positions in the state's civil service. The Court acknowledged the state's "substantial" interest in "having an employee of undivided loyalty" in significant policy-making positions, but concluded that the statute covered mostly menial employees. Several years later, relying on the "policy-making" exception that the Court had suggested in *Sugarman*, the Court declined to apply strict scrutiny to a state policy excluding aliens from employment as state troopers. *Foley v. Connelie*, 435 U.S.

291 (1978). The Court declared that "to require every statutory exclusion of aliens to clear the high hurdle of 'strict scrutiny' [would] obliterate all the distinctions between citizens and aliens, and thus depreciate the historic values of citizenship." The Court noted that police officers "are clothed with authority to exercise an almost infinite variety of discretionary powers." The Court upheld the policy, concluding that "[i]n the enforcement and execution of the laws the police function is one where citizenship bears a rational relationship to the special demands of the particular position."

After *Graham*, *Sugarman*, and *Foley*, what is the appropriate level of scrutiny for classifications based upon citizenship status?

b. Defining the Political Community

The Court has struggled in many contexts with the states' efforts to define their political communities. It seems widely accepted that states can deny the right to vote to persons who are not citizens. Why is that denial less problematic than the denial at issue in *Graham*?

Is the amount of time that one spends in a community a relevant criteria in defining the political community? In *Graham*, the states sought to limit public benefits to those who were citizens, or at least (in the case of Arizona) to those who had been legal residents for a long time. In Chapter 1, we considered the Court's response to a state statute that limited newly arrived residents to the level of welfare benefits that they would have received in their prior states of residence. In *Saenz v. Roe*, the Court invalidated the statute, relying on the Privileges or Immunities Clause of the Fourteenth Amendment. Why didn't the Court rely on that provision in *Graham*? What limits, if any, should there be on the ability of the states to exclude persons from their political communities? Should those limits apply with equal force to the federal government?

c. Aliens Who Were Not Lawfully Admitted

Aliens who were not lawfully admitted to the United States plainly are "persons," they lack political power (indeed, they lack the right to vote), and they are often the targets of hostility. Can states withhold benefits from them? If so, why are such classifications different from the classifications at issue in *Graham*?

2. Parents' Marital Status

CLARK V. JETER
486 U.S. 456 (1988)

JUSTICE O'CONNOR delivered the opinion of the Court.

Under Pennsylvania law, an illegitimate child must prove paternity before seeking support from his or her father, and a suit to establish paternity ordinarily must be brought within six years of an illegitimate child's birth. By contrast, a legitimate child may seek support from his or her parents at any time. [Ten years after her illegitimate daughter's birth, Cherlyn Clark filed a complaint on her daughter's behalf seeking to compel Gene Jeter, the alleged father, to pay support. Although a blood test demonstrated a 99.3% probability that Jeter was the father, the court entered judgment for Jeter based on the six-year statute of limitations.]

Between [the] extremes of rational basis review and strict scrutiny lies a level of intermediate scrutiny, which generally has been applied to discriminatory classifications based on sex or illegitimacy. To withstand intermediate scrutiny, a statutory classification must be substantially related to an important governmental objective. Consequently we have invalidated classifications that burden illegitimate children for the sake of punishing the illicit relations of their parents, because "visiting this condemnation on the head of an infant is illogical and unjust." *Weber v. Aetna Casualty & Surety Co.,* 406 U.S. 164, 175 (1972). Yet, in the seminal case concerning the child's right to support, this Court acknowledged that it might be appropriate to treat illegitimate children differently in the support context because of "lurking problems with respect to proof of paternity." *Gomez v. Perez,* 409 U.S. 535, 538 (1973).

[W]e conclude that Pennsylvania's 6-year statute of limitations violates the Equal Protection Clause. Even six years does not necessarily provide a reasonable opportunity to assert a claim on behalf of an illegitimate child. "The unwillingness of the mother to file a paternity action on behalf of her child, which could stem from her relationship with the natural father or [from] the emotional strain of having an illegitimate child, or even from the desire to avoid community and family disapproval, may continue years after the child is born. The problem may be exacerbated if, as often happens, the mother herself is a minor." *Mills v. Habluetzel,* 456 U.S. 91, 105 n.4 (1982) (O'CONNOR, J., concurring). Not all of these difficulties are likely to abate in six years. A mother might realize only belatedly "a loss of income attributable to the need to care for the child." Furthermore, financial difficulties are likely to increase as the child matures and incurs expenses for clothing, school, and medical care. Thus it is questionable whether a State acts reasonably when it requires most paternity and support actions to be brought within six years of an illegitimate child's birth.

We do not rest our decision on this ground, however, for it is not entirely evident that six years would necessarily be an unreasonable limitations period for child support actions involving illegitimate children. We are, however, confident that the 6-year statute of limitations is not substantially related to Pennsylvania's interest in avoiding the litigation of stale or fraudulent claims. In a number of circumstances, Pennsylvania permits the issue of paternity to be litigated more than six years after the birth of an illegitimate child. The statute itself permits a suit to be brought more than six years after the child's birth if it is brought within two years of a support payment made by the father. And in other types of suits, Pennsylvania places no limits on when the issue of paternity may be litigated. For example, the intestacy statute, 20 Pa. Cons. Stat. § 2107(3) (1982), permits a child born out of wedlock to establish paternity as long as "there is clear and convincing evidence that the man was the father of the child." Likewise, no statute of limitations applies to a father's action to establish paternity. [In addition, increasingly] sophisticated tests for genetic markers permit the exclusion of over 99% of those who might be accused of paternity, regardless of the age of the child. This scientific evidence is available throughout the child's minority.

We conclude that the Pennsylvania statute does not withstand heightened scrutiny under the Equal Protection Clause.

POINTS FOR DISCUSSION

a. Illegitimate Children as a Suspect Class

Are illegitimate children a "discrete and insular minority"? Are they the victims of societal prejudice? Is there reason to think that they will not be protected by the ordinary operation of the political process? And is the "status" of illegitimacy immutable? If so, then why doesn't the Court apply strict, as opposed to intermediate, scrutiny for classifications that burden people whose parents were not married?

Is the real concern with such classifications that they visit the "sins" of the parents on their children? In this regard, consider Article III, section 3, clause 2, which provides that "no Attainder of Treason shall work Corruption of Blood." Corruption of Blood was an old British practice by which the family of a person convicted of treason was prohibited from

> **Make the Connection**
>
> We will consider this question in Chapter 6, when we discuss *Plyler v. Doe* and state efforts to deny public education to the children of illegal immigrants.

inheriting his property. Does this provision stand for the broader proposition that it is constitutionally suspect to punish children for the actions of their parents?

b.   Application of Intermediate Scrutiny

Was the defect in the Pennsylvania statute invalidated in *Clark* that the state did not have an important interest? Or that the shorter statute of limitations was not sufficiently related to that interest? What other interests, if any, might justify classifying on the basis of a person's parents' marital status? Would an interest in upholding traditional family values and the sanctity of marriage be sufficiently important? Is there a countervailing state interest in granting men repose from the possibility of paternity suits?

3.   Age

MASSACHUSETTS BD. OF RETIREMENT V. MURGIA
427 U.S. 307 (1976)

PER CURIAM.

This case presents the question whether the provision of Mass.Gen.Laws Ann. c. 32, § 26(3)(a) (1969), that a uniformed state police officer "shall be retired [upon] his attaining age fifty," denies appellee police officer equal protection of the laws in violation of the Fourteenth Amendment. [Appellee, a police officer, was forced to retire on his 50th birthday, despite being in excellent physical and mental health. He brought suit claiming that his forced retirement violated the Equal Protection Clause.]

[S]trict scrutiny is not the proper test for determining whether the mandatory retirement provision denies appellee equal protection. [E]qual protection analysis requires strict scrutiny of a legislative classification only when the classification impermissibly interferes with the exercise of a fundamental right or operates to the peculiar disadvantage of a suspect class. Mandatory retirement at age 50 under the Massachusetts statute involves neither situation.

> **Make the Connection**
>
> We will discuss the relationship between the Equal Protection Clause and "fundamental rights" in Chapter 6.

This Court's decisions give no support to the proposition that a right of governmental employment per se is fundamental. * * * Nor does the class of uniformed state police officers over 50 constitute a suspect class for purposes of equal protection analysis. [A] suspect class is one "saddled with such disabilities, or subjected to such a history of purposeful unequal treatment, or relegated to such a position of political powerlessness as to command extraordinary protection from the majoritarian political process." *San Antonio School District v. Rodriguez*, 411 U.S. 1, 16 (1973). While the treatment of the aged in this Nation has not been wholly free of discrimination, such persons, unlike, say, those who have been discriminated against on the basis of race or national origin, have not experienced a "history of purposeful unequal treatment" or been subjected to unique disabilities on the basis of stereotyped characteristics not truly indicative of their abilities. * * * Even if the statute could be said

> **Take Note**
>
> The statute distinguishes between police officers who are older than 50 years and those who are younger than 50. Does the statute discriminate against the *elderly*? What if the statute excluded from service persons older than 40? Or persons older than 30? Conversely, what if it excluded only people older than 70? Would there be a stronger argument then that it burdened a suspect class?

to impose a penalty upon a class defined as the aged, it would not impose a distinction sufficiently akin to those classifications that we have found suspect to call for strict judicial scrutiny. Under the circumstances, it is unnecessary to subject the State's resolution of competing interests in this case to the degree of critical examination that our cases under the Equal Protection Clause recently have characterized as "strict judicial scrutiny."

We turn then to examine this state classification under the rational-basis standard. [T]he Massachusetts statute clearly meets the requirements of the Equal Protection Clause, for the State's classification rationally furthers the purpose identified by the State: Through mandatory retirement at age 50, the legislature seeks to protect the public by assuring physical preparedness of its uniformed police. Since physical ability generally declines with age, mandatory retirement at 50 serves to remove from police service those whose fitness for uniformed work presumptively has diminished with age. This clearly is rationally related to the State's objective. There is no indication that [the statute] has the effect of excluding from service so few officers who are in fact unqualified as to render age 50 a criterion wholly unrelated to the objective of the statute.

> **FYI**
>
> In addition to requiring retirement at age 50, the statute also required police officers to pass comprehensive physical examinations biennially until age 40, and then annually until age 50. In light of this requirement, what interest does the mandatory retirement age advance?

That the State chooses not to determine fitness more precisely through individualized testing after age 50 is not to say that the objective of assuring physical fitness is not rationally furthered by a maximum-age limitation. It is only to say that with regard to the interest of all concerned, the State perhaps has not chosen the best means to accomplish this purpose. But where rationality is the test, a

State "does not violate the Equal Protection Clause merely because the classifications made by its laws are imperfect." *Dandridge v. Williams*, 397 U.S. 471, 485 (1970).

We do not make light of the substantial economic and psychological effects premature and compulsory retirement can have on an individual; nor do we denigrate the ability of elderly citizens to continue to contribute to society. * * * We decide only that the system enacted by the Massachusetts Legislature does not deny appellee equal protection of the laws.

MR. JUSTICE MARSHALL, dissenting.

While depriving any government employee of his job is a significant deprivation, it is particularly burdensome when the person deprived is an older citizen. Once terminated, the elderly cannot readily find alternative employment. The lack of work is not only economically damaging, but emotionally and physically draining. Deprived of his status in the community and of the opportunity for meaningful activity, fearful of becoming dependent on others for his support, and lonely in his new-found isolation, the involuntarily retired person is susceptible to physical and emotional ailments as a direct consequence of his enforced idleness. Ample clinical evidence supports the conclusion that mandatory retirement poses a direct threat to the health and life expectancy of the retired person * * *. Thus, an older person deprived of his job by the government loses not only his right to earn a living, but, too often, his health as well * * *. Not only are the elderly denied important benefits when they are terminated on the basis of age, but the classification of older workers is itself one that merits judicial attention. Whether older workers constitute a "suspect" class or not, it cannot be disputed that they constitute a class subject to repeated and arbitrary discrimination in employment.

FYI

In 1967, Congress passed the Age Discrimination in Employment Act, 29 U.S.C. § 621(a), which prohibits discrimination on the basis of age in employment against persons who are at least 40 years old, except where age "is a bona fide occupational qualification reasonably necessary to the normal operation of the particular business." Does this legislation support Justice Marshall's view that the elderly are deserving of heightened judicial protection, or the Court's view that they are not?

Of course, [the] elderly are protected not only by certain anti-discrimination legislation, but by legislation that provides them with positive benefits not enjoyed by the public at large. Moreover, the elderly are not isolated in society, and discrimination against them is not pervasive but is centered primarily in employment. The advantage of a flexible equal protection standard, however, is that it can readily accommodate such variables. The elderly are undoubtedly discriminated against

[when] legislation denies them an important benefit. [I] conclude that to sustain the legislation appellants must show a reasonably substantial interest and a scheme reasonably closely tailored to achieving that interest.

[I] agree that the purpose of the mandatory retirement law is legitimate, and indeed compelling[;] the Commonwealth has every reason to assure that its state police officers are of sufficient physical strength and health to perform their jobs. In my view, however, the means chosen, the forced retirement of officers at age 50, is so over-inclusive that it must fall. [T]he Commonwealth is in the position of already individually testing its police officers for physical fitness, conceding that such testing is adequate to determine the physical ability of an officer to continue on the job, and conceding that that ability may continue after age 50. In these circumstances, I see no reason at all for automatically terminating those officers who reach the age of 50; indeed, that action seems the height of irrationality.

POINTS FOR DISCUSSION

a. Age as a Suspect Basis for Classification

Should age be a suspect basis for classification? Few people would dispute that the government should be able to draw distinctions that burden children because of their youth, such as a requirement that a person be at least sixteen years old to obtain a driver's license. But is it problematic when the government draws distinctions that burden the elderly? Are the elderly victims of prejudice who are not adequately protected by the political process?

Recall that Justice Scalia suggested in his separate opinion in *Cruzan v. Director, Missouri Department of Health*, which we considered in Chapter 2, that the elderly and infirm are protected by the Equal Protection Clause, "which requires the democratic majority to accept for themselves and their loved ones what they impose on you and me." Does the "golden rule," combined with the possibility that we may all be old one day, mean that there is no need for judicial protection for the elderly?

b. Tiers of Scrutiny

The Court concluded in *Murgia* that age is not a suspect basis for classification, and it accordingly subjected the challenged statute to rational-basis review. Justice Marshall urged a more nuanced approach to judicial scrutiny, one that would abandon the separate tiers of scrutiny and instead "accommodate" the various state and individual interests implicated by the state's regulation. What are the merits of such an approach? What are its drawbacks? The case that follows raises the same questions.

4.   Disability

CLEBURNE V. CLEBURNE LIVING CENTER
473 U.S. 432 (1985)

JUSTICE WHITE delivered the opinion of the Court.

A Texas city denied a special use permit for the operation of a group home for the mentally retarded, acting pursuant to a municipal zoning ordinance requiring permits for such homes. The Court of Appeals for the Fifth Circuit held that mental retardation is a "quasi-suspect" classification and that the ordinance violated the Equal Protection Clause because it did not substantially further an important governmental purpose. We hold that a lesser standard of scrutiny is appropriate, but conclude that under that standard the ordinance is invalid as applied in this case.

The general rule is that legislation is presumed to be valid and will be sustained if the classification drawn by the statute is rationally related to a legitimate state interest. * * * [W]here individuals in the group affected by a law have distinguishing characteristics relevant to interests the State has the authority to implement, the courts have been very reluctant, as they should be in our federal system and with our respect for the separation of powers, to closely scrutinize legislative choices as to whether, how, and to what extent those interests should be pursued. In such cases, the Equal Protection Clause requires only a rational means to serve a legitimate end.

[W]e conclude for several reasons that the Court of Appeals erred in holding mental retardation a quasi-suspect classification calling for a more exacting standard of judicial review than is normally accorded economic and social legislation. First, it is undeniable, and it is not argued otherwise here, that those who are mentally retarded have a reduced ability to cope with and function in the everyday world. Nor are they all cut from the same pattern: as the testimony in this record indicates, they range from those whose disability is not immediately evident to those who must be constantly cared for. They are thus different, immutably so, in relevant respects, and the States' interest in dealing with and providing for them is plainly a legitimate one. How this large and diversified group is to be treated under the law is a difficult and often a technical matter, very much a task for legislators guided by qualified professionals and not by the perhaps ill-informed opinions of the judiciary. Heightened scrutiny inevitably involves substantive judgments about legislative decisions, and we doubt that the predicate for such judicial oversight is present where the classification deals with mental retardation.

Second, the distinctive legislative response, both national and state, to the plight of those who are mentally retarded demonstrates not only that they have unique problems, but also that the lawmakers have been addressing their difficulties in a manner that belies a continuing antipathy or prejudice and a corresponding need for more intrusive oversight by the judiciary. * * * Third, the legislative response, which could hardly have occurred and survived without public support, negates any claim that the mentally retarded are politically powerless in the sense that they have no ability to attract the attention of the lawmakers.

Fourth, if the large and amorphous class of the mentally retarded were deemed quasi-suspect, it would be difficult to find a principled way to distinguish a variety of other groups who have perhaps immutable

> **FYI**
>
> The Rehabilitation Act of 1973, 29 U.S.C. § 794, prohibits discrimination by federally funded programs against persons with disabilities, and several other federal statutes confer on the mentally retarded rights to equal educational opportunities and humane treatment facilities. Several years after the Court's decision in *Cleburne*, Congress enacted the Americans with Disabilities Act, 42 U.S.C. § 12101 et seq., which provides additional protections for the disabled in general and for the mentally retarded in particular. Do these statutes suggest that the mentally retarded are protected by the political process, or instead that government felt compelled to intervene to protect the mentally retarded from pervasive private prejudice and animus?

disabilities setting them off from others, who cannot themselves mandate the desired legislative responses, and who can claim some degree of prejudice from at least part of the public at large.

Our refusal to recognize the retarded as a quasi-suspect class does not leave them entirely unprotected from invidious discrimination. To withstand equal protection review, legislation that distinguishes between the mentally retarded and others must be rationally related to a legitimate governmental purpose. This standard, we believe, affords government the latitude necessary both to pursue policies designed to assist the retarded in realizing their full potential, and to freely and efficiently engage in activities that burden the retarded in what is essentially an incidental manner. The State may not rely on a classification whose relationship to an asserted goal is so attenuated as to render the distinction arbitrary or irrational.

The city does not require a special use permit [for] apartment houses, multiple dwellings, boarding and lodging houses, fraternity or sorority houses, dormitories, apartment hotels, hospitals, sanitariums, nursing homes for convalescents or the aged (other than for the insane or feebleminded or alcoholics or drug addicts), private clubs or fraternal orders, and other specified uses. * * *

May the city require the permit for [facilities for the mentally retarded] when other care and multiple-dwelling facilities are freely permitted? [T]he record does not reveal any rational basis for believing that [the home] would pose any special threat to the city's legitimate interests * * *.

The District Court found that the City Council's insistence on the permit rested on several factors. First, the Council was concerned with the negative attitude of the majority of property owners located within 200 feet of the [facility], as well as with the fears of elderly residents of the neighborhood. But mere negative attitudes, or fear, unsubstantiated by factors which are properly cognizable in a zoning proceeding, are not permissible bases for treating a home for the mentally retarded differently from apartment houses, multiple dwellings, and the like. * * *

Second, the Council [was] concerned that the facility was across the street from a junior high school, and it feared that the students might harass the occupants of the [home]. But the school itself is attended by about 30 mentally retarded students, and denying a permit based on such vague, undifferentiated fears is again permitting some portion of the community to validate what would otherwise be an equal protection violation. The other objection to the home's location was that it was located on "a five hundred year flood plain." This concern with the possibility of a flood, however, can hardly be based on a distinction between the [home] and, for example, nursing homes, homes for convalescents or the aged, or sanitariums or hospitals, any of which could be located on the [site] without obtaining a special use permit. The same may be said of another concern of the Council—doubts about the legal responsibility for actions which the mentally retarded might take. If there is no concern about legal responsibility with respect to other uses that would be permitted in the area, such as boarding and fraternity houses, it is difficult to believe that the groups of mildly or moderately mentally retarded individuals who would live at [the facility] would present any different or special hazard.

> **Take Note**
>
> The Court dismisses the reasons that the Council offered for the permit requirement. Is the Court's treatment of these interests consistent with rational-basis review?

Fourth, the Council was concerned with the size of the home and the number of people that would occupy it. [T]here would be no restrictions on the number of people who could occupy this home as a boarding house, nursing home, family dwelling, fraternity house, or dormitory. The question is whether it is rational to treat the mentally retarded differently. It is true that they suffer disability not shared by others; but why this difference warrants a density regulation that others need not observe is not at all apparent.

The short of it is that requiring the permit in this case appears to us to rest on an irrational prejudice against the mentally retarded, including those who would occupy the [facility] and who would live under the closely supervised and highly regulated conditions expressly provided for by state and federal law. The judgment of the Court of Appeals is affirmed insofar as it invalidates the zoning ordinance as applied to the [home].

JUSTICE STEVENS, with whom THE CHIEF JUSTICE joins, concurring.

The Court of Appeals disposed of this case as if a critical question to be decided were which of three clearly defined standards of equal protection review should be applied to a legislative classification discriminating against the mentally retarded. In fact, our cases have not delineated three—or even one or two—such well-defined standards. Rather, our cases reflect a continuum of judgmental responses to differing classifications which have been explained in opinions by terms ranging from "strict scrutiny" at one extreme to "rational basis" at the other. I have never been persuaded that these so-called "standards" adequately explain the decisional process. Cases involving classifications based on alienage, illegal residency, illegitimacy, gender, age, or—as in this case—mental retardation do not fit well into sharply defined classifications.

In my own approach to these cases, I have always asked myself whether I could find a "rational basis" for the classification at issue. The term "rational," of course, includes a requirement that an impartial lawmaker could logically believe that the classification would serve a legitimate public purpose that transcends the harm to the members of the disadvantaged class. Thus, the word "rational—for me at least—includes elements of legitimacy and neutrality that must always characterize the performance of the sovereign's duty to govern impartially.

In every equal protection case, we have to ask certain basic questions. What class is harmed by the legislation, and has it been subjected to a "tradition of disfavor" by our laws? What is the public purpose that is being served by the law? What is the characteristic of the disadvantaged class that justifies the disparate treatment? In most cases the answer to these questions will tell us whether the statute has a "rational basis." The answers will result in the virtually automatic invalidation of racial classifications and in the validation of most economic classifications, but they will provide differing results in cases involving classifications based on alienage, gender, or illegitimacy. But that is not because we apply an "intermediate standard of review" in these cases; rather it is because the characteristics of these groups are sometimes relevant and sometimes irrelevant to a valid public purpose, or, more specifically, to the purpose that the challenged laws purportedly intended to serve.

Every law that places the mentally retarded in a special class is not presumptively irrational. The differences between mentally retarded persons and those with greater mental capacity are obviously relevant to certain legislative decisions. [But] the mentally retarded "have been subjected to a history of unfair and often grotesque mistreatment." [The record in this case] convinces me that this permit was required because of the irrational fears of neighboring property owners, rather than for the protection of the mentally retarded persons who would reside in respondent's home.

JUSTICE MARSHALL, with whom JUSTICE BRENNAN and JUSTICE BLACKMUN join, concurring in the judgment in part and dissenting in part.

[The majority's discussion of the rational-basis test is] puzzling given that Cleburne's ordinance is invalidated only after being subjected to precisely the sort of probing inquiry associated with heightened scrutiny. To be sure, the Court does not label its handiwork heightened scrutiny, and perhaps the method employed must hereafter be called "second order" rational-basis review rather than "heightened scrutiny." But however labeled, the rational basis test invoked today is most assuredly not the rational-basis test of *Williamson v. Lee Optical of Oklahoma, Inc.,* 348 U.S. 483 (1955).

> **Make the Connection**
>
> We considered the Court's decision in *Williamson* in Chapter 2.

The refusal to acknowledge that something more than minimum rationality review is at work here is, in my view, unfortunate in at least two respects. The suggestion that the traditional rational-basis test allows this sort of searching inquiry creates precedent for this Court and lower courts to subject economic and commercial classifications to similar and searching "ordinary" rational-basis review—a small and regrettable step back toward the days of *Lochner*. Moreover, by failing to articulate the factors that justify today's "second order" rational-basis review, the Court provides no principled foundation for determining when more searching inquiry is to be invoked. Lower courts are thus left in the dark on this important question, and this Court remains unaccountable for its decisions employing, or refusing to employ, particularly searching scrutiny.

I have long believed the level of scrutiny employed in an equal protection case should vary with "the constitutional and societal importance of the interest adversely affected and the recognized invidiousness of the basis upon which the particular classification is drawn." When a zoning ordinance works to exclude the retarded from all residential districts in a community, these two considerations require that the ordinance be convincingly justified as substantially furthering legitimate and important purposes. First, the interest of the retarded in establishing group homes is substantial. The right to "establish a home" has long been cherished as one of the fundamental liberties embraced by the Due Process Clause. * * * Second, the mentally retarded have been subject to a "lengthy and tragic history" [of] segregation and discrimination that can only be called grotesque.

> **Make the Connection**
>
> For some of the history on which Justice Marshall relies, recall the Court's decision in *Skinner v. Oklahoma* (and the decision in *Buck v. Bell*, which preceded it). We considered those decisions in Chapter 2.

[Cleburne's] vague generalizations for classifying the "feeble-minded" with drug addicts, alcoholics, and the insane, and excluding them where the elderly, the ill, the boarder, and the transient are allowed, are not substantial or important enough to overcome the suspicion that the ordinance rests on impermissible assumptions or outmoded and perhaps invidious stereotypes.

[The Court points to] legislative action that is said to "beli[e] a continuing antipathy or prejudice." * * * It is natural that evolving standards of equality come to be embodied in legislation. When that occurs, courts should look to the fact of such change as a source of guidance on evolving principles of equality. * * * Moreover, even when judicial action *has* catalyzed legislative change, that change certainly does not eviscerate the underlying constitutional principle. The Court, for example, has never suggested that race-based classifications became any less suspect once extensive legislation had been enacted on the subject. For the retarded, just as for Negroes and women, much has changed in recent years, but much remains the same; out-dated statutes are still on the books, and irrational fears or ignorance, traceable to the prolonged social and cultural isolation of the retarded, continue to stymie recognition of the dignity and individuality of retarded people. Heightened judicial scrutiny of action appearing to impose unnecessary barriers to the retarded is required in light of increasing recognition that such barriers are inconsistent with evolving principles of equality embedded in the Fourteenth Amendment. * * * In light of the scrutiny that should be applied here, Cleburne's ordinance sweeps too broadly to dispel the suspicion that it rests on a bare desire to treat the retarded as outsiders, pariahs who do not belong in the community.

POINTS FOR DISCUSSION

a. Levels of Scrutiny

The Court's opinion in *Cleburne* was premised on the view that there are different tiers of scrutiny, and that the Court's role varies greatly depending upon which tier applies to a given government action. Justice Stevens, in contrast, urged the abandonment of an approach based on discrete tiers of scrutiny, offering a more searching (and perhaps literal) form of rational-basis review in its place. And Justice Marshall asserted that "[t]he formal label under which an equal protection claim is reviewed is less important than careful identification of the interest at stake and the extent to which society recognizes the classification as an invidious one," apparently suggesting that the Court should adopt a more flexible, sliding-scale approach to review under the Equal Protection Clause.

Which approach makes the most sense? Does the formal system of different levels of scrutiny limit the Court's authority to second-guess legislative and political judgments only to those circumstances in which it is most warranted? Or does it simply require arbitrary line-drawing in resolving the threshold question about what level of scrutiny a particular type of classification should receive? Has the tiered approach led to consistent and acceptable results? Conversely, are the more flexible approaches that Justice Stevens and Justice Marshall proposed likely to lead to judicial candor about the competing interests implicated in any given case? Or are they simply invitations for judicial legislation?

Regardless of the merits of the competing approaches, do you agree that the Court in *Cleburne* adhered to the tiered system of review under the Equal Protection Clause?

b. Discrimination on the Basis of Mental Retardation or Disability

After *Cleburne*, what is the appropriate standard of review for state action that distinguishes between the mentally retarded and others? As a matter of constitutional law, can a state withhold driver's licenses from the mentally retarded? Can it refuse to hire the mentally retarded to serve in all sorts of civil service positions? Might rational bases exist for these actions? Does their constitutionality depend upon the government's actual motivation in taking them?

What about classifications that burden people with other physical disabilities? In *Board of Trustees of University of Alabama v. Garrett*, 531 U.S. 356 (2001), in which the Court considered Congress's power to enforce the Fourteenth Amendment, the Court stated, "the result of *Cleburne* is that States are not required by the Fourteenth Amendment to make special accommodations for *the disabled*, so long as their actions toward such individuals are rational." (Emphasis added.)

c.   **Rational Basis "with Bite"**

Commentators have referred to the Court's approach in *Cleburne* as rational-basis review "with bite"—an approach pursuant to which the Court is "less willing to supply justifying rationales by exercising its imagination," assesses the means "in terms of legislative purposes that have substantial basis in actuality, not merely in conjecture," and gauges the "reasonableness of questionable means on the basis of materials that are offered to the Court, rather than resorting to rationalizations created by perfunctory judicial hypothesizing." Gerald Gunther, *Foreword: In Search of Evolving Doctrine on a Changing Court: A Model for a Newer Equal Protection*, 86 Harv. L. Rev. 1 (1972). Is this approach preferable to the highly deferential form of rational-basis review that emerged post-1937? Is it at least appropriate for some forms of classifications, even if not all innocuous classifications?

Cleburne is not the only case in which the Court has purported to apply rational-basis review but in fact reviewed the challenged policy more searchingly. In *United States Department of Agriculture v. Moreno*, 413 U.S. 528 (1973), for example, the Court invalidated a provision of the Food Stamp Act of 1964 that excluded from participation in the program any household containing an individual unrelated to any other member of the household. The appellee shared an apartment with another woman on public assistance to whom she was not related, in order to save money on living expenses. The Court, in an opinion by Justice Brennan, concluded that the exclusion failed to satisfy rational-basis review. The Court reasoned that the classification (which treated persons living in group homes differently from people living in households only with family members) did not advance Congress's stated purpose in raising levels of nutrition in low-income households. Moreover, the Court concluded that the purpose suggested by the legislative history—that Congress sought "to prevent so-called 'hippies' and 'hippie communes' from participating in the food stamp program"—was insufficient, because the "bare congressional desire to harm a politically unpopular group cannot constitute a *legitimate* governmental interest." Justice Rehnquist, joined by Chief Justice Burger, dissented, reasoning that limiting assistance to households consisting of related individuals "provides a guarantee which is not provided by households containing unrelated individuals that the household exists for some purpose other than to collect federal food stamps." Did the classification at issue in *Moreno* warrant judicial scrutiny more searching than conventional rational-basis review?

5. Sexual Orientation

ROMER V. EVANS
517 U.S. 620 (1996)

JUSTICE KENNEDY delivered the opinion of the Court.

The enactment challenged in this case is an amendment to the Constitution of the State of Colorado, adopted in a 1992 statewide referendum. The parties and the state courts refer to it as "Amendment 2," its designation when submitted to the voters. The impetus for the amendment [came] in large part from ordinances that had been passed in various Colorado municipalities [banning discrimination on the basis of sexual orientation]. Amendment 2 repeals these ordinances [and] prohibits all legislative, executive or judicial action at any level of state or local government designed to protect [homosexual] persons or gays and lesbians. The amendment reads [in relevant part]:

> "Neither the State of Colorado, through any of its branches or departments, nor any of its agencies, political subdivisions, municipalities or school districts, shall enact, adopt or enforce any statute, regulation, ordinance or policy whereby homosexual, lesbian or bisexual orientation, conduct, practices or relationships shall constitute or otherwise be the basis of or entitle any person or class of persons to have or claim any minority status, quota preferences, protected status or claim of discrimination."

[A gay municipal employee in Denver filed suit claiming that Amendment 2 was unconstitutional.]

The State's principal argument in defense of Amendment 2 is that it [does] no more than deny homosexuals special rights. This reading of the amendment's language is implausible. * * * Homosexuals, by state decree, are put in a solitary class with respect to transactions and relations in both the private and governmental spheres. The amendment withdraws from homosexuals, but no others, specific legal protection from the injuries caused by discrimination, and it forbids reinstatement of these laws and policies. [A]mendment 2 bars homosexuals from securing protection against the injuries that [many municipal] public-accommodations laws address [and] nullifies specific legal protections for this targeted class in all transactions in housing, sale of real estate, insurance, health and welfare services, private education, and employment. Not confined to the private sphere, Amendment 2 also operates to repeal and forbid all laws or policies providing specific protection for gays or lesbians from discrimination by every level of Colorado government.

[W]e cannot accept the view that Amendment 2's prohibition on specific legal protections does no more than deprive homosexuals of special rights. To the contrary, the amendment imposes a special disability upon those persons alone. [Homosexuals] can obtain specific protection against discrimination only by enlisting the citizenry of Colorado to amend the State Constitution * * *. This is so no matter how local or discrete the harm, no matter how public and widespread the injury. We find nothing special in the protections Amendment 2 withholds. These are protections taken for granted by most people either because they already have them or do not need them; these are protections against exclusion from an almost limitless number of transactions and endeavors that constitute ordinary civic life in a free society.

The Fourteenth Amendment's promise that no person shall be denied the equal protection of the laws must coexist with the practical necessity that most legislation classifies for one purpose or another, with resulting disadvantage to various groups or persons. We have attempted to reconcile the principle with the reality by stating that, if a law neither burdens a fundamental right nor targets a suspect class, we will uphold the legislative classification so long as it bears a rational relation to some legitimate end.

Amendment 2 fails, indeed defies, even this conventional inquiry. First, the amendment has the peculiar property of imposing a broad and undifferentiated disability on a single named group, an exceptional and, as we shall explain, invalid form of legislation. Second, its sheer breadth is so discontinuous with the reasons offered for it that the amendment seems inexplicable by anything but animus toward the class it affects; it lacks a rational relationship to legitimate state interests.

Taking the first point, even in the ordinary equal protection case calling for the most deferential of standards, we insist on knowing the relation between the classification adopted and the object to be attained. * * * By requiring that the classification bear a rational relationship to an independent and legitimate legislative

Take Note

The Court states that the purpose of rational-basis review is to ensure that classifications are not drawn for the purpose of "disadvantaging" the group "burdened" by the law. Isn't the group "burdened" by the law by definition "disadvantaged" by it? For example, a law permitting only persons younger than 50 years old to serve as police officers "advantages" people who are relatively young only because it excludes people who are relatively older. Isn't the point of rational-basis review simply to ensure that government classifications are not entirely arbitrary?

end, we ensure that classifications are not drawn for the purpose of disadvantaging the group burdened by the law.

Amendment 2 confounds this normal process of judicial review. It is at once too narrow and too broad. It identifies persons by a single trait and then denies them protection across the board. The resulting disqualification of a class of persons from the right to seek specific protection from the law is unprecedented in our jurisprudence. * * * It is not within our constitutional tradition to enact laws of this sort. Central both to the idea of the rule of law and to our own Constitution's guarantee of equal protection is the principle that government and each of its parts remain open on impartial terms to all who seek its assistance. * * * A law declaring that in general it shall be more difficult for one group of citizens than for all others to seek aid from the government is itself a denial of equal protection of the laws in the most literal sense.

A second and related point is that laws of the kind now before us raise the inevitable inference that the disadvantage imposed is born of animosity toward the class of persons affected. "[I]f the constitutional conception of 'equal protection of the laws' means anything, it must at the very least mean that a bare [desire] to harm a politically unpopular group cannot constitute a *legitimate* governmental interest." *United States Department of Agriculture v. Moreno*, 413 U.S. 528, 534 (1973). * * * Amendment 2, however, in making a general announcement that gays and lesbians shall not have any particular protections from the law, inflicts on them immediate, continuing, and real injuries that outrun and belie any legitimate justifications that may be claimed for it.

> **Take Note**
>
> Is the Court's suggestion here that Colorado's asserted interests are not legitimate, or is it instead that the classification does not bear any rational relationship to those interests? Is either of those conclusions consistent with the Court's ordinary approach in cases applying rational-basis review? Is the Court applying rational-basis review?

The primary rationale the State offers for Amendment 2 is respect for other citizens' freedom of association, and in particular the liberties of landlords or employers who have personal or religious objections to homosexuality. Colorado also cites its interest in conserving resources to fight discrimination against other groups. The breadth of the amendment is so far removed from these particular justifications that we find it impossible to credit them. We cannot say that Amendment 2 is directed to any identifiable legitimate purpose or discrete objective. It is a status-based enactment divorced from any factual context from which we could discern a relationship to legitimate state interests; it is a classification of persons undertaken for its own sake, something the Equal Protection Clause does not permit.

We must conclude that Amendment 2 classifies homosexuals not to further a proper legislative end but to make them unequal to everyone else. This Colorado cannot do. A State cannot so deem a class of persons a stranger to its laws.

JUSTICE SCALIA, with whom THE CHIEF JUSTICE and JUSTICE THOMAS join, dissenting.

The Court has mistaken a Kulturkampf for a fit of spite. The constitutional amendment before us here is not the manifestation of a "bare [desire] to harm" homosexuals, but is rather a modest attempt by seemingly tolerant Coloradans to preserve traditional sexual mores against the efforts of a politically powerful minority to revise those mores through use of the laws. That objective, and the means chosen to achieve it, are not only unimpeachable under any constitutional doctrine hitherto pronounced (hence the opinion's heavy reliance upon principles of righteousness rather than judicial holdings); they have been specifically approved by [this] Court.

> **Definition**
>
> The German word "Kulturkampf" literally means "conflict of cultures." Justice Scalia is suggesting that the Court has no business intervening in the culture wars. But does the mere fact that challenged legislation is the product of one side's victory in a public battle over values automatically immunize it from judicial scrutiny? Wasn't the law invalidated in *Loving*, which we considered earlier in this chapter, a product of a "culture war," as well?

In holding that homosexuality cannot be singled out for disfavorable treatment, the Court contradicts a decision, unchallenged here, pronounced only 10 years ago, see *Bowers v. Hardwick,* 478 U.S. 186 (1986), and places the prestige of this institution behind the proposition that opposition to homosexuality is as reprehensible as racial or religious bias. Whether it is or not is *precisely* the cultural debate that gave rise to the Colorado constitutional amendment (and to the preferential laws against which the amendment was directed). Since the Constitution of the United States says nothing about this subject, it

> **Make the Connection**
>
> Several years after the decision in *Romer*, the Court overruled *Bowers*, in *Lawrence v. Texas*. We considered *Lawrence* in Chapter 2.

is left to be resolved by normal democratic means, including the democratic adoption of provisions in state constitutions. This Court has no business imposing upon all Americans the resolution favored by the elite class from which the Members of this institution are selected, pronouncing that "animosity" toward homosexuality [is] evil.

[Amendment 2] prohibits *special treatment* of homosexuals, and nothing more. * * * The only denial of equal treatment [the Court] contends homosexuals have suffered is this: They may not obtain *preferential* treatment without amending the State Constitution. That is to say, the principle underlying the Court's opinion is that one who is accorded equal treatment under the laws, but cannot as readily as others obtain *preferential* treatment under the laws, has been denied equal protection of the laws. If merely stating this alleged "equal protection" violation does not suffice to refute it, our constitutional jurisprudence has achieved terminal silliness.

> **Take Note**
>
> Colorado law (and the laws in many of the municipalities whose ordinances were repealed by Amendment 2) prohibited discrimination on many bases, including age, marital or family status, veterans' status, and even whether the person engaged in lawful behavior, such as smoking tobacco, in his spare time. In light of this, do you agree that the repealed ordinances' additional prohibition of discrimination on the basis of sexual orientation amounted to "special treatment"?

What [Colorado] has done is not only unprohibited, but eminently reasonable * * *. The Court's opinion contains grim, disapproving hints that Coloradans have been guilty of "animus" or "animosity" toward homosexuality, as though that has been established as un-American. Of course it is our moral heritage that one should not hate any human being or class of human beings. But I had thought that one could consider certain conduct reprehensible—murder, for example, or polygamy, or cruelty to animals—and could exhibit even "animus" toward such conduct. Surely that is the only sort of "animus" at issue here: moral disapproval of homosexual conduct, the same sort of moral disapproval that produced the centuries-old criminal laws that we held constitutional in *Bowers*. The Colorado amendment does not, to speak entirely precisely, prohibit giving favored status to people who are *homosexuals;* they can be favored for many reasons—for example, because they are senior citizens or members of racial minorities. But it prohibits giving them favored status *because of their homosexual conduct*—that is, it prohibits favored status *for homosexuality*.

But though Coloradans [are] *entitled* to be hostile toward homosexual conduct, the [Court's] portrayal of Coloradans as a society

> **Take Note**
>
> Justice Scalia distinguishes between homosexuality as an orientation and homosexual "conduct." In his dissent in *Lawrence*, he advanced a similar view, referring not to homosexuals but instead to "persons who openly engage in homosexual conduct." There is, to be sure, continuing social debate over whether sexual orientation is biological or instead a choice. But if scientists were conclusively to demonstrate that sexual orientation is an immutable, biological characteristic, would Justice Scalia's view be tenable as a matter of constitutional law?

fallen victim to pointless, hate-filled "gay-bashing" is so false as to be comical. Colorado [was one of the first states to repeal its] anti-sodomy laws. But the society that eliminates criminal punishment for homosexual acts does not necessarily abandon the view that homosexuality is morally wrong and socially harmful; often, abolition simply reflects the view that enforcement of such criminal laws involves unseemly intrusion into the intimate lives of citizens. * * * Amendment 2 is designed to prevent piecemeal deterioration of the sexual morality favored by a majority of Coloradans, and is not only an appropriate means to that legitimate end, but a means that Americans have employed before. Striking it down is an act, not of judicial judgment, but of political will.

POINTS FOR DISCUSSION

a. Sexual Orientation as a Suspect Basis for Classification

Under the *Carolene Products* test, are gays and lesbians a suspect class deserving of heightened judicial protection? Notice that Justice Scalia referred to gays and lesbians as a "politically powerful minority." Was he thereby suggesting that they do not meet the *Carolene Products* test?

Did the Court in *Romer* conclude that laws that discriminate on the basis of sexual orientation are subject to heightened scrutiny? What level of scrutiny did the Court apply?

b. Legitimate State Interests

The Court stated in *Romer* that the challenged Amendment was explainable only as a manifestation of animus towards gays and lesbians, and it suggested that animus is never a legitimate basis for a classification. But can this really be true? What about laws disadvantaging ex-felons, such as laws withholding from ex-felons the right to vote? To be sure, such laws might serve a variety of objectives, but assuming that they are based on animus towards ex-felons (and the acts that they committed), does that make them unconstitutional?

Romer raised the question whether discrimination on the basis of sexual orientation is suspect and thus triggers heightened scrutiny, much in the same way that discrimination on the basis of race or sex does. The Court, however, did not squarely answer that question. The question took on renewed importance in the decade following the Court's decision in *Romer*, when the debate over the constitutionality of same-sex marriage began in earnest. Did the Court's decision in *Romer* suggest that state laws or constitutional provisions prohibiting same-sex marriage violate the Equal Protection Clause? In 2003, the Massachusetts

Supreme Judicial Court invalidated state laws that limited the right to marry to opposite-sex couples. *Goodridge v. Department of Public Health*, 798 N.E.2d 941 (Mass. 2003). Although the Court relied on the state, rather than the federal, constitution, it cited the Supreme Court's decision in *Romer* (and the Court's decision in *Lawrence v. Texas*). In the wake of the decision in *Goodridge*, twenty-nine states approved amendments to their constitutions to limit the right to marry to opposite-sex couples. Courts in several of those states, including California, then held that so limiting marriage violates their states' constitutions. See *In re Marriage Cases*, 183 P.3d 384 (Cal. 2008); *Kerrigan v. Commissioner of Pub. Health*, 957 A.2d 407 (Conn. 2008); *Varnum v. Brien*, 763 N.W.2d 862 (Iowa 2009).

Voters in California responded to the state Supreme Court's decision in *In re Marriage Cases* by approving Proposition 8, which amended the state constitution to exclude same-sex couples from marriage. See Cal. Const. art. I, § 7.5. A federal district court in California in 2010 invalidated Proposition 8, holding that it violates the Due Process and Equal Protection Clauses of the Fourteenth Amendment, *Perry v. Schwarzenegger*, 704 F.Supp.2d 921 (N.D. Cal. 2010), and the court of appeals, relying heavily on *Romer*, affirmed in *Perry v. Brown*, 671 F.3d 1052 (9th Cir. 2013).

The case reached the Supreme Court under the name of *Hollingsworth v. Perry*, 570 U.S. 693 (2013). The Governor and other local officials who had been named as defendants in the suit declined to defend the constitutionality of Proposition 8. The Supreme Court held that the proponents of the initiative, who had intervened to defend the law, lacked standing to appeal the district court's order. The Court therefore did not address the respondents' claims that the ban on same-sex marriage violates the Due Process and Equal Protection Clauses.

On the same day, however, the Supreme Court decided *United States v. Windsor*, 570 U.S. 744 (2013), which addressed the constitutionality of Section 3 the federal Defense of Marriage Act ("DOMA"). That provision defined "marriage" and "spouse," for the purposes of all federal legislation using those terms, to exclude same-sex marriages. The respondent, Edith Windsor, married her same-sex partner, and New York recognized the validity of their marriage. When Windsor's partner died, she left her entire estate to Windsor. Because DOMA denied federal recognition to same-sex spouses, Windsor did not qualify for the marital exemption from the federal estate tax, which excludes from taxation "any interest in property which passes or has passed from the decedent to his surviving spouse." After paying the tax, Windsor filed suit seeking a tax refund, contending that DOMA violated the equal protection component of the Fifth Amendment's Due Process Clause.

The Court invalidated the provision in a 5–4 decision, in an opinion by Justice Kennedy. The Court began by discussing "the extent of the state power and authority over marriage as a matter of history and tradition." The Court then explained:

> [T]he State's decision to give this class of persons the right to marry conferred upon them a dignity and status of immense import. When the State used its historic and essential authority to define the marital relation in this way, its role and its power in making the decision enhanced the recognition, dignity, and protection of the class in their own community. * * * For same-sex couples who wished to be married, the State acted to give their lawful conduct a lawful status. This status is a far-reaching legal acknowledgment of the intimate relationship between two people, a relationship deemed by the State worthy of dignity in the community equal with all other marriages. It reflects both the community's considered perspective on the historical roots of the institution of marriage and its evolving understanding of the meaning of equality.

The Court then asserted that "DOMA seeks to injure the very class New York seeks to protect." It continued:

> By doing so it violates basic due process and equal protection principles applicable to the Federal Government. See U.S. Const., Amdt. 5; *Bolling v. Sharpe*, 347 U.S. 497 (1954). The Constitution's guarantee of equality "must at the very least mean that a bare congressional desire to harm a politically unpopular group cannot" justify disparate treatment of that group. *Department of Agriculture v. Moreno*, 413 U.S. 528, 534–535 (1973). In determining whether a law is motivated by an improper animus or purpose, "[d]iscriminations of an unusual character" especially require careful consideration. DOMA cannot survive under these principles. The responsibility of the States for the regulation of domestic relations is an important indicator of the substantial societal impact the State's classifications have in the daily lives and customs of its people. DOMA's unusual deviation from the usual tradition of recognizing and accepting state definitions of marriage here operates to deprive same-sex couples of the benefits and responsibilities that come with the federal recognition of their marriages. This is strong evidence of a law having the purpose and effect of disapproval of that class. The avowed purpose and practical effect of the law here in question are to impose a disadvantage, a separate status, and so a stigma upon all who

enter into same-sex marriages made lawful by the unquestioned authority of the States.

The history of DOMA's enactment and its own text demonstrate that interference with the equal dignity of same-sex marriages, a dignity conferred by the States in the exercise of their sovereign power, was more than an incidental effect of the federal statute. It was its essence. The House Report announced its conclusion that "it is both appropriate and necessary for Congress to do what it can to defend the institution of traditional heterosexual marriage. . . . H.R. 3396 is appropriately entitled the 'Defense of Marriage Act.' The effort to redefine 'marriage' to extend to homosexual couples is a truly radical proposal that would fundamentally alter the institution of marriage." H.R. Rep. No. 104–664, pp. 12–13 (1996). The House concluded that DOMA expresses "both moral disapproval of homosexuality, and a moral conviction that heterosexuality better comports with traditional (especially Judeo-Christian) morality." Id., at 16 (footnote deleted). The stated purpose of the law was to promote an "interest in protecting the traditional moral teachings reflected in heterosexual-only marriage laws." Ibid. * * *

DOMA's operation in practice confirms this purpose. * * * DOMA writes inequality into the entire United States Code. The particular case at hand concerns the estate tax, but DOMA is more than a simple determination of what should or should not be allowed as an estate tax refund. Among the over 1,000 statutes and numerous federal regulations that DOMA controls are laws pertaining to Social Security, housing, taxes, criminal sanctions, copyright, and veterans' benefits.

DOMA's principal effect is to identify a subset of state-sanctioned marriages and make them unequal. The principal purpose is to impose inequality, not for other reasons like governmental efficiency. * * * By creating two contradictory marriage regimes within the same State, DOMA forces same-sex couples to live as married for the purpose of state law but unmarried for the purpose of federal law, thus diminishing the stability and predictability of basic personal relations the State has found it proper to acknowledge and protect. * * * This places same-sex couples in an unstable position of being in a second-tier marriage. The differentiation demeans the couple, whose moral and sexual choices the Constitution protects, see Lawrence, 539 U.S. 558, and whose relationship the State has sought to dignify. * * *

The Court then concluded that because "the principal purpose and the necessary effect of this law are to demean those persons who are in a lawful same-sex marriage," DOMA "is unconstitutional as a deprivation of the liberty of the person protected by the Fifth Amendment of the Constitution." The Court explained:

> The liberty protected by the Fifth Amendment's Due Process Clause contains within it the prohibition against denying to any person the equal protection of the laws. See *Bolling*, 347 U.S., at 499–500; *Adarand Constructors, Inc. v. Peña*, 515 U.S. 200, 217–218 (1995). While the Fifth Amendment itself withdraws from Government the power to degrade or demean in the way this law does, the equal protection guarantee of the Fourteenth Amendment makes that Fifth Amendment right all the more specific and all the better understood and preserved.

> The class to which DOMA directs its restrictions and restraints are those persons who are joined in same-sex marriages made lawful by the State. DOMA singles out a class of persons deemed by a State entitled to recognition and protection to enhance their own liberty. It imposes a disability on the class by refusing to acknowledge a status the State finds to be dignified and proper. * * * The federal statute is invalid, for no legitimate purpose overcomes the purpose and effect to disparage and to injure those whom the State, by its marriage laws, sought to protect in personhood and dignity. By seeking to displace this protection and treating those persons as living in marriages less respected than others, the federal statute is in violation of the Fifth Amendment.

Chief Justice Roberts dissented, asserting that the interests in "uniformity and stability amply justified Congress's decision to retain the definition of marriage that, at that point, had been adopted by every State in our Nation, and every nation in the world." He also stated: "The Court does not have before it, and the logic of its opinion does not decide, the distinct question whether the States, in the exercise of their 'historic and essential authority to define the marital relation' may continue to utilize the traditional definition of marriage."

Justice Scalia also dissented. He responded to the Court's focus on equality:

> [I]f this is meant to be an equal-protection opinion, it is a confusing one. The opinion does not resolve and indeed does not even mention what had been the central question in this litigation: whether, under the Equal Protection Clause, laws restricting marriage to a man and a woman are reviewed for more than mere rationality. That is the issue

that divided the parties and the court below. In accord with my previously expressed skepticism about the Court's "tiers of scrutiny" approach, I would review this classification only for its rationality. See *United States v. Virginia*, 518 U.S. 515, 567–570 (1996) (SCALIA, J., dissenting). As nearly as I can tell, the Court agrees with that; its opinion does not apply strict scrutiny, and its central propositions are taken from rational-basis cases like *Moreno*. But the Court certainly does not apply anything that resembles that deferential framework.

Justice Scalia also criticized "the Court's nonspecific hand-waving" suggesting that DOMA is invalid because "it is motivated by a 'bare . . . desire to harm' couples in same-sex marriages." In his view, "the Constitution does not forbid the government to enforce traditional moral and sexual norms." But he asserted that "there are many perfectly valid—indeed, downright boring— justifying rationales for this legislation."

> **Take Note**
>
> A "choice-of-law issue" is an issue about which state's laws govern an activity. Choice-of-law issues arises because many activities concern more than one state. If state law governs these activities, and the concerned states have different legal rules, a court must decide which state's laws control.

To choose just one of these defenders' arguments, DOMA avoids difficult choice-of-law issues that will now arise absent a uniform federal definition of marriage. Imagine a pair of women who marry in Albany and then move to Alabama, which does not "recognize as valid any marriage of parties of the same sex." Ala.Code § 30–1–19(e) (2011). When the couple files their next federal tax return, may it be a joint one? Which State's law controls, for federal-law purposes: their State of celebration (which recognizes the marriage) or their State of domicile (which does not)? (Does the answer depend on whether they were just visiting in Albany?) * * * DOMA avoided all of this uncertainty by specifying which marriages would be recognized for federal purposes. That is a classic purpose for a definitional provision.

Further, DOMA preserves the intended effects of prior legislation against then-unforeseen changes in circumstance. When Congress provided (for example) that a special estate-tax exemption would exist for spouses, this exemption reached only opposite-sex spouses—those being the only sort that were recognized in any State at the time of DOMA's passage. When it became clear that changes in state law might one day alter that balance, DOMA's definitional section was enacted to ensure that state-level experimentation did not automatically alter the basic operation of federal law, unless and until Congress made the further judgment to do so on its own. That is not animus—just stabilizing prudence.

Justice Alito also dissented. He asserted that "[i]t is beyond dispute that the right to same-sex marriage is not deeply rooted in this Nation's history and tradition. In this country, no State permitted same-sex marriage until the Massachusetts Supreme Judicial Court held in 2003 that limiting marriage to opposite-sex couples violated the State Constitution. * * * What Windsor and the United States seek, therefore, is not the protection of a deeply rooted right but the recognition of a very new right, and they seek this innovation not from a legislative body elected by the people, but from unelected judges. Faced with such a request, judges have cause for both caution and humility."

Two years after the Court's decision in *Windsor*, it decided *Obergefell v. Hodges*, 576 U.S. 644 (2015), which held that state bans on same-sex marriage violate the Due Process Clause of the Fourteenth Amendment. Because the Court's opinion in *Obergefell* focused primarily on the Due Process Clause of the Fourteenth Amendment and its protection of a fundamental right to marry, we considered the Court's decision in Chapter 2.

The Court in *Obergefell* also declared that the bans at issue violated the Equal Protection Clause because "same-sex couples are denied all the benefits afforded to opposite-sex couples and are barred from exercising a fundamental right." (You might find it useful at this point to review the Court's opinion.) Is this analysis consistent with your understanding of what the Court's cases involving the Equal Protection Clause require? Wasn't the question whether discrimination on the basis of sexual orientation triggers heightened scrutiny and, if so, whether the states' refusal to permit gay couples to marry could be justified under that level of scrutiny? If that were the question, then how should the Court have answered it? In thinking about this question, note that Justice Kennedy twice referred in passing to sexual orientation as an "immutable characteristic"; to a history of prejudice against gays and lesbians; and to the need that many gays and lesbians historically felt to keep their sexual orientation secret. Do these assertions suggest that the Court effectively concluded that gays and lesbians are a suspect class entitled to heightened judicial protection from discrimination?

Either way, how would state bans on same-sex marriage have fared if subjected to either rational-basis review or heightened scrutiny under the Equal Protection Clause? What state interests do such bans advance? Are the bans rationally related to those interests? Substantially related to them? Narrowly tailored to advance them?

Executive Summary of This Chapter

"[A]ll legal restrictions which curtail the civil rights of a single racial group are immediately suspect." *Korematsu v. United States* (1944). As such, laws, regulations, and policies that discriminate against racial minorities on the basis of race or national origin are subject to **strict scrutiny**—that is, they "must serve a **compelling governmental interest**, and must be **narrowly tailored** to further that interest." *Adarand Constructors, Inc. v. Peña* (1995). This rule applies to the states by the force of the Equal Protection Clause of the Fourteenth Amendment, *Strauder v. West Virginia* (1879), and to the federal government by the force of the Due Process Clause of the Fifth Amendment, *Bolling v. Sharpe* (1954).

Strict scrutiny applies to laws that discriminate on the basis of race or national origin on their face, *Strauder v. West Virginia* (1879), to laws that are motivated by discriminatory animus against persons based on their race or national origin, *Hunter v. Underwood* (1985), and to the discriminatory application, based on race or national origin, of otherwise facially neutral laws, *Yick Wo v. Hopkins* (1886). "Standing alone," however, a racially disproportionate *impact* "does not trigger the rule that racial classifications are to be subjected to the strictest scrutiny and are justifiable only by the weightiest of considerations." *Washington v. Davis* (1976).

Laws that classify on the basis of race but are facially symmetrical—that is, laws that impose equal burdens on persons of different races—are also subject to strict scrutiny. Accordingly, laws prohibiting inter-racial marriage, *Loving v. Virginia* (1967), and laws providing for "separate but equal" public facilities, *Brown v. Board of Education of Topeka* (1954), are unconstitutional.

"[T]he standard of review under the Equal Protection Clause is not dependent on the race of those burdened or benefited by a particular classification." *City of Richmond v. J.A. Croson Co.* (1989). Accordingly, strict scrutiny applies to government consideration of race even when it is designed to benefit, rather than burden, racial minorities. *Adarand Constructors, Inc. v. Peña* (1995). This rule applies to affirmative action programs in government contracting, *City of Richmond v. J.A. Croson Co.* (1989), and school admissions, *Grutter v. Bollinger* (2003), and to legislative apportionment schemes for which race was a "predominant" factor in the drawing of district lines, *Shaw v. Reno* (1993); *Miller v. Johnson* (1995).

The Court has emphasized, however, that some race-conscious decision-making can satisfy strict scrutiny. In particular, because public institutions of higher education have a "compelling interest in attaining a diverse student body," admissions policies that seek to achieve a "critical mass" of minority students by considering race or ethnicity "flexibly as a 'plus' factor in the context of individualized consideration of each and every applicant" can survive strict scrutiny. *Grutter v. Bollinger* (2003). It is expected that, in the future, racial preferences will no longer be necessary, and therefore permissible, to further the government's interest in attaining a diverse student body. *Id.* In reviewing a university's admissions program that takes race into account, a court must apply strict scrutiny and cannot simply ask whether the university acted in good faith and cannot defer to the university in deciding whether the program is narrowly tailored. *Fisher v. University of Texas at Austin* (2013).

However, policies that "establish quotas for members of certain racial groups or put members of those groups on separate admissions tracks" fail strict scrutiny. *Gratz v. Bollinger* (2003). In addition, schools that have already achieved unitary status after desegregation efforts, or that were never segregated *de jure*, may not rely upon race to determine which schools children may attend. *Parents Involved in Community Schools v. Seattle School District No. 1* (2007).

Government decisions that classify on the basis of **sex** are subject to **intermediate scrutiny**. This level of scrutiny requires a justification that is "exceedingly persuasive" and will be upheld only if the government can demonstrate that "the [challenged] classification serves **important governmental objectives** and that the discriminatory means employed are **substantially related** to the achievement of those objectives." *United States v. Virginia* (1996). This rule applies both to laws that burden women, *id.*, and to laws that burden men, *Craig v. Boren* (1976). Neutral laws that were not motivated by discriminatory animus do not receive intermediate scrutiny simply because they have a disproportionate impact on persons of a particular sex. *Personnel Administrator of Massachusetts v. Feeney* (1979).

Laws and policies that distinguish between conditions that are uniquely associated with one sex do not on that basis alone necessarily trigger intermediate scrutiny. *Geduldig v. Aiello* (1974). Laws or policies that treat men and women differently because of "real" differences between the sexes might survive intermediate scrutiny, *Michael M. v. Superior Court of Sonoma County* (1981), but not if the lines are drawn based on mere gender stereotypes, *Orr v. Orr* (1979); *Mississippi Univ. for Women v. Hogan* (1982).

Classifications on the basis of **alienage** are subject to strict scrutiny. *Graham v. Richardson* (1971). However, policies excluding aliens from employment in "policy-making" positions are subject only to rational-basis review. *Foley v. Connelie* (1978).

Laws that discriminate on the basis of one's **parents' marital status** are subject to intermediate scrutiny. *Clark v. Jeter* (1988). Laws may classify on this basis in matters related to the establishment of paternity, but to survive intermediate scrutiny they must be substantially related to that end.

The elderly are not a suspect class. Accordingly, laws that classify on the basis of **age** are subject only to rational-basis review. *Massachusetts Board of Retirement v. Murgia* (1976).

Laws that discriminate on the basis of **disability** are subject to rational-basis review. In assessing such laws, however, the Court has sometimes applied a form of rational-basis review that is substantially more searching than the ordinary version of that approach. *Cleburne v. Cleburne Living Center* (1985).

It is not entirely clear what level of scrutiny applies to laws that discriminate on the basis of **sexual orientation**. The Court has, however, invalidated a state constitutional provision that prevented the government from extending its laws to protect persons from discrimination on the basis of sexual orientation. *Romer v. Evans* (1996). At least one member of the Court, moreover, has concluded that a law that criminalizes homosexual sex (but not heterosexual sex) violates the Equal Protection Clause. *Lawrence v. Texas* (2003). The Constitution's guarantee of equality prevents the disparate treatment of a "politically unpopular group," such as gay men and women, merely because Congress desires to harm the group. *United States v. Windsor* (2013). The Court has also held that the Equal Protection Clause, in conjunction with the Due Process Clause, prohibits states from denying marriage licenses to same-sex couples. *Obergefell v. Hodges* (2015).

CHAPTER 6

Equal Protection and Fundamental Rights

INTRODUCTION

We have now seen both the cases addressing "fundamental rights"—generally under the rubric of substantive due process, which we considered in Chapter 2—and the cases concerning equal protection, which we considered in Chapter 5. Although we have treated them as separate topics, in some of the cases that we saw the Court in fact relied on both concepts.

For example, in some of the fundamental rights cases that we considered in Chapter 2—such as the Court's decisions on constitutional protections for marital and family rights—the Court relied on the Equal Protection Clause, rather than (or in addition to) the Due Process Clause, to invalidate state laws that interfered with those rights. For instance, the Court's decision in *Loving v. Virginia*, which invalidated Virginia's ban on inter-racial marriages, was based both on the right to marry and the prohibition on state laws that discriminate on the basis of race. In *Skinner v. Oklahoma*, which invalidated a state law requiring the sterilization of persons convicted three times of crimes of moral turpitude, the Court seemed to rely both on the Equal Protection Clause—concluding that the statute's exemption of white-collar crimes amounted to unequal treatment—and the constitutional protection accorded to reproductive rights. And in *Lawrence v. Texas*, which invalidated Texas's ban on gay sex, Justice Kennedy's opinion for the Court relied on substantive due process, while Justice O'Connor's concurring opinion relied on the Equal Protection Clause.

In this chapter, we explore the relationship between fundamental rights and the Equal Protection Clause more systematically. We defer until later chapters the Court's treatment of laws that interfere with rights specifically identified in the Bill of Rights. In those cases, as we will see, the Court generally analyzes the challenged law according to the specific tests that apply to the specific right at issue. This

411

chapter, as did Chapter 2, concerns rights that are not specifically enumerated in the Constitution. Several questions will recur in the cases that follow, even if the Court does not always address them directly. First, if the Constitution (explicitly or implicitly) deems a right to be "fundamental," then isn't the government largely precluded from abridging it (assuming it cannot satisfy heightened scrutiny) regardless of whether it abridges it only for some people? Phrased another way, if the government abridges a fundamental constitutional right, why is the Equal Protection Clause even relevant? (In Chapter 2, for example, we saw that in substantive due process cases the inquiry for the Court was generally whether a person had been denied an important right, not whether the right had been denied only to some class of individuals.)

Second, it is clear that the Equal Protection Clause sometimes prohibits state action even when the state does not abridge a fundamental right. For example, even if there is no constitutional right to a state-provided education—a question we will take up in this chapter in *San Antonio Independent School District v. Rodriguez*— the state plainly cannot make education available only to citizens of one particular race.

But what if the state denies eligibility for a particular benefit based on membership in a class that is not "suspect" under the Court's Equal Protection cases? Are there some "benefits" that the state is not constitutionally obligated to provide, but that are sufficiently important that the state—once it decides to provide them—may not provide them *selectively* only to some classes of citizens?

As you read the cases that follow, keep these questions in mind.

A. THE FRANCHISE

One of the areas in which the interaction between fundamental rights and the equal protection principle has been most frequent is in matters related to the franchise. In this section, we consider two related issues: the right of citizens to vote, and "apportionment"—that is, the process by which elected officials draw the electoral maps that define the districts in which they will then seek office.

1.   The Right to Vote

Law students are always surprised to learn that the Constitution does not explicitly protect an undifferentiated right to vote. To be sure, there are provisions of the Constitution that arguably recognize such a right. For example, the Guarantee Clause in Article IV provides that the United States shall guarantee the states a "Republican"—that is, representative—form of government. And the

Fifteenth, Nineteenth, and Twenty-Sixth Amendments protect the "right" to vote against discrimination on the basis of race, gender, or (in some cases) age. But the Court has long suggested that the somewhat cryptic Guarantee Clause is non-justiciable, and the Amendments do not explicitly require the grant of the franchise; they seem to require only that, once a state grants the right to vote, the right may not be withheld selectively on one of the impermissible bases. Is it conceivable that the Constitution does not in fact protect a right to vote? The case that follows considers that question.

HARPER V. VIRGINIA STATE BD. OF ELECTIONS
383 U.S. 663 (1966)

MR. JUSTICE DOUGLAS delivered the opinion of the Court.

These are suits by Virginia residents to have declared unconstitutional Virginia's poll tax. * * * While the right to vote in federal elections is conferred by Art. I, § 2 of the Constitution, the right to vote in state elections is nowhere expressly mentioned. It is argued that the right to vote in state elections is implicit, particularly by reason of the First Amendment and that it may not constitutionally be conditioned upon the payment of a tax or fee. We do not stop to canvass the relation between voting and political expression. For it is enough to say that once the franchise is granted to the electorate, lines may not

Election workers in Virginia check that voters have paid their poll tax before providing ballots
Library of Congress

be drawn which are inconsistent with the Equal Protection Clause of the Fourteenth Amendment. That is to say, the right of suffrage "is subject to the imposition of state standards which are not discriminatory and which do not contravene any restriction that Congress, acting pursuant to its constitutional powers, has imposed." *Lassiter v. Northampton County Board of Elections*, 360 U.S. 45, 51 (1959).

FYI

The Twenty-Fourth Amendment, which was ratified in 1964, provides that the right to vote in elections for *federal* offices "shall not be denied or abridged by the United States or any State by reason of failure to pay any poll tax or other tax." It does not address the permissibility of poll taxes in elections for state offices. What does that suggest about the question presented here?

> **Take Note**
>
> The Court states that the "right to vote" in federal elections is conferred by Article I, § 2, cl. 1, which provides that "The House of Representatives shall be composed of Members chosen every second Year by the People of the several States, and the Electors in each State shall have the Qualifications requisite for Electors of the most numerous Branch of the State Legislature." But does that provision require the states to extend the franchise to *any particular portion* of the electorate? What if a state permits only college-educated adult males to vote for members of the state legislature?

We conclude that a State violates the Equal Protection Clause of the Fourteenth Amendment whenever it makes the affluence of the voter or payment of any fee an electoral standard. Voter qualifications have no relation to wealth nor to paying or not paying this or any other tax. Our cases demonstrate that the Equal Protection Clause of the Fourteenth Amendment restrains the States from fixing voter qualifications which invidiously discriminate.

Long ago in *Yick Wo v. Hopkins*, 118 U.S. 356, 370 (1886), the Court referred to "the political franchise of voting" as a "fundamental political right, because preservative of all rights." * * * The Equal Protection Clause demands no less than substantially equal state legislative representation for all citizens, of all places as well as of all races. *Reynolds v. Sims*, 377 U.S. 533, 568 (1964). We say the same whether the citizen, otherwise qualified to vote, has $1.50 in his pocket or nothing at all, pays the fee or fails to pay it. The principle that denies the State the right to dilute a citizen's vote on account of his economic status or other such factors by analogy bars a system which excludes those unable to pay a fee to vote or who fail to pay.

It is argued that a State may exact fees from citizens for many different kinds of licenses; that if it can demand from all an equal fee for a driver's license, it can demand from all an equal poll tax for voting. But we must remember that the interest of the State, when it comes to voting, is limited to the power to fix qualifications. Wealth, like race, creed, or color, is not germane to one's ability to participate intelligently in the electoral process. Lines drawn on the basis of wealth or property, like those of race, are traditionally disfavored.

> **Food for Thought**
>
> Does the Court invalidate the poll tax because it impermissibly discriminates among citizens on the basis of wealth? If that is a basis for invalidation, then are higher marginal tax rates for the wealthy, or fees for driver's licenses, also unconstitutional? Is the poll tax unconstitutional because there is a fundamental right to vote? If so, then why is the Equal Protection Clause relevant?

To introduce wealth or payment of a fee as a measure of a voter's qualifications is to introduce a capricious or irrelevant factor.

[The] Equal Protection Clause is not shackled to the political theory of a particular era. In determining what lines are unconstitutionally discriminatory, we have never been confined to historic notions of equality, any more than we have restricted due process to a fixed catalogue of what was at a given time deemed to be the limits of fundamental rights. Notions of what constitutes equal treatment for purposes of the Equal Protection Clause do change. * * * See *Brown v. Board of Education*, 347 U.S. 483 (1954).

We have long been mindful that where fundamental rights and liberties are asserted under the Equal Protection Clause, classifications which might invade or restrain them must be closely scrutinized and carefully confined. Those principles apply here. For to repeat, wealth or fee paying has, in our view, no relation to voting qualifications; the right to vote is too precious, too fundamental to be so burdened or conditioned.

MR. JUSTICE BLACK, dissenting.

It should be pointed out at once that the Court's decision is to no extent based on a finding that the Virginia law as written or as applied is being used as a device or mechanism to deny Negro citizens of Virginia the right to vote on account of their color. Apparently the Court agrees with the District Court below [that] this record would not support any finding that the Virginia poll tax law the Court invalidates has any such effect. If the record could support a finding that the law as written or applied has such an effect, the law would of course be unconstitutional as a violation of the Fourteenth and Fifteenth Amendments * * *.

All voting laws treat some persons differently from others in some respects. Some bar a person from voting who is under 21 years of age; others bar those under 18. Some bar convicted felons or the insane, and some have attached a freehold or other property qualification for voting. * * * The equal protection cases carefully analyzed boil down to the principle that distinctions drawn and even discriminations imposed by state laws do not violate the Equal Protection Clause so long as these distinctions and discriminations are not "irrational," "irrelevant," "unreasonable," "arbitrary," or "invidious." * * * State poll tax legislation can "reasonably," "rationally" and without an "invidious" or evil purpose to injure anyone be found to rest on a number of state policies including (1) the State's desire to collect its revenue, and (2) its belief that voters who pay a poll tax will be interested in furthering the State's welfare when they vote.

I can only conclude that the primary, controlling, predominate, if not the exclusive reason for declaring the Virginia law unconstitutional is the Court's deep-seated hostility and antagonism, which I share, to making payment of a tax a prerequisite to voting. * * * [When] a "political theory" embodied in our Constitution becomes outdated, it seems to me that a majority of the nine members of this Court are not only without constitutional power but are far less qualified to choose a new constitutional political theory than the people of this country proceeding in the manner provided by Article V.

Moreover, the people, in § 5 of the Fourteenth Amendment, designated the governmental tribunal they wanted to provide additional rules to enforce the guarantees of that Amendment. The branch of Government they chose was not the Judicial Branch but the Legislative. I have no doubt at all that Congress has the power under § 5 to pass legislation to abolish the poll tax in order to protect the citizens of this country if it believes that the poll tax is being used as a device to deny voters equal protection of the laws. * * * But for us to undertake in the guise of constitutional interpretation to decide the constitutional policy question of this case amounts, in my judgment, to a plain exercise of power which the Constitution has denied us but has specifically granted to Congress.

> **Make the Connection**
>
> If the poll tax does not violate the Fourteenth Amendment, can Congress really be said to be "enforcing" the Amendment by "appropriate legislation" if it prohibits the poll tax? We will consider this question—and Congress's power to enforce the provisions of the Reconstruction Amendments—in Chapter *7*.

MR. JUSTICE HARLAN, whom MR. JUSTICE STEWART joins, dissenting.

The Court's analysis of the equal protection issue goes no further than to say that the electoral franchise is "precious" and "fundamental," and to conclude that "[t]o introduce wealth or payment of a fee as a measure of a voter's qualifications is to introduce a capricious or irrelevant factor." These are of course captivating phrases, but they are wholly inadequate to satisfy the standard governing adjudication of the equal protection issue: Is there a rational basis for Virginia's poll tax as a voting qualification? I think the answer to that question is undoubtedly "yes."

For example, it is certainly a rational argument that payment of some minimal poll tax promotes civic responsibility, weeding out those who do not care enough about public affairs to pay $1.50 or thereabouts a year for the exercise of the franchise. It is also arguable, indeed it was probably accepted as sound political theory by a large percentage of Americans through most of our history, that people with some property have a deeper stake in community affairs, and are consequently more responsible, more educated, more knowledgeable, more worthy of confidence, than those without means, and that the community and Nation would be better managed if the franchise were restricted to such citizens.

These viewpoints, to be sure, ring hollow on most contemporary ears. * * * Property and poll-tax qualifications, very simply, are not in accord with current egalitarian notions of how a modern democracy should be organized. It is of course entirely fitting that legislatures should modify the law to reflect such changes in popular attitudes. However, it is all wrong, in my view, for the Court to adopt the political doctrines popularly accepted at a particular moment of our history and to declare all others to be irrational and invidious, barring them from the range of choice by reasonably minded people acting through the political process.

POINTS FOR DISCUSSION

a.   Level of Scrutiny

In their dissents, Justices Black and Harlan urged the Court to apply rational-basis review to the poll taxes in question (and, as a result, to uphold the constitutionality of the taxes). Although he obviously disagreed about the constitutionality of the taxes, Justice Douglas, writing for the Court, declared that wealth is a "capricious" and "irrelevant" factor in the grant of the franchise. Does this terminology indicate that Justice Douglas was in fact applying rational-basis review? Or was he applying some heightened level of scrutiny? If so, why?

b.   Fundamental Rights and "Discrimination"

Did the Court invalidate the poll tax because it abridged the right to vote, or because it classified voters on some impermissible basis? That is, did the Court conclude that the problem with the poll tax was that it impaired the exercise of a fundamental right of some—any—voters, or did it conclude that the problem was that it treated different classes of citizens differently without an adequate justification? There is evidence for both conclusions. On the one hand, the Court described the right to vote as "fundamental"—and thus different from other state-conferred benefits, such as the right to drive a car. On the other hand, the Court declared that "[l]ines drawn on the basis of wealth or property, like those of race, are traditionally disfavored," suggesting that the problem with the poll tax was that it discriminated on the basis of wealth.

Of course, if the right to vote is fundamental, it seems to follow that the right cannot be withheld from people who are poor, just as it cannot be withheld from people who were born in August or people who are too near-sighted to drive. But perhaps the right is not "fundamental" in the sense that the right to privacy in one's intimate relationships is fundamental, in that it can indeed be permissibly abridged in many ways—by, for example, rules that prohibit people who did not register 60 days before an election from voting. Yet even in that case, perhaps it is still sufficiently important that it cannot be withheld on the basis of wealth, which bears little relationship to the ability to vote responsibly. Assuming that the Court in *Harper* was correct to invalidate the poll tax, which basis for decision do you find more compelling? Is it possible even to distinguish between the fundamental rights and equal protection approaches?

c. Assessing Burdens

The Court concluded its opinion in *Harper* by stating that "wealth or fee paying has [no] relation to voting qualifications; the right to vote is too precious, too fundamental to be so burdened or conditioned." As in other cases involving fundamental rights, the Court in *Harper* thus seemed to suggest that the relevant inquiry involved weighing the state's interest in the regulation against the burden imposed on the right.

How should a Court measure the burden in a case challenging a voting regulation? Is the question whether the regulation makes it more difficult for a particular class of voters to vote? Must the class of voters be a protected class under Equal Protection doctrine? If so, then why does it matter that the right to vote is fundamental? Or is it enough for one (or a few) voters to allege that their ability to vote has been substantially impaired?

In *Crawford v. Marion County Election Board*, 553 U.S. 181 (2008), the Court considered a challenge to Indiana's "Voter ID" law, which required the presentation of photo identification issued by the government as a prerequisite to voting. The plaintiffs argued that the law imposed a substantial burden on elderly, disabled, poor, and minority voters, who are less likely to have the requisite forms of identification. The Court upheld the law, although no opinion attracted a majority of the Court. Justice Stevens, joined by Chief Justice Roberts and Justice Kennedy, noted that "evenhanded restrictions that protect the integrity and reliability of the electoral process itself" are not invidious and satisfy the standard set forth in *Harper*. Justice Stevens concluded that the state's interest in deterring voter fraud and promoting confidence in the electoral process were legitimate and important interests, and that the burden imposed on voters without photo IDs was not substantial—and plainly not sufficient to justify facial invalidation of the statute.

Justice Scalia, joined by Justices Thomas and Alito, asserted that "what petitioners view as the law's several light and heavy burdens are no more than the different *impacts* of the single burden that the law uniformly imposes on all voters. To vote in person in Indiana, *everyone* must have and present a photo identification that can be obtained for free." The law, he stated, thus "is a generally applicable, nondiscriminatory voting regulation." Accordingly, in Justice Scalia's view, a "voter complaining about [the] law's effect on him has no valid equal-protection claim because, without proof of discriminatory intent, a generally applicable law with disparate impact is not unconstitutional. [The] Fourteenth Amendment does not regard neutral laws as invidious ones, *even when their burdens purportedly fall disproportionately on a protected class. A fortiori* it does not do so when, as here, the classes complaining of disparate impact are not even protected."

After *Crawford*, what is the relevance of the Equal Protection Clause in assessing laws that are alleged to burden the right to vote?

BUSH V. GORE

531 U.S. 98 (2000)

PER CURIAM.

On November 8, 2000, the day following the Presidential election, the Florida Division of Elections reported that petitioner Bush had received 2,909,135 votes, and respondent Gore had received 2,907,351 votes, a margin of 1,784 for Governor Bush. Because Governor Bush's margin of victory was less than "one-half of a percent [of] the votes cast," an automatic machine recount was conducted under [the Florida] election code, the results of which showed Governor Bush still winning the race but by a diminished margin. [Gore then sought manual recounts in four counties. After litigation, the Florida Supreme Court ordered the Florida Secretary of State to include in the certified election results the totals produced by the manual recounts if they were submitted by 5:00 pm on November 26. Some of the counties requested a brief extension, which the Secretary of State denied. The Secretary of State then certified Bush as the winner by 537 votes.]

> **Take Note**
>
> The President of the United States is not elected by the popular vote of the entire nation. Instead, as specified in the Twelfth Amendment, the President is elected by "electors" from the states. The number of electors from each state equals the number of the state's senators and representatives. The District of Columbia has 3 electors. In total, there are 538 electors (collectively called the "electoral college"). To win the presidency, a candidate needs 270 electors. In 2000, Florida had 25 electoral votes. As in most states, the presidential candidate who had the majority of popular votes in Florida would receive all of the state's electoral votes.

On November 27, Vice President Gore, pursuant to Florida's contest provisions, filed a complaint in Leon County Circuit Court contesting the certification. He sought relief pursuant to [Fla. Stat.] § 102.168(3)(c), which provides that "[r]eceipt of a number of illegal votes or rejection of a number of legal votes sufficient to change or place in doubt the result of the election" shall be grounds for a contest. * * * A "legal vote," as determined by the [Florida] Supreme Court, is "one in which there is a 'clear indication of the intent of the voter.' " [The Florida trial court held that

Gore had not demonstrated a "reasonable probability" that the election results would have been different if not for the rejection of some legal votes, but on December 8 the Florida Supreme Court reversed.] Observing that the contest provisions vest broad discretion in the circuit judge to "provide any relief appropriate under such circumstances," § 102.168(8), the Supreme Court further held that the Circuit Court could order "the Supervisor of Elections and the Canvassing Boards, as well as the necessary public officials, in all counties that have not conducted a manual recount or tabulation of the undervotes [to] do so forthwith, said tabulation to take place in the individual counties where the ballots are located." [The Florida Supreme Court also directed the lower court to include in the certified results votes that had been counted during the manual recounts in Palm Beach and Miami-Dade Counties but that had not been accepted by the Secretary of State. A few hours later, the Florida trial court ordered manual recounts and set a deadline of December 10. The next morning, the Supreme Court granted Bush's petition for certiorari and granted a stay of the counting of votes.]

The individual citizen has no federal constitutional right to vote for electors for the President of the United States unless and until the state legislature chooses a statewide election as the means to implement its power to appoint members of the electoral college. * * * History has now favored the voter, and in each of the several States the citizens themselves vote for Presidential electors. When the state legislature vests the right to vote for President in its people, the right to vote as the legislature has prescribed is fundamental; and one source of its fundamental nature lies in the equal weight accorded to each vote and the equal dignity owed to each voter. * * * Equal protection applies as well to the manner of its exercise. Having once granted the right to vote on equal terms, the State may not, by later arbitrary and disparate treatment, value one person's vote over that of another. See, e.g., *Harper v. Virginia Bd. of Elections*, 383 U.S. 663 (1966).

The question before us [is] whether the recount procedures the Florida Supreme Court has adopted are consistent with its obligation to avoid arbitrary and disparate treatment of the members of its electorate. Much of the controversy seems to revolve around ballot cards designed to be perforated by a stylus but which, either through error or deliberate omission, have not been perforated with sufficient precision for a machine to register the perforations. In some cases a piece of the card—a chad—is hanging, say, by two corners. In other cases there is no separation at all, just an indentation. * * * Florida's basic command for the count of legally cast votes is to consider the "intent of the voter." This is unobjectionable as an abstract proposition and a starting principle. The problem inheres in the absence of specific standards to ensure its equal application. The formulation of uniform rules to determine intent based on these recurring circumstances is practicable and, we conclude, necessary.

The want of those rules here has led to unequal evaluation of ballots in various respects. * * * A monitor in Miami-Dade County testified at trial that he observed that three members of the county canvassing board applied different standards in defining a legal vote. And testimony at trial also revealed that at least one county changed its evaluative standards during the counting process. * * * This is not a process with sufficient guarantees of equal treatment. The State Supreme Court ratified this uneven treatment. It mandated that the recount totals from [the counties in question] be included in the certified total. * * * Yet each of the counties used varying standards to determine what was a legal vote. Broward County used a more forgiving standard than Palm Beach County, and uncovered almost three times as many new votes, a result markedly disproportionate to the difference in population between the counties. * * * The recount process, in its features here described, is inconsistent with the minimum procedures necessary to protect the fundamental right of each voter in the special instance of a statewide recount under the authority of a single state judicial officer. Our consideration is limited to the present circumstances, for the problem of equal protection in election processes generally presents many complexities. * * * When a court orders a statewide remedy, there must be at least some assurance that the rudimentary requirements of equal treatment and fundamental fairness are satisfied.

> **Food for Thought**
>
> The Court declares that its "consideration is limited to the present circumstances." Does that mean that the equal protection analysis in the decision will not serve as binding precedent in future controversies? If so, does the Court's decision itself satisfy the concept of equal protection on which its conclusion is based?

Upon due consideration of the difficulties identified to this point, it is obvious that the recount cannot be conducted in compliance with the requirements of equal protection and due process without substantial additional work. It would require not only the adoption (after opportunity for argument) of adequate statewide standards for determining what is a legal vote, and practicable procedures to implement them, but also orderly judicial review of any disputed matters that might arise.

The Supreme Court of Florida has said that the legislature intended the State's electors to "participat[e] fully in the federal electoral process," as provided in 3 U.S.C. § 5. That statute, in turn, requires that any controversy or contest that is designed to lead to a conclusive selection of electors be completed by December

12. That date is upon us, and there is no recount procedure in place under the State Supreme Court's order that comports with minimal constitutional standards. Because it is evident that any recount seeking to meet the December 12 date will be unconstitutional for the reasons we have discussed, we reverse the judgment of the Supreme Court of Florida ordering a recount to proceed.

None are more conscious of the vital limits on judicial authority than are the Members of this Court, and none stand more in admiration of the Constitution's design to leave the selection of the President to the people, through their legislatures, and to the political sphere. When contending parties invoke the process of the courts, however, it becomes our unsought responsibility to resolve the federal and constitutional issues the judicial system has been forced to confront. The judgment of the Supreme Court of Florida is reversed, and the case is remanded for further proceedings not inconsistent with this opinion.

CHIEF JUSTICE REHNQUIST, with whom JUSTICE SCALIA and JUSTICE THOMAS join, concurring.

Article II, § 1, cl. 2 provides that "[e]ach State shall appoint, in such Manner as the *Legislature* thereof may direct," electors for President and Vice President. (Emphasis added.) Thus, the text of the election law itself, and not just its interpretation by the courts of the States, takes on independent significance. * * * A significant departure from the legislative scheme for appointing Presidential electors presents a federal constitutional question.

Isolated sections of the [Florida election] code may well admit of more than one interpretation, but the general coherence of the legislative scheme may not be altered by judicial interpretation so as to wholly change the statutorily provided apportionment of responsibility among [the Secretary of State and the state circuit courts]. * * * [T]he Florida Supreme Court's interpretation of the Florida election laws impermissibly distorted them beyond what a fair reading required, in violation of Article II.

JUSTICE STEVENS, with whom JUSTICE GINSBURG and JUSTICE BREYER join, dissenting.

Admittedly, the use of differing substandards for determining voter intent in different counties employing similar voting systems may raise serious concerns. [But] "[t]he interpretation of constitutional principles must not be too literal. We must remember that the machinery of government would not work if it were not allowed a little play in its joints." *Bain Peanut Co. of Tex. v. Pinson*, 282 U.S. 499, 501 (1931) (Holmes, J.). If it were otherwise, Florida's decision to leave to each county the determination of what balloting system to employ—despite enormous differences in accuracy—might run afoul of equal protection. So, too, might the similar decisions of the vast majority of state legislatures to delegate to local authorities certain decisions with respect to voting systems and ballot design.

Even assuming that aspects of the remedial scheme might ultimately be found to violate the Equal Protection Clause, I could not subscribe to the majority's disposition of the case. * * * Under their own reasoning, the appropriate course of action would be to remand to allow more specific procedures for implementing the legislature's uniform general standard to be established.

[T]he Florida Supreme Court [did not] make any substantive change in Florida electoral law. Its decisions were rooted in long-established precedent and were consistent with the relevant statutory provisions, taken as a whole. It did what courts do—it decided the case before it in light of the legislature's intent to leave no legally cast vote uncounted. * * * What must underlie petitioners' entire federal assault on the Florida election procedures is an unstated lack of confidence in the impartiality and capacity of the state judges who would make the critical decisions if the vote count were to proceed. * * * The endorsement of that position by the majority of this Court can only lend credence to the most cynical appraisal of the work of judges throughout the land. It is confidence in the men and women who administer the judicial system that is the true backbone of the rule of law. Time will one day heal the wound to that confidence that will be inflicted by today's decision. One thing, however, is certain. Although we may never know with complete certainty the identity of the winner of this year's Presidential election, the identity of the loser is perfectly clear. It is the Nation's confidence in the judge as an impartial guardian of the rule of law.

JUSTICE SOUTER, with whom JUSTICE BREYER joins, and with whom JUSTICE STEVENS and JUSTICE GINSBURG join as to all but Part III, dissenting.

[III] It is true that the Equal Protection Clause does not forbid the use of a variety of voting mechanisms within a jurisdiction, even though different mechanisms will have different levels of effectiveness in recording voters' intentions; local variety can be justified by concerns about cost, the potential value of innovation, and so on. But evidence in the record here suggests that a different order of disparity obtains under rules for determining a voter's intent that have been applied (and could continue to be applied) to identical types of ballots used in identical brands of machines and exhibiting identical physical characteristics (such as "hanging" or "dimpled" chads). I can conceive of no legitimate state interest served by these differing treatments of the expressions of voters' fundamental rights. The differences appear wholly arbitrary.

In deciding what to do about this, we should take account of the fact that electoral votes are due to be cast in six days. I would therefore remand the case to the courts of Florida with instructions to establish uniform standards for evaluating the several types of ballots that have prompted differing treatments, to be applied within and among counties when passing on such identical ballots in any further recounting (or successive recounting) that the courts might order. Unlike the majority, I see no warrant for this Court to assume that Florida could not possibly comply with this requirement before the date set for the meeting of electors, December 18. * * * To recount these manually would be a tall order, but before this Court stayed the effort to do that the courts of Florida were ready to do their best to get that job done. There is no justification for denying the State the opportunity to try to count all disputed ballots now.

JUSTICE GINSBURG, with whom JUSTICE STEVENS joins, and with whom JUSTICE SOUTER and JUSTICE BREYER join as to Part I, dissenting.

[II]   Ideally, perfection would be the appropriate standard for judging the recount. But we live in an imperfect world, one in which thousands of votes have not been counted. I cannot agree that the recount adopted by the Florida court, flawed as it may be, would yield a result any less fair or precise than the certification that preceded that recount. Even if there were an equal protection violation, I would agree with Justice STEVENS, Justice SOUTER, and Justice BREYER that the Court's concern about "the December 12 deadline" is misplaced. Time is short in part because of the Court's entry of a stay on December 9, several hours after an able circuit judge in Leon County had begun to superintend the recount process. More fundamentally, the Court's reluctance to let the recount go forward—despite its suggestion that "[t]he search for intent can be confined by specific rules designed to ensure uniform treatment"— ultimately turns on its own judgment about the practical realities of implementing a recount, not the judgment of those much closer to the process.

JUSTICE BREYER, with whom JUSTICE STEVENS and JUSTICE GINSBURG join except as to Part I-A-1, and with whom JUSTICE SOUTER joins as to Part I, dissenting.

[I-A-2]   By halting the manual recount, and thus ensuring that the uncounted legal votes will not be counted under any standard, this Court crafts a remedy out of proportion to the asserted harm. And that remedy harms the very fairness interests the Court is attempting to protect. The manual recount would itself redress a problem of unequal treatment of ballots. * * *

[II] Of course, the selection of the President is of fundamental national importance. But that importance is political, not legal. And this Court should resist the temptation unnecessarily to resolve tangential legal disputes, where doing so threatens to determine the outcome of the election. * * * Justice Brandeis once said of the Court, "The most important thing we do is not doing." What it does today, the Court should have left undone. I would repair the damage done as best we now can, by permitting the Florida recount to continue under uniform standards.

POINTS FOR DISCUSSION

a.   Counting the Votes (on the Court)

How many Justices concluded that the recount procedures violated the Equal Protection Clause? What was the rationale for this conclusion? Did the Court properly apply *Harper*'s test? Did any of the Justices conclude that the procedures did not violate the Equal Protection Clause? The Court's ruling on the Equal Protection issue has provoked strong but differing academic opinions. A leading article condemning the decision is Laurence H. Tribe, *Erog v. Hsub and its Disguises: Freeing Bush v. Gore from its Hall of Mirrors*, 115 Harv. L. Rev. 170 (2001), in which the author concludes that the skeptics of the decision are correct to proclaim "EQUAL PROTECTION, MY ASS!" For a response, see Nelson Lund, *"Equal Protection, My Ass!"?: Bush v. Gore and Laurence Tribe's Hall of Mirrors*, 19 Const. Comment. 543 (2002).

b.   Elections and the Judicial Role

The Court's decision in *Bush v. Gore* effectively ended the recount in Florida, which resulted in George Bush's being certified the winner of Florida's electoral votes (and thus the Presidency). Did the Court properly intervene in this election dispute? Is there a difference between prospectively identifying constitutional standards for the exercise of the franchise and the administration of elections—as the Court did in *Harper*—and retrospectively reviewing the state's adherence to such standards?

Two days before the Court issued its decision in the case, it granted a stay of the recount, which prevented the counting of votes pending the Court's decision on the merits. Justice Stevens, joined by Justices Souter, Ginsburg, and Breyer, dissented from the order, arguing that Bush had failed to establish a likelihood of irreparable harm, a traditional prerequisite to the grant of a stay, because "[c]ounting every legally cast vote cannot constitute irreparable harm." Indeed, he asserted, "[p]reventing the recount from being completed will inevitably cast a cloud on the legitimacy of the election." Justice Scalia wrote separately to respond to Justice Stevens, asserting that the "counting of votes that are of questionable legality does in my view threaten irreparable harm to petitioner Bush, and to the country, by casting a cloud upon what he claims to be the legitimacy of his election." What do these competing views of irreparable harm suggest about the Justices' views of the judicial role in election disputes?

c. Equal Protection and Voting

What are the implications for voting practices of the Court's equal protection analysis? Can different counties in the same state (or precincts in the same county) use different vote-counting technologies? Must each precinct have the same voter-to-machine ratio? What should we (and lower courts entertaining challenges to election procedures) make of the Court's statement that its "consideration is limited to the present circumstances"?

d. Equal Protection and Remedies

If the defect under the Equal Protection Clause was that the recounts were being conducted in different counties pursuant to different standards, then why wasn't the remedy to require the counting of votes statewide pursuant to a uniform—even judicially declared—standard? Why was the only remedy for this problem not to count the votes at all?

After the Supreme Court's controversial decision to end the recount, a consortium of eight news organizations, including the *New York Times*, the *Wall Street Journal*, and the *Washington Post*, decided to undertake an unofficial recount. The consortium's systematic recounting process took 10 months. In the end, the consortium concluded: "Contrary to what many partisans of former Vice President Al Gore have charged, the United States Supreme Court did not award an election to Mr. Bush that otherwise would have been won by Mr. Gore. A close examination of the ballots found that Mr. Bush would have retained a slender margin over Mr. Gore if the Florida court's order to recount more than 43,000 ballots had not been reversed by the United States Supreme Court." Ford Fessenden and John M. Broder, *Study Finds Justices Did Not Cast the Deciding Vote*, N.Y. Times, Nov. 12, 2001, at A1. Does either the result of the consortium's recount or the duration of the recounting process affect your assessment of the Supreme Court's decision in this case?

2. Apportionment and Gerrymandering

In *Baker v. Carr*, 369 U.S. 186 (1962), which we considered in Volume 1, the Court held that the Equal Protection Clause provides discoverable and manageable standards for use by lower courts in determining the constitutionality of a state legislative apportionment scheme. In the case that follows, the Court announced what those standards are.

REYNOLDS V. SIMS

377 U.S. 533 (1964)

MR. CHIEF JUSTICE WARREN delivered the opinion of the Court.

[In 1961, Alabama voters brought a class-action lawsuit against state and political party officials responsible for conducting state elections, alleging that the apportionment of the Alabama legislature violated their rights under the Equal Protection Clause. The parties did not dispute that there were significant representative disparities among Alabama legislative districts that tended to favor rural areas over urban areas. For example, the largest district in the Alabama Senate had 46 times as many voters as the smallest, and the largest district in the state House of Representatives had 16 times as many voters as the smallest. The record demonstrated that approximately 25% of the state population could elect a majority of members in both houses. Although the Alabama Constitution required reapportionment every ten years, the legislature had not been reapportioned since 1901.]

Undeniably the Constitution of the United States protects the right of all qualified citizens to vote, in state as well as in federal elections. * * * The right to vote freely for the candidate of one's choice is of the essence of a democratic society, and any restrictions on that right strike at the heart of representative government. And the right of suffrage can be denied by a debasement or dilution of the weight of a citizen's vote just as effectively as by wholly prohibiting the free exercise of the franchise.

[Our cases demonstrate that the] fundamental principle of representative government in this country is one of equal representation for equal numbers of people, without regard to race, sex, economic status, or place of residence within a State. Our problem, then, is to ascertain, in the instant cases, whether there are any constitutionally cognizable principles which would justify departures

> **Take Note**
>
> Alabama was not anomalous in its apportionment scheme. Yet the Court declares that "equal representation for equal numbers of people" is the "fundamental principle" governing state apportionment schemes. If actual state practice before *Reynolds* regularly deviated from this principle, then how "fundamental" could it really be?

from the basic standard of equality among voters in the apportionment of seats in state legislatures.

Legislators represent people, not trees or acres. Legislators are elected by voters, not farms or cities or economic interests. As long as ours is a representative form of government, and our legislatures are those instruments of government elected directly by and directly representative of the people, the right to elect legislators in a free and unimpaired fashion is a bedrock of our political system. * * * It could hardly be gainsaid that a constitutional claim had been asserted by an allegation that certain otherwise qualified voters had been entirely prohibited from voting for members of their state legislature. And, if a State should provide that the votes of citizens in one part of the State should be given two times, or five times, or 10 times the weight of votes of citizens in another part of the State, it could hardly be contended that the right to vote of those residing in the disfavored areas had not been effectively diluted. * * * The resulting discrimination against those individual voters living in disfavored areas is easily demonstrable mathematically. * * * Two, five, or 10 of them must vote before the effect of their voting is equivalent to that of their favored neighbor.

Since legislatures are responsible for enacting laws by which all citizens are to be governed, they should be bodies which are collectively responsive to the popular will. With respect to the allocation of legislative representation, all voters, as citizens of a State, stand in the same relation regardless of where they live. Any suggested criteria for the differentiation of citizens are insufficient to justify any discrimination, as to the weight of their votes, unless relevant to the permissible purposes of legislative apportionment. * * * Since the achieving of fair and effective representation for all citizens is concededly the basic aim of legislative apportionment, we conclude that the Equal Protection Clause guarantees the opportunity for equal participation by all voters in the election of state legislators.

We are told that the matter of apportioning representation in a state legislature is a complex and many-faceted one [and we] are cautioned about the dangers of entering into political thickets and mathematical quagmires. Our answer is this: a denial of constitutionally protected rights demands judicial protection; our oath and our office require no less of us. * * * To the extent that a citizen's right to vote is debased, he is that much less a citizen. The fact that an individual lives here or there is not a legitimate reason for overweighting or diluting the efficacy of his vote. We hold that, as a basic constitutional standard, the Equal Protection Clause requires that the seats in both houses of a bicameral state legislature must be apportioned on a population basis.

Food for Thought

Article IV, § 4 provides that the "United States shall guarantee to every State in this Union a Republican Form of Government." In common parlance, "republican" government means "representative" government. Wouldn't this be a more sensible basis for the Court's holding? The Court has traditionally avoided claims under the Guarantee Clause, however, usually concluding that they are not justiciable. See, e.g., *New York v. United States*, 505 U.S. 144, 183–86 (1992).

Simply stated, an individual's right to vote for state legislators is unconstitutionally impaired when its weight is in a substantial fashion diluted when compared with votes of citizens living in other parts of the State. [The current apportionment accordingly is constitutionally invalid.]

Much has been written since our decision in *Baker v. Carr* about the applicability of the so-called federal analogy to state legislative apportionment arrangements. * * * Arising from unique historical circumstances, [the states' equal representation in the Senate] is based on the consideration that in establishing our type of federalism a group of formerly independent States bound themselves together under one national government. [A]t the time of the inception of the system of representation in the Federal Congress, a compromise between the larger and smaller States on this matter averted a deadlock in the Constitutional Convention which had threatened to abort the birth of our Nation. * * * Since we find the so-called federal analogy inapposite to a consideration of the constitutional validity of state legislative apportionment schemes, we necessarily hold that the Equal Protection Clause requires both houses of a state legislature to be apportioned on a population basis.

By holding that as a federal constitutional requisite both houses of a state legislature must be apportioned on a population basis, we mean that the Equal Protection Clause requires that a State make an honest and good faith effort to construct districts, in both houses of its legislature, as nearly of equal population as is practicable. We realize that it is a practical impossibility to arrange legislative districts so

> **Take Note**
>
> Most of the Equal Protection cases we have seen have involved claims of discrimination against minorities. Is the Court's holding in *Reynolds* designed to protect minorities? Or instead is it majorities who benefit from the decision?

that each one has an identical number of residents, or citizens, or voters. Mathematical exactness or precision is hardly a workable constitutional requirement. * * * Lower courts can and assuredly will work out more concrete and specific standards for evaluating state legislative apportionment schemes in the context of actual litigation.

MR. JUSTICE HARLAN, dissenting.

Under the Court's ruling it is bound to follow that the legislatures in all but a few of the other [States] will meet the same fate. [The Court's decision has] the effect of placing basic aspects of state political systems under the pervasive overlordship of the federal judiciary.

[T]he Equal Protection Clause was never intended to inhibit the States in choosing any democratic method they pleased for the apportionment of their legislatures. * * * I am unable to understand the Court's utter disregard of the second section [of the Fourteenth Amendment,] which expressly recognizes the States' power to deny "or in any way" abridge the right of their inhabitants to vote for "the members of the (State) Legislature," and its express provision of a remedy for such denial or abridgment. The comprehensive scope of the second section and its particular reference to the state legislatures preclude the suggestion that the first section was intended to have the result reached by the Court today.

Of the 23 loyal States which ratified the Amendment before 1870, five had constitutional provisions for apportionment of at least one house of their respective legislatures which wholly disregarded the spread of population. Ten more had constitutional provisions which gave primary emphasis to population, but which applied also other principles, such as partial ratios and recognition of political subdivisions, which were intended to favor sparsely settled areas. Can it be seriously contended that the legislatures of these States, almost two-thirds of those concerned, would have ratified an amendment which might render their own States' constitutions unconstitutional?

[A]fter the adoption of the [F]ourteenth [A]mendment, it was deemed necessary to adopt a [F]ifteenth * * *. The [F]ourteenth [A]mendment had already provided that no State should make or enforce any law which should abridge the privileges or immunities of citizens of the United States. If suffrage was one of these privileges or immunities, why amend the Constitution to prevent its being denied on account of race, &c.? [U]nless one takes the highly implausible view that the Fourteenth Amendment controls methods of apportionment but leaves the right to vote itself unprotected, the conclusion is inescapable that the Court has, for purposes of these cases, relegated the Fifteenth and Nineteenth Amendments to the same limbo of constitutional anachronisms to which the second section of the Fourteenth Amendment has been assigned.

[The Court's decision gives] support to a current mistaken view of the Constitution and the constitutional function of this Court. This view, in a nutshell, is that every major social ill in this country can find its cure in some constitutional "principle." [This Court] does not serve its high purpose when it exceeds its authority, even to satisfy justified impatience with the slow workings of the political process. For when, in the name of constitutional interpretation, the Court adds something to the Constitution that was deliberately excluded from it, the Court in reality substitutes its view of what should be so for the amending process.

POINTS FOR DISCUSSION

a. "One Person, One Vote"

The same term that it decided *Reynolds*, the Court applied the "one-person, one-vote" principle to districting for the United States House of Representatives. See *Wesberry v. Sanders*, 376 U.S. 1 (1964). Since that time, the Court has applied the principle to local governments, as well. See, e.g., *Avery v. Midland County*, 390 U.S. 474 (1968) (county commission).

The principle of one person, one vote requires that legislators (or other elected representatives) represent districts of equal sizes, so that no person's vote is worth "more" than any other's. Although the Court stated in *Reynolds* that it would not insist on "mathematical exactness," since that time it has tolerated only very small deviations from the principle of one person, one vote. See, e.g., *Karcher v. Daggett*, 462 U.S. 725 (1983) (invalidating districting for the House of Representatives with deviation among districts of 0.7 percent, where state could offer no justification for the deviation).

Does the one-person, one-vote principle apply to the United States Senate? (In the United States Senate, Wyoming, which has under 600,000 residents, and California, which has roughly 38 million residents, are represented by the same number of Senators, which means that each resident of Wyoming has considerably more influence than does each resident of California over who is elected to the Senate from the state.) If the one-person, one-vote principle does not apply in the Senate, then can it truly be a principle of constitutional importance?

b. Vote Dilution

Justice Harlan asserted in dissent in *Reynolds* that the Constitution does not prohibit the states from apportioning legislatures on principles other than one person, one vote, assuming that there is no invidious discrimination on the basis of race or gender. If Justice Harlan's view had prevailed, could a state conduct at-large elections for the state legislature—that is, eliminate individual districts and let the voters in the state choose from a slate to fill all of the legislative seats—and give some citizens—say, rural residents—ten votes to spread among candidates while giving other citizens only one? Could it give 100 votes to some citizens and only one to others? (The effect, of course, would be the same as the apportionment at issue in *Reynolds*.) Could it deny the vote to all urban residents or citizens who do not own property? Cf. *Harper v. Virginia State Bd. of Elections*, which we considered earlier in this chapter.

c. Remedies

Putting aside the question of the appropriate *standard* for apportionment, what *remedy* should a district court grant for a valid claim of unconstitutional apportionment? Can it order the state legislature to redraw the legislative map? Would such a remedy be consistent with *New York v. United States*, which we considered in Volume 1? Can the district court draw the lines itself?

———————

In Chapter 5, we considered the extent to which legislators may consider race when drawing the election map. In *Shaw v. Reno*, the Court concluded that strict scrutiny applies to the use of race in redistricting, even when race has been used to increase the likelihood that minority groups will be able to elect the candidate of their choice. Accordingly, claims of "racial gerrymandering"—the drawing of legislative district lines to benefit voters based on their race—not only are justiciable, but they also challenge a practice that is presumptively unconstitutional.

Does the same approach apply to efforts to draw electoral maps to benefit other definable groups? In *Davis v. Bandemer*, 478 U.S. 109 (1986), the Court considered a challenge by Indiana Democrats to a reapportionment plan passed by the Republican-controlled legislature and signed by the Republican Governor. The plaintiffs contended that the plan constituted an impermissible **political gerrymander** intended to disadvantage Democrats, but the Court rejected their challenge. A six-member majority of the Court, after considering the factors identified in *Baker v. Carr*, concluded that the claim was justiciable. But no standard for assessing the plaintiffs' claims received five votes. Justice White, joined by Justices Brennan, Marshall, and Blackmun, began by rejecting "any claim that the Constitution requires proportional representation or that legislatures in reapportioning must draw district lines to come as near as possible to allocating seats to the contending parties in proportion to what their anticipated statewide vote will be." In Justice White's view, plaintiffs could prevail only by proving both intentional discrimination against an identifiable political group and an actual discriminatory effect on that group. But he was unwilling to find the requisite effects in that case: "unconstitutional discrimination occurs only when the electoral system is arranged in a manner that will consistently degrade a voter's or a group of voters' influence on the political process as a whole."

Justice Powell, joined by Justice Stevens, agreed that the claim was justiciable, but proposed a multi-factored test for determining when a political gerrymander violates the Constitution: "The most important of these factors are the shapes of voting districts and adherence to established political subdivision boundaries. Other relevant considerations include the nature of the legislative procedures by which the apportionment law was adopted and legislative history reflecting contemporaneous legislative goals." In Justice Powell's view, "[n]o one factor should be dispositive."

Justice O'Connor, joined by Chief Justice Burger and Justice Rehnquist, wrote separately to assert that political gerrymandering claims should be non-justiciable: "[T]he legislative business of apportionment is fundamentally a political affair, and challenges to the manner in which an apportionment has been carried out—by the very parties that are responsible for this process—present a political question in the truest sense of the term." Justice O'Connor asserted that there is a "fundamental distinction between state action that inhibits an individual's right to vote and state action that affects the political strength of various groups that compete for leadership in a democratically governed community."

The Court revisited the issue in *Vieth v. Jubelirer*, 541 U.S. 267 (2004), which involved a challenged to Pennsylvania legislation apportioning the state's federal congressional districts. Justice Scalia's plurality opinion concluded that, because there were no judicially discernable and manageable standards to govern claims of undue partisanship in redistricting, such claims are non-justiciable. Justice Scalia noted that, in the 18 years since the Court's decision in *Bandemer*, no administrable test had emerged. He also observed that the fact that the dissenters in the case had "come up with three different standards—all of them different from the two proposed in *Bandemer* and the one proposed here by appellants—goes a long way to establishing that there is no constitutionally discernible standard." Justice Kennedy concurred in the judgment, but made clear that he "would not foreclose all possibility of judicial relief if some limited and precise rationale were found to correct an established violation of the Constitution in some redistricting cases." Justice Stevens, Justice Souter (joined by Justice Ginsburg), and Justice Breyer dissented separately, each proposing a different test to address the constitutionality of partisan redistricting plans.

In *Gill v. Whitford*, 138 S.Ct. 1916 (2018), the Court considered a challenge to Wisconsin's redistricting plan, under which Republican candidates for the state Assembly received a much higher percentage of seats in the legislature than they did of the state-wide two-party vote. The plaintiffs contended that the plan intentionally diluted Democratic votes, and they offered a test for unconstitutional political gerrymanders. The plaintiffs argued that the degree to which a redistricting plan has favored one political party over another can be measured by an "efficiency gap" that compares each party's respective "wasted" votes—that is, votes cast for a losing candidate or for a winning candidate in excess of what that candidate needs to win—across all legislative districts. The plaintiffs claimed that the Wisconsin redistricting plan generated an excess of wasted Democratic votes, in violation of their First Amendment right of association and their Fourteenth Amendment right to equal protection. But the Court declined to address the merits of the plaintiffs' claims, concluding that the plaintiffs lacked standing because they could not show that the specific districts in which they lived would have had different boundaries under a politically neutral plan.

The Court finally addressed the viability of claims of impermissible partisan gerrymander in the case that follows.

RUCHO V. COMMON CAUSE
139 S.Ct. 2984 (2019)

CHIEF JUSTICE ROBERTS delivered the opinion of the Court.

These cases require us to consider once again whether claims of excessive partisanship in districting are "justiciable"—that is, properly suited for resolution by the federal courts. * * * The districting plans at issue here are highly partisan, by any measure. The question is whether the courts below appropriately exercised judicial power when they found them unconstitutional as well.

The first case involves a challenge to the congressional redistricting plan enacted by the Republican-controlled North Carolina General Assembly in 2016. The Republican legislators leading the redistricting effort instructed their mapmaker to use political data to draw a map that would produce a congressional delegation of ten Republicans and three [Democrats, even though as recently as 2012 Democratic congressional candidates had received more votes on a statewide basis than Republican candidates.] As one of the two Republicans chairing the redistricting committee stated, "I think electing Republicans is better than electing Democrats. So I drew this map to help foster what I think is better for the country." He further explained that the map was drawn with the aim of electing ten Republicans and three Democrats because he did "not believe it [would be] possible to draw a map with 11 Republicans and 2 Democrats." [After the General Assembly approved the Plan in a party-line vote, Republican candidates won 10 of the 13 congressional districts. The North Carolina Democratic Party, Common Cause (a nonprofit organization), and 14 individual North Carolina voters filed suit challenging the constitutionality of the redistricting plan. A three-judge district court concluded that 12 of the 13 districts violated the Equal Protection Clause and the First Amendment.]

[The second case involved the plan enacted by the Democratic-controlled Maryland Legislature. The Governor later testified that his aim was to "use the redistricting process to change the overall composition of Maryland's congressional delegation to 7 Democrats and 1 Republican by flipping" one district. The Plan accomplished that goal by reducing the number of registered Republicans in the district by about 66,000 and increasing the number of registered Democrats by about 24,000. A Democrat has held the seat ever since. Three Maryland voters filed suit challenging the plan. The District Court concluded that the plaintiffs' claims were justiciable, and that the Plan violated the First Amendment by diminishing their "ability to elect their candidate of choice" because of their party affiliation and voting history.]

Chief Justice Marshall famously wrote that it is "the province and duty of the judicial department to say what the law is." *Marbury v. Madison*, 1 Cranch 137, 177 (1803). Sometimes, however, "the law is that the judicial department has no business entertaining the claim of unlawfulness—because the question is entrusted to one of the political branches or involves no judicially enforceable rights." *Vieth v. Jubelirer*, 541 U. S. 267, 277 (2004) (plurality opinion). In such a case the claim is said to present a "political question" and to be nonjusticiable—outside the courts' competence and therefore beyond the courts' jurisdiction. *Baker v. Carr*, 369 U. S. 186, 217

> **Make the Connection**
>
> We considered the political question doctrine, and *Baker v. Carr*, in Volume 1.

(1962). Among the political question cases the Court has identified are those that lack "judicially discoverable and manageable standards for resolving [them]." *Ibid.*
* * *

Partisan gerrymandering is nothing new. Nor is frustration with it. The practice was known in the Colonies prior to Independence, and the Framers were familiar with it at the time of the drafting and ratification of the Constitution. See *Vieth*, 541 U. S., at 274 (plurality opinion). * * * The Framers addressed the election of Representatives to Congress in the Elections Clause. Art. I, § 4, cl. 1. That provision assigns to state legislatures the power to prescribe the "Times, Places and Manner of holding Elections" for Members of Congress, while giving Congress the power to "make or alter" any such regulations. * * * The Framers were aware of electoral districting problems and considered what to do about them. They settled on a characteristic approach, assigning the issue to the state legislatures, expressly checked and balanced by the Federal Congress. * * * At no point was there a suggestion that the federal courts had a role to play. Nor was there any indication that the Framers had ever heard of courts doing such a thing.

Courts have nevertheless been called upon to resolve a variety of questions surrounding districting. * * * In the leading case of *Baker* v. *Carr*, [the Court held that an apportionment scheme] predicated on a 60-year-old census that no longer reflected the distribution of population in the State * * * violated the Equal Protection Clause of the Fourteenth Amendment. [The Court concluded that there were judicially discoverable and manageable standards] under basic equal protection principles. In *Wesberry v. Sanders*, 376 U.S. 1, 8 (1964), the Court extended its ruling to malapportionment of congressional districts, holding that Article I, § 2, required that "one man's vote in a congressional election is to be worth as much as another's."

Another line of challenges to districting plans has focused on race. Laws that explicitly discriminate on the basis of race, as well as those that are race neutral on their face but are unexplainable on grounds other than race, are of course presumptively invalid. The Court applied those principles to electoral boundaries in *Gomillion* v. *Lightfoot*, concluding that a challenge to an "uncouth twenty-eight sided" municipal boundary line that excluded black voters from city elections stated a constitutional claim. 364 U. S. 339, 340 (1960). In *Wright v. Rockefeller*, 376 U. S. 52 (1964), the Court extended the reasoning of *Gomillion* to congressional districting. * * *

Partisan gerrymandering claims have proved far more difficult to adjudicate. The basic reason is that, while it is illegal for a jurisdiction to depart from the one-person, one-vote rule, or to engage in racial discrimination in districting, "a jurisdiction may engage in constitutional political gerrymandering." *Hunt v. Cromartie*, 526 U. S. 541, 551 (1999). * * * To hold that legislators cannot take partisan interests into account when drawing district lines would essentially countermand the Framers' decision to entrust districting to political entities. The "central problem" is not determining whether a jurisdiction has engaged in partisan gerrymandering. It is "determining when political gerrymandering has gone too far." *Vieth*, 541 U. S., at 296 (plurality opinion).

Partisan gerrymandering claims rest on an instinct that groups with a certain level of political support should enjoy a commensurate level of political power and influence. Explicitly or implicitly, a districting map is alleged to be unconstitutional because it makes it too difficult for one party to translate statewide support into seats in the legislature. * * * Partisan gerrymandering claims invariably sound in a desire for proportional representation. * * * "Our cases, however, clearly foreclose any claim that the Constitution requires proportional representation or that legislatures in reapportioning must draw district lines to come as near as possible to allocating seats to the contending parties in proportion to what their anticipated statewide vote will be." *Bandemer*, 487 U.S., at 130 (plurality opinion). See *Mobile* v. *Bolden*, 446 U. S. 55, 75–76 (1980) (plurality opinion) ("The Equal Protection Clause of the Fourteenth Amendment does not require proportional representation as an imperative of political organization.").

Unable to claim that the Constitution requires proportional representation outright, plaintiffs inevitably ask the courts to make their own political judgment about how much representation particular political parties *deserve*—based on the votes of their supporters—and to rearrange the challenged districts to achieve that end. But federal courts are not equipped to apportion political power as a matter of fairness, nor is there any basis for concluding that they were authorized to do so. * * *

The initial difficulty in settling on a "clear, manageable and politically neutral" test for fairness is that it is not even clear what fairness looks like in this context. There is a large measure of "unfairness" in any winner-take-all system. Fairness may mean a greater number of competitive districts. Such a claim seeks to undo packing and cracking so that supporters of the disadvantaged party have a better shot at electing their preferred candidates. But making as many districts as possible more competitive could be a recipe for disaster for the disadvantaged party. As Justice White has pointed out, "[i]f all or most of the districts are

> **FYI**
>
> "Packing" a district means to fill it with a supermajority of a given group or party. "Cracking" involves the splitting of a group or party among several districts to deny that group or party a majority in any of those districts.

competitive ... even a narrow statewide preference for either party would produce an overwhelming majority for the winning party in the state legislature." *Bandemer*, 478 U. S., at 130 (plurality opinion).

On the other hand, perhaps the ultimate objective of a "fairer" share of seats in the congressional delegation is most readily achieved by yielding to the gravitational pull of proportionality and engaging in cracking and packing, to ensure each party its "appropriate" share of "safe" seats. See *id.*, at 130–131 ("To draw district lines to maximize the representation of each major party would require creating as many safe seats for each party as the demographic and predicted political characteristics of the State would permit."). Such an approach, however, comes at the expense of competitive districts and of individuals in districts allocated to the opposing party.

Or perhaps fairness should be measured by adherence to "traditional" districting criteria, such as maintaining political subdivisions, keeping communities of interest together, and protecting incumbents. But protecting incumbents, for example, enshrines a particular partisan distribution. And the "natural political geography" of a State—such as the fact that urban electoral districts are often dominated by one political party—can itself lead to inherently packed districts. [A] decision under these standards would unavoidably have significant political effect, whether intended or not." *Vieth*, 541 U. S., at 308–309 (opinion concurring in judgment). * * *

Deciding among just these different visions of fairness (you can imagine many others) poses basic questions that are political, not legal. There are no legal standards discernible in the Constitution for making such judgments, let alone limited and precise standards that are clear, manageable, and politically neutral. * * * And it is only after determining how to define fairness that you can even begin to answer the determinative question: "How much is too much?" At what point does permissible partisanship become unconstitutional? If compliance with traditional districting criteria is the fairness touchstone, for example, how much deviation from those criteria is constitutionally acceptable and how should mapdrawers prioritize competing criteria? * * * A court would have to rank the relative importance of [the] traditional criteria and weigh how much deviation from each to allow. If a court instead focused on the respective number of seats in the legislature, it would have to decide the ideal number of seats for each party and determine at what point deviation from that balance went too far. * * *

Appellees contend that if we can adjudicate one-person, one-vote claims, we can also assess partisan gerrymandering claims. But the one-person, one-vote rule is relatively easy to administer as a matter of math. The same cannot be said of partisan gerrymandering claims, because the Constitution supplies no objective measure for assessing whether a districting map treats a political party fairly. It hardly follows from the principle that each person must have an equal say in the election of representatives that a person is entitled to have his political party achieve representation in some way commensurate to its share of statewide support.

More fundamentally, "vote dilution" in the one-person, one-vote cases refers to the idea that each vote must carry equal weight. In other words, each representative must be accountable to (approximately) the same number of constituents. That requirement does not extend to political parties. It does not mean that each party must be influential in proportion to its number of supporters. * * * Nor do our racial gerrymandering cases provide an appropriate standard for assessing partisan gerrymandering. * * * Unlike partisan gerrymandering claims, a racial gerrymandering claim does not ask for a fair share of political power and influence, with all the justiciability conundrums that entails. It asks instead for the elimination of a racial classification. A partisan gerrymandering claim cannot ask for the elimination of partisanship.

Appellees and the dissent propose a number of "tests" for evaluating partisan gerrymandering claims, but none meets the need for a limited and precise standard that is judicially discernible and manageable. * * *

The [District Court] concluded that all but one of the districts in North Carolina's 2016 Plan violated the Equal Protection Clause by intentionally diluting the voting strength of Democrats. [The court considered, among other things, whether the legislature's "predominant purpose" in drawing district lines was to "subordinate adherents of one political party and entrench a rival party in power"; and whether the cracking or packing "is likely to persist in subsequent elections such that an elected representative from the favored party in the district will not feel a need to be responsive to constituents who support the disfavored party."]

But determining that lines were drawn on the basis of partisanship does not indicate that the districting was improper. A permissible intent—securing partisan advantage—does not become constitutionally impermissible, like racial discrimination, when that permissible intent "predominates." * * * And the test [requires] a far more nuanced prediction than simply who would prevail in future political contests. Judges must forecast with unspecified certainty whether a prospective winner will have a margin of victory sufficient to permit him to ignore the supporters of his defeated opponent (whoever that may turn out to be). Judges not only have to pick the winner—they have to beat the point spread.

* * * Experience proves that accurately predicting electoral outcomes is not so simple, either because the plans are based on flawed assumptions about voter preferences and behavior or because demographics and priorities change over time. In our two leading partisan gerrymandering cases themselves, the predictions of durability proved to be dramatically wrong. In 1981, Republicans controlled both houses of the Indiana Legislature as well as the governorship. Democrats challenged the state legislature districting map enacted by the Republicans. This Court in *Bandemer* rejected that challenge, and just months later the Democrats increased their share of House seats in the 1986 elections. Two years later the House was split 50–50 between Democrats and Republicans, and the Democrats took control of the chamber in 1990. Democrats also challenged the Pennsylvania congressional districting plan at issue in *Vieth*. Two years after that challenge failed, they gained four seats in the delegation, going from a 12–7 minority to an 11–8 majority. * * *

The District Courts also found partisan gerrymandering claims justiciable under the First Amendment, coalescing around a basic three-part test: proof of intent to burden individuals based on their voting history or party affiliation; an actual burden on political speech or associational rights; and a causal link between the invidious intent and actual burden. * * * [But the] First Amendment test simply describes the act of districting for partisan advantage. It provides no standard for determining when partisan activity goes too far.

The dissent proposes using a State's own districting criteria as a neutral baseline from which to measure how extreme a partisan gerrymander is. The dissent would have us line up all the possible maps drawn using those criteria according to the partisan distribution they would produce. Distance from the "median" map would indicate whether a particular districting plan harms supporters of one party to an unconstitutional extent.

As an initial matter, it does not make sense to use criteria that will vary from State to State and year to year as the baseline for determining whether a gerrymander violates the Federal Constitution. The degree of partisan advantage that the Constitution tolerates should not turn on criteria offered by the gerrymanderers themselves. * * * Even if we were to accept the dissent's proposed baseline, it would return us to "the original unanswerable question (How much political motivation and effect is too much?)." *Vieth*, 541 U. S., at 296–297 (plurality opinion). Would twenty percent away from the median map be okay? Forty percent? Sixty percent? Why or why not? * * * The dissent's answer says it all: "This much is too much." That is not even trying to articulate a standard or rule.

Excessive partisanship in districting leads to results that reasonably seem unjust. But the fact that such gerrymandering is "incompatible with democratic principles" does not mean that the solution lies with the federal judiciary. We conclude that partisan gerrymandering claims present political questions beyond the reach of the federal courts. Federal judges have no license to reallocate political power between the two major political parties, with no plausible grant of authority in the Constitution, and no legal standards to limit and direct their decisions. * * *

Our conclusion does not condone excessive partisan gerrymandering. Nor does our conclusion condemn complaints about districting to echo into a void. The States, for example, are actively addressing the issue on a number of fronts. In 2015, the Supreme Court of Florida struck down that State's congressional districting plan as a violation of the Fair Districts Amendment to the Florida Constitution. *League of Women Voters of Florida v. Detzner*, 172 So. 3d 363 (2015). * * * [I]n November 2018, voters in Colorado and Michigan approved constitutional amendments creating multimember commissions that will be responsible in whole or in part for creating and approving district maps for congressional and state legislative districts. * * * Voters [in Missouri] overwhelmingly approved the creation of a new position—state demographer—to draw state legislative district lines. Mo. Const., Art. III, § 3. * * *

As noted, the Framers gave Congress the power to do something about partisan gerrymandering in the Elections Clause. The first bill introduced in the 116th Congress would require States to create 15-member independent commissions to draw congressional districts and would establish certain redistricting criteria, including protection for communities of interest, and ban partisan gerrymandering. H. R. 1, 116th Cong., 1st Sess., §§ 2401, 2411 (2019). Dozens of other bills have been introduced to limit reliance on political considerations in redistricting. * * * We express no view on any of these pending proposals. We simply note that the avenue for reform established by the Framers, and used by Congress in the past, remains open.

No one can accuse this Court of having a crabbed view of the reach of its competence. But we have no commission to allocate political power and influence in the absence of a constitutional directive or legal standards to guide us in the exercise of such authority. "It is emphatically the province and duty of the judicial department to say what the law is." *Marbury* v. *Madison*, 1 Cranch, at 177. In this rare circumstance, that means our duty is to say "this is not law." [Vacated and remanded with instructions to dismiss for lack of jurisdiction.]

JUSTICE KAGAN, with whom JUSTICE GINSBURG, JUSTICE BREYER, and JUSTICE SOTOMAYOR join, dissenting.

* * * The partisan gerrymanders in these cases deprived citizens of the most fundamental of their constitutional rights: the rights to participate equally in the political process, to join with others to advance political beliefs, and to choose their political representatives. In so doing, the partisan gerrymanders here debased and dishonored our democracy, turning upside-down the core American idea that all governmental power derives from the people. These gerrymanders enabled politicians to entrench themselves in office as against voters' preferences. They promoted partisanship above respect for the popular will. They encouraged a politics of polarization and dysfunction. If left unchecked, gerrymanders like the ones here may irreparably damage our system of government.

And checking them is *not* beyond the courts. The majority's abdication comes just when courts across the country, including those below, have coalesced around manageable judicial standards to resolve partisan gerrymandering claims. Those standards satisfy the majority's own benchmarks. They do not require—indeed, they do not permit—courts to rely on their own ideas of electoral fairness, whether proportional representation or any other. And they limit courts to correcting only egregious gerrymanders, so judges do not become omnipresent players in the political process. But yes, the standards used here do allow—as well they should—judicial intervention in the worst-of-the-worst cases of democratic subversion, causing blatant constitutional harms. In other words, they allow courts to undo partisan gerrymanders of the kind we face today from North Carolina and Maryland. In giving such gerrymanders a pass from judicial review, the majority goes tragically wrong.

* * * If there is a single idea that made our Nation (and that our Nation commended to the world), it is this one: The people are sovereign. * * * Free and fair and periodic elections are the key to that vision. The people get to choose their representatives. And then they get to decide, at regular intervals, whether to keep them. * * * And partisan gerrymandering can make it meaningless. * * * By drawing districts to maximize the power of some voters and minimize the power of others, a party in office at the right time can entrench itself there for a decade or more, no matter what the voters would prefer. * * * The "core principle of republican government," this Court has recognized, is "that the voters should choose their representatives, not the other way around." *Arizona State Legislature* v. *Arizona Independent Redistricting Comm'n*, 135 S.Ct. 2652, 2677 (2015). * * *

* * * The majority disputes none of what I have said (or will say) about how gerrymanders undermine democracy. Indeed, the majority concedes (really, how could it not?) that gerrymandering is "incompatible with democratic principles." * * * That recognition would seem to demand a response. The majority offers two ideas that might qualify as such. One is that the political process can deal with the problem—a proposition so dubious on its face that I feel secure in delaying my answer for some time. The other is that political gerrymanders have always been with us. To its credit, the majority does not frame that point as an originalist constitutional argument. After all (as the majority rightly notes), racial and residential gerrymanders were also once with us, but the Court has done something about that fact. The majority's idea instead seems to be that if we have lived with partisan gerrymanders so long, we will survive.

That complacency has no cause. Yes, partisan gerrymandering goes back to the Republic's earliest days. (As does vociferous opposition to it.) But big data and modern technology—of just the kind that the mapmakers in North Carolina and Maryland used—make today's gerrymandering altogether different from the crude linedrawing of the past. Old-time efforts, based on little more than guesses, sometimes led to so-called dummymanders—gerrymanders that went spectacularly wrong. Not likely in today's world. Mapmakers now have access to more granular data about party preference and voting behavior than ever before.

* * * Just as important, advancements in computing technology have enabled mapmakers to put that information to use with unprecedented efficiency and precision. * * * The effect is to make gerrymanders far more effective and durable than before, insulating politicians against all but the most titanic shifts in the political tides. These are not your grandfather's—let alone the Framers'—gerrymanders.

Partisan gerrymandering of the kind before us not only subverts democracy (as if that weren't bad enough). It violates individuals' constitutional rights as well. * * * Partisan gerrymandering operates through vote dilution—the devaluation of one citizen's vote as compared to others. A mapmaker draws district lines to "pack" and "crack" voters likely to support the disfavored party. * * * In short, the mapmaker [makes] some votes count for less, because they are likely to go for the other party. That practice implicates the Fourteenth Amendment's Equal Protection Clause, [which] "guarantees the opportunity for equal participation by all voters in the election" of legislators. *Reynolds v. Sims*, 377 U. S. 533, 566 (1964). * * * And partisan gerrymandering implicates the First Amendment [too, by subjecting] certain voters to "disfavored treatment"—again, counting their votes for less—precisely because of "their voting history [and] their expression of political views." *Vieth*, 541 U. S., at 314 (opinion of Kennedy, J.). * * *

The majority gives two reasons for thinking that the adjudication of partisan gerrymandering claims is beyond judicial capabilities. First and foremost, the majority says, it cannot find a neutral baseline—one not based on contestable notions of political fairness—from which to measure injury. * * * And second, the majority argues that even after establishing a baseline, a court would have no way to answer "the determinative question: 'How much is too much?'" * * * [I agree that judges] should not be apportioning political power based on their own vision of electoral fairness, [and that] judges should not be striking down maps left, right, and center, on the view that every smidgen of politics is a smidgen too much. Respect for state legislative processes—and restraint in the exercise of judicial authority—counsels intervention in only egregious cases.

But in throwing up its hands, the majority misses something under its nose: What it says can't be done *has* been done. Over the past several years, federal courts across the country—including, but not exclusively, in the decisions below—have largely converged on a standard for adjudicating partisan gerrymandering claims (striking down both Democratic and Republican districting plans in the process). And that standard does what the majority says is impossible. The standard does not use any judge-made conception of electoral fairness—either proportional representation or any other; instead, it takes as its baseline a State's *own* criteria of fairness, apart from partisan gain. And by requiring plaintiffs to make difficult showings relating to both purpose and effects, the standard invalidates the most extreme, but only the most extreme, partisan gerrymanders.

Start with the standard the lower courts used. * * * First, the plaintiffs challenging a districting plan must prove that state officials' "predominant purpose" in drawing a district's lines was to "entrench [their party] in power" by diluting the votes of citizens favoring its rival. Second, the plaintiffs must establish that the lines drawn in fact have the intended effect by "substantially" diluting their votes. And third, if the plaintiffs make those showings, the State must come up with a legitimate, non-partisan justification to save its map. If you are a lawyer, you know that this test looks utterly ordinary. It is the sort of thing courts work with every day.

* * * The majority does not contest the lower courts' findings [that the North Carolina and Maryland districters had the predominant purpose of entrenching their own party in power]; how could it? Instead, the majority says that state officials' intent to entrench their party in power is perfectly "permissible," even when it is the predominant factor in drawing district lines. But that is wrong. True enough, that the intent to inject "political considerations" into districting may not raise any constitutional concerns. In *Gaffney v. Cummings*, 412 U. S. 735 (1973), for example, we thought it non-problematic when state officials used political data to ensure rough proportional representation between the two parties. * * * But when political actors have a specific and predominant intent to entrench themselves in power by manipulating district lines, that goes too far. * * *

The majority fails to discuss most of the evidence the District Courts relied on to find that the plaintiffs [proved that the districting plans substantially dilute their votes]. But that evidence—particularly from North Carolina—is the key to understanding both the problem these cases present and the solution to it they offer. * * * [In the North Carolina case,] the plaintiffs demonstrated the districting plan's effects mostly by relying on what might be called the "extreme outlier approach." * * * [The approach] begins by using advanced computing technology to randomly generate a large collection of districting plans that incorporate the State's physical and political geography and meet its declared districting criteria, *except for* partisan gain. For each of those maps, the method then uses actual precinct-level votes from past elections to determine a partisan outcome (*i.e.,* the number of Democratic and Republican seats that map produces). Suppose we now have 1,000 maps, each with a partisan outcome attached to it. We can line up those maps on a continuum—the most favorable to Republicans on one end, the most favorable to Democrats on the other. We can then find the median outcome—that is, the outcome smack dab in the center—in a world with no partisan manipulation. And we can see where the State's actual plan falls on the spectrum—at or near the median or way out on one of the tails? The further out on the tail, the more extreme the partisan distortion and the more significant the vote dilution.

Using that approach, the North Carolina plaintiffs offered a boatload of alternative districting plans—all showing that the State's map was an out-out-out-outlier. One expert produced 3,000 maps, adhering in the way described above to the districting criteria that the North Carolina redistricting committee had used, other than partisan advantage. * * * Every single one of the 3,000 maps would have produced at least one more Democratic House Member than the State's actual map, and 77% would have elected three or four more. * * * Because the Maryland gerrymander involved just one district, the evidence in that case was far simpler—but no less powerful for that. * * * In what was once a party stronghold, Republicans now have little or no chance to elect their preferred candidate.

The majority claims all these findings are mere "prognostications" about the future, in which no one "can have any confidence." But the [courts' findings] about these gerrymanders' effects on voters—both in the past and predictably in the future—were evidence-based, data-based, statistics-based. Knowledge-based, one might say. * * * They did not bet America's future—as today the majority does—on the idea that maps constructed with so much expertise and care to make electoral outcomes impervious to voting would somehow or other come apart. They looked at the evidence—at the facts about how these districts operated—and they could reach only one conclusion. By substantially diluting the votes of citizens favoring their rivals, the politicians of one party had succeeded in entrenching themselves in office. They had beat democracy.

The majority's broadest claim, as I've noted, is that this is a price we must pay because judicial oversight of partisan gerrymandering cannot be "politically neutral" or "manageable." * * * Contrary to the majority's suggestion, the District Courts did not have to—and in fact did not—choose among competing visions of electoral fairness. That is because they did not try to compare the State's actual map to an "ideally fair" one (whether based on proportional representation or some other criterion). Instead, they looked at the difference between what the State did and what the State would have done if politicians hadn't been intent on partisan gain. * * *

The majority's "how much is too much" critique fares no better than its neutrality argument. How about the following for a first-cut answer: This much is too much. By any measure, a map that produces a greater partisan skew than any of 3,000 randomly generated maps (all with the State's political geography and districting criteria built in) reflects "too much" partisanship. Think about what I just said: The absolute worst of 3,001 possible maps. The *only one* that could produce a 10–3 partisan split even as Republicans got a bare majority of the statewide vote. And again: How much is too much? This much is too much: A map that without any evident non-partisan districting reason (to the contrary) shifted the composition of a district from 47% Republicans and 36% Democrats to 33% Republicans and 42% Democrats. * * *

This Court has long understood that it has a special responsibility to remedy violations of constitutional rights resulting from politicians' districting decisions. * * * Those harms arise because politicians want to stay in office. No one can look to them for effective relief. The majority disagrees, concluding its opinion with a paean to congressional bills limiting partisan gerrymanders. "Dozens of [those] bills have been introduced," the majority says. [But] what all these *bills* have in common is that they are not *laws*. The politicians who benefit from partisan gerrymandering are unlikely to change partisan gerrymandering. And because those politicians maintain themselves in office through partisan gerrymandering, the chances for legislative reform are slight.

No worries, the majority says; it has another idea. The majority notes that voters themselves have recently approved ballot initiatives to put power over districting in the hands of independent commissions or other non-partisan actors. * * * Fewer than half the States offer voters an opportunity to put initiatives to direct vote; in all the rest (including North Carolina and Maryland), voters are dependent on legislators to make electoral changes (which for all the reasons already given, they are unlikely to do). And even when voters have a mechanism they can work themselves, legislators often fight their efforts tooth and nail. * * *

The majority's most perplexing "solution" is to look to state courts. * * * But [if state courts] can develop and apply neutral and manageable standards to identify unconstitutional gerrymanders, why couldn't we? * * * That is not to deny, of course, that these cases have great political consequence. They do. * * * These artificially drawn districts shift influence from swing voters to party-base voters who participate in primaries; make bipartisanship and pragmatic compromise politically difficult or impossible; and drive voters away from an ever more dysfunctional political process. * * * Gerrymandering, in short, helps create the polarized political system so many Americans loathe.

Of all times to abandon the Court's duty to declare the law, this was not the one. The practices challenged in these cases imperil our system of government.

Part of the Court's role in that system is to defend its foundations. None is more important than free and fair elections. With respect but deep sadness, I dissent.

POINTS FOR DISCUSSION

a.   Districting, Geography, and Partisanship

As the dissent noted, there is widespread agreement that partisan gerrymandering is at best unseemly and at worst fundamentally incompatible with democracy. But are you confident you can spot a partisan gerrymander?

One of the challenges of reviewing redistricting plans is that the geographical distribution of a political party's supporters can negatively impact the party's ability to gain a number of seats proportional to its statewide support. For example, imagine that a state has one million voters and ten congressional districts. 50% of the voters in the state are loyal Democrats, and the other 50% are loyal Republicans. But a high percentage of the Democrats live in dense urban areas where there are very few Republican voters. (Imagine that each of the two urban congressional districts has 90,000 Democrats and 10,000 Republicans.) The Democrats will of course win the seats in those urban areas. But if the remaining Democratic voters in the state are distributed evenly among the other eight seats, the Republicans will win all of them. (There will be 60,000 Republicans in each of the remaining seats, and only 40,000 Democrats.) Should this outcome—an 8–2 congressional delegation in favor of Republicans in an evenly divided state—be constitutionally problematic? Would it matter if the state legislature drew the district lines in order to produce a Republican-dominated congressional delegation?

Can you think of alternatives that would produce a more even split in the state's congressional delegation? If so, should courts insist that states adopt those alternatives?

b.   Judicially Manageable Standards

The principal debate between the Court and the dissent was over whether it is possible to articulate judicially manageable standards to identify unconstitutional partisan gerrymanders. The Court feared that any standard that a court applies would not be neutral and would present impossible line-drawing problems. The dissent responded by asserting that it is possible to identify the worst of the worst in partisan gerrymandering. Is it clear to you that the standards proposed by the lower courts and adopted by the dissent are any less determinate or manageable than the standards applied in other cases involving constitutional rights? If not, what is different about this context? And if the dissent is correct that there is a manageable standard, do you agree that the one that it proposed is the right one? Or should it have proposed a standard that would have rendered an even greater number of redistricting plans suspect—that is, not just the worst of the worst?

c. Political Gerrymandering v. Racial Gerrymandering

Although in recent years cases involving racial gerrymandering have challenged districting that seeks to benefit, rather than harm, racial minorities, it was not too long ago that state legislatures drew district lines with the intent to impair—generally through dilution—the voting strength of racial minorities. The Court has made clear that such districting plans violate the Fourteenth Amendment. See, e.g., *Rogers v. Lodge,* 458 U.S. 613 (1982) (invalidating at-large voting system that was maintained for the invidious purpose of diluting the voting strength of African Americans). If claims challenging racial gerrymandering are justiciable, why isn't it clear that claims challenging political gerrymandering are, too? What is the Court's answer to that question? Do you find it convincing?

d. Remedies and Institutional Logic

The Court noted that the Framers gave Congress power to "alter" the "[m]anner" of elections "prescribed in each State by the Legislature thereof." U.S. Const., art. I, § 4. Is there reason to think that members of Congress will be any more willing to address partisan gerrymanders than are members of state legislatures? Isn't the problem with partisan gerrymanders that they eliminate the incentive for elected legislators to act in a way that represents the will of a majority of the voters? If so, isn't there a strong argument for judicial intervention?

B. WELFARE AND EDUCATION

DANDRIDGE V. WILLIAMS
397 U.S. 471 (1970)

MR. JUSTICE STEWART delivered the opinion of the Court.

[Maryland computed the standard of need for each eligible family under the federal Aid to Families with Dependent Children Program (AFDC) based on the number of children in the family and the circumstances under which the family lived. But the state imposed an upper limit on the total amount of money any one family unit was eligible to receive. In general, the standard of need increased with each additional person in the household, but the increments became proportionately smaller. The suit was filed by recipients who had large families—and whose standards of need thus substantially exceeded the maximum grants available—to enjoin Maryland's rule on the ground that it was in conflict with the Equal Protection Clause. The District Court held that the regulation "is invalid on its face for overreaching."]

[Here] we deal with state regulation in the social and economic field, not affecting freedoms guaranteed by the Bill of Rights, and claimed to violate the Fourteenth Amendment only because the regulation results in some disparity in grants of welfare payments to the largest AFDC families. For this Court to approve the invalidation of state economic or social regulation as "overreaching" would be far too reminiscent of an era when the Court thought the Fourteenth Amendment gave it power to strike down state laws "because they may be unwise, improvident, or out of harmony with a particular school of thought."

> **Food for Thought**
>
> Does the fact that a state chooses to regulate "social or economic" matters automatically exempt it from heightened scrutiny under the Equal Protection Clause? Isn't the real question whether the challenged program discriminates on some impermissible basis? Is wealth or family size such a basis? And wouldn't regulation in this area be problematic if it abridged some fundamental right to which the Court has extended protection? Is there such a right here?

Williamson v. Lee Optical Co., 348 U.S. 483 (1955). That era long ago passed into history. In the area of economics and social welfare, a State does not violate the Equal Protection Clause merely because the classifications made by its laws are imperfect. If the classification has some "reasonable basis," it does not offend the Constitution simply because the classification "is not made with mathematical nicety or because in practice it results in some inequality."

Under this long-established meaning of the Equal Protection Clause, it is clear that the Maryland Maximum grant regulation is constitutionally valid. We need not explore all the reasons that the State advances in justification of the regulation. It is enough that a solid foundation for the regulation can be found in the State's legitimate interest in encouraging employment and in avoiding discrimination between welfare families and the families of the working poor. By combining a limit on the recipient's grant with permission to retain money earned, without reduction in the amount of the grant, Maryland provides an incentive to seek gainful employment. And by keying the maximum family AFDC grants to the minimum wage a steadily employed head of a household receives, the State maintains some semblance of an equitable balance between families on welfare and those supported by an employed breadwinner.

> **Make the Connection**
>
> We considered the Court's decision in *Goldberg* in Chapter 3, in our unit on Procedural Due Process.

[T]he intractable economic, social, and even philosophical problems presented by public welfare assistance programs are not the business of this Court. The Constitution may impose certain procedural safeguards upon systems of welfare administration, *Goldberg v.*

Kelly, 397 U.S. 254 (1970), [but] the Constitution does not empower this Court to second-guess state officials charged with the difficult responsibility of allocating limited public welfare funds among the myriad of potential recipients.

MR. JUSTICE HARLAN, concurring.

Except with respect to racial classifications, to which unique historical considerations apply, I believe the constitutional provisions assuring equal protection of the laws impose a standard of rationality of classification, long applied in the decisions of this Court, that does not depend upon the nature of the classification or interest involved. It is on this basis, and not because this case involves only interests in "the area of economics and social welfare," that I join the Court's constitutional holding.

[JUSTICE DOUGLAS's dissent, which asserted that Maryland's rule was inconsistent with the federal Social Security Act, is omitted.]

MR. JUSTICE MARSHALL, whom MR. JUSTICE BRENNAN joins, dissenting.

[T]he operative effect [of the maximum grant regulation] is to create two classes of needy children and two classes of eligible families: those small families and their members who receive payments to cover their subsistence needs and those large families who do not. * * * The class of individuals with respect to whom payments are actually made (the first four or five eligible dependent children in a family), is grossly underinclusive in terms of the class that the AFDC program was designed to assist, namely, all needy dependent children.

It is the individual interests here at stake that [most] clearly distinguish this case from the "business regulation" equal protection cases. AFDC support to needy dependent children provides the stuff that sustains those children's lives: food, clothing, shelter. And this Court has already recognized several times that when a benefit, even a "gratuitous" benefit, is necessary to sustain life, stricter constitutional standards, both procedural and substantive, are applied to the deprivation of that benefit.

> **Make the Connection**
>
> Is under-inclusiveness a defect under rational-basis review? Recall the Court's discussion in the *Railway Express* case, which we considered in Chapter 4. Does this mean that Justice Marshall is applying something other than rational-basis review?

The asserted state interests in the maintenance of the maximum grant regulation, on the other hand, are hardly clear. * * * Maryland, with the encouragement and assistance of the Federal Government, has elected to provide assistance at a subsistence level for those in particular need—the aged, the blind, the infirm, and the unemployed and unemployable, and their children. The only question presented here is whether, having once undertaken such a program, the State may arbitrarily select from among the concededly eligible those to whom it will provide benefits. [To] the extent there is a legitimate state interest in encouraging heads of AFDC households to find employment, application of the maximum grant regulation [is] grossly underinclusive because it singles out and affects only large families. * * * There is simply no indication whatever that heads of large families, as opposed to heads of small families, are particularly prone to refuse to seek or to maintain employment.

Appellees are not a gas company or an optical dispenser; they are needy dependent children and families who are discriminated against by the State. The basis of that discrimination—the classification of individuals into large and small families—is too arbitrary and too unconnected to the asserted rationale, the impact on those discriminated against—the denial of even a subsistence existence—too great, and the supposed interests served too contrived and attenuated to meet the requirements of the Constitution. In my view Maryland's maximum grant regulation is invalid under the Equal Protection Clause of the Fourteenth Amendment.

POINTS FOR DISCUSSION

a. Level of Scrutiny and "Fundamental Rights"

The majority in *Dandridge* applied rational-basis review, implicitly suggesting that there is no fundamental right to welfare. Did Justice Marshall assert that there is in fact a constitutional right to welfare? If there is such a right, is the Equal Protection Clause a sensible textual basis for it? And if there is such a right, what is the proper level of scrutiny by which to review the regulation at issue in *Dandridge*?

b. Wealth and Classifications

The regulation at issue in *Dandridge* distinguished among poor families, not between rich and poor families. In light of this fact, did the case present the Court with an opportunity to decide whether the poor are a suspect class? The Court largely avoided the issue there, but the question was more squarely presented in the case that follows.

SAN ANTONIO INDEPENDENT SCHOOL DIST. V. RODRIGUEZ
411 U.S. 1 (1973)

MR. JUSTICE POWELL delivered the opinion of the Court.

[At the time of this litigation, approximately 40% of Texas's state education budget came from local property taxes. Texas law also imposed a ceiling on the local property-tax rate that any locality could assess. Mexican-American parents whose children attended the public schools of Edgewood Independent School District in San Antonio, Texas, brought suit against various state officials challenging the funding scheme. Because Edgewood was in a district with low property values, it raised only $26 per student in local funds and spent $356 per student during the 1967–68 school year. In contrast, Alamo Heights Independent School District, which was also in San Antonio, raised substantially more money from property taxes and spent $594 per student. The District Court held that the funding scheme violated the Equal Protection Clause.]

Our task must be to ascertain whether [the] Texas system has been shown to discriminate on [the basis of wealth] and, if so, whether the resulting classification may be regarded as suspect. * * * The individuals, or groups of individuals, who constituted the class discriminated against in our prior cases [involving the indigent] shared two distinguishing characteristics: because of their impecunity they were completely unable to pay for some desired benefit, and as a consequence, they sustained an absolute deprivation of a meaningful opportunity to enjoy that benefit. In *Griffin v. Illinois,* 351 U.S. 12 (1956), and its progeny, the Court invalidated state laws that prevented an indigent criminal defendant from acquiring a transcript, or an adequate substitute for a transcript, for use at several stages of the trial and appeal process. * * * Likewise, [*Douglas v. California,* 372 U.S. 353 (1963), established] an indigent defendant's right to court-appointed counsel on direct appeal.

[N]either of the two distinguishing characteristics of wealth classifications can be found here. First, [there] is no basis on the record in this case for assuming that the poorest people—defined by reference to any level of absolute impecunity—are concentrated in the poorest districts. Second, [lack] of personal resources has not occasioned an absolute deprivation of the desired benefit. The argument here is not that the children in districts having relatively low assessable property values are receiving no public education; rather, it is that they are receiving a poorer quality education than that available to children in districts having more assessable wealth. [A]t least where wealth is involved, the Equal Protection Clause does not require absolute equality or precisely equal advantages.

Food for Thought

Is the Court suggesting here that "true" wealth classifications are suspect—that is, that classifications that actually single out the poor (and only the poor) are problematic—but that the challenged policy here is not such a classification?

[A]ppellees' suit asks this Court to extend its most exacting scrutiny to review a system that allegedly discriminates against a large, diverse, and amorphous class, unified only by the common factor of residence in districts that happen to have less taxable wealth than other districts. The system of alleged discrimination and the class it defines have none of the traditional indicia of suspectness: the class is not saddled with such disabilities, or subjected to such a history of purposeful unequal treatment, or relegated to such a position of political powerlessness as to command extraordinary protection from the majoritarian political process.

We thus conclude that the Texas system does not operate to the peculiar disadvantage of any suspect class. But [appellees] also assert that the State's system impermissibly interferes with the exercise of a "fundamental" right and that accordingly the prior decisions of this Court require the application of the strict standard of judicial review. * * * In *Brown v. Board of Education*, 347 U.S. 483 (1954), a unanimous Court recognized that "education is perhaps the most important function of state and local governments." * * * But the importance of a service performed by the State does not determine whether it must be regarded as fundamental for purposes of examination under the Equal Protection Clause. Education, of course, is not among the rights afforded explicit protection under our Federal Constitution. Nor do we find any basis for saying it is implicitly so protected.

It is appellees' contention, however, that education is distinguishable from other services and benefits provided by the State because it bears a peculiarly close relationship to other rights and liberties accorded protection under the Constitution. Specifically, they insist that education is itself a fundamental personal right because it is essential to the effective exercise of First Amendment freedoms and to intelligent utilization of the right to vote. * * * That these may be desirable goals of a system of freedom of expression and of a representative form of government is not to be doubted. [But] they are not values to be implemented by judicial instruction into otherwise legitimate state activities.

Even if it were conceded that some identifiable quantum of education is a constitutionally protected prerequisite to the meaningful exercise of either right, * * * no charge fairly could be made that [Texas's] system fails to provide each child with an opportunity to acquire the basic minimal skills necessary for the enjoyment of the rights of speech and of full participation in the political process. Furthermore, the logical limitations on appellees' nexus theory are difficult to perceive. How, for instance, is education to be distinguished from the significant personal interests in the basics of decent food and shelter? Empirical examination might well buttress an assumption that the ill-fed, ill-clothed, and ill-housed are among the most ineffective participants in the political process, and that they derive the least enjoyment from the benefits of the First Amendment. If so, appellees' thesis would cast serious doubt on the authority of *Dandridge v. Williams*. [In addition,] it would be difficult to imagine a case having a greater potential impact on our federal system than the one now before us, in which we are urged to abrogate systems of financing public education presently in existence in virtually every State.

The foregoing considerations buttress our conclusion that Texas' system of public school finance is an inappropriate candidate for strict judicial scrutiny. These same considerations are relevant to the determination whether that system, with its conceded imperfections, nevertheless bears some rational relationship to a legitimate state purpose. * * * While assuring a basic education for every child in the State, [the Texas system of school financing] permits and encourages a large measure of participation in and control of each district's schools at the local level. * * * Pluralism [affords] opportunity for experimentation, innovation, and a healthy competition for educational excellence. * * * Moreover, if local taxation for local expenditures were an unconstitutional method of providing for education then it might be an equally impermissible means of providing other necessary services customarily financed largely from local property taxes, including local police and fire protection, public health and hospitals, and public utility facilities of various kinds. We perceive no justification for such a severe denigration of local property taxation and control as would follow from appellees' contentions.

In sum, to the extent that the Texas system of school financing results in unequal expenditures between children who happen to reside in different districts, we cannot say that such disparities are the product of a system that is so irrational as to be invidiously discriminatory. * * * The constitutional standard under the Equal Protection Clause is whether the challenged state action rationally furthers a legitimate state purpose or interest. We hold that the Texas plan abundantly satisfies this standard.

[JUSTICE STEWART's concurring opinion and JUSTICE BRENNAN's dissenting opinion are omitted.]

MR. JUSTICE WHITE, with whom MR. JUSTICE DOUGLAS and MR. JUSTICE BRENNAN join, dissenting.

In [districts with low property values], the Texas system utterly fails to extend a realistic choice to parents because the property tax, which is the only revenue-raising mechanism extended to school districts, is practically and legally unavailable. * * * In order to equal the [tax revenues of Alamo Heights, which taxes at a rate of 68¢ per $100 of assessed valuation,] Edgewood would be required to tax at the prohibitive rate of $5.76 per $100. But state law places a $1.50 per $100 ceiling on the maintenance tax rate, a limit that would surely be reached long before Edgewood attained an equal yield. Edgewood is thus precluded in law, as well as in fact, from achieving a yield even close to that of some other districts. * * * If the State aims at maximizing local initiative and local choice, by permitting school districts to resort to the real property tax if they choose to do so, it utterly fails in achieving its purpose in districts with property tax bases so low that there is little if any opportunity for interested parents, rich or poor, to augment school district revenues. Requiring the State to establish only that unequal treatment is in furtherance of a permissible goal, without also requiring the State to show that the means chosen to effectuate that goal are rationally related to its achievement, makes equal protection analysis no more than an empty gesture. In my view, the parents and children in Edgewood, and in like districts, suffer from an invidious discrimination violative of the Equal Protection Clause.

> **Food for Thought**
>
> Justice White states that this case involves "invidious" discrimination. Must the plaintiffs demonstrate that the discrimination is intentional—that is, that the state intentionally deprived poor districts of adequate resources or mechanisms to secure adequate resources? Or is evidence of the discriminatory effects of the policy sufficient for Justice White?

MR. JUSTICE MARSHALL, with whom MR. JUSTICE DOUGLAS concurs, dissenting.

The Court today decides, in effect, that a State may constitutionally vary the quality of education which it offers its children in accordance with the amount of taxable wealth located in the school districts within which they reside. * * * In my judgment, the right of every American to an equal start in life, so far as the provision of a state service as important as education is concerned, is far too vital to permit state discrimination on grounds as tenuous as those presented by this record. Nor can I accept the notion that it is sufficient to remit these appellees to the vagaries of the political process which, contrary to the majority's suggestion, has proved singularly unsuited to the task of providing a remedy for this discrimination. I, for one, am unsatisfied with the hope of an ultimate "political" solution sometime in the indefinite future while, in the meantime, countless children unjustifiably receive inferior educations that may affect their hearts and minds in a way unlikely ever to be undone.

It is an inescapable fact that if one district has more funds available per pupil than another district, the former will have greater choice in educational planning than will the latter. In this regard, I believe the question of discrimination in educational quality must be deemed to be an objective one that looks to what the State provides its children, not to what the children are able to do with what they receive. [The] Equal Protection Clause is not addressed to the minimal sufficiency but rather to the unjustifiable inequalities of state action. It mandates nothing less than that "all persons similarly circumstanced shall be treated alike."

[In addition, I cannot] accept the majority's labored efforts to demonstrate that fundamental interests, which call for strict scrutiny of the challenged classification, encompass only established rights which we are somehow bound to recognize from the text of the Constitution itself. * * * The task in every case should be to determine the extent to which constitutionally guaranteed rights are dependent on interests not mentioned in the Constitution. As the nexus between the specific constitutional guarantee and the nonconstitutional interest draws closer, the nonconstitutional interest becomes more fundamental and the degree of judicial scrutiny applied when the interest is infringed on a discriminatory basis must be adjusted accordingly. * * * Education directly affects the ability of a child to exercise his First Amendment rights, both as a source and as a receiver of information and ideas, whatever interests he may pursue in life.

POINTS FOR DISCUSSION

a. Wealth Classifications

Should the Court treat the poor as a suspect class? Consider the framework that the Court suggested in its famous footnote in *United States v. Carolene Products Co.*, 304 U.S. 144, 152 n.4 (1938), which we considered in Chapters 2 and 4. There, the Court suggested that heightened scrutiny might be warranted when "prejudice against discrete and insular minorities may be a special condition, which tends seriously to curtail the operation of those political processes ordinarily to be relied upon to protect minorities." Are poor people a "discrete and insular minority" and the victims of prejudice? Poverty certainly is not immutable in the same sense that race and national origin are, but are the poor politically powerless? Are the existence of welfare programs and progressive taxation evidence to the contrary?

Did Justice White treat the poor as a suspect class? What level of scrutiny did he apply in his dissent? Was it rational-basis review or something else?

b.   Education as a Fundamental Right

Did Justice Marshall suggest that the Constitution protects a fundamental right to a quality education? If so, what in his view is the source of that right? Is it the Equal Protection Clause? Is it implicit in other provisions of the Constitution, such as the First Amendment? Regardless of its constitutional source, if there is a fundamental right to a state-provided education, what level of scrutiny did Justice Marshall believe should apply to impairments of the right? Compare Susan H. Bitensky, *Theoretical Foundations for a Right to Education Under the United States Constitution*, 86 Nw. U. L. Rev. 550 (1992), with Gregory E. Maggs, *Innovation in Constitutional Law: The Right to Education and the Tricks of the Trade*, 86 Nw. U. L. Rev. 1038 (1992).

c.   Is Equal Spending the Answer?

Even if the Supreme Court had concluded that everyone has a right to an equal education, would this conclusion necessarily have required all school districts to spend the same amount of money per student? Or are expenditures per pupil an incomplete measure of equality? A review of New York City's school districts found this startling result: "The amount of money spent per pupil is inversely related to academic performance, according to an analysis of spending in the city's 32 community school districts by *The New York Times*. The analysis * * * found that the best schools spent the least per pupil and had the most crowded classrooms." John Tierney, *"Money Per Pupil" Is an Incomplete Response*, N.Y. Times, Jun. 21, 2000, at B4. What might explain this result? How should governments promote equality in education if not through spending equal amounts of money?

If the Constitution does not protect a fundamental right to education, then presumably a state could constitutionally decline to provide it. But clearly it couldn't provide education to some but withhold it from others on the basis of their membership in a suspect class. Indeed, *Brown v. Board of Education* essentially held as much. But the Court has not recognized very many suspect classes. On what bases can a state withhold an education that it otherwise provides? The following case addresses whether a state can withhold an education from the children of undocumented immigrants.

PLYLER V. DOE

457 U.S. 202 (1982)

JUSTICE BRENNAN delivered the opinion of the Court.

The question presented by these cases is whether, consistent with the Equal Protection Clause of the Fourteenth Amendment, Texas may deny to undocumented school-age children the free public education that it provides to children who are citizens of the United States or legally admitted aliens. [Plaintiffs filed this class action on behalf of school-age children of Mexican origin who could not establish that they had been legally admitted into the United States.]

Food for Thought

Article III of the Constitution prohibits Congress from effecting a "Corruption of Blood," which means to withhold from the children of condemned adults the right to inherit property. Does this principle, broadly construed, apply here?

Persuasive arguments support the view that a State may withhold its beneficence from those whose very presence within the United States is the product of their own unlawful conduct. These arguments do not apply with the same force to classifications imposing disabilities on the minor *children* of such illegal entrants. [L]egislation directing the onus of a parent's misconduct against his children does not comport with fundamental conceptions of justice. * * * It is thus difficult to conceive of a rational justification for penalizing these children for their presence within the United States. Yet that appears to be precisely the effect of [Texas law].

Public education is not a "right" granted to individuals by the Constitution. *San Antonio Independent School Dist. v. Rodriguez,* 411 U.S. 1 (1973). But neither is it merely some governmental "benefit" indistinguishable from other forms of social welfare legislation. [E]ducation has a fundamental role in maintaining the fabric of our society. We cannot ignore the significant social costs borne by our Nation when select groups are denied the means to absorb the values and skills upon which our social order rests. In addition to the pivotal role of education in sustaining our political and cultural heritage, denial of education to some isolated group of children poses an affront to one of the goals of the Equal Protection Clause: the abolition of governmental barriers presenting unreasonable obstacles to advancement on the basis of individual merit. Paradoxically, by depriving the children of any disfavored group of an education, we foreclose the means by which that group might raise the level of esteem in which it is held by the majority. * * * By denying these children a basic education, we deny them the ability to live within the structure of our civic institutions, and foreclose any realistic possibility that they will contribute in even the smallest way to the progress of our Nation.

Undocumented aliens cannot be treated as a suspect class because their presence in this country in violation of federal law is not a "constitutional irrelevancy." Nor is education a fundamental right; a State need not justify by compelling necessity every variation in the manner in which education is provided to its population. [But in] determining the rationality of [Texas's education policy], we may appropriately take into account its costs to the Nation and to the innocent children who are its victims. In light of these countervailing costs, the discrimination [can] hardly be considered rational unless it furthers some substantial goal of the State.

We discern three colorable state interests that might support [the Texas policy.] First, appellants appear to suggest that the State may seek to protect itself from an influx of illegal immigrants. While a State might have an interest in mitigating the potentially harsh economic effects of sudden shifts in population, [the Texas policy] hardly offers an effective method of dealing with an urgent demographic or economic problem. * * * The dominant incentive for illegal entry into the State of Texas is the availability of employment; few if any illegal immigrants come to this country, or presumably to the State of Texas, in order to avail themselves of a free education. [Second,] appellants suggest that undocumented children are appropriately singled out for exclusion because of the special burdens they impose on the State's ability to provide high-quality public education. [But] even if improvement in the quality of education were a likely result of barring some *number* of children from the schools of the State, the State must support its selection of *this* group as the appropriate target for exclusion.

Finally, appellants suggest that undocumented children are appropriately singled out because their unlawful presence within the United States renders them less likely than other children to remain within the boundaries of the State, and to put their education to productive social or political use within the State. Even assuming that such an interest is legitimate, it is an interest that is most difficult to quantify. The State has no assurance that any child, citizen or not, will employ the education provided by the State within the confines of the State's borders. It is difficult to understand precisely what the State hopes to achieve by promoting the creation and perpetuation of a subclass of illiterates within our boundaries, surely adding to the problems and costs of unemployment, welfare, and crime. If the State is to deny a discrete group of innocent children the free public education that it offers to other children residing within its borders, that denial must be justified by a showing that it furthers some substantial state interest. No such showing was made here.

[The separate concurring opinions of JUSTICES MARSHALL, BLACKMUN, and POWELL are omitted.]

CHIEF JUSTICE BURGER, with whom JUSTICE WHITE, JUSTICE REHNQUIST, and JUSTICE O'CONNOR join, dissenting.

[T]he Court expressly—and correctly—rejects any suggestion that illegal aliens are a suspect class or that education is a fundamental right. Yet by patching together bits and pieces of what might be termed quasi-suspect-class and quasi-fundamental-rights analysis, the Court spins out a theory custom-tailored to the facts of these cases. * * * If ever a court was guilty of an unabashedly result-oriented approach, this case is a prime example.

[The] Equal Protection Clause does not preclude legislators from classifying among persons on the basis of factors and characteristics over which individuals may be said to lack "control." [A] state legislature is not barred from considering, for example, relevant differences between the mentally healthy and the mentally ill [simply] because these may be factors unrelated to individual choice or to any "wrongdoing." The Equal Protection Clause protects against arbitrary and irrational classifications, and against invidious discrimination stemming from prejudice and hostility; it is not an all-encompassing "equalizer" designed to eradicate every distinction for which persons are not "responsible."

The second strand of the Court's analysis rests on the premise that, although public education is not a constitutionally guaranteed right, "neither is it merely some governmental 'benefit' indistinguishable from other forms of social welfare legislation." Whatever meaning or relevance this opaque observation might have in some other context, it simply has no bearing on the issues at hand. * * * In *San Antonio Independent School Dist.*, [we] expressly rejected the proposition that state laws dealing with public education are subject to special scrutiny under the Equal Protection Clause. Moreover, the Court points to no meaningful way to distinguish between education and other governmental benefits in this context. Is the Court suggesting that education is more "fundamental" than food, shelter, or medical care? The Equal Protection Clause guarantees similar treatment of similarly situated persons, but it does not mandate a constitutional hierarchy of governmental services.

Once it is conceded—as the Court does—that illegal aliens are not a suspect class, and that education is not a fundamental right, our inquiry should focus on and be limited to whether the legislative classification at issue bears a rational relationship to a legitimate state purpose. * * * Without laboring what will undoubtedly seem obvious to many, it simply is not "irrational" for a state to conclude that it does not have the same responsibility to provide benefits for persons whose very presence in the state and this country is illegal as it does to provide for persons lawfully present. By definition, illegal aliens have no right whatever to be here, and the state may reasonably, and constitutionally, elect not to provide them with governmental services at the expense of those who are lawfully in the state.

Denying a free education to illegal alien children is not a choice I would make were I a legislator. Apart from compassionate considerations, the long-range costs of excluding any children from the public schools may well outweigh the costs of educating them. But that is not the issue; the fact that there are sound *policy* arguments against the Texas Legislature's choice does not render that choice an unconstitutional one. * * * Today's [decision], I regret to say, present[s] yet another example of unwarranted judicial action which in the long run tends to contribute to the weakening of our political processes.

POINTS FOR DISCUSSION

a.   Level of Scrutiny

What level of scrutiny did the Court apply in *Phyler*? The Court purported to measure the rationality of the challenged policy, but it also seemed to require that the classification further a "substantial state interest." Rational-basis review, in contrast, typically requires only that the policy bear a rational relationship to some legitimate state interest. Is the Court effectively applying heightened scrutiny, as it does in the context of gender discrimination? If so, is it because of the group disadvantaged by the classification? Or because education is a uniquely important benefit?

The three concurring opinions (which have been omitted here) advanced varying rationales for invalidating the policy. Justice Marshall emphasized his view that "an individual's interest in education is fundamental." Justice Blackmun compared the absolute deprivation of education, as opposed to the arguably inferior education that nevertheless was provided in *Rodriguez*, to a denial of the right to vote, and he asserted that "the State must offer something more than a rational basis for its classification." Justice Powell wrote to "emphasize the unique character" of the case before the Court, substantially agreeing with the analysis of the majority.

Does it make sense to view challenged state regulation as falling along a continuum, rather than as falling into fixed categories (such as rational-basis review or strict scrutiny) that virtually pre-ordain the outcome? Recall Justice Marshall's and Justice Stevens's opinions in *Cleburne v. Cleburne Living Center*, which we considered in Chapter 5. Is the Court effectively adopting their suggested approach without actually saying so?

b.   Immigration and the Constitution

The Constitution grants Congress the power to "establish an uniform Rule of Naturalization." Art. I., § 8, cl. 4. The Court has long held that there are strong reasons to conclude that Congress's authority over matters of immigration is not only plenary, but also exclusive:

The Federal Government, representing as it does the collective interests of [the] states, is entrusted with full and exclusive responsibility for the conduct of affairs with foreign sovereignties. * * * One of the most important and delicate of all international relationships, recognized immemorially as a responsibility of government, has to do with the protection of the just rights of a country's own nationals when those nationals are in another country. * * * Legal imposition of distinct, unusual and extraordinary burdens and obligations upon aliens [thus] bears an inseparable relationship to the welfare and tranquility of all the states, and not merely to the welfare and tranquility of one.

Hines v. Davidowitz, 312 U.S. 52 (1941).

Could the Court have resolved *Plyler* on this basis, by concluding that the Texas policy in effect impermissibly attempted to regulate matters—the status and rights of aliens—that are within the exclusive authority of Congress? This approach might have answered Chief Justice Burger's contention that the Court was "weakening our political process," because the appropriate political process for resolving matters relating to aliens is the one at the national level, not the ones in the individual states. But there would also be problems with this approach. For example, if the Court had taken such an approach, would Congress then have had authority to withhold federal education funds from states that permit children of undocumented aliens to attend public school? If so, would that conclusion be consistent with the Court's frequent assertion that "[e]qual protection analysis in the Fifth Amendment area is the same as that under the Fourteenth Amendment"? *Buckley v. Valeo,* 424 U.S. 1 (1976).

> **Make the Connection**
>
> We considered the application of the equal protection principle to the federal government, and the Court's decision in *Bolling v. Sharpe*, in Chapter 4.

c. Parents and Children

In treating illegitimate children as a suspect class under the Equal Protection Clause, the Court has reasoned that it is impermissible for a state to punish children for the actions of their parents. Do these cases provide support for the Court's conclusion in *Plyler?* Or would a better

> **Make the Connection**
>
> We considered discrimination on the basis of parents' marital status, and the Court's decision in *Clark v. Jeter*, in Chapter 5.

analogy be the state's presumed authority to deny welfare benefits to families—including families with children—as a result of the actions of the parents? Cf. *Dandridge v. Williams.*

C. ACCESS TO THE COURTS

Dandridge and *Rodriguez* seem to stand for the proposition that wealth is not a suspect basis for classification under the Equal Protection Clause. Yet *Harper,* which we considered earlier in this chapter, held that the state cannot condition the right to vote on the payment of a poll tax, because wealth "as a measure of a voter's qualifications" is "a capricious or irrelevant factor." The following case addresses whether a state can condition the availability of a civil appeal on the appellant's advance payment of costs. As you read the case, consider whether it is about wealth classifications, access to court, or instead something else.

M. L. B. v. S. L. J.

519 U.S. 102 (1996)

JUSTICE GINSBURG delivered the opinion of the Court.

Petitioner M. L. B. and respondent S. L. J. are, respectively, the [unmarried] biological mother and father of two children. [After S. L. J. married respondent J. P. J., they] filed suit in Chancery Court in Mississippi, seeking to terminate the parental rights of M. L. B. and to gain court approval for adoption of the children by their stepmother, J. P. J. [T]he Chancellor [terminated] all parental rights of the natural mother [and] approved the adoption. * * * Mississippi grants civil litigants a right to appeal, but conditions that right on prepayment of costs. * * * Unable to pay $2,352.36, M. L. B. sought leave to appeal *in forma pauperis*. The Supreme Court of Mississippi denied her application.

> **Definition**
>
> *In forma pauperis* means "in the manner of a pauper" and describes the permission given to an indigent person to proceed without liability for court fees or costs.

[T]he Court's decisions concerning access to judicial processes reflect both equal protection and due process concerns. The equal protection concern relates to the legitimacy of fencing out would-be appellants based solely on their inability to pay [costs]. The due process concern homes in on the essential fairness of the state-ordered proceedings anterior to adverse state action. * * * Nevertheless, "[m]ost decisions in this area [rest] on an equal protection framework," [for] due process does not independently require that the State provide a right to appeal. We place this case within the framework established by our past decisions in this area. In line with those decisions, we inspect the character and intensity of the individual interest at stake, on the one hand, and the State's justification for its exaction, on the other.

[T]he stakes for petitioner M. L. B.—forced dissolution of her parental rights—are large, "more substantial than mere loss of money." * * * And the risk of error, Mississippi's experience shows, is considerable. [Mississippi] has, by statute, adopted a "clear and convincing proof" standard for parental status termination cases. Nevertheless, the Chancellor's termination order in this case

Make the Connection

We considered the Constitution's protections for marriage and family in Chapter 2. If the petitioner's interest is in preserving a familial relationship, then isn't (substantive) Due Process a more appropriate basis for the Court's decision?

simply recites statutory language; it describes no evidence, and otherwise details no reasons for finding M. L. B. "clear[ly] and convincing[ly]" unfit to be a parent.

Mississippi urges, as the justification for its appeal cost prepayment requirement, the State's legitimate interest in offsetting the costs of its court system. But in the tightly circumscribed category of parental status termination cases, appeals are few, and not likely to impose an undue burden on the State. [W]e do not question the general rule [that] fee requirements ordinarily are examined only for rationality. The State's need for revenue to offset costs, in the mine run of cases, satisfies the rationality requirement. * * * But our cases solidly establish two exceptions to that general rule. The basic right to participate in political processes as voters and candidates cannot be limited to those who can pay for a license. [See *Harper v. Virginia Bd. of Elections*, 383 U.S. 663, 664 (1966).] Nor may access to judicial processes in cases criminal or "quasi criminal in nature" turn on ability to pay. [See *Griffin v. Illinois*, 351 U.S. 12, 16 (1956) (invalidating Illinois rule that conditioned appeals from criminal convictions on the defendant's procurement of a transcript of trial proceedings).] [W]e place decrees forever terminating parental rights in the category of cases in which the State may not "bolt the door to equal justice." * * * Accordingly, we reverse the judgment of the Supreme Court of Mississippi and remand the case for further proceedings not inconsistent with this opinion.

Food for Thought

Is this a case where the state is actively depriving a person of some important right, or instead a case where the state is simply declining to facilitate (or subsidize) a person's exercise of an important right? That is, does this case involve government action or government inaction? Should anything turn on that characterization?

JUSTICE KENNEDY, concurring in the judgment.

[In my view,] due process is quite a sufficient basis for our holding. I acknowledge the authorities do not hold that an appeal is required, even in a criminal case; but given the existing appellate structure in Mississippi, the realities of the litigation process, and the fundamental interests at stake in this particular proceeding, the State may not erect a bar in the form of transcript and filing costs beyond this petitioner's means.

JUSTICE THOMAS, with whom JUSTICE SCALIA joins, and with whom THE CHIEF JUSTICE joins [in relevant part], dissenting.

If neither [the Due Process or Equal Protection] Clause affords petitioner the right to a free, civil-appeal transcript, I assume that no amalgam of the two does. The majority reaffirms that due process does not require an appeal. * * * Due process has never compelled an appeal where, as here, its rigors are satisfied by an adequate hearing.

[W]e have regularly required more of an equal protection claimant than a showing that state action has a harsher effect on him or her than on others. * * * I see no principled difference between a facially neutral rule that serves in some cases to prevent persons from availing themselves of state employment, or a state-funded education, or a state-funded abortion—each of which the State may, but is not required to, provide—and a facially neutral rule that prevents a person from taking an appeal that is available only because the State chooses to provide it.

Mississippi's requirement of prepaid transcripts in civil appeals seeking to contest the sufficiency of the evidence adduced at trial is facially neutral; it creates no classification. The transcript rule reasonably obliges would-be appellants to bear the costs of availing themselves of a service that the State chooses, but is not constitutionally required, to provide. Any adverse impact that the transcript requirement has on any person seeking to appeal arises not out of the State's action, but out of factors entirely unrelated to it.

> **Food for Thought**
>
> Anatole France, a French writer, once quipped, "The law, in its majestic equality, forbids the rich as well as the poor to sleep under bridges, to beg in the streets, and to steal bread." Is that the sense in which the state's rule here is "facially neutral"? Is there a sense in which it is not neutral at all?

POINTS FOR DISCUSSION

a. Due Process v. Equal Protection

Does the Court base its decision on the Equal Protection Clause or the Due Process Clause? What if the underlying litigation had concerned a run-of-the-mill tort claim and the party who lost at trial was unable to appeal because of a cost-prepayment requirement? Would there be a constitutional problem then? If so, why? See *Pennzoil Co. v. Texaco, Inc.*, 481 U.S. 1, 7 & n. 6 (1987) (describing, but abstaining from deciding, a Due Process claim by oil giant Texaco that alleged that the company was effectively barred from appealing a massive tort judgment because the Texas courts would not stay the execution of a judgment lien, pending Texaco's appeal, unless Texaco secured a $13 billion bond).

b.   Wealth and Access to the Courts

As we saw above, the Court in *Dandridge* and *Rodriguez* effectively held that the poor are not a suspect class, or at least that wealth classifications ordinarily will not receive strict scrutiny. Is *M. L. B.* consistent with *Dandridge* and *Rodriguez?*

Executive Summary of This Chapter

As we saw in Chapter 2, the Court sometimes relies on the Due Process Clause to identify and protect "fundamental rights." The Court also sometimes relies on the Equal Protection Clause to assess the constitutionality of regulations that selectively affect the exercise of important or fundamental rights.

Because the **right to vote** is "fundamental," a state violates the Equal Protection Clause when it denies the right to vote on the basis of wealth or the voter's failure to pay a poll tax. *Harper v. Virginia State Board of Elections* (1966). The Equal Protection Clause might also require uniform standards for counting votes during recounts. *Bush v. Gore* (2000).

The Equal Protection Clause requires electoral districts at the local, state, and federal level to be apportioned based on the principle of **one person, one vote**. *Reynolds v. Sims* (1964). But claims that district lines have been drawn solely for the sake of partisan advantage—that is, claims of **political gerrymandering**—are non-justiciable political questions. *Rucho v. Common Cause* (2019).

A state does not violate the Equal Protection Clause when it limits the amount of welfare benefits that a large family may receive. *Dandridge v. Williams* (1970). Nor does a state violate the Equal Protection Clause when it creates a scheme that results in substantially less funding for poorer school districts than for wealthier school districts. *San Antonio Independent School District v. Rodriguez* (1973). These cases suggest that **classifications on the basis of wealth** are subject only to rational-basis review, and that there is no fundamental right to welfare or a free public school education.

A state does, however, violate the Equal Protection Clause when it denies a free public school education to undocumented children. *Phyler v. Doe* (1982). And a state violates the Equal Protection Clause when it conditions an indigent person's right to appeal an order terminating her parental rights on her ability to pre-pay the costs of the appeal. *M. L. B. v. S. L. J.* (1996).

PART III

Legislative Protection of Individual Rights

In Volume 1, we considered Congress's affirmative powers under Article I of the Constitution. We paid particularly close attention to the power to regulate interstate commerce, the power to spend for the general welfare, and the power to tax. In addition, we saw that Congress has power under the Necessary and Proper Clause to select the means for carrying into execution not only the affirmative powers granted to Congress, but also "all other Powers vested by this Constitution in the Government of the United States, or in any Department or Officer thereof." In considering the scope of these powers, the principal question was whether particular constructions of the provisions granting those powers impermissibly encroached on the powers of the states; the limits on Congress's power, in other words, were a function of federalism.

In the last several chapters, however, we have seen how the Constitution, through its rights-granting provisions, limits not only the power of the federal government but also the power of the state governments. Indeed, the Fourteenth Amendment, which has been our principal focus in the last six chapters, is an express limitation on the power of the states; it prohibits states from abridging the privileges or immunities of citizens of the United States, depriving any person of life, liberty, or property without due process of law, or denying equal protection of the laws. At the same time that it limits the powers of the states, the Fourteenth Amendment (in Section 5) confers on Congress the power "to enforce, by appropriate legislation, the provisions of this article."

In a very important sense, therefore, the Fourteenth Amendment—and, indeed, the Thirteenth and Fifteenth Amendments, the other two "Reconstruction Amendments"—are about federalism, as well. But the balance that the Reconstruction Amendments contemplate between state and federal authority appears to be quite different from the balance created in 1789. In many respects this is unsurprising, particularly when one considers the historical

Definition

The "Reconstruction Amendments" acquired their name because they were adopted during the Reconstruction Era, in which the Union was reconstituted after the Civil War.

background of the Amendments. The Thirteenth Amendment, which abolished slavery, was a sharp rebuke of the choice of Southern states before the Civil War to permit slavery. The Fourteenth Amendment was ratified three years after the Thirteenth, after it had become clear that the formal abolition of slavery had not stopped the former slave states from using legal means to subjugate Americans of African descent. And the Fifteenth Amendment was ratified two years after the Fourteenth, to prohibit those states from continuing to exclude former slaves from the political process to which they should have been welcomed upon the abolition of slavery. All three of the Reconstruction Amendments also authorized Congress to enforce their substantive provisions by "appropriate legislation." Viewed in this context, it seems plain that the Reconstruction Amendments worked a significant change in the relationship between the states and the federal government.

But just how significant a change was it? Is Congress's power under those Amendments plenary, notwithstanding the limits imposed on its powers by the original provisions of the Constitution? Does the Tenth Amendment modify the Reconstruction Amendments, serving as a rule of construction that makes clear that Congress shall have only those powers necessary to enforce the Amendments' substantive provisions? Or, conversely, do the Reconstruction Amendments modify the Tenth, effectively legitimating the vast expansion of federal power that the Court permitted in the middle of the twentieth century? And can Congress, acting pursuant to its power to enforce the Reconstruction Amendments, effectively define new rights and provide them with legislative protection? Or is the notion of "appropriate" enforcement legislation limited by the Court's interpretation of the rights protected by the substantive provisions of the Amendments? As we will see, these last two questions are as much about the separation of powers as they are about federalism. Indeed, although our consideration of the Reconstruction Amendments thus far has been principally about individual rights rather than structural arrangements, federalism and the

Make the Connection

Recall that the Court in the *Slaughter-House* Cases, which we considered in Chapter 1, interpreted the Privileges or Immunities Clause of the Fourteenth Amendment narrowly, effectively concluding that the Amendment did not work a significant change in the balance between state and federal power. Keep that view in mind as you explore the materials in this part.

separation of powers will never be far from the surface in our discussion here of Congress's power under those Amendments.

CHAPTER 7

Congress's Power to Enforce the Reconstruction Amendments

A. THE THIRTEENTH AMENDMENT

On January 1, 1863, President Lincoln issued the Emancipation Proclamation, an executive order that famously declared that "all persons held as slaves" in the states engaged in "rebellion against the United States" were "thenceforward [and] forever free." The Proclamation, however, did not fully accomplish the objective of ending slavery. First, there was some doubt as to the legal validity of the order, issued unilaterally by the President pursuant to his authority as Commander in Chief, and by its terms applying only to states that did not (at the time) recognize the authority of the United States. Second, the Proclamation applied only to those slave states that were engaged in rebellion against the United States, and thus did not provide protection to slaves in the border slave states that had remained loyal to the United States or in states that had seceded but had since been brought under Union control. Third, the Confederate States ignored the Proclamation during the war, and even after the war had ended, the former slave states enacted so-called "Black Codes," which imposed severe restrictions on the former slaves' freedom, thereby creating a new legal institution nearly tantamount to slavery.

In response, Congress enacted, and the states ratified, the Thirteenth Amendment to abolish formally and finally the institution of slavery and its equivalents. The southern states were required to ratify it as a condition of re-entry to the Union.

U.S. Constitution, Amendment XIII

Section 1.   Neither slavery nor involuntary servitude, except as a punishment for crime whereof the party shall have been duly convicted, shall exist within the United States, or any place subject to their jurisdiction.

Section 2.   Congress shall have power to enforce this article by appropriate legislation.

The Thirteenth Amendment is the only provision in the Constitution (with the possible exception of the Treason Clause in Article III, § 3) that regulates private, as opposed to governmental, conduct. It does not merely forbid state legal regimes that tolerate slavery, but also any form of slavery or involuntary servitude—which "shall not exist within the United States."

At the time of its ratification, the Thirteenth Amendment was unique for another reason: it was the first provision added since the ratification of the original document that expressly conferred a new power on Congress. Note that Section 2 of the Amendment authorizes Congress to "enforce" Section 1 of the Amendment "by appropriate legislation." Because Section 1 of the Amendment prohibits private action, Congress presumably has at least some authority under Section 2 to regulate some forms of private action. What limits are there on the scope of that power?

In 1866, shortly after the ratification of the Thirteenth Amendment, Congress enacted the Civil Rights Act over the veto of President Andrew Johnson, who asserted that the Act was unconstitutional. The next case, decided more than 100 years after the enactment of that law, raised the question of the scope of Congress's power under Section 2 of the Thirteenth Amendment.

JONES V. ALFRED H. MAYER CO.
392 U.S. 409 (1968)

MR. JUSTICE STEWART delivered the opinion of the Court.

In this case we are called upon to determine the scope and constitutionality of [part of the Civil Rights Act of 1866,] 42 U.S.C. § 1982, which provides that: "All citizens of the United States shall have the same right, in every State and Territory, as is enjoyed by white citizens thereof to inherit, purchase, lease, sell, hold, and convey real and personal property." [T]he petitioners [alleged] that the respondents had refused to sell them a home [for] the sole reason that petitioner Joseph Lee Jones is a Negro. Relying in part upon § 1982, the petitioners sought injunctive and other relief. The District Court sustained the respondents' motion to dismiss the complaint, and the Court of Appeals for the Eighth Circuit affirmed, concluding that § 1982 applies only to state action and does not reach private refusals to sell.

[The right to purchase and lease property] can be impaired as effectively by "those who place property on the market" as by the State itself. * * * So long as a Negro citizen who wants to buy or rent a home can be turned away simply because he is not white, he cannot be said to enjoy "the same right [as] is enjoyed by white citizens [to] purchase [and] lease [real] and personal property." On its face, therefore, § 1982 appears to prohibit all discrimination against Negroes in the sale or rental of property—discrimination by private owners as well as discrimination by public authorities. [Our] examination of the relevant history [persuades] us that Congress meant exactly what it said.

The remaining question is whether Congress has power under the Constitution to * * * prohibit all racial discrimination, private and public, in the sale and rental of property. Our starting point is the Thirteenth Amendment, for it was pursuant to that constitutional provision that Congress originally enacted what is now § 1982. * * * As its text reveals, the Thirteenth Amendment "is not a mere prohibition of state laws establishing or upholding slavery, but an absolute declaration that slavery or involuntary servitude shall not exist in any part of the United States." *Civil Rights Cases*, 109 U.S. 3, 20 (1883). It has never been doubted, therefore, "that the power vested in Congress to enforce the article by appropriate legislation" [includes] the power to enact laws "direct and primary, operating upon the acts of individuals, whether sanctioned by state legislation or not."

If Congress has power under the Thirteenth Amendment to eradicate conditions that prevent Negroes from buying and renting property because of their race or color, then no federal statute calculated to achieve that objective can be thought to exceed the constitutional power of Congress simply because it reaches beyond state action to regulate the conduct of private individuals. The constitutional question in this case, therefore, comes to this: Does the authority of Congress to enforce the Thirteenth Amendment "by appropriate legislation" include the power to eliminate all racial barriers to the acquisition of real and personal property? We think the answer to that question is plainly yes.

"By its own unaided force and effect," the Thirteenth Amendment "abolished slavery, and established universal freedom." Whether or not the Amendment itself did any more than that—a question not involved in this case— it is at least clear that the Enabling Clause of that Amendment empowered Congress to do much more. For that clause clothed "Congress with power to pass *all laws necessary and proper for abolishing all badges and incidents of slavery in the United*

Definition

The Court uses the term "badges and incidents of slavery" to capture the important idea that slavery was not merely a system in which slaves were owned as property. On the contrary, slaves lacked almost all civil and political rights enjoyed by non-slaves. They could not make contracts, marry, seek paid employment, and so forth. All of these disabilities are badges and incidents of slavery.

States." Civil Rights Cases, 109 U.S. at 20. * * * Surely Congress has the power under the Thirteenth Amendment rationally to determine what are the badges and the incidents of slavery, and the authority to translate that determination into effective legislation. Nor can we say that the determination Congress has made is an irrational one. For this Court recognized long ago that, whatever else they may have encompassed, the badges and incidents of slavery—its "burdens and disabilities"— included restraints upon "those fundamental rights which are the essence of civil freedom, namely, the same right [to] inherit, purchase, lease, sell and convey property, as is enjoyed by white citizens." [*Civil Rights Cases.*] Just as the Black Codes, enacted after the Civil War to restrict the free exercise of those rights, were substitutes for the slave system, so the exclusion of Negroes from white communities became a substitute for the Black Codes. And when racial discrimination herds men into ghettos and makes their ability to buy property turn on the color of their skin, then it too is a relic of slavery.

Negro citizens, North and South, who saw in the Thirteenth Amendment a promise of freedom—freedom to "go and come at pleasure" and to "buy and sell when they please"—would be left with "a mere paper guarantee" if Congress were powerless to assure that a dollar in the hands of a Negro will purchase the same thing as a dollar in the hands of a white man. At the very least, the freedom that Congress is empowered to secure under the Thirteenth Amendment includes the freedom to buy whatever a white man can buy, the right to live wherever a white man can live. If Congress cannot say

FYI

In 1865, all of the Southern former slave states adopted "Black Codes" that severely limited the civil, social, and political rights of former slaves. Among other things, the Codes typically defined the types of employment that blacks could hold and the terms under which they could hold their jobs, restrictions so severe in many cases that they amounted to a form of de facto slavery. Blacks were also denied the vote. In response to the Codes, Congress placed the South under military rule in 1866 to enforce "Reconstruction" and proposed the Fourteenth Amendment. For more information about the Black Codes and the reconstruction era, read Chapter 7 of the U.S. State Department's online Outline of U.S. History.

that being a free man means at least this much, then the Thirteenth Amendment made a promise the Nation cannot keep. [Reversed.]

[JUSTICE DOUGLAS's concurring opinion is omitted.]

In 1865, all of the Southern former slave states adopted "Black Codes" that severely limited the civil, social, and political rights of former slaves. Among other things, the Codes typically defined the types of employment that blacks could hold and the terms under which they could hold their jobs, restrictions so severe in many cases that they amounted to a form of de facto slavery. Blacks were also denied the vote. In response to the Codes, Congress placed the South under military rule in 1866 to enforce "Reconstruction" and proposed the Fourteenth Amendment. For more information about the Black Codes and the reconstruction era, read Chapter 7 of the U.S. State Department's online Outline of U.S. History.

MR. JUSTICE HARLAN, whom MR. JUSTICE WHITE joins, dissenting.

I believe that the Court's construction of § 1982 as applying to purely private action is almost surely wrong, and at the least is open to serious doubt. The [issue] of the constitutionality of § 1982, as construed by the Court, [also presents] formidable difficulties. Moreover, the political processes of our own era have, since the date of oral argument in this case, given birth to [the Civil Rights Act of 1968, which contains] "fair housing" provisions which would at the end of this year make available to others, though apparently not to the petitioners themselves, the type of relief which the petitioners now seek. It seems to me that this latter factor so diminishes the public importance of this case

> **Take Note**
>
> Justice Harlan seems implicitly to suggest here that the Civil Rights Act of 1968's regulation of private housing arrangements was within Congress's authority to enact. If that is true—either under Section 2 of the Thirteenth Amendment or the Commerce Clause—then why isn't § 1982, as well?

that by far the wisest course would be for this Court to refrain from decision and to dismiss the writ as improvidently granted.

POINTS FOR DISCUSSION

a. The Thirteenth Amendment and Civil Rights Legislation

> **Make the Connection**
>
> We consider *Heart of Atlanta Motel* and *McClung*, and Congress's power under the Commerce Clause to enact the Civil Rights Act of 1964, in Volume 1.

The Court concludes that Congress's power to enforce the Thirteenth Amendment includes the authority to eliminate the "badges and incident of slavery," which includes the power to enact civil rights legislation regulating certain types of private conduct. Recall that the Court held that provisions of the Civil Rights Act of 1964 that applied to private conduct were valid exercises of Congress's authority under the Commerce Clause. After *Jones*, isn't Section 2 of the Thirteenth Amendment a sufficient basis for all such legislation?

b.   The Thirteenth Amendment and Protected Groups

Conversely, in discussing the "Black Codes" and pervasive discrimination against blacks in the mid-twentieth century, does *Jones* suggest that Congress's power to enforce the Thirteenth Amendment is considerably less robust when what is at issue is discrimination against persons other than African Americans? Section 1 of the Amendment plainly prohibits slavery, regardless of the race of the servant and the master. See *Slaughter-House Cases*, 83 U.S. 36, 72 (1872) ("Undoubtedly while negro slavery alone was in the mind of the Congress which proposed the thirteenth article, it forbids any other kind of slavery, now or hereafter."). But is the scope of *Congress's* power under *Section 2* broader when providing remedies for discrimination against African Americans due to their prior condition of servitude?

B. THE FOURTEENTH AND FIFTEENTH AMENDMENTS

President Johnson's veto of the Civil Rights Act of 1866 reflected concerns over the scope of Congress's power to enforce the Thirteenth Amendment. In response, Congress proposed the Fourteenth Amendment in June 1866, and it achieved the requisite number of state ratifications two years later. As we have seen in some detail, the Fourteenth Amendment included the Privileges or Immunities, Due Process, and Equal Protection Clauses. In addition, in February 1869, Congress passed the Fifteenth Amendment, which would prohibit denying or abridging the right to vote on the basis of race, and it reached the requisite number of state ratifications one year later. As did the Thirteenth Amendment, both Amendments expressly authorized Congress to enforce their substantive provisions.

U.S. Constitution, Amendment XIV

Section 5.   The Congress shall have the power to enforce, by appropriate legislation, the provisions of this article.

U.S. Constitution, Amendment XV

Section 1.   The right of citizens of the United States to vote shall not be denied or abridged by the United States or by any State on account of race, color, or previous condition of servitude.

> **Section 2.**   The Congress shall have the power to enforce this article by appropriate legislation.

Unlike the Thirteenth Amendment, however, the Fourteenth and Fifteenth Amendments appear to address their substantive limitations only to the states. Indeed, the Court held shortly after the ratification of the Fourteenth Amendment that its provisions limit only state, and not private, action. (Accordingly, the Fourteenth Amendment does not prohibit, for example, a private employer from refusing to hire a person solely because of her race, although state and federal laws generally do prohibit such conduct.) Although the "state action doctrine" is controversial, it has important implications for the scope of Congress's power under the Fourteenth and Fifteenth Amendments. If those Amendments do not prohibit private action, can Congress invoke its power to enforce those Amendments to regulate private action?

> **Make the Connection**
>
> We consider the Court's decision in the *Civil Rights Cases*, 109 U.S. 3, 20 (1883), and the state-action requirement, in Volume 1.

UNITED STATES V. GUEST
383 U.S. 745 (1966)

MR. JUSTICE STEWART delivered the opinion of the Court.

The six defendants in this case were indicted by a United States grand jury in the Middle District of Georgia for criminal conspiracy in violation of 18 U.S.C. § 241 (1964 ed.), [which makes it a crime for "two or more persons [to] conspire to injure, oppress, threaten, or intimidate any citizen in the free exercise or enjoyment of any right or privilege secured to him by the Constitution or laws of the United States, or because of his having so exercised the same." The defendants had been prosecuted, but acquitted by an all-white jury, in state court for the murder of Lemuel Penn, an African-American reserve officer in the military who was shot while returning from active duty to Washington, D.C., where he was a teacher. Federal prosecutors then successfully obtained the indictment in question, charging the defendants with conspiring to deprive blacks of the right to use public state-owned and state-operated facilities in Athens, Georgia. The district court dismissed the indictment.]

[T]he indictment in the present case names no person alleged to have acted in any way under the color of state law. * * * It is a commonplace that rights under the Equal Protection Clause itself arise only where there has been involvement of the State or of one acting under the color of its authority.

This is not to say, however, that the involvement of the State need be either exclusive or direct. In a variety of situations the Court has found state action of a nature sufficient to create rights under the Equal Protection Clause even though the participation of the State was peripheral, or its action was only one of several co-operative forces leading to the constitutional violation. See, e.g., *Shelley v. Kraemer*, 334 U.S. 1 (1948). This case, however, requires no determination of the threshold level that state action must attain in order to create rights under the Equal Protection Clause. This is so because, contrary to the argument of the

> **Make the Connection**
>
> We discuss the Court's decision in *Shelley* in Volume 1.

litigants, the indictment in fact contains an express allegation of state involvement sufficient at least to require the denial of a motion to dismiss. One of the means of accomplishing the object of the conspiracy, according to the indictment, was "By causing the arrest of Negroes by means of false reports that such Negroes had committed criminal acts." [T]he allegation is broad enough to cover a charge of active connivance by agents of the State in the making of the "false reports," or other conduct amounting to official discrimination clearly sufficient to constitute denial of rights protected by the Equal Protection Clause. Although it is possible that a bill of particulars,

> **Definition**
>
> A "bill of particulars" is a "formal, detailed statement of the claims or charges brought by a plaintiff or a prosecutor, [usually] filed in response to the defendant's request for a more specific complaint." *Black's Law Dictionary* (10th ed. 2014).

or the proof if the case goes to trial, would disclose no co-operative action of that kind by officials of the State, the allegation is enough to prevent dismissal of this branch of the indictment. [Reversed and remanded.]

MR. JUSTICE CLARK, with whom MR. JUSTICE BLACK and MR. JUSTICE FORTAS join, concurring.

The Court's interpretation of the indictment clearly avoids the question whether Congress, by appropriate legislation, has the power to punish private conspiracies that interfere with Fourteenth Amendment rights, such as the right to utilize public facilities. [I]t is, I believe, both appropriate and necessary under the circumstances here to say that there now can be no doubt that the specific language of § 5 empowers the Congress to enact laws punishing all conspiracies—with or without state action—that interfere with Fourteenth Amendment rights.

MR. JUSTICE HARLAN, concurring in part and dissenting in part.

As a general proposition it seems to me very dubious that the Constitution was intended to create certain rights of private individuals as against other private individuals. The Constitutional Convention was called to establish a nation, not to reform the common law. Even the Bill of Rights, designed to protect personal liberties, was directed at rights against governmental authority, not other individuals. * * * I would sustain this aspect of the indictment only on the premise that it sufficiently alleges state interference with [constitutional rights], and on no other ground.

MR. JUSTICE BRENNAN, with whom THE CHIEF JUSTICE and MR. JUSTICE DOUGLAS join, concurring in part and dissenting in part.

I do not agree [that] a conspiracy to interfere with the exercise of the right to equal utilization of state facilities is not, within the meaning of § 241, a conspiracy to interfere with the exercise of a "right [secured] by the Constitution" unless discriminatory conduct by state officers is involved in the alleged conspiracy. * * * I believe that § 241 reaches [the private conspiracy alleged in the indictment], not because the Fourteenth Amendment of its own force prohibits such a conspiracy, but because § 241, as an exercise of congressional power under § 5 of that Amendment, prohibits *all* conspiracies to interfere with the exercise of a "right [secured] by the Constitution." [T]he right to use state facilities without discrimination on the basis of race is, within the meaning of § 241, a right created by, arising under and dependent upon the Fourteenth Amendment and hence is a right "secured" by that Amendment. * * *

My view as to the scope of § 241 requires that I reach the question of constitutional power—whether § 241 or legislation indubitably designed to punish entirely private conspiracies to interfere with the exercise of Fourteenth Amendment rights constitutes a permissible exercise of the power granted to Congress by § 5 * * *. A majority of the members of the Court expresses the view today that § 5 empowers Congress to enact laws punishing *all* conspiracies to interfere with the exercise of Fourteenth Amendment rights, whether or not state officers or others acting under the color of state law are implicated in the conspiracy. Although the Fourteenth Amendment itself, according to established doctrine, "speaks to the State or to those acting under the color of its authority," [§ 5] authorizes Congress to make laws that it concludes are reasonably necessary to protect a right created by and arising under that Amendment; and Congress is thus fully

> **Take Note**
>
> Justice Brennan states that a majority of the Court agrees that Section 5 of the Fourteenth Amendment empowers Congress to punish private, as opposed to state, action. (Two other Justices joined Justice Clark's concurring opinion to that effect.) After the Court's decision in *Guest*, must the government, in a prosecution under 18 U.S.C. § 241, prove state involvement in the conspiracy?

7

empowered to determine that punishment of private conspiracies interfering with the exercise of such a right is necessary to its full protection.

Viewed in its proper perspective, § 5 of the Fourteenth Amendment appears as a positive grant of legislative power, authorizing Congress to exercise its discretion in fashioning remedies to achieve civil and political equality for all citizens. No one would deny that Congress could enact legislation directing state officials to provide Negroes with equal access to state schools, parks and other facilities owned or operated by the State. Nor could it be denied that Congress has the power to punish state officers who, in excess of their authority and in violation of state law, conspire to threaten, harass and murder Negroes for attempting to use these facilities. And I can find no principle of federalism nor word of the Constitution that denies Congress power to determine that in order adequately to protect the right to equal utilization of state facilities, it is also appropriate to punish other individuals—not state officers themselves and not acting in concert with state officers—who engage in the same brutal conduct for the same misguided purpose.

POINTS FOR DISCUSSION

a.   The Fourteenth Amendment and Private Conduct

As noted above (and explored in more detail in Volume 1), the *Civil Rights Cases* held that Section 1 of the Fourteenth Amendment limits only state, as opposed to private, action. Assuming that the Court in that case properly interpreted the Fourteenth Amendment, does it follow that Congress cannot regulate purely private conduct pursuant to its authority to "enforce" Section 1 by "appropriate" legislation? Did the Court resolve that question in *Guest*? We will revisit this question later in this chapter, when we consider the Court's decision in *United States v. Morrison*.

b.   Other Sources of Authority

Would Congress's power to enforce the Thirteenth Amendment, which (we saw above) does apply to private action, be sufficient to prohibit private conspiracies of the type at issue in *Guest*, even if Congress lacks such power under Section 5 of the Fourteenth Amendment? How would 18 U.S.C. § 241 fare under the Court's approach in *Jones*?

The Thirteenth and Fourteenth Amendments are not the only conceivable sources of congressional authority to regulate private action to deprive individuals of constitutional rights. Recall that Congress enacted the Civil Rights Act of 1964 pursuant to its authority to regulate interstate commerce, and the Court upheld that assertion of authority in *Heart of Atlanta* and *McClung*.

> **Make the Connection**
>
> Recall that at least two Justices in *Heart of Atlanta* and *McClung* would have held that Congress had power to enact the provisions of the Civil Rights Act of 1964 that applied to places of public accommodations pursuant to its authority to enforce the Fourteenth Amendment. As you read the cases that follow, consider whether that view has prevailed.

Whatever limits exist on the scope of Congress's power to regulate *private* conduct pursuant to Section 5 of the Fourteenth Amendment, it clearly has power to create remedies for actual *state* violations of the substantive provisions of the Amendment. As the following case suggests, moreover, the Court has interpreted the enforcement provision of the Fifteenth Amendment in the same fashion that it has interpreted the analogous provision of the Fourteenth Amendment. What limits, if any, does the Constitution impose on Congress's power to regulate state action pursuant to those sources of authority?

SOUTH CAROLINA V. KATZENBACH

383 U.S. 301 (1966)

MR. CHIEF JUSTICE WARREN delivered the opinion of the Court.

South Carolina [seeks] a declaration that selected provisions of the Voting Rights Act of 1965 violate the Federal Constitution. * * * The Voting Rights Act was designed by Congress to banish the blight of racial discrimination in voting, which has infected the electoral process in parts of our country for nearly a century. * * * Congress assumed the power to prescribe these remedies from § 2 of the Fifteenth Amendment, which authorizes the National Legislature to effectuate by "appropriate" measures the constitutional prohibition against racial discrimination in voting. We hold that the sections of the Act which are properly before us are an appropriate means for carrying out Congress' constitutional responsibilities and are consonant with all other provisions of the Constitution.

Before enacting the measure, Congress explored with great care the problem of racial discrimination in voting. The House and Senate Committees on the Judiciary each held hearings for nine days and received testimony from a total of 67 witnesses. * * * Two points emerge vividly from the voluminous legislative history of the Act contained in the committee hearings and floor debates. First:

Congress felt itself confronted by an insidious and pervasive evil which had been perpetuated in certain parts of our country through unremitting and ingenious defiance of the Constitution. Second: Congress concluded that the unsuccessful remedies which it had prescribed in the past would have to be replaced by sterner and more elaborate measures in order to satisfy the clear commands of the Fifteenth Amendment.

[B]eginning in 1890, the States of Alabama, Georgia, Louisiana, Mississippi, North Carolina, South Carolina, and Virginia enacted tests still in use which were specifically designed to prevent Negroes from voting. Typically, they made the ability to read and write a registration qualification and also required completion of a registration form. These laws were based on the fact that as of 1890 in each of the named States, more than two-thirds of the adult Negroes were illiterate while less than one-quarter of the adult whites were unable to read or write. At the same time, alternate tests were prescribed in all of the named States to assure that white illiterates would not be deprived of the franchise. These included grandfather clauses, property qualifications, "good character" tests, and the requirement that registrants "understand" or "interpret" certain matter. [D]iscriminatory application of voting tests [is] now the principal method used to bar Negroes from the polls.

> **FYI**
>
> The obstacles that states imposed to voting as a means of disenfranchising blacks often, if applied neutrally, would have excluded many poor white voters, as well. "Grandfather clauses" exempted voters from these obstacles to voting if their grandfathers had voted. Because blacks (but not whites) were wholly disenfranchised two generations before the imposition of these tests, the grandfather clauses permitted poor whites to vote but not blacks.

The heart of the [Voting Rights Act] is a complex scheme of stringent remedies aimed at areas where voting discrimination has been most flagrant. [Among other things, the Act created a formula defining the states and political subdivisions—mainly places with a history of voting discrimination—to which these new remedies would apply; suspended literacy tests and similar voting qualifications for a period of five years; suspended all new voting regulations pending review by federal authorities to determine whether their use would perpetuate voting discrimination; and broadly prohibited, in all jurisdictions, the use of voting rules to abridge exercise of the franchise on racial grounds.]

These provisions of the Voting Rights Act of 1965 are challenged on the fundamental ground that they exceed the powers of Congress and encroach on an area reserved to the States by the Constitution. * * * The ground rules for resolving this question are clear. [As] against the reserved powers of the States,

Congress may use any rational means to effectuate the constitutional prohibition of racial discrimination in voting. * * * The Court [has] echoed [Chief Justice Marshall's language from *McCulloch v. Maryland*] in describing each of the Civil War Amendments: "Whatever legislation is appropriate, that is, adapted to carry out the objects the amendments have in view, whatever tends to enforce submission to the prohibitions they contain, and to secure to all persons the enjoyment of perfect equality of civil rights and the equal protection of the laws against State denial or invasion, if not prohibited, is brought within the domain of congressional power." *Ex parte Virginia*, 100 U.S. 339, 345–346 (1880). * * * We therefore reject South Carolina's argument that Congress may appropriately do no more than to forbid violations of the Fifteenth Amendment in general terms— that the task of fashioning specific remedies or of applying them to particular localities must necessarily be left entirely to the courts.

> **Take Note**
>
> The Court declares here that Congress's power to enforce the Fifteenth Amendment authorizes it to prohibit state actions that themselves would not violate Section 1 of the Amendment. Can you articulate why some of the practices prohibited by the Act do not violate the Fifteenth Amendment? Can Congress really be said to "enforce" the Amendment when it prohibits conduct that the Amendment itself permits?

South Carolina assails the temporary suspension of existing voting qualifications, reciting the rule laid down by *Lassiter v. Northampton County Bd. of Elections*, 360 U.S. 45 (1959), that literacy tests and related devices are not in themselves contrary to the Fifteenth Amendment. In that very case, however, the Court went on to say, "Of course a literacy test, fair on its face, may be employed to perpetuate that discrimination which the Fifteenth Amendment was designed to uproot." *Id.* at 53. The record shows that in most of the States covered by the Act, including South Carolina, various tests and devices have been instituted with the purpose of disenfranchising Negroes, have been framed in such a way as to facilitate this aim, and have been administered in a discriminatory fashion for many years. Under these circumstances, the Fifteenth Amendment has clearly been violated.

> **Food for Thought**
>
> Under the Court's view of Congress's enforcement powers, is it necessary that the literacy tests have been adopted for discriminatory purposes or administered in a discriminatory fashion? Under the Court's test, could Congress ban *all* voter-qualification tests, even those adopted for benign and legitimate purposes?

The Act suspends literacy tests and similar devices for a period of five years from the last occurrence of substantial voting discrimination. * * * Congress knew that continuance of the tests and devices in use at the present time, no matter how fairly administered in the future, would freeze the effect of past discrimination in favor of unqualified white registrants. Congress permissibly rejected the alternative of requiring a complete re-registration of all voters, believing that this would be too harsh on many whites who had enjoyed the franchise for their entire adult lives.

[The provision suspending new voting regulations pending scrutiny by federal authorities] may have been an uncommon exercise of congressional power, as South Carolina contends, but the Court has recognized that exceptional conditions can justify legislative measures not otherwise appropriate. Congress knew that some of the States covered by [the Act] had resorted to the extraordinary stratagem of contriving new rules of various kinds for the sole purpose of perpetuating voting discrimination in the face of adverse federal court decrees. Congress had reason to suppose that these States might try similar maneuvers in the future in order to evade the remedies for voting discrimination contained in the Act itself. Under the compulsion of these unique circumstances, Congress responded in a permissibly decisive manner.

After enduring nearly a century of widespread resistance to the Fifteenth Amendment, Congress has marshalled an array of potent weapons against the evil, with authority in the Attorney General to employ them effectively. We here hold that the portions of the Voting Rights Act properly before us are a valid means for carrying out the commands of the Fifteenth Amendment. Hopefully, millions of non-white Americans will now be able to participate for the first time on an equal basis in the government under which they live.

MR. JUSTICE BLACK, concurring [in part] and dissenting [in part].

I agree [that Section 2 of the Fifteenth Amendment] unmistakably gives Congress specific power to go further and pass appropriate legislation to protect [the] right to vote against any method of abridgement no matter how subtle. [I think, however, that the provision preventing a covered state from amending] its constitution or laws relating to voting without first trying to persuade the Attorney General of the United States or the Federal District Court for the District of Columbia that the new proposed laws do not have the purpose and will not have the effect of denying the right to vote to citizens on account of their race or color [is unconstitutional.]

[This provision], by providing that some of the States cannot pass state laws or adopt state constitutional amendments without first being compelled to beg federal authorities to approve their policies, so distorts our constitutional structure of government as to render any distinction drawn in the Constitution between state and federal power almost meaningless. One of the most basic premises upon which our structure of government was founded was that the Federal Government was to have certain specific and limited powers and no others, and all other power was to be reserved either "to the States respectively, or to the people." [If these premises] are to mean anything, they mean at least that the States have power to pass laws and amend their constitutions without first sending their officials hundreds of miles away to beg federal authorities to approve them. * * * It is inconceivable to me that such a radical degradation of state power was intended in any of the provisions of our Constitution or its Amendments.

The proceedings of the original Constitutional Convention show beyond all doubt that the power to veto or negative state laws was denied Congress. * * * The refusal to give Congress this extraordinary power to veto state laws was based on the belief that if such power resided in Congress the States would be helpless to function as effective governments. * * * Since that time neither the Fifteenth Amendment nor any other Amendment to the Constitution has given the slightest indication of a purpose to grant Congress the power to veto state laws either by itself or its agents. Nor does any provision in the Constitution endow the federal courts with power to participate with state legislative bodies in determining what state policies shall be enacted into law. * * * I would hold [the pre-clearance provision] invalid for the reasons stated above with full confidence that the Attorney General has ample power to give vigorous, expeditious and effective protection to the voting rights of all citizens.

POINTS FOR DISCUSSION

a. The Reconstruction Amendments and Federalism

The Voting Rights Act of 1965, of course, is addressed to the issue of discrimination in the grant of the franchise. But South Carolina argued its challenge to the Act largely in the language of federalism. The Fourteenth and Fifteenth Amendments contain express limitations on state authority and expressly confer additional powers upon Congress. How helpful are our understandings of the system of federalism created by the original Constitution in interpreting the Reconstruction Amendments?

Justice Black appeared to assert that the Fifteenth Amendment should be read in light of the Tenth Amendment and principles of federalism. But the Fifteenth Amendment was ratified later in time, after an era in which federalism was thought to give inadequate protection to racial minorities. In light of this fact, would it be more appropriate to read the Tenth Amendment in light of the Fifteenth Amendment? Or does the inclusion of express, new powers in the Thirteenth, Fourteenth, and

Fifteenth Amendments suggest an understanding that basic principles of federalism still prevailed and that the states would retain any powers not granted to Congress?

For example, we saw in Volume 1 that the Court has held that Congress lacks authority to compel the states to enact or administer a federal regulatory program. See *New York v. United States*; *Printz v. United States*. Does the Voting Rights Act violate this principle? If so, does that principle limit Congress's power to enforce the Reconstruction Amendments? Can you think of reasons why it should not?

b.   Selective Application

Some of the most stringent provisions of the Voting Rights Act apply only to states that had a history of discrimination in voting. Are there any limits on Congress's ability to apply legal norms to some states but not to others? Is there a risk that a majority of states will "gang up" on a small number of states? Or is the limited geographical application of some provisions of the Act evidence that it is more modest in scope, and thus more "appropriate" remedial legislation?

c.   Purpose and Effect

Recall that the Court has held that state action that has a racially discriminatory *effect* is not unconstitutional absent evidence of a discriminatory *purpose*. Under the Court's decision in *Katzenbach*, does Congress have authority under Section 2 of the Fifteenth Amendment to prohibit practices that were not adopted with a discriminatory purpose but that nevertheless have a discriminatory effect? Can legislation be said to "enforce" the Amendment when it prohibits conduct that is permissible under the substantive provisions of the Amendment?

Make the Connection

We considered discriminatory purpose and effect, and the Court's decision in *Washington v. Davis*, in Chapter 5.

The Court in *Katzenbach* upheld Section 5 of the Voting Rights Act, which requires all changes in election procedures in states where racial discrimination in voting was most pronounced to be pre-cleared by a three-judge federal district court or the Attorney General. Specifically, Section 5 applied to all election changes in states that had used a forbidden test or device in November 1964 and had less than 50% voter registration or turnout in the 1964 Presidential election. Section 5 was designed to ensure that states and localities with a history of discrimination could not change their election procedures to abridge the right to vote on the basis of race. As originally enacted, Section 5 was to remain in effect for only five years, but Congress extended the provision several times. The formula for determining which states are subject to the pre-clearance requirement remained the same, but Congress changed the pertinent date for assessing those criteria from 1964 to 1972. Most recently, in 2006 Congress extended Section 5 for another 25 years. The 2006 extension retained 1972 as the last baseline year for triggering coverage under Section 5.

Does Congress's power to enforce the Fifteenth Amendment authorize it to require pre-clearance *indefinitely* in states that historically discriminated on the basis of race? In *Northwest Austin Municipal Utility District Number One v. Holder*, 557 U.S. 193 (2009), a utility district in Texas, one of the states that is subject to the requirements under Section 5, filed suit seeking relief from the pre-clearance requirement. The Court acknowledged that the "historic accomplishments of the Voting Rights Act are undeniable," but it also noted that "[s]ome of the conditions that we relied upon in upholding this statutory scheme in *Katzenbach* [have] unquestionably improved." The Court noted that, in light of these changes, the Act's "preclearance requirements and its coverage formula raise serious constitutional questions." The Court declined to decide whether Section 5 of the Voting Rights Act was unconstitutional, however, because it concluded that a "bailout" provision in Section 5 allowed for the release of the utility district from the pre-clearance requirement. Four years later, the Court decided the case that follows, which squarely presented the question whether Section 5 is still constitutional.

SHELBY COUNTY, ALABAMA V. HOLDER
570 U.S. 529 (2013)

CHIEF JUSTICE ROBERTS delivered the opinion of the Court.

The Voting Rights Act of 1965 employed extraordinary measures to address an extraordinary problem. Section 5 of the Act required States to obtain federal permission before enacting any law related to voting—a drastic departure from basic principles of federalism. And § 4 of the Act applied that requirement only to some States—an equally dramatic departure from the principle that all States enjoy equal sovereignty. * * * The question is whether the Act's extraordinary measures, including its disparate treatment of the States, continue to satisfy constitutional requirements. As we put it a short time ago, "the Act imposes current burdens

Jurisdictions Covered by Section 4(b)
of the Voters Rights Act
House Judiciary Committee

and must be justified by current needs." *Northwest Austin Municipal Util. Dist. No. One v. Holder,* 557 U.S. 193, 203 (2009).

The Fifteenth Amendment was ratified in 1870, in the wake of the Civil War. It provides that "[t]he right of citizens of the United States to vote shall not be denied or abridged by the United States or by any State on account of race, color, or previous condition of servitude," and it gives Congress the "power to enforce this article by appropriate legislation."

"The first century of congressional enforcement of the Amendment, however, can only be regarded as a failure." *Id.,* at 197. In the 1890s, Alabama, Georgia, Louisiana, Mississippi, North Carolina, South Carolina, and Virginia began to enact literacy tests for voter registration and to employ other methods designed to prevent African-Americans from voting. *South Carolina v. Katzenbach,* 383 U.S. 301, 310 (1966). Congress passed statutes outlawing some of these practices and facilitating litigation against them, but litigation remained slow and expensive, and the States came up with new ways to discriminate as soon as existing ones were struck down. Voter registration of African-Americans barely improved. *Id.,* at 313–314.

Inspired to action by the civil rights movement, Congress responded in 1965 with the Voting Rights Act. Section 2 was enacted to forbid, in all 50 States, any * * * "standard, practice, or procedure" that "results in a denial or abridgement of the right of any citizen of the United States to vote on account of race or color." 42 U.S.C. § 1973(a). * * * Section 2 is permanent, applies nationwide, and is not at issue in this case.

Other sections targeted only some parts of the country. At the time of the Act's passage, these "covered" jurisdictions were those States or political subdivisions that had maintained a test or device as a prerequisite to voting as of November 1, 1964, and had less than 50 percent voter registration or turnout in the 1964 Presidential election. § 4(b), 79 Stat. 438. Such tests or devices included literacy and knowledge tests, good moral character requirements, the need for vouchers from registered voters, and the like. § 4(c), *id.,* at 438–439. A covered jurisdiction could "bail out" of coverage if it had not used a test or device in the preceding five years "for the purpose or with the effect of denying or abridging the right to vote on account of race or color." § 4(a), *id.,* at 438. In 1965, the covered States included Alabama, Georgia, Louisiana, Mississippi, South Carolina, and Virginia. The additional covered subdivisions included 39 counties in North Carolina and one in Arizona. See 28 CFR pt. 51, App. (2012).

In those jurisdictions, § 4 of the Act banned all such tests or devices. § 4(a), 79 Stat. 438. Section 5 provided that no change in voting procedures could take effect until it was approved by federal authorities in Washington, D.C.—either the Attorney General or a court of three judges. *Id.,* at 439. A jurisdiction could obtain such "preclearance" only by proving that the change had neither "the purpose [nor] the effect of denying or abridging the right to vote on account of race or color." *Ibid.*

Sections 4 and 5 were intended to be temporary; they were set to expire after five years. See § 4(a), *id.,* at 438. In *South Carolina v. Katzenbach,* we upheld the 1965 Act against constitutional challenge, explaining that it was justified to address "voting discrimination where it persists on a pervasive scale." 383 U.S., at 308. In 1970, Congress reauthorized the Act for another five years, and extended the coverage formula in § 4(b) to jurisdictions that had a voting test and less than 50 percent voter registration or turnout as of 1968. Voting Rights Act Amendments of 1970, §§ 3–4, 84 Stat. 315. That swept in several counties in California, New Hampshire, and New York. * * * In 1975, Congress reauthorized the Act for seven more years, and extended its coverage to jurisdictions that had a voting test and less than 50 percent voter registration or turnout as of 1972. Voting Rights Act Amendments of 1975, §§ 101, 202, 89 Stat. 400, 401. Congress also amended the definition of "test or device" to include the practice of providing English-only voting materials in places where over five percent of voting-age citizens spoke a single language other than English. § 203, *id.,* at 401–402. As a result of these amendments, the States of Alaska, Arizona, and Texas, as well as several counties in California, Florida, Michigan, New York, North Carolina, and South Dakota, became covered jurisdictions. * * * In 1982, Congress reauthorized the Act for 25 years, but did not alter its coverage formula. See Voting Rights Act Amendments, 96 Stat. 131. * * * We upheld each of these reauthorizations against constitutional challenge. See *Georgia v. United States,* 411 U.S. 526 (1973); *City of Rome v. United States,* 446 U.S. 156 (1980); *Lopez v. Monterey County,* 525 U.S. 266 (1999).

In 2006, Congress again reauthorized the Voting Rights Act for 25 years, again without change to its coverage formula. 120 Stat. 577. Congress also amended § 5 to prohibit more conduct than before. Section 5 now forbids voting changes with "any discriminatory purpose" as well as voting changes that diminish the ability of citizens, on account of race, color, or language minority status, "to elect their preferred candidates of choice." 42 U.S.C. §§ 1973c(b)–(d).

Shelby County is located in Alabama, a covered jurisdiction. It has not sought bailout, as the Attorney General has recently objected to voting changes proposed from within the county. Instead, in 2010, the county sued the Attorney General

---

Food for Thought

The Court notes that recently proposed voting changes in Shelby County had triggered concerns under section 5 of the Voting Rights Act, which permitted pre-clearance only of voting changes that do not have the purpose or effect of denying or abridging the right to vote on the basis of race. In light of this recent history, would the County have prevailed in an as-applied challenge to the coverage formula under section 4? If not, should it have been permitted to maintain a facial challenge against the provision?

---

in Federal District Court in Washington, D.C., seeking a declaratory judgment that sections 4(b) and 5 of the Voting Rights Act are facially unconstitutional, as well as a permanent injunction against their enforcement. The District Court ruled against the county and [the Court of Appeals affirmed].

The Constitution and laws of the United States are "the supreme Law of the Land." U.S. Const., Art. VI, cl. 2. State legislation may not contravene federal law. The Federal Government does not, however, have a general right to review and veto state enactments before they go into effect. A proposal to grant such authority to "negative" state laws was considered at the Constitutional Convention, but rejected in favor of allowing state laws to take effect, subject to later challenge under the Supremacy Clause. See 1 Records of the Federal Convention of 1787, pp. 21, 164–168 (M. Farrand ed.1911); 2 *id.,* at 27–29, 390–392.

Outside the strictures of the Supremacy Clause, States retain broad autonomy in structuring their governments and pursuing legislative objectives. * * * More specifically, " 'the Framers of the Constitution intended the States to keep for themselves, as provided in the Tenth Amendment, the power to regulate elections.' " *Gregory v. Ashcroft,* 501 U.S. 452, 461–462 (1991). Of course, the Federal Government retains significant control over federal elections. [See, e.g., Art. I, § 4, cl. 1.] But States have "broad powers to determine the conditions under which the right of suffrage may be exercised." *Carrington v. Rash,* 380 U.S. 89, 91 (1965). And "[e]ach State has the power to prescribe the qualifications of its officers and the manner in which they shall be chosen." *Boyd v. Nebraska ex rel. Thayer,* 143 U.S. 135, 161 (1892). Drawing lines for congressional districts is likewise "primarily the duty and responsibility of the State." *Perry v. Perez,* 132 S.Ct. 934, 940 (2012) (*per curiam*).

Not only do States retain sovereignty under the Constitution, there is also a "fundamental principle of *equal* sovereignty" among the States. *Northwest Austin, supra,* at 203. Over a hundred years ago, this Court explained that our Nation "was and is a union of States, equal in power, dignity and authority." *Coyle v. Smith,* 221 U.S. 559, 567 (1911). Indeed, "the constitutional equality of the States is essential to the harmonious operation of the scheme upon which the Republic was organized." *Id.,* at 580. *Coyle* concerned the admission of new States, and *Katzenbach* rejected the notion that the principle operated as a *bar* on differential treatment outside that context. 383 U.S., at 328–329. At the same time, as we made clear in *Northwest Austin,* the fundamental principle of equal sovereignty remains highly pertinent in assessing subsequent disparate treatment of States. 557 U.S., at 203.

The Voting Rights Act sharply departs from these basic principles. It suspends "*all* changes to state election law—however innocuous—until they have been precleared by federal authorities in Washington, D. C." *Id.,* at 202. States must beseech the Federal Government for permission to implement laws that they would otherwise have the right to enact and execute on their own, subject of course to any injunction in a § 2 action. The Attorney General has 60 days to object to a preclearance request, longer if he requests more information. If a State seeks preclearance from a three-judge court, the process can take years.

And despite the tradition of equal sovereignty, the Act applies to only nine States (and several additional counties). While one State waits months or years and expends funds to implement a validly enacted law, its neighbor can typically put the same law into effect immediately, through the normal legislative process. * * *

In 1966, we found these departures from the basic features of our system of government justified. The "blight of racial discrimination in voting" had "infected the electoral process in parts of our country for nearly a century." *Katzenbach,* 383 U.S., at 308. Several States had enacted a variety of requirements and tests "specifically designed to prevent" African-Americans from voting. *Id.,* at 310. Case-by-case litigation had proved inadequate to prevent such racial discrimination in voting, in part because States "merely switched to discriminatory devices not covered by the federal decrees," "enacted difficult new tests," or simply "defied and evaded court orders." *Id.,* at 314. Shortly before enactment of the Voting Rights Act, only 19.4 percent of African-Americans of voting age were registered to vote in Alabama, only 31.8 percent in Louisiana, and only 6.4 percent in Mississippi. *Id.,* at 313. Those figures were roughly 50 percentage points or more below the figures for whites. *Ibid.*

In short, we concluded that "[u]nder the compulsion of these unique circumstances, Congress responded in a permissibly decisive manner." *Id.,* at 334, 335. * * * At the time, the coverage formula—the means of linking the exercise of the unprecedented authority with the problem that warranted it—made sense. We found that "Congress chose to limit its attention to the geographic areas where immediate action seemed necessary." *Katzenbach,* 383 U.S., at 328. The areas where Congress found "evidence of actual voting discrimination" shared two characteristics: "the use of tests and devices for voter registration, and a voting rate in the 1964 presidential election at least 12 points below the national average." *Id.,* at 330. We explained that "[t]ests and devices are relevant to voting discrimination because of their long history as a tool for perpetrating the evil; a low voting rate is pertinent for the obvious reason that widespread disenfranchisement must inevitably affect the number of actual voters." *Ibid.* We therefore concluded that "the coverage formula [was] rational in both practice and theory." *Ibid.* * * *

Nearly 50 years later, things have changed dramatically. Shelby County contends that the preclearance requirement, even without regard to its disparate coverage, is now unconstitutional. Its arguments have a good deal of force. In the covered jurisdictions, "[v]oter turnout and registration rates now approach parity. Blatantly discriminatory evasions of federal decrees are rare. And minority candidates hold office at unprecedented levels." *Northwest Austin,* 557 U.S., at 202. The tests and devices that blocked access to the ballot have been forbidden nationwide for over 40 years.

Census Bureau data from the most recent election indicate that African-American voter turnout exceeded white voter turnout in five of the six States originally covered by § 5, with a gap in the sixth State of less than one half of one percent. The preclearance statistics are also illuminating. In the first decade after enactment of § 5, the Attorney General objected to 14.2 percent of proposed voting changes. In the last decade before reenactment, the Attorney General objected to a mere 0.16 percent.

There is no doubt that these improvements are in large part *because of* the Voting Rights Act. The Act has proved immensely successful at redressing racial discrimination and integrating the voting process. * * * Problems [remain], but there is no denying that, due to the Voting Rights Act, our Nation has made great strides. Yet the Act has not eased the restrictions in § 5 or narrowed the scope of the coverage formula in § 4(b) along the way. Those extraordinary and unprecedented features were reauthorized—as if nothing had changed. In fact, the Act's unusual remedies have grown even stronger. * * *

Respondents do not deny that there have been improvements on the ground, but argue that much of this can be attributed to the deterrent effect of § 5, which dissuades covered jurisdictions from engaging in discrimination that they would resume should § 5 be struck down. Under this theory, however, § 5 would be effectively immune from scrutiny; no matter how "clean" the record of covered jurisdictions, the argument could always be made that it was deterrence that accounted for the good behavior.

The provisions of § 5 apply only to those jurisdictions singled out by § 4. * * * When upholding the constitutionality of the coverage formula in 1966, we concluded that it was "rational in both practice and theory." *Katzenbach,* 383 U.S., at 330. The formula looked to cause (discriminatory tests) and effect (low voter registration and turnout), and tailored the remedy (preclearance) to those jurisdictions exhibiting both. By 2009, however, we concluded that the "coverage formula raise[d] serious constitutional questions." *Northwest Austin,* 557 U.S., at 204. As we explained, a statute's "current burdens" must be justified by "current needs," and any "disparate geographic coverage" must be "sufficiently related to the problem that it targets." *Id.,* at 203. The coverage formula met that test in 1965, but no longer does so.

Coverage today is based on decades-old data and eradicated practices. * * * In 1965, the States could be divided into two groups: those with a recent history of voting tests and low voter registration and turnout, and those without those characteristics. Congress based its coverage formula on that distinction. Today the Nation is no longer divided along those lines, yet the Voting Rights Act continues to treat it as if it were.

The Government [argues] that because the formula was relevant in 1965, its continued use is permissible so long as any discrimination remains in the States Congress identified back then—regardless of how that discrimination compares to discrimination in States unburdened by coverage. This argument does not look to "current political conditions," *Northwest Austin, supra,* at 203, but instead relies on a comparison between the States in 1965. That comparison reflected the different histories of the North and South. It was in the South that slavery was upheld by law until uprooted by the Civil War, that the reign of Jim Crow denied African-Americans the most basic freedoms, and that state and local governments worked tirelessly to disenfranchise citizens on the basis of race. The Court invoked that history—rightly so—in sustaining the disparate coverage of the Voting Rights Act in 1966.

But history did not end in 1965. By the time the Act was reauthorized in 2006, there had been 40 more years of it. In assessing the "current need[ ]" for a preclearance system that treats States differently from one another today, that history cannot be ignored. During that time, largely because of the Voting Rights Act, voting tests were abolished, disparities in voter registration and turnout due to race were erased, and African-Americans attained political office in record numbers. And yet the coverage formula that Congress reauthorized in 2006 ignores these developments, keeping the focus on decades-old data relevant to decades-old problems, rather than current data reflecting current needs. The

Fifteenth Amendment * * * is not designed to punish for the past; its purpose is to ensure a better future. To serve that purpose, Congress—if it is to divide the States—must identify those jurisdictions to be singled out on a basis that makes sense in light of current conditions. It cannot rely simply on the past. * * *

In defending the coverage formula, the Government, the intervenors, and the dissent also rely heavily on data from the record that they claim justify disparate coverage. Congress compiled thousands of pages of evidence before reauthorizing the Voting Rights Act. The court below and the parties have debated what that record shows * * *. Regardless of how to look at the record, however, no one can fairly say that it shows anything approaching the "pervasive," "flagrant," "widespread," and "rampant" discrimination that faced Congress in 1965, and that clearly distinguished the covered jurisdictions from the rest of the Nation at that time. *Katzenbach, supra,* at 308, 315, 331.

But a more fundamental problem remains: Congress did not use the record it compiled to shape a coverage formula grounded in current conditions. It instead reenacted a formula based on 40-year-old facts having no logical relation to the present day. The dissent relies on "second-generation barriers," which are not impediments to the casting of ballots, but rather electoral arrangements that affect the weight of minority votes. That does not cure the problem. Viewing the preclearance requirements as targeting such efforts simply highlights the irrationality of continued reliance on the § 4 coverage formula, which is based on voting tests and access to the ballot, not vote dilution. We cannot pretend that we are reviewing an updated statute, or try our hand at updating the statute ourselves, based on the new record compiled by Congress. Contrary to the dissent's contention, we are not ignoring the record; we are simply recognizing that it played no role in shaping the statutory formula before us today.

* * * If Congress had started from scratch in 2006, it plainly could not have enacted the present coverage formula. It would have been irrational for Congress to distinguish between States in such a fundamental way based on 40-year-old data, when today's statistics tell an entirely different story. And it would have been irrational to base coverage on the use of voting tests 40 years ago, when such tests have been illegal since that time. But that is exactly what Congress has done.

Striking down an Act of Congress "is the gravest and most delicate duty that this Court is called on to perform." *Blodgett v. Holden,* 275 U.S. 142, 148 (1927) (Holmes, J., concurring). We do not do so lightly. That is why, in 2009, we took care to avoid ruling on the constitutionality of the Voting Rights Act when asked to do so, and instead resolved the case then before us on statutory grounds. But in issuing that decision, we expressed our broader concerns about the constitutionality of the Act. Congress could have updated the coverage formula at that time, but did not do so. Its failure to act leaves us today with no choice but to declare § 4(b) unconstitutional. The formula in that section can no longer be used as a basis for subjecting jurisdictions to preclearance.

Our decision in no way affects the permanent, nationwide ban on racial discrimination in voting found in § 2. We issue no holding on § 5 itself, only on the coverage formula. Congress may draft another formula based on current conditions. * * * Our country has changed, and while any racial discrimination in voting is too much, Congress must ensure that the legislation it passes to remedy that problem speaks to current conditions. [Reversed.]

JUSTICE THOMAS, concurring.

I join the Court's opinion in full but write separately to explain that I would find § 5 of the Voting Rights Act unconstitutional as well. * * * "The extensive pattern of discrimination that led the Court to previously uphold § 5 as enforcing the Fifteenth Amendment no longer exists." *Northwest Austin, supra,* at 226 (THOMAS, J., concurring in judgment in part and dissenting in part). Section 5 is, thus, unconstitutional. * * * By leaving the inevitable conclusion unstated, the Court needlessly prolongs the demise of that provision. For the reasons stated in the Court's opinion, I would find § 5 unconstitutional.

JUSTICE GINSBURG, with whom JUSTICE BREYER, JUSTICE SOTOMAYOR, and JUSTICE KAGAN join, dissenting.

In the Court's view, the very success of § 5 of the Voting Rights Act demands its dormancy. Congress was of another mind. Recognizing that large progress has been made, Congress determined, based on a voluminous record, that the scourge of discrimination was not yet extirpated. The question this case presents is who decides whether, as currently operative, § 5 remains justifiable,[1] this Court, or a Congress charged with the obligation to enforce the post-Civil War Amendments "by appropriate legislation." With overwhelming support in both Houses, Congress concluded that, for two prime reasons, § 5 should continue in force, unabated. First, continuance would facilitate completion of the impressive gains thus far made; and second, continuance would guard against backsliding. Those assessments were well within Congress' province to make and should elicit this Court's unstinting approbation.

* * * Although the VRA wrought dramatic changes in the realization of minority voting rights, the Act, to date, surely has not eliminated all vestiges of

---

[1]   The Court purports to declare unconstitutional only the coverage formula set out in § 4(b). But without that formula, § 5 is immobilized.

discrimination against the exercise of the franchise by minority citizens. Jurisdictions covered by the preclearance requirement continued to submit, in large numbers, proposed changes to voting laws that the Attorney General declined to approve, auguring that barriers to minority voting would quickly resurface were the preclearance remedy eliminated. *City of Rome v. United States,* 446 U.S. 156, 181 (1980). Congress also found that as "registration and voting of minority citizens increas[ed], other measures may be resorted to which would dilute increasing minority voting strength." *Ibid.* Efforts to reduce the impact of minority votes, in contrast to direct attempts to block access to the ballot, are aptly described as "second-generation barriers" to minority voting.

Second-generation barriers come in various forms. One of the blockages is racial gerrymandering, the redrawing of legislative districts in an "effort to segregate the races for purposes of voting." *Id.,* at 642. Another is adoption of a system of at-large voting in lieu of district-by-district voting in a city with a sizable black minority. By switching to at-large voting, the overall majority could control the election of each city council member, effectively eliminating the potency of the minority's votes. * * * Whatever the device employed, this Court has long recognized that vote dilution, when adopted with a discriminatory purpose, cuts down the right to vote as certainly as denial of access to the ballot.

In response to evidence of these substituted barriers, Congress reauthorized the VRA for five years in 1970, for seven years in 1975, and for 25 years in 1982. Each time, this Court upheld the reauthorization as a valid exercise of congressional power. As the 1982 reauthorization approached its 2007 expiration date, Congress again considered whether the VRA's preclearance mechanism remained an appropriate response to the problem of voting discrimination in covered jurisdictions. Congress did not take this task lightly. * * * The House and Senate Judiciary Committees held 21 hearings, heard from scores of witnesses, received a number of investigative reports and other written documentation of continuing discrimination in covered jurisdictions. In all, the legislative record Congress compiled filled more than 15,000 pages. * * *

After considering the full legislative record, Congress made the following findings: The VRA has directly caused significant progress in eliminating first-generation barriers to ballot access, leading to a marked increase in minority voter registration and turnout and the number of minority elected officials. 2006 Reauthorization § 2(b)(1). But despite this progress, "second generation barriers constructed to prevent minority voters from fully participating in the electoral process" continued to exist, as well as racially polarized voting in the covered jurisdictions, which increased the political vulnerability of racial and language minorities in those jurisdictions. §§ 2(b)(2)–(3), 120 Stat. 577. * * * The overall record demonstrated to the federal lawmakers that, "without the continuation of the Voting Rights Act of 1965 protections, racial and language minority citizens will be deprived of the opportunity to exercise their right to vote, or will have their votes diluted, undermining the significant gains made by minorities in the last 40 years." § 2(b)(9), *id.,* at 578.

Based on these findings, Congress reauthorized preclearance for another 25 years, while also undertaking to reconsider the extension after 15 years to ensure that the provision was still necessary and effective. 42 U.S.C. § 1973b(a)(7), (8) (2006 ed., Supp. V). The question before the Court is whether Congress had the authority under the Constitution to act as it did.

* * * It is well established that Congress' judgment regarding exercise of its power to enforce the Fourteenth and Fifteenth Amendments warrants substantial deference. * * * The basis for this deference is firmly rooted in both constitutional text and precedent. The Fifteenth Amendment, which targets precisely and only racial discrimination in voting rights, states that, in this domain, "Congress shall have power to enforce this article by appropriate legislation." In choosing this language, the Amendment's framers invoked Chief Justice Marshall's formulation of the scope of Congress' powers under the Necessary and Proper Clause:

> "Let the end be legitimate, let it be within the scope of the constitution, and *all means which are appropriate, which are plainly adapted to that end,* which are not prohibited, but consist with the letter and spirit of the constitution, are constitutional." *McCulloch v. Maryland,* 4 Wheat. 316, 421 (1819) (emphasis added).

[W]hen Congress acts to enforce the right to vote free from racial discrimination, we ask not whether Congress has chosen the means most wise, but whether Congress has rationally selected means appropriate to a legitimate end. [*South Carolina v. Katzenbach,* 383 U.S., at 324; *City of Rome,* 446 U.S., at 178.]

The 2006 reauthorization of the Voting Rights Act fully satisfies [this] standard * * *. The surest way to evaluate whether that remedy remains in order is to see if preclearance is still effectively preventing discriminatory changes to voting laws. On that score, the record before Congress was huge. In fact, Congress found there were *more* DOJ objections between 1982 and 2004 (626) than there were between 1965 and the 1982 reauthorization (490). All told, between 1982 and 2006, DOJ objections blocked over 700 voting changes based on a determination that the changes were discriminatory. Congress found that the majority of DOJ objections included findings of discriminatory intent, and that the changes blocked by preclearance were "calculated decisions to keep minority voters from fully participating in the political process." H.R. Rep. 109–478, at 21. On top of that, over the same time period the DOJ and private plaintiffs succeeded in more than 100 actions to enforce the § 5 preclearance requirements. * * * The number of discriminatory changes blocked or deterred by the preclearance requirement suggests that the state of voting rights in the covered jurisdictions would have been significantly different absent this remedy.

There is no question, moreover, that the covered jurisdictions have a unique history of problems with racial discrimination in voting. Consideration of this long history, still in living memory, was altogether appropriate. The Court criticizes Congress for failing to recognize that "history did not end in 1965." But the Court ignores that "what's past is prologue." W. Shakespeare, The Tempest, act 2, sc. 1. And "[t]hose who cannot remember the past are condemned to repeat it." 1 G. Santayana, The Life of Reason 284 (1905). Congress was especially mindful of the need to reinforce the gains already made and to prevent backsliding.

Of particular importance, even after 40 years and thousands of discriminatory changes blocked by preclearance, conditions in the covered jurisdictions demonstrated that the formula was still justified by "current needs." *Northwest Austin,* 557 U.S., at 203. Congress learned of these conditions through a report, known as the Katz study, that looked at § 2 suits between 1982 and 2004.

> **FYI**
>
> Section 2 of the Voting Rights Act applies nationwide and prohibits voting rules or requirements that deny or abridge the right to vote on the basis of race. Section 2 is generally enforced in court proceedings initiated by voters claiming disenfranchisement or by the United States. Unlike Section 5, it is enforced after the voting requirement has been enacted or imposed.

* * * Although covered jurisdictions account for less than 25 percent of the country's population, the Katz study revealed that they accounted for 56 percent of successful § 2 litigation since 1982. Controlling for population, there were nearly *four* times as many successful § 2 cases in covered jurisdictions as there were in noncovered jurisdictions. The Katz study further found that § 2 lawsuits are more likely to succeed when they are filed in covered jurisdictions than in noncovered jurisdictions. From these findings—ignored by the Court—Congress reasonably concluded that the coverage formula continues to identify the jurisdictions of greatest concern.

The case for retaining a coverage formula that met needs on the ground was therefore solid. Congress might have been charged with rigidity had it afforded covered jurisdictions no way out or ignored jurisdictions that needed superintendence. Congress, however, responded to this concern [by including] statutory provisions allowing jurisdictions to "bail out" of pre-clearance, and for court-ordered "bail ins." [These features expose] the inaccuracy of the Court's portrayal of the Act as static, unchanged since 1965. * * * True, many covered jurisdictions have not been able to bail out due to recent acts of noncompliance with the VRA, but that truth reinforces the congressional judgment that these jurisdictions were rightfully subject to preclearance, and ought to remain under that regime.

For the reasons stated, I would affirm the judgment of the Court of Appeals.

POINTS FOR DISCUSSION

a.   Pre-Clearance

Section 5 of the Voting Rights Act required pre-clearance of changes to voting rules in covered jurisdictions. As the Court noted, such a requirement is highly unusual in our federal system. The Court, however, purported to invalidate only Section 4 of the Voting Rights Act, which established the formula for identifying the jurisdictions subject to the pre-clearance requirement. After the Court's decision, what is the status of the pre-clearance requirement in Section 5? More generally, after the Court's decision, when (if ever) can Congress require states to pre-clear legislation or other actions with the federal government?

b.   Coverage

The Court reasoned that the formula for determining the jurisdictions subject to the pre-clearance requirement was constitutionally infirm because it did not reflect "current needs." Yet the Court had previously upheld the coverage formula several times. At what point did the formula become unconstitutional? How can the Court tell when that line has been crossed? In making that determination, how much deference should the Court grant to Congress? How much deference did the Court grant in this case?

The Court also reasoned that "the fundamental principle of equal sovereignty remains highly pertinent in assessing" legislation that imposes burdens on only some, rather than all, States. What is the origin and basis for this rule? When is Congress justified in singling out certain states for disfavored (or favored) treatment?

Notwithstanding the Court's decision in *Shelby County*, there is little doubt that the enforcement clauses of the Fourteenth and Fifteenth Amendments empower Congress to create statutory remedies—such as criminal prohibitions or civil claims—for the violation of rights protected by the substantive clauses of those Amendments. Congress, for example, can authorize individuals to sue state officials who have violated their due process or equal protection rights. See, e.g., 42 U.S.C. § 1983. And in *Katzenbach*, the Court suggested that Congress is not limited simply to providing remedies for actual violations of the Amendments. But just how far does Congress's enforcement power reach? Can Congress create remedies for state actions that, in Congress's view, are inconsistent with the values protected by the Amendments, but that the Court has already concluded do not actually violate the Amendments? If so, what is the necessary relationship between the Amendments' protections and Congress's remedy? Consider the cases that follow.

KATZENBACH V. MORGAN

384 U.S. 641 (1966)

MR. JUSTICE BRENNAN delivered the opinion of the Court.

These cases concern the constitutionality of § 4(e) of the Voting Rights Act of 1965. That law [provides] that no person who has successfully completed the sixth primary grade in a public school in, or a private school accredited by, the Commonwealth of Puerto Rico in which the language of instruction was other than English shall be denied the right to vote in any election because of his inability to read or write English. Appellees, registered voters in New York City, brought this suit to challenge the constitutionality of § 4(e) insofar as [it] prohibits the enforcement of the election laws of New York requiring an ability to read and write English as a condition of voting. * * * We hold that, in the application challenged in these cases, § 4(e) is a proper exercise of the powers granted to Congress by § 5 of the Fourteenth Amendment * * *.

The Attorney General of the State of New York argues that * * * § 4(e) cannot be sustained as appropriate legislation to enforce the Equal Protection Clause unless the judiciary decides—even with the guidance of a congressional judgment—that the application of the English literacy requirement prohibited by § 4(e) is forbidden by the Equal Protection Clause itself. We disagree. * * * A construction of § 5 that would require a judicial determination that the enforcement of the state law precluded by Congress violated the Amendment, as a condition of sustaining the congressional enactment, would depreciate both congressional resourcefulness and congressional responsibility for implementing the Amendment. It would confine the legislative power in this context to the insignificant role of abrogating only those state laws that the judicial branch was prepared to adjudge unconstitutional, or of merely informing the judgment of the judiciary by particularizing the "majestic generalities" of § 1 of the Amendment.

Thus our task in this case is not to determine whether the New York English literacy requirement as applied to deny the right to vote to a person who successfully completed the sixth grade in a Puerto Rican school violates the Equal Protection Clause. Accordingly, our decision in *Lassiter v. Northampton County Bd. of Election*, 360 U.S. 45 (1959), sustaining the North Carolina English literacy requirement as not in all circumstances prohibited by the first sections of the Fourteenth and Fifteenth Amendments, is inapposite. *Lassiter* did not present the question before us here: Without regard to whether the judiciary would find that the Equal Protection Clause itself nullifies New York's English literacy requirement as so applied, could Congress prohibit the enforcement of the state law by legislating under § 5 of the Fourteenth Amendment? In answering this question, our task is limited to determining whether such legislation is, as required by § 5, appropriate legislation to enforce the Equal Protection Clause.

By including § 5 the draftsmen sought to grant to Congress, by a specific provision applicable to the Fourteenth Amendment, the same broad powers expressed in the Necessary and Proper Clause, Art. I, s 8, cl. 18. The classic formulation of the reach of those powers was established by Chief Justice Marshall in *McCulloch v. Maryland*, 4 Wheat. 316, 421 (1819). * * * Correctly viewed, § 5 is a positive grant of legislative power authorizing Congress to exercise its discretion in determining whether and what legislation is needed to secure the guarantees of the Fourteenth Amendment. We therefore proceed to the consideration whether § 4(e) is "appropriate legislation" to enforce the Equal Protection Clause, that is, under the *McCulloch* standard, whether § 4(e) may be regarded as an enactment to enforce the Equal Protection Clause, whether it is "plainly adapted to that end" and whether it is not prohibited by but is consistent with "the letter and spirit of the constitution."[10]

There can be no doubt that § 4(e) may be regarded as an enactment to enforce the Equal Protection Clause. * * * § 4(e) may be viewed as a measure to secure for the Puerto Rican community residing in New York nondiscriminatory treatment by government—both in the imposition of voting qualifications and the provision or administration of governmental services, such as public schools, public housing and law enforcement. Section 4(e) may be readily seen as "plainly adapted" to furthering these aims of the Equal Protection Clause. The practical

---

[10] Contrary to the suggestion of the dissent, § 5 does not grant Congress power to exercise discretion in the other direction and to enact "statutes so as in effect to dilute equal protection and due process decisions of this Court." We emphasize that Congress' power under § 5 is limited to adopting measures to enforce the guarantees of the Amendment; § 5 grants Congress no power to restrict, abrogate, or dilute these guarantees. Thus, for example, an enactment authorizing the States to establish racially segregated systems of education would not be—as required by § 5—a measure "to enforce" the Equal Protection Clause since that clause of its own force prohibits such state laws.

effect of § 4(e) is to prohibit New York from denying the right to vote to large segments of its Puerto Rican community. * * * This enhanced political power will be helpful in gaining nondiscriminatory treatment in public services for the entire Puerto Rican community. * * * It was well within congressional authority to say that this need of the Puerto Rican minority for the vote warranted federal intrusion upon any state interests served by the English literacy requirement. It was for Congress, as the branch that made this judgment, to assess and weigh the various conflicting considerations—the risk or pervasiveness of the discrimination in governmental services, the effectiveness of eliminating the state restriction on the right to vote as a means of dealing with the evil, the adequacy or availability of alternative remedies, and the nature and significance of the state interests that would be affected by the nullification of the English literacy requirement as applied to residents who have successfully completed the sixth grade in a Puerto Rican school. It is not for us to review the congressional resolution of these factors. It is enough that we be able to perceive a basis upon which the Congress might resolve the conflict as it did. There plainly was such a basis to support § 4(e) in the application in question in this case.

The result is no different if we confine our inquiry to the question whether § 4(e) was merely legislation aimed at the elimination of an invidious discrimination in establishing voter qualifications. We are told that New York's English literacy requirement originated in the desire to provide an incentive for non-English speaking immigrants to learn the English language and in order to assure the intelligent exercise of the franchise. Yet Congress might well have questioned, in light of the many exemptions provided, and some evidence suggesting that prejudice played a prominent role in the enactment of the requirement, whether these were actually the interests being served. Congress might have also questioned whether denial of a right deemed so precious and fundamental in our society was a necessary or appropriate means of encouraging persons to learn English, or of furthering the goal of an intelligent exercise of the franchise. Finally, Congress might well have concluded that as a means of furthering the intelligent exercise of the franchise, an ability to read or understand Spanish is as effective as ability to read English for those to whom Spanish-language newspapers and Spanish-language radio and television programs are available to inform them of election issues and governmental affairs. [It] was Congress' prerogative to weigh these competing considerations. Here again, it is enough that we perceive a basis upon which Congress might predicate a judgment that the application of New York's English literacy requirement * * * constituted an invidious discrimination in violation of the Equal Protection Clause.

There remains the question whether the congressional remedies adopted in § 4(e) constitute means which are not prohibited by, but are consistent "with the letter and spirit of the constitution." [Appellees contend that § 4(e)] itself works an invidious discrimination in violation of the Fifth Amendment by prohibiting the enforcement of the English literacy requirement only for those educated in American-flag schools (schools located within United States jurisdiction) in which the language of instruction was other than English, and not for those educated in schools beyond the territorial limits of the United States in which the language of instruction was also other than English. * * * Section 4(e) does not restrict or deny the franchise but in effect extends the franchise to persons who otherwise would be denied it by state law. * * * [W]e are guided by the familiar [principle] that "reform may take one step at a time, addressing itself to the phase of the problem which seems most acute to the legislative mind." *Williamson v. Lee Optical Co.*, 348 U.S. 483, 489 (1955). * * * [T]he congressional choice to limit the relief effected in § 4(e) may, for example, reflect Congress' greater familiarity with the quality of instruction in American-flag schools, a recognition of the unique historic relationship between the Congress and the Commonwealth of Puerto Rico, an awareness of the Federal Government's acceptance of the desirability of the use of Spanish as the language of instruction in Commonwealth schools, and the fact that Congress has fostered policies encouraging migration from the Commonwealth to the States. We have no occasion to determine in this case whether such factors would justify a similar distinction embodied in a voting-qualification law that denied the franchise to persons educated in non-American-flag schools. We hold only that the limitation on relief effected in § 4(e) does not constitute a forbidden discrimination since these factors might well have been the basis for the decision of Congress to go "no farther than it did."

[JUSTICE DOUGLAS's concurring opinion is omitted.]

MR. JUSTICE HARLAN, whom MR. JUSTICE STEWART joins, dissenting.

Worthy as its purposes may be thought by many, I do not see how [§ 4(e)] can be sustained except at the sacrifice of fundamentals in the American constitutional system—the separation between the legislative and judicial function and the boundaries between federal and state political authority. * * * Although § 5 [of the Fourteenth Amendment] most certainly does give to the Congress wide powers in the field of devising remedial legislation to effectuate the Amendment's prohibition on arbitrary state action, I believe the Court has confused the issue of how much enforcement power Congress possesses under § 5 with the distinct issue of what questions are appropriate for congressional determination and what questions are essentially judicial in nature. When recognized state violations of federal constitutional standards have occurred, Congress is of course empowered by § 5 to take appropriate remedial measures to redress and prevent the wrongs. But it is a judicial question whether the condition with which Congress has thus sought to deal is in truth an infringement of the Constitution, something that is the necessary prerequisite to bringing the § 5 power into play at all.

The question here is not whether the statute is appropriate remedial legislation to cure an established violation of a constitutional command, but whether there has in fact been an infringement of that constitutional command, that is, whether a particular state practice or, as here, a statute is so arbitrary or irrational as to offend the command of the Equal Protection Clause of the Fourteenth Amendment. That question is one for the judicial branch ultimately to determine. Were the rule otherwise, Congress would be able to qualify this Court's constitutional decisions under the Fourteenth and Fifteenth Amendments let alone those under other provisions of the Constitution, by resorting to congressional power under the Necessary and Proper Clause. In view of this Court's holding in *Lassiter* that an English literacy test is a permissible exercise of state supervision over its franchise, I do not think it is open to Congress to limit the effect of that decision as it has undertaken to do by § 4(e). In effect the Court reads § 5 of the Fourteenth Amendment as giving Congress the power to define the substantive scope of the Amendment. If that indeed be the true reach of § 5, then I do not see why Congress should not be able as well to exercise its § 5 "discretion" by enacting statutes so as in effect to dilute equal protection and due process decisions of this Court. In all such cases there is room for reasonable men to differ as to whether or not a denial of equal protection or due process has occurred, and the final decision is one of judgment. Until today this judgment has always been one for the judiciary to resolve.

I do not mean to suggest in what has been said that a legislative judgment of the type incorporated in § 4(e) is without any force whatsoever. * * * To the extent "legislative facts" are relevant to a judicial determination, Congress is well equipped to investigate them, and such determinations are of course entitled to due respect. [See *South Carolina v. Katzenbach*; *Heart of Atlanta Motel, Inc. v. United States*, 379 U.S. 241 (1964).] But no such factual data provide a legislative record supporting § 4(e) by way of showing that Spanish-speaking citizens are fully as capable of making informed decisions in a New York election as are English-speaking citizens. Nor was there any showing whatever to support the Court's alternative argument that § 4(e) should be viewed as but a remedial measure designed to cure or assure against unconstitutional discrimination of other varieties * * * to which Puerto Rican minorities might be subject in such communities as New York. * * * Thus, we have here not a matter of giving deference to a congressional estimate, based on its determination of legislative facts, bearing upon the validity *vel non* of a statute, but rather what can at most be called a legislative announcement that Congress believes a state law to entail an unconstitutional deprivation of equal protection. Although this

> **Definition**
>
> The Latin term "*vel non*" means "or not."

kind of declaration is of course entitled to the most respectful consideration, coming as it does from a concurrent branch and one that is knowledgeable in matters of popular political participation, I do not believe it lessens our responsibility to decide the fundamental issue of whether in fact the state enactment violates federal constitutional rights.

To hold, on this record, that § 4(e) overrides the New York literacy requirement seems to me tantamount to allowing the Fourteenth Amendment to swallow the State's constitutionally ordained primary authority in this field. For if

> **Definition**
>
> The Latin term "*ipse dixit*," which means "he himself said it," refers to a statement made without supporting authority.

Congress by what, as here, amounts to mere *ipse dixit* can set that otherwise permissible requirement partially at naught I see no reason why it could not also substitute its judgment for that of the States in other fields of their exclusive primary competence as well.

After *Morgan*, can Congress create, define, and protect rights pursuant to its power to enforce the Fourteenth Amendment? The case that follows addresses this question directly.

CITY OF BOERNE V. FLORES
521 U.S. 507 (1997)

JUSTICE KENNEDY delivered the opinion of the Court.

[The Archbishop of San Antonio applied for a building permit for construction to enlarge a church in the parish. City authorities, relying on a historic-preservation ordinance, denied the application. The Archbishop brought suit, relying on the Religious Freedom Restoration Act of 1993 (RFRA), 42 U.S.C. § 2000bb *et seq*. The City contended that the Act exceeded the scope of Congress's power under § 5 of the Fourteenth Amendment.]

Congress enacted RFRA in direct response to the Court's decision in *Employment Div., Dept. of Human Resources of Oregon v. Smith*, 494 U.S. 872 (1990), [which] held that neutral, generally applicable laws may be applied to religious practices even when not supported by a compelling governmental interest. * * * RFRA prohibits "[g]overnment" from "substantially burden[ing]" a person's exercise of religion even if the burden results from a rule of general applicability unless the government can demonstrate [that] the burden "(1) is in furtherance of a compelling governmental interest; and (2) is the least restrictive means of furthering that compelling governmental interest."

Legislation which deters or remedies constitutional violations can fall within the sweep of Congress' enforcement power even if in the process it prohibits conduct which is not itself unconstitutional and intrudes into "legislative spheres of autonomy previously reserved to the States." [See *South Carolina v. Katzenbach,* 383 U.S. 301, 308 (1966); *Katzenbach v. Morgan,* 384 U.S. 641 (1966).] Congress' power under § 5, however, extends only to "enforc[ing]" the provisions of the Fourteenth Amendment. The Court has described this power as "remedial." The design of the Amendment and the text of § 5 are

inconsistent with the suggestion that Congress has the power to decree the substance of the Fourteenth Amendment's restrictions on the States. Legislation which alters the meaning of the Free Exercise Clause cannot be said to be enforcing the Clause. Congress does not enforce a constitutional right by changing what the right is.

While the line between measures that remedy or prevent unconstitutional actions and measures that make a substantive change in the governing law is not easy to discern, and Congress must have wide latitude in determining where it lies, the distinction exists and must be observed. There must be a congruence and proportionality between the injury to be prevented or remedied and the means adopted to that end. Lacking such a connection, legislation may become substantive in operation and effect. History and our case law support drawing the distinction, one apparent from the text of the Amendment.

In February [1866], Republican Representative John Bingham of Ohio reported the following draft Amendment to the House of Representatives on behalf of the Joint Committee: "The Congress shall have power to make all laws which shall be necessary and proper to secure to the citizens of each State all privileges and immunities of citizens in the several States, and to all persons in the several States equal protection in the rights of life, liberty, and property." The proposal encountered immediate opposition, which continued through three days of debate. Members of Congress from across the political spectrum criticized the Amendment [on the ground that it] gave Congress too much legislative power at the expense of the existing constitutional structure. * * * As a result of these objections, [the] Joint Committee [drafted a revised proposal under which] Congress' power was no longer plenary but remedial. Congress was granted the power to make the substantive constitutional prohibitions against the States effective.

There is language in our opinion in *Katzenbach v. Morgan,* 384 U.S. 641 (1966), which could be interpreted as acknowledging a power in Congress to enact legislation that expands the rights contained in § 1 of the Fourteenth Amendment. This is not a necessary interpretation, however, or even the best one. In *Morgan,* [the Court's] rationales for upholding § 4(e) rested on unconstitutional discrimination by New York and Congress' reasonable attempt to combat it.

> **Take Note**
>
> The Court does not address the statements in *Morgan* suggesting that Congress has power to expand the class of protected rights beyond those identified by the Court in interpreting the Fourteenth Amendment. Is the Court effectively overruling *Morgan* without saying so?

If Congress could define its own powers by altering the Fourteenth Amendment's meaning, no longer would the Constitution be "superior paramount law, unchangeable by ordinary means." It would be "on a level with ordinary legislative acts, and, like other acts, [alterable] when the legislature shall please to alter it." *Marbury v. Madison,* 1 Cranch, at 177. Under this approach, it is difficult to conceive of a principle that would limit congressional power. Shifting legislative majorities could change the Constitution and effectively circumvent the difficult and detailed amendment process contained in Article V.

Respondent contends that RFRA is a proper exercise of Congress' remedial or preventive power. [He argues that it] prevents and remedies laws which are enacted with the unconstitutional object of targeting religious beliefs and practices. While preventive rules are sometimes appropriate remedial measures, there must be a congruence between the means used and the ends to be achieved. The appropriateness of remedial measures must be considered in light of the evil presented. Strong measures appropriate to address one harm may be an unwarranted response to another, lesser one.

Make the Connection

Although the Court held in *Smith* that neutral, generally applicable laws that burden the free exercise of religion do not violate the First Amendment, it has since made clear that laws that appear neutral on their face but in fact were enacted with the object of burdening particular religious practices must satisfy heightened scrutiny. See *Church of Lukumi Babalu Aye, Inc. v. Hialeah*, 508 U.S. 520, 533 (1993). We will consider these developments in Chapter 11.

A comparison between RFRA and the Voting Rights Act is instructive. In contrast to the record which confronted Congress and the Judiciary in the voting rights cases, RFRA's legislative record lacks examples of modern instances of generally applicable laws passed because of religious bigotry. [T]he emphasis of the hearings was on laws of general applicability which place incidental burdens on religion. * * * Congress' concern was with the incidental burdens imposed, not the object or purpose of the legislation.

Regardless of the state of the legislative record, RFRA cannot be considered remedial, preventive legislation, if those terms are to have any meaning. RFRA is so out of proportion to a supposed remedial or preventive object that it cannot be understood as responsive to, or designed to prevent, unconstitutional behavior. It appears, instead, to attempt a substantive change in constitutional protections. Preventive measures prohibiting certain types of laws may be appropriate when there is reason to believe that many of the laws affected by the congressional enactment have a significant likelihood of being unconstitutional. * * * RFRA is not so confined. Sweeping coverage ensures its intrusion at every level of government, displacing laws and prohibiting official actions of almost every description and regardless of subject matter. * * * Any law is subject to challenge at any time by any individual who alleges a substantial burden on his or her free exercise of religion.

The stringent test RFRA demands of state laws reflects a lack of proportionality or congruence between the means adopted and the legitimate end to be achieved. * * * Requiring a State to demonstrate a compelling interest and show that it has adopted the least restrictive means of achieving that interest is the most demanding test known to constitutional law. Laws valid under *Smith* would fall under RFRA without regard to whether they had the object of stifling or punishing free exercise. * * * Simply put, RFRA is not designed to identify and counteract state laws likely to be unconstitutional because of their treatment of religion. In most cases, the state laws to which RFRA applies are not ones which will have been motivated by religious bigotry.

When the Court has interpreted the Constitution, it has acted within the province of the Judicial Branch, which embraces the duty to say what the law is. *Marbury.* When the political branches of the Government act against the background of a judicial interpretation of the Constitution already issued, it must be understood that in later cases and controversies the Court will treat its precedents with the respect due them under settled principles, including *stare decisis,* and contrary expectations must be disappointed. RFRA was designed to control cases and controversies, such as the one before us; but as the provisions of the federal statute here invoked are beyond congressional authority, it is this Court's precedent, not RFRA, which must control.

[The separate concurring opinions of JUSTICES STEVENS, SCALIA, O'CONNOR, SOUTER, and BREYER, which concerned the validity of the Court's holding in *Smith,* are omitted.]

POINTS FOR DISCUSSION

a. Congruence and Proportionality

The Court emphasized in *Flores* that Congress has authority under Section 5 of the Fourteenth Amendment to prohibit some conduct that is not actually unconstitutional under the substantive provisions of the Amendment. But when Congress does so, there must be a "congruence and proportionality" between the potential constitutional violation and Congress's remedy. Is this a judicially manageable standard? How should the Court apply that standard? Does it give Congress sufficient guidance? Does it give Congress sufficient leeway to legislate prophylactically to prevent the violation of Fourteenth Amendment rights? Can that standard be reconciled with the Court's reasoning in *Morgan*?

b. Judicial Supremacy Redux?

In enacting RFRA, Congress effectively attempted to overrule a Supreme Court decision. Is the real point of the Court's decision in *Flores* that Congress simply lacks power to do so, regardless of which source of authority it invokes? Recall our discussion in Volume 1 of the notion of judicial supremacy, and in particular of the Court's decisions in *Cooper v. Aaron* and *Dickerson v. United States.* Whatever one thinks about the general view that the Court's interpretation of the Constitution binds the other branches, is there any reason to argue that matters should be different under the Reconstruction Amendments?

In Volume 1, we considered another excerpt from the case that follows for its discussion of Congress's power under the Commerce Clause. The case involved a challenge to the Violence Against Women Act, 42 U.S.C. § 13981(a), which created a civil right of action for victims of gender-motivated violence against their attackers. In enacting the statute, Congress explicitly relied not only on the Commerce Clause, but also on its "affirmative power [under] section 5 of the Fourteenth Amendment to the Constitution." 42 U.S.C. § 13981(a). The government defended the Act as a valid exercise of that power. Please review the facts and reasoning presented there before continuing.

UNITED STATES V. MORRISON
529 U.S. 598 (2000)

CHIEF JUSTICE REHNQUIST delivered the opinion of the Court.

Petitioners' § 5 argument is founded on an assertion that there is pervasive bias in various state justice systems against victims of gender-motivated violence. This assertion is supported by a voluminous congressional record. Specifically, Congress received evidence that many participants in state justice systems are perpetuating an array of erroneous stereotypes and assumptions. Congress concluded that these discriminatory stereotypes often result in insufficient investigation and prosecution of gender-motivated crime, inappropriate focus on the behavior and credibility of the victims of that crime, and unacceptably lenient punishments for those who are actually convicted of gender-motivated violence. See H.R. Conf. Rep. No. 103–711, at 385–386; S.Rep. No. 103–138, at 38, 41–55; S.Rep. No. 102–197, at 33–35, 41, 43–47. Petitioners contend that this bias denies victims of gender-motivated violence the equal protection of the laws and that Congress therefore acted appropriately in enacting a private civil remedy against the perpetrators of gender-motivated violence to both remedy the States' bias and deter future instances of discrimination in the state courts.

> **Make the Connection**
>
> We discussed the Court's decision in *United States v. Virginia*, and the topic of gender discrimination, in Chapter 5.

As our cases have established, state-sponsored gender discrimination violates equal protection unless it serves "important governmental objectives and [the] discriminatory means employed" are "substantially related to the achievement of those objectives." *United States v. Virginia*, 518 U.S. 515, 533 (1996). However, the language and purpose of the Fourteenth Amendment place certain limitations on the manner in which Congress may attack discriminatory conduct. These limitations are necessary to prevent the Fourteenth Amendment from obliterating the Framers' carefully crafted balance of power between the States and the National Government. Foremost among these limitations is the time-honored principle that the Fourteenth Amendment, by its very terms, prohibits only state action.

Shortly after the Fourteenth Amendment was adopted, we decided two cases interpreting the Amendment's provisions, *United States v. Harris,* 106 U.S. 629 (1883), and the *Civil Rights Cases,* 109 U.S. 3 (1883). In *Harris,* the Court considered a challenge to § 2 of the Civil Rights Act of 1871. That section sought to punish "private persons" for "conspiring to deprive any one of the equal protection of the laws enacted by the State." 106 U.S., at 639. We concluded that this law exceeded Congress' § 5 power because the law was "directed exclusively against the action of private persons, without reference to the laws of the State, or their administration by her officers." *Id.,* at 640. * * * We reached a similar conclusion in the *Civil Rights Cases.* In those consolidated cases, we held that the public accommodation provisions of the Civil Rights Act of 1875, which applied to purely private conduct, were beyond the scope of the § 5 enforcement power. 109 U.S., at 11.

The force of the doctrine of *stare decisis* behind these decisions stems not only from the length of time they have been on the books, but also from the insight attributable to the Members of the Court at that time. Every Member had been appointed by President Lincoln, Grant, Hayes, Garfield, or Arthur— and each of their judicial appointees obviously had intimate knowledge and familiarity with the events surrounding the adoption of the Fourteenth Amendment.

Petitioners [rely] on *United States v. Guest,* 383 U.S. 745 (1966), for the proposition that the rule laid down in the *Civil Rights Cases* is no longer good law. In *Guest,* the Court reversed the construction of an indictment under 18 U.S.C. § 241, saying in the course of its opinion that "we deal here with issues of statutory construction, not with issues of constitutional power." 383 U.S., at 749. Three Members of the Court, in a separate opinion by Justice Brennan, expressed the view that the *Civil Rights Cases* were wrongly decided, and that Congress could under § 5 prohibit actions by private individuals. Three other Members of the Court, who joined the opinion of the Court, joined a separate opinion by Justice Clark which in two or three sentences stated the conclusion that Congress could "punis[h] all conspiracies—with or without state action—that interfere with Fourteenth

---

Food for Thought

Why does the Court identify the Presidents who appointed the Justices who served on the Court in 1883? The five Presidents were all Republicans, the party that provided most of the support for Reconstruction. Is that fact relevant here? Should the Court consider the partisan identification of the Justices, let alone the partisan identification of the Presidents who appointed them, in deciding whether to adhere to their decisions?

> **Food for Thought**
>
> In *Guest*, which we considered earlier in this chapter, a majority of the Justices signed Justice Stewart's opinion for the Court on the question of statutory construction. But a majority also expressed the view that Congress can regulate private conduct pursuant to Section 5. What is the precedential value of the separate opinions? Does the Court here fairly dismiss them?

Amendment rights." *Id.,* at 762. * * * Though [these] Justices saw fit to opine on matters not before the Court in *Guest,* the Court had no occasion to revisit the *Civil Rights Cases* and *Harris,* having determined "the indictment [charging private individuals with conspiring to deprive blacks of equal access to state facilities] in fact contain[ed] an express allegation of state involvement." 383 U.S., at 756. * * * To accept petitioners' argument, moreover, one must add to the three Justices joining Justice Brennan's reasoned explanation for his belief that the *Civil Rights Cases* were wrongly decided, the three Justices joining Justice Clark's opinion who gave no explanation whatever for their similar view. This is simply not the way that reasoned constitutional adjudication proceeds.

Petitioners alternatively argue that, unlike the situation in the *Civil Rights Cases,* here there has been gender-based disparate treatment by state authorities, whereas in those cases there was no indication of such state action. [But] prophylactic legislation under § 5 must have a "congruence and proportionality between the injury to be prevented or remedied and the means adopted to that end." *Florida Prepaid Postsecondary Ed. Expense Bd. v. College Savings Bank,* 527 U.S. 627, 639 (1999). Section 13981 is not aimed at proscribing discrimination by officials which the Fourteenth Amendment might not itself proscribe; it is directed not at any State or state actor, but at individuals who have committed criminal acts motivated by gender bias.

In the present cases, for example, § 13981 visits no consequence whatever on any Virginia public official involved in investigating or prosecuting Brzonkala's assault. The section is, therefore, unlike any of the § 5 remedies that we have previously upheld. [See *Katzenbach v. Morgan,* 384 U.S. 641 (1966); *South Carolina v. Katzenbach,* 383 U.S. 301 (1966).] Section 13981 is also different from these previously upheld remedies in that it applies uniformly throughout the Nation. * * * By contrast, the § 5 remedy upheld in *Katzenbach v. Morgan* was directed only to the State where the evil found by Congress existed, and in *South Carolina v. Katzenbach,* the remedy was directed only to those States in which Congress found that there had been discrimination. For these reasons, we conclude that Congress' power under § 5 does not extend to the enactment of § 13981.

JUSTICE BREYER, with whom JUSTICE STEVENS joins, and with whom JUSTICE SOUTER and JUSTICE GINSBURG join as to Part I-A, dissenting.

[II] Given my conclusion [that VAWA is a valid exercise of Congress's power under the Commerce Clause,] I need not consider Congress' authority under § 5 of the Fourteenth Amendment. Nonetheless, I doubt the Court's reasoning rejecting that source of authority. * * * The Federal Government's argument [is] that Congress used § 5 to remedy the actions of *state actors,* namely, those States which, through discriminatory design or the discriminatory conduct of their officials, failed to provide adequate (or any) state remedies for women injured by gender-motivated violence—a failure that the States, and Congress, documented in depth. Neither *Harris* nor the *Civil Rights Cases* considered this kind of claim.

The Court responds directly to the relevant "state actor" claim by finding that the present law lacks "congruence and proportionality" to the state discrimination that it purports to remedy [because the law] is not "directed [at] any State or state actor." But why can Congress not provide a remedy against private actors? Those private actors, of course, did not themselves violate the Constitution. But this Court has held that Congress at least sometimes can enact remedial "[l]egislation [that] prohibits conduct which is not itself unconstitutional." *Flores.* The statutory remedy does not in any sense purport to "determine what constitutes a constitutional violation." [*Id.*] It intrudes little upon either States or private parties. It may lead state actors to improve their own remedial systems, primarily through example. It restricts private actors only by imposing liability for private conduct that is, in the main, already forbidden by state law. Why is the remedy "disproportionate"? And given the relation between remedy and violation—the creation of a federal remedy to substitute for constitutionally inadequate state remedies—where is the lack of "congruence"? * * * Despite my doubts about the majority's § 5 reasoning, I need not, and do not, answer the § 5 question, which I would leave for more thorough analysis if necessary on another occasion.

POINTS FOR DISCUSSION

a. State v. Private Conduct

The Violence Against Women Act authorized the victims of gender-motivated violence (whether male or female) to sue their attackers, even when those attackers were private citizens. Because of the state action doctrine, it is clear that such private attacks, however loathsome, do not violate the Fourteenth Amendment. In light of this fact, how did the plaintiff and the government defend the Act as a valid exercise of Section 5 authority? Was Congress responding to private conduct in creating the

<table>
<tr><td>

Make the Connection

In *DeShaney v. Winnebago County Department of Social Services*, which we considered in Chapter 2 in our consideration of substantive due process, the Court held that the Due Process Clause does not impose an obligation on the states to protect their citizens from private violence. The Court reached a similar conclusion in *Town of Castle Rock v. Gonzales*, which we considered in Chapter 3 in our unit on procedural due process.

</td></tr>
</table>

civil remedy? Or was it responding to state conduct? If the latter, what was the state conduct at issue? Did that conduct violate the Fourteenth Amendment?

b. State Acts v. State Omissions

The government argued in *Morrison* that the states' failure to protect the victims of gender-motivated violence was a sufficient predicate for the exercise of Congress's Section 5 power. Can government inaction ever violate the Constitution? Even if the government generally has no affirmative constitutional obligation to act to protect individuals, is it possible that a systemic failure to act could itself be motivated by sexist views about the respective roles of men and women? If so, would that constitute a sufficient predicate for at least some remedy under Section 5?

c. Congruence and Proportionality

Under the Court's approach, can a remedy against *private* individuals ever be congruent and proportional to the injury inflicted by *state* actors? Should Congress ever have authority to create such remedies?

If nothing else, the test presumably permits Congress to regulate at least some state action that does not itself violate Section 1 of the Fourteenth Amendment. But how much? In *Tennessee v. Lane*, 541 U.S. 509 (2004), the Court held that Congress had authority under Section 5 to enact Title II of the Americans with Disabilities Act of 1990, 42 U.S.C. § 12132, at least insofar as it required reasonable access to courts. That section provides that "no qualified individual with a disability shall, by reason of such disability, be excluded from participation in or be denied the benefits of the services, programs or activities of a public entity, or be subjected to discrimination by any such entity." In his opinion for the Court, Justice Stevens emphasized that the Due Process Clause of the Fourteenth Amendment guarantees a "right of access to the courts," and that Congress had enacted Title II "against a backdrop of pervasive unequal treatment" that led to the exclusion of disabled persons "from courthouses and court proceedings by reason of their disabilities." The Court reasoned that Congress's remedy for this "pattern of exclusion and discrimination"—Title II's requirement of program accessibility—was "congruent and proportional to its object of enforcing the right of access to the courts." The Court noted that the "unequal treatment of disabled persons in the administration of judicial services has a long history, and has persisted despite several legislative efforts to remedy the problem of disability discrimination." In addition, the Court stressed that Title II's remedy was "a limited one," requiring only "reasonable modifications" to existing facilities, a standard that permitted consideration of costs and other factors.

Chief Justice Rehnquist, joined by Justices Kennedy and Thomas, dissented, asserting that there was "nothing in the legislative record or statutory findings to indicate that disabled persons were systematically denied" the right of access to courts. Absent a constitutional violation, he reasoned, Congress could not act pursuant to Section 5 to impose the remedy in Title II. He also objected to the Court's decision to review Title II's constitutionality only as applied to a claim of right of access to the courts, stating that the "effect is to rig the congruence-and-proportionality test by artificially constricting the scope of the statute to closely mirror a recognized constitutional right."

In his separate dissent, Justice Scalia urged the Court to abandon the congruence and proportionality standard. He declared that the standard, "like all such flabby tests, is a standing invitation to judicial arbitrariness and policy-driven decisionmaking." He continued:

> Worse still, it casts this Court in the role of Congress's taskmaster. Under it, the courts (and ultimately this Court) must regularly check Congress's homework to make sure that it has identified sufficient constitutional violations to make its remedy congruent and proportional. As a general matter, we are ill advised to adopt or adhere to constitutional rules that bring us into constant conflict with a coequal branch of Government. And when conflict is unavoidable, we should not come to do battle with the United States Congress armed only with a test ("congruence and proportionality") that has no demonstrable basis in the text of the Constitution and cannot objectively be shown to have been met or failed.

Justice Scalia would have replaced the test with one that clearly prohibits Congress from going "*beyond* the provisions of the Fourteenth Amendment to proscribe, prevent, or 'remedy' conduct that does not *itself* violate any provision of the Fourteenth Amendment," because "[s]o-called 'prophylactic legislation' is reinforcement rather than enforcement." He declared, however, that "principally for reasons of *stare decisis*" he would continue to "apply the permissive *McCulloch* standard" applied in *Morgan* "to congressional measures designed to remedy racial discrimination by the States."

Do you agree that the congruence and proportionality test is effectively devoid of content? Or is it a sensible response to a constitutional text that itself calls for a judgment about whether particular legislation is "appropriate"?

Executive Summary of This Chapter

The **Thirteenth Amendment** prohibits slavery and involuntary servitude. The provision applies to both state action and private action. It also empowers Congress to enforce its provisions by "appropriate legislation." Pursuant to that power, Congress can pass laws that it rationally believes are necessary and proper for abolishing all of the "badges and incidents of slavery in the United States." *Jones v. Alfred H. Mayer Co.* (1968); *Civil Rights Cases* (1883). In exercising this power, Congress may prohibit some forms of private conduct. *Jones v. Alfred H. Mayer Co.* (1968).

The **Fourteenth and Fifteenth Amendments** include provisions empowering Congress to enforce their substantive provisions "by appropriate legislation." Pursuant to these sources of authority, Congress not only has power to outlaw state violations of the Amendments and provide for civil and criminal remedies for those violations, but also has power to act prophylactically to prevent violations of the Amendments. *South Carolina v. Katzenbach* (1966). However, in enforcing the Fifteenth Amendment's guarantee of voting, Congress may depart from basic principles of federalism and equal sovereignty among the states only so long as the departure "makes sense in light of current conditions." *Shelby County, Alabama v. Holder* (2013).

When Congress seeks to exercise those powers to regulate state conduct that does not violate the substantive provisions of the Amendments, however, there must be a **congruence and proportionality** between the injury to be prevented or remedied and the means adopted to that end. *City of Boerne v. Flores* (1997). Congressional efforts that seek to redefine the Amendments' substantive provisions exceed the scope of the enforcement powers. *Id.*

Because the substantive provisions of the Fourteenth Amendment prohibit only state, as opposed to private, action, *Civil Rights Cases* (1883), Congress's power under the Fourteenth Amendment to regulate private conduct is highly circumscribed. *United States v. Morrison* (2000); *United States v. Guest* (1966).

POINT-COUNTERPOINT

Should the Reconstruction Amendments be read in light of the Tenth Amendment?

POINT: PETER J. SMITH

In the first 75 years of the nation's history, the phrase "the United States" was often used as a plural noun, suggesting that the union was in fact a collection of largely independent states. To be sure, there is, as we saw in Volume 1, continuing debate over the extent to which this view was consistent with the original meaning of the Constitution. But even assuming that the Constitution's protections were as robust as proponents of serious limits on federal power assert, the events leading up to the Civil War—and in particular the southern states' repeated invocations of state sovereignty to defend their embrace of the institution of slavery—demonstrated that there were serious drawbacks to the conception of the United States as a loose union of independent states.

The Civil War itself was obviously the most immediate response to this problem, but the principal *legal* remedy was the ratification of the Reconstruction Amendments. It is difficult to overstate the transformative nature of their adoption. The original Constitution expressly imposed only a few limits on state authority—principally those included in Article I, section 10, and in the Supremacy Clause—and impliedly imposed only a few others—such as the bar on state taxation of federal instrumentalities that the Court announced in *McCulloch v. Maryland*, 17 U.S. (4 Wheat.) 316 (1819). (The Bill of Rights, as we saw in *Barron v. Baltimore*, 32 U.S. (7 Pet.) 243 (1833), in Chapter 1, was not originally understood to limit state action.) In this scheme, the Tenth Amendment's rule of construction—that powers not granted to the United States expressly or by necessary implication remained with the states—stated a central structural principle.

The Reconstruction Amendments, in contrast, by their terms imposed substantial limits on state authority. The Equal Protection, Due Process, and Privileges or Immunities Clauses of the Fourteenth Amendment made clear that the states no longer had authority to engage in various forms of discrimination or to interfere with (at least some) individual rights. And the Amendments expressly authorized Congress to enforce their provisions "by appropriate legislation," language strongly reminiscent of the Necessary and Proper Clause, which itself had long been construed as a potent source of congressional authority.

In light of this history and text, it is inappropriate to read the Tenth Amendment as a limit on Congress's authority to enforce the Reconstruction Amendments. The Tenth Amendment—which was designed to confirm limits on federal authority and reiterate the breadth of state authority—seems singularly inapposite in interpreting provisions that were designed fundamentally to *alter* the relationship between the federal government and the states, and between the states and their citizens. Indeed, for this reason there is a strong argument that the *Tenth Amendment* should now be construed *in light of the Reconstruction Amendments*. At a minimum, however, the fact that the Reconstruction Amendments came later in time than did the Tenth Amendment suggests that their conception of the scope of state and federal authority should prevail with respect to matters within the scope of the Reconstruction Amendments.

————————————

COUNTERPOINT: GREGORY E. MAGGS

The Tenth Amendment says that the federal government has only the powers delegated to it in the Constitution. Congress, for example, cannot regulate non-economic intrastate activities that do not have a substantial effect on interstate commerce because nothing in the Constitution gives Congress this power. Therefore, Congress cannot regulate guns in schools or gender-motivated violence, or at least not as it tried to regulate these subjects in *United States v. Lopez*, 514 U.S. 549 (1995), and *United States v. Morrison*, 529 U.S. 598 (2000).

New amendments to the Constitution conceivably could declare that federalism is dead and that Congress has plenary legislative power. But the Thirteenth, Fourteenth, and Fifteenth Amendments do not do anything like this. Although they were added to the Constitution after the Tenth Amendment, their text and structure make clear that they were not intended to alter the principle that Congress may act only according to its delegated powers.

Consider what the Amendments say. They each include important new prohibitions, but they do not stop at that. Each also concludes by saying: "The Congress shall have power to enforce this article by appropriate legislation." Why were these words added? The Amendments evidently rest on the premise that Congress only has the powers granted by the Constitution, just as the Tenth Amendment says. The drafters of the Amendments understood that Congress would lack power to enforce them without newly delegated powers.

Contemporaneous court decisions and subsequent amendments to the Constitution confirm that the Thirteenth, Fourteenth, and Fifteenth Amendments did not undercut the Tenth Amendment. For example, in the *Civil Rights Cases*, 109 U.S. 3 (1883), the Supreme Court emphasized that the last section of the Fourteenth Amendment was added because otherwise Congress could not enforce the Equal Protection requirement. Similarly, the Sixteenth, Eighteenth, and Nineteenth Amendments also include sections granting additional powers to Congress. The Court and the drafters of the Amendments recognized that new grants of power were necessary because the Tenth Amendment's principles remained effective.

True, the prohibitions of the Thirteenth, Fourteenth, and Fifteenth Amendments strike deeply into what was formerly a sphere of state prerogative.

But it would be an incorrect overgeneralization to conclude that because these Amendments reduced state power and increased federal power over certain subjects, they also decreased state power and increased federal power in additional respects. The Amendments go as far as they go, but no further.

While Congress may use its new power under the Thirteenth Amendment to enforce the prohibition on slavery, it cannot regulate all matters concerning race. Similarly, Congress can employ its power under the Fourteenth Amendment to pass laws preventing the states from denying anyone due process, but Congress cannot regulate all aspects of state government. And Congress can enforce the prohibition on discrimination in voting rights in the Fifteenth Amendment, but it cannot dictate all aspects of state elections. The Tenth Amendment continues to leave the powers not specifically granted in the Thirteenth, Fourteenth, and Fifteenth Amendments to the states.

PART IV

The First Amendment

The First Amendment is the source of several of our most prized and fundamental rights: the freedom of speech, the press, and religion, and the rights to assemble and to petition the government for a redress of grievances.

> ### U.S. Constitution, Amendment I
>
> Congress shall make no law respecting an establishment of religion, or prohibiting the free exercise thereof; or abridging the freedom of speech, or of the press; or the right of the people peaceably to assemble, and to petition the Government for a redress of grievances.

→ Freedom to associate = implied

There is a vast body of decisions interpreting the various provisions in the First Amendment. Many colleges and law schools have classes devoted solely to the First Amendment; indeed, many have separate classes for the freedom of speech and the freedom of religion. Our task here is to provide an overview of the doctrine that the Court has developed to govern all of these rights, in a book devoted to all of American constitutional law.

In the chapters that follow, we focus on four discrete—but related—rights that the Court has protected under the First Amendment. In Chapter 8, we take up the freedom of speech. In Chapter 9, we consider the freedom of the press. In Chapter 10, we address the freedom of association, which the Court has held is essential to the rights expressly protected by the Amendment. And in Chapter 11, we discuss the "Religion Clauses"—that is, the prohibition on the "establishment" of religion and the protection for the free exercise of religion. Although we separately address each of these freedoms protected by the First Amendment, be mindful of the common themes in the Court's approach to those different freedoms.

Freedom of Speech

INTRODUCTION

The freedom of speech as we now know it did not exist in the colonial era. For example, as a means of controlling public discourse, English laws required printers to obtain a license from the government. English laws also made "seditious libel"—the printing of words aimed at undermining government authority—a serious crime. Justice Hugo Black, a great champion of the freedom of speech, described some of this pre-Revolutionary history as follows:

> The obnoxious press licensing law of England, which was also enforced on the Colonies was due in part to the knowledge that exposure of the names of printers, writers and distributors would lessen the circulation of literature critical of the government. The old seditious libel cases in England show the lengths to which government had to go to find out who was responsible for books that were obnoxious to the rulers. John Lilburne was whipped, pilloried and fined for refusing to answer questions designed to get evidence to convict him or someone else for the secret distribution of books in England. Two Puritan Ministers, John Penry and John Udal, were sentenced to death on charges that they were responsible for writing, printing or publishing books. Before the Revolutionary War colonial patriots frequently had to conceal their authorship or distribution of literature that easily could have brought down on them prosecutions by English-controlled courts.

Talley v. California, 362 U.S. 60, 64–65 (1960).

Yet despite this history of oppression, the original Constitution contained no provision expressly guaranteeing a right of free speech. We saw in Chapter 1 how some delegates at the Constitutional Convention refused to sign the document because it did not include a Bill of Rights, 2 *The Records of the Federal Convention of 1787* 646–47, 649 (Max Farrand, ed. 1911), and how Anti-Federalist opponents of the Constitution demanded an express bill of rights to identify protected liberties, including the right to free speech.

Recall that the Federalists initially responded to this objection during the ratification debates by asserting that a Bill of Rights was neither necessary nor a good idea. As we have seen, the Federalists' arguments were not ultimately convincing, and several states, upon ratifying the Constitution, passed resolutions specifically urging the adoption of a Bill of Rights. See 2 Francis Newton Thorpe, *The Constitutional History of the United States* 198 (1902). By the end of 1791, the states had ratified the ten proposed amendments that we now call the "Bill of Rights."

The First Amendment says, in relevant part, that "Congress shall make no law * * * abridging the freedom of speech." Two aspects of this language require

---

Make the Connection

We addressed the "incorporation doctrine" in Chapter 1.

---

comment. First, the Amendment does not define "the freedom of speech." Accordingly, many cases have arisen over what the phrase means. Second, although the Amendment refers to "Congress," the Supreme Court has held that this provision applies to the states through the Fourteenth Amendment. See *Grosjean v. American Press Co.*, 297 U.S. 233, 244 (1936).

In this chapter, we will consider how the Supreme Court has interpreted the First Amendment's protection for the freedom of speech. If we were starting from scratch, one possible view would be that the freedom of speech is "absolute"— that is, that no government interest can justify abridgment of the freedom in cases to which it extends. Justice Black famously advanced this view, arguing that "the men who drafted our Bill of Rights did all the 'balancing' that was to be done in this field." *Konigsberg v. State Bar of California*, 366 U.S. 36, 61 (1961) (Black, J., dissenting). But the Court has never accepted this view. Instead, the Court has repeatedly stated that the freedom of speech is not absolute. See, e.g., *Virginia v. Black*, 538 U.S. 343, 358 (2003). The government does not have to allow a person to say anything he wishes, in any manner, at any place, at any time. On the contrary, some regulation of speech is possible. So the basic question throughout this chapter is: What kind of government regulations are allowed, and what kinds are not? Answering this question in a pragmatic fashion, the Supreme Court has adopted a number of standards that essentially weigh the value of free speech against the importance of governmental regulation. As you read the materials that follow, consider whether the Court's tests properly accommodate these competing interests, and whether the Court has properly applied those tests in its cases.

POINTS FOR DISCUSSION

a. "*The* Freedom of Speech"

The First Amendment does not protect "freedom of speech"; it protects "*the* freedom of speech." The use of a definite article (i.e., "the") before the word "freedom" has led some to conclude that a freedom of speech pre-existed the First Amendment, and that the First Amendment serves to preserve this freedom rather than to expand or otherwise redefine it. For example, in an academic lecture, Justice John Paul Stevens said: "[T]he definite article suggests that the draftsmen intended to immunize a previously identified category or subset of speech. That category could not have been co-extensive with the category of oral communications that are commonly described as 'speech' in ordinary usage. For it is obvious that the Framers did not intend to provide constitutional protection for false testimony under oath, or for oral contracts that are against public policy, such as wagers or conspiracies * * *." John Paul Stevens, *The Freedom of Speech: Address at the Inaugural Ralph Gregory Elliot First Amendment Lecture*, 102 Yale L.J. 1293, 1296 (1993). What implications would this theory have for interpreting the First Amendment?

b. A Debate over the Original Meaning of "Freedom of Speech"

A common view of American history is that the Framers protected the freedom of speech because they knew first hand the value of being able to express dissenting opinions. The Framers had felt oppressed by England before the Revolution, and they wanted to secure complete freedom for their descendants. According to this view, we are to understand the freedom of speech as a right, at a minimum, to be free from the many kinds of restrictions that England had placed on the colonists during the colonial period. Writing for the Court, for example, Justice Scalia has asserted:

> The First Amendment's guarantee of "the freedom of speech, or of the press" prohibits a wide assortment of government restraints upon expression, but the core abuse against which it was directed was the scheme of licensing laws implemented by the monarch and Parliament to contain the "evils" of the printing press in 16th- and 17-century England.

Thomas v. Chicago Park District, 534 U.S. 316, 320 (2002).

The late Leonard W. Levy, a renowned scholar of constitutional history, has contested this account of the original meaning of the freedom of speech. In a lengthy book describing the freedom of speech in the newly formed United States, he writes:

> The persistent image of colonial America as a society in which freedom of expression was cherished is an hallucination of sentiment that ignores history. The evidence provides little comfort for the notion that the colonies hospitably received advocates of obnoxious or detestable ideas on

matters that counted. * * * The American people simply did not understand that freedom of thought and expression means equal freedom for the other fellow, especially the one with hated ideas.

Leonard W. Levy, *Legacy of Suppression: Freedom of Speech and Press in Early American History* 18 (1960). How would Levy's alternative view, if accepted, affect interpretation of the First Amendment from an originalist perspective?

c.   What Counts as "Speech"? – more than words

There is little doubt that the First Amendment's protection for the freedom of speech extends to a person's attempt to give a speech on a soap box, or to a pamphlet that a person publishes to convince the public that the President has made an unwise decision. But what else counts as "speech" under the First Amendment? As it turns out, there is no easy answer to this question.

What speeches and pamphlets have in common is their use in conveying a message. Does this mean that every act that conveys a message counts as speech? Music often conveys a message, as do symbolic acts, such as bowing one's head and holding one's right fist above the head, or even the burning of a flag or a draft card at a protest rally. These acts have an obvious expressive content. And, as we will see, the First Amendment is principally concerned with expression. But many other acts that do not seem principally expressive—such as the assassination of a political leader—also make a statement, and sometimes are committed in large part for that purpose. Surely such acts are not immune from punishment simply because they contain an expressive element.

As you read the cases in this chapter, consider whether it is possible to discern a test for when a particular act that conveys a message counts as "speech" within the meaning of the First Amendment.

d.   The Theory of the Freedom of Speech

What is the basic theory of the First Amendment's protection for the freedom of speech? One possibility, suggested by the history recounted above, is that the freedom of speech is designed to ensure that government remains accountable and responsive to the will of the people. These ends are obviously substantially undermined by prohibitions on criticism of the government.

Another possibility is that the freedom of speech aids in the quest for the truth by creating a robust marketplace of ideas. As Justice Brandeis famously stated, "freedom to think as you will and to speak as you think are means indispensable to the discovery and spread of political truth." *Whitney v. California*, 274 U.S. 357, 375 (1927) (Brandeis, J., concurring). On this view, speech is protected because the expression of every possible view permits individuals to assess the relative merits of competing views and to decide which view is worthy of adherence. As Justice Holmes put it, "the ultimate good desired is better reached by free trade in ideas—[the] best test of truth is the power of the thought to get itself accepted in the competition of the market, and that truth is the only ground upon which their wishes safely can be carried out." *Abrams v. United States*, 250 U.S. 616, 630 (1919) (Holmes, J., dissenting).

On both of these views—the "government accountability" theory and the "marketplace of ideas" theory—the freedom of speech is largely instrumental—that is, it is important because it permits the advancement of *other* important goals. Is there a value to the freedom of speech—to the ability to express oneself freely—wholly aside from its potential to enhance the democratic process or aid in the search for truth?

As you read the materials in this chapter, consider which theory (or theories) of the First Amendment the Court embraces, and the implications of those choices for First Amendment doctrines.

A. GENERAL PRINCIPLES AND RULES FOR REGULATING SPEECH

In interpreting the First Amendment, the Supreme Court has developed a number of distinct doctrines and rules. These doctrines and rules basically fall into two general categories. Some concern the various types of regulations that the government wants to impose on speech. Others focus on the kinds of speech that the government wants to regulate. This chapter's organization follows this same division.

In this section, we consider the following types of governmental regulations on speech: (1) content-based restrictions; (2) reasonable time, place, and manner restrictions; (3) generally applicable regulations that incidentally affect expression; (4) prior restraints; (5) vague or overbroad restrictions; and (6) unconstitutional conditions. In Section B, we take up doctrines and rules pertaining to particular classes of speech.

1. Content-Based Restrictions

The first general principle concerns **content-based restrictions** on speech. A content-based restriction on speech is a restraint based on the content of what is being said. For example, in *Boos v. Barry*, 485 U.S. 312 (1988), the Supreme Court considered the constitutionality of a District of Columbia statute making it unlawful to "display [any] placard" within 500 feet of an embassy if the placard was "designed [to] bring into public odium any foreign government [or] to bring into public disrepute political, social, or economic acts, views, or purposes of any foreign government." The Court concluded that this statute was a content-based restriction on speech because it prohibited only placards that contained messages critical of foreign governments, while permitting ones that contained supportive messages. For example, under the statute, a person could permissibly hold a sign outside the United Kingdom's embassy saying, "Princess Diana, Forever in our Hearts, May She Rest in Peace," but could not display a placard saying, "Unite Ireland! British Oppressors Out of Belfast Now!"

A "freedom" of speech that nevertheless allowed the government to restrict the content of what people may say would not be much of a freedom at all. (Recall automaker Henry Ford's famous joke that his customers could buy the Model-T in any color they want, "so long as it is black.") And if the government could ban unpopular speech—and if the First Amendment protected only the expression of popular views—then there really wouldn't be any *need* for the First Amendment, as the majority would be unlikely to ban views that they hold and wish to express.

> **Make the Connection**
>
> We saw strict scrutiny, among other places, in Chapter 2, in our consideration of fundamental rights, and in Chapter 5, in our consideration of discrimination on the basis of race and national origin.

For this reason, the Supreme Court subjects content-based restrictions to strict scrutiny: The government may enforce a content-based restriction on speech in a public forum only if the regulation is necessary to serve a compelling state interest and the regulation is narrowly drawn to achieve that end. The term "public forum" refers to government property that "by long tradition or by government fiat," has been "devoted to assembly and debate." *Arkansas Educ. Television Comm'n v. Forbes*, 523 U.S. 666, 677 (1998). Typical examples are parks or sidewalks. A compelling state interest is an "extremely important justification." *Denver Area Educ. Telecommunications Consortium, Inc. v. F.C.C.*, 518 U.S. 727, 743 (1996). The Supreme Court, for example, has held that the government has a compelling state interest in taking measures "to protect children from exposure to patently offensive sex-related material." *Id.* A regulation is "narrowly tailored" if it restricts only the speech which the government has a compelling interest in restricting; regulations are not narrowly tailored if they are "overinclusive" (i.e., they restrict speech that the government does not have an interest in regulating) or "underinclusive" (i.e., they fail to regulate enough speech to further the government's interest). See *Simon & Schuster, Inc. v. Members of New York State Crime Victims Bd.*, 502 U.S. 105, 121 & n.* (1991). As we have seen elsewhere in this book, strict scrutiny is the most searching form of review that the Court applies, and challenged government actions rarely survive such judicial inquiries.

Note that a regulation need not discriminate among competing *viewpoints* in order to be considered content based. To be sure, such regulations constitute a particularly pernicious form of content-based restriction: a law that prohibits statements supporting Republican (but not Democratic) candidates for public office not only is based on the content of the proscribed speech—matters concerning electoral politics—but is also based on the particular viewpoint that the speaker expresses. But the Court has made clear that a regulation that "does not favor either side of a political controversy" nevertheless imposes a content-based restriction if it prohibits "public discussion of an entire topic." *Consolidated Edison Co. v. Public Service Comm'n,* 447 U.S. 530, 537 (1980). Accordingly, a law that prohibits statements in favor of *any* candidate for political office, regardless of political party, is also content based and thus is subject to strict scrutiny.

In *Boos v. Barry,* the Supreme Court struck down the District of Columbia law regarding placards outside of embassies. The law, as explained, was clearly a content-based restriction. The District of Columbia argued that the law served to protect the dignity of foreign diplomats. Without deciding whether this was a compelling interest, the Court concluded that the law was not narrowly tailored to achieve the government's goal, because there were other ways to protect the dignity of ambassadors without banning negative messages. See *id.* at 329.

In contrast, government regulations that affect speech but that do not single out disfavored speech based upon its content do not generally trigger such searching scrutiny. For example, a law that prohibits the use of megaphones on residential streets does not single out particular messages—based solely on their content—for disfavored treatment. Instead, it applies regardless of the message conveyed by the user of the megaphone—it applies, that is, equally to a person announcing a sale at the local general store, a person trying to get people to attend a political rally sponsored by the mayor, and a person seeking to register voters to oppose the current mayor. Such "content-neutral" regulations do not run the same risk of government censorship as do content-based restrictions, and they accordingly raise fewer concerns. But they nevertheless impose some burdens on the ability of individuals to convey their messages. Accordingly, as we will see, they are permitted if they are narrowly tailored to serve a significant governmental interest and leave open ample alternative channels for communication.

Such "time, place, or manner" restrictions directly regulate expressive activities but are generally thought to be reasonable regulations of those activities. It is also possible (and, indeed, not uncommon) for a generally applicable, content-neutral regulation that is not limited in its application to expressive activities nevertheless to impose burdens on expressive activities. For example, the creation of a no-parking zone in a downtown area might affect the business of a bookstore located in the area. Such regulations do not generally have as their aim the suppression (or even the regulation) of expressive activities protected by the First Amendment, but they might nevertheless have some effect on such activities—in the example, by making it more difficult to distribute ideas. Although the Court's cases in this area are not easy to summarize, the Court generally will uphold such regulations if they further "an important or substantial governmental interest; if the governmental interest is unrelated to the suppression of free expression; and if the incidental restriction on alleged First Amendment freedoms is no greater than is essential to the furtherance of that interest." *United States v. O'Brien,* 391 U.S. 367 (1968).

Content-neutral regulations, in other words, are subject to a less searching level of scrutiny than are content-based regulations. Given the different levels of scrutiny triggered by the different types of government regulation, the threshold question—whether the challenged regulation is content based or instead content neutral—takes on great significance in cases concerning the freedom of speech. But as the cases that follow demonstrate, that question is not always easy to answer.

REED V. TOWN OF GILBERT, ARIZONA
576 U.S. 155 (2015)

JUSTICE THOMAS delivered the opinion of the Court.

The town of Gilbert, Arizona (or Town), has adopted a comprehensive code governing the manner in which people may display outdoor signs. Gilbert, Ariz., Land Development Code, ch. 1, § 4.402 (2005). The Sign Code identifies various categories of signs based on the type of information they convey, then subjects each category to different restrictions. * * * We hold that these provisions are content-based regulations of speech that cannot survive strict scrutiny.

The Sign Code prohibits the display of outdoor signs anywhere within the Town without a permit, but it then exempts 23 categories of signs from that requirement. * * * Three categories of exempt signs are particularly relevant here. The first is "Ideological Sign[s]." This category includes any "sign communicating a message or ideas for noncommercial purposes that is not a Construction Sign, Directional Sign, Temporary Directional Sign Relating to a Qualifying Event, Political Sign, Garage Sale Sign, or a sign owned or required by a governmental agency." Of the three categories discussed here, the Code treats ideological signs most favorably, allowing them to be up to 20 square feet in area and to be placed in all "zoning districts" without time limits. § 4.402(J).

The second category is "Political Sign[s]." This includes any "temporary sign designed to influence the outcome of an election called by a public body." Glossary 23.[2] The Code treats these signs less favorably than ideological signs. The Code allows the placement of political signs up to 16 square feet on residential property and up to 32 square feet on nonresidential property, undeveloped municipal property, and "rights-of-way." § 4.402(I). These signs may be displayed up to 60 days before a primary election and up to 15 days following a general election. *Ibid.*

The third category is "Temporary Directional Signs Relating to a Qualifying Event." This includes any "Temporary Sign intended to direct pedestrians, motorists, and other passersby to a 'qualifying event.' " A "qualifying event" is defined as any "assembly, gathering, activity, or meeting sponsored, arranged, or promoted by a religious, charitable, community service, educational, or other similar non-profit organization." *Ibid.* The Code treats temporary directional signs even less favorably than political signs. Temporary directional signs may be no larger than six square feet. § 4.402(P). They may be placed on private property or on a public right-of-way, but no more than four signs may be placed on a single property at any time. *Ibid.* And, they may be displayed no more than 12 hours before the "qualifying event" and no more than 1 hour afterward. *Ibid.*

Petitioners Good News Community Church [and] its pastor, Clyde Reed, wish to advertise the time and location of their Sunday church services. The Church is a small, cash-strapped entity that owns no building, so it holds its services at elementary schools or other locations in or near the Town. In order to inform the public about its services, which are held in a variety of different locations, the Church began placing 15 to 20 temporary signs around the Town, frequently in the public right-of-way abutting the street. The signs typically displayed the Church's name, along with the time and location of the upcoming service. Church members would post the signs early in the day on Saturday and then remove them around midday on Sunday. The display of these signs requires little money and manpower, and thus has proved to be an economical and effective way for the Church to let the community know where its services are being held each week.

This practice caught the attention of the Town's Sign Code compliance manager, who twice cited the Church for violating the Code. * * * His efforts proved unsuccessful. The Town's Code compliance manager informed the

---

[2] A "Temporary Sign" is a "sign not permanently attached to the ground, a wall or a building, and not designed or intended for permanent display." Glossary 25.

Church that there would be "no leniency under the Code" and promised to punish any future violations.

Shortly thereafter, petitioners filed a complaint in the United States District Court for the District of Arizona, arguing that the Sign Code abridged their freedom of speech in violation of the First and Fourteenth Amendments. [The District Court granted summary judgment in favor of the town, concluding that the Code's sign categories were content neutral, and the Court of Appeals affirmed, reasoning that the Town "did not adopt its regulation of speech because it disagreed with the message conveyed" and its "interests in regulat[ing] temporary signs are unrelated to the content of the sign," 707 F.3d 1057, 1071–72 (9th Cir. 2013).]

The First Amendment, applicable to the States through the Fourteenth Amendment, prohibits the enactment of laws "abridging the freedom of speech." U.S. Const., Amdt. 1. Under that Clause, a government, including a municipal government vested with state authority, "has no power to restrict expression because of its message, its ideas, its subject matter, or its content." *Police Dept. of Chicago v. Mosley*, 408 U.S. 92, 95 (1972). Content-based laws—those that target speech based on its communicative content—are presumptively unconstitutional and may be justified only if the government proves that they are narrowly tailored to serve compelling state interests. *R.A.V. v. St. Paul*, 505 U.S. 377, 395 (1992); *Simon & Schuster, Inc. v. Members of N.Y. State Crime Victims Bd.*, 502 U.S. 105, 115, 118 (1991).

Government regulation of speech is content based if a law applies to particular speech because of the topic discussed or the idea or message expressed. *E.g., Carey v. Brown*, 447 U.S. 455, 462 (1980). This commonsense meaning of the phrase "content based" requires a court to consider whether a regulation of speech "on its face" draws distinctions based on the message a speaker conveys. Some facial distinctions based on a message are obvious, defining regulated speech by particular subject matter, and others are more subtle, defining regulated speech by its function or purpose. Both are distinctions drawn based on the message a speaker conveys, and, therefore, are subject to strict scrutiny. Our precedents have also recognized a separate and additional category of laws that, though facially content neutral, will be considered content-based regulations of speech: laws that cannot be "justified without reference to the content of the regulated speech," or that were adopted by the government "because of disagreement with the message [the speech] conveys," *Ward v. Rock Against Racism*, 491 U.S. 781, 791 (1989). Those laws, like those that are content based on their face, must also satisfy strict scrutiny.

The Town's Sign Code is content based on its face. It defines "Temporary Directional Signs" on the basis of whether a sign conveys the message of directing the public to church or some other "qualifying event." It defines "Political Signs" on the basis of whether a sign's message is "designed to influence the outcome of an election." And it defines "Ideological Signs" on the basis of whether a sign "communicat[es] a message or ideas" that do not fit within the Code's other categories. It then subjects each of these categories to different restrictions.

The restrictions in the Sign Code that apply to any given sign thus depend entirely on the communicative content of the sign. If a sign informs its reader of the time and place a book club will discuss John Locke's Two Treatises of Government, that sign will be treated differently from a sign expressing the view that one should vote for one of Locke's followers in an upcoming election, and both signs will be treated differently from a sign expressing an ideological view rooted in Locke's theory of government. More to the point, the Church's signs inviting people to attend its worship services are treated differently from signs conveying other types of ideas. On its face, the Sign Code is a content-based regulation of speech. We thus have no need to consider the government's justifications or purposes for enacting the Code to determine whether it is subject to strict scrutiny.

In reaching the contrary conclusion, the Court of Appeals offered several theories to explain why the Town's Sign Code should be deemed content neutral. None is persuasive. The Court of Appeals first determined that the Sign Code was content neutral because the Town "did not adopt its regulation of speech [based on] disagree[ment] with the message conveyed," and its justifications for regulating temporary directional signs were "unrelated to the content of the sign." 707 F.3d, at 1071–1072. * * *

But this analysis skips the crucial first step in the content-neutrality analysis: determining whether the law is content neutral on its face. A law that is content based on its face is subject to strict scrutiny regardless of the government's benign motive, content-neutral justification, or lack of "animus toward the ideas contained" in the regulated speech. *Cincinnati v. Discovery Network, Inc.*, 507 U.S. 410, 429 (1993). We have thus made clear that "[i]llicit legislative intent is not the *sine qua non* of a violation of the First Amendment," and a party opposing the government "need adduce 'no evidence of an improper censorial motive.' " *Simon & Schuster, supra,* at 117. Although "a content-based purpose may be sufficient in certain circumstances to show that a regulation is content based, it is not necessary." *Turner Broadcasting System, Inc. v. FCC*, 512 U.S. 622, 642 (1994). In other words, an innocuous justification cannot transform a facially content-based law into one that is content neutral. * * * Because strict scrutiny applies either when a law is content based on its face or when the purpose and justification for the law are content based, a court must evaluate each question before it concludes that the law is content neutral and thus subject to a lower level of scrutiny.

* * * Innocent motives do not eliminate the danger of censorship presented by a facially content-based statute, as future government officials may one day wield such statutes to suppress disfavored speech. * * * [O]ne could easily imagine a Sign Code compliance manager who disliked the Church's substantive teachings deploying the Sign Code to make it more difficult for the Church to inform the public of the location of its services. Accordingly, we have repeatedly "rejected the argument that 'discriminatory ... treatment is suspect under the First Amendment only when the legislature intends to suppress certain ideas.' " *Discovery Network,* 507 U.S., at 429.

The Court of Appeals next reasoned that the Sign Code was content neutral because it "does not mention any idea or viewpoint, let alone single one out for differential treatment." 587 F.3d, at 977. It reasoned that, for the purpose of the Code provisions, "[i]t makes no difference which candidate is supported, who sponsors the event, or what ideological perspective is asserted." 707 F.3d, at 1069. * * * This analysis conflates two distinct but related limitations that the First Amendment places on government regulation of speech. Government discrimination among viewpoints—or the regulation of speech based on "the specific motivating ideology or the opinion or perspective of the speaker"—is a "more blatant" and "egregious form of content discrimination." *Rosenberger v. Rector and Visitors of Univ. of Va.,* 515 U.S. 819, 829 (1995). But it is well established that "[t]he First Amendment's hostility to content-based regulation extends not only to restrictions on particular viewpoints, but also to prohibition of public discussion of an entire topic." *Consolidated Edison Co. of N.Y. v. Public Serv. Comm'n of N. Y.,* 447 U.S. 530, 537 (1980).

Thus, a speech regulation targeted at specific subject matter is content based even if it does not discriminate among viewpoints within that subject matter. For example, a law banning the use of sound trucks for political speech—and only political speech—would be a content-based regulation, even if it imposed no limits on the political viewpoints that could be expressed. The Town's Sign Code likewise singles out specific subject matter for differential treatment, even if it does not target viewpoints within that subject matter. Ideological messages are given more favorable treatment than messages concerning a political candidate, which are themselves given more favorable treatment than messages announcing an assembly of like-minded individuals. That is a paradigmatic example of content-based discrimination.

Finally, the Court of Appeals characterized the Sign Code's distinctions as turning on "the content-neutral elements of who is speaking through the sign and whether and when an event is occurring." 707 F.3d, at 1069. That analysis is mistaken on both factual and legal grounds. To start, the Sign Code's distinctions are not speaker based. The restrictions for political, ideological, and temporary event signs apply equally no matter who sponsors them. * * * In any case, the fact that a distinction is speaker based does not, as the Court of Appeals seemed to believe, automatically render the distinction content neutral. Because "[s]peech restrictions based on the identity of the speaker are all too often simply a means to control content," *Citizens United v. Federal Election Comm'n*, 558 U.S. 310, 340 (2010), we have insisted that "laws favoring some speakers over others demand strict scrutiny when the legislature's speaker preference reflects a content preference," *Turner*, 512 U.S., at 658.

Nor do the Sign Code's distinctions hinge on "whether and when an event is occurring." The Code does not permit citizens to post signs on any topic whatsoever within a set period leading up to an election, for example. Instead, come election time, it requires Town officials to determine whether a sign is "designed to influence the outcome of an election" (and thus "political") or merely "communicating a message or ideas for noncommercial purposes" (and thus "ideological"). That obvious content-based inquiry does not evade strict scrutiny review simply because an event (*i.e.,* an election) is involved. * * * A regulation that targets a sign because it conveys an idea about a specific event is no less content based than a regulation that targets a sign because it conveys some other idea. Here, the Code singles out signs bearing a particular message: the time and location of a specific event. This type of ordinance may seem like a perfectly rational way to regulate signs, but a clear and firm rule governing content neutrality is an essential means of protecting the freedom of speech, even if laws that might seem "entirely reasonable" will sometimes be "struck down because of their content-based nature." *City of Ladue v. Gilleo*, 512 U.S. 43, 60 (1994) (O'Connor, J., concurring).

Because the Town's Sign Code imposes content-based restrictions on speech, those provisions can stand only if they survive strict scrutiny, "which requires the Government to prove that the restriction furthers a compelling interest and is narrowly tailored to achieve that interest," *Arizona Free Enterprise Club's Freedom Club PAC v. Bennett*, 564 U.S. 721, 734 (2011). Thus, it is the Town's burden to demonstrate that the Code's differentiation between temporary directional signs and other types of signs, such as political signs and ideological signs, furthers a compelling governmental interest and is narrowly tailored to that end. The Town cannot do so. It has offered only two governmental interests in support of the distinctions the Sign Code draws: preserving the Town's aesthetic appeal and traffic safety. Assuming for the sake of argument that those are compelling governmental interests, the Code's distinctions fail as hopelessly underinclusive.

Starting with the preservation of aesthetics, temporary directional signs are "no greater an eyesore," *Discovery Network,* 507 U.S., at 425, than ideological or political ones. Yet the Code allows unlimited proliferation of larger ideological signs while strictly limiting the number, size, and duration of smaller directional ones. The Town cannot claim that placing strict limits on temporary directional signs is necessary to beautify the Town while at the same time allowing unlimited numbers of other types of signs that create the same problem. The Town similarly has not shown that limiting temporary directional signs is necessary to eliminate threats to traffic safety, but that limiting other types of signs is not. The Town has offered no reason to believe that directional signs pose a greater threat to safety than do ideological or political signs. If anything, a sharply worded ideological sign seems more likely to distract a driver than a sign directing the public to a nearby church meeting.

Take Note

The Court concludes here that the Sign Code is not narrowly tailored to advance a compelling government interest. Can you articulate why the Code is under-inclusive, and why under-inclusivity means that the Code is not narrowly tailored?

In light of this underinclusiveness, the Town has not met its burden to prove that its Sign Code is narrowly tailored to further a compelling government interest. Because a "law cannot be regarded as protecting an interest of the highest order, and thus as justifying a restriction on truthful speech, when it leaves appreciable damage to that supposedly vital interest unprohibited," *Republican Party of Minn. v. White,* 536 U.S. 765, 780 (2002), the Sign Code fails strict scrutiny.

Our decision today will not prevent governments from enacting effective sign laws. The Town asserts that an "absolutist" content-neutrality rule would render "virtually all distinctions in sign laws . . . subject to strict scrutiny," Brief for Respondents 34–35, but that is not the case. Not "all distinctions" are subject to strict scrutiny, only *content-based* ones are. Laws that are *content neutral* are instead subject to lesser scrutiny. See *Clark,* 468 U.S., at 295. The Town has ample content-neutral options available to resolve problems with safety and aesthetics. For example, its current Code regulates many aspects of signs that have nothing to do with a sign's message: size, building materials, lighting, moving parts, and portability. And on public property, the Town may go a long way toward entirely forbidding the posting of signs, so long as it does so in an evenhanded, content-neutral manner. See *Members of City Council of Los Angeles v. Taxpayers for Vincent*, 466 U.S. 789, 817 (1984) (upholding content-neutral ban against posting signs on public property).

We acknowledge that a city might reasonably view the general regulation of signs as necessary because signs "take up space and may obstruct views, distract motorists, displace alternative uses for land, and pose other problems that legitimately call for regulation." *City of Ladue*, 512 U.S., at 48. At the same time, the presence of certain signs may be essential, both for vehicles and pedestrians, to guide traffic or to identify hazards and ensure safety. A sign ordinance narrowly tailored to the challenges of protecting the safety of pedestrians, drivers, and passengers—such as warning signs marking hazards on private property, signs directing traffic, or street numbers associated with private houses—well might survive strict scrutiny. The signs at issue in this case, including political and ideological signs and signs for events, are far removed from those purposes.

We reverse the judgment of the Court of Appeals and remand the case for proceedings consistent with this opinion.

[JUSTICE ALITO's concurring opinion has been omitted.]

JUSTICE BREYER, concurring in the judgment.

* * * To use content discrimination to trigger strict scrutiny sometimes makes perfect sense. There are cases in which the Court has found content discrimination an unconstitutional method for suppressing a viewpoint. *E.g., Boos v. Barry*, 485 U.S. 312, 318–319 (1988) (plurality opinion) (applying strict scrutiny where the line between subject matter and viewpoint was not obvious). And there are cases where the Court has found content discrimination to reveal that rules governing a traditional public forum are, in fact, not a neutral way of fairly managing the forum in the interest of all speakers. *Police Dept. of Chicago v. Mosley*, 408 U.S. 92, 96 (1972). In these types of cases, strict scrutiny is often appropriate, and content discrimination has thus served a useful purpose.

But content discrimination, while helping courts to identify unconstitutional suppression of expression, cannot and should not *always* trigger strict scrutiny. * * * Regulatory programs almost always require content discrimination. And to hold that such content discrimination triggers strict scrutiny is to write a recipe for judicial management of ordinary government regulatory activity. Consider a few examples of speech regulated by government that inevitably involve content discrimination, but where a strong presumption against constitutionality has no place. Consider governmental regulation of securities, *e.g.,* 15 U.S.C. § 781 (requirements for content that must be included in a registration statement); of energy conservation labeling-practices, *e.g.,* 42 U.S.C. § 6294 (requirements for content that must be included on labels of certain consumer electronics); of prescription drugs, *e.g.,* 21 U.S.C. § 353(b)(4)(A) (requiring a prescription drug label to bear the symbol "Rx only"); * * * of signs at petting zoos, *e.g.,* N.Y. Gen. Bus. Law Ann. § 399–ff(3) (West Cum. Supp. 2015) (requiring petting zoos to post a sign at every exit "strongly recommend[ing] that persons wash their hands upon exiting the petting zoo area"); and so on.

* * * The better approach is to generally treat content discrimination as a strong reason weighing against the constitutionality of a rule where a traditional public forum, or where viewpoint discrimination, is threatened, but elsewhere treat it as a rule of thumb, finding it a helpful, but not determinative legal tool, in an appropriate case, to determine the strength of a justification. I would use content discrimination as a supplement to a more basic analysis, which, tracking most of our First Amendment cases, asks whether the regulation at issue works harm to First Amendment interests that is disproportionate in light of the relevant regulatory objectives. Answering this question requires examining the seriousness of the harm to speech, the importance of the countervailing objectives, the extent to which the law will achieve those objectives, and whether there are other, less restrictive ways of doing so. Admittedly, this approach does not have the simplicity of a mechanical use of categories. But it does permit the government to regulate speech in numerous instances where the voters have authorized the government to regulate and where courts should hesitate to substitute judicial judgment for that of administrators.

Here, [there] is no traditional public forum nor do I find any general effort to censor a particular viewpoint. Consequently, the specific regulation at issue does not warrant "strict scrutiny." Nonetheless, for the reasons that Justice KAGAN sets forth, I believe that the Town of Gilbert's regulatory rules violate the First Amendment. I consequently concur in the Court's judgment only.

JUSTICE KAGAN, with whom JUSTICE GINSBURG and JUSTICE BREYER join, concurring in the judgment.

Countless cities and towns across America have adopted ordinances regulating the posting of signs, while exempting certain categories of signs based on their subject matter. For example, some municipalities generally prohibit illuminated signs in residential neighborhoods, but lift that ban for signs that identify the address of a home or the name of its owner or occupant. In other municipalities, safety signs such as "Blind Pedestrian Crossing" and "Hidden Driveway" can be posted without a permit, even as other permanent signs require one. Elsewhere, historic site markers—for example, "George Washington Slept Here"—are also exempt from general regulations. And similarly, the federal Highway Beautification Act limits signs along interstate highways unless, for instance, they direct travelers to "scenic and historical attractions" or advertise free coffee. See 23 U.S.C. §§ 131(b), (c)(1), (c)(5).

Given the Court's analysis, many sign ordinances of that kind are now in jeopardy. * * * Says the majority: When laws "single[ ] out specific subject matter," they are "facially content based"; and when they are facially content based, they are automatically subject to strict scrutiny. And although the majority holds out hope that some sign laws with subject-matter exemptions "might survive" that stringent review, the likelihood is that most will be struck down. After all, it is the "rare case[ ] in which a speech restriction withstands strict scrutiny." *Williams-Yulee v. Florida Bar*, 135 S.Ct. 1656, 1666 (2015). * * * The consequence—unless courts water down strict scrutiny to something unrecognizable—is that our communities will find themselves in an unenviable bind: They will have to either repeal the exemptions that allow for helpful signs on streets and sidewalks, or else lift their sign restrictions altogether and resign themselves to the resulting clutter.

Although the majority insists that applying strict scrutiny to all such ordinances is "essential" to protecting First Amendment freedoms, I find it challenging to understand why that is so. This Court's decisions articulate two important and related reasons for subjecting content-based speech regulations to the most exacting standard of review. The first is "to preserve an uninhibited marketplace of ideas in which truth will ultimately prevail." *McCullen v. Coakley*, 134 S.Ct. 2518, 2529 (2014). The second is to ensure that the government has not regulated speech "based on hostility—or favoritism—towards the underlying message expressed." *R.A.V. v. St. Paul*, 505 U.S. 377, 386 (1992). Yet the subject-matter exemptions included in many sign ordinances do not implicate those concerns. Allowing residents, say, to install a light bulb over "name and address" signs but no others does not distort the marketplace of ideas. Nor does that different treatment give rise to an inference of impermissible government motive.

We apply strict scrutiny to facially content-based regulations of speech, in keeping with the rationales just described, when there is any "realistic possibility that official suppression of ideas is afoot." *Davenport v. Washington Ed. Assn.*, 551 U.S. 177, 189 (2007). That is always the case when the regulation facially differentiates on the basis of viewpoint. See *Rosenberger v. Rector and Visitors of Univ. of Va.*, 515 U.S. 819, 829 (1995). It is also the case (except in non-public or limited public forums) when a law restricts "discussion of an entire topic" in public debate. *Consolidated Edison Co. of N.Y. v. Public Serv. Comm'n of N.Y.*, 447 U.S. 530, 537, 539–540 (1980) (invalidating a limitation on speech about nuclear power). * * * And we have recognized that such subject-matter restrictions, even though viewpoint-neutral on their face, may "suggest[ ] an attempt to give one side of a debatable public question an advantage in expressing its views to the people." *First Nat. Bank of Boston v. Bellotti*, 435 U.S. 765, 785 (1978). Subject-matter regulation, in other words, may have the intent or effect of favoring some ideas over others. When that is realistically possible—when the restriction "raises the specter that the Government may effectively drive certain ideas or viewpoints from the marketplace"—we insist that the law pass the most demanding constitutional test. *R.A.V.*, 505 U.S., at 387.

But when that is not realistically possible, we may do well to relax our guard so that "entirely reasonable" laws imperiled by strict scrutiny can survive. * * * To do its intended work, of course, the category of content-based regulation triggering strict scrutiny must sweep more broadly than the actual harm; that category exists to create a buffer zone guaranteeing that the government cannot favor or disfavor certain viewpoints. But that buffer zone need not extend forever. We can administer our content-regulation doctrine with a dose of common sense, so as to leave standing laws that in no way implicate its intended function.

And indeed we have done just that: Our cases have been far less rigid than the majority admits in applying strict scrutiny to facially content-based laws—including in cases just like this one. * * * In *Members of City Council of Los Angeles v. Taxpayers for Vincent*, 466 U.S. 789 (1984), the Court declined to apply strict scrutiny to a municipal ordinance that exempted address numbers and markers commemorating "historical, cultural, or artistic event[s]" from a generally applicable limit on sidewalk signs. And [in] *City of Ladue v. Gilleo*, 512 U.S. 43 (1994), the Court assumed *arguendo* that a sign ordinance's exceptions for address signs, safety signs, and for-sale signs in residential areas did not trigger strict scrutiny. We did not need to, and so did not, decide the level-of-scrutiny question because the law's breadth made it unconstitutional under any standard.

The majority could easily have taken *Ladue*'s tack here. The Town of Gilbert's defense of its sign ordinance—most notably, the law's distinctions between directional signs and others—does not pass strict scrutiny, or intermediate scrutiny, or even the laugh test. The Town, for example, provides no reason at all for prohibiting more than four directional signs on a property while placing no limits on the number of other types of signs. See Gilbert, Ariz., Land Development Code, ch. I, §§ 4.402(J), (P)(2) (2014). Similarly, the Town offers no coherent justification for restricting the size of directional signs to 6 square feet while allowing other signs to reach 20 square feet. See §§ 4.402(J), (P)(1). The best the Town could come up with at oral argument was that directional signs "need to be smaller because they need to guide travelers along a route." Tr. of Oral Arg. 40. Why exactly a smaller sign better helps travelers get to where they are going is left a mystery. The absence of any sensible basis for these and other distinctions dooms the Town's ordinance under even the intermediate scrutiny that the Court typically applies to "time, place, or manner" speech regulations. Accordingly, there is no need to decide in this case whether strict scrutiny applies to every sign ordinance in every town across this country containing a subject-matter exemption.

I suspect this Court and others will regret the majority's insistence today on answering that question in the affirmative. As the years go by, courts will discover that thousands of towns have such ordinances, many of them "entirely reasonable." And as the challenges to them mount, courts will have to invalidate one after the other. (This Court may soon find itself a veritable Supreme Board of Sign Review.) And courts will strike down those democratically enacted local laws even though no one—certainly not the majority—has ever explained why the vindication of First Amendment values requires that result. Because I see no reason why such an easy case calls for us to cast a constitutional pall on reasonable regulations quite unlike the law before us, I concur only in the judgment.

POINTS FOR DISCUSSION

a. Understanding the Decision

The Court explained that a regulation is content based if, on its face, the regulation "applies to particular speech because of the topic discussed or the idea or message expressed." This is true—and strict scrutiny therefore applies—regardless of whether the government adopted the regulation based on its disagreement with the particular message conveyed. In *Renton v. Playtime Theatres*, which follows, the Court concluded that a regulation that prohibited adult movie theaters—defined as theaters that present movies depicting certain sexual activities—from locating in certain areas was not content based because it was "aimed not at the content of the films shown," but rather at "the secondary effects of such theaters on the surrounding community." Is *Renton* still good law after *Reed?*

b. Rules and Standards

As Justices Kagan and Breyer noted in their separate opinions, many laws and regulations that are common around the country—such as laws that prohibit all signs except street numbers and for-sale signs on residential property—are suspect under the Court's approach, even though such laws do not seem clearly to implicate the values that the First Amendment is designed to serve. Justice Breyer suggested that the Court apply a balancing test, and Justice Kagan proposed that the Court "relax [its] guard" in such cases. Is the Court's approach misguided because it lacks nuance? Or is its virtue that it is clear and easy to administer?

c. Alternatives to the Sign Code

Can you think of content-neutral regulations that the town could have enacted that would have achieved its goals? Would those regulations have been equally effective in achieving the town's goals of preserving aesthetics and promoting traffic safety?

d. Time, Place, or Manner Restrictions

The conclusion that a regulation of speech is content neutral does not end the inquiry under the First Amendment. As we will see, content-neutral regulations of the time, place, or manner of speech must still be narrowly tailored to serve the government's legitimate interests and must leave open ample alternative channels for communication. Even though that standard is less stringent in practice than the strict scrutiny that the Court applies to content-based regulations, the Court has invalidated some content-neutral regulations under that standard.

———————

The Court in *Reed* held that a facially content-based regulation triggers strict scrutiny regardless of the legislature's motive in adopting it. But is that always true? Consider the following case, in which the Court focused on the legislature's motive in adopting the regulation at issue. As you read the Court's opinion, consider whether the legislature's motive was relevant because it was not clear on the statute's face whether it was content based, or instead because it suggested that a statute that *was* content based on its face nevertheless should not be treated as such.

RENTON V. PLAYTIME THEATRES, INC.
475 U.S. 41 (1986)

JUSTICE REHNQUIST delivered the opinion of the Court.

In May 1980, the Mayor of Renton, a city of approximately 32,000 people located just south of Seattle, suggested to the Renton City Council that it consider the advisability of enacting zoning legislation dealing with adult entertainment uses. No such uses existed in the city at that time. Upon the Mayor's suggestion, the City Council referred the matter to the city's Planning and Development

Committee. The Committee held public hearings, reviewed the experiences of Seattle and other cities, and received a report from the City Attorney's Office advising as to developments in other cities. The City Council, meanwhile, adopted Resolution No. 2368, which imposed a moratorium on the licensing of "any business [which] has as its primary purpose the selling, renting or showing of sexually explicit materials." The resolution contained a clause explaining that such businesses "would have a severe impact upon surrounding businesses and residences."

In April 1981, acting on the basis of the Planning and Development Committee's recommendation, the City Council enacted Ordinance No. 3526. The ordinance prohibited any "adult motion picture theater" from locating within 1,000 feet of any residential zone, single- or multiple-family dwelling, church, or park, and within one mile of any school. The term "adult motion picture theater" was defined as "[a]n enclosed building used for presenting motion picture films, video cassettes, cable television, or any other such visual media, distinguished or characteri[zed] by an emphasis on matter depicting, describing or relating to 'specified sexual activities' or 'specified anatomical areas' [for] observation by patrons therein."

In early 1982, respondents acquired two existing theaters in downtown Renton, with the intention of using them to exhibit feature-length adult films. The theaters were located within the area proscribed by Ordinance No. 3526. At about the same time, respondents filed [a] lawsuit challenging the ordinance on First and Fourteenth Amendment grounds, and seeking declaratory and injunctive relief. While the federal action was pending, the City Council amended the ordinance in several respects, adding a statement of reasons for its enactment and reducing the minimum distance from any school to 1,000 feet. [The lower courts held that the ordinance did not violate the First Amendment.]

In our view, the resolution of this case is largely dictated by our decision in *Young v. American Mini Theatres, Inc.,* 427 U.S. 50 (1976). There, although five Members of the Court did not agree on a single rationale for the decision, we held that the city of Detroit's zoning ordinance, which prohibited locating an adult theater within 1,000 feet of any two other "regulated uses" or within 500 feet of any residential zone, did not violate the First and Fourteenth Amendments. The Renton ordinance, like the one in *American Mini Theatres,* does not ban adult

> **Take Note**
>
> We will consider "time, place, and manner" regulations in the section that follows. For now, note that such regulations trigger a form of scrutiny less searching than strict scrutiny only if they are content neutral. How does the Court go about deciding whether the ordinance at issue here is content neutral?

theaters altogether, but merely provides that such theaters may not be located within 1,000 feet of any residential zone, single- or multiple-family dwelling, church, park, or school. The ordinance is therefore properly analyzed as a form of time, place, and manner regulation.

Describing the ordinance as a time, place, and manner regulation is, of course, only the first step in our inquiry. This Court has long held that regulations enacted for the purpose of restraining speech on the basis of its content presumptively violate the First Amendment. See *Carey v. Brown,* 447 U.S. 455, 462–463 & n. 7 (1980); *Police Dept. of Chicago v. Mosley,* 408 U.S. 92, 95, 98–99 (1972). On the other hand, so-called "content-neutral" time, place, and manner regulations are acceptable so long as they are designed to serve a substantial governmental interest and do not unreasonably limit alternative avenues of communication. See *Clark v. Community for Creative Non-Violence,* 468 U.S. 288, 293 (1984).

At first glance, the Renton ordinance, like the ordinance in *American Mini Theatres,* does not appear to fit neatly into either the "content-based" or the "content-neutral" category. To be sure, the ordinance treats theaters that specialize in adult films differently from other kinds of theaters. Nevertheless, as the District Court concluded, the Renton ordinance is aimed not at the *content* of the films shown at "adult motion picture theatres," but rather at the *secondary effects* of such theaters on the surrounding community. The District Court found that the City Council's "*predominate* concerns" were with the secondary effects of adult theaters, and not with the content of adult films themselves. * * *

The District Court's finding as to "predominate" intent, left undisturbed by the Court of Appeals, is more than adequate to establish that the city's pursuit of its zoning interests here was unrelated to the suppression of free expression. The ordinance by its terms is designed to prevent crime, protect the city's retail trade, maintain property values, and generally "protec[t] and preserv[e] the quality of [the city's] neighborhoods, commercial districts, and the quality of urban life," not to suppress the expression of unpopular views. As Justice POWELL observed in *American Mini Theatres,* "[i]f [the city] had been concerned with restricting the message purveyed by adult theaters, it would have tried to close them or restrict their number rather than circumscribe their choice as to location." 427 U.S. at 82, n. 4.

In short, the Renton ordinance is completely consistent with our definition of "content-neutral" speech regulations as those that "are *justified* without reference to the content of the regulated speech." *Virginia Pharmacy Board v. Virginia Citizens Consumer Council, Inc.,* 425 U.S. 748, 771 (1976) (emphasis added). The ordinance does not contravene the fundamental principle that underlies our concern about "content-based" speech regulations: that "government may not grant the use of a forum to people whose views it finds acceptable, but deny use to those wishing to express less favored or more controversial views." *Mosley,* 408 U.S., at 95–96.

The appropriate inquiry in this case, then, is whether the Renton ordinance is designed to serve a substantial governmental interest and allows for reasonable alternative avenues of communication. [The Court then answered both questions in the affirmative.]

JUSTICE BLACKMUN concurs in the result.

JUSTICE BRENNAN, with whom JUSTICE MARSHALL joins, dissenting.

The fact that adult movie theaters may cause harmful "secondary" land-use effects may arguably give Renton a compelling reason to regulate such establishments; it does not mean, however, that such regulations are content neutral. Because the ordinance imposes special restrictions on certain kinds of speech on the basis of content, I cannot simply accept, as the Court does, Renton's claim that the ordinance was not designed to suppress the content of adult movies.

The ordinance discriminates on its face against certain forms of speech based on content. Movie theaters specializing in "adult motion pictures" may not be located within 1,000 feet of any residential zone, single- or multiple-family dwelling, church, park, or school. Other motion picture theaters, and other forms of "adult entertainment," such as bars, massage parlors, and adult bookstores, are not subject to the same restrictions. This selective treatment strongly suggests that Renton was interested not in controlling the "secondary effects" associated with adult businesses, but in discriminating against adult theaters based on the content of the films they exhibit.

Rather than speculate about Renton's motives for adopting such measures, our cases require the conclusion that the ordinance, like any other content-based restriction on speech, is constitutional "only if the [city] can show that [it] is a precisely drawn means of serving a compelling [governmental] interest." *Consolidated Edison Co. v. Public Service Comm'n of N.Y.,* 447 U.S. 530, 540 (1980). Only this strict approach can insure that cities will not use their zoning powers as a pretext for suppressing constitutionally protected expression.

POINTS FOR DISCUSSION

a. Secondary Effects

In *Renton*, much turned on the Court's characterization of the challenged ordinance. If the ordinance was content based, it would be subject to strict scrutiny and thus would likely be invalid. The challenged ordinance on its face provided disfavored treatment only to theaters that showed films about a particular subject. Doesn't that mean by definition that it was a content-based regulation?

In concluding that it was not, the Court's theory appeared to be that the City of Renton did not care what an adult theater might show on its screens; it cared only about the "secondary effects" of the presence of theaters showing such films. Are these considerations entirely distinct? Aren't most content-based restrictions on speech imposed because of a fear of the consequences of the speech? Consider the Court's discussion in *Boos v. Barry*, 485 U.S. 312 (1988):

> Listeners' reactions to speech are not the type of "secondary effects" we referred to in *Renton*. To take an example factually close to *Renton*, if the ordinance there was justified by the city's desire to prevent the psychological damage it felt was associated with viewing adult movies, then analysis of the measure as a content-based statute would have been appropriate. The hypothetical regulation targets the direct impact of a particular category of speech, not a secondary feature that happens to be associated with that type of speech.

Can you articulate the distinction between "listeners' reactions" and "secondary effects"? Suppose a city council bans the display of political bumper stickers on cars. It justifies the ban as follows: "When we banned the political bumper stickers, it was not because of their political content; we just thought that people seeing them might vote for our opponents. We were worried about this secondary effect." Would that argument be successful? If not, why was the ordinance in *Renton* different?

b. Content-Based Regulation and Municipal Zoning

In *City of Los Angeles v. Alameda Books, Inc.*, 535 U.S. 425, 448 (2002), Justice O'Connor suggested, in a plurality opinion joined by three other Justices, that *Renton*'s reasoning should be confined to the zoning context:

> The Court [in *Renton*] appeared to recognize [that] the designation ["content neutral"] was something of a fiction, which, perhaps, is why it kept the phrase in quotes. After all, whether a statute is content neutral or content based is something that can be determined on the face of it; if the statute describes speech by content then it is content based. * * * The fiction that this sort of ordinance is content neutral [is] perhaps more confusing than

helpful * * *. It is also not a fiction that has commanded our consistent adherence. See *Thomas v. Chicago Park Dist.*, 534 U.S. 316, 322, and n. 2 (2002) (suggesting that a licensing scheme targeting only those businesses purveying sexually explicit speech is not content neutral). These ordinances are content based, and we should call them so.

Nevertheless, [the] central holding of *Renton* is sound: A zoning restriction that is designed to decrease secondary effects and not speech should be subject to intermediate rather than strict scrutiny. [Z]oning regulations do not automatically raise the specter of impermissible content discrimination, even if they are content based, because they have a prima facie legitimate purpose: to limit the negative externalities of land use. As a matter of common experience, these sorts of ordinances are more like a zoning restriction on slaughterhouses and less like a tax on unpopular newspapers. The zoning context provides a built-in legitimate rationale, which rebuts the usual presumption that content-based restrictions are unconstitutional.

Is there a reason to treat the zoning context differently? If so, does that suggest that the "secondary effects" rationale will have little application outside of that context? Either way, can the decision in *Renton* survive the Court's decision in *Reed*?

Problem

After public outrage over several highly publicized instances in which persons convicted of crimes profited by writing books about their crimes, the state legislature enacted a statute that required publishers that published books by persons accused or convicted of a crime to deposit in an escrow account all income from works describing those crimes. Funds in the account were then made available to crime victims who obtained civil judgments against the convicted authors. A publisher of a tell-all book by a person convicted of a crime has challenged the law under the First and Fourteenth Amendments. How should the Court rule?

---

2. Reasonable Time, Place, or Manner Restrictions

The second general principle is that the government may impose **reasonable restrictions on the time, place, or manner of speech**, even in public forums, if the restrictions: (1) are content neutral; (2) are narrowly tailored to serve a significant governmental interest; and (3) leave open ample alternative channels for communication of the information. The Supreme Court devised this rule as a means of balancing free speech rights against important public needs, recognizing that allowing anyone to speak at any time and in any manner might be intolerable.

The case of *Kovacs v. Cooper*, 336 U.S. 77 (1949), is a classic example of this approach. The City of Trenton, New Jersey, enacted an ordinance generally barring sound-amplification devices from its streets. The Supreme Court held that the city could apply this ordinance to prohibit a truck from playing music and announcements from loud speakers on city roads. The regulation was content neutral because it applied to all sound amplification, regardless of the message being broadcast. The regulation also served significant government interests in promoting safety and controlling noise pollution. Justice Reed explained: "On the business streets of cities like Trenton, with its more than 125,000 people, such distractions would be dangerous to traffic at all hours useful for the dissemination of information, and in the residential thoroughfares the quiet and tranquility so desirable for city dwellers would likewise be at the mercy of advocates of particular religious, social or political persuasions." Finally, the prohibition restricted only one of many different ways of communicating with the public.

How different from strict scrutiny is this form of review for time, place, and manner restrictions? Consider the case that follows.

WARD V. ROCK AGAINST RACISM
491 U.S. 781 (1989)

JUSTICE KENNEDY delivered the opinion of the Court.

In the southeast portion of New York City's Central Park, about 10 blocks upward from the park's beginning point at 59th Street, there is an amphitheater and stage structure known as the Naumburg Acoustic Bandshell. The bandshell faces west across the remaining width of the park. In close proximity to the bandshell, and lying within the directional path of its sound, is a grassy open area called the Sheep Meadow. The city has designated the Sheep Meadow as a quiet area for passive recreations like reclining, walking, and reading. Just beyond the park, and also within the potential sound range of the bandshell, are the apartments and residences of Central Park West.

> **FYI**
>
> You can view the Naumburg Acoustic Bandshell at https://www.centralpark.com/things-to-do/attractions/naumburg-bandshell/.

This case arises from the city's attempt to regulate the volume of amplified music at the bandshell so the performances are satisfactory to the audience without intruding upon those who use the Sheep Meadow or live on Central Park West and in its vicinity. The city's regulation requires bandshell performers to use sound-amplification equipment and a sound technician provided by the city. The challenge to this volume control technique comes from the sponsor of a rock concert. * * *

Over the years, the city received numerous complaints about excessive sound amplification at respondent's concerts from park users and residents of areas adjacent to the park. * * * The city considered various solutions to the sound-amplification problem. The idea of a fixed decibel limit for all performers using the bandshell was rejected because the impact on listeners of a single decibel level is not constant, but varies in response to changes in air temperature, foliage, audience size, and like factors. The city also rejected the possibility of employing a sound technician to operate the equipment provided by the various sponsors of bandshell events, because the city's technician might have had difficulty satisfying the needs of sponsors while operating unfamiliar, and perhaps inadequate, sound equipment. Instead, the city concluded that the most effective way to achieve adequate but not excessive sound amplification would be for the city to furnish high quality sound equipment and retain an independent, experienced sound technician for all performances at the bandshell. After an extensive search the city hired a private sound company capable of meeting the needs of all the varied users of the bandshell.

Music is one of the oldest forms of human expression. From Plato's discourse in the Republic to the totalitarian state in our own times, rulers have known its capacity to appeal to the intellect and to the emotions, and have censored musical compositions to serve the needs of the state. The Constitution prohibits any like attempts in our own legal order. Music, as a form of expression and communication, is protected under the First Amendment. In the case before us the performances apparently consisted of remarks by speakers, as well as rock music, but the case has been presented as one in which the constitutional challenge is to the city's regulation of the musical aspects of the concert; and, based on the principle we have stated, the city's guideline must meet the demands of the First Amendment. The parties do not appear to dispute that proposition.

Our cases make clear [that] even in a public forum the government may impose reasonable restrictions on the time, place, or manner of protected speech, provided the restrictions "are justified without reference to the content of the regulated speech, that they are narrowly tailored to serve a significant

> **Food for Thought**
>
> It is not difficult to see why some musical performances are protected as speech under the First Amendment; consider, for example, songs parodying the government or encouraging listeners to donate money for relief efforts. But why is all music—even music without lyrics—protected? Why does any form of "expression," as opposed to any form of "communication," count as "speech"?

governmental interest, and that they leave open ample alternative channels for communication of the information." *Clark v. Community for Creative Non-Violence,* 468 U.S. 288, 293 (1984). We consider these requirements in turn.

The principal inquiry in determining content neutrality, in speech cases generally and in time, place, or manner cases in particular, is whether the government has adopted a regulation of speech because of disagreement with the message it conveys. The government's purpose is the controlling consideration. A regulation that serves purposes unrelated to the content of expression is deemed neutral, even if it has an incidental effect on some speakers or messages but not others. See *Renton v. Playtime Theatres, Inc.,* 475 U.S. 41, 47–48 (1986). * * * The principal justification for the sound-amplification guideline is the city's desire to control noise levels at bandshell events, in order to retain the character of the Sheep Meadow and its more sedate activities, and to avoid undue intrusion into residential areas and other areas of the park. This justification for the guideline "ha[s] nothing to do with content," *Boos v. Barry,* 485 U.S. 312, 320 (1988), and it satisfies the requirement that time, place, or manner regulations be content neutral.

The only other justification offered below was the city's interest in "ensur[ing] the quality of sound at Bandshell events." Respondent urges that this justification is not content neutral because it is based upon the quality, and thus the content, of the speech being regulated. In respondent's view, the city is seeking to assert artistic control over performers at the bandshell by enforcing a bureaucratically determined, value-laden conception of good sound. That all performers who have used the city's sound equipment have been completely satisfied is of no moment, respondent argues, because "[t]he First Amendment does not permit and cannot tolerate state control of artistic expression merely because the State claims that [its] efforts will lead to 'top-quality' results."

While respondent's arguments that the government may not interfere with artistic judgment may have much force in other contexts, they are inapplicable to the facts of this case. The city has disclaimed in express terms any interest in imposing its own view of appropriate sound mix on performers. To the contrary, as the District Court found, the city requires its sound technician to defer to the wishes of event sponsors concerning sound mix. On this record, the city's concern with sound quality extends only to the clearly content-neutral goals of ensuring adequate sound amplification and avoiding the volume problems associated with inadequate sound mix. Any governmental attempt to serve purely esthetic goals by imposing subjective standards of acceptable sound mix on performers would raise serious First Amendment concerns, but this case provides us with no opportunity to address those questions. As related above, the District Court found that the city's equipment and its sound technician could meet all of the standards requested by the performers, including [respondent].

The city's regulation is also "narrowly tailored to serve a significant governmental interest." *Community for Creative Non-Violence*, 468 U.S., at 293. Despite respondent's protestations to the contrary, it can no longer be doubted that government "ha[s] a substantial interest in protecting its citizens from unwelcome noise." *City Council of Los Angeles v. Taxpayers for Vincent*, 466 U.S. 789, 806 (1984). This interest is perhaps at its greatest when government seeks to protect "the well-being, tranquility, and privacy of the home," *Frisby v. Schultz*, 487 U.S. 474, 484 (1988) (quoting *Carey v. Brown*, 447 U.S. 455, 471 (1980)), but it is by no means limited to that context, for the government may act to protect even such traditional public forums as city streets and parks from excessive noise. *Kovacs v. Cooper*, 336 U.S. 77, 86–87 (1988) (opinion of Reed, J.).

We think it also apparent that the city's interest in ensuring the sufficiency of sound amplification at bandshell events is a substantial one. The record indicates that inadequate sound amplification has had an adverse [effect] on the ability of some audiences to hear and enjoy performances at the bandshell. The city enjoys a substantial interest in ensuring the ability of its citizens to enjoy whatever benefits the city parks have to offer, from amplified music to silent meditation.

The city's second content-neutral justification for the guideline, that of ensuring "that the sound amplification [is] sufficient to reach all listeners within the defined concertground," also supports the city's choice of regulatory methods. By providing competent sound technicians and adequate amplification equipment, the city eliminated the problems of inexperienced technicians and insufficient sound volume that had plagued some bandshell performers in the past. No doubt this concern is not applicable to respondent's concerts, which apparently were characterized by more-than-adequate sound amplification. But that fact is beside the point, for the validity of the regulation depends on the relation it bears to the overall problem the government seeks to correct, not on the extent to which it furthers the government's interests in an individual case. Here, the regulation's effectiveness must be judged by considering all the varied groups that use the bandshell, and it is valid so long as the city could reasonably have determined that its interests overall would be served less effectively without the sound-amplification guideline than with it. Considering these proffered justifications together, therefore, it is apparent that the guideline directly furthers the city's legitimate governmental interests and that those interests would have been less well served in the absence of the sound-amplification guideline.

The final requirement, that the guideline leave open ample alternative channels of communication, is easily met. Indeed, in this respect the guideline is far less restrictive than regulations we have upheld in other cases, for it does not attempt to ban any particular manner or type of expression at a given place or time. Rather, the guideline continues to permit expressive activity in the bandshell, and has no effect on the quantity or content of that expression beyond regulating the extent of amplification. That the city's limitations on volume may reduce to some degree the potential audience for respondent's speech is of no consequence, for there has been no showing that the remaining avenues of communication are inadequate.

The city's sound-amplification guideline is narrowly tailored to serve the substantial and content-neutral governmental interests of avoiding excessive sound volume and providing sufficient amplification within the bandshell concert ground, and the guideline leaves open ample channels of communication. Accordingly, it is valid under the First Amendment as a reasonable regulation of the place and manner of expression.

JUSTICE BLACKMUN concurs in the result.

JUSTICE MARSHALL, with whom JUSTICE BRENNAN and JUSTICE STEVENS join, dissenting.

No one can doubt that government has a substantial interest in regulating the barrage of excessive sound that can plague urban life. Unfortunately, the majority plays to our shared impatience with loud noise to obscure the damage that it does to our First Amendment rights. Until today, a key safeguard of free speech has been government's obligation to adopt the least intrusive restriction necessary to achieve its goals. * * *

Government's interest in avoiding loud sounds cannot justify giving government total control over sound equipment, any more than its interest in avoiding litter could justify a ban on handbill distribution. In both cases, government's legitimate goals can be effectively and less intrusively served by directly punishing the evil—the persons responsible for excessive sounds and the persons who litter. Indeed, the city concedes that it has an ordinance generally limiting noise but has chosen not to enforce it.[5]

---

[5] Significantly, the National Park Service relies on the very methods of volume control rejected by the city—monitoring sound levels on the perimeter of an event, communicating with event sponsors, and, if necessary, turning off the power. In light of the Park Service's "experienc[e] with thousands of events over the years," the city's claims that these methods of monitoring excessive sound are ineffective and impracticable are hard to accept.

POINTS FOR DISCUSSION

a.   Reasonable Restrictions

As described above, reasonable time, place, and manner restrictions are permissible if they are content neutral, are narrowly tailored to serve a substantial state interest, and leave open ample alternative means of communication. *Ward* concerned a challenge to regulations about sound amplification at a city bandshell. Would the First Amendment have prevented the city from demolishing the bandshell and replacing it with a ball field? If not, then how could the challenged regulation, which *permitted* concerts in the space, not be a reasonable restriction? Doesn't the greater power here to get rid of the bandshell necessarily include the lesser power to regulate sound amplification at the bandshell?

b.   Position of the Dissent

The dissent agreed that the government has a substantial interest in controlling noise, but concluded that it cannot advance that interest by actually asserting control over amplification equipment and thus over private expression itself. Does this view provide an answer to the "greater-includes-the-lesser" argument in favor of the challenged regulation? If you were arguing the case for the plaintiffs, what analogy might you offer to support this view?

Problem

After receiving many complaints about the unsightliness of signs and advertisements on telephone poles and along sidewalks, the Los Angeles City Council adopted an ordinance that prohibits the posting of any signs on public property. A candidate for elected public office has filed a lawsuit alleging that the ordinance prevents him from promoting his candidacy and seeking a declaration that the ordinance violates the First and Fourteenth Amendments. At the same time, the City Council of Ladue, a suburb of St. Louis, adopted an ordinance that prohibits the display of all signs (other than "for sale" signs or signs displaying a house's street address) on residential property. A person who wants to display a sign stating "End the War" filed a suit seeking to enjoin enforcement of the ordinance on the ground that it violates the First and Fourteenth Amendments. The Supreme Court has decided to review both ordinances. How should the Court rule in the two cases?

3. Generally Applicable Regulations of Conduct That Incidentally Affect Expression

As we have just seen, time, place, and manner restrictions directly regulate expressive activities: limitations on the permissible volume at which trucks can broadcast messages or musicians can amplify their music at public concerts, to take the examples we have just considered, by design apply to activities that are squarely protected by the First Amendment. But it is also possible for a government regulation that is *not* directed at protected expressive activities nevertheless to affect those activities. In this section, we consider how the Court reviews challenges to such regulations.

As a general matter, the Court will uphold a regulation of conduct that incidentally affects speech if "it furthers an important or substantial governmental interest; if the governmental interest is unrelated to the suppression of free expression; and if the incidental restriction on alleged First Amendment freedoms is no greater than is essential to the furtherance of that interest." *United States v. O'Brien*, 391 U.S. 367 (1968). For example, in *Clark v. Community for Creative Non-Violence*, 468 U.S. 288, 299–300 & n.8 (1984), the Supreme Court upheld a government ban on sleeping in a park across from the White House even though the ban made it more difficult for a group to carry out its plan to hold demonstrations and protests around the clock. The Court recognized that this ban on conduct (i.e., sleeping) had an incidental effect on speech (i.e., making a long protest more difficult) but agreed that the ban furthered "a substantial Government interest in conserving park property." *Id.* at 300. This test, however, is sometimes more easily stated than applied, as the following cases demonstrate.

UNITED STATES V. O'BRIEN

391 U.S. 367 (1968)

MR. CHIEF JUSTICE WARREN delivered the opinion of the Court.

On the morning of March 31, 1966, David Paul O'Brien and three companions burned their Selective Service registration certificates on the steps of the South Boston Courthouse. A sizable crowd, including several agents of the Federal Bureau of Investigation, witnessed the event. Immediately after the burning, members of the crowd began attacking O'Brien and his companions. An FBI agent ushered O'Brien to safety inside the courthouse. After he was advised of his right to counsel and to silence, O'Brien stated to FBI agents that he had burned his registration certificate because of his beliefs, knowing that he was violating federal law. He produced the charred remains of the certificate, which, with his consent, were photographed.

> **FYI**
>
> Some opponents of the war in Vietnam burned their draft cards as a means of protesting the United States' involvement in the war. Destroying draft cards was illegal. But prosecuting draft card burning cases was difficult because the prosecutor had to prove the defendant in fact burned his draft card and not something else. Usually only ashes remained, which were insufficient as evidence. The record of trial reveals that David O'Brien was unlucky in this regard. A corner of his card—the corner by which he held it—did not burn, and that corner happened to contain his signature.

For this act, O'Brien was indicted, tried, convicted, and sentenced in the United States District Court for the District of Massachusetts. He did not contest the fact that he had burned the certificate. He stated in argument to the jury that he burned the certificate publicly to influence others to adopt his antiwar beliefs, as he put it, "so that other people would reevaluate their positions with Selective Service, with the armed forces, and reevaluate their place in the culture of today, to hopefully consider my position."

[A 1965 Amendment to the Universal Military Training and Service Act of 1948 made it an offense knowingly to destroy or mutilate a selective service registration certificate, also known as a draft card. Prior to enactment of the Amendment, regulations required registrants to keep their certificates in their "personal possession at all times."] O'Brien first argues that the 1965 Amendment is unconstitutional as applied to him because his act of burning his registration certificate was protected "symbolic speech" within the First Amendment. His argument is that the freedom of expression which the First Amendment

Vietnam War Era Draft Card
National Archives

guarantees includes all modes of "communication of ideas by conduct," and that his conduct is within this definition because he did it in "demonstration against the war and against the draft."

We cannot accept the view that an apparently limitless variety of conduct can be labeled "speech" whenever the person engaging in the conduct intends thereby to express an idea. However, even on the assumption that the alleged communicative element in O'Brien's conduct is sufficient to bring into play the First Amendment, it does not necessarily follow that the destruction of a registration certificate is constitutionally protected activity. This Court has held that when "speech" and "nonspeech" elements are combined in the same course of conduct, a sufficiently important governmental interest in regulating the nonspeech element can justify incidental limitations on First Amendment freedoms. To characterize the quality of the governmental interest which must appear, the Court has employed a variety of descriptive terms: compelling; substantial; subordinating; paramount; cogent; strong. Whatever imprecision inheres in these terms, we think it clear that a government regulation is sufficiently justified if it is within the constitutional power of the Government; if it furthers an important or substantial governmental interest; if the governmental interest is unrelated to the suppression of free expression; and if the incidental restriction on alleged First Amendment freedoms is no greater than is essential to the furtherance of that interest. We find that the 1965 Amendment to § 12(b)(3) of the Universal Military Training and Service Act meets all of these requirements, and consequently that O'Brien can be constitutionally convicted for violating it.

Make the Connection

We will consider the extent to which "expressive conduct" is protected by the First Amendment later in this chapter, when we discuss the Court's treatment of a law prohibiting flag burning.

The power of Congress to classify and conscript manpower for military service is "beyond question." *Lichter v. United States*, 334 U.S. 742, 755–758 (1948). Pursuant to this power, Congress may establish a system of registration for individuals liable for training and service, and may require such individuals within reason to cooperate in the registration system. The issuance of certificates indicating the registration and eligibility classification of individuals is a legitimate and substantial administrative aid in the functioning of this system. And legislation to insure the continuing availability of issued certificates serves a legitimate and substantial purpose in the system's administration.

O'Brien's argument to the contrary is necessarily premised upon his unrealistic characterization of Selective Service certificates. He essentially adopts the position that such certificates are so many pieces of paper designed to notify registrants of their registration or classification, to be retained or tossed in the wastebasket according to the convenience or taste of the registrant. Once the registrant has received notification, according to this view, there is no reason for him to retain the certificates. O'Brien notes that most of the information on a registration certificate serves no notification purpose at all; the registrant hardly needs to be told his address and physical characteristics. We agree that the registration certificate contains much information of which the registrant needs no notification. This circumstance, however, does not lead to the conclusion that the certificate serves no purpose, but that, like the classification certificate, it serves purposes in addition to initial notification. Many of these purposes would be defeated by the certificates' destruction or mutilation. Among these are:

1.   The registration certificate serves as proof that the individual described thereon has registered for the draft. The classification certificate shows the eligibility classification of a named but undescribed individual. Voluntarily displaying the two certificates is an easy and painless way for a young man to dispel a question as to whether he might be delinquent in his Selective Service obligations. Correspondingly, the availability of the certificates for such display relieves the Selective Service System of the administrative burden it would otherwise have in verifying the registration and classification of all suspected delinquents. * * *

2.   The information supplied on the certificates facilitates communication between registrants and local boards, simplifying the system and benefiting all concerned. To begin with, each certificate bears the address of the registrant's local board, an item unlikely to be committed to memory. Further, each card bears the registrant's Selective Service number, and a registrant who has his number readily available so that he can communicate it to his local board when he supplies

or requests information can make simpler the board's task in locating his file. Finally, a registrant's inquiry, particularly through a local board other than his own, concerning his eligibility status is frequently answerable simply on the basis of his classification certificate; whereas, if the certificate were not reasonably available and the registrant were uncertain of his classification, the task of answering his questions would be considerably complicated.

3.   Both certificates carry continual reminders that the registrant must notify his local board of any change of address, and other specified changes in his status. The smooth functioning of the system requires that local boards be continually aware of the status and whereabouts of registrants, and the destruction of certificates deprives the system of a potentially useful notice device.

4.   The regulatory scheme involving Selective Service certificates includes clearly valid prohibitions against the alteration, forgery, or similar deceptive misuse of certificates. The destruction or mutilation of certificates obviously increases the difficulty of detecting and tracing abuses such as these. Further, a mutilated certificate might itself be used for deceptive purposes.

The many functions performed by Selective Service certificates establish beyond doubt that Congress has a legitimate and substantial interest in preventing their wanton and unrestrained destruction and assuring their continuing availability by punishing people who knowingly and wilfully destroy or mutilate them. And we are unpersuaded that the pre-existence of the nonpossession regulations in any way negates this interest.

[B]oth the governmental interest and the operation of the 1965 Amendment are limited to the noncommunicative aspect of O'Brien's conduct. The governmental interest and the scope of the 1965 Amendment are limited to preventing harm to the smooth and efficient functioning of the Selective Service System. When O'Brien deliberately rendered unavailable his registration certificate, he wilfully frustrated this governmental interest. For this noncommunicative impact of his conduct, and for nothing else, he was convicted. The case at bar is therefore unlike one where the alleged governmental interest in regulating conduct arises in some measure because the communication allegedly integral to the conduct is itself thought to be harmful. In *Stromberg v. People of State of California*, 283 U.S. 359 (1931), for example, this Court struck down a statutory phrase which punished people who expressed their "opposition to organized government" by displaying "any flag, badge, banner, or device." Since the statute there was aimed at suppressing communication it could not be sustained as a regulation of noncommunicative conduct. [Here,] a sufficient governmental interest has been shown to justify O'Brien's conviction.

O'Brien finally argues that the 1965 Amendment is unconstitutional as enacted because what he calls the "purpose" of Congress was "to suppress freedom of speech." We reject this argument because under settled principles the purpose of Congress, as O'Brien uses that term, is not a basis for declaring this legislation unconstitutional. It is a familiar principle of constitutional law that this Court will not strike down an otherwise constitutional statute on the basis of an alleged illicit legislative motive. * * * Inquiries into congressional motives or purposes are a hazardous matter. When the issue is simply the interpretation of legislation, the Court will look to statements by legislators for guidance as to the purpose of the legislature, because the benefit to sound decision-making in this circumstance is thought sufficient to risk the possibility of misreading Congress' purpose. It is entirely a different matter when we are asked to void a statute that is, under well-settled criteria, constitutional on its face, on the basis of what fewer than a handful of Congressmen said about it. What motivates one legislator to make a speech about a statute is not necessarily what motivates scores of others to enact it, and the stakes are sufficiently high for us to eschew guesswork. We decline to void essentially on the ground that it is unwise legislation which Congress had the undoubted power to enact and which could be reenacted in its exact form if the same or another legislator made a "wiser" speech about it. * * * Accordingly, we [reinstate] the judgment and sentence of the District Court.

MR. JUSTICE HARLAN, concurring.

I wish to make explicit my understanding that [the Court's decision] does not foreclose consideration of First Amendment claims in those rare instances when an "incidental" restriction upon expression, imposed by a regulation which furthers an "important or substantial" governmental interest and satisfies the Court's other criteria, in practice has the effect of entirely preventing a "speaker" from reaching a significant audience with whom he could not otherwise lawfully communicate. This is not such a case, since O'Brien manifestly could have conveyed his message in many ways other than by burning his draft card.

[JUSTICE DOUGLAS's dissenting opinion is omitted.]

POINTS FOR DISCUSSION

a.   "Incidental Limitations on First Amendment Freedoms"

Is it clear that the statute prohibiting the destruction of a draft card imposed only an "incidental" limitation on O'Brien's ability to express his opposition to the war? After all, it prohibited the *exact* expressive conduct in which he engaged to protest the war. Is the point that O'Brien's conduct only tangentially conveyed a message, and thus was not entitled to robust protection under the First Amendment? Or that he could have found some other way to protest the war and thus communicate his message? We will consider the conundrum posed by "expressive conduct" later in this chapter.

b.   "Unrelated to the Suppression of Free Expression"

The *O'Brien* test applies, by its terms, only when the government's interest is "unrelated to the suppression of free expression." Accordingly, *O'Brien* scrutiny does not apply to content-based regulations. Could the government prohibit the burning of a draft card if "done for the specific purpose of protesting the draft"? Or would such a statute be content based and thus subject to strict scrutiny?

Is it clear that the *actual* statute at issue was content neutral? Suppose that upon receiving his draft card in the mail, O'Brien, upset by being drafted, threw his draft card in the trash. If the government had somehow learned of this act—for example, when O'Brien responded to a routine summons to the local draft board—do you think that he would have been prosecuted under the 1965 Amendment to the Universal Military Training and Service Act of 1948? If not, what does that suggest about whether the government interest was "related to the suppression of free expression"?

c.   The *O'Brien* Test and Reasonable Time, Place, or Manner Restrictions

Is there a difference between the *O'Brien* test and the test for time, place, or manner restrictions? Both require that the challenged regulation be content neutral, supported by a substantial governmental interest, and narrowly tailored to avoid burdening more expression than is necessary. In *Clark v. Community for Creative Non-Violence*, 468 U.S. 288 (1984), the Court suggested that the inquiries are essentially the same.

In practice, however, the scrutiny that the Court applies in cases involving time, place, or manner restrictions has had more bite. The Court, applying that level of scrutiny, has invalidated several time, place, or manner restrictions. See, e.g., *McCullen v. Coakley*, 573 U.S. 464 (2014); *City of Ladue v. Gilleo*, 512 U.S. 43 (1992). Yet the Court, applying *O'Brien* scrutiny, has never invalidated a genuinely content-neutral, generally applicable regulation of conduct alleged to have an incidental effect on expression. Indeed, the Court has sometimes not applied any scrutiny at all under the First Amendment in cases claiming that content-neutral, generally applicable regulations of conduct incidentally burden expression. See, e.g., *Arcara v. Cloud Books, Inc.*, 478 U.S. 697 (1987) (declining to apply *O'Brien* scrutiny to order closing down bookstore because solicitations of prostitution had taken place in store).

———————

Under the *O'Brien* test, content-neutral laws that have an incidental effect on activities protected under the First Amendment are subject to an intermediate form of scrutiny. In the case that follows, consider whether (1) the challenged law was in fact content neutral and (2) whether, if so, the Court properly concluded that it was constitutionally valid.

BARNES V. GLEN THEATRE, INC.

501 U.S. 560 (1991)

CHIEF JUSTICE REHNQUIST delivered the opinion of the Court.

Respondents are two establishments in South Bend, Indiana, that wish to provide totally nude dancing as entertainment, and individual dancers who are employed at these establishments. They claim that the First Amendment's guarantee of freedom of expression prevents the State of Indiana from enforcing its public indecency law to prevent this form of dancing. [That law, Ind.Code § 35–45–4–1 (1988), made it a misdemeanor for any person to "knowingly or intentionally, in a public place * * * [appear] in a state of nudity." We] hold that the Indiana statutory requirement that the dancers in the establishments involved in this case must wear pasties and G-strings does not violate the First Amendment.

> **Take Note**
>
> Although the case report says that "Chief Justice Rehnquist delivered the opinion of the Court," this statement is inaccurate. Chief Justice Rehnquist announced the judgment of the court and delivered an opinion, in which Justice O'Connor and Justice Kennedy joined.

Several of our cases contain language suggesting that nude dancing of the kind involved here is expressive conduct protected by the First Amendment. *Schad v. Mount Ephraim,* 452 U.S. 61, 66 (1981). * * * These statements support the conclusion of the Court of Appeals that nude dancing of the kind sought to be performed here is expressive conduct within the outer perimeters of the First Amendment, though we view it as only marginally so. This, of course, does not end our inquiry. We must determine [whether] the Indiana statute is an impermissible infringement of that protected activity.

Indiana, of course, has not banned nude dancing as such, but has proscribed public nudity across the board. The Supreme Court of Indiana has construed the Indiana statute to preclude nudity in what are essentially places of public accommodation such as the Glen Theatre and the Kitty Kat Lounge.

Applying the four-part *O'Brien* [test], we find that Indiana's public indecency statute is justified despite its incidental limitations on some expressive activity.

The public indecency statute is clearly within the constitutional power of the State and furthers substantial governmental interests. It is impossible to discern, other than from the text of the statute, exactly what governmental interest the Indiana legislators had in mind when they enacted this statute, for Indiana does not record legislative history, and the State's highest court has not shed additional light on the statute's purpose. Nonetheless, the statute's purpose of protecting societal order and morality is clear from its text and history. Public indecency statutes of this sort are of ancient origin and presently exist in at least 47 States. Public indecency, including nudity, was a criminal offense at common law, and [p]ublic

> **Definition**
>
> An act *malum in se* is an act that is wrong in and of itself, wholly aside from whether it is formally prohibited by law.

nudity was considered an act *malum in se. Le Roy v. Sidley,* 1 Sid. 168, 82 Eng.Rep. 1036 (K.B.1664). Public indecency statutes such as the one before us reflect moral disapproval of people appearing in the nude among strangers in public places.

The traditional police power of the States is defined as the authority to provide for the public health, safety, and morals, and we have upheld such a basis for legislation. * * * Thus, the public indecency statute furthers a substantial government interest in protecting order and morality.

This interest is unrelated to the suppression of free expression. * * * It can be argued, of course, that almost limitless types of conduct—including appearing in the nude in public—are "expressive," and in one sense of the word this is true. People who go about in the nude in public may be expressing something about themselves by so doing. But the court rejected this expansive notion of "expressive conduct" in *O'Brien* * * *.

Respondents contend that even though prohibiting nudity in public generally may not be related to suppressing expression, prohibiting the performance of nude dancing is related to expression because the State seeks to prevent its erotic message. Therefore, they reason that the application of the Indiana statute to the nude dancing in this case violates the First Amendment * * *. But we do not think that when Indiana applies its statute to the nude dancing in these nightclubs it is proscribing nudity because of the erotic message conveyed by the dancers. Presumably numerous other erotic performances are presented at these establishments and similar clubs without any interference from the State, so long as the performers wear a scant amount of clothing. Likewise, the requirement that the dancers don pasties and G-strings does not deprive the dance of whatever erotic message it conveys; it simply makes the message slightly less graphic. The perceived evil that Indiana seeks to address is not erotic dancing, but public nudity.

The appearance of people of all shapes, sizes and ages in the nude at a beach, for example, would convey little if any erotic message, yet the State still seeks to prevent it. Public nudity is the evil the State seeks to prevent, whether or not it is combined with expressive activity.

The statutory prohibition is not a means to some greater end, but an end in itself. It is without cavil that the public indecency statute is "narrowly tailored"; Indiana's requirement that the dancers wear at least pasties and G-strings is modest, and the bare minimum necessary to achieve the State's purpose.

JUSTICE SCALIA, concurring in the judgment.

In my view, [the] challenged regulation must be upheld, not because it survives some lower level of First Amendment scrutiny, but because, as a general law regulating conduct and not specifically directed at expression, it is not subject to First Amendment scrutiny at all. * * * On its face, [Indiana's] law is not directed at expression in particular. * * * The intent to convey a "message of eroticism" (or any other message) is not a necessary element of the statutory offense of public indecency; nor does one commit that statutory offense by conveying the most explicit "message of eroticism," so long as he does not [engage in public nudity] in the process. * * * Were it the case that Indiana *in practice* targeted only expressive nudity, while turning a blind eye to nude beaches and unclothed purveyors of hot dogs and machine tools, it might be said that what posed as a regulation of conduct in general was in reality a regulation of only communicative conduct. Respondents have adduced no evidence of that.

The dissent confidently asserts that the purpose of restricting nudity in public places in general is to protect nonconsenting parties from offense; and argues that since only consenting, admission-paying patrons see respondents dance, that purpose cannot apply and the only remaining purpose must relate to the communicative elements of the performance. Perhaps the dissenters believe that "offense to others" *ought* to be the only reason for restricting nudity in public places generally, but there is no basis for thinking that our society has ever shared that Thoreauvian "you-may-do-what-you-like-so-long-as-it-does-not-injure-someone-else" beau ideal—much less for thinking that it was written into the Constitution. The purpose of Indiana's nudity law would be violated, I think, if 60,000 fully consenting adults crowded into the Hoosier Dome to display their genitals to one another, even if there were not an offended innocent in the crowd. Our society prohibits, and all human societies have prohibited, certain activities not because they harm others but because they are considered, in the traditional phrase, "*contra bonos mores*," *i.e.,* immoral. In American society, such prohibitions have included, for example, sadomasochism, cockfighting, bestiality, suicide, drug use, prostitution, and sodomy. While there may be great diversity of view on whether various of these prohibitions should exist (though I have found few ready to abandon, in principle, all of them), there is no doubt that, absent specific constitutional protection for the conduct involved, the Constitution does not prohibit them simply because they regulate "morality." See *Bowers v. Hardwick*, 478 U.S. 186 (1986). The purpose of the Indiana statute, as both its text and the manner of its enforcement demonstrate, is to enforce the traditional moral belief that people should not expose their private parts indiscriminately, regardless of whether those who see them are disedified. Since that is so, the dissent has no basis for positing that, where only thoroughly edified adults are present, the purpose must be repression of communication.

Since the Indiana regulation is a general law not specifically targeted at expressive conduct, its application to such conduct does not in my view implicate the First Amendment. The First Amendment explicitly protects "the freedom of speech [and] of the press"—oral and written speech—not "expressive conduct." When any law restricts speech, even for a purpose that has nothing to do with the suppression of communication, * * * we insist that it meet the high, First-Amendment standard of justification. But virtually *every* law restricts conduct, and virtually *any* prohibited conduct can be performed for an expressive purpose—if only expressive of the fact that the actor disagrees with the prohibition. It cannot reasonably be demanded, therefore, that every restriction of expression incidentally produced by a general law regulating conduct pass normal First Amendment scrutiny, or even—as some of our cases have suggested, *see, e.g., United States v. O'Brien*, 391 U.S. 367, 377 (1968)—that it be justified by an "important or substantial" government interest. Nor do our holdings require such justification: We have never invalidated the application of a general law simply because the conduct that it reached was being engaged in for expressive purposes and the government could not demonstrate a sufficiently important state interest.

This is not to say that the First Amendment affords no protection to expressive conduct. Where the government prohibits conduct *precisely because of its communicative attributes*, we hold the regulation unconstitutional. See, *e.g., Texas v. Johnson*, 491 U.S. 397 (1989) [(burning flag)]; *Tinker v. Des Moines Independent Community School Dist.*, 393 U.S. 503 (1969) (wearing black arm bands). In each of the foregoing cases, we explicitly found that suppressing communication was the object of the regulation of conduct. Where that has not been the case, however—where suppression of communicative use of the conduct was merely the incidental effect of forbidding the conduct for other reasons—we have allowed the regulation to stand. *O'Brien*, 391 U.S., at 377. * * * Such a regime ensures that the government does not act to suppress communication, without requiring that all conduct-restricting regulation (which means in effect all regulation) survive an enhanced level of scrutiny.

JUSTICE SOUTER, concurring in the judgment.

I agree with the plurality and the dissent that an interest in freely engaging in the nude dancing at issue here is subject to a degree of First Amendment protection. * * * I nonetheless write separately to rest my concurrence in the judgment, not on the possible sufficiency of society's moral views to justify the limitations at issue, but on the State's substantial interest in combating the secondary effects of adult entertainment establishments of the sort typified by respondents' establishments.

In my view, the interest asserted by petitioners in preventing prostitution, sexual assault, and other criminal activity, although presumably not a justification for all applications of the statute, is sufficient under *O'Brien* to justify the State's enforcement of the statute against the type of adult entertainment at issue here. * * * The type of entertainment respondents seek to provide is plainly of the same character as that at issue in *Renton v. Playtime Theatres, Inc.,* 475 U.S. 41 (1986). It therefore is no leap to say that live nude dancing of the sort at issue here is likely to produce the same pernicious secondary effects as the adult films displaying "specified anatomical areas" at issue in *Renton.* * * * Because the State's interest in banning nude dancing results from a simple correlation of such dancing with other evils, rather than from a relationship between the other evils and the expressive component of the dancing, the interest is unrelated to the suppression of free expression.

JUSTICE WHITE, with whom JUSTICE MARSHALL, JUSTICE BLACKMUN, and JUSTICE STEVENS join, dissenting.

Both the plurality and Justice Scalia in his opinion concurring in the judgment overlook a fundamental and critical aspect of our cases upholding the States' exercise of their police powers. None of the cases they rely upon, including *O'Brien* and *Bowers,* involved anything less than truly *general* proscriptions on individual conduct. * * * By contrast, in this case Indiana does not suggest that its statute applies to, or could be applied to, nudity wherever it occurs, including the home. We do not understand the plurality or Justice Scalia to be suggesting that Indiana could constitutionally enact such an intrusive prohibition, nor do we think such a suggestion would be tenable * * *. As a result, the plurality and Justice Scalia's simple references to the State's general interest in promoting societal order and morality are not sufficient justification for a statute which concededly reaches a significant amount of protected expressive activity.

Legislators do not just randomly select certain conduct for proscription; they have reasons for doing so and those reasons illuminate the purpose of the law that is passed. Indeed, a law may have multiple purposes. The purpose of forbidding people to appear nude in parks, beaches, hot dog stands, and like public places is to protect others from offense. But that could not possibly be the purpose of preventing nude dancing in theaters and barrooms since the viewers are exclusively consenting adults who pay money to see these dances. The purpose of the proscription in these contexts is to protect the viewers from what the State believes is the harmful message that nude dancing communicates.

In arriving at its conclusion, the plurality concedes that nude dancing conveys an erotic message and concedes that the message would be muted if the dancers wore pasties and G-strings. Indeed, the emotional or erotic impact of the dance is intensified by the nudity of the performers. * * * The sight of a fully clothed, or even a partially clothed, dancer generally will have a far different impact on a spectator than that of a nude dancer, even if the same dance is performed. The nudity is itself an expressive component of the dance, not merely incidental "conduct."

This being the case, it cannot be that the statutory prohibition is unrelated to expressive conduct. Since the State permits the dancers to perform if they wear pasties and G-strings but forbids nude dancing, it is precisely because of the distinctive, expressive content of the nude dancing performances at issue in this case that the State seeks to apply the statutory prohibition. It is only because nude dancing performances may generate emotions and feelings of eroticism and sensuality among the spectators that the State seeks to regulate such expressive activity, apparently on the assumption that creating or emphasizing such thoughts and ideas in the minds of the spectators may lead to increased prostitution and the degradation of women. But generating thoughts, ideas, and emotions is the essence of communication.

That fact dictates the level of First Amendment protection to be accorded the performances at issue here. * * * Content based restrictions "will be upheld only if narrowly drawn to accomplish a compelling governmental interest." * * * The plurality and Justice SOUTER do not go beyond saying that the state interests asserted here are important and substantial. But even if there were compelling interests, the Indiana statute is not narrowly drawn. If the State is genuinely concerned with prostitution and associated evils, * * * it can adopt restrictions that do not interfere with the expressiveness of nonobscene nude dancing performances. * * * Banning an entire category of expressive activity, however, generally does not satisfy the narrow tailoring requirement of strict First Amendment scrutiny.

POINTS FOR DISCUSSION

a.   Content Neutral or Content Based?

Part of the disagreement between the dissent, on the one hand, and the plurality and Justice Scalia, on the other, was over whether Indiana's public indecency law's application to the nude dancing establishments was "unrelated to the suppression of free expression"—that is, content neutral. Assuming a state can ban nudity in public generally—which the dissent did not seem to question—is it clear that the application of such a ban to nude dancing has nothing to do with the expressive elements of the dancing? What was the dissent's reasoning in asserting that it does? What was the plurality's response?

b.   Conduct v. Speech

Another source of disagreement in the case was the extent to which nude dancing falls within the scope of the First Amendment at all. The plurality conceded that it does, although "only marginally so," and Justice Souter and the four dissenters likewise concluded that it is an activity protected by the First Amendment. In what way is nude dancing a form of "expression"? What is the "message" that is communicated by nude dancing? In what way does the "message" it communicates differ from the message that dancing while fully clothed communicates? For that matter, in what way does the message communicated by nude dancing differ from the "message" communicated by walking down a public street in the nude?

Clearly not all conduct is protected by the First Amendment. But it seems just as clear that some conduct contains strong expressive elements. Justice Scalia, for example, cited *Tinker v. Des Moines Independent Community School Dist.*, 393 U.S. 503 (1969). In that case, the Court held that a school policy forbidding the wearing of black arm bands—which some students had done as a form of protest against the Vietnam War—violated the First Amendment. There was little doubt that the wearing of the arm bands—whatever one thinks of the message—was a means (and apparently a potent one, given the school's response) of conveying a message.

Can you articulate a test for identifying when "conduct" contains sufficiently strong expressive elements that it is entitled to protection under the First Amendment? We will consider this question further later in this chapter.

c.   The *O'Brien* Test and Laws of General Applicability

In his separate opinion, Justice Scalia asserted that content-neutral laws of general applicability should not be subject to scrutiny under the First Amendment at all, even when they incidentally burden expression. He has expressed a similar view

> **Make the Connection**
>
> We will consider the First Amendment's protection for the free exercise of religion, and the Court's decision in *Smith*, in Chapter 11.

in the context of the First Amendment's protection for the free exercise of religion, and in that context a majority of the Court agreed. See *Employment Div., Dept. of Human Resources of Ore. v. Smith*, 494 U.S. 872 (1990). What are the virtues of such an approach? What are the costs?

4.   Prior Restraints

A **prior restraint on speech** is an executive or judicial order prohibiting a communication before it has occurred. See *Alexander v. United States*, 509 U.S. 544, 550 (1993). For example, in *Nebraska Press Association v. Stuart*, 427 U.S. 539 (1976), a state court was worried that pretrial publicity might frustrate the ability of a defendant charged with a triple murder to receive a fair trial. To address this concern, the state court issued an injunction barring the press from publishing accounts of the defendant's alleged confession and other facts. This order was a prior restraint because it blocked the publication of speech (i.e., news reports) before it occurred. The Supreme Court held the order was unconstitutional in part because the trial court had made "no finding that alternative measures would not have protected [the defendant's] rights." *Id.* at 565.

The Court has long held that the First Amendment provides more protection against prior restraints on speech than it does against subsequent liability for speech. For example, the Supreme Court has held that the First Amendment would not allow a state to enjoin a publisher in advance from publishing a "malicious, scandalous and defamatory newspaper, magazine or other periodical," *Near v. Minnesota ex rel. Olson*, 283 U.S. 697, 707 (1931), even if the state could constitutionally provide a remedy for libel after publication, *id.* at 714. The Supreme Court has explained its concern over prior restraints concisely: "It is always difficult to know in advance what an

> **FYI**
>
> The general counsel of *The New York Times* summarized the case that follows in this way: "In 1971, the Pentagon Papers—the Defense Department's top-secret study of the growth of United States military involvement in Vietnam—were leaked by a government official to *The New York Times*. On June 13 of that year, the newspaper began publishing articles based on the documents. When the government learned of this, the Department of Justice asked for a temporary restraining order, which was granted." The following litigation ensued.

individual will say, and the line between legitimate and illegitimate speech is often so finely drawn that the risks of freewheeling censorship are formidable." *Southeastern Promotions, Ltd. v. Conrad,* 420 U.S. 546, 558–559 (1975).

The following case is a leading decision on the issue of whether the prohibition on prior restraints is absolute. As you read the various opinions in the case, consider whether there are any exceptions to the rule against prior restraints, and if so when they can be applied.

NEW YORK TIMES CO. V. UNITED STATES

403 U.S. 713 (1971)

PER CURIAM.

We granted certiorari in these cases in which the United States seeks to enjoin the New York Times and the Washington Post from publishing the contents of a classified study entitled "History of U.S. Decision-Making Process on Viet Nam Policy."

"Any system of prior restraints of expression comes to this Court bearing a heavy presumption against its constitutional validity." *Bantam Books, Inc. v. Sullivan,* 372 U.S. 58, 70 (1963). The Government "thus carries a heavy burden of showing justification for the

> **Definition**
>
> *Per curiam* means by the court. *Black's Law Dictionary* (9th ed. 2009). In this case, a majority of the Supreme Court agreed on the ultimate judgment in the case, but the individual justices in the majority could not agree on the reasoning. They therefore issued an opinion for the Court, and then wrote separate concurring opinions offering their different reasons for the judgment.

imposition of such a restraint." *Organization for a Better Austin v. Keefe,* 402 U.S. 415, 419 (1971). The District Court for the Southern District of New York in the New York Times case, and the District Court for the District of Columbia and the Court of Appeals for the District of Columbia Circuit, in the Washington Post case held that the Government had not met that burden. We agree. So ordered.

MR. JUSTICE BLACK, with whom MR. JUSTICE DOUGLAS joins, concurring.

> **Make the Connection**
>
> We will consider the freedom of the press, and the extent to which that protection is different from the freedom of speech, in Chapter 9.

In seeking injunctions against these newspapers and in its presentation to the Court, the Executive Branch seems to have forgotten the essential purpose and history of the First Amendment. * * * Both the history and language of the First Amendment support the view that the press must be left free to publish news, whatever the source, without censorship, injunctions, or prior restraints.

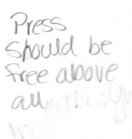

* * * In my view, far from deserving condemnation for their courageous reporting, the New York Times, the Washington Post, and other newspapers should be commended for serving the purpose that the Founding Fathers saw so clearly. In revealing the workings of government that led to the Vietnam war, the newspapers nobly did precisely that which the Founders hoped and trusted they would do.

The Government's case here is based on premises entirely different from those that guided the Framers of the First Amendment. * * * [T]he Government argues in its brief that in spite of the First Amendment, "[t]he authority of the Executive Department to protect the nation against publication of information whose disclosure would endanger the national security stems from two interrelated sources: the constitutional power of the President over the conduct of foreign affairs and his authority as Commander-in-Chief."

In other words, we are asked to hold that despite the First Amendment's emphatic command, the Executive Branch, the Congress, and the Judiciary can make laws enjoining publication of current news and abridging freedom of the press in the name of "national security." The Government does not even attempt to rely on any act of Congress. * * * To find that the President has "inherent power" to halt the publication of news by resort to the courts would wipe out the First Amendment and destroy the fundamental liberty and security of the very people the Government hopes to make "secure." No one can read the history of the adoption of the First Amendment without being convinced beyond any doubt that it was injunctions like those sought here that Madison and his collaborators intended to outlaw in this Nation for all time.

Make the Connection

We consider the President's "inherent" constitutional powers, and the President's powers over foreign affairs and as Commander in Chief, in Volume 1.

MR. JUSTICE DOUGLAS, with whom MR. JUSTICE BLACK joins, concurring.

The dominant purpose of the First Amendment was to prohibit the widespread practice of governmental suppression of embarrassing information. It is common knowledge that the First Amendment was adopted against the widespread use of the common law of seditious libel to punish the dissemination of material that is embarrassing to the powers-that-be. See T. Emerson, The System of Freedom of Expression, c. V (1970); Z. Chafee, Free Speech in the United States, c. XIII (1941). The present cases will, I think, go down in history as the most dramatic illustration of that principle. A debate of large proportions goes on in the Nation over our posture in Vietnam. That debate antedated the disclosure of the contents of the present documents. The latter are highly relevant to the debate in progress.

Secrecy in government is fundamentally anti-democratic, perpetuating bureaucratic errors. Open debate and discussion of public issues are vital to our national health. On public questions there should be "uninhibited, robust, and wide-open" debate. *New York Times Co. v. Sullivan*, 376 U.S. 254, 269–270 (1964).

MR. JUSTICE BRENNAN, concurring.

The error that has pervaded these cases from the outset was the granting of any injunctive relief whatsoever, interim or otherwise. The entire thrust of the Government's claim throughout these cases has been that publication of the material sought to be enjoined "could," or "might," or "may" prejudice the national interest in various ways. But the First Amendment tolerates absolutely no prior judicial restraints of the press predicated upon surmise or conjecture that untoward consequences may result. Our cases, it is true, have indicated that there is a single, extremely narrow class of cases in which the First Amendment's ban on prior judicial restraint may be overridden. Our cases have thus far indicated that such cases may arise only when the Nation "is at war," *Schenck v. United States*, 249 U.S. 47, 52 (1919), during which times "[n]o one would question but that a government might prevent actual obstruction to its recruiting service or the publication of the sailing dates of transports or the number and location of troops." *Near v. Minnesota ex rel. Olson*, 283 U.S. 697, 716 (1931). Even if the present world situation were assumed to be tantamount to a time of war, or if the power of presently available armaments would justify even in peacetime the suppression of information that would set in motion a nuclear holocaust, in neither of these actions has the Government presented or even alleged that publication of items from or based upon the material at issue would cause the happening of an event of that nature. [O]nly governmental allegation and proof that publication must inevitably, directly, and immediately cause the occurrence of an event kindred to imperiling the safety of a transport already at sea can support even the issuance of an interim restraining order. In no event may mere conclusions be sufficient: for if the Executive Branch seeks judicial aid in preventing publication, it must inevitably submit the basis upon which that aid is sought to scrutiny by the judiciary. And therefore, every restraint issued in this case, whatever its form, has violated the First Amendment—and not less so because that restraint was justified as necessary to afford the courts an opportunity to examine the claim more thoroughly. Unless and until the Government has clearly made out its case, the First Amendment commands that no injunction may issue.

MR. JUSTICE WHITE, with whom MR. JUSTICE STEWART joins, concurring.

I concur in today's judgments, but only because of the concededly extraordinary protection against prior restraints enjoyed by the press under our constitutional system. I do not say that in no circumstances would the First Amendment permit an injunction against publishing information about government plans or operations. Nor, after examining the materials the Government characterizes as the most sensitive and destructive, can I deny that revelation of these documents will do substantial damage to public interests. Indeed, I am confident that their disclosure will have that result. But I nevertheless agree that the United States has not satisfied the very heavy burden that it must meet to warrant an injunction against publication in these cases, at least in the absence of express and appropriately limited congressional authorization for prior restraints in circumstances such as these.

The Government's position is simply stated: The responsibility of the Executive for the conduct of the foreign affairs and for the security of the Nation is so basic that the President is entitled to an injunction against publication of a newspaper story whenever he can convince a court that the information to be revealed threatens "grave and irreparable" injury to the public interest; and the injunction should issue whether or not the material to be published is classified, whether or not publication would be lawful under relevant criminal statutes enacted by Congress, and regardless of the circumstances by which the newspaper came into possession of the information.

At least in the absence of legislation by Congress, based on its own investigations and findings, I am quite unable to agree that the inherent powers of the Executive and the courts reach so far as to authorize remedies having such sweeping potential for inhibiting publications by the press. Much of the difficulty inheres in the "grave and irreparable danger" standard suggested by the United States. If the United States were to have judgment under such a standard in these cases, our decision would be of little guidance to other courts in other cases, for the material at issue here would not be available from the Court's opinion or from public records, nor would it be published by the press. Indeed, even today where we hold that the United States has not met its burden, the material remains sealed in court records and it is properly not discussed in today's opinions. Moreover, because the material poses substantial dangers to national interests and because of the hazards of criminal sanctions, a responsible press may choose never to publish the more sensitive materials. To sustain the Government in these cases would start the courts down a long and hazardous road that I am not willing to travel, at least without congressional guidance and direction.

MR. JUSTICE MARSHALL, concurring.

It would [be] utterly inconsistent with the concept of separation of powers for this Court to use its power of contempt to prevent behavior that Congress has specifically declined to prohibit. There would be a similar damage to the basic concept of these co-equal branches of Government if when the Executive Branch has adequate authority granted by Congress to protect "national security" it can choose instead to invoke the contempt power of a court to enjoin the threatened conduct. The Constitution provides that Congress shall make laws, the President execute laws, and courts interpret laws. *Youngstown Sheet & Tube Co. v. Sawyer*, 343 U.S. 579 (1952). * * *

MR. CHIEF JUSTICE BURGER, dissenting.

In these cases, the imperative of a free and unfettered press comes into collision with another imperative, the effective functioning of a complex modern government and specifically the effective exercise of certain constitutional powers of the Executive. Only those who view the First Amendment as an absolute in all circumstances—a view I respect, but reject—can find such cases as these to be simple or easy.

MR. JUSTICE HARLAN, with whom THE CHIEF JUSTICE and MR. JUSTICE BLACKMUN join, dissenting.

With all respect, I consider that the Court has been almost irresponsibly feverish in dealing with these cases. Both the Court of Appeals for the Second Circuit and the Court of Appeals for the District of Columbia Circuit rendered judgment on June 23. The New York Times' petition for certiorari, its motion for accelerated consideration thereof, and its application for interim relief were filed in this Court on June 24 at about 11 a.m. The application of the United States for interim relief in the Post case was also filed here on June 24 at about 7:15 p.m. This Court's order setting a hearing before us on June 26 at 11 a.m., a course which I joined only to avoid the possibility of even more peremptory action by the Court, was issued less than 24 hours before. The record in the Post case was filed with the Clerk shortly before 1 p.m. on June 25; the record in the Times case did not arrive until 7 or 8 o'clock that same night. The briefs of the parties were received less than two hours before argument on June 26.

This frenzied train of events took place in the name of the presumption against prior restraints created by the First Amendment. Due regard for the extraordinarily important and difficult questions involved in these litigations should have led the Court to shun

> **FYI**
> The Court issued its decision in this case on June 30, 1971, four days after the argument.

such a precipitate timetable. * * * Forced as I am to reach the merits of these cases, I dissent from the opinion and judgments of the Court. Within the severe limitations imposed by the time constraints under which I have been required to operate, I can only state my reasons in telescoped form, even though in different circumstances I would have felt constrained to deal with the cases in the fuller sweep indicated above.

It is plain to me that the scope of the judicial function in passing upon the activities of the Executive Branch of the Government in the field of foreign affairs is very narrowly restricted. This view is, I think, dictated by the concept of separation of powers upon which our constitutional system rests. * * * See *United States v. Curtiss-Wright Export Corp.*, 299 U.S. 304, 319–321 (1936), collecting authorities.

From this constitutional primacy in the field of foreign affairs, it seems to me that certain conclusions necessarily follow. * * * The power to evaluate [what President Washington called] the "pernicious influence" of premature disclosure [of sensitive materials related to foreign affairs] is not [lodged] in the Executive alone. I agree that, in performance of its duty to protect the values of the First Amendment against political pressures, the judiciary must review the initial Executive determination to the point of satisfying itself that the subject matter of the dispute does lie within the proper compass of the President's foreign relations power. * * * Moreover the judiciary may properly insist that the determination that disclosure of the subject matter would irreparably impair the national security be made by the head of the Executive Department concerned—here the Secretary of State or the Secretary of Defense—after actual personal consideration by that officer. This safeguard is required in the analogous area of executive claims of privilege for secrets of state. But in my judgment the judiciary may not properly go beyond these two inquiries and redetermine for itself the probable impact of disclosure on the national security.

Even if there is some room for the judiciary to override the executive determination, it is plain that the scope of review must be exceedingly narrow. I can see no indication in the opinions of either the District Court or the Court of Appeals in the Post litigation that the conclusions of the Executive were given even the deference owing to an administrative agency, much less that owing to a co-equal branch of the Government operating within the field of its constitutional prerogative.

MR. JUSTICE BLACKMUN, dissenting.

The First Amendment [is] only one part of an entire Constitution. Article II of the great document vests in the Executive Branch primary power over the conduct of foreign affairs and places in that branch the responsibility for the Nation's safety. Each provision of the Constitution is important, and I cannot subscribe to a doctrine of unlimited absolutism for the First Amendment at the cost of downgrading other provisions. * * * What is needed here is a weighing, upon properly developed standards, of the broad right of the press to print and of the very narrow right of the Government to prevent. Such standards are not yet developed. The parties here are in disagreement as to what those standards should be. But even the newspapers concede that there are situations where restraint is in order and is constitutional. * * *

I strongly urge, and sincerely hope, that these two newspapers will be fully aware of their ultimate responsibilities to the United States of America. Judge Wilkey, dissenting in the District of Columbia case, after a review of only the affidavits before his court (the basic papers had not then been made available by either party), concluded that there were a number of examples of documents that, if in the possession of the Post, and if published, "could clearly result in great harm to the nation," and he defined "harm" to mean "the death of soldiers, the destruction of alliances, the greatly increased difficulty of negotiation with our enemies, the inability of our diplomats to negotiate * * *." I, for one, have now been able to give at least some cursory study not only to the affidavits, but to the material itself. I regret to say that from this examination I fear that Judge Wilkey's statements have possible foundation. * * * I hope that damage has not already been done. If, however, damage has been done, and if, with the Court's action today, these newspapers proceed to publish the critical documents and there results therefrom [the consequences that Judge Wilkey feared,] to which list I might add the factors of prolongation of the war and of further delay in the freeing of United States prisoners, then the Nation's people will know where the responsibility for these sad consequences rests.

POINTS FOR DISCUSSION

a.   Prior Restraint on Publication v. Punishment After Publication

If releasing classified documents would violate a federal criminal law, would the First Amendment bar the government from prosecuting the newspapers for publishing the Pentagon Papers? The Court did not reach this question. But in omitted portions of the opinions excerpted above, four justices mentioned this issue. Why would subsequent prosecution differ from prior restraint? Why wouldn't a federal law prohibiting the publication of sensitive government documents itself violate the First Amendment?

In any event, wouldn't a person who is willing to violate a federal statute prohibiting the communication of certain information, even though the statute authorizes punishment for the disclosure, also be willing to violate a judicial order prohibiting the communication of the same information? In thinking about this question, consider the relative status of laws and judicial orders. If the person believes that the statute prohibiting the communication violates the First Amendment, on its face or as applied, then he can assert such a defense in the course of the prosecution. And if he is correct, then the First Amendment defense will shield him from punishment. Is the same true of judicial orders? Can a court punish a person who violates a judicial order, even if the order turns out to have been an unconstitutional prior restraint?

b.   Justifying Prior Restraints

How many Justices concluded that prior restraints are permissible under at least some circumstances? In the view of those Justices, when is a prior restraint justified? Do those circumstances exist only when the President or an officer of the Executive Branch seeks the restraint, or might they also apply when a state official, such as a prosecutor or Governor, seeks a restraint?

c.   Licensing and Prior Restraints

The Pentagon Papers case involved a judicial order that would have prevented publication of particular subject matter. But prior restraints can come in other forms, as well. For example, imagine that a local ordinance requires any group that wishes to hold a parade on public streets first to obtain a permit from the chief of police. If the chief of police denies an application for a permit to hold a parade celebrating gay rights, does that decision constitute a prior restraint on speech? In one sense, it seems strange to say that a town cannot require a permit before a group can conduct a noisy and potentially disruptive event on downtown streets. But a decision denying a permit would be an executive order preventing expressive activity before it occurs, which is the very definition of a prior restraint.

The Court, recognizing this tension, has held that the government may require permits or licenses before certain expressive activities take place in public, but only if there is some important reason for requiring a permit; there are clear standards leaving almost no discretion for the government official charged with administering the scheme; and there are procedural safeguards, including the right to a prompt judicial determination of the validity of the denial of a permit, to ensure that an application was not denied arbitrarily or because of the content of the desired expression. See *City of Lakewood v. Plain Dealer Publishing Co.*, 486 U.S. 750 (1988).

> ### Problem
>
> In World War II, Allied Forces devised an elaborate plan, Operation Overlord, for launching an amphibious invasion of France to fight the occupying Nazi forces. The success of the plan depended to a large extent on keeping the exact date and location of the invasion secret from the German forces. Tens of thousands of lives were at stake in the immediate battle, and failure by the Allies may have changed the outcome of the war. We now know, of course, that the Allies planned the invasion for June 6, 1944, also known as "D-Day." Suppose that the *New York Times* had learned the details of the invasion in advance. Would a court have had authority to enjoin the newspaper from publishing this information? Or would such a prior restraint have violated the First Amendment?

5. Vague or Overbroad Restrictions

We will see later in this chapter that some kinds of speech do not have full protection under the First Amendment. The government, for example, may pass laws restricting libel, fighting words, and obscenity. But if not artfully phrased, a legislature's attempts to regulate these kinds of speech may suffer from two common problems in the First Amendment area.

First, the government might pass a law that is **overbroad**, meaning that it reaches both protected and unprotected speech. For example, the federal Child Pornography Prevention Act of 1996 outlawed possession not only of actual pictures of children, but also of "any visual depiction, including any photograph, film, video, picture, or computer or computer-generated image or picture" that "is, or appears to be, of a minor engaging in sexually explicit conduct." The Supreme Court held that this statute violated the First Amendment because it was overbroad. It concluded that, although the government may regulate actual child pornography and obscenity, it cannot ban any image merely because it appears to involve children. "Pictures of what appear to be 17-year-olds engaging in sexually explicit activity," the Court said, "do not in every case contravene community standards [of obscenity]." See *Ashcroft v. Free Speech Coalition*, 535 U.S. 234 (2002).

Second, the government might enact a law that suffers from **vagueness**, meaning that the law does not make clear to a reasonable person what it prohibits and what it does not. For example, a Nevada Supreme Court rule prohibited a lawyer from making extrajudicial statements to the media that would have a "substantial likelihood of materially prejudicing" a pending case, but the prohibition was subject to an exception allowing the lawyer to "state without

elaboration [the] general nature of [the] defense." The Supreme Court recognized
that a state court may, consistently with the First Amendment, limit what lawyers
can say about a pending case, but it nevertheless held that the challenged rule was
void for vagueness. The Court said: "A lawyer seeking to avail himself of [the
exception] must guess at its contours. The right to explain the 'general' nature of
the defense without 'elaboration' provides insufficient guidance because 'general'
and 'elaboration' are both classic terms of degree." *Gentile v. State Bar of Nevada*,
501 U.S. 1030, 1048–49 (1991).

> **Make the Connection**
>
> We briefly discuss the difference
> between as-applied and facial
> challenges in Volume 1, when we
> consider cases concerning the
> scope of Congress's power under
> the Commerce Clause.

A special and important procedural rule
applies to lawsuits claiming that a law violates
the First Amendment because of overbreadth
or vagueness. In general, when claiming that
a law is unconstitutional, a plaintiff can assert
either an **"as-applied challenge"** or a
"facial challenge" to the law. In an as-
applied challenge, the plaintiff claims that the
law is unconstitutional as applied to the facts of his or her case. In a typical facial
challenge, by contrast, the plaintiff claims that the law is "invalid *in toto*—and
therefore incapable of any valid application." *Steffel v. Thompson*, 415 U.S. 452, 474
(1974).

In the First Amendment context, however, the standard for facial challenges
on the ground of overbreadth and vagueness is relaxed. The Supreme Court has
held that any law that is "substantially overbroad" in its application to protected
speech may be invalidated on its face. *Members of City Council of Los Angeles v.
Taxpayers for Vincent*, 466 U.S. 789, 800 (1984). In other words, the plaintiff does
not have to show that the law is unconstitutional in every case, or even that it
would be unconstitutional as applied to the facts of his or her case. Similarly, a
plaintiff can challenge a law on its face as being void for vagueness if the law "fails
to draw reasonably clear lines between" what is permitted or not, *Smith v. Goguen*,
415 U.S. 566, 569 (1974), or if the law "encourages arbitrary enforcement by
failing to describe with sufficient particularity" what is permitted and what is not,
Kolender v. Lawson, 461 U.S. 352 (1983). The standards for facial challenges are
relaxed because an overbroad or vague law may have a **"chilling effect"** on
protected speech; unless the law's constitutionality is clarified, speakers worried
about liability under the laws may censor their speech more than is constitutionally
required. See *Law Students Civil Rights Research Council, Inc. v. Wadmond*, 401 U.S.
154, 158–159 (1971).

The two cases that follow concern the doctrines of vagueness and overbreadth.

NAACP v. Button
371 U.S. 415 (1963)

MR. JUSTICE BRENNAN delivered the opinion of the Court.

The NAACP was formed in 1909 and incorporated under New York law as a nonprofit membership corporation in 1911. It maintains its headquarters in New York and presently has some 1,000 active unincorporated branches throughout the Nation. * * * The basic aims and purposes of NAACP are to secure the elimination of all racial barriers which deprive Negro citizens of the privileges and burdens of equal citizenship rights in the United States. To this end the Association engages in extensive educational and lobbying activities. It also devotes much of its funds and energies to an extensive program of assisting certain kinds of litigation on behalf of its declared purposes. For more than 10 years, the Virginia Conference has concentrated upon financing litigation aimed at ending racial segregation in the public schools of the Commonwealth.

The members of the legal staff of the Virginia Conference and other NAACP or Defense Fund lawyers called in by the staff to assist are drawn into litigation in various ways. One is for an aggrieved Negro to apply directly to the Conference or the legal staff for assistance. His application is referred to the Chairman of the legal staff. The Chairman, with the concurrence of the President of the Conference, is authorized to agree to give legal assistance in an appropriate case. In litigation involving public school segregation, the procedure tends to be different. Typically, a local NAACP branch will invite a member of the legal staff to explain to a meeting of parents and children the legal steps necessary to achieve desegregation. The staff member will bring printed forms to the meeting authorizing him, and other NAACP or Defense Fund attorneys of his designation, to represent the signers in legal proceedings to achieve desegregation. On occasion, blank forms have been signed by litigants, upon the understanding that a member or members of the legal staff, with or without assistance from other NAACP lawyers, or from the Defense Fund, would handle the case. It is usual, after obtaining authorizations, for the staff lawyer to bring into the case the other staff members in the area where suit is to be brought, and sometimes to bring in lawyers from the national organization or the Defense Fund. In effect, then, the prospective litigant retains not so much a particular attorney as the "firm" of NAACP and Defense Fund lawyers, which has a corporate reputation for expertness in presenting and arguing the difficult questions of law that frequently arise in civil rights litigation.

Statutory regulation of unethical and nonprofessional conduct by attorneys has been in force in Virginia since 1849. These provisions outlaw, inter alia,

> **Definition**
>
> The terms "running" and "capping" describe the act of soliciting clients for a legal practice, usually in personal injury cases.

solicitation of legal business in the form of "running" or "capping." Prior to 1956, however, no attempt was made to proscribe under such regulations the activities of the NAACP, which had been carried on openly for many years in substantially the manner

described. In 1956, however, the legislature amended, by the addition of Chapter 33, the provisions of the Virginia Code forbidding solicitation of legal business by a "runner" or "capper" to include, in the definition of "runner" or "capper," an agent for an individual or organization which retains a lawyer in connection with an action to which it is not a party and in which it has no pecuniary right or liability. The Virginia Supreme Court of Appeals held that the chapter's purpose "was to strengthen the existing statutes to further control the evils of solicitation of legal business * * *." The court held that the activities of NAACP, the Virginia Conference, the Defense Fund, and the lawyers furnished by them, fell within, and could constitutionally be proscribed by, the chapter's expanded definition of improper solicitation of legal business, and also violated Canons 35 and 47 of the American Bar Association's Canons of Professional Ethics, which the court had adopted in 1938. Specifically the court held that, under the expanded definition, such activities on the part of NAACP, the Virginia Conference, and the Defense Fund constituted "fomenting and soliciting legal business in which they are not parties and have no pecuniary right or liability, and which they channel to the enrichment of certain lawyers employed by them, at no cost to the litigants and over which the litigants have no control." * * *

Petitioner challenges the decision of the Supreme Court of Appeals on many grounds. But we reach only one: that Chapter 33 as construed and applied abridges the freedoms of the First Amendment, protected against state action by the Fourteenth. More specifically, petitioner claims that the chapter infringes the right of the NAACP and its members and lawyers to associate for the purpose of assisting persons

> **Make the Connection**
>
> We consider the First Amendment's protection for the freedom of association in Chapter 10.

who seek legal redress for infringements of their constitutionally guaranteed and other rights. * * *

We meet at the outset the contention that "solicitation" is wholly outside the area of freedoms protected by the First Amendment. To this contention there are two answers. The first is that a State cannot foreclose the exercise of constitutional rights by mere labels. The second is that abstract discussion is not the only species of communication which the Constitution protects; the First Amendment also protects vigorous advocacy, certainly of lawful ends, against governmental intrusion. In the context of NAACP objectives, litigation is not a technique of resolving private differences; it is a means for achieving the lawful objectives of equality of treatment by all government, federal, state and local, for the members of the Negro community in this country. It is thus a form of political expression. Groups which find themselves unable to achieve their objectives through the ballot frequently turn to the courts. Just as it was true of the opponents of New Deal legislation during the 1930's, for example, no less is it true of the Negro minority today. And under the conditions of modern government, litigation may well be the sole practicable avenue open to a minority to petition for redress of grievances.

* * * If the line drawn by the decree between the permitted and prohibited activities of the NAACP, its members and lawyers is an ambiguous one, we will not presume that the statute curtails constitutionally protected activity as little as possible. For standards of permissible statutory vagueness are strict in the area of free expression. See *Smith v. California*, 361 U.S. 147, 151 (1959). Furthermore, the instant decree may be invalid if it prohibits privileged exercises of First Amendment rights whether or not the record discloses that the petitioner has engaged in privileged conduct. For in appraising a statute's inhibitory effect upon such rights, this Court has not hesitated to take into account possible applications of the statute in other factual contexts besides that at bar. *Thornhill v. Alabama*, 310 U.S. 88, 97–98 (1940). It makes no difference that the instant case was not a criminal prosecution and not based on a refusal to comply with a licensing requirement. The objectionable quality of vagueness and overbreadth does not depend upon absence of fair notice to a criminally accused or upon unchanneled delegation of legislative powers, but upon the danger of tolerating, in the area of First Amendment freedoms, the existence of a penal statute susceptible of sweeping and improper application. Cf. *Marcus v. Search Warrant*, 367 U.S. 717, 733 (1961). These freedoms are delicate and vulnerable, as well as supremely precious in our society. The threat of sanctions may deter their exercise almost as potently as the actual application of sanctions. Cf. *Smith v. California*, 361 U.S. at 151–154. Because First Amendment freedoms need breathing space to survive, government may regulate in the area only with narrow specificity. *Cantwell v. Connecticut*, 310 U.S. 296, 311 (1940).

We read the decree of the Virginia Supreme Court of Appeals in the instant case as proscribing any arrangement by which prospective litigants are advised to seek the assistance of particular attorneys. No narrower reading is plausible. We cannot accept the reading suggested on behalf of the Attorney General of Virginia on the second oral argument that the Supreme Court of Appeals construed Chapter 33 as proscribing control only of the actual litigation by the NAACP after it is instituted. In the first place, upon a record devoid of any evidence of interference by the NAACP in the actual conduct of litigation, or neglect or harassment of clients, the court nevertheless held that petitioner, its members, agents and staff attorneys had practiced criminal solicitation. Thus, simple referral to or recommendation of a lawyer may be solicitation within the meaning of Chapter 33. In the second place, the decree does not seem to rest on the fact that the attorneys were organized as a staff and paid by petitioner. The decree expressly forbids solicitation on behalf of "any particular attorneys" in addition to attorneys retained or compensated by the NAACP. In the third place, although Chapter 33 purports to prohibit only solicitation by attorneys or their "agents," it defines agent broadly as anyone who "represents" another in his dealings with a third person. Since the statute appears to depart from the common-law concept of the agency relationship and since the Virginia court did not clarify the statutory definition, we cannot say that it will not be applied with the broad sweep which the statutory language imports.

We conclude that under Chapter 33, as authoritatively construed by the Supreme Court of Appeals, a person who advises another that his legal rights have been infringed and refers him to a particular attorney or group of attorneys (for example, to the Virginia Conference's legal staff) for assistance has committed a crime, as has the attorney who knowingly renders assistance under such circumstances. There thus inheres in the statute the gravest danger of smothering all discussion looking to the eventual institution of litigation on behalf of the rights of members of an unpopular minority. Lawyers on the legal staff or even mere NAACP members or sympathizers would understandably hesitate, at an NAACP meeting or on any other occasion, to do what the decree purports to allow, namely, acquaint "persons with what they believe to be their legal rights and * * * (advise) them to assert their rights by commencing or further prosecuting a suit * * *." For if the lawyers, members or sympathizers also appeared in or had any connection with any litigation supported with NAACP funds contributed under the provision of the decree by which the NAACP is not prohibited "from contributing money to persons to assist them in commencing or further prosecuting such suits," they plainly would risk (if lawyers) disbarment proceedings and, lawyers and nonlawyers alike, criminal

> **Take Note**
>
> In this paragraph, the Court explains that a vague or overbroad statute may be challenged even if it has not been applied to protected speech. What reason does the Court give for this rule?

prosecution for the offense of "solicitation," to which the Virginia court gave so broad and uncertain a meaning. It makes no difference whether such prosecutions or proceedings would actually be commenced. It is enough that a vague and broad statute lends itself to selective enforcement against unpopular causes. We cannot close our eyes to the fact that the militant Negro civil rights movement has engendered the intense resentment and opposition of the politically dominant white community of Virginia; litigation assisted by the NAACP has been bitterly fought. In such circumstances, a statute broadly curtailing group activity leading to litigation may easily become a weapon of oppression, however evenhanded its terms appear. Its mere existence could well freeze out of existence all such activity on behalf of the civil rights of Negro citizens.

It is apparent, therefore, that Chapter 33 as construed limits First Amendment freedoms. As this Court said in *Thomas v. Collins*, 323 U.S. 516, 537 (1945), "Free trade in ideas means free trade in the opportunity to persuade to action, not merely to describe facts." * * * [T]he Association and its members were advocating lawful means of vindicating legal rights.

> **Definition**
>
> Barratry is "[v]exatious incitement to litigation," while maintenance and champerty consist of assisting in the litigation of a case in which one has no legal interest. *Black's Law Dictionary* (9th ed. 2009). Why would a state ban the latter practices?

* * * However valid may be Virginia's interest in regulating the traditionally illegal practices of barratry, maintenance and champerty, that interest does not justify the prohibition of the NAACP activities disclosed by this record. Malicious intent was of the essence of the common-law offenses of fomenting or stirring up litigation. And whatever may be or may have been true of suits

against government in other countries, the exercise in our own, as in this case, of First Amendment rights to enforce constitutional rights through litigation, as a matter of law, cannot be deemed malicious. Even more modern, subtler regulations of unprofessional conduct or interference with professional relations, not involving malice, would not touch the activities at bar; regulations which reflect hostility to stirring up litigation have been aimed chiefly at those who urge recourse to the courts for private gain, serving no public interest. Hostility still exists to stirring up private litigation where it promotes the use of legal machinery to oppress: as, for example, to sow discord in a family; to expose infirmities in land titles, as by hunting up claims of adverse possession; to harass large companies through a multiplicity of small claims; or to oppress debtors as by seeking out unsatisfied judgments. For a member of the bar to participate, directly or through intermediaries, in such misuses of the legal process is conduct traditionally condemned as injurious to the public. And beyond this, for a lawyer to attempt to reap gain by urging another to engage in private litigation has also been condemned: that seems to be the import of Canon 28, which the Virginia Supreme Court of Appeals has adopted as one of its Rules.

We conclude that although the petitioner has amply shown that its activities fall within the First Amendment's protections, the State has failed to advance any substantial regulatory interest, in the form of substantive evils flowing from petitioner's activities, which can justify the broad prohibitions which it has imposed. Nothing that this record shows as to the nature and purpose of NAACP activities permits an inference of any injurious intervention in or control of litigation which would constitutionally authorize the application of Chapter 33 to those activities. A fortiori, nothing in this record justifies the breadth and vagueness of the Virginia Supreme Court of Appeals' decree. Reversed.

MR. JUSTICE HARLAN, whom MR. JUSTICE CLARK and MR. JUSTICE STEWART join, dissenting.

In my opinion the litigation program of the NAACP, as shown by this record, falls within an area of activity which a State may constitutionally regulate. (Whether it was wise for Virginia to exercise that power in this instance is not, of course, for us to say.) * * *

The regulation before us has its origins in the long-standing common-law prohibitions of champerty, barratry, and maintenance, the closely related prohibitions in the Canons of Ethics against solicitation and intervention by a lay intermediary, and statutory provisions forbidding the unauthorized practice of law. The Court recognizes this formidable history, but puts it aside in the present case on the grounds that there is here no element of malice or of pecuniary gain, that the interests of the NAACP are not to be regarded as substantially different from those of its members, and that we are said to be dealing here with a matter that transcends mere legal ethics—the securing of federally guaranteed rights. But these distinctions are too facile. They do not account for the full scope of the State's legitimate interest in regulating professional conduct. For although these professional standards may have been born in a desire to curb malice and self-aggrandizement by those who would use clients and the courts for their own pecuniary ends, they have acquired a far broader significance during their long development.

POINTS FOR DISCUSSION

a.   Vagueness or Overbreadth?

Did the law at issue in *Button* violate the First Amendment because it was vague or because it was overbroad? Or did it suffer from both defects? Can you articulate why the law was arguably vague and overbroad?

b.   Litigation as a Protected Activity

Former Judge Patricia Wald has written that *Button* is one of the Warren Court's most important decisions because it "recognized public interest litigation as a valid form of political advocacy." Patricia Wald *et al.*, *Remembering a Constitutional Hero*, 43 N.Y.L. Sch. L. Rev. 13, 32 (1999). Public interest litigation has brought about many very important changes since the 1950s. If the states could have regulated lawyers as Virginia had sought to regulate them in this case, much of this public interest litigation might not have occurred. Is the First Amendment right at stake in public interest litigation the right to free speech? The freedom of association? Or the right to petition the government for the redress of grievances?

c.   State Regulation of Lawyers and the First Amendment

Does state regulation of lawyers' solicitation of clients in more mundane cases violate the First Amendment? The Court's decisions in this area do not admit of easy synthesis, but the short answer is "sometimes." The Court has invalidated some such restrictions on the ground that they violate the freedom of speech, see, e.g., *Shapero v. Kentucky Bar Assn.*, 486 U.S. 466 (1988); *Zauderer v. Office of Disciplinary Counsel of Supreme Court of Ohio*, 471 U.S. 626 (1985); *In re R.M.J.*, 455 U.S. 191, 202 (1982), but upheld others against First Amendment challenges, see *Florida Bar v. Went For It, Inc.*, 515 U.S. 618 (1995). These cases concern the doctrine of "commercial speech," which we will consider later in this chapter.

SCHAD V. BOROUGH OF MOUNT EPHRAIM
452 U.S. 61 (1981)

JUSTICE WHITE delivered the opinion of the Court.

In 1973, appellants began operating an adult bookstore in the commercial zone in the Borough of Mount Ephraim in Camden County, N. J. The store sold adult books, magazines, and films. Amusement licenses shortly issued permitting the store to install coin-operated devices by virtue of which a customer could sit in a booth, insert a coin, and watch an adult film. In 1976, the store introduced an additional coin-operated mechanism permitting the customer to watch a live dancer, usually nude, performing behind a glass panel. Complaints were soon filed against appellants charging that the bookstore's exhibition of live dancing violated § 99–15B of Mount Ephraim's zoning ordinance, which described the permitted uses in a commercial zone, in which the store was located, as follows:

(1)   Offices and banks; taverns; restaurants and luncheonettes for sit-down dinners only and with no drive-in facilities; automobile sales; retail stores, such as but not limited to food, wearing apparel, millinery, fabrics, hardware, lumber, jewelry, paint, wallpaper, appliances, flowers, gifts, books, stationery, pharmacy, liquors, cleaners, novelties, hobbies and toys; repair shops for shoes, jewels, clothes and appliances; barbershops and beauty salons; cleaners and laundries; pet stores; and nurseries. Offices may, in addition, be permitted to a group of four (4) stores or more without additional parking, provided the offices do not exceed the equivalent of twenty percent (20%) of the gross floor area of the stores.

(2)   Motels.

Mount Ephraim Code § 99–15B(1), (2) (1979). Section 99–4 of the Borough's code provided that "[a]ll uses not expressly permitted in this chapter are prohibited."

Appellants were found guilty in the Municipal Court and fines were imposed. * * * Appellants appealed to this Court. Their principal claim is that the imposition of criminal penalties under an ordinance prohibiting all live entertainment, including nonobscene, nude dancing, violated their rights of free expression guaranteed by the First and Fourteenth Amendments of the United States Constitution. * * *

As the Mount Ephraim Code has been construed by the New Jersey courts—a construction that is binding upon us—"live entertainment," including nude dancing, is "not a permitted use in any establishment" in the Borough of Mount Ephraim. By excluding live entertainment throughout the Borough, the Mount Ephraim ordinance prohibits a wide range of expression that has long been held to be within the protections of the First and Fourteenth Amendments. Entertainment, as well as political and ideological speech, is protected; motion pictures, programs broadcast by radio and television, and live entertainment, such as musical and dramatic works fall within the First Amendment guarantee. Nor may an entertainment program be prohibited solely because it displays the nude human figure. "[N]udity alone" does not place otherwise protected material outside the mantle of the First Amendment. *Jenkins v. Georgia*, 418 U.S. 153 (1974). Furthermore, as the state courts in this case recognized, nude dancing is not without its First Amendment protections from official regulation.

Whatever First Amendment protection should be extended to nude dancing, live or on film, however, the Mount Ephraim ordinance prohibits all live entertainment in the Borough: no property in the Borough may be principally used for the commercial production of plays, concerts, musicals, dance, or any other form of live entertainment. Because appellants' claims are rooted in the First Amendment, they are entitled to rely on the impact of the ordinance on the expressive activities of others as well as their own. "Because overbroad laws, like vague ones, deter privileged activit[ies], our cases firmly establish appellant's standing to raise an overbreadth challenge." *Grayned v. City of Rockford*, 408 U.S. 104, 114 (1972).

The power of local governments to zone and control land use is undoubtedly broad and its proper exercise is an essential aspect of achieving a satisfactory quality of life in both urban and rural communities. But the zoning power is not infinite and unchallengeable; it "must be exercised within constitutional limits." *Moore v. East Cleveland*, 431 U.S. 494, 514 (1977) (STEVENS, J., concurring in judgment). * * *

In this [case], Mount Ephraim has not adequately justified its substantial restriction of protected activity. None of the justifications asserted in this Court was articulated by the state courts and none of them withstands scrutiny. First, the Borough contends that permitting live entertainment would conflict with its plan to create a commercial area that caters only to the "immediate needs" of its residents and that would enable them to purchase at local stores the few items they occasionally forgot to buy outside the Borough. No evidence was introduced below to support this assertion, and it is difficult to reconcile this characterization of the Borough's commercial zones with the provisions of the ordinance. Section 99–15A expressly states that the purpose of creating commercial zones was to provide areas for "local and *regional* commercial operations." (Emphasis added.) The range of permitted uses goes far beyond providing for the "immediate needs" of the residents. Motels, hardware stores, lumber stores, banks, offices, and car showrooms are permitted in commercial zones. The list of permitted "retail stores" is nonexclusive, and it includes such services as beauty salons, barbershops, cleaners, and restaurants. Virtually the only item or service that may not be sold in a commercial zone is entertainment, or at least live entertainment. The Borough's first justification is patently insufficient.

Second, Mount Ephraim contends that it may selectively exclude commercial live entertainment from the broad range of commercial uses permitted in the Borough for reasons normally associated with zoning in commercial districts, that is, to avoid the problems that may be associated with live entertainment, such as parking, trash, police protection, and medical facilities. The Borough has presented no evidence, and it is not immediately apparent as a matter of experience, that live entertainment poses problems of this nature more significant than those associated with various permitted uses; nor does it appear that the Borough's zoning authority has arrived at a defensible conclusion that unusual problems are presented by live entertainment. We do not find it self-evident that a theater, for example, would create greater parking problems than would a restaurant. Even less apparent is what unique problems would be posed by exhibiting live nude dancing in connection with the sale of adult books and films, particularly since the bookstore is licensed to exhibit nude dancing on films. It

> **Food for Thought**
>
> In this passage, the Court explains why the Borough's restrictions are overbroad. How could they have been rewritten to survive this challenge?

may be that some forms of live entertainment would create problems that are not associated with the commercial uses presently permitted in Mount Ephraim. Yet this ordinance is not narrowly drawn to respond to what might be the distinctive problems arising from certain types of live entertainment, and it is not clear that a more selective approach would fail to address those unique problems if any there are. The Borough has not established that its interests could not be met by restrictions that are less intrusive on protected forms of expression.

Accordingly, the convictions of these appellants are infirm, and the judgment of the Appellate Division of the Superior Court of New Jersey is reversed and the case is remanded for further proceedings not inconsistent with this opinion.

JUSTICE STEVENS, concurring in the judgment.

The difficulty in this case is that we are left to speculate as to the Borough's reasons for proceeding against appellants' business, and as to the justification for the distinction the Borough has drawn between live and other forms of entertainment. While a municipality need not persuade a federal court that its zoning decisions are correct as a matter of policy, when First Amendment interests are implicated it must at least be able to demonstrate that a uniform policy in fact exists and is applied in a content-neutral fashion. Presumably, municipalities may regulate expressive activity—even protected activity—

pursuant to narrowly drawn content-neutral standards; however, they may not regulate protected activity when the only standard provided is the unbridled discretion of a municipal official. Compare *Saia v. New York*, 334 U.S. 558 (1948), with *Kovacs v. Cooper*, 336 U.S. 77 (1949). Because neither the text of the zoning ordinance nor the evidence in the record indicates that Mount Ephraim applied narrowly drawn content-neutral standards to the appellants' business, for me this case involves a criminal prosecution of appellants simply because one of their employees has engaged in expressive activity that has been assumed, *arguendo*, to be protected by the First Amendment. Accordingly, and without endorsing the overbreadth analysis employed by the Court, I concur in its judgment.

CHIEF JUSTICE BURGER, with whom JUSTICE REHNQUIST joins, dissenting.

The Court depicts Mount Ephraim's ordinance as a ban on live entertainment. But, in terms, it does not mention any kind of entertainment. As applied, it operates as a ban on nude dancing in appellants' "adult" bookstore, and for that reason alone it is here. Thus, the issue *in the case that we have before us* is not whether Mount Ephraim may ban traditional live entertainment, but whether it may ban nude dancing, which is used as the "bait" to induce customers into the appellants' bookstore. When, and if, this ordinance is used to prevent a high school performance of "The Sound of Music," for example, the Court can deal with that problem.

> **Definition**
>
> "The Sound of Music" is a wholesome musical drama in which an Austrian family and their lovely governess oppose the Nazis' rise to power in the 1930s. A film version made in 1965 won 5 Oscars.

POINTS FOR DISCUSSION

a. Overbreadth

The Court concluded that the challenged ordinance was overbroad because it prohibited an entire class of expressive activities. In reaching this conclusion, the Court considered the other possible applications of the ordinance, regardless of whether the Borough had authority to prohibit live, nude dancing. With which feature of the overbreadth doctrine, as described above, did the dissent disagree? Does it make sense for the Court to invalidate a statute that could constitutionally have been applied to the person raising the challenge?

b. Nude Dancing and the First Amendment

Did the Court conclude that live, nude dancing is protected by the First Amendment? Did it need to decide that question, in light of its conclusion that the zoning ordinance was overbroad? As we have seen, ten years after the Court's decision in *Schad*, a divided Court in *Barnes v. Glen Theatre, Inc.*, 501 U.S. 560 (1991), upheld an Indiana statute that prohibited nudity in public places as applied to an establishment very similar to the one that brought the challenge in *Schad*. A majority of the Court, however, agreed that nude dancing "is expressive conduct" under the First Amendment, although the Justices disagreed about the extent of protection that the First Amendment offers that activity and the constitutionality of the statute as applied in the case. Does the Court's decision in *Barnes* strengthen or undermine the Court's conclusion in *Schad*?

6. Unconstitutional Conditions

As we saw in Volume 1, the government sometimes uses conditional spending to accomplish ends that it cannot achieve through direct regulation. For example, in *South Dakota v. Dole*, 483 U.S. 203 (1987), Congress threatened to withhold certain federal highway funds unless states set the drinking age at 21. A long-standing question is whether and how the First Amendment limits Congress's spending power. For example, suppose that the First Amendment plainly would prevent Congress from passing a statute barring an individual from discussing a particular topic. May the government use conditional spending to accomplish the same objective—by stating, in effect, "You will receive a payment from the government unless you discuss the particular topic"?

> **Make the Connection**
>
> We briefly considered the unconstitutional conditions doctrine, and the Court's decision in *Sindermann*, in Chapter 3.

The Supreme Court has addressed this issue with two doctrines. On the one hand, the **unconstitutional conditions** doctrine says that the "the government 'may not deny a benefit to a person on a basis that infringes his constitutionally protected * * * freedom of speech' even if he has no entitlement to that benefit." *Board of Commissioners, Wabaunsee County v. Umbehr*, 518 U.S. 668, 674 (1996) (quoting *Perry v. Sindermann*, 408 U.S. 593, 597 (1972)). For example, in *Umbehr*, the Supreme Court held that a county violated the free speech rights of a trash hauler. The trash hauler had an at-will employment contract, and the county board fired him after he made critical statements about the board. The Court held that even though the county did not have to hire the trash hauler, and even though he could be fired for essentially no reason at all, it could not fire him for criticizing the government. The county, in other words, could not condition his continued employment on his willingness to refrain from criticizing the government.

On the other hand, as we will see in the following case, the Supreme Court has said: "The Government can, without violating the Constitution, **selectively**

fund a program to encourage certain activities it believes to be in the public interest, without at the same time funding an alternative program which seeks to deal with the problem in another way." *Rust v. Sullivan,* 500 U.S. 173, 194 (1991). The funding of the program may be conditional. For example, in *United States v. American Library Association,* 539 U.S. 194 (2003), the federal government gave libraries subsidies to provide internet access to their patrons. But the subsidies came only on the condition that the libraries agree to install internet filters to block pornography. The Supreme Court held that this restriction did not violate the Constitution, explaining that the government could choose not to provide subsidies for pornography.

Are these two doctrines in tension? Consider the case that follows.

RUST V. SULLIVAN
500 U.S. 173 (1991)

CHIEF JUSTICE REHNQUIST delivered the opinion of the Court.

In 1970, Congress enacted Title X of the Public Health Service Act (Act), 84 Stat. 1506, as amended, 42 U.S.C. §§ 300–399a–6, which provides federal funding for family-planning services. The Act authorizes the Secretary to "make grants to and enter into contracts with public or nonprofit private entities to assist in the establishment and operation of voluntary family planning projects which shall offer a broad range of acceptable and effective family planning methods and services." § 300(a). Grants and contracts under Title X must "be made in accordance with such regulations as the Secretary may promulgate." § 300a–4(a). Section 1008 of the Act, however, provides that "[n]one of the funds appropriated under this subchapter shall be used in programs where abortion is a method of family planning." § 300a–6. That restriction was intended to ensure that Title X funds would "be used only to support preventive family planning services, population research, infertility services, and other related medical, informational, and educational activities." H.R. Conf. Rep. No. 91–1667, p. 8 (1970). [The Secretary promulgated regulations prohibiting recipients of Title X funds from, among other things, discussing abortion with their clients and patients.]

Petitioners contend that the regulations violate the First Amendment by impermissibly discriminating based on viewpoint because they prohibit "all discussion about abortion as a lawful option—including counseling, referral, and the provision of neutral and accurate information about ending a pregnancy—while compelling the clinic or counselor to provide information that promotes continuing a pregnancy to term." They assert that the regulations violate the "free speech rights of private health care organizations that receive Title X funds, of their staff, and of their patients" by impermissibly imposing "viewpoint-discriminatory conditions on government subsidies" and thus "penaliz[e] speech funded with non-Title X monies." Because "Title X continues to fund speech ancillary to pregnancy testing in a manner that is not evenhanded with respect to views and information about abortion, it invidiously discriminates on the basis of viewpoint." Relying on *Regan v. Taxation with Representation of Wash.*, 461 U.S. 540 (1983), and *Arkansas Writers' Project, Inc. v. Ragland,* 481 U.S. 221, 234 (1987), petitioners also assert that while the Government may place certain conditions on the receipt of federal subsidies, it may not "discriminate invidiously in its subsidies in such a way as to 'ai[m] at the suppression of dangerous ideas.' " *Regan, supra,* 461 U.S., at 548 (quoting *Cammarano v. United States,* 358 U.S. 498, 513 (1959)).

There is no question but that the statutory prohibition contained in § 1008 is constitutional. In *Maher v. Roe,* 432 U.S. 464 (1977), we upheld a state welfare regulation under which Medicaid recipients received payments for services related to childbirth, but not for nontherapeutic abortions. The Court rejected the claim that this unequal subsidization worked a violation of the Constitution. We held that the government may "make a value judgment favoring childbirth over abortion, [and] implement that judgment by the allocation of public funds." *Id.,* 432 U.S., at 474. Here the Government is exercising the authority it possesses under *Maher* and *Harris v. McRae,* 448 U.S. 297 (1980), to subsidize family planning services which will lead to conception and childbirth, and declining to "promote or encourage abortion." The Government can, without violating the Constitution, selectively fund a program to encourage certain activities it believes to be in the public interest, without at the same time funding an alternative program which seeks to deal with the problem in another way. In so doing, the Government has not discriminated on the basis of viewpoint; it has merely chosen to fund one activity to the exclusion of the other. "[A] legislature's decision not to subsidize the exercise of a fundamental right does not infringe the right." *Regan, supra,* 461 U.S., at 549. See also *Buckley v. Valeo,* 424 U.S. 1 (1976). "A refusal to fund protected activity, without more, cannot be equated with the imposition of a 'penalty' on that activity." *McRae,* 448 U.S., at 317, n.19. "There is a basic difference between direct state interference with a protected activity and state encouragement of an alternative activity consonant with legislative policy." *Maher,* 432 U.S., at 475.

The challenged regulations implement the statutory prohibition by prohibiting counseling, referral, and the provision of information regarding abortion as a method of family planning. They are designed to ensure that the limits of the federal program are observed. The Title X program is designed not for prenatal care, but to encourage family planning. A doctor who wished to offer prenatal care to a project patient who became pregnant could properly be prohibited from doing so because such service is outside the scope of the federally funded program. The regulations prohibiting abortion counseling and referral are of the same ilk; "no funds appropriated for the project may be used in programs where abortion is a method of family planning," and a doctor employed by the

> **Take Note**
>
> The Court explains here why the restrictions imposed on recipients of the federal funds do not violate the First Amendment. Is there a difference between declining to spend federal funds to subsidize a particular activity and providing funds only on the condition that the recipients refrain from discussing certain matters with patients?

project may be prohibited in the course of his project duties from counseling abortion or referring for abortion. This is not a case of the Government "suppressing a dangerous idea," but of a prohibition on a project grantee or its employees from engaging in activities outside of the project's scope.

To hold that the Government unconstitutionally discriminates on the basis of viewpoint when it chooses to fund a program dedicated to advance certain permissible goals, because the program in advancing those goals necessarily discourages alternative goals, would render numerous Government programs constitutionally suspect. When Congress established a National Endowment for Democracy to encourage other countries to adopt democratic principles, 22 U.S.C. § 4411(b), it was not constitutionally required to fund a program to encourage competing lines of political philosophy such as communism and fascism. Petitioners' assertions ultimately boil down to the position that if the government chooses to subsidize one protected right, it must subsidize analogous counterpart rights. But the Court has soundly rejected that proposition. Within far broader limits than petitioners are willing to concede, when the Government appropriates public funds to establish a program it is entitled to define the limits of that program.

JUSTICE BLACKMUN, with whom JUSTICE MARSHALL joins, with whom JUSTICE STEVENS joins as to Parts II and III, and with whom JUSTICE O'CONNOR joins as to Part I, dissenting.

[II]

Until today, the Court never has upheld viewpoint-based suppression of speech simply because that suppression was a condition upon the acceptance of public funds. Whatever may be the Government's power to condition the receipt of its largess upon the relinquishment of constitutional rights, it surely does not extend to a condition that suppresses the recipient's cherished freedom of speech based solely upon the content or viewpoint of that speech. * * *

Nothing in the Court's opinion in *Regan v. Taxation with Representation of Washington,* 461 U.S. 540 (1983), can be said to challenge this long-settled understanding. In *Regan,* the Court upheld a content-neutral provision of the Internal Revenue Code, 26 U.S.C. § 501(c)(3), that disallowed a particular tax-exempt status to organizations that "attempt[ed] to influence legislation," while affording such status to veterans' organizations irrespective of their lobbying activities. [T]he Court explained: "The case would be different if Congress were to discriminate invidiously in its subsidies in such a way as to "ai[m] at the suppression of dangerous ideas. . . . We find no indication that the statute was intended to suppress any ideas or any demonstration that it has had that effect." 461 U.S., at 548. The separate concurrence in *Regan* joined the Court's opinion precisely "[b]ecause 26 U.S.C. § 501's discrimination between veterans' organizations and charitable organizations is not based on the content of their speech." 461 U.S., at 551.

It cannot seriously be disputed that the counseling and referral provisions at issue in the present cases constitute content-based regulation of speech. Title X grantees may provide counseling and referral regarding any of a wide range of family planning and other topics, save abortion.

> **Take Note**
>
> Justice Blackmun asserts here that the challenged regulations are both content based and viewpoint based. Can you articulate the difference between content-based and viewpoint-based restrictions? Would it be possible for a challenged regulation in this context to be content based but not viewpoint based? Would that make the regulations any more likely to be upheld?

The regulations are also clearly viewpoint based. While suppressing speech favorable to abortion with one hand, the Secretary compels antiabortion speech with the other. For example, the Department of Health and Human Services' own description of the regulations makes plain that "Title X projects are *required* to facilitate access to prenatal care and social services, including adoption services, that might be needed by the pregnant client to promote her well-being and that of her child, while making it abundantly clear that the project is not permitted to promote abortion by facilitating access to abortion through the referral process." 53 Fed.Reg. 2927 (1988) (emphasis added).

Moreover, the regulations command that a project refer for prenatal care each woman diagnosed as pregnant, irrespective of the woman's expressed desire to continue or terminate her pregnancy. 42 CFR § 59.8(a)(2) (1990). If a client asks directly about abortion, a Title X physician or counselor is required to say, in essence, that the project does not consider abortion to be an appropriate method of family planning. § 59.8(b)(4). Both requirements are antithetical to the First Amendment. See *Wooley v. Maynard*, 430 U.S. 705, 714 (1977).

The regulations pertaining to "advocacy" are even more explicitly viewpoint based. These provide: "A Title X project may not *encourage, promote or advocate* abortion as a method of family planning." § 59.10 (emphasis added). They explain: "This requirement prohibits actions to *assist* women to obtain abortions or *increase* the availability or accessibility of abortion for family planning purposes." § 59.10(a) (emphasis added). The regulations do not, however, proscribe or even

> **FYI**
>
> In *Wooley*, the Court held that New Hampshire could not compel a person who sought to register a car to use a license plate that said, "Live Free or Die." The Court reasoned that such compulsion violated the "right to refrain from speaking," by effectively requiring the appellees "to use their private property as a 'mobile billboard' for the State's ideological message."

regulate anti-abortion advocacy. These are clearly restrictions aimed at the suppression of "dangerous ideas."

The Court concludes that the challenged regulations do not violate the First Amendment rights of Title X staff members because any limitation of the employees' freedom of expression is simply a consequence of their decision to accept employment at a federally funded project. But it has never been sufficient to justify an otherwise unconstitutional condition upon public employment that the employee may escape the condition by relinquishing his or her job. It is beyond question "that a government may not require an individual to relinquish rights guaranteed him by the First Amendment as a condition of public employment." *Abood v. Detroit Bd. of Ed.,* 431 U.S. 209, 234 (1977). * * * Under the majority's reasoning, the First Amendment could be read to tolerate *any* governmental restriction upon an employee's speech so long as that restriction is limited to the funded workplace. This is a dangerous proposition, and one the Court has rightly rejected in the past.

Finally, it is of no small significance that the speech the Secretary would suppress is truthful information regarding constitutionally protected conduct of vital importance to the listener. One can imagine no legitimate governmental interest that might be served by suppressing such information. Concededly, the abortion debate is among the most divisive and contentious issues that our Nation has faced in recent years. "But freedom to differ is not limited to things that do not matter much. That would be a mere shadow of freedom. The test of its substance is the right to differ as to things that touch the heart of the existing order." *West Virginia Bd. of Ed. v. Barnette,* 319 U.S. 624, 642 (1943).

POINTS FOR DISCUSSION

a.   The "Gag Rule"

Many critics of the *Rust* decision have referred to the Reagan Administration's regulations implementing § 1008 as the "gag rule." *Get Rid of the Gag Rule*, N.Y. Times, Jul. 13, 1991, at 1:20. Is this moniker an appropriate nickname for the regulations? Has the government prevented anyone from speaking about any subject? What could a doctor who wished to have unfettered discretion to discuss abortion with her patients have done to avoid the restrictions imposed by the regulations? Would that be a realistic option?

b.   Executive Suspension

Although the Supreme Court upheld the regulations implementing the conditional spending program, President Clinton (on his first day in office) ordered the Secretary of Health and Human Services to suspend their enforcement. See The Title X "Gag Rule," Memorandum from President William J. Clinton to Secretary of Health and Human Services, 58 Fed. Reg. 7455 (1993). Was this action within the President's power? Does it matter that the challenged regulations were themselves promulgated by the Secretary of Health and Human Services in a prior Administration?

c.   Withholding Funds from Organizations Based upon Their Views

Can a state university withhold funds that it gives to some groups from religious student groups, on the ground that it has limited funds and does not want to fund religious organizations? In *Rosenberger v. Rector and Visitors of University of Virginia*, 515 U.S. 819 (1995), the Court held that scarcity of funds does not permit a public university to discriminate on the basis of viewpoint. Is this decision consistent with *Rust*? Is this decision consistent with the Establishment Clause?

> **Make the Connection**
>
> We will consider the Establishment Clause, and the limits that it imposes on state aid to religion, in Chapter 11.

d.   Government Speech

In *Rosenberger v. Rector and Visitors of University of Virginia*, 515 U.S. 819 (1995), described above, the state argued that *Rust* stands for the proposition that "content-based funding decisions are both inevitable and lawful." Writing for the Court, Justice Kennedy disagreed, stating that in *Rust*, "the government did not create a program to encourage private speech but instead used private speakers to transmit specific information pertaining to its own program." He continued:

> We recognized [in *Rust*] that when the government appropriates public funds to promote a particular policy of its own it is entitled to say what it

wishes. When the government disburses public funds to private entities to convey a governmental message, it may take legitimate and appropriate steps to ensure that its message is neither garbled nor distorted by the grantee. It does not follow, however, [that] viewpoint-based restrictions are proper when the [government] does not itself speak or subsidize transmittal of a message it favors but instead expends funds to encourage a diversity of views from private speakers.

Do you agree that the Court's decision in *Rust* turned on the fact that the government itself was seeking to speak? Didn't the challenged regulations simply prohibit the doctors and other program participants from communicating a message that they might otherwise have thought was appropriate?

What is the status of "government speech" under the First Amendment? Does the government have the same right to communicate a message that private actors enjoy? In *Pleasant Grove City, Utah v. Summum*, 555 U.S. 460 (2009), the Court held that a city's decision to place a donated monument in a public park—and to refuse to place in the park a monument that a different group wished to donate to communicate a different message—was a form of government speech and thus not subject to scrutiny under the Free Speech Clause of the First Amendment. The Court reasoned:

> The Free Speech Clause restricts government regulation of private speech; it does not regulate government speech. Indeed, it is not easy to imagine how government could function if it lacked this freedom. "If every citizen were to have a right to insist that no one paid by public funds express a view with which he disagreed, debate over issues of great concern to the public would be limited to those in the private sector, and the process of government as we know it radically transformed." *Keller v. State Bar of Cal.*, 496 U.S. 1, 12–13 (1990). * * * A government entity may exercise this same freedom to express its views when it receives assistance from private sources for the purpose of delivering a government-controlled message.

When the government provides funds to private actors who then speak (or refrain from speaking)—or when private actors donate monuments designed to express a particular point of view—how can the Court tell whether it is the government or instead the private actor who is speaking?

B. CATEGORIES OF SPEECH

In the previous materials, we considered doctrines that the Supreme Court has developed for analyzing different types of regulations that the federal and state governments have attempted to place on speech. Most of those doctrines require a reviewing court to consider whether the governmental interests advanced by the regulation justify the interference with the freedom of speech. Recall that Justice Black believed that such balancing is inappropriate when a law abridges the freedom of speech—in essence, that the First Amendment's reference to "no law" means what it says. Would that view mean that the government simply cannot regulate in any fashion that impairs expression or communication?

Our intuition tells us that this cannot always be the case, at least as a matter of existing practice, and that there must be some categories of speech that are beyond the protection of the First Amendment. Indeed, in our legal culture we routinely permit prosecution and conviction for many forms of speech. For example, false statements under oath can be punished as perjury, even though those statements clearly count as "speech" within the general understanding of the term. The same is true of speech soliciting a bribe—such as when a public official says, "I will vote for this bill if you give me $10,000"—and blackmail—such as when a person says, "Give me $10,000 or I will tell your wife that you're having an affair."

In a famous passage in *Chaplinsky v. State of New Hampshire*, 315 U.S. 568 (1942), which we will consider later in this section, the Court declared:

> Allowing the broadest scope to the language and purpose of the Fourteenth Amendment, it is well understood that the right of free speech is not absolute at all times and under all circumstances. There are certain well-defined and narrowly limited classes of speech, the prevention and punishment of which has never been thought to raise any Constitutional problem. These include the lewd and obscene, the profane, the libelous, and the insulting or "fighting" words—those which by their very utterance inflict injury or tend to incite an immediate breach of the peace. It has been well observed that such utterances are no essential part of any exposition of ideas, and are of such slight social value as a step to truth that any benefit that may be derived from them is clearly outweighed by the social interest in order and morality.

As we will see, the Court has frequently quoted this language when deciding whether to exclude a particular category of speech from the protection of the First Amendment.

But it is easier to note that some categories of speech have long been treated as beyond the protection of the First Amendment than it is to develop a coherent theory about *why* those categories are excluded from protection—and thus why *other* categories might be, as well. Indeed, in light of what we have seen about the danger of content-based regulation, it seems particularly important to develop such a coherent (and perhaps limiting) theory for when the Court can declare that an entire category of speech, defined by its content, is beyond the protection of the First Amendment.

So how exactly does the Court identify exceptions to the general rule against content-based restrictions? Are those categories excluded from protection because of some historical tradition that declines to treat such utterances as "speech"? Are they excluded because the speech itself is dangerous or of low value? Are they excluded because the government's interest in regulating such speech is so strong that it essentially always justifies regulation? Or is there simply no coherent theory that can explain the exclusion of certain categories of speech from the protection of the First Amendment?

We explore these questions in the materials that follow in this section. The materials are organized by category of speech. These categories include: (1) incitement and advocacy of crime; (2) defamation, (3) obscenity; (4) symbolic conduct; (5) provocative speech; (6) commercial speech; (7) campaign contributions and expenditures; and (8) the speech of public employees.

As you read these materials, consider how the Court goes about deciding whether a particular category of speech should be subject to distinctive rules, whether such an inquiry is itself consistent with the First Amendment, and, if so, whether the Court has done a good job in identifying those categories and the special rules that apply.

1. Incitement and Advocacy of Crime

In what circumstances does the First Amendment permit the government to punish a person merely for advocating the commission of crimes (without actually committing them)? This question has a long and frequently discussed history, at least in part because it was one of the first questions that the Court decided respecting the freedom of speech. The Court concisely summarized much of this history in the following excerpt from *Dennis v. United States*, 341 U.S. 494 (1951):

> **FYI**
>
> The Criminal Espionage Act of 1917 was enacted during World War I. The Act imposed severe criminal penalties for spying, interfering with the draft, encouraging disloyalty, and other acts thought to harm the war effort.

> No important case involving free speech was decided by this Court prior to *Schenck v. United States*, 249 U.S. 47 (1919). * * * That case involved a conviction under the Criminal Espionage Act, 40 Stat. 217 (1917).

The question the Court faced was whether the evidence was sufficient to sustain the conviction. Writing for a unanimous Court, Justice Holmes stated that the "question in every case is whether the words used are used in such circumstances and are of such a nature as to create a clear and present danger that they will bring about the substantive evils that Congress has a right to prevent." 249 U.S. at 52. * * * The charge was causing and attempting to cause insubordination in the military forces and obstruct recruiting. The objectionable document denounced conscription and its most inciting sentence was, "You must do your share to maintain, support and uphold the rights of the people of this country." *Id.* at 51. Fifteen thousand copies were printed and some circulated. This insubstantial gesture toward insubordination in 1917 during war was held to be a clear and present danger of bringing about the evil of military insubordination.

In several later cases involving convictions under the Criminal Espionage Act, the nub of the evidence the Court held sufficient to meet the "clear and present danger" test enunciated in *Schenck* was as follows: *Frohwerk v. United States*, 249 U.S. 204 (1919)—publication of twelve newspaper articles attacking the war; *Debs v. United States*, 249 U.S. 211 (1919)—one speech attacking the United States' participation in the war; *Abrams v. United States*, 250 U.S. 616 (1919)—circulation of copies of two different socialist circulars attacking the war; *Schaefer v. United States*, 251 U.S. 466 (1920)—publication of a German-language newspaper with allegedly false articles, critical of capitalism and the war; *Pierce v. United States*, 252 U.S. 239 (1920)—circulation of copies of a four-page pamphlet written by a clergyman, attacking the purposes of the war and United States' participation therein. * * *

The rule we deduce from these cases is that where an offense is specified by a statute in nonspeech or nonpress terms, a conviction relying upon speech or press as evidence of violation may be sustained only when the speech or publication created a "clear and present danger" of attempting or accomplishing the prohibited crime, e. g., interference with enlistment. * * *

The next important case before the Court in which free speech was the crux of the conflict was *Gitlow v. New York*, 268 U.S. 652 (1925). There New York had made it a crime to advocate "the necessity or propriety of overthrowing . . . organized government by force." The evidence of violation of the statute was that the defendant had published a Manifesto attacking the Government and capitalism. The convictions were sustained, Justices Holmes and Brandeis dissenting. The majority refused to apply the "clear and present danger" test to the specific utterance. Its reasoning was as follows: The "clear and present danger" test was applied to the utterance itself in *Schenck* because the question was merely one of sufficiency of evidence under an admittedly constitutional statute. *Gitlow*, however, presented a different question. There a legislature had found that a certain kind of speech was, itself, harmful and unlawful. The constitutionality of such a state statute had to be adjudged by this Court just as it determined the constitutionality of any state statute, namely, whether the statute was "reasonable." Since it was entirely reasonable for a state to attempt to protect itself from violent overthrow, the statute was perforce reasonable. The only question remaining in the case became whether there was evidence to support the conviction, a question which gave the majority no difficulty. * * * This approach was emphasized in *Whitney v. California*, 274 U.S. 357 (1927), where the Court was

> **Definition**
>
> The term "criminal syndicalism" refers to a radical political doctrine that "advocates or teaches the use of illegal methods to change industrial or political control," such as workers taking over factories by force. *Black's Law Dictionary* (9th ed. 2009).

confronted with a conviction under the California Criminal Syndicalist statute. The Court sustained the conviction * * *.

The cases discussed in this excerpt from *Dennis* arose under a variety of circumstances. The earliest cases were decided while (or shortly after) the United States was involved in World War I. The cases from the 1920s—*Gitlow* and *Whitney*—involved statutes that were enacted in response to the perceived "Red Scare," the fear that radicals would import the Russian Revolution to American shores. And *Dennis* involved a prosecution under the Smith Act of 1940, which made it a crime to conspire to overthrow the government of the United States by force and violence, and which was increasingly used against communist sympathizers at the beginning of the Cold War. In all of these cases, the Court permitted the conviction of the defendants on the basis of their authorship or distribution of leaflets, pamphlets, and the like that advocated the overthrow of the government, or on the basis of their membership in organizations, such as the Communist Party, that espoused similar aims.

In virtually all of the cases described in *Dennis* (and in *Dennis* itself), there were strong dissents (or at least separate concurring opinions). The most enduring were Justice Holmes's dissent in *Abrams* and Justice Brandeis's concurrence in *Whitney*. In *Abrams*, which permitted a conviction for the distribution of a pamphlet calling on workers in factories to stop making ammunition and to "unite in the fight against capitalism," Justice Holmes stated in dissent:

> It is only the present danger of immediate evil or an intent to bring it about that warrants Congress in setting a limit to the expression of opinion where private rights are not concerned. Congress certainly cannot forbid all effort to change the mind of the country. * * * In this case sentences of twenty years imprisonment have been imposed for the publishing of two leaflets that I believe the defendants had as much right to publish as the Government has to publish the Constitution of the United States now vainly invoked by them. Even if I am technically wrong and enough can be squeezed from these poor and puny anonymities to turn the color of legal litmus paper, [the] most nominal punishment seems to me all that possibly could be inflicted, unless the defendants are to be made to suffer not for what the indictment alleges but for the creed that they avow * * *.
>
> Persecution for the expression of opinions seems to me perfectly logical. If you have no doubt of your premises or your power and want a certain result with all your heart you naturally express your wishes in law and sweep away all opposition. To allow opposition by speech seems to indicate that you think the speech impotent, as when a man says that he has squared the circle, or that you do not care whole heartedly for the result, or that you doubt either your power or your premises. But when men have realized that time has upset many fighting faiths, they may come to believe even more than they believe the very foundations of their own conduct that the ultimate good desired is better reached by free trade in ideas—that the best test of truth is the power of the thought to get itself accepted in the competition of the market, and that truth is the only ground upon which their wishes safely can be carried out. That at any rate is the theory of our Constitution. It is an experiment, as all life is an experiment. * * * While that experiment is part of our system I think that we should be eternally vigilant against attempts to check the expression of opinions that we loathe and believe to be fraught with death, unless they so imminently threaten immediate interference with the lawful and pressing purposes of the law that an immediate check is required to save the country.

250 U.S. at 628–30 (HOLMES, J., dissenting)

Justice Holmes was not the only Justice who advanced a different view of the First Amendment. In *Whitney*, which involved the conviction of Anita Whitney, the niece of Justice Stephen Field and a member of the Communist Party who was arrested after giving a speech criticizing race-based lynching, Justice Brandeis stated the following in his separate opinion:

Those who won our independence believed that the final end of the state was to make men free to develop their faculties, and that in its government the deliberative forces should prevail over the arbitrary. They valued liberty both as an end and as a means. * * * They believed that freedom to think as you will and to speak as you think are means indispensable to the discovery and spread of political truth; that without free speech and assembly discussion would be futile; that with them, discussion affords ordinarily adequate protection against the dissemination of noxious doctrine; that the greatest menace to freedom is an inert people; that public discussion is a political duty; and that this should be a fundamental principle of the American government. They recognized the risks to which all human institutions are subject. But they knew that order cannot be secured merely through fear of punishment for its infraction; that it is hazardous to discourage thought, hope and imagination; that fear breeds repression; that repression breeds hate; that hate menaces stable government; that the path of safety lies in the opportunity to discuss freely supposed grievances and proposed remedies; and that the fitting remedy for evil counsels is good ones. Believing in the power of reason as applied through public discussion, they eschewed silence coerced by law—the argument of force in its worst form. Recognizing the occasional tyrannies of governing majorities, they amended the Constitution so that free speech and assembly should be guaranteed.

Fear of serious injury cannot alone justify suppression of free speech and assembly. Men feared witches and burnt women. It is the function of speech to free men from the bondage of irrational fears. To justify suppression of free speech there must be reasonable ground to fear that serious evil will result if free speech is practiced. There must be reasonable ground to believe that the danger apprehended is imminent. There must be reasonable ground to believe that the evil to be prevented is a serious one. * * * But even advocacy of violation, however reprehensible morally, is not a justification for denying free speech where the advocacy falls short of incitement and there is nothing to indicate that the advocacy would be immediately acted on.

274 U.S. at 375–76 (BRANDEIS, J., concurring).

POINTS FOR DISCUSSION

a.   Theory of the First Amendment

The cases about the government's power to punish the advocacy of crime provide a stark context in which to discern the basic theory (or theories) of the First Amendment. On which theory did the Court rely from World War I until the 1950s? What was Justice Holmes's theory of the First Amendment? Was it different from Justice Brandeis's theory? What are the costs of the Court's approach from this era? What are the costs of Justices Holmes's and Brandeis's approaches?

b.   War and Exigent Circumstances

Does the First Amendment by necessity permit greater government regulation of speech advocating its overthrow during times of stress or war? If so, how can we determine when such times exist, and whether circumstances are sufficiently exigent to justify such regulation?

In the case that follows, the Court developed the modern test for when the government can punish a person for advocating the commission of a crime or inciting violence.

BRANDENBURG V. OHIO
395 U.S. 444 (1969)

PER CURIAM.

The appellant, a leader of a Ku Klux Klan group, was convicted under the Ohio Criminal Syndicalism statute for "advocat[ing] * * * the duty, necessity, or propriety of crime, sabotage, violence, or unlawful methods of terrorism as a means of accomplishing industrial or political reform" and for "voluntarily assembl[ing] with any society, group, or assemblage of persons formed to teach or advocate the doctrines of criminal syndicalism." Ohio Rev. Code Ann. § 2923.13. He was fined $1,000 and sentenced to one to 10 years' imprisonment. * * *

The record shows that a man, identified at trial as the appellant, telephoned an announcer-reporter on the staff of a Cincinnati television station and invited him to come to a Ku Klux Klan "rally" to be held at a farm in Hamilton County.

With the cooperation of the organizers, the reporter and a cameraman attended the meeting and filmed the events. Portions of the films were later broadcast on the local station and on a national network.

The prosecution's case rested on the films and on testimony identifying the appellant as the person who communicated with the reporter and who spoke at the rally. The State also introduced into evidence several articles appearing in the film, including a pistol, a rifle, a shotgun, ammunition, a Bible, and a red hood worn by the speaker in the films.

One film showed 12 hooded figures, some of whom carried firearms. They were gathered around a large wooden cross, which they burned. No one was present other than the participants and the newsmen who made the film. Most of the words uttered during the scene were incomprehensible when the film was projected, but scattered phrases could be understood that were derogatory of Negroes and, in one instance, of Jews. Another scene on the same film showed the appellant, in Klan regalia, making a speech. The speech, in full, was as follows:

> "This is an organizers' meeting. We have had quite a few members here today which are—we have hundreds, hundreds of members throughout the State of Ohio. I can quote from a newspaper clipping from the Columbus, Ohio Dispatch, five weeks ago Sunday morning. The Klan has more members in the State of Ohio than does any other organization. We're not a revengent organization, but if our President, our Congress, our Supreme Court, continues to suppress the white, Caucasian race, it's possible that there might have to be some revengeance taken. We are marching on Congress July the Fourth, four hundred thousand strong. From there we are dividing into two groups, one group to march on St. Augustine, Florida, the other group to march into Mississippi. Thank you."

The second film showed six hooded figures one of whom, later identified as the appellant, repeated a speech very similar to that recorded on the first film. The reference to the possibility of "revengeance" was omitted, and one sentence was added [that contained a racial epithet and stated appellant's belief that black people] "should be returned to Africa, [and] the Jew returned to Israel." Though some of the figures in the films carried weapons, the speaker did not.

The Ohio Criminal Syndicalism Statute was enacted in 1919. From 1917 to 1920, identical or quite similar laws were adopted by 20 States and two territories. In 1927, this Court sustained the constitutionality of California's Criminal Syndicalism Act, the text of which is quite similar to that of the laws of Ohio.

Whitney v. California, 274 U.S. 357 (1927). The Court upheld the statute on the ground that, without more, "advocating" violent means to effect political and economic change involves such danger to the security of the State that the State may outlaw it. But *Whitney* has been thoroughly discredited by later decisions. See *Dennis v. United States*, 341 U.S. 494, 507 (1951). These later decisions have fashioned the principle that the constitutional guarantees of free speech and free press do not permit a State to forbid or proscribe advocacy of the use of force or of law violation except where such advocacy is directed to inciting or producing imminent lawless action and is likely to incite or produce such action. As we said in *Noto v. United States*, 367 U.S. 290, 297–298 (1961), "the mere abstract teaching * * * of the moral propriety or even moral necessity for a resort to force and violence, is not the same as preparing a group for violent action and steeling it to such action." A statute which fails to draw this distinction impermissibly intrudes upon the freedoms guaranteed by the First and Fourteenth Amendments. It sweeps within its condemnation speech which our Constitution has immunized from governmental control.

> **Take Note**
>
> In this passage, the Court specifies the standard for when the government may restrict advocacy of crime. In what way does the standard differ from the approach of the older cases?

Measured by this test, Ohio's Criminal Syndicalism Act cannot be sustained. The Act punishes persons who "advocate or teach the duty, necessity, or propriety" of violence "as a means of accomplishing industrial or political reform"; or who publish or circulate or display any book or paper containing such advocacy; or who "justify" the commission of violent acts "with intent to exemplify, spread or advocate the propriety of the doctrines of criminal syndicalism"; or who "voluntarily assemble" with a group formed "to teach or advocate the doctrines of criminal syndicalism." Neither the indictment nor the trial judge's instructions to the jury in any way refined the statute's bald definition of the crime in terms of mere advocacy not distinguished from incitement to imminent lawless action.

Accordingly, we are here confronted with a statute which, by its own words and as applied, purports to punish mere advocacy and to forbid, on pain of criminal punishment, assembly with others merely to advocate the described type of action. Such a statute falls within the condemnation of the First and Fourteenth Amendments. The contrary teaching of *Whitney v. California* cannot be supported, and that decision is therefore overruled.

POINTS FOR DISCUSSION

a.   Incitement of Imminent Lawless Action

The Court in *Brandenburg* held that the government may restrict advocacy of crime only where "advocacy is directed to inciting or producing imminent lawless action and is likely to incite or produce such action." As a practical matter, how would the government know when advocacy of crime is "likely to incite" lawless action? Is it ever possible for the mere delivery of a speech, authorship of a book or pamphlet, or membership in an organization to satisfy that standard?

b.   Crime and Speech

The Court in *Brandenburg* did not go so far as to hold that a person can *never* be punished for his speech, even if a person could constitutionally be punished for actually engaging in conduct, such as armed insurrection or mob violence, that the state legitimately has criminalized. Should the Court have done so, on the ground that any other approach effectively chills some speech?

Or did the Court go too far in *Brandenburg*, and perhaps even in its older "clear and present danger" cases? Robert Bork, for example, argued that the First Amendment provides *no* protection for speech advocating the violation of the law. See Robert H. Bork, *Neutral Principles and Some First Amendment Problems*, 47 Ind. L. J. 1 (1971). On this view, is advocacy of crime unprotected because of the strong government interest in preventing crime, or because such speech simply isn't worthy of protection? Would the speeches of Martin Luther King, Jr., regularly have subjected him to criminal punishment for advocating "crime," in the form of civil disobedience?

c.   Serious Lawless Action

The *Brandenburg* standard permits the government to restrict advocacy of crime only if the advocacy is directed to inciting or producing, and is likely to incite or produce, "imminent lawless action." Does any lawless action count for purposes of the test? For example, does explicitly urging your brother to jaywalk count as punishable incitement? The Court in *Brandenburg* did not limit the category of unprotected incitement only to incitement of *serious* lawless action, and the Supreme Court has never directly held that the category is so limited. But common sense suggests that the government's interest in limiting speech is much greater when it acts to prevent serious harm. In addition, Justice Brandeis's view, on which the *Brandenburg* standard was based, would have permitted the government to punish incitement only in cases of advocacy of serious lawless action. *Whitney v. California*, 274 U.S. 357 (1927) (Brandeis, J., concurring) ("To justify suppression of free speech there must be reasonable ground to fear that serious evil will result if free speech is practiced. There must be reasonable ground to believe that the danger apprehended is imminent. There must be reasonable ground to believe that the evil to be prevented is a serious one."). Most people assume that the *Brandenburg* test incorporates this requirement, as well.

2. Defamation and Related Torts

Under the tort law of most states, a person may incur liability for libel or slander by making "a false and defamatory statement concerning another." Restatement (Second) of the Law of Torts § 558. A statement is "defamatory if it tends so to harm the reputation of another as to lower him in the estimation of the community or to deter third persons from associating or dealing with him." *Id.* § 559. The tort of libel generally consists of the "publication of defamatory matter by written or printed words," while the tort of slander typically consists of "the publication of defamatory matter by spoken words." *Id.* § 568.

Imposing liability for defamatory statements is, in some senses, a limitation on the freedom of speech. For example, in one case (fortunately not involving either of the co-authors of this textbook), a court required a professor to pay $50,000 in damages for saying that one of his colleagues was "a liar, deceitful, absolutely useless, and does not have a Ph.D., and was a fraud * * *." *Raymond U v. Duke University*, 371 S.E.2d 701, 709 (N.C. App. 1988). Judgments like this one certainly limit the freedom of people to say whatever they think about other people, and they are imposed and enforced by courts, which are clearly governmental actors.

The Supreme Court has held that the First Amendment does not absolutely bar the imposition of tort liability for defamatory statements. See *Beauharnais v. People of State of Illinois*, 343 U.S. 250, 266 (1952). But the First Amendment does impose some important restrictions. Two of the most important are as follows. First, a **public official, political candidate, or public figure** may not recover in tort for a defamatory statement relating to his official conduct or a matter of public concern unless the statement was both false and made with "actual malice." See *New York Times Co. v. Sullivan*, 376 U.S. 254 (1964), which follows. The person seeking to recover for defamation bears the burden of proving falsity and absolute malice by clear and convincing evidence. Second, a private figure may not recover for a defamatory statement regarding **a matter of public concern** unless the statement was both false and made knowingly or at least negligently. See *Gertz v. Robert Welch, Inc.*, 418 U.S. 323 (1974). The person seeking to recover for defamation bears the burden of proving falsity, by the conventional preponderance of the evidence standard.

To understand these two rules, several terms require explanation. The Supreme Court has said that "actual malice" is "a term of art denoting deliberate or reckless falsification." *Masson v. New Yorker Magazine, Inc.*, 501 U.S. 496, 499 (1991). The term "public official" includes "at the very least * * * those among the hierarchy of government employees who have, or appear to the public to have, substantial responsibility for or control over the conduct of governmental affairs." *Rosenblatt v. Baer*, 383 U.S. 75 (1966). The Court in *Rosenblatt* also stated that a public official is a person who holds a position of such "apparent importance that the public has an independent interest in the qualifications and performance of the person who holds it." A "public figure" is generally someone, such as a movie star or other celebrity, who has voluntarily become the subject of public attention; the term does not include a person who has merely become "involved in or associated with a matter that attracts public attention," like a mere criminal suspect. *Wolston v. Reader's Digest Ass'n, Inc.*, 443 U.S. 157, 167 (1979). The term "matter of public concern" does not have a precise definition, but the Supreme Court has said that the term refers to "something that is a subject of legitimate news interest; that is, a subject of general interest and of value and concern to the public at the time of publication." *City of San Diego v. Roe*, 543 U.S. 77, 83–84 (2004).

POINTS FOR DISCUSSION

a. Competing Interests

The rules reflect an attempt to strike a balance between the interest in protecting reputations and the interest in free speech. In thinking about this balance, consider these two questions.

First, if the First Amendment protects the freedom of speech, why should a state be allowed to impose *any* liability for statements a person might make, even if they are defamatory? One commentator writes:

> No matter how much it values speech, [a] civilized society cannot refuse to protect reputation. Some form of libel law is as essential to the health of the commonweal and the press as it is to the victims of defamation. Without libel law, the credibility of the press would be at the mercy of the least scrupulous among it, and public discourse would have no necessary anchor in truth.

David A. Anderson, *Is Libel Law Worth Reforming*, 140 U. Penn. L. Rev. 487, 490 (1991). Can you think of hypothetical examples of negative consequences that might flow from the abolition of libel laws? Do you agree that prohibitions on defamation, regardless of their desirability, are consistent with the First Amendment? Does it matter that libel laws were common at the time that the First Amendment was ratified?

Second, on the other hand, why should the First Amendment restrict tort liability for defamatory statements at all? For example, should a newspaper be able to publish an editorial falsely implicating an innocent government scientist in terrorist attacks, absolutely ruin his career, but then escape liability if the scientist cannot show that the newspaper acted with actual malice? Cf. *Hatfill v. New York Times*, 532 F.3d 312 (4th Cir. 2008) (similar facts). What policies could justify excusing this real harm to an individual? Are these policies of constitutional significance? Could a newspaper escape tort liability if one of its reporters negligently ran over a pedestrian on the way to interview someone for a news story? Why is defamation different?

b.   Matter of Public Concern

What is a matter of public concern? Can it be anything that, if included in a newspaper, will attract public attention? Doesn't the very fact that it was in a newspaper by definition guarantee that it will be a matter of public concern, even if it wasn't before?

c.   Public Figures

If in fact the interest in free speech is paramount, why are First Amendment limits on liability for defamation mostly limited to cases involving "public figures"? Is speech about public figures more valuable than speech about people that no one has heard of? Are courts capable of applying principled standards to distinguish public figures from everyone else?

As you read the case that follows, consider whether the Court satisfactorily answered the questions that we have just raised.

NEW YORK TIMES CO. V. SULLIVAN
376 U.S. 254 (1964)

MR. JUSTICE BRENNAN delivered the opinion of the Court.

We are required in this case to determine for the first time the extent to which the constitutional protections for speech and press limit a State's power to award damages in a libel action brought by a public official against critics of his official conduct.

Respondent L. B. Sullivan is one of the three elected Commissioners of the City of Montgomery, Alabama. He testified that he was "Commissioner of Public Affairs and the duties are supervision of the Police Department, Fire Department, Department of Cemetery and Department of Scales." He brought this civil libel action against the four individual petitioners, who are Negroes and Alabama clergymen, and against petitioner the New York Times Company, a New York corporation which publishes the New York Times, a daily newspaper. A jury in the Circuit Court of Montgomery County awarded him damages of $500,000, the full amount claimed, against all the petitioners, and the Supreme Court of Alabama affirmed.

Respondent's complaint alleged that he had been libeled by statements in a full-page advertisement that was carried in the New York Times on March 29, 1960. Entitled "Heed Their Rising Voices," the advertisement began by stating that "As the whole world knows by now, thousands of Southern Negro students are engaged in widespread non-violent demonstrations in positive affirmation of the right to live in human dignity as guaranteed by the U.S. Constitution and the Bill of Rights." It went on to charge that "in their efforts to uphold these guarantees, they are being met by an unprecedented wave of terror by those who would deny and negate that document which the whole world looks upon as setting the pattern for modern freedom. * * *" Succeeding paragraphs purported to illustrate the "wave of terror" by describing certain alleged events. The text concluded with an appeal for funds for three purposes: support of the student movement, "the struggle for the right-to-vote," and the legal defense of Dr. Martin Luther King, Jr., leader of the movement, against a perjury indictment then pending in Montgomery.

> **Definition**
>
> "Perjury" is the crime of "deliberately making material false or misleading statements while under oath." *Black's Law Dictionary* (10th ed. 2014).

Of the 10 paragraphs of text in the advertisement, the third and a portion of the sixth were the basis of respondent's claim of libel. They read as follows:

> Third paragraph: "In Montgomery, Alabama, after students sang 'My Country, 'Tis of Thee' on the State Capitol steps, their leaders were expelled from school, and truckloads of police armed with shotguns and tear-gas ringed the Alabama State College Campus. When the entire student body protested to state authorities by refusing to re-register, their dining hall was padlocked in an attempt to starve them into submission."

> Sixth paragraph: "Again and again the Southern violators have answered Dr. King's peaceful protests with intimidation and violence. They have bombed his home almost killing his wife and child. They have assaulted his person. They have arrested him seven times—for 'speeding,' 'loitering' and similar 'offenses.' And now they have charged him with

'perjury'—a felony under which they could imprison him for ten years.
* * *"

Although neither of these statements mentions respondent by name, he contended that the word "police" in the third paragraph referred to him as the Montgomery Commissioner who supervised the Police Department, so that he was being accused of "ringing" the campus with police. He further claimed that the paragraph would be read as imputing to the police, and hence to him, the padlocking of the dining hall in order to starve the students into submission. As to the sixth paragraph, he contended that since arrests are ordinarily made by the police, the statement "They have arrested (Dr. King) seven times" would be read as referring to him; he further contended that the "They" who did the arresting would be equated with the "They" who committed the other described acts and with the 'Southern violators.' Thus, he argued, the paragraph would be read as accusing the Montgomery police, and hence him, of answering Dr. King's protests with "intimidation and violence," bombing his home, assaulting his person, and charging him with perjury. Respondent and six other Montgomery residents testified that they read some or all of the statements as referring to him in his capacity as Commissioner.

It is uncontroverted that some of the statements contained in the two paragraphs were not accurate descriptions of events which occurred in Montgomery. Although Negro students staged a demonstration on the State Capital steps, they sang the National Anthem and not "My Country, 'Tis of Thee." Although nine students were expelled by the State Board of Education, this was not for leading the demonstration at the Capitol, but for demanding service at a lunch counter in the Montgomery County Courthouse on another day. Not the entire student body, but most of it, had protested the expulsion, not by refusing to register, but by boycotting classes on a single day; virtually all the students did register for the ensuing semester. The campus dining hall was not padlocked on any occasion, and the only students who may have been barred from eating there were the few who had neither signed a preregistration application nor requested temporary meal tickets. Although the police were deployed near the campus in large numbers on three occasions, they did not at any time "ring" the campus, and they were not called to the campus in connection with the demonstration on the State Capitol steps, as the third paragraph implied. Dr. King had not been arrested seven times, but only four; and although he claimed to have been assaulted some years earlier in connection with his arrest for loitering outside a courtroom, one of the officers who made the arrest denied that there was such an assault.

On the premise that the charges in the sixth paragraph could be read as referring to him, respondent was allowed to prove that he had not participated in the events described. Although Dr. King's home had in fact been bombed twice when his wife and child were there, both of these occasions antedated respondent's tenure as Commissioner, and the police were not only not implicated in the bombings, but had made every effort to apprehend those who were. Three of Dr. King's four arrests took place before respondent became Commissioner. Although Dr. King had in fact been indicted (he was subsequently acquitted) on two counts of perjury, each of which carried a possible five-year sentence, respondent had nothing to do with procuring the indictment.

Approximately 394 copies of the edition of the Times containing the advertisement were circulated in Alabama. Of these, about 35 copies were distributed in Montgomery County. The total circulation of the Times for that day was approximately 650,000 copies.

Under Alabama law as applied in this case, a publication is "libelous per se" if the words "tend to injure a person * * * in his reputation" or to "bring [him] into public contempt"; the trial court stated that the standard was met if the words are such as to "injure him in his public office, or impute misconduct to him in his office, or want of official integrity, or want of fidelity to a public trust * * *." The jury must find that the words were published "of and concerning" the plaintiff, but where the plaintiff is a public official his place in the governmental hierarchy is sufficient evidence to support a finding that his reputation has been affected by statements that reflect upon the agency of which he is in charge. Once "libel per se" has been established, the defendant has no defense as to stated facts unless he can persuade the jury that they were true in all their particulars. His privilege of "fair comment" for expressions of opinion depends on the truth of the facts upon which the comment is based. Unless he can discharge the burden of proving truth, general damages are presumed, and may be awarded without proof of pecuniary injury. A showing of actual malice is apparently a prerequisite to recovery of punitive damages, and the defendant may in any event forestall a punitive award by a retraction meeting the statutory requirements. Good motives and belief in truth do not negate an inference of malice, but are relevant only in mitigation of punitive damages if the jury chooses to accord them weight.

The question before us is whether this rule of liability, as applied to an action brought by a public official against critics of his official conduct, abridges the freedom of speech and of the press that is guaranteed by the First and Fourteenth Amendments.

Respondent relies heavily, as did the Alabama courts, on statements of this Court to the effect that the Constitution does not protect libelous publications. Those statements do not foreclose our inquiry here. None of the cases sustained the use of libel laws to impose sanctions upon expression critical of the official conduct of public officials. * * * In the only previous case that did present the question of constitutional limitations upon the power to award damages for libel of a public official, the Court was equally divided and the question was not decided. *Schenectady Union Pub. Co. v. Sweeney*, 316 U.S. 642 (1942). In deciding the question now, we are compelled by neither precedent nor policy to give any more weight to the epithet "libel" than we have to other "mere labels" of state law. *N.A.A.C.P. v. Button*, 371 U.S. 415 (1963). Like insurrection, contempt, advocacy of unlawful acts, breach of the peace, obscenity, solicitation of legal business, and the various other formulae for the repression of expression that have been challenged in this Court, libel can claim no talismanic immunity from constitutional limitations. It must be measured by standards that satisfy the First Amendment.

The general proposition that freedom of expression upon public questions is secured by the First Amendment has long been settled by our decisions. The constitutional safeguard, we have said, "was fashioned to assure unfettered interchange of ideas for the bringing about of political and social changes desired by the people." *Roth v. United States*, 354 U.S. 476, 484 (1957). * * *

Thus we consider this case against the background of a profound national commitment to the principle that debate on public issues should be uninhibited, robust, and wide-open, and that it may well include vehement, caustic, and sometimes unpleasantly sharp attacks on government and public officials. The present advertisement, as an expression of grievance and protest on one of the major public issues of our time, would seem clearly to qualify for the constitutional protection. The question is whether it forfeits that protection by the falsity of some of its factual statements and by its alleged defamation of respondent.

Authoritative interpretations of the First Amendment guarantees have consistently refused to recognize an exception for any test of truth—whether administered by judges, juries, or administrative officials—and especially one that puts the burden of proving truth on the speaker. The constitutional protection does not turn upon "the truth, popularity, or social utility of the ideas and beliefs which are offered." *N.A.A.C.P. v. Button*, 371 U.S. at 445. As Madison said, "Some degree of abuse is inseparable from the proper use of every thing; and in no instance is this more true than in that of the press." 4 Elliot's Debates on the Federal Constitution (1876), p. 571. * * *

A rule compelling the critic of official conduct to guarantee the truth of all his factual assertions—and to do so on pain of libel judgments virtually unlimited in amount— leads to a comparable "self-censorship." Allowance of the defense of truth, with the burden of proving it on the defendant, does not mean that only false speech will be deterred. Even courts accepting this defense as an adequate safeguard have recognized the difficulties of adducing legal proofs that the alleged libel was true in all its factual particulars. Under such a rule, would-be critics of official conduct may be deterred from

> **Take Note**
>
> The Court here declares that a rule permitting judgments by public figures in defamation cases unless the critic can demonstrate the truth of the statements is insufficient under the First Amendment. Is this because the First Amendment protects even untrue statements? Is it because courts (and juries) are ill-suited to determine the truth? Or is it because a truth standard would tend to chill true speech, even though false speech is not protected?

voicing their criticism, even though it is believed to be true and even though it is in fact true, because of doubt whether it can be proved in court or fear of the expense of having to do so. They tend to make only statements which "steer far wider of the unlawful zone." *Speiser v. Randall*, 357 U.S. 513, 526 (1958). The rule thus dampens the vigor and limits the variety of public debate. It is inconsistent with the First and Fourteenth Amendments.

The constitutional guarantees require, we think, a federal rule that prohibits a public official from recovering damages for a defamatory falsehood relating to his official conduct unless he proves that the statement was made with "actual malice"—that is, with knowledge that it was false or with reckless disregard of whether it was false or not. * * * We conclude that such a privilege is required by the First and Fourteenth Amendments.

standard/ test

Applying these standards, we consider that the proof presented to show actual malice lacks the convincing clarity which the constitutional standard demands, and hence that it would not constitutionally sustain the judgment for respondent under the proper rule of law. * * * Even assuming that [the individual petitioners] could constitutionally be found to have authorized the use of their names on the advertisement, there was no evidence whatever that they were aware of any erroneous statements or were in any way reckless in that regard. * * * We think the evidence against the Times supports at most a finding of negligence in failing to discover the misstatements, and is constitutionally insufficient to show the recklessness that is required for a finding of actual malice.

We also think the evidence was constitutionally defective in another respect: it was incapable of supporting the jury's finding that the allegedly libelous statements were made "of and concerning" respondent. * * * There was no reference to respondent in the advertisement, either by name or official position. [The Supreme Court of Alabama relied] on the bare fact of respondent's official position. * * * Raising as it does the possibility that a good-faith critic of government will be penalized for his criticism, the proposition relied on by the Alabama courts strikes at the very center of the constitutionally protected area of free expression. We hold that such a proposition may not constitutionally be utilized to establish that an otherwise impersonal attack on governmental operations was a libel of an official responsible for those operations. Since it was relied on exclusively here, and there was no other evidence to connect the statements with respondent, the evidence was constitutionally insufficient to support a finding that the statements referred to respondent. [Reversed.]

MR. JUSTICE BLACK, with whom MR. JUSTICE DOUGLAS joins, concurring.

I base my vote to reverse on the belief that the First and Fourteenth Amendments not merely "delimit" a State's power to award damages to "public officials against critics of their official conduct" but completely prohibit a State from exercising such a power. * * * The requirement that malice be proved provides at best an evanescent protection for the right critically to discuss public affairs and certainly does not measure up to the sturdy safeguard embodied in the First Amendment. Unlike the Court, therefore, I vote to reverse exclusively on the ground that the Times and the individual defendants had an absolute, unconditional constitutional right to publish in the Times advertisement their criticisms of the Montgomery agencies and officials. * * * This Nation, I suspect, can live in peace without libel suits based on public discussions of public affairs and public officials. But I doubt that a country can live in freedom where its people can be made to suffer physically or financially for criticizing their government, its actions, or its officials. * * * An unconditional right to say what one pleases about public affairs is what I consider to be the minimum guarantee of the First Amendment.

MR. JUSTICE GOLDBERG, with whom MR. JUSTICE DOUGLAS joins, concurring in the result.

In my view, the First and Fourteenth Amendments to the Constitution afford to the citizen and to the press an absolute, unconditional privilege to criticize official conduct despite the harm which may flow from excesses and abuses. * * * This is not to say that the Constitution protects defamatory statements directed against the private conduct of a public official or private citizen. * * * Purely private defamation has little to do with the political ends of a self-governing society. The imposition of liability for private defamation does not abridge the freedom of public speech or any other freedom protected by the First Amendment. This, of course, cannot be said "where public officials are concerned or where public matters are involved. * * *"

POINTS FOR DISCUSSION

a.   The Importance of *Sullivan*

Professor Harry Kalven Jr., a noted scholar of the First Amendment, predicted that *New York Times v. Sullivan* would "prove to be the best and most important" decision that the Supreme Court "has ever produced in the realm of Freedom of Speech." Harry Kalven Jr., *The New York Times Case: A Note on "The Central Meaning of the First Amendment,"* 1964 Sup. Ct. Rev. 191, 193–94. He correctly anticipated that the rule of the case would expand from protecting speech about public officials to protecting speech about other matters in the public interest. *Id.* at 221. Why is the right of newspapers to publish false stories without fearing tort liability so important?

b.   The Theory of *Sullivan*

Did the Court in *Sullivan* conclude that all false and defamatory speech is nevertheless speech, and thus entitled to protection under the First Amendment? Or did it instead conclude that, although false and defamatory speech is outside of the protection of the First Amendment, the interests served by the Amendment require some limits on the authority of courts to impose liability for such speech? And if the latter, did the Court simply attempt to strike a balance between First Amendment interests and the individual interest in reputation?

In *Gertz v. Robert Welch, Inc.*, 418 U.S. 323 (1974), the Court held that a private figure may not recover for a defamatory statement regarding a matter of public concern unless the statement was both false and made knowingly or at least negligently, a lesser standard than the one that the Court announced in *Sullivan.* Two things about the Court's decision in *Gertz* are particularly notable here. First, the Court stated:

> Under the First Amendment there is no such thing as a false idea. However pernicious an opinion may seem, we depend for its correction not on the conscience of judges and juries but on the competition of other ideas. But there is no constitutional value in false statements of fact. Neither the intentional lie nor the careless error materially advances society's interest in "uninhibited, robust, and wide-open" debate on public issues. They belong to that category of utterances which "are no essential part of any exposition of ideas, and are of such slight social value as a step to truth that any benefit that may be derived from them is clearly outweighed by the social interest

in order and morality." *Chaplinsky v. New Hampshire*, 315 U.S. 568, 572 (1942).

Second, the Court in *Gertz* declared that the *Sullivan* standard was not "justified solely by reference to the interest of the press and broadcast media in immunity from liability," but instead "states an accommodation between this concern and the limited state interest present in the context of libel actions brought by public persons." The Court then declared that a different "balance between the needs of the press and the individual's claim to compensation for wrongful injury" should apply for statements about private figures on matters of public concern. The Court noted that "[p]ublic officials and public figures usually enjoy significantly greater access to the channels of effective communication and hence have a more realistic opportunity to counteract false statements than private individuals normally enjoy," whereas "private individuals will [likely] lack effective opportunities for rebuttal." In addition, the Court stated that, by virtue of their positions, public officials and public figures "must accept certain necessary consequences of [their] involvement in public affairs" and effectively have "voluntarily exposed themselves to increased risk of injury from defamatory falsehood concerning them." In contrast, "[n]o such assumption is justified with respect to a private individual."

Is it appropriate for the Court to permit some liability for speech based on, as the Court in *Gertz* described it, an explicit "accommodation of the competing values at stake in defamation suits"? Doesn't the First Amendment strike a balance in favor of speech? Or, conversely, would it make more sense for the Court simply to conclude that the First Amendment has nothing to say about defamation claims, which were historically considered appropriate notwithstanding their chilling effect on speech?

c. Limiting *Sullivan*

Sullivan and related cases make clear that the First Amendment requires special rules for the imposition of tort liability in cases involving statements about public officials and public figures and in cases involving claims by private figures arising from statements on matters of public concern. Does the First Amendment impose any limits on the authority of a court to impose liability for a statement about a private figure on a matter of private concern? In *Dun & Bradstreet, Inc. v. Greenmoss Builders, Inc.*, 472 U.S. 749 (1985), the Court held that a state rule permitting the recovery of presumed and punitive damages in defamation cases—that is, permitting recovery without a showing of actual harm and damages—absent a showing of actual malice did not violate the First Amendment when the defamatory statements were about a private figure and did not involve matters of public concern. The Court applied the "approach approved in *Gertz* and balance[d] the State's interest in compensating private individuals for injury to their reputation against the First Amendment interest in protecting this type of expression." The Court noted that the state interest in protecting the reputation of private figures was "identical to the one weighed in *Gertz*," but that "speech on matters of purely private concern is of less First Amendment concern" than the speech on matters of public concern at issue in *Gertz*. The Court also reasoned that the common-law rule permitting the award of damages even absent proof of actual damage "furthers the state interest in providing remedies for defamation by ensuring that those remedies are effective." The Court concluded: "In light of the reduced constitutional value of speech involving no matters of public concern, we hold that the state interest adequately supports awards of presumed and punitive damages—even absent a showing of 'actual malice.' " Justice Brennan, joined by three other Justices, dissented, asserting (among other things) that "unrestrained presumed and punitive damages" rules violate the First Amendment.

Does the Court's decision in *Dun & Bradstreet* mean that the First Amendment imposes no limits on the states' authority to permit liability for defamatory statements about private figures on matters of private concern?

d.   Extending *Sullivan*

As we noted above, the Court eventually extended First Amendment protection to speech about public figures (not just public officials) and to cases involving claims by private figures arising from speech on matters of public concern. Does the approach in *Sullivan* also apply to tort claims other than those sounding in defamation?

In *Hustler Magazine, Inc. v. Falwell*, 485 U.S. 46 (1988), Jerry Falwell, a prominent minister and televangelist, sued a magazine after it published a parody depicting Falwell having a drunken sexual encounter with his mother in an outhouse. Falwell asserted claims for invasion of privacy, libel, and intentional infliction of emotional distress. The jury found against him on the first two claims, but in his favor on the last one. (Under Virginia law at the time of the case, to prevail on a tort claim for intentional infliction of emotional distress, a plaintiff had to show that "the defendant's conduct (1) [was] intentional or reckless; (2) offend[ed] generally accepted standards of decency or morality; (3) [was] causally connected with the plaintiff's emotional distress; and (4) caused emotional distress that was severe." *Id.* at 50.) The Supreme Court reversed. The Court noted that, historically, "graphic depictions and satirical cartoons have played a prominent role in public and political debate." Relying on *Sullivan*, the Court held that "public figures and public officials may not recover for the tort of intentional infliction of emotional distress by reason of publications such as the one here at issue without showing in addition that the publication contains a false statement of fact which was made with 'actual malice' * * *." If the Court had reached the opposite conclusion, would public figures be able effectively to recover for injured reputations by asserting claims for intentional infliction of emotional distress?

e.   False Statements

In *United States v. Alvarez*, 567 U.S. 709 (2012), the Court invalidated the Stolen Valor Act of 2005, 18 U.S.C. § 704, which made it a crime falsely to represent oneself "to have been awarded any decoration or medal authorized by Congress for the Armed Forces of the United States." Justice Kennedy, in an opinion for himself and three other Justices, listed the categories of speech that are beyond the protection of the First Amendment and then stated: "Absent from those few categories where the law allows content-based regulation of speech is any general exception to the First Amendment for false statements." Justice Kennedy acknowledged the language above from *Gertz* and other cases, but he reasoned that those "quotations all derive from cases discussing defamation, fraud, or some other legally cognizable harm associated with a false statement, such as an invasion of privacy or the costs of vexatious litigation. In those decisions the falsity of the speech at issue was not irrelevant to our analysis, but neither was it determinative." He stressed that the Court "has never endorsed the categorical rule the Government advances: that false statements receive no First Amendment protection." Justice Kennedy rejected the government's attempt to "convert a rule that limits liability even in defamation cases where the law permits recovery for tortious wrongs into a rule that expands liability in a different, far greater realm of discourse and expression. That inverts the rationale for the exception. The requirements of a knowing falsehood or reckless disregard for the truth as the condition for recovery in certain defamation cases exists to allow more speech, not less. A rule designed to tolerate certain speech ought not blossom to become a rationale for a rule restricting it." Justice Kennedy distinguished well-established criminal prohibitions on perjury and false statements to government officials, reasoning that such bans "protect the integrity of Government processes" and thus "do not establish a principle that all proscriptions of false statements are exempt from exacting First Amendment scrutiny."

Justice Breyer, joined by Justice Kagan, concurred in the judgment. He acknowledged that the Court "has frequently said or implied that false factual statements enjoy little First Amendment protection." But he concluded that "these judicial statements cannot be read to mean 'no protection at all,'" because "[f]alse factual statements can serve useful human objectives" and because "the threat of criminal prosecution for making a false statement can inhibit the speaker from making true statements, thereby 'chilling' a kind of speech that lies at the First Amendment's heart." Applying something akin to intermediate scrutiny, Justice Breyer concluded that the statute violated the First Amendment.

Justice Alito, joined by Justices Scalia and Thomas, dissented. He concluded that "false statements of fact merit no First Amendment protection in their own right" and that, in any event, "the Stolen Valor Act presents no risk at all that valuable speech will be suppressed" because the "speech punished by the Act is not only verifiably false and entirely lacking in intrinsic value, but it also fails to serve any instrumental purpose that the First Amendment might protect."

After the decision in *Alvarez*, what is the status under the First Amendment of false statements? And after *Alvarez*, is strict scrutiny the appropriate level of scrutiny for content-based restrictions on speech?

SNYDER V. PHELPS

562 U.S. 443 (2011)

CHIEF JUSTICE ROBERTS delivered the opinion of the Court.

A jury held members of the Westboro Baptist Church liable for millions of dollars in damages for picketing near a soldier's funeral service. The picket signs reflected the church's view that the United States is overly tolerant of sin and that God kills American soldiers as punishment. The question presented is whether the First Amendment shields the church members from tort liability for their speech in this case.

Fred Phelps founded the Westboro Baptist Church in Topeka, Kansas, in 1955. The church's congregation believes that God hates and punishes the United States for its tolerance of homosexuality, particularly in America's military. The church frequently communicates its views by picketing, often at military funerals. In the more than 20 years that the members of Westboro Baptist have publicized their message, they have picketed nearly 600 funerals.

Marine Lance Corporal Matthew Snyder was killed in Iraq in the line of duty. Lance Corporal Snyder's father selected the Catholic church in the Snyders' hometown of Westminster, Maryland, as the site for his son's funeral. Local newspapers provided notice of the time and location of the service. Phelps became aware of Matthew Snyder's funeral and decided to travel to Maryland with six other Westboro Baptist parishioners (two of his daughters and four of his grandchildren) to picket. On the day of the memorial service, the Westboro congregation members picketed on public land adjacent to public streets near the Maryland State House, the United States Naval Academy, and Matthew Snyder's funeral. The Westboro picketers carried signs that were largely the same at all three locations. They stated, for instance: "God Hates the USA/Thank God for 9/11," "America is Doomed," "Don't Pray for the USA," "Thank God for IEDs," "Thank God for Dead Soldiers," "Pope in Hell," "Priests Rape Boys," "God Hates Fags," "You're Going to Hell," and "God Hates You."

The church had notified the authorities in advance of its intent to picket at the time of the funeral, and the picketers complied with police instructions in staging their demonstration. The picketing took place within a 10-by 25-foot plot of public land adjacent to a public street, behind a temporary fence. That plot was approximately 1,000 feet from the church where the funeral was held. Several buildings separated the picket site from the church. The Westboro picketers displayed their signs for about 30 minutes before the funeral began and sang hymns and recited Bible verses. None of the picketers entered church property or went to the cemetery. They did not yell or use profanity, and there was no violence associated with the picketing. The funeral procession passed within 200 to 300 feet of the picket site. Although Snyder testified that he could see the tops of the picket signs as he drove to the funeral, he did not see what was written on the signs until later that night, while watching a news broadcast covering the event.[1]

FYI

To succeed on a claim for intentional infliction of emotional distress in Maryland, a plaintiff must demonstrate that the defendant intentionally or recklessly engaged in extreme and outrageous conduct that caused the plaintiff to suffer severe emotional distress. Under Maryland Law, a "civil conspiracy is a combination of two or more persons by an agreement or understanding to accomplish an unlawful act." *Green v. Washington Suburban Sanitary Commission*, 269 A.2d 815, 824 (Md. 1970). A defendant is entitled to "judgment as a matter of law," notwithstanding a jury's verdict for the plaintiff, if the evidence presented raised no material issue that the jury could decide in the plaintiff's favor.

Snyder filed suit against Phelps, Phelps's daughters, and the Westboro Baptist Church (collectively Westboro or the church) [alleging] five state tort law claims: defamation, publicity given to private life, intentional infliction of emotional distress, intrusion upon seclusion, and civil conspiracy. Westboro moved for summary judgment contending, in part, that the church's speech was insulated from liability by the First Amendment. The District Court awarded Westboro summary judgment on Snyder's claims for defamation and publicity given to private life, concluding that Snyder could not prove the necessary elements of those torts. A trial was held on the remaining claims. At trial, Snyder described the

---

[1] A few weeks after the funeral, one of the picketers posted a message on Westboro's Web site discussing the picketing and containing religiously oriented denunciations of the Snyders, interspersed among lengthy Bible quotations. Snyder discovered the posting, referred to by the parties as the "epic," during an Internet search for his son's name. The epic is not properly before us and does not factor in our analysis. Although the epic was submitted to the jury and discussed in the courts below, Snyder never mentioned it in his petition for certiorari. Nor did Snyder respond to the statement in the opposition to certiorari that "[t]hough the epic was asserted as a basis for the claims at trial, the petition . . . appears to be addressing only claims based on the picketing." Snyder devoted only one paragraph in the argument section of his opening merits brief to the epic. Given the foregoing and the fact that an Internet posting may raise distinct issues in this context, we decline to consider the epic in deciding this case.

severity of his emotional injuries. He testified that he is unable to separate the thought of his dead son from his thoughts of Westboro's picketing, and that he often becomes tearful, angry, and physically ill when he thinks about it. Expert witnesses testified that Snyder's emotional anguish had resulted in severe depression and had exacerbated pre-existing health conditions.

A jury found for Snyder on the intentional infliction of emotional distress, intrusion upon seclusion, and civil conspiracy claims, and held Westboro liable for $2.9 million in compensatory damages and $8 million in punitive damages. Westboro filed several post-trial motions, including a motion contending that the jury verdict was grossly excessive and a motion seeking judgment as a matter of law on all claims on First Amendment grounds. The District Court remitted the punitive damages award to $2.1 million, but left the jury verdict otherwise intact. [The Court of Appeals reversed, concluding that Westboro's statements were entitled to First Amendment protection.]

Whether the First Amendment prohibits holding Westboro liable for its speech in this case turns largely on whether that speech is of public or private concern, as determined by all the circumstances of the case. "[S]peech on 'matters of public concern' . . . is 'at the heart of the First Amendment's protection.' " *Dun & Bradstreet, Inc. v. Greenmoss Builders, Inc.*, 472 U.S. 749, 758–759 (1985) (opinion of Powell, J.). * * * That is because "speech concerning public affairs is more than self-expression; it is the essence of self-government." *Garrison v. Louisiana*, 379 U.S. 64, 74–75 (1964). * * * "[N]ot all speech is of equal First Amendment importance," however, and where matters of purely private significance are at issue, First Amendment protections are often less rigorous. *Hustler Magazine, Inc. v. Falwell*, 485 U.S. 46, 56 (1988). That is because restricting speech on purely private matters does not implicate the same constitutional concerns as limiting speech on matters of public interest: "[T]here is no threat to the free and robust debate of public issues; there is no potential interference with a meaningful dialogue of ideas"; and the "threat of liability" does not pose the risk of "a reaction of self-censorship" on matters of public import. *Dun & Bradstreet, supra*, at 760.

[Although] "the boundaries of the public concern test are not well defined," *San Diego v. Roe*, 543 U.S. 77, 83 (2004), we have articulated some guiding principles, principles that accord broad protection to speech to ensure that courts themselves do not become inadvertent censors. Speech deals with matters of public concern when it can "be fairly considered as relating to any matter of political, social, or other concern to the community," *Connick v. Myers*, 461 U.S. 138, 146 (1983), or when it "is a subject of legitimate news interest; that is, a subject of general interest and of value and concern to the public," *San Diego, supra*, at 83–84. The arguably "inappropriate or controversial character of a statement is irrelevant to the question whether it deals with a matter of public concern." *Rankin v. McPherson,* 483 U.S. 378, 387 (1987). * * * Deciding whether speech is of public or private concern requires us to examine the "content, form, and context" of that speech, "as revealed by the whole record." *Dun & Bradstreet, supra,* at 761. * * * In considering content, form, and context, no factor is dispositive, and it is necessary to evaluate all the circumstances of the speech, including what was said, where it was said, and how it was said.

The "content" of Westboro's signs plainly relates to broad issues of interest to society at large, rather than matters of "purely private concern." *Dun & Bradstreet, supra,* at 759. The placards read "God Hates the USA/Thank God for 9/11," "America is Doomed," "Don't Pray for the USA," "Thank God for IEDs," "Fag Troops," "Semper Fi Fags," "God Hates Fags," "Maryland Taliban," "Fags Doom Nations," "Not Blessed Just Cursed," "Thank God for Dead Soldiers," "Pope in Hell," "Priests Rape Boys," "You're Going to Hell," and "God Hates You." While these messages may fall short of refined social or political commentary, the issues they highlight—the political and moral conduct of the United States and its citizens, the fate of our Nation, homosexuality in the military, and scandals involving the Catholic clergy—are matters of public import. The signs certainly convey Westboro's position on those issues, in a manner designed, unlike the private speech in *Dun & Bradstreet,* to reach as broad a public audience as possible. And even if a few of the signs—such as "You're Going to Hell" and "God Hates You"—were viewed as containing messages related to Matthew Snyder or the Snyders specifically, that would not change the fact that the overall thrust and dominant theme of Westboro's demonstration spoke to broader public issues.

Apart from the content of Westboro's signs, Snyder contends that the "context" of the speech—its connection with his son's funeral—makes the speech a matter of private rather than public concern. The fact that Westboro spoke in connection with a funeral, however, cannot by itself transform the nature of Westboro's speech. Westboro's signs, displayed on public land next to a public street, reflect the fact that the church finds much to condemn in modern society. Its speech is "fairly characterized as constituting speech on a matter of public concern," *Connick,* 461 U.S., at 146, and the funeral setting does not alter that conclusion.

Snyder argues that the church members in fact mounted a personal attack on Snyder and his family, and then attempted to "immunize their conduct by claiming that they were actually protesting the United States' tolerance of homosexuality or the supposed evils of the Catholic Church." We are not concerned in this case that Westboro's speech on public matters was in any way contrived to insulate speech on a private matter from liability. Westboro had been actively engaged in speaking on the subjects addressed in its picketing long before it became aware of Matthew Snyder, and there can be no serious claim that Westboro's picketing did not represent its "honestly believed" views on public issues. There was no pre-existing relationship or conflict between Westboro and Snyder that might suggest Westboro's speech on public matters was intended to mask an attack on Snyder over a private matter.

Snyder goes on to argue that Westboro's speech should be afforded less than full First Amendment protection "not only because of the words" but also because the church members exploited the funeral "as a platform to bring their message to a broader audience." There is no doubt that Westboro chose to stage its picketing at the Naval Academy, the Maryland State House, and Matthew Snyder's funeral to increase publicity for its views and because of the relation between those sites and its views—in the case of the military funeral, because Westboro believes that God is killing American soldiers as punishment for the Nation's sinful policies. Westboro's choice to convey its views in conjunction with Matthew Snyder's funeral made the expression of those views particularly hurtful to many, especially to Matthew's father. The record makes clear that the applicable legal term—"emotional distress"—fails to capture fully the anguish Westboro's choice added to Mr. Snyder's already incalculable grief. But Westboro conducted its picketing peacefully on matters of public concern at a public place adjacent to a public street. Such space occupies a "special position in terms of First Amendment protection." *United States v. Grace*, 461 U.S. 171, 180 (1983). "[W]e have repeatedly referred to public streets as the archetype of a traditional public forum," noting that " '[t]ime out of mind' public streets and sidewalks have been used for public assembly and debate." *Frisby v. Schultz*, 487 U.S. 474, 480 (1988).

That said, "[e]ven protected speech is not equally permissible in all places and at all times." *Id.,* at 479. Westboro's choice of where and when to conduct its picketing is not beyond the Government's regulatory reach—it is "subject to reasonable time, place, or manner restrictions" that are consistent with the standards announced in this Court's precedents. Maryland now has a law imposing restrictions on funeral picketing, Md.Crim. Law Code Ann. § 10–205 (Lexis Supp.2010), as do 43 other States

> **Food for Thought**
>
> The new Maryland law prohibits picketing within 100 feet of a funeral service or funeral procession. Is that statute (and others like it) a valid time, place, or manner restriction? We considered such regulations earlier in this chapter.

and the Federal Government. To the extent these laws are content neutral, they raise very different questions from the tort verdict at issue in this case. Maryland's law, however, was not in effect at the time of the events at issue here, so we have no occasion to consider how it might apply to facts such as those before us, or whether it or other similar regulations are constitutional.

We have identified a few limited situations where the location of targeted picketing can be regulated under provisions that the Court has determined to be content neutral. In *Frisby,* for example, we upheld a ban on such picketing "before or about" a particular residence, 487 U.S., at 477. In *Madsen v. Women's Health Center, Inc.,* we approved an injunction requiring a buffer zone between protesters and an abortion clinic entrance. 512 U.S. 753, 768 (1994). The facts here are obviously quite different, both with respect to the activity being regulated and the means of restricting those activities. Simply put, the church members had the right to be where they were. Westboro alerted local authorities to its funeral protest and fully complied with police guidance on where the picketing could be staged. The picketing was conducted under police supervision some 1,000 feet from the church, out of the sight of those at the church. The protest was not unruly; there was no shouting, profanity, or violence.

The record confirms that any distress occasioned by Westboro's picketing turned on the content and viewpoint of the message conveyed, rather than any interference with the funeral itself. A group of parishioners standing at the very spot where Westboro stood, holding signs that said "God Bless America" and "God Loves You," would not have been subjected to liability. It was what Westboro said that exposed it to tort damages.

Given that Westboro's speech was at a public place on a matter of public concern, that speech is entitled to "special protection" under the First Amendment. Such speech cannot be restricted simply because it is upsetting or arouses contempt. "If there is a bedrock principle underlying the First Amendment, it is that the government may not prohibit the expression of an idea simply because society finds the idea itself offensive or disagreeable." *Texas v. Johnson,* 491 U.S. 397, 414 (1989). Indeed, "the point of all speech protection . . . is to shield just those choices of content that in someone's eyes are misguided, or even hurtful." *Hurley v. Irish-American Gay, Lesbian and Bisexual Group of Boston, Inc.,* 515 U.S. 557, 574 (1995).

The jury here was instructed that it could hold Westboro liable for intentional infliction of emotional distress based on a finding that Westboro's picketing was "outrageous." "Outrageousness," however, is a highly malleable standard with "an inherent subjectiveness about it which would allow a jury to impose liability on the basis of the jurors' tastes or views, or perhaps on the basis of their dislike of a particular expression." *Hustler*, 485 U.S., at 55. In a case such as this, a jury is "unlikely to be neutral with respect to the content of [the] speech," posing "a real danger of becoming an instrument for the suppression of . . . 'vehement, caustic, and sometimes unpleasan[t]' " expression. *Bose Corp. v. Consumers Union of the United States, Inc.,* 466 U.S. 485, 510 (1984). Such a risk is unacceptable; "in public debate [we] must tolerate insulting, and even outrageous, speech in order to provide adequate 'breathing space' to the freedoms protected by the First Amendment." *Boos v. Barry,* 485 U.S. 312, 322 (1988). What Westboro said, in the whole context of how and where it chose to say it, is entitled to "special protection" under the First Amendment, and that protection cannot be overcome by a jury finding that the picketing was outrageous. For all these reasons, the jury verdict imposing tort liability on Westboro for intentional infliction of emotional distress must be set aside.

The jury also found Westboro liable for the state law torts of intrusion upon seclusion and civil conspiracy. * * * Snyder argues that even assuming Westboro's speech is entitled to First Amendment protection generally, the church is not immunized from liability for intrusion upon seclusion because Snyder was a member of a captive audience at his son's funeral. We do not agree. * * * As a general matter, we have applied the captive audience doctrine only sparingly to protect unwilling listeners from protected speech. For example, we have upheld a statute allowing a homeowner to restrict the delivery of offensive mail to his home, see *Rowan v. Post Office Dept.,* 397 U.S. 728, 736–738 (1970), and an ordinance prohibiting picketing "before or about" any individual's residence, *Frisby,* 487 U.S., at 484–485. Here, Westboro stayed well away from the memorial service. Snyder could see no more than the tops of the signs when driving to the funeral. And there is no indication that the picketing in any way interfered with the funeral service itself. We decline to expand the captive audience doctrine to the circumstances presented here.

Because we find that the First Amendment bars Snyder from recovery for intentional infliction of emotional distress or intrusion upon seclusion—the alleged unlawful activity Westboro conspired to accomplish—we must likewise hold that Snyder cannot recover for civil conspiracy based on those torts.

Our holding today is narrow. We are required in First Amendment cases to carefully review the record, and the reach of our opinion here is limited by the particular facts before us. * * * Westboro believes that America is morally flawed; many Americans might feel the same about Westboro. Westboro's funeral picketing is certainly hurtful and its contribution to public discourse may be negligible. But Westboro addressed matters of public import on public property, in a peaceful manner, in full compliance with the guidance of local officials. The speech was indeed planned to coincide with Matthew Snyder's funeral, but did not itself disrupt that funeral, and Westboro's choice to conduct its picketing at that time and place did not alter the nature of its speech.

Speech is powerful. It can stir people to action, move them to tears of both joy and sorrow, and—as it did here—inflict great pain. On the facts before us, we cannot react to that pain by punishing the speaker. As a Nation we have chosen a different course—to protect even hurtful speech on public issues to ensure that we do not stifle public debate. That choice requires that we shield Westboro from tort liability for its picketing in this case. *Affirmed.*

JUSTICE ALITO, dissenting.

Our profound national commitment to free and open debate is not a license for the vicious verbal assault that occurred in this case. Petitioner Albert Snyder is not a public figure. He is simply a parent whose son, Marine Lance Corporal Matthew Snyder, was killed in Iraq. Mr. Snyder wanted what is surely the right of any parent who experiences such an incalculable loss: to bury his son in peace. But respondents, members of the Westboro Baptist Church, deprived him of that elementary right. They first issued a press release and thus turned Matthew's funeral into a tumultuous media event. They then appeared at the church, approached as closely as they could without trespassing, and launched a malevolent verbal attack on Matthew and his family at a time of acute emotional vulnerability. As a result, Albert Snyder suffered severe and lasting emotional injury. The Court now holds that the First Amendment protected respondents' right to brutalize Mr. Snyder. I cannot agree.

Respondents and other members of their church have strong opinions on certain moral, religious, and political issues, and the First Amendment ensures that they have almost limitless opportunities to express their views. They may write and distribute books, articles, and other texts; they may create and disseminate video and audio recordings; they may circulate petitions; they may speak to individuals and groups in public forums and in any private venue that wishes to accommodate them; they may picket peacefully in countless locations; they may appear on television and speak on the radio; they may post messages on the Internet and send out e-mails. And they may express their views in terms that are "uninhibited," "vehement," and "caustic." *New York Times Co. v. Sullivan,* 376 U.S. 254, 270 (1964).

It does not follow, however, that they may intentionally inflict severe emotional injury on private persons at a time of intense emotional sensitivity by launching vicious verbal attacks that make no contribution to public debate. To protect against such injury, "most if not all jurisdictions" permit recovery in tort for the intentional infliction of emotional distress (or IIED). This is a very narrow tort with requirements that "are rigorous, and difficult to satisfy." W. Keeton, D. Dobbs, R. Keeton, & D. Owen, Prosser and Keeton on Law of Torts § 12, p. 61 (5th ed.1984). To recover, a plaintiff must show that the conduct at issue caused harm that was truly severe. * * * A plaintiff must also establish that the defendant's conduct was "so outrageous in character, and so extreme in degree, as to go beyond all possible bounds of decency, and to be regarded as atrocious, and utterly intolerable in a civilized community." *Harris v. Jones,* 281 Md. 560, 567 (1977).

[R]espondents long ago abandoned any effort to show that those tough standards were not satisfied here. * * * Instead, they maintained that the First Amendment gave them a license to engage in such conduct. They are wrong. * * * It is well established that a claim for the intentional infliction of emotional distress can be satisfied by speech. * * * And although this Court has not decided the question, I think it is clear that the First Amendment does not entirely preclude liability for the intentional infliction of emotional distress by means of speech. This Court has recognized that words may "by their very utterance inflict injury" and that the First Amendment does not shield utterances that form "no essential part of any exposition of ideas, and are of such slight social value as a step to truth that any benefit that may be derived from them is clearly outweighed by the social interest in order and morality." *Chaplinsky v. New Hampshire,* 315 U.S. 568, 572 (1942); see also *Cantwell v. Connecticut,* 310 U.S. 296, 310 (1940) ("[P]ersonal abuse is not in any proper sense communication of information or opinion safeguarded by the Constitution"). When grave injury is intentionally inflicted by means of an attack like the one at issue here, the First Amendment should not interfere with recovery.

> **Food for Thought**
>
> Justice Alito cites *Chaplinsky*, which involved "fighting words." Can the state assign liability for the speech at issue in this case on the ground that it constituted unprotected fighting words? If not, why not?

The Court concludes that respondents' speech was protected by the First Amendment for essentially three reasons, but none is sound. First—and most important—the Court finds that "the overall thrust and dominant theme of [their] demonstration spoke to" broad public issues. As I have attempted to show, this portrayal is quite inaccurate; respondents' attack on Matthew was of central importance. But in any event, I fail to see why actionable speech should be immunized simply because it is interspersed with speech that is protected. The First Amendment allows recovery for defamatory statements that are interspersed with nondefamatory statements on matters of public concern, and there is no good reason why respondents' attack on Matthew Snyder and his family should be treated differently.

Second, the Court suggests that respondents' personal attack on Matthew Snyder is entitled to First Amendment protection because it was not motivated by a private grudge, but I see no basis for the strange distinction that the Court appears to draw. Respondents' motivation—"to increase publicity for its views"—did not transform their statements attacking the character of a private figure into statements that made a contribution to debate on matters of public concern. Nor did their publicity-seeking motivation soften the sting of their attack. And as far as culpability is concerned, one might well think that wounding statements uttered in the heat of a private feud are less, not more, blameworthy than similar statements made as part of a cold and calculated strategy to slash a stranger as a means of attracting public attention.

Third, the Court finds it significant that respondents' protest occurred on a public street, but this fact alone should not be enough to preclude IIED liability. To be sure, statements made on a public street may be less likely to satisfy the elements of the IIED tort than statements made on private property, but there is no reason why a public street in close proximity to the scene of a funeral should be regarded as a free-fire zone in which otherwise actionable verbal attacks are shielded from liability. If the First Amendment permits the States to protect their residents from the harm inflicted by such attacks—and the Court does not hold otherwise—then the location of the tort should not be dispositive. * * * Neither classic "fighting words" nor defamatory statements are immunized when they occur in a public place, and there is no good reason to treat a verbal assault based on the conduct or character of a private figure like Matthew Snyder any differently.

[F]unerals are unique events at which special protection against emotional assaults is in order. At funerals, the emotional well-being of bereaved relatives is particularly vulnerable. Exploitation of a funeral for the purpose of attracting public attention "intrud[es] upon their . . . grief," and may permanently stain their memories of the final moments before a loved one is laid to rest. Allowing family members to have a few hours of peace without harassment does not undermine public debate. I would therefore hold that, in this setting, the First Amendment permits a private figure to recover for the intentional infliction of emotional distress caused by speech on a matter of private concern. * * * I therefore respectfully dissent.

[JUSTICE BREYER's concurring opinion has been omitted.]

POINTS FOR DISCUSSION

a.   Public Concern, Private Figure

In *New York Times v. Sullivan* and its progeny, which we considered earlier in this chapter, the Court considered both the substance of the speech at issue—that is, whether it involved a matter of public or instead private concern—and the notoriety of the plaintiff—that is, whether the victim or target of the speech was a public or instead private figure. Under those cases, the constitutional protection for speech varies depending on the public or private character of the speech and the plaintiff; accordingly, there is less constitutional protection for defamatory speech about a private figure than there is for defamatory speech about a public figure. In *Hustler Magazine, Inc. v. Falwell*, 485 U.S. 46, 56 (1988), for example, the Court's conclusion that Jerry Falwell, a prominent religious leader, could not recover for intentional infliction of emotional distress for the publication of a cartoon that depicted him in an unflattering light was based in part on the fact that Falwell was a public figure.

Was the plaintiff (or the subject of the controversial speech) in *Snyder* a public or instead private figure? Did the Court seek to answer that question? If not, why not? After *Hustler Magazine* and *Snyder*, is it possible for anyone to recover for intentional infliction of emotional distress for public speech that concerns a matter of public importance?

b.   Opinion and Fact

In *Sullivan*, *Hustler*, and other cases, the Court has permitted liability in tort for speech only when the speaker knowingly lied or acted with reckless disregard for the truth. These cases thus can be read to stand for the proposition that the First Amendment might not protect false speech uttered with knowledge of its falsity, but that it generally protects truthful speech. Whatever one can say about the speech at issue in *Snyder*, however, it would be difficult to subject it to a standard of truth or falsity. Could such speech—which mostly expresses opinions, however misguided— ever give rise to liability under such a standard?

3. Obscenity

The Supreme Court has held that the First Amendment does not protect "obscenity." See *Roth v. United States*, 354 U.S. 476 (1957), which we consider below. The government, therefore, can regulate and even ban obscene materials, including those that might appear in magazines, movies, internet sites, and so forth. From this principle, two key questions arise: What is obscenity? And why does it receive no First Amendment protection?

Obscenity is notoriously hard to define. But since 1973, the basic test has remained the same. The Supreme Court has said:

> The basic guidelines for the trier of fact must be: (a) whether the average person, applying contemporary community standards would find that the work, taken as a whole, appeals to the prurient interest; (b) whether the work depicts or describes, in a patently offensive way, sexual conduct specifically defined by the applicable state law; and (c) whether the work, taken as a whole, lacks serious literary, artistic, political, or scientific value.

Miller v. California, 413 U.S. 15, 24 (1973). The word "prurient" is an adjective meaning "[c]haracterized by or arousing inordinate or unusual sexual desire." *Black's Law Dictionary* (9th ed. 2009). Note, then, that under the Court's test for obscenity, the material in question must both arouse (that is, appeal to the prurient interest) and disgust (that is, be "offensive"). Is this a sensible or manageable test?

The Supreme Court has relied on historical and originalist arguments, among others, in concluding that the First Amendment does not protect obscenity. In *Roth*, the Court explained that the history reveals "the rejection of obscenity as utterly without redeeming social importance." And as Justice Scalia has concisely put it: "There is no doubt, for example, that laws against [obscenity] do not violate 'the freedom of speech' to which the First Amendment refers; they existed and were universally approved in 1791." *McIntyre v. Ohio Elections Com'n*, 514 U.S. 334, 372 (1995) (Scalia, J., dissenting).

As you read the materials that follow, consider whether the Court has properly excluded obscenity from the protection of the First Amendment, and whether the Court's test for identifying obscenity is sensible and manageable.

ROTH V. UNITED STATES
354 U.S. 476 (1957)

MR. JUSTICE BRENNAN delivered the opinion of the Court.

The constitutionality of a criminal obscenity statute is the question in each of these cases. In *Roth*, the primary constitutional question is whether the federal obscenity statute[1] violates the provision of the First Amendment that "Congress shall make no law * * * abridging the freedom of speech, or of the press * * *." In *Alberts*, [a companion case,] the primary constitutional question is whether the obscenity provisions of the California Penal Code[2] invade the freedoms of speech and press as they may be incorporated in the liberty protected from state action by the Due Process Clause of the Fourteenth Amendment.

Roth conducted a business in New York in the publication and sale of books, photographs and magazines. He used circulars and advertising matter to solicit sales. He was convicted by a jury in the District Court for the Southern District of New York upon 4 counts of a 26-count indictment charging him with mailing obscene circulars and advertising, and an obscene book, in violation of the federal obscenity statute. * * * Alberts conducted a mail-order business from Los Angeles. He was convicted by the Judge of the Municipal Court of the Beverly Hills Judicial District (having waived a jury trial) under a misdemeanor complaint which charged him with lewdly keeping for sale obscene and indecent books, and with writing, composing and publishing an obscene advertisement of them, in violation of the California Penal Code. * * *

The dispositive question is whether obscenity is utterance within the area of protected speech and press. Although this is the first time the question has been squarely presented to this Court, either under the First Amendment or under the Fourteenth Amendment, expressions found in numerous opinions indicate that

---

[1] The federal obscenity statute provided, in pertinent part: "Every obscene, lewd, lascivious, or filthy book, pamphlet, picture, paper, letter, writing, print, or other publication of an indecent character; and [e]very written or printed card, letter, circular, book, pamphlet, advertisement, or notice of any kind giving information, directly or indirectly, where, or how, or from whom, or by what means any of such mentioned matters, articles, or things may be obtained or made, * * * whether sealed or unsealed * * * [i]s declared to be nonmailable matter and shall not be conveyed in the mails or delivered from any post office or by any letter carrier. Whoever knowingly deposits for mailing or delivery, anything declared by this section to be nonmailable, or knowingly takes the same from the mails for the purpose of circulating or disposing thereof, or of aiding in the circulation or disposition thereof, shall be fined not more than $5,000 or imprisoned not more than five years, or both." 18 U.S.C. § 1461. * * *

[2] "Every person who wilfully and lewdly, either: * * * 3. Writes, composes, stereotypes, prints, publishes, sells, distributes, keeps for sale, or exhibits any obscene or indecent writing, paper, or book; or designs, copies, draws, engraves, paints, or otherwise prepares any obscene or indecent picture or print; or molds, cuts, casts, or otherwise makes any obscene or indecent figure; or * * *, 4. Writes, composes, or publishes any notice or advertisement of any such writing, paper, book, picture, print or figure; * * * is guilty of a misdemeanor * * *." West's Cal. Penal Code Ann., 1955 § 311.

this Court has always assumed that obscenity is not protected by the freedoms of speech and press.

The guaranties of freedom of expression in effect in 10 of the 14 States which by 1792 had ratified the Constitution, gave no absolute protection for every utterance. Thirteen of the 14 States provided for the prosecution of libel, and all of those States made either blasphemy or profanity, or both, statutory crimes. As early as 1712, Massachusetts made it criminal to publish "any filthy, obscene, or profane song, pamphlet, libel or mock sermon" in imitation or mimicking of religious services. Acts and Laws of the Province of Mass. Bay, c. CV, § 8 (1712), Mass. Bay Colony Charters & Laws 399 (1814). Thus, profanity and obscenity were related offenses.

In light of this history, it is apparent that the unconditional phrasing of the First Amendment was not intended to protect every utterance. This phrasing did not prevent this Court from concluding that libelous utterances are not within the area of constitutionally protected speech. *Beauharnais v. People of State of Illinois*, 343 U.S. 250, 266 (1952). At the time of the adoption of the First Amendment, obscenity law was not as fully developed as libel law, but there is sufficiently contemporaneous evidence to show that obscenity, too, was outside the protection intended for speech and press.

The protection given speech and press was fashioned to assure unfettered interchange of ideas for the bringing about of political and social changes desired by the people. * * * All ideas having even the slightest redeeming social importance—unorthodox ideas, controversial ideas, even ideas hateful to the prevailing climate of opinion—have the full protection of the guaranties, unless excludable because they encroach upon the limited area of more important interests. But implicit in the history of the First Amendment is the rejection of obscenity as utterly without redeeming social importance. This rejection for that reason is mirrored in the universal judgment that obscenity should be restrained, reflected in the international agreement of over 50 nations, in the obscenity laws of all of the 48 States, and in the 20 obscenity laws enacted by the Congress from 1842 to 1956. This is the same judgment expressed by this Court in *Chaplinsky v. New Hampshire*, 315 U.S. 568, 571–572 (1942):

> * * * There are certain well-defined and narrowly limited classes of speech, the prevention and punishment of which have never been thought to raise any Constitutional problem. These include the lewd and obscene * * *. It has been well observed that such utterances are no essential part of any exposition of ideas, and are of such slight social

value as a step to truth that any benefit that may be derived from them is clearly outweighed by the social interest in order and morality * * *.

We hold that obscenity is not within the area of constitutionally protected speech or press.

It is strenuously urged that these obscenity statutes offend the constitutional guaranties because they punish incitation to impure sexual *thoughts*, not shown to be related to any overt antisocial conduct which is or may be incited in the persons stimulated to such *thoughts*. * * * However, sex and obscenity are not synonymous. Obscene material is material which deals with sex in a manner appealing to prurient interest.[20] The portrayal of sex, e.g., in art, literature and scientific works, is not itself sufficient reason to deny material the constitutional protection of freedom of speech and press. Sex, a great and mysterious motive force in human life, has indisputably been a subject of absorbing interest to mankind through the ages; it is one of the vital problems of human interest and public concern.

> **Take Note**
>
> The Court decides that the First Amendment does not protect obscenity. But it then gives obscenity a somewhat narrow definition. Although the definition of obscenity has varied over time, this basic approach to obscenity has not. Does the Court's approach mean that courts will repeatedly be called upon to decide what depictions of sex sufficiently appeal to the "prurient interest" to fall outside the scope of the First Amendment's protection?

The fundamental freedom of speech and press have contributed greatly to the development and well-being of our free society and are indispensable to its continued growth. Ceaseless vigilance is the watchword to prevent their erosion by Congress or by the States. The door barring federal and state intrusion into this area cannot be left ajar; it must be kept tightly closed and opened only the slightest crack necessary to prevent encroachment upon more important interests. It is therefore vital that the standards for judging obscenity safeguard the protection of freedom of speech and press for material which does not treat sex in a manner appealing to prurient interest.

The early leading standard of obscenity allowed material to be judged merely by the effect of an isolated excerpt upon particularly susceptible persons. *Regina v. Hicklin*, (1868) L.R. 3 Q.B. 360. Some American courts adopted this standard but later decisions have rejected it and substituted this test: whether to the average person, applying contemporary community standards, the dominant theme of the

---

[20] I.e., material having a tendency to excite lustful thoughts. Webster's New International Dictionary (Unabridged, 2d ed., 1949) defines prurient, in pertinent part, as follows: "Itching; longing; uneasy with desire or longing; of persons, having itching, morbid, or lascivious longings; of desire, curiosity, or propensity, lewd."

material taken as a whole appeals to prurient interest. The *Hicklin* test, judging obscenity by the effect of isolated passages upon the most susceptible persons, might well encompass material legitimately treating with sex, and so it must be rejected as unconstitutionally restrictive of the freedoms of speech and press. On the other hand, the substituted standard provides safeguards adequate to withstand the charge of constitutional infirmity. Both trial courts below sufficiently followed the proper standard. Both courts used the proper definition of obscenity. [Affirmed.]

[JUSTICE HARLAN'S dissenting opinion is omitted.]

MR. JUSTICE DOUGLAS, with whom MR. JUSTICE BLACK concurs, dissenting.

When we sustain these convictions, we make the legality of a publication turn on the purity of thought which a book or tract instills in the mind of the reader. I do not think we can approve that standard and be faithful to the command of the First Amendment, which by its terms is a restraint on Congress and which by the Fourteenth is a restraint on the States.

Any test that turns on what is offensive to the community's standards is too loose, too capricious, too destructive of freedom of expression to be squared with the First Amendment. Under that test, juries can censor, suppress, and punish what they don't like, provided the matter relates to "sexual impurity" or has a tendency "to excite lustful thoughts." This is community censorship in one of its worst forms. It creates a regime where in the battle between the literati and the Philistines, the Philistines are certain to win.

> **Definitions**
>
> "Literati" are "persons interested in literature or the arts," and a philistine (a word taken from the name of a Biblical people) is a "person who is guided by materialism and is usually disdainful of intellectual or artistic values." *Merriam-Webster's Online Dictionary* (2017).

I can understand (and at times even sympathize) with programs of civic groups and church groups to protect and defend the existing moral standards of the community. * * * When speech alone is involved, I do not think that government, consistently with the First Amendment, can become the sponsor of any of these movements. I do not think that government, consistently with the First Amendment, can throw its weight behind one school or another. Government should be concerned with antisocial conduct, not with utterances. Thus, if the First Amendment guarantee of freedom of speech and press is to mean anything in this field, it must allow protests even against the moral code that the standard of the day sets for the community. In other words, literature should not be suppressed merely because it offends the moral code of the censor. * * *

[T]he test that suppresses a cheap tract today can suppress a literary gem tomorrow. All it need do is to incite a lascivious thought or arouse a lustful desire. The list of books that judges or juries can place in that category is endless.

I would give the broad sweep of the First Amendment full support. I have the same confidence in the ability of our people to reject noxious literature as I have in their capacity to sort out the true from the false in theology, economics, politics, or any other field.

POINTS FOR DISCUSSION

a.   Examples

The Court says that the "portrayal of sex, e.g., in art, literature and scientific works," is not necessarily obscenity. Can you think of specific examples of such portrayals that are not obscene? Are you confident that your peers would share your assessment?

What does count as obscenity? In *Miller v. California*, 413 U.S. 15, 25 (1973), the Court suggested that a state could define obscenity to include "[p]atently offensive representations or descriptions of ultimate sexual acts, normal or perverted, actual or simulated" and "[p]atently offensive representation or descriptions of masturbation, excretory functions, and lewd exhibition of the genitals." How would you decide what is "patently offensive"? Can you think of books that contain descriptions or movies that contain scenes that fall within these tests for obscenity but that nevertheless should be protected as speech under the First Amendment?

b.   The Court's Reasoning

Although the Supreme Court had previously suggested in dicta that the Constitution does not protect obscenity, *Roth* was the first case in which the Court actually decided the issue. What reasoning did the Court use to reach its decision? If the Court applied this reasoning in all First Amendment cases, what other types of speech or expression would be beyond the protection of the First Amendment?

c.   Excluding Categories of Speech from First Amendment Protection

Doesn't the Court have to "weigh" the value of speech in order to decide that it and other similar speech is not worthy of protection under the First Amendment? Are you confident that the Court can identify categories of speech that are beyond the protection of the First Amendment without, in the process, effectively acting as a censor itself? Note, in this regard, that the statutes at issue in *Roth* and the companion case were quintessentially content-based regulations.

Consider the test that the Court established in *Miller*, which requires the Court to determine "whether the work, taken as a whole, lacks serious literary, artistic, political, or scientific value." How does a court make such an assessment? Would that inquiry be acceptable for other categories of speech?

d.   Vagueness and Overbreadth

Even if obscenity is not protected by the First Amendment, didn't the statutes at issue in *Roth* and the companion case suffer from problems of vagueness and overbreadth, which we considered earlier in this chapter? Can you formulate an argument that the Court should have invalidated the convictions on those grounds? Is the Court's own test for obscenity itself subject to attack on those grounds?

Although Justice Brennan wrote the opinion in *Roth*, he subsequently changed his mind about the viability of the Court's obscenity doctrine because of the Court's inability to formulate a workable standard. Consider the view that he expressed in dissent in *Paris Adult Theatre I v. Slaton*, 413 U.S. 49 (1973), a companion case to *Miller v. California*, 413 U.S. 15, 25 (1973):

> Our experience with the *Roth* approach has certainly taught us that the outright suppression of obscenity cannot be reconciled with the fundamental principles of the First and Fourteenth Amendments. For we have failed to formulate a standard that sharply distinguishes protected from unprotected speech, and out of necessity, we have resorted to [an] approach [that] resolves cases as between the parties, but offers only the most obscure guidance to legislation, adjudication by other courts, and primary conduct. * * * It comes as no surprise that judicial attempts to follow our lead conscientiously have often ended in hopeless confusion.

> Of course, the vagueness problem would be largely of our own creation if it stemmed primarily from our failure to reach a consensus on any one standard. But after 16 years of experimentation and debate I am reluctantly forced to the conclusion that none of the available formulas, including the one announced today, can reduce the vagueness to a tolerable level while at the same time striking an acceptable balance between the protections of the First and Fourteenth Amendments, on the one hand, and on the other the asserted state interest in regulating the dissemination of certain sexually oriented materials. Any effort to draw a constitutionally acceptable boundary on state power must resort to such indefinite concepts as "prurient interest," "patent offensiveness," "serious literary value," and the like. The meaning of these concepts necessarily varies with the experience, outlook, and even idiosyncrasies of the person defining them. Although we have assumed that obscenity does exist and that we "know it when (we) see it," *Jacobellis v. Ohio*, 378 U.S., at 197 (Stewart, J., concurring), we are

manifestly unable to describe it in advance except by reference to concepts so elusive that they fail to distinguish clearly between protected and unprotected speech.

Is the problem that any test that is clear and workable would also run the risk of permitting the banning of material that is entitled to First Amendment protection under any theory of the Amendment?

NEW YORK V. FERBER

458 U.S. 747 (1982)

JUSTICE WHITE delivered the opinion of the Court.

At issue in this case is the constitutionality of a New York criminal statute which prohibits persons from knowingly promoting sexual performances by children under the age of 16 by distributing material which depicts such performances.

This case arose when Paul Ferber, the proprietor of a Manhattan bookstore specializing in sexually oriented products, sold two films to an undercover police officer. The films are devoted almost exclusively to depicting young boys masturbating. Ferber was indicted on two counts of violating § 263.10 and two counts of violating § 263.15, the two New York laws controlling dissemination of child pornography. After a jury trial, Ferber was acquitted of the two counts of promoting an obscene sexual performance, but found guilty of the two counts under § 263.15, which did not require proof that the films were obscene. Ferber's convictions were affirmed without opinion by the Appellate Division of the New York State Supreme Court. The New York Court of Appeals reversed, holding that § 263.15 violated the First Amendment. * * *

[This] Court squarely held in *Roth v. United States*, 354 U.S. 476 (1957), that "obscenity is not within the area of constitutionally protected speech or press." The Court recognized that "rejection of obscenity as utterly without redeeming social importance" was implicit in the history of the First Amendment * * *. *Roth* was followed by 15 years during which this Court struggled with "the intractable obscenity problem." *Interstate Circuit, Inc. v. Dallas*, 390 U.S. 676, 704 (1968) (opinion of Harlan, J.). Despite considerable vacillation over the proper definition of obscenity, a majority of the Members of the Court remained firm in the position that "the States have a legitimate interest in prohibiting dissemination or exhibition of obscene material when the mode of dissemination carries with it a significant danger of offending the sensibilities of unwilling recipients or of exposure to juveniles." *Miller v. California*, 413 U.S. 15, 18–19 (1973).

Throughout this period, we recognized "the inherent dangers of undertaking to regulate any form of expression." Consequently, our difficulty was not only to assure that statutes designed to regulate obscene materials sufficiently defined what was prohibited, but also to devise substantive limits on what fell within the permissible scope of regulation. In *Miller*, a majority of the Court agreed that a "state offense must also be limited to works which, taken as a whole, appeal to the prurient interest in sex, which portray sexual conduct in a patently offensive way, and which, taken as a whole, do not have serious literary, artistic, political, or scientific value." *Id.*, at 24. Over the past decade, we have adhered to the guidelines expressed in *Miller*, which subsequently has been followed in the regulatory schemes of most States.

The *Miller* standard, like its predecessors, was an accommodation between the State's interests in protecting the "sensibilities of unwilling recipients" from exposure to pornographic material and the dangers of censorship inherent in unabashedly content-based laws. Like obscenity statutes, laws directed at the dissemination of child pornography run the risk of suppressing protected expression by allowing the hand of the censor to become unduly heavy. For the following reasons, however, we are persuaded that the States are entitled to greater leeway in the regulation of pornographic depictions of children.

First. It is evident beyond the need for elaboration that a State's interest in "safeguarding the physical and psychological well-being of a minor" is "compelling." *Globe Newspaper Co. v. Superior Court*, 457 U.S. 596, 607 (1982). "A democratic society rests, for its continuance, upon the healthy, well-rounded growth of young people into full maturity as citizens." *Prince v. Massachusetts*, 321 U.S. 158, 168 (1944). Accordingly, we have sustained legislation aimed at protecting the physical and emotional well-being of youth even when the laws have operated in the sensitive area of constitutionally protected rights. In *Prince*, the Court held that a statute prohibiting use of a child to distribute literature on the street was valid notwithstanding the statute's effect on a First Amendment activity. In *Ginsberg v. New York*, 390 U.S. 629 (1968), we sustained a New York law protecting children from exposure to nonobscene literature. Most recently, we held that the Government's interest in the "well-being of its youth" justified special treatment of indecent broadcasting received by adults as well as children. *FCC v. Pacifica Foundation*, 438 U.S. 726 (1978).

The prevention of sexual exploitation and abuse of children constitutes a government objective of surpassing importance. * * * Suffice it to say that virtually all of the States and the United States have passed legislation proscribing the production of or otherwise combating "child pornography." The legislative judgment, as well as the judgment found in the relevant literature, is that the use of children as subjects of pornographic materials is harmful to the physiological, emotional, and mental health of the child. That judgment, we think, easily passes muster under the First Amendment.

Second. The distribution of photographs and films depicting sexual activity by juveniles is intrinsically related to the sexual abuse of children in at least two ways. First, the materials produced are a permanent record of the children's participation and the harm to the child is exacerbated by their circulation. Second, the distribution network for child pornography must be closed if the production of material which requires the sexual exploitation of children is to be effectively controlled. Indeed, there is no serious contention that the legislature was unjustified in believing that it is difficult, if not impossible, to halt the exploitation of children by pursuing only those who produce the photographs and movies. While the production of pornographic materials is a low-profile, clandestine industry, the need to market the resulting products requires a visible apparatus of distribution. The most expeditious if not the only practical method of law enforcement may be to dry up the market for this material by imposing severe criminal penalties on persons selling, advertising, or otherwise promoting the product. Thirty-five States and Congress have concluded that restraints on the distribution of pornographic materials are required in order to effectively combat the problem, and there is a body of literature and testimony to support these legislative conclusions.

Respondent does not contend that the State is unjustified in pursuing those who distribute child pornography. Rather, he argues that it is enough for the State to prohibit the distribution of materials that are legally obscene under the *Miller* test. While some States may find that this approach properly accommodates its interests, it does not follow that the First Amendment prohibits a State from going further. The *Miller* standard, like all general definitions of what may be banned as obscene, does not reflect the State's particular and more compelling interest in prosecuting those who promote the sexual exploitation of children. Thus, the question under the *Miller* test of whether a work, taken as a whole, appeals to the prurient interest of the average person bears no connection to the issue of whether a child has been physically or psychologically harmed in the production of the work. Similarly, a sexually explicit depiction need not be "patently offensive" in order to have required the sexual exploitation of a child for its production. In addition, a work which, taken on the whole, contains serious literary, artistic, political, or scientific value may nevertheless embody the hardest core of child pornography. "It is irrelevant to the child [who has been abused] whether or not the material [has] a literary, artistic, political or social value." Memorandum of Assemblyman Lasher in Support of § 263.15. We therefore cannot conclude that the *Miller* standard is a satisfactory solution to the child pornography problem.

Third. The advertising and selling of child pornography provide an economic motive for and are thus an integral part of the production of such materials, an activity illegal throughout the Nation. "It rarely has been suggested that the constitutional freedom for speech and press extends its immunity to speech or writing used as an integral part of conduct in violation of a valid criminal statute." *Giboney v. Empire Storage & Ice Co.*, 336 U.S. 490, 498 (1949). We note that were the statutes outlawing the employment of children in these films and photographs fully effective, and the constitutionality of these laws has not been questioned, the First Amendment implications would be no greater than that presented by laws against distribution: enforceable production laws would leave no child pornography to be marketed.

Fourth. The value of permitting live performances and photographic reproductions of children engaged in lewd sexual conduct is exceedingly modest, if not *de minimis*. We consider it unlikely that visual depictions of children performing sexual acts or lewdly exhibiting their genitals would often constitute an important and necessary part of a literary performance or scientific or educational work. As a state judge in this case observed, if it were necessary for literary or artistic value, a person over the statutory age who perhaps looked younger could be utilized. Simulation outside of the prohibition of the statute could provide another alternative. Nor is there any question here of censoring a particular literary theme or portrayal of sexual activity. The First Amendment interest is limited to that of rendering the portrayal somewhat more "realistic" by utilizing or photographing children.

> **Make the Connection**
>
> We will consider the "fighting words" doctrine, and the Court's decision in *Chaplinsky*, later in this chapter. We considered the libel cases earlier in this chapter.

Fifth. Recognizing and classifying child pornography as a category of material outside the protection of the First Amendment is not incompatible with our earlier decisions. * * * "[I]t is the content of [an] utterance that determines whether it is a protected epithet or an unprotected 'fighting comment.'" See *Chaplinsky v. New Hampshire*, 315 U.S. 568 (1942). Leaving aside the special considerations when public officials are the target, *New York Times Co. v. Sullivan*, 376 U.S. 254 (1964), a libelous publication is not protected by the Constitution. *Beauharnais v. Illinois*, 343 U.S. 250 (1952). Thus, it is not rare that a content-based classification of speech has been accepted because it may be appropriately generalized that within the confines of the given classification, the evil to be restricted so overwhelmingly outweighs the expressive interests, if any, at stake, that no process of case-by-case adjudication is required. When a definable class of material, such as that covered by § 263.15, bears so heavily and pervasively on the welfare of children engaged in its production, we think the balance of competing interests is clearly struck and that it is permissible to consider these materials as without the protection of the First Amendment.

There are, of course, limits on the category of child pornography which, like obscenity, is unprotected by the First Amendment. As with all legislation in this sensitive area, the conduct to be prohibited must be adequately defined by the applicable state law, as written or authoritatively construed. Here the nature of the harm to be combated requires that the state offense be limited to works that *visually* depict sexual conduct by children below a specified age. The category of "sexual conduct" proscribed must also be suitably limited and described.

The test for child pornography is separate from the obscenity standard enunciated in *Miller*, but may be compared to it for the purpose of clarity. The *Miller* formulation is adjusted in the following respects: A trier of fact need not find that the material appeals to the prurient interest of the average person; it is not required that sexual conduct portrayed be done so in a patently offensive manner; and the material at issue need not be considered as a whole. We note that the distribution of descriptions or other depictions of sexual conduct, not otherwise obscene, which do not involve live performance or photographic or other visual reproduction of live performances, retains First Amendment protection. As with obscenity laws, criminal responsibility may not be imposed without some element of scienter on the part of the defendant.

We hold that § 263.15 sufficiently describes a category of material the production and distribution of which is not entitled to First Amendment protection. It is therefore clear that there is nothing unconstitutionally "underinclusive" about a statute that singles out this category of material for proscription.[18]

Reversed and remanded.

JUSTICE O'CONNOR, concurring.

Although I join the Court's opinion, I write separately to stress that the Court does not hold that New York must except "material with serious literary,

---

[18] * * * Today, we hold that child pornography as defined in § 263.15 is unprotected speech subject to content-based regulation. Hence, it cannot be underinclusive or unconstitutional for a State to do precisely that.

scientific, or educational value" from its statute. * * * The compelling interests identified in today's opinion suggest that the Constitution might in fact permit New York to ban knowing distribution of works depicting minors engaged in explicit sexual conduct, regardless of the social value of the depictions. * * * The audience's appreciation of the depiction is simply irrelevant to New York's asserted interest in protecting children from psychological, emotional, and mental harm.

JUSTICE BRENNAN, with whom JUSTICE MARSHALL joins, concurring in the judgment.

I agree with much of what is said in the Court's opinion. * * * But in my view application of § 263.15 or any similar statute to depictions of children that in themselves do have serious literary, artistic, scientific, or medical value, would violate the First Amendment. * * * The First Amendment value of depictions of children that are in themselves serious contributions to art, literature, or science, is, by definition, simply not "de minimis." At the same time, the State's interest in suppression of such materials is likely to be far less compelling. For the Court's assumption of harm to the child resulting from the "permanent record" and "circulation" of the child's "participation" lacks much of its force where the depiction is a serious contribution to art or science. * * * With this understanding, I concur in the Court's judgment in this case.

[JUSTICE STEVENS's opinion concurring in the judgment is omitted.]

POINTS FOR DISCUSSION

a.   Obscenity v. Child Pornography

The opinion makes clear that child pornography and obscenity are two separate categories of speech, though neither is protected by the First Amendment. Was this distinction necessary for deciding the case? Given the facts of the case, could the Court have held that the child pornography at issue was obscene?

b.   Defining Child Pornography

What exactly is the Court's definition of child pornography? Would Vladimir Nabokov's famous novel *Lolita*, which is about a man who becomes obsessed with, and has a sexual relationship with, a twelve-year-old girl, count as child pornography, such that a state could ban its sale and possession? Could a state ban Stanley Kubrick's critically acclaimed film adaptation of the novel?

c.   **Virtual Child Pornography**

How would the Court's theory for why child pornography is not protected apply to computer-generated virtual child pornography? In *Ashcroft v. Free Speech Coalition*, 535 U.S. 234, 251 (2002), the Supreme Court held that the First Amendment prohibits the government from banning non-obscene, virtual child pornography. But in *United States v. Williams*, 553 U.S. 285, 300 (2008), the Court held that the government may punish a person for distributing virtual child pornography as though it were real child pornography. What is the distinction between the two cases?

4.   Symbolic Conduct

The First Amendment explicitly protects only "speech." The Amendment, for example, does not mention marching in a parade, participating in a sit-down strike, burning a flag or other emblem, wearing an arm band as a sign of protest, and other forms of expressive conduct. A question thus arises whether these activities count as "speech." Can the government regulate these communicative activities without violating the First Amendment?

The Supreme Court has concluded that conduct may be "sufficiently imbued with elements of communication to fall within the scope of the First and Fourteenth Amendments." *Spence v. Washington*, 418 U.S. 405, 409 (1974). For example, in *Tinker v. Des Moines Independent Community School Dist.*, 393 U.S. 503 (1969), the Court held that a school regulation prohibiting students from wearing arm bands violated the First Amendment. The school had adopted the regulation only after learning that a group of students had decided to wear the arm bands to protest the Vietnam War. The Court concluded that the school had acted "to punish petitioners for a silent, passive expression of opinion, unaccompanied by any disorder or disturbance on the part of petitioners," and that "undifferentiated fear or apprehension of disturbance is not enough" to justify such a content-based regulation of expressive activity. Accordingly, when the government seeks to regulate "conduct" *because of* the expressive elements of that conduct, the Court applies searching scrutiny.

But we have also already seen important cases in which the Court seemed to conclude that expressive conduct receives less protection than other speech. In *United States v. O'Brien*, 391 U.S. 367 (1968), which we considered earlier in this chapter, the Court noted that "when 'speech' and 'nonspeech' elements are combined in the same course of conduct, a sufficiently important governmental interest in regulating the nonspeech element can justify incidental limitations on First Amendment freedoms." Under the Court's approach in *O'Brien*, the government may regulate expressive conduct if four conditions are met: (1) the regulation is within the constitutional power of the Government; (2) the regulation furthers an important or substantial governmental interest; (3) the governmental interest is unrelated to the suppression of free expression; and (4) the incidental restriction on alleged First Amendment freedoms is no greater than is essential to the furtherance of that interest. Significantly, the *O'Brien* test is not strict scrutiny; under the test, the government does not need to have a compelling interest to justify burdens on speech, but instead merely must advance an important or substantial interest.

Does the *O'Brien* test apply to all government attempts to regulate "expressive conduct"? By its own terms, it requires, at a minimum, that the governmental interest in the regulation be "unrelated to the suppression of free expression"—that is, that the regulation not be content based, and thus not be directed at the suppression of the very message expressed by the regulated conduct. As you read the following case, consider (1) whether the government's interest in the challenged regulation makes the case more like *Tinker* or instead more like *O'Brien*, and (2) whether a distinction between "conduct" and "speech" is a useful device in assessing claims under the First Amendment.

TEXAS V. JOHNSON

491 U.S. 397 (1989)

JUSTICE BRENNAN delivered the opinion of the Court.

After publicly burning an American flag as a means of political protest, Gregory Lee Johnson was convicted of desecrating a flag in violation of Texas law. This case presents the question whether his conviction is consistent with the First Amendment. We hold that it is not.

While the Republican National Convention was taking place in Dallas in 1984, respondent Johnson participated in a political demonstration dubbed the "Republican War Chest Tour." As explained in literature distributed by the demonstrators and in speeches made by them, the purpose of this event was to protest the policies of the Reagan administration and of certain Dallas-based corporations. The demonstrators marched through the Dallas streets, chanting political slogans and stopping at several corporate locations to stage "die-ins" intended to dramatize the consequences of nuclear war. On several occasions they spray-painted the walls of buildings and overturned potted plants, but Johnson himself took no part in such activities. He did, however, accept an American flag handed to him by a fellow protestor who had taken it from a flagpole outside one of the targeted buildings.

The demonstration ended in front of Dallas City Hall, where Johnson unfurled the American flag, doused it with kerosene, and set it on fire. While the flag burned, the protestors chanted: "America, the red, white, and blue, we spit on you." After the demonstrators dispersed, a witness to the flag burning collected the flag's remains and buried them in his backyard. No one was physically injured or threatened with injury, though several witnesses testified that they had been seriously offended by the flag burning.

Of the approximately 100 demonstrators, Johnson alone was charged with a crime. The only criminal offense with which he was charged was the desecration of a venerated object in violation of Tex. Penal Code Ann. § 42.09(a)(3) (1989).[1] [The Texas Court of Criminal Appeals reversed the conviction on the ground that it violated the First Amendment.]

The First Amendment literally forbids the abridgment only of "speech," but we have long recognized that its protection does not end at the spoken or written word. While we have rejected "the view that an apparently limitless variety of conduct can be labeled 'speech' whenever the person engaging in the conduct intends thereby to express an idea," *United States v. O'Brien,* 391 U.S. 367, 376 (1968), we have acknowledged that conduct may be "sufficiently imbued with elements of communication to fall within the scope of the First and Fourteenth Amendments," *Spence v. Washington,* 418 U.S. 405, 409 (1974).

In deciding whether particular conduct possesses sufficient communicative elements to bring the First Amendment into play, we have asked whether "[a]n intent to convey a particularized message was present, and [whether] the likelihood was great that the message would be understood by those who viewed it." 418 U.S., at 410–411. Hence, we have recognized the expressive nature of students' wearing of black armbands to protest American military involvement in Vietnam, *Tinker v. Des Moines Independent Community School Dist.,* 393 U.S. 503, 505 (1969); of a sit-in by blacks in a "whites only" area to protest segregation, *Brown v. Louisiana,* 383 U.S. 131, 141–142 (1966); of the wearing of American military uniforms in a dramatic presentation criticizing American involvement in Vietnam, *Schacht v. United States,* 398 U.S. 58 (1970); and of picketing about a wide variety of causes, *see, e.g., Food Employees v. Logan Valley Plaza, Inc.,* 391 U.S. 308, 313–314 (1968).

---

[1] Texas Penal Code Ann. § 42.09 (1989) provides in full: "§ 42.09. Desecration of Venerated Object. (a) A person commits an offense if he intentionally or knowingly desecrates: (1) a public monument; (2) a place of worship or burial; or (3) a state or national flag. (b) For purposes of this section, 'desecrate' means deface, damage, or otherwise physically mistreat in a way that the actor knows will seriously offend one or more persons likely to observe or discover his action. (c) An offense under this section is a Class A misdemeanor."

Especially pertinent to this case are our decisions recognizing the communicative nature of conduct relating to flags. Attaching a peace sign to the flag, *Spence, supra,* at 409–410; refusing to salute the flag, *West Virginia Board of Education v. Barnette,* 319 U.S. 624, 632 (1943); and displaying a red flag, *Stromberg v. California,* 283 U.S. 359, 368–369 (1931), we have held, all may find shelter under the First Amendment. That we have had little difficulty identifying an expressive element in conduct relating to flags should not be surprising. The very purpose of a national flag is to serve as a symbol of our country; it is, one might say, "the one visible manifestation of two hundred years of nationhood." *Smith v. Goguen,* 415 U.S. 566, 603 (1974) (REHNQUIST, J., dissenting). Thus, we have observed:

"[T]he flag salute is a form of utterance. Symbolism is a primitive but effective way of communicating ideas. The use of an emblem or flag to symbolize some system, idea, institution, or personality, is a short cut from mind to mind. Causes and nations, political parties, lodges and ecclesiastical groups seek to knit the loyalty of their followings to a flag or banner, a color or design." *Barnette, supra,* at 632.

[A]lthough we have recognized that where " 'speech' and 'nonspeech' elements are combined in the same course of conduct, a sufficiently important governmental interest in regulating the nonspeech element can justify incidental limitations on First Amendment freedoms," *O'Brien, supra,* at 376, we have limited the applicability of *O'Brien*'s relatively lenient standard to those cases in which "the governmental interest is unrelated to the suppression of free expression." *Id.* at 377. In stating, moreover, that *O'Brien*'s test "in the last analysis is little, if any, different from the standard applied to time, place, or manner restrictions," *Clark v. Community for Creative Non-Violence,* 468 U.S. 288, 298 (1984), we have highlighted the requirement that the governmental interest in question be unconnected to expression in order to come under *O'Brien*'s less demanding rule.

> **Take Note**
>
> Beginning here, the Court reviews the interests that Texas claims to have in the enforcement of its law. How does the Court decide whether these interests are sufficient? Does it measure them against the standard from *O'Brien*? If not, what level of scrutiny does it apply?

Texas claims that its interest in preventing breaches of the peace justifies Johnson's conviction for flag desecration. However, no disturbance of the peace actually occurred or threatened to occur because of Johnson's burning of the flag. * * * The State's position, therefore, amounts to a claim that an audience that takes serious offense at particular expression is necessarily likely to disturb the peace and that the expression may be prohibited on this basis. Our precedents do not countenance such a presumption. On the contrary, they recognize that a principal "function of free speech under our system of government is to invite dispute. It may indeed best serve its high purpose when it induces a condition of unrest, creates dissatisfaction with conditions as they are, or even stirs people to anger." *Terminiello v. Chicago,* 337 U.S. 1, 4 (1949). * * *

Thus, we have not permitted the government to assume that every expression of a provocative idea will incite a riot, but have instead required careful consideration of the actual circumstances surrounding such expression, asking whether the expression "is directed to inciting or producing imminent lawless action and is likely to incite or produce such action." *Brandenburg v. Ohio,* 395 U.S. 444, 447 (1969). To accept Texas' arguments that it need only demonstrate "the potential for a breach of the peace," and that every flag burning necessarily possesses that potential, would be to eviscerate our holding in *Brandenburg.* This we decline to do. * * * We thus conclude that the State's interest in maintaining order is not implicated on these facts.

The State also asserts an interest in preserving the flag as a symbol of nationhood and national unity. * * * We [are] persuaded that this interest is related to expression in the case of Johnson's burning of the flag. The State, apparently, is concerned that such conduct will lead people to believe either that the flag does not stand for nationhood and national unity, but instead reflects other, less positive concepts, or that the concepts reflected in the flag do not in fact exist, that is, that we do not enjoy unity as a Nation. These concerns blossom only when a person's treatment of the flag communicates some message, and thus are related "to the suppression of free expression" within the meaning of *O'Brien.* We are thus outside of *O'Brien*'s test altogether.

[handwritten: strict scrutiny]

It remains to consider whether the State's interest in preserving the flag as a symbol of nationhood and national unity justifies Johnson's conviction. * * * Johnson was prosecuted because he knew that his politically charged expression would cause "serious offense." If he had burned the flag as a means of disposing of it because it was dirty or torn, he would not have been convicted of flag desecration under this Texas law: federal law designates burning as the preferred means of disposing of a flag "when it is in such condition that it is no longer a fitting emblem for display," 36 U.S.C. § 176(k), and Texas has no quarrel with this means of disposal. The Texas law is thus not aimed at protecting the physical integrity of the flag in all circumstances, but is designed instead to protect it only against impairments that would cause serious offense to others.

Whether Johnson's treatment of the flag violated Texas law thus depended on the likely communicative impact of his expressive conduct. * * * Johnson's political expression [thus] was restricted because of the content of the message he conveyed. We must therefore subject the State's asserted interest in preserving the special symbolic character of the flag to "the most exacting scrutiny." *Boos v. Barry,* 485 U.S. 312, 321 (1988).

Texas argues that its interest in preserving the flag as a symbol of nationhood and national unity survives this close analysis. Quoting extensively from the writings of this Court chronicling the flag's historic and symbolic role in our society, the State emphasizes the "special place" reserved for the flag in our Nation. The State's argument is not that it has an interest simply in maintaining the flag as a symbol of *something,* no matter what it symbolizes; indeed, if that were the State's position, it would be difficult to see how that interest is endangered by highly symbolic conduct such as Johnson's. Rather, the State's claim is that it has an interest in preserving the flag as a symbol of *nationhood* and *national unity,* a symbol with a determinate range of meanings. According to Texas, if one physically treats the flag in a way that would tend to cast doubt on either the idea that nationhood and national unity are the flag's referents or that national unity actually exists, the message conveyed thereby is a harmful one and therefore may be prohibited.

If there is a bedrock principle underlying the First Amendment, it is that the government may not prohibit the expression of an idea simply because society finds the idea itself offensive or disagreeable. * * * We have not recognized an exception to this principle even where our flag has been involved. In *Street v. New York,* 394 U.S. 576 (1969), we held that a State may not criminally punish a person for uttering words critical of the flag. Rejecting the argument that the conviction could be sustained on the ground that Street had "failed to show the respect for our national symbol which may properly be demanded of every citizen," we concluded that "the constitutionally guaranteed 'freedom to be intellectually . . . diverse or even contrary,' and the 'right to differ as to things that touch the heart of the existing order,' encompass the freedom to express publicly one's opinions about our flag, including those opinions which are defiant or contemptuous." *Id.,* at 593, quoting *Barnette,* 319 U.S., at 642. Nor may the government, we have held, compel conduct that would evince respect for the flag. "To sustain the compulsory flag salute we are required to say that a Bill of Rights which guards the individual's right to speak his own mind, left it open to public authorities to compel him to utter what is not in his mind." *Id.,* at 634.

There is, moreover, no indication—either in the text of the Constitution or in our cases interpreting it—that a separate juridical category exists for the American flag alone. Indeed, we would not be surprised to learn that the persons who framed our Constitution and wrote the Amendment that we now construe were not known for their reverence for the Union Jack. The First Amendment does not guarantee that other concepts virtually sacred to our Nation as a whole—such as the principle that discrimination on the basis of race is odious and destructive—will go unquestioned in the marketplace of ideas. See *Brandenburg v. Ohio,* 395 U.S. 444 (1969). We decline, therefore, to create for the flag an exception to the joust of principles protected by the First Amendment.

It is not the State's ends, but its means, to which we object. It cannot be gainsaid that there is a special place reserved for the flag in this Nation, and thus we do not doubt that the government has a legitimate interest in making efforts to "preserv[e] the national flag as an unalloyed symbol of our country." *Spence,* 418 U.S., at 412. We reject the suggestion, urged at oral argument by counsel for Johnson, that the government lacks "any state interest whatsoever" in regulating the manner in which the flag may be displayed. Congress has, for example, enacted precatory regulations describing the proper treatment of the flag, see 36 U.S.C. §§ 173–177, and we cast no doubt on the legitimacy of its interest in making such recommendations. To say that the government has an interest in encouraging proper treatment of the flag, however, is not to say that it may criminally punish a person for burning a flag as a means of political protest. "National unity as an end which officials may foster by persuasion and example is not in question. The problem is whether under our Constitution compulsion as here employed is a permissible means for its achievement." *Barnette,* 319 U.S., at 640. *Affirmed.*

JUSTICE KENNEDY, concurring.

I write not to qualify the words Justice BRENNAN chooses so well, for he says with power all that is necessary to explain our ruling. I join his opinion without reservation, but with a keen sense that this case, like others before us from time to time, exacts its personal toll.

The hard fact is that sometimes we must make decisions we do not like. We make them because they are right, right in the sense that the law and the Constitution, as we see them, compel the result. And so great is our commitment to the process that, except in the rare case, we do not pause to express distaste for the result, perhaps for fear of undermining a valued principle that dictates the decision. This is one of those rare cases.

Our colleagues in dissent advance powerful arguments why respondent may be convicted for his expression, reminding us that among those who will be dismayed by our holding will be some who have had the singular honor of carrying the flag in battle. And I agree that the flag holds a lonely place of honor in an age when absolutes are distrusted and simple truths are burdened by unneeded apologetics.

With all respect to those views, I do not believe the Constitution gives us the right to rule as the dissenting Members of the Court urge, however painful this judgment is to announce. Though symbols often are what we ourselves make of them, the flag is constant in expressing beliefs Americans share, beliefs in law and peace and that freedom which sustains the human spirit. The case here today forces recognition of the costs to which those beliefs commit us. It is poignant but fundamental that the flag protects those who hold it in contempt.

For all the record shows, this respondent was not a philosopher and perhaps did not even possess the ability to comprehend how repellent his statements must be to the Republic itself. But whether or not he could appreciate the enormity of the offense he gave, the fact remains that his acts were speech, in both the technical and the fundamental meaning of the Constitution. So I agree with the Court that he must go free.

CHIEF JUSTICE REHNQUIST, with whom JUSTICE WHITE and JUSTICE O'CONNOR join, dissenting.

In holding this Texas statute unconstitutional, the Court ignores Justice Holmes' familiar aphorism that "a page of history is worth a volume of logic." *New York Trust Co. v. Eisner*, 256 U.S. 345, 349 (1921). For more than 200 years, the American flag has occupied a unique position as the symbol of our Nation, a uniqueness that justifies a governmental prohibition against flag burning in the way respondent Johnson did here.

The flag symbolizes the Nation in peace as well as in war. It signifies our national presence on battleships, airplanes, military installations, and public buildings from the United States Capitol to the thousands of county courthouses and city halls throughout the country. Two flags are prominently placed in our courtroom. Countless flags are placed by the graves of loved ones each year on what was first called Decoration Day, and is now called Memorial Day. The flag is traditionally placed on the casket of deceased members of the Armed Forces, and it is later given to the deceased's family. 10 U.S.C. §§ 1481, 1482. Congress has provided that the flag be flown at half-staff upon the death of the President, Vice President, and other government officials "as a mark of respect to their memory." 36 U.S.C. § 175(m).

The American flag, then, throughout more than 200 years of our history, has come to be the visible symbol embodying our Nation. It does not represent the views of any particular political party, and it does not represent any particular political philosophy. The flag is not simply another "idea" or "point of view" competing for recognition in the marketplace of ideas. Millions and millions of Americans regard it with an almost mystical reverence regardless of what sort of social, political, or philosophical beliefs they may have. I cannot agree that the First Amendment invalidates the Act of Congress, and the laws of 48 of the 50 States, which make criminal the public burning of the flag.

In *Chaplinsky v. New Hampshire*, 315 U.S. 568 (1942), a unanimous Court said:

"Allowing the broadest scope to the language and purpose of the Fourteenth Amendment, it is well understood that the right of free speech is not absolute at all times and under all circumstances. There are certain well-defined and narrowly limited classes of speech, the prevention and punishment of which have never been thought to raise any Constitutional problem. These include the lewd and obscene, the profane, the libelous, and the insulting or 'fighting' words—those which by their very utterance inflict injury or tend to incite an immediate breach of the peace. It has been well observed that such utterances are no essential part of any exposition of ideas, and are of such slight social value as a step to truth that any benefit that may be derived from them is clearly outweighed by the social interest in order and morality." *Id.*, at 571–572.

Here it may equally well be said that the public burning of the American flag by Johnson was no essential part of any exposition of ideas, and at the same time it had a tendency to incite a breach of the peace. Johnson was free to make any verbal denunciation of the flag that he wished; indeed, he was free to burn the flag in private. He could publicly burn other symbols of the Government or effigies of political leaders. He did lead a march through the streets of Dallas, and conducted a rally in front of the Dallas City Hall. He engaged in a "die-in" to protest nuclear weapons. He shouted out various slogans during the march * * *. For none of these acts was he arrested or prosecuted; it was only when he proceeded to burn publicly an American flag stolen from its rightful owner that he violated the Texas statute.

Johnson's public burning of the flag * * * obviously did convey [his] bitter dislike of his country. But his act * * * conveyed nothing that could not have been conveyed and was not conveyed just as forcefully in a dozen different ways. As with "fighting words," so with flag burning, for purposes of the First Amendment: It is "no essential part of any exposition of ideas, and [is] of such slight social value as a step to truth that any benefit that may be derived from [it] is clearly outweighed" by the public interest in avoiding a probable breach of the peace.

The Court decides that the American flag is just another symbol, about which not only must opinions pro and con be tolerated, but for which the most minimal public respect may not be enjoined. The government may conscript men into the Armed Forces where they must fight and perhaps die for the flag, but the government may not prohibit the public burning of the banner under which they fight. I would uphold the Texas statute as applied in this case.

JUSTICE STEVENS, dissenting.

The value of the flag as a symbol cannot be measured. Even so, I have no doubt that the interest in preserving that value for the future is both significant and legitimate. Conceivably that value will be enhanced by the Court's conclusion that our national commitment to free expression is so strong that even the United States as ultimate guarantor of that freedom is without power to prohibit the desecration of its unique symbol. But I am unpersuaded. The creation of a federal right to post bulletin boards and graffiti on the Washington Monument might enlarge the market for free expression, but at a cost I would not pay. Similarly, in my considered judgment, sanctioning the public desecration of the flag will tarnish its value—both for those who cherish the ideas for which it waves and for those who desire to don the robes of martyrdom by burning it. That tarnish is not justified by the trivial burden on free expression occasioned by requiring that an available, alternative mode of expression—including uttering words critical of the flag, see *Street v. New York,* 394 U.S. 576 (1969)—be employed.

Respondent was prosecuted because of the method he chose to express his dissatisfaction with those policies. Had he chosen to spray-paint * * * his message of dissatisfaction on the facade of the Lincoln Memorial, there would be no question about the power of the Government to prohibit his means of expression. The prohibition would be supported by the legitimate interest in preserving the quality of an important national asset. Though the asset at stake in this case is intangible, given its unique value, the same interest supports a prohibition on the desecration of the American flag.

POINTS FOR DISCUSSION

a.   Comparison to *O'Brien*

How does this case differ from *United States v. O'Brien*? Note that both involved "symbolic conduct" that led to criminal punishment. Why did the Court permit O'Brien's conviction for his conduct but prohibit the state from punishing Johnson?

b. Reasoning by Analogy

Justice Stevens suggested in his dissent that the statute under which Johnson was convicted was no different from a statute prohibiting a person from spray-painting a message on the Lincoln Memorial. Is there a difference between convicting a person under an anti-graffiti ordinance for spray-painting a message critical of the government on the side of a government building, on the one hand, and convicting Johnson under Texas's flag desecration law, on the other?

In answering this question, consider whether it would have violated the Texas statute if Johnson had been camping in the wilderness, became lost, and burned a flag—the only cloth he had other than his clothes—in order to stay warm. If such an act would not have run afoul of the Texas statute, what does it say about whether the statute was directed at a particular message? Is the same true of an ordinance prohibiting all graffiti on public buildings?

c. Carving out a Category for Flag Desecration

In his dissent, Chief Justice Rehnquist acknowledged that there is an expressive element to flag burning of the sort at issue in *Johnson*, but he urged the Court to treat it as a category of expression that, like obscenity, is outside the scope of First Amendment protection. Do you agree that the Court should exclude this form of symbolic conduct—or any other forms of symbolic conduct—from the protection of the First Amendment? What considerations are relevant in deciding whether to create such a category of expression? Are you satisfied that any such considerations argue here for exclusion?

d. Response by Congress

Congress responded to *Texas v. Johnson* by passing the Flag Protection Act of 1989. This federal act prohibited knowingly mutilating, defacing, defiling, burning, or trampling on a flag, without regard to whether the conduct might offend someone else. How is that different from the Texas law? Is the difference enough to make the federal law constitutional? The Court concluded that it was not. See *United States v. Eichman*, 496 U.S. 310 (1990). Can you make an argument that the Act should have survived scrutiny under the principles announced in *Johnson*?

Since the Court's decision in *Eichman*, Congress has on several occasions considered a proposed constitutional amendment that provides: "The Congress shall have power to prohibit the physical desecration of the flag of the United States." Although the House of Representatives has passed the Amendment by the requisite super-majority vote several times, the Senate has not, although it fell only one vote short one of the times that it considered it. Do you think that it would be a good idea to amend the Constitution to prohibit this form of conduct?

5. Provocative Speech

Can the government prohibit a person from saying something, not because the government specifically disapproves of the speech, but instead because the words might offend others and possibly lead to violence or other disruption? The answer is not so clear. We have already seen—in *Texas v. Johnson*, the flag desecration case—how the First Amendment imposes limits on the government's ability to criminalize expressive conduct solely because it might tend to offend others. How far do those limits extend? Can the government act when the offense is likely to be so great that it might provoke a violent response?

In this section, we consider several categories of offensive and provocative speech. We consider speech that is likely to provoke the listener to respond with violence against the speaker, otherwise known as "fighting words"; profanity; hate speech; and threats. As you read the materials that follow, consider whether these are separate categories that ought to be treated by their own distinctive rules, or instead whether there are broader themes that justify uniform treatment.

In the following case, the Supreme Court held that the First Amendment does not protect "insulting or 'fighting' words—those which by their very utterance inflict injury or tend to incite an immediate breach of the peace." Although the Court has never overruled the case, in no subsequent case has the Supreme Court upheld a government restriction on fighting words. As you read the case, consider whether it remains viable today, and whether, in light of the Court's decision in *Brandenburg*, it adds anything to the doctrine.

CHAPLINSKY V. STATE OF NEW HAMPSHIRE
315 U.S. 568 (1942)

MR. JUSTICE MURPHY delivered the opinion of the Court.

Appellant, a member of the sect known as Jehovah's Witnesses, was convicted in the municipal court of Rochester, New Hampshire, for violation of Chapter 378, Section 2, of the Public Laws of New Hampshire: "No person shall address any offensive, derisive or annoying word to any other person who is lawfully in any street or other public place, nor call him by any offensive or derisive name, nor make any noise or exclamation in his presence and hearing with intent to deride, offend or annoy him, or to prevent him from pursuing his lawful business or occupation."

The complaint charged that appellant "with force and arms, in a certain public place in said city of Rochester, to wit, on the public sidewalk on the easterly side of Wakefield Street, near unto the entrance of the City Hall, did unlawfully repeat, the words following, addressed to the complainant, that is to say, 'You are a God damned racketeer' and 'a damned Fascist and the whole government of Rochester are Fascists or agents of Fascists' the same being offensive, derisive and annoying words and names."

There is no substantial dispute over the facts. Chaplinsky was distributing the literature of his sect on the streets of Rochester on a busy Saturday afternoon. Members of the local citizenry complained to the City Marshal, Bowering, that Chaplinsky was denouncing all religion as a "racket." Bowering told them that Chaplinsky was lawfully engaged, and then warned Chaplinsky that the crowd was getting restless. Some time later a disturbance occurred and the traffic officer on duty at the busy intersection started with Chaplinsky for the police station, but did not inform him that he was under arrest or that he was going to be arrested. On the way they encountered Marshal Bowering who had been advised that a riot was under way and was therefore hurrying to the scene. Bowering repeated his earlier warning to Chaplinsky who then addressed to Bowering the words set forth in the complaint.

Chaplinsky's version of the affair was slightly different. He testified that when he met Bowering, he asked him to arrest the ones responsible for the disturbance. In reply Bowering cursed him and told him to come along. Appellant admitted that he said the words charged in the complaint with the exception of the name of the Deity.

Allowing the broadest scope to the language and purpose of the Fourteenth Amendment, it is well understood that the right of free speech is not absolute at all times and under all circumstances. There are certain well-defined and narrowly limited classes of speech, the prevention and punishment of which has never been thought to raise any Constitutional problem. These include the lewd and obscene, the profane, the libelous, and the insulting or "fighting" words—those which by their very utterance inflict injury or tend to incite an immediate breach of the peace. It has been well observed that such utterances are no essential part of any exposition of ideas, and are of such slight social value as a step to truth that any benefit that may be derived from them is clearly outweighed by the social interest in order and morality. "Resort to epithets or personal abuse is not in any proper sense communication of information or opinion safeguarded by the Constitution, and its punishment as a criminal act would raise no question under that instrument." *Cantwell v. Connecticut*, 310 U.S. 296, 309, 310 (1940).

The state statute here challenged comes to us authoritatively construed by the highest court of New Hampshire. * * * On the authority of its earlier decisions, the state court declared that the statute's purpose was to preserve the public peace, no words being "forbidden except such as have a direct tendency to cause acts of violence by the person to whom, individually, the remark is addressed." It was further said: "The word 'offensive' is not to be defined in terms of what a particular addressee thinks. * * * The test is what men of common intelligence would understand would be words likely to cause an average addressee to fight. * * * The English language has a number of words and expressions which by general consent are 'fighting words' when said without a disarming smile. * * * Such words, as ordinary men know, are likely to cause a fight. * * *"

> **Take Note**
>
> The highest court of each state makes the final determination of the meaning of state law. The Supreme Court makes the final determination of the meaning of federal law, including the U.S. Constitution. Accordingly, when the Supreme Court reviews the constitutionality of a state law, it accepts the meaning of the law adopted by the state courts, but determines for itself whether the law is unconstitutional.

We are unable to say that the limited scope of the statute as thus construed contravenes the constitutional right of free expression. It is a statute narrowly drawn and limited to define and punish specific conduct lying within the domain of state power, the use in a public place of words likely to cause a breach of the peace. This conclusion necessarily disposes of appellant's contention that the statute is so vague and indefinite as to render a conviction thereunder a violation of due process. A statute punishing verbal acts, carefully drawn so as not unduly to impair liberty of expression, is not too vague for a criminal law.

Nor can we say that the application of the statute to the facts disclosed by the record substantially or unreasonably impinges upon the privilege of free speech. Argument is unnecessary to demonstrate that the appellations "damn racketeer" and "damn Fascist" are epithets likely to provoke the average person to retaliation, and thereby cause a breach of the peace. Affirmed.

POINTS FOR DISCUSSION

a. Understanding the Decision

The Court gives several distinct reasons for concluding that fighting words lack First Amendment protection. Can you identify them? Is the Court's reasoning consistent with other cases that we have seen? Note that the Court cited *Chaplinsky* in *Roth v. United States*, which concluded that obscenity is not protected by the First

Amendment, and Chief Justice Rehnquist cited it in his dissent in *Texas v. Johnson*, the flag-burning case.

b. Alternative Rationale

Could the Supreme Court have reached the same conclusion by a different method of reasoning? For example, could the Court have said that Chaplinsky's words were protected by the First Amendment, but that New Hampshire could impose reasonable restrictions on the time, place, and manner in which Chaplinsky uttered them? Consider the following suggestion by Judge Richard Posner: "[W]hile the First Amendment surely prevents the government from interfering with the dissemination of offensive ideas, it is less clear why it should be thought to privilege their dissemination by means that show an intent not to persuade, but instead to incite a violent reaction either from ordinarily peaceable people or from extremists at the other end of the political spectrum * * *." *Church of American Knights of Ku Klux Klan v. City of Gary, Indiana*, 334 F.3d 676, 684 (7th Cir. 2003). Do you agree that the New Hampshire statute would survive scrutiny as a reasonable time, place, and manner restriction? Was it content neutral?

Regardless of the Court's reasoning in 1942, is the "fighting words" exception really just a specific application today of the *Brandenburg* doctrine about incitement? In the Court's view, aren't fighting words just an invitation to engage in assault and battery?

c. Fighting Words

Putting aside the problems of vagueness, which the Court in *Chaplinsky* rejected, do you agree that there are words or epithets that are "likely to provoke the average person to retaliation"? To *physical* retaliation? Under the Court's view of the First Amendment, is it not just sticks and stones that lead to broken bones, but also words? In answering that question, consider that the Supreme Court has not upheld a conviction under the fighting words doctrine since 1942, when it decided *Chaplinsky*.

———————

The Court did not offer very specific guidance in *Chaplinsky* about what counts as fighting words, other than to conclude that calling someone a "damn racketeer" and "damn Fascist" apparently can be sufficient. The case that followed concerned more colorful language. Even if profanity is not alone always enough to amount to fighting words, should profanity simply be considered another category outside of the protection of the First Amendment?

COHEN V. CALIFORNIA

403 U.S. 15 (1971)

MR. JUSTICE HARLAN delivered the opinion of the Court.

This case may seem at first blush too inconsequential to find its way into our books, but the issue it presents is of no small constitutional significance. Appellant Paul Robert Cohen was convicted in the Los Angeles Municipal Court of violating that part of California Penal Code § 415 which prohibits "maliciously and willfully disturb[ing] the peace or quiet of any neighborhood or person [by] offensive conduct * * *." He was given 30 days' imprisonment. The facts upon which his conviction rests are detailed in the opinion of the Court of Appeal of California, Second Appellate District, as follows:

> On April 26, 1968, the defendant was observed in the Los Angeles County Courthouse in the corridor outside of division 20 of the municipal court wearing a jacket bearing the words "Fuck the Draft" which were plainly visible. There were women and children present in the corridor. The defendant was arrested. The defendant testified that he wore the jacket knowing that the words were on the jacket as a means of informing the public of the depth of his feelings against the Vietnam War and the draft.

> The defendant did not engage in, nor threaten to engage in, nor did anyone as the result of his conduct in fact commit or threaten to commit any act of violence. The defendant did not make any loud or unusual noise, nor was there any evidence that he uttered any sound prior to his arrest.

The conviction quite clearly rests upon the asserted offensiveness of the words Cohen used to convey his message to the public. The only "conduct" which the State sought to punish is the fact of communication. Thus, we deal here with a conviction resting solely upon "speech," not upon any separately identifiable conduct which allegedly was intended by Cohen to be perceived by others as expressive of particular views but which, on its face, does not necessarily convey any message and hence arguably could be regulated without effectively repressing Cohen's ability to express himself. *Cf. United States v. O'Brien*, 391 U.S. 367 (1968). Further, the State certainly lacks power to punish Cohen for the underlying content of the message the inscription conveyed. At least so long as there is no showing of an intent to incite disobedience to or disruption of the draft, Cohen could not, consistently with the First and Fourteenth Amendments, be punished for asserting the evident position on the inutility or immorality of the draft his jacket reflected.

Appellant's conviction, then, rests squarely upon his exercise of the "freedom of speech" protected from arbitrary governmental interference by the Constitution and can be justified, if at all, only as a valid regulation of the manner in which he exercised that freedom, not as a permissible prohibition on the substantive message it conveys. * * *

This Court has * * * held that the States are free to ban the simple use, without a demonstration of additional justifying circumstances, of so-called "fighting words," those personally abusive epithets which, when addressed to the ordinary citizen, are, as a matter of common knowledge, inherently likely to provoke violent reaction. *Chaplinsky v. New Hampshire*, 315 U.S. 568 (1942). While the four-letter word displayed by Cohen in relation to the draft is not uncommonly employed in a personally provocative fashion, in this instance it was clearly not "directed to the person of the hearer." *Cantwell v. Connecticut*, 310 U.S. 296, 309 (1940). No individual actually or likely to be present could reasonably have regarded the words on appellant's jacket as a direct personal insult. Nor do we have here an instance of the exercise of the State's police power to prevent a speaker from intentionally provoking a given group to hostile reaction. There is, as noted above, no showing that anyone who saw Cohen was in fact violently aroused or that appellant intended such a result.

Finally, in arguments before this Court much has been made of the claim that Cohen's distasteful mode of expression was thrust upon unwilling or unsuspecting viewers, and that the State might therefore legitimately act as it did in order to protect the sensitive from otherwise unavoidable exposure to appellant's crude form of protest. Of course, the mere presumed presence of unwitting listeners or viewers does not serve automatically to justify curtailing all speech capable of giving offense. While this Court has recognized that government may properly act in many situations to prohibit intrusion into the privacy of the home of unwelcome views and ideas which cannot be totally banned from the public dialogue, e.g., *Rowan v. United States Post Office Dept.*, 397 U.S. 728 (1970), we have at the same time consistently stressed that "we are often 'captives' outside the sanctuary of the home and subject to objectionable speech." *Id.* at 738. The ability of government, consonant with the Constitution, to shut off discourse solely to protect others from hearing it is, in other words, dependent upon a showing that substantial privacy interests are being invaded in an essentially intolerable manner. Any broader view of this authority would effectively empower a majority to silence dissidents simply as a matter of personal predilections.

In this regard, persons confronted with Cohen's jacket were in a quite different posture than, say, those subjected to the raucous emissions of sound trucks blaring outside their residences. Those in the Los Angeles courthouse could effectively avoid further bombardment of their sensibilities simply by averting their eyes. * * *

Against this background, the issue flushed by this case stands out in bold relief. It is whether California can excise, as "offensive conduct," one particular scurrilous epithet from the public discourse, either upon the theory of the court below that its use is inherently likely to cause violent reaction or upon a more general assertion that the States, acting as guardians of public morality, may properly remove this offensive word from the public vocabulary.

We have been shown no evidence that substantial numbers of citizens are standing ready to strike out physically at whoever may assault their sensibilities with execrations like that uttered by Cohen. There may be some persons about with such lawless and violent proclivities, but that is an insufficient base upon which to erect, consistently with constitutional values, a governmental power to force persons who wish to ventilate their dissident views into avoiding particular forms of expression. The argument amounts to little more than the self-defeating proposition that to avoid physical censorship of one who has not sought to provoke such a response by a hypothetical coterie of the violent and lawless, the States may more appropriately effectuate that censorship themselves.

Admittedly, it is not so obvious that the First and Fourteenth Amendments must be taken to disable the States from punishing public utterance of this unseemly expletive in order to maintain what they regard as a suitable level of discourse within the body politic. We think, however, that examination and reflection will reveal the shortcomings of a contrary viewpoint. * * * The constitutional right of free expression is powerful medicine in a society as diverse and populous as ours. It is designed and intended to remove governmental restraints from the arena of public discussion, putting the decision as to what views shall be voiced largely into the hands of each of us, in the hope that use of such freedom will ultimately produce a more capable citizenry and more perfect polity and in the belief that no other approach would comport with the premise of individual dignity and choice upon which our political system rests. See *Whitney v. California*, 274 U.S. 357, 375–377 (1927) (Brandeis, J., concurring).

To many, the immediate consequence of this freedom may often appear to be only verbal tumult, discord, and even offensive utterance. These are, however, within established limits, in truth necessary side effects of the broader enduring values which the process of open debate permits us to achieve. That the air may at times seem filled with verbal cacophony is, in this sense not a sign of weakness but of strength. We cannot lose sight of the fact that, in what otherwise might seem a trifling and annoying instance of individual distasteful abuse of a privilege, these fundamental societal values are truly implicated.

Against this perception of the constitutional policies involved, we discern certain more particularized considerations that peculiarly call for reversal of this conviction. First, the principle contended for by the State seems inherently boundless. How is one to distinguish this from any other offensive word? Surely the State has no right to cleanse public debate to the point where it is grammatically palatable to the most squeamish among us. Yet no readily ascertainable general principle exists for stopping short of that result were we to affirm the judgment below. For, while the particular four-letter word being litigated here is perhaps more distasteful than most others of its genre, it is nevertheless often true that one man's vulgarity is another's lyric. Indeed, we think it is largely because governmental officials cannot make principled distinctions in this area that the Constitution leaves matters of taste and style so largely to the individual.

Additionally, we cannot overlook the fact, because it is well illustrated by the episode involved here, that much linguistic expression serves a dual communicative function: it conveys not only ideas capable of relatively precise, detached explication, but otherwise inexpressible emotions as well. In fact, words are often chosen as much for their emotive as their cognitive force. We cannot sanction the view that the Constitution, while solicitous of the cognitive content of individual speech has little or no regard for that emotive function which practically speaking, may often be the more important element of the overall message sought to be communicated.

Finally, and in the same vein, we cannot indulge the facile assumption that one can forbid particular words without also running a substantial risk of suppressing ideas in the process. Indeed, governments might soon seize upon the censorship of particular words as a convenient guise for banning the expression of unpopular views.

It is, in sum, our judgment that, absent a more particularized and compelling reason for its actions, the State may not, consistently with the First and Fourteenth Amendments, make the simple public display here involved of this single four-letter expletive a criminal offense. Because that is the only arguably sustainable rationale for the conviction here at issue, the judgment below must be reversed.

MR. JUSTICE BLACKMUN, with whom THE CHIEF JUSTICE and MR. JUSTICE BLACK join.

I dissent * * *.

Cohen's absurd and immature antic, in my view, was mainly conduct and little speech. * * * Further, the case appears to me to be well within the sphere of *Chaplinsky v. New Hampshire*, 315 U.S. 568 (1942), where Mr. Justice Murphy, a known champion of First Amendment freedoms, wrote for a unanimous bench. As a consequence, this Court's agonizing over First Amendment values seem misplaced and unnecessary.

POINTS FOR DISCUSSION

a. The Value of Words

The Court in *Cohen* gave several reasons why the state could not punish the defendant for the words on his jacket. Can you articulate those reasons? Under the Court's reasoning, are there *any* words that are so offensive or likely to cause the listener to fight that the state can ban their use? If so, what are they? How can the court identify which words are proscribable and which are not?

b. Comparing *Cohen* and *Chaplinsky*

In the Court's view, *Cohen*, unlike *Chaplinsky*, did not involve "words likely to cause an average addressee to fight." But *Chaplinsky* also gave other rationales for banning fighting words, namely that they formed "no essential part of any exposition of ideas" and that "by their very utterance [they] inflict injury." Was the same true for the words on Cohen's jacket? If not, is it because the words at issue in *Cohen* were different in kind, or instead because the Court in *Chaplinsky* under-valued the importance of the words at issue there?

Problem

Pursuant to a federal statute prohibiting "obscene, indecent, or profane" language on the airwaves, the Federal Communications Commission adopted a policy to impose penalties for "fleeting expletives"—that is, the occasional utterance of expletives during a live broadcast. A television network ordered to pay a substantial fine under the policy challenged the order as violating the First Amendment. How should the Court rule? (We will consider special rules that apply to television broadcasters in Chapter 9, when we take up the freedom of the press.)

Can the government ban "hate speech"—that is, speech that communicates hatred on the basis of race or some other status-based criterion—that is likely to cause the listener to fight? The Court took up that question in the case that follows.

R.A.V. v. CITY OF ST. PAUL, MINN.
505 U.S. 377 (1992)

JUSTICE SCALIA delivered the opinion of the Court.

In the predawn hours of June 21, 1990, petitioner and several other teenagers allegedly assembled a crudely made cross by taping together broken chair legs. They then allegedly burned the cross inside the fenced yard of a black family that lived across the street from the house where petitioner was staying. Although this conduct could have been punished under any of a number of laws, one of the two provisions under which respondent city of St. Paul chose to charge petitioner (then a juvenile) was the St. Paul Bias-Motivated Crime Ordinance, which provides:

> Whoever places on public or private property a symbol, object, appellation, characterization or graffiti, including, but not limited to, a burning cross or Nazi swastika, which one knows or has reasonable grounds to know arouses anger, alarm or resentment in others on the basis of race, color, creed, religion or gender commits disorderly conduct and shall be guilty of a misdemeanor.]→ also protects 1 side of arg. more

Petitioner moved to dismiss this count on the ground that the St. Paul ordinance was substantially overbroad and impermissibly content based and therefore facially invalid under the First Amendment. * * *

In construing the St. Paul ordinance, we are bound by the construction given to it by the Minnesota court. Accordingly, we accept the Minnesota Supreme Court's authoritative statement that the ordinance reaches only those expressions that constitute "fighting words" within the meaning of *Chaplinsky v. New Hampshire*, 315 U.S. 568, 572 (1942). Petitioner and his *amici* urge us to modify the scope of the *Chaplinsky* formulation, thereby invalidating the ordinance as "substantially overbroad," *Broadrick v. Oklahoma*, 413 U.S. 601, 610 (1973). We find it unnecessary to consider this issue. Assuming, *arguendo*, that all of the expression reached by the ordinance is proscribable under the "fighting words" doctrine, we nonetheless conclude that the ordinance is facially unconstitutional in that it prohibits otherwise permitted speech solely on the basis of the subjects the speech addresses.

The First Amendment generally prevents government from proscribing speech, *see, e.g., Cantwell v. Connecticut,* 310 U.S. 296, 309–311 (1940), or even expressive conduct, *see, e.g., Texas v. Johnson,* 491 U.S. 397, 406 (1989), because of disapproval of the ideas expressed. Content-based regulations are presumptively invalid. *Simon & Schuster, Inc. v. Members of N.Y. State Crime Victims Bd.,* 502 U.S. 105, 115 (1991). From 1791 to the present, however, our society, like other free but civilized societies, has permitted restrictions upon the content of speech in a few limited areas, which are "of such slight social value as a step to truth that any benefit that may be derived from them is clearly outweighed by the social interest in order and morality." *Chaplinsky,* 315 U.S., at 572. We have recognized that "the freedom of speech" referred to by the First Amendment does not include a freedom to disregard these traditional limitations. See, *e.g., Roth v. United States,* 354 U.S. 476 (1957) (obscenity); *Beauharnais v. Illinois,* 343 U.S. 250 (1952) (defamation); *Chaplinsky v. New Hampshire, supra* (" 'fighting' words"). Our decisions since the 1960s have narrowed the scope of the traditional categorical exceptions for defamation, but a limited categorical approach has remained an important part of our First Amendment jurisprudence.

We have sometimes said that these categories of expression are "not within the area of constitutionally protected speech," *Roth v. United States,* 354 U.S. 476, 483 (1957), or that the "protection of the First Amendment does not extend" to them, *Bose Corp. v. Consumers Union of United States, Inc.,* 466 U.S. 485, 504 (1984). Such statements must be taken in context, however * * *. What they mean is that these areas of speech can, consistently with the First Amendment, be regulated *because of their constitutionally proscribable content* (obscenity, defamation, etc.)—not that they are categories of speech entirely invisible to the Constitution, so that they may be made the vehicles for content discrimination unrelated to their distinctively proscribable content. Thus, the government may proscribe libel; but it may not make the further content discrimination of proscribing *only* libel critical of the government.

Our cases surely do not establish the proposition that the First Amendment imposes no obstacle whatsoever to regulation of particular instances of such proscribable expression, so that the government "may regulate [them] freely." That would mean that a city council could enact an ordinance prohibiting only those legally obscene works that contain criticism of the city government or, indeed, that do not include endorsement of the city government. Such a simplistic, all-or-nothing-at-all approach to First Amendment protection is at odds with common sense and with our jurisprudence as well. It is not true that "fighting words" have at most a "*de minimis*" expressive content, or that their content is *in all respects* "worthless and undeserving of constitutional protection"; sometimes they are quite expressive indeed. We have not said that they constitute "*no* part of the expression of ideas," but only that they constitute "no *essential* part of any exposition of ideas." *Chaplinsky*, 315 U.S., at 572 (emphasis added).

The proposition that a particular instance of speech can be proscribable on the basis of one feature (*e.g.*, obscenity) but not on the basis of another (*e.g.*, opposition to the city government) is commonplace and has found application in many contexts. We have long held, for example, that nonverbal expressive activity can be banned because of the action it entails, but not because of the ideas it expresses—so that burning a flag in violation of an ordinance against outdoor fires could be punishable, whereas burning a flag in violation of an ordinance against dishonoring the flag is not. See *Johnson*, 491 U.S., at 406–407. Similarly, we have upheld reasonable "time, place, or manner" restrictions, but only if they are "justified without reference to the content of the regulated speech." *Ward v. Rock Against Racism*, 491 U.S. 781, 791 (1989) (internal quotation marks omitted). And just as the power to proscribe particular speech on the basis of a noncontent element (*e.g.*, noise) does not entail the power to proscribe the same speech on the basis of a content element; so also, the power to proscribe it on the basis of *one* content element (*e.g.*, obscenity) does not entail the power to proscribe it on the basis of *other* content elements.

The concurrences describe us as setting forth a new First Amendment principle that prohibition of constitutionally proscribable speech cannot be "underinclusiv[e]"—a First Amendment "absolutism" whereby "[w]ithin a particular 'proscribable' category of expression, [a] government must either proscribe all speech or no speech at all." That easy target is of the concurrences' own invention. In our view, the First Amendment imposes not an "underinclusiveness" limitation but a "content discrimination" limitation upon a State's prohibition of proscribable speech. There is no problem whatever, for example, with a State's prohibiting obscenity (and other forms of proscribable expression) only in certain media or markets, for although that prohibition would be "underinclusive," it would not discriminate on the basis of content.

Even the prohibition against content discrimination that we assert the First Amendment requires is not absolute. It applies differently in the context of proscribable speech than in the area of fully protected speech. * * * When the basis for the content discrimination consists entirely of the very reason the entire class of speech at issue is proscribable, no significant danger of idea or viewpoint discrimination exists. Such a reason, having been adjudged neutral enough to support exclusion of the entire class of speech from First Amendment protection, is also neutral enough to form the basis of distinction within the class. To illustrate: A State might choose to prohibit only that obscenity which is the most patently offensive *in its prurience*—i.e., that which involves the most lascivious displays of sexual activity. But it may not prohibit, for example, only that obscenity which includes offensive *political* messages. And the Federal Government can criminalize only those threats of violence that are directed against the President, see 18 U.S.C. § 871—since the reasons why threats of violence are outside the First Amendment (protecting individuals from the fear of violence, from the disruption that fear engenders, and from the possibility that the threatened violence will occur) have special force when applied to the person of the President. See *Watts v. United States*, 394 U.S. 705, 707 (1969). But the Federal Government may not criminalize only those threats against the President that mention his policy on aid to inner cities.

Another valid basis for according differential treatment to even a content-defined subclass of proscribable speech is that the subclass happens to be associated with particular "secondary effects" of the speech, so that the regulation is "justified without reference to the content of the . . . speech," *Renton v. Playtime Theatres, Inc.*, 475 U.S. 41, 48 (1986). A State could, for example, permit all obscene live performances except those involving minors. Moreover, since words can in some circumstances violate laws directed not against speech but against conduct (a law against treason, for example, is violated by telling the enemy the Nation's defense secrets), a particular content-based subcategory of a proscribable class of speech can be swept up incidentally within the reach of a statute directed at conduct rather than speech. Thus, for example, sexually derogatory "fighting words," among other words, may produce a violation of Title VII's general prohibition against sexual discrimination in employment practices. Where the government does not target conduct on the basis of its expressive content, acts are not shielded from regulation merely because they express a discriminatory idea or philosophy. [In addition,] it may not even be necessary to identify any particular "neutral" basis, so long as the nature of the content discrimination is such that there is no realistic possibility that official suppression of ideas is afoot.

Applying these principles to the St. Paul ordinance, we conclude that, even as narrowly construed by the Minnesota Supreme Court, the ordinance is facially unconstitutional. Although the phrase in the ordinance, "arouses anger, alarm or resentment in others," has been limited by the Minnesota Supreme Court's construction to reach only those symbols or displays that amount to "fighting words," the remaining, unmodified terms make clear that the ordinance applies only to "fighting words" that insult, or provoke violence, "on the basis of race, color, creed, religion or gender." Displays containing abusive invective, no matter how vicious or severe, are permissible unless they are addressed to one of the specified disfavored topics. Those who wish to use "fighting words" in connection with other ideas—to express hostility, for example, on the basis of political affiliation, union membership, or homosexuality—are not covered. The First Amendment does not permit St. Paul to impose special prohibitions on those speakers who express views on disfavored subjects.

In its practical operation, moreover, the ordinance goes even beyond mere content discrimination, to actual viewpoint discrimination. Displays containing some words—odious racial epithets, for example—would be prohibited to proponents of all views. But "fighting words" that do not themselves invoke race, color, creed, religion, or gender—aspersions upon a person's mother, for example—would seemingly be usable *ad libitum* in the placards of those arguing in favor of racial, color, etc., tolerance and equality, but could not be used by those speakers' opponents. One could hold up a sign saying, for example, that all "anti-Catholic bigots" are misbegotten; but not that all "papists" are, for that would insult and provoke violence "on the basis of religion." St. Paul has no such authority to license one side of a debate to fight freestyle, while requiring the other to follow Marquis of Queensberry rules.

* * * Justice STEVENS suggests that [the ordinance] is directed, [not] to speech of a particular content, but to particular "injur[ies]" that are "qualitatively different" from other injuries. This is wordplay. What makes the anger, fear, sense of dishonor, etc., produced by violation of this ordinance distinct from the anger, fear, sense of dishonor, etc., produced by other fighting words is nothing other than the fact that it is caused by a distinctive idea, conveyed by a distinctive message. The First Amendment cannot be evaded that easily.

The content-based discrimination reflected in the St. Paul ordinance comes within neither any of the specific exceptions to the First Amendment prohibition we discussed earlier nor a more general exception for content discrimination that does not threaten censorship of ideas. It assuredly does not fall within the exception for content discrimination based on the very reasons why the particular class of speech at issue (here, fighting words) is proscribable. * * * St. Paul has not singled out an especially offensive mode of expression—it has not, for example, selected for prohibition only those fighting words that communicate ideas in a threatening (as opposed to a merely obnoxious) manner. Rather, it has proscribed fighting words of whatever manner that communicate messages of racial, gender, or religious intolerance. Selectivity of this sort creates the possibility that the city is seeking to handicap the expression of particular ideas.

St. Paul [argues that], even if the ordinance regulates expression based on hostility towards its protected ideological content, this discrimination is nonetheless justified because it is narrowly tailored to serve compelling state interests. Specifically, they assert that the ordinance helps to ensure the basic human rights of members of groups that have historically been subjected to discrimination, including the right of such group members to live in peace where they wish. We do not doubt that these interests are compelling, and that the ordinance can be said to promote them. But [the ordinance's content discrimination is not] reasonably necessary to achieve St. Paul's compelling interests * * *. An ordinance not limited to the favored topics, for example, would have precisely the same beneficial effect. In fact the only interest distinctively served by the content limitation is that of displaying the city council's special hostility towards the particular biases thus singled out. That is precisely what the First Amendment forbids. The politicians of St. Paul are entitled to express that hostility—but not through the means of imposing unique limitations upon speakers who (however benightedly) disagree.

JUSTICE WHITE, with whom JUSTICE BLACKMUN and JUSTICE O'CONNOR join, and with whom JUSTICE STEVENS joins except as to Part I-A, concurring in the judgment.

This Court's decisions have plainly stated that expression falling within certain limited categories so lacks the values the First Amendment was designed to protect that the Constitution affords no protection to that expression. * * * Thus, [this] Court has long held certain discrete categories of expression [including child pornography, obscenity, and some forms of libel] to be proscribable on the basis of their content. * * * All of these categories are content based. But the Court has held that the First Amendment does not apply to them because their expressive content is worthless or of de minimis value to society. *Chaplinsky v. New Hampshire*, 315 U.S. 568, 571–572 (1942). We have not departed from this principle, emphasizing repeatedly that, "within the confines of [these] given classification[s], the evil to be restricted so overwhelmingly outweighs the expressive interests, if any, at stake, that no process of case-by-case adjudication is required." *New York v. Ferber*, 458 U.S. 747, 763–764 (1982). This categorical approach has provided a principled and narrowly focused means for distinguishing between expression that the government may regulate freely and that which it may regulate on the basis of content only upon a showing of compelling need.

It is inconsistent to hold that the government may proscribe an entire category of speech because the content of that speech is evil, but that the government may not treat a subset of that category differently without violating the First Amendment; the content of the subset is by definition worthless and undeserving of constitutional protection. * * * Fighting words are not a means of exchanging views, rallying supporters, or registering a protest; they are directed against individuals to provoke violence or to inflict injury. *Chaplinsky*, 315 U.S., at 572. Therefore, a ban on all fighting words or on a subset of the fighting words category would restrict only the social evil of hate speech, without creating the danger of driving viewpoints from the marketplace. * * * Any contribution of [the Court's] holding to First Amendment jurisprudence is surely a negative one, since it necessarily signals that expressions of violence, such as the message of intimidation and racial hatred conveyed by burning a cross on someone's lawn, are of sufficient value to outweigh the social interest in order and morality that has traditionally placed such fighting words outside the First Amendment.

In a second break with precedent, the Court refuses to sustain the ordinance even though it would survive under the strict scrutiny applicable to other protected expression. * * * The Court expressly concedes that [St. Paul's] interest is compelling and is promoted by the ordinance. Nevertheless, the Court treats strict scrutiny analysis as irrelevant to the constitutionality of the legislation. * * * Under the majority's view, a narrowly drawn, content-based ordinance could never pass constitutional muster if the object of that legislation could be accomplished by banning a wider category of speech. This appears to be a general renunciation of strict scrutiny review, a fundamental tool of First Amendment analysis.

[The Court also creates an exception to] its newly announced First Amendment rule: Content-based distinctions may be drawn within an unprotected category of speech if the basis for the distinctions is "the very reason the entire class of speech at issue is proscribable." * * * The exception swallows the majority's rule. Certainly, it should apply to the St. Paul ordinance * * *. A prohibition on fighting words [is] a ban on a class of speech that conveys an overriding message of personal injury and imminent violence, a message that is at its ugliest when directed against groups that have long been the targets of discrimination. Accordingly, the ordinance falls within the first exception to the majority's theory.

Although I disagree with the Court's analysis, I do agree with its conclusion: The St. Paul ordinance is unconstitutional. * * * Although the ordinance as construed reaches categories of speech that are constitutionally unprotected, it also criminalizes a substantial amount of expression that—however repugnant— is shielded by the First Amendment. * * * The mere fact that expressive activity causes hurt feelings, offense, or resentment does not render the expression unprotected. * * * The ordinance is therefore fatally overbroad and invalid on its face. * * * I join the judgment, but not the folly of the opinion.

JUSTICE BLACKMUN, concurring in the judgment.

I fear that the Court has been distracted from its proper mission by the temptation to decide the issue over "politically correct speech" and "cultural diversity," neither of which is presented here. * * *

I see no First Amendment values that are compromised by a law that prohibits hoodlums from driving minorities out of their homes by burning crosses on their lawns, but I see great harm in preventing the people of Saint Paul from specifically punishing the race-based fighting words that so prejudice their community. I concur in the judgment, however, because I agree with Justice WHITE that this particular ordinance reaches beyond fighting words to speech protected by the First Amendment.

JUSTICE STEVENS, with whom JUSTICE WHITE and JUSTICE BLACKMUN join as to Part I, concurring in the judgment.

[W]hile the Court rejects the "all-or-nothing-at-all" nature of the categorical approach, it promptly embraces an absolutism of its own: Within a particular "proscribable" category of expression, the Court holds, a government must either proscribe *all* speech or no speech at all. * * * This new absolutism in the prohibition of content-based regulations severely contorts the fabric of settled First Amendment law.

Although I agree with much of Justice WHITE's analysis, I have reservations about the "categorical approach" to the First Amendment. * * * Admittedly, the categorical approach to the First Amendment has some appeal: Either expression is protected or it is not—the categories create safe harbors for governments and speakers alike. But this approach sacrifices subtlety for clarity and is, I am convinced, ultimately unsound. As an initial matter, the concept of "categories" fits poorly with the complex reality of expression. Few dividing lines in First Amendment law are straight and unwavering, and efforts at categorization inevitably give rise only to fuzzy boundaries. Our definitions of "obscenity" * * * illustrate this all too well. * * * Moreover, [the] history of the categorical approach is largely the history of narrowing the categories of unprotected speech. * * * This evolution, I believe, indicates that the categorical approach is unworkable and the quest for absolute categories of "protected" and "unprotected" speech ultimately futile.

Unlike the Court, I do not believe that all content-based regulations are equally infirm and presumptively invalid; unlike Justice WHITE, I do not believe that fighting words are wholly unprotected by the First Amendment. To the contrary, I believe our decisions establish a more complex and subtle analysis, one that considers the content and context of the regulated speech, and the nature and scope of the restriction on speech. Applying this analysis and assuming, *arguendo*, (as the Court does) that the St. Paul ordinance is *not* overbroad, I conclude that such a selective, subject-matter regulation on proscribable speech is constitutional.

[T]he ordinance (by hypothesis) regulates *only* fighting words. * * * By hypothesis, then, the St. Paul ordinance restricts speech in confrontational and potentially violent situations. * * * Significantly, the St. Paul ordinance regulates speech not on the basis of its subject matter or the viewpoint expressed, but rather on the basis of the *harm* the speech causes. [J]ust as the ordinance would prohibit a Muslim from hoisting a sign claiming that all Catholics were misbegotten, so the ordinance would bar a Catholic from hoisting a similar sign attacking Muslims.

Finally, it is noteworthy that the St. Paul ordinance is, as construed by the Court today, quite narrow. The St. Paul ordinance does not ban all "hate speech," nor does it ban, say, all cross burnings or all swastika displays. Rather it only bans a subcategory of the already narrow category of fighting words. Such a limited ordinance leaves open and protected a vast range of expression on the subjects of racial, religious, and gender equality. * * * Taken together, these several considerations persuade me that the St. Paul ordinance is not an unconstitutional content-based regulation of speech. Thus, were the ordinance not overbroad, I would vote to uphold it.

POINTS FOR DISCUSSION

a.   Content-Based Restrictions on Unprotected Speech

In *New York v. Ferber*, 458 U.S. 747, 765 n.18 (1982), which we discussed above, the Supreme Court held that "child pornography [is] unprotected speech subject to content-based regulation. Hence, it cannot be underinclusive or unconstitutional for a State to do precisely that." But in *R.A.V.*, although the Court recognized that fighting words are unprotected speech, it concluded that fighting words cannot be subjected to content-based restrictions. Does this inconsistency call *Ferber* into doubt, or is there an explanation for it? Logically speaking, if a particular category of speech is unprotected, should the government be able to impose content-based restrictions on it? Does the greater power here include the lesser power?

b.   Solving All Problems at Once

In other First Amendment cases, the Court has said that the government "need not deal with every problem at once." *Denver Area Educational Telecommunications Consortium, Inc. v. F.C.C.*, 518 U.S. 727, 757 (1996). Was the Court effectively saying in *R.A.V.* that, if a state wants to ban fighting words, it must ban them in all contexts at once? Must a state address the problems of fighting words concerning "political affiliation, union membership, or homosexuality" at the same time that it addresses the problem of fighting words concerning "race, color, creed, religion or gender?" What if only some of the problems have actually arisen in the state?

c.   Threats

When one person threatens another—particularly when he does so in words— he communicates a message. Are threats protected speech, or are they instead outside of the protection of the First Amendment? In *R.A.V.*, the Court suggested that they were not. And, indeed, in *Watts v. United States*, 394 U.S. 705 (1969), which involved a statute (18 U.S.C. § 871) that criminalizes threats of violence directed against the President, the Court implied that genuine threats are not protected speech. The petitioner had been convicted for stating, "I have already received my draft classification as 1-A and I have got to report for my physical this Monday coming. I am not going. If they ever make me carry a rifle the first man I want to get in my sights is L.B.J. * * * They are not going to make me kill my black brothers." In its brief opinion, the Court reversed the petitioner's conviction. The Court stated:

> Certainly the statute under which petitioner was convicted is constitutional on its face. The Nation undoubtedly has a valid, even an overwhelming, interest in protecting the safety of its Chief Executive and in allowing him to perform his duties without interference from threats of physical violence. Nevertheless, a statute such as this one, which makes criminal a form of pure speech, must be interpreted with the commands of the First Amendment clearly in mind. What is a threat must be distinguished from what is constitutionally protected speech.

The Court reversed the petitioner's conviction because "the statute initially requires the Government to prove a true 'threat.' We do not believe that the kind of political hyperbole indulged in by petitioner fits within that statutory term." Does the Court's decision mean that all genuine threats are simply beyond the protection of the First Amendment? If so, why? And if they are unprotected speech, after *R.A.V.* can the government decide to criminalize only some threats, defined by the content of the threats?

In *Virginia v. Black*, 538 U.S. 343 (2003), the Court considered a Virginia statute that made it a crime to burn a cross with "the intent to intimidate a person or group of persons." The Court first traced the history of cross burning and noted that it is a "symbol of hate" that is often used to convey a message of intimidation. The Court then declared, citing *Watts*, that the First Amendment "permits a State to ban a 'true threat,' " which it defined as a statement "where the speaker means to communicate a serious expression of an intent to commit an act of unlawful violence to a particular individual or group of individuals." The Court noted that "a prohibition on true threats 'protect[s] individuals from the fear of violence' and 'from the disruption that fear engenders,' in addition to protecting people 'from the possibility that the threatened violence will occur.' " The Court also stated that "some cross burnings fit within this meaning of intimidating speech."

The Court also disagreed with the conclusion of the Supreme Court of Virginia, which had relied on *R.A.V.*, that "even if it is constitutional to ban cross burning in a content-neutral manner, the Virginia cross-burning statute is unconstitutional because it discriminates on the basis of content and viewpoint." The Court reasoned that, under *R.A.V.*, the government can engage in content discrimination in banning a subset of speech in an unprotected category when "the basis for the content discrimination consists entirely of the very reason the entire class of speech at issue is proscribable." The Court then stated:

> The First Amendment permits Virginia to outlaw cross burnings done with the intent to intimidate because burning a cross is a particularly virulent form of intimidation. Instead of prohibiting all intimidating messages, Virginia may choose to regulate this subset of intimidating messages in light of cross burning's long and pernicious history as a signal of impending violence. Thus, just as a State may regulate only that obscenity which is the most obscene due to its prurient content, so too may a State choose to prohibit only those forms of intimidation that are most likely to inspire fear of bodily harm.

The Court, however, invalidated a provision of the statute that treated any cross burning as "prima facie evidence of an intent to intimidate a person or group of persons," reasoning that the provision "strips away the very reason why a State may ban cross burning with the intent to intimidate" and instead "permits the Commonwealth to arrest, prosecute, and convict a person based solely on the fact of cross burning itself." Justice O'Connor reasoned that "a burning cross is not always intended to intimidate," but instead sometimes "is a statement of ideology, a symbol of group solidarity." Accordingly, the provision "chill[ed] constitutionally protected political speech because of the possibility that the Commonwealth [would] prosecute—and potentially convict—somebody engaging only in lawful political speech at the core of what the First Amendment is designed to protect."

Do you agree that cross burning should sometimes be considered a form of protected speech? And if not, is it because it is a "true threat" or instead for some other reason?

6. Commercial Speech

Commercial speech consists of advertising and other business communications. Until 1976, the Court viewed commercial speech as a category of speech entirely outside the protection of the First Amendment. See, e.g., *Valentine v. Chrestensen*, 316 U.S. 52 (1942) (stating that although government may not "unduly burden or proscribe" the freedom of communicating information and disseminating opinion on public streets, "the Constitution imposes no such restraint on government as respects purely commercial advertising"); *Breard v. Alexandria*, 341 U.S. 622 (1951) (upholding conviction for violation of an ordinance prohibiting door-to-door solicitation of magazine subscriptions because of the "commercial feature" of the act).

In *Virginia State Bd. of Pharmacy v. Virginia Citizens Consumer Council, Inc.*, 425 U.S. 748 (1976), however, the Court invalidated a Virginia law prohibiting pharmacists from advertising the prices of prescription drugs. The Court concluded that commercial speech—that is, speech that "does no more than propose a commercial transaction"—is protected by the First Amendment. The Court noted that "speech does not lose its First Amendment protection because money is spent to project it, as in a paid advertisement of one form or another. Speech likewise is protected even though it is carried in a form that is 'sold' for profit," as occurs with books and movies. The Court also noted that the "consumer's interest in the free flow of commercial information * * * may be as keen, if not keener by far, than his interest in the day's most urgent political debate." The Court stated that "[s]o long as we preserve a predominantly free enterprise economy, the allocation of our resources in large measure will be made through numerous private economic decisions. It is a matter of public interest that those decisions, in the aggregate, be intelligent and well informed. To this end, the free flow of commercial information is indispensable." The Court concluded:

[T]he State's protectiveness of its citizens rests in large measure on the advantages of their being kept in ignorance. * * * There is, of course, an alternative to this highly paternalistic approach. That alternative is to assume that this information is not in itself harmful, that people will perceive their own best interests if only they are well enough informed, and that the best means to that end is to open the channels of communication rather than to close them.

The Court in *Virginia State Board of Pharmacy* did not identify a level of scrutiny for reviewing claims that the government has impermissibly regulated commercial speech. The Court did observe, however, that "[s]ome forms of commercial speech regulation are surely permissible." Most important, the Court noted that "[u]ntruthful speech, commercial or otherwise, has never been protected for its own sake," and that the First Amendment "does not prohibit the State from insuring that the stream of commercial information flow cleanly as well as freely." The Court stated, moreover, that

> [t]he truth of commercial speech [may] be more easily verifiable by its disseminator than [news] reporting or political commentary * * *. Also, [s]ince advertising is the Sine qua non of commercial profits, there is little likelihood of its being chilled by proper regulation and forgone entirely. Attributes such as these, the greater objectivity and hardiness of commercial speech, may make it less necessary to tolerate inaccurate statements for fear of silencing the speaker.

The Court therefore suggested that commercial speech might be subject to greater regulation than other forms of speech.

Several years after the Court's decision in *Virginia State Board of Pharmacy*, the Court settled on an approach for reviewing regulations of commercial speech. Under the leading case of *Central Hudson Gas & Electric Corp. v. Public Service Comm'n of New York*, 447 U.S. 557 (1980), the Supreme Court divided commercial speech into two categories. First, commercial speech that concerns an unlawful activity or that is fraudulent or misleading has no First Amendment protection. For example, the government may completely prohibit businesses from discussing the formation of horizontal price-fixing conspiracies that would violate the antitrust laws. See *North Texas Specialty Physicians v. FTC*, 528 F.3d 346, 372 (5th Cir. 2008). Second, regulation of other commercial speech is reviewed by a form of intermediate scrutiny. The government may regulate it if the government has a substantial interest, the regulation directly furthers the interest, and the regulation restrains speech only to the extent necessary to further the interest. Note that, under this test, a compelling governmental interest is not required. The Court, however, has struggled to apply this standard, and several Justices on the current Court have urged the Court to abandon it.

POINTS FOR DISCUSSION

a.   Protecting Commercial Speech

What is the Court's rationale for protecting commercial speech? Is it that protection is necessary to preserve the marketplace of ideas? That the First Amendment embodies a general principle against government paternalism? That consumers, as "listeners," have a First Amendment right to *receive* the information? Or is it that the courts have no way to distinguish between commercial speech and other forms of speech? What do these various rationales suggest about the extent of the protection that the Court should provide to commercial speech?

b.   Limits on Protection for Commercial Speech

Do you agree that commercial speech is more readily "verifiable," and less subject to a chilling effect, than other forms of speech? If so, is this an argument for a lower level of scrutiny under the First Amendment for commercial speech regulations, or instead an argument that commercial speech should not be protected at all?

> **FYI**
>
> Puerto Rico is a self-governing, unincorporated territory of the United States. 28 U.S.C. § 1258(2) specifically authorizes an appeal to the Supreme Court from a decision of the Supreme Court of Puerto Rico "where is drawn in question the validity of a statute of the Commonwealth of Puerto Rico on the ground of its being repugnant to the Constitution, treaties, or laws of the United States, and the decision is in favor of its validity."

In the years after the Court announced the *Central Hudson* standard, the Court struggled to apply it consistently. For example, in *Posadas de Puerto Rico Associates v. Tourism Co. of Puerto Rico*, 478 U.S. 328 (1986), the Court upheld the constitutionality of a Puerto Rico statute and regulations restricting advertising of casino gambling. The Court reasoned that Puerto Rico had a substantial interest in protecting the health, safety, and welfare of its citizens, and that the legislature's belief that advertising for casino gambling would increase the demand for the product—and thus potentially lead to an "increase in local crime, the fostering of prostitution, the development of corruption, and the infiltration of organized crime"—was a "reasonable one." The Court rejected the appellant's contention that the ban was impermissibly under-inclusive because advertising for other forms of gambling—including horse racing, cockfighting, and the lottery—was legal. The Court reasoned that the legislature permissibly concluded that "the risks associated with casino gambling were significantly greater than those associated with the more traditional kinds of gambling in Puerto Rico." The Court also stated that "the greater power to completely ban casino gambling necessarily includes the lesser power to ban advertising of casino gambling."

Many commentators read the Court's opinion in *Posadas*, which seemed to apply a more deferential version of intermediate scrutiny than it applies in other contexts, to suggest, at a minimum, that the government has more leeway to regulate commercial speech that promotes traditional "vices." Less than ten years later, however, the Court in *Rubin v. Coors Brewing Co.*, 514 U.S. 476 (1995), squarely rejected the government's argument that "legislatures have broader latitude to regulate speech that promotes socially harmful activities, such as alcohol consumption, than they have to regulate other types of speech." The Court in *Rubin* held that a federal statute prohibiting beer labels from displaying alcohol content violated the First Amendment.

One year after the Court's decision in *Rubin*, it decided the case that follows. As you will see, although the Court was unanimous in invalidating the challenged laws—a pair of Rhode Island statutes prohibiting the advertising of the price of alcoholic beverages except by tags and signs in liquor stores—the Justices divided sharply on the rationale and on the appropriate level of scrutiny.

44 LIQUORMART, INC. V. RHODE ISLAND
517 U.S. 484 (1996)

[This case involved a challenge to two Rhode Island laws that together prohibited advertising of the price of alcoholic beverages "in any manner whatsoever," except by tags or signs inside liquor stores. Among other things, the laws thus banned advertisements in print and broadcast media stating a price for alcoholic beverages. The plaintiffs were discount liquor retailers that wanted to advertise their low prices for alcoholic beverages but had previously been fined for print advertisements that implied (without identifying) low prices for alcoholic beverages. For example, one advertisement included the word "WOW" in large letters next to pictures of vodka and rum bottles. The state argued that the statutes advanced its interest in reducing alcohol consumption. Justice Stevens announced the judgment of the Court, but no opinion commanded a majority.]

JUSTICE STEVENS [joined by JUSTICE KENNEDY and JUSTICE GINSBURG].

Advertising has been a part of our culture throughout our history. * * * In accord with the role that commercial messages have long played, the law has developed to ensure that advertising provides consumers with accurate information about the availability of goods and services. * * * On the basis of [the principles announced in *Virginia State Bd. of Pharmacy v. Virginia Citizens Consumer*

Council, Inc., 425 U.S. 748 (1976)], our early cases uniformly struck down several broadly based bans on truthful, nonmisleading commercial speech, each of which served ends unrelated to consumer protection. * * * At the same time, our early cases recognized that the State may regulate some types of commercial advertising more freely than other forms of protected speech. Specifically, we explained that the State may require commercial messages to "appear in such a form, or include such additional information, warnings, and disclaimers, as are necessary to prevent its being deceptive," *Virginia Bd. of Pharmacy*, 425 U.S., at 772, n. 24, and that it may restrict some forms of aggressive sales practices that have the potential to exert "undue influence" over consumers, see *Bates v. State Bar of Ariz.*, 433 U.S. 350, 366 (1977). * * * Our decision [in *Central Hudson Gas & Elec. Corp. v. Public Serv. Comm'n of N.Y.*, 447 U.S. 557 (1980),] acknowledged the special features of commercial speech but identified the serious First Amendment concerns that attend blanket advertising prohibitions that do not protect consumers from commercial harms.

Rhode Island errs in concluding that *all* commercial speech regulations are subject to a similar form of constitutional review simply because they target a similar category of expression. The mere fact that messages propose commercial transactions does not in and of itself dictate the constitutional analysis that should apply to decisions to suppress them.

When a State regulates commercial messages to protect consumers from misleading, deceptive, or aggressive sales practices, or requires the disclosure of beneficial consumer information, the purpose of its regulation is consistent with the reasons for according constitutional protection to commercial speech and therefore justifies less than strict review. However, when a State entirely prohibits the dissemination of truthful, nonmisleading commercial messages for reasons unrelated to the preservation of a fair bargaining process, there is far less reason to depart from the rigorous review that the First Amendment generally demands. * * *

Sound reasons justify reviewing the latter type of commercial speech regulation more carefully. Most obviously, complete speech bans, unlike content-neutral restrictions on the time, place, or manner of expression, see

> **Take Note**
>
> Justice Stevens suggests here that bans on the "dissemination of truthful, nonmisleading commercial messages for reasons unrelated to the preservation of a fair bargaining process" should receive "the rigorous review that the First Amendment generally demands." Does this mean that he believes that strict scrutiny should apply to such regulations? If so, is there a conceivable argument that the challenged laws would survive scrutiny?

Kovacs v. Cooper, 336 U.S. 77, 89 (1949), are particularly dangerous because they all but foreclose alternative means of disseminating certain information.

The special dangers that attend complete bans on truthful, nonmisleading commercial speech cannot be explained away by appeals to the "commonsense distinctions" that exist between commercial and noncommercial speech. *Virginia Bd. of Pharmacy*, 425 U.S., at 771, n. 24. Regulations that suppress the truth are no less troubling because they target objectively verifiable information, nor are they less effective because they aim at durable messages. As a result, neither the "greater objectivity" nor the "greater hardiness" of truthful, nonmisleading commercial speech justifies reviewing its complete suppression with added deference. *Ibid.*

It is the State's interest in protecting consumers from "commercial harms" that provides "the typical reason why commercial speech can be subject to greater governmental regulation than noncommercial speech." *Cincinnati v. Discovery Network, Inc.*, 507 U.S. 410, 426 (1993). Yet bans that target truthful, nonmisleading commercial messages rarely protect consumers from such harms. Instead, such bans often serve only to obscure an "underlying governmental policy" that could be implemented without regulating speech. *Central Hudson*, 447 U.S., at 566, n. 9. In this way, these commercial speech bans not only hinder consumer choice, but also impede debate over central issues of public policy.

Precisely because bans against truthful, nonmisleading commercial speech rarely seek to protect consumers from either deception or overreaching, they usually rest solely on the offensive assumption that the public will respond "irrationally" to the truth. The First Amendment directs us to be especially skeptical of regulations that seek to keep people in the dark for what the government perceives to be their own good. That teaching applies equally to state attempts to deprive consumers of accurate information about their chosen products * * *.

In this case, there is no question that Rhode Island's price advertising ban constitutes a blanket prohibition against truthful, nonmisleading speech about a lawful product. There is also no question that the ban serves an end unrelated to consumer protection. Accordingly, we must review the price advertising ban with "special care," *Central Hudson*, 447 U.S., at 566, n. 9, mindful that speech prohibitions of this type rarely survive constitutional review.

> **Take Note**
>
> Justices Kennedy, Souter, and Ginsburg joined the next four paragraphs of Justice Stevens's opinion.

The State argues that the price advertising prohibition should nevertheless be upheld because it directly advances the State's substantial interest in promoting temperance, and because it is no more extensive than necessary. * * * [T]he State bears the burden of showing not merely that its regulation will advance its interest, but also that it will do so "to a material degree." The need for the State to make such a showing is particularly great given the drastic nature of its chosen means— the wholesale suppression of truthful, nonmisleading information. Accordingly, we must determine whether the State has shown that the price advertising ban will *significantly* reduce alcohol consumption.

We can agree that common sense supports the conclusion that a prohibition against price advertising, like a collusive agreement among competitors to refrain from such advertising, will tend to mitigate competition and maintain prices at a higher level than would prevail in a completely free market. Despite the absence of proof on the point, we can even agree with the State's contention that it is reasonable to assume that demand, and hence consumption throughout the market, is somewhat lower whenever a higher, noncompetitive price level prevails. However, [the] State has presented no evidence to suggest that its speech prohibition will *significantly* reduce marketwide consumption. Indeed, the District Court's considered and uncontradicted finding on this point is directly to the contrary. Moreover, the evidence suggests that the abusive drinker will probably not be deterred by a marginal price increase, and that the true alcoholic may simply reduce his purchases of other necessities. * * * [A]ny conclusion that elimination of the ban would significantly increase alcohol consumption would require us to engage in the sort of "speculation or conjecture" that is an unacceptable means of demonstrating that a restriction on commercial speech directly advances the State's asserted interest.

The State also cannot satisfy the requirement that its restriction on speech be no more extensive than necessary. It is perfectly obvious that alternative forms of regulation that would not involve any restriction on speech would be more likely to achieve the State's goal of promoting temperance. As the State's own expert conceded, higher prices can be maintained either by direct regulation or by increased taxation. Per capita purchases could be limited as is the case with prescription drugs. Even educational campaigns focused on the problems of excessive, or even moderate, drinking might prove to be more effective. As a result, even under the less than strict standard that generally applies in commercial speech cases,

> **Take Note**
>
> Justices Kennedy, Thomas, and Ginsburg joined the next three paragraphs of Justice Stevens's opinion.

the State has failed to establish a "reasonable fit" between its abridgment of speech and its temperance goal. It necessarily follows that the price advertising ban cannot survive the more stringent constitutional review that *Central Hudson* itself concluded was appropriate for the complete suppression of truthful, nonmisleading commercial speech.

Relying on the *Central Hudson* analysis set forth in *Posadas de Puerto Rico Associates v. Tourism Co. of P. R.*, 478 U.S. 328 (1986), and *United States v. Edge Broadcasting Co.*, 509 U.S. 418 (1993), Rhode Island [argues] that, because expert opinions as to the effectiveness of the price advertising ban "go both ways," the Court of Appeals correctly concluded that the ban constituted a "reasonable choice" by the legislature. The State next contends that precedent requires us to give particular deference to that legislative choice because the State could, if it chose, ban the sale of alcoholic beverages outright. Finally, the State argues that deference is appropriate because alcoholic beverages are so-called "vice" products. * * * The reasoning in *Posadas* does support the State's argument, but, on reflection, we are now persuaded that *Posadas* erroneously performed the First Amendment analysis. * * * [W]e conclude that a state legislature does not have the broad discretion to suppress truthful, nonmisleading information for paternalistic purposes that the *Posadas* majority was willing to tolerate.

We also cannot accept the State's second contention, which is premised entirely on the "greater-includes-the-lesser" reasoning [in] *Posadas*, [because that argument] is inconsistent with both logic and well-settled doctrine. * * * [W]e think it quite clear that banning speech may sometimes prove far more intrusive than banning conduct. * * * The text of the First Amendment makes clear that the Constitution presumes that attempts to regulate speech are more dangerous than attempts to regulate conduct.

Finally, we find unpersuasive the State's contention that [the] price advertising ban should be upheld because it targets commercial speech that pertains to a "vice" activity. * * * Our decision last Term striking down an alcohol-related advertising restriction effectively rejected the very contention respondents now make. See *Rubin v. Coors Brewing Co.*, 514 U.S. 476, 478, 482 n.2 (1995). * * * Moreover, the scope of any "vice" exception to the protection afforded by the First Amendment would be difficult, if not impossible, to define.

JUSTICE SCALIA, concurring in part and concurring in the judgment.

I share Justice THOMAS's discomfort with the *Central Hudson* test, which seems to me to have nothing more than policy intuition to support it. I also share Justice STEVENS's aversion towards paternalistic governmental policies that

684   Chapter 8

prevent men and women from hearing facts that might not be good for them. On the other hand, it would also be paternalism for us to prevent the people of the States from enacting laws that we consider paternalistic, unless we have good reason to believe that the Constitution itself forbids them. I will take my guidance as to what the Constitution forbids, with regard to a text as indeterminate as the First Amendment's preservation of "the freedom of speech," and where the core offense of suppressing particular political ideas is not at issue, from the long accepted practices of the American people. The briefs and arguments of the parties in the present case provide no illumination on * * * the state legislative practices prevalent at the time the First Amendment was adopted [and] at the time the Fourteenth Amendment was adopted.

Since I do not believe we have before us the wherewithal to declare *Central Hudson* wrong—or at least the wherewithal to say what ought to replace it—I must resolve this case in accord with our existing jurisprudence, which all except Justice THOMAS agree would prohibit the challenged regulation.

JUSTICE THOMAS, concurring [in part] and concurring in the judgment.

In cases such as this, in which the government's asserted interest is to keep legal users of a product or service ignorant in order to manipulate their choices in the marketplace, the balancing test adopted in *Central Hudson* should not be applied, in my view. Rather, such an "interest" is *per se* illegitimate and can no more justify regulation of "commercial" speech than it can justify regulation of "noncommercial" speech. * * * Faulting the State for failing to show that its price advertising ban decreases alcohol consumption "significantly," as Justice STEVENS does, seems to imply that if the State had been more successful at keeping consumers ignorant and thereby decreasing their consumption, then the restriction might have been upheld. This contradicts *Virginia Bd. of Pharmacy*'s rationale for protecting "commercial" speech in the first instance.

Both Justice STEVENS and Justice O'CONNOR appear to adopt a stricter, more categorical interpretation of the fourth prong of *Central Hudson* than that suggested in some of our other opinions, one that could, as a practical matter, go a long way toward the position I take. * * * [Their] opinions would appear to commit the courts to striking down restrictions on speech whenever a direct regulation (i.e., a regulation involving no restriction on speech regarding lawful activity at all) would be an equally effective method of dampening demand by legal users. But it would seem that directly banning a product (or rationing it, taxing it, controlling its price, or otherwise restricting its sale in specific ways) would virtually always be at least as effective in discouraging consumption as merely restricting advertising regarding the product would be, and thus virtually all restrictions with such a purpose would fail the fourth prong of the *Central Hudson* test. * * * I welcome this outcome; but, rather than "applying" the fourth prong of *Central Hudson* to reach the inevitable result that all or most such advertising restrictions must be struck down, I would adhere to the doctrine adopted in *Virginia Bd. of Pharmacy* [that] all attempts to dissuade legal choices by citizens by keeping them ignorant are impermissible.

JUSTICE O'CONNOR, with whom THE CHIEF JUSTICE, JUSTICE SOUTER, and JUSTICE BREYER join, concurring in the judgment.

I agree with the Court that Rhode Island's price-advertising ban is invalid. I would resolve this case more narrowly, however, by applying our established *Central Hudson* test to determine whether this commercial speech regulation survives First Amendment scrutiny.

Rhode Island's regulation [is] more extensive than necessary to serve the State's interest. * * * Rhode Island offers one, and only one, justification for its ban on price advertising. Rhode Island says that the ban is intended to keep alcohol prices high as a way to keep consumption low. * * * The fit between Rhode Island's method and this particular goal is not reasonable. * * * The State has other methods at its disposal—methods that would more directly accomplish this stated goal without intruding on sellers' ability to provide truthful, nonmisleading information to customers. * * * A [sales] tax, for example, is not normally very difficult to administer and would have a far more certain and direct effect on prices, without any restriction on speech. The principal opinion suggests further alternatives * * *. The ready availability of such alternatives—at least some of which would far more effectively achieve Rhode Island's only professed goal, at comparatively small additional administrative cost—demonstrates that the fit between ends and means is not narrowly tailored. * * * Because Rhode Island's regulation fails even the less stringent standard set out in *Central Hudson*, nothing here requires adoption of a new analysis for the evaluation of commercial speech regulation.

POINTS FOR DISCUSSION

a.   Level of Scrutiny

The Justices in *44 Liquormart* divided over the proper level of scrutiny for restrictions on commercial speech. Justices Stevens, Kennedy, and Ginsburg apparently would have applied strict scrutiny to prohibitions on the "dissemination of truthful, nonmisleading commercial messages for reasons unrelated to the preservation of a fair bargaining process." Justice Thomas would have gone even further, subjecting such regulations to a rule of *per se* invalidity. Justice Scalia concluded that the law was invalid under the Court's precedents, but would have preferred the Court to apply an originalist approach. He did not say what standard such an approach likely would produce for commercial speech regulation, because the Court had no evidence of historic legislative practices before it. And Justices O'Connor, Souter, and Breyer and Chief Justice Rehnquist concluded that the *Central Hudson* test was the appropriate level of scrutiny. What level of scrutiny should the Court apply to regulations of commercial speech? Does it matter whether the regulated speech is "truthful" and "non-misleading"? Are courts competent to determine when in fact speech is "truthful" or "non-misleading"?

In its verbal formulation, the *Central Hudson* test sounds very much like the other forms of intermediate scrutiny that we have seen in this chapter, including the test for reasonable time, place, or manner restrictions, see *Ward v. Rock Against Racism*, 491 U.S. 781 (1989), and the test for generally applicable laws that incidentally burden expression, see *United States v. O'Brien,* 391 U.S. 367 (1968). Is that test sufficiently protective of commercial speech? Conversely, is it too protective? More important, is the *Central Hudson* test still the appropriate standard for commercial speech regulation after *44 Liquormart*? In fact, the Court has applied the *Central Hudson* test in cases decided since *44 Liquormart*, see, e.g., *Thompson v. Western States Med. Ctr.*, 535 U.S. 357 (2002), though some Justices have continued to express the view that the Court should abandon the test, see *id.* (Thomas, J., concurring). What test should replace the *Central Hudson* test, if the Court does abandon it?

b.   Identifying Commercial Speech

The Court in *Virginia State Board of Pharmacy* defined commercial speech as a communication that "does no more than propose a commercial transaction." Even assuming that commercial speech should receive a different degree of protection under the First Amendment than other forms of speech, is that the appropriate test for what counts as commercial speech? And if it is the appropriate test, does it provide sufficient guidance for distinguishing between commercial speech and other forms of speech? Suppose, for example, that an athletic apparel company broadcasts a television commercial that consists simply of girls, dressed in the company's athletic apparel, stating, "I am an athlete," and ends with a depiction of the company's logo. Would such an advertisement be commercial speech? After all, it would be designed (among other things) to encourage prospective customers to buy the company's products. Would it be problematic to say that the government can regulate the content of such an advertisement?

c.   Commercial Speech and the Original Meaning

Is there an originalist argument for giving commercial speech less protection than other forms of speech? Judge Alex Kozinski and Stuart Banner note that "[t]he argument would go like this: The Framers evidenced absolutely no interest in protecting commercial speech, so it would be a gross misinterpretation of the first amendment to construe it to afford commercial speech the same level of protection as political speech." In their view, however, "this argument proves too much. The Framers never expressed an interest in protecting literature either, but the idea that the first amendment protects artistic expression is not one that attracts much opposition." Alex Kozinski & Stuart Banner, *Who's Afraid of Commercial Speech?*, 76 Va. L. Rev. 627 (1990). They argue that the same is true for proselytizing, nude dancing, and so forth. Ultimately, they reason, there is little in the text or history of the First Amendment to suggest that commercial speech should be treated differently from political speech.

What inference about the original meaning should be drawn given this lack of evidence? Is the problem that the only clear evidence we have of the First Amendment's original meaning provides clues of its meaning only at a very high level of generality?

7.   Campaign Contributions and Expenditures

Candidates running for political office usually must spend large amounts of money for television, radio, internet, and other advertising. Restricting these expenditures would hamper their ability to convey their political messages to potential voters, a very important form of free speech. But permitting unfettered campaign spending might also permit wealthy or well-financed candidates effectively to swamp the messages of less well-financed candidates.

Of course, spending money is only half of what a candidate ordinarily must do in order to get out his message. In order to spend money on campaigning, most candidates (all but the very wealthy) must first obtain the funds from contributors. Accordingly, limits on campaign contributions affect candidates' ability to convey their political messages, as well. But if contributions are totally unregulated, political candidates in effect might be unduly influenced—"bought"—by wealthy donors. In light of these competing interests, can the government regulate campaign spending and contributions?

The Court developed two rules in the case that follows. The first is that the First Amendment generally prohibits the federal government from regulating how much money a political candidate is permitted to spend. The second is that the First Amendment generally permits the government to impose reasonable restrictions on the right to contribute to a political campaign. In reading the case, try to identify the Court's rationale for each rule.

BUCKLEY V. VALEO

424 U.S. 1 (1976)

PER CURIAM.

These appeals present constitutional challenges to the key provisions of the Federal Election Campaign Act of 1971 (Act), and related provisions of the Internal Revenue Code of 1954, all as amended in 1974. [The Act imposed a variety of restrictions on campaign contributions and expenditures. Among the most important were limitations prohibiting individuals from contributing more than $25,000 in a single year or more than $1,000 to any single candidate for an election campaign and from spending more than $1,000 a year "relative to a clearly identified candidate." The Act also restricted candidates' use of personal and family resources in their campaigns and limited the amount that they could spend on a campaign for federal office. The plaintiffs, who included political candidates and political parties, challenged the contribution and spending limitations under the First Amendment.]

> **Take Note**
>
> What follows is only a brief excerpt from an extremely long opinion touching upon numerous issues. We briefly consider this case in Volume 1, when we discuss the Constitution's provisions for the appointment of officers of the United States.

The Act's contribution and expenditure limitations operate in an area of the most fundamental First Amendment activities. Discussion of public issues and debate on the qualifications of candidates are integral to the operation of the system of government established by our Constitution. The First Amendment affords the broadest protection to such political expression in order "to assure (the) unfettered interchange of ideas for the bringing about of political and social changes desired by the people." *Roth v. United States*, 354 U.S. 476, 484 (1957). Although First Amendment protections are not confined to "the exposition of ideas," *Winters v. New York*, 333 U.S. 507, 510 (1948), "there is practically universal agreement that a major purpose of that Amendment was to protect the free discussion of governmental affairs [of] course includ(ing) discussions of candidates." *Mills v. Alabama*, 384 U.S. 214, 218 (1966). This no more than reflects our "profound national commitment to the principle that debate on public issues should be uninhibited, robust, and wide-open," *New York Times Co. v. Sullivan*, 376 U.S. 254, 270 (1964). In a republic where the people are sovereign, the ability of the citizenry to make informed choices among candidates for office is essential, for the identities of those who are elected will inevitably shape the course that we follow as a nation. As the Court observed in *Monitor Patriot Co. v. Roy*, 401 U.S. 265, 272 (1971), "it can hardly be doubted that the constitutional guarantee has its fullest and most urgent application precisely to the conduct of campaigns for political office."

The First Amendment protects political association as well as political expression. The constitutional right of association explicated in *NAACP v. Alabama*, 357 U.S. 449, 460 (1958), stemmed from the Court's recognition that "[e]ffective advocacy of both public and private points of view, particularly controversial ones, is undeniably enhanced by group association." Subsequent decisions have made clear that the First and Fourteenth Amendments guarantee "freedom to associate with others for the common advancement of political beliefs and ideas," a freedom that encompasses "[t]he right to associate with the political party of one's choice." *Kusper v. Pontikes*, 414 U.S. 51, 56, 57 (1973), quoted in *Cousins v. Wigoda*, 419 U.S. 477, 487 (1975).

> **Make the Connection**
>
> We will consider the First Amendment's protection for the freedom of association in Chapter 10.

It is with these principles in mind that we consider the primary contentions of the parties with respect to the Act's limitations upon the giving and spending of money in political campaigns. Those conflicting contentions could not more sharply define the basic issues before us. Appellees contend that what the Act regulates is conduct, and that its effect on speech and association is incidental at most. Appellants respond that contributions and expenditures are at the very core of political speech, and that the Act's limitations thus constitute restraints on First Amendment liberty that are both gross and direct.

In upholding the constitutional validity of the Act's contribution and expenditure provisions on the ground that those provisions should be viewed as regulating conduct, not speech, the Court of Appeals relied upon *United States v. O'Brien*, 391 U.S. 367 (1968). * * * We cannot share the view that the present Act's contribution and expenditure limitations are comparable to the restrictions on conduct upheld in *O'Brien*. The expenditure of money simply cannot be equated with such conduct as destruction of a draft card. Some forms of communication made possible by the giving and spending of money involve speech alone, some involve conduct primarily, and some involve a combination of the two. Yet this Court has never suggested that the dependence of a communication on the expenditure of money operates itself to introduce a nonspeech element or to reduce the exacting scrutiny required by the First Amendment. * * *

Even if the categorization of the expenditure of money as conduct were accepted, the limitations challenged here would not meet the *O'Brien* test because the governmental interests advanced in support of the Act involve "suppressing communication." The interests served by the Act include restricting the voices of people and interest groups who have money to spend and reducing the overall scope of federal election campaigns. Although the Act does not focus on the ideas expressed by persons or groups subject to its regulations, it is aimed in part at equalizing the relative ability of all voters to affect electoral outcomes by placing a ceiling on expenditures for political expression by citizens and groups. Unlike *O'Brien*, where the Selective Service System's administrative interest in the preservation of draft cards was wholly unrelated to their use as a means of communication, it is beyond dispute that the interest in regulating the alleged "conduct" of giving or spending money "arises in some measure because the communication allegedly integral to the conduct is itself thought to be harmful." 391 U.S., at 382.

Nor can the Act's contribution and expenditure limitations be sustained, as some of the parties suggest, by reference to the constitutional principles reflected in such decisions as * * * *Kovacs v. Cooper*, 336 U.S. 77 (1949). Those cases stand for the proposition that the government may adopt reasonable time, place, and manner regulations, which do not discriminate among speakers or ideas, in order to further an important governmental interest unrelated to the restriction of communication. * * * The critical difference between this case and [the] time, place, and manner cases is that the present Act's contribution and expenditure limitations impose direct quantity restrictions on political communication and association by persons, groups, candidates, and political parties in addition to any reasonable time, place, and manner regulations otherwise imposed.

A restriction on the amount of money a person or group can spend on political communication during a campaign necessarily reduces the quantity of expression by restricting the number of issues discussed, the depth of their exploration, and the size of the audience reached. This is because virtually every means of communicating ideas in today's mass society requires the expenditure of money. The distribution of the humblest handbill or leaflet entails printing, paper, and circulation costs. Speeches and rallies generally necessitate hiring a hall and publicizing the event. The electorate's increasing dependence on television, radio, and other mass media for news and information has made these expensive modes of communication indispensable instruments of effective political speech.

The expenditure limitations contained in the Act represent substantial rather than merely theoretical restraints on the quantity and diversity of political speech. The $1,000 ceiling on spending "relative to a clearly identified candidate" would appear to exclude all citizens and groups except candidates, political parties, and the institutional press from any significant use of the most effective modes of communication. Although the Act's limitations on expenditures by campaign organizations and political parties provide substantially greater room for discussion and debate, they would have required restrictions in the scope of a number of past congressional and Presidential campaigns and would operate to constrain campaigning by candidates who raise sums in excess of the spending ceiling.

By contrast with a limitation upon expenditures for political expression, a limitation upon the amount that any one person or group may contribute to a candidate or political committee entails only a marginal restriction upon the contributor's ability to engage in free communication. A contribution serves as a general expression of support for the candidate and his views, but does not communicate the underlying basis for the support. The quantity of communication by the contributor does not increase perceptibly with the size of his contribution, since the expression rests solely on the undifferentiated, symbolic act of contributing. At most, the size of the contribution provides a very rough index of the intensity of the contributor's support for the candidate. A limitation on the amount of money a person may give to a candidate or campaign organization thus involves little direct restraint on his political communication, for it permits the symbolic expression of support evidenced by a contribution but does not in any way infringe the contributor's freedom to discuss candidates and issues. While contributions may result in political expression if spent by a candidate or an association to present views to the voters, the transformation of contributions into political debate involves speech by someone other than the contributor.

Given the important role of contributions in financing political campaigns, contribution restrictions could have a severe impact on political dialogue if the limitations prevented candidates and political committees from amassing the resources necessary for effective advocacy. There is no indication, however, that the contribution limitations imposed by the Act would have any dramatic adverse effect on the funding of campaigns and political associations. The overall effect of the Act's contribution ceilings is merely to require candidates and political committees to raise funds from a greater number of persons and to compel people who would otherwise contribute amounts greater than the statutory limits to expend such funds on direct political expression, rather than to reduce the total amount of money potentially available to promote political expression.

In sum, although the Act's contribution and expenditure limitations both implicate fundamental First Amendment interests, its expenditure ceilings impose significantly more severe restrictions on protected freedoms of political expression and association than do its limitations on financial contributions.

[T]he primary First Amendment problem raised by the Act's contribution limitations is their restriction of one aspect of the contributor's freedom of political association. * * * Yet [even] a " 'significant interference' with protected rights of political association" may be sustained if the State demonstrates a sufficiently important interest and employs means closely drawn to avoid unnecessary abridgment of associational freedoms.

It is unnecessary to look beyond the Act's primary purpose to limit the actuality and appearance of corruption resulting from large individual financial contributions in order to find a constitutionally sufficient justification for the $1,000 contribution limitation. * * * To the extent that large contributions are given to secure a political quid pro quo from current and potential office holders, the integrity of our system of representative democracy is undermined. Although the scope of such pernicious practices can never be reliably ascertained, the deeply disturbing examples surfacing after the 1972 election demonstrate that the problem is not an illusory one. Of

FYI

Congress enacted the challenged provision in part in response to disclosures that President Nixon's campaign had illegally solicited large donations, often from corporations. We will consider the right of corporations to spend money in political campaigns later in this section.

almost equal concern as the danger of actual quid pro quo arrangements is the impact of the appearance of corruption stemming from public awareness of the opportunities for abuse inherent in a regime of large individual financial contributions.

Appellants contend that the contribution limitations must be invalidated because bribery laws and narrowly drawn disclosure requirements constitute a less restrictive means of dealing with "proven and suspected quid pro quo arrangements." But laws making criminal the giving and taking of bribes deal with only the most blatant and specific attempts of those with money to influence governmental action. * * * Congress was surely entitled to conclude that disclosure was only a partial measure, and that contribution ceilings were a necessary legislative concomitant to deal with the reality or appearance of corruption * * *. We find that, under the rigorous standard of review established by our prior decisions, the weighty interests served by restricting the size of financial contributions to political candidates are sufficient to justify the limited effect upon First Amendment freedoms caused by the $1,000 contribution ceiling.

The Act's expenditure ceilings impose direct and substantial restraints on the quantity of political speech. * * * We find that the governmental interest in preventing corruption and the appearance of corruption is inadequate to justify [the Act's limits on expenditures "relative to a clearly identified candidate."] * * * [The] parties defending [the limits] contend that it is necessary to prevent would-be contributors from avoiding the contribution limitations by the simple expedient of paying directly for media advertisements or for other portions of the candidate's campaign activities. * * * Yet such controlled or coordinated expenditures are treated as contributions rather than expenditures under the Act. * * * By contrast, [the provision at issue] limits expenditures for express advocacy of candidates made totally independently of the candidate and his campaign. * * * The absence of prearrangement and coordination of an expenditure with the candidate or his agent not only undermines the value of the expenditure to the candidate, but also alleviates the danger that expenditures will be given as a quid pro quo for improper commitments from the candidate. * * * While the independent expenditure ceiling thus fails to serve any substantial governmental interest in stemming the reality or appearance of corruption in the electoral process, it heavily burdens core First Amendment expression.

It is argued, however, that the ancillary governmental interest in equalizing the relative ability of individuals and groups to influence the outcome of elections serves to justify the limitation on express advocacy of the election or defeat of candidates * * *. But the concept that government may restrict the speech of some elements of our society in order to enhance the relative voice of others is wholly foreign to the First Amendment, which was designed "to secure 'the widest possible dissemination of information from diverse and antagonistic sources,' " and "to assure unfettered interchange of ideas for the bringing about of political and social changes desired by the people." *Sullivan*, 376 U.S., at 266, 269. The First Amendment's protection against governmental abridgment of free expression cannot properly be made to depend on a person's financial ability to engage in public discussion. * * * [W]e conclude that [the] independent expenditure limitation is unconstitutional under the First Amendment.

The Act also sets limits on expenditures by a candidate "from his personal funds, or the personal funds of his immediate family, in connection with his campaigns during any calendar year." * * * The candidate, no less than any other person, has a First Amendment right to engage in the discussion of public issues and vigorously and tirelessly to advocate his own election and the election of other candidates. * * * The primary governmental interest served by the Act—the prevention of actual and apparent corruption of the political process—does not support the limitation on the candidate's expenditure of his own personal funds. * * * Indeed, the use of personal funds reduces the candidate's dependence on outside contributions and thereby counteracts the coercive pressures and attendant risks of abuse to which the Act's contribution limitations are directed. * * * The ancillary interest in equalizing the relative financial resources of candidates competing for elective office [is] clearly not sufficient to justify the provision's infringement of fundamental First Amendment rights. First, the limitation may fail to promote financial equality among candidates. A candidate who spends less of his personal resources on his campaign may nonetheless outspend his rival as a result of more successful fundraising efforts. * * * Second, and more fundamentally, the First Amendment simply cannot tolerate [the Act's] restriction upon the freedom of a candidate to speak without legislative limit on behalf of his own candidacy. We therefore hold that the restriction on a candidate's personal expenditures is unconstitutional.

[The Act] places limitations on overall campaign expenditures by candidates seeking nomination for election and election to federal office. * * * No governmental interest that has been suggested is sufficient to justify the restriction on the quantity of political expression imposed by [these limits]. * * * The interest in alleviating the corrupting influence of large contributions is served by the Act's contribution limitations and disclosure provisions * * *. The interest in equalizing the financial resources of candidates competing for federal office is no more convincing a justification for restricting the scope of federal election campaigns. Given the limitation on the size of outside contributions, the financial resources available to a candidate's campaign, like the number of volunteers recruited, will normally vary with the size and intensity of the candidate's support. There is nothing invidious, improper, or unhealthy in permitting such funds to be spent to carry the candidate's message to the electorate.

The campaign expenditure ceilings appear to be designed primarily to serve the governmental interests in reducing the allegedly skyrocketing costs of political campaigns. * * * The First Amendment denies government the power to determine that spending to promote one's political views is wasteful, excessive, or unwise. In the free society ordained by our Constitution it is not the government, but the people individually as citizens and candidates and collectively as associations and political committees who must retain control over the quantity and range of debate on public issues in a political campaign.

MR. CHIEF JUSTICE BURGER, concurring in part and dissenting in part.

I agree fully with that part of the Court's opinion that holds unconstitutional the limitations the Act puts on campaign expenditures * * *. Yet when it approves similarly stringent limitations on contributions, the Court ignores the reasons it finds so persuasive in the context of expenditures. For me contributions and expenditures are two sides of the same First Amendment coin.

By limiting campaign contributions, the Act restricts the amount of money that will be spent on political activity and does so directly. Appellees argue, as the Court notes, that these limits will "act as a brake on the skyrocketing cost of political campaigns." * * * Limiting contributions, as a practical matter, will limit expenditures and will put an effective ceiling on the amount of political activity and debate that the Government will permit to take place. The argument that the ceiling is not, after all, very low as matters now stand gives little comfort for the future, since the Court elsewhere notes the rapid inflation in the cost of political campaigning.

MR. JUSTICE WHITE, concurring in part and dissenting in part.

I am [in] agreement with the Court's judgment upholding the limitations on contributions. I dissent, however, from the Court's view that the expenditure limitations [violate] the First Amendment. * * * Since the contribution and expenditure limitations are neutral as to the content of speech and are not motivated by fear of the consequences of the political speech of particular candidates or of political speech in general, this case depends on whether the nonspeech interests of the Federal Government in regulating the use of money in political campaigns are sufficiently urgent to justify the incidental effects that the limitations visit upon the First Amendment interests of candidates and their supporters.

The Court [accepts] the congressional judgment that the evils of unlimited contributions are sufficiently threatening to warrant restriction regardless of the impact of the limits on the contributor's opportunity for effective speech and in turn on the total volume of the candidate's political communications by reason of his inability to accept large sums from those willing to give. The congressional judgment, which I would also accept, was that other steps must be taken to counter the corrosive effects of money in federal election campaigns. One of these steps is [the Act's limits on expenditures in support of a candidate]. * * * It would make little sense to me, and apparently made none to Congress, to limit the amounts an individual may give to a candidate or spend with his approval but fail to limit the amounts that could be spent on his behalf. Yet the Court permits the former while striking down the latter limitation. * * * I would take the word of those who know that limiting independent expenditures is essential to prevent transparent and widespread evasion of the contribution limits.

The Court also rejects Congress' judgment [that] the federal interest in limiting total campaign expenditures by individual candidates justifies the incidental effect on their opportunity for effective political speech. * * * In this posture of the case, there is no sound basis for invalidating the expenditure limitations, so long as the purposes they serve are legitimate and sufficiently substantial, which in my view they are. In the first place, expenditure ceilings reinforce the contribution limits and help eradicate the hazard of corruption. [In addition,] expenditure limits have their own potential for preventing the corruption of federal elections themselves. [T]he corrupt use of money by candidates is as much to be feared as the corrosive influence of large contributions. * * * I have little doubt in addition that limiting the total that can be spent will ease the candidate's understandable obsession with fundraising, and so free him and his staff to communicate in more places and ways unconnected with the fundraising function. * * * It is also important to restore and maintain public confidence in federal elections. It is critical to obviate or dispel the impression that federal elections are purely and simply a function of money, that federal offices are bought and sold or that political races are reserved for those who have the facility and the stomach for doing whatever it takes to bring together those interests, groups, and individuals that can raise or contribute large fortunes in order to prevail at the polls.

The ceiling on candidate expenditures represents the considered judgment of Congress that elections are to be decided among candidates none of whom has overpowering advantage by reason of a huge campaign war chest. At least so long as the ceiling placed upon the candidates is not plainly too low, elections are not to turn on the difference in the amounts of money that candidates have to spend. This seems an acceptable purpose and the means chosen a common-sense way to achieve it.

I also disagree with the Court's judgment that [the Act's limit on the amount of money that a candidate or his family may spend on his campaign] violates the Constitution. Although it is true that this provision does not promote any interest in preventing the corruption of candidates, the provision [helps] to assure that only individuals with a modicum of support from others will be viable candidates. This in turn would tend to discourage any notion that the outcome of elections is primarily a function of money. Similarly, [the limit] tends to equalize access to the political arena, encouraging the less wealthy, unable to bankroll their own campaigns, to run for political office.

[JUSTICE MARSHALL's, REHNQUIST's, and BLACKMUN's separate opinions concurring in part and dissenting in part have been omitted.]

POINTS FOR DISCUSSION

a.   Campaign Finance Laws and Level of Scrutiny

What level of scrutiny did the Court apply to the challenged provisions? Are statutory limitations on contributions to and expenditures by political campaigns content based? (Did Congress impose similar limits on contributions to charitable organizations or expenditures by companies to promote their business?) If the limitations were content based, what does that suggest about the appropriate level of scrutiny? Assuming they were content based, is there something distinct about the regulated category of speech that justifies distinctive rules?

What government interests were advanced by the expenditure and contribution limitations? The per curiam opinion found that the "Act's primary purpose to limit the actuality and appearance of corruption resulting from large individual financial contributions" was a "sufficient justification for the $1,000 contribution limitation." Is that interest compelling? Wouldn't the criminalization of bribery and graft advance that interest without placing such a burden on expression? Conversely, why wasn't that interest sufficient to justify the limits on individuals' expenditures, as well?

b.   Inequality

If candidates can spend as much money as they want, but are limited in how much money they can receive, are all candidates treated equally? Or are incumbents favored because they have an advantage, based on name-recognition, in raising contributions from a large number of people and an advantage, based on incumbency itself, in raising contributions from those with interests in pending and future legislation? And aren't rich candidates systematically favored over poor candidates because they can spend their own money? (If you belonged to a minority party, would you want to nominate a wealthy candidate or one who would have to raise funds from donations?) Is inequality of this kind a concern of the First Amendment?

c.   *Buckley*'s Theory of the First Amendment

At the beginning of this chapter, we suggested several visions of the theory of the First Amendment. On which theory did the Court rely in *Buckley*? Does the decision promote the marketplace of ideas, or instead make it more likely that only one or a few ideas will be available in that marketplace? Does the decision promote the ideal of accountable government, or does it instead make it more likely that electoral checks will *not* operate effectively?

d.   Distinction Between Contributions and Expenditures

Although the Supreme Court continues to conclude that the government has more leeway to regulate campaign contributions than it does to regulate campaign expenditures, see, e.g., *Nixon v. Shrink Missouri Government PAC*, 528 U.S. 377 (2000), some of the Justices disagree with that approach. Justice Thomas writes:

> [U]nlike the *Buckley* Court, I believe that contribution limits infringe as directly and as seriously upon freedom of political expression and association as do expenditure limits. The protections of the First Amendment do not depend upon so fine a line as that between spending money to support a candidate or group and giving money to the candidate or group to spend for the same purpose. In principle, people and groups give money to candidates and other groups for the same reason that they spend money in support of those candidates and groups: because they share social, economic, and political beliefs and seek to have those beliefs affect governmental policy.

Colorado Republican Federal Campaign Comm. v. Federal Election Comm'n, 518 U.S. 604 (1996) (Thomas, J., concurring in part and dissenting in part). If the Court adopted this view, what alternatives would be available to Congress to limit the influence of rich donors who make large campaign contributions?

In any event, the Court in recent years has not been willing to uphold all restrictions even on campaign contributions. In *McCutcheon v. Federal Election Commission*, 572 U.S. 185 (2014), the Court invalidated a provision of a federal statute that restricted how much money a person could contribute in total to all candidates or committees. 2 U.S.C. § 441a(a)(3). The Court explained:

> [W]hile preventing corruption or its appearance is a legitimate objective, Congress may target only a specific type of corruption—"*quid pro quo*" corruption. As *Buckley v. Valeo*, 424 U.S. 1, 26 (1976), explained, Congress may permissibly seek to rein in "large contributions [that] are given to secure a political *quid pro quo* from current and potential office holders." In addition to "actual *quid pro quo* arrangements," Congress may permissibly limit "the appearance of corruption stemming from public awareness of the opportunities for abuse inherent in a regime of large individual financial contributions" to particular candidates. *Id.*, at 27.

Spending large sums of money in connection with elections, but not in connection with an effort to control the exercise of an officeholder's official duties, does not give rise to such *quid pro quo* corruption. Nor does the possibility that an individual who spends large sums may garner "influence over or access to" elected officials or political parties. *Id.*, at 359; see *McConnell v. Federal Election Comm'n*, 540 U.S. 93, 297 (2003) (Kennedy, J., concurring in judgment in part and dissenting in part). And because the Government's interest in preventing the appearance of corruption is equally confined to the appearance of *quid pro quo* corruption, the Government may not seek to limit the appearance of mere influence or access.

Do you agree that the government has a compelling interest only in preventing quid pro quo corruption, rather than preventing individual donors from gaining substantial influence over the government?

After the decision in *Buckley*, federal law allowed candidates for federal office to spend an unlimited amount of money on their own campaigns, but limited how much money they may receive in campaign contributions from donors. In addition, the decision in *Buckley* opened the door to other significant expenditures, at least if they did not relate to a clearly identified candidate. After the decision in *Buckley*, did Congress have any authority to limit certain types of independent expenditures? In particular, after *Buckley*, does the First Amendment prevent Congress from limiting the influence of corporations and unions in the federal elections process?

The federal and state governments can create "corporations," which are artificial entities that have certain legal rights. For example, the New York Times Company, the publisher of a popular newspaper, is a corporation chartered by the State of New York. The New York Times can enter into contracts, such as employment contracts with its reporters and contracts to buy paper and ink from various suppliers. One constitutional question is whether corporations and other associations, like labor unions, can assert constitutional rights just like individuals. For example, suppose Congress passed a law prohibiting the New York Times from endorsing political candidates in their editorials. Could the New York Times assert that the law violates its freedom of speech under the First Amendment? For many years, most legal scholars believed that the First Amendment protected corporate speech of this kind. But decisions concerning election contributions raised doubt about this issue.

In 2003, in *McConnell v. Federal Election Comm'n*, 540 U.S. 93 (2003), the Court upheld a provision of federal law prohibiting corporations and unions from using their general treasury funds to make independent expenditures for speech defined as an "electioneering communication" or for speech expressly advocating the election or defeat of a candidate. 2 U.S.C. § 441b. The Court revisited that holding in the case that follows.

CITIZENS UNITED V. FEDERAL ELECTION COMMISSION
558 U.S. 310 (2010)

JUSTICE KENNEDY delivered the opinion of the Court.

Citizens United is a nonprofit corporation [with] an annual budget of about $12 million. Most of its funds are from donations by individuals; but, in addition, it accepts a small portion of its funds from for-profit corporations. In January 2008, Citizens United released a film entitled *Hillary: The Movie*, [a] 90-minute documentary about then-Senator Hillary Clinton, who was a candidate in the Democratic Party's 2008 Presidential primary elections. * * * *Hillary* was released in theaters and on DVD, but Citizens United wanted to increase distribution by making it available through video-on-demand. [To] promote the film, it produced two 10-second ads and one 30-second ad for *Hillary*. Each ad includes a short (and, in our view, pejorative) statement about Senator Clinton, followed by the name of the movie and the movie's Website address. Citizens United desired to promote the video-on-demand offering by running advertisements on broadcast and cable television.

Before the Bipartisan Campaign Reform Act of 2002 (BCRA), federal law prohibited—and still does prohibit—corporations and unions from using general treasury funds to make direct contributions to candidates or independent expenditures that expressly advocate the election or defeat of a candidate, through any form of media, in connection with certain qualified federal elections. 2 U.S.C. § 441b (2000 ed.). BCRA amended § 441b to prohibit any "electioneering communication" as well. 2 U.S.C. § 441b(b)(2) (2006 ed.). An electioneering communication is defined as "any broadcast, cable, or satellite communication" that "refers to a clearly identified candidate for Federal office" and is made within 30 days of a primary or 60 days of a general election. § 434(f)(3)(A). * * * Corporations and unions are barred from using their general treasury funds for express advocacy or electioneering communications. They may establish, however, a "separate segregated fund" (known as a political action committee, or PAC) for these purposes. 2 U.S.C. § 441b(b)(2). The moneys received by the segregated fund are limited to donations from stockholders and employees of the corporation or, in the case of unions, members of the union. *Ibid.*

Citizens United wanted to make *Hillary* available through video-on-demand within 30 days of the 2008 primary elections. It feared, however, that both the film and the ads would be covered by § 441b's ban on corporate-funded independent expenditures, thus subjecting the corporation to civil and criminal penalties under § 437g. In December 2007, Citizens United sought declaratory and injunctive relief against the FEC [arguing that the ban violated the First

Amendment. A three-judge district court impaneled under BCRA granted the FEC's motion for summary judgment.]

[*Hillary,*] in essence, is a feature-length negative advertisement that urges viewers to vote against Senator Clinton for President. In light of historical footage, interviews with persons critical of her, and voiceover narration, the film would be understood by most viewers as an extended criticism of Senator Clinton's character and her fitness for the office of the Presidency. * * * [T]he film qualifies as the functional equivalent of express advocacy [against a specific candidate, and thus falls within § 441b].

The law before us is an outright ban, backed by criminal sanctions. Section 441b makes it a felony for all corporations—including nonprofit advocacy corporations—either to expressly advocate the election or defeat of candidates or to broadcast electioneering communications within 30 days of a primary election and 60 days of a general election. * * * Section 441b is a ban on corporate speech notwithstanding the fact that a PAC created by a corporation can still speak. A PAC is a separate association from the corporation. So the PAC exemption from § 441b's expenditure ban does not allow corporations to speak. Even if a PAC could somehow allow a corporation to speak, [the] option to form PACs does not alleviate the First Amendment problems with § 441b. PACs are burdensome alternatives; they are expensive to administer and subject to extensive regulations. * * * This might explain why fewer than 2,000 of the millions of corporations in this country have PACs. * * * Section 441b's prohibition on corporate independent expenditures is thus a ban on speech.

[N]ot until 1947 did Congress first prohibit independent expenditures by corporations and labor unions in § 304 of the Labor Management Relations Act 1947 (codified at 2 U.S.C. § 251 (1946 ed., Supp. I)). * * * For almost three decades thereafter, the Court did not reach the question whether restrictions on corporate and union expenditures are constitutional.

In *Buckley v. Valeo,* 424 U.S. 1 (1976), the Court [invalidated an independent expenditure ban, 18 U.S.C. § 608(e) (1970 ed., Supp. V), that applied to individuals as well as corporations and labor unions. The Court in *Buckley* did not consider a different provision of the Federal Election Campaign Act, 18 U.S.C. § 610, that banned corporate and union independent expenditures.] Had § 610 been challenged in the wake of *Buckley,* however, it could not have been squared with the reasoning and analysis of that precedent. Notwithstanding this precedent, Congress recodified § 610's corporate and union expenditure ban at 2 U.S.C. § 441b four months after *Buckley* was decided. Section 441b is the independent expenditure restriction challenged here.

Less than two years after *Buckley, First Nat. Bank of Boston v. Bellotti*, 435 U.S. 765 (1978), * * * struck down a state-law prohibition on corporate independent expenditures related to referenda issues. * * *

Take Note

Some of the cases that we have seen so far in this chapter involved protected speech by corporations. See, e.g., *New York Times Co. v. Sullivan*, 376 U.S. 254 (1964). In what way did the First Amendment claims in those cases differ from the claim in this case?

[T]he reasoning and holding of *Bellotti* [rested] on the principle that the Government lacks the power to ban corporations from speaking. *Bellotti* did not address the constitutionality of the State's [separate] ban on corporate independent expenditures to support candidates. In our view, however, that restriction would have been unconstitutional under *Bellotti*'s central principle: that the First Amendment does not allow political speech restrictions based on a speaker's corporate identity.

Thus the law stood until *Austin v. Michigan Chamber of Commerce*, 494 U.S. 652 (1990). * * * There, the Michigan Chamber of Commerce sought to use general treasury funds to run a newspaper ad supporting a specific candidate. Michigan law, however, prohibited corporate independent expenditures that supported or opposed any candidate for state office. * * * The Court sustained the speech prohibition. To bypass *Buckley* and *Bellotti*, the *Austin* Court * * * found a compelling governmental interest in preventing "the corrosive and distorting effects of immense aggregations of wealth that are accumulated with the help of the corporate form and that have little or no correlation to the public's support for the corporation's political ideas."

As for *Austin*'s antidistortion rationale, the Government does little to defend it. And with good reason, for the rationale cannot support § 441b. If the First Amendment has any force, it prohibits Congress from fining or jailing citizens, or associations of citizens, for simply engaging in political speech. If the antidistortion rationale were to be accepted, however, it would permit Government to ban political speech simply because the speaker is an association that has taken on the corporate form. * * * If *Austin* were correct, the Government could prohibit a corporation from expressing political views in media beyond those presented here, such as by printing books.

Austin sought to defend the antidistortion rationale as a means to prevent corporations from obtaining "an unfair advantage in the political marketplace" by using "resources amassed in the economic marketplace." 494 U.S., at 659. But *Buckley* rejected the premise that the Government has an interest "in equalizing the relative ability of individuals and groups to influence the outcome of elections." 424 U.S., at 48. * * * The rule that political speech cannot be limited based on a speaker's wealth is a necessary consequence of the premise that the First Amendment generally prohibits the suppression of political speech based on the speaker's identity.

Austin's antidistortion rationale would produce the dangerous, and unacceptable, consequence that Congress could ban political speech of media corporations. Media corporations are now exempt from § 441b's ban on corporate expenditures. See 2 U.S.C. §§ 431(9)(B)(i), 434(f)(3)(B)(i). Yet media corporations accumulate wealth with the help of the corporate form, the largest media

> **Food for Thought**
>
> Where does the principle that the government may not suppress speech based on the speaker's identity come from? Is such regulation necessarily tantamount to content-based regulation? If not, why is it problematic?

corporations have "immense aggregations of wealth," and the views expressed by media corporations often "have little or no correlation to the public's support" for those views. Thus, under the Government's reasoning, wealthy media corporations could have their voices diminished to put them on par with other media entities. * * * The law's exception for media corporations is, on its own terms, all but an admission of the invalidity of the antidistortion rationale.

There is simply no support for the view that the First Amendment, as originally understood, would permit the suppression of political speech by media corporations. * * * The First Amendment [was] understood as a response to the repression of speech and the press that had existed in England and the heavy taxes on the press that were imposed in the colonies. * * * The Framers may have been unaware of certain types of speakers or forms of communication, but that does not mean that those speakers and media are entitled to less First Amendment protection than those types of speakers and media that provided the means of communicating political ideas when the Bill of Rights was adopted.

[T]he Government falls back on the argument that corporate political speech can be banned in order to prevent corruption or its appearance. In *Buckley,* the Court found this interest "sufficiently important" to allow limits on contributions but did not extend that reasoning to expenditure limits. [W]e now conclude that independent expenditures, including those made by corporations, do not give rise to corruption or the appearance of corruption. * * * [I]ndependent expenditures do not lead to, or create the appearance of, *quid pro quo* corruption. In fact, there is only scant evidence that independent expenditures even ingratiate. Ingratiation and access, in any event, are not corruption.

If elected officials succumb to improper influences from independent expenditures; if they surrender their best judgment; and if they put expediency before principle, then surely there is cause for concern. * * * The remedies enacted by law, however, must comply with the First Amendment; and, it is our law and our tradition that more speech, not less, is the governing rule. * * * Here Congress has created categorical bans on speech that are asymmetrical to preventing *quid pro quo* corruption.

> **Definition**
>
> "*Quid pro quo*" is Latin for "something for something." An example of *quid pro quo* corruption is bribery of politician in exchange for some government benefit.

Austin should be and now is overruled. We return to the principle established in *Buckley* and *Bellotti* that the Government may not suppress political speech on the basis of the speaker's corporate identity. * * * Section 441b's restrictions on corporate independent expenditures are therefore invalid and cannot be applied to *Hillary*. Given our conclusion we are further required to overrule the part of *McConnell* that upheld [BCRA's] extension of § 441b's restrictions on corporate independent expenditures.

[The Court rejected the petitioner's challenge to BCRA's disclaimer provision, which requires televised electioneering communications funded by anyone other than a candidate to identify clearly who is responsible for the communication, 2 U.S.C. § 441d(d)(2), and BCRA's disclosure provision, which requires any person who spends more than $10,000 on electioneering communications within a calendar year to file a statement with the FEC identifying the person making the expenditure, the amount of the expenditure, the election to which the communication was directed, and the names of certain contributors, 2 U.S.C. § 434(f)(1) & (2). The Court concluded, "Disclaimer and disclosure requirements may burden the ability to speak, but they 'impose no ceiling on campaign-related activities,' and 'do not prevent anyone from speaking.' "*]

[CHIEF JUSTICE ROBERTS's concurring opinion is omitted.]

JUSTICE SCALIA, with whom JUSTICE ALITO joins, and with whom JUSTICE THOMAS joins in part, concurring.

I write separately to address Justice STEVENS' [dissent, which] purports to show that today's decision is not supported by the original understanding of the First Amendment. The dissent attempts this demonstration, however, in splendid

---

* Justice Thomas joined all of the Court's opinion except the part upholding the disclaimer and disclosure requirements, which he concluded "abridge the right to anonymous speech."—*Eds.*

isolation from the text of the First Amendment. It never shows why "the freedom of speech" that was the right of Englishmen did not include the freedom to speak in association with other individuals, including association in the corporate form.

Instead of taking this straightforward approach to determining the Amendment's meaning, the dissent embarks on a detailed exploration of the Framers' views about the "role of corporations in society." The Framers didn't like corporations, the dissent concludes, and therefore it follows (as night the day) that corporations had no rights of free speech. Of course the Framers' personal affection or disaffection for corporations is relevant only insofar as it can be thought to be reflected in the understood meaning of the text they enacted—not, as the dissent suggests, as a freestanding substitute for that text.

[In any event, despite] the corporation-hating quotations the dissent has dredged up, it is far from clear that by the end of the 18th century corporations were despised. If so, how came there to be so many of them? * * * There were approximately 335 charters issued to business corporations in the United States by the end of the 18th century. [W]hat seems like a small number by today's standards surely does not indicate the relative importance of corporations when the Nation was considerably smaller. * * * Even if we thought it proper to apply the dissent's approach of excluding from First Amendment coverage what the Founders disliked, and even if we agreed that the Founders disliked founding-era corporations; modern corporations might not qualify for exclusion. Most of the Founders' resentment towards corporations was directed at the state-granted monopoly privileges that individually chartered corporations enjoyed. Modern corporations do not have such privileges, and would probably have been favored by most of our enterprising Founders—excluding, perhaps, Thomas Jefferson and others favoring perpetuation of an agrarian society. Moreover, [a]t the time of the founding, religious, educational, and literary corporations were incorporated under general incorporation statutes, much as business corporations are today. * * * Were all of these silently excluded from the protections of the First Amendment?

The dissent says that when the Framers "constitutionalized the right to free speech in the First Amendment, it was the free speech of individual Americans that they had in mind." That is no doubt true. All the provisions of the Bill of Rights set forth the rights of individual men and women—not, for example, of trees or polar bears. But the individual person's right to speak includes the right to speak *in association with other individual persons*. Surely the dissent does not believe that speech by the Republican Party or the Democratic Party can be censored because it is not the speech of "an individual American." It is the speech of many individual Americans, who have associated in a common cause, giving the leadership of the party the right to speak on their behalf. The association of individuals in a business corporation is no different—or at least it cannot be denied the right to speak on the simplistic ground that it is not "an individual American."

[The First Amendment] is written in terms of "speech," not speakers. Its text offers no foothold for excluding any category of speaker, from single individuals to partnerships of individuals, to unincorporated associations of individuals, to incorporated associations of individuals—and the dissent offers no evidence about the original meaning of the text to support any such exclusion.

We are therefore simply left with the question whether the speech at issue in this case is "speech" covered by the First Amendment. No one says otherwise. A documentary film critical of a potential Presidential candidate is core political speech, and its nature as such does not change simply because it was funded by a corporation.

JUSTICE STEVENS, with whom JUSTICE GINSBURG, JUSTICE BREYER, and JUSTICE SOTOMAYOR join, concurring in part and dissenting in part.

Pervading the Court's analysis is the ominous image of a "categorical ba[n]" on corporate speech. * * * This characterization is highly misleading, and needs to be corrected. * * * Under BCRA, any corporation's "stockholders and their families and its executive or administrative personnel and their families" can pool their resources [in a PAC] to finance electioneering communications. 2 U.S.C. § 441b(b)(4)(A)(i). A significant and growing number of corporations avail themselves of this option; during the most recent election cycle, corporate and union PACs raised nearly a billion dollars. Administering a PAC entails some administrative burden, but so does complying with the disclaimer, disclosure, and reporting requirements that the Court today upholds, and no one has suggested that the burden is severe for a sophisticated for-profit corporation. * * * [T]he majority's incessant talk of a "ban" aims at a straw man.

The second pillar of the Court's opinion is its assertion that "the Government cannot restrict political speech based on the speaker's . . . identity." * * * Apart perhaps from measures designed to protect the press, [the text of the First Amendment] might seem to permit no distinctions of any kind. Yet in a variety of contexts, we have held that speech can be regulated differentially on account of the speaker's identity, when identity is understood in categorical or institutional terms. The Government routinely places special restrictions on the speech rights of students, prisoners, members of the Armed Forces, foreigners, and its own employees. When such restrictions are justified by a legitimate governmental interest, they do not necessarily raise constitutional problems.

> **Make the Connection**
>
> We will consider the speech of government employees later in this chapter.

The same logic applies to this case with additional force because it is the identity of corporations, rather than individuals, that the Legislature has taken into account. * * * Campaign finance distinctions based on corporate identity tend to be less worrisome [because] the "speakers" are not natural persons, much less members of our political community, and the governmental interests are of the highest order. Furthermore, when corporations, as a class, are distinguished from noncorporations, as a class, there is a lesser risk that regulatory distinctions will reflect invidious discrimination or political favoritism.

A third fulcrum of the Court's opinion is the idea that *Austin* and *McConnell* are radical outliers, "aberration[s]," in our First Amendment tradition. The Court has it exactly backwards. It is today's holding that is the radical departure from what had been settled First Amendment law. * * * To the extent that the Framers' views are discernible and relevant to the disposition of this case, they would appear to cut strongly against the majority's position.

This is not only because the Framers and their contemporaries conceived of speech more narrowly than we now think of it, but also because they held very different views about the nature of the First Amendment right and the role of corporations in society. Those few corporations that existed at the founding were authorized by grant of a special legislative charter. * * * Corporations were created, supervised, and conceptualized as quasi-public entities, "designed to serve a social function for the state." The individualized charter mode of incorporation reflected the "cloud of disfavor under which corporations labored" in the early years of this Nation. Thomas Jefferson famously fretted that corporations would subvert the Republic. General incorporation statutes, and widespread acceptance of business corporations as socially useful actors, did not emerge until the 1800's.

The Framers thus took it as a given that corporations could be comprehensively regulated in the service of the public welfare. Unlike our colleagues, they had little trouble distinguishing corporations from human beings, and when they constitutionalized the right to free speech in the First Amendment, it was the free speech of individual Americans that they had in mind. While individuals might join together to exercise their speech rights, business corporations, at least, were plainly not seen as facilitating such associational or expressive ends. In light of these background practices and understandings, it seems to me implausible that the Framers believed "the freedom of speech" would extend equally to all corporate speakers, much less that it would preclude legislatures from taking limited measures to guard against corporate capture of elections.

In fairness, our campaign finance jurisprudence has never attended very closely to the views of the Framers, whose political universe differed profoundly from that of today. [But] in light of the Court's effort to cast itself as guardian of ancient values, it pays to remember that nothing in our constitutional history dictates today's outcome. To the contrary, [a] century of more recent history puts to rest any notion that today's ruling is faithful to our First Amendment tradition. At the federal level, the express distinction between corporate and individual political spending on elections stretches back to 1907, when Congress passed the Tillman Act banning all corporate contributions to candidates.

In the Court's view, *Buckley* and *Bellotti* decisively rejected the possibility of distinguishing corporations from natural persons in the 1970's. [But it] is implausible to think, as the majority suggests, that *Buckley* covertly invalidated FECA's separate corporate and union campaign expenditure restriction, even though that restriction had been on the books for decades before *Buckley* and would remain on the books, undisturbed, for decades after. [And] *Bellotti* ruled, in an explicit limitation on the scope of its holding, that "our consideration of a corporation's right to speak on issues of general public interest implies no comparable right in the quite different context of participation in a political campaign for election to public office." 435 U.S., at 788, n. 26. * * * The *Bellotti* Court confronted a dramatically different factual situation from the one that confronts us in this case: a state statute that barred business corporations' expenditures on some referenda but not others. * * * *Bellotti* thus involved a *viewpoint-discriminatory* statute, created to effect a particular policy outcome. * * * *Austin* and *McConnell*, then, sit perfectly well with *Bellotti*.

[I] come at last to the interests that are at stake. Undergirding the majority's approach to the merits is the claim that the only "sufficiently important governmental interest in preventing corruption or the appearance of corruption" is one that is "limited to *quid pro quo* corruption." [But corruption] operates along a spectrum, and the majority's apparent belief that *quid pro quo* arrangements can be neatly demarcated from other improper influences does not accord with the theory or reality of politics. It certainly does not accord with the record Congress developed in passing BCRA, a record that stands as a remarkable testament to the energy and ingenuity with which corporations, unions, lobbyists, and politicians may go about scratching each other's backs—and which amply supported Congress' determination to target a limited set of especially destructive practices. * * * Starting today, corporations with large war chests to deploy on electioneering may find democratically elected bodies becoming much more attuned to their interests.

The majority seems oblivious to the simple truth that laws such as [§ 441b] do not merely pit the anticorruption interest against the First Amendment, but also pit competing First Amendment values against each other. * * * The Court's blinkered and aphoristic approach to the First Amendment may well promote corporate power at the cost of the individual and collective self-expression the Amendment was meant to serve.

At bottom, the Court's opinion is [a] rejection of the common sense of the American people, who have recognized a need to prevent corporations from undermining self-government since the founding, and who have fought against the distinctive corrupting potential of corporate electioneering since the days of Theodore Roosevelt. It is a strange time to repudiate that common sense. While American democracy is imperfect, few outside the majority of this Court would have thought its flaws included a dearth of corporate money in politics.

POINTS FOR DISCUSSION

a. Theory of the First Amendment

What is the Court's theory of the First Amendment? Is the Court concerned with the corporate speaker's right to communicate or with the public's right to hear the speaker's message? Is there a difference? If so, does Justice Stevens have a different vision of the First Amendment?

b. The Reach of the Ban on Corporate Speech

Many advocacy organizations from across the political spectrum—including the Sierra Club, the National Rifle Association, and the American Civil Liberties Union—are organized as non-profit corporations. The provision at issue in *Citizens United* thus prohibited such organizations from expressly advocating the election or defeat of a candidate within 60 days of an election (or 30 days of a primary election). Does this fact strengthen the Court's conclusion, or instead justify Congress's decision to limit corporate independent expenditures?

c. State of the Union Address

At the 2010 State of the Union address, President Obama criticized the Court's decision in *Citizens United,* saying: "With all due deference to the separation of powers, last week the Supreme Court reversed a century of law that I believe will open the floodgates for special interests—including foreign corporations—to spend without limit in our elections." Justice Alito, who was in the audience, appeared to mouth the words, "Not true." Who was correct? Was either comment inappropriate?

8. Speech of Public Employees

Suppose that an employee makes comments that his or her employer does not like. For example, the employee might criticize the employer's management style or say negative things about his co-workers' performance. If the employer is a private business, the employer generally may fire the employee for these comments without violating the First Amendment. As we noted in Volume 1, under the state action doctrine, the First Amendment applies to government institutions and officials, but does not apply to non-state actors like private businesses.

When the employer is the government, the situation is more complicated. Under the First Amendment, the government generally cannot take adverse actions against individuals based upon the content of their speech. In addition, as we saw in the first part of this chapter, "the government 'may not deny a benefit to a person on a basis that infringes his constitutionally protected * * * freedom of speech' even if he has no entitlement to that benefit." *Board of Commissioners, Wabaunsee County v. Umbehr,* 518 U.S. 668, 674 (1996). The Court thus has, at least as a matter of theory, rejected the absolutist premise behind Justice Holmes's famous statement, in a case upholding the termination of a police officer for engaging in political activities, that the "petitioner may have a constitutional right to talk politics, but he has no constitutional right to be a policeman." *McAuliffe v. New Bedford,* 29 N.E. 517 (Mass. 1892).

Yet the government—like a private employer—needs some ability to control the speech and conduct of its employees. The Supreme Court balanced these competing concerns in *Connick v. Myers,* 461 U.S. 138 (1983). In that case, a district attorney fired an assistant district attorney after she prepared and distributed a questionnaire soliciting the views of other staff on office morale, confidence in supervisors, and other subjects. The assistant district attorney claimed that her firing violated the First Amendment. In assessing her claim, the Supreme Court drew a distinction. Adverse personnel actions based upon speech about private concerns generally do not implicate the First Amendment. But if an employee speaks on matters of public concern, the government may take an adverse action only if the government's needs as an employer exceed the employee's interest in free speech. The Court pursued this balancing approach in other cases, as well. See, e.g., *Pickering v. Board of Ed. of Township High School Dist. 205, Will Cty.,* 391 U.S. 563, 568 (1968).

In the following case, the Supreme Court further refined this test. It held that speech about matters of public concern is protected only if the employee is speaking in a private capacity. In reading the case, think carefully about what this new limitation means.

GARCETTI V. CEBALLOS

547 U.S. 410 (2006)

JUSTICE KENNEDY delivered the opinion of the Court.

It is well settled that "a State cannot condition public employment on a basis that infringes the employee's constitutionally protected interest in freedom of expression." *Connick v. Myers,* 461 U.S. 138, 142 (1983). The question presented by the instant case is whether the First Amendment protects a government employee from discipline based on speech made pursuant to the employee's official duties.

Respondent Richard Ceballos has been employed since 1989 as a deputy district attorney for the Los Angeles County District Attorney's Office. During the period relevant to this case, Ceballos was a calendar deputy in the office's Pomona branch, and in this capacity he exercised certain supervisory responsibilities over other lawyers. In February 2000, a defense attorney contacted Ceballos about a pending criminal case. The defense attorney said there were inaccuracies in an affidavit used to obtain a critical search warrant. The attorney informed Ceballos that he had filed a motion to traverse, or challenge, the warrant, but he also wanted Ceballos to review the case. According to Ceballos, it was not unusual for defense attorneys to ask calendar deputies to investigate aspects of pending cases.

After examining the affidavit and visiting the location it described, Ceballos determined the affidavit contained serious misrepresentations. The affidavit called a long driveway what Ceballos thought should have been referred to as a separate roadway. Ceballos also questioned the affidavit's statement that tire tracks led from a stripped-down truck to the premises covered by the warrant. His doubts arose from his conclusion that the roadway's composition in some places made it difficult or impossible to leave visible tire tracks.

Ceballos spoke on the telephone to the warrant affiant, a deputy sheriff from the Los Angeles County Sheriff's Department, but he did not receive a satisfactory explanation for the perceived inaccuracies. He relayed his findings to his supervisors, petitioners Carol Najera and Frank Sundstedt, and followed up by preparing a disposition memorandum. The memo explained Ceballos' concerns and recommended dismissal of the case. On March 2, 2000, Ceballos submitted the memo to Sundstedt for his review. * * *

Despite Ceballos' concerns, Sundstedt decided to proceed with the prosecution, pending disposition of the defense motion to traverse. The trial court held a hearing on the motion. Ceballos was called by the defense and recounted his observations about the affidavit, but the trial court rejected the challenge to the warrant.

Ceballos claims that in the aftermath of these events he was subjected to a series of retaliatory employment actions. The actions included reassignment from his calendar deputy position to a trial deputy position, transfer to another courthouse, and denial of a promotion. [Ceballos claimed that the petitioners violated the First and Fourteenth Amendments by retaliating against him based on his memo of March 2.]

The Court has made clear that public employees do not surrender all their First Amendment rights by reason of their employment. Rather, the First Amendment protects a public employee's right, in certain circumstances, to speak as a citizen addressing matters of public concern. See, *e.g. Pickering v. Board of Ed. of Township High School Dist. 205, Will Cty.,* 391 U.S. 563, 568 (1968).

Pickering provides a useful starting point in explaining the Court's doctrine. There the relevant speech was a teacher's letter to a local newspaper addressing issues including the funding policies of his school board. "The problem in any case," the Court stated, "is to arrive at a balance between the interests of the teacher, as a citizen, in commenting upon matters of public concern and the interest of the State, as an employer, in promoting the efficiency of the public services it performs through its employees." *Id.* at 568. The Court found the teacher's speech "neither [was] shown nor can be presumed to have in any way either impeded the teacher's proper performance of his daily duties in the classroom or to have interfered with the regular operation of the schools generally." *Id.* at 568. Thus, the Court concluded that "the interest of the school administration in limiting teachers' opportunities to contribute to public debate is not significantly greater than its interest in limiting a similar contribution by any member of the general public." *Id.* at 573.

Pickering and the cases decided in its wake identify two inquiries to guide interpretation of the constitutional protections accorded to public employee speech. The first requires determining whether the employee spoke as a citizen on a matter of public concern. If the answer is no, the employee has no First Amendment cause of action based on his or her employer's reaction to the speech. *See Connick,* 461 U.S. at 147. If the answer is yes, then the possibility of a First Amendment claim arises. The question becomes whether the relevant government entity had an adequate justification for treating the employee differently from any other member of the general public. *See Pickering,* 391 U.S., at 568. This consideration reflects the importance of the relationship between the speaker's expressions and employment. A government entity has broader discretion to restrict speech when it acts in its role as employer, but the restrictions it imposes must be directed at speech that has some potential to affect the entity's operations.

When a citizen enters government service, the citizen by necessity must accept certain limitations on his or her freedom. Government employers, like private employers, need a significant degree of control over their employees' words and actions; without it, there would be little chance for the efficient provision of public services. Public employees, moreover, often occupy trusted positions in society. When they speak out, they can express views that contravene governmental policies or impair the proper performance of governmental functions.

> **Food for Thought**
>
> The government can speak only through the individuals who work for it. Does the government have an independent interest in controlling its own speech? If so, is that interest protected by the First Amendment, or is it merely an interest relevant to determining whether the government has violated the Amendment?

At the same time, the Court has recognized that a citizen who works for the government is nonetheless a citizen. The First Amendment limits the ability of a public employer to leverage the employment relationship to restrict, incidentally or intentionally, the liberties employees enjoy in their capacities as private citizens. So long as employees are speaking as citizens about matters of public concern, they must face only those speech restrictions that are necessary for their employers to operate efficiently and effectively. *See, e.g., Connick,* 461 U.S. at 147 ("Our responsibility is to ensure that citizens are not deprived of fundamental rights by virtue of working for the government").

With these principles in mind we turn to the instant case. Respondent Ceballos believed the affidavit used to obtain a search warrant contained serious misrepresentations. He conveyed his opinion and recommendation in a memo to his supervisor. That Ceballos expressed his views inside his office, rather than publicly, is not dispositive. Employees in some cases may receive First Amendment protection for expressions made at work. *See, e.g., Givhan v. Western Line Consol. School Dist.,* 439 U.S. 410, 414 (1979). Many citizens do much of their talking inside their respective workplaces, and it would not serve the goal of treating public employees like "any member of the general public," *Pickering,* 391 U.S., at 573, to hold that all speech within the office is automatically exposed to restriction.

The memo concerned the subject matter of Ceballos' employment, but this, too, is nondispositive. The First Amendment protects some expressions related to the speaker's job. As the Court noted in *Pickering*: "Teachers are, as a class, the members of a community most likely to have informed and definite opinions as to how funds allotted to the operation of the schools should be spent. Accordingly, it is essential that they be able to speak out freely on such questions without fear of retaliatory dismissal." 391 U.S., at 572. The same is true of many other categories of public employees.

The controlling factor in Ceballos' case is that his expressions were made pursuant to his duties as a calendar deputy. That consideration—the fact that Ceballos spoke as a prosecutor fulfilling a responsibility to advise his supervisor about how best to proceed with a pending case—distinguishes Ceballos' case from those in which the First Amendment provides protection against discipline. We hold that when public employees make statements pursuant to their official duties, the employees are not speaking as citizens for First Amendment purposes, and the Constitution does not insulate their communications from employer discipline.

Ceballos wrote his disposition memo because that is part of what he, as a calendar deputy, was employed to do. It is immaterial whether he experienced some personal gratification from writing the memo; his First Amendment rights do not depend on his job satisfaction. The significant point is that the memo was written pursuant to Ceballos' official duties. Restricting speech that owes its existence to a public employee's professional responsibilities does not infringe any liberties the employee might have enjoyed as a private citizen. It simply reflects the exercise of employer control over what the employer itself has commissioned or created. * * *

JUSTICE STEVENS, dissenting.

The proper answer to the question "whether the First Amendment protects a government employee from discipline based on speech made pursuant to the employee's official duties," is "Sometimes," not "Never." Of course a supervisor may take corrective action when such speech is "inflammatory or misguided." But what if it is just unwelcome speech because it reveals facts that the supervisor would rather not have anyone else discover?*

JUSTICE SOUTER, with whom JUSTICE STEVENS and JUSTICE GINSBURG join, dissenting.

I agree with the majority that a government employer has substantial interests in effectuating its chosen policy and objectives, and in demanding competence, honesty, and judgment from employees who speak for it in doing their work. But I would hold that private and public interests in addressing official wrongdoing and threats to health and safety can outweigh the government's stake in the efficient implementation of policy, and when they do public employees who speak on these matters in the course of their duties should be eligible to claim First Amendment protection.

JUSTICE BREYER, dissenting.

[In this case, the] respondent, a government lawyer, complained of retaliation, in part, on the basis of speech contained in his disposition memorandum that he says fell within the scope of his obligations under *Brady v. Maryland*, 373 U.S. 83 (1963). The facts present two special circumstances that together justify First Amendment review.

> **FYI**
>
> In *Brady*, the Court held that prosecutors must disclose to the defense evidence that is material to guilt or punishment. We consider *Brady* in Chapter 14.

First, the speech at issue is professional speech—the speech of a lawyer. Such speech is subject to independent regulation by canons of the profession. Those canons provide an obligation to speak in certain instances. And where that is so,

---

* See, *e.g.*, *Branton v. Dallas*, 272 F.3d 730 (5th Cir. 2001) (police internal investigator demoted by police chief after bringing the false testimony of a fellow officer to the attention of a city official); *Miller v. Jones*, 444 F.3d 929, 936 (7th Cir. 2006) (police officer demoted after opposing the police chief's attempt to "us[e] his official position to coerce a financially independent organization into a potentially ruinous merger"); *Delgado v. Jones*, 282 F.3d 511 (7th Cir. 2002) (police officer sanctioned for reporting criminal activity that implicated a local political figure who was a good friend of the police chief); *Herts v. Smith*, 345 F.3d 581 (8th Cir. 2003) (school district official's contract was not renewed after she gave frank testimony about the district's desegregation efforts); *Kincade v. Blue Springs*, 64 F.3d 389 (8th Cir. 1995) (engineer fired after reporting to his supervisors that contractors were failing to complete dam-related projects and that the resulting dam might be structurally unstable); *Fox v. District of Columbia*, 83 F.3d 1491, 1494 (D.C. Cir. 1996) (D.C. Lottery Board security officer fired after informing the police about a theft made possible by "rather drastic managerial ineptitude").

the government's own interest in forbidding that speech is diminished. * * * Second, the Constitution itself here imposes speech obligations upon the government's professional employee. A prosecutor has a constitutional obligation to learn of, to preserve, and to communicate with the defense about exculpatory and impeachment evidence in the government's possession. * * *

Where professional and special constitutional obligations are both present, the need to protect the employee's speech is augmented, the need for broad government authority to control that speech is likely diminished, and administrable standards are quite likely available. Hence, I would find that the Constitution mandates special protection of employee speech in such circumstances. Thus I would apply the *Pickering* balancing test here.

POINTS FOR DISCUSSION

a.   Official Capacity v. Private Capacity

Under the Court's approach in *Garcetti*, public employees' statements pursuant to their official duties are not protected by the First Amendment. How does the Court tell whether a particular statement was made in that capacity? Suppose, for example, that Mr. Ceballos had talked to a reporter or sent a letter to the editor of a local newspaper at the same time that he prepared the memo in question, and that he had then been fired. Would he have been fired for speaking in his capacity as a private citizen or in his official capacity? How would a court make that determination?

b.   Whistleblowers

Does the Court's decision in *Garcetti* make it more difficult for "whistleblowers" publicly to disclose government wrongdoing? If so, is the Court's decision consistent with the theory that the First Amendment is designed to ensure, among other things, the means for citizens to hold their government accountable for bad decision-making and wrongdoing?

Problem

Most college deans are professors who serve in the role of dean at the pleasure of the university president. The president of the university, in other words, can ask a dean at any time to step down and assume a non-leadership position on the faculty. Suppose that the dean of a college at a state university writes a well-researched but controversial article on a sensitive political topic. Unhappy with what the dean has written, and fearing condemnation by donors, the president of the university asks the dean to step down. Has the university president violated the dean's First Amendment rights?

9. Other Categories?

In this section, we have considered whether there are categories of speech, defined by their content, that are outside of the protection of the First Amendment. Are there other such categories that the Court has not yet identified? If so, how will the Court go about identifying them? Consider the case that follows.

UNITED STATES V. STEVENS
559 U.S. 460 (2010)

CHIEF JUSTICE ROBERTS delivered the opinion of the Court.

18 U.S.C. § 48 establishes a criminal penalty of up to five years in prison for anyone who knowingly "creates, sells, or possesses a depiction of animal cruelty," if done "for commercial gain" in interstate or foreign commerce. § 48(a). A depiction of "animal cruelty" is defined as one "in which a living animal is intentionally maimed, mutilated, tortured, wounded, or killed," if that conduct violates federal or state law where "the creation, sale, or possession takes place." § 48(c)(1). In what is referred to as the "exceptions clause," the law exempts from prohibition any depiction "that has serious religious, political, scientific, educational, journalistic, historical, or artistic value." § 48(b).

The legislative background of § 48 focused primarily on the interstate market for "crush videos." According to the House Committee Report on the bill, such videos feature the intentional torture and killing of helpless animals, including cats, dogs, monkeys, mice, and hamsters. H.R.Rep. No. 106–397, p. 2 (1999). Crush videos often depict women slowly crushing animals to death "with their bare feet or while wearing high heeled shoes," sometimes while "talking to the animals in a kind of dominatrix patter" over "[t]he cries and squeals of the animals, obviously in great pain." *Ibid.* Apparently these depictions "appeal to persons with a very specific sexual fetish who find them sexually arousing or otherwise exciting." *Id.,* at 2–3. The acts depicted in crush videos are typically prohibited by the animal cruelty laws enacted by all 50 States and the District of Columbia. But crush videos rarely disclose the participants' identities, inhibiting prosecution of the underlying conduct.

This case, however, involves an application of § 48 to depictions of animal fighting. * * * Respondent Robert J. Stevens ran a business, "Dogs of Velvet and Steel," and an associated Web site, through which he sold videos of pit bulls engaging in dogfights and attacking other animals. Among these videos were Japan Pit Fights and Pick-A-Winna: A Pit Bull Documentary, which include contemporary footage of dogfights in Japan (where such conduct is allegedly legal) as well as footage of American dogfights from the 1960's and 1970's. A third video, Catch Dogs and Country Living, depicts the use of pit bulls to hunt wild boar, as well as a "gruesome" scene of a pit bull attacking a domestic farm pig. On the basis of these videos, Stevens was indicted on three counts of violating § 48. Stevens moved to dismiss the indictment, arguing that § 48 is facially invalid under the First Amendment. [The Court of Appeals held that Section 48 was facially invalid.]

The Government's primary submission is that § 48 necessarily complies with the Constitution because the banned depictions of animal cruelty, as a class, are categorically unprotected by the First Amendment. We disagree.

"[A]s a general matter, the First Amendment means that government has no power to restrict expression because of its message, its ideas, its subject matter, or its content." *Ashcroft v. American Civil Liberties Union*, 535 U.S. 564, 573 (2002). Section 48 explicitly regulates expression based on content: The statute restricts "visual [and] auditory depiction[s]," such as photographs, videos, or sound recordings, depending on whether they depict conduct in which a living animal is intentionally harmed. As such, § 48 is " 'presumptively invalid,' and the Government bears the burden to rebut that presumption." *United States v. Playboy Entertainment Group, Inc.*, 529 U.S. 803, 817 (2000) (quoting *R.A.V. v. St. Paul*, 505 U.S. 377, 382 (1992)).

"From 1791 to the present," however, the First Amendment has "permitted restrictions upon the content of speech in a few limited areas" * * *. *Id.*, at 382–383. These "historic and traditional categories long familiar to the bar"—including obscenity, defamation, fraud, incitement, and speech integral to criminal conduct—are "well-defined and narrowly limited classes of speech, the prevention and punishment of which have never been thought to raise any Constitutional problem." *Chaplinsky v. New Hampshire*, 315 U.S. 568, 571–572 (1942).

The Government argues that "depictions of animal cruelty" should be added to the list. * * * As the Government notes, the prohibition of animal cruelty itself has a long history in American law, starting with the early settlement of the Colonies. But we are unaware of any similar tradition excluding *depictions* of animal cruelty from "the freedom of speech" codified in the First Amendment, and the Government points us to none. The Government contends that * * * categories of speech may be exempted from the First Amendment's protection without any long-settled tradition of subjecting that speech to regulation. Instead, the Government * * * proposes that a claim of categorical exclusion should be considered under a simple balancing test: "Whether a given category of speech enjoys First Amendment protection depends upon a categorical balancing of the value of the speech against its societal costs." Brief for United States 8.

As a free-floating test for First Amendment coverage, that sentence is startling and dangerous. The First Amendment's guarantee of free speech does not extend only to categories of speech that survive an ad hoc balancing of relative social costs and benefits. The First Amendment itself reflects a judgment by the American people that the benefits of its restrictions on the Government outweigh the costs. Our Constitution forecloses any attempt to revise that judgment simply on the basis that some speech is not worth it.

To be fair to the Government, its view did not emerge from a vacuum. As the Government correctly notes, this Court has often *described* historically unprotected categories of speech as being "of such slight social value as a step to truth that any benefit that may be derived from them is clearly outweighed by the social interest in order and morality." *R.A.V.*, 505 U.S. at 383 (quoting *Chaplinsky*, 315 U.S. at 572). In *New York v. Ferber*, 458 U.S. 747 (1982), we noted that within these categories of unprotected speech, "the evil to be restricted so overwhelmingly outweighs the expressive interests, if any, at stake, that no process of case-by-case adjudication is required," because "the balance of competing interests is clearly struck." The Government derives its proposed test from these descriptions in our precedents.

But such descriptions are just that—descriptive. They do not set forth a test that may be applied as a general matter to permit the Government to imprison any speaker so long as his speech is deemed valueless or unnecessary, or so long as an ad hoc calculus of costs and benefits tilts in a statute's favor.

When we have identified categories of speech as fully outside the protection of the First Amendment, it has not been on the basis of a simple cost-benefit analysis. In *Ferber*, for example, we classified child pornography as such a category. We noted that the State of New York had a compelling interest in protecting children from abuse, and that the value of using children

> **FYI**
>
> *Giboney* involved the application of a state antitrust law to a union that was picketing—and thus engaged in expressive activity—as a means to restrain trade.

in these works (as opposed to simulated conduct or adult actors) was *de minimis*. But our decision did not rest on this "balance of competing interests" alone. *Id.,* at 764. We made clear that [the] market for child pornography was "intrinsically related" to the underlying abuse, and was therefore "an integral part of the production of such materials, an activity illegal throughout the Nation." *Id.,* at 759.

As we noted, "[i]t rarely has been suggested that the constitutional freedom for speech and press extends its immunity to speech or writing used as an integral part of conduct in violation of a valid criminal statute." *Id.,* at 761–762 (quoting *Giboney v. Empire Storage & Ice Co.,* 336 U.S. 490, 498 (1949)). *Ferber* thus grounded its analysis in a previously recognized, long-established category of unprotected speech * * *.

Our decisions in *Ferber* and other cases cannot be taken as establishing a freewheeling authority to declare new categories of speech outside the scope of the First Amendment. Maybe there are some categories of speech that have been historically unprotected, but have not yet been specifically identified or discussed as such in our case law. But if so, there is no evidence that "depictions of animal cruelty" is among them. We need not foreclose the future recognition of such additional categories to reject the Government's highly manipulable balancing test as a means of identifying them.

Because we decline to carve out from the First Amendment any novel exception for § 48, we review Stevens's First Amendment challenge under our existing doctrine. [The Court concluded that Section 48 creates "a criminal prohibition of alarming breadth" and is "substantially overbroad, and therefore invalid under the First Amendment."]

[JUSTICE ALITO's dissenting opinion is omitted.]

POINTS FOR DISCUSSION

a. Identifying Excluded Categories

According to the Court, what is the appropriate test for determining if a category of speech is excluded from the protection of the First Amendment? Is it based only on history? If so, do the other categories of speech that the Court has excluded obviously satisfy the test?

b. Child Pornography and Animal Cruelty

The Court stated that its conclusion in *Ferber* that non-obscene child pornography is outside of the protection of the First Amendment was "grounded" in the excluded category of speech used as an "integral part of conduct in violation of a valid criminal statute." Do you agree that this was the basis of the Court's decision in *Ferber?* Even if it was, in what way does that distinguish it from this case? After all, just as the related criminal "conduct" in *Ferber* was the actual exploitation of children (rather than the distribution of the videos that chronicled the exploitation), the statute in *Stevens* applied only to videos that depicted animal cruelty that violates state or federal law. Is this a fair basis for treating "crush videos" differently?

c.   **"Crush Videos" and Obscenity**

The statute at issue in *Stevens* exempted from the prohibition any depiction "that has serious religious, political, scientific, educational, journalistic, historical, or artistic value," a standard that Congress obviously based on the Court's obscenity doctrine. Why wasn't this exemption sufficient to protect the statute from a First Amendment challenge?

Executive Summary of This Chapter

Basic Ideas

The First Amendment says, in part, that "Congress shall make no law * * * abridging the freedom of speech." The amendment does not define "the freedom of speech."

The Supreme Court has said in many cases that the freedom is not absolute. See, e.g., *Virginia v. Black*, 538 U.S. 343, 358 (2003). On the contrary, some regulation of speech is possible. The central question therefore is: What kind of government regulations are allowed, and what kinds are not? In answering this question, the Supreme Court has adopted a number of standards that essentially weigh the value of free speech against the importance of governmental regulations.

Although the First Amendment refers to "Congress," the Supreme Court has held that the protection of freedom of speech applies to the states through the Fourteenth Amendment under the incorporation doctrine. *Grosjean v. American Press Co.*, 297 U.S. 233, 244 (1936).

In interpreting the First Amendment, the Supreme Court has developed a number of distinct doctrines and rules. These doctrines and rules basically fall into two general categories. Some concern the types of regulation that the government wants to impose on speech. Others focus on the kinds of speech that the government wants to regulate.

Types of Regulations on Speech

The Supreme Court subjects **content-based restrictions** to strict scrutiny: The government may enforce a content-based restriction on speech that does not fall into a recognized exception only if the regulation is necessary to serve a compelling state interest and the regulation is narrowly drawn to achieve that end. *Reed v. Town of Gilbert, Arizona*, 576 U.S. 155 (2015).

The government may impose **reasonable restrictions on the time, place, or manner of speech**, even in public forums, if the restrictions (1) are content neutral; (2) are narrowly tailored to serve a significant governmental interest; and

(3) leave open ample alternative channels for communication of the information. *Ward v. Rock Against Racism*, 491 U.S. 781, 791 (1989).

The government may enforce a **generally applicable regulation**, even when it incidentally burdens expressive activities, if "it furthers an important or substantial governmental interest; if the governmental interest is unrelated to the suppression of free expression; and if the incidental restriction on alleged First Amendment freedoms is no greater than is essential to the furtherance of that interest." *United States v. O'Brien*, 391 U.S. 367 (1968).

A **prior restraint on speech** is an executive or judicial order prohibiting a communication before it has occurred. The First Amendment provides more protection against prior restraints on speech than it does against subsequent liability for speech. Although the Court has suggested that the First Amendment does not absolutely bar prior restraints, and that exceptions might exist, it has not fully specified what these exceptions might be. *New York Times Co. v. United States*, 403 U.S. 713 (1971).

A law regulating speech is **overbroad** if it reaches both protected and unprotected speech. A law is **vague** if it does not make clear to a reasonable person what it prohibits and what it does not. In the First Amendment context, overbroad and vague laws may be challenged either **as applied** to the actual facts of a particular case or **on their face** without regard to the particular facts. The standards for facial challenges are relaxed because overbroad or vague laws may have a **chilling effect** on protected speech; unless the constitutionality is clarified, speakers worried about liability under the laws may censor their speech more than is constitutionally required. *NAACP v. Button*, 371 U.S. 415 (1963); *Schad v. Borough of Mount Ephraim*, 452 U.S. 61 (1981).

The **unconstitutional conditions** doctrine says that the government may not grant or deny benefits to a person based on whether the person engages in speech protected by the First Amendment. But the government can **selectively fund programs** and does not have to pay for all speech. *Rust v. Sullivan*, 500 U.S. 173, 194 (1991).

Categories of Speech

The First Amendment does not allow the government to proscribe **advocacy of crime** except where such advocacy is directed to inciting or producing imminent lawless action and is likely to incite or produce such action. *Brandenburg v. Ohio*, 395 U.S. 444 (1969).

The First Amendment does not absolutely prohibit liability for defamatory statements. Generally speaking, a plaintiff may recover for the torts of slander and libel. *Beauharnais v. People of State of Illinois*, 343 U.S. 250, 266 (1952). But the First Amendment does impose some important restrictions. First, a **public official, political candidate, or public figure** may not recover in tort for a defamatory statement unless the statement was both false and made with actual malice. *New York Times Co. v. Sullivan*, 376 U.S. 254 (1964). Second, a private figure may not recover for a defamatory statement regarding **a matter of public concern** unless the statement was both false and made with at least negligence. A statement is made with **actual malice** if it is deliberately false or if the speaker was reckless with regard to its falsity. A **"public figure"** is generally someone, like a movie star or other celebrity, who has voluntarily become the subject of public attention. A **"matter of public concern"** is something that has significant news value.

The First Amendment does not protect **obscenity**. *Roth v. United States*, 354 U.S. 476 (1957). Whether speech is obscene depends on the following factors:

(a) whether the average person, applying contemporary community standards would find that the work, taken as a whole, appeals to the prurient interest; (b) whether the work depicts or describes, in a patently offensive way, sexual conduct specifically defined by the applicable state law; and (c) whether the work, taken as a whole, lacks serious literary, artistic, political, or scientific value.

Miller v. California, 413 U.S. 15, 24 (1973) (internal quotation marks and citations omitted). The First Amendment also does not protect **child pornography**, regardless of whether it is obscene. *New York v. Ferber*, 458 U.S. 747 (1982).

The First Amendment protects **expressive conduct** if it is "sufficiently imbued with elements of communication." *Spence v. Washington*, 418 U.S. 405 (1974). The government may regulate expressive conduct if four conditions are met: (1) the regulation is within the constitutional power of the Government; (2) the regulation furthers an important or substantial governmental interest; (3) the governmental interest is unrelated to the suppression of free expression; and (4) the incidental restriction on alleged First Amendment freedoms is no greater than is essential to the furtherance of that interest. *United States v. O'Brien*, 391 U.S. 367 (1968). Government regulation of conduct that is directed at the expressive elements of the conduct, however, fails the third factor of the test and accordingly is subject to strict scrutiny. *Texas v. Johnson*, 491 U.S. 397 (1989).

The First Amendment does not protect **fighting words**, which are words "which by their very utterance inflict injury or tend to incite an immediate breach of the peace." *Chaplinsky v. State of New Hampshire*, 315 U.S. 568 (1942). Words that are merely offensive and not likely to provoke a fight are not fighting words. *Cohen* *v. California*, 403 U.S. 15 (1971). The government may not impose certain content-based restrictions on fighting words. *R.A.V. v. City of St. Paul, Minn.*, 505 U.S. 377 (1992). Speech made at a public place on a matter of public concern, however, cannot be restricted simply because it is upsetting or arouses contempt. *Snyder v. Phelps*, 562 U.S. 443 (2011).

Commercial speech consists of advertising and other business communications. Under the leading case of *Central Hudson Gas & Electric Corp. v. Public Service Comm'n of New York*, 447 U.S. 557 (1980), the Supreme Court has divided commercial speech into two categories. First, commercial speech that concerns an unlawful activity or that is fraudulent or misleading has no First Amendment protection. Second, other commercial speech may be regulated if the government has a substantial interest, the regulation directly furthers the interest, and the regulations restrain speech only to the extent necessary to further the interest. *Posadas de Puerto Rico Associates v. Tourism Co. of Puerto Rico*, 478 U.S. 328 (1986).

The First Amendment applies to **campaign financing**. It prohibits the government from regulating how much money a political candidate can spend, but permits the government to regulate campaign contributions to avoid corruption or the appearance of corruption. *Buckley v. Valeo*, 424 U.S. 1 (1976). The First Amendment also prohibits the government from limiting the right of corporations to spend money to support candidates for political office. *Citizens United v. Federal Election Comm'n*, 558 U.S. 310 (2010). Although Congress may restrict the total amount of money a donor may contribute to any one candidate, Congress may not restrict the aggregate amount of money a donor may contribute to all candidates. *McCutcheon v. Federal Election Comm'n*, 572 U.S. 185 (2014).

The First Amendment also applies to some speech of **government employees**. The government may take adverse personnel actions based on speech about private concerns. But if an employee speaks on matters of public concern, the government may take an adverse action only if the government's needs as an employer exceed the employee's interest in free speech. *Connick v. Myers*, 461 U.S. 138 (1983). In addition, speech about matters of public concern is protected only if the employee is speaking in a private capacity. *Garcetti v. Ceballos*, 547 U.S. 410 (2006).

CHAPTER 9

Freedom of the Press

INTRODUCTION

Before the Revolution, John Hancock, John Adams, and other dissidents published articles in newspapers and journals criticizing British rule over the colonies. Through their articles, they helped to spread revolutionary ideas. In writing their missives, these authors typically used pseudonyms to conceal their identities. They feared imprisonment for the content of their writing because a general freedom of the press did not exist. See Clyde Augustus Duniway, *The Development of Freedom of the Press in Massachusetts* 123 (1906).

In Virginia, after the royal governor dissolved the House of Burgesses (the colonial legislature), a number of revolutionary figures held a series of meetings called the Virginia Conventions. At the convention held in June of 1776, the members adopted the Virginia Declaration of Rights. This document, drafted principally by George Mason, later influenced both the Declaration of Independence and the Bill of Rights. In addition to addressing various other liberties, the document announced that "the Freedom of the Press is one of the great Bulwarks of Liberty, and can never be restrained but by despotick Governments."

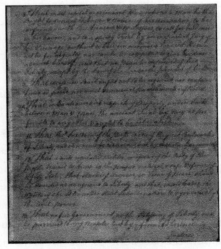

Virginia Declaration of Rights, Section 12
Library of Virginia

The original Constitution contained no mention of a freedom of the press. During the ratification period, Anti-Federalists criticized the Constitution for this omission. One of the leading Anti-Federalists, writing under the pseudonym Federal Farmer, argued: "All parties apparently agree, that the freedom of the press is a fundamental right, and ought not to be restrained by any taxes, duties, or in any manner whatever. Why should not the people, in adopting a federal constitution, declare this, even if there are only doubts about it." Federal Farmer, No. 16 (Jan. 20, 1788) (reprinted in *The Complete Anti-Federalist* (Herbert J. Storing ed. 1981), and *The Founders' Constitution* (Philip B. Kurland & Ralph Lerner eds. 1986)). Although this sentiment did not prevent ratification of the Constitution, it did prevail when Congress and the states added the Bill of Rights. The First Amendment provides in part that "Congress shall make no law * * * abridging the freedom of speech, or of the press." The Supreme Court has held that the prohibition against abridging the freedom of the press applies not just to Congress, but also to the states under the incorporation doctrine. *Gitlow v. People of State of New York*, 268 U.S. 652, 666 (1925); *Near v. Minnesota ex rel. Olson*, 283 U.S. 697, 707 (1931).

POINTS FOR DISCUSSION

a. Freedom of the Press and Freedom of Speech

Is there a difference between the freedom of "the press" and the freedom of "speech"? Are the protections that the First Amendment affords for the press and speech duplicative? When "the press" publishes views that are critical of the government, isn't it—or the publisher or journalist responsible for the content of the article—engaging in the act of "speech"? Does the separate inclusion of a specific freedom of the press suggest that the press is entitled to even greater protection for its "speech" than ordinary citizens?

b. Meaning of "Press"

A "metonymy" is a figure of speech in which the name of one thing stands for another thing associated with it. For example, in the phrase "the White House opposes the legislation," the term "White House" is a metonymy for the President. When the First Amendment refers to the freedom "of the press," the term "press" clearly is, at a minimum, a metonymy for those who traditionally used printing presses, such as the publishers of books, magazines, and newspapers. But does the term "press" also extend to publishers who use non-print media, such as radio and television broadcasters? Does the term include journalists as well as publishers? Does it also include internet bloggers? The Supreme Court has never answered these questions in any detail. As the following cases will show, the Court generally has viewed the freedom of the press to be coextensive with the freedom of speech. Because (as we will see later in this part) everyone enjoys the freedom of speech, the Court generally has not had to make distinctions between "the press" and others who seek to disseminate their views through non-traditional means. Should any special rules apply to the press?

A. APPLICABILITY OF GENERAL LAWS TO THE PRESS

In a variety of cases, members of the press have claimed that the First Amendment grants them special exemptions from the operation of generally applicable laws. As the cases that follow demonstrate, this issue involves competing considerations. On the one hand, enforcing general laws sometimes has the effect of impeding the work of journalists. For example, in the following case, *Branzburg v. Hayes*, 408 U.S. 665 (1972), reporters sought to avoid giving testimony before a grand jury about what their sources had told them. They feared that the sources might refuse to talk to them in the future if they could not speak confidentially. On the other hand, attempting to recognize exceptions for the press might prove a very difficult judicial task. Courts would have to decide who counts as "the press" and whether there are any exceptions to the general sweep of the term. Perhaps to avoid these difficult questions, the Supreme Court has held that "generally applicable laws do not offend the First Amendment simply because their enforcement against the press has incidental effects on its ability to gather and report the news." *Cohen v. Cowles Media Co.*, 501 U.S. 663 (1991), which we consider below. This conclusion, however, does not mean that the press *must* be treated the same as everyone else. On the contrary, Congress and the states can use legislation to grant the media exemptions from general laws. As you read the following case, consider whether the Constitution itself should be interpreted to exempt "the press" from the impact of some generally applicable laws.

BRANZBURG V. HAYES

408 U.S. 665 (1972)

Opinion of the Court by MR. JUSTICE WHITE, announced by THE CHIEF JUSTICE.

The issue in these cases is whether requiring newsmen to appear and testify before state or federal grand juries abridges the freedom of speech and press guaranteed by the First Amendment. We hold that it does not.

The writ of certiorari in No. 70–85, *Branzburg v. Hayes and Meigs*, brings before us two judgments of the Kentucky Court of Appeals, both involving petitioner Branzburg, a staff reporter for the Courier-Journal, a daily newspaper published in Louisville, Kentucky.

On November 15, 1969, the Courier-Journal carried a story under petitioner's by-line describing in detail his observations of two young residents of Jefferson County synthesizing hashish from marihuana, an activity which, they asserted, earned them about $5,000 in three weeks. The article included a photograph of a pair of hands working above a laboratory table on which was a substance identified by the caption as hashish. The article stated that petitioner had promised not to reveal the identity of the two hashish makers. Petitioner was shortly subpoenaed by the Jefferson County grand jury; he appeared, but refused to identify the individuals he had seen possessing marihuana or the persons he had seen making hashish from marihuana. * * *

The second case involving petitioner Branzburg arose out of his later story published on January 10, 1971, which described in detail the use of drugs in Frankfort, Kentucky. The article reported that in order to provide a comprehensive survey of the "drug scene" in Frankfort, petitioner had "spent two weeks

Definition

A "subpoena" is a "writ or order commanding a person to appear before a court or other tribunal, subject to a penalty for failing to comply." *Black's Law Dictionary* (10th ed. 2014).

interviewing several dozen drug users in the capital city" and had seen some of them smoking marihuana. A number of conversations with and observations of several unnamed drug users were recounted. Subpoenaed to appear before a Franklin County grand jury "to testify in the matter of violation of statutes concerning use and sale of drugs," petitioner Branzburg moved to quash the summons; the motion was denied * * *.

In re Pappas, No. 70–94, originated when petitioner Pappas, a television newsman-photographer working out of the Providence, Rhode Island, office of a New Bedford, Massachusetts, television station, was called to New Bedford on July 30, 1970, to report on civil disorders there which involved fires and other turmoil. He intended to cover a Black Panther news conference at that group's headquarters in a boarded-up store. Petitioner found the streets around the store barricaded, but he ultimately gained entrance to the area and recorded and photographed a prepared statement read by one of the Black Panther leaders at about 3 p.m. He then asked for and received permission to re-enter the area. Returning at about 9 o'clock, he was allowed to enter and remain inside Panther headquarters. As a condition of entry, Pappas agreed not to disclose anything he saw or heard inside the store except an anticipated police raid, which Pappas, "on his own," was free to photograph and report as he wished. Pappas stayed inside the headquarters for about three hours, but there was no police raid, and petitioner wrote no story and did not otherwise reveal what had occurred in the store while he was there. Two months later, petitioner was summoned before the Bristol County Grand Jury and appeared, answered questions as to his name, address, employment, and what he had seen and heard outside Panther headquarters, but refused to answer any questions about what had taken place inside headquarters while he was there, claiming that the First Amendment afforded him a privilege to protect confidential informants and their information. * * *

United States v. Caldwell, No. 70–57, arose from subpoenas issued by a federal grand jury in the Northern District of California to respondent Earl Caldwell, a reporter for the New York Times assigned to cover the Black Panther Party and other black militant groups. A subpoena duces tecum was served on respondent on February 2, 1970, ordering him to appear before the grand jury to testify and to bring with him notes and tape recordings of interviews given him for publication by officers and spokesmen of the Black Panther Party concerning the aims, purposes, and activities of that organization. * * * Respondent and his employer, the New York Times, moved to quash on the ground that the unlimited breadth of the subpoenas and the fact that Caldwell would have to appear in secret before the grand jury would destroy his working relationship with the Black Panther Party and "suppress vital First Amendment freedoms [by] driving a wedge of distrust and silence between the news media and the militants." * * *

> **Definition**
>
> A *subpoena duces tecum* is a "subpoena ordering the witness to appear in court and to bring specified documents, records, or things." *Black's Law Dictionary* (9th ed. 2009).

Petitioners Branzburg and Pappas and respondent Caldwell press First Amendment claims that may be simply put: that to gather news it is often necessary to agree either not to identify the source of information published or to publish only part of the facts revealed, or both; that if the reporter is nevertheless forced to reveal these confidences to a grand jury, the source so identified and other confidential sources of other reporters will be measurably deterred from furnishing publishable information, all to the detriment of the free flow of information protected by the First Amendment. Although the newsmen in these cases do not claim an absolute privilege against official interrogation in all

> **Practice Pointer**
>
> The journalists did not assert an absolute privilege in this case, but instead asserted only a qualified privilege. Why do you think they made that choice?

circumstances, they assert that the reporter should not be forced either to appear or to testify before a grand jury or at trial until and unless sufficient grounds are shown for believing that the reporter possesses information relevant to a crime the grand jury is investigating, that the information the reporter has is unavailable from other sources, and that the need for the information is sufficiently compelling to override the claimed invasion of First Amendment interests occasioned by the disclosure. Principally relied upon are prior cases emphasizing the importance of the First Amendment guarantees to individual development and to our system of representative government, decisions requiring that official action with adverse impact on First Amendment rights be justified by a public interest that is "compelling" or "paramount," and those precedents establishing the principle that justifiable governmental goals may not be achieved by unduly broad means having an unnecessary impact on protected rights of speech, press, or association. The heart of the claim is that the burden on news gathering resulting from compelling reporters to disclose confidential information outweighs any public interest in obtaining the information.

We do not question the significance of free speech, press, or assembly to the country's welfare. Nor is it suggested that news gathering does not qualify for First Amendment protection; without some protection for seeking out the news, freedom of the press could be eviscerated. But these cases involve no intrusions upon speech or assembly, no prior restraint or restriction on what the press may publish, and no express or implied command that the press publish what it prefers to withhold. No exaction or tax for the privilege of publishing, and no penalty, civil or criminal, related to the content of published material is at issue here. The use of confidential sources by the press is not forbidden or restricted; reporters remain free to seek news from any source by means within the law. No attempt is made to require the press to publish its sources of information or indiscriminately to disclose them on request.

The sole issue before us is the obligation of reporters to respond to grand jury subpoenas as other citizens do and to answer questions relevant to an investigation into the commission of crime. Citizens generally are not constitutionally immune from grand jury subpoenas; and neither the First

Amendment nor any other constitutional provision protects the average citizen from disclosing to a grand jury information that he has received in confidence. The claim is [that] reporters are exempt from these obligations * * *.

It is clear that the First Amendment does not invalidate every incidental burdening of the press that may result from the enforcement of civil or criminal statutes of general applicability. Under prior cases, otherwise valid laws serving substantial public interests may be enforced against the press as against others, despite the possible burden that may be imposed. The Court has emphasized that "[t]he publisher of a newspaper has no special immunity from the application of general laws. He has no special privilege to invade the rights and liberties of others." *Associated Press v. NLRB*, 301 U.S. 103, 132–133 (1937). It was there held that the Associated Press, a news-gathering and disseminating organization, was not exempt from the requirements of the National Labor Relations Act. The holding was reaffirmed in *Oklahoma Press Publishing Co. v. Walling*, 327 U.S. 186, 192–193 (1946), where the Court rejected the claim that applying the Fair Labor Standards Act to a newspaper publishing business would abridge the freedom of press guaranteed by the First Amendment. *Associated Press v. United States*, 326 U.S. 1 (1945), similarly overruled assertions that the First Amendment precluded application of the Sherman Act to a news-gathering and disseminating organization. Likewise, a newspaper may be subjected to nondiscriminatory forms of general taxation. *Grosjean v. American Press Co.*, 297 U.S. 233, 250 (1936).

The prevailing view is that the press is not free to publish with impunity everything and anything it desires to publish. Although it may deter or regulate what is said or published, the press may not circulate knowing or reckless falsehoods damaging to private reputation without subjecting itself to liability for damages, including punitive damages, or even criminal prosecution. See *New York Times Co. v. Sullivan*, 376 U.S. 254, 279–280 (1964). A newspaper or a journalist may also be punished for contempt of court, in appropriate circumstances. *Craig v. Harney*, 331 U.S. 367, 377–378 (1947).

It has generally been held that the First Amendment does not guarantee the press a constitutional right of special access to information not available to the public generally. In *Zemel v. Rusk*, 381 U.S. 1, 16–17 (1965), for example, the Court sustained the Government's refusal to validate passports to Cuba even though that restriction "render[ed] less than wholly free the flow of information concerning that country." The ban on travel was held constitutional, for "[t]he right to speak and publish does not carry with it the unrestrained right to gather information."

Despite the fact that news gathering may be hampered, the press is regularly excluded from grand jury proceedings, our own conferences, the meetings of other official bodies gathered in executive session, and the meetings of private organizations. Newsmen have no constitutional right of access to the scenes of crime or disaster when the general public is excluded, and they may be prohibited from attending or publishing information about trials if such restrictions are necessary to assure a defendant a fair trial before an impartial tribunal. In *Sheppard v. Maxwell*, 384 U.S. 333 (1966), for example, the Court reversed a state court conviction where the trial court failed to adopt "stricter rules governing the use of the courtroom by newsmen, as Sheppard's counsel requested," neglected to insulate witnesses from the press, and made no "effort to control the release of leads, information, and gossip to the press by police officers, witnesses, and the counsel for both sides." *Id.*, at 358. "[T]he trial court might well have proscribed extrajudicial statements by any lawyer, party, witness, or court official which divulged prejudicial matters." *Id.*, at 361.

> **Make the Connection**
>
> Does the First Amendment impose limits on the ability of the government—and the courts in particular—to exclude the press from its proceedings? Could the government declare that all criminal trials will occur in secrecy, without permitting members of the press to attend? We will take up this question later in this chapter when we consider the Court's decision in *Richmond Newspapers, Inc. v. Virginia*.

It is thus not surprising that the great weight of authority is that newsmen are not exempt from the normal duty of appearing before a grand jury and answering questions relevant to a criminal investigation. * * *

A number of States have provided newsmen a statutory privilege of varying breadth, but the majority have not done so, and none has been provided by federal statute. Until now the only testimonial privilege for unofficial witnesses that is rooted in the Federal Constitution is the Fifth Amendment privilege against compelled self-incrimination. We are asked to create another by interpreting the First Amendment to grant newsmen a testimonial privilege that other citizens do not enjoy. This we decline to do. Fair and effective law enforcement aimed at providing security for the person and property of the individual is a fundamental function of government, and the grand jury plays an important, constitutionally mandated role in this process. On the records now before us, we perceive no basis for holding

> **FYI**
>
> We briefly saw the privilege against self-incrimination in Chapter 1, when we discussed the incorporation doctrine and the Court's decision in *Adamson v. California*. We consider the privilege in detail in Chapter 14.

that the public interest in law enforcement and in ensuring effective grand jury proceedings is insufficient to override the consequential, but uncertain, burden on news gathering that is said to result from insisting that reporters, like other citizens, respond to relevant questions put to them in the course of a valid grand jury investigation or criminal trial.

MR. JUSTICE STEWART, with whom MR. JUSTICE BRENNAN and MR. JUSTICE MARSHALL join, dissenting.

The reporter's constitutional right to a confidential relationship with his source stems from the broad societal interest in a full and free flow of information to the public. It is this basic concern that underlies the Constitution's protection of a free press because the guarantee is "not for the benefit of the press so much as for the benefit of all of us." *Time, Inc. v. Hill*, 385 U.S. 374, 389 (1967).

Enlightened choice by an informed citizenry is the basic ideal upon which an open society is premised, and a free press is thus indispensable to a free society. Not only does the press enhance personal self-fulfillment by providing the people with the widest possible range of fact and opinion, but it also is an incontestable precondition of self-government. The press "has been a mighty catalyst in awakening public interest in governmental affairs, exposing corruption among public officers and employees and generally informing the citizenry of public events and occurrences * * *." *Estes v. Texas*, 381 U.S. 532, 539 (1965). As private and public aggregations of power burgeon in size and the pressures for conformity necessarily mount, there is obviously a continuing need for an independent press to disseminate a robust variety of information and opinion through reportage, investigation, and criticism, if we are to preserve our constitutional tradition of maximizing freedom of choice by encouraging diversity of expression.

A corollary of the right to publish must be the right to gather news. The full flow of information to the public protected by the free-press guarantee would be severely curtailed if no protection whatever were afforded to the process by which news is assembled and disseminated. * * * The right to gather news implies, in turn, a right to a confidential relationship between a reporter and his source. This proposition follows as a matter of simple logic once three factual predicates are recognized: (1) newsmen require informants to gather news; (2) confidentiality—the promise or understanding that names or certain aspects of communications will be kept off the record—is essential to the creation and maintenance of a news-gathering relationship with informants; and (3) an unbridled subpoena power—the absence of a constitutional right protecting, in any way, a confidential relationship from compulsory process—will either deter sources from divulging information or deter reporters from gathering and publishing information.

It is obvious that informants are necessary to the news-gathering process as we know it today. If it is to perform its constitutional mission, the press must do far more than merely print public statements or publish prepared handouts. Familiarity with the people and circumstances involved in the myriad background activities that result in the final product called "news" is vital to complete and responsible journalism, unless the press is to be a captive mouthpiece of "newsmakers."

POINTS FOR DISCUSSION

a.   Rationale

The Court acknowledged the journalists' argument that if "forced to respond to subpoenas and identify their sources or disclose other confidences, their informants will refuse or be reluctant to furnish newsworthy information in the future." Why did the Court conclude that this argument was insufficient to justify a journalist's privilege not to testify before a grand jury? Did the Court conclude that there is a "privilege," but that it was overcome by "the public interest in law enforcement and in ensuring effective grand jury proceedings"? Or did it conclude that there is no privilege at all, regardless of the circumstances surrounding the subpoena?

b.   Constitutional Privileges

The Court stated that "the only testimonial privilege for unofficial witnesses that is rooted in the Federal Constitution is the Fifth Amendment privilege against compelled self-incrimination," and it declined to "create" another. Two years after the Court's decision in *Branzburg*, the Court held in *United States v. Nixon* that the

> **Make the Connection**
>
> We discuss the Court's decision in *Nixon* in Volume 1, during our consideration of the federal executive power.

Constitution protects an "executive privilege," which permits the President (at least under certain circumstances) to protect confidential communications from disclosure. Does the Court's subsequent decision in *Nixon* suggest a greater willingness of the Court to find implied evidentiary privileges from more general constitutional text? Is the argument for a journalist's privilege to protect confidential sources stronger than the argument for executive privilege, or weaker?

c.   Legislation

Congress and the states presumably have authority to enact legislation that would create an evidentiary privilege giving journalists the right not to disclose information about their sources. The privilege would be similar to the attorney-client privilege, which protects confidential communications between lawyers and their clients from disclosure. Would creating a journalist's privilege be a good idea? How exactly would you phrase the legislation? In particular, how would you define a "journalist" or describe the kinds of communications to which the privilege would apply? Would it be a qualified privilege or an absolute one?

d. Journalists' Ethics

Should journalists make promises of confidentiality to their sources when they do not have the lawful power to keep these promises? If a journalist has promised confidentiality to a source, should the journalist refuse to testify before a grand jury even if it means spending time in jail on charges of contempt? Judith Miller, a former *New York Times* reporter, thought that going to prison was the proper course. A judge jailed her after she refused to answer questions about her sources of information in writing about the CIA's decision to send Joe Wilson, the husband of a CIA employee, Valerie Plame, to Africa to investigate the potential sale of uranium to Iraq. Upon her release from prison, Miller said: "I went to jail to preserve the time-honored principle that a journalist must respect a promise not to reveal the identity of a confidential source. * * * I am leaving jail today because my source has now voluntarily and personally released me from my promise of confidentiality regarding our conversations relating to the Wilson-Plame matter." Neil A. Lewis & Scott Shane, *Reporter Who Was Jailed Testifies in Libby Case*, N.Y. Times, Jan. 31, 2007, at A1. Did Miller owe an obligation to anyone other than her source?

ZURCHER V. STANFORD DAILY
436 U.S. 547 (1978)

MR. JUSTICE WHITE delivered the opinion of the Court.

Late in the day on Friday, April 9, 1971, officers of the Palo Alto Police Department and of the Santa Clara County Sheriff's Department responded to a call from the director of the Stanford University Hospital requesting the removal of a large group of demonstrators who had seized the hospital's administrative offices and occupied them since the previous afternoon. After several futile efforts to persuade the demonstrators to leave peacefully, more drastic measures were employed. The demonstrators had barricaded the doors at both ends of a hall adjacent to the administrative offices. The police chose to force their way in at the west end of the corridor. As they did so, a group of demonstrators emerged through the doors at the east end and, armed with sticks and clubs, attacked the group of nine police officers stationed there. One officer was knocked to the floor and struck repeatedly on the head; another suffered a broken shoulder. All nine were injured. There were no police photographers at the east doors, and most bystanders and reporters were on the west side. The officers themselves were able to identify only two of their assailants, but one of them did see at least one person photographing the assault at the east doors.

On Sunday, April 11, a special edition of the Stanford Daily (Daily), a student newspaper published at Stanford University, carried articles and photographs devoted to the hospital protest and the violent clash between demonstrators and police. The photographs carried the byline of a Daily staff member and indicated that he had been at the east end of the hospital hallway where he could have photographed the assault on the nine officers. The next day, the Santa Clara County District Attorney's Office secured a warrant from the Municipal Court for an immediate search of the Daily's offices for negatives, film, and pictures showing the events and occurrences at the hospital on the evening of April 9. The warrant issued on a finding of "just, probable and reasonable cause for believing that: Negatives and photographs and films, evidence material and relevant to the identity of the perpetrators of felonies, to wit, Battery on a Peace Officer, and Assault with Deadly Weapon, will be located [on the premises of the Daily]." The warrant affidavit contained no allegation or indication that members of the Daily staff were in any way involved in unlawful acts at the hospital.

The search pursuant to the warrant was conducted later that day by four police officers and took place in the presence of some members of the Daily staff. The Daily's photographic laboratories, filing cabinets, desks, and wastepaper baskets were searched. Locked drawers and rooms were not opened. The officers apparently had opportunity to read notes and correspondence during the search; but, contrary to claims of the staff, the officers denied that they had exceeded the limits of the warrant. They had not been advised by the staff that the areas they were searching contained confidential materials. The search revealed only the photographs that had already been published on April 11, and no materials were removed from the Daily's office.

A month later the Daily and various members of its staff, respondents here, brought a civil action in the United States District Court for the Northern District of California seeking declaratory and injunctive relief under 42 U.S.C. § 1983 against the police officers who conducted the search, the chief of police, the district attorney and one of his deputies, and the judge who had issued the warrant. The complaint alleged that the search of the Daily's office had deprived respondents under color of state law of rights secured to them by the First, Fourth, and Fourteenth Amendments of the United States Constitution.

The issue here is how the Fourth Amendment is to be construed and applied to the "third party" search, the recurring situation where state authorities have probable cause to believe that fruits, instrumentalities, or other evidence of crime is located on identified property but do not then have probable cause to believe that the owner or possessor of the property is himself implicated in the crime that has occurred or is occurring. [Addressing this Fourth Amendment issue, the Court reasoned that "the State's interest in enforcing the criminal law and recovering evidence is the same whether the third party is culpable or not" and that "[t]he critical element in a reasonable search is not that the owner of the property is suspected of crime but that there is reasonable cause to believe that the specific 'things' to be searched for and seized are located on the property to which entry is sought." The Court therefore held that the premises of a third-party could be searched upon a showing of probable cause. The Court then turned to the First Amendment.]

The District Court held, and respondents assert here, that whatever may be true of third-party searches generally, where the third party is a newspaper, there are additional factors derived from the First Amendment that justify a nearly *per se* rule forbidding the search warrant and permitting only the subpoena *duces tecum*. The general submission is that searches of newspaper offices for evidence of crime reasonably believed to be on the premises will

> **Take Note**
>
> What exactly do the respondents claim is prohibited by the First Amendment? Do they argue that they can withhold relevant evidence from the police or the prosecutor? Or simply that the police may not obtain that evidence during a search pursuant to a warrant?

seriously threaten the ability of the press to gather, analyze, and disseminate news. This is said to be true for several reasons: First, searches will be physically disruptive to such an extent that timely publication will be impeded. Second, confidential sources of information will dry up, and the press will also lose opportunities to cover various events because of fears of the participants that press files will be readily available to the authorities. Third, reporters will be deterred from recording and preserving their recollections for future use if such information is subject to seizure. Fourth, the processing of news and its dissemination will be chilled by the prospects that searches will disclose internal editorial deliberations. Fifth, the press will resort to self-censorship to conceal its possession of information of potential interest to the police.

It is true that the struggle from which the Fourth Amendment emerged "is largely a history of conflict between the Crown and the press," *Stanford v. Texas*, 379 U.S. 476, 482 (1965), and that in issuing warrants and determining the reasonableness of a search, state and federal magistrates should be aware that "unrestricted power of search and seizure could also be an instrument for stifling liberty of expression." *Marcus v. Search Warrant*, 367 U.S. 717, 729 (1961). Where the materials sought to be seized may be protected by the First Amendment, the requirements of the Fourth Amendment must be applied with "scrupulous exactitude." *Stanford v. Texas*, 379 U.S., at 485. "A seizure reasonable as to one type of material in one setting may be unreasonable in a different setting or with respect to another kind of material." *Roaden v. Kentucky*, 413 U.S. 496, 501 (1973). Hence, in *Stanford v. Texas*, the Court invalidated a warrant authorizing the search of a private home for all books, records, and other materials relating to the Communist Party, on the ground that whether or not the warrant would have been sufficient in other contexts, it authorized the searchers to rummage among and make judgments about books and papers and was the functional equivalent of a general warrant, one of the principal targets of the Fourth Amendment. Where presumptively protected materials are sought to be seized, the warrant requirement should be administered to leave as little as possible to the discretion or whim of the officer in the field.

Neither the Fourth Amendment nor the cases requiring consideration of First Amendment values in issuing search warrants, however, call for imposing the regime ordered by the District Court. Aware of the long struggle between Crown and press and desiring to curb unjustified official intrusions, the Framers took the enormously important step of subjecting searches to the test of reasonableness and to the general rule requiring search warrants issued by neutral magistrates. They nevertheless did not forbid warrants where the press was involved, did not require special showings that subpoenas would be impractical, and did not insist that the owner of the place to be searched, if connected with the press, must be shown to be implicated in the offense being investigated. Further, the prior cases do no more than insist that the courts apply the warrant requirements with particular exactitude when First Amendment interests would be endangered by the search. As we see it, no more than this is required where the warrant requested is for the seizure of criminal evidence reasonably believed to be on the premises occupied by a newspaper. Properly administered, the preconditions for a warrant—probable cause, specificity with respect to the place to be searched and the things to be seized, and overall reasonableness—should afford sufficient protection against the harms that are assertedly threatened by warrants for searching newspaper offices.

There is no reason to believe, for example, that magistrates cannot guard against searches of the type, scope, and intrusiveness that would actually interfere with the timely publication of a newspaper. Nor, if the requirements of specificity and reasonableness are properly applied, policed, and observed, will there be any occasion or opportunity for officers to rummage at large in newspaper files or to intrude into or to deter normal editorial and publication decisions. The warrant issued in this case authorized nothing of this sort. Nor are we convinced, any more than we were in *Branzburg v. Hayes*, 408 U.S. 665 (1972), that confidential sources will disappear and that the press will suppress news because of fears of warranted searches. Whatever incremental effect there may be in this regard if search warrants, as well as subpoenas, are permissible in proper circumstances, it does not make a constitutional difference in our judgment.

> **Food for Thought**
>
> The Court sees no reason to believe that the prospect of searches pursuant to properly issued warrants will affect journalistic decisions or cause sources to refuse to talk to the press. Do you agree? Can you think of any hypothetical searches in which a newspaper's journalistic decisions might be affected?

MR. JUSTICE STEWART, with whom MR. JUSTICE MARSHALL joins, dissenting.

It seems to me self-evident that police searches of newspaper offices burden the freedom of the press. The most immediate and obvious First Amendment injury caused by such a visitation by the police is physical disruption of the operation of the newspaper. Policemen occupying a newsroom and searching it thoroughly for what may be an extended period of time will inevitably interrupt its normal operations, and thus impair or even temporarily prevent the processes of newsgathering, writing, editing, and publishing. By contrast, a subpoena would afford the newspaper itself an opportunity to locate whatever material might be requested and produce it.

But there is another and more serious burden on a free press imposed by an unannounced police search of a newspaper office: the possibility of disclosure of information received from confidential sources, or of the identity of the sources themselves. Protection of those sources is necessary to ensure that the press can fulfill its constitutionally designated function of informing the public, because important information can often be obtained only by an assurance that the source will not be revealed. *Branzburg v. Hayes,* 408 U.S. 665, 725–736 (dissenting opinion). And the Court has recognized that "without some protection for seeking out the news, freedom of the press could be eviscerated." *Pell v. Procunier,* 417 U.S. 817, 833 (1974).

Today the Court does not question the existence of this constitutional protection, but says only that it is not "convinced [that] confidential sources will disappear and that the press will suppress news because of fears of warranted searches." This facile conclusion seems to me to ignore common experience. It requires no blind leap of faith to understand that a person who gives information to a journalist only on condition that his identity will not be revealed will be less likely to give that information if he knows that, despite the journalist's assurance his identity may in fact be disclosed. And it cannot be denied that confidential information may be exposed to the eyes of police officers who execute a search warrant by rummaging through the files, cabinets, desks, and wastebaskets of a newsroom. Since the indisputable effect of such searches will thus be to prevent a newsman from being able to promise confidentiality to his potential sources, it seems obvious to me that a journalist's access to information, and thus the public's will thereby be impaired.

A search warrant allows police officers to ransack the files of a newspaper, reading each and every document until they have found the one named in the warrant, while a subpoena would permit the newspaper itself to produce only the specific documents requested. A search, unlike a subpoena, will therefore lead to the needless exposure of confidential information completely unrelated to the purpose of the investigation. The knowledge that police officers can make an unannounced raid on a newsroom is thus bound to have a deterrent effect on the availability of confidential news sources. The end result, wholly inimical to the First Amendment, will be a diminishing flow of potentially important information to the public.

POINTS FOR DISCUSSION

a.   Comparison to *Branzburg v. Hayes*

Zurcher and *Branzburg* both held that the press does not have any exemption from generally applicable laws. In which case do you think the press had a stronger argument for seeking an exception? Given the decision in *Branzburg*, does the majority's view in *Zurcher* necessarily follow?

b.   Federal Legislation

Congress responded to the *Zurcher* decision by enacting the Privacy Protection Act of 1980, 42 U.S.C. § 2000aa, which restricts the ability of the police to search newsrooms for evidence of crimes committed by third-parties. Subject to various exceptions, the act makes it "unlawful for a government officer or employee, in connection with the investigation or prosecution of a criminal offense, to search for or seize any work product materials possessed by a person reasonably believed to have a purpose to disseminate to the public a newspaper, book, broadcast, or other similar form of public communication, in or affecting interstate or foreign commerce." One exception is for when "there is probable cause to believe that the person possessing such materials has committed or is committing the criminal offense to which the materials relate." Does this statute address all of the concerns expressed by Justice Stewart in *Zurcher*?

COHEN V. COWLES MEDIA CO.

501 U.S. 663 (1991)

JUSTICE WHITE delivered the opinion of the Court.

During the closing days of the 1982 Minnesota gubernatorial race, Dan Cohen, an active Republican associated with Wheelock Whitney's Independent-Republican gubernatorial campaign, approached reporters from the St. Paul Pioneer Press Dispatch (Pioneer Press) and the Minneapolis Star and Tribune (Star Tribune) and offered to provide documents relating to a candidate in the upcoming election. Cohen made clear to the reporters that he would provide the information only if he was given a promise of confidentiality. Reporters from both papers promised to keep Cohen's identity anonymous and Cohen turned over copies of two public court records concerning Marlene Johnson, the Democratic-Farmer-Labor candidate for Lieutenant Governor. The first record indicated that Johnson had been charged in 1969 with three counts of unlawful assembly, and the second that she had been convicted in 1970 of petit theft. Both newspapers interviewed Johnson for her explanation and one reporter tracked down the person who had found the records for Cohen. As it turned out, the unlawful assembly charges arose out of Johnson's participation in a protest of an alleged failure

> **FYI**
>
> Negative information about a candidate released just before an election is sometimes called an "October Surprise" because elections generally occur at the start of November. Do you recall any famous October surprises? See Carey Goldberg, *The Tipster: Maine Lawyer Delights in Leaking Bush's Arrest*, N.Y. Times, Nov. 4, 2000, at A14 (describing how a lawyer active in the Democratic Party revealed news just before the 2000 election that presidential candidate George W. Bush was convicted of drunk driving in 1976).

to hire minority workers on municipal construction projects, and the charges were eventually dismissed. The petit theft conviction was for leaving a store without paying for $6 worth of sewing materials. The incident apparently occurred at a time during which Johnson was emotionally distraught, and the conviction was later vacated.

After consultation and debate, the editorial staffs of the two newspapers independently decided to publish Cohen's name as part of their stories concerning Johnson. In their stories, both papers identified Cohen as the source of the court records, indicated his connection to the Whitney campaign, and included denials by Whitney campaign officials of any role in the matter. The same day the stories appeared, Cohen was fired by his employer.

[Cohen sued the newspapers' publishers, claiming that they had violated their promises of confidentiality. A jury awarded him $200,000, concluding that the promises were enforceable on a theory of promissory estoppel. The Minnesota Supreme Court vacated the judgment, concluding that "in this case enforcement of the promise of confidentiality under a promissory estoppel theory would violate defendants' First Amendment rights."]

Respondents rely on the proposition that "if a newspaper lawfully obtains truthful information about a matter of public significance then state officials may not constitutionally punish publication of the information, absent a need to further a state interest of the highest order." *Smith v. Daily Mail Publishing Co.*, 443 U.S. 97, 103 (1979). That proposition is unexceptionable, and it has been applied in various cases that have found insufficient the asserted state interests in preventing publication of truthful, lawfully obtained information.

This case, however, is not controlled by this line of cases but, rather, by the equally well-established line of decisions holding that generally applicable laws do not offend the First Amendment simply because their enforcement against the press has incidental effects on its ability to gather and report the news. As the cases relied on by respondents recognize, the truthful information sought to be published must have been lawfully acquired. The press may not with impunity break and enter an office or dwelling to gather news.

> **Take Note**
>
> The Court announces here the rule that the press is subject to generally applicable laws notwithstanding the First Amendment. From the cases we have seen so far, are there any exceptions to this general rule? Does the First Amendment impose any limits on the application of generally applicable rules to the press?

Neither does the First Amendment relieve a newspaper reporter of the obligation shared by all citizens to respond to a grand jury subpoena and answer questions relevant to a criminal investigation, even though the reporter might be required to reveal a confidential source. *Branzburg v. Hayes*, 408 U.S. 665 (1972). The press, like others interested in publishing, may not publish copyrighted material without obeying the copyright laws. See *Zacchini v. Scripps-Howard Broadcasting Co.*, 433 U.S. 562, 576–579 (1977). Similarly, the media must obey the National Labor Relations Act, *Associated Press v. NLRB*, 301 U.S. 103 (1937), and the Fair Labor Standards Act, *Oklahoma Press Publishing Co. v. Walling*, 327 U.S. 186, 192–193 (1946); may not restrain trade in violation of the antitrust laws, *Associated Press v. United States*, 326 U.S. 1 (1945); and must pay non-discriminatory taxes, *Murdock v. Pennsylvania*, 319 U.S. 105, 112

(1943). It is, therefore, beyond dispute that "[t]he publisher of a newspaper has no special immunity from the application of general laws. He has no special privilege to invade the rights and liberties of others." *Associated Press v. NLRB, supra*, 301 U.S., at 132–133. Accordingly, enforcement of such general laws against the press is not subject to stricter scrutiny than would be applied to enforcement against other persons or organizations.

There can be little doubt that the Minnesota doctrine of promissory estoppel is a law of general applicability. It does not target or single out the press. Rather, insofar as we are advised, the doctrine is generally applicable to the daily transactions of all the citizens of Minnesota. The First Amendment does not forbid its application to the press. * * * Accordingly, the judgment of the Minnesota Supreme Court is reversed, and the case is remanded for further proceedings not inconsistent with this opinion.

JUSTICE BLACKMUN, with whom JUSTICE MARSHALL and JUSTICE SOUTER join, dissenting.

* * * I regard our decision in *Hustler Magazine, Inc. v. Falwell*, 485 U.S. 46 (1988), to be precisely on point. There, we found that the use of a claim of intentional infliction of emotional distress to impose liability for the publication of a satirical critique violated the First Amendment. There was no doubt that Virginia's tort of intentional infliction of emotional distress was "a law of general applicability" unrelated to the suppression of speech. Nonetheless, a unanimous Court found that, when used to penalize the expression of opinion, the law was subject to the strictures of the First Amendment. In applying that principle, we concluded that "public figures and public officials may not recover for the tort of intentional infliction of emotional distress by reason of publications such as the one here at issue without showing in addition that the publication contains a false statement of fact which was made with 'actual malice,'" as defined by *New York Times Co. v. Sullivan*, 376 U.S. 254 (1964). In so doing, we rejected the argument that Virginia's interest in protecting its citizens from emotional distress was sufficient to remove from First Amendment protection a "patently offensive" expression of opinion.

Make the Connection

We considered some of the limits that the First Amendment imposes on common-law rights of action—and in particular claims for defamation—in Chapter 8, when we considered *New York Times v. Sullivan.*

* * * I perceive no meaningful distinction between a statute that penalizes published speech in order to protect the individual's psychological well being or reputational interest and one that exacts the same penalty in order to compensate

the loss of employment or earning potential. Certainly, our decision in *Hustler* recognized no such distinction.

JUSTICE SOUTER, with whom JUSTICE MARSHALL, JUSTICE BLACKMUN, and JUSTICE O'CONNOR join, dissenting.

* * * [G]eneral laws [that] entail effects on the content of speech, like the one in question, may of course be found constitutional, but only, as Justice Harlan observed,

> when [such effects] have been found justified by subordinating valid governmental interests, a prerequisite to constitutionality which has necessarily involved a weighing of the governmental interest involved. * * * Whenever, in such a context, these constitutional protections are asserted against the exercise of valid governmental powers a reconciliation must be effected, and that perforce requires an appropriate weighing of the respective interests involved.

Konigsberg v. State Bar of California, 366 U.S. 36, 51 (1961). Because I believe the State's interest in enforcing a newspaper's promise of confidentiality insufficient to outweigh the interest in unfettered publication of the information revealed in this case, I respectfully dissent.

POINTS FOR DISCUSSION

a.   Defamation v. Promissory Estoppel

Is there a meaningful difference between a claim that a newspaper's publication of information damaged a person's reputation or emotional psyche, on the one hand, and a claim that a newspaper's publication of information violated a promise not to disclose that information, on the other? If so, what is the difference? Is it sufficient to justify different rules under the First Amendment? Didn't the decisions in *Sullivan* and *Falwell*, which we considered in Chapter 8, favor the press because they involved public figures, and thus called for the application of a special rule? Was the same true in *Cohen*? Does it turn on whether Mr. Cohen was a public figure?

b.   Rules v. Standards

Justice Souter's dissent calls for a balancing of interests—specifically, the balancing of the need for the general enforcement of laws against the needs of the media. What might be the benefits of a balancing test in comparison to the categorical rule adopted by the Court? Would a balancing test have any drawbacks?

B. REQUIRING THE PRESS TO PROVIDE MEDIA ACCESS TO OTHERS

The freedom of the press is often justified as a means to an end. If the media are free to publish whatever they wish, the reasoning goes, all good ideas will be heard. This logic, however, rests on an assumption that the press actually will use its freedom to promote all ideas. There is a significant question whether this assumption accords with reality. Over forty years ago, Professor Jerome Barron (later the dean of the George Washington University Law School) addressed this issue in a highly influential article. He observed that:

> Our constitutional theory is in the grip of a romantic conception of free expression, a belief that the "marketplace of ideas" is freely accessible. But if ever there were a self-operating marketplace of ideas, it has long ceased to exist. The mass media's development of an antipathy to ideas requires legal intervention if novel and unpopular ideas are to be assured a forum—unorthodox points of view which have no claim on broadcast time and newspaper space as a matter of right are in poor position to compete with those aired as a matter of grace.

Jerome Barron, *Access to the Press—A New First Amendment Right*, 80 Harv. L. Rev. 1641, 1641 (1967).

The following two landmark cases involved government regulations that attempted to require "balance" in what the press publishes. The regulations at issue did not prohibit media outlets from saying anything. But they each required (or attempted to require) publishers to devote some of their news content to opposing views. The Supreme Court upheld the regulation in the case of radio programming, but not newspaper publishing. In reading the two cases, attempt to discern what justifies the difference in results.

RED LION BROADCASTING CO. V. F.C.C.

395 U.S. 367 (1969)

MR. JUSTICE WHITE delivered the opinion of the Court.

The Federal Communications Commission has for many years imposed on radio and television broadcasters the requirement that discussion of public issues be presented on broadcast stations, and that each side of those issues must be given fair coverage. This is known as the fairness doctrine, which originated very early in the history of broadcasting and has maintained its present outlines for some time. It is an obligation whose content has been defined in a long series of FCC rulings in particular cases, and which is distinct from the statutory requirement of § 315 of the Communications Act that equal time be allotted all qualified candidates for public office. Two aspects of the fairness doctrine, relating to personal attacks in the context of controversial public issues and to political editorializing, were codified more precisely in the form of FCC regulations in 1967. The two cases before us now, which were decided separately below, challenge the constitutional and statutory bases of the doctrine and component rules. [One] involves the application of the fairness doctrine to a particular broadcast, and [the other] arises as an action to review the FCC's 1967 promulgation of the personal attack and political editorializing regulations, which were laid down after the Red Lion litigation had begun.

The Red Lion Broadcasting Company is licensed to operate a Pennsylvania radio station, WGCB. On November 27, 1964, WGCB carried a 15-minute broadcast by the Reverend Billy James Hargis as part of a "Christian Crusade" series. A book by Fred J. Cook entitled "Goldwater—Extremist on the Right" was discussed by Hargis, who said that Cook had been fired by a newspaper for making false charges against city officials; that Cook had then worked for a Communist-affiliated publication; that he had defended Alger Hiss and attacked J. Edgar Hoover and the Central Intelligence Agency; and that he had now written a "book to smear and destroy Barry Goldwater." When Cook heard of the broadcast he concluded that he had been personally attacked and demanded free reply time, which the station refused. After an exchange of letters among Cook, Red Lion, and the FCC, the FCC declared that the Hargis broadcast constituted a personal attack on Cook [and] that Red Lion had failed to meet its obligation under the fairness doctrine * * *.

> **FYI**
>
> Senator Barry Goldwater of Arizona was the Republican nominee for president in the 1964 election. One of his famous quotations from the campaign was: "I would remind you that extremism in the defense of liberty is no vice! And let me remind you also that moderation in the pursuit of justice is no virtue!"

Before 1927, the allocation of frequencies was left entirely to the private sector, and the result was chaos. It quickly became apparent that broadcast frequencies constituted a scarce resource whose use could be regulated and rationalized only by the Government. Without government control, the medium would be of little use because of the cacophony of competing voices, none of which could be clearly and predictably heard. Consequently, the Federal Radio

Commission was established to allocate frequencies among competing applicants in a manner responsive to the public "convenience, interest, or necessity."

Very shortly thereafter the Commission expressed its view that the "public interest requires ample play for the free and fair competition of opposing views, and the commission believes that the principle applies [to] all discussions of issues of importance to the public." *Great Lakes Broadcasting Co.*, 3

> **Make the Connection**
>
> Is Congress's charge to the Commission (later the FCC) to distribute licenses in a manner consistent with public "convenience, interest, or necessity," 47 U.S.C. § 303 & § 303(r), consistent with the non-delegation doctrine? We briefly address that doctrine—and the Court's decision to uphold the delegation of authority to the FCC— in Volume 1.

F.R.C. Ann. Rep. 32, 33 (1929), rev'd on other grounds, 37 F.2d 993 (D.C. Cir. 1929), *cert. dismissed*, 281 U.S. 706 (1930). * * *

There is a twofold duty laid down by the FCC's decisions and described by the 1949 Report on Editorializing by Broadcast Licensees, 13 F.C.C. 1246 (1949). The broadcaster must give adequate coverage to public issues, *United Broadcasting Co.*, 10 F.C.C. 515 (1945), and coverage must be fair in that it accurately reflects the opposing views. *New Broadcasting Co.,* 6 P & F Radio Reg. 258 (1950). This must be done at the broadcaster's own expense if sponsorship is unavailable. *Cullman Broadcasting Co.*, 25 P & F Radio Reg. 895 (1963). Moreover, the duty must be met by programming obtained at the licensee's own initiative if available from no other source. *John J. Dempsey*, 6 P & F Radio Reg. 615 (1950). * * *

When a personal attack has been made on a figure involved in a public issue both [FCC doctrine, established case by case, and] the 1967 regulations [require] that the individual attacked himself be offered an opportunity to respond. Likewise, where one candidate is endorsed in a political editorial, the other candidates must themselves be offered reply time to use personally or through a spokesman. These obligations differ from the general fairness requirement that issues be presented, and presented with coverage of competing views, in that the broadcaster does not have the option of presenting the attacked party's side himself or choosing a third party to represent that side. But insofar as there is an obligation of the broadcaster to see that both sides are presented, and insofar as that is an affirmative obligation, the personal attack doctrine and regulations do not differ from the preceding fairness doctrine. The simple fact that the attacked men or unendorsed candidates may respond themselves or through agents is not a critical distinction, and indeed, it is not unreasonable for the FCC to conclude that the objective of adequate presentation of all sides may best be served by allowing those most closely affected to make the response, rather than leaving the response in the hands of the station which has attacked their candidacies, endorsed their opponents, or carried a personal attack upon them.

The broadcasters challenge the fairness doctrine and its specific manifestations in the personal attack and political editorial rules on conventional First Amendment grounds, alleging that the rules abridge their freedom of speech and press. Their contention is that the First Amendment protects their desire to use their allotted frequencies continuously to broadcast whatever they choose, and to exclude whomever they choose from ever using that frequency. No man may be prevented from saying or publishing what he thinks, or from refusing in his speech or other utterances to give equal weight to the views of his opponents. This right, they say, applies equally to broadcasters.

> **Food for Thought**
>
> Do you agree that the regulation at issue here is analogous to an ordinance limiting the volume at which (or the places in which) "sound trucks" may amplify certain messages? Wouldn't the proper analogy be an ordinance requiring sound trucks to play not only their chosen message (at whatever volume) but also messages with which the sound truck operator disagrees?

Although broadcasting is clearly a medium affected by a First Amendment interest, *United States v. Paramount Pictures, Inc.,* 334 U.S. 131, 166 (1948), differences in the characteristics of new media justify differences in the First Amendment standards applied to them. For example, the ability of new technology to produce sounds more raucous than those of the human voice justifies restrictions on the sound level, and on the hours and places of use, of sound trucks so long as the restrictions are reasonable and applied without discrimination. *Kovacs v. Cooper,* 336 U.S. 77 (1949).

Just as the Government may limit the use of sound-amplifying equipment potentially so noisy that it drowns out civilized private speech, so may the Government limit the use of broadcast equipment. The right of free speech of a broadcaster, the user of a sound truck, or any other individual does not embrace a right to snuff out the free speech of others.

When two people converse face to face, both should not speak at once if either is to be clearly understood. But the range of the human voice is so limited that there could be meaningful communications if half the people in the United States were talking and the other half listening. Just as clearly, half the people might publish and the other half read. But the reach of radio signals is incomparably greater than the range of the human voice and the problem of interference is a massive reality. The lack of know-how and equipment may keep many from the air, but only a tiny fraction of those with resources and intelligence can hope to communicate by radio at the same time if intelligible communication is to be had, even if the entire radio spectrum is utilized in the present state of commercially acceptable technology.

It was this fact, and the chaos which ensued from permitting anyone to use any frequency at whatever power level he wished, which made necessary the enactment of the Radio Act of 1927 and the Communications Act of 1934, as the Court has noted at length before. *National Broadcasting Co. v. United States,* 319 U.S. 190, 210–214 (1943). It was this reality which at the very least necessitated first the division of the radio spectrum into portions reserved respectively for public broadcasting and for other important radio uses such as amateur operation, aircraft, police, defense, and navigation; and then the subdivision of each portion, and assignment of specific frequencies to individual users or groups of users. Beyond this, however, because the frequencies reserved for public broadcasting were limited in number, it was essential for the Government to tell some applicants that they could not broadcast at all because there was room for only a few.

Where there are substantially more individuals who want to broadcast than there are frequencies to allocate, it is idle to posit an unabridgeable First Amendment right to broadcast comparable to the right of every individual to speak, write, or publish. If 100 persons want broadcast licenses but there are only 10 frequencies to allocate, all of them may have the same "right" to a license; but if there is to be any effective communication by radio, only a few can be licensed and the rest must be barred from the airwaves. It would be strange if the First Amendment, aimed at protecting and furthering communications, prevented the Government from making radio communication possible by requiring licenses to broadcast and by limiting the number of licenses so as not to overcrowd the spectrum.

By the same token, as far as the First Amendment is concerned those who are licensed stand no better than those to whom licenses are refused. A license permits broadcasting, but the licensee has no constitutional right to be the one who holds the license or to monopolize a radio frequency to the exclusion of his fellow citizens. There is nothing in the First Amendment which prevents the Government from requiring a licensee to share his frequency with others and to conduct himself as a proxy or fiduciary with obligations to present those views and voices

> **Make the Connection**
>
> In Chapter 8, we considered the "unconstitutional conditions" doctrine. Is the Court's suggestion here—that the government can compel broadcasters to present views with which they disagree because the broadcasters have no "right" to their broadcast licenses— consistent with that doctrine?

which are representative of his community and which would otherwise, by necessity, be barred from the airwaves.

This is not to say that the First Amendment is irrelevant to public broadcasting. On the contrary, it has a major role to play as the Congress itself recognized in § 326, which forbids FCC interference with "the right of free speech by means of radio communication." Because of the scarcity of radio frequencies, the Government is permitted to put restraints on licensees in favor of others whose views should be expressed on this unique medium. But the people as a whole retain their interest in free speech by radio and their collective right to have the medium function consistently with the ends and purposes of the First Amendment. It is the right of the viewers and listeners, not the right of the broadcasters, which is paramount. It is the purpose of the First Amendment to preserve an uninhibited marketplace of ideas in which truth will ultimately prevail, rather than to countenance monopolization of that market, whether it be by the Government itself or a private licensee. It is the right of the public to receive suitable access to social, political, esthetic, moral, and other ideas and experiences which is crucial here. That right may not constitutionally be abridged either by Congress or by the FCC.

> **Take Note**
>
> The Court suggests here that the First Amendment protects the "right of the viewers and listeners, not the right of the broadcasters." Is this consistent with the view of the First Amendment that we saw in Chapter 8? Is it a sensible view of the First Amendment's protections for speech and the press?

Rather than confer frequency monopolies on a relatively small number of licensees, in a Nation of 200,000,000, the Government could surely have decreed that each frequency should be shared among all or some of those who wish to use it, each being assigned a portion of the broadcast day or the broadcast week. The ruling and regulations at issue here do not go quite so far. They assert that under specified circumstances, a licensee must offer to make available a reasonable amount of broadcast time to those who have a view different from that which has already been expressed on his station. The expression of a political endorsement, or of a personal attack while dealing with a controversial public issue, simply triggers this time sharing. As we have said, the First Amendment confers no right on licensees to prevent others from broadcasting on "their" frequencies and no right to an unconditional monopoly of a scarce resource which the Government has denied others the right to use.

It is strenuously argued, however, that if political editorials or personal attacks will trigger an obligation in broadcasters to afford the opportunity for expression to speakers who need not pay for time and whose views are unpalatable to the licensees, then broadcasters will be irresistibly forced to self-censorship and their coverage of controversial public issues will be eliminated or at least rendered wholly ineffective. Such a result would indeed be a serious matter, for should licensees actually eliminate their coverage of controversial issues, the purposes of the doctrine would be stifled.

At this point, however, as the Federal Communications Commission has indicated, that possibility is at best speculative. The communications industry, and in particular the networks, have taken pains to present controversial issues in the past, and even now they do not assert that they intend to abandon their efforts in this regard. It would be better if the FCC's encouragement were never necessary to induce the broadcasters to meet their responsibility. And if experience with the administration of those doctrines indicates that they have the net effect of reducing rather than enhancing the volume and quality of coverage, there will be time enough to reconsider the constitutional implications. The fairness doctrine in the past has had no such overall effect.

In view of the scarcity of broadcast frequencies, the Government's role in allocating those frequencies, and the legitimate claims of those unable without governmental assistance to gain access to those frequencies for expression of their views, we hold the regulations and ruling at issue here are both authorized by statute and constitutional.

POINTS FOR DISCUSSION

a. The Fairness Doctrine

Did the Supreme Court, in referring to the rights of "viewers and listeners," suggest in *Red Lion* that the First Amendment *required* the fairness doctrine, or instead only that the fairness doctrine did not violate the First Amendment? Note that the FCC decided to abolish the fairness doctrine in 1989, a decision that was upheld in subsequent litigation. See *Syracuse Peace Council v. FCC*, 867 F.2d 654, 665 (D.C. Cir. 1989). Would the fairness doctrine, which applied only to the "broadcast spectrum," be constitutional in an era when most people watch cable television and a large number of people obtain their news from numerous sources on the internet?

b. Theories of First Amendment Protection

What is the purpose of the First Amendment's protections for the press (and for speech)? One common theory is that it promotes democracy by enabling the electorate to become informed. See, e.g., Owen Fiss, *Free Speech and Social Structure*, 71

Iowa L. Rev. 1405 (1986). Is *Red Lion* based on this view of the First Amendment? If so, in what way?

Problem

Rush Limbaugh was the most popular radio talk show host in the United States in the late 1980s and early 1990s. Millions of listeners tuned in to his 3-hour radio program every day to hear his conservative commentary. In 1993, Congress considered enacting a statute to reinstate the fairness doctrine. Opponents dubbed the proposed legislation the "Hush Rush" bill. *The Hush Rush Law*, Wall St. J., Sept. 1, 1993, at A14. They reasoned that no radio station could afford to deliver Limbaugh's program every day if the station also had to broadcast a 3-hour program espousing contrary (and presumably less popular) views. Commentators predicted that radio stations "would certainly eliminate [Rush's program] rather than carve out three additional hours for a liberal political show." *"Fairness" Not Fair to Electronic Media*, South Fl. Sun-Sent., Oct. 19, 1993, at 1E. If the purpose of recreating the fairness doctrine was to silence Rush Limbaugh, would the law be constitutional under *Red Lion*? What if the purpose was to diversify the marketplace of ideas, but the likely effect was to silence Limbaugh and similar programs?

The Court in *Red Lion* upheld the fairness doctrine as applied to a radio station. Does the First Amendment permit its application to newspapers, as well? The following case considered that question.

MIAMI HERALD PUBLISHING CO. V. TORNILLO
418 U.S. 241 (1974)

MR. CHIEF JUSTICE BURGER delivered the opinion of the Court.

The issue in this case is whether a state statute granting a political candidate a right to equal space to reply to criticism and attacks on his record by a newspaper violates the guarantees of a free press. In the fall of 1972, appellee, Executive Director of the Classroom Teachers Association, apparently a teachers' collective-bargaining agent, was a candidate for the Florida House of Representatives. On September 20, 1972, and again on September 29, 1972, appellant printed editorials critical of appellee's candidacy. In response to these editorials appellee demanded that appellant print verbatim his replies, defending the role of the Classroom Teachers Association and the organization's accomplishments for the citizens of Dade County. Appellant declined to print the appellee's replies and appellee brought suit in Circuit Court, Dade County, seeking declaratory and injunctive relief and actual and punitive damages in excess of $5,000. The action was premised on Florida Statute § 104.38 (1973), a "right of reply" statute which provides that if a candidate for nomination or election is assailed regarding his personal character or official record by any newspaper, the candidate has the right to demand that the newspaper print, free of cost to the candidate, any reply the candidate may make to the newspaper's charges. The reply must appear in as conspicuous a place and in the same kind of type as the charges which prompted the reply, provided it does not take up more space than the charges. Failure to comply with the statute constitutes a first-degree misdemeanor.

Appellant contends the statute is void on its face because it purports to regulate the content of a newspaper in violation of the First Amendment. Alternatively it is urged that the statute is void for vagueness since no editor could know exactly what words would call the statute into operation. It is also contended that the statute fails to distinguish between critical comment which is and which is not defamatory.

> **Make the Connection**
>
> We considered vagueness as a ground for facial invalidation of a statute under the First Amendment, and the constitutional status of defamatory speech, in Chapter 8.

The appellee and supporting advocates of an enforceable right of access to the press vigorously argue that government has an obligation to ensure that a wide variety of views reach the public.[8] The contentions of access proponents will be set out in some detail. It is urged that at the time the First Amendment to the Constitution was ratified in 1791 as part of our Bill of Rights the press was broadly representative of the people it was serving. While many of the newspapers were intensely partisan and narrow in their views, the press collectively presented a broad range of opinions to readers. Entry into publishing was inexpensive; pamphlets and books provided meaningful alternatives to the organized press for the expression of unpopular ideas and often treated events and expressed views not covered by conventional newspapers. A true marketplace of ideas existed in which there was relatively easy access to the channels of communication.

Access advocates submit that although newspapers of the present are superficially similar to those of 1791 the press of today is in reality very different from that known in the early years of our national existence. In the past half century a communications revolution has seen the introduction of radio and television into our lives, the promise of a global community through the use of communications satellites, and the spectre of a "wired" nation by means of an

---

[8] *See generally* Jerome Barron, *Access to the Press—A New First Amendment Right*, 80 Harv. L. Rev. 1641 (1967).

expanding cable television network with two-way capabilities. The printed press, it is said, has not escaped the effects of this revolution. Newspapers have become big business and there are far fewer of them to serve a larger literate population. Chains of newspapers, national newspapers, national wire and news services, and one-newspaper towns, are the dominant features of a press that has become noncompetitive and enormously powerful and influential in its capacity to manipulate popular opinion and change the course of events. Major metropolitan newspapers have collaborated to establish news services national in scope. Such national news organizations provide syndicated "interpretive reporting" as well as syndicated features and commentary, all of which can serve as part of the new school of "advocacy journalism."

The elimination of competing newspapers in most of our large cities, and the concentration of control of media that results from the only newspaper's being owned by the same interests which own a television station and a radio station, are important components of this trend toward concentration of control of outlets to inform the public.

The result of these vast changes has been to place in a few hands the power to inform the American people and shape public opinion. Much of the editorial opinion and commentary that is printed is that of syndicated columnists distributed nationwide and, as a result, we are told, on national and world issues there tends to be a homogeneity of editorial opinion, commentary, and interpretive analysis. The abuses of bias and manipulative reportage are, likewise, said to be the result of the vast accumulations of unreviewable power in the modern media empires. In effect, it is claimed, the public has lost any ability to respond or to contribute in a meaningful way to the debate on issues. The monopoly of the means of communication allows for little or no critical analysis of the media except in professional journals of very limited readership.

The obvious solution, which was available to dissidents at an earlier time when entry into publishing was relatively inexpensive, today would be to have additional newspapers. But the same economic factors which have caused the disappearance of vast numbers of metropolitan newspapers, have made entry into the marketplace of ideas served by the print media almost impossible. It is urged that the claim of newspapers to be "surrogates for the public" carries with it a concomitant fiduciary obligation to account for that stewardship. From this premise it is reasoned that the only effective way to insure fairness and accuracy and to provide for some accountability is for government to take affirmative action. The First Amendment interest of the public in being informed is said to be in peril because the "marketplace of ideas" is today a monopoly controlled by the owners of the market.

However much validity may be found in these arguments, at each point the implementation of a remedy such as an enforceable right of access necessarily calls for some mechanism, either governmental or consensual. If it is governmental coercion, this at once brings about a confrontation with the express provisions of the First Amendment and the judicial gloss on that Amendment developed over the years.

The Court foresaw the problems relating to government-enforced access as early as its decision in *Associated Press v. United States*, 326 U.S. 1 (1945). There it carefully contrasted the private "compulsion to print" called for by the Association's bylaws with the provisions of the District Court decree against appellants which "does not compel AP or its members to permit publication of anything which their 'reason' tells them should not be published." *Id.*, at 20. In *Branzburg v. Hayes*, 408 U.S. 665, 681 (1972), we emphasized that the cases then before us "involve no intrusions upon speech or assembly, no prior restraint or restriction on what the press may publish, and no express or implied command that the press publish what it prefers to withhold." In *Columbia Broadcasting System, Inc. v. Democratic National Committee*, 412 U.S. 94, 117 (1973), the plurality opinion [noted]:

> The power of a privately owned newspaper to advance its own political, social, and economic views is bounded by only two factors: first, the acceptance of a sufficient number of readers—and hence advertisers— to assure financial success; and, second, the journalistic integrity of its editors and publishers.

[Beginning] with *Associated Press*, the Court has expressed sensitivity as to whether a restriction or requirement constituted the compulsion exerted by government on a newspaper to print that which it would not otherwise print. The clear implication has been that any such compulsion to publish that which " 'reason' tells them should not be published" is unconstitutional. A responsible press is an undoubtedly desirable goal, but press responsibility is not mandated by the Constitution and like many other virtues it cannot be legislated.

Appellee's argument that the Florida statute does not amount to a restriction of appellant's right to speak because "the statute in question here has not prevented the Miami Herald from saying anything it wished" begs the core question. Compelling editors or publishers to publish that which "reason tells them should not be published" is what is at issue in this case. The Florida statute operates as a command in the same sense as a statute or regulation forbidding appellant to publish specified matter. Governmental restraint on publishing need not fall into familiar or traditional patterns to be subject to constitutional limitations on governmental powers. *Grosjean v. American Press Co.*, 297 U.S. 233, 244–245 (1936). The Florida statute exacts a penalty on the basis of the content of a newspaper. The first phase of the penalty resulting from the compelled printing of a reply is exacted in terms of the cost in printing and composing time and materials and in taking up space that could be devoted to other material the newspaper may have preferred to print. It is correct, as appellee contends, that a newspaper is not subject to the finite technological limitations of time that confront a broadcaster but it is not correct to say that, as an economic reality, a newspaper can proceed to infinite expansion of its column space to accommodate the replies that a government agency determines or a statute commands the readers should have available.

> **Take Note**
>
> The Court explains in these passages how the Florida statute imposes a burden on newspapers and, consequently, why the statute might chill protected speech. Is the Court's point that a regulation *mandating* the inclusion of particular content is tantamount to a regulation *prohibiting* the inclusion of other content? Or that any government interference with editorial choices are suspect, regardless of whether it mandates coverage or prohibits coverage?

Faced with the penalties that would accrue to any newspaper that published news or commentary arguably within the reach of the right-of-access statute, editors might well conclude that the safe course is to avoid controversy. Therefore, under the operation of the Florida statute, political and electoral coverage would be blunted or reduced. Government-enforced right of access inescapably "dampens the vigor and limits the variety of public debate." *New York Times Co. v. Sullivan*, 376 U.S. 254, 279 (1964). * * *

Even if a newspaper would face no additional costs to comply with a compulsory access law and would not be forced to forgo publication of news or opinion by the inclusion of a reply, the Florida statute fails to clear the barriers of the First Amendment because of its intrusion into the function of editors. A newspaper is more than a passive receptacle or conduit for news, comment, and advertising. The choice of material to go into a newspaper, and the decisions made as to limitations on the size and content of the paper, and treatment of public issues and public officials—whether fair or unfair—constitute the exercise of editorial control and judgment. It has yet to be demonstrated how governmental regulation of this crucial process can be exercised consistent with First

Amendment guarantees of a free press as they have evolved to this time. Accordingly, the judgment of the Supreme Court of Florida is reversed.

POINTS FOR DISCUSSION

a.   Newspapers and Broadcasters

The Supreme Court oddly did not cite *Red Lion* in *Tornillo*, even though the two cases involved similar issues. Are the two cases inconsistent or are they distinguishable?

b.   Theory of the First Amendment's Protections

What theory of the First Amendment's protections did the Court advance in *Tornillo*? Did the court reject the "marketplace of ideas" theory that seemed central to the Court's decision in *Red Lion*? Or did the Court simply conclude that the challenged statute did not ultimately advance that theory of the First Amendment? If the former, what interests did the Court think that the First Amendment serves?

C. PRESS ACCESS TO GOVERNMENT PROCEEDINGS

Newspapers and broadcast media cannot publish informed accounts of important developments unless their reporters have access to the sources of the news. Does the freedom of the press guarantee journalists a right of access to government proceedings, to crime and accident scenes, and to other places where news is made? The Supreme Court has not attempted to give a general answer to this question. Instead, the Court has given some context-specific answers. The following case considers whether the media have a right to attend criminal trials.

RICHMOND NEWSPAPERS, INC. V. VIRGINIA
448 U.S. 555 (1980)

MR. CHIEF JUSTICE BURGER announced the judgment of the Court and delivered an opinion, in which MR. JUSTICE WHITE and MR. JUSTICE STEVENS joined.

[Stevenson was tried and convicted in state court in Virginia in July 1976 of second-degree murder, but the Virginia Supreme Court reversed after concluding that a bloodstained shirt purportedly belonging to Stevenson had been improperly admitted into evidence. Stevenson was retried in the same court, but

> **Take Note**
>
> This is a plurality opinion. Consider what that means for the analysis contained in this opinion and in those by the other Justices.

the second trial ended in a mistrial in May 1978 when a juror asked to be excused after trial had begun and no alternate was available. A third trial one month later in the same court also ended in a mistrial, apparently because a prospective juror had read about the previous trials in a newspaper and had told other prospective jurors about the case before the retrial began.]

Stevenson was tried in the same court for a fourth time beginning on September 11, 1978. Present in the courtroom when the case was called were appellants Wheeler and McCarthy, reporters for appellant Richmond Newspapers, Inc. Before the trial began, counsel for the defendant moved that it be closed to the public [on the ground that persons who observed the prior trials might shuffle information "back and forth when we have a recess as to what—who testified to what."] The trial judge, who had presided over two of the three previous trials, asked if the prosecution had any objection to clearing the courtroom. The prosecutor stated he had no objection and would leave it to the discretion of the court. Presumably [relying on] Va. Code § 19.2–266 (Supp.1980), the trial judge then [ordered] "that the Courtroom be kept clear of all parties except the witnesses when they testify." The record does not show that any objections to the closure order were made by anyone present at the time, including appellants Wheeler and McCarthy.

Later that same day, however, appellants sought a hearing on a motion to vacate the closure order. The trial judge granted the request and scheduled a hearing to follow the close of the day's proceedings. When the hearing began, the court ruled that the hearing was to be treated as part of the trial; accordingly, he again ordered the reporters to leave the courtroom, and they complied.

At the closed hearing, counsel for appellants observed that no evidentiary findings had been made by the court prior to the entry of its closure order and pointed out that the court had failed to consider any other, less drastic measures within its power to ensure a fair trial. Counsel for appellants argued that constitutional considerations mandated that before ordering closure, the court should first decide that the rights of the defendant could be protected in no other way.

Counsel for defendant Stevenson pointed out that this was the fourth time he was standing trial. He also referred to "difficulty with information between the jurors," and stated that he "didn't want information to leak out," be published by the media, perhaps inaccurately, and then be seen by the jurors. Defense counsel argued that these things, plus the fact that "this is a small community," made this a proper case for closure. The court denied the motion to vacate and ordered the trial to continue the following morning "with the press and public excluded."

What transpired when the closed trial resumed the next day was disclosed in the following manner by an order of the court entered September 12, 1978:

> [I]n the absence of the jury, the defendant by counsel made a Motion that a mistrial be declared, which motion was taken under advisement. At the conclusion of the Commonwealth's evidence, the attorney for the defendant moved the Court to strike the Commonwealth's evidence on grounds stated to the record, which Motion was sustained by the Court. And the jury having been excused, the Court doth find the accused NOT GUILTY of Murder, as charged in the Indictment, and he was allowed to depart.

[The newspapers appealed the denial of their motion. The Court considered the possibility that the case was now moot because the trial was over. But the Court decided to grant review on grounds that "it is reasonably foreseeable that other trials may be closed by other judges" and "criminal trials will be of sufficiently short duration that a closure order" will evade review.]

We have found nothing to suggest that the presumptive openness of the trial, which English courts were later to call "one of the essential qualities of a court of justice," *Daubney v. Cooper*, 10 B. & C. 237, 240, 109 Eng. Rep. 438, 440 (K. B. 1829), was not also an attribute of the judicial systems of colonial America. In Virginia, for example, such records as there are of early criminal trials indicate that they were open, and nothing to the contrary has been cited. *See* A. Scott, Criminal Law in Colonial Virginia 128–129 (1930); Reinsch, The English Common Law in the Early American Colonies, in 1 Select Essays in Anglo-American Legal History 367, 405 (1907). * * * In some instances, the openness of trials was explicitly recognized as part of the fundamental law of the Colony. The 1677 Concessions and Agreements of West New Jersey, for example, provided:

> That in all publick courts of justice for tryals of causes, civil or criminal, any person or persons, inhabitants of the said Province may freely come into, and attend the said courts, and hear and be present, at all or any such tryals as shall be there had or passed, that justice may not be done in a corner nor in any covert manner." Reprinted in Sources of Our Liberties 188 (R. Perry ed. 1959). See also 1 B. Schwartz, The Bill of Rights: A Documentary History 129 (1971).

The Pennsylvania Frame of Government of 1682 also provided "[t]hat all courts shall be open * * *," Sources of Our Liberties, *supra*, at 217; 1 Schwartz, *supra*, at 140, and this declaration was reaffirmed in § 26 of the Constitution adopted by Pennsylvania in 1776. See 1 Schwartz, *supra*, at 271.

> **FYI**
>
> The Sixth Amendment guarantees a right to a "public trial." In *Gannett*, however, the Court concluded that this right belongs only to the accused criminal defendant. The Court held that the press and members of the public have no right under the Sixth Amendment to attend criminal trials. In what way is the claim here different?

As we have shown, and as was shown in both the Court's opinion and the dissent in *Gannett Co. v. DePasquale*, 443 U.S. 368, 384, 386, n. 15 (1979), the historical evidence demonstrates conclusively that at the time when our organic laws were adopted, criminal trials both here and in England had long been presumptively open. The question is whether anyone else can insist on a public trial if the defendant waives that right. This is no quirk of history; rather, it has long been recognized as an indispensable attribute of an Anglo-American trial. Both Hale in the 17th century and Blackstone in the 18th saw the importance of openness to the proper functioning of a trial; it gave assurance that the proceedings were conducted fairly to all concerned, and it discouraged perjury, the misconduct of participants, and decisions based on secret bias or partiality. *See, e. g.*, M. Hale, The History of the Common Law of England 343–345 (6th ed. 1820); 3 W. Blackstone, Commentaries *372–*373. * * * From this unbroken, uncontradicted history, supported by reasons as valid today as in centuries past, we are bound to conclude that a presumption of openness inheres in the very nature of a criminal trial under our system of justice.

> **FYI**
>
> Sir Matthew Hale (1609–1676) wrote *The History of the Common Law of England* in 1713. He later became the Chief Justice of the Court of the King's Bench. Sir William Blackstone (1723–1780), a member of Parliament and later a judge of the Court of Common Pleas, published an influential four-volume treatise called *Commentaries on the Laws of England* between 1765–1769. The Supreme Court often cites these works for authoritative statements of the common law prior to the Constitution.

The First Amendment, in conjunction with the Fourteenth, prohibits governments from "abridging the freedom of speech, or of the press; or the right of the people peaceably to assemble, and to petition the Government for a redress of grievances." These expressly guaranteed freedoms share a common core purpose of assuring freedom of communication on matters relating to the functioning of government. Plainly it would be difficult to single out any aspect of government of higher concern and importance to the people than the manner in which criminal trials are conducted; as we have shown, recognition of this pervades the centuries-old history of open trials and the opinions of this Court.

The Bill of Rights was enacted against the backdrop of the long history of trials being presumptively open. Public access to trials was then regarded as an important aspect of the process itself; the conduct of trials "before as many of the people as chuse to attend" was regarded as one of "the inestimable advantages of a free English constitution of government." 1 Journals 106, 107. In guaranteeing freedoms such as those of speech and press, the First Amendment can be read as protecting the right of everyone to attend trials so as to give meaning to those explicit guarantees. "[T]he First Amendment goes beyond protection of the press and the self-expression of individuals to prohibit government from limiting the stock of information from which members of the public may draw." *First National Bank of Boston v. Bellotti*, 435 U.S. 765, 783 (1978). Free speech carries with it some freedom to listen. "In a variety of contexts this Court has referred to a First Amendment right to 'receive information and ideas.' " *Kleindienst v. Mandel*, 408 U.S. 753, 762 (1972). What this means in the context of trials is that the First Amendment guarantees of speech and press, standing alone, prohibit government from summarily closing courtroom doors which had long been open to the public at the time that Amendment was adopted. "For the First Amendment does not speak equivocally. [It] must be taken as a command of the broadest scope that explicit language, read in the context of a liberty-loving society, will allow." *Bridges v. California*, 314 U.S. 252, 263 (1941).

It is not crucial whether we describe this right to attend criminal trials to hear, see, and communicate observations concerning them as a "right of access" or a "right to gather information," for we have recognized that "without some protection for seeking out the news, freedom of the press could be eviscerated." *Branzburg v. Hayes*, 408 U.S. 665, 681 (1972). The explicit, guaranteed rights to speak and to publish concerning what takes place at a trial would lose much meaning if access to observe the trial could, as it was here, be foreclosed arbitrarily.

The State argues that the Constitution nowhere spells out a guarantee for the right of the public to attend trials, and that accordingly no such right is protected. The possibility that such a contention could be made did not escape the notice of the Constitution's draftsmen; they were concerned that some important rights might be thought disparaged because not specifically guaranteed. It was even argued that because of this danger no Bill of Rights should be adopted. See, *e. g.*, The Federalist No. 84 (A. Hamilton). In a letter to Thomas Jefferson in October 1788, James Madison [stated] that "there is great reason to fear that a positive declaration of some of the most essential rights could not be obtained in the requisite latitude." 5 Writings of James Madison 271 (G. Hunt ed. 1904).[15]

> **Make the Connection**
>
> The plurality here compares the right to attend criminal trials to other unenumerated rights that the Court has recognized. Is the Court's approach here consistent with the approach that it took in other cases involving unenumerated rights that we considered in Chapter 2?

Notwithstanding the appropriate caution against reading into the Constitution rights not explicitly defined, the Court has acknowledged that certain unarticulated rights are implicit in enumerated guarantees. For example, the rights of association and of privacy, the right to be presumed innocent, and the right to be judged by a standard of proof beyond a reasonable doubt in a criminal trial, as well as the right to travel, appear nowhere in the Constitution or Bill of Rights. Yet these important but unarticulated rights have nonetheless been found to share constitutional protection in common with explicit guarantees. The concerns expressed by Madison and others have thus been resolved; fundamental rights, even though not expressly guaranteed, have been recognized by the Court as indispensable to the enjoyment of rights explicitly defined.

We hold that the right to attend criminal trials is implicit in the guarantees of the First Amendment; without the freedom to attend such trials, which people have exercised for centuries, important aspects of freedom of speech and "of the press could be eviscerated." *Branzburg*, 408 U.S., at 681.

Having concluded there was a guaranteed right of the public under the First and Fourteenth Amendments to attend the trial of Stevenson's case, we return to the closure order challenged by appellants. Despite the fact that this was the fourth trial of the accused, the trial judge made no findings to support closure; no inquiry was made as to whether alternative solutions would have met the need to ensure fairness; there was no recognition of any right under the Constitution for the public or press to attend the trial. [T]here exist in the context of

> **Take Note**
>
> Note that the plurality's conclusion here appears to extend the right to attend trials not only to the press, but also to the public. Does that suggest that the First Amendment's protection for the freedom of the press is not central to the resolution of the case? Whatever the weight of the public's general interest in open trials, does the press have a special claim of access to criminal trials?

---

[15] Madison's comments in Congress also reveal the perceived need for some sort of constitutional "saving clause," which, among other things, would serve to foreclose application to the Bill of Rights of the maxim that the affirmation of particular rights implies a negation of those not expressly defined. See 1 Annals of Cong. 438–440 (1789). See also, e.g., 2 J. Story, Commentaries on the Constitution of the United States 651 (5th ed. 1891). Madison's efforts, culminating in the Ninth Amendment, served to allay the fears of those who were concerned that expressing certain guarantees could be read as excluding others.

the trial itself various tested alternatives to satisfy the constitutional demands of fairness. There was no suggestion that any problems with witnesses could not have been dealt with by their exclusion from the courtroom or their sequestration during the trial. Nor is there anything to indicate that sequestration of the jurors would not have guarded against their being subjected to any improper information. All of the alternatives admittedly present difficulties for trial courts, but none of the factors relied on here was beyond the realm of the manageable. Absent an overriding interest articulated in findings, the trial of a criminal case must be open to the public. * * * *Reversed.*

MR. JUSTICE BRENNAN, with whom MR. JUSTICE MARSHALL joins, concurring in the judgment.

Gannett Co. v. DePasquale, 443 U.S. 368 (1979), held that the Sixth Amendment right to a public trial was personal to the accused, conferring no right of access to pretrial proceedings that is separately enforceable by the public or the press. The instant case raises the question whether the First Amendment, of its own force and as applied to the States through the Fourteenth Amendment, secures the public an independent right of access to trial proceedings. Because I believe that the First Amendment—of itself and as applied to the States through the Fourteenth Amendment—secures such a public right of access, I agree with those of my Brethren who hold that, without more, agreement of the trial judge and the parties cannot constitutionally close a trial to the public.

Secrecy is profoundly inimical to [the] demonstrative purpose of the trial process. Open trials assure the public that procedural rights are respected, and that justice is afforded equally. Closed trials breed suspicion of prejudice and arbitrariness, which in turn spawns disrespect for law. Public access is essential, therefore, if trial adjudication is to achieve the objective of maintaining public confidence in the administration of justice.

But the trial is more than a demonstrably just method of adjudicating disputes and protecting rights. It plays a pivotal role in the entire judicial process, and, by extension, in our form of government. * * * While individual cases turn upon the controversies between parties, or involve particular prosecutions, court rulings impose official and practical consequences upon members of society at large. Moreover, judges bear responsibility for the vitally important task of construing and securing constitutional rights. Thus, so far as the trial is the mechanism for judicial factfinding, as well as the initial forum for legal decisionmaking, it is a genuine governmental proceeding. * * * It follows that the conduct of the trial is pre-eminently a matter of public interest. More importantly, public access to trials acts as an important check, akin in purpose to the other checks and balances that infuse our system of government. * * *

Since in the present case the trial judge appears to have given no recognition to the right of representatives of the press and members of the public to be present at the Virginia murder trial over which he was presiding, the judgment under review must be reversed. * * *

MR. JUSTICE BLACKMUN, concurring in the judgment.

My opinion and vote in partial dissent last Term in *Gannett Co. v. DePasquale*, 443 U.S. 368, 406 (1979), compels my vote to reverse the judgment of the Supreme Court of Virginia. The Court, however, has eschewed the Sixth Amendment route. The plurality turns to other possible constitutional sources and invokes a veritable potpourri of them—the Speech Clause of the First Amendment, the Press Clause, the Assembly Clause, the Ninth Amendment, and a cluster of penumbral guarantees recognized in past decisions. This course is troublesome, but it is the route that has been selected and, at least for now, we must live with it. * * *

Having said all this, and with the Sixth Amendment set to one side in this case, I am driven to conclude, as a secondary position, that the First Amendment must provide some measure of protection for public access to the trial. The opinion in partial dissent in *Gannett* explained that the public has an intense need and a deserved right to know about the administration of justice in general; about the prosecution of local crimes in particular; about the conduct of the judge, the prosecutor, defense counsel, police officers, other public servants, and all the actors in the judicial arena; and about the trial itself. See 443 U.S., at 413, and n.2, 414, 428–429, 448. It is clear and obvious to me, on the approach the Court has chosen to take, that, by closing this criminal trial, the trial judge abridged these First Amendment interests of the public.

MR. JUSTICE REHNQUIST, dissenting.

For the reasons stated in my separate concurrence in *Gannett Co. v. DePasquale*, 443 U.S. 368, 403 (1979), I do not believe that either the First or Sixth Amendment, as made applicable to the States by the Fourteenth, requires that a State's reasons for denying public access to a trial, where both the prosecuting attorney and the defendant have consented to an order of closure approved by the judge, are subject to any additional constitutional review at our hands. And I most certainly do not believe that the Ninth Amendment confers upon us any such power to review orders of state trial judges closing trials in such situations.

The issue here is not whether the "right" to freedom of the press conferred by the First Amendment to the Constitution overrides the defendant's "right" to a fair trial conferred by other Amendments to the Constitution; it is instead whether any provision in the Constitution may fairly be read to prohibit what the trial judge in the Virginia state-court system did in this case. Being unable to find any such prohibition in the First, Sixth, Ninth, or any other Amendment to the United States Constitution, or in the Constitution itself, I dissent.

POINTS FOR DISCUSSION

a.   Views of the Justices

On what ground did the plurality decision rest? Why did the concurrences agree with the result but not the rationale? Was their dispute with the Court's interpretive methodology? Or simply with the particular provisions of the Constitution on which the plurality relied? How was the dissent's position different from the positions expressed in the other opinions?

Consider the following hypothetical case: A prominent businessman and supporter of the mayor is implicated in a bribery scandal. He is indicted by a prosecutor who is loyal to the mayor. Shortly after the mayor is defeated in an election but before the new mayor takes office, an elected trial judge from the outgoing mayor's party enters an order announcing his plan to hold a closed trial. The local newspaper challenges the order, arguing that the judge might direct a judgment of acquittal to ensure that the businessman is protected by the double jeopardy provision of the Fifth Amendment. (A judge can direct that a defendant be found not guilty if the government fails to provide evidence that could support a charge. Once a defendant is found not guilty, the defendant cannot be tried again.) How would the claim be resolved under the Court's approach? Under the dissent's approach? Would we need to know other facts, as well?

b.   Right of Access to Prisons

In *Pell v. Procunier*, 417 U.S. 817 (1974), the Supreme Court rejected a claim by journalists that they had a constitutional right to interview a particular inmate in a prison. In what ways is a prison different from a criminal trial?

Executive Summary of This Chapter

The First Amendment expressly prohibits Congress from abridging the **freedom of the press**. The Supreme Court has held that this prohibition also applies to the states under the incorporation doctrine. *Gitlow v. People of State of New York*, 268 U.S. 652, 666 (1925).

One question is whether the freedom of the press gives the press (e.g., newspapers, radio and television news producers, journalists, etc.) **special rights or special exemptions from generally applicable laws** beyond the free speech rights generally enjoyed by everyone. The Supreme Court has answered this question in the negative by holding that "generally applicable laws do not offend the First Amendment simply because their enforcement against the press has incidental effects on its ability to gather and report the news." *Cohen v. Cowles Media Co.,* 501 U.S. 663 (1991). Cases in this chapter provide several illustrations. The freedom of the press does not give journalists a right to refuse to appear and testify before grand juries. *Branzburg v. Hayes,* 408 U.S. 665 (1972). The freedom of the press does not immunize newspaper offices from search warrants or exempt newspaper offices from complying with otherwise lawful subpoenas to turn over evidence of crimes. *Zurcher v. Stanford Daily,* 436 U.S. 547 (1978). And the freedom of the press does not prevent the enforcement of a reporter's promises to a source under the doctrine of promissory estoppel. *Cohen.*

A second question is whether the freedom of the press prevents the government from requiring news providers to give outsiders **access to their media** (e.g., column space in a newspaper or airtime during a radio or television broadcast). The Supreme Court's answer to this question has depended upon the context. The Court has held that the freedom of the press does not prevent the government from requiring radio and television broadcasters to discuss public issues and to give fair coverage to each side of the issues. *Red Lion Broadcasting Co. v. F.C.C.,* 395 U.S. 367 (1969). But the Court has held that the government cannot require a newspaper to give political candidates space to reply to criticism printed in a newspaper. *Miami Herald Publishing Co. v. Tornillo,* 418 U.S. 241 (1974). A possible rationale for why the government may require broadcasters to publish contrary views but not newspapers is that anyone can start a newspaper but the number of radio and television stations is limited because the airwaves can physically carry only so many radio and television broadcasts.

A third question is whether the freedom of the press gives the media **special rights of access to government proceedings**. The Supreme Court has not announced a general rule with respect to this issue. But a plurality of the Court concluded that the First Amendment gives the press, and the general public, a right to attend criminal trials. *Richmond Newspapers, Inc. v. Virginia,* 448 U.S. 555 (1980).

CHAPTER 10

Freedom of Association

INTRODUCTION

The text of the Constitution does not expressly mention a "freedom of association." So what is this freedom and where does it come from? The Supreme Court offered a concise explanation in *Roberts v. U.S. Jaycees*, 468 U.S. 609, 617–618 (1984):

> Our decisions have referred to constitutionally protected "freedom of association" in two distinct senses. In one line of decisions, the Court has concluded that choices to enter into and maintain certain intimate human relationships must be secured against undue intrusion by the State because of the role of such relationships in safeguarding the individual freedom that is central to our constitutional scheme. In this respect, freedom of association receives protection as a fundamental element of personal liberty. In another set of decisions, the Court has recognized a right to associate for the purpose of engaging in those activities protected by the First Amendment—speech, assembly, petition for the redress of grievances, and the exercise of religion. The Constitution guarantees freedom of association of this kind as an indispensable means of preserving other individual liberties.

In other words, the Supreme Court has developed two distinct "freedom of association" doctrines. Under the first doctrine, freedom of association is a fundamental right, protected under the theory of substantive due process. This freedom of association may encompass, for example, "a right to maintain certain familial relationships, including association among members of an

> **Make the Connection**
>
> We addressed the doctrine of substantive due process—the idea that the Due Process Clauses in the Fifth and Fourteenth Amendments confer substantive rights (as opposed to procedural rights)—and protected rights of family and intimate association in Chapter 2.

immediate family and association between grandchildren and grandparents."
Overton v. Bazzetta, 539 U.S. 126, 131 (2003). In recent years, the Supreme Court
has said fairly little about the freedom of association protected by the Due Process
Clauses, perhaps because of continuing controversy over the concept of
substantive due process. *Collins v. Harker Heights*, 503 U.S. 115, 125 (1992) ("As a
general matter, the Court has always been reluctant to expand the concept of
substantive due process because guideposts for responsible decisionmaking in this
unchartered area are scarce and open-ended.").

Under the second doctrine, the Court has treated the protection of freedom
of association as a necessary means for securing rights guaranteed by the First
Amendment. The reasoning behind this doctrine is as follows: The First
Amendment protects freedom of speech. The government therefore must allow
a dissenter to speak. But a single voice speaking alone often goes unheard.
Therefore, if the government can prevent a dissenter from associating with
others—say, at a rally or in a parade—the government effectively could stifle the
dissenter's message. The First Amendment, accordingly, must protect the
dissenter's freedom to associate with others who may wish to express similar
views.

The idea that speakers can propagate ideas more effectively when they act
with others is not new. Recounting American history, the Supreme Court has said:

> [T]he practice of persons sharing common views banding together to
> achieve a common end is deeply embedded in the American political
> process. The 18th-century * * * pamphleteers were early examples of
> this phenomen[on] and the *Federalist Papers* were perhaps the most
> significant and lasting example. The tradition of volunteer committees
> for collective action has manifested itself in myriad community and
> public activities; in the political process it can focus on a candidate or
> on a ballot measure. Its value is that by collective effort individuals can
> make their views known, when, individually, their voices would be faint
> or lost.

Citizens Against Rent Control/Coalition for Fair Housing v. City of Berkeley, 454 U.S. 290,
294 (1981). Thus, even though the Constitution does not expressly mention a
freedom of association, recognition of such a right appears to be consistent with
the original understanding of what freedom of speech requires. See Robert H.
Bork, *Neutral Principles and Some First Amendment Problems*, 47 Ind. L.J. 1, 17 (1971)
(arguing that deriving "secondary rights" in this manner "is essential to the
interpretation of the first amendment"). In any event, the Court has consistently
accorded it protection.

In this chapter, we are concerned with the freedom of association that derives from the First Amendment. We will consider three main issues: (1) the extent to which the government may penalize a person for being a member of a group; (2) the extent to which the government may force a group or organization to divulge the identities of its members; and (3) the extent to which the government may force groups to associate with individuals with whom they do not wish to associate.

POINTS FOR DISCUSSION

a. Freedom of Association and Religion

The justification that we considered above for a derivative First Amendment right of freedom of association is based primarily on the need to protect the freedom of speech and assembly. Can you construct an argument that freedom of association is also necessary if the First Amendment is to provide meaningful protection for the free exercise of *religion*? See *Salvation Army v. Department of Community Affairs*, 919 F.2d 183, 198–201 (3d Cir. 1990) (discussing the constitutional right to associate for religious purposes). We will consider the freedom of religion in Chapter 11.

b. Activity Not Protected by the First Amendment

In the quotation from *Roberts* above, the Supreme Court indicated that protecting freedom of association is "an indispensable means of preserving" First Amendment rights. A corollary of this logic is that the Court will not recognize a right of association when the association is not a means of engaging in conduct protected by the First Amendment. A good illustration of this corollary appears in *City of Chicago v. Morales*, 527 U.S. 41 (1999). The City of Chicago enacted an ordinance that prohibits "criminal street gang members" from loitering in public places. Although the Supreme Court invalidated the ordinance on other grounds, it concluded that the ordinance did not violate the freedom of association. It stated:

> The ordinance does not prohibit speech. Because the term "loiter" is defined as remaining in one place "with no apparent purpose," it is also clear that it does not prohibit any form of conduct that is apparently intended to convey a message. By its terms, the ordinance is inapplicable to assemblies that are designed to demonstrate a group's support of, or opposition to, a particular point of view. Its impact on the social contact between gang members and others does not impair the First Amendment "right of association" that our cases have recognized.

Id. at 53. In other words, the gang members' First Amendment freedom of association was not impaired because loitering is not an activity protected by the First

Amendment. Can you make an argument that all decisions about whom to associate with implicate First Amendment values, even when the activities that the individuals engage in together do not communicate a message?

c.   Protecting Association as an End in Itself?

The Supreme Court has treated the freedom of association largely instrumentally, as a means to secure the rights expressly protected by the First Amendment. Do you agree that the freedom of association is not an end in itself, but merely a means to ensure protection of other rights? See David Cole, *Hanging with the Wrong Crowd: Of Gangs, Terrorists, and the Right of Association*, 1999 Sup. Ct. Rev. 203 (arguing that freedom of association should be seen as an end in itself, and not just a means to other ends).

A. PENALIZING INDIVIDUALS FOR JOINING GROUPS

In general, the government cannot impose civil or criminal liability on a person merely because he or she has decided to associate with others. As the court explained in *Scales v. United States*, 367 U.S. 203, 229 (1961), allowing the government to prohibit group memberships would raise "a real danger that legitimate political expression or association would be impaired." For example, suppose a number of students at a state university want to debate politics. The First Amendment clearly would prohibit the university from forbidding any of the individual students to speak on political matters. So too, the First Amendment must prevent the university from forbidding the students to form and join a political debating society at which they argue politics with each other. Debates cannot occur unless the students can form the society and thus have debating partners.

This general rule, however, has an important exception. The government does not have to permit individuals to associate with each other for the purpose of undertaking unlawful activities that are not themselves protected by the First Amendment. Because bank robbery is illegal, for example, the government can outlaw conspiracies to commit bank robbery. This exception may apply even when a group is political in nature. In *Scales,* for example, the Court upheld the conviction of an individual for his membership in a communist party organization where evidence showed that he specifically intended to accomplish the criminal aims of the organization, namely, the overthrow of the U.S. government "by resort to violence." *Id.* at 229. In a different case decided the same day, however, the Court reversed the conviction of an individual who had joined a communist organization but who did not advocate or intend illegal action. See *Noto v. United States*, 367 U.S. 290, 299 (1961).

The federal and state governments have generally taken to heart the rule that they cannot ban membership in groups that do not have illegal purposes, and accordingly have rarely enacted laws that expressly seek to accomplish that end. But what is the constitutional status of a law that does not directly ban membership in a group that engages in protected First Amendment activities, but still indirectly discourages individuals from joining the group? For example, imagine a state law that provides: "Membership in political debating societies on state university campuses is permitted. But if any member of a political debating society shall make a slanderous remark, all members of the debating society will be liable." This law surely would discourage membership in the political debating society because few potential members would want to risk incurring liability for the slanderous remarks of another.

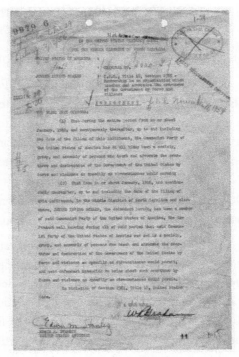

Indictment of Junius Irving Scales. Scales was the first person charged with violating 18 U.S.C. § 2385, a federal statute (still in force) that criminalizes membership in an organization that teaches and advocates the overthrow of the Government by force and violence. A jury found that Scales was a member of the Communist Party of the United States of America and that this organization taught and advocated the overthrow of the Government by force and violence. Professor Douglas Maggs (the grandfather of one of the authors of this book) worked unsuccessfully for Scales's defense. See Junius Irving Scales & Richard Nickson, *Cause at Heart: A Former Communist Remembers* 278 (1987).
National Archives

The following case suggests that such a law would be unconstitutional. Although the state may impose liability on a person who commits slander, it may not impose this liability on others merely because they associated with the person.

NAACP v. CLAIBORNE HARDWARE CO.

458 U.S. 886 (1982)

JUSTICE STEVENS delivered the opinion of the Court.

In March 1966, black citizens of Port Gibson, Miss., and other areas of Claiborne County presented white elected officials with a list of particularized demands for racial equality and integration. The complainants did not receive a satisfactory response and, at a local National Association for the Advancement of Colored People (NAACP) meeting at the First Baptist Church, several hundred black persons voted to place a boycott on white merchants in the area. On October 31, 1969, several of the merchants filed suit in state court to recover losses caused by the boycott and to enjoin future boycott activity. * * *

The complaint [named] two corporations and 146 individuals as defendants: the NAACP, a New York membership corporation; Mississippi Action for Progress (MAP), a Mississippi corporation that implemented the federal "Head Start" program; Aaron Henry, the President of the Mississippi State Conference of the NAACP; Charles Evers, the Field Secretary of the NAACP in Mississippi; and 144 other individuals who had participated in the boycott. The complaint sought injunctive relief and an attachment of property, as well as damages. * * *

[The Mississippi Supreme Court held that most of the defendants, including the NAACP, were jointly and severally liable under Mississippi law for the tort of malicious interference with the plaintiffs' businesses.] After reviewing the chancellor's recitation of the facts, the court quoted the following finding made by the trial court:

> In carrying out the agreement and design [of the boycott], certain of the defendants, acting for all others, engaged in acts of physical force and violence against the persons and property of certain customers and prospective customers. Intimidation, threats, social ostracism, vilification, and traduction were some of the devices used by the defendants to achieve the desired results. Most effective, also, was the stationing of guards ("enforcers," "deacons," or "black hats") in the vicinity of white-owned businesses. Unquestionably, the evidence shows that the volition of many black persons was overcome out of sheer fear, and they were forced and compelled against their personal wills to withhold their trade and business intercourse from the complainants.

On the basis of this finding, the court concluded that the entire boycott was unlawful. "If any of these factors—force, violence, or threats—is present, then the boycott is illegal regardless of whether it is primary, secondary, economical, political, social or other." * * *

The First Amendment * * * restricts the ability of the State to impose liability on an individual solely because of his association with another. In *Scales v. United States*, 367 U.S. 203, 229 (1961), the Court noted that a "blanket prohibition of association with a group having both legal and illegal aims" would present "a real danger that legitimate political expression or association would be impaired." The Court suggested that to punish association with such a group, there must be "clear proof that a defendant 'specifically intend[s] to accomplish [the aims of the organization] by resort to violence.' " *Ibid.* (quoting *Noto v. United States*, 367 U.S. 290, 299 (1961)). Moreover, in *Noto* the Court emphasized that this intent must be judged "according to the strictest law," for "otherwise there is a danger that one in sympathy with the legitimate aims of such an organization, but not specifically intending to accomplish them by resort to violence, might be punished for his adherence to lawful and constitutionally protected purposes, because of other and unprotected purposes which he does not necessarily share." *Id.* at 299–300.

In *Healy v. James*, 408 U.S. 169 (1972), the Court applied these principles in a noncriminal context. In that case the Court held that a student group could not be denied recognition at a state-supported college merely because of its affiliation with a national organization associated with disruptive and violent campus activity. It noted that "the Court has consistently disapproved governmental action imposing criminal sanctions or denying rights and privileges solely because of a citizen's association with an unpopular organization." *Id.*, at 185–186. The Court stated that "it has been established that 'guilt by association alone, without [establishing] that an individual's association poses the threat feared by the Government,' is an impermissible basis upon which to deny First Amendment rights." *Id.*, at 186 (quoting *United States v. Robel*, 389 U.S. 258, 265 (1967)). "The government has the burden of establishing a knowing affiliation with an organization possessing unlawful aims and goals, and a specific intent to further those illegal aims." 408 U.S., at 186.

The principles announced in *Scales, Noto,* and *Healy* are relevant to this case. Civil liability may not be imposed merely because an individual belonged to a group, some members of which committed acts of violence. For liability to be imposed by reason of association alone, it is necessary to establish that the group itself possessed unlawful goals and that the individual held a specific intent to further those illegal aims.

[Reversed.]

POINTS FOR DISCUSSION

a.   An Individual's Liability for Belonging to an Organization

A significant part of the Court's discussion in *Claiborne Hardware* is addressed to the problem under the First Amendment of "guilt by association"—that is, the imposition of criminal liability on one person solely because of the actions of a person with whom he associates. Isn't imposing guilt by association problematic wholly aside from any First Amendment concerns? Doesn't the imposition of criminal liability for actions taken by another (and not fairly attributed to the defendant) violate basic notions of Due Process, under which the government must demonstrate beyond a reasonable doubt that the defendant committed the charged offense? Does it matter whether the Court grounds a presumption against guilt by association in the First Amendment or instead in the Due Process Clause? Did it matter in this case, where the guilt by association had been imposed on an organization, rather than on an individual?

b.   An Organization's Liability for Acts of Its Members

Another portion of the Court's opinion, not quoted above, addressed the issue of whether the NAACP as an organization could be liable because of the acts of some of its members. The Court said: "To impose liability without a finding that the NAACP authorized—either actually or apparently—or ratified unlawful conduct would impermissibly burden the rights of political association that are protected by the First Amendment." What might happen to an organization like the NAACP if it were held liable for the acts of some (or any) of its members? Can you articulate why those consequences might raise particular concerns under the First Amendment?

The preceding case concerned the possibility that imposing civil liability on members of a group might discourage membership in the group. A state law also could discourage membership in groups by denying legal or other privileges to persons who belong to groups or who refuse to provide information about them. The following case addresses the constitutionality of such a law.

BAIRD V. STATE BAR OF ARIZONA
401 U.S. 1 (1971)

MR. JUSTICE BLACK announced the judgment of the Court and delivered an opinion in which MR. JUSTICE DOUGLAS, MR. JUSTICE BRENNAN, and MR. JUSTICE MARSHALL join.

This is one of two cases now before us from two different States in which applicants have been denied admission to practice law solely because they refused to answer questions about their personal beliefs or their affiliations with organizations that advocate certain ideas about government. Sharp conflicts and close divisions have arisen in this Court concerning the power of States to refuse to permit applicants to practice law in cases where bar examiners have been suspicious about applicants' loyalties and their views on Communism and revolution. This has been an increasingly divisive and bitter issue for some years, especially since Senator Joseph McCarthy from Wisconsin stirred up anti-Communist feelings and fears by his "investigations" in the early 1950's. One applicant named Raphael Konigsberg was denied admission in California and this Court reversed. *Konigsberg v. State Bar*, 353 U.S. 252 (1957). The State nevertheless denied him admission a second time, and this Court then affirmed by a 5-to-4 decision. 366 U.S. 36 (1961). An applicant named Rudolph Schware was denied admission in New Mexico and this Court reversed, with five Justices agreeing on one opinion, three Justices on another opinion, and one not participating. *Schware v. Board of Bar Examiners*, 353 U.S. 232 (1957). In another case an applicant named George Anastaplo was denied admission in Illinois on grounds similar to those involved in *Konigsberg* and *Schware*, and the denial was affirmed by a 5-to-4 margin. *In re Anastaplo*, 366 U.S. 82 (1961). With sharp divisions in this Court, our docket and those of the Courts of Appeals have been filled for years with litigation involving inquisitions about beliefs and associations and refusals to let people practice law and hold public or even private jobs solely because public authorities have been suspicious of their ideas. Usually these denials of employment have not been based on any overt acts of misconduct or lawlessness, and the litigation has continued to raise serious questions of alleged violations of the First Amendment and other guarantees of the Bill of Rights.

The foregoing cases and others contain thousands of pages of confusing formulas, refined reasonings, and puzzling holdings that touch on the same suspicions and fears about citizenship and loyalty. However we have concluded the best way to handle this case is to narrate its simple facts and then relate them to the 45 words that make up the First Amendment.

These are the facts. The petitioner, Sara Baird, graduated from law school at Stanford University in California in 1967. So far as the record shows there is not now and never has been a single mark against her moral character. She has taken the examination prescribed by Arizona, and the answer of the State admits that she satisfactorily passed it. Among the questions she answered was No. 25, which called on her to reveal all organizations with which she had been associated since she reached 16 years of age. This question she answered to the satisfaction of the Arizona Bar Committee. * * * In addition, however, she was asked [in question

27] to state whether she had ever been a member of the Communist Party or any organization "that advocates overthrow of the United States Government by force or violence." When she refused to answer this question, the Committee declined to process her application further or recommend her admission to the bar. The Arizona Supreme Court then denied her petition for an order to the Committee to show cause why she should not be admitted to practice law. We granted certiorari.

In Arizona it is perjury to answer the bar committee's questions falsely, and perjury is punishable as a felony. In effect this young lady was asked by the State to make a guess as to whether any organization to which she ever belonged "advocates overthrow of the United States Government by force or violence." There may well be provisions of the Federal Constitution other than the First Amendment that would protect an applicant to a state bar from being subjected to a question potentially so hazardous to her liberty. But whether or not there are other provisions that protect her, we think the First Amendment does so here.

> **Food for Thought**
>
> In what way might answering Question 27 have been "hazardous to [Baird's] liberty"? Does the answer to that question help to identify another provision of the Constitution that might give Baird a right to decline to answer?

The First Amendment's protection of association prohibits a State from excluding a person from a profession or punishing him solely because he is a member of a particular political organization or because he holds certain beliefs. *United States v. Robel*, 389 U.S. 258, 266 (1967). Similarly, when a State attempts to make inquiries about a person's beliefs or associations, its power is limited by the First Amendment. Broad and sweeping state inquiries into these protected areas, as Arizona has engaged in here, discourage citizens from exercising rights protected by the Constitution.

When a State seeks to inquire about an individual's beliefs and associations a heavy burden lies upon it to show that the inquiry is necessary to protect a legitimate state interest. Of course Arizona has a legitimate interest in determining whether petitioner has the qualities of character and the professional competence requisite to the practice of law. But here petitioner has already supplied the Committee with extensive personal and professional information to assist its determination. By her answers to questions other than No. 25, and her listing of former employers, law school professors, and other references, she has made available to the Committee the information relevant to her fitness to practice law. And whatever justification may be offered, a State may not inquire about a man's views or associations solely for the purpose of withholding a right or benefit because of what he believes.

Much has been written about the application of the First Amendment to cases where penalties have been imposed on people because of their beliefs. Some of what has been written is reconcilable with what we have said here and some of it is not. Without detailed reference to all prior cases, it is sufficient to say we hold that views and beliefs are immune from bar association inquisitions designed to lay a foundation for barring an applicant from the practice of law. Clearly Arizona has engaged in such questioning here.

> **Take Note**
>
> Justice Black concludes here that the First Amendment precluded Arizona from asking Question 27 because the question improperly delved into Sara Baird's views and beliefs. Justice Black, however, was joined by only three other Justices. What is the rule that emerges from this case?

The practice of law is not a matter of grace, but of right for one who is qualified by his learning and his moral character. This record is wholly barren of one word, sentence, or paragraph that tends to show this lady is not morally and professionally fit to serve honorably and well as a member of the legal profession. It was error not to process her application and not to admit her to the Arizona Bar. The judgment of the Arizona Supreme Court is reversed and the case remanded for further proceedings not inconsistent with this opinion.

MR. JUSTICE STEWART, concurring in judgment.

The Court has held that under some circumstances simple inquiry into present or past Communist Party membership of an applicant for admission to the Bar is not as such unconstitutional. *Konigsberg v. State Bar*, 366 U.S. 36 (1957); *In re Anastaplo*, 366 U.S. 82 (1961). Question 27, however, goes further and asks applicants whether they have ever belonged to any organization "that advocates overthrow of the United States Government by force or violence." Our decisions have made clear that such inquiry must be confined to knowing membership to satisfy the First and Fourteenth Amendments. It follows from these decisions that mere membership in an organization can never, by itself, be sufficient ground for a State's imposition of civil disabilities or criminal punishment. Such membership can be quite different from knowing membership in an organization advocating the overthrow of the

> **Take Note**
>
> Justice Stewart concludes here that Arizona could not ask Question 27 because it did not ask whether Sara Baird "knowingly" belonged to an organization that advocates the overthrow of the United States Government by force or violence. Why does the phrasing of the question matter?

Government by force or violence, on the part of one sharing the specific intent to further the organization's illegal goals.

There is a further constitutional infirmity in Arizona's Question 27. The respondent State Bar is the agency entrusted with the administration of the standards for admission to practice law in Arizona. And the respondent's explanation of its purpose in asking the question makes clear that the question must be treated as an inquiry into political beliefs. For the respondent explicitly states that it would recommend denial of admission solely because of an applicant's beliefs that the respondent found objectionable. Yet the First and Fourteenth Amendments bar a State from acting against any person merely because of his beliefs.

MR. JUSTICE BLACKMUN, with whom THE CHIEF JUSTICE, MR. JUSTICE HARLAN, and MR. JUSTICE WHITE join, dissenting.

In my view, applicant Baird vastly overstates her case. * * * No one is in a better position to know the aim and purpose and advocacy of an organization than a member. Certainly the Committee and the Arizona Supreme Court, which have other things to do, are not equipped for the task of checking out the identity of every named organization, especially one which might follow the standard of the less said and known, the better. And Mrs. Baird would place this burden on the Committee by submitting partial answers. She gives the appearance of playing a game. The importance of the subject deserves better than that.

POINTS FOR DISCUSSION

a.   The Holding

In a companion case, *Law Students Civil Rights Research Council v. Wadmond*, 401 U.S. 154 (1971), the Supreme Court found no constitutional defect with a question that asked bar applicants if they had ever belonged to an organization that they "knew was advocating or teaching that the government of the United States or any state or any political subdivision thereof should be overthrown or overturned by force." Justice Stewart wrote the majority opinion, and Justice Black wrote a dissent. What does that suggest about the governing rule?

b.   The Rationale

How does the rationale in Justice Black's opinion for the plurality differ from the rationale in Justice Stewart's concurrence in judgment? Which opinion is more consistent with the analysis in *NAACP v. Claiborne Hardware*? If the state can deny a person a valuable benefit (such as bar membership) for knowingly belonging to an organization that merely advocates—but does not necessarily take actions to bring about—the overthrow of the government, then isn't the government effectively punishing that person for her views? Is Justice Stewart's view that the government *can* punish people for holding such views, as long as it is sure that the person actually *does* hold the views? If so, then what role, if any, did he believe the freedom of association played in the analysis? If so, is it consistent with the Court's decision in *Brandenburg v. Ohio*, 395 U.S. 444 (1969), which we considered in Chapter 8?

B. DISCLOSURE OF MEMBERSHIP LISTS

May the government require a private group to divulge the identities of its members, or would required disclosure violate the members' freedom of association? This question does not have an easy answer. The following case concludes that the government may require disclosure, but only if the government has a compelling interest in knowing the identities of the group's members.

NAACP v. State of Alabama ex rel. Patterson
357 U.S. 449 (1958)

MR. JUSTICE HARLAN delivered the opinion of the Court.

We review [a] judgment of civil contempt entered against petitioner, the National Association for the Advancement of Colored People, in the courts of Alabama. The question presented is whether Alabama, consistently with the Due Process Clause of the Fourteenth Amendment, can compel petitioner to reveal to the State's Attorney General the names and addresses of all its Alabama members and agents, without regard to their positions or functions in the Association. The judgment of contempt was based upon petitioner's refusal to comply

> **Definition**
>
> The term *ex rel.* (an abbreviation for the Latin *ex relatione*) means "by or on the relation of." In some cases, the government litigates upon the invitation of a private person, called the relator. In other cases, a private party conducts the litigation on behalf of the government. (We consider an example of this in *McCulloch v. Maryland* in Volume 1.) In this case, John Patterson, the Alabama Attorney General, litigated on behalf of the state government of Alabama.

fully with a court order requiring in part the production of membership lists. Petitioner's claim is that the order, in the circumstances shown by this record, violated rights assured to petitioner and its members under the Constitution.

Alabama has a statute similar to those of many other States which requires a foreign corporation, except as exempted, to qualify before doing business by filing its corporate charter with the Secretary of State and designating a place of business and an agent to receive service of process. The statute imposes a fine on a corporation transacting intrastate business before qualifying and provides for criminal prosecution of officers of such a corporation. The National Association for the Advancement of Colored People is a nonprofit membership corporation organized under the laws of New York. Its purposes, fostered on a nationwide basis, are those indicated by its name, and it operates through chartered affiliates which are independent unincorporated associations, with membership therein equivalent to membership in petitioner. The first Alabama affiliates were chartered in 1918. Since that time the aims of the Association have been advanced through activities of its affiliates, and in 1951 the Association itself opened a regional office in Alabama, at which it employed two supervisory persons and one clerical worker. The Association has never complied with the qualification statute, from which it considered itself exempt.

In 1956 the Attorney General of Alabama brought an equity suit in the State Circuit Court, Montgomery County, to enjoin the Association from conducting further activities within, and to oust it from, the State. Among other things the bill in equity alleged that the Association had opened a regional office and had organized various affiliates in Alabama; had recruited members and solicited contributions within the State; had given financial support and furnished legal assistance to Negro students seeking admission to the state university; and had supported a Negro boycott of the bus lines in Montgomery to compel the seating of passengers without regard to race. The bill recited that the Association, by continuing to do business in Alabama without complying with the qualification statute, was "causing irreparable injury to the property and civil rights of the residents and citizens of the State of Alabama for which criminal prosecution and civil actions at law afford no adequate relief." On the day the complaint was filed, the Circuit Court issued ex parte an order restraining the Association, *pendente lite*, from engaging in further activities within the State and forbidding it to take any steps to qualify itself to do business therein.

> **Definition**
>
> The Latin term *pendente lite* means "during the litigation."

Petitioner demurred to the allegations of the bill and moved to dissolve the restraining order. It contended that its activities did not subject it to the qualification requirements of the statute and that in any event what the State sought to accomplish by its suit would violate rights to freedom of speech and assembly guaranteed under the Fourteenth Amendment to the Constitution of the United States. Before the date set for a hearing on this motion, the State moved for the production of a large number of the Association's records and papers, including bank statements, leases, deeds, and records containing the names and addresses of all Alabama "members" and "agents" of the Association. It alleged that all such documents were necessary for adequate preparation for the hearing, in view of petitioner's denial of the conduct of intrastate business within the meaning of the qualification statute. Over petitioner's objections, the court ordered the production of a substantial part of the requested records, including the membership lists, and postponed the hearing on the restraining order to a date later than the time ordered for production.

* * * Thereafter petitioner filed its answer to the bill in equity. It admitted its Alabama activities substantially as alleged in the complaint and that it had not qualified to do business in the State. Although still disclaiming the statute's application to it, petitioner offered to qualify if the bar from qualification made part of the restraining order were lifted, and it submitted with the answer an executed set of the forms required by the statute. However petitioner did not comply with the production order, and for this failure was adjudged in civil contempt and fined $10,000. The contempt judgment provided that the fine would be subject to reduction or remission if compliance were forthcoming within five days but otherwise would be increased to $100,000. [When the NAACP did not comply with the production order, the court held it in contempt.]

We thus reach petitioner's claim that the production order in the state litigation trespasses upon fundamental freedoms protected by the Due Process Clause of the Fourteenth Amendment. Petitioner argues that in view of the facts and circumstances shown in the record, the effect of compelled disclosure of the membership lists will be to abridge the rights of its rank-and-file members to engage in lawful association in support of their common beliefs. It contends that governmental action which, although not directly suppressing association, nevertheless carries this consequence, can be justified only upon some overriding valid interest of the State.

Effective advocacy of both public and private points of view, particularly controversial ones, is undeniably enhanced by group association, as this Court has more than once recognized by remarking upon the close nexus between the freedoms of speech and assembly. *De Jonge v. Oregon*, 299 U.S. 353, 364 (1937); *Thomas v. Collins*, 323 U.S. 516, 530 (1945). It is beyond debate that freedom to engage in association for the advancement of beliefs and ideas is an inseparable aspect of the "liberty" assured by the Due Process Clause of the Fourteenth Amendment, which embraces freedom of speech. Of course, it is immaterial whether the beliefs sought to be advanced by association pertain to political, economic, religious or cultural matters, and state action which may have the effect of curtailing the freedom to associate is subject to the closest scrutiny.

The fact that Alabama, so far as is relevant to the validity of the contempt judgment presently under review, has taken no direct action to restrict the right of petitioner's members to associate freely, does not end inquiry into the effect of the production order. See *American Communications Ass'n v. Douds*, 339 U.S. 382, 402 (1950). In the domain of these indispensable liberties, whether of speech, press, or association, the decisions of this Court recognize that abridgement of such rights, even though unintended, may inevitably follow from varied forms of governmental action. Thus in *Douds*, the Court stressed that the legislation there challenged, which on its face sought to regulate labor unions and to secure stability in interstate commerce, would have the practical effect "of discouraging" the exercise of constitutionally protected political rights, and it upheld that statute only after concluding that the reasons advanced for its enactment were constitutionally sufficient to justify its possible deterrent effect upon such freedoms. * * *

We think that the production order, in the respects here drawn in question, must be regarded as entailing the likelihood of a substantial restraint upon the exercise by petitioner's members of their right to freedom of association. Petitioner has made an uncontroverted showing that on past occasions revelation of the identity of its rank-and-file members has exposed these members to economic reprisal, loss of employment, threat of physical coercion, and other manifestations of public hostility. Under these circumstances, we think it apparent that compelled disclosure of petitioner's Alabama membership is likely to affect adversely the ability of petitioner and its members to pursue their collective effort to foster beliefs which they admittedly have the right to advocate, in that it may induce members to withdraw from the Association and dissuade others from joining it because of fear of exposure of their beliefs shown through their associations and of the consequences of this exposure.

We turn to the final question whether Alabama has demonstrated an interest in obtaining the disclosures it seeks from petitioner which is sufficient to justify the deterrent effect which we have concluded these disclosures may well have on the free exercise by petitioner's members of their constitutionally protected right of association. Such a "subordinating interest of the State must be compelling," *Sweezy v. New Hampshire*, 354 U.S. 234, 265 (1957) (concurring opinion). It is not of moment that the State has here acted solely through its judicial branch, for whether legislative or judicial, it is still the application of state power which we are asked to scrutinize.

* * * During the course of a hearing before the Alabama Circuit Court on a motion of petitioner to set aside the production order, the State Attorney General

presented at length, under examination by petitioner, the State's reason for requesting the membership lists. The exclusive purpose was to determine whether petitioner was conducting intrastate business in violation of the Alabama foreign corporation registration statute, and the membership lists were expected to help resolve this question. The issues in the litigation commenced by Alabama by its bill in equity were whether the character of petitioner and its activities in Alabama had been such as to make petitioner subject to the registration statute, and whether the extent of petitioner's activities without qualifying suggested its permanent ouster from the State. Without intimating the slightest view upon the merits of these issues, we are unable to perceive that the disclosure of the names of petitioner's rank-and-file members has a substantial bearing on either of them. As matters stand in the state court, petitioner (1) has admitted its presence and conduct of activities in Alabama since 1918; (2) has offered to comply in all respects with the state qualification statute, although preserving its contention that the statute does not apply to it; and (3) has apparently complied satisfactorily with the production order, except for the membership lists, by furnishing the Attorney General with varied business records, its charter and statement of purposes, the names of all of its directors and officers, and with the total number of its Alabama members and the amount of their dues. These last items would not on this record appear subject to constitutional challenge and have been furnished, but whatever interest the State may have in obtaining names of ordinary members has not been shown to be sufficient to overcome petitioner's constitutional objections to the production order.

We hold that the immunity from state scrutiny of membership lists which the Association claims on behalf of its members is here so related to the right of the members to pursue their lawful private interests privately and to associate freely with others in so doing as to come within the protection of the Fourteenth Amendment. And we conclude that Alabama has fallen short of showing a controlling justification for the deterrent effect on the free enjoyment of the right to associate which disclosure of membership lists is likely to have. Accordingly, the judgment of civil contempt and the $100,000 fine which resulted from petitioner's refusal to comply with the production order in this respect must fall.

Reversed.

POINTS FOR DISCUSSION

a.   Substantial Burden on the Freedom of Association

Notice that this case arose at a time when the NAACP was a central figure in efforts to challenge segregation in the South, and particularly in Alabama. The Court appeared to give weight to this fact. In concluding that disclosure of the organization's membership lists would impose a substantial burden on the freedom of association, the Court noted that "on past occasions revelation of the identity of its rank-and-file members has exposed these members to economic reprisal, loss of employment, threat of physical coercion, and other manifestations of public hostility." Does the Court's reliance on these circumstances suggest that state requests for the membership lists of private organizations under different circumstances are not as likely to impose a substantial restraint on the freedom of association?

Consider the Court's treatment of disclosure requirements in other contexts. Federal election laws require political campaigns to disclose a list of their contributors. Litigants challenged this requirement in *Buckley v. Valeo*, 424 U.S. 1 (1976). Relying on *NAACP v. Alabama ex rel. Patterson*, the litigants argued that requiring disclosure of the names of contributors violates the freedom of association. The Supreme Court, however, upheld the federal law. The Court explained:

> There could well be a case, similar to those before the Court in *NAACP v. Alabama* * * *, where the threat to the exercise of First Amendment rights is so serious and the state interest furthered by disclosure so insubstantial that the Act's requirements cannot be constitutionally applied. But no appellant in this case has tendered record evidence of the sort proffered in *NAACP v. Alabama*. Instead, appellants primarily rely on "the clearly articulated fears of individuals, well experienced in the political process." At best they offer the testimony of several minor-party officials that one or two persons refused to make contributions because of the possibility of disclosure. On this record, the substantial public interest in disclosure identified by the legislative history of this Act outweighs the harm generally alleged.

Id. at 71–72. What is the government's interest in requiring disclosure of the identities of campaign contributors? Does the reasoning in the passage leave open the possibility that a litigant might succeed in challenging the required disclosure of the identities of campaign contributors in the future?

In *Citizens United v. Federal Election Comm'n*, 558 U.S. 310 (2010), which we considered in Chapter 8, the Court upheld federal statutory provisions requiring (1) televised electioneering communications funded by anyone other than a candidate to include a disclaimer identifying the person or entity that was responsible for the content and funding of the advertisement and (2) a person or entity who spends more than $10,000 on electioneering communications within a calendar year to file a disclosure statement with the Federal Election Commission identifying the person making the expenditure, the amount of the expenditure, the election to which the communication was directed, and the names of certain contributors. The Court reasoned that the requirements were justified by a "governmental interest in providing information to the electorate," and that "disclosure is a less restrictive alternative to more comprehensive regulations of speech." The Court concluded by noting that the "transparency" fostered by disclosure and disclaimer requirements "enables the electorate to make informed decisions and give proper weight to different speakers and messages."

b. The State's Interest

What interest did the state assert as a reason for requiring disclosure? Did the Court conclude that the state's interest in requiring disclosure was not compelling, or that the request for disclosure did not sufficiently advance that interest? If the former, what sorts of state interests in disclosure would count as compelling?

C. FREEDOM NOT TO ASSOCIATE WITH OTHERS

Does the freedom of association include not only a freedom to associate with others but also **a freedom to choose not to associate** with others? In other words, may the government tell an organization that it must accept members that the organization does not want to admit? If so, may the organization object to members based on race, sex, sexual orientation, or other such factors? The Supreme Court addressed this question in the leading case of *Roberts v. United States Jaycees*, 468 U.S. 609 (1984).

In *Roberts*, the state of Minnesota sued the Jaycees, a national organization of young men interested in business, claiming that the Jaycees' refusal to admit women violated the state's anti-discrimination laws. In deciding the case, the Court established (or at least clarified) three important principles. First, the freedom of association generally gives an organization a right to choose its members. Second, the government may regulate this freedom if the state has "compelling state interests * * * that cannot be achieved through means significantly less restrictive of associational freedoms." *Id.* at 623. But third, the government may not prohibit an organization from discriminating in its selection of members if the regulation would significantly affect the organization's "intimate association" or "expressive activity." *Id.*

Applying these factors to the case, the Court recognized that the Jaycees in general had a right to decide who could join their organization and who could not. But the Court held that preventing discrimination against women was a compelling state interest. And the Court concluded that the Jaycees could not object to the anti-discrimination law because the Jaycees, as a very large organization, could not claim that discrimination was necessary for intimate association (given the large size of the organization), and because the Jaycees did not claim that having women members would affect any message they wished to convey. The Court thus held that the state could apply the anti-discrimination legislation to the organization.

The Supreme Court applied the *Roberts* standard in the following three cases. In the first, the Court considered whether anti-discrimination legislation, even if it otherwise advances a compelling governmental interest, would impair an organization's expressive activities.

HURLEY V. IRISH-AMERICAN GAY, LESBIAN AND BISEXUAL GROUP OF BOSTON
515 U.S. 557 (1995)

JUSTICE SOUTER delivered the opinion of the Court.

The issue in this case is whether Massachusetts may require private citizens who organize a parade to include among the marchers a group imparting a message the organizers do not wish to convey. We hold that such a mandate violates the First Amendment.

[The South Boston Allied War Veterans Council is an unincorporated association of individuals elected from various South Boston veterans groups. Every year since 1947, the Council has held a parade in Boston on March 17 to celebrate St. Patrick's Day. The Council obtains a permit from the City of Boston to conduct the parade. The Council allows numerous groups to join the parade, which has included as many as 20,000 marchers. More than one million spectators typically watch the parade. In 1992 and 1993, the Irish-American Gay, Lesbian and Bisexual Group of Boston (GLIB) asked the Council for permission to join the parade, but in both years the Council denied the request.]

In 1993, after the Council had again refused to admit GLIB to the upcoming parade, the organization and some of its members filed this suit against the Council, the individual petitioner John J. "Wacko" Hurley, and the city of Boston, alleging violations of the State and Federal Constitutions and of the state public accommodations law, which prohibits "any distinction, discrimination or restriction on account [of] sexual orientation

> **Take Note**
>
> The trial court interpreted the Massachusetts statute to require the Council to associate with GLIB. For this reason, the Council argued that the statute was unconstitutional. Did GLIB have any argument that the exclusion itself violated the Constitution? Was the defendant a state (or instead a private) actor?

[relative] to the admission of any person to, or treatment in any place of public accommodation, resort or amusement." Mass. Gen. Laws § 272:98 (1992). After finding that "[f]or at least the past 47 years, the Parade has traveled the same basic route along the public streets of South Boston, providing entertainment, amusement, and recreation to participants and spectators alike," the state trial court ruled that the parade fell within the statutory definition of a public accommodation, which includes "any place [which] is open to and accepts or solicits the patronage of the general public and, without limiting the generality of this definition, whether or not it be . . . (6) a boardwalk or other public highway [or] (8) a place of public amusement, recreation, sport, exercise or entertainment," Mass. Gen. Laws § 272:92A (1992). The court found that the Council had no written criteria and employed no particular procedures for admission, voted on new applications in batches, had occasionally admitted groups who simply showed up at the parade without having submitted an application, and did "not generally inquire into the specific messages or views of each applicant." The court consequently rejected the Council's contention that the parade was "private" (in the sense of being exclusive), holding instead that "the lack of genuine selectivity in choosing participants and sponsors demonstrates that the Parade is a public event." It found the parade to be "eclectic," containing a wide variety of "patriotic, commercial, political, moral, artistic, religious, athletic, public service, trade union, and eleemosynary themes," as well as conflicting messages. While noting that the Council had indeed excluded the Ku Klux Klan and ROAR (an antibusing group), it attributed little significance to these facts, concluding ultimately that "[t]he only common theme among the participants and sponsors is their public involvement in the Parade." [The Massachusetts Supreme Judicial Court affirmed.]

*** Real "[p]arades are public dramas of social relations, and in them performers define who can be a social actor and what subjects and ideas are available for communication and consideration." S. Davis, Parades and Power: Street Theatre in Nineteenth-Century Philadelphia 6 (1986). Hence, we use the word "parade" to indicate marchers who are making some sort of collective point, not just to each other but to bystanders along the way. Indeed, a parade's dependence on watchers is so extreme that nowadays, as with Bishop Berkeley's celebrated tree, "if a parade or demonstration receives no media coverage, it may as well not have happened." Parades are thus a form of expression, not just motion, and the inherent expressiveness of marching to make a point explains our cases involving protest marches. In *Gregory v. Chicago,* 394 U.S. 111, 112 (1969), for example, petitioners had taken part in a procession to express their grievances to the city government, and we held that such a "march, if peaceful and orderly, falls well within the sphere of conduct protected by the First Amendment." Similarly, in *Edwards v. South Carolina,* 372 U.S. 229, 235 (1963), where petitioners had joined in a march of protest and pride, carrying placards and singing The Star Spangled Banner, we held that the activities "reflect an exercise of these basic constitutional rights in their most pristine and classic form."

The protected expression that inheres in a parade is not limited to its banners and songs, however, for the Constitution looks beyond written or spoken words as mediums of expression. Noting that "[s]ymbolism is a primitive but effective way of communicating ideas," *West Virginia Bd. of Ed. v. Barnette,* 319 U.S. 624, 632 (1943), our cases have recognized that the First Amendment shields such acts as saluting a flag (and refusing to do so), *id.* at 632, wearing an armband to protest a war, *Tinker v. Des Moines Independent Community School Dist.,* 393 U.S. 503, 505–506 (1969), displaying a red flag, *Stromberg v. California,* 283 U.S. 359, 369 (1931), and even "[m]arching, walking or

> **Make the Connection**
>
> We considered the status of symbolic conduct under the First Amendment in Chapter 8.

parading" in uniforms displaying the swastika, *National Socialist Party of America v. Skokie,* 432 U.S. 43 (1977). As some of these examples show, a narrow, succinctly articulable message is not a condition of constitutional protection, which if confined to expressions conveying a "particularized message" would never reach the unquestionably shielded painting of Jackson Pollock, music of Arnold Schöenberg, or Jabberwocky verse of Lewis Carroll.

Not many marches, then, are beyond the realm of expressive parades, and the South Boston celebration is not one of them. Spectators line the streets; people march in costumes and uniforms, carrying flags and banners with all sorts of messages (*e.g.,* "England get out of Ireland," "Say no to drugs"); marching bands and pipers play; floats are pulled along; and the whole show is broadcast over Boston television. To be sure, we agree with the state courts that in spite of excluding some applicants, the Council is rather lenient in admitting participants.

But a private speaker does not forfeit constitutional protection simply by combining multifarious voices, or by failing to edit their themes to isolate an exact message as the exclusive subject matter of the speech. Nor, under our precedent, does First Amendment protection require a speaker to generate, as an original matter, each item featured in the communication. Cable operators, for example, are engaged in protected speech activities even when they only select programming originally produced by others. *Turner Broadcasting System, Inc. v. FCC,* 512 U.S. 622, 636 (1994). For that matter, the presentation of an edited compilation of speech generated by other persons is a staple of most newspapers' opinion pages, which, of course, fall squarely within the core of First Amendment security, *Miami Herald Publishing Co. v. Tornillo,* 418 U.S. 241, 258 (1974), as does even the simple selection of a paid noncommercial advertisement for inclusion in a daily paper, see *New York Times v. Sullivan,* 376 U.S. 254, 265–266 (1964). The selection of contingents to make a parade is entitled to similar protection.

Respondents' participation as a unit in the parade was equally expressive. GLIB was formed for the very purpose of marching in it, as the trial court found, in order to celebrate its members' identity as openly gay, lesbian, and bisexual descendants of the Irish immigrants, to show that there are such individuals in the community, and to support the like men and women who sought to march in the New York parade. The organization distributed a fact sheet describing the members' intentions, and the record otherwise corroborates the expressive nature of GLIB's participation. In 1993, members of GLIB marched behind a shamrock-strewn banner with the simple inscription "Irish American Gay, Lesbian and Bisexual Group of Boston." GLIB understandably seeks to communicate its ideas as part of the existing parade, rather than staging one of its own.

Petitioners disclaim any intent to exclude homosexuals as such, and no individual member of GLIB claims to have been excluded from parading as a member of any group that the Council has approved to march. Instead, the disagreement goes to the admission of GLIB as its own parade unit carrying its own banner. Since every participating unit affects the message conveyed by the private organizers, the state courts' application of the statute produced an order essentially requiring petitioners to alter the expressive content of their parade. Although the state courts spoke of the parade as a place of public accommodation, once the expressive character of both the parade and the marching GLIB contingent is understood, it becomes apparent that the state courts' application of the statute had the effect of declaring the sponsors' speech itself to be the public accommodation. Under this approach any contingent of protected individuals with a message would have the right to participate in petitioners' speech, so that the communication produced by the private organizers would be shaped by all those protected by the law who wished to join in with some expressive demonstration of their own. But this use of the State's power violates the fundamental rule of protection under the First Amendment, that a speaker has the autonomy to choose the content of his own message.

Petitioners' claim to the benefit of this principle of autonomy to control one's own speech is as sound as the South Boston parade is expressive. Rather like a composer, the Council selects the expressive units of the parade from potential participants, and though the score may not produce a particularized message, each contingent's expression in the Council's eyes comports with what merits celebration on that day. Even if this view gives the Council credit for a more considered judgment than it actively made, the Council clearly decided to exclude a message it did not like from the communication it chose to make, and that is enough to invoke its right as a private speaker to shape its expression by speaking on one subject while remaining silent on another. The message it disfavored is not difficult to identify. Although GLIB's point (like the Council's) is not wholly articulate, a contingent marching behind the organization's banner would at least bear witness to the fact that some Irish are gay, lesbian, or bisexual, and the presence of the organized marchers would suggest their view that people of their sexual orientations have as much claim to unqualified social acceptance as heterosexuals and indeed as members of parade units organized around other identifying characteristics. The parade's organizers may not believe these facts about Irish sexuality to be so, or they may object to unqualified social acceptance of gays and lesbians or have some other reason for wishing to keep GLIB's message out of the parade. But whatever the reason, it boils down to the choice of a speaker not to propound a particular point of view, and that choice is presumed to lie beyond the government's power to control.

> **Take Note**
>
> In this passage, the Court explains why requiring the parade organizers to include GLIB would affect the parade organizers' speech. In *Roberts v. United States Jaycees*, by contrast, the Court held that the state could prevent the private organization from discriminating. In what ways were the two cases different?

Our holding today rests not on any particular view about the Council's message but on the Nation's commitment to protect freedom of speech. Disapproval of a private speaker's statement does not legitimize use of the Commonwealth's power to compel the speaker to alter the message by including one more acceptable to others. Accordingly, the judgment of the Supreme Judicial

Court is reversed, and the case is remanded for proceedings not inconsistent with this opinion.

POINTS FOR DISCUSSION

a.   Pattern of Argumentation

The three principles explained in *Roberts v. United States Jaycees* give rise to a pattern of argumentation apparent in this case and others like it. The parade organizers argued that they had a First Amendment right to choose not to associate with GLIB. GLIB responded that the freedom not to associate was not absolute, and that the state had a compelling interest in preventing discrimination. But the parade organizers replied that even if the state ordinarily has a compelling interest in preventing discrimination, in this case—unlike in *Roberts*—the discrimination was integral to their expressive activity. The Court in *Roberts* agreed with the persons who had been excluded; the Court in *Hurley* agreed with the organization.

Doesn't every organization convey some message—even if only implicitly—by its membership choices? For example, a private school that chose in 1955 to accept students of all races plainly made a statement about the importance of racial integration, as did a private school at that time that chose to accept only white children. If these actions are therefore "expressive," then was the Court's decision in *Roberts* correct? If not, was the Court's decision in *Hurley* nevertheless correct?

b.   Condoning Discrimination

In *Hurley*, the Supreme Court essentially held that the First Amendment permits an organization to discriminate against a group based on the group's views on sexual orientation. Is allowing this kind of discrimination objectionable? Is it inconsistent with the spirit of the Fourteenth Amendment? (Recall that the Court has held that the Fourteenth Amendment applies only to state, as opposed to private, action.) Or is it an unfortunate but necessary consequence of protecting free speech?

In answering these questions, does it help to consider how you might respond to the converse set of circumstances? That is, should the organizers of a Gay Pride march have to include in their parade a religious group known for its opposition to homosexuality?

c.   Discrimination Against a Group's Members

In this case, the parade organization expressed a willingness to allow individual members of GLIB to join the parade, just not GLIB as a group. Suppose the facts had been different and that the parade organizers had decided to exclude any members of GLIB—or, for that matter, any person who was homosexual—from marching. Under those circumstances, could Massachusetts have enforced its anti-discrimination laws to require the parade organizers to include the gay marchers? If so, would the parade organizers nevertheless have been permitted to refuse to allow any members of the Ku Klux Klan to join in its parade? If so, why would the organizers have the right to exclude racists but not to exclude gays?

———————

In *Hurley*, the Court unanimously concluded that a private organization's parade involves a quintessential form of expressive activity and thus cannot be regulated by anti-discrimination legislation. Can the state apply such legislation to groups that do not engage in expressive activity as obvious as a parade?

BOY SCOUTS OF AMERICA V. DALE
530 U.S. 640 (2000)

JUSTICE REHNQUIST delivered the opinion of the Court.

Petitioners are the Boy Scouts of America and the Monmouth Council, a division of the Boy Scouts of America (collectively, Boy Scouts). The Boy Scouts is a private, not-for-profit organization engaged in instilling its system of values in young people. The Boy Scouts asserts that homosexual conduct is inconsistent with the values it seeks to instill. Respondent is James Dale, a former Eagle Scout whose adult membership in the Boy Scouts was revoked when the Boy Scouts learned that he is an avowed homosexual and gay rights activist. The New Jersey Supreme Court held that New Jersey's public accommodations law requires that the Boy Scouts readmit Dale. This case presents the question whether applying New Jersey's public accommodations law in this way violates the Boy Scouts' First Amendment right of expressive association. We hold that it does.

Dale applied for adult membership in the Boy Scouts in 1989. The Boy Scouts approved his application for the position of assistant scoutmaster of Troop 73. Around the same time, Dale left home to attend Rutgers University. After arriving at Rutgers, Dale first acknowledged to himself and others that he is gay. He quickly became involved with, and eventually became the co-president of, the Rutgers University Lesbian/Gay Alliance. In 1990, Dale attended a seminar addressing the psychological and health needs of lesbian and gay teenagers. A newspaper covering the event interviewed Dale about his advocacy of homosexual teenagers' need for gay role models. In early July 1990, the newspaper published the interview and Dale's photograph over a caption identifying him as the co-president of the Lesbian/Gay Alliance.

Later that month, Dale received a letter from Monmouth Council Executive James Kay revoking his adult membership. Dale wrote to Kay requesting the reason for Monmouth Council's decision. Kay responded by letter that the Boy Scouts "specifically forbid membership to homosexuals."

In 1992, Dale filed a complaint against the Boy Scouts in the New Jersey Superior Court. The complaint alleged that the Boy Scouts had violated New Jersey's public accommodations statute and its common law by revoking Dale's membership based solely on his sexual orientation. New Jersey's public accommodations statute prohibits, among other things, discrimination on the basis of sexual orientation in places of public accommodation. N.J. Stat. Ann. §§ 10:5–4 and 10:5–5 (West Supp. 2000). * * * The New Jersey Supreme Court [held] that the Boy Scouts was a place of public accommodation subject to the public accommodations law, that the organization was not exempt from the law under any of its express exceptions, and that the Boy Scouts violated the law by revoking Dale's membership based on his avowed homosexuality. * * * [The New Jersey Supreme Court rejected the Boy Scouts' claim that applying the public accommodations law to the Boy Scouts would violate the Boy Scouts' First Amendment right of freedom of association.]

In *Roberts v. United States Jaycees,* 468 U.S. 609, 622 (1984), we observed that "implicit in the right to engage in activities protected by the First Amendment" is "a corresponding right to associate with others in pursuit of a wide variety of political, social, economic, educational, religious, and cultural ends." This right is crucial in preventing the majority from imposing its views on groups that would rather express other, perhaps unpopular, ideas. Government actions that may unconstitutionally burden this freedom may take many forms, one of which is "intrusion into the internal structure or affairs of an association" like a "regulation that forces the group to accept members it does not desire." *Id.,* at 623. Forcing a group to accept certain members may impair the ability of the group to express those views, and only those views, that it intends to express. Thus, "[f]reedom of association [plainly] presupposes a freedom not to associate." *Ibid.*

The forced inclusion of an unwanted person in a group infringes the group's freedom of expressive association if the presence of that person affects in a significant way the group's ability to advocate public or private viewpoints. But the freedom of expressive association, like many freedoms, is not absolute. We have held that the freedom could be overridden "by regulations adopted to serve compelling state interests, unrelated to the suppression of ideas, that cannot be achieved through means significantly less restrictive of associational freedoms." *Ibid.*

To determine whether a group is protected by the First Amendment's expressive associational right, we must determine whether the group engages in "expressive association." The First Amendment's protection of expressive association is not reserved for advocacy groups. But to come within its ambit, a group must engage in some form of expression, whether it be public or private.

The record reveals the following. The Boy Scouts is a private, nonprofit organization. According to its mission statement:

> It is the mission of the Boy Scouts of America to serve others by helping to instill values in young people and, in other ways, to prepare them to make ethical choices over their lifetime in achieving their full potential.

The values we strive to instill are based on those found in the Scout Oath and Law:

Scout Oath

On my honor I will do my best
To do my duty to God and my country
and to obey the Scout Law;
To help other people at all times;
To keep myself physically strong,
mentally awake, and morally straight.

Scout Law

A Scout is:

Trustworthy.	Obedient.
Loyal.	Cheerful.
Helpful.	Thrifty.
Friendly.	Brave.
Courteous.	Clean.
Kind.	Reverent.

Thus, the general mission of the Boy Scouts is clear: "[T]o instill values in young people." The Boy Scouts seeks to instill these values by having its adult leaders spend time with the youth members, instructing and engaging them in activities like camping, archery, and fishing. During the time spent with the youth members, the scoutmasters and assistant scoutmasters inculcate them with the Boy Scouts' values—both expressly and by example. It seems indisputable that an association that seeks to transmit such a system of values engages in expressive activity.

Given that the Boy Scouts engages in expressive activity, we must determine whether the forced inclusion of Dale as an assistant scoutmaster would significantly affect the Boy Scouts' ability to advocate

> **Food for Thought**
>
> In *Hurley*, there was little doubt that the parade was a form of expressive activity, and that the parade's message was conveyed to people—one million spectators— outside of the parade itself. Is the Court suggesting here that the Boy Scouts' activity is also intended to convey a message to persons outside of the organization? Or instead that the message is intended for persons—specifically, the Scouts themselves—*inside* the organization? If the latter, is this distinction relevant?

public or private viewpoints. This inquiry necessarily requires us first to explore, to a limited extent, the nature of the Boy Scouts' view of homosexuality.

The values the Boy Scouts seeks to instill are "based on" those listed in the Scout Oath and Law. The Boy Scouts explains that the Scout Oath and Law provide "a positive moral code for living;" they are a list of "do's" rather than "don'ts." The Boy Scouts asserts that homosexual conduct is inconsistent with the values embodied in the Scout Oath and Law, particularly with the values represented by the terms "morally straight" and "clean."

Obviously, the Scout Oath and Law do not expressly mention sexuality or sexual orientation. And the terms "morally straight" and "clean" are by no means self-defining. Different people would attribute to those terms very different meanings. For example, some people may believe that engaging in homosexual conduct is not at odds with being "morally straight" and "clean." And others may believe that engaging in homosexual conduct is contrary to being "morally straight" and "clean." The Boy Scouts says it falls within the latter category.

The New Jersey Supreme Court analyzed the Boy Scouts' beliefs and found that the "exclusion of members solely on the basis of their sexual orientation is inconsistent with Boy Scouts' commitment to a diverse and 'representative' membership [and] contradicts Boy Scouts' overarching objective to reach 'all eligible youth.'" The court concluded that the exclusion of members like Dale "appears antithetical to the organization's goals and philosophy." But our cases reject this sort of inquiry; it is not the role of the courts to reject a group's expressed values because they disagree with those values or find them internally inconsistent. See *Democratic Party of United States v. Wisconsin ex rel. La Follette,* 450 U.S. 107, 124 (1981) ("[A]s is true of all expressions of First Amendment freedoms, the courts may not interfere on the ground that they view a particular expression as unwise or irrational"); see also *Thomas v. Review Bd. of Indiana Employment Security Div.,* 450 U.S. 707, 714 (1981) ("[R]eligious beliefs need not be acceptable, logical, consistent, or comprehensible to others in order to merit First Amendment protection.").

The Boy Scouts asserts that it "teach[es] that homosexual conduct is not morally straight," Brief for Petitioners 39, and that it does "not want to promote homosexual conduct as a legitimate form of behavior," Reply Brief for Petitioners 5. We accept the Boy Scouts' assertion. We need not inquire further to determine the nature of the Boy Scouts' expression with respect to homosexuality. * * *

We must then determine whether Dale's presence as an assistant scoutmaster would significantly burden the Boy Scouts' desire to not "promote homosexual conduct as a legitimate form of behavior." As we give deference to an association's assertions regarding the nature of its expression, we must also give deference to an association's view of what would impair its expression. That is not to say that an expressive association can erect a shield against antidiscrimination laws simply by asserting that mere acceptance of a member from a particular group would impair its message. But here Dale, by his own admission, is one of a group of gay Scouts who have "become leaders in their community and are open and honest about their sexual orientation." Dale was the co-president of a gay and lesbian organization at college and remains a gay rights activist. Dale's presence in the Boy Scouts would, at the very least, force the organization to send a message, both to the youth members and the world, that the Boy Scouts accepts homosexual conduct as a legitimate form of behavior.

> **Take Note**
>
> Here the Court defers to the Boy Scouts' assertion about the message that it wants to convey. Is this approach consistent with the Court's decisions in *Roberts* and *Hurley,* or should the Court have delved more deeply into the sincerity of the Boy Scouts' position?

Hurley v. Irish-American Gay, Lesbian and Bisexual Group of Boston, Inc., 515 U.S. 557 (1995), is illustrative on this point. There we [held that Massachusetts could not require the organizers of a private St. Patrick's Day parade to include among the marchers an Irish-American gay, lesbian, and bisexual group, GLIB.] We observed:

[T]he presence of the organized marchers would suggest their view that people of their sexual orientations have as much claim to unqualified social acceptance as heterosexuals .... The parade's organizers may [object] to unqualified social acceptance of gays and lesbians or have some other reason for wishing to keep GLIB's message out of the parade. [W]hatever the reason, it boils down to the choice of a speaker not to propound a particular point of view, and that choice is presumed to lie beyond the government's power to control.

515 U.S., at 574–575.

Here, we have found that the Boy Scouts believes that homosexual conduct is inconsistent with the values it seeks to instill in its youth members; it will not "promote homosexual conduct as a legitimate form of behavior." Reply Brief for Petitioners 5. As the presence of GLIB in Boston's St. Patrick's Day parade would have interfered with the parade organizers' choice not to propound a particular point of view, the presence of Dale as an assistant scoutmaster would just as surely interfere with the Boy Scouts' choice not to propound a point of view contrary to its beliefs. [Reversed.]

JUSTICE STEVENS, with whom JUSTICE SOUTER, JUSTICE GINSBURG, and JUSTICE BREYER join, dissenting.

[T]he right to associate does not mean "that in every setting in which individuals exercise some discrimination in choosing associates, their selective process of inclusion and exclusion is protected by the Constitution." *New York State Club Assn., Inc. v. City of New York,* 487 U.S. 1, 13 (1988). For example, we have routinely and easily rejected assertions of this right by expressive organizations with discriminatory membership policies, such as private schools, law firms, and labor organizations. In fact, until today, we have never once found a claimed right to associate in the selection of members to prevail in the face of a State's antidiscrimination law. To the contrary, we have squarely held that a State's antidiscrimination law does not violate a group's right to associate simply because the law conflicts with that group's exclusionary membership policy.

Several principles are made perfectly clear by *Jaycees.* First, to prevail on a claim of expressive association in the face of a State's antidiscrimination law, it is not enough simply to engage in *some kind* of expressive activity. * * * Second, it is not enough to adopt an openly avowed exclusionary membership policy. * * * Third, it is not sufficient merely to articulate *some* connection between the group's expressive activities and its exclusionary policy. * * * The relevant question is whether the mere inclusion of the person at issue would "impose any serious burden," "affect in any significant way," or be "a substantial restraint upon" the organization's "shared goals," "basic goals," or "collective effort to foster beliefs." Accordingly, it is necessary to examine what, exactly, are BSA's shared goals and the degree to which its expressive activities would be burdened, affected, or restrained by including homosexuals.

* * * The evidence before this Court makes it exceptionally clear that BSA has, at most, simply adopted an exclusionary membership policy and has no shared goal of disapproving of homosexuality. BSA's mission statement and federal charter say nothing on the matter; its official membership policy is silent; its Scout Oath and Law—and accompanying definitions—are devoid of any view on the topic; its guidance for Scouts and Scoutmasters on sexuality declare that such matters are "not construed to be Scouting's proper area," but are the province of a Scout's parents and pastor; and BSA's posture respecting religion tolerates a wide variety of views on the issue of homosexuality. Moreover, there is simply no evidence that BSA otherwise teaches anything in this area, or that it instructs Scouts on matters involving homosexuality in ways not conveyed in the Boy Scout or Scoutmaster Handbooks. In short, Boy Scouts of America is simply silent on homosexuality. There is no shared goal or collective effort to foster a belief about homosexuality at all—let alone one that is significantly burdened by admitting homosexuals.

Surely there are instances in which an organization that truly aims to foster a belief at odds with the purposes of a State's antidiscrimination laws will have a First Amendment right to association that precludes forced compliance with those laws. But that right * * * is an implicit right designed to protect the enumerated rights of the First Amendment, not a license to act on any discriminatory impulse. To prevail in asserting a right of expressive association as a defense to a charge of violating an antidiscrimination law, the organization must at least show it has adopted and advocated an unequivocal position inconsistent with a position advocated or epitomized by the person whom the organization seeks to exclude. If this Court were to defer to whatever position an organization is prepared to assert in its briefs, there would be no way to mark the proper boundary between genuine exercises of the right to associate, on the one hand, and sham claims that are simply attempts to insulate nonexpressive private discrimination, on the other hand.

The majority's argument relies exclusively on *Hurley v. Irish-American Gay, Lesbian and Bisexual Group of Boston, Inc.,* 515 U.S. 557 (1995). * * * Though *Hurley* has a superficial similarity to the present case, a close inspection reveals a wide gulf between that case and the one before us today. First, it was critical to our analysis that GLIB was actually conveying a message by participating in the parade—otherwise, the parade organizers could hardly claim that they were being forced to include any unwanted message at all. * * * Second, we found it relevant that GLIB's message "would likely be perceived" as the parade organizers' own speech. * * * Dale's inclusion in the Boy Scouts is nothing like the case in *Hurley*. His participation sends no cognizable message to the Scouts or to the world. Unlike GLIB, Dale did not carry a banner or a sign; he did not distribute any factsheet; and he expressed no intent to send any message. If there is any kind of message being sent, then, it is by the mere act of joining the Boy Scouts. Such an act does not constitute an instance of symbolic speech under the First Amendment.

Unfavorable opinions about homosexuals "have ancient roots." *Bowers v. Hardwick*, 478 U.S. 186, 192 (1986). * * * That such prejudices are still prevalent and that they have caused serious and tangible harm to countless members of the class New Jersey seeks to protect are established matters of fact that neither the Boy Scouts nor the Court disputes. That harm can only be aggravated by the creation of a constitutional shield for a policy that is itself the product of a habitual way of thinking about strangers. As Justice Brandeis so wisely advised, "we must be ever on our guard, lest we erect our prejudices into legal principles."

POINTS FOR DISCUSSION

a. Burdening Expressive Activity

The Court concludes that, on these facts, inclusion of Dale as an adult member of the Boy Scouts would "significantly burden" the Boy Scouts' right to control the content of its own speech. Can you imagine a hypothetical situation in which including Dale would not significantly burden the Boy Scouts' speech?

b. Limits on the Freedom of Association

If the Boy Scouts engages in expressive activity because of its desire to "transmit its values" to its members, then does a large business similarly engage in expressive activity if it requires its employees to act in a "morally straight" way? If so, are employers immune from state anti-discrimination laws, as well? Similarly, are the members of a country club engaging in expression when they decide to limit membership only to white men? If not, why are those associations different from the Boy Scouts?

c. Understanding the Dissent

Did the dissent object to the content of the Boy Scouts' asserted message, disagree about the sincerity of the message, or both? Should the freedom of association under the First Amendment turn on either consideration? Or did the dissent conclude that the Boy Scouts was not engaged in expressive activity at all?

Problem

Until 1993, the United States military excluded gays and lesbians from service. In 1993, the federal government adopted a new policy that continued to exclude gays and lesbians from service if they were open about their sexual orientation. In protest of that policy, some law schools began restricting the access of military recruiters to their students. Congress responded by enacting the Solomon Amendment, 10 U.S.C. § 983, which specified that if any part of an institution of higher education denied military recruiters access equal to that provided other recruiters, the entire institution would lose certain federal funds. An association of law schools and law faculties filed suit, claiming that the Solomon Amendment violated the First Amendment. How should the court rule? This problem is based on *Rumsfeld v. Forum for Academic and Institutional Rights, Inc.*, 547 U.S. 47 (2006).

Does it violate the freedom of association to require persons to subsidize the speech of others with whom they disagree? If so, is that what happens when a person is forced to join a union? Consider the case that follows.

JANUS V. AMERICAN FEDERATION OF STATE, COUNTY, & MUNICIPAL EMPLOYEES
138 S.Ct. 2438 (2018)

JUSTICE ALITO delivered the opinion of the Court.

Under Illinois law, public employees are forced to subsidize a union, even if they choose not to join and strongly object to the positions the union takes in collective bargaining and related activities. We conclude that this arrangement violates the free speech rights of nonmembers by compelling them to subsidize private speech on matters of substantial public concern.

We upheld a similar law in *Abood v. Detroit Bd. of Ed.*, 431 U.S. 209 (1977), and we recognize the importance of following precedent unless there are strong reasons for not doing so. But there are very strong reasons in this case. Fundamental free speech rights are at stake. *Abood* was poorly reasoned. It has led to practical problems and abuse. It is inconsistent with other First Amendment cases and has been undermined by more recent decisions. Developments since *Abood* was handed down have shed new light on the issue of agency fees, and no reliance interests on the part of public-sector unions are sufficient to justify the perpetuation of the free speech violations that *Abood* has countenanced for the past 41 years. *Abood* is therefore overruled.

* * * As illustrated by the record in this case, unions charge nonmembers, not just for the cost of collective bargaining *per se,* but also for many other supposedly connected activities. Here, the nonmembers were told that they had to pay for "[l]obbying," "[s]ocial and recreational activities," "advertising," "[m]embership meetings and conventions," and "litigation," as well as other unspecified "[s]ervices" that "may ultimately inure to the benefit of the members of the local bargaining unit." The total chargeable amount for nonmembers was 78.06% of full union dues.

Petitioner Mark Janus is employed by the Illinois Department of Healthcare and Family Services as a child support specialist. The employees in his unit are among the 35,000 public employees in Illinois who are represented by respondent American Federation of State, County, and Municipal Employees, Council 31 (Union). Janus refused to join the Union because he opposes "many of the public policy positions that [it] advocates," including the positions it takes in collective bargaining. Janus believes that the Union's "behavior in bargaining does not appreciate the current fiscal crises in Illinois and does not reflect his best interests or the interests of Illinois citizens." Therefore, if he had the choice, he "would not pay any fees or otherwise subsidize [the Union]." Under his unit's collective-bargaining agreement, however, he was required to pay an agency fee of $44.58 per month—which would amount to about $535 per year.

The First Amendment, made applicable to the States by the Fourteenth Amendment, forbids abridgment of the freedom of speech. We have held time and again that freedom of speech "includes both the right to speak freely and the right to refrain from speaking at all." *Wooley v. Maynard,* 430 U.S. 705, 714 (1977); see *Miami Herald Publishing Co. v. Tornillo,* 418 U.S. 241, 256–257 (1974). The right to eschew association for expressive purposes is likewise protected. *Roberts v. United States Jaycees,* 468 U.S. 609, 623 (1984) ("Freedom of association ... plainly presupposes a freedom not to associate"). As Justice Jackson memorably put it: "If there is any fixed star in our constitutional constellation, it is that no official, high or petty,

> **Food for Thought**
>
> Is this a case of freedom of speech or a case of freedom of association or both?

can prescribe what shall be orthodox in politics, nationalism, religion, or other matters of opinion or *force citizens to confess by word or act their faith therein.*" *West Virginia Bd. of Ed. v. Barnette,* 319 U.S. 624, 642 (1943) (emphasis added).

Compelling individuals to mouth support for views they find objectionable violates that cardinal constitutional command, and in most contexts, any such effort would be universally condemned. Suppose, for example, that the State of Illinois required all residents to sign a document expressing support for a particular set of positions on controversial public issues—say, the platform of one of the major political parties. No one, we trust, would seriously argue that the First Amendment permits this.

Perhaps because such compulsion so plainly violates the Constitution, most of our free speech cases have involved restrictions on what can be said, rather than laws compelling speech. But measures compelling speech are at least as threatening.

Free speech serves many ends. It is essential to our democratic form of government, see, *e.g., Garrison v. Louisiana,* 379 U.S. 64, 74–75 (1964), and it furthers the search for truth, see, *e.g., Thornhill v. Alabama,* 310 U.S. 88, 95 (1940). Whenever the Federal Government or a State prevents individuals from saying what they think on important matters or compels them to voice ideas with which they disagree, it undermines these ends.

When speech is compelled, however, additional damage is done. In that situation, individuals are coerced into betraying their convictions. Forcing free and independent individuals to endorse ideas they find objectionable is always demeaning, and for this reason, one of our landmark free speech cases said that a law commanding "involuntary affirmation" of objected-to beliefs would require "even more immediate and urgent grounds" than a law demanding silence. *Barnette, supra,* at 633.

Compelling a person to *subsidize* the speech of other private speakers raises similar First Amendment concerns. As Jefferson famously put it, "to compel a man to furnish contributions of money for the propagation of opinions which he disbelieves and abhor[s] is sinful and tyrannical." A Bill for Establishing Religious Freedom, in 2 Papers of Thomas Jefferson 545 (J. Boyd ed. 1950). We have therefore recognized that a "significant impingement on First Amendment rights" occurs when public employees are required to provide financial support for a union that "takes many positions during collective bargaining that have powerful political and civic consequences." Knox v. Service Employees, 567 U.S. 298, 310–311 (2012) (quoting *Ellis v. Railway Clerks,* 466 U.S. 435, 455 (1984)).

Because the compelled subsidization of private speech seriously impinges on First Amendment rights, it cannot be casually allowed. Our free speech cases have identified "levels of scrutiny" to be applied in different contexts, and in three recent cases, we have considered the standard that should be used in judging the constitutionality of agency fees.

In *Knox,* the first of these cases, we found it sufficient to hold that the conduct in question was unconstitutional under even the test used for the compulsory subsidization of commercial speech. 567 U.S., at 309–310, 321–322. Even though commercial speech has been thought to enjoy a lesser degree of protection, see, *e.g., Central Hudson Gas & Elec. Corp. v. Public Serv. Comm'n of N. Y.,* 447 U.S. 557, 562–563 (1980), prior precedent in that area * * * had applied what we characterized as "exacting" scrutiny, *Knox,* 567 U.S., at 310, a less demanding test than the "strict" scrutiny that might be thought to apply outside the commercial sphere. Under "exacting" scrutiny, we noted, a compelled subsidy must "serve a compelling state interest that cannot be achieved through means significantly less restrictive of associational freedoms." *Ibid.*

In *Harris v. Quinn,* 573 U.S. 616 (2014), the second of these cases, we again found that an agency-fee requirement failed "exacting scrutiny." But we questioned whether that test provides sufficient protection for free speech rights, since "it is apparent that the speech compelled" in agency-fee cases "is not commercial speech."

Picking up that cue, petitioner in the present case contends that the Illinois law at issue should be subjected to "strict scrutiny." The dissent, on the other hand, proposes that we apply what amounts to rational-basis review, that is, that we ask only whether a government employer could reasonably believe that the exaction of agency fees serves its interests. This form of minimal scrutiny is foreign to our free-speech jurisprudence, and we reject it here. At the same time, we again find it unnecessary to decide the issue of strict scrutiny because the Illinois scheme cannot survive under even the more permissive standard applied in *Knox* and *Harris.*

* * * It might be argued that a State has a compelling interest in requiring the payment of agency fees because (1) unions would otherwise be unwilling to represent nonmembers or (2) it would be fundamentally unfair to require unions to provide fair representation for nonmembers if nonmembers were not required to pay. Neither of these arguments is sound.

First, it is simply not true that unions will refuse to serve as the exclusive representative of all employees in the unit if they are not given agency fees. As noted, unions represent millions of public employees in jurisdictions that do not permit agency fees. No union is ever compelled to seek that designation. On the contrary, designation as exclusive representative is avidly sought. * * *

What about the representation of nonmembers in grievance proceedings? Unions do not undertake this activity solely for the benefit of nonmembers—which is why Illinois law gives a public-sector union the right to send a representative to such proceedings even if the employee declines union representation. § 315/6(b). Representation of nonmembers furthers the union's interest in keeping control of the administration of the collective-bargaining agreement, since the resolution of one employee's grievance can affect others. And when a union controls the grievance process, it may, as a practical matter, effectively subordinate "the interests of [an] individual employee ... to the collective interests of all employees in the bargaining unit." *Alexander v. Gardner-Denver Co.,* 415 U.S. 36, 58, n. 19 (1974).

In any event, whatever unwanted burden is imposed by the representation of nonmembers in disciplinary matters can be eliminated "through means significantly less restrictive of associational freedoms" than the imposition of agency fees. *Harris.* Individual nonmembers could be required to pay for that service or could be denied union representation altogether. Thus, agency fees cannot be sustained on the ground that unions would otherwise be unwilling to represent nonmembers.

Nor can such fees be justified on the ground that it would otherwise be unfair to require a union to bear the duty of fair representation. That duty is a necessary concomitant of the authority that a union seeks when it chooses to serve as the exclusive representative of all the employees in a unit. As explained, designating a union as the exclusive representative of nonmembers substantially restricts the nonmembers' rights. Protection of their interests is placed in the hands of the union, and if the union were free to disregard or even work against those interests, these employees would be wholly unprotected. That is why we said many years ago that serious "constitutional questions [would] arise" if the union were *not* subject to the duty to represent all employees fairly. *Steele v. Louisville & N.R. Co.,* 323 U.S. 192, 198 (1944).

In sum, we do not see any reason to treat the free-rider interest any differently in the agency-fee context than in any other First Amendment context. We therefore hold that agency fees cannot be upheld on free-rider grounds.

For the reasons given above, we conclude that public-sector agency-shop arrangements violate the First Amendment, and *Abood* erred in concluding otherwise. There remains the question whether *stare decisis* nonetheless counsels against overruling *Abood.* It does not.

Our cases identify factors that should be taken into account in deciding whether to overrule a past decision. Five of these are most important here: the quality of *Abood*'s reasoning, the workability of the rule it established, its consistency with other related decisions, developments since the decision was handed down, and reliance on the decision. After analyzing these factors, we conclude that *stare decisis* does not require us to retain *Abood*. [The Court's extensive discussion of *stare decisis* is omitted.]

[JUSTICE SOTOMAYOR's dissenting opinion is omitted.]

JUSTICE KAGAN, with whom JUSTICE GINSBURG, JUSTICE BREYER, and JUSTICE SOTOMAYOR join, dissenting.

For over 40 years, *Abood v. Detroit Bd. of Ed.*, 431 U.S. 209 (1977), struck a stable balance between public employees' First Amendment rights and government entities' interests in running their workforces as they thought proper. Under that decision, a government entity could require public employees to pay a fair share of the cost that a union incurs when negotiating on their behalf over terms of employment. But no part of that fair-share payment could go to any of the union's political or ideological activities.

That holding fit comfortably with this Court's general framework for evaluating claims that a condition of public employment violates the First Amendment. The Court's decisions have long made plain that government entities have substantial latitude to regulate their employees' speech—especially about terms of employment—in the interest of operating their workplaces effectively. *Abood* allowed governments to do just that. While protecting public employees' expression about non-

> **Make the Connection**
>
> We considered the speech of government employees under the First Amendment in Chapter 8.

workplace matters, the decision enabled a government to advance important managerial interests—by ensuring the presence of an exclusive employee representative to bargain with. Far from an "anomaly," the *Abood* regime was a paradigmatic example of how the government can regulate speech in its capacity as an employer.

Not any longer. Today, the Court succeeds in its 6-year campaign to reverse *Abood*. See *Friedrichs v. California Teachers Assn.*, 578 U.S. ___ (2016) (*per curiam*); *Harris v. Quinn*, 573 U.S. 616 (2014); *Knox v. Service Employees*, 567 U.S. 298 (2012). Its decision will have large-scale consequences. Public employee unions will lose a secure source of financial support. State and local governments that thought fair-share provisions furthered their interests will need to find new ways of managing their workforces. Across the country, the relationships of public employees and employers will alter in both predictable and wholly unexpected ways.

Rarely if ever has the Court overruled a decision—let alone one of this import—with so little regard for the usual principles of *stare decisis*. There are no special justifications for reversing *Abood*. It has proved workable. No recent developments have eroded its underpinnings. And it is deeply entrenched, in both the law and the real world. More than 20 States have statutory schemes built on the decision. Those laws underpin thousands of ongoing contracts involving millions of employees. Reliance interests do not come any stronger than those surrounding *Abood*. And likewise, judicial disruption does not get any greater than what the Court does today. I respectfully dissent.

POINTS FOR DISCUSSION

a.   Freedom of Speech or Freedom of Association?

Does the Court base its decision on the free speech rights of objecting government employees or on their rights to the freedom of association? The Court discusses "compelled speech," noting that it is odious for the government to require a person to subsidize the speech of others with whom he disagrees. But aren't we all inevitably forced to do that when we pay taxes? After all, few people agree with everything the government says and does. Why is this context different? Or is the Court's point that it is inappropriate to force an employee who disagrees with a union's positions to "associate" with the union (and its members)?

b.   The Government's (and the Union's) Interests

Does the dissent disagree with the majority's view that the required agency fees burden the public employees who do not want to support unions or does the dissent instead believe that there are burdens but that the burdens are permissible given the strength of the governmental interests? What are the governmental interests? The editors of the *Wall Street Journal* supported the *Janus* decision, asserting that the asserted government interests could not be especially strong because public sector unions exist in 28 states that prohibit mandatory agency fees by statute. See *The Supreme Court's Banner Year*, Wall St. J., June 28, 2018, at A16. How can you explain this argument? What is a possible counter argument?

Executive Summary of This Chapter

The Supreme Court has developed two distinct **freedom of association** doctrines. Under one doctrine, freedom of association is a right of substantive due process. This freedom of association encompasses rights such as the right to maintain familial relationships. Under the other doctrine, the Court has treated protection of freedom of association as a necessary means for securing rights guaranteed by the First Amendment. The theory is that associating with others may strengthen the ability to communicate. This chapter concerns the latter doctrine.

Civil or Criminal Liability for Associating with Others

In general, the government cannot impose civil or criminal liability on a person merely because he or she has decided to associate with others. This general rule, however, has an important exception. The government does not have to allow individuals to associate with each other for the purpose of undertaking unlawful activities. *Scales v. United States*, 367 U.S. 203, 229 (1961).

The government may not discourage membership in a group by imposing vicarious liability on non-culpable group members, *NAACP v. Claiborne Hardware Co.*, 458 U.S. 886 (1982), or by denying legal or other privileges to persons who belong to groups or who refuse to provide information about them, *Baird v. State Bar of Arizona*, 401 U.S. 1 (1971).

Disclosure of Membership Lists

The government may require a group to disclose its membership only if the government has a compelling interest in knowing the identities of the group's members. *NAACP v. State of Alabama ex rel. Patterson*, 357 U.S. 449 (1958); *Buckley v. Valeo*, 424 U.S. 1 (1976).

Freedom Not to Associate with Others

The freedom of association generally gives an organization a right to choose its members. The government, however, may pass laws that regulate this freedom if the state has a compelling interest that cannot be achieved through means significantly less restrictive of associational freedoms. But government regulations may not prohibit an organization from discriminating in its membership if the regulations would significantly affect "intimate association" or "expressive activity." *Roberts v. United States Jaycees*, 468 U.S. 609 (1984).

Applying this test, the Supreme Court has held that a state may prevent a large group of businessmen from excluding women where the exclusion of women would not affect the group's message. *Roberts v. United States Jaycees*, 468 U.S. 609 (1984).

But the Supreme Court has held that a state may not prevent the organizers of a parade from excluding a gay-rights group where inclusion of the group would affect the parade organizer's message. *Hurley v. Irish-American Gay, Lesbian and Bisexual Group of Boston*, 515 U.S. 557 (1995). Similarly, a state may not prevent the Boy Scouts from excluding a homosexual scout leader where his inclusion would affect the Boy Scouts' expressive activity. *Boy Scouts of America v. Dale*, 530 U.S. 640 (2000).

"Exacting scrutiny" applies when the government forces public employees to provide financial support for a union with whose positions they disagree. *Janus v. American Federation of State, County & Municipal Employees*, 138 S.Ct. 2438 (2018). Under "exacting" scrutiny, compelled subsidy must "serve a compelling state interest that cannot be achieved through means significantly less restrictive of associational freedoms." *Id.*

Freedom of Religion

The original Constitution addressed freedom of religion in just one clause. Article VI, clause 3 says that "no religious Test shall ever be required as a Qualification to any Office or public Trust under the United States." This clause has a clear purpose. As Justice Joseph Story explained in his influential treatise on constitutional law, "It is easy to foresee, that without some prohibition of religious tests, a successful sect, in our country, might, by once possessing power, pass test-laws, which would secure to themselves a monopoly of all the offices of trust and profit, under the national government." 3 Joseph Story, *Commentaries on the Constitution of the United States* § 1843 (1833).

The First Amendment substantially augments the protection of religious freedom. The Amendment begins by saying: "Congress shall make no law respecting an establishment of religion, or prohibiting the free exercise thereof * * *." The two clauses in this phrase have become known, respectively, as the **Establishment Clause** and the **Free Exercise Clause**. Although on their faces these clauses refer only to Congress, the Supreme Court has held that the Due Process Clause of the Fourteenth Amendment makes both of these clauses applicable to the states, as well. See *Cantwell v. Connecticut*, 310 U.S. 296, 303 (1940). This chapter considers the meaning and application of these two clauses.

> **Make the Connection**
>
> We addressed the incorporation doctrine, which makes certain provisions of the Bill of Rights applicable to the states, in Chapter 1.

A. THE ESTABLISHMENT CLAUSE

At the time of the Revolution, twelve of the thirteen colonies had established religions or churches. See *Engel v. Vitale*, 370 U.S. 421, 428 (1962). Justice Scalia has described some of what the establishment of religion in these colonies customarily entailed:

Typically, attendance at the state church was required; only clergy of the official church could lawfully perform sacraments; and dissenters, if tolerated, faced an array of civil disabilities. Thus, for example, in the Colony of Virginia, where the Church of England had been established, ministers were required by law to conform to the doctrine and rites of the Church of England; and all persons were required to attend church and observe the Sabbath, were tithed for the public support of Anglican ministers, and were taxed for the costs of building and repairing churches.

Lee v. Weisman, 505 U.S. 577, 640–641 (1992) (Scalia, J., dissenting) (citations omitted).

The Supreme Court has held that the Establishment Clause prohibits all of these practices: "Neither a state nor the Federal Government can * * * force nor influence a person to go to or to remain away from church against his will or force him to profess a belief or disbelief in any religion. No person can be punished for entertaining or professing religious beliefs or disbeliefs, for church attendance or non-attendance * * *." *Everson v. Board of Education of Ewing Township,* 330 U.S. 1, 15–16 (1947).

More difficult questions concern the extent to which the government may take other actions pertaining to religion. The following sections consider two broad topics: government aid to religious institutions and religion within government institutions. Most modern Establishment Clause challenges involve one of these topics.

POINTS FOR DISCUSSION

a.   The "Separation of Church and State"

In *Reynolds v. United States,* 98 U.S. 145, 164 (1878), the Supreme Court asserted that the First Amendment implements the "separation of church and state." This phrase, which the Supreme Court has used many times since *Reynolds,* refers to a civic ideal in which the government and religion operate in separate spheres: the government is secular, and the clergy and their congregations have no formal political authority. The Supreme Court has recognized that the mere invocation of the phrase "separation of church and state" cannot answer all questions that arise under the Establishment Clause, but the Court

> **FYI**
>
> *Reynolds* involved a Mormon's Free Exercise challenge to a federal law banning polygamy.

still views the phrase as "a useful figure of speech." See *Lynch v. Donnelly*, 465 U.S. 668, 673 (1984).

In *Reynolds*, the Supreme Court relied on a now-famous letter that Thomas Jefferson wrote to a religious congregation in 1802. In the letter, Jefferson stated:

> Believing with you that religion is a matter which lies solely between man and his God, that he owes account to none other for his faith or his worship, that the legislative powers of government reach actions only, and not opinions, I contemplate with sovereign reverence that act of the whole American people which declared that their legislature should "make no law respecting an establishment of religion, or prohibiting the free exercise thereof," *thus building a wall of separation between Church and State.*

Letter from Thomas Jefferson to Danbury Baptist Association, reprinted in 5 *The Founders' Constitution* 58 (Philip B. Kurland & Ralph Lerner eds. 1987) (emphasis added).

More than 150 years before Jefferson articulated his view, Roger Williams, a Christian clergyman who had been exiled from Salem, Massachusetts, for resisting the establishment of a state church, helped to found the colony of Rhode Island as a place where religious minorities could live in peace and tolerance. In 1644, a few years before the colony obtained a royal charter ensuring religious liberty, Williams warned about the risks of creating an opening "in the hedge, or wall of separation, between the garden of the church and the wilderness of the world."

James Madison advanced a similar view in his famous "Memorial and Remonstrance," which he wrote in 1785 to oppose a Bill (proposed by Patrick Henry) in the Virginia legislature to impose a tax to support "teachers of the Christian religion." After providing a robust defense of the freedom of religion, he argued:

> Who does not see that the same authority which can establish Christianity, in exclusion of all other Religions, may establish with the same ease any particular sect of Christians, in exclusion of all other Sects? That the same authority which can force a citizen to contribute three pence only of his property for the support of any one establishment, may force him to conform to any other establishment in all cases whatsoever? * * * Whilst we assert for ourselves a freedom to embrace, to profess and to observe the Religion which we believe to be of divine origin, we cannot deny an equal freedom to those whose minds have not yet yielded to the evidence which has convinced us. * * *
>
> During almost fifteen centuries has the legal establishment of Christianity been on trial. What have been its fruits? More or less in all places, pride and indolence in the Clergy, ignorance and servility in the laity,

in both, superstition, bigotry and persecution. * * * Rulers who wished to subvert the public liberty, may have found an established Clergy convenient auxiliaries. A just Government instituted to secure & perpetuate it needs them not. Such a Government will be best supported by protecting every Citizen in the enjoyment of his Religion with the same equal hand which protects his person and his property; by neither invading the equal rights of any Sect, nor suffering any Sect to invade those of another.

This view—sometimes called "separationism" because of its central premise that there ought to be a separation between church and state—thus has a significant historical pedigree. Some scholars have asserted, moreover, that the Establishment Clause incorporated this view, and thus that the Clause not only prohibits the government from establishing an official church but also prohibits the government from, among other things, preferring religion over non-religion. See, e.g., Douglas Laycock, *"Nonpreferential" Aid to Religion: A False Claim About Original Intent*, 27 Wm. & Mary L. Rev. 875 (1986).

Not everyone shares the view, however, that the Establishment Clause requires an absolute separation of church and state. In 1985, then-Justice William Rehnquist asserted in a lengthy dissent in *Wallace v. Jaffree*, 472 U.S. 38 (1985), that the Clause does not require "neutrality on the part of government between religion and irreligion." Instead, he concluded, after an extensive review of the drafting history of the Establishment Clause and early government practice, that the Clause merely "forbade establishment of a national religion, and forbade preference among religious sects or denominations." Accordingly, he reasoned that the Clause does not prohibit the government from "providing nondiscriminatory aid to religion." Justice Rehnquist's opinion, with his support for these assertions, appears later in this chapter. His view is typically referred to as "non-preferentialism," because it asserts that the Establishment Clause requires only that the government not prefer one religion over another, not that the government be neutral between religion and non-religion.

In an influential book, Professor Phillip Hamburger reaches a similar conclusion. See Phillip Hamburger, *Separation of Church and State* (2002). He argues that the Establishment Clause was originally intended only to prevent the government from discriminating based on religion. See *id.* at 14. A desire for separation of church and state, he contends, arose much later in United States history, based on "ideals of individual independence, fears of Catholicism, and various types of specialization." *Id.* Hamburger concluded: "Americans gradually transformed their understanding of religious liberty. Increasingly, Americans conceived their freedom to require an independence from churches and they feared the demands of one church in particular. To limit such threats, Americans called for a separation of church and state, and eventually the U.S. Supreme Court gave their new conception of religious liberty the force of law." *Id.* at 17.

Despite this criticism, the ideal of separation of church and state remains an important influence in the Supreme Court's interpretation of the Establishment Clause. Does the historical ambiguity mean that originalism cannot answer which view better captures the meaning of the Establishment Clause? If originalism is the appropriate approach, what weight should be given to the views of figures such as Jefferson, Madison, and Williams? As we consider the cases in this section, consider the extent to which the Supreme Court has accepted the pure view of separation.

b. Who Is Protected by the Establishment Clause?

Most of the provisions in the Bill of Rights are designed to protect minority rights against majoritarian incursion. The protections in the Fourth, Fifth, Sixth, and Eighth Amendments, for example, serve to ensure that unpopular persons—that is, persons accused of crimes—receive process that an angry majority might otherwise be reluctant to provide. Similarly, as we saw in Chapter 8, the Free Speech Clause of the First Amendment protects dissenters and others with unpopular views from retribution by the majority. Indeed, the provisions in the Bill of Rights typically matter only because they provide protections for minorities; the majority, after all, rarely needs protection from the majoritarian political process.

Is the Establishment Clause such a provision, as well? If so, whom does it protect? Those who support the separationist view generally assert that the Establishment Clause protects several groups: (1) adherents of minority religions, who would face ostracism and coercion if adherents of the dominant religion could impose their religious views by law; (2) those who do not subscribe to any religion or hold any religious beliefs, for much the same reason; and (3) religious institutions and organizations, such as organized churches, which would inevitably be corrupted by the political process and the resulting desire to attain and consolidate power. See, e.g., James Madison, Memorial and Remonstrance, reprinted in *Everson v. Board of Education of Ewing Township*, 330 U.S. 1, 67 (1947).

Whom does the Establishment Clause protect under the non-preferentialist view, which Justice Rehnquist advanced in the excerpt above and which (we will see in this chapter) has become increasingly popular on the Court? Does it protect adherents of minority religions, on the theory that they can receive the same aid from the government that adherents of the dominant religion can receive? Does it protect religious organizations, by giving them access to government aid and the public square? What is its view of the rights of non-believers? As you read the materials in this chapter, consider the justifications for and implications of the competing views of the Establishment Clause.

c.   **Application of the Establishment Clause to the States**

Although the Supreme Court has squarely held that the Establishment Clause applies to the states as a result of the clause's incorporation by the Due Process Clause of the Fourteenth Amendment, *Cantwell v. Connecticut,* 310 U.S. 296, 303 (1940), some Justices in recent years have expressed a willingness to revisit the issue. Justice Clarence Thomas articulated this view in a separate opinion in *Elk Grove Unified School Dist. v. Newdow,* 542 U.S. 1, 45 (2004) (Thomas, J., concurring in judgment):

> As a textual matter, [the Establishment] Clause probably prohibits Congress from establishing a national religion. *But see* P. Hamburger, *Separation of Church and State* 106, n. 40 (2002). Perhaps more importantly, the Clause made clear that Congress could not interfere with state establishments, notwithstanding any argument that could be made based on Congress' power under the Necessary and Proper Clause. *See* A. Amar, *The Bill of Rights* 36–39 (1998).
>
> Nothing in the text of the Clause suggests that it reaches any further. The Establishment Clause does not purport to protect individual rights. By contrast, the Free Exercise Clause plainly protects individuals against congressional interference with the right to exercise their religion, and the remaining Clauses within the First Amendment expressly disable Congress from "abridging [particular] *freedom[s]*." (Emphasis added.) This textual analysis is consistent with the prevailing view that the Constitution left religion to the States. *See, e.g.,* 2 J. Story, *Commentaries on the Constitution of the United States* § 1873 (5th ed. 1891); *see also* Amar, *The Bill of Rights,* at 32–42; *id.,* at 246–257. History also supports this understanding: At the founding, at least six States had established religions, see McConnell, *The Origins and Historical Understanding of Free Exercise of Religion,* 103 Harv. L.Rev. 1409, 1437 (1990). Nor has this federalism point escaped the notice of Members of this Court. See, *e.g., Zelman v. Simmons-Harris,* 536 U.S. 639, 677–680 (2002) (THOMAS, J., concurring); *Lee v. Weisman,* 505 U.S. 577, 641 (1992) (Scalia, J., dissenting).
>
> Quite simply, the Establishment Clause is best understood as a federalism provision—it protects state establishments from federal interference but does not protect any individual right. These two features independently make incorporation of the Clause difficult to understand. The best argument in favor of incorporation would be that, by disabling Congress from establishing a national religion, the Clause protected an individual right, enforceable against the Federal Government, to be free from coercive federal establishments. * * *

Under Justice Thomas's view, the Establishment Clause would prohibit Congress from establishing a national church or religion, but it would not impose any limits on the authority of the states to do the same. Accordingly, under this view, a bill today similar to the 1785 Bill in Virginia to impose a tax to support "teachers of the Christian religion," which prompted Madison to write his "Memorial and Remonstrance," would not violate the Establishment Clause, notwithstanding the doctrine of incorporation. Does the fact that many states had established churches or religions before the ratification of the Constitution support Justice Thomas's conclusion, or does it shed light on the reasons why the First Amendment was proposed and ratified?

Consider the competing view, which Justice Brennan expressed in a concurring opinion in *School Dist. of Abington Twp. v. Schempp*, 374 U.S. 203 (1963):

> It has been suggested, with some support in history, that [incorporation of the Establishment Clause] is conceptually impossible because the Framers meant the Establishment Clause also to foreclose any attempt by Congress to disestablish the existing official state churches. Whether or not such was the understanding of the Framers and whether such a purpose would have inhibited the absorption of the Establishment Clause at the threshold of the Nineteenth Century are questions not dispositive of our present inquiry. For it is clear on the record of history that the last of the formal state establishments was dissolved more than three decades before the Fourteenth Amendment was ratified, and thus the problem of protecting official state churches from federal encroachments could hardly have been any concern of those who framed the post-Civil War Amendments. Any such objective of the First Amendment, having become historical anachronism by 1868, cannot be thought to have deterred the absorption of the Establishment Clause to any greater degree than it would, for example, have deterred the absorption of the Free Exercise Clause. That no organ of the Federal Government possessed in 1791 any power to restrain the interference of the States in religious matters is indisputable. It is equally plain, on the other hand, that the Fourteenth Amendment created a panoply of new federal rights for the protection of citizens of the various States [including] freedom from such state governmental involvement in the affairs of religion as the Establishment Clause had originally foreclosed on the part of Congress.
>
> It has also been suggested that [the Establishment Clause is not incorporated] because that clause is not one of the provisions of the Bill of Rights which in terms protects a "freedom" of the individual. The fallacy in this contention, I think, is that it underestimates the role of the

Establishment Clause as a coguarantor, with the Free Exercise Clause, of religious liberty. The Framers did not entrust the liberty of religious beliefs to either clause alone.

Finally, it has been contended that absorption of the Establishment Clause is precluded by the absence of any intention on the part of the Framers of the Fourteenth Amendment to circumscribe the residual powers of the States to aid religious activities and institutions in ways which fell short of formal establishments. * * * Even if we assume that the draftsmen of the Fourteenth Amendment saw no immediate connection between its protections against state action infringing personal liberty and the guarantees of the First Amendment, it is certainly too late in the day to suggest that their assumed inattention to the question dilutes the force of these constitutional guarantees in their application to the States. It is enough to conclude that the religious liberty embodied in the Fourteenth Amendment would not be viable if the Constitution were interpreted to forbid only establishments ordained by Congress.

Was Justice Brennan suggesting that the understanding of the states' role in matters of religion had changed between 1791 and 1868 such that the Establishment principle held by the Supreme Court to be incorporated by the Fourteenth Amendment is different from the principle in the original First Amendment? Or was he suggesting that the meaning of the Establishment principle has evolved since its incorporation in 1868?

The majority of the cases that follow in this part involve challenges to state, as opposed to federal, laws. As you read them, consider what the results would have been if the Supreme Court had accepted Justice Thomas's view of the reach of the Establishment Clause.

1.   Government Aid to Religious Institutions

To what extent does the Establishment Clause prevent the federal and state governments from providing aid to religious institutions? Although the Supreme Court has addressed this question in many cases, a simple answer has not emerged. The Court has concluded that some forms of aid are permissible, but that other forms are not. Exactly what distinguishes the two categories, however, remains unsettled.

Consider, for example, cases involving governmental aid to parochial schools (i.e., private schools with a religious affiliation). On the one hand, the Supreme Court has said that the government cannot supplement the salary of teachers in parochial schools, *Lemon v. Kurtzman*, 403 U.S. 602 (1971), or conduct classes in parochial schools, *School District of the City of Grand Rapids v. Ball*, 473 U.S. 373 (1985). Under current doctrine, these actions violate the Establishment Clause. On the other hand, the Supreme Court has held that the government may provide tax credits to parents for tuition paid to parochial schools, *Mueller v. Allen*, 463 U.S. 388 (1983), loan textbooks to parochial

> **For More Information**
>
> For lists of more examples of cases that have upheld and struck down governmental programs under the Establishment Clause, see *Van Orden v. Perry*, 545 U.S. 677, 685 nn. 3 & 4 (2005) (plurality opinion).

schools, *Board of Education v. Allen*, 392 U.S. 236 (1968), and reimburse the cost of transportation to parochial schools, *Everson v. Board of Education of Ewing Township*, 330 U.S. 1 (1947). Under current doctrine, these actions do not violate the

> **Definition**
>
> Januslike means like the Roman god Janus, who had two faces looking in opposite directions.

Establishment Clause. As Chief Justice William Rehnquist aptly put it: "Our cases, Januslike, point in two directions in applying the Establishment Clause." *Van Orden v. Perry*, 545 U.S. 677, 685 (2005) (plurality opinion).

In the following case, the Court announced at least two principles. First, the Court, echoing the separationist view described above, declared that the Establishment Clause "was intended to erect 'a wall of separation between Church and State' " and thus that "[n]o tax in any amount, large or small, can be levied to support any religious activities or institutions * * *." Second, the Court announced what might be called a general neutrality principle. This principle states that the Establishment Clause "requires the state to be a neutral in its relations with groups of religious believers and non-believers." The government may provide benefits to religious believers if it does so in a neutral fashion—that is, if, generally speaking, it does not favor religious individuals or organizations over the non-religious. As you read the case, ask yourself whether (1) these principles are sensible interpretations of the Establishment Clause, (2) they are reconcilable, and (3) the Court applied them correctly in the case.

EVERSON V. BOARD OF EDUCATION OF EWING TOWNSHIP
330 U.S. 1 (1947)

MR. JUSTICE BLACK delivered the opinion of the Court.

A New Jersey statute authorizes its local school districts to make rules and contracts for the transportation of children to and from schools. The [appellee] acting pursuant to this statute authorized reimbursement to parents of money expended by them for the bus transportation of their children on regular busses operated by the public transportation system. Part of this money was for the payment of transportation of some children in the community to Catholic parochial schools. These church schools give their students, in addition to secular education, regular religious instruction conforming to the religious tenets and modes of worship of the Catholic Faith. The superintendent of these schools is a Catholic priest.

The appellant, in his capacity as a district taxpayer, filed suit in a State court challenging the right of the Board to reimburse parents of parochial school students. He contended that the statute and the resolution passed pursuant to it violated both the State and the Federal Constitutions. * * *[2]

Make the Connection

Under current standing doctrine, which we discuss in Volume 1, did the plaintiff in this suit have standing? What was his injury? Should that be a cognizable injury under Article III? We consider this question later in this chapter.

A large proportion of the early settlers of this country came here from Europe to escape the bondage of laws which compelled them to support and attend government favored churches. The centuries immediately before and contemporaneous with the colonization of America had been filled with turmoil, civil strife, and persecutions, generated in large part by established sects determined to maintain their absolute political and religious supremacy. With the power of government supporting them, at various times and places, Catholics had persecuted Protestants, Protestants had persecuted Catholics, Protestant sects had persecuted other Protestant sects, Catholics of one shade of belief had persecuted Catholics of another shade of belief, and all of these had from time to time persecuted Jews. In efforts to force loyalty to whatever religious group happened to be on top and in league with the government of a particular time and place, men and women had been fined, cast in jail, cruelly tortured, and killed. Among the offenses for which these punishments had been inflicted were such things as speaking disrespectfully of the views of ministers of government-established churches, nonattendance at those churches, expressions of non-belief in their doctrines, and failure to pay taxes and tithes to support them.

These practices of the old world were transplanted to and began to thrive in the soil of the new America. The very charters granted by the English Crown to the individuals and companies designated to make the laws which would control the destinies of the colonials authorized these individuals and companies to erect religious establishments which all, whether believers or non-believers, would be

---

2   * * * Although the township resolution authorized reimbursement only for parents of public and Catholic school pupils, appellant does not allege, nor is there anything in the record which would offer the slightest support to an allegation, that there were any children in the township who attended or would have attended, but for want of transportation, any but public and Catholic schools. * * *

required to support and attend. An exercise of this authority was accompanied by a repetition of many of the old world practices and persecutions. Catholics found themselves hounded and proscribed because of their faith; Quakers who followed their conscience went to jail; Baptists were peculiarly obnoxious to certain dominant Protestant sects; men and women of varied faiths who happened to be in a minority in a particular locality were persecuted because they steadfastly persisted in worshipping God only as their own consciences dictated. And all of these dissenters were compelled to pay tithes and taxes to support government-sponsored churches whose ministers preached inflammatory sermons designed to strengthen and consolidate the established faith by generating a burning hatred against dissenters.

These practices became so commonplace as to shock the freedom-loving colonials into a feeling of abhorrence. The imposition of taxes to pay ministers' salaries and to build and maintain churches and church property aroused their indignation. It was these feelings which found expression in the First Amendment. No one locality and no one group throughout the Colonies can rightly be given entire credit for having aroused the sentiment that culminated in adoption of the Bill of Rights' provisions embracing religious liberty. But Virginia, where the established church had achieved a dominant influence in political affairs and where many excesses attracted wide public attention, provided a great stimulus and able leadership for the movement. The people there, as elsewhere, reached the conviction that individual religious liberty could be achieved best under a government which was stripped of all power to tax, to support, or otherwise to assist any or all religions, or to interfere with the beliefs of any religious individual or group.

The movement toward this end reached its dramatic climax in Virginia in 1785–86 when the Virginia legislative body was about to renew Virginia's tax levy for the support of the established church. Thomas Jefferson and James Madison led the fight against this tax. Madison wrote his great Memorial and Remonstrance against the law. In it, he eloquently argued that a true religion did not need the support of law; that no person, either believer or non-believer, should be taxed to support a religious institution of any kind; that the best interest of a society required that the minds of men always be wholly free; and that cruel persecutions were the inevitable result of government-established religions. Madison's Remonstrance received

> **Go Online**
>
> For more history of this struggle for religious freedom in Virginia and for images and transcripts of Madison's and Jefferson's documents, visit the Library of Congress's online exhibition on Religion and the Founding of the American Republic.

strong support throughout Virginia, and the Assembly postponed consideration of the proposed tax measure until its next session. When the proposal came up for consideration at that session, it not only died in committee, but the Assembly enacted the famous "Virginia Bill for Religious Liberty" originally written by Thomas Jefferson. The preamble to that Bill stated among other things that

> Almighty God hath created the mind free; that all attempts to influence it by temporal punishments, or burthens, or by civil incapacitations, tend only to beget habits of hypocrisy and meanness, and are a departure from the plan of the Holy author of our religion who being Lord both of body and mind, yet chose not to propagate it by coercions on either . . .; that to compel a man to furnish contributions of money for the propagation of opinions which he disbelieves, is sinful and tyrannical; that even the forcing him to support this or that teacher of his own religious persuasion, is depriving him of the comfortable liberty of giving his contributions to the particular pastor, whose morals he would make his pattern. * * *

And the statute itself enacted

> That no man shall be compelled to frequent or support any religious worship, place, or ministry whatsoever, nor shall be enforced, restrained, molested, or burthened, in his body or goods, nor shall otherwise suffer on account of his religious opinions or belief. . . .

This Court has previously recognized that the provisions of the First Amendment, in the drafting and adoption of which Madison and Jefferson played such leading roles, had the same objective and were intended to provide the same protection against governmental intrusion on religious liberty as the Virginia statute. *Reynolds v. United States*, 98 U.S. 145, 164 (1878). Prior to the adoption of the Fourteenth Amendment, the First Amendment did not apply as a restraint against the states. Most of them did soon provide similar constitutional protections for religious liberty. But some states persisted for about half a century in imposing restraints upon the free exercise of religion and in discriminating against particular religious groups. In recent years, so far as the provision against the establishment of a religion is concerned, the question has most frequently arisen in connection with proposed state aid to church schools and efforts to carry on religious teachings in the public schools in accordance with the tenets of a particular sect. Some churches have either sought or accepted state financial support for their schools. Here again the efforts to obtain state aid or acceptance of it have not been limited to any one particular faith. The state courts, in the main, have remained faithful to the language of their own constitutional provisions designed to protect religious freedom and to separate religious and governments. Their decisions, however, show the difficulty in drawing the line between tax legislation which provides funds for the welfare of the general public and that which is designed to support institutions which teach religion.

The "establishment of religion" clause of the First Amendment means at least this: Neither a state nor the Federal Government can set up a church. Neither can pass laws which aid one religion, aid all religions, or prefer one religion over another. Neither can force nor influence a person to go to or to remain away from church against his will or force him to profess a belief or disbelief in any religion. No person can be punished for entertaining or professing religious beliefs or disbeliefs, for church attendance or non-attendance. No tax in any amount, large or small, can be levied to support any religious activities or institutions, whatever they may be called, or whatever form they may adopt to teach or practice religion. Neither a state nor the Federal Government can, openly or secretly, participate in the affairs of any religious organizations or groups and vice versa. In the words of Jefferson, the clause against establishment of religion by law was intended to erect "a wall of separation between Church and State." *Reynolds v. United States*, 98 U.S. at 164.

> **Take Note**
>
> The Court here announces a series of principles that derive from the Establishment Clause. How many of these principles are implicated by the practice challenged in this case? Assuming that not all are, is most of this passage simply dicta? Or is it essential to the Court's reasoning and interpretation of the First Amendment?

We must consider the New Jersey statute in accordance with the foregoing limitations imposed by the First Amendment. * * * New Jersey cannot consistently with the "establishment of religion" clause of the First Amendment contribute tax-raised funds to the support of an institution which teaches the tenets and faith of any church. On the other hand, other language of the amendment commands that New Jersey cannot hamper its citizens in the free exercise of their own religion. Consequently, it cannot exclude individual Catholics, Lutherans, Mohammedans, Baptists, Jews, Methodists, Non-believers, Presbyterians, or the members of any other faith, because of their faith, or lack of it, from receiving the benefits of public welfare legislation. While we do not mean to intimate that a state could not provide transportation only to children attending public schools, we must be careful, in protecting the citizens of New Jersey against state-established churches, to be sure that we do not inadvertently prohibit New Jersey from extending its general State law benefits to all its citizens without regard to their religious belief.

Measured by these standards, we cannot say that the First Amendment prohibits New Jersey from spending tax raised funds to pay the bus fares of parochial school pupils as a part of a general program under which it pays the fares of pupils attending public and other schools. It is undoubtedly true that children are helped to get to church schools. There is even a possibility that some of the children might not be sent to the church schools if the parents were compelled to pay their children's bus fares out of their own pockets when transportation to a public school would have been paid for by the State. The same possibility exists where the state requires a local transit company to provide reduced fares to school children including those attending parochial schools, or where a municipally owned transportation system undertakes to carry all school children free of charge. Moreover, state-paid policemen, detailed to protect children going to and from church schools from the very real hazards of traffic, would serve much the same purpose and accomplish much the same result as state provisions intended to guarantee free transportation of a kind which the state deems to be best for the school children's welfare. And parents might refuse to risk their children to the serious danger of traffic accidents going to and from parochial schools, the approaches to which were not protected by policemen. Similarly, parents might be reluctant to permit their children to attend schools which the state had cut off from such general government services as ordinary police and fire protection, connections for sewage disposal, public highways and sidewalks. Of course, cutting off church schools from these services, so separate and so indisputably marked off from the religious function, would make it far more difficult for the schools to operate. But such is obviously not the purpose of the First Amendment. That Amendment requires the state to be a neutral in its relations with groups of religious believers and non-believers; it does not require the state to be their adversary. State power is no more to be used so as to handicap religions, than it is to favor them.

> **Take Note**
>
> In this passage, the Court states a test of neutrality between religion and non-religion. In what way is the law in this case neutral? Is there an argument that it is not neutral? Is the challenged policy different in any meaningful way from a policy that provides police and fire protection to religious institutions?

The First Amendment has erected a wall between church and state. That wall must be kept high and impregnable. We could not approve the slightest breach. New Jersey has not breached it here.

MR. JUSTICE JACKSON, [joined by MR. JUSTICE FRANKFURTER,] dissenting.

I find myself, contrary to first impressions, unable to join in this decision. I have a sympathy, though it is not ideological, with Catholic citizens who are compelled by law to pay taxes for public schools, and also feel constrained by conscience and discipline to support other schools for their own children. Such relief to them as this case involves is not in itself a serious burden to taxpayers and I had assumed it to be as little serious in principle. Study of this case convinces me otherwise. The Court's opinion marshals every argument in favor of state aid and puts the case in its most favorable light, but much of its reasoning confirms my conclusions that there are no good grounds upon which to support the present legislation. In fact, the undertones of the opinion, advocating complete and uncompromising separation of Church from State, seem utterly discordant with its conclusion yielding support to their commingling in educational matters. * * *

It seems to me that the basic fallacy in the Court's reasoning, which accounts for its failure to apply the principles it avows, is in ignoring the essentially religious test by which beneficiaries of this expenditure are selected. A policeman protects a Catholic, of course—but not because he is a Catholic; it is because he is a man and a member of our society. The fireman protects the Church school—but not because it is a Church school; it is because it is property, part of the assets of our society. Neither the fireman nor the policeman has to ask before he renders aid "Is this man or building identified with the Catholic Church." But before these school authorities draw a check to reimburse for a student's fare they must ask just that question, and if the school is a Catholic one they may render aid because it is such, while if it is of any other faith or is run for profit, the help must be withheld. To consider the converse of the Court's reasoning will best disclose its fallacy. That there is no parallel between police and fire protection and this plan

of reimbursement is apparent from the incongruity of the limitation of this Act if applied to police and fire service. Could we sustain an Act that said police shall protect pupils on the way to or from public schools and Catholic schools but not while going to and coming from other schools, and firemen shall extinguish a blaze in public or Catholic school buildings but shall not put out a blaze in Protestant Church schools or private schools operated for profit? That is the true analogy to the case we have before us and I should think it pretty plain that such a scheme would not be valid.

> **Take Note**
>
> Is Justice Jackson's objection to the challenged statute that it is not neutral between religion and *non-*religion, or that it is not neutral among *different* religions? Under Justice Jackson's reasoning, what would be the constitutional status of a law that used taxpayer funds to pay for bus transportation to all schools, public and private, secular and religious of any denomination? As you consider this question, note that Justice Jackson also joined Justice Rutledge's opinion, which follows.

MR. JUSTICE RUTLEDGE, with whom MR. JUSTICE FRANKFURTER, MR. JUSTICE JACKSON and MR. JUSTICE BURTON agree, dissenting.

Believers of all faiths, and others who do not express their feeling toward ultimate issues of existence in any creedal form, pay the New Jersey tax. When the money so raised is used to pay for transportation to religious schools, the Catholic taxpayer to the extent of his proportionate share pays for the transportation of Lutheran, Jewish and otherwise religiously affiliated children to receive their non-Catholic religious instruction. Their parents likewise pay proportionately for the transportation of Catholic children to receive Catholic instruction. Each thus contributes to "the propagation of opinions which he disbelieves" in so far as their religions differ, as do others who accept no creed without regard to those differences. Each thus pays taxes also to support the teaching of his own religion, an exaction equally forbidden since it denies "the comfortable liberty" of giving one's contribution to the particular agency of instruction he approves.

New Jersey's action therefore exactly fits the type of exaction and the kind of evil at which Madison and Jefferson struck. Under the test they framed it cannot be said that the cost of transportation is no part of the cost of education or of the religious instruction given. That it is a substantial and a necessary element is shown most plainly by the continuing and increasing demand for the state to assume it. Nor is there pretense that it relates only to the secular instruction given in religious schools or that any attempt is or could be made toward allocating proportional shares as between the secular and the religious instruction. It is precisely because the instruction is religious and relates to a particular faith, whether one or another, that parents send their children to religious schools * * *. And the very purpose of the state's contribution is to defray the cost of conveying the pupil to the place where he will receive not simply secular, but also and primarily religious, teaching and guidance.

POINTS FOR DISCUSSION

a.   Identifying the Rule

Which one of the Establishment Clause principles that the Court announced in *Everson* governed the outcome of the case? Did the policy authorizing reimbursement to parents permit the use of tax funds "to support any religious activities or institutions"? If so, in what way? And if so, then why was the policy nevertheless consistent with the Constitution?

The Court declared that the policy was constitutional because it was consistent with the "neutrality principle." Where did this rule come from? Is it based on the history that the Court discussed earlier in the opinion? Is it based on a political or philosophical theory about the role of government in matters of conscience? If so, do you agree with that theory? Or is it based on other Clauses in the Constitution (or even in the First Amendment)?

b. Satisfying the Rule of Neutrality

The Court held in *Everson* that a local board of education does not violate the rule of neutrality when it pays for transporting children to schools, even if some of the schools are private Catholic schools. Yet, as Justice Jackson observed, the policy (at least in practice) paid costs *only* for children attending public schools and Catholic schools; children (if any) attending other private religious schools were not covered. Does this suggest that the policy was not neutral towards religion and non-religion? Or only that it was not neutral among religions? If the latter, is that a defect under the Establishment Clause? Under the Equal Protection Clause? Under the Free Exercise Clause?

Even if the policy had paid transportation costs to *all* schools, including private religious schools of all denominations, is there an argument that the policy was nevertheless inconsistent with the Establishment Clause? Justice Rutledge asserted that the policy was unconstitutional because it effectively provided a government subsidy for religious instruction. In his view, what exactly was wrong with such a subsidy? Did he reject the rule of neutrality as insufficient under the Establishment Clause, or did he simply think that the rule was not satisfied in this case? Would his view require the conclusion that a state cannot provide police or fire protection for religious institutions? If not, why was this case different?

Assuming that the Court was correct in its conclusion that the challenged policy was neutral, what sorts of policies would fail the Court's test? Can you think of hypothetical examples of policies that would provide payment for transportation to Catholic schools but that would not be neutral?

c. Other Forms of Aid to Parochial Schools

How important was the fact that the aid at issue in *Everson* was provided to individuals rather than to the religious schools themselves? Obviously, the aid benefitted the schools, in that it made it more likely that students would choose to enroll. But is such aid different in kind from aid provided directly to religious institutions?

For example, could a public school board of education pay for the costs of field trips taken by students at religious schools if it also pays for the cost of field trips taken at public schools? Would such a law be "neutral"? If so, is neutrality enough? The Supreme Court initially held that a board of education could not pay for field trips even under a neutral policy. In *Wolman v. Walter*, 433 U.S. 229, 253–254 (1977), the Court explained:

> [A]lthough a trip may be to a location that would be of interest to those in public schools, it is the individual teacher who makes a field trip meaningful. The experience begins with the study and discussion of the place to be visited; it continues on location with the teacher pointing out items of interest and stimulating the imagination; and it ends with a discussion of the experience. The field trips are an integral part of the educational experience, and where the teacher works within and for a sectarian institution, an unacceptable risk of fostering of religion is an inevitable byproduct.

Accordingly, the Court concluded in *Wolman* that neutrality is not enough to satisfy scrutiny under the Establishment Clause; the governmental action also must not "foster" religion. But the Court overruled *Wolman* in *Mitchell v. Helms*, 530 U.S. 793 (2000). In *Mitchell*, the Court held that a policy permitting the use of public funds to pay for library books, computers, laboratory equipment, and other educational items at religious schools did not violate the Establishment Clause. The plurality opinion asserted that neutral aid to religious schools is permissible so long as no "religious indoctrination that occurs in those schools could reasonably be attributed to governmental action." *Id.* at 809.

How can a court tell whether public funds provided to religious institutions are used for "religious indoctrination"? Assuming that the religious institution has other, non-governmental sources of funds, isn't all of the money fungible? That is, doesn't any government aid to a religious institution free up the institution's other funds to be used for religious indoctrination?

d.   Dissatisfaction with Neutrality

To the extent that the dissenters in *Everson* disagreed with the neutrality principle, the source of their disagreement was the conviction that the principle did not *adequately constrain* the power of government to subsidize religious practice. As we will see in the materials that follow, however, in more recent years several members of the Supreme Court have disagreed with the neutrality principle on the ground that it *unduly* constrains the power of the government to affirm and support religious practices.

> **Make the Connection**
>
> We will consider the Ten Commandments cases—*McCreary* and *Van Orden v. Perry*, 545 U.S. 677 (2005), a companion case—later in this chapter.

Justice Scalia, writing for himself and two others, recently expressed his opposition to the neutrality principle in a dissenting opinion in *McCreary County, Ky. v. American Civil Liberties Union of Ky.*, 545 U.S. 844, 888–891 (2005), which held that a display of the Ten Commandments in a courthouse violates the Establishment Clause:

> Presidents continue to conclude the Presidential oath with the words "so help me God." Our legislatures, state and national, continue to open their sessions with prayer led by official chaplains. The sessions of this Court continue to open with the prayer "God save the United States and this Honorable Court." Invocation of the Almighty by our public figures, at all levels of government, remains commonplace. Our coinage bears the motto, "IN GOD WE TRUST." And our Pledge of Allegiance contains the acknowledgment that we are a Nation "under God." * * *

> With all of this reality (and much more) staring it in the face, how can the Court *possibly* assert that the "First Amendment mandates governmental neutrality between . . . religion and nonreligion," and that "[m]anifesting a purpose to favor [adherence] to religion generally," is unconstitutional? Who says so? Surely not the words of the Constitution. Surely not the history and traditions that reflect our society's constant understanding of those words. * * * Nothing stands behind the Court's assertion that governmental affirmation of the society's belief in God is unconstitutional except the Court's own say-so, citing as support only the unsubstantiated say-so of earlier Courts going back no further than the mid-20th century. * * * And [the Court's practice] is discredited because the Court has not had the courage (or the foolhardiness) to apply the neutrality principle consistently.

Is it clear that "history and tradition" demonstrate that the neutrality principle is incorrect? One commentator has argued that Justice Scalia "selectively [drew] upon the historical record to give the appearance of a historical consensus that did not exist," holding out as "unambiguous evidence of a universally understood original meaning actions that, in fact, many of the Framers themselves strongly condemned as unconstitutional":

> For instance, James Madison—who originally proposed the Establishment Clause—fought the First Congress's decision to hire a legislative chaplain, and condemned it as "a palpable violation [of] Constitutional principles." Similarly, Thomas Jefferson refused to issue Thanksgiving prayers because he understood them to violate the Establishment Clause's prohibition against governmental "recommendation" of religion. Madison also refused during his early years in office to issue calls for Thanksgiving prayer. Later, during the politically contentious War of 1812, he did issue such calls, but he subsequently confessed that his doing so had violated the Constitution. * * * [T]he text, historical antecedents, drafting history, and debate

surrounding the adoption of the Establishment Clause all provide compelling, though perhaps not conclusive, evidence that the clause was intended and originally understood to preclude government preference for particular religions or for religion over nonreligion, as the Court has long understood.

Thomas B. Colby, *A Constitutional Hierarchy of Religions? Justice Scalia, the Ten Commandments, and the Establishment Clause*, 100 Nw. U. L. Rev. 1097 (2006). There remains, in other words, substantial debate about the neutrality rule announced in *Everson*.

After the decision in *Everson*, the Supreme Court struggled to reconcile the neutrality principle with the principle that the government should not use tax funds to support religion. In the following landmark case, the Court attempted to address this difficulty by devising a multi-factor analysis for deciding whether a law violates the Establishment Clause. The case created the so-called ***Lemon* test**, by which the courts consider (1) whether the challenged law has a secular purpose; (2) whether the principal or primary effect of the law is to advance or inhibit religion; and (3) whether the law excessively entangles the government and religion. The *Lemon* test quickly became the operative standard in Establishment Clause cases. In the two and a half decades that followed the decision, about 2000 state and federal cases applied the *Lemon* test. As you read the case, consider whether the test sensibly implements Establishment Clause principles.

LEMON V. KURTZMAN

403 U.S. 602 (1971)

MR. CHIEF JUSTICE BURGER delivered the opinion of the Court.

These two appeals raise questions as to Pennsylvania and Rhode Island statutes providing state aid to church-related elementary and secondary schools. * * * The Rhode Island Salary Supplement Act was enacted in 1969. It rests on the legislative finding that the quality of education available in nonpublic elementary schools has been jeopardized by the rapidly rising salaries needed to attract competent and dedicated teachers. The Act authorizes state officials to supplement the salaries of teachers of secular subjects in nonpublic elementary schools by paying directly to a teacher an amount not in excess of 15% of his current annual salary. As supplemented, however, a nonpublic school teacher's salary cannot exceed the maximum paid to teachers in the State's public schools, and the recipient must be certified by the state board of education in substantially the same manner as public school teachers.

The Pennsylvania Nonpublic Elementary and Secondary Education Act was passed in 1968 in response to a crisis that the Pennsylvania Legislature found existed in the State's nonpublic schools due to rapidly rising costs. * * * The statute authorizes appellee state Superintendent of Public Instruction to "purchase" specified "secular educational services" from nonpublic schools. Under the "contracts" authorized by the statute, the State directly reimburses nonpublic schools solely for their actual expenditures for teachers' salaries, textbooks, and instructional materials. A school seeking reimbursement must maintain prescribed accounting procedures that identify the "separate" cost of the "secular educational service." * * * Reimbursement is limited to courses "presented in the curricula of the public schools." It is further limited "solely" to courses in the following "secular" subjects: mathematics, modern foreign languages, physical science, and physical education. Textbooks and instructional materials included in the program must be approved by the state Superintendent of Public Instruction. Finally, the statute prohibits reimbursement for any course that contains "any subject matter expressing religious teaching, or the morals or forms of worship of any sect."

> **Food for Thought**
>
> Before reading further, ask yourself how you would attempt to defend these programs based on the principles announced in *Everson v. Board of Education*. In what way were Rhode Island and Pennsylvania arguably acting neutrally in supplementing or reimbursing the teachers' salaries? Even if the laws were neutral, was there anything else wrong with them?

Candor compels acknowledgment [that] we can only dimly perceive the lines of demarcation in this extraordinarily sensitive area of constitutional law. The language of the Religion Clauses of the First Amendment is at best opaque, particularly when compared with other portions of the Amendment. Its authors did not simply prohibit the establishment of a state church or a state religion, an area history shows they regarded as very important and fraught with great dangers. Instead they commanded that there should be "no law respecting an establishment of religion." A law may be one "respecting" the forbidden objective while falling short of its total realization. * * * A given law might not establish a state religion but nevertheless be one "respecting" that end in the sense of being a step that could lead to such establishment and hence offend the First Amendment.

In the absence of precisely stated constitutional prohibitions, we must draw lines with reference to the three main evils against which the Establishment Clause was intended to afford protection: "sponsorship, financial support, and active involvement of the sovereign in religious activity." *Walz v. Tax Commission*, 397 U.S. 664, 668 (1970).

Every analysis in this area must begin with consideration of the cumulative criteria developed by the Court over many years. Three such tests may be gleaned from our cases. First, the statute must have a secular legislative purpose; second, its principal or primary effect must be one that neither advances nor inhibits religion, *Board of Education v. Allen*, 392 U.S. 236, 243 (1968); finally, the statute must not foster "an excessive government entanglement with religion." *Walz, supra*, at 674.

Inquiry into the legislative purposes of the Pennsylvania and Rhode Island statutes affords no basis for a conclusion that the legislative intent was to advance religion. On the contrary, the statutes themselves clearly state that they are intended to enhance the quality of the secular education in all schools covered by the compulsory attendance laws. There is no reason to believe the legislatures meant anything else. A State always has a legitimate concern for maintaining minimum standards in all schools it allows to operate. * * * The legislatures of Rhode Island and Pennsylvania have concluded that secular and religious education are identifiable and separable. In the abstract we have no quarrel with this conclusion.

The two legislatures, however, have also recognized that church-related elementary and secondary schools have a significant religious mission and that a substantial portion of their activities is religiously oriented. They have therefore sought to create statutory restrictions designed to guarantee the separation between secular and religious educational functions and to ensure that State financial aid supports only the former. * * * We need not decide whether these legislative precautions restrict the principal or primary effect of the programs to the point where they do not offend the Religion Clauses, for we conclude that the cumulative impact of the entire relationship arising under the statutes in each State involves excessive entanglement between government and religion.

In order to determine whether the government entanglement with religion is excessive, we must examine the character and purposes of the institutions that are benefited, the nature of the aid that the State provides, and the resulting relationship between the government and the religious authority. Mr. Justice Harlan, in a separate opinion in *Walz*, echoed the classic warning as to "programs, whose very nature is apt to entangle the state in details of administration." Here we find that both statutes foster an impermissible degree of entanglement.

The church schools involved in the program are located close to parish churches. This understandably permits convenient access for religious exercises since instruction in faith and morals is part of the total educational process. The school buildings contain identifying religious symbols such as crosses on the exterior and crucifixes, and religious paintings and statutes either in the classrooms or hallways. Although only approximately 30 minutes a day are devoted to direct religious instruction, there are religiously oriented extracurricular activities. Approximately two-thirds of the teachers in these schools are nuns of various religious orders. Their dedicated efforts provide an atmosphere in which religious instruction and religious vocations are natural and proper parts of life in such schools. * * *

The dangers and corresponding entanglements are enhanced by the particular form of aid that the Rhode Island Act provides. * * * The Rhode Island Roman Catholic elementary schools are under the general supervision of the Bishop of Providence and his appointed representative, the Diocesan Superintendent of Schools. In most cases, each individual parish, however, assumes the ultimate financial responsibility for the school, with the parish priest authorizing the allocation of parish funds. * * * Religious authority necessarily pervades the school system.

The schools are governed by the standards set forth in a "Handbook of School Regulations," which has the force of synodal law in the diocese. It emphasizes the role and importance of the teacher in parochial schools: "The prime factor for the success or the failure of the school is the spirit and personality, as well as the professional competency, of the teacher . . . ." The Handbook also states that: "Religious formation is not confined to formal courses; nor is it restricted to a single subject area." Finally, the Handbook advises teachers to stimulate interest in religious vocations and missionary work. Given the mission of the church school, these instructions are consistent and logical.

We need not and do not assume that teachers in parochial schools will be guilty of bad faith or any conscious design to evade the limitations imposed by the statute and the First Amendment. We simply recognize that a dedicated religious person, teaching in a school affiliated with his or her faith and operated to inculcate its tenets, will inevitably experience great difficulty in remaining religiously neutral. Doctrines and faith are not inculcated or advanced by neutrals. With the best of intentions such a teacher would find it hard to make a total separation between secular teaching and religious doctrine. What would appear to some to be essential to good citizenship might well for others border on or constitute instruction in religion. Further difficulties are inherent in the combination of religious discipline and the possibility of disagreement between teacher and religious authorities over the meaning of the statutory restrictions.

There is another area of entanglement in the Rhode Island program that gives concern. The statute excludes teachers employed by nonpublic schools whose average per-pupil expenditures on secular education equal or exceed the comparable figures for public schools. In the event that the total expenditures of an otherwise eligible school exceed this norm, the program requires the government to examine the school's records in order to determine how much of the total expenditures is attributable to secular education and how much to religious activity. This kind of state inspection and evaluation of the religious content of a religious organization is fraught with the sort of entanglement that the Constitution forbids. It is a relationship pregnant with dangers of excessive government direction of church schools and hence of churches. [W]e cannot ignore here the danger that pervasive modern governmental power will ultimately intrude on religion and thus conflict with the Religion Clauses.

> **Food for Thought**
>
> Who is the "separation" between church and state designed to benefit? Those who practice minority religions or no religion at all? Those who follow the dominant religion (or one of the dominant religions)? Religious institutions themselves? Or is it designed to protect all of them? What does the Court's analysis here suggest about this question?

The Pennsylvania statute also provides state aid to church-related schools for teachers' salaries. The complaint describes an educational system that is very similar to the one existing in Rhode Island. According to the allegations, the church-related elementary and secondary schools are controlled by religious organizations, have the purpose of propagating and promoting a particular religious faith, and conduct their operations to fulfill that purpose. Since this complaint was dismissed for failure to state a claim for relief, we must accept these allegations as true for purposes of our review.

> **Take Note**
>
> A plaintiff initiates a lawsuit by filing a complaint. The complaint alleges the facts that support the plaintiff's legal claim against the defendant. The defendant sometimes responds by asking the court to dismiss the complaint for "failure to state a claim." The defendant essentially argues that even if the facts that the plaintiff has alleged are true (which the defendant does not necessarily admit), they do not establish any legal liability. When a court evaluates such a motion by the defendant, the court assumes that the plaintiff could prove all the facts.

As we noted earlier, the very restrictions and surveillance necessary to ensure that teachers play a strictly non-ideological role give rise to entanglements between church and state. The Pennsylvania statute, like that of Rhode Island, fosters this kind of relationship. Reimbursement is not only limited to courses offered in the public schools and materials approved by state officials, but the statute excludes "any subject matter expressing religious teaching, or the morals or forms of worship of any sect." In addition, schools seeking reimbursement must maintain accounting procedures that require the State to establish the cost of the secular as distinguished from the religious instruction.

The Pennsylvania statute, moreover, has the further defect of providing state financial aid directly to the church-related schools. This factor distinguishes both *Everson* and *Allen*, for in both those cases the Court was careful to point out that state aid was provided to the student and his parents—not to the church-related school.

> **FYI**
>
> In *Allen*, the Court upheld a New York law that required school districts to purchase textbooks and to loan them to students enrolled in public, private, and parochial schools.

In *Walz*, the Court warned of the dangers of direct payments to religious organizations:

> Obviously a direct money subsidy would be a relationship pregnant with involvement and, as with most governmental grant programs, could encompass sustained and detailed administrative relationships for enforcement of statutory or administrative standards * * *.

A broader base of entanglement of yet a different character is presented by the divisive political potential of these state programs. In a community where such a large number of pupils are served by church-related schools, it can be assumed that state assistance will entail considerable political activity. Partisans of parochial schools, understandably concerned with rising costs and sincerely dedicated to both the religious and secular educational missions of their schools, will inevitably champion this cause and promote political action to achieve their goals. Those who oppose state aid, whether for constitutional, religious, or fiscal reasons, will inevitably respond and employ all of the usual political campaign techniques to prevail. Candidates will be forced to declare and voters to choose. It would be unrealistic to ignore the fact that many people confronted with issues of this kind will find their votes aligned with their faith. * * * The potential for political divisiveness related to religious belief and practice is aggravated in these two statutory programs by the need for continuing annual appropriations and the likelihood of larger and larger demands as costs and populations grow.

Finally, nothing we have said can be construed to disparage the role of church-related elementary and secondary schools in our national life. Their contribution has been and is enormous. Nor do we ignore their economic plight in a period of rising costs and expanding need. Taxpayers generally have been spared vast sums by the maintenance of these educational institutions by religious organizations, largely by the gifts of faithful adherents.

The merit and benefits of these schools, however, are not the issue before us in these cases. The sole question is whether state aid to these schools can be squared with the dictates of the Religion Clauses. Under our system the choice has been made that government is to be entirely excluded from the area of religious instruction and churches excluded from the affairs of government. The Constitution decrees that religion must be a private matter for the individual, the family, and the institutions of private choice, and that while some involvement and entanglement are inevitable, lines must be drawn.

POINTS FOR DISCUSSION

a.   Understanding the *Lemon* Test

The Court described three factors for deciding whether a government action (including a policy or statute) violates the Establishment Clause. The first factor is whether the action has a secular (i.e., non-religious) legislative purpose. In *Everson*, the purpose of reimbursing transportation fares was to enable children to travel to school where they could be educated. Phrased as such, the policy appeared to have a secular purpose. (Can you think of a way to characterize the purpose of the policy that suggests that it was not entirely secular?) By contrast, if a city announced that it would subsidize bus fares to services at a church, mosque, or synagogue, it seems clear that the policy would not have a secular purpose.

The second factor asks whether the principal or primary effect of the policy is one that neither advances nor inhibits religion. In *Board of Education v. Allen*, 392 U.S. 236 (1968), cited in *Lemon*, the Court upheld a New York statute requiring school districts to loan textbooks to all students, regardless of whether they were enrolled in public or private schools, including private parochial schools. The Court there explained: "The express purpose of [the statute] was stated by the New York Legislature to be furtherance of the educational opportunities available to the young. Appellants have shown us nothing about the necessary effects of the statute that is contrary to its stated purpose. The law merely makes available to all children the benefits of a general program to lend school books free of charge." *Id.* at 243. Should the Court simply defer to such a statement of legislative purpose? How would this factor have been applied if the New York statute had required school districts to buy and distribute Bibles to all school children? (Would it have mattered in which class— say, history or theology—the students were using the Bibles?)

The third factor asks whether the statute fosters "an excessive government entanglement with religion." In *Walz v. Tax Commission*, 397 U.S. 664 (1970), the Court upheld a New York law that provided a tax exemption for property used exclusively for religious purposes. The Court observed that any tax policy would entangle government and churches to some extent. Without the exemption, the government would benefit fiscally from the churches; with the exemption, the government might have to monitor the use of the property to ensure that the exemption was properly claimed. The Court said: "In analyzing either alternative the questions are whether the involvement is excessive, and whether it is a continuing one calling for official and continuing surveillance leading to an impermissible degree of entanglement." The Court ultimately concluded that the entanglement was not excessive: "The exemption creates only a minimal and remote involvement between church and state and far less than taxation of churches." How can a Court determine what counts as "excessive" in this context?

b. Criticism of the *Lemon* Test

Critics maintain that the *Lemon* test is problematic for two reasons. First, the parts of the test are rather vague and open-ended. For example, how does a court know when governmental entanglement with religion is "excessive"? And how does the Court determine whether the "principal" or "primary" effect of a policy is to advance or inhibit religion, when most controversial policies have both secular and religious implications? Second, perhaps even more troubling, the second and third factors tend in practice to point in opposite directions. Dean Jesse Choper elaborates on this problem in the context of aid to religious schools:

> The Court began with a critical premise: the mission of church related elementary and secondary schools is to teach religion, and all subjects either are, or carry the potential of being, permeated with religion. Therefore, if the government were to help fund any subjects in these schools, the effect would aid religion unless public officials monitored the situation to see to it that those courses were not infused with religious doctrine. But if public officials did engage in adequate surveillance—this is the other horn of the dilemma—there would be excessive entanglement between government and religion, the image being government spies regularly or periodically sitting in the classes conducted in parochial schools.

Jesse H. Choper, *The Establishment Clause and Aid to Parochial Schools—An Update*, 75 Cal. L. Rev. 5 (1987). Does this suggest that the Court should abandon the *Lemon* test? Or is ambiguity and nuance inevitable in this area of the law, given the Court's adherence both to the principle that the government should not spend tax money to support religion and to the neutrality principle?

c. The Elusive Death of the *Lemon* Test

Criticism of the *Lemon* test seems to have influenced the Supreme Court. In the last few decades, the Supreme Court did not consistently follow the *Lemon* test. In *Lee v. Weisman*, 505 U.S. 577, 586–587 (1992), which we consider below, the Supreme

Court declined to apply the *Lemon* test in determining whether a clergyman's benediction at a high school graduation violated the Establishment Clause. But the following year, in *Lamb's Chapel v. Center Moriches Union Free School Dist.*, 508 U.S. 384 (1993), the Court applied the test to determine whether allowing a church to use school facilities for showing a film violated the Establishment Clause. The citation of *Lemon* caused Justice Scalia to write the following statement in his concurrence in the judgment:

> Like some ghoul in a late-night horror movie that repeatedly sits up in its grave and shuffles abroad, after being repeatedly killed and buried, *Lemon* stalks our Establishment Clause jurisprudence once again, frightening the little children and school attorneys of Center Moriches Union Free School District. Its most recent burial, only last Term, was, to be sure, not fully six feet under: Our decision in *Lee v. Weisman*, 505 U.S. 577, 586–587 (1992), conspicuously avoided using the supposed "test" but also declined the invitation to repudiate it. Over the years, however, no fewer than five of the currently sitting Justices have, in their own opinions, personally driven pencils through the creature's heart (the author of today's opinion repeatedly), and a sixth has joined an opinion doing so.
>
> The secret of the *Lemon* test's survival, I think, is that it is so easy to kill. It is there to scare us (and our audience) when we wish it to do so, but we can command it to return to the tomb at will. When we wish to strike down a practice it forbids, we invoke it, see, *e.g., Aguilar v. Felton*, 473 U.S. 402 (1985) (striking down state remedial education program administered in part in parochial schools); when we wish to uphold a practice it forbids, we ignore it entirely, see *Marsh v. Chambers*, 463 U.S. 783 (1983) (upholding state legislative chaplains). Sometimes, we take a middle course, calling its three prongs "no more than helpful signposts," *Hunt v. McNair*, 413 U.S. 734, 741 (1973). Such a docile and useful monster is worth keeping around, at least in a somnolent state; one never knows when one might need him.

In Justice Scalia's view, what is most problematic about the *Lemon* test? Is it the way that the Court has applied it? Or is it the test itself?

In *American Legion v. American Humanist Ass'n.*, 139 S.Ct. 2067 (2019), which we consider later in this chapter, a majority of the Justices concluded that the *Lemon* test should be discarded in the context of religious displays and symbols on government property, and some Justices wrote separately to urge the Court to abandon the *Lemon* test in all contexts. The Court has not addressed the applicability of the *Lemon* test in cases involving funding of religious organizations since its decision in *American Legion*.

The *Lemon* test did not resolve the tension between the competing principles that the Court announced in *Everson*, but instead merely incorporated it. (Notice that a law violates the second prong of the test if its principal or primary effect is *either* to "advance *or* inhibit religion.") It thus is unsurprising that in the years after the decision in *Lemon*, the Court continued to struggle with challenges to government policies that conferred financial benefits on religious institutions. For example, in *Mueller v. Allen*, 463 U.S. 388 (1983), the Court considered the constitutionality of a Minnesota law that permitted taxpayers to deduct expenses incurred for tuition, textbooks, and transportation for the education of their children. Because the law permitted parents to deduct (among other things) the cost of tuition and other expenses incurred in sending children to private religious schools, it had the practical effect of conferring a financial benefit on those schools. The Court, however, applied the *Lemon* test and upheld the law. The Court concluded that the primary effect of the policy was not to advance "the sectarian aims of the nonpublic schools." The Court stressed that the deduction was "available for educational expenses incurred by *all* parents, including those whose children attend public schools and those whose children attend non-sectarian private schools or sectarian private schools." In addition, the Court reasoned that "by channeling whatever assistance it may provide to parochial schools through individual parents, Minnesota has reduced the Establishment Clause objections to which its action is subject," because "under Minnesota's arrangement public funds become available only as a result of numerous, private choices of individual parents of school-age children." Justice Marshall, joined by three others, dissented, asserting that the Establishment Clause "prohibits a State from subsidizing religious education, whether it does so directly or indirectly," and thus forbids "any tax benefit, including the tax deduction at issue here, which subsidizes tuition payments to sectarian schools."

Twelve years later, in *Rosenberger v. Rector and Visitors of the University of Virginia*, 515 U.S. 819 (1995), the Court considered a public university's refusal to use funds derived from student activities fees to pay printing costs for the newspaper of an evangelical Christian

> **Make the Connection**
>
> We briefly considered the Court's decision in *Rosenberger*, and its view of the freedom of speech, in Chapter 8.

student group, Wide Awake Productions ("WAP"), even though the University authorized payment for printing costs for other student-authored publications. WAP challenged the exclusion as a violation of its freedom of speech. The state defended the exclusion on the ground that it would violate the Establishment Clause to use the funds, which it said were tantamount to tax revenues, to support sectarian proselytizing. The Court rejected this claim and held that the exclusion constituted impermissible viewpoint discrimination in violation of WAP's freedom of speech.

Writing for the Court, Justice Kennedy stated:

The governmental program here is neutral toward religion. There is no suggestion that the University created it to advance religion or adopted some ingenious device with the purpose of aiding a religious cause. The object of the [student activities fund] is to open a forum for speech and to support various student enterprises, including the publication of newspapers, in recognition of the diversity and creativity of student life. * * * The neutrality of the program distinguishes the student fees from a tax levied for the direct support of a church or group of churches.

Government neutrality is apparent in the State's overall scheme in a further meaningful respect. * * * The University has taken pains to disassociate itself from the private speech involved in this case. * * * We do not confront a case where, even under a neutral program that includes nonsectarian recipients, the government is making direct money payments to an institution or group that is engaged in religious activity. * * * It does not violate the Establishment Clause for a public university to grant access to its facilities on a religion-neutral basis to a wide spectrum of student groups * * *. There is no difference in logic or principle, and no difference of constitutional significance, between a school using its funds to operate a facility to which students have access, and a school paying a third-party contractor to operate the facility on its behalf. The latter occurs here. * * * [Moreover, by] paying outside printers, the University in fact attains a further degree of separation from the student publication, for it avoids the duties of supervision, escapes the costs of upkeep, repair, and replacement attributable to student use, and has a clear record of costs.

Justice Souter, joined by Justices Stevens, Ginsburg, and Breyer, dissented. He would have concluded that providing funds to the religious student group to publish its newspaper would violate the Establishment Clause, and thus that the University was justified in withholding its funds. Justice Souter noted that WAP's newspaper contained "nothing other than the preaching of the word, which (along with the sacraments) is what most branches of Christianity offer those called to the religious life." He then declared, "Using public funds for the direct subsidization of preaching the word is categorically forbidden under the Establishment Clause, and if the Clause was meant to accomplish nothing else, it was meant to bar this use of public money." Justice Souter reasoned that the mere fact that a funding program is neutral, "in the formal sense that it makes funds available on an evenhanded basis to secular and sectarian applicants alike, * * * does not alone satisfy the requirements of the Establishment Clause. * * * [W]henever affirmative government aid ultimately benefits religion, the Establishment Clause requires some justification beyond evenhandedness on the government's part * * *." He then sought to explain the relative importance of the separation principle and the neutrality principle:

> [T]he relationship between the prohibition on direct aid and the requirement of evenhandedness when affirmative government aid does result in some benefit to religion reflects the relationship between basic rule and marginal criterion. At the heart of the Establishment Clause stands the prohibition against direct public funding, but that prohibition does not answer the questions that occur at the margins of the Clause's application. Is any government activity that provides any incidental benefit to religion likewise unconstitutional? Would it be wrong to put out fires in burning churches, wrong to pay the bus fares of students on the way to parochial schools, wrong to allow a grantee of special education funds to spend them at a religious college? These are the questions that call for drawing lines, and it is in drawing them that evenhandedness becomes important. However the Court may in the past have phrased its line-drawing test, the question whether such benefits are provided on an evenhanded basis has been relevant, for the question addresses one aspect of the issue whether a law is truly neutral with respect to religion (that is, whether the law either "advance[s] [or] inhibit[s] religion." * * * In the doubtful cases (those not involving direct public funding), where there is initially room for argument about a law's effect, evenhandedness serves to weed out those laws that impermissibly advance religion by channelling aid to it exclusively. Evenhandedness is therefore a prerequisite to further enquiry into the constitutionality of a doubtful law, but evenhandedness goes no further. It does not guarantee success under Establishment Clause scrutiny.

Justice Souter also disagreed with the Court's suggestion that funding for WAP's publication was permissible because the University paid the funds directly to the printer: "The formalism of distinguishing between payment to Wide Awake so it can pay an approved bill and payment of the approved bill itself cannot be the basis of a decision of constitutional law. If this indeed were a critical distinction, the Constitution would permit a State to pay all the bills of any religious institution * * *."

The decisions in *Mueller* and *Rosenberger* suggest that the Court has increasingly relied on the neutrality principle over the "no support" (or separation) principle. That trend continued in the case that follows, one of the Court's most important recent decisions about the limits that the Establishment Clause imposes on the ability of government to provide aid that benefits religious institutions. The case involved the constitutionality of a program providing parents with vouchers that could be used to cover the cost of tuition at private schools, including religious schools. As you read the case, consider what it suggests about the Court's likely approach in the future to questions that arise in this area.

ZELMAN V. SIMMONS-HARRIS
536 U.S. 639 (2002)

CHIEF JUSTICE REHNQUIST delivered the opinion of the Court.

There are more than 75,000 children enrolled in the Cleveland City School District. The majority of these children are from low-income and minority families. Few of these families enjoy the means to send their children to any school other than an inner-city public school. For more than a generation, however, Cleveland's public schools have been among the worst performing public schools in the Nation. * * * It is against this backdrop that Ohio enacted, among other initiatives, its Pilot Project Scholarship Program, Ohio Rev. Code Ann. §§ 3313.974–3313.979. * * * The program [provides] tuition aid for students in kindergarten through third grade, expanding each year through eighth grade, to attend a participating public or private school of their parent's choosing. * * * Any private school, whether religious or nonreligious, may participate in the program and accept program students so long as the school is located within the boundaries of a covered district and meets statewide educational standards. * * * Any public school located in a school district adjacent to the covered district may also participate in the program [and is] eligible to receive a $2,250 tuition grant for each program student accepted in addition to the full amount of per-pupil state funding attributable to each additional student. * * * Tuition aid is distributed to parents according to financial need. * * * If parents choose a private school, checks are made payable to the parents who then endorse the checks over to the chosen school. § 3313.979.

The program has been in operation within the Cleveland City School District since the 1996–1997 school year. In the 1999–2000 school year, 56 private schools participated in the program, 46 (or 82%) of which had a religious affiliation. None of the public schools in districts adjacent to Cleveland have elected to participate. More than 3,700 students participated in the scholarship program, most of whom

(96%) enrolled in religiously affiliated schools. [Ohio taxpayers filed this suit seeking to enjoin the program on the ground that it violated the Establishment Clause.]

The Establishment Clause of the First Amendment, applied to the States through the Fourteenth Amendment, prevents a State from enacting laws that have the "purpose" or "effect" of advancing or inhibiting religion. *Agostini v. Felton,* 521 U.S. 203, 222–223 (1997). There is no dispute that the program challenged here was enacted for the valid secular purpose of providing educational assistance to poor children in a demonstrably failing public school system. Thus, the question presented is whether the Ohio program nonetheless has the forbidden "effect" of advancing or inhibiting religion.

To answer that question, our decisions have drawn a consistent distinction between government programs that provide aid directly to religious schools and programs of true private choice, in which government aid reaches religious schools only as a result of the genuine and independent choices of private individuals. * * * Three times we have confronted Establishment Clause challenges to neutral government programs that provide aid directly to a broad class of individuals, who, in turn, direct the aid to religious schools or institutions of their own choosing. Three times we have rejected such challenges.

> **Take Note**
>
> The Court's statement of the test under the Establishment Clause omits the third prong of the *Lemon* test—whether the challenged policy fosters an excessive entanglement between church and state. In *Agostini,* a five-Justice majority treated this factor as an aspect of the inquiry into the second factor—the effects of the challenged policy. Do you agree with the Court's reasoning in that case that the considerations relevant to assessing whether an entanglement is "excessive" are similar to the considerations used to determine the challenged policy's "effect"?

In *Mueller v. Allen,* 463 U.S. 388 (1983), we rejected an Establishment Clause challenge to a Minnesota program authorizing tax deductions for various educational expenses, including private school tuition costs, even though the great majority of the program's beneficiaries (96%) were parents of children in religious schools. We began by focusing on the class of beneficiaries, [which] included "*all* parents," including parents with "children [who] attend nonsectarian private schools or sectarian private schools," 463 U.S., at 397. * * * Then, viewing the program as a whole, we emphasized the principle of private choice, noting that public funds were made available to religious schools "only as a result of numerous, private choices of individual parents of school-age children." 463 U.S., at 399–400. [We] thus found it irrelevant to the constitutional inquiry that the vast majority of beneficiaries were parents of children in religious schools * * *.

In *Witters v. Washington Dept. of Servs. for Blind,* 474 U.S. 481 (1986), we used identical reasoning to reject an Establishment Clause challenge to a vocational scholarship program that provided tuition aid to a student studying at a religious institution to become a pastor. * * * Finally, in *Zobrest v. Catalina Foothills School Dist.,* 509 U.S. 1 (1993), we applied *Mueller* and *Witters* to reject an Establishment Clause challenge to a federal program that permitted sign-language interpreters to assist deaf children enrolled in religious schools.

Mueller, Witters, and *Zobrest* thus make clear that where a government aid program is neutral with respect to religion, and provides assistance directly to a broad class of citizens who, in turn, direct government aid to religious schools wholly as a result of their own genuine and independent private choice, the program is not readily subject to challenge under the Establishment Clause. A program that shares these features permits government aid to reach religious institutions only by way of the deliberate choices of numerous individual recipients. The incidental advancement of a religious mission, or the perceived endorsement of a religious message, is reasonably attributable to the individual recipient, not to the government, whose role ends with the disbursement of benefits. * * * It is precisely for these reasons that we have never found a program of true private choice to offend the Establishment Clause.

We believe that the program challenged here is a program of true private choice [and] thus constitutional. [The] Ohio program is neutral in all respects toward religion. It is part of a general and multifaceted undertaking by the State of Ohio to provide educational opportunities to the children of a failed school district. It confers educational assistance directly to a broad class of individuals defined without reference to religion, *i.e.,* any parent of a school-age child who resides in the Cleveland City School District. The program permits the participation of *all* schools within the district, religious or nonreligious. Adjacent public schools also may participate and have a financial incentive to do so. Program benefits are available to participating families on neutral terms, with no reference to religion.

There are no "financial incentives" that "skew" the program toward religious schools. * * * The program here in fact creates financial *dis*incentives for religious schools, with private schools receiving only half the government assistance given to community schools and one-third the assistance given to magnet schools. Adjacent public schools, should any choose to accept program students, are also eligible to receive two to three times the state funding of a private religious school. [In addition, parents] that choose to participate in the scholarship program and then to enroll their children in a private school (religious or nonreligious) must copay a portion of the school's tuition. Families that choose a community school, magnet school, or traditional public school pay nothing. Although such features of the program are not necessary to its constitutionality, they clearly dispel the claim that the program "creates [financial] incentives for parents to choose a sectarian school." *Zobrest,* 509 U.S., at 10.

Food for Thought

As the Court noted, over 80% of the private schools participating in the challenged program had a religious affiliation, and over 90% of the students participating used the vouchers to attend religious schools. In light of this fact, can you make an argument that the program was not in fact "neutral" toward religion?

Respondents suggest that even without a financial incentive for parents to choose a religious school, the program creates a "public perception that the State is endorsing religious practices and beliefs." But [no] reasonable observer would think a neutral program of private choice, where state aid reaches religious schools solely as a result of the numerous independent decisions of private individuals, carries with it the *imprimatur* of government endorsement. * * * Any objective observer familiar with the full history and context of the Ohio program would reasonably view it as one aspect of a broader undertaking to assist poor children in failed schools, not as an endorsement of religious schooling in general.

There also is no evidence that the program fails to provide genuine opportunities for Cleveland parents to select secular educational options for their school-age children. Cleveland schoolchildren enjoy a range of educational choices: They may remain in public school as before, remain in public school with publicly funded tutoring aid, obtain a scholarship and choose a religious school, obtain a scholarship and choose a nonreligious private school, enroll in a community school, or enroll in a magnet school. That 46 of the 56 private schools now participating in the program are religious schools does not condemn it as a violation of the Establishment Clause.

Justice SOUTER speculates that because more private religious schools currently participate in the program, the program itself must somehow discourage the participation of private nonreligious schools. * * * It is true that 82% of Cleveland's participating private schools are religious schools, but it is also true that 81% of private schools in Ohio are religious schools. To attribute constitutional significance to this figure, moreover, would lead to the absurd result that a neutral school-choice program might be permissible in some parts of Ohio, such as Columbus, where a lower percentage of private schools are religious schools, but not in inner-city Cleveland, where Ohio has deemed such programs most sorely needed, but where the preponderance of religious schools happens to be greater.

Respondents and Justice SOUTER claim that even if we do not focus on the number of participating schools that are religious schools, we should attach constitutional significance to the fact that 96% of scholarship recipients have enrolled in religious schools. [But the] constitutionality of a neutral educational aid program simply does not turn on whether and why, in a particular area, at a particular time, most private schools are run by religious organizations, or most recipients choose to use the aid at a religious school. [In any event, the] 96% figure upon which respondents and Justice SOUTER rely discounts entirely (1) the more than 1,900 Cleveland children enrolled in alternative community schools, (2) the more than 13,000 children enrolled in alternative magnet schools, and (3) the more than 1,400 children enrolled in traditional public schools with tutorial assistance. Including some or all of these children in the denominator of children enrolled in nontraditional schools during the 1999–2000 school year drops the percentage enrolled in religious schools from 96% to under 20%.

In sum, the Ohio program is entirely neutral with respect to religion. It provides benefits directly to a wide spectrum of individuals, defined only by financial need and residence in a particular school district. It permits such individuals to exercise genuine choice among options public and private, secular and religious. The program is therefore a program of true private choice. In keeping with an unbroken line of decisions rejecting challenges to similar programs, we hold that the program does not offend the Establishment Clause.

JUSTICE O'CONNOR, concurring.

These cases are different from prior indirect aid cases in part because a significant portion of the funds appropriated for the voucher program reach religious schools without restrictions on the use of these funds. The share of public resources that reach religious schools is not, however, as significant as respondents suggest. * * * Even if one assumes that all voucher students came from low-income families and that each voucher student used up the entire $2,250 voucher, at most $8.2 million of public funds flowed to religious schools under the voucher program in 1999–2000. [In contrast,] the State spent over $1 million more—$9.4 million—on students in community schools than on students in religious private schools because per-pupil aid to community schools is more than double the per-pupil aid to private schools under the voucher program. Moreover, the amount spent on religious private schools is minor compared to the $114.8 million the State spent on students in the Cleveland magnet schools.

Although $8.2 million is no small sum, it pales in comparison to the amount of funds that federal, state, and local governments already provide religious institutions. Religious organizations may qualify for exemptions from the federal corporate income tax, the corporate income tax in many States, and property taxes in all 50 States * * *. In addition, the Federal Government provides individuals, corporations, trusts, and estates a tax deduction for charitable contributions to qualified religious groups [and] tax credits for educational expenses, many of which are spent on education at religious schools. [These tax policies] confer a significant relative benefit on religious institutions. [In addition, federal] dollars also reach religiously affiliated organizations through public health programs such as Medicare and Medicaid, through educational programs such as the Pell Grant program, and the G.I. Bill of Rights, and through childcare programs * * *. A significant portion of the funds appropriated for these programs reach religiously affiliated institutions, typically without restrictions on its subsequent use. * * * Against this background, the support that the Cleveland voucher program provides religious institutions is neither substantial nor atypical of existing government programs.

> **Food for Thought**
>
> Justice O'Connor suggests here that the program is permissible because the government routinely provides various forms of aid to religious institutions. If in fact the Establishment Clause was designed to prevent such direct aid, is it convincing to note that the government has been systematically engaged in the provision of such aid?

There is little question in my mind that the Cleveland voucher program is neutral as between religious schools and nonreligious schools. * * * In looking at the voucher program, all the choices available to potential beneficiaries of the government program should be considered. * * * That inquiry requires an evaluation of all reasonable educational options Ohio provides the Cleveland school system, regardless of whether they are formally made available in the same section of the Ohio Code as the voucher program. * * * I am persuaded that the Cleveland voucher program affords parents of eligible children genuine nonreligious options and is consistent with the Establishment Clause.

[JUSTICE THOMAS's concurring opinion is omitted.]

JUSTICE SOUTER, with whom JUSTICE STEVENS, JUSTICE GINSBURG, and JUSTICE BREYER join, dissenting.

The applicability of the Establishment Clause to public funding of benefits to religious schools was settled in *Everson v. Board of Ed. of Ewing*, 330 U.S. 1 (1947), which inaugurated the modern era of establishment doctrine. The Court stated the principle in words from which there was no dissent: "No tax in any amount, large or small, can be levied to support any religious activities or institutions, whatever they may be called, or whatever form they may adopt to teach or practice religion." The Court has never in so many words repudiated this statement, let alone, in so many words, overruled *Everson*.

Today, however, the majority holds that the Establishment Clause is not offended by Ohio's Pilot Project Scholarship Program, under which students may be eligible to receive as much as $2,250 in the form of tuition vouchers transferable to religious schools. In the city of Cleveland the overwhelming proportion of large appropriations for voucher money must be spent on religious schools if it is to be spent at all, and will be spent in amounts that cover almost all of tuition. The money will thus pay for eligible students' instruction not only in secular subjects but in religion as well, in schools that can fairly be characterized as founded to teach religious doctrine and to imbue teaching in all subjects with a religious dimension. Public tax money will pay at a systemic level for teaching the covenant with Israel and Mosaic law in Jewish schools, the primacy of the Apostle Peter and the Papacy in Catholic schools, the truth of reformed Christianity in Protestant schools, and the revelation to the Prophet in Muslim schools, to speak only of major religious groupings in the Republic. * * * It is only by ignoring *Everson* that the majority can claim to rest on traditional law in its invocation of neutral aid provisions and private choice to sanction the Ohio law. It is, moreover, only by ignoring the meaning of neutrality and private choice themselves that the majority can even pretend to rest today's decision on those criteria.

Neutrality in this sense refers, of course, to evenhandedness in setting eligibility as between potential religious and secular recipients of public money. * * * In order to apply the neutrality test, then, it makes sense to focus on a category of aid that may be directed to religious as well as secular schools, and ask whether the scheme favors a religious direction. Here, one would ask whether the voucher provisions, allowing for as much as $2,250 toward private school tuition (or a grant to a public school in an adjacent district), were written in a way that skewed the scheme toward benefiting religious schools. * * * This, however, is not what the majority asks. The majority looks not to the provisions for tuition vouchers, but to every provision for educational opportunity. * * * The illogic is patent. [T]he majority's reasoning would find neutrality in a scheme of vouchers available for private tuition in districts with no secular private schools at all. "Neutrality" as the majority employs the term is, literally, verbal and nothing more.

The majority addresses the issue of choice the same way it addresses neutrality, by asking whether recipients or potential recipients of voucher aid have a choice of public schools among secular alternatives to religious schools. [But the] majority's view that all educational choices are comparable for purposes of choice [ignores] the whole point of the choice test: it is a criterion for deciding whether indirect aid to a religious school is legitimate because it passes through private hands that can spend or use the aid in a secular school. The question is whether the private hand is genuinely free to send the money in either a secular direction or a religious one. The majority now has transformed this question about private choice in channeling aid into a question about selecting from examples of state spending (on education) including direct spending on magnet and community public schools that goes through no private hands and could never reach a religious school under any circumstance. When the choice test is transformed from where to spend the money to where to go to school, it is cut loose from its very purpose. [I]f the majority wishes to claim that choice is a criterion, it must define choice in a way that can function as a criterion with a practical capacity to screen something out.

If, contrary to the majority, we ask the right question about genuine choice to use the vouchers, the answer shows that something is influencing choices in a way that aims the money in a religious direction * * *. Evidence shows [that] almost two out of three families using vouchers to send their children to religious schools did not embrace the religion of those schools. The families made it clear they had not chosen the schools because they wished their children to be proselytized in a religion not their own, or in any religion, but because of educational opportunity. * * * The [fact that] 96.6% [of students participating in the program enrolled in religious schools] reflects [the] fact that too few nonreligious school desks are available and few but religious schools can afford to accept more than a handful of voucher students. [For] the overwhelming number of children in the voucher scheme, the only alternative to the public schools is religious.

I do not dissent merely because the majority has misapplied its own law, for even if I assumed *arguendo* that the majority's formal criteria were satisfied on the facts, today's conclusion would be profoundly at odds with the Constitution. * * * [First, the] scale of the aid to religious schools approved today is unprecedented, both in the number of dollars and in the proportion of systemic school expenditure supported. * * * [The] majority makes no pretense that substantial amounts of tax money are not systematically underwriting religious practice and indoctrination.

[Second,] every objective underlying the prohibition of religious establishment is betrayed by this scheme * * *. [The first, respect for freedom of conscience,] has simply been lost in the majority's formalism. As for the second objective, to save religion from its own corruption, Madison wrote of the "experience [that] ecclesiastical establishments, instead of maintaining the purity and efficacy of Religion, have had a contrary operation." Memorial and Remonstrance ¶ 7, reprinted in *Everson,* 330 U.S., at 67. In [the] 21st century, the risk is one of "corrosive secularism" to religious schools, and the specific threat is to the primacy of the schools' mission to educate the children of the faithful according to the unaltered precepts of their faith.

The risk is already being realized. In Ohio, for example, a condition of receiving government money under the program is that participating religious schools may not "discriminate on the basis [of] religion," Ohio Rev. Code Ann. § 3313.976(A)(4), which means the school may not give admission preferences to children who are members of the patron faith; children of a parish are generally consigned to the same admission lotteries as non-believers. * * * Indeed, a separate condition that "[t]he school [not] teach hatred of any person or group on the basis [of] religion," § 3313.976(A)(6), could be understood (or subsequently broadened) to prohibit religions from teaching traditionally legitimate articles of faith as to the error, sinfulness, or ignorance of others, if they want government money for their schools. * * * For perspective on this foot-in-the-door of religious regulation, it is well to remember that the money has barely begun to flow. * * * When government aid goes up, so does reliance on it; the only thing likely to go down is independence. * * * A day will come when religious schools will learn what political leverage can do, just as Ohio's politicians are now getting a lesson in the leverage exercised by religion.

Increased voucher spending is not, however, the sole portent of growing regulation of religious practice in the school, for state mandates to moderate religious teaching may well be the most obvious response to the third concern behind the ban on establishment, its inextricable link with social conflict. *Everson,* 330 U.S., at 8–11. As appropriations for religious subsidy rise, competition for the money will tap sectarian religion's capacity for discord. * * * [I]t is enough to say that the intensity of the expectable friction can be gauged by realizing that the scramble for money will energize not only contending sectarians, but taxpayers who take their liberty of conscience seriously. Religious teaching at taxpayer expense simply cannot be cordoned from taxpayer politics, and every major religion currently espouses social positions that provoke intense opposition. [Such views] have been safe in the sectarian pulpits and classrooms of this Nation not only because the Free Exercise Clause protects them directly, but because the ban on supporting religious establishment has protected free exercise, by keeping it relatively private. With the arrival of vouchers in religious schools, that privacy will go, and along with it will go confidence that religious disagreement will stay moderate.

[The dissenting opinions of JUSTICE BREYER and JUSTICE STEVENS have been omitted.]

POINTS FOR DISCUSSION

a.   The Test for Government Aid to Religious Institutions

After *Zelman*, what is the test for determining the constitutionality of government aid to religious institutions? Is neutrality the rule? If so, how is neutrality determined? What else, if anything, must be true for neutral policies to survive scrutiny? What is the status of the "no support" (or separation) principle?

Did the Court apply the *Lemon* test in *Zelman*? If so, did it apply the same test that we have seen in prior cases? Consider Justice O'Connor's view that the Court's approach involved a "refinement" of the *Lemon* test:

> The Court's opinion in [this case] focuses on a narrow question related to the *Lemon* test: how to apply the primary effects prong in indirect aid cases? * * * What the Court clarifies in [this case] is that the Establishment Clause [requires] that state aid flowing to religious organizations through the hands of beneficiaries must do so only at the direction of those beneficiaries.

Do you agree that this is the import of the Court's decision? If so, do you agree that it represents simply a "refinement" of the *Lemon* test? What did Justice Souter think was the appropriate test?

As noted above, in *American Legion v. American Humanist Association*, 139 S.Ct. 2067 (2019), which we will consider later in this chapter, a majority of the Justices joined opinions asserting that the *Lemon* test is misguided, at least in cases involving religious displays on government property. The Court has not decided a case since *American Legion* involving government financial support for religion or religious organizations.

b.   "True Private Choice"

How important to the Court's conclusion was the ability of the voucher recipients to choose which school to attend? Consider this view:

> *Zelman* represents the most recent and dramatic move away from Separationism. By holding in no uncertain terms that the Cleveland school voucher program satisfies constitutional requirements, the Supreme Court has opened the door for a wide range of relationships, once thought impermissible, between government and religious institutions. The key to these new relationships, the Court held, is the concept of "true," "genuine," and "independent" private choice to partake of services offered by religious entities.

Ira C. Lupu & Robert W. Tuttle, Zelman*'s Future: Vouchers, Sectarian Providers, and the Next Round of Constitutional Battles*, 78 Notre Dame L. Rev. 917 (2003).

Do you agree that the recipients' choice under the challenged program was "genuine"? The Court reasoned that it was genuine because, at least as a formal matter, there were non-religious schools—including community and magnet schools—to which the parents could send their children. But was the parents' choice really unfettered? Again, consider the view of Professors Lupu and Tuttle:

> Parents might prefer School A over School B on grounds of academic quality, value emphasis, and/or physical safety, but prefer B over A because of the religious teaching at A. Parents in such circumstances are squeezed by the set of trade-offs presented to them. The comparative quality or safety of the various schools may generate pressure on parents to send their children to religious schools, calling into question the "genuineness" of their choice of a particular religious element to their child's education. The Court's opinion, however, evinces no concern for their plight.

Is there an argument that the voucher program effectively *coerced* parents—at least, that is, parents hoping to find better educational options for their children—to send their children to religious schools?

Problem

Imagine that Congress recently enacted the "Level Playing Field Act," which provides that "faith-based" providers of social services—such as drug-addiction treatment programs and welfare programs administered by churches and other religious organizations—are eligible to compete for (and receive) federal funds. The Act protects the "right of religious organizations to maintain their religious identities while providing social services" funded by the government and permits those organizations to "provide a preference in hiring to persons who share their religious beliefs." There is no provision in the Act forbidding participating faith-based organizations to engage in religious proselytizing or instruction in the programs funded by the government. A suit has been filed challenging the program under the Establishment Clause. How should the Court rule?

A Note on Standing and Establishment Clause Challenges

We noted in our consideration of *Everson* that the plaintiff had filed the challenge "in his capacity as a district taxpayer." The plaintiff presumably objected to the government's decision to use tax revenues to pay the cost of transportation to religious schools. But is this a cognizable injury under the Court's Article III standing doctrine, which we considered in Volume 1? Recall that the Court has "repeatedly held that an asserted right to have the Government act in accordance with law is not sufficient, standing alone, to confer jurisdiction on a federal court." *Allen v. Wright*, 468 U.S. 737 (1984). In addition, the Court has held that, as a general matter, the interest of a federal taxpayer in seeing that government funds are spent in accordance with the Constitution does not constitute a cognizable "injury in fact." *Frothingham v. Mellon*, 262 U.S. 447, 488 (1923). Should matters be any different when the challenge alleges that government spending violates the Establishment Clause?

In *Flast v. Cohen*, 392 U.S. 83 (1968), the Court held that "a taxpayer will have standing [when] he alleges that congressional action under the taxing and spending clause is in derogation of those constitutional provisions which operate to restrict the exercise of the taxing and spending power." The Court concluded that the Establishment Clause was such a provision:

> Our history vividly illustrates that one of the specific evils feared by those who drafted the Establishment Clause and fought for its adoption was that the taxing and spending power would be used to favor one religion over another or to support religion in general. * * * The Establishment Clause was designed as a specific bulwark against such potential abuses of governmental power, and that clause of the First Amendment operates as a specific constitutional limitation upon the exercise by Congress of the taxing and spending power.

Many Establishment Clause challenges—including most of those that we have considered so far in this chapter—have been maintained on the basis of taxpayer standing under the theory announced in *Flast*.

More recently, however, the Court has questioned the consistency of *Flast* with its standing doctrine more generally. In *Hein v. Freedom From Religion Foundation, Inc.*, 551 U.S. 587 (2007), the Court held that a taxpayer lacked standing to challenge the President's expenditure of funds from a general appropriation for day-to-day activities. Writing for himself and Chief Justice Roberts and Justice Kennedy, Justice Alito concluded that *Flast* authorized taxpayer standing only in suits challenging *specific* congressional appropriations of funds for activities that are alleged to violate the Establishment Clause. Because the challenge in *Hein* was to an executive decision to spend funds without any specific congressional direction that they be spent for those purposes, Justice Alito found *Flast* inapposite and accordingly declined to reconsider it. Justice Scalia, joined by Justice Thomas, asserted in his opinion concurring in the judgment that *Flast* is inconsistent with the Court's standing doctrine and should be overruled. Justice Souter, joined by Justices Stevens, Ginsburg, and Breyer, asserted in dissent that *Flast* was correct and authorized standing in the case.

Under Justice Alito's or Justice Scalia's approach in *Hein*—under which taxpayer standing will be either more difficult or impossible to establish—is it likely that there will be *any* plaintiff with standing to challenge government programs that provide direct aid to religious organizations? If not, what does that suggest about the various approaches in *Hein*? About the future of Establishment Clause litigation itself?

2. Religion in Governmental Institutions

Visit the U.S. Supreme Court to hear an oral argument in December and you will pass a large Christmas tree in the main hall on your way into the courtroom. After sitting down, you might study the elaborate frieze encircling the top of the courtroom. In the frieze, you can see a depiction of Moses with the Ten Commandments and other religious images. The Court's marshal will announce the start of the day's sessions by stating, "God save this Honorable Court!" If the Court is admitting new attorneys to its bar, the Clerk of Court may ask them to take an oath of admission, which they may accomplish by solemnly swearing to conduct themselves uprightly.

Does the Establishment Clause permit these religious displays in a public courthouse? The answer to this question, under decisions of the Supreme Court, appears to be yes. Religion is not completely banned in government institutions. But surely there are *some* limits on the ability of government to engage in religious activities. After all, if nothing else, Congress cannot create a national church. That prohibition, moreover, presumably extends beyond a formal congressional declaration creating such a church to other actions promoting religion. The difficult task, therefore, is to determine precisely what limits the Establishment Clause imposes on the government's ability to promote religion or engage in religious activities or displays.

The Supreme Court has held that the Establishment Clause does not bar all religious activities—including prayer—in public institutions. The Court has occasionally permitted some such activities, outside of the public primary and secondary school context, if they are deeply embedded in the history and tradition of the country. In addition, the Court has held that the Establishment Clause does not prevent the display of religious symbols on government property if the symbols have a secular purpose and do not amount to an endorsement of a particular religion or religion in general. Determining when that standard is satisfied, however, has proved to be no easy task.

The Court has also had many opportunities to decide how the Establishment Clause applies to religious acts in public schools. The Establishment Clause bars prayer in public schools if the prayer is an official or approved part of school activities. Indeed, official prayer is banned in schools whether the students say the prayer or merely hear the prayer, whether the prayer is denominational or non-denominational, whether the prayer is silent or spoken, and whether student participation in the prayer is voluntary or involuntary. The following cases explore these rules.

We begin with the Court's decisions concerning religious activities in public schools. As you read them, consider whether there is something special about schools, or instead whether this context should be considered paradigmatic.

As with the cases we saw in our unit on government funding for religious activities, the Court's decisions concerning religious activities in public schools have often revealed competing visions of the scope and meaning of the Establishment Clause. For example, in *Illinois ex rel. McCollum v. Board of Education*, 333 U.S. 203 (1948), the Court invalidated a local school board's policy of permitting teachers employed by private religious groups "to come weekly into the school buildings during the regular hours set apart for secular teaching, and then and there for a period of thirty minutes substitute their religious teaching for the secular education provided under the compulsory education law." Classes were offered "by Protestant teachers, Catholic priests, and a Jewish rabbi" and "conducted in the regular classrooms of the school building. Students who did not choose to take the religious instruction were not released from public school duties; they were required to leave their classrooms and go to some other place in the school building for pursuit of their secular studies. On the other hand, students who were released from secular study for the religious instructions were required to be present at the religious classes." Writing for the Court, Justice Black reasoned that the policy violated the Establishment Clause because it amounted to "a utilization of the tax-established and tax-supported public school system to aid religious groups to spread their faith." Justice Black also concluded that the policy impermissibly "afford[ed] sectarian groups an invaluable aid in that it help[ed] to provide pupils for their religious classes through use of the state's compulsory public school machinery." Both of these features of the policy, Justice Black concluded, were inconsistent with the principle of separation of church and state. Only Justice Reed dissented.

The Court's decision in *McCollum* provoked a strong reaction in many parts of the country. Four years later, the Court in *Zorach v. Clauson*, 343 U.S. 306 (1952), upheld a public school policy permitting the release of children from school during school hours to attend sectarian classes outside the public schools. The

Court concluded that the challenged policy did not violate the Establishment Clause. Writing for the Court, Justice Douglas first observed that, under the program, "[n]o one is forced to go to the religious classroom and no religious exercise or instruction is brought to the classrooms of the public schools. A student need not take religious instruction. He is left to his own desires as to the manner or time of his religious devotions, if any." Justice Douglas declared that "[t]here cannot be the slightest doubt that the First Amendment reflects the philosophy that Church and State should be separated." But, he asserted, "[w]e would have to press the concept of separation of Church and State [to] extremes to condemn the present law on constitutional grounds," because such a conclusion also perhaps would require school officials to deny permission to religious students who asked to be excused for the observance of religious holiday or other reasonable accommodations. Justice Douglas rejected this view of separation, declaring:

> We are a religious people whose institutions presuppose a Supreme Being. We guarantee the freedom to worship as one chooses. We make room for as wide a variety of beliefs and creeds as the spiritual needs of man deem necessary. We sponsor an attitude on the part of government that shows no partiality to any one group and that lets each flourish according to the zeal of its adherents and the appeal of its dogma. When the state encourages religious instruction or cooperates with religious authorities by adjusting the schedule of public events to sectarian needs, it follows the best of our traditions. For it then respects the religious nature of our people and accommodates the public service to their spiritual needs. To hold that it may not would be to find in the Constitution a requirement that the government show a callous indifference to religious groups. That would be preferring those who believe in no religion over those who do believe. Government may not finance religious groups nor undertake religious instruction nor blend secular and sectarian education nor use secular institutions to force one or some religion on any person. * * * The government must be neutral when it comes to competition between sects. * * * It may not coerce anyone to attend church, to observe a religious holiday, or to take religious instruction. But it can close its doors or suspend its operations as to those who want to repair to their religious sanctuary for worship or instruction. No more than that is undertaken here.

Justice Douglas distinguished *McCollum* by noting that in that case "the classrooms were used for religious instruction and the force of the public school was used to promote that instruction," whereas in *Zorach* "the public schools do no more than accommodate their schedules to a program of outside religious instruction."

Justice Black dissented, finding no meaningful difference between the challenged policy and the policy at issue in *McCollum*, which he read to stand for the proposition that the state cannot "constitutionally manipulate the compelled classroom hours of its compulsory school machinery so as to channel children into sectarian classes." Justice Jackson also dissented, reasoning that the challenged program was impermissibly "founded upon a use of the State's power of coercion." He stated:

> Stripped to its essentials, the plan has two stages, first, that the State compel each student to yield a large part of his time for public secular education and, second, that some of it be "released" to him on condition that he devote it to sectarian religious purposes. No one suggests that the Constitution would permit the State directly to require this "released" time to be spent "under the control of a duly constituted religious body." This program accomplishes that forbidden result by indirection. If public education were taking so much of the pupils' time as to injure the public or the students' welfare by encroaching upon their religious opportunity, simply shortening everyone's school day would facilitate voluntary and optional attendance at Church classes. But that suggestion is rejected upon the ground that if they are made free many students will not go to the Church. Hence, they must be deprived of freedom for this period, with Church attendance put to them as one of the two permissible ways of using it. * * * Here schooling is more or less suspended during the "released time" so the nonreligious attendants will not forge ahead of the churchgoing absentees. But it serves as a temporary jail for a pupil who will not go to Church. It takes more subtlety of mind than I possess to deny that this is governmental constraint in support of religion. It is as unconstitutional, in my view, when exerted by indirection as when exercised forthrightly.

Justice Jackson found the Court's attempt to distinguish *McCollum* "trivial, almost to the point of cynicism." He concluded by declaring, "The wall which the Court was professing to erect [in *McCollum*] between Church and State has become even more warped and twisted than I expected," and he warned that the "day that this country ceases to be free for irreligion it will cease to be free for religion—except for the sect that can win political power."

The decisions in *McCollum* and *Zorach* reflect competing visions of the Establishment Clause. How should the Court apply the principles in those decisions to policies requiring or permitting prayer in school? Consider the cases that follow.

ENGEL V. VITALE

370 U.S. 421 (1962)

MR. JUSTICE BLACK delivered the opinion of the Court.

The respondent Board of Education of Union Free School District No. 9, New Hyde Park, New York, acting in its official capacity under state law, directed the School District's principal to cause the following prayer to be said aloud by each class in the presence of a teacher at the beginning of each school day: "Almighty God, we acknowledge our dependence upon Thee, and we beg Thy blessings upon us, our parents, our teachers and our Country."

This daily procedure was adopted on the recommendation of the State Board of Regents, a governmental agency created by the State Constitution to which the New York Legislature has granted broad supervisory, executive, and legislative powers over the State's public school system. These state officials composed the prayer which they recommended and published as a part of their "Statement on Moral and Spiritual Training in the Schools," saying: "We believe that this Statement will be subscribed to by all men and women of good will, and we call upon all of them to aid in giving life to our program."

Shortly after the practice of reciting the Regents' prayer was adopted by the School District, the parents of ten pupils brought this action in a New York State Court insisting that use of this official prayer in the public schools was contrary

Take Note

Before this case came to the Supreme Court, the New York courts concluded that no student could be compelled to recite the challenged prayer. One of the questions for the Supreme Court, therefore, was whether the "voluntary" nature of the prayer eliminated any concerns under the Establishment Clause.

to the beliefs, religions, or religious practices of both themselves and their children. Among other things, these parents challenged the constitutionality of both the state law authorizing the School District to direct the use of prayer in public schools and the School District's regulation ordering the recitation of this particular prayer on the ground that these actions of official governmental agencies violate [the First and Fourteenth Amendments.] The New York Court of Appeals * * * sustained an order of the lower state courts which had upheld the power of New York to use the Regents' prayer as a part of the daily procedures of its public schools so long as the schools did not compel any pupil to join in the prayer over his or his parents' objection. * * *

We think that by using its public school system to encourage recitation of the Regents' prayer, the State of New York has adopted a practice wholly inconsistent with the Establishment Clause. There can, of course, be no doubt that New York's program of daily classroom invocation of God's blessings as prescribed in the Regents' prayer is a religious activity. It is a solemn avowal of divine faith and supplication for the blessings of the Almighty. * * *

It is a matter of history that this very practice of establishing governmentally composed prayers for religious services was one of the reasons which caused many of our early colonists to leave England and seek religious freedom in America. The *Book of Common Prayer*, which was created under governmental direction and which was approved by Acts of Parliament in 1548 and 1549, set out in minute detail the accepted form and content of prayer and other religious ceremonies to be used in the established, tax-supported Church of England. The controversies over the Book and what should be its content repeatedly threatened to disrupt the peace of that country as the accepted forms of prayer in the established church changed with the views of the particular ruler that happened to be in control at the time. Powerful groups representing some of the varying religious views of the people struggled among themselves to impress their particular views upon the Government and obtain amendments of the Book more suitable to their respective notions of how religious services should be conducted in order that the official religious establishment would advance their particular religious beliefs. Other groups, lacking the necessary political power to influence the Government on the matter, decided to leave England and its established church and seek freedom in America from England's governmentally ordained and supported religion.

It is an unfortunate fact of history that when some of the very groups which had most strenuously opposed the established Church of England found themselves sufficiently in control of colonial governments in this country to write their own prayers into law, they passed laws making their own religion the official religion of their respective colonies. Indeed, as late as the time of the Revolutionary War, there were established churches in at least eight of the thirteen former colonies and established religions in at least four of the other five. But the successful Revolution against English political domination was shortly followed by intense opposition to the practice of establishing religion by law. This opposition crystallized rapidly into an effective political force in Virginia where the minority religious groups such as Presbyterians, Lutherans, Quakers and

Baptists had gained such strength that the adherents to the established Episcopal Church were actually a minority themselves. In 1785–1786, those opposed to the established Church, led by James Madison and Thomas Jefferson, who, though themselves not members of any of these dissenting religious groups, opposed all religious establishments by law on grounds of principle, obtained the enactment of the famous "Virginia Bill for Religious Liberty" by which all religious groups were placed on an equal footing so far as the State was concerned. Similar though less far-reaching legislation was being considered and passed in other States.

By the time of the adoption of the Constitution, our history shows that there was a widespread awareness among many Americans of the dangers of a union of Church and State. These people knew, some of them from bitter personal experience that one of the greatest dangers to the freedom of the individual to worship in his own way lay in the Government's placing its official stamp of approval upon one particular kind of prayer or one particular form of religious services. They knew the anguish, hardship and bitter strife that could come when zealous religious groups struggled with one another to obtain the Government's stamp of approval from each King, Queen, or Protector that came to temporary power. The Constitution was intended to avert a part of this danger by leaving the government of this country in the hands of the people rather than in the hands of any monarch. But this safeguard was not enough. Our Founders were no more willing to let the content of their prayers and their privilege of praying whenever they pleased be influenced by the ballot box than they were to let these vital matters of personal conscience depend upon the succession of monarchs. The First Amendment was added to the Constitution to stand as a guarantee that neither the power nor the prestige of the Federal Government would be used to control, support or influence the kinds of prayer the American people can say— that the people's religions must not be subjected to the pressures of government for change each time a new political administration is elected to office. Under that Amendment's prohibition against governmental establishment of religion, as reinforced by the provisions of the Fourteenth Amendment, government in this country, be it state or federal, is without power to prescribe by law any particular form of prayer which is to be used as an official prayer in carrying on any program of governmentally sponsored religious activity.

There can be no doubt that New York's state prayer program officially establishes the religious beliefs embodied in the Regents' prayer. The respondents' argument to the contrary, which is largely based upon the contention that the Regents' prayer is "nondenominational" and the fact that the program, as modified and approved by state courts, does not require all pupils to recite the prayer but permits those who wish to do so to remain silent or be excused from the room, ignores the essential nature of the program's constitutional defects. Neither the fact that the prayer may be denominationally neutral nor the fact that its observance on the part of the students is voluntary can serve to free it from the limitations of the Establishment Clause, as it might from the Free Exercise Clause, of the First Amendment, both of which are operative against the States by virtue of the Fourteenth Amendment. Although these two clauses may in certain instances overlap, they forbid two quite different kinds of governmental encroachment upon religious freedom. The Establishment Clause, unlike the Free Exercise Clause, does not depend upon any showing of direct governmental compulsion and is violated by the enactment of laws which establish an official religion whether those laws operate directly to coerce nonobserving individuals or not. This is not to say, of course, that laws officially prescribing a particular form of religious worship do not involve coercion of such individuals. When the power, prestige and financial support of government is placed behind a particular religious belief, the indirect coercive pressure upon religious minorities to conform to the prevailing officially approved religion is plain. But the purposes underlying the Establishment Clause go much further than that. Its first and most immediate purpose rested on the belief that a union of government and religion tends to destroy government and to degrade religion. * * * Another purpose of the Establishment Clause rested upon an awareness of the historical fact that governmentally established religions and religious persecutions go hand in hand. * * * It was in large part to get completely away from this sort of systematic religious persecution that the Founders brought into being our Nation, our Constitution, and our Bill of Rights with its prohibition against any governmental establishment of religion. The New York laws officially prescribing the Regents' prayer are inconsistent both with the purposes of the Establishment Clause and with the Establishment Clause itself.

It has been argued that to apply the Constitution in such a way as to prohibit state laws respecting an establishment of religious services in public schools is to indicate a hostility toward religion or toward prayer. Nothing, or course, could be more wrong. * * * It is neither sacrilegious nor antireligious to say that each separate government in this country should stay out of the business of writing or sanctioning official prayers and leave that purely religious function to the people themselves and to those the people choose to look to for religious guidance. [Reversed.]

MR. JUSTICE STEWART, dissenting.

With all respect, I think the Court has misapplied a great constitutional principle. I cannot see how an "official religion" is established by letting those who want to say a prayer say it. On the contrary, I think that to deny the wish of these school children to join in reciting this prayer is to deny them the opportunity of sharing in the spiritual heritage of our Nation.

POINTS FOR DISCUSSION

a. Scope of the Decision

In response to hearing that the Supreme Court had banned school prayer in *Engel*, someone quipped in disbelief: "As long as there are math tests, there will be prayer in school." (Perhaps your personal educational experience confirms this truth.) The observation, although offered as humor, raises important questions about the exact scope and theory of the Court's decision. The Court held that New York had violated the Establishment Clause even though the state had not mandated that students join in the Regents' prayer. Does the Court's decision mean that all voluntary prayer in school is unconstitutional? In other words, if a student in a public middle school said a prayer before an algebra test, would that violate the Establishment Clause? Or does the decision bar only government-authorized or approved prayer?

b. Reach of the Decision

The prayer at issue in *Engel* had been composed and approved by the state. One year after *Engel*, the Court held in *School Dist. of Abington Twp. v. Schempp*, 374 U.S. 203 (1963), that the Establishment Clause also prohibits state laws and policies "requiring the selection and reading at the opening of the school day of verses from the Holy Bible and the recitation of the Lord's Prayer by the students in unison." The challenged Pennsylvania law required that "[a]t least ten verses from the Holy Bible" be read each day, though it permitted children to be excused from the reading upon the written request of their parents. The Court held that the law was unconstitutional because the prayers were "prescribed as part of the curricular activities of students who are required by law to attend school" and were "held in the school buildings under the supervision and with the participation of teachers employed in those schools." The Court emphasized that "[n]othing we have said here indicates that such study of the Bible or of religion, when presented objectively as part of a secular program of education, may not be effected consistently with the First Amendment," but the Court concluded that the "exercises here do not fall into those categories."

c. Theory of the Decision

The Court's insistence that the Regents' prayer was unconstitutional even though students could abstain is particularly notable in light of an earlier, seminal First

Amendment case. In *West Virginia State Board of Education v. Barnette*, 319 U.S. 624 (1943), the Court concluded that the state could not require students to salute the flag and recite the pledge of allegiance. The Court reasoned:

> To sustain the compulsory flag salute we are required to say that a Bill of Rights which guards the individual's right to speak his own mind, left it open to public authorities to compel him to utter what is not in his mind. * * * Struggles to coerce uniformity of sentiment in support of some end thought essential to their time and country have been waged by many good as well as by evil men. [As] first and moderate methods to attain unity have failed, those bent on its accomplishment must resort to an ever-increasing severity. * * * Those who begin coercive elimination of dissent soon find themselves exterminating dissenters. Compulsory unification of opinion achieves only the unanimity of the graveyard.
>
> It seems trite but necessary to say that the First Amendment to our Constitution was designed to avoid these ends by avoiding these beginnings. There is no mysticism in the American concept of the State or of the nature or origin of its authority. We set up government by consent of the governed, and the Bill of Rights denies those in power any legal opportunity to coerce that consent. Authority here is to be controlled by public opinion, not public opinion by authority. * * * If there is any fixed star in our constitutional constellation, it is that no official, high or petty, can prescribe what shall be orthodox in politics, nationalism, religion, or other matters of opinion or force citizens to confess by word or act their faith therein. If there are any circumstances which permit an exception, they do not now occur to us.

If coercion was the defect of the policy at issue in *Barnette*, under which students were required to recite the pledge of allegiance, then why wasn't the defect of the Regents' prayer addressed by the New York Court's decision that the prayer was optional? Is there a difference between the pledge of allegiance (which in 1943 did not include the phrase "under God") and the prayer at issue in *Engel*? Was coercion the only defect in *Engel*?

> **Make the Connection**
>
> We will consider the extent to which claims under the Establishment Clause require a showing of governmental coercion later in this chapter, when we consider the Court's decision in *Lee v. Weisman*.

In response to *Engel*, some states and school districts eliminated public prayers but left a time in the day for school children to pray silently if they so chose. In the following case, the Supreme Court considered whether providing a "moment of silence" in schools violates the Constitution.

WALLACE V. JAFFREE
472 U.S. 38 (1985)

JUSTICE STEVENS delivered the opinion of the Court.

[Alabama Code § 16–1–20, as initially enacted in 1978, provided: "At the commencement of the first class each day in the first through the sixth grades in all public schools, the teacher in charge of the room in which each such class is held shall announce that a period of silence, not to exceed one minute in duration, shall be observed for meditation, and during any such period silence shall be maintained and no activities engaged in." Alabama Code § 16–1–20 (Supp.1984). Three years later, the Alabama legislature enacted a statute authorizing teachers to provide a period of silence "for meditation or voluntary prayer," during which "no other activities shall be engaged in." Alabama Code § 16–1–20.1 (Supp.1984). And in 1982, the legislature authorized teachers to lead "willing students" in a prescribed prayer to "Almighty God * * * the Creator and Supreme Judge of the world." Alabama Code § 16–1–20.2 (Supp.1984).

Appellee Ishmael Jaffree, the father of three children in Alabama public schools, brought a lawsuit claiming that the statutes violated the Establishment Clause. In an earlier order, the Supreme Court summarily affirmed the court of appeals' conclusion, based on *School Dist. Abington v. Schempp,* 374 U.S. 203 (1963), that the 1982 statute was unconstitutional. *See Wallace v. Jaffree,* 466 U.S. 924 (1984). Before the Supreme Court, appellee did not argue that § 16–1–20 was unconstitutional, leaving only his claim that § 16–1–20.1, which authorized a period of silence for meditation or voluntary prayer, violated the Establishment Clause.]

When the Court has been called upon to construe the breadth of the Establishment Clause, it has examined the criteria developed over a period of many years. Thus, in *Lemon v. Kurtzman,* 403 U.S. 602 (1971), we [announced a three-factor test]: "First, the statute must have a secular legislative purpose; second, its principal or primary effect must be one that neither advances nor inhibits religion; finally, the statute must not foster 'an excessive government entanglement with religion.'"

Food for Thought

We have regularly noted in this book the difficulty of determining the motivation or purpose of a multi-member legislative body. Yet the *Lemon* test requires the Court to discern a legislative purpose. Is this a problem with the *Lemon* test? Or is the problem unavoidable in this context, where legislative purpose must be a relevant—and sometimes dispositive—criterion? Even if legislative purpose is relevant here, is evidence of the views of one legislator sufficient?

It is the first of these three criteria that is most plainly implicated by this case. As the District Court correctly recognized, no consideration of the second or third criteria is necessary if a statute does not have a clearly secular purpose. For even though a statute that is motivated in part by a religious purpose may satisfy the first criterion, the First Amendment requires that a statute must be invalidated if it is entirely motivated by a purpose to advance religion.

The sponsor of the bill that became § 16–1–20.1, Senator Donald Holmes, inserted into the legislative record—apparently without dissent—a statement indicating that the legislation was an "effort to return voluntary prayer" to the public schools. Later Senator Holmes confirmed this purpose before the District Court. In response to the question whether he had any purpose for the legislation other than returning voluntary prayer to public schools, he stated: "No, I did not have no other purpose in mind." The State did not present evidence of *any* secular purpose.

We must, therefore, conclude that the Alabama Legislature * * * enacted § 16–1–20.1 [for] the sole purpose of expressing the State's endorsement of prayer activities for one minute at the beginning of each schoolday. The addition of "or voluntary prayer" indicates that the State intended to characterize prayer as a favored practice. Such an endorsement is not consistent with the established principle that the government must pursue a course of complete neutrality toward religion.

The importance of that principle does not permit us to treat this as an inconsequential case involving nothing more than a few words of symbolic speech on behalf of the political majority. For whenever the State itself speaks on a religious subject, one of the questions that we must ask is "whether the government intends to convey a message of endorsement or disapproval of religion." The well-supported concurrent findings of the District Court and the Court of Appeals—that § 16–1–20.1 was intended to convey a message of state approval of prayer activities in the public schools—make it unnecessary, and indeed inappropriate, to evaluate the practical significance of the addition of the words "or voluntary prayer" to the statute. Keeping in mind, as we must, "both the fundamental place held by the Establishment Clause in our constitutional scheme and the myriad, subtle ways in which Establishment Clause values can be eroded," *Lynch v. Donnelly*, 465 U.S. 668, 694 (1984) (O'CONNOR, J., concurring), we conclude that § 16–1–20.1 violates the First Amendment.

JUSTICE O'CONNOR, concurring in the judgment.

* * * It once appeared that the Court had developed a workable standard by which to identify impermissible government establishments of religion. *See Lemon v. Kurtzman,* 403 U.S. 602 (1971). Under the now familiar *Lemon* test, statutes must have both a secular legislative purpose and a principal or primary effect that neither advances nor inhibits religion, and in addition they must not foster excessive government entanglement with religion. Despite its initial promise, the *Lemon* test has proved problematic. The required inquiry into "entanglement" has been modified and questioned, *see Mueller v. Allen,* 463 U.S. 388, 403, n. 11 (1983), and in one case we have upheld state action against an Establishment Clause challenge without applying the *Lemon* test at all. *Marsh v. Chambers,* 463 U.S. 783 (1983). The author of *Lemon* himself apparently questions the test's general applicability. *See Lynch v. Donnelly,* 465 U.S. 668, 679 (1984). * * *

Perhaps because I am new to the struggle, I am not ready to abandon all aspects of the *Lemon* test. I do believe, however, that the standards announced in *Lemon* should be reexamined and refined in order to make them more useful in achieving the underlying purpose of the First Amendment. * * * Last Term, I proposed a refinement of the *Lemon* test with this goal in mind. *Lynch v. Donnelly,* 465 U.S., at 687–689 (concurring opinion). [I] suggested that the religious liberty protected by the Establishment Clause is infringed when the government makes

Make the Connection

We will consider the Court's decision in *Lynch* later in this chapter.

adherence to religion relevant to a person's standing in the political community. Direct government action endorsing religion or a particular religious practice is invalid under this approach because it "sends a message to nonadherents that they are outsiders, not full members of the political community, and an accompanying message to adherents that they are insiders, favored members of the political community." *Id.,* at 688. Under this view, *Lemon*'s inquiry as to the purpose and effect of a statute requires courts to examine whether government's purpose is to endorse religion and whether the statute actually conveys a message of endorsement.

The endorsement test is useful because of the analytic content it gives to the *Lemon*-mandated inquiry into legislative purpose and effect. In this country, church and state must necessarily operate within the same community. Because of this coexistence, it is inevitable that the secular interests of government and the religious interests of various sects and their adherents will frequently intersect, conflict, and combine. A statute that ostensibly promotes a secular interest often has an incidental or even a primary effect of helping or hindering a sectarian belief. Chaos would ensue if every such statute were invalid under the Establishment Clause. For example, the State could not criminalize murder for fear that it would thereby promote the Biblical command against killing. The task for the Court is to sort out those statutes and government practices whose purpose and effect go against the grain of religious liberty protected by the First Amendment.

The endorsement test does not preclude government from acknowledging religion or from taking religion into account in making law and policy. It does preclude government from conveying or attempting to convey a message that religion or a particular religious belief is favored or preferred. Such an endorsement infringes the religious liberty of the nonadherent, for "[w]hen the power, prestige and financial support of government is placed behind a particular religious belief, the indirect coercive pressure upon religious minorities to conform to the prevailing officially approved religion is plain." *Engel v. Vitale*, 370 U.S., at 431. At issue today is whether state moment of silence statutes in general, and Alabama's moment of silence statute in particular, embody an impermissible endorsement of prayer in public schools.

* * * The sole purpose reflected in the official history is "to return voluntary prayer to our public schools." Nor does anything in the legislative history contradict an intent to encourage children to choose prayer over other alternatives during the moment of silence. * * * In light of the legislative history and the findings of the courts below, I agree with the Court that the State intended § 16–1–20.1 to convey a message that prayer was the endorsed activity during the state-prescribed moment of silence. * * *

CHIEF JUSTICE BURGER, dissenting.

Some who trouble to read the opinions in these cases will find it ironic—perhaps even bizarre—that on the very day we heard arguments in the cases, the Court's session opened with an invocation for Divine protection. Across the park a few hundred yards away, the House of Representatives and the Senate regularly open each session with a prayer. These legislative prayers are not just one minute in duration, but are extended, thoughtful invocations and prayers for Divine guidance. They are given, as they have been since 1789, by clergy appointed as official chaplains and paid from the Treasury of the United States. Congress has also provided chapels in the Capitol, at public expense, where Members and others may pause for prayer, meditation—or a moment of silence.

* * * The Alabama Legislature has no more "endorsed" religion than a state or the Congress does when it provides for legislative chaplains, or than this Court does when it opens each session with an invocation to God. * * *

JUSTICE REHNQUIST, dissenting.

It is impossible to build sound constitutional doctrine upon a mistaken understanding of constitutional history, but unfortunately the Establishment Clause has been expressly freighted with Jefferson's misleading metaphor [of "a wall of separation between church and State"] for nearly 40 years. Thomas Jefferson was of course in France at the time the constitutional Amendments known as the Bill of Rights were passed by Congress and ratified by the States. [The letter in which he stated the wall metaphor] was a short note of courtesy, written 14 years after the Amendments were passed by Congress. He would seem to any detached observer as a less than ideal source of contemporary history as to the meaning of the Religion Clauses of the First Amendment. [In contrast,] James Madison [was] present in the United States, and he was a leading Member of the First Congress. But when we turn to the record of the proceedings in the First Congress leading up to the adoption of the Establishment Clause of the Constitution, including Madison's significant contributions thereto, we see a far different picture of its purpose than the highly simplified "wall of separation between church and State."

The language Madison proposed for what ultimately became the Religion Clauses of the First Amendment was this: "The civil rights of none shall be abridged on account of religious belief or worship, nor shall any national religion be established, nor shall the full and equal rights of conscience be in any manner, or on any pretext, infringed." * * * [During the floor debate on a Select Committee's revision of the proposal, Madison stated] that "he apprehended the meaning of the words to be, that Congress should not establish a religion, and enforce the legal observation of it by law, nor compel men to worship God in any manner contrary to their conscience." 1 Annals of Cong. 730. [In response to concerns that this language might "be taken in such latitude as to be extremely hurtful to the cause of religion," Madison emphasized the word "national" before the word "religion."] "He believed that the people feared one sect might obtain a pre-eminence, or two combine together, and establish a religion to which they would compel others to conform. He thought that if the word 'national' was introduced, it would point the amendment directly to the object it was intended to prevent." *Id.*, at 731.

The following week, without any apparent debate, the House voted to alter the language of the Religion Clauses to read "Congress shall make no law establishing religion, or to prevent the free exercise thereof, or to infringe the rights of conscience." *Id.*, at 766. The floor debates in the Senate were secret, and therefore not reported in the Annals. * * * The House refused to accept the Senate's changes in the Bill of Rights and asked for a conference; the version which emerged from the conference was that which ultimately found its way into the Constitution as a part of the First Amendment.

On the basis of the record of these proceedings in the House of Representatives, James Madison was undoubtedly the most important architect among the Members of the House of the Amendments which became the Bill of Rights, but it was James Madison speaking as an advocate of sensible legislative compromise, not as an advocate of incorporating the Virginia Statute of Religious Liberty into the United States Constitution. During the ratification debate in the Virginia Convention, Madison had actually opposed the idea of any Bill of Rights. His sponsorship of the Amendments in the House was obviously not that of a zealous believer in the necessity of the Religion Clauses, but of one who felt it might do some good, could do no harm, and would satisfy those who had ratified the Constitution on the condition that Congress propose a Bill of Rights. His original language "nor shall any national religion be established" obviously does not conform to the "wall of separation" between church and State idea which latter-day commentators have ascribed to him. His explanation on the floor of the meaning of his language * * * is of the same ilk.

It seems indisputable from these glimpses of Madison's thinking, as reflected by actions on the floor of the House in 1789, that he saw the Amendment as designed to prohibit the establishment of a national religion, and perhaps to prevent discrimination among sects. He did not see it as requiring neutrality on the part of government between religion and irreligion. Thus the Court's opinion in *Everson*—while correct in bracketing Madison and Jefferson together in their exertions in their home State leading to the enactment of the Virginia Statute of Religious Liberty—is totally incorrect in suggesting that Madison carried these views onto the floor of the United States House of Representatives when he proposed the language which would ultimately become the Bill of Rights.

None of the other Members of Congress who spoke during the [congressional] debate expressed the slightest indication that they thought the language before them from the Select Committee, or the evil to be aimed at, would require that the Government be absolutely neutral as between religion and irreligion. The evil to be aimed at, so far as those who spoke were concerned, appears to have been the establishment of a national church, and perhaps the preference of one religious sect over another; but it was definitely not concerned about whether the Government might aid all religions evenhandedly.

The actions of the First Congress * * * confirm the view that Congress did not mean that the Government should be neutral between religion and irreligion. * * * On the day after the House of Representatives voted to adopt the form of the First Amendment Religion Clauses which was ultimately proposed and ratified, Representative Elias Boudinot proposed a resolution asking President George Washington to issue a Thanksgiving Day Proclamation. Boudinot said he "could not think of letting the session pass over without offering an opportunity to all the citizens of the United States of joining with one voice, in returning to Almighty God their sincere thanks for the many blessings he had poured down upon them." 1 Annals of Cong. 914 (1789). * * * George Washington responded [by issuing a proclamation that recommended that the day "be devoted by the people of these States to the service of that great and glorious Being who is the beneficent author of all the good that was, that is, or that will be" and that "we may then unite in most humbly offering our prayers and supplications to the great Lord and Ruler of Nations, and beseech Him to pardon our national and other transgressions."] John Adams [and] James Madison also issued Thanksgiving Proclamations * * *.

[In the nineteenth century, Congress on several occasions appropriated money for the aid of religion.] It would seem from this evidence that the Establishment Clause of the First Amendment had acquired a well-accepted meaning: it forbade establishment of a national religion, and forbade preference among religious sects or denominations. * * * The Establishment Clause did not require government neutrality between religion and irreligion nor did it prohibit the Federal Government from providing nondiscriminatory aid to religion. There is simply no historical foundation for the proposition that the Framers intended to build the "wall of separation" that was constitutionalized in *Everson*.

Notwithstanding the absence of a historical basis for this theory of rigid separation, the wall idea might well have served as a useful albeit misguided analytical concept, had it led this Court to unified and principled results in Establishment Clause cases. The opposite, unfortunately, has been true; in the 38 years since *Everson* our Establishment Clause cases have been neither principled nor unified. * * * Whether due to its lack of historical support or its practical unworkability, the *Everson* "wall" has proved all but useless as a guide to sound constitutional adjudication. * * * But the greatest injury of the "wall" notion is its mischievous diversion of judges from the actual intentions of the drafters of the Bill of Rights. * * * [The "wall" metaphor] should be frankly and explicitly abandoned.

[T]he *Lemon* test has no more grounding in the history of the First Amendment than does the wall theory upon which it rests. The three-part test represents a determined effort to craft a workable rule from a historically faulty doctrine; but the rule can only be as sound as the doctrine it attempts to service. * * * [N]othing in the Establishment Clause requires government to be strictly neutral between religion and irreligion, nor does that Clause prohibit Congress or the States from pursuing legitimate secular ends through nondiscriminatory sectarian means.

It would come as much of a shock to those who drafted the Bill of Rights as it will to a large number of thoughtful Americans today to learn that the Constitution, as construed by the majority, prohibits the Alabama Legislature from "endorsing" prayer. George Washington himself, at the request of the very Congress which passed the Bill of Rights, proclaimed a day of "public thanksgiving and prayer, to be observed by acknowledging with grateful hearts the many and signal favors of Almighty God." History must judge whether it was the Father of his Country in 1789, or a majority of the Court today, which has strayed from the meaning of the Establishment Clause.

[The concurring opinion of JUSTICE POWELL and the dissenting opinion of JUSTICE WHITE are omitted.]

POINTS FOR DISCUSSION

a. Religious Purpose

In this case, the Alabama statute expressly made the moment of silence a time for "voluntary prayer," and the state acknowledged that the purpose was to encourage prayer. Would the case have come out differently if the statute merely provided for "a moment of silence for reflection" without mentioning prayer and if the legislative history also did not say anything about prayer? For example, every year on September 11, many schools and public institutions hold a moment of silence in memory of the victims of the terrorist attacks of 2001. Certainly many people use this time for prayer. Is this moment of silence unconstitutional?

b.　Justice O'Connor's Proposed Endorsement Test

The Supreme Court has not replaced the *Lemon* test with an endorsement test such as the one that Justice O'Connor proposed in her separate opinion. But the Court in subsequent cases has recognized endorsement as a factor relevant to determining the constitutionality of actions challenged under the Establishment Clause. In *County of Allegheny v. ACLU*, 492 U.S. 573, 593–94 (1989), the Court said:

> Whether the key word is "endorsement," "favoritism," or "promotion," the essential principle remains the same. The Establishment Clause, at the very least, prohibits government from appearing to take a position on questions of religious belief or from "making adherence to a religion relevant in any way to a person's standing in the political community." *Lynch v. Donnelly*, 465 U.S., at 687 (O'CONNOR, J., concurring).

c.　Non-Preferentialism

Justice Rehnquist asserted that the Establishment Clause does not require neutrality "between religion and irreligion" and does not prohibit "nondiscriminatory aid to religion." He thus rejected the separation principle that the Court had announced in *Everson* and proposed in its place a principle that merely forbids the government from preferring one religion to another. What is the source of this principle? Are you convinced by Justice Rehnquist's historical argument? If Madison's views are largely dispositive, then isn't it also important that he concluded that presidential Thanksgiving proclamations invoking God violate the Establishment Clause? See *Lee v. Weisman*, 505 U.S. 577 (1992) (Souter, J., concurring). Also, is it possible for the government to endorse or provide aid to religion generally without preferring some religions to others?

In the previous two cases, schools provided time for students to pray at school during the school day. Is the Establishment Clause violated if schools offer, and students hear, non-denominational prayers at graduation ceremonies?

LEE V. WEISMAN
505 U.S. 577 (1992)

JUSTICE KENNEDY the opinion of the Court.

Deborah Weisman graduated from Nathan Bishop Middle School, a public school in Providence, at a formal ceremony in June 1989. She was about 14 years old. For many years it has been the policy of the Providence School Committee and the Superintendent of Schools to permit principals to invite members of the clergy to give invocations and benedictions at middle school and high school graduations. Many, but not all, of the principals elected to include prayers as part of the graduation ceremonies. Acting for himself and his daughter, Deborah's father, Daniel Weisman, objected to any prayers at Deborah's middle school graduation, but to no avail. The school principal, petitioner Robert E. Lee, invited a rabbi to deliver prayers at the graduation exercises for Deborah's class. Rabbi Leslie Gutterman, of the Temple Beth El in Providence, accepted.*

* * * It is beyond dispute that, at a minimum, the Constitution guarantees that government may not coerce anyone to support or participate in religion or its exercise, or otherwise act in a way which "establishes a [state] religion or religious faith, or tends to do so." *Lynch v. Donnelly*, 465 U.S. 668, 678 (1984). The State's involvement in the school prayers challenged today violates these central principles.

That involvement is as troubling as it is undenied. A school official, the principal, decided that an invocation and a benediction should be given; this is a choice attributable to the State, and from a constitutional perspective it is as if a state statute decreed that the prayers must occur. The principal chose the religious participant, here a rabbi, and that choice is also attributable to the State. The reason for the choice of a rabbi is not disclosed by the record, but the potential for divisiveness over the choice of a particular member of the clergy to conduct the ceremony is apparent.

The State's role did not end with the decision to include a prayer and with the choice of a clergyman. Principal Lee provided Rabbi Gutterman with a copy of the "Guidelines for Civic Occasions," and advised him that his prayers should be nonsectarian. Through these means the principal directed and controlled the content of the prayers. Even if the only sanction for ignoring the instructions were that the rabbi would not be invited back, we think no religious representative who valued his or her continued reputation and effectiveness in the community would

---

* Rabbi Gutterman's invocation was as follows: "God of the Free, Hope of the Brave: For the legacy of America where diversity is celebrated and the rights of minorities are protected, we thank You. May these young men and women grow up to enrich it. For the liberty of America, we thank You. May these new graduates grow up to guard it. For the political process of America in which all its citizens may participate, for its court system where all may seek justice we thank You. May those we honor this morning always turn to it in trust. For the destiny of America we thank You. May the graduates of Nathan Bishop Middle School so live that they might help to share it. May our aspirations for our country and for these young people, who are our hope for the future, be richly fulfilled." In his benediction, he stated: "O God, we are grateful to You for having endowed us with the capacity for learning which we have celebrated on this joyous commencement. Happy families give thanks for seeing their children achieve an important milestone. Send Your blessings upon the teachers and administrators who helped prepare them. The graduates now need strength and guidance for the future, help them to understand that we are not complete with academic knowledge alone. We must each strive to fulfill what You require of us all: To do justly, to love mercy, to walk humbly. We give thanks to You, Lord, for keeping us alive, sustaining us and allowing us to reach this special, happy occasion."—*Eds.*

incur the State's displeasure in this regard. It is a cornerstone principle of our Establishment Clause jurisprudence that "it is no part of the business of government to compose official prayers for any group of the American people to recite as a part of a religious program carried on by government," *Engel v. Vitale,* 370 U.S. 421, 425 (1962), and that is what the school officials attempted to do.

Petitioners argue, and we find nothing in the case to refute it, that the directions for the content of the prayers were a good-faith attempt by the school to ensure that the sectarianism which is so often the flashpoint for religious animosity be removed from the graduation ceremony. The concern is understandable, as a prayer which uses ideas or images identified with a particular religion may foster a different sort of sectarian rivalry than an invocation or benediction in terms more neutral. The school's explanation, however, does not resolve the dilemma caused by its participation. The question is not the good faith of the school in attempting to make the prayer acceptable to most persons, but the legitimacy of its undertaking that enterprise at all when the object is to produce a prayer to be used in a formal religious exercise which students, for all practical purposes, are obliged to attend.

The degree of school involvement here made it clear that the graduation prayers bore the imprint of the State and thus put school-age children who objected in an untenable position. We turn our attention now to consider the position of the students, both those who desired the prayer and she who did not.

As we have observed before, there are heightened concerns with protecting freedom of conscience from subtle coercive pressure in the elementary and secondary public schools. Our decisions in *Engel v. Vitale,* 370 U.S. 421 (1962), and *School Dist. Abington v. Schempp,* 374 U.S. 203 (1963), recognize, among other things, that prayer exercises in public schools carry a particular risk of indirect coercion. The concern may not be limited to the context of schools, but it is most pronounced there. What to most believers may seem nothing more than a reasonable request that the nonbeliever respect their religious practices, in a school context may appear to the nonbeliever or dissenter to be an attempt to employ the machinery of the State to enforce a religious orthodoxy.

We need not look beyond the circumstances of this case to see the phenomenon at work. The undeniable fact is that the school district's supervision and control of a high school graduation ceremony places public pressure, as well as peer pressure, on attending students to stand as a group or, at least, maintain respectful silence during the invocation and benediction. This pressure, though subtle and indirect, can be as real as any overt compulsion. Of course, in our culture standing or remaining silent can signify adherence to a view or simple respect for the views of others. And no doubt some persons who have no desire to join a prayer have little objection to standing as a sign of respect for those who do. But for the dissenter of high school age, who has a reasonable perception that she is being forced by the State to pray in a manner her conscience will not allow, the injury is no less real. There can be no doubt that for many, if not most, of the students at the graduation, the act of standing or remaining silent was an expression of participation in the rabbi's prayer. That was the very point of the religious exercise. It is of little comfort to a dissenter, then, to be told that for her the act of standing or remaining in silence signifies mere respect, rather than participation. What matters is that, given our social conventions, a reasonable dissenter in this milieu could believe that the group exercise signified her own participation or approval of it.

Finding no violation under these circumstances would place objectors in the dilemma of participating, with all that implies, or protesting. We do not address whether that choice is acceptable if the affected citizens are mature adults, but we think the State may not, consistent with the Establishment Clause, place primary and secondary school children in this position. Research in psychology supports the common assumption that adolescents are often susceptible to pressure from their peers towards conformity, and that the influence is strongest in matters of social convention. Brittain, Adolescent Choices and Parent-Peer Cross-Pressures, 28 Am. Sociological Rev. 385 (June 1963); Clasen & Brown, The Multidimensionality of Peer Pressure in Adolescence, 14 J. of Youth and Adolescence 451 (Dec.1985); Brown, Clasen, & Eicher, Perceptions of Peer Pressure, Peer Conformity Dispositions, and Self-Reported Behavior Among Adolescents, 22 Developmental Psychology 521 (July 1986). To recognize that the choice imposed by the State constitutes an unacceptable constraint only acknowledges that the government may no more use social pressure to enforce orthodoxy than it may use more direct means.

> **Food for Thought**
>
> We will see later in this chapter that the Court has upheld the practice of prayer at legislative sessions. *Marsh v. Chambers*, 463 U.S. 783, 790 (1983). Does the Court's discussion here suggest a reason to treat such practices differently? Or are the "pressures" on a non-believing, elected member of the legislature at least as great, if not greater?

There was a stipulation in the District Court that attendance at graduation and promotional ceremonies is voluntary. Petitioners and the United States, as *amicus,* made this a center point of the case, arguing that the option of not attending the graduation excuses any inducement or coercion in the ceremony itself. The argument lacks all persuasion. Law reaches past formalism. And to say a teenage student has a real choice not to attend her high school graduation is formalistic in the extreme. True, Deborah could elect not to attend commencement without renouncing her diploma; but we shall not allow the case to turn on this point. Everyone knows that in our society and in our culture high school graduation is one of life's most significant occasions. A school rule which excuses attendance is beside the point. Attendance may not be required by official decree, yet it is apparent that a student is not free to absent herself from the graduation exercise in any real sense of the term "voluntary," for absence would require forfeiture of those intangible benefits which have motivated the student through youth and all her high school years. Graduation is a time for family and those closest to the student to celebrate success and express mutual wishes of gratitude and respect, all to the end of impressing upon the young person the role that it is his or her right and duty to assume in the community and all of its diverse parts.

The [school district and the United States contend] that the prayers are an essential part of these ceremonies because for many persons an occasion of this significance lacks meaning if there is no recognition, however brief, that human achievements cannot be understood apart from their spiritual essence. [This argument] fails to acknowledge that what for many of Deborah's classmates and their parents was a spiritual imperative was for Daniel and Deborah Weisman religious conformance compelled by the State. * * * The essence of the Government's position is that with regard to a civic, social occasion of this importance it is the objector, not the majority, who must take unilateral and private action to avoid compromising religious scruples, hereby electing to miss the graduation exercise. This turns conventional First Amendment analysis on its head. It is a tenet of the First Amendment that the State cannot require one of its citizens to forfeit his or her rights and benefits as the price of resisting conformance to state-sponsored religious practice. To say that a student must remain apart from the ceremony at the opening invocation and closing benediction is to risk compelling conformity in an environment analogous to the classroom setting, where we have said the risk of compulsion is especially high.

We do not hold that every state action implicating religion is invalid if one or a few citizens find it offensive. People may take offense at all manner of religious as well as nonreligious messages, but offense alone does not in every case show a violation. We know too that sometimes to endure social isolation or even anger may be the price of conscience or nonconformity. But, by any reading of our cases, the conformity required of the student in this case was too high an exaction to withstand the test of the Establishment Clause. The prayer exercises in this case are especially improper because the State has in every practical sense compelled attendance and participation in an explicit religious exercise at an event of singular importance to every student, one the objecting student had no real alternative to avoid. * * * *Affirmed.*

JUSTICE BLACKMUN, with whom JUSTICE STEVENS and JUSTICE O'CONNOR join, concurring.

I join the Court's opinion today because I find nothing in it inconsistent with the essential precepts of the Establishment Clause developed in our precedents. The Court holds that the graduation prayer is unconstitutional because the State "in effect required participation in a religious exercise." Although our precedents make clear that proof of government coercion is not necessary to prove an Establishment Clause violation, it is sufficient. Government pressure to participate in a religious activity is an obvious indication that the government is endorsing or promoting religion.

But it is not enough that the government restrain from compelling religious practices: It must not engage in them either. The Court repeatedly has recognized that a violation of the Establishment Clause is not predicated on coercion. The Establishment Clause proscribes public schools from "conveying or attempting to convey a message that religion or a particular religious belief is *favored* or *preferred*," *County of Allegheny v. American Civil Liberties Union, Greater Pittsburgh Chapter*, 492 U.S. 573, 593 (1989), even if the schools do not actually "impos[e] pressure upon a student to participate in a religious activity." *Board of Ed. of Westside Community Schools (Dist. 66) v. Mergens*, 496 U.S. 226, 261 (1990) (Kennedy, J., concurring in part and concurring in judgment).

There is no doubt that attempts to aid religion through government coercion jeopardize freedom of conscience. Even subtle pressure diminishes the right of each individual to choose voluntarily what to believe. * * * Our decisions have gone beyond prohibiting coercion, however, because the Court has recognized that "the fullest possible scope of religious liberty" entails more than freedom from coercion. * * * The mixing of government and religion can be a threat to free government, even if no one is forced to participate. When the government puts its *imprimatur* on a particular religion, it conveys a message of exclusion to all those who do not adhere to the favored beliefs. A government cannot be premised on the belief that all persons are created equal when it asserts that God prefers some.

It is these understandings and fears that underlie our Establishment Clause jurisprudence. We have believed that religious freedom cannot exist in the absence of a free democratic government, and that such a government cannot endure when there is fusion between religion and the political regime. We have believed that religious freedom cannot thrive in the absence of a vibrant religious community and that such a community cannot prosper when it is bound to the secular. And we have believed that these were the animating principles behind the adoption of the Establishment Clause. To that end, our cases have prohibited government endorsement of religion, its sponsorship, and active involvement in religion, whether or not citizens were coerced to conform.

JUSTICE SOUTER, with whom JUSTICE STEVENS and JUSTICE O'CONNOR join, concurring.

Since *Everson,* we have consistently held the [Establishment] Clause applicable no less to governmental acts favoring religion generally than to acts favoring one religion over others. * * * Some have challenged this precedent by reading the Establishment Clause to permit "nonpreferential" state promotion of religion. The challengers argue that, as originally understood by the Framers, "[t]he Establishment Clause did not require government neutrality between religion and irreligion nor did it prohibit the Federal Government from providing nondiscriminatory aid to religion." *Wallace v. Jaffree,* 472 U.S. 38, 106 (1985) (REHNQUIST, J., dissenting). While a case has been made for this position, it is not so convincing as to warrant reconsideration of our settled law; indeed, I find in the history of the Clause's textual development a more powerful argument supporting the Court's jurisprudence following *Everson.* * * *

> **Go Online**
>
> In the full text of his opinion, Justice Souter provided a detailed account of the drafting history of the Establishment Clause. You can read his discussion, in Section I.B of his opinion, at https://www.law.cornell.edu/supremecourt/text/505/577.

While [this history is], for me, sufficient to reject the nonpreferentialist position, one further concern animates my judgment. In many contexts, including this one, nonpreferentialism requires some distinction between "sectarian" religious practices and those that would be, by some measure, ecumenical enough to pass Establishment Clause muster. Simply by requiring the enquiry, nonpreferentialists invite the courts to engage in comparative theology. I can hardly imagine a subject less amenable to the competence of the federal judiciary, or more deliberately to be avoided where possible. * * * Nor does it solve the problem to say that the State should promote a "diversity" of religious views; that position would necessarily compel the government and, inevitably, the courts to make wholly inappropriate judgments about the number of religions the State should sponsor and the relative frequency with which it should sponsor each.

Petitioners rest most of their argument on a theory that, whether or not the Establishment Clause permits extensive nonsectarian support for religion, it does not forbid the state to sponsor affirmations of religious belief that coerce neither support for religion nor participation in religious observance. * * * But we could not adopt that reading without abandoning our settled law, a course that, in my view, the text of the Clause would not readily permit. * * * Over the years, this Court has declared the invalidity of many noncoercive state laws and practices conveying a message of religious endorsement. For example, [in] *Wallace v. Jaffree*, 472 U.S. 38 (1985), we struck down a state law requiring a moment of silence in public classrooms not because the statute coerced students to participate in prayer (for it did not), but because the manner of its enactment "convey[ed] a message of state approval of prayer activities in the public schools." * * * Our precedents may not always have drawn perfectly straight lines. They simply cannot, however, support the position that a showing of coercion is necessary to a successful Establishment Clause claim.

[Petitioners also cannot] easily square that claim with the constitutional text. The First Amendment forbids not just laws "respecting an establishment of religion," but also those "prohibiting the free exercise thereof." Yet laws that coerce nonadherents to "support or participate in any religion or its exercise" would virtually by definition violate their right to religious free exercise. Thus, a literal application of the coercion test would render the Establishment Clause a virtual nullity * * *.

Petitioners contend that because the early Presidents included religious messages in their inaugural and Thanksgiving Day addresses, the Framers could not have meant the Establishment Clause to forbid noncoercive state endorsement of religion. The argument ignores the fact, however, that * * * President Jefferson, for example, steadfastly refused to issue Thanksgiving proclamations of any kind, in part because he thought they violated the Religion Clauses. * * * He accordingly construed the Establishment Clause to forbid not simply state coercion, but also state endorsement, of religious belief and observance. * * * During his first three years in office, James Madison also refused to call for days of thanksgiving and prayer, though later, amid the political turmoil of the War of 1812, he did so on four separate occasions. Upon retirement, in an essay condemning as an unconstitutional "establishment" the use of public money to support congressional and military chaplains, he concluded that "[r]eligious proclamations by the Executive recommending thanksgivings & fasts are shoots from the same root with the legislative acts reviewed."

To be sure, the leaders of the young Republic engaged in some of the practices that separationists like Jefferson and Madison criticized. The First Congress did hire institutional chaplains, and Presidents Washington and Adams unapologetically marked days of "public thanksgiving and prayer." Yet in the face of the separationist dissent, those practices prove, at best, that the Framers simply did not share a common understanding of the Establishment Clause, and, at worst, that they, like other politicians, could raise constitutional ideals one day and turn their backs on them the next. * * * Sometimes the National Constitution fared no better. Ten years after proposing the First Amendment, Congress passed the Alien and Sedition Acts, measures patently unconstitutional by modern standards. If the early Congress's political actions were determinative, and not merely relevant, evidence of constitutional meaning, we would have to gut our current First Amendment doctrine to make room for political censorship.

While the Establishment Clause's concept of neutrality is not self-revealing, our recent cases have invested it with specific content: the State may not favor or endorse either religion generally over nonreligion or one religion over others. * * * [T]he government's sponsorship of prayer at the graduation ceremony is most reasonably understood as an official endorsement of religion and, in this instance, of theistic religion.

Petitioners would deflect this conclusion by arguing that graduation prayers are no different from Presidential religious proclamations and similar official "acknowledgments" of religion in public life. But religious invocations in Thanksgiving Day addresses and the like, rarely noticed, ignored without effort, conveyed over an impersonal medium, and directed at no one in particular, inhabit a pallid zone worlds apart from official prayers delivered to a captive audience of public school students and their families. When public school officials, armed with the State's authority, convey an endorsement of religion to their students, they strike near the core of the Establishment Clause. However "ceremonial" their messages may be, they are flatly unconstitutional.

JUSTICE SCALIA, with whom THE CHIEF JUSTICE, JUSTICE WHITE, and JUSTICE THOMAS join, dissenting.

In holding that the Establishment Clause prohibits invocations and benedictions at public-school graduation ceremonies, the Court—with nary a mention that it is doing so—lays waste a tradition that is as old as public-school graduation ceremonies themselves, and that is a component of an even more longstanding American tradition of nonsectarian prayer to God at public celebrations generally. As its instrument of destruction, the bulldozer of its social engineering, the Court invents a boundless, and boundlessly manipulable, test of psychological coercion * * *. Today's opinion shows more forcefully than volumes of argumentation why our Nation's protection, that fortress which is our Constitution, cannot possibly rest upon the changeable philosophical predilections of the Justices of this Court, but must have deep foundations in the historic practices of our people. The history and tradition of our Nation are replete with public ceremonies featuring prayers of thanksgiving and petition. Illustrations of this point have been amply provided in our prior opinions, see, *e.g., Lynch v. Donnelly,* 465 U.S. 668, 673 (1984); *Marsh v. Chambers,* 463 U.S. 783, 790 (1983) * * *.

From our Nation's origin, prayer has been a prominent part of governmental ceremonies and proclamations. The Declaration of Independence, the document marking our birth as a separate people, "appeal[ed] to the Supreme Judge of the world for the rectitude of our intentions" and avowed "a firm reliance on the protection of divine Providence." In his first inaugural address, after swearing his oath of office on a Bible, George Washington deliberately made a prayer a part of his first official act as President:

> "[I]t would be peculiarly improper to omit in this first official act my fervent supplications to that Almighty Being who rules over the universe, who presides in the councils of nations, and whose providential aids can supply every human defect, that His benediction may consecrate to the liberties and happiness of the people of the United States a Government instituted by themselves for these essential purposes." Inaugural Addresses of the Presidents of the United States, S.Doc. 101–10, p. 2 (1989).

Our national celebration of Thanksgiving likewise dates back to President Washington. [Our] tradition of Thanksgiving Proclamations—with their religious theme of prayerful gratitude to God—has been adhered to by almost every President. * * * The other two branches of the Federal Government also have a long-established practice of prayer at public events. [C]ongressional sessions have opened with a chaplain's prayer ever since the First Congress. And this Court's own sessions have opened with the invocation "God save the United States and this Honorable Court" since the days of Chief Justice Marshall. In addition to this general tradition of prayer at public ceremonies, there exists a more specific tradition of invocations and benedictions at public school graduation exercises. By one account, the first public high school graduation ceremony took place in Connecticut in July 1868—the very month, as it happens, that the Fourteenth Amendment (the vehicle by which the Establishment Clause has been applied against the States) was ratified—when "15 seniors from the Norwich Free

Academy marched in their best Sunday suits and dresses into a church hall and waited through majestic music and long prayers."

The Court presumably would separate graduation invocations and benedictions from other instances of public "preservation and transmission of religious beliefs" on the ground that they involve "psychological coercion." [But a] few citations of "[r]esearch in psychology" that have no particular bearing upon the precise issue here cannot disguise the fact that the Court has gone beyond the realm where judges know what they are doing. The Court's argument that state officials have "coerced" students to take part in the invocation and benediction at graduation ceremonies is, not to put too fine a point on it, incoherent.

The Court's notion that a student who simply *sits* in "respectful silence" during the invocation and benediction (when all others are standing) has somehow joined—or would somehow be perceived as having joined—in the prayers is nothing short of ludicrous. We indeed live in a vulgar age. But surely "our social conventions" have not coarsened to the point that anyone who does not stand on his chair and shout obscenities can reasonably be deemed to have assented to everything said in his presence. Since the Court does not dispute that students exposed to prayer at graduation ceremonies retain (despite "subtle coercive pressures") the free will to sit, there is absolutely no basis for the Court's decision. It is fanciful enough to say that "a reasonable dissenter," standing head erect in a class of bowed heads, "could believe that the group exercise signified her own participation or approval of it." It is beyond the absurd to say that she could entertain such a belief while pointedly declining to rise.

But let us assume the very worst, that the nonparticipating graduate is "subtly coerced" . . . to stand! Even that [does] not remotely establish a "participation" (or an "appearance of participation") in a religious exercise. [I]f it is a permissible inference that one who is standing is doing so simply out of respect for the prayers of others that are in progress, then how can it possibly be said that a "reasonable dissenter could believe that the group exercise signified her own participation or approval"? * * * I may add, moreover, that maintaining respect for the religious observances of others is a fundamental civic virtue that government (including the public schools) can and should cultivate—so that even if it were the case that the displaying of such respect might be mistaken for taking part in the prayer, I would deny that the dissenter's interest in avoiding *even the false appearance of participation* constitutionally trumps the government's interest in fostering respect for religion generally.

The deeper flaw in the Court's opinion does not lie in its wrong answer to the question whether there was state-induced "peer-pressure" coercion; it lies,

rather, in the Court's making violation of the
Establishment Clause hinge on such a precious
question. The coercion that was a hallmark of
historical establishments of religion was
coercion of religious orthodoxy and of
financial support *by force of law and threat of
penalty.* * * * The Establishment Clause was
adopted to prohibit such an establishment of
religion at the federal level (and to protect state
establishments of religion from federal
interference). I will further acknowledge for
the sake of argument that, as some scholars
have argued, by 1790 the term "establishment"
had acquired an additional meaning—

> **Food for Thought**
>
> Justice Scalia suggests here that
> the Establishment Clause was
> designed, among other things, to
> "protect state establishments of
> religion from federal interference."
> On this view, would incorporation
> of the Establishment Clause make
> any sense? Would it mean that
> states can in fact establish state
> churches and coerce religious
> orthodoxy? For a more detailed
> account of this view, see Akhil R.
> Amar, *The Bill of Rights as a
> Constitution,* 100 Yale L.J. 1131,
> 1157 (1991).

"financial support of religion generally, by public taxation"—that reflected the
development of "general or multiple" establishments, not limited to a single
church. But that would still be an establishment coerced *by force of law.* And I will
further concede that our constitutional tradition, from the Declaration of
Independence and the first inaugural address of Washington, quoted earlier, down
to the present day, has, with a few aberrations, see *Church of Holy Trinity v. United
States,* 143 U.S. 457 (1892), ruled out of order government-sponsored
endorsement of religion—even when no legal coercion is present, and indeed
even when no ersatz, "peer-pressure" psycho-coercion is present—where the
endorsement is sectarian, in the sense of specifying details upon which men and
women who believe in a benevolent, omnipotent Creator and Ruler of the world
are known to differ (for example, the divinity of Christ). But there is simply no
support for the proposition that the officially sponsored nondenominational
invocation and benediction read by Rabbi Gutterman—with no one legally
coerced to recite them—violated the Constitution of the United States. To the
contrary, they are so characteristically American they could have come from the
pen of George Washington or Abraham Lincoln himself.

Thus, while I have no quarrel with the Court's general proposition that the
Establishment Clause "guarantees that government may not coerce anyone to
support or participate in religion or its exercise," I see no warrant for expanding
the concept of coercion beyond acts backed by threat of penalty—a brand of
coercion that, happily, is readily discernible to those of us who have made a career
of reading the disciples of Blackstone rather than of Freud. The Framers were
indeed opposed to coercion of religious worship by the National Government;
but, as their own sponsorship of nonsectarian prayer in public events

demonstrates, they understood that "[s]peech is not coercive; the listener may do as he likes." *American Jewish Congress v. Chicago,* 827 F.2d 120, 132 (1987) (Easterbrook, J., dissenting).

The Court relies on our "school prayer" cases. But whatever the merit of those cases, they do not support, much less compel, the Court's psycho-journey. In the first place, *Engel* and *Schempp* do not constitute an exception to the rule, distilled from historical practice, that public ceremonies may include prayer; rather, they simply do not fall within the scope of the rule (for the obvious reason that school instruction is not a public ceremony). Second, we have made clear our understanding that school prayer occurs within a framework in which legal coercion to attend school (*i.e.,* coercion under threat of penalty) provides the ultimate backdrop. [O]ur school prayer cases turn in part on the fact that the classroom is inherently an instructional setting, and daily prayer there—where parents are not present to counter "the students' emulation of teachers as role models and the children's susceptibility to peer pressure," *Edwards v. Aguillard,* 482 U.S. 578, 584 (1987)—might be thought to raise special concerns regarding state interference with the liberty of parents to direct the religious upbringing of their children * * *. Voluntary prayer at graduation—a one-time ceremony at which parents, friends, and relatives are present—can hardly be thought to raise the same concerns.

Given the odd basis for the Court's decision, invocations and benedictions will be able to be given at public school graduations next June, as they have for the past century and a half, so long as school authorities make clear that anyone who abstains from screaming in protest does not necessarily participate in the prayers. All that is seemingly needed is an announcement, or perhaps a written insertion at the beginning of the graduation program, to the effect that, while all are asked to rise for the invocation and benediction, none is compelled to join in them, nor will be assumed, by rising, to have done so. That obvious fact recited, the graduates and their parents may proceed to thank God, as Americans have always done, for the blessings He has generously bestowed on them and on their country.

The reader has been told much in this case about the personal interest of Mr. Weisman and his daughter, and very little about the personal interests on the other side. They are not inconsequential. Church and state would not be such a difficult subject if religion were, as the Court apparently thinks it to be, some purely personal avocation that can be indulged entirely in secret, like pornography, in the privacy of one's room. For most believers it is *not* that, and has never been. Religious men and women of almost all denominations have felt it necessary to acknowledge and beseech the blessing of God as a people, and not just as individuals * * *. One can believe in the effectiveness of such public worship, or one can deprecate and deride it. But the longstanding American tradition of prayer at official ceremonies displays with unmistakable clarity that the Establishment Clause does not forbid the government to accommodate it.

I must add one final observation: The Founders of our Republic knew the fearsome potential of sectarian religious belief to generate civil dissension and civil strife. And they also knew that nothing, absolutely nothing, is so inclined to foster among religious believers of various faiths a toleration—no, an affection—for one another than voluntarily joining in prayer together, to the God whom they all worship and seek. Needless to say, no one should be compelled to do that, but it is a shame to deprive our public culture of the opportunity, and indeed the encouragement, for people to do it voluntarily. * * * To deprive our society of that important unifying mechanism, in order to spare the nonbeliever what seems to me the minimal inconvenience of standing or even sitting in respectful nonparticipation, is as senseless in policy as it is unsupported in law.

POINTS FOR DISCUSSION

a.   A Question of Tolerance?

Erwin Griswold, the dean of Harvard Law School and later the Solicitor General of the United States, asserted that although religious believers in the majority should respect the views of a non-believer in the minority, a non-believer should reciprocate. In his view, so long as prayers are voluntary, the non-believer "too has the opportunity to be tolerant. He [should allow] the majority of the group to follow their own tradition, perhaps coming to understand and respect what they feel is significant to them." Erwin Griswold, *Absolute in the Dark: A Discussion of the Approach of the Supreme Court to Constitutional Questions*, 8 Utah L. Rev. 167, 177 (1963) (quoted in Erwin Chemerinsky, *Constitutional Law: Principles and Policies* 1221 (3d ed. 2006)). In *Lee*, Justice Kennedy answered this line of reasoning by saying: "What to most believers may seem nothing more than a reasonable request that the nonbeliever respect their religious practices, in a school context may appear to the nonbeliever or dissenter to be an attempt to employ the machinery of the State to enforce a religious orthodoxy." If the believer and non-believer see the matter in different ways, must the non-believer's view prevail? What, if anything, does the Establishment Clause tell us about the answer to this question?

b. Non-Preferentialism and Non-Sectarianism

At the beginning of this chapter, we considered several different views of the Establishment Clause. Recall that one view, which the Court appeared to endorse in *Everson* and subsequent cases, is sometimes called "separationism." Under this view, the Establishment Clause requires a firm separation between church and state. Another view, which then-Justice Rehnquist advanced in his dissent in *Wallace*, is usually called "non-preferentialism." Under this view, the government need not remain neutral as between religion and non-religion, but instead merely must refrain from preferring one religion over another.

The school in *Lee* argued that the graduation prayer was permissible because it was non-sectarian and non-denominational. The school thus advanced a non-preferentialist view of the Establishment Clause. The Court concluded that even such prayers are impermissible in this context, in part because they (by definition) do not include, at the very least, the views of those who adhere to no religion at all. The Court therefore advanced a separationist view of the Establishment Clause.

If the Court had reached the opposite conclusion—if, for example, it had accepted the non-preferentialist view of the Establishment Clause—then how would it have determined whether a challenged prayer in fact was non-sectarian and non-denominational? Is it clear that the prayer at issue in *Lee* was truly non-sectarian and non-denominational? Did it, for example, embrace the views of adherents of religions, such as some forms of Hinduism, that believe that there is more than one God? What religions "count" for these purposes? Should courts be engaged in such an inquiry?

c. Prayer in School and Free Speech

The foregoing cases show that the government may not require or approve official prayer on public school grounds. Does this mean that government also may (or must) ban all voluntary prayer or religious speech on school grounds? Or would such a ban itself violate the First Amendment? In *Good News Club v. Milford*, 533 U.S. 98 (2001), a public school allowed various community groups to use its building after school hours, but prohibited the petitioner from using the school because it was a religious organization. The Supreme Court held that the ban violated the First Amendment's protection for the freedom of speech because the ban constituted viewpoint discrimination, and that such discrimination was not required to avoid violating the Establishment Clause. See also *Rosenberger v. Rector and Visitors of the University of Virginia*, 515 U.S. 819 (1995), which we considered earlier in this chapter.

d. Student-Led Prayer at School Events

In *Lee*, the prayer at an official school event was led by a member of the clergy. In *Santa Fe Independent School District v. Doe*, 530 U.S. 290 (2000), the Court considered a public high school's program authorizing the student body to vote each year on whether to choose a student to deliver, before each varsity football game, a "brief invocation and/or message [to] solemnize the event," and to vote on who the student should be. The program replaced an earlier program under which a student "chaplain" led prayers before each football game. (That program was enjoined after the Court's decision in *Lee.*) The Court held that the program violated the Establishment Clause, concluding that the "specific purpose of the policy was to preserve a popular state-sponsored religious practice." The Court rejected the argument that the program was valid because it simply permitted the private speech of students rather than official speech, noting that the program was "authorized by a government policy," took place "on governmental property at government-sponsored school-related events," and relied on a "majoritarian process" that guaranteed "by definition [that] minority candidates will never prevail and that their views will be effectively silenced."

Everyone who has read or seen Jerome Lawrence's and Robert Edwin Lee's play *Inherit the Wind,* which recounted the "Scopes trial" and the legal battle over Tennessee's "monkey law," knows that many states once banned the teaching in public schools of the theory of evolution. In *Epperson v. Arkansas,* 393 U.S. 97 (1968), the Court held that an Arkansas law forbidding the teaching of evolution in public schools and universities violated the First and Fourteenth Amendments. The Court began by asserting:

> Government in our democracy, state and national, must be neutral in matters of religious theory, doctrine, and practice. It may not be hostile to any religion or to the advocacy of [non]-religion; and it may not aid, foster, or promote one religion or religious theory against another or even against the militant opposite. The First Amendment mandates governmental neutrality between religion and religion, and between religion and nonreligion.

The Court then invalidated the statute as a violation of those principles:

> [T]here can be no doubt that Arkansas has sought to prevent its teachers from discussing the theory of evolution because it is contrary to the belief of some that the Book of Genesis must be the exclusive source of doctrine as to the origin of man. No suggestion has been made that Arkansas' law may be justified by considerations of state policy other than the religious views of some of its citizens. It is clear that fundamentalist sectarian conviction was and is the law's reason for existence. Its antecedent, Tennessee's "monkey law," candidly stated its purpose: to make it unlawful "to teach any theory that denies the story of the Divine Creation of man as taught in the Bible, and to teach instead

that man has descended from a lower order of animals." Perhaps the sensational publicity attendant upon the Scopes trial induced Arkansas to adopt less explicit language. It eliminated Tennessee's reference to "the story of the Divine Creation of man" as taught in the Bible, but there is no doubt that the motivation for the law was the same: to suppress the teaching of a theory which, it was thought, "denied" the divine creation of man.

Arkansas' law cannot be defended as an act of religious neutrality. Arkansas did not seek to excise from the curricula of its schools and universities all discussion of the origin of man. The law's effort was confined to an attempt to blot out a particular theory because of its supposed conflict with the Biblical account, literally read.

In the decades after the Court's decision in *Epperson*, several states sought to include in their public school curricula consideration of "creationism"—that is, the study of the Biblical account of the creation of the earth and all of its species— alongside consideration of the theory of evolution. Do such policies satisfy the approach that the Court followed in *Epperson*? The case that follows addresses that question.

EDWARDS V. AGUILLARD
482 U.S. 578 (1987)

JUSTICE BRENNAN delivered the opinion of the Court.

The question for decision is whether Louisiana's "Balanced Treatment for Creation-Science and Evolution-Science in Public School Instruction" Act (Creationism Act), La.Rev.Stat.Ann. §§ 17:286.1–17:286.7, is facially invalid as violative of the Establishment Clause of the First Amendment. The Creationism Act forbids the teaching of the theory of evolution in public schools unless accompanied by instruction in "creation science." § 17:286.4A. No school is required to teach evolution or creation science. If either is taught, however, the other must also be taught. The theories of evolution and creation science are statutorily defined as "the scientific evidences for [creation or evolution] and inferences from those scientific evidences." §§ 17.286.3(2) and (3). Appellees, who include parents of children attending Louisiana public schools, Louisiana teachers, and religious leaders, challenged the constitutionality of the Act * * *.

The Court has applied [the three-pronged *Lemon* test] to determine whether legislation comports with the Establishment Clause. * * * *Lemon*'s first prong focuses on the purpose that animated adoption of the Act. * * * In this case, appellants have identified no clear secular purpose for the Louisiana Act. True, the Act's stated purpose is to protect academic freedom. La.Rev.Stat.Ann. § 17:286.2. * * * While the Court is normally deferential to a State's articulation of a secular purpose, it is required that the statement of such purpose be sincere and not a sham. [R]equiring schools to teach creation science with evolution does not advance academic freedom. The Act does not grant teachers a flexibility that they did not already possess to supplant the present science curriculum with the presentation of theories, besides evolution, about the origin of life.

> **Take Note**
>
> The Court asserts that the Act creates a "discriminatory preference" in favor of creation science. Can you articulate in what way the Act "discriminates" against the teaching of evolution? Do you agree that the statute "discriminates"?

Furthermore, the goal of basic "fairness" is hardly furthered by the Act's discriminatory preference for the teaching of creation science and against the teaching of evolution.

If the Louisiana Legislature's purpose was solely to maximize the comprehensiveness and effectiveness of science instruction, it would have encouraged the teaching of all scientific theories about the origins of humankind. But under the Act's requirements, teachers who were once free to teach any and all facets of this subject are now unable to do so. * * * Thus we agree with the Court of Appeals' conclusion that the Act does not serve to protect academic freedom, but has the distinctly different purpose of discrediting "evolution by counterbalancing its teaching at every turn with the teaching of creationism." 765 F.2d, at 1257.

[W]e need not be blind in this case to the legislature's preeminent religious purpose in enacting this statute. There is a historic and contemporaneous link between the teachings of certain religious denominations and the teaching of evolution. [See *Epperson v. Arkansas,* 393 U.S. 97 (1968).] The preeminent purpose of the Louisiana Legislature was clearly to advance the religious viewpoint that a supernatural being created humankind. * * * The legislative history [reveals] that the term "creation science," as contemplated by the legislature that adopted this Act, embodies the religious belief that a supernatural creator was responsible for the creation of humankind.

Furthermore, it is not happenstance that the legislature required the teaching of a theory that coincided with this religious view. The legislative history documents that the Act's primary purpose was to change the science curriculum of public schools in order to provide persuasive advantage to a particular religious doctrine that rejects the factual basis of evolution in its entirety. The sponsor of the Creationism Act, Senator Keith, explained during the legislative hearings that his disdain for the theory of evolution resulted from the support that evolution supplied to views contrary to his own religious beliefs. [He] repeatedly stated that scientific evidence supporting his religious views should be included in the public

> **Food for Thought**
>
> The Court relies heavily on the views expressed by the sponsor of the bill in the state senate. Is it appropriate to put such heavy reliance on the views of one legislator? Isn't it possible that other members of the legislature voted for the bill for entirely different reasons? If so, can you think of any secular reasons that one might have had for supporting the bill?

school curriculum to redress the fact that the theory of evolution incidentally coincided with what he characterized as religious beliefs antithetical to his own. The legislation therefore sought to alter the science curriculum to reflect endorsement of a religious view that is antagonistic to the theory of evolution.

[Accordingly,] the Creationism Act is designed *either* to promote the theory of creation science which embodies a particular religious tenet by requiring that creation science be taught whenever evolution is taught *or* to prohibit the teaching of a scientific theory disfavored by certain religious sects by forbidding the teaching of evolution when creation science is not also taught. The Establishment Clause, however, "forbids *alike* the preference of a religious doctrine *or* the prohibition of theory which is deemed antagonistic to a particular dogma." *Epperson*, 393 U.S. at 106–107 (emphasis added). Because the primary purpose of the Creationism Act is to advance a particular religious belief, the Act endorses religion in violation of the First Amendment.

We do not imply that a legislature could never require that scientific critiques of prevailing scientific theories be taught. [T]eaching a variety of scientific theories about the origins of humankind to schoolchildren might be validly done with the clear secular intent of enhancing the effectiveness of science instruction. But because the primary purpose of the Creationism Act is to endorse a particular religious doctrine, the Act furthers religion in violation of the Establishment Clause.

[JUSTICE POWELL's concurring opinion and JUSTICE WHITE's opinion concurring in the judgment are omitted.]

JUSTICE SCALIA, with whom THE CHIEF JUSTICE joins, dissenting.

I doubt whether [the] "purpose" requirement of *Lemon* is a proper interpretation of the Constitution; but even if it were, I could not agree with the Court's assessment that the requirement was not satisfied here. * * * We have relatively little information upon which to judge the motives of those who supported the Act. * * * Nevertheless, there is ample evidence that the majority is wrong in holding that the Balanced Treatment Act is without secular purpose. * * * Senator Keith and his witnesses

> **Food for Thought**
>
> Does the question whether the enacting legislature had a secular purpose turn on the validity of the evidence on which the legislature relied? Must creation science be a "legitimate" science in order to attribute the secular purpose that Justice Scalia says existed? If so, are courts competent to make such judgments?

testified essentially: (1) There are two and only two scientific explanations for the beginning of life—evolution and creation science. * * * Since there are only two possible explanations of the origin of life, any evidence that tends to disprove the theory of evolution necessarily tends to prove the theory of creation science, and vice versa. (2) The body of scientific evidence supporting creation science is as strong as that supporting evolution. * * * Evolution is not a scientific "fact," since it cannot actually be observed in a laboratory. Rather, evolution is merely a scientific theory or "guess" [and] a very bad guess at that. (3) Students exposed to [creation science] better understand the current state of scientific evidence about the origin of life. (4) Although creation science is educationally valuable and strictly scientific, it is now being censored from or misrepresented in the public schools. (5) The censorship of creation science [deprives] students of knowledge of one of the two scientific explanations for the origin of life and leads them to believe that evolution is proven fact; thus, their education suffers and they are wrongly taught that science has proved their religious beliefs false.

We have no way of knowing, of course, how many legislators believed the testimony of Senator Keith and his witnesses. But in the absence of evidence to the contrary, we have to assume that many of them did. Given that assumption, the Court today plainly errs in holding that the Louisiana Legislature passed the Balanced Treatment Act for exclusively religious purposes.

I can only attribute [the Court's rejection of this legislative history and the Act's stated purpose] to an intellectual predisposition created by the facts and the legend of *Scopes v. State,* 154 Tenn. 105 (1927)—an instinctive reaction that any governmentally imposed requirements bearing upon the teaching of evolution must be a manifestation of Christian fundamentalist repression. In this case, however, it seems to me the Court's position is the repressive one. The people of Louisiana, including those who are Christian fundamentalists, are quite entitled, as a secular matter, to have whatever scientific evidence there may be against evolution presented in their schools, just as Mr. Scopes was entitled to present whatever scientific evidence there was for it. * * * Because I believe that the Balanced Treatment Act had a secular purpose, which is all the first component of the *Lemon* test requires, I would reverse the judgment of the Court of Appeals and remand for further consideration.

I have to this point assumed the validity of the *Lemon* "purpose" test. In fact, however, I think [it] is "a constitutional theory [that] has no basis in the history of the amendment it seeks to interpret, is difficult to apply and yields unprincipled results." *Wallace v. Jaffree*, 472 U.S. 38, 112 (1985) (REHNQUIST, J., dissenting). * * * Our cases interpreting and applying the purpose test have made such a maze of the Establishment Clause that even the most conscientious governmental officials can only guess what motives will be held unconstitutional.

But the difficulty of knowing what vitiating purpose one is looking for is as nothing compared with the difficulty of knowing how or where to find it. For while it is possible to discern the objective "purpose" of a statute (*i.e.,* the public good at which its provisions appear to be directed), or even the formal motivation for a statute where that is explicitly set forth (as it was, to no avail, here), discerning the subjective motivation of those enacting the statute is, to be honest, almost always an impossible task. The number of possible motivations, to begin with, is not binary, or indeed even finite. * * * To look for *the sole purpose* of even a single legislator is probably to look for something that does not exist. * * * Putting that problem aside, however, where ought we to look for the individual legislator's purpose? * * * Legislative histories can be contrived and sanitized, favorable media coverage orchestrated, and postenactment recollections conveniently distorted. [And we] must still confront the question (yet to be addressed in any of our cases) how *many* of them must have the invalidating intent. Because there are no good answers to these questions, this Court has recognized [that] determining the subjective intent of legislators is a perilous enterprise.

In the past we have attempted to justify our embarrassing Establishment Clause jurisprudence on the ground that it "sacrifices clarity and predictability for flexibility." *Committee for Public Education & Religious Liberty v. Regan,* 444 U.S. 646, 662 (1980). * * * I think it time that we sacrifice some "flexibility" for "clarity and predictability." Abandoning *Lemon*'s purpose test [would] be a good place to start.

POINTS FOR DISCUSSION

a.   Teaching Creationism

The Court in *Epperson* invalidated a state law prohibiting the teaching of the theory of evolution. Is a statute requiring the teaching of creationism equivalent, for Establishment Clause purposes, to a statute banning the teaching of evolution? Could a state constitutionally enact a statute that permits, but does not require, science teachers to teach creationism? (Can you articulate how such a statute would be different from the statute at issue in *Edwards*?) Similarly, in the absence of any statutory guidance, could a teacher in a public school science class constitutionally teach his or her students that the account in Genesis, and not the theory of evolution, explains the origin of the human species? If not, then how could the statute at issue in *Edwards* be constitutional?

b.   Purpose and the *Lemon* Test

The Court in *Edwards* considered only the first prong of the *Lemon* test, invalidating the statute as lacking a valid secular purpose. Justice Scalia asserted that (at least) this prong of the *Lemon* test should be abandoned. Do you agree that it is usually impossible to determine the "actual" purpose that motivated a legislature to enact a statute? Even if you agree with Justice Scalia that the inquiry is fraught with difficulties, is there an argument that the inquiry nevertheless is essential in the Establishment Clause context?

c.   Teaching "Intelligent Design"

After the decision in *Edwards*, advocates of teaching creationism in public schools began an effort to encourage the teaching of the theory of "intelligent design," which posits that there are natural systems that cannot be adequately explained by undirected natural forces and that thus must be the product of design by some intelligent agent. Does the teaching in public schools of the theory of intelligent design—either alone or alongside the theory of evolution—violate the Establishment Clause? The only court to address the question concluded that it does. See *Kitzmiller v. Dover Area School District*, 400 F.Supp. 2d 707 (M.D. Pa. 2005). Do you agree?

So far, the cases that we have considered in this section have involved the public school context. Is that context unique? Or do the rules that the Court has announced for religious activities in public schools apply equally to governmental actions outside of the school context?

MARSH V. CHAMBERS
463 U.S. 783 (1983)

CHIEF JUSTICE BURGER delivered the opinion of the Court.

The Nebraska Legislature begins each of its sessions with a prayer offered by a chaplain who is chosen biennially by the Executive Board of the Legislative Council and paid out of public funds. Robert E. Palmer, a Presbyterian minister, has served as chaplain since 1965 at a salary of $319.75 per month for each month the legislature is in session.

Ernest Chambers is a member of the Nebraska Legislature and a taxpayer of Nebraska. Claiming that the Nebraska Legislature's chaplaincy practice violates the Establishment Clause of the First Amendment, he brought this action under 42 U.S.C. § 1983, seeking to enjoin enforcement of the practice. * * *

The opening of sessions of legislative and other deliberative public bodies with prayer is deeply embedded in the history and tradition of this country. From colonial times through the founding of the Republic and ever since, the practice of legislative prayer has coexisted with the principles of disestablishment and religious freedom. In the very courtrooms in which the United States District Judge and later three Circuit Judges heard and decided this case, the proceedings opened with an announcement that concluded, "God save the United States and this Honorable Court." The same invocation occurs at all sessions of this Court.

The tradition in many of the colonies was, of course, linked to an established church, but the Continental Congress, beginning in 1774, adopted the traditional procedure of opening its sessions with a prayer offered by a paid chaplain. See *e.g.,* 1 J. of the Continental Cong. 26 (1774). Although prayers were not offered during the Constitutional Convention, the First Congress, as one of its early items of business, adopted the policy of selecting a chaplain to open each session with prayer. Thus, on April 7, 1789, the Senate appointed a committee "to take under consideration the manner of electing Chaplains." J. of the Sen. 10. On April 9, 1789, a similar committee was appointed by the House of Representatives. On

> **FYI**
>
> Ernie Chambers, one of the longest serving members of the Nebraska legislature, initially protested the opening prayer by leaving the chamber before the prayer started. But one day the governor and the chaplain conspired to play a trick on him. They started the session a few minutes early so that he did not have time to leave. Chambers later brought this lawsuit. See Duke Law School, Video Interview of Rev. Robert Palmer. Despite winning the case, the Nebraska legislature subsequently changed its practices. Instead of paying a chaplain, it set up a system of volunteers.

April 25, 1789, the Senate elected its first chaplain, J. of the Sen. 16; the House followed suit on May 1, 1789, J. of the H.R. 26. A statute providing for the payment of these chaplains was enacted into law on Sept. 22, 1789. 2 Annals of Cong. 2180; 1 Stat. 71.

On Sept. 25, 1789, three days after Congress authorized the appointment of paid chaplains, final agreement was reached on the language of the Bill of Rights, J. of the Sen. 88; J. of the H.R. 121. Clearly the men who wrote the First Amendment Religion Clause did not view paid legislative chaplains and opening prayers as a violation of that Amendment, for the practice of opening sessions with prayer has continued without interruption ever since that early session of Congress. It has also been followed consistently in most of the states, including Nebraska, where the institution of opening legislative sessions with prayer was adopted even before the State attained statehood. Nebraska Journal of the Council at the First Regular Session of the General Assembly 16 (Jan. 22, 1855).

Standing alone, historical patterns cannot justify contemporary violations of constitutional guarantees, but there is far more here than simply historical patterns. In this context, historical evidence sheds light not only on what the draftsmen intended the Establishment Clause to mean, but also on how they thought that Clause applied to the practice authorized by the First Congress— their actions reveal their intent. An act "passed by the first Congress assembled under the Constitution, many of whose members had taken part in framing that instrument, [is] contemporaneous and weighty evidence of its true meaning." *Wisconsin v. Pelican Ins. Co.,* 127 U.S. 265, 297 (1888).

No more is Nebraska's practice of over a century, consistent with two centuries of national practice, to be cast aside. It can hardly be thought that in the same week Members of the First Congress voted to appoint and to pay a Chaplain for each House and also voted to approve the draft of the First Amendment for submission to the States, they intended the Establishment Clause of the Amendment to forbid what they had just declared acceptable. In applying the First Amendment to the states through the Fourteenth Amendment, it would be incongruous to interpret that clause as

> **Food for Thought**
>
> The First Congress passed the Bill of Rights and submitted it to the states for ratification. Is it possible that the Bill of Rights prohibits some of the actions in which the First Congress engaged? If the original meaning is the touchstone of constitutional meaning, should the Court consider what members of the First Congress intended, or should it instead consider what the words would objectively have meant to the ratifiers? And is there a difference between how the drafters and ratifiers *expected* a provision to apply and how it does apply to modern circumstances?

imposing more stringent First Amendment limits on the States than the draftsmen imposed on the Federal Government.

This unique history leads us to accept the interpretation of the First Amendment draftsmen who saw no real threat to the Establishment Clause arising from a practice of prayer similar to that now challenged. We conclude that legislative prayer presents no more potential for establishment than the provision of school transportation, *Everson v. Board of Education,* 330 U.S. 1 (1946), beneficial grants for higher education, *Tilton v. Richardson,* 403 U.S. 672 (1971), or tax exemptions for religious organizations, *Walz v. Tax Comm'n,* 397 U.S. 664, 678 (1970).

JUSTICE BRENNAN, with whom JUSTICE MARSHALL joins, dissenting.

The most commonly cited formulation of prevailing Establishment Clause doctrine is found in *Lemon v. Kurtzman,* 403 U.S. 602 (1971):

> "First, the statute [at issue] must have a secular legislative purpose; second, its principal or primary effect must be one that neither advances nor inhibits religion; finally, the statute must not foster 'an excessive government entanglement with religion.' "

That the "purpose" of legislative prayer is preeminently religious rather than secular seems to me to be self-evident. "To invoke Divine guidance on a public body entrusted with making the laws," is nothing but a religious act. Moreover, whatever secular functions legislative prayer might play—formally opening the legislative session, getting the members of the body to quiet down, and imbuing them with a sense of seriousness and high purpose—could so plainly be performed in a purely nonreligious fashion that to claim a secular purpose for the prayer is an insult to the perfectly honorable individuals who instituted and continue the practice.

The "primary effect" of legislative prayer is also clearly religious. * * * More importantly, invocations in Nebraska's legislative halls explicitly link religious belief and observance to the power and prestige of the State. "[T]he mere appearance of a joint exercise of legislative authority by Church and State provides a significant symbolic benefit to religion in the minds of some by reason of the power conferred." *Larkin v. Grendel's Den,* 459 U.S. 116 (1982).

Finally, there can be no doubt that the practice of legislative prayer leads to excessive "entanglement" between the State and religion. *Lemon* pointed out that "entanglement" can take two forms: First, a state statute or program might involve the state impermissibly in monitoring and overseeing religious affairs. In the case of legislative prayer, the process of choosing a "suitable" chaplain, whether on a permanent or rotating basis, and insuring that the chaplain limits himself or herself to "suitable" prayers, involves precisely the sort of supervision that agencies of government should if at all possible avoid.

Second, excessive "entanglement" might arise out of "the divisive political potential" of a state statute or program. * * * In this case, this second aspect of entanglement is also clear. The controversy between Senator Chambers and his colleagues, which had reached the stage of difficulty and rancor long before this lawsuit was brought, has split the Nebraska Legislature precisely on issues of religion and religious conformity. The record in this case also reports a series of instances, involving legislators other than Senator Chambers, in which invocations by Reverend Palmer and others led to controversy along religious lines. And in general, the history of legislative prayer has been far more eventful—and divisive—than a hasty reading of the Court's opinion might indicate.

JUSTICE STEVENS, dissenting.

In a democratically elected legislature, the religious beliefs of the chaplain tend to reflect the faith of the majority of the lawmakers' constituents. Prayers may be said by a Catholic priest in the Massachusetts Legislature and by a Presbyterian minister in the Nebraska Legislature, but I would not expect to find a Jehovah's Witness or a disciple of Mary Baker Eddy or the Reverend Moon serving as the official chaplain in any state legislature. Regardless of the motivation of the majority that exercises the power to appoint the chaplain, it seems plain to me that the designation of a member of one religious faith to serve as the sole official chaplain of a state legislature for a period of 16 years constitutes the preference of one faith over another in violation of the Establishment Clause of the First Amendment.

POINTS FOR DISCUSSION

a. School Prayer and Legislative Prayer

Although the Supreme Court held in *Marsh* that Nebraska can begin its legislative sessions with a prayer, we have also seen that it has concluded that the Establishment Clause bars almost all kinds of official authorized or approved prayers in public elementary and secondary schools. The Court decided the seminal case concerning prayer in schools—*Engel v. Vitale*—more than twenty years before it decided *Marsh*. The majority in *Marsh*, however, did not cite *Engel* in its opinion. Should the Court in *Marsh* have concluded that *Engel* was controlling?

Was there anything in the Court's opinion in *Engel* or its progeny to suggest that the school context is unique? For example, are schools different because they teach impressionable children? Or because school attendance is generally mandatory? Or because schools form a traditional melting pot for society? Consider the view that Justice Brennan expressed in *Edwards v. Aguillard*, several years after the decision in *Marsh*:

> The Court has been particularly vigilant in monitoring compliance with the Establishment Clause in elementary and secondary schools. Families entrust public schools with the education of their children, but condition their trust on the understanding that the classroom will not purposely be used to advance religious views that may conflict with the private beliefs of the student and his or her family. Students in such institutions are impressionable and their attendance is involuntary. The State exerts great authority and coercive power through mandatory attendance requirements, and because of the students' emulation of teachers as role models and the children's susceptibility to peer pressure.

Edwards v. Aguillard, 482 U.S. 578 (1987).

Did the Court in *Marsh* have an obligation to specify that schools are in fact different? If you conclude that there is no meaningful difference between the school context and the legislative context, does that mean that the school cases were decided incorrectly? Or was it *Marsh* that was decided incorrectly? In any event, if evidence emerged that prayer was common in public schools as a matter of history and tradition, would the decision in *Marsh* require the Court to overrule *Engel*?

b.   The Rule of *Marsh*

The Court stated in *Marsh* that legislative prayers are "deeply embedded in the history and tradition of this country." Does this language suggest that any religious activities in governmental institutions that have a long history and tradition are constitutional under the Establishment Clause? Must the tradition extend to the time before the First Amendment (or Fourteenth Amendment, in the case of actions by the states) was ratified? Are history and tradition relevant because they help us to determine the original meaning of the Establishment Clause? Or are they relevant because, regardless of the original meaning of the Clause, a consistently observed tradition can become constitutional simply by virtue of its repetition?

What history and traditions should the Court consider in deciding the constitutionality of practices under the Establishment Clause? Consider Justice Souter's view in *Lee v. Weisman*, which we considered earlier in this chapter:

> To be sure, the leaders of the young Republic engaged in some of the practices that separationists like Jefferson and Madison criticized. The First Congress did hire institutional chaplains, and Presidents Washington and Adams unapologetically marked days of "public thanksgiving and prayer."

Yet in the face of the separationist dissent, those practices prove, at best, that the Framers simply did not share a common understanding of the Establishment Clause, and, at worst, that they, like other politicians, could raise constitutional ideals one day and turn their backs on them the next. * * * Ten years after proposing the First Amendment, Congress passed the Alien and Sedition Acts, measures patently unconstitutional by modern standards. If the early Congress's political actions were determinative, and not merely relevant, evidence of constitutional meaning, we would have to gut our current First Amendment doctrine to make room for political censorship.

Lee v. Weisman, 505 U.S. 577 (1992) (Souter, J., concurring). Can the Court tell the difference between history that shows the exception and history that shows the rule?

c.   History v. the *Lemon* Test

Chief Justice Burger's opinion resolved this case based upon the original meaning (or perhaps intent) of the Establishment Clause, and he did not attempt to apply the *Lemon* test (which, you might recall, he had authored). Justice Brennan, by contrast, relied on the *Lemon* test. Was his application of the *Lemon* test correct? If the *Lemon* test produces results that are inconsistent with history, tradition, or the original expected application of the Establishment Clause, then is the *Lemon* test problematic?

d.   Separationism v. Non-Preferentialism

Justice Brennan's dissent in *Marsh* advanced the classic view of separationism— that is, he asserted that the Establishment Clause prohibits the government from preferring or endorsing religion. Justice Stevens's dissent, by contrast, rejected the practice as inconsistent with even a non-preferentialist view—that is, he asserted that the Establishment Clause at least requires the government to refrain from preferring one religion over another. Which view of the Establishment Clause did Chief Justice Burger advance?

e.   The Continuing Vitality of *Marsh*

In *McCreary County, Kentucky v. American Civil Liberties Union, Kentucky*, 545 U.S. 844 (2005), which we will consider later in this chapter, the Court held that a public display of the Ten Commandments violated the Establishment Clause. In his opinion for the Court, Justice Souter stated:

At least since *Everson v. Board of Ed. of Ewing*, 330 U.S. 1 (1947), it has been clear that Establishment Clause doctrine lacks the comfort of categorical absolutes. In special instances we have found good reason to hold governmental action legitimate even where its manifest purpose was presumably religious. See, *e.g., Marsh v. Chambers*, 463 U.S. 783 (1983) (upholding legislative prayer despite its religious nature). No such reasons present themselves here.

Does this suggest that the approach of the Court in *Marsh* is confined to "special" (and thus presumably rare) instances? Or are similar examples of religion in governmental institutions—such as the friezes, oaths, and prayers at the Supreme Court described at the start of this section—so clearly unproblematic that they are seldom litigated?

In *Town of Greece v. Galloway*, 572 U.S. 565 (2014), the Court rejected a challenge to a New York town's practice of opening its monthly board meetings with a prayer. The respondents, town residents who attended board meetings, contended that the town preferred Christian prayer givers and that the prayers often were sectarian in nature. The Court, in an opinion by Justice Kennedy, began by asserting that "*Marsh* must not be understood as permitting a practice that would amount to a constitutional violation if not for its historical foundation." Instead, "*Marsh* stands for the proposition that it is not necessary to define the precise boundary of the Establishment Clause where history shows that the specific practice is permitted. Any test the Court adopts must acknowledge a practice that was accepted by the Framers and has withstood the critical scrutiny of time and political change. A test that would sweep away what has so long been settled would create new controversy and begin anew the very divisions along religious lines that the Establishment Clause seeks to prevent."

The Court therefore sought to "determine whether the prayer practice [fits] within the tradition long followed in Congress and the state legislatures." The Court concluded that it did, notwithstanding the respondents' assertion that the prayers were sectarian. The Court reasoned that to "hold that invocations must be nonsectarian would force the legislatures that sponsor prayers and the courts that are asked to decide these cases to act as supervisors and censors of religious speech. * * * Once it invites prayer into the public sphere, government must permit a prayer giver to address his or her own God or gods as conscience dictates, unfettered by what an administrator or judge considers to be nonsectarian." The Court concluded that "[p]rayer that reflects beliefs specific to only some creeds can still serve to solemnize the occasion, so long as the practice over time is not 'exploited to proselytize or advance any one, or to disparage any other, faith or belief.' " In a section of the opinion joined by only Chief Justice Roberts and Justice Alito, Justice Kennedy also rejected the respondents' claim that the town's prayer practice, at board meetings regularly attended by ordinary citizens, coerced participation by nonadherents. Although he stated that the inquiry "is a fact-sensitive one that considers both the setting in which the prayer arises and the audience to whom it is directed," he was "not persuaded that the [town], through the act of offering a brief, solemn, and respectful prayer to open its monthly meetings, compelled its citizens to engage in a religious observance." He concluded that the "analysis would be different if town board members directed the public to participate in the prayers, singled out dissidents for opprobrium, or indicated that their decisions might be influenced by a person's acquiescence in the prayer opportunity." Justices Breyer, Ginsburg, Kagan, and Sotomayor dissented.

———————

The cases that we have considered so far in this section have concerned religious activities by government or government actors. The following cases concern a particular manifestation of this phenomenon: the placement of religious symbols on government property. As you will see, the early cases apply the *Lemon* test, while the later cases are less likely to do so. But it is still possible to discern rules from the cases. For the most part, the Court has held that religious symbols are permissible if they have a secular purpose and do not endorse a specific religion or religion in general. As you read the cases, consider (1) whether this is a sensible approach and (2) whether the Court has faithfully and consistently followed this approach.

LYNCH V. DONNELLY

465 U.S. 668 (1984)

THE CHIEF JUSTICE delivered the opinion of the Court.

Each year, in cooperation with the downtown retail merchants' association, the City of Pawtucket, Rhode Island, erects a Christmas display as part of its observance of the Christmas holiday season. The display is situated in a park owned by a nonprofit organization and located in the heart of the shopping district. The display is essentially like those to be found in hundreds of towns or cities across the Nation—often on public grounds—during the Christmas season. The Pawtucket display comprises many of the figures and decorations traditionally associated with Christmas, including, among other things, a Santa Claus house, reindeer pulling Santa's sleigh, candy-striped poles, a Christmas tree, carolers, cutout figures representing such characters as a clown, an elephant, and a teddy bear, hundreds of colored lights, a large banner that reads "SEASONS GREETINGS," and the crèche at issue here. All components of this display are owned by the City.

The crèche, which has been included in the display for 40 or more years, consists of the traditional figures, including the Infant Jesus, Mary and Joseph, angels, shepherds, kings, and animals, all ranging in height from 5" to 5'. In 1973, when the present crèche was acquired, it cost the City $1365; it now is valued at

$200. The erection and dismantling of the crèche costs the City about $20 per year; nominal expenses are incurred in lighting the crèche. No money has been expended on its maintenance for the past 10 years.

Respondents, Pawtucket residents and individual members of the Rhode Island affiliate of the American Civil Liberties Union, and the affiliate itself, brought this action [claiming that] the crèche in the display violates the Establishment Clause which is binding on the states through the Fourteenth Amendment. * * *

This Court has explained that the purpose of the Establishment and Free Exercise Clauses of the First Amendment is "to prevent, as far as possible, the intrusion of either [the church or the state] into the precincts of the other." *Lemon v. Kurtzman,* 403 U.S. 602, 614 (1971). At the same time, however, the Court has recognized that "total separation is not possible in an absolute sense. Some relationship between government and religious organizations is inevitable." *Ibid.* In every Establishment Clause case, we must reconcile the inescapable tension between the objective of preventing unnecessary intrusion of either the church or the state upon the other, and the reality that, as the Court has so often noted, total separation of the two is not possible.

There is an unbroken history of official acknowledgment by all three branches of government of the role of religion in American life from at least 1789. * * * Beginning in the early colonial period long before Independence, a day of Thanksgiving was celebrated as a religious holiday to give thanks for the bounties of Nature as gifts from God. * * * Executive Orders and other official announcements of Presidents and of the Congress have proclaimed both Christmas and Thanksgiving National Holidays in religious terms. And, by Acts of Congress, it has long been the practice that federal employees are released from duties on these National Holidays, while being paid from the same public revenues that provide the compensation of the Chaplains of the Senate and the House and the military services. Thus, it is clear that Government has long recognized—indeed it has subsidized—holidays with religious significance. Other examples of reference to our religious heritage are found in the statutorily prescribed national motto "In God We Trust," 36 U.S.C. § 186, which Congress and the President mandated for our currency, see 31 U.S.C. § 324, and in the language "One nation under God," as part of the Pledge of Allegiance to the American flag. * * * Art galleries supported by public revenues display religious paintings of the 15th and 16th centuries, predominantly inspired by one religious faith. * * * One cannot look at even this brief resume without finding that our history is pervaded by expressions of religious beliefs * * *. Equally pervasive is the evidence of accommodation of all faiths and all forms of religious expression, and hostility toward none.

This history may help explain why the Court consistently has declined to take a rigid, absolutist view of the Establishment Clause. * * * Rather than mechanically invalidating all governmental conduct or statutes that confer benefits or give special recognition to religion in general or to one faith—as an absolutist approach would dictate—the Court has scrutinized challenged legislation or official conduct to determine whether, in reality, it establishes a religion or religious faith, or tends to do so. In each case, the inquiry calls for line drawing; no fixed, *per se* rule can be framed.

In the line-drawing process we have often found it useful to inquire whether the challenged law or conduct has a secular purpose, whether its principal or primary effect is to advance or inhibit religion, and whether it creates an excessive entanglement of government with religion. *Lemon.* But, we have repeatedly emphasized our unwillingness to be confined to any single test or criterion in this sensitive area. * * * We did not, for example, consider that analysis relevant in *Marsh v. Chambers,* 463 U.S. 783 (1983). * * *

The District Court inferred from the religious nature of the crèche that the City has no secular purpose for the display. In so doing, it rejected the City's claim that its reasons for including the crèche are essentially the same as its reasons for sponsoring the display as a whole. The District Court plainly erred by focusing almost exclusively on the crèche. When viewed in the proper context of the Christmas Holiday season, it is apparent that, on this record, there is insufficient evidence to establish that the inclusion of the crèche is a purposeful or surreptitious effort to express some kind of subtle governmental advocacy of a particular religious message. In a pluralistic society a variety of motives and purposes are implicated. The City, like the Congresses and Presidents, however, has principally taken note of a significant historical religious event long celebrated in the Western World. The crèche in the display depicts the historical origins of this traditional event long recognized as a National Holiday.

Take Note

The Court concludes here that the display of the crèche has the legitimate secular purpose of celebrating and depicting the origins of Christmas. Must the Court rely, in reaching this conclusion, on the premise that Christmas is not a religious holiday? If so, do you agree? By contrast, if the Court views Christmas as a religious holiday, then how can official governmental celebration of the holiday have a secular purpose?

The narrow question is whether there is a secular purpose for Pawtucket's display of the crèche. The display is sponsored by the City to celebrate the Holiday and to depict the origins of that Holiday. These are legitimate secular purposes. The District Court's inference, drawn from the religious nature of the crèche, that the City has no secular purpose was, on this record, clearly erroneous.

The District Court found that the primary effect of including the crèche is to confer a substantial and impermissible benefit on religion in general and on the Christian faith in particular. Comparisons of the relative benefits to religion of different forms of governmental support are elusive and difficult to make. But to conclude that the primary effect of including the crèche is to advance religion in violation of the Establishment Clause would require that we view it as more beneficial to and more an endorsement of religion, for example, than expenditure of large sums of public money for textbooks supplied throughout the country to students attending church-sponsored schools, *Board of Education v. Allen,* 392 U.S. 236 (1968); expenditure of public funds for transportation of students to church-sponsored schools, *Everson v. Board of Education,* 330 U.S. 1 (1947); federal grants for college buildings of church-sponsored institutions of higher education combining secular and religious education, *Tilton v. Richardson,* 403 U.S. 672 (1971); noncategorical grants to church-sponsored colleges and universities, *Roemer v. Board of Public Works,* 426 U.S. 736 (1976); and the tax exemptions for church properties sanctioned in *Walz v. Tax Commission,* 397 U.S. 664, 671 (1970). It would also require that we view it as more of an endorsement of religion

---

Food for Thought

Most (though not all) of the cases that the Court cites here involved government aid to religious institutions, rather than religious displays by government institutions. Is there a difference in the way that those types of activities appear to "endorse" religion?

---

than the Sunday Closing Laws upheld in *McGowan v. Maryland,* 366 U.S. 420 (1961); the release time program for religious training in *Zorach v. Clauson,* 343 U.S. 306, 314, 315 (1952); and the legislative prayers upheld in *Marsh.*

We are unable to discern a greater aid to religion deriving from inclusion of the crèche than from these benefits and endorsements previously held not violative of the Establishment Clause. What was said about the legislative prayers in *Marsh* and implied about the Sunday Closing Laws in *McGowan* is true of the City's inclusion of the crèche: its "reason or effect merely happens to coincide or harmonize with the tenets of [some] religions."

The dissent asserts some observers may perceive that the City has aligned itself with the Christian faith by including a Christian symbol in its display and that this serves to advance religion. We can assume, *arguendo*, that the display advances religion in a sense; but our precedents plainly contemplate that on occasion some advancement of religion will result from governmental action. * * * Here, whatever benefit to one faith or religion or to all religions, is indirect, remote and incidental; display of the crèche is no more an advancement or endorsement of religion than the Congressional and Executive recognition of the origins of the Holiday itself as "Christ's Mass," or the exhibition of literally hundreds of religious paintings in governmentally supported museums.

The District Court found that there had been no administrative entanglement between religion and state resulting from the City's ownership and use of the crèche. But it went on to hold that some political divisiveness was engendered by this litigation. Coupled with its finding of an impermissible sectarian purpose and effect, this persuaded the court that there was "excessive entanglement." The Court of Appeals expressly declined to accept the District Court's finding that inclusion of the crèche has caused political divisiveness along religious lines, and noted that this Court has never held that political divisiveness alone was sufficient to invalidate government conduct.

Entanglement is a question of kind and degree. In this case, however, there is no reason to disturb the District Court's finding on the absence of administrative entanglement. There is no evidence of contact with church authorities concerning the content or design of the exhibit prior to or since Pawtucket's purchase of the crèche. No expenditures for maintenance of the crèche have been necessary; and since the City owns the crèche, now valued at $200, the tangible material it contributes is *de minimis*. In many respects the display requires far less ongoing, day-to-day interaction between church and state than religious paintings in public galleries. There is nothing here, of course, like the "comprehensive, discriminating, and continuing state surveillance" or the "enduring entanglement" present in *Lemon*.

We are satisfied that the City has a secular purpose for including the crèche, that the City has not impermissibly advanced religion, and that including the crèche does not create excessive entanglement between religion and government.

The display engenders a friendly community spirit of good will in keeping with the season. * * * It would be ironic [if] the inclusion of a single symbol of a particular historic religious event, as part of a celebration acknowledged in the Western World for 20 centuries, and in this country by the people, by the Executive Branch, by the Congress, and the courts for two centuries, would so "taint" the City's exhibit as to render it violative of the Establishment Clause. To forbid the use of this one passive symbol—the crèche—at the very time people are taking note of the season with Christmas hymns and carols in public schools and other public places, and while the Congress and Legislatures open sessions with prayers by paid chaplains would be a stilted over-reaction contrary to our history and to our holdings. If the presence of the crèche in this display violates the Establishment Clause, a host of other forms of taking official note of Christmas, and of our religious heritage, are equally offensive to the Constitution. * * * Any notion that these symbols pose a real danger of establishment of a state church is far-fetched indeed.

We hold that, notwithstanding the religious significance of the crèche, the City of Pawtucket has not violated the Establishment Clause of the First Amendment.

JUSTICE O'CONNOR, concurring.

The Establishment Clause prohibits government from making adherence to a religion relevant in any way to a person's standing in the political community. Government can run afoul of that prohibition in two principal ways. One is excessive entanglement with religious institutions * * *. The second and more direct infringement is government endorsement or disapproval of religion. Endorsement sends a message to nonadherents that they are outsiders, not full members of the political community, and an accompanying message to adherents that they are insiders, favored members of the political community. Disapproval sends the opposite message.

Our prior cases have used the three-part [*Lemon* test] as a guide to detecting these two forms of unconstitutional government action. It has never been entirely clear, however, how the three parts of the test relate to the principles enshrined in the Establishment Clause. Focusing on institutional entanglement and on endorsement or disapproval of religion clarifies the *Lemon* test as an analytical device.

In this case, as even the District Court found, there is no institutional entanglement. * * * The central issue [is] whether Pawtucket has endorsed Christianity by its display of the crèche. To answer that question, we must examine both what Pawtucket intended to communicate in displaying the crèche and what message the City's display actually conveyed. The purpose and effect prongs of the *Lemon* test represent these two aspects of the meaning of the City's action. * * * The purpose prong [asks] whether government's actual purpose is to endorse or disapprove of religion. The effect prong asks whether, irrespective of government's actual purpose, the practice under review in fact conveys a message of endorsement or disapproval.

Applying that formulation to this case, I would find that Pawtucket did not intend to convey any message of endorsement of Christianity or disapproval of non-Christian religions. The evident purpose of including the crèche in the larger display was not promotion of the religious content of the crèche but celebration of the public holiday through its traditional symbols. Celebration of public holidays, which have cultural significance even if they also have religious aspects, is a legitimate secular purpose.

Focusing on the evil of government endorsement or disapproval of religion makes clear that the effect prong of the *Lemon* test is properly interpreted not to require invalidation of a government practice merely because it in fact causes, even as a primary effect, advancement or inhibition of religion. * * * What is crucial is that a government practice not have the effect of communicating a message of government endorsement or disapproval of religion. It is only practices having that effect, whether intentionally or unintentionally, that make religion relevant, in reality or public perception, to status in the political community.

Pawtucket's display of its crèche, I believe, does not communicate a message that the government intends to endorse the Christian beliefs represented by the crèche. Although the religious and indeed sectarian significance of the crèche, as the district court found, is not neutralized by the setting, the overall holiday setting changes what viewers may fairly understand to be the purpose of the display—as a typical museum setting, though not neutralizing the religious content of a religious painting, negates any message of endorsement of that content. The display celebrates a public holiday, and no one contends that declaration of that holiday is understood to be an endorsement of religion. The holiday itself has very strong secular components and traditions. Government celebration of the holiday, which is extremely common, generally is not understood to endorse the religious content of the holiday, just as government celebration of Thanksgiving is not so understood. The crèche is a traditional symbol of the holiday that is very commonly displayed along with purely secular symbols, as it was in Pawtucket.

These features combine to make the government's display of the crèche in this particular physical setting no more an endorsement of religion than such governmental "acknowledgments" of religion as legislative prayers of the type approved in *Marsh v. Chambers*, 463 U.S. 783 (1983), government declaration of Thanksgiving as a public holiday, printing of "In God We Trust" on coins, and opening court sessions with "God save the United States and this honorable court." Those government acknowledgments of religion serve, in the only ways reasonably possible in our culture, the legitimate secular purposes of solemnizing public occasions, expressing confidence in the future, and encouraging the recognition of what is worthy of appreciation in society. For that reason, and because of their history and ubiquity, those practices are not understood as conveying government approval of particular religious beliefs. The display of the crèche likewise * * * cannot fairly be understood to convey a message of government endorsement of religion.

JUSTICE BRENNAN, with whom JUSTICE MARSHALL, JUSTICE BLACKMUN and JUSTICE STEVENS join, dissenting.

Applying the three-part [*Lemon*] test to Pawtucket's crèche, I am persuaded that the City's inclusion of the crèche in its Christmas display simply does not reflect a "clearly secular purpose." * * * Plainly, the City's interest in celebrating the holiday and in promoting both retail sales and goodwill are fully served by the elaborate display of Santa Claus, reindeer, and wishing wells that are already a part of Pawtucket's annual Christmas display. More importantly, the nativity scene, unlike every other element of the Hodgson Park display, reflects a sectarian exclusivity that the avowed purposes of celebrating the holiday season and promoting retail commerce simply do not encompass. To be found constitutional, Pawtucket's seasonal celebration must at least be non-denominational and not serve to promote religion. The inclusion of a distinctively religious element like the crèche, however, demonstrates that a narrower sectarian purpose lay behind the decision to include a nativity scene. That the crèche retained this religious character for the people and municipal government of Pawtucket is suggested by the Mayor's testimony at trial in which he stated that for him, as well as others in the City, the effort to eliminate the nativity scene from Pawtucket's Christmas celebration "is a step towards establishing another religion, non-religion that it may be." Plainly, the City and its leaders understood that the inclusion of the crèche in its display would serve the wholly religious purpose of "keep[ing] 'Christ in Christmas.' " From this record, therefore, it is impossible to say * * * that a wholly secular goal predominates.

The "primary effect" of including a nativity scene in the City's display [is] to place the government's imprimatur of approval on the particular religious beliefs exemplified by the crèche. Those who believe in the message of the nativity receive the unique and exclusive benefit of public recognition and approval of their views. For many, the City's decision to include the crèche as part of its extensive and costly efforts to celebrate Christmas can only mean that the prestige of the government has been conferred on the beliefs associated with the crèche, thereby providing "a significant symbolic benefit to religion." *Larkin v. Grendel's Den, Inc.,* 459 U.S., at 125. The effect on minority religious groups, as well as on those who may reject all religion, is to convey the message that their views are not similarly worthy of public recognition nor entitled to public support.

Finally, it is evident that Pawtucket's inclusion of a crèche as part of its annual Christmas display does pose a significant threat of fostering "excessive entanglement." * * * [A]fter today's decision, * * * Jews and other non-Christian groups * * * can be expected to press government for inclusion of their symbols, and faced with such requests, government will have to become involved in accommodating the various demands. More importantly, although no political divisiveness was apparent in Pawtucket prior to the filing of respondents' lawsuit, that act, as the District Court found, unleashed powerful emotional reactions which divided the City along religious lines.

The Court, by focusing on the holiday "context" in which the nativity scene appeared, seeks to explain away the clear religious import of the crèche * * *. The effect of the crèche, of course, must be gauged not only by its inherent religious significance but also by the overall setting in which it appears. But it blinks reality to claim, as the Court does, that by including such a distinctively religious object as the crèche in its Christmas display, Pawtucket has done no more than make use of a "traditional" symbol of the holiday, and has thereby purged the crèche of its religious content and conferred only an "incidental and indirect" benefit on religion. * * * [E]ven in the context of Pawtucket's seasonal celebration, the crèche retains a specifically Christian religious meaning. * * * It is the chief symbol of the characteristically Christian belief that a divine Savior was brought into the world and that the purpose of this miraculous birth was to illuminate a path toward salvation and redemption. For Christians, that path is exclusive, precious and holy. But for those who do not share these beliefs, the symbolic re-enactment of the birth of a divine being who has been miraculously incarnated as a man stands as a dramatic reminder of their differences with Christian faith. * * * To be so excluded on religious grounds by one's elected government is an insult and an injury that, until today, could not be countenanced by the Establishment Clause.

The Court also attempts to justify the crèche by entertaining a beguilingly simple, yet faulty syllogism. * * * The Court apparently believes that once it finds that the designation of Christmas as a public holiday is constitutionally acceptable, it is then free to conclude that virtually every form of governmental association with the celebration of the holiday is also constitutional. The vice of this dangerously superficial argument is that it overlooks the fact that the Christmas holiday in our national culture contains both secular and sectarian elements. To say that government may recognize the holiday's traditional, secular elements of giftgiving, public festivities and community spirit, does not mean that government may indiscriminately embrace the distinctively sectarian aspects of the holiday.

> **Make the Connection**
>
> Does the government have an obligation, under the Free Exercise Clause of the First Amendment, to accommodate people who observe Christmas? We will consider questions of this sort later in this chapter.

When government decides to recognize Christmas day as a public holiday, it does no more than accommodate the calendar of public activities to the plain fact that many Americans will expect on that day to spend time visiting with their families, attending religious services, and perhaps enjoying some respite from pre-holiday activities. * * * Because it is clear that the celebration of Christmas has both secular and sectarian elements, it may well be that by taking note of the holiday, the government is simply seeking to serve [wholly] secular goals [such as] promoting goodwill and a common day of rest * * *. If public officials go further and participate in the *secular* celebration of Christmas—by, for example, decorating public places with such secular images as wreaths, garlands or Santa Claus figures—they move closer to the limits of their constitutional power but nevertheless remain within the boundaries set by the Establishment Clause. But when those officials participate in or appear to endorse the distinctively religious elements of this otherwise secular event, they encroach upon First Amendment freedoms. For it is at that point that the government brings to the forefront the theological content of the holiday, and places the prestige, power and financial support of a civil authority in the service of a particular faith.

The inclusion of a crèche in Pawtucket's otherwise secular celebration of Christmas clearly violates these principles. Unlike such secular figures as Santa Claus, reindeer and carolers, a nativity scene represents far more than a mere "traditional" symbol of Christmas. The essence of the crèche's symbolic purpose and effect is to prompt the observer to experience a sense of simple awe and wonder appropriate to the contemplation of one of the central elements of Christian dogma—that God sent His son into the world to be a Messiah. Contrary to the Court's suggestion, the crèche is far from a mere representation of a "particular historic religious event." It is, instead, best understood as a mystical re-creation of an event that lies at the heart of Christian faith. To suggest, as the

Court does, that such a symbol is merely "traditional" and therefore no different from Santa's house or reindeer is not only offensive to those for whom the crèche has profound significance, but insulting to those who insist for religious or personal reasons that the story of Christ is in no sense a part of "history" nor an unavoidable element of our national "heritage."

The Court's opinion [also] asserts, without explanation, that Pawtucket's inclusion of a crèche in its annual Christmas display poses no more of a threat to Establishment Clause values than [other] official "acknowledgments" of religion. * * * [T]he Court has never comprehensively addressed the extent to which government may acknowledge religion by, for example, incorporating religious references into public ceremonies and proclamations, and I do not presume to offer a comprehensive approach. Nevertheless, it appears from our prior decisions that at least three principles [may] be identified. First, although the government may not be compelled to do so by the Free Exercise Clause, it may, consistently with the Establishment Clause, act to accommodate to some extent the opportunities of individuals to practice their religion. * * * [F]or me that principle would justify government's decision to declare December 25th a public holiday.

Second, our cases recognize that while a particular governmental practice may have derived from religious motivations and retain certain religious connotations, it is nonetheless permissible for the government to pursue the practice when it is continued today solely for secular reasons. * * * Thanksgiving Day, in my view, fits easily within this principle, for despite its religious antecedents, the current practice of celebrating Thanksgiving is unquestionably secular and patriotic. * * * Finally, we have noted that government cannot be completely prohibited from recognizing in its public actions the religious beliefs and practices of the American people as an aspect of our national history and culture. While I remain uncertain about these questions, I would suggest that such practices as the designation of "In God We Trust" as our national motto, or the references to God contained in the Pledge of Allegiance can best be understood [as] a form a "ceremonial deism," protected from Establishment Clause scrutiny chiefly because they have lost through rote repetition any significant religious content. Moreover, these references are uniquely suited to serve such wholly secular purposes as solemnizing public occasions, or inspiring commitment to meet some national challenge in a manner that simply could not be fully served in our culture if government were limited to purely non-religious phrases. The practices by which the government has long acknowledged religion are therefore probably necessary to serve certain secular functions, and that necessity, coupled with their long history, gives those practices an essentially secular meaning.

The crèche fits none of these categories. Inclusion of the crèche is not necessary to accommodate individual religious expression. * * * Nor is the inclusion of the crèche necessary to serve wholly secular goals; it is clear that the City's secular purposes of celebrating the Christmas holiday and promoting retail commerce can be fully served without the crèche. And the crèche, because of its unique association with Christianity, is clearly more sectarian than those references to God that we accept in ceremonial phrases or in other contexts that assure neutrality.

The Court today [insists] that Pawtucket has done nothing more than include a "traditional" symbol of Christmas in its celebration of this national holiday, thereby muting the religious content of the crèche. But the City's action should be recognized for what it is: a coercive, though perhaps small, step toward establishing the sectarian preferences of the majority at the expense of the minority, accomplished by placing public facilities and funds in support of the religious symbolism and theological tidings that the crèche conveys.

[JUSTICE BLACKMUN's dissenting opinion is omitted.]

POINTS FOR DISCUSSION

a.   Neutrality

The dispute in *Lynch* was over whether the inclusion of a crèche—a scene depicting the birth of Jesus Christ—in the town's Christmas display violated the Establishment Clause. Do you agree that the City had a secular purpose for including this symbol in the display?

Do you agree that the inclusion of the crèche did not "impermissibly advance" religion (to use the majority's approach) or "endorse" religion (to use Justice O'Connor's approach)? In answering those questions, from whose perspective should we view the display? From the perspective of an observant Christian who celebrates both the religious and secular aspects of Christmas? From the perspective of someone who celebrates the secular aspects of Christmas but not the religious aspects? From the perspective of someone who is not Christian and does not celebrate the holiday in any of its aspects?

b.   Non-Preferentialism

In his dissent, Justice Brennan criticized the Court for, in his view, failing to adhere to the rule of separation. But regardless of the Court's adherence to that rule, did the Court at least ensure that the City did not prefer one religious denomination over others? After all, even the non-preferentialist view—which a majority of the Court has never explicitly adopted—generally prohibits the government from discriminating among different religious sects. *Wallace v. Jaffree*, 472 U.S. 38 (1985) (Rehnquist, J., dissenting). Didn't the challenged display prefer Christianity over all other religions?

c. Subsequent Developments

After the Supreme Court's decision in *Lynch*, lawsuits continued regarding municipal holiday decorations. Some disputes concerned the degree to which displays conveyed secular, as opposed to non-secular, messages. Judge Frank Easterbrook, unsettled by the view that *Lynch* requires this kind of analysis, wrote: "It would be appalling to conduct litigation under the Establishment Clause as if it were a trademark case, with experts testifying about whether one display is really like another, and witnesses testifying that they were offended—but would have been less so were the crèche five feet closer to the jumbo candy cane." *American Jewish Congress v. City of Chicago*, 827 F.2d 120, 130 (7th Cir. 1987) (Easterbrook, J., dissenting).

Two years later, in *County of Allegheny v. American Civil Liberties Union*, 492 U.S. 573 (1989), a divided Court allowed a city to display a menorah because it was accompanied by a Christmas tree and a sign extolling liberty, but did not allow the city to display a crèche because it was unaccompanied by other religious and non-secular symbols. Does this case suggest that Judge Easterbrook's apprehensions have come to pass? Does the case suggest a way that municipalities may display religious symbols without violating the Constitution?

Menorah display held not to violate the Establishment Clause
County of Allegheny v. ACLU Greater Pittsburgh Chapter, 492 U.S. 573, 621 (2014) (appendix to opinion)

Problem

Every day, public schools throughout the United States request students to stand and recite the Pledge of Allegiance, which states: "I pledge allegiance to the flag of the United States of America and to the republic for which it stands, one nation under God, indivisible, with liberty and justice for all." The pledge dates to the late nineteenth century, but the phrase "under God" did not become part of the pledge until 1954. In *Elk Grove Unified School Dist. v. Newdow*, 542 U.S. 1 (2004), the father of an elementary school student sued, claiming that a public school's practice of having a teacher lead the pledge violated the Establishment Clause. The Supreme Court granted certiorari in the case, but did not reach the merits of the constitutional claim because it held that the father lacked standing to bring the challenge. (Justice Antonin Scalia recused himself from *Newdow* because he had previously made a public speech in which he specifically criticized the lower court decision holding that the pledge was unconstitutional. See Linda Greenhouse, *Supreme Court to Consider Case on "Under God" in Pledge to Flag,* N.Y. Times, Oct. 15, 2003, at A1.) If the question had properly been before the Court, what would have been the best arguments on both sides of the constitutional issue?

In addition to litigation over holiday displays, the Supreme Court in several cases has addressed the question whether government institutions may display the

> **FYI**
>
> The books of Exodus and Deuteronomy do not enumerate the Ten Commandments, but instead describe various obligations in narrative prose. Based on this prose, Jewish, Catholic, and Protestant religious orders identify and list the Ten Commandments in different ways.

Ten Commandments, a set of moral imperatives found in the Bible at Exodus 20:2–17 and Deuteronomy 5:6–21. As it turns out, this question has no single answer. The Court has held that schools may not display the Ten Commandments, reasoning that the Commandments "are undeniably a sacred text in the Jewish and Christian faiths." *Stone v. Graham,* 449 U.S. 39 (1980) *(per curiam).* But the Court has issued dueling opinions about the constitutionality of displays of the Ten Commandments on government property. As you read the following two cases, which were decided on the same day, consider what principles govern the Court's analysis, whether the cases can be reconciled, and whether they are consistent with the cases that we have already seen.

McCREARY COUNTY, KENTUCKY V. AMERICAN CIVIL LIBERTIES UNION OF KENTUCKY

545 U.S. 844 (2005)

JUSTICE SOUTER delivered the opinion of the Court.

[In 1999, two counties in Kentucky put up in their courthouses large, gold-framed copies of an abridged text of the King James version of the Ten Commandments. After lawsuits were filed to challenge the displays under the Establishment Clause,] the legislative body of each County authorized a second, expanded display, by nearly identical resolutions reciting that the Ten Commandments are "the precedent legal code upon which the civil and criminal codes [of] Kentucky are founded," and stating several grounds for taking that position: that "the Ten Commandments are codified in Kentucky's civil and criminal laws"; that the Kentucky House of Representatives had in 1993 "voted unanimously [to] adjourn 'in remembrance and honor of Jesus Christ, the Prince of Ethics' "; and that the "Founding Father[s] [had an] explicit understanding of the duty of elected officials to publicly acknowledge God as the source of America's strength and direction."

As directed by the resolutions, the Counties expanded the displays of the Ten Commandments in their locations [to include] eight other documents in smaller frames, each either having a religious theme or excerpted to highlight a religious element. [After a District Court issued an injunction prohibiting the revised displays, the counties installed new displays consisting of] nine framed documents of equal size, one of them setting out the Ten Commandments explicitly identified as the "King James Version" at Exodus 20:3–17 [and] quoted at greater length than before. * * * Assembled with the Commandments are framed copies of the Magna Carta, the Declaration of Independence, the Bill of Rights, the lyrics of the Star Spangled Banner, the Mayflower Compact, the National Motto, the Preamble to the Kentucky Constitution, and a picture of Lady Justice. The collection is entitled "The Foundations of American Law and Government Display" and each document comes with a statement about its historical and legal significance.

Ever since *Lemon* summarized the three familiar considerations for evaluating Establishment Clause claims, looking to whether government action has "a secular legislative purpose" has been a common, albeit seldom dispositive, element of our cases. The touchstone for our analysis is the principle that the "First Amendment mandates governmental neutrality between religion and religion, and between religion and nonreligion." *Epperson v. Arkansas,* 393 U.S. 97, 104 (1968); *Everson v. Board of Ed. of Ewing,* 330 U.S. 1, 15–16 (1947). When the government acts with the ostensible and predominant purpose of advancing religion, it violates that central Establishment Clause value of official religious neutrality, there being no neutrality when the government's ostensible object is to take sides. * * *

Despite the intuitive importance of official purpose to the realization of Establishment Clause values, the Counties ask us to abandon *Lemon*'s purpose test, or at least to truncate any enquiry into purpose here. [A]ccording to them, true "purpose" is unknowable, and its search merely an excuse for courts to act selectively and unpredictably in picking out evidence of subjective intent. The assertions are as seismic as they are unconvincing.

Examination of purpose is [a] key element of a good deal of constitutional doctrine, *e.g., Washington v. Davis,* 426 U.S. 229 (1976). * * * [S]crutinizing purpose does make practical sense, as in Establishment Clause analysis, where an understanding of official objective emerges from readily discoverable fact, without any judicial psychoanalysis of a drafter's heart of hearts. * * * The cases with findings of a predominantly religious purpose point to the straightforward nature of the test. In *Wallace v. Jaffree*, 472 U.S. 38, 58–60 (1985), for example, we inferred purpose from a change of wording from an earlier statute to a later one, each dealing with prayer in schools. And in *Edwards v. Aguillard*, 482 U.S. 578, 586–588 (1987), we relied on a statute's text and the detailed public comments of its sponsor, when we sought the purpose of a state law requiring creationism to be taught alongside evolution. In other cases, the government action itself bespoke the purpose, as in *School Dist. of Abington Township v. Schempp*, 374 U.S. 203 (1963), where the object of required Bible study in public schools was patently religious. * * * In each case, the government's action was held unconstitutional only because openly available data supported a commonsense conclusion that a religious objective permeated the government's action.

The Counties would read the cases as if the purpose enquiry were so naive that any transparent claim to secularity would satisfy it * * *. [T]he Court often does accept governmental statements of purpose, in keeping with the respect owed in the first instance to such official claims. But in those unusual cases where the claim was an apparent sham, or the secular purpose secondary, the unsurprising results have been findings of no adequate secular object, as against a predominantly religious one. * * * [The Counties also] argue that purpose in a case like this one should be inferred, if at all, only from the latest news about the last in a series of governmental actions, however close they may all be in time and subject. But the world is not made brand new every morning, and the Counties are simply asking us to ignore perfectly probative evidence; they want an absentminded objective observer, not one presumed to be familiar with the history of the government's actions and competent to learn what history has to show. The Counties' position just bucks common sense: reasonable observers have reasonable memories, and our precedents sensibly forbid an observer "to turn a blind eye to the context in which [the] policy arose."

[T]he Commandments [are] a central point of reference in the religious and moral history of Jews and Christians. They proclaim the existence of a monotheistic god (no other gods). They regulate details of religious obligation (no graven images, no sabbath breaking, no vain oath swearing). And they unmistakably rest even the universally accepted prohibitions (as against murder, theft, and the like) on the sanction of the divinity proclaimed at the beginning of the text. Displaying that text is thus different from a symbolic depiction, like tablets with 10 roman numerals, which could be seen as alluding to a general notion of law, not a sectarian conception of faith. Where the text is set out, the insistence of the religious message is hard to avoid in the absence of a context plausibly suggesting a message going beyond an excuse to promote the religious point of view.

[There was no such context for the original exhibits here.] [A]t the [original] ceremony for posting the framed Commandments in Pulaski County, the county executive was accompanied by his pastor, who testified to the certainty of the existence of God. The reasonable observer could only think that the Counties meant to emphasize and celebrate the Commandments' religious message. [The second version of the exhibits included] a series of American historical documents with theistic and Christian references * * *. The display's unstinting focus was on

religious passages, showing that the Counties were posting the Commandments precisely because of their sectarian content. That demonstration of the government's objective was enhanced by serial religious references and the accompanying resolution's claim about the embodiment of ethics in Christ. Together, the display and resolution presented an indisputable, and undisputed, showing of an impermissible purpose. Today, the Counties make no attempt to defend their undeniable objective, but

> **Take Note**
>
> The Court here considers the original exhibits (which were no longer on display) to determine the purpose behind the current exhibits. Given that, as the Court acknowledges, there are plausible secular motives to support posting the Ten Commandments in public buildings under some circumstances, does it make sense to consider the purpose that motivated the posting of the original versions of the exhibits?

instead hopefully describe version two as "dead and buried." Their refusal to defend the second display is understandable, but the reasonable observer could not forget it.

[After mounting the third display, the counties] cited several new purposes * * *, including a desire "to educate the citizens of the county regarding some of the documents that played a significant role in the foundation of our system of law and government." * * * These new statements of purpose were presented only as a litigating position, there being no further authorizing action by the Counties' governing boards. And although repeal of the earlier county authorizations would not have erased them from the record of evidence bearing on current purpose, the extraordinary resolutions for the second display passed just months earlier were not repealed or otherwise repudiated. Indeed, the sectarian spirit of the common resolution found enhanced expression in the third display, which quoted more of the purely religious language of the Commandments than the first two displays had done. No reasonable observer could swallow the claim that the Counties had cast off the objective so unmistakable in the earlier displays.

Nor did the selection of posted material suggest a clear theme that might prevail over evidence of the continuing religious object. In a collection of documents said to be "foundational" to American government, it is at least odd to include a patriotic anthem, but to omit the Fourteenth Amendment * * *. And it is no less baffling to leave out the original Constitution of 1787 while quoting the 1215 Magna Carta even to the point of its declaration that "fish-weirs shall be removed from the Thames." If an observer found these choices and omissions perplexing in isolation, he would be puzzled for a different reason when he read the Declaration of Independence seeking confirmation for the Counties' posted explanation that the Ten Commandments' "influence is clearly seen in the Declaration"; in fact the observer would find that the Commandments are sanctioned as divine imperatives, while the Declaration of Independence holds that the authority of government to enforce the law derives "from the consent of the governed." If the observer had not thrown up his hands, he would probably suspect that the Counties were simply reaching for any way to keep a religious document on the walls of courthouses constitutionally required to embody religious neutrality.

[W]e do not decide that the Counties' past actions forever taint any effort on their part to deal with the subject matter. We hold only that purpose needs to be taken seriously under the Establishment Clause and needs to be understood in light of context; an implausible claim that governmental purpose has changed should not carry the day in a court of law any more than in a head with common sense. Nor do we have occasion here to hold that a sacred text can never be integrated constitutionally into a governmental display on the subject of law, or American history. We do not forget, and in this litigation have frequently been reminded, that our own courtroom frieze was deliberately designed in the exercise of governmental authority so as to include the figure of Moses holding tablets exhibiting a portion of the Hebrew text of the later, secularly phrased Commandments; in the company of 17 other lawgivers, most of them secular figures, there is no risk that Moses would strike an observer as evidence that the National Government was violating neutrality in religion.

[The principle of neutrality] responds to one of the major concerns that prompted adoption of the Religion Clauses. The Framers and the citizens of their time intended not only to protect the integrity of individual conscience in religious matters, but to guard against the civic divisiveness that follows when the government weighs in on one side of religious debate; nothing does a better job of roiling society, a point that needed no explanation to the descendants of English Puritans and Cavaliers (or Massachusetts Puritans and Baptists).

The dissent, however, puts forward a limitation on the application of the neutrality principle, with citations to historical evidence said to show that the Framers understood the ban on establishment of religion as sufficiently narrow to allow the government to espouse submission to the divine will. * * * But the dissent's argument for the original understanding is flawed from the outset by its failure to consider the full range of evidence showing what the Framers believed. The dissent is certainly correct in putting forward evidence that some of the Framers thought some endorsement of religion was compatible with the establishment ban * * *. [But] there is also evidence supporting the proposition that the Framers intended the Establishment Clause to require governmental neutrality in matters of religion, including neutrality in statements acknowledging religion. The very language of the Establishment Clause represented a significant departure from early drafts that merely prohibited a single national religion, and the final language instead "extended [the] prohibition to state support for 'religion' in general." See *Lee v. Weisman*, 505 U.S. 577, 614–615 (1992) (SOUTER, J., concurring). The historical record, moreover, is complicated beyond the dissent's account by the writings and practices of figures no less influential than Thomas Jefferson and James Madison. Jefferson, for example, refused to issue Thanksgiving Proclamations because he believed that they violated the Constitution. And Madison, whom the dissent claims as supporting its thesis, criticized Virginia's general assessment tax not just because it required people to donate "three pence" to religion, but because "it is itself a signal of persecution. It degrades from the equal rank of Citizens all those whose opinions in Religion do not bend to those of the Legislative authority."

[The dissent also says] that the deity the Framers had in mind was the God of monotheism, with the consequence that government may espouse a tenet of traditional monotheism. This is truly a remarkable view. Other Members of the Court have dissented on the ground that the Establishment Clause bars nothing more than governmental preference for one religion over another, *e.g.*, *Wallace*, 472 U.S., at 98–99 (REHNQUIST, J.,

> **FYI**
>
> In the St. Bartholomew's Day massacre, a mob of French Catholics killed thousands of French Protestants over a period of several days in 1572. The treatment of heretics in early Massachusetts is famously chronicled in Arthur Miller's play *The Crucible*.

dissenting), but at least religion has previously been treated inclusively. Today's dissent, however, apparently means that government should be free to approve the core beliefs of a favored religion over the tenets of others, a view that should trouble anyone who prizes religious liberty. * * * We are centuries away from the St. Bartholomew's Day massacre and the treatment of heretics in early

Massachusetts, but the divisiveness of religion in current public life is inescapable. This is no time to deny the prudence of understanding the Establishment Clause to require the Government to stay neutral on religious belief, which is reserved for the conscience of the individual.

[The Court affirmed the district court's grant of a preliminary injunction against the challenged displays.]

JUSTICE O'CONNOR, concurring.

Given the history of this particular display of the Ten Commandments, the Court correctly finds an Establishment Clause violation. The purpose behind the counties' display is relevant because it conveys an unmistakable message of endorsement to the reasonable observer. It is true that many Americans find the Commandments in accord with their personal beliefs. But we do not count heads before enforcing the First Amendment. Nor can we accept the theory that Americans who do not accept the Commandments' validity are outside the First Amendment's protections. There is no list of approved and disapproved beliefs appended to the First Amendment—and the Amendment's broad terms ("free exercise," "establishment," "religion") do not admit of such a cramped reading. It is true that the Framers lived at a time when our national religious diversity was neither as robust nor as well recognized as it is now. They may not have foreseen the variety of religions for which this Nation would eventually provide a home. They surely could not have predicted new religions, some of them born in this country. But they did know that line-drawing between religions is an enterprise that, once begun, has no logical stopping point. * * * The Religion Clauses, as a result, protect adherents of all religions, as well as those who believe in no religion at all.

JUSTICE SCALIA, with whom THE CHIEF JUSTICE and JUSTICE THOMAS join, and with whom JUSTICE KENNEDY joins as to Parts II and III, dissenting.

[O]ne model of the relationship between church and state [is the] model spread across Europe by the armies of Napoleon, and reflected in the Constitution of France, which begins, "France is [a] secular Republic." Religion is to be strictly excluded from the public forum. This is not, and never was, the model adopted by America. * * * George Washington added to the form of Presidential oath prescribed by Art. II, § 1, cl. 8, of the Constitution, the concluding words "so help me God." The Supreme Court under John Marshall opened its sessions with the prayer, "God save the United States and this Honorable Court." The First Congress instituted the practice of beginning its legislative sessions with a prayer. The same week that Congress submitted the Establishment Clause as part of the

Bill of Rights for ratification by the States, it enacted legislation providing for paid chaplains in the House and Senate. The day after the First Amendment was proposed, the same Congress that had proposed it requested the President to proclaim "a day of public thanksgiving and prayer, to be observed, by acknowledging, with grateful hearts, the many signal favours of Almighty God." H.R. Jour., 1st Cong., 1st Sess., 123 (1826 ed.). * * * And of course the First Amendment itself accords religion (and no other manner of belief) special constitutional protection.

These actions of our First President and Congress and the Marshall Court were not idiosyncratic; they reflected the beliefs of the period. Those who wrote the Constitution believed that morality was essential to the well-being of society and that encouragement of religion was the best way to foster morality. * * * Nor have the views of our people on this matter significantly changed. Presidents continue to conclude the Presidential oath with the words "so help me God." Our legislatures, state and national, continue to open their sessions with prayer led by official chaplains. The sessions of this Court continue to open with the prayer "God save the United States and this Honorable Court." Invocation of the Almighty by our public figures, at all levels of government, remains commonplace. Our coinage bears the motto, "IN GOD WE TRUST." And our Pledge of Allegiance contains the acknowledgment that we are a Nation "under God." As one of our Supreme Court opinions rightly observed, "We are a religious people whose institutions presuppose a Supreme Being." *Zorach v. Clauson*, 343 U.S. 306, 313 (1952).

With all of this reality (and much more) staring it in the face, how can the Court *possibly* assert that the "First Amendment mandates governmental neutrality between [religion] and nonreligion," and that "[m]anifesting a purpose to favor [adherence] to religion generally," is unconstitutional? Who says so? Surely not the words of the Constitution. Surely not the history and traditions that reflect our society's constant understanding of those words. * * * Nothing stands behind the Court's assertion that governmental affirmation of the society's belief in God is unconstitutional except the Court's own say-so, citing as support only the unsubstantiated say-so of earlier Courts going back no further than the mid-20th century. * * * And it is, moreover, a thoroughly discredited say-so. It is discredited [because] a majority of the Justices on the current Court (including at least one Member of today's majority) have, in separate opinions, repudiated the brain-spun "*Lemon* test" that embodies the supposed principle of neutrality between religion and irreligion. And it is discredited because the Court has not had the courage (or the foolhardiness) to apply the neutrality principle consistently.

Besides appealing to the demonstrably false principle that the government cannot favor religion over irreligion, today's opinion suggests that the posting of the Ten Commandments violates the principle that the government cannot favor one religion over another. That is indeed a valid principle where public aid or assistance to religion is concerned, see *Zelman v. Simmons-Harris,* 536 U.S. 639, 652 (2002), or where the free exercise of religion is at issue, but it necessarily applies in a more limited sense to public acknowledgment of the Creator. If religion in the public forum had to be entirely nondenominational, there could be no religion in the public forum at all. One cannot say the word "God," or "the Almighty," one cannot offer public supplication or thanksgiving, without contradicting the beliefs of some people that there are many gods, or that God or the gods pay no attention to human affairs. With respect to public acknowledgment of religious belief, it is entirely clear from our Nation's historical practices that the Establishment Clause permits this disregard of polytheists and believers in unconcerned deities, just as it permits the disregard of devout atheists.

Historical practices [demonstrate] that there is a distance between the acknowledgment of a single Creator and the establishment of a religion. * * * The three most popular religions in the United States, Christianity, Judaism, and Islam—which combined account for 97.7% of all believers—are monotheistic. All of them, moreover (Islam included), believe that the Ten Commandments were given by God to Moses, and are divine prescriptions for a virtuous life. Publicly honoring the Ten Commandments is thus indistinguishable, insofar as discriminating against other religions is concerned, from publicly honoring God. Both practices are recognized across such a broad and diverse range of the population—from Christians to Muslims—that they cannot be reasonably understood as a government endorsement of a particular religious viewpoint.

* * * I must respond to Justice STEVENS' assertion [in his dissent in *Van Orden v. Perry,* 545 U.S. 677, 719, n. 18 (2005), the companion case,] that I would "marginaliz[e] the belief systems of more than 7 million Americans" who adhere to religions that are not monotheistic. Surely that is a gross exaggeration. The beliefs of those citizens are entirely protected by the Free Exercise Clause, and by those aspects of the Establishment Clause that do not relate to government acknowledgment of the Creator. Invocation of God despite their beliefs is permitted not because nonmonotheistic religions cease to be religions recognized by the Religion Clauses of the First Amendment, but because governmental invocation of God is not an establishment. Justice STEVENS fails to recognize that in the context of public acknowledgments of God there are legitimate *competing* interests: On the one hand, the interest of that minority in not feeling "excluded";

but on the other, the interest of the overwhelming majority of religious believers in being able to give God thanks and supplication *as a people*, and with respect to our national endeavors. Our national tradition has resolved that conflict in favor of the majority.

Acknowledgment of the contribution that religion has made to our Nation's legal and governmental heritage partakes of a centuries-old tradition. * * * Display of the Ten Commandments is well within the mainstream of this practice of acknowledgment. * * * The Supreme Court Building itself includes depictions of Moses with the Ten Commandments in the Courtroom and on the east pediment of the building * * *. Similar depictions of the Decalogue appear on public buildings and monuments throughout our Nation's Capital. The frequency of these displays testifies to the popular understanding that the Ten Commandments are a foundation of the rule of law, and a symbol of the role that religion played, and continues to play, in our system of government.

VAN ORDEN V. PERRY

545 U.S. 677 (2005)

CHIEF JUSTICE REHNQUIST announced the judgment of the Court and delivered an opinion, in which JUSTICE SCALIA, JUSTICE KENNEDY, and JUSTICE THOMAS join.

> **Take Note**
> This case does not have a majority opinion.

The 22 acres surrounding the Texas State Capitol contain 17 monuments and 21 historical markers commemorating the "people, ideals, and events that compose Texan identity."[1] Tex. H. Con. Res. 38, 77th Leg., Reg.Sess. (2001). The monolith challenged here stands 6-feet high and 3 1/2-feet wide. It is located to the north of the Capitol building, between the Capitol and the Supreme Court building. Its primary content is the text of the Ten Commandments. An eagle

---

[1] The monuments are: Heroes of the Alamo, Hood's Brigade, Confederate Soldiers, Volunteer Fireman, Terry's Texas Rangers, Texas Cowboy, Spanish-American War, Texas National Guard, Ten Commandments, Tribute to Texas School Children, Texas Pioneer Woman, The Boy Scouts' Statue of Liberty Replica, Pearl Harbor Veterans, Korean War Veterans, Soldiers of World War I, Disabled Veterans, and Texas Peace Officers.

Monument inscribed with the Ten Commandments on the Texas State Capitol grounds
Van Orden v. Perry, 545 U.S. 677, 736 (2005) (appendix to opinion of Justice Stevens)

grasping the American flag, an eye inside of a pyramid, and two small tablets with what appears to be an ancient script are carved above the text of the Ten Commandments. Below the text are two Stars of David and the superimposed Greek letters Chi and Rho, which represent Christ. The bottom of the monument bears the inscription "PRESENTED TO THE PEOPLE AND YOUTH OF TEXAS BY THE FRATERNAL ORDER OF EAGLES OF TEXAS 1961." * * * The Eagles paid the cost of erecting the monument, the dedication of which was presided over by two state legislators.

Our cases, Januslike, point in two directions in applying the Establishment Clause. One face looks toward the strong role played by religion and religious traditions throughout our Nation's history. * * * The other face looks toward the principle that governmental intervention in religious matters can itself endanger religious freedom.

This case, like all Establishment Clause challenges, presents us with the difficulty of respecting both faces. Our institutions presuppose a Supreme Being, yet these institutions must not press religious observances upon their citizens. One face looks to the past in acknowledgment of our Nation's heritage, while the other looks to the present in demanding a separation between church and state. Reconciling these two faces requires that we neither abdicate our responsibility to maintain a division between church and state nor evince a hostility to religion by disabling the government from in some ways recognizing our religious heritage * * *.

These two faces are evident in representative cases both upholding and invalidating laws under the Establishment Clause. Over the last 25 years, we have sometimes pointed to *Lemon v. Kurtzman*, 403 U.S. 602 (1971), as providing the governing test in Establishment Clause challenges. Yet [m]any of our recent cases simply have not applied the *Lemon* test. * * * Whatever may be the fate of the *Lemon* test in the larger scheme of Establishment Clause jurisprudence, we think it not useful in dealing with the sort of passive monument that Texas has erected on its Capitol grounds. Instead, our analysis is driven both by the nature of the monument and by our Nation's history.

In this case we are faced with a display of the Ten Commandments on government property outside the Texas State Capitol. Such acknowledgments of the role played by the Ten Commandments in our Nation's heritage are common throughout America. We need only look within our own Courtroom. Since 1935, Moses has stood, holding two tablets that reveal portions of the Ten Commandments written in Hebrew, among other lawgivers in the south frieze. [In addition,] a large statue of Moses holding the Ten Commandments, alongside a statue of the Apostle Paul, has overlooked the rotunda of the Library of Congress' Jefferson Building since 1897. And the Jefferson Building's Great Reading Room contains a sculpture of a woman beside the Ten Commandments with a quote above her from the Old Testament (Micah 6:8). A medallion with two tablets depicting the Ten Commandments decorates the floor of the National Archives. Inside the Department of Justice, a statue entitled "The Spirit of Law" has two tablets representing the Ten Commandments lying at its feet. In front of the Ronald Reagan Building is another sculpture that includes a depiction of the Ten Commandments. So too a 24-foot-tall sculpture, depicting, among other things, the Ten Commandments and a cross, stands outside the federal courthouse that houses both the Court of Appeals and the District Court for the District of Columbia. * * *

Of course, the Ten Commandments are religious—they were so viewed at their inception and so remain. The monument, therefore, has religious significance. According to Judeo-Christian belief, the Ten Commandments were given to Moses by God on Mt. Sinai. But Moses was a lawgiver as well as a religious leader. And the Ten Commandments have an undeniable historical meaning, as the foregoing examples demonstrate. Simply having religious content or promoting a message consistent with a religious doctrine does not run afoul of the Establishment Clause. See *Lynch v. Donnelly*, 465 U.S. 668, 687 (1984).

There are, of course, limits to the display of religious messages or symbols. For example, we held unconstitutional a Kentucky statute requiring the posting of the Ten Commandments in every public schoolroom. *Stone v. Graham*, 449 U.S. 39 (1980) *(per curiam)*. * * * As evidenced by *Stone's* almost exclusive reliance upon two of our school prayer cases, *id.*, at 41–42 (citing *School Dist. of Abington Township v. Schempp*, 374 U.S. 203 (1963), and *Engel v. Vitale*, 370 U.S. 421 (1962)), it stands as an example of the fact that we have "been particularly vigilant in monitoring compliance with the Establishment Clause in elementary and secondary schools," *Edwards v. Aguillard*, 482 U.S. 578, 583–584 (1987). * * *

The placement of the Ten Commandments monument on the Texas State Capitol grounds is a far more passive use of those texts than was the case in *Stone,* where the text confronted elementary school students every day. * * * The monument is therefore also quite different from the prayers involved in *Schempp* and *Lee v. Weisman.* Texas has treated its Capitol grounds monuments as representing the several strands in the State's political and legal history. The inclusion of the Ten Commandments monument in this group has a dual significance, partaking of both religion and government. We cannot say that Texas' display of this monument violates the Establishment Clause of the First Amendment.

JUSTICE SCALIA, concurring.

I join the opinion of THE CHIEF JUSTICE because I think it accurately reflects our current Establishment Clause jurisprudence—or at least the Establishment Clause jurisprudence we currently apply some of the time. I would prefer to reach the same result by adopting an Establishment Clause jurisprudence that is in accord with our Nation's past and present practices, and that can be consistently applied—the central relevant feature of which is that there is nothing unconstitutional in a State's favoring religion generally, honoring God through public prayer and acknowledgment, or, in a nonproselytizing manner, venerating the Ten Commandments.

JUSTICE THOMAS, concurring.

This case would be easy if the Court were willing to abandon the inconsistent guideposts it has adopted for addressing Establishment Clause challenges, and return to the original meaning of the Clause. I have previously suggested that the Clause's text and history "resis[t] incorporation" against the States. See *Elk Grove Unified School Dist. v. Newdow,* 542 U.S. 1, 45–46 (2004) (opinion concurring in judgment). If the Establishment Clause does not restrain the States, then it has no application here, where only state action is at issue.

Even if the Clause is incorporated, or if the Free Exercise Clause limits the power of States to establish religions, our task would be far simpler if we returned to the original meaning of the word "establishment" than it is under the various approaches this Court now uses. The Framers understood an establishment "necessarily [to] involve actual legal coercion." *Newdow,* 542 U.S. at 52 (THOMAS, J., concurring in judgment). * * * There is no question that, based on the original meaning of the Establishment Clause, the Ten Commandments display at issue here is constitutional. In no sense does Texas compel petitioner Van Orden to do anything. The only injury to him is that he takes offense at seeing the monument as he passes it on his way to the Texas Supreme Court Library. He need not stop to read it or even to look at it, let alone to express support for it or adopt the Commandments as guides for his life. The mere presence of the monument along his path involves no coercion and thus does not violate the Establishment Clause.

Returning to the original meaning would do more than simplify our task. It also would avoid the pitfalls present in the Court's current approach to such challenges. This Court's precedent elevates the trivial to the proverbial "federal case," by making benign signs and postings subject to challenge. Yet even as it does so, the Court's precedent attempts to avoid declaring all religious symbols and words of longstanding tradition unconstitutional, by counterfactually declaring them of little religious significance. Even when the Court's cases recognize that such symbols have religious meaning, they adopt an unhappy compromise that fails fully to account for either the adherent's or the nonadherent's beliefs, and provides no principled way to choose between them. Even worse, the incoherence of the Court's decisions in this area renders the Establishment Clause impenetrable and incapable of consistent application. * * * While the Court correctly rejects the challenge to the Ten Commandments monument on the Texas Capitol grounds, a more fundamental rethinking of our Establishment Clause jurisprudence remains in order.

JUSTICE BREYER, concurring in the judgment.

If the relation between government and religion is one of separation, but not of mutual hostility and suspicion, one will inevitably find difficult borderline cases. And in such cases, I see no test-related substitute for the exercise of legal judgment. * * * While the Court's prior tests provide useful guideposts—and might well lead to the same result the Court reaches today, see, *e.g., Lemon v. Kurtzman,* 403 U.S. 602, 612–613 (1971)—no exact formula can dictate a resolution to such fact-intensive cases.

The case before us is a borderline case. * * * On the one hand, the Commandments' text undeniably has a religious message, invoking, indeed emphasizing, the Deity. On the other hand, focusing on the text of the Commandments alone cannot conclusively resolve this case. Rather, to determine the message that the text here conveys, we must examine how the text is *used.* And that inquiry requires us to consider the context of the display.

In certain contexts, a display of the tablets of the Ten Commandments can convey not simply a religious message but also a secular moral message (about proper standards of social conduct). And in certain contexts, a display of the tablets can also convey a historical message (about a historic relation between those standards and the law)—a fact that helps to explain the display of those tablets in dozens of courthouses throughout the Nation, including the Supreme Court of the United States.

Here the tablets have been used as part of a display that communicates not simply a religious message, but a secular message as well. The circumstances surrounding the display's placement on the capitol grounds and its physical setting suggest that the State itself intended the latter, nonreligious aspects of the tablets' message to predominate. And the monument's 40-year history on the Texas state grounds indicates that that has been its effect.

The group that donated the monument, the Fraternal Order of Eagles, a private civic (and primarily secular) organization, while interested in the religious aspect of the Ten Commandments, sought to highlight the Commandments' role in shaping civic morality as part of that organization's efforts to combat juvenile delinquency. The Eagles' consultation with a committee composed of members of several faiths in order to find a nonsectarian text underscores the group's ethics-based motives. The tablets, as displayed on the monument, prominently acknowledge that the Eagles donated the display, a factor which, though not sufficient, thereby further distances the State itself from the religious aspect of the Commandments' message.

The physical setting of the monument, moreover, suggests little or nothing of the sacred. The monument sits in a large park containing 17 monuments and 21 historical markers, all designed to illustrate the "ideals" of those who settled in Texas and of those who have lived there since that time. The setting does not readily lend itself to meditation or any other religious activity. But it does provide a context of history and moral ideals. It (together with the display's inscription about its origin) communicates to visitors that the State sought to reflect moral principles, illustrating a relation between ethics and law that the State's citizens, historically speaking, have endorsed. That is to say, the context suggests that the State intended the display's moral message—an illustrative message reflecting the historical "ideals" of Texans—to predominate.

If these factors provide a strong, but not conclusive, indication that the Commandments' text on this monument conveys a predominantly secular message, a further factor is determinative here. As far as I can tell, 40 years passed in which the presence of this monument, legally speaking, went unchallenged (until the single legal objection raised by petitioner). And I am not aware of any evidence suggesting that this was due to a climate of intimidation. Hence, those 40 years suggest more strongly than can any set of formulaic tests that few individuals, whatever their system of beliefs, are likely to have understood the monument as amounting, in any significantly detrimental way, to a government effort to favor a particular religious sect, primarily to promote religion over nonreligion, to "engage in" any "religious practic[e]," to "compel" any "religious practic[e]," or to "work deterrence" of any "religious belief." *School Dist. of Abington Township v. Schempp,* 374 U.S. 203, 305 (1963) (Goldberg, J., concurring).

This display has stood apparently uncontested for nearly two generations. That experience helps us understand that as a practical matter of *degree* this display is unlikely to prove divisive. And this matter of degree is, I believe, critical in a borderline case such as this one.

JUSTICE STEVENS, with whom JUSTICE GINSBURG joins, dissenting.

The sole function of the monument on the grounds of Texas' State Capitol is to display the full text of one version of the Ten Commandments. The monument is not a work of art and does not refer to any event in the history of the State. It is significant because, and only because, it communicates the [message of the monument's text]. * * * The message transmitted by Texas' chosen display is quite plain: This State endorses the divine code of the "Judeo-Christian" God.

In my judgment, at the very least, the Establishment Clause has created a strong presumption against the display of religious symbols on public property. * * * Government's obligation to avoid divisiveness and exclusion in the religious sphere is compelled by the Establishment and Free Exercise Clauses, which together erect a wall of separation between church and state. This metaphorical wall protects principles long recognized and often recited in this Court's cases. The first and most fundamental of these principles, one that a majority of this Court today affirms, is that the Establishment Clause demands religious neutrality—government may not exercise a preference for one religious faith over another. This essential command, however, is not merely a prohibition against the government's differentiation among religious sects. We have repeatedly reaffirmed that neither a State nor the Federal Government "can constitutionally pass laws or impose requirements which aid all religions as against non-believers, and neither can aid those religions based on a belief in the existence of God as against those religions founded on different beliefs." *Torcaso v. Watkins,* 367 U.S. 488, 495 (1961).

In restating this principle, I do not discount the importance of avoiding an overly strict interpretation of the metaphor so often used to define the reach of the Establishment Clause. * * * The wall that separates the church from the State does not prohibit the government from acknowledging the religious beliefs and practices of the American people, nor does it require governments to hide works of art or historic memorabilia from public view just because they also have religious significance.

This case, however, is not about historic preservation or the mere recognition of religion. * * * The monolith displayed on Texas Capitol grounds cannot be discounted as a passive acknowledgment of religion, nor can the State's refusal to remove it upon objection be explained as a simple desire to preserve a historic relic. * * * When the Ten Commandments monument was donated to the State of Texas in 1961, it was not for the purpose of commemorating a noteworthy event in Texas history, signifying the Commandments' influence on the development of secular law, or even denoting the religious beliefs of Texans at that time. To the contrary, the donation was only one of over a hundred largely identical monoliths, and of over a thousand paper replicas, distributed to state and local governments throughout the Nation over the course of several decades. This ambitious project was the work of the Fraternal Order of Eagles, a well-respected benevolent organization * * * motivated by a desire to "inspire the youth" and curb juvenile delinquency by providing children with a "code of conduct or standards by which to govern their actions."

Though the State of Texas may genuinely wish to combat juvenile delinquency, and may rightly want to honor the Eagles for their efforts, it cannot effectuate these admirable purposes through an explicitly religious medium. The State may admonish its citizens not to lie, cheat, or steal, to honor their parents, and to respect their neighbors' property * * *. The message at issue in this case, however, is fundamentally different from either a bland admonition to observe generally accepted rules of behavior or a general history lesson.

The reason this message stands apart is that the Decalogue is a venerable religious text. * * * The profoundly sacred message embodied by the text inscribed on the Texas monument is emphasized by the especially large letters that identify its author: "I AM the LORD thy God." It commands present worship of Him and no other deity. It directs us to be guided by His teaching in the current and future conduct of all of our affairs. It instructs us to follow a code of divine law, some of which has informed and been integrated into our secular legal code ("Thou shalt not kill"), but much of which has not ("Thou shalt not make to thyself any graven images . . . . Thou shalt not covet"). Moreover, despite the Eagles' best efforts to choose a benign nondenominational text, the Ten Commandments display projects not just a religious, but an inherently sectarian, message. There are many distinctive versions of the Decalogue, ascribed to by different religions and even different denominations within a particular faith; to a pious and learned observer, these differences may be of enormous religious significance. In choosing to display this version of the Commandments, Texas tells the observer that the State supports this side of the doctrinal religious debate.

Even if, however, the message of the monument, despite the inscribed text, fairly could be said to represent the belief system of all Judeo-Christians, it would still run afoul of the Establishment Clause by prescribing a compelled code of conduct from one God, namely a Judeo-Christian God, that is rejected by prominent polytheistic sects, such as Hinduism, as well as nontheistic religions, such as Buddhism. And, at the very least, the text of the Ten Commandments impermissibly commands a preference for religion over irreligion. * * *

The plurality relies heavily on the fact that our Republic was founded, and has been governed since its nascence, by leaders who spoke then (and speak still) in plainly religious rhetoric. * * * [But] when public officials deliver public speeches, we recognize that their words are not exclusively a transmission from the government because those oratories have embedded within them the inherently personal views of the speaker as an individual member of the polity. The permanent placement of a textual religious display on state property is different in kind; it amalgamates otherwise discordant individual views into a collective statement of government approval.

The plurality's reliance on early religious statements and proclamations made by the Founders is also problematic * * *. Notably absent from their historical snapshot is the fact that Thomas Jefferson refused to issue the Thanksgiving proclamations that Washington had so readily embraced based on the argument that to do so would violate the Establishment Clause. THE CHIEF JUSTICE and Justice Scalia disregard the substantial debates that took place regarding the constitutionality of the early proclamations and acts they cite, and paper over the fact that Madison more than once repudiated the views attributed to him by many * * *. [In addition,] many of the Framers understood the word "religion" in the Establishment Clause to encompass only the various sects of Christianity. * * * The original understanding of the type of "religion" that qualified for constitutional protection under the Establishment Clause likely did not include those followers of Judaism and Islam who are among the preferred "monotheistic" religions Justice Scalia has embraced in his *McCreary County* opinion. * * * Justice Scalia's inclusion of Judaism and Islam is a laudable act of religious tolerance, but it is one that is unmoored from the Constitution's history and text, and moreover one that is patently arbitrary in its inclusion of some, but exclusion of other (*e.g.*, Buddhism), widely practiced non-Christian religions.

A reading of the First Amendment dependent on either of the purported original meanings expressed above would eviscerate the heart of the

Establishment Clause. It would replace Jefferson's "wall of separation" with a perverse wall of exclusion—Christians inside, non-Christians out. It would permit States to construct walls of their own choosing—Baptists inside, Mormons out; Jewish Orthodox inside, Jewish Reform out. A Clause so understood might be faithful to the expectations of some of our Founders, but it is plainly not worthy of a society whose enviable hallmark over the course of two centuries has been the continuing expansion of religious pluralism and tolerance.

It is our duty, therefore, to interpret the [Establishment Clause] * * * not by merely asking what those words meant to observers at the time of the founding, but instead by deriving from the Clause's text and history the broad principles that remain valid today. * * * The principle that guides my analysis is neutrality. * * * As religious pluralism has expanded, so has our acceptance of what constitutes valid belief systems. * * * The Establishment Clause thus [prohibits] Texas from displaying the Ten Commandments monument the plurality so casually affirms.

[JUSTICE O'CONNOR's dissenting opinion has been omitted.]

JUSTICE SOUTER, with whom JUSTICE STEVENS and JUSTICE GINSBURG join, dissenting.

The Ten Commandments constitute a religious statement, [their] message is inherently religious, and [the] purpose of singling them out in a display is clearly the same. * * * Thus, a pedestrian happening upon the monument at issue here needs no training in religious doctrine to realize that the statement of the Commandments, quoting God himself, proclaims that the will of the divine being is the source of obligation to obey the rules, including the facially secular ones. In this case, moreover, the text is presented to give particular prominence to the Commandments' first sectarian reference, "I am the Lord thy God." That proclamation is centered on the stone and written in slightly larger letters than the subsequent recitation. * * * What follows, of course, are the rules against other gods, graven images, vain swearing, and Sabbath breaking.

Nothing on the monument, in fact, detracts from its religious nature, and the plurality does not suggest otherwise. It would therefore be difficult to miss the point that the government of Texas is telling everyone who sees the monument to live up to a moral code because God requires it, with both code and conception of God being rightly understood as the inheritances specifically of Jews and Christians.

POINTS FOR DISCUSSION

a.   Reconciling *McCreary County* and *Van Orden*

Four of the five Justices who agreed that the display in *McCreary County* violated the Establishment Clause dissented in *Van Orden*; only Justice Breyer was on the winning side in both cases, although he did not join Chief Justice Rehnquist's opinion in *Van Orden*. What was Justice Breyer's reasoning in concluding that the displays in *McCreary County* were unconstitutional, but that the monument in *Van Orden* was not?

Was it the context in which the Commandments were displayed? If so, then why wasn't the inclusion in the final version of the Kentucky displays of other, secular documents sufficient to render them constitutional? Was it instead that the Kentucky displays were of recent vintage? If so, does that mean essentially that any already-existing displays are likely to survive challenge but that newly created ones will not? What would be the basis of such a rule?

b.   The Test Under the Establishment Clause

After *McCreary* and *Van Orden*, what is the test for determining the constitutionality of religious displays on government property? Is neutrality still the governing principle? (How many Justices subscribed to that view in the two cases?) Is the proper test the one announced in *Lemon*? Note that Justice Souter based his opinion in *McCreary* on the purpose of the displays, which of course is the first prong of the traditional inquiry under *Lemon*. But in *Van Orden*, Chief Justice Rehnquist (who did not write for a majority) did not appear to apply the test. Is the proper test simply a multi-factored inquiry of the sort applied by Justice Breyer, or the "endorsement" test applied by Justice O'Connor in her separate opinion in *Lynch*? If so, are those approaches preferable to the *Lemon* test?

c.   Legal Advice

Suppose that you are counsel to a local government. The government wants to display a religious symbol—perhaps the Ten Commandments, perhaps something else—without violating the Establishment Clause. What practical steps could you advise the government to take?

d.   The Supreme Court

At the beginning of this section, we described various manifestations of religion that one might encounter on an ordinary day at the Supreme Court. Having read the cases in this section, can you explain why the Court's Christmas tree, its frieze depicting Moses and the Ten Commandments, and its customary prayer to save the Court are consistent with the Establishment Clause? Do you agree with this conclusion?

AMERICAN LEGION v. AMERICAN HUMANIST ASSOCIATION

139 S.Ct. 2067 (2019)

JUSTICE ALITO announced the judgment of the Court and delivered the opinion of the Court with respect to Parts I, II-B, II-C, III, and IV, and an opinion with respect to Parts II-A and II-D, in which THE CHIEF JUSTICE, JUSTICE BREYER, and JUSTICE KAVANAUGH join.

Bladensburg Peace Cross
American Legion v. American Humanist Assoc.,
139 S. Ct. 2067, 2113 (2019) (photograph
included in the appendix to the
Supreme Court's opinion)

Since 1925, the Bladensburg Peace Cross (Cross) has stood as a tribute to 49 area soldiers who gave their lives in the First World War. Eighty-nine years after the dedication of the Cross, respondents filed this lawsuit, claiming that they are offended by the sight of the memorial on public land and that its presence there and the expenditure of public funds to maintain it violate the Establishment Clause of the First Amendment. * * *

I

The cross came into widespread use as a symbol of Christianity by the fourth century, and it retains that meaning today. But there are many contexts in which the symbol has also taken on a secular meaning. * * * The image used in the Bladensburg memorial—a plain Latin cross—[took] on new meaning after World War I. "During and immediately after the war, the army marked soldiers' graves with temporary wooden crosses or Stars of David"—a departure from the prior practice of marking graves in American military cemeteries with uniform rectangular slabs. G. Piehler, Remembering War the American Way 101 (1995). The vast majority of these grave markers consisted of crosses, and thus when Americans saw photographs of these cemeteries, what struck them were rows and rows of plain white crosses. As a result, the image of a simple white cross "developed into a 'central symbol' " of the conflict. *Ibid.* * * *

After the 1918 armistice, the War Department announced plans to replace the wooden crosses and Stars of David with uniform marble slabs like those previously used in American military cemeteries. But the public outcry against that proposal was swift and fierce. * * * When the American Battle Monuments Commission took over the project of designing the headstones, it responded to this public sentiment by opting to replace the wooden crosses and Stars of David with marble versions of those symbols. * * * This * * * confirmed the cross's widespread resonance as a symbol of sacrifice in the war.

* * * In late 1918, residents of Prince George's County, Maryland, formed a committee for the purpose of erecting a memorial for the county's fallen soldiers. * * * Although we do not know precisely why the committee chose the cross, it is unsurprising that the committee—and many others commemorating World War I—adopted a symbol so widely associated with that wrenching event. [After the committee ran out of funds, the] local post of the American Legion took over the project, and the monument was finished in 1925.

The completed monument is a 32-foot tall Latin cross that sits on a large pedestal. The American Legion's emblem is displayed at its center, and the words "Valor," "Endurance," "Courage," and "Devotion" are inscribed at its base, one on each of the four faces. The pedestal also features a 9- by 2.5-foot bronze plaque explaining that the monument is "Dedicated to the heroes of Prince George's County, Maryland who lost their lives in the Great War for the liberty of the world." The plaque lists the names of 49 local men, both Black and White, who died in the war. It identifies the dates of American involvement, and quotes President Woodrow Wilson's request for a declaration of war: "The right is more precious than peace. We shall fight for the things we have always carried nearest our hearts. To such a task we dedicate our lives."

At the dedication ceremony, a local Catholic priest offered an invocation. United States Representative Stephen W. Gambrill delivered the keynote address, honoring the "men of Prince George's County" who "fought for the sacred right of all to live in peace and security." He encouraged the community to look to the "token of this cross, symbolic of Calvary," to "keep fresh the memory of our boys who died for a righteous cause." The ceremony closed with a benediction offered by a Baptist pastor.

Since its dedication, the Cross has served as the site of patriotic events honoring veterans, including gatherings on Veterans Day, Memorial Day, and Independence Day. * * * Over the years, memorials honoring the veterans of other conflicts have been added to the surrounding area, which is now known as Veterans Memorial Park. * * * In 1961, the Maryland-National Capital Park and Planning Commission (Commission) acquired the Cross and the land on which it sits in order to preserve the monument and address traffic-safety concerns. The American Legion reserved the right to continue using the memorial to host a variety of ceremonies, including events in memory of departed veterans. * * *

In 2012, nearly 90 years after the Cross was dedicated and more than 50 years after the Commission acquired it, the American Humanist Association (AHA) [and three residents of Washington, D.C., and Maryland] sued the Commission in the District Court for the District of Maryland, [raising claims under Establishment Clause]. The AHA sought declaratory and injunctive relief requiring "removal or demolition of the Cross, or removal of the arms from the Cross to form a non-religious slab or obelisk." The American Legion intervened to defend the Cross.

The District Court granted summary judgment for the Commission and the American Legion. The Cross, the District Court held, satisfies both the three-pronged test announced in Lemon v. Kurtzman, 403 U. S. 602 (1971), and the analysis applied by Justice BREYER in upholding the Ten Commandments monument at issue in Van Orden v. Perry, 545 U.S. 677 (2005). * * * A divided panel of the Court of Appeals for the Fourth Circuit reversed. * * * While recognizing that the Commission acted for a secular purpose, the court held that the Bladensburg Cross failed *Lemon*'s "effects" prong because a reasonable observer would view the Commission's ownership and maintenance of the monument as an endorsement of Christianity. The court emphasized the cross's "inherent religious meaning" as the "preeminent symbol of Christianity." Although conceding that the monument had several "secular elements," the court asserted that they were "overshadow[ed]" by the Cross's size and Christian connection * * *.

II

A

The Establishment Clause of the First Amendment provides that "Congress shall make no law respecting an establishment of religion." While the concept of a formally established church is straightforward, pinning down the meaning of a "law respecting an establishment of religion" has proved to be a vexing problem. * * * After grappling with [difficult] cases for more than 20 years, *Lemon* ambitiously attempted to distill from the Court's existing case law a test that would bring order and predictability to Establishment Clause decisionmaking. That test * * * called on courts to examine the purposes and effects of a challenged government action, as well as any entanglement with religion that it might entail. The Court later elaborated that the "effect[s]" of a challenged action should be assessed by asking whether a "reasonable observer" would conclude that the action constituted an "endorsement" of religion. County of Allegheny v. American Civil Liberties Union, Greater Pittsburgh Chapter, 492 U.S. 573, 592 (1989); *id.,* at 630 (O'Connor, J., concurring in part and concurring in judgment).

If the *Lemon* Court thought that its test would provide a framework for all future Establishment Clause decisions, its expectation has not been met. In many cases, this Court has either expressly declined to apply the test or has simply ignored it. * * * This pattern is a testament to the *Lemon* test's shortcomings. * * * The test has been harshly criticized by Members of this Court, lamented by lower court judges, and questioned by a diverse roster of scholars.

For at least four reasons, the *Lemon* test presents particularly daunting problems in cases, including the one now before us, that involve the use, for ceremonial, celebratory, or commemorative purposes, of words or symbols with religious associations. Together, these considerations counsel against efforts to evaluate such cases under *Lemon* and toward application of a presumption of constitutionality for longstanding monuments, symbols, and practices.

B

First, these cases often concern monuments, symbols, or practices that were first established long ago, and in such cases, identifying their original purpose or purposes may be especially difficult. * * * *Second*, as time goes by, the purposes associated with an established monument, symbol, or practice often multiply. * * * Even if the original purpose of a monument was infused with religion, the passage of time may obscure that sentiment. As our society becomes more and more religiously diverse, a community may preserve such monuments, symbols, and practices for the sake of their historical significance or their place in a common cultural heritage.

Third, just as the purpose for maintaining a monument, symbol, or practice may evolve, "[t]he 'message' conveyed . . . may change over time." *Pleasant Grove City v. Summum*, 555 U.S. 460, 477 (2009). * * * With sufficient time, religiously expressive monuments, symbols, and practices can become embedded features of a community's landscape and identity. The community may come to value them without necessarily embracing their religious roots. * * * Religion undoubtedly motivated those who named Bethlehem, Pennsylvania; Las Cruces, New Mexico; Providence, Rhode Island; Corpus Christi, Texas; Nephi, Utah, and the countless other places in our country with names that are rooted in religion. Yet few would argue that this history requires that these names be erased from the map. Or take a motto like Arizona's, *"Ditat Deus"* ("God enriches"), which was adopted in 1864, or a flag like Maryland's, which has included two crosses since 1904. Familiarity itself can become a reason for preservation.

Fourth, when time's passage imbues a religiously expressive monument, symbol, or practice with this kind of familiarity and historical significance, removing it may no longer appear neutral, especially to the local community for which it has taken on particular meaning. A government that roams the land, tearing down monuments with religious symbolism and scrubbing away any reference to the divine will strike many as aggressively hostile to religion. * * *

> **Take Note**
>
> Is the Court suggesting here that new monuments that resemble the one at issue in this case might be unconstitutional? If so, do you agree with the Court's conclusion that older monuments are constitutional?

These four considerations show that retaining established, religiously expressive monuments, symbols, and practices is quite different from erecting or adopting new ones. The passage of time gives rise to a strong presumption of constitutionality.

C

The role of the cross in World War I memorials is illustrative of each of the four preceding considerations. * * * In the wake of the war, the United States adopted the cross as part of its military honors, establishing the Distinguished Service Cross and the Navy Cross in 1918 and 1919, respectively. And as already noted, the fallen soldiers' final resting places abroad were marked by white crosses or Stars of David. The solemn image of endless rows of white crosses became inextricably linked with and symbolic of the ultimate price paid by 116,000 soldiers. And this relationship between the cross and the war undoubtedly influenced the design of the many war memorials that sprang up across the Nation.

This is not to say that the cross's association with the war was the sole or dominant motivation for the inclusion of the symbol in every World War I memorial that features it. But today, it is all but impossible to tell whether that was so. The passage of time means that testimony from those actually involved in the decisionmaking process is generally unavailable, and attempting to uncover their motivations invites rampant speculation. And no matter what the original purposes for the erection of a monument, a community may wish to preserve it for very different reasons, such as the historic preservation and traffic-safety concerns the Commission has pressed here.

[The AHA argues that the cross at issue in this case is different from the crosses commemorating World War I in Arlington National Cemetery because their location in a cemetery] gives them a closer association with individual gravestones and interred soldiers. But a memorial's placement in a cemetery is not necessary to create such a connection. The parents and other relatives of many of the war dead lacked the means to travel to Europe to visit their graves, and the bodies of approximately 4,400 American soldiers were either never found or never identified. Thus, for many grieving relatives and friends, memorials took the place of gravestones. * * * Whether in a cemetery or a city park, a World War I cross remains a memorial to the fallen.

Finally, as World War I monuments have endured through the years and become a familiar part of the physical and cultural landscape, requiring their removal would not be viewed by many as a neutral act. And an alteration like the one entertained by the Fourth Circuit—amputating the arms of the Cross—would be seen by many as profoundly disrespectful. [A] campaign to obliterate items with religious associations may evidence hostility to religion even if those religious associations are no longer in the forefront.

D

While the *Lemon* Court ambitiously attempted to find a grand unified theory of the Establishment Clause, in later cases, we have taken a more modest approach that focuses on the particular issue at hand and looks to history for guidance. Our cases involving prayer before a legislative session are an example.

In *Marsh v. Chambers*, 463 U.S. 783 (1983), the Court upheld the Nebraska Legislature's practice of beginning each session with a prayer by an official chaplain, and in so holding, the Court conspicuously ignored *Lemon* and did not respond to Justice Brennan's argument in dissent that the legislature's practice could not satisfy the *Lemon* test. Instead, the Court found it highly persuasive that Congress for more than 200 years had opened its sessions with a prayer and that many state legislatures had followed suit. We took a similar approach more recently in *Town of Greece*, [declaring that] "the Establishment Clause must be interpreted 'by reference to historical practices and understandings.' " * * *

* * * This practice was designed to solemnize congressional meetings, unifying those in attendance as they pursued a common goal of good governance. [To] achieve that purpose, legislative prayer needed to be inclusive rather than divisive * * *. Over time, the members of the clergy invited to offer prayers at the opening of a session grew more and more diverse. * * * The practice begun by the First Congress stands out as an example of respect and tolerance for differing views, an honest endeavor to achieve inclusivity and nondiscrimination, and a recognition of the important role that religion plays in the lives of many Americans. Where categories of monuments, symbols, and practices with a longstanding history follow in that tradition, they are likewise constitutional.

III

Applying these principles, we conclude that the Bladensburg Cross does not violate the Establishment Clause. As we have explained, the Bladensburg Cross carries special significance in commemorating World War I. Due in large part to the image of the simple wooden crosses that originally marked the graves of American soldiers killed in the war, the cross became a symbol of their sacrifice, and the design of the Bladensburg Cross must be understood in light of that background. That the cross originated as a Christian symbol and retains that meaning in many contexts does not change the fact that the symbol took on an added secular meaning when used in World War I memorials.

Not only did the Bladensburg Cross begin with this meaning, but with the passage of time, it has acquired historical importance. It reminds the people of Bladensburg and surrounding areas of the deeds of their predecessors and of the sacrifices they made in a war fought in the name of democracy. * * * And the monument has acquired additional layers of historical meaning in subsequent years. The Cross now stands among memorials to veterans of later wars. It has become part of the community.

The monument would not serve that role if its design had deliberately disrespected area soldiers who perished in World War I. More than 3,500 Jewish soldiers gave their lives for the United States in that conflict, and some have wondered whether the names of any Jewish soldiers from the area were deliberately left off the list on the memorial or whether the names of any Jewish soldiers were included on the Cross against the wishes of their families. There is no evidence that either thing was done, and we do know that one of the local American Legion leaders responsible for the Cross's construction was a Jewish veteran.

Finally, it is surely relevant that the monument commemorates the death of particular individuals. It is natural and appropriate for those seeking to honor the deceased to invoke the symbols that signify what death meant for those who are memorialized * * *—the same symbol that marks the graves of so many of their comrades near the battlefields where they fell.

IV

The cross is undoubtedly a Christian symbol, but that fact should not blind us to everything else that the Bladensburg Cross has come to represent. For some, that monument is a symbolic resting place for ancestors who never returned home. For others, it is a place for the community to gather and honor all veterans and their sacrifices for our Nation. For others still, it is a historical landmark. For many of these people, destroying or defacing the Cross that has stood undisturbed for nearly a century would not be neutral and would not further the ideals of respect and tolerance embodied in the First Amendment. For all these reasons, the Cross does not offend the Constitution. We reverse the judgment of the Court of Appeals for the Fourth Circuit and remand the cases for further proceedings.

JUSTICE BREYER, with whom JUSTICE KAGAN joins, concurring.

I have long maintained that there is no single formula for resolving Establishment Clause challenges. See *Van Orden v. Perry*, 545 U.S. 677, 698 (2005) (opinion concurring in judgment). The Court must instead consider each case in light of the basic purposes that the Religion Clauses were meant to serve: assuring religious liberty and tolerance for all, avoiding religiously based social conflict, and maintaining that separation of church and state that allows each to flourish in its "separate spher[e]." *Ibid.*; see also *Zelman v. Simmons-Harris*, 536 U.S. 639, 717–723 (2002) (BREYER, J., dissenting).

I agree with the Court that allowing the State of Maryland to display and maintain the Peace Cross poses no threat to those ends. * * * The case would be different, in my view, if there were evidence that the organizers had "deliberately disrespected" members of minority faiths or if the Cross had been erected only recently, rather than in the aftermath of World War I. But those are not the circumstances presented to us here, and I see no reason to order *this* cross torn down simply because *other* crosses would raise constitutional concerns.

Nor do I understand the Court's opinion today to adopt a "history and tradition test" that would permit any newly constructed religious memorial on public land. The Court appropriately "looks to history for guidance," but it upholds the constitutionality of the Peace Cross only after considering its particular historical context and its long-held place in the community. A newer memorial, erected under different circumstances, would not necessarily be permissible under this approach.

JUSTICE KAVANAUGH, concurring.

Consistent with the Court's case law, the Court today applies a history and tradition test in examining and upholding the constitutionality of the Bladensburg Cross. As this case again demonstrates, this Court no longer applies the old test articulated in *Lemon v. Kurtzman*, 403 U. S. 602 (1971). * * * If *Lemon* guided this Court's understanding of the Establishment Clause, then many of the Court's Establishment Clause cases over the last 48 years would have been decided differently * * *.

[The] cases together lead to an overarching set of principles: If the challenged government practice is not coercive *and* if it (i) is rooted in history and tradition; or (ii) treats religious people, organizations, speech, or activity equally to comparable secular people, organizations, speech, or activity; or (iii) represents a permissible legislative accommodation or exemption from a generally applicable law, then there ordinarily is no Establishment Clause violation. * * * The practice of displaying religious memorials, particularly religious war memorials, on public land is not coercive and is rooted in history and tradition. * * *

JUSTICE KAGAN, concurring in part.

I fully agree with the Court's reasons for allowing the Bladensburg Peace Cross to remain as it is, and so join Parts I, II-B, II-C, III, and IV of its opinion, as well as Justice BREYER's concurrence. Although I agree that rigid application of the *Lemon* test does not solve every Establishment Clause problem, I think that test's focus on purposes and effects is crucial in evaluating government action in this sphere—as this very suit shows. I therefore do not join Part II-A. I do not join Part II-D out of perhaps an excess of caution. Although I too "look[ ] to history for guidance," I prefer at least for now to do so case-by-case, rather than to sign on to any broader statements about history's role in Establishment Clause analysis. But I find much to admire in this section of the opinion—particularly, its emphasis on whether longstanding monuments, symbols, and practices reflect "respect and tolerance for differing views, an honest endeavor to achieve inclusivity and nondiscrimination, and a recognition of the important role that religion plays in the lives of many Americans." Here, as elsewhere, the opinion shows sensitivity to and respect for this Nation's pluralism, and the values of neutrality and inclusion that the First Amendment demands.

JUSTICE THOMAS, concurring in the judgment.

The text and history of [the Establishment] Clause suggest that it should not be incorporated against the States. Even if the Clause expresses an individual right enforceable against the States, it is limited by its text to "law[s]" enacted by a legislature, so it is unclear whether the Bladensburg Cross would implicate any incorporated right. And even if it did, this religious display does not involve the type of actual legal coercion that was a hallmark of historical establishments of religion. Therefore, the Cross is clearly constitutional.

As to the long-discredited test set forth in *Lemon v. Kurtzman*, 403 U.S. 602, 612–613 (1971), * * * the plurality rightly rejects its relevance to claims, like this one, involving "religious references or imagery in public monuments, symbols, mottos, displays, and ceremonies." * * * I would take the logical next step and overrule the *Lemon* test in all contexts. First, that test has no basis in the original meaning of the Constitution. Second, "since its inception," it has "been manipulated to fit whatever result the Court aimed to achieve." *McCreary County v. American Civil Liberties Union of Ky.*, 545 U.S. 844, 900 (2005) (Scalia, J., dissenting).

Third, it continues to cause enormous confusion in the States and the lower courts. * * * *Lemon* does not provide a sound basis for judging Establishment Clause claims. * * * It is our job to say what the law is, and because the *Lemon* test is not good law, we ought to say so.

JUSTICE GORSUCH, with whom JUSTICE THOMAS joins, concurring in the judgment.

The American Humanist Association wants a federal court to order the destruction of a 94 year-old war memorial because its members are offended. Today, the Court explains that the plaintiffs are not entitled to demand the destruction of longstanding monuments, and I find much of its opinion compelling. In my judgment, however, it follows from the Court's analysis that suits like this one should be dismissed for lack of standing. * * *

> **Make the Connection**
>
> We considered standing doctrine, and the *Lujan* case, in Volume 1, and we considered standing in Establishment Clause cases earlier in this chapter.

* * * This "offended observer" theory of standing has no basis in law. * * * If individuals and groups could invoke the authority of a federal court to forbid what they dislike for no more reason than they dislike it, we would risk exceeding the judiciary's limited constitutional mandate and infringing on powers committed to other branches of government. Courts would start to look more like legislatures, responding to social pressures rather than remedying concrete harms, in the process supplanting the right of the people and their elected representatives to govern themselves.

Proceeding on these principles, this Court has held offense alone insufficient to convey standing in analogous—and arguably more sympathetic— circumstances. [See *Allen v. Wright*, 468 U.S. 737 (1984).] [Under the Association's standing theory, an] African-American offended by a Confederate flag atop a state capitol would lack standing to sue under the Equal Protection Clause, but an atheist who is offended by the cross on the same flag could sue under the Establishment Clause. Who really thinks *that* could be the law?

* * * Lower courts invented offended observer standing for Establishment Clause cases in the 1970s in response to this Court's decision in *Lemon v. Kurtzman*, 403 U.S. 602 (1971), [which] this Court came to understand as prohibiting the government from doing anything that a "reasonable observer" might perceive as "endorsing" religion, *County of Allegheny v. American Civil Liberties Union, Greater Pittsburgh Chapter*, 492 U.S. 573, 620–621 (1989) (opinion of Blackmun, J.); *id.*, at 631 (O'Connor, J., concurring in part and concurring in judgment). * * * With

Lemon now shelved, little excuse will remain for the anomaly of offended observer standing, and the gaping hole it tore in standing doctrine in the courts of appeals should now begin to close. * * * [T]his will bring with it the welcome side effect of rescuing the federal judiciary from the sordid business of having to pass aesthetic judgment, one by one, on every public display in this country for its perceived capacity to give offense. * * *

JUSTICE GINSBURG, with whom JUSTICE SOTOMAYOR joins, dissenting.

The Latin cross is the foremost symbol of the Christian faith, embodying the "central theological claim of Christianity: that the son of God died on the cross, that he rose from the dead, and that his death and resurrection offer the possibility of eternal life." Brief for Baptist Joint Committee for Religious Liberty et al. as *Amici Curiae* 7. Precisely because the cross symbolizes these sectarian beliefs, it is a common marker for the graves of Christian soldiers. For the same reason, using the cross as a war memorial does not transform it into a secular symbol * * *. Just as a Star of David is not suitable to honor Christians who died serving their country, so a cross is not suitable to honor those of other faiths who died defending their nation. Soldiers of all faiths "are united by their love of country, but they are not united by the cross." Brief for Jewish War Veterans of the United States of America, Inc., as *Amicus Curiae* 3.

In cases challenging the government's display of a religious symbol, the Court has tested fidelity to the principle of neutrality by asking whether the display has the "effect of 'endorsing' religion." *County of Allegheny*, 492 U.S. at 592. * * * As I see it, when a cross is displayed on public property, the government may be presumed to endorse its religious content. The venue is surely associated with the State; the symbol and its meaning are just as surely associated exclusively with Christianity. * * * To non-Christians, nearly 30% of the population of the United States, Pew Research Center, America's Changing Religious Landscape 4 (2015), the State's choice to display the cross on public buildings or spaces conveys a message of exclusion: It tells them they "are outsiders, not full members of the political community," *County of Allegheny*, 492 U.S. at 625 (O'Connor, J., concurring in part and concurring in judgment).

A presumption of endorsement, of course, may be overcome. A display does not run afoul of the neutrality principle if its "setting . . . plausibly indicates" that the government has not sought "either to adopt [a] religious message or to urge its acceptance by others." *Van Orden*, 545 U.S. at 737 (Souter, J., dissenting). * * * The Peace Cross, however, is not of that genre. "For nearly two millennia," the Latin cross has been the "defining symbol" of Christianity, R. Jensen, The Cross: History, Art, and Controversy ix (2017), evoking the foundational claims of that faith. * * * Christians wear crosses, not as an ecumenical symbol, but to proclaim their adherence to Christianity. An exclusively Christian symbol, the Latin cross is not emblematic of any other faith. The principal symbol of Christianity around the world should not loom over public thoroughfares, suggesting official recognition of that religion's paramountcy.

The Commission urges in defense of its monument that "when used in the context of a war memorial," the cross becomes "a universal symbol of the sacrifices of those who fought and died." * * * [But the] asserted commemorative meaning of the cross rests on—and is inseparable from—its Christian meaning: "the crucifixion of Jesus Christ and the redeeming benefits of his passion and death," specifically, "the salvation of man." *American Civil Liberties Union of Illinois v. St. Charles*, 794 F.2d 265, 273 (7th Cir. 1986).

Because of its sacred meaning, the Latin cross has been used to mark Christian deaths since at least the fourth century. The cross on a grave "says that a Christian is buried here," Brief for *Amici* Christian and Jewish Organizations 8, and "commemorates [that person's death] by evoking a conception of salvation and eternal life reserved for Christians," Brief for *Amicus* Jewish War Veterans 7. * * * The cross affirms that, thanks to the soldier's embrace of Christianity, he will be rewarded with eternal life. * * *

The Peace Cross is no exception. That was evident from the start. At the dedication ceremony, the keynote speaker analogized the sacrifice of the honored soldiers to that of Jesus Christ, calling the Peace Cross "symbolic of Calvary," where Jesus was crucified. * * * The character of the monument has not changed with the passage of time. The Commission nonetheless urges that the Latin cross is a "well-established" secular symbol commemorating, in particular, "military valor and sacrifice [in] World War I." [The] Commission overlooks this reality: The cross was never perceived as an appropriate headstone or memorial for Jewish soldiers and others who did not adhere to Christianity.

Recognizing that a Latin cross does not belong on a public highway or building does not mean the monument must be "torn down." "[L]ike the determination of the violation itself," the "proper remedy . . . is necessarily context specific." *Salazar v. Buono*, 559 U.S. 700, 755, n. 11 (2010) (Stevens, J., dissenting). In some instances, the violation may be cured by relocating the monument to private land or by transferring ownership of the land and monument to a private party.

POINTS FOR DISCUSSION

a.   Evaluating the Memorial Under the *Lemon* Test

If the Court had applied the *Lemon* test, would it have upheld the memorial? Was there a secular purpose for erecting a cross at the site of the memorial? Would the primary effect of such a display be to advance particular religious beliefs? Would a reasonable observer conclude that the government had endorsed Christianity by including a large cross in the memorial?

b.   Evaluating the *Lemon* Test

Do you agree with the plurality—and a majority of the Justices—that the *Lemon* test is misguided? On the one hand, it is difficult to explain many of the Court's Establishment Clause cases—including *Marsh* and *Town of Greece*—under the test. The test, after all, was devised to address cases involving government funding of religious organizations and practices, and it might not translate easily to the context of religious displays. On the other hand, is there a good reason to consider the government's purpose and the effect of a religious display in deciding whether the government has run afoul of core Establishment Clause principles? Is the problem that the members of the Court simply do not agree about what those core principles are?

c.   The Standard for Religious Displays—and Other Establishment Clause Challenges

What is the standard for evaluating the constitutionality of religious displays after *American Legion*? Is it the historical practices test of *Marsh*? The *Lemon* test? Some combination of the two? And what does the Court's opinion tell us about the test for other Establishment Clause challenges—such as challenges to the use of prayer in public schools or government funding of religion or religious organizations? What did the plurality mean when it said that practices that demonstrate an "honest endeavor to achieve inclusivity and nondiscrimination" are constitutional even when they include a "recognition of the important role that religion plays in the lives of many Americans"? What other practices fall in that category?

B. THE FREE EXERCISE CLAUSE

Many colonists came to the United States from England because they wanted freedom to practice their religions. At the time, England was notorious for suppressing practices outside of the established Church of England (also called the Anglican Church). Justice Story reminded his readers

> that the laws of England merely tolerated protestant dissenters [i.e., protestants who were not Anglicans] in their public worship upon certain conditions, at once irritating and degrading; that the test and

corporation acts excluded them from public and corporate offices, both of trust and profit, * * * in common with Turks, Jews, heretics, papists, and other sectaries; that to deny the Trinity, however conscientiously disbelieved, was a public offence, punishable by fine and imprisonment; and that, in the rear of all these disabilities and grievances, came the long list of acts against papists, by which they were reduced to a state of political and religious slavery, and cut off from some of the dearest privileges of mankind.

3 Joseph Story, *Commentaries on the Constitution of the United States* § 1872 (1833).

The First Amendment responds to such practices. It provides: "Congress shall make no law respecting an establishment of religion, *or prohibiting the free exercise thereof* * * *." What exactly is the scope of that provision? The answer is not perfectly clear, at least in part because the Court has decided many fewer Free Exercise Clause cases than Establishment Clause cases. But certain principles are widely accepted.

First, the government cannot punish people solely for holding particular religious beliefs. It clearly would violate the Free Exercise Clause for the government to require all people to declare a belief in a particular conception of God, or to require all people to renounce a belief in a competing conception of God. As the Court has stated, the "freedom to hold religious beliefs and opinions is absolute." *Braunfeld v. Brown*, 366 U.S. 599, 603 (1961).

As a corollary to this principle, the government cannot impose special disabilities on the basis of religious belief or religious status. Accordingly, the Court invalidated a state constitutional provision that excluded ministers from serving as legislators or delegates to the state's constitutional convention. *McDaniel v. Paty*, 435 U.S. 618 (1978). Similarly, in *Torcaso v. Watkins*, 367 U.S. 488 (1961), the Court invalidated a provision in the Maryland Constitution that required state officials to declare their belief in the existence of God. The Court reasoned that the government may not force a person to "profess a belief or disbelief in any religion." Another corollary of the principle that the freedom to hold religious beliefs is absolute is that the government cannot punish the expression of religious doctrines it believes to be false. In *United States v. Ballard*, 322 U.S. 78, 86–88 (1944), for example, the Court reviewed a mail fraud indictment of the widow and son of the founder of the "I am" religion after they claimed that they had the power to cure diseases. The Court held that the jury could not be permitted to determine the truth or falsity of the defendants' religious beliefs.

Second, the Free Exercise Clause by its terms protects the free "exercise" of religion, which suggests that the Clause protects more than simply the right to believe. It is clear that the government cannot outlaw religious worship, such as by making it a crime to attend services at, say, a Jewish temple or Catholic church.

But government action seeking to interfere directly with the "freedom to believe," *Cantwell v. Connecticut*, 310 U.S. 296 (1940), or expressly to prohibit religious worship is rare. Instead, most cases arising under the Free Exercise Clause involve claims that government regulations of conduct interfere with the ability to practice one's religion. Sometimes the claim is that a law prohibits conduct that a person's religion requires. The first Supreme Court decision involving the Free Exercise Clause, for example, involved a claim that a law prohibiting polygamy abridged a Mormon's right to exercise his religion, which he claimed required him to marry more than one woman. See *Reynolds v. United States*, 98 U.S. 145 (1878) (rejecting challenge). Other times, the claim is that a law requires conduct that a person's religion forbids. For example, in *United States v. Lee*, 455 U.S. 252 (1982), the Court considered (and rejected) a claim by Amish employees that the imposition of Social Security taxes interfered with their free exercise rights because the payment of taxes violated their religious beliefs.

These cases require the Supreme Court to mediate between competing principles. On the one hand, the Free Exercise Clause guarantees that individuals generally may practice their religions freely. In general, they should have an unburdened right to pray, fast, sing hymns, keep kosher, tithe, attend religious services, and so forth. On the other hand, the Free Exercise Clause cannot mean that individuals may take any actions that they choose in the name of religion. The government, for example, must be able to criminalize murder and theft even if a person might claim that he engages in these acts out of religious obligation. Indeed, as the Supreme Court has said, "the very concept of ordered liberty precludes allowing every person to make his own standards on matters of conduct in which society as a whole has important interests." *Wisconsin v. Yoder*, 406 U.S. 205, 215-216 (1972).

The current standard, developed in *Employment Division, Dept. of Human Resources of Oregon v. Smith*, 494 U.S. 872 (1990), and *Church of the Lukumi Babalu Aye, Inc. v. City of Hialeah*, 508 U.S. 520 (1993), is as follows: The government may enforce a law that burdens a particular religious practice only if (1) the law is both neutral and of general applicability; or (2) the government has a compelling interest for imposing the burden and the law is narrowly tailored to advance that interest. A law is not neutral if the object of the law is to infringe upon or restrict practices because of their religious motivation. A law lacks general applicability if it is underinclusive, applying to religious practices but not to similar non-religious practices.

By way of example, contrast two hypothetical laws. The first bars the consumption of all alcoholic beverages (as some counties in the United States still do) for the purpose of reducing alcoholism, domestic violence, and drunk driving. This law may have an effect on religious practices; for example, a Catholic church could not use wine in a communion service. But under current doctrine, the law would not violate the Free Exercise Clause because it would be neutral (given its secular purposes) and of general applicability (given that it applies to all consumption of alcoholic beverages). The second bans the consumption of wine only in churches, in order to discourage Catholic congregations from settling in the area. This second law is neither neutral—because its purpose is to burden religious practice—nor of general applicability—because it bans the consumption of wine in only limited (and religious) contexts.

In the cases that follow, we explore the path that the Supreme Court took to arrive at this particular approach. Perhaps because of the competing impulses in this area—that is, the desire to accommodate religious freedom, on the one hand, and the desire to ensure that the government can regulate conduct according to consistently applied standards, on the other—the Court's path has not been an even one.

In some of the older cases, the Court refused to require exemptions from generally applicable laws to accommodate religious practices or beliefs. In *Braunfeld v. Brown*, 366 U.S. 599, 603 (1961), for example, the Court considered a claim by Orthodox Jews that a law requiring all businesses to close on Sundays interfered with the free exercise of their religion. The appellants argued that because their religious beliefs required them to close their businesses on Saturdays, which was their Sabbath, the effect of the law was to require them to close their businesses two days every week. The law thus put them to a choice between giving up a basic tenet of their faith, on the one hand, and facing serious economic disadvantage and the potential loss of livelihood, on the other.

The Court rejected their claim. The Court declared that "the freedom to act, even when the action is in accord with one's religious convictions, is not totally free from legislative restrictions." The Court noted that the statute at issue "does not make unlawful any religious practices of appellants * * *. To strike down, without the most critical scrutiny, legislation which imposes only an indirect burden on the exercise of religion, i.e., legislation which does not make unlawful the religious practice itself, would radically restrict the operating latitude of the legislature." The Court noted that the State had "power to provide a weekly respite from all labor and, at the same time, to set one day of the week apart from the others as a day of rest, repose, recreation and tranquility." It then stated: "[I]f the State regulates conduct by enacting a general law within its power, the purpose and effect of which is to advance the State's secular goals, the statute is valid despite its indirect burden on religious observance unless the State may accomplish its purpose by means which do not impose such a burden." Because a system of exemptions from the one uniform day of rest might give economic advantages to a different set of businesses, and might require the State to assess the sincerity of the religious beliefs of applicants for an exemption, the Court concluded that the State was not required to adopt such a system. Justices Brennan, Stewart, and Douglas dissented.

Only two years after the decision in *Braunfeld*, however, the Court decided the case that follows. As you will see, the Court's approach in that case was different from the approach in *Braunfeld*. In addition, the outcome did not turn on whether the challenged regulation was neutral and generally applicable. In this respect, its approach was quite different from the Court's later approach in *Employment Division v. Smith*, which we will get to shortly.

SHERBERT V. VERNER
374 U.S. 398 (1963)

MR. JUSTICE BRENNAN delivered the opinion of the Court.

Appellant, a member of the Seventh-day Adventist Church was discharged by her South Carolina employer because she would not work on Saturday, the Sabbath Day of her faith. When she was unable to obtain other employment because from conscientious scruples she would not take Saturday work, she filed a claim for unemployment compensation benefits under the South Carolina Unemployment Compensation Act. That law provides that, to be eligible for benefits, a claimant must be "able to work and [is] available for work"; and, further, that a claimant is ineligible for benefits "[if] he has failed, without good cause [to] accept available suitable work when offered him by the employment office or the employer." The appellee Employment Security Commission, in administrative proceedings under the statute, found that appellant's restriction upon her availability for Saturday work brought her within the provision disqualifying for benefits insured workers who fail, without good cause, to accept "suitable work when offered [by] the employment office or the employer."

The door of the Free Exercise Clause stands tightly closed against any governmental regulation of religious beliefs as such. Government may neither compel affirmation of a repugnant belief, nor penalize or discriminate against individuals or groups because they hold religious views abhorrent to the authorities, nor employ the taxing power to inhibit the dissemination of particular religious views. On the other hand, the Court has rejected challenges under the Free Exercise Clause to governmental regulation of certain overt acts prompted by religious beliefs or principles, for "even when the action is in accord with one's religious convictions, [it] is not totally free from legislative restrictions." *Braunfeld v. Brown*, 366 U.S. 599, 603 (1961). The conduct or actions so regulated have invariably posed some substantial threat to public safety, peace or order.

Plainly enough, appellant's conscientious objection to Saturday work constitutes no conduct prompted by religious principles of a kind within the reach of state legislation. If, therefore, the decision of the South Carolina Supreme Court is to withstand appellant's constitutional challenge, it must be either because her disqualification as a beneficiary represents no infringement by the State of her constitutional rights of free exercise, or because any incidental burden on the free exercise of appellant's religion may be justified by a "compelling state interest in the regulation of a subject within the State's constitutional power to regulate." *NAACP v. Button*, 371 U.S. 415 (1963).

We turn first to the question whether the disqualification for benefits imposes any burden on the free exercise of appellant's religion. We think it is clear that it does. In a sense the consequences of such a disqualification to religious principles and practices may be only an indirect result of welfare legislation within the State's general competence to enact; it is true that no criminal sanctions directly compel appellant to work a six-day week. But this is only the beginning, not the end, of our inquiry. For "[i]f the purpose or effect of a law is to impede the observance of one or all religions or is to discriminate invidiously between religions, that law is constitutionally invalid even though the burden may be characterized as being only indirect." *Braunfield v. Braun*, 366 U.S., at 607. Here not only is it apparent that appellant's declared ineligibility for benefits derives solely from the practice of her religion, but

> **Take Note**
>
> The Court describes here the substantial burden imposed by the law. What is the burden? Is it relevant that the appellant is seeking employment benefits, which are generally available not as a matter of constitutional right but instead as a matter of legislative grace? That is, does it matter that what she seeks is a "privilege," not a right? We briefly considered the significance of that difference (to the extent that there is one) in Chapter 3, when we considered Procedural Due Process, and in Chapter 8, when we considered the "unconstitutional conditions" doctrine.

the pressure upon her to forego that practice is unmistakable. The ruling forces her to choose between following the precepts of her religion and forfeiting benefits, on the one hand, and abandoning one of the precepts of her religion in order to accept work, on the other hand. Governmental imposition of such a choice puts the same kind of burden upon the free exercise of religion as would a fine imposed against appellant for her Saturday worship.

We must next consider whether some compelling state interest enforced in the eligibility provisions of the South Carolina statute justifies the substantial infringement of appellant's First Amendment right. It is basic that no showing merely of a rational relationship to some colorable state interest would suffice; in this highly sensitive constitutional area, "[o]nly the gravest abuses, endangering paramount interest, give occasion for permissible limitation," *Thomas v. Collins*, 323 U.S. 516, 530 (1945). No such abuse or danger has been advanced in the present case. The appellees suggest no more than a possibility that the filing of fraudulent claims by unscrupulous claimants feigning religious objections to Saturday work might not only dilute the unemployment compensation fund but also hinder the scheduling by employers of necessary Saturday work. But that possibility is not apposite here because no such objection appears to have been made before the South Carolina Supreme Court, and we are unwilling to assess the importance of an asserted state interest without the views of the state court. Nor, if the contention had been made below, would the record appear to sustain it; there is no proof whatever to warrant such fears of malingering or deceit as those which the respondents now advance. Even if consideration of such evidence is not foreclosed by the prohibition against judicial inquiry into the truth or falsity of religious beliefs—a question as to which we intimate no view since it is not before us—it is highly doubtful whether such evidence would be sufficient to warrant a substantial infringement of religious liberties. For even if the possibility of spurious claims did threaten to dilute the fund and disrupt the scheduling of work, it would plainly be incumbent upon the appellees to demonstrate that no alternative forms of regulation would combat such abuses without infringing First Amendment rights.

> **Practice Pointer**
>
> What was the state interest that South Carolina advanced here? Can you think of any other state interest that would have been more compelling?

In these respects, then, the state interest asserted in the present case is wholly dissimilar to the interests which were found to justify the less direct burden upon religious practices in *Braunfeld v. Brown*. [The statute at issue in that case was] saved by a countervailing factor which finds no equivalent in the instant case— a strong state interest in providing one uniform day of rest for all workers. That secular objective could be achieved, the Court found, only by declaring Sunday to be that day of rest. Requiring exemptions for Sabbatarians, while theoretically possible, appeared to present an administrative problem of such magnitude, or to afford the exempted class so great a competitive advantage, that such a requirement would have rendered the entire statutory scheme unworkable. In the present case no such justifications underlie the determination of the state court that appellant's religion makes her ineligible to receive benefits.

In holding as we do, plainly we are not fostering the "establishment" of the Seventh-day Adventist religion in South Carolina, for the extension of unemployment benefits to Sabbatarians in common with Sunday worshippers reflects nothing more than the governmental obligation of neutrality in the face of religious differences, and does not represent that involvement of religious with secular institutions which it is the object of the Establishment Clause to forestall. Nor does the recognition of the appellant's right to unemployment benefits under the state statute serve to abridge any other person's religious liberties. Nor do we, by our decision today, declare the existence of a constitutional right to unemployment benefits on the part of all persons whose religious convictions are the cause of their unemployment. This is not a case in which an employee's religious convictions serve to make him a nonproductive member of society. Finally, nothing we say today constrains the States to adopt any particular form or scheme of unemployment compensation. Our holding today is only that South Carolina may not constitutionally apply the eligibility provisions so as to constrain a worker to abandon his religious convictions respecting the day of rest. This holding but reaffirms a principle that we announced a decade and a half ago, namely that no State may "exclude individual Catholics, Lutherans, Mohammedans, Baptists, Jews, Methodists, Non-believers, Presbyterians, or the members of any other faith, because of their faith, or lack of it, from receiving the benefits of public welfare legislation." *Everson v. Board of Education*, 330 U.S. 1, 16 (1947).

MR. JUSTICE STEWART, concurring in the result.

Because the appellant refuses to accept available jobs which would require her to work on Saturdays, South Carolina has declined to pay unemployment compensation benefits to her. Her refusal to work on Saturdays is based on the tenets of her religious faith. The Court says that South Carolina cannot under these circumstances declare her to be not "available for work" within the meaning of its statute because to do so would violate her constitutional right to the free exercise of her religion.

Yet what this Court has said about the Establishment Clause must inevitably lead to a diametrically opposite result. If the appellant's refusal to work on Saturdays were based on indolence, or on a compulsive desire to watch the Saturday television programs, no one would say that South Carolina could not hold that she was not "available for work" within the meaning of its statute. That being so, the Establishment Clause as construed by this Court not only permits but affirmatively requires South Carolina equally to deny the appellant's claim for unemployment compensation when her refusal to work on Saturdays is based upon her religious creed. For, as said in *Everson v. Board of Education*, 330 U.S. 1, 11 (1943), the Establishment Clause bespeaks "a government [stripped] of all power [to] support, or otherwise to assist any or all religions," and no State "can pass laws which aid one religion." *Id.* at 30. * * *

> **Take Note**
>
> Do you agree that, under *Everson*'s principle of neutrality, the Establishment Clause requires South Carolina to decline to pay benefits under the circumstances here? Isn't it a neutral, generally applicable law? Or is Justice Stewart's point that a state cannot, consistently with that principle, grant an *exemption* only to adherents of a particular religious faith? If so, do you agree?

To require South Carolina to so administer its laws as to pay public money to the appellant under the circumstances of this case is thus clearly to require the State to violate the Establishment Clause as construed by this Court. This poses no problem for me, because I think the Court's mechanistic concept of the Establishment Clause is historically unsound and constitutionally wrong. I think the process of constitutional decision in the area of the relationships between government and religion demands considerably more than the invocation of broad-brushed rhetoric of the kind I have quoted. And I think that the guarantee of religious liberty embodied in the Free Exercise Clause affirmatively requires government to create an atmosphere of hospitality and accommodation to individual belief or disbelief. In short, I think our Constitution commands the positive protection by government of religious freedom—not only for a minority, however small—not only for the majority, however large—but for each of us.

MR. JUSTICE HARLAN, whom MR. JUSTICE WHITE joins, dissenting.

Since virtually all of the mills in the Spartanburg area were operating on a six-day week, the appellant was "unavailable for work," and thus ineligible for benefits, when personal considerations prevented her from accepting employment on a full-time basis in the industry and locality in which she had worked. * * * [I]n no proper sense can it be said that the State discriminated against the appellant on the basis of her religious beliefs or that she was denied benefits *because* she was a Seventh-day Adventist. She was denied benefits just as any other claimant would be denied benefits who was not "available for work" for personal reasons.

What the Court is holding is that if the State chooses to condition unemployment compensation on the applicant's availability for work, it is constitutionally compelled to carve out an exception—and to provide benefits— for those whose unavailability is due to their religious convictions. Such a holding has particular significance in two respects.

First, despite the Court's protestations to the contrary, the decision necessarily overrules *Braunfeld* * * *. [J]ust as in *Braunfeld*—where exceptions to the Sunday closing laws for Sabbatarians would have been inconsistent with the purpose to achieve a uniform day of rest and would have required case-by-case inquiry into religious beliefs—so here, an exception to the rules of eligibility based on religious convictions would necessitate judicial examination of those convictions and would be at odds with the limited purpose of the statute to smooth out the economy during periods of industrial instability.

Second, [under the Court's holding the] State [must] single out for financial assistance those whose behavior is religiously motivated, even though it denies such assistance to others whose identical behavior (in this case, inability to work on Saturdays) is not religiously motivated. It has been suggested that such singling out of religious conduct for special treatment may violate the constitutional limitations on state action. * * * My own view [is] that at least under the circumstances of this case it would be a permissible accommodation of religion for the State, if it chose to do so, to create an exception to its eligibility requirements for persons like the appellant. The constitutional obligation of "neutrality" is not so narrow a channel that the slightest deviation from an absolutely straight course leads to condemnation. * * * For very much the same reasons, however, I cannot subscribe to the conclusion that the State is constitutionally compelled to carve out an exception to its general rule of eligibility in the present case. Those situations in which the Constitution may require special treatment on account of religion are, in my view, few and far between, and this view is amply supported by the course of constitutional litigation in this area.

POINTS FOR DISCUSSION

a. Strict Scrutiny?

In requiring the state to articulate a "compelling interest" before applying a neutral law to burden an individual's religious freedom, is the Court effectively applying strict scrutiny to such applications of state regulation? Does it make sense to apply such searching scrutiny to laws that not only are neutral and generally applicable, but also do not appear to have been applied with any invidious purpose? In *Sherbert*, for example, there was no contention that South Carolina had intentionally singled out the appellant for adverse treatment because of her religious beliefs; to the contrary, the claim was that South Carolina's presumably neutral application of a neutral law happened to burden appellant because of her particular beliefs. Is this the type of government action that, in other contexts, triggers strict scrutiny? Is it consistent with the Court's approach in *Washington v. Davis*, 426 U.S. 229 (1976), which (we saw in Chapter 5) held that neutral laws that disproportionately affect persons of a particular race are not subject to strict scrutiny under the Equal Protection Clause? Is it consistent with the Court's approach in *United States v. O'Brien*, 391 U.S. 367 (1968), which (we saw in Chapter 8) held that content-neutral, generally applicable regulations of conduct that incidentally burden expression are not subject to strict scrutiny under the First Amendment?

How much of the outcome in *Sherbert* turned on the importance of the public benefit at stake? Can we expect other neutral, generally applicable laws to survive this form of scrutiny when they do not provide something as desirable as unemployment compensation? Notice that, upon finding a "substantial burden" on appellant's religious freedom, the Court insisted upon a compelling interest. Under other neutral, generally applicable laws, is there reason to think that the burden on religious freedom will be less substantial than the burden at issue in *Sherbert*?

b. Compelling State Interest

What would be an example of a compelling state interest that could justify a substantial burden on religious freedom? This question is difficult to answer. Not surprisingly, the Supreme Court in most cases has not been clear on the subject. In *Goldman v. Weinberger*, 475 U.S. 503 (1986), for example, the Supreme Court held that the Air Force's interest in uniformity of appearance and other factors justified a regulation prohibiting an officer from wearing a yarmulke while on duty. But the Court did not specifically describe the Air Force's interest as "compelling." Is the Air Force's interest in uniformity more "compelling" than a state's interest in ensuring that only those who have sought work and could not find it are eligible to receive benefits from a limited pot of state funds?

———————

In the following case, which also pre-dated the Court's decision in *Employment Division v. Smith*, the Court did not apply the *Smith* standard for determining when a law may permissibly burden a religious practice. After you have read *Smith*, consider whether *Yoder* is still good law. If nothing else, note that the case established the principle that the Free Exercise Clause protects only practices that are rooted in religious belief.

WISCONSIN V. YODER
406 U.S. 205 (1972)

MR. CHIEF JUSTICE BURGER delivered the opinion of the Court.

Respondents Jonas Yoder and Wallace Miller are members of the Old Order Amish religion, and respondent Adin Yutzy is a member of the Conservative Amish Mennonite Church. They and their families are residents of Green County, Wisconsin. Wisconsin's compulsory school-attendance law required them to cause their children to attend public or private school until reaching age 16 but the respondents declined to send their children, ages 14 and 15, to public school after they complete the eighth grade. The children were not enrolled in any private school, or within any recognized exception to the compulsory-attendance law, and they are conceded to be subject to the Wisconsin statute.

On complaint of the school district administrator for the public schools, respondents were charged, tried, and convicted of violating the compulsory-attendance law in Green County Court and were fined the sum of $5 each. Respondents defended on the ground that the application of the compulsory-attendance law violated their rights under the First and Fourteenth Amendments. The trial testimony showed that respondents believed, in accordance with the tenets of Old Order Amish communities generally, that their children's attendance at high school, public or private, was contrary to the Amish religion and way of life. They believed that by sending their children to high school, they would not only expose themselves to the danger of the censure of the church community, but, as found by the county court, also endanger their own salvation and that of their children. The State stipulated that respondents' religious beliefs were sincere.

There is no doubt as to the power of a State, having a high responsibility for education of its citizens, to impose reasonable regulations for the control and duration of basic education. *See, e.g., Pierce v. Society of Sisters*, 268 U.S. 510, 534 (1925). Providing public schools ranks at the very apex of the function of a State. Yet even this paramount responsibility was, in *Pierce*, made to yield to the right of parents to provide an equivalent education in a privately operated system. There the Court held that Oregon's statute compelling attendance in a public school from age eight to age 16 unreasonably interfered with the interest of parents in directing the rearing of their

> **Make the Connection**
>
> We considered the Court's decision in *Pierce*, and the right of parents to control the upbringing of their children, in Chapter 2.

off-spring, including their education in church-operated schools. As that case suggests, the values of parental direction of the religious upbringing and education of their children in their early and formative years have a high place in our society. Thus, a State's interest in universal education, however highly we rank it, is not totally free from a balancing process when it impinges on fundamental rights and interests, such as those specifically protected by the Free Exercise Clause of the First Amendment, and the traditional interest of parents with respect to the religious upbringing of their children so long as they, in the words of *Pierce*, "prepare [them] for additional obligations." 268 U.S. at 535.

It follows that in order for Wisconsin to compel school attendance beyond the eighth grade against a claim that such attendance interferes with the practice of a legitimate religious belief, it must appear either that the State does not deny the free exercise of religious belief by its requirement, or that there is a state interest of sufficient magnitude to override the interest claiming protection under the Free Exercise Clause. Long before there was general acknowledgment of the need for universal formal education, the Religion Clauses had specifically and firmly fixed the right to free exercise of religious beliefs, and buttressing this fundamental right was an equally firm, even if less explicit, prohibition against the establishment of any religion by government. The values underlying these two provisions relating to religion have been zealously protected, sometimes even at the expense of other interests of admittedly high social importance. The invalidation of financial aid to parochial schools by government grants for a salary subsidy for teachers is but one example of the extent to which courts have gone in this regard, notwithstanding that such aid programs were legislatively determined to be in the public interest and the service of sound educational policy by States and by Congress. *Lemon v. Kurtzman*, 403 U.S. 602 (1971).

> **Take Note**
>
> In this passage, the Court explains that, to be protected by the Free Exercise Clause, a practice must be rooted in a legitimate "religious belief." The Clause accordingly does not protect acts undertaken solely for secular reasons. The state in this case conceded that the respondents were motivated by "sincere" religious beliefs. What would the Court's inquiry have been like if the state had not made that concession?

We come then to the quality of the claims of the respondents concerning the alleged encroachment of Wisconsin's compulsory school-attendance statute on their rights and the rights of their children to the free exercise of the religious beliefs they and their forbears have adhered to for almost three centuries. In evaluating those claims we must be careful to determine whether the Amish religious faith and their mode of life are, as they claim, inseparable and interdependent. A way of life, however virtuous and admirable, may not be interposed as a barrier to reasonable state regulation of education if it is based on purely secular considerations; to have the protection of the Religion Clauses, the claims must be rooted in religious belief. Although a determination of what is a "religious" belief or practice entitled to constitutional protection may present a most delicate question, the very concept of ordered liberty precludes allowing every person to make his own standards on matters of conduct in which society as a whole has important interests. Thus, if the Amish asserted their claims because of their subjective evaluation and rejection of the contemporary secular values accepted by the majority, much as Thoreau rejected the social values of his time and isolated himself at Walden Pond, their claims would not rest on a religious basis. Thoreau's choice was philosophical and personal rather than religious, and such belief does not rise to the demands of the Religion Clauses.

Giving no weight to such secular considerations, however, we see that the record in this case abundantly supports the claim that the traditional way of life of the Amish is not merely a matter of personal preference, but one of deep religious conviction, shared by an organized group, and intimately related to daily living. That the Old Order Amish daily life and religious practice stem from their faith is shown by the fact that it is in response to their literal interpretation of the Biblical injunction from the Epistle of Paul to the Romans, "be not conformed to this world." This command is fundamental to the Amish faith. Moreover, for the Old Order

> **Take Note**
>
> The trial in this case included testimony from experts who described Amish religious beliefs. What if the state had offered experts to rebut that testimony? Could the judge find one set of experts not credible? Misinformed?

Amish, religion is not simply a matter of theocratic belief. As the expert witnesses explained, the Old Order Amish religion pervades and determines virtually their entire way of life, regulating it with the detail of the Talmudic diet through the strictly enforced rules of the church community.

The impact of the compulsory-attendance law on respondents' practice of the Amish religion is not only severe, but inescapable, for the Wisconsin law affirmatively compels them, under threat of criminal sanction, to perform acts undeniably at odds with fundamental tenets of their religious beliefs. Nor is the impact of the compulsory-attendance law confined to grave interference with important Amish religious tenets from a subjective point of view. It carries with it precisely the kind of objective danger to the free exercise of religion that the First Amendment was designed to prevent. As the record shows, compulsory school attendance to age 16 for Amish children carries with it a very real threat of undermining the Amish community and religious practice as they exist today; they must either abandon belief and be assimilated into society at large, or be forced to migrate to some other and more tolerant region.

In sum, the unchallenged testimony of acknowledged experts in education and religious history, almost 300 years of consistent practice, and strong evidence of a sustained faith pervading and regulating respondents' entire mode of life support the claim that enforcement of the State's requirement of compulsory formal education after the eighth grade would gravely endanger if not destroy the free exercise of respondents' religious beliefs.

The State advances two primary arguments in support of its system of compulsory education. It notes, as Thomas Jefferson pointed out early in our history, that some degree of education is necessary to prepare citizens to participate effectively and intelligently in our open political system if we are to preserve freedom and independence. Further, education prepares individuals to be self-reliant and self-sufficient participants in society. We accept these propositions.

> **Take Note**
>
> In this passage, the Court applies a form of "means-ends analysis" for determining whether the state can apply its law to the respondents. The Court concludes that the means chosen by the state (i.e., compulsory education until age 16) is not necessary to achieve the state's ends (i.e., preparing individuals to participate in society). Under the Court's approach, how weighty must the state's interest be? How closely tailored to achieving that interest must the challenged regulation be?

However, the evidence adduced by the Amish in this case is persuasively to the effect that an additional one or two years of formal high school for Amish children in place of their long-established program of informal vocational education would do little to serve those interests. Respondents' experts testified at trial, without challenge, that the value of all education must be assessed in terms of its capacity to prepare the child for life. It is one thing to say that compulsory education for a year or two beyond the eighth grade may be necessary when its goal is the preparation of the child for life in modern society as the majority live, but it is quite another if the goal of education be viewed as the preparation of the child for life in the separated agrarian community that is the keystone of the Amish faith.

The State attacks respondents' position as one fostering "ignorance" from which the child must be protected by the State. No one can question the State's duty to protect children from ignorance but this argument does not square with the facts disclosed in the record. Whatever their idiosyncrasies as seen by the majority, this record strongly shows that the Amish community has been a highly successful social unit within our society, even if apart from the conventional "mainstream." Its members are productive and very law-abiding members of society; they reject public welfare in any of its usual modern forms. The Congress itself recognized their self-sufficiency by authorizing exemption of such groups as the Amish from the obligation to pay social security taxes.

There is nothing in this record to suggest that the Amish qualities of reliability, self-reliance, and dedication to work would fail to find ready markets in today's society. Absent some contrary evidence supporting the State's position, we are unwilling to assume that persons possessing such valuable vocational skills and habits are doomed to become burdens on society should they determine to leave the Amish faith, nor is there any basis in the record to warrant a finding that an additional one or two years of formal school education beyond the eighth grade would serve to eliminate any such problem that might exist.

For the reasons stated we hold, with the Supreme Court of Wisconsin, that the First and Fourteenth Amendments prevent the State from compelling respondents to cause their children to attend formal high school to age 16. Our disposition of this case, however, in no way alters our recognition of the obvious fact that courts are not school boards or legislatures, and are ill-equipped to determine the "necessity" of discrete aspects of a State's program of compulsory education. This should suggest that courts must move with great circumspection in performing the sensitive and delicate task of weighing a State's legitimate social concern when faced with religious claims for exemption from generally applicable education requirements. It cannot be overemphasized that we are not dealing with a way of life and mode of education by a group claiming to have recently discovered some "progressive" or more enlightened process for rearing children for modern life.

MR. JUSTICE DOUGLAS, dissenting in part.

I agree with the Court that the religious scruples of the Amish are opposed to the education of their children beyond the grade schools, yet I disagree with the Court's conclusion that the matter is within the dispensation of parents alone. The Court's analysis assumes that the only interests at stake in the case are those of the Amish parents on the one hand, and those of the State on the other. The difficulty with this approach is that, despite the Court's claim, the parents are seeking to vindicate not only their own free exercise claims, but also those of their high-school-age children.

On this important and vital matter of education, I think the children should be entitled to be heard. While the parents, absent dissent, normally speak for the entire family, the education of the child is a matter on which the child will often have decided views. He may want to be a pianist or an astronaut or an oceanographer. To do so he will have to break from the Amish tradition.

It is the future of the student, not the future of the parents, that is imperiled by today's decision. If a parent keeps his child out of school beyond the grade school, then the child will be forever barred from entry into the new and amazing world of diversity that we have today. The child may decide that that is the preferred course, or he may rebel. It is the student's judgment, not his parents', that is essential if we are to give full meaning to what we have said about the Bill of Rights and of the right of students to be masters of their own destiny. * * * [But the] views of the two children in question were not canvassed by the Wisconsin courts. The matter should be explicitly reserved so that new hearings can be held on remand of the case.

POINTS FOR DISCUSSION

a. Neutral and Generally Applicable Laws?

Was the law at issue in *Yoder* neutral—that is, did it have a purpose neither to advance nor inhibit religious practice? Was it a law of general applicability—that is, did it apply evenly to the religious and the non-religious alike? If so, then why did the Court hold that it could not be applied to the respondents? Must courts grant exemptions from such laws for every person who sincerely asserts that his religious beliefs preclude compliance, assuming he can substantiate the genuineness of his religious convictions? Or is the form of scrutiny that the Court applied in *Yoder*— something very much like strict scrutiny, although the court did not explicitly call it that—flexible enough to ensure that truly important laws are enforced uniformly?

Imagine, for example, a person who adheres to a sect of Christianity that teaches that the only acceptable "tax" in God's eyes is a tithe to the Church, and that any other form of tax—including federal income taxes—violates the Biblical injunction against "false idols." Does the Court's approach in *Yoder* require the government to exempt him from the obligation to pay income taxes? If not, why? Because the government has a more compelling interest in raising revenues than it does in ensuring an educated polity? Or because there is no other way to advance its interest? Or is it simply impossible to draw a principled distinction?

b. What Is a Religious Belief?

If the Free Exercise Clause protects only practices rooted in religious beliefs, courts presumably must distinguish religious beliefs from other kinds of beliefs. The Supreme Court has never devised a clear definition. How should religion be defined?

Should it be a function of the adherent's sincerity? The number of adherents to the religion? The extent to which the beliefs seem within the plausible range of acceptable views? Isn't the very inquiry in tension with the idea of free exercise of religion?

Consider the view of then-Dean (and now Judge) Guido Calabresi:

> There may be some beliefs which are considered *so* outlandish that they do not count as religions at all, even for purposes of the [religion clauses]. In fact that is a subterfuge—for no principled distinction can be made between cults and religions. It may, nonetheless, be a useful—if dangerous—lie * * *. By denying that some cults are religions at all, we may be able to give full protection in the face of majoritarian pressures to any number of other religions which are *not* "acceptable," but which could not be termed non-religious under any reasonable definition of religion.

Guido Calabresi, *Ideals, Beliefs, Attitudes, and the Law* 60–61 (1985). Do you agree that there is no "principled" way to distinguish among claims of religious beliefs? If so, is Judge Calabresi's approach defensible?

In the following case, the Court appeared to depart from *Sherbert* and *Yoder* to establish a new standard for claims under the Free Exercise Clause. Consider carefully what the Court says about its precedents, and whether the standard it articulates—new or not—is sensible.

EMPLOYMENT DIV., DEPT. OF HUMAN RESOURCES OF OREGON V. SMITH
494 U.S. 872 (1990)

JUSTICE SCALIA delivered the opinion of the Court.

Oregon law prohibits the knowing or intentional possession of a "controlled substance" unless the substance has been prescribed by a medical practitioner. The law defines "controlled substance" as a drug classified in Schedules I through V of the Federal Controlled Substances Act, as modified by the State Board of Pharmacy. Persons who violate this provision by possessing a controlled substance listed on Schedule I are "guilty of a Class B felony." As compiled by the State Board of Pharmacy under its statutory authority, Schedule I contains the drug peyote, a hallucinogen derived from the plant *Lophophora williamsii Lemaire*.

Respondents Alfred Smith and Galen Black (hereinafter respondents) were fired from their jobs with a private drug rehabilitation organization because they ingested peyote for sacramental purposes at a ceremony of the Native American Church, of which both are members. When respondents applied to petitioner

Employment Division (hereinafter petitioner) for unemployment compensation, they were determined to be ineligible for benefits because they had been discharged for work-related "misconduct." * * * [The Oregon Supreme Court confirmed that Oregon law prohibits the religious use of peyote. The issue now is whether that prohibition is permissible under the Free Exercise Clause.]

The free exercise of religion means, first and foremost, the right to believe and profess whatever religious doctrine one desires. Thus, the First Amendment obviously excludes all "governmental regulation of religious *beliefs* as such." *Sherbert v. Verner,* 374 U.S. 398, 402 (1963). The government may not compel affirmation of religious belief, see *Torcaso v. Watkins,* 367 U.S. 488 (1961), punish the expression of religious doctrines it believes to be false, *United States v. Ballard,* 322 U.S. 78, 86–88 (1944), impose special disabilities on the basis of religious views or religious status, see *McDaniel v. Paty,* 435 U.S. 618 (1978), or lend its power to one or the other side in controversies over religious authority or dogma, see *Presbyterian Church in U.S. v. Mary Elizabeth Blue Hull Memorial Presbyterian Church,* 393 U.S. 440, 445–452 (1969).

But the "exercise of religion" often involves not only belief and profession but the performance of (or abstention from) physical acts: assembling with others for a worship service, participating in sacramental use of bread and wine, proselytizing, abstaining from certain foods or certain modes of transportation. It would be true, we think (though no case of ours has involved the point), that a State would be "prohibiting the free exercise [of religion]" if it sought to ban such

> **Make the Connection**
>
> The case that follows—*Church of the Lukumi Babalu Aye, Inc. v. City of Hialeah*—involved (in the Court's view) just such a statute.

acts or abstentions only when they are engaged in for religious reasons, or only because of the religious belief that they display. It would doubtless be unconstitutional, for example, to ban the casting of "statues that are to be used for worship purposes," or to prohibit bowing down before a golden calf.

Respondents in the present case, however, seek to carry the meaning of "prohibiting the free exercise [of religion]" one large step further. They contend that their religious motivation for using peyote places them beyond the reach of a criminal law that is not specifically directed at their religious practice, and that is concededly constitutional as applied to those who use the drug for other reasons. They assert, in other words, that "prohibiting the free exercise [of religion]" includes requiring any individual to observe a generally applicable law that requires (or forbids) the performance of an act that his religious belief forbids (or requires). As a textual matter, we do not think the words must be given that meaning. It is no more necessary to regard the collection of a general tax, for example, as "prohibiting the free exercise [of religion]" by those citizens who believe support of organized government to be sinful, than it is to regard the same tax as "abridging the freedom [of] the press" of those publishing companies that must pay the tax as a condition of staying in business. It is a permissible reading of the text, in the one case as in the other, to say that if prohibiting the exercise of religion (or burdening the activity of printing) is not the object of the tax but merely the incidental effect of a generally applicable and otherwise valid provision, the First Amendment has not been offended.

Our decisions reveal that the latter reading is the correct one. We have never held that an individual's religious beliefs excuse him from compliance with an otherwise valid law prohibiting conduct that the State is free to regulate. On the contrary, the record of more than a century of our free exercise jurisprudence contradicts that proposition. As described succinctly by Justice Frankfurter in *Minersville School Dist. Bd. of Ed. v. Gobitis,* 310 U.S. 586, 594–595 (1940): "Conscientious

> **FYI**
>
> In *Gobitis*, the Court rejected a free exercise challenge to a requirement that school children recite the pledge of allegiance. The Court overruled *Gobitis*, however, in *West Virginia State Board of Education v. Barnette*, 319 U.S. 624 (1943). In light of that fact, should the Court rely on *Gobitis* here?

scruples have not, in the course of the long struggle for religious toleration, relieved the individual from obedience to a general law not aimed at the promotion or restriction of religious beliefs. The mere possession of religious convictions which contradict the relevant concerns of a political society does not relieve the citizen from the discharge of political responsibilities." We first had occasion to assert that principle in *Reynolds v. United States,* 98 U.S. 145 (1878), where we rejected the claim that criminal laws against polygamy could not be constitutionally applied to those whose religion commanded the practice. "Laws," we said, "are made for the government of actions, and while they cannot interfere with mere religious belief and opinions, they may with practices. [Can] a man excuse his practices to the contrary because of his religious belief? To permit this would be to make the professed doctrines of religious belief superior to the law of the land, and in effect to permit every citizen to become a law unto himself." *Id.* at 166–167.

Our most recent decision involving a neutral, generally applicable regulatory law that compelled activity forbidden by an individual's religion was *United States v. Lee,* 455 U.S. 252, 258–261 (1982). There, an Amish employer, on behalf of himself and his employees, sought exemption from collection and payment of

Social Security taxes on the ground that the Amish faith prohibited participation in governmental support programs. We rejected the claim that an exemption was constitutionally required. There would be no way, we observed, to distinguish the Amish believer's objection to Social Security taxes from the religious objections that others might have to the collection or use of other taxes. "If, for example, a religious adherent believes war is a sin, and if a certain percentage of the federal budget can be identified as devoted to war-related activities, such individuals would have a similarly valid claim to be exempt from paying that percentage of the income tax. The tax system could not function if denominations were allowed to challenge the tax system because tax payments were spent in a manner that violates their religious belief." *Id.* at 260.

The only decisions in which we have held that the First Amendment bars application of a neutral, generally applicable law to religiously motivated action have involved not the Free Exercise Clause alone, but the Free Exercise Clause in conjunction with other constitutional protections, such as freedom of speech and of the press, see *Cantwell v. Connecticut,* 310 U.S. 296, 304–307 (1940) (invalidating a licensing system for religious and charitable solicitations under which the administrator had discretion to deny a license to any cause he deemed nonreligious); *Murdock v. Pennsylvania,* 319 U.S. 105 (1943) (invalidating a flat tax on solicitation as applied to the dissemination of religious ideas); or the right of parents, acknowledged in *Pierce v. Society of Sisters,* 268 U.S. 510 (1925), to direct the education of their children, see *Wisconsin v. Yoder,* 406 U.S. 205 (1972) (invalidating compulsory school-attendance laws as applied to Amish parents who refused on religious grounds to send their children to school). * * *

Take Note

The Court here distinguishes *Yoder* on the ground that it involved the constitutional right of parents to direct the education of their children. Having read *Yoder,* do you agree that this fact was central to the decision?

The present case does not present such a hybrid situation, but a free exercise claim unconnected with any communicative activity or parental right. Respondents urge us to hold, quite simply, that when otherwise prohibitable conduct is accompanied by religious convictions, not only the convictions but the conduct itself must be free from governmental regulation. We have never held that, and decline to do so now. There being no contention that Oregon's drug law represents an attempt to regulate religious beliefs, the communication of religious beliefs, or the raising of one's children in those beliefs, the rule to which we have adhered ever since *Reynolds* plainly controls. "Our cases do not at their farthest reach support the proposition that a stance of conscientious opposition relieves an objector from any colliding duty fixed by a democratic government." *Gillette v. United States,* 401 U.S. 437, 461 (1971).

Respondents argue that even though exemption from generally applicable criminal laws need not automatically be extended to religiously motivated actors, at least the claim for a religious exemption must be evaluated under the balancing test set forth in *Sherbert v. Verner,* 374 U.S. 398 (1963). Under the *Sherbert* test, governmental actions that substantially burden a religious practice must be justified by a compelling governmental interest. Applying that test we have, on three occasions, invalidated state unemployment compensation rules that conditioned the availability of benefits upon an applicant's willingness to work under conditions forbidden by his religion. See *Sherbert; Thomas v. Review Bd. of Indiana Employment Security Div.,* 450 U.S. 707 (1981); *Hobbie v. Unemployment Appeals Comm'n of Florida,* 480 U.S. 136 (1987). We have never invalidated any governmental action on the basis of the *Sherbert* test except the denial of

> **Take Note**
>
> In this passage, the Court states that the *Sherbert* test, which requires a compelling state interest for laws that burden religious practices, has been applied only in cases involving claims for unemployment compensation. Isn't *Smith* just such a case? The Court seems to suggest that the neutral, generally applicable law at issue here is the criminal prohibition on the possession of a controlled substance. But isn't the challenge here to the state's refusal to provide unemployment compensation? Is the Court effectively overruling *Sherbert* without explicitly saying so?

unemployment compensation. Although we have sometimes purported to apply the *Sherbert* test in contexts other than that, we have always found the test satisfied, see *United States v. Lee,* 455 U.S. 252 (1982); *Gillette v. United States,* 401 U.S. 437 (1971). In recent years we have abstained from applying the *Sherbert* test (outside the unemployment compensation field) at all. In *Bowen v. Roy,* 476 U.S. 693 (1986), we declined to apply *Sherbert* analysis to a federal statutory scheme that required benefit applicants and recipients to provide their Social Security numbers. The plaintiffs in that case asserted that it would violate their religious beliefs to obtain and provide a Social Security number for their daughter. We held the statute's application to the plaintiffs valid regardless of whether it was necessary to effectuate a compelling interest. In *Lyng v. Northwest Indian Cemetery Protective Assn.,* 485 U.S. 439 (1988), we declined to apply *Sherbert* analysis to the Government's logging and road construction activities on lands used for religious purposes by several Native American Tribes, even though it was undisputed that the activities "could have devastating effects on traditional Indian religious practices," 485 U.S., at 451. In *Goldman v. Weinberger,* 475 U.S. 503 (1986), we rejected application of the *Sherbert* test to military dress regulations that forbade the wearing of yarmulkes.

* * *

Even if we were inclined to breathe into *Sherbert* some life beyond the unemployment compensation field, we would not apply it to require exemptions from a generally applicable criminal law. The *Sherbert* test, it must be recalled, was developed in a context that lent itself to individualized governmental assessment of the reasons for the relevant conduct. [A] distinctive feature of unemployment compensation programs is that their eligibility criteria invite consideration of the particular circumstances behind an applicant's unemployment * * *. [O]ur decisions in the unemployment cases stand for the proposition that where the State has in place a system of individual exemptions, it may not refuse to extend that system to cases of "religious hardship" without compelling reason. *Bowen v. Roy*, 476 U.S., at 708.

Whether or not the decisions are that limited, they at least have nothing to do with an across-the-board criminal prohibition on a particular form of conduct. Although, as noted earlier, we have sometimes used the *Sherbert* test to analyze free exercise challenges to such laws, we have never applied the test to invalidate one. We conclude today that the sounder approach, and the approach in accord with the vast majority of our precedents, is to hold the test inapplicable to such challenges. The government's ability to enforce generally applicable prohibitions of socially harmful conduct, like its ability to carry out other aspects of public policy, "cannot depend on measuring the effects of a governmental action on a religious objector's spiritual development." *Lyng*, 485 U.S., at 451. To make an individual's obligation to obey such a law contingent upon the law's coincidence with his religious beliefs, except where the State's interest is "compelling"— permitting him, by virtue of his beliefs, "to become a law unto himself," *Reynolds v. United States*, 98 U.S., at 167—contradicts both constitutional tradition and common sense.

The "compelling government interest" requirement seems benign, because it is familiar from other fields. But using it as the standard that must be met before the government may accord different treatment on the basis of race or before the government may regulate the content of speech is not remotely comparable to using it for the purpose asserted here. What it produces in those other fields— equality of treatment and an unrestricted flow of contending speech—are constitutional norms; what it would produce here—a private right to ignore generally applicable laws—is a constitutional anomaly.[3]

---

[3]   * * * Just as we subject to the most exacting scrutiny laws that make classifications based on race, so too we strictly scrutinize governmental classifications based on religion, see *McDaniel v. Paty*, 435 U.S. 618 (1978). But we have held that race-neutral laws that have the effect of disproportionately disadvantaging a particular racial group do not thereby become subject to compelling-interest analysis under the Equal Protection Clause, see *Washington v. Davis*, 426 U.S. 229 (1976); and we have held that generally applicable laws

Nor is it possible to limit the impact of respondents' proposal by requiring a "compelling state interest" only when the conduct prohibited is "central" to the individual's religion. It is no more appropriate for judges to determine the "centrality" of religious beliefs before applying a "compelling interest" test in the free exercise field, than it would be for them to determine the "importance" of ideas before applying the "compelling interest" test in the free speech field. What principle of law or logic can be brought to bear to contradict a believer's assertion that a particular act is "central" to his personal faith? * * * Repeatedly and in many different contexts, we have warned that courts must not presume to determine the place of a particular belief in a religion or the plausibility of a religious claim. See, *e.g.*, *United States v. Ballard*, 322 U.S. 78, 85–87 (1944).

If the "compelling interest" test is to be applied at all, then, it must be applied across the board, to all actions thought to be religiously commanded. Moreover, if "compelling interest" really means what it says (and watering it down here would subvert its rigor in the other fields where it is applied), many laws will not meet the test. Any society adopting such a system would be courting anarchy, but that danger increases in direct proportion to the society's diversity of religious beliefs, and its determination to coerce or suppress none of them. Precisely because "we are a cosmopolitan nation made up of people of almost every conceivable religious preference," and precisely because we value and protect that religious divergence, we cannot afford the luxury of deeming *presumptively invalid*, as applied to the religious objector, every regulation of conduct that does not protect an interest of the highest order. The rule respondents favor would open the prospect of constitutionally required religious exemptions from civic obligations of almost every conceivable kind—ranging from compulsory military service, *Gillette v. United States*, 401 U.S. 437 (1971), to the payment of taxes; to health and safety regulation such as manslaughter and child neglect laws, compulsory vaccination laws, drug laws, and traffic laws; to social welfare legislation such as minimum wage laws, child labor laws, animal cruelty laws, environmental protection laws, and laws providing for equality of opportunity for the races, see, *e.g.*, *Bob Jones University v. United States*, 461 U.S. 574, 603–604 (1983). The First Amendment's protection of religious liberty does not require this.

Because respondents' ingestion of peyote was prohibited under Oregon law, and because that prohibition is constitutional, Oregon may, consistent with the

---

unconcerned with regulating speech that have the effect of interfering with speech do not thereby become subject to compelling-interest analysis under the First Amendment, see *Citizen Publishing Co. v. United States*, 394 U.S. 131, 139 (1969) (antitrust laws). Our conclusion that generally applicable, religion-neutral laws that have the effect of burdening a particular religious practice need not be justified by a compelling governmental interest is the only approach compatible with these precedents.

Free Exercise Clause, deny respondents unemployment compensation when their dismissal results from use of the drug.

JUSTICE O'CONNOR, with whom JUSTICE BRENNAN, JUSTICE MARSHALL, and JUSTICE BLACKMUN join as to Parts I and II, concurring in the judgment.

Although I agree with the result the Court reaches in this case, I cannot join its opinion. In my view, today's holding dramatically departs from well-settled First Amendment jurisprudence, appears unnecessary to resolve the question presented, and is incompatible with our Nation's fundamental commitment to individual religious liberty.

The First Amendment [does] not distinguish between laws that are generally applicable and laws that target particular religious practices. Indeed, few States would be so naive as to enact a law directly prohibiting or burdening a religious practice as such. Our free exercise cases have all concerned generally applicable laws that had the effect of significantly burdening a religious practice. If the First Amendment is to have any vitality, it ought not be construed to cover only the extreme and hypothetical situation in which a State directly targets a religious practice.

To say that a person's right to free exercise has been burdened, of course, does not mean that he has an absolute right to engage in the conduct. Under our established First Amendment jurisprudence, we have recognized that the freedom to act, unlike the freedom to believe, cannot be absolute. Instead, we have respected both the First Amendment's express textual mandate and the governmental interest in regulation of conduct by requiring the government to justify any substantial burden on religiously motivated conduct by a compelling state interest and by means narrowly tailored to achieve that interest.

The Court endeavors to escape from our decisions in *Cantwell* and *Yoder* by labeling them "hybrid" decisions, but there is no denying that both cases expressly relied on the Free Exercise Clause, see *Cantwell*, 310 U.S., at 303–307; *Yoder*, 406 U.S., at 219–229, and that we have consistently regarded those cases as part of the mainstream of our free exercise jurisprudence. Moreover, in each of the other cases cited by the Court to support its categorical rule, we rejected the particular constitutional claims before us only after carefully weighing the competing interests. That we rejected the free exercise claims in those cases hardly

---

FYI

In *Cantwell*, the Court reversed a conviction under a statute that required a person to obtain a license before soliciting money for religious causes. The Court relied on the First Amendment's protections for the freedom of speech and the free exercise of religion.

calls into question the applicability of First Amendment doctrine in the first place. Indeed, it is surely unusual to judge the vitality of a constitutional doctrine by looking to the win-loss record of the plaintiffs who happen to come before us.

In my view, [the] essence of a free exercise claim is relief from a burden imposed by government on religious practices or beliefs, whether the burden is imposed directly through laws that prohibit or compel specific religious practices, or indirectly through laws that, in effect, make abandonment of one's own religion or conformity to the religious beliefs of others the price of an equal place in the civil community. A State that makes criminal an individual's religiously motivated conduct burdens that individual's free exercise of religion in the severest manner possible * * *. I would have thought it beyond argument that such laws implicate free exercise concerns. Indeed, we have never distinguished between cases in which a State conditions receipt of a benefit on conduct prohibited by religious beliefs and cases in which a State affirmatively prohibits such conduct.

Once it has been shown that a government regulation or criminal prohibition burdens the free exercise of religion, we have consistently asked the government to demonstrate that unbending application of its regulation to the religious objector "is essential to accomplish an overriding governmental interest," *Lee*, 455 U.S., at 257–258, or represents "the least restrictive means of achieving some compelling state interest." *Thomas*, 450 U.S., at 718. To me, the sounder approach—the approach more consistent with our role as judges to decide each case on its individual merits—is to apply this test in each case to determine whether the burden on the specific plaintiffs before us is constitutionally significant and whether the particular criminal interest asserted by the State before us is compelling. Even if, as an empirical matter, a government's criminal laws might usually serve a compelling interest in health, safety, or public order, the First Amendment at least requires a case-by-case determination of the question, sensitive to the facts of each particular claim.

The Court today gives no convincing reason to depart from settled First Amendment jurisprudence. There is nothing talismanic about neutral laws of general applicability or general criminal prohibitions, for laws neutral toward religion can coerce a person to violate his religious conscience or intrude upon his religious duties just as effectively as laws aimed at religion. * * * As the language of the [Free Exercise] Clause itself makes clear, an individual's free exercise of religion is a preferred constitutional activity. A law that makes criminal such an activity therefore triggers constitutional concern—and heightened judicial scrutiny—even if it does not target the particular religious conduct at issue. Our free speech cases similarly recognize that neutral regulations that affect free speech values are subject to a balancing, rather than categorical, approach. See, *e.g., United States v. O'Brien*, 391 U.S. 367, 377 (1968). The Court's parade of horribles not only fails as a reason for discarding the compelling interest test, it instead demonstrates just the opposite: that courts have been quite capable of applying our free exercise jurisprudence to strike sensible balances between religious liberty and competing state interests.

[T]he Court today suggests that the disfavoring of minority religions is an "unavoidable consequence" under our system of government and that accommodation of such religions must be left to the political process. In my view, however, the First Amendment was enacted precisely to protect the rights of those whose religious practices are not shared by the majority and may be viewed with hostility. The history of our free exercise doctrine amply demonstrates the harsh impact majoritarian rule has had on unpopular or emerging religious groups such as the Jehovah's Witnesses and the Amish. Indeed, "[t]he very purpose of a Bill of Rights was to withdraw certain subjects from the vicissitudes of political controversy, to place them beyond the reach of majorities and officials and to establish them as legal principles to be applied by the courts." *West Virginia State Bd. of Educ. v. Barnette*, 319 U.S., at 638. * * * The compelling interest test reflects the First Amendment's mandate of preserving religious liberty to the fullest extent possible in a pluralistic society. For the Court to deem this command a "luxury" is to denigrate "[t]he very purpose of a Bill of Rights."

The Court's holding today not only misreads settled First Amendment precedent; it appears to be unnecessary to this case. I would reach the same result applying our established free exercise jurisprudence. I believe that granting a selective exemption in this case would seriously impair Oregon's compelling interest in prohibiting possession of peyote by its citizens. Under such circumstances, the Free Exercise Clause does not require the State to accommodate respondents' religiously motivated conduct. * * * Accordingly, I concur in the judgment of the Court.

JUSTICE BLACKMUN, with whom JUSTICE BRENNAN and JUSTICE MARSHALL join, dissenting.

I agree with Justice O'CONNOR's analysis of the applicable free exercise doctrine * * *. As she points out, "the critical question in this case is whether exempting respondents from the State's general criminal prohibition will unduly interfere with fulfillment of the governmental interest." I do disagree, however, with her specific answer to that question.

In weighing the clear interest of respondents Smith and Black (hereinafter respondents) in the free exercise of their religion against Oregon's asserted interest in enforcing its drug laws, it is important to articulate in precise terms the state interest involved. It is not the State's broad interest in fighting the critical "war on drugs," [but] the State's narrow interest in refusing to make an exception for the religious, ceremonial use of peyote. * * * Oregon has never sought to prosecute respondents, and does not claim that it has made significant enforcement efforts against other religious users of peyote. The State's asserted interest thus amounts only to the symbolic preservation of an unenforced prohibition.

The State proclaims an interest in protecting the health and safety of its citizens from the dangers of unlawful drugs. It offers, however, no evidence that the religious use of peyote has ever harmed anyone. * * * The fact that peyote is classified as a Schedule I controlled substance does not, by itself, show that any and all uses of peyote, in any circumstance, are inherently harmful and dangerous. The Federal Government, which created the classifications of unlawful drugs from which Oregon's drug laws are derived, apparently does not find peyote so dangerous as to preclude an exemption for religious use. [21 CFR § 1307.31 (1989).]

The carefully circumscribed ritual context in which respondents used peyote is far removed from the irresponsible and unrestricted recreational use of unlawful drugs. * * * Not only does the church's doctrine forbid nonreligious use of peyote; it also generally advocates self-reliance, familial responsibility, and abstinence from alcohol. * * * Far from promoting the lawless and irresponsible use of drugs, Native American Church members' spiritual code exemplifies values that Oregon's drug laws are presumably intended to foster.

Finally, the State argues that granting an exception for religious peyote use would erode its interest in the uniform, fair, and certain enforcement of its drug laws. The State fears that, if it grants an exemption for religious peyote use, a flood of other claims to religious exemptions will follow. It would then be placed in a dilemma, it says, between allowing a patchwork of exemptions that would hinder its law enforcement efforts, and risking a violation of the Establishment Clause by arbitrarily limiting its religious exemptions. * * * The State's apprehension of a flood of other religious claims is purely speculative. Almost half the States, and the Federal Government, have maintained an exemption for religious peyote use for many years, and apparently have not found themselves overwhelmed by claims to other religious exemptions. * * * The unusual circumstances that make the religious use of peyote compatible with the State's interests in health and safety and in preventing drug trafficking would not apply to other religious claims. Some religions, for example, might not restrict drug use to a limited ceremonial context, as does the Native American Church. * * * That the State might grant an exemption for religious peyote use, but deny other religious claims arising in different circumstances, would not violate the Establishment Clause. Though the State must treat all religions equally, and not favor one over another, this obligation is fulfilled by the uniform application of the "compelling interest" test to all free exercise claims, not by reaching uniform *results* as to all claims.

Finally, although I agree with Justice O'CONNOR that courts should refrain from delving into questions whether, as a matter of religious doctrine, a particular practice is "central" to the religion, I do not think this means that the courts must turn a blind eye to the severe impact of a State's restrictions on the adherents of a minority religion. Respondents believe, and their sincerity has *never* been at issue, that the peyote plant embodies their deity, and eating it is an act of worship and communion. Without peyote, they could not enact the essential ritual of their religion.

For these reasons, I conclude that Oregon's interest in enforcing its drug laws against religious use of peyote is not sufficiently compelling to outweigh respondents' right to the free exercise of their religion. Since the State could not constitutionally enforce its criminal prohibition against respondents, the interests underlying the State's drug laws cannot justify its denial of unemployment benefits.

POINTS FOR DISCUSSION

a.   The Theory of *Smith*

What is the theoretical basis of the Court's decision in *Smith* that the Free Exercise Clause does not require exemptions from neutral laws of general applicability? Is it the practical intuition that government cannot operate effectively when its laws cannot apply to those who object to their content? Is it the institutional concern that judges are ill suited to weigh the state's interest in its regulations against individuals' religious imperatives? Is it the commitment to democratic majoritarianism, which necessarily means that law will impose more burdens on religious minorities than on those who adhere to the majority faith?

Consider the view that Justice Stevens advanced in his concurring opinion in *Goldman v. Weinberger*, 475 U.S. 503 (1986), which the Court cited in *Smith* and which held that the Free Exercise Clause did not require the Air Force to exempt an observant Jew who wished to wear a yarmulke from a regulation prohibiting the wearing of headgear:

Captain Goldman presents an especially attractive case for an exception from the uniform regulations that are applicable to all other Air Force personnel. His devotion to his faith is readily apparent. The yarmulke is a familiar and accepted sight. In addition to its religious significance for the wearer, the yarmulke may evoke the deepest respect and admiration—the symbol of a distinguished tradition and an eloquent rebuke to the ugliness of anti-Semitism. Captain Goldman's military duties are performed in a setting in which a modest departure from the uniform regulation creates almost no danger of impairment of the Air Force's military mission.

[However, the] very strength of Captain Goldman's claim creates the danger that a similar claim on behalf of a Sikh or a Rastafarian might readily be dismissed as "so extreme, so unusual, or so faddish an image that public confidence in his ability to perform his duties will be destroyed." If exceptions from dress code regulations are to be granted on the basis of a multifactored test * * *, inevitably the decisionmaker's evaluation of the character and the sincerity of the requester's faith—as well as the probable reaction of the majority to the favored treatment of a member of that faith—will play a critical part in the decision. For the difference between a turban or a dreadlock on the one hand, and a yarmulke on the other, is not merely a difference in "appearance"—it is also the difference between a Sikh or a Rastafarian, on the one hand, and an Orthodox Jew on the other. The Air Force has no business drawing distinctions between such persons when it is enforcing commands of universal application.

Is the real force of *Smith*'s rule the insight that the alternative—the compelling interest approach of *Sherbert*—is much worse, because it will require courts to become embroiled in disputes over which religions should "count"?

b. ***Smith* and Precedent**

To what extent did *Smith* change the law as articulated in *Yoder* and *Sherbert*? To what extent does *Smith* merely conform the articulated legal rules to the actual results of Free Exercise Clause precedents, including *Reynolds* and *Goldman*?

c. Constitutional Interpretation

We have seen that Justice Scalia, who wrote the opinion for the Court in *Smith*, is an avowed originalist. Was his approach to constitutional interpretation in *Smith* originalist? Did he focus on historical understandings of the meaning of the Free Exercise Clause? (Recall that the closest he came to an analysis of the meaning of the text was to suggest that the one the Court adopted was "a permissible reading.") If not, why is the Free Exercise Clause different from other constitutional provisions?

What rule would an originalist approach have yielded? Scholars have disagreed on the answer to this question. Professor Michael McConnell has argued that the approach of the Court in *Sherbert* was "more consistent with the original understanding" than the approach of the Court in *Smith*. Michael W. McConnell, *Free Exercise Revisionism and the* Smith *Decision*, 57 U. Chi. L. Rev. 1109 (1990). Professor Philip Hamburger, however, has disputed that conclusion. See Philip A. Hamburger, *A Constitutional Right of Religious Exemption: An Historical Perspective*, 60 Geo. Wash. L. Rev. 915 (1992).

d. Religious Freedom Restoration Act

In 1993, Congress passed the Religious Freedom Restoration Act, 42 U.S.C. § 2000bb, in an effort to overrule *Smith*. The initial section of this act declares:

The purposes of this chapter are—

(1)   to restore the compelling interest test as set forth in *Sherbert v. Verner*, 374 U.S. 398 (1963) and *Wisconsin v. Yoder*, 406 U.S. 205 (1972) and to guarantee its application in all cases where free exercise of religion is substantially burdened; and

(2)   to provide a claim or defense to persons whose religious exercise is substantially burdened by government.

Id. § 2000bb(b). The key operative section of the act then provides:

(a)   In general. Government shall not substantially burden a person's exercise of religion even if the burden results from a rule of general applicability, except as provided in subsection (b).

(b)   Exception. Government may substantially burden a person's exercise of religion only if it demonstrates that application of the burden to the person—

(1)   is in furtherance of a compelling governmental interest; and

(2)   is the least restrictive means of furthering that compelling governmental interest.

(c)   Judicial relief. A person whose religious exercise has been burdened in violation of this section may assert that violation as a claim or defense in a judicial proceeding and obtain appropriate relief against a government. Standing to assert a claim or defense under this section shall be governed by the general rules of standing under article III of the Constitution.

Id. § 2000bb–1.

The portion of the act that applied to state (as opposed to federal) action was short-lived. In *City of Boerne v. Flores*, 521 U.S. 507 (1997), the Supreme Court held that Congress lacked the power to pass this act, at least as it applied to state laws. Although the Court has not squarely

> **Make the Connection**
>
> We considered *City of Boerne*, and Congress's power to enforce the Fourteenth Amendment, in Chapter *7*.

addressed the constitutionality of RFRA as applied to federal law, the Court has applied it to grant exemptions under federal law. See *Gonzales v. O Centro Espirita Beneficente Uniao do Vegetal*, 546 U.S. 418 (2006).

The Supreme Court in *Smith* held that the government does not need a compelling state interest to justify the burden that a neutral law of general applicability imposes on religious practice, but the Court did not specify what test should apply to a law that is not of general applicability or that is targeted at religious practices. In the following case, the Court concluded that the compelling interest test remains in effect for such laws.

CHURCH OF THE LUKUMI BABALU AYE, INC. V. CITY OF HIALEAH

508 U.S. 520 (1993)

JUSTICE KENNEDY delivered the opinion of the Court, except as to Part II-A-2.*

I

Petitioner Church of the Lukumi Babalu Aye, Inc. (Church), is a not-for-profit corporation organized under Florida law in 1973. The Church and its congregants practice the Santeria religion. The president of the Church is petitioner Ernesto Pichardo, who is also the Church's priest and holds the religious title of *Italero,* the second highest in the Santeria faith. In April 1987, the Church leased land in the City of Hialeah, Florida, and announced plans to establish a house of worship as well as a school, cultural center, and museum. Pichardo indicated that the Church's goal was to bring the practice of the Santeria faith, including its ritual of animal sacrifice, into the open. The Church began the process of obtaining utility service and receiving the necessary licensing, inspection, and zoning approvals. Although the Church's efforts at obtaining the necessary licenses and permits were far from smooth, it appears that it received all needed approvals by early August 1987.

---

* THE CHIEF JUSTICE, Justice SCALIA, and Justice THOMAS join all but Part II-A-2 of this opinion. Justice WHITE joins all but Part II-A of this opinion. Justice SOUTER joins only Parts I, III, and IV of this opinion.

The prospect of a Santeria church in their midst was distressing to many members of the Hialeah community, and the announcement of the plans to open a Santeria church in Hialeah prompted the city council to hold an emergency public session on June 9, 1987. * * * In September 1987, the city council adopted three substantive ordinances addressing the issue of religious animal sacrifice. Ordinance 87–52 defined "sacrifice" as "to unnecessarily kill, torment, torture, or mutilate an animal in a public or private ritual or ceremony not for the primary purpose of food consumption," and prohibited owning or possessing an animal "intending to use such animal for food purposes." It restricted application of this prohibition, however, to any individual or group that "kills, slaughters or sacrifices animals for any type of ritual, regardless of whether or not the flesh or blood of the animal is to be consumed." The ordinance contained an exemption for slaughtering by "licensed establishment[s]" of animals "specifically raised for food purposes." Declaring, moreover, that the city council "has determined that the sacrificing of animals within the city limits is contrary to the public health, safety, welfare and morals of the community," the city council adopted Ordinance 87–71. That ordinance defined sacrifice as had Ordinance 87–52, and then provided that "[i]t shall be unlawful for any person, persons, corporations or associations to sacrifice any animal within the corporate limits of the City of Hialeah, Florida." The final Ordinance, 87–72, defined "slaughter" as "the killing of animals for food" and prohibited slaughter outside of areas zoned for slaughterhouse use. The ordinance provided an exemption, however, for the slaughter or processing for sale of "small numbers of hogs and/or cattle per week in accordance with an exemption provided by state law." All ordinances and resolutions passed the city council by unanimous vote. Violations of each of the four ordinances were punishable by fines not exceeding $500 or imprisonment not exceeding 60 days, or both.

II

The city does not argue that Santeria is not a "religion" within the meaning of the First Amendment. Nor could it. Although the practice of animal sacrifice may seem abhorrent to some, "religious beliefs need not be acceptable, logical, consistent, or comprehensible to others in order to merit First Amendment protection." *Thomas v. Review Bd. of Indiana Employment Security Div.,* 450 U.S. 707, 714 (1981). Given the historical association between animal sacrifice and religious worship, petitioners' assertion that animal sacrifice is an integral part of their religion "cannot be deemed bizarre or incredible." *Frazee v. Illinois Dept. of Employment Security,* 489 U.S. 829, 834, n. 2 (1989). Neither the city nor the courts below, moreover, have questioned the sincerity of petitioners' professed desire to conduct animal sacrifices for religious reasons. We must consider petitioners' First Amendment claim.

In addressing the constitutional protection for free exercise of religion, our cases establish the general proposition that a law that is neutral and of general applicability need not be justified by a compelling governmental interest even if the law has the incidental effect of burdening a particular religious practice. *Employment Div., Dept. of Human Resources of Ore. v. Smith,* 494 U.S. 872 (1990). Neutrality and general applicability are interrelated, and, as becomes apparent in this case, failure to satisfy one requirement is a likely indication that the other has not been satisfied. A law failing to satisfy these requirements must be justified by a compelling governmental interest and must be narrowly tailored to advance that interest. These ordinances fail to satisfy the *Smith* requirements. We begin by discussing neutrality.

A

At a minimum, the protections of the Free Exercise Clause pertain if the law at issue discriminates against some or all religious beliefs or regulates or prohibits conduct because it is undertaken for religious reasons. See, *e.g., Braunfeld v. Brown,* 366 U.S. 599, 607 (1961) (plurality opinion). Indeed, it was "historical instances of religious persecution and intolerance that gave concern to those who drafted the Free Exercise Clause." *Bowen v. Roy,* 476 U.S. 693, 703 (1986) (opinion of Burger, C.J.).

1

Although a law targeting religious beliefs as such is never permissible, if the object of a law is to infringe upon or restrict practices because of their religious motivation, the law is not neutral, and it is invalid unless it is justified by a compelling interest and is narrowly tailored to advance that interest. There are, of course, many ways of demonstrating that the object or purpose of a law is the suppression of religion or religious conduct. To determine the object of a law, we must begin with its text, for the minimum requirement of neutrality is that a law not discriminate on its face. A law lacks facial neutrality if it refers to a religious practice without a secular meaning discernable from the language or context. Petitioners contend that three of the ordinances fail this test of facial neutrality because they use the words "sacrifice" and "ritual," words with strong religious connotations. We agree that these words are consistent with the claim of facial discrimination, but the argument is not conclusive. The words "sacrifice" and "ritual" have a religious origin, but current use admits also of secular meanings. See Webster's Third New International Dictionary 1961, 1996 (1971). See also 12

Encyclopedia of Religion, at 556 ("[T]he word *sacrifice* ultimately became very much a secular term in common usage"). The ordinances, furthermore, define "sacrifice" in secular terms, without referring to religious practices.

We reject the contention advanced by the city that our inquiry must end with the text of the laws at issue. * * * Official action that targets religious conduct for distinctive treatment cannot be shielded by mere compliance with the requirement of facial neutrality. The Free Exercise Clause protects against governmental hostility which is masked, as well as overt.

The record in this case compels the conclusion that suppression of the central element of the Santeria worship service was the object of the ordinances. * * * Apart from the text, the effect of a law in its real operation is strong evidence of its object. * * * The subject at hand does implicate, of course, multiple concerns unrelated to religious animosity, for example, the suffering or mistreatment visited upon the sacrificed animals and health hazards from improper disposal. But the ordinances when considered together disclose an object remote from these legitimate concerns.

It is a necessary conclusion that almost the only conduct subject to Ordinances 87-40, 87-52, and 87-71 is the religious exercise of Santeria church members. The texts show that they were drafted in tandem to achieve this result. We begin with Ordinance 87-71. * * * The definition [of "sacrifice"] excludes almost all killings of animals except for religious sacrifice, and the primary purpose requirement narrows the proscribed category even further, in particular by exempting kosher slaughter. We need not discuss whether this differential treatment of two religions is itself an independent constitutional violation. It suffices to recite this feature of the law as support for our conclusion that Santeria alone was the exclusive legislative concern. The net result [is] that few if any killings of animals are prohibited other than Santeria sacrifice, which is proscribed because it occurs during a ritual or ceremony and its primary purpose is to make an offering to the *orishas,* not food consumption. Indeed, careful drafting ensured that, although Santeria sacrifice is prohibited, killings that are no more necessary or humane in almost all other circumstances are unpunished.

Operating in similar fashion is Ordinance 87-52, which prohibits the "possess[ion], sacrifice, or slaughter" of an animal with the "inten[t] to use such animal for food purposes." This prohibition, extending to the keeping of an animal as well as the killing itself, applies if the animal is killed in "any type of ritual" and there is an intent to use the animal for food, whether or not it is in fact consumed for food. The ordinance exempts, however, "any licensed [food] establishment" with regard to "any animals which are specifically raised for food purposes," if the activity is permitted by zoning and other laws. This exception, too, seems intended to cover kosher slaughter. Again, the burden of the ordinance, in practical terms, falls on Santeria adherents but almost no others * * *.

Ordinance 87-40 incorporates the Florida animal cruelty statute, Fla. Stat. § 828.12 (1987). Its prohibition is broad on its face, punishing "[w]hoever . . . unnecessarily . . . kills any animal." The city claims that this ordinance is the epitome of a neutral prohibition. The problem, however, is the interpretation given to the ordinance by respondent and the Florida attorney general. Killings for religious reasons are deemed unnecessary, whereas most other killings fall outside the prohibition. The city, on what seems to be a *per se* basis, deems hunting, slaughter of animals for food, eradication of insects and pests, and euthanasia as necessary. * * * Respondent's application of the ordinance's test of necessity devalues religious reasons for killing by judging them to be of lesser import than nonreligious reasons. Thus, religious practice is being singled out for discriminatory treatment.

2

That the ordinances were enacted " 'because of,' not merely 'in spite of,' " their suppression of Santeria religious practice, *Personnel Administrator of Mass. v. Feeney*, 442 U.S. 256, 279, n. 24 (1979), is revealed by the events preceding their enactment. Although respondent claimed at oral argument that it had experienced significant problems resulting from the

> **Take Note**
> This section did not receive the support of a majority of the Court.

sacrifice of animals within the city before the announced opening of the Church, the city council made no attempt to address the supposed problem before its meeting in June 1987, just weeks after the Church announced plans to open. The minutes and taped excerpts of the June 9 session, both of which are in the record, evidence significant hostility exhibited by residents, members of the city council, and other city officials toward the Santeria religion and its practice of animal sacrifice. The public crowd that attended the June 9 meetings interrupted statements by council members critical of Santeria with cheers and the brief comments of Pichardo with taunts. When Councilman Martinez, a supporter of the ordinances, stated that in prerevolution Cuba "people were put in jail for practicing this religion," the audience applauded. * * * Other statements by members of the city council were in a similar vein. For example, * * * Councilman Cardoso said that Santeria devotees at the Church "are in violation of everything this country stands for." Councilman Mejides [stated,] "The Bible says we are

allowed to sacrifice an animal for consumption [but] for any other purposes, I
don't believe that the Bible allows that." The president of the city council,
Councilman Echevarria, asked: "What can we do to prevent the Church from
opening?"

Various Hialeah city officials made comparable comments. The chaplain of
the Hialeah Police Department told the city council that Santeria was a sin,
"foolishness," "an abomination to the Lord," and the worship of "demons." He
advised the city council: "We need to be helping people and sharing with them
the truth that is found in Jesus Christ." He concluded: "I would exhort you . . .
not to permit this Church to exist." The city attorney commented that Resolution
87–66 indicated: "This community will not tolerate religious practices which are
abhorrent to its citizens . . . ." * * * This history discloses the object of the
ordinances to target animal sacrifice by Santeria worshippers because of its
religious motivation.

3

In sum, the neutrality inquiry leads to one conclusion: The ordinances had as
their object the suppression of religion. The pattern we have recited discloses
animosity to Santeria adherents and their religious practices; the ordinances by
their own terms target this religious exercise; the texts of the ordinances were
gerrymandered with care to proscribe religious killings of animals but to exclude
almost all secular killings; and the ordinances suppress much more religious
conduct than is necessary in order to achieve the legitimate ends asserted in their
defense. These ordinances are not neutral, and the court below committed clear
error in failing to reach this conclusion.

B

We turn next to a second requirement of the Free Exercise Clause, the rule
that laws burdening religious practice must be of general applicability. *Smith*, 494
U.S., at 879–881. All laws are selective to some extent, but categories of selection
are of paramount concern when a law has the incidental effect of burdening
religious practice. The Free Exercise Clause "protect[s] religious observers against
unequal treatment," *Hobbie v. Unemployment Appeals Comm'n of Fla.*, 480 U.S. 136,
148 (1987) (STEVENS, J., concurring in judgment), and inequality results when a
legislature decides that the governmental interests it seeks to advance are worthy
of being pursued only against conduct with a religious motivation.

Respondent claims that Ordinances 87-40, 87-52, and 87-71 advance two
interests: protecting the public health and preventing cruelty to animals. The
ordinances are underinclusive for those ends. They fail to prohibit nonreligious

conduct that endangers these interests in a similar or greater degree than Santeria sacrifice does. The underinclusion is substantial, not inconsequential. Despite the city's proffered interest in preventing cruelty to animals, the ordinances are drafted with care to forbid few killings but those occasioned by religious sacrifice. Many types of animal deaths or kills for nonreligious reasons are either not prohibited or approved by express provision. * * *

The ordinances are also underinclusive with regard to the city's interest in public health, which is threatened by the disposal of animal carcasses in open public places and the consumption of uninspected meat. Neither interest is pursued by respondent with regard to conduct that is not motivated by religious conviction. The city does not [prohibit] hunters from bringing their kill to their houses, nor does it regulate disposal after their activity, [and] restaurants are outside the scope of the ordinances.

Ordinance 87-72, which prohibits the slaughter of animals outside of areas zoned for slaughterhouses, is underinclusive on its face. The ordinance includes an exemption for "any person, group, or organization" that "slaughters or processes for sale, small numbers of hogs and/or cattle per week in accordance with an exemption provided by state law." See Fla. Stat. § 828.24(3) (1991). Respondent has not explained why commercial operations that slaughter "small numbers" of hogs and cattle do not implicate its professed desire to prevent cruelty to animals and preserve the public health. Although the city has classified Santeria sacrifice as slaughter, subjecting it to this ordinance, it does not regulate other killings for food in like manner.

We conclude, in sum, that each of Hialeah's ordinances pursues the city's governmental interests only against conduct motivated by religious belief. The ordinances "ha[ve] every appearance of a prohibition that society is prepared to impose upon [Santeria worshippers] but not upon itself." *Florida Star v. B.J.F.*, 491 U.S. 524, 542 (1989) (Scalia, J., concurring in part and concurring in judgment). This precise evil is what the requirement of general applicability is designed to prevent.

III

A law burdening religious practice that is not neutral or not of general application must undergo the most rigorous of scrutiny. To satisfy the commands of the First Amendment, a law restrictive of religious practice must advance "interests of the highest order" and must be narrowly tailored in pursuit of those interests. *McDaniel v. Paty*, 435 U.S. 618, 628 (1978), quoting *Wisconsin v. Yoder*, 406 U.S. 205, 215 (1972). * * * A law that targets religious conduct for distinctive treatment or advances legitimate governmental interests only against conduct with a religious motivation will survive strict scrutiny only in rare cases. It follows from what we have already said that these ordinances cannot withstand this scrutiny.

[E]ven were the governmental interests compelling, the ordinances are not drawn in narrow terms to accomplish those interests. As we have discussed, all four ordinances are overbroad or underinclusive in substantial respects. The proffered objectives are not pursued with respect to analogous non-religious conduct, and those interests could be achieved by narrower ordinances that burdened religion to a far lesser degree. The absence of narrow tailoring suffices to establish the invalidity of the ordinances.

JUSTICE SCALIA, with whom THE CHIEF JUSTICE joins, concurring in part and concurring in the judgment.

I join the judgment of the Court and all of its opinion except section 2 of Part II-A. I do not join that section because it departs from the opinion's general focus on the object of the *laws* at issue to consider the subjective motivation of the *lawmakers, i.e.,* whether the Hialeah City Council actually *intended* to disfavor the religion of Santeria. As I have noted elsewhere, it is virtually impossible to determine the singular "motive" of a collective legislative body, see, *e.g., Edwards v. Aguillard,* 482 U.S. 578, 636–639 (1987) (dissenting opinion), and this Court has a long tradition of refraining from such inquiries, see, *e.g., Fletcher v. Peck,* 6 Cranch (10 U.S.) 87, 130–131 (1810) (Marshall, C.J.); *United States v. O'Brien,* 391 U.S. 367, 383–384 (1968).

JUSTICE BLACKMUN, with whom JUSTICE O'CONNOR joins, concurring in the judgment.

The Court holds today that the city of Hialeah violated the First and Fourteenth Amendments when it passed a set of restrictive ordinances explicitly directed at petitioners' religious practice. With this holding I agree. I write separately to emphasize that the First Amendment's protection of religion extends beyond those rare occasions on which the government explicitly targets religion (or a particular religion) for disfavored treatment, as is done in this case. * * * I continue to believe that *Smith* was wrongly decided, because it ignored the value of religious freedom as an affirmative individual liberty and treated the Free Exercise Clause as no more than an antidiscrimination principle.

[JUSTICE SOUTER's opinion concurring in part and concurring in the judgment has been omitted.]

POINTS FOR DISCUSSION

a.   Triggering the Compelling Interest Test

The Court in *Church of the Lukumi Babalu Aye* announced a familiar test for laws that burden religious practice and that are not neutral or not of general application: such laws must advance a compelling interest and be narrowly tailored in pursuit of those interests. How exactly does the Court determine whether a law is neutral or of general applicability? Is there a difference between "neutrality" and "general applicability"? Can you think of a statute that is neutral but not generally applicable? Or a law that is generally applicable but not neutral?

b.   Assessing Purpose

Justice Scalia declined to join the section of the Court's opinion finding a discriminatory purpose behind the challenged ordinances. Suppose that shortly after the Court's decision, the City enacted a new ordinance providing criminal penalties for the "killing of an animal by any person, group, or establishment who does not intend to eat the animal or sell the animal as food," and exempting from the prohibition "the killing of animals in the course of recreational hunting or fishing." Suppose further that at the session at which the City Council enacted the ordinance, every member of the Council declared that they were voting for it "to get around the Court's ruling."

Under Justice Scalia's approach, would this ordinance be constitutional? Is there a way to find that it impermissibly "targets" religious practice without referring to evidence of purpose? If it would be constitutional under Justice Scalia's approach, what does this suggest about his approach?

c.   Another View

Professor Lino Graglia, a confirmed skeptic of judicial review, viewed this case in a different light. He began his article, *Church of the Lukumi Babalu Aye: Of Animal Sacrifice and Religious Persecution*, 85 Geo. L.J. 1 (1996), as follows:

> In recent years, residents of South Florida found themselves faced with a new and unsettling problem. The remains of animals, often accompanied by what appeared to be religious paraphernalia, were frequently encountered in public places. Carcasses were found in or along rivers and canals, at intersections, under trees, on lawns and doorsteps; a goat cut in two was found at a major Miami Beach intersection. * * * Surely it was not to be expected that such spectacles would be tolerated in a modern American city, and the people of Hialeah quickly enacted ordinances specifically prohibiting them. It is a self-assigned function of intellectuals, however, to expand the boundaries of the expected and the tolerable * * *.

Thus, in *Church of the Lukumi Babalu Aye v. City of Hialeah*, the Justices of the Supreme Court, intellectuals all, could find no explanation for Hialeah's attempt to ban animal sacrifice other than religious prejudice.

What exactly is the basis for Professor Graglia's criticism: that the Court was wrong to conclude that the laws at issue were not neutral, that the city had a compelling interest in the laws, or that any legal rule that would produce the result in this case must be flawed?

Problem

As a matter of religious practice, some Muslim women cover their heads with scarves when in public places. Suppose that the Transportation Safety Administration issues a regulation requiring all passengers wearing headscarves to remove them when going through airport security lines. Is this regulation consistent with the Free Exercise Clause? Would you need any other information to conduct that inquiry? What if the regulation did not require the removal of other forms of headwear, such as yarmulkes or turbans? What if it required the removal of those, as well, but not the removal of baseball caps?

As we have seen, the Establishment Clause and the Free Exercise Clause both protect religious freedom, but they do so in different ways. In the first part of the chapter, we saw that the Establishment Clause protects religious freedom by ensuring that adherents of the majority religion cannot "force [or] influence a person to go to or to remain away from church against his will or force him to profess a belief or disbelief in any religion." *Everson v. Board of Education of Ewing Township*, 330 U.S. 1 (1947). The Free Exercise Clause appears to accomplish this goal even more directly.

Do the requirements imposed by the two Clauses ever conflict with each other? Sometimes, the government will defend against an Establishment Clause challenge by contending that it permissibly sought to accommodate religious practice. In *Board of Education of Kiryas Joel Village School District v. Grumet*, 512 U.S. 687 (1994), for example, the Court considered the constitutionality of a state decision to create a school district that embraced only adherents of one sect of Judaism, so that disabled students in the community would not have to attend public schools with children from outside of their religious community. The state contended that it had sought to accommodate the unique circumstances of one particular religious group, but the Court held that the policy violated the Establishment Clause.

Other times, the government will defend against a Free Exercise claim by arguing that it was seeking to avoid violating the Establishment Clause. Under what circumstances can the government rely on such an interest to defeat a Free Exercise claim? Consider the cases that follow.

LOCKE V. DAVEY

540 U.S. 712 (2004)

CHIEF JUSTICE REHNQUIST delivered the opinion of the Court.

The State of Washington established the Promise Scholarship Program to assist academically gifted students with postsecondary education expenses. In accordance with the State Constitution, students may not use the scholarship at an institution where they are pursuing a degree in devotional theology. We hold that such an exclusion from an otherwise inclusive aid program does not violate the Free Exercise Clause of the First Amendment.

Respondent, Joshua Davey, was awarded a Promise Scholarship, and chose to attend [a] private, Christian college affiliated with the Assemblies of God denomination * * *. [H]e decided to pursue a double major in pastoral ministries and business management/administration. [After he learned that he could not use his scholarship to pursue a devotional theology degree, he filed suit challenging the state's refusal to permit him to use the scholarship for such studies.]

[T]he Establishment Clause and the Free Exercise Clause [are] frequently in tension. Yet we have long said that "there is room for play in the joints" between them. *Walz v. Tax Comm'n of City of New York,* 397 U.S. 664, 669 (1970). In other words, there are some state actions permitted by the Establishment Clause but not required by the Free Exercise Clause.

Under our Establishment Clause precedent, the link between government funds and religious training is broken by the independent and private choice of recipients. See *Zelman v. Simmons-Harris,* 536 U.S. 639, 652 (2002). As such, there is no doubt that the State could, consistent with the Federal Constitution, permit Promise Scholars to pursue a degree in devotional theology * * *. The question before us, however, is whether Washington, pursuant to its own constitution, which has been authoritatively interpreted as prohibiting even indirectly funding religious instruction

> **Make the Connection**
>
> We considered the significance of the "independent and private choice of recipients" of government funds to decide how to spend those funds earlier in this chapter, in *Zelman v. Simmons-Harris.*

that will prepare students for the ministry, can deny them such funding without violating the Free Exercise Clause.

Davey urges us to answer that question in the negative. He contends that under the rule we enunciated in *Church of Lukumi Babalu Aye, Inc. v. Hialeah,* 508 U.S. 520 (1993), the program is presumptively unconstitutional because it is not facially neutral with respect to religion. We reject his claim of presumptive unconstitutionality, however; to do otherwise would extend the *Lukumi* line of cases well beyond not only their facts but their reasoning. In *Lukumi,* the city of Hialeah * * * sought to suppress ritualistic animal sacrifices of the Santeria religion. In the present case, the State's disfavor of religion (if it can be called that) is of a far milder kind. It imposes neither criminal nor civil sanctions on any type of religious service or rite. It does not deny to ministers the right to participate in the political affairs of the community. And it does not require students to choose between their religious beliefs and receiving a government benefit. The State has merely chosen not to fund a distinct category of instruction.

Justice Scalia argues, however, that generally available benefits are part of the "baseline against which burdens on religion are measured." Because the Promise Scholarship Program funds training for all secular professions, Justice Scalia contends the State must also fund training for religious professions. But training for religious professions and training for secular professions are not fungible. Training someone to lead a congregation is an essentially religious endeavor. Indeed, majoring in devotional theology is akin to a religious calling as well as an academic pursuit. And the subject of religion is one in which both the United States and state constitutions embody distinct views—in favor of free exercise, but opposed to establishment—that find no counterpart with respect to other callings or professions. That a State would deal differently with religious education for the ministry than with education for other callings is a product of these views, not evidence of hostility toward religion.

We can think of few areas in which a State's antiestablishment interests come more into play. Since the founding of our country, there have been popular uprisings against procuring taxpayer funds to support church leaders, which was one of the hallmarks of an "established" religion. * * * Most states that sought to avoid an establishment of religion around the time of the founding placed in their constitutions formal prohibitions against using tax funds to support the ministry. The plain text of these constitutional provisions prohibited *any* tax dollars from supporting the clergy. * * * That early state constitutions saw no problem in explicitly excluding *only* the ministry from receiving state dollars reinforces our conclusion that religious instruction is of a different ilk.

Far from evincing the hostility toward religion which was manifest in *Lukumi*, we believe that the entirety of the Promise Scholarship Program goes a long way toward including religion in its benefits. The program permits students to attend pervasively religious schools, so long as they are accredited. * * * And under the Promise Scholarship Program's current guidelines, students are still eligible to take devotional theology courses. * * * In short, we find neither in the history or text of [the] Washington Constitution, nor in the operation of the Promise Scholarship Program, anything that suggests animus toward religion. Given the historic and substantial state interest at issue, we therefore cannot conclude that the denial of funding for vocational religious instruction alone is inherently constitutionally suspect.

Without a presumption of unconstitutionality, Davey's claim must fail. The State's interest in not funding the pursuit of devotional degrees is substantial and the exclusion of such funding places a relatively minor burden on Promise Scholars. If any room exists between the two Religion Clauses, it must be here. We need not venture further into this difficult area in order to uphold the Promise Scholarship Program as currently operated by the State of Washington.

JUSTICE SCALIA, with whom JUSTICE THOMAS joins, dissenting.

In *Lukumi*, the [Court] held that "[a] law burdening religious practice that is not neutral . . . must undergo the most rigorous of scrutiny," and that "the minimum requirement of neutrality is that a law not discriminate on its face." [*Lukumi* is] irreconcilable with today's decision, which sustains a public benefits program that facially discriminates against religion.

When the State makes a public benefit generally available, that benefit becomes part of the baseline against which burdens on religion are measured; and when the State withholds that benefit from some individuals solely on the basis of religion, it violates the Free Exercise Clause no less than if it had imposed a special tax. That is precisely what the State of Washington has done here. It has created a generally available public benefit, whose receipt is conditioned only on academic performance, income, and attendance at an accredited school. It has then carved out a solitary course of study for exclusion: theology. No field of study but religion is singled out for disfavor in this fashion.

The Court's reference to historical "popular uprisings against procuring taxpayer funds to support church leaders" is therefore quite misplaced. That history involved not the inclusion of religious ministers in public benefits programs like the one at issue here, but laws that singled them out for financial aid. * * * One can concede the Framers' hostility to funding the clergy *specifically*, but that says nothing about whether the clergy had to be excluded from benefits the State made available to all.

The Court does not dispute that the Free Exercise Clause places some constraints on public benefits programs, but finds none here, based on a principle of "play in the joints." I use the term "principle" loosely, for that is not so much a legal principle as a refusal to apply *any* principle when faced with competing constitutional directives. * * * Even if "play in the joints" were a valid legal principle, surely it would apply only when it was a close call whether complying with one of the Religion Clauses would violate the other. But that is not the case here. It is not just that "the State could, consistent with the Federal Constitution, permit Promise Scholars to pursue a degree in devotional theology." The establishment question *would not even be close* * * *. Perhaps some formally neutral public benefits programs are so gerrymandered and devoid of plausible secular purpose that they might raise specters of state aid to religion, but an evenhanded Promise Scholarship Program is not among them.

[T]he interest to which the Court defers is not fear of a conceivable Establishment Clause violation, budget constraints, avoidance of endorsement, or substantive neutrality—none of these. It is a pure philosophical preference: the State's opinion that it would violate taxpayers' freedom of conscience *not* to discriminate against candidates for the ministry. This sort of protection of "freedom of conscience" has no logical limit and can justify the singling out of religion for exclusion from public programs in virtually any context. The Court never says whether it deems this interest compelling (the opinion is devoid of any mention of standard of review) but, self-evidently, it is not.

The Court makes no serious attempt to defend the program's neutrality, and instead identifies two features thought to render its discrimination less offensive. The first is the lightness of Davey's burden. The Court offers no authority for approving facial discrimination against religion simply because its material consequences are not severe. * * * The Court has not required proof of "substantial" concrete harm with other forms of discrimination, see, *e.g., Brown v. Board of Education,* 347 U.S. 483, 493–495 (1954); cf. *Craig v. Boren,* 429 U.S. 190 (1976), and it should not do so here.

The other reason the Court thinks this particular facial discrimination less offensive is that the scholarship program was not motivated by animus toward religion. The Court does not explain why the legislature's motive matters, and I fail to see why it should. * * * It is sufficient that the citizen's rights have been infringed.

Let there be no doubt: This case is about discrimination against a religious minority. Most citizens of this country identify themselves as professing some religious belief, but the State's policy poses no obstacle to practitioners of only a tepid, civic version of faith. Those the statutory exclusion actually affects—those whose belief in their religion is so strong that they dedicate their study and their lives to its ministry—are a far narrower set. One need not delve too far into modern popular culture to perceive a trendy disdain for deep religious conviction. In an era when the Court is so quick to come to the aid of other disfavored groups, see, *e.g., Romer v. Evans,* 517 U.S. 620, 635 (1996), its indifference in this case, which involves a form of discrimination to which the Constitution actually speaks, is exceptional.

Today's holding is limited to training the clergy, but its logic is readily extendible, and there are plenty of directions to go. What next? Will we deny priests and nuns their prescription-drug benefits on the ground that taxpayers' freedom of conscience forbids medicating the clergy at public expense? * * * When the public's freedom of conscience is invoked to justify denial of equal treatment, benevolent motives shade into indifference and ultimately into repression. Having accepted the justification in this case, the Court is less well equipped to fend it off in the future. I respectfully dissent.

[JUSTICE THOMAS's dissenting opinion is omitted.]

POINTS FOR DISCUSSION

a. Free Exercise Clause

The Court reasoned that the challenged policy did not violate the Free Exercise Clause because it did not impose "criminal [or] civil sanctions," did not "deny to ministers the right to participate in the political affairs of the community," and did not "require students to choose between their religious beliefs and receiving a government benefit." Is this the test that we have seen for whether a challenged policy violates the Free Exercise Clause? Was the challenged policy similar to the law at issue in *Lukumi*? Is there a difference between singling out one particular religion for disfavored treatment (as in *Lukumi*) and treating all religious education regardless of denomination as a disfavored subject of instruction?

b. Establishment Clause

The Court concluded that it would not violate the Establishment Clause for the state to provide funding, on a neutral basis, to students who wish to pursue studies in devotional theology. Can you make an argument that the Court should conclude that such funding violates the Establishment Clause? Should it matter that the funds would be used for actual religious indoctrination? Given the Court's conclusion that it would not violate the Establishment Clause to fund such education, how could the state's interest in avoiding an Establishment Clause violation justify the exclusion at issue?

TRINITY LUTHERAN CHURCH OF COLUMBIA, INC. V. COMER
137 S.Ct. 2012 (2017)

CHIEF JUSTICE ROBERTS delivered the opinion of the Court, except as to footnote 3.

The Trinity Lutheran Church Child Learning Center is a preschool and daycare center open throughout the year to serve working families in Boone County, Missouri, and the surrounding area. Established as a nonprofit organization in 1980, the Center merged with Trinity Lutheran Church in 1985 and operates under its auspices on church property. * * * The Center includes a playground that is equipped with the basic playground essentials: slides, swings, jungle gyms, monkey bars, and sandboxes. Almost the entire surface beneath and surrounding the play equipment is coarse pea gravel. Youngsters, of course, often fall on the playground or tumble from the equipment. And when they do, the gravel can be unforgiving.

In 2012, the Center sought to replace a large portion of the pea gravel with a pour-in-place rubber surface by participating in Missouri's Scrap Tire Program. Run by the State's Department of Natural Resources to reduce the number of used tires destined for landfills and dump sites, the program offers reimbursement grants to qualifying nonprofit organizations that purchase playground surfaces made from recycled tires. * * * Due to limited resources, the Department cannot offer grants to all applicants and so awards them on a competitive basis to those scoring highest based on several criteria, such as the poverty level of the population in the surrounding area and the applicant's plan to promote recycling. When the Center applied, the Department had a strict and express policy of denying grants to any applicant owned or controlled by a church, sect, or other religious entity. That policy, in the Department's view, was compelled by Article I, Section 7 of the Missouri Constitution, which provides:

> "That no money shall ever be taken from the public treasury, directly or indirectly, in aid of any church, sect or denomination of religion, or in aid of any priest, preacher, minister or teacher thereof, as such; and that no preference shall be given to nor any discrimination made against any church, sect or creed of religion, or any form of religious faith or worship."

In its application, the Center disclosed its status as a ministry of Trinity Lutheran Church and specified that the Center's mission was "to provide a safe, clean, and attractive school facility in conjunction with an educational program structured to allow a child to grow spiritually, physically, socially, and cognitively." After describing the playground and the safety hazards posed by its current surface, the Center detailed the anticipated benefits of the proposed project * * *. The Center ranked fifth among the 44 applicants in the 2012 Scrap Tire Program. But despite its high score, the Center was deemed categorically ineligible to receive a grant. In a letter rejecting the Center's application, the program director explained that, [because] the Center was operated by Trinity Lutheran Church, it did not receive a grant.

Trinity Lutheran sued the Director of the Department in Federal District Court. The Church alleged that the Department's failure to approve the Center's application, pursuant to its policy of denying grants to religiously affiliated applicants, violates the Free Exercise Clause of the First Amendment. * * * The District Court granted the Department's motion to dismiss. * * * Finding the present case "nearly indistinguishable from *Locke v. Davey,* 540 U.S. 712 (2004)," the District Court held that the Free Exercise Clause did not require the State to make funds available under the Scrap Tire Program to religious institutions like Trinity Lutheran. The Court of Appeals for the Eighth Circuit affirmed.

The parties agree that the Establishment Clause of that Amendment does not prevent Missouri from including Trinity Lutheran in the Scrap Tire Program. That does not, however, answer the question under the Free Exercise Clause, because we have recognized that there is "play in the joints" between what the Establishment Clause permits and the Free Exercise Clause compels. *Locke,* 540 U.S., at 718 (internal quotation marks omitted).

The Free Exercise Clause "protect[s] religious observers against unequal treatment" and subjects to the strictest scrutiny laws that target the religious for "special disabilities" based on their "religious status." *Church of Lukumi Babalu Aye, Inc. v. Hialeah,* 508 U.S. 520, 533, 542 (1993) (internal quotation marks omitted). Applying that basic principle, this Court has repeatedly confirmed that denying a generally available benefit solely

---

Food for Thought

In this case, Missouri declined to provide funding directly to a church. Is it obvious to you that the Establishment Clause would have permitted Missouri to provide the funds under the circumstances in this case? Why didn't Missouri defend on the ground that the decision to decline funds was required by the Establishment Clause? We considered the Establishment Clause's application to government funding for religious institutions and activities in the first part of this chapter.

on account of religious identity imposes a penalty on the free exercise of religion that can be justified only by a state interest "of the highest order." *McDaniel v. Paty,* 435 U.S. 618, 628 (1978) (plurality opinion).

[I]n *McDaniel,* the Court struck down under the Free Exercise Clause a Tennessee statute disqualifying ministers from serving as delegates to the State's constitutional convention. Writing for the plurality, Chief Justice Burger [concluded] that the statute discriminated against McDaniel by denying him a benefit solely because of his "status as a 'minister.'" 435 U.S., at 627. McDaniel could not seek to participate in the convention while also maintaining his role as a minister; to pursue the one, he would have to give up the other. In this way, said Chief Justice Burger, the Tennessee law "effectively penalizes the free exercise of [McDaniel's] constitutional liberties." Id., at 626 (quoting *Sherbert v. Verner,* 374 U.S. 398, 406 (1963); internal quotation marks omitted). * * * [I]n *Church of Lukumi Babalu Aye, Inc. v. Hialeah,* we struck down three facially neutral city ordinances that outlawed certain forms of animal slaughter. * * * [We] restated the now-familiar refrain: The Free Exercise Clause protects against laws that "impose[ ] special disabilities on the basis of . . . religious status." 508 U.S., at 533.

The Department's policy expressly discriminates against otherwise eligible recipients by disqualifying them from a public benefit solely because of their religious character. If the cases just described make one thing clear, it is that such a policy imposes a penalty on the free exercise of religion that triggers the most exacting scrutiny. This conclusion is unremarkable in light of our prior decisions.

The Department contends that merely declining to extend funds to Trinity Lutheran does not *prohibit* the Church from engaging in any religious conduct or otherwise exercising its religious rights. In this sense, says the Department, its policy is unlike the ordinances struck down in *Lukumi,* which outlawed rituals central to Santeria. Here the Department has simply declined to allocate to Trinity Lutheran a subsidy the State had no obligation to provide in the first place. * * *

Trinity Lutheran is not claiming any entitlement to a subsidy. It instead asserts a right to participate in a government benefit program without having to disavow its religious character. * * * The express discrimination against religious exercise here is not the denial of a grant, but rather the refusal to allow the Church—solely because it is a church—to compete with secular organizations for a grant. Trinity Lutheran is a member of the community too, and the State's decision to exclude it for purposes of this public program must withstand the strictest scrutiny.

The Department attempts to get out from under the weight of our precedents by arguing that the free exercise question in this case is instead controlled by our decision in *Locke v. Davey*. It is not. In *Locke*, * * * Davey was not denied a scholarship because of who he *was*; he was denied a scholarship because of what he proposed *to do*—use the funds to prepare for the ministry. Here there is no question that Trinity Lutheran was denied a grant simply because of what it is—a church.

The Court in *Locke* also stated that Washington's choice was in keeping with the State's antiestablishment interest in not using taxpayer funds to pay for the training of clergy * * *. The claimant in *Locke* sought funding for an "essentially religious endeavor . . . akin to a religious calling as well as an academic pursuit," and opposition to such funding "to support church leaders" lay at the historic core of the Religion Clauses. *Id.*, at 721–722. Here nothing of the sort can be said about a program to use recycled tires to resurface playgrounds.

Relying on *Locke*, the Department nonetheless emphasizes Missouri's similar constitutional tradition of not furnishing taxpayer money directly to churches. But *Locke* took account of Washington's antiestablishment interest only after determining [that] the scholarship program did not "require students to choose between their religious beliefs and receiving a government benefit." 540 U.S., at 720–721. * * * Students in the program were free to use their scholarships at "pervasively religious schools." *Ibid.* Davey could use his scholarship to pursue a secular degree at one institution while studying devotional theology at another. He could also use his scholarship money to attend a religious college and take devotional theology courses there. The only thing he could not do was use the scholarship to pursue a degree in that subject.

> **Take Note**
>
> What does footnote 3 mean? What is the difference between religious "identity" and religious "use"? And is there something special about funding for playgrounds that would make this case different from other funding cases? Note that only a plurality of the Court joined the footnote.

In this case, there is no dispute that Trinity Lutheran *is* put to the choice between being a church and receiving a government benefit. The rule is simple: No churches need apply.[3]

The State in this case expressly requires Trinity Lutheran to renounce its religious character in order to participate in an otherwise generally available public benefit program, for which it is fully qualified. Our cases make clear that such a condition imposes a penalty on the free exercise of religion that must be subjected to the "most rigorous" scrutiny. *Lukumi*, 508 U.S., at 546. Under that stringent

---

[3]   This case involves express discrimination based on religious identity with respect to playground resurfacing. We do not address religious uses of funding or other forms of discrimination.

standard, only a state interest "of the highest order" can justify the Department's discriminatory policy. *McDaniel,* 435 U.S., at 628. Yet the Department offers nothing more than Missouri's policy preference for skating as far as possible from religious establishment concerns. In the face of the clear infringement on free exercise before us, that interest cannot qualify as compelling. As we said when considering Missouri's same policy preference on a prior occasion, "the state interest asserted here—in achieving greater separation of church and State than is already ensured under the Establishment Clause of the Federal Constitution—is limited by the Free Exercise Clause." *Widmar v. Vincent,* 454 U.S. 263, 276 (1981).

The State has pursued its preferred policy to the point of expressly denying a qualified religious entity a public benefit solely because of its religious character. Under our precedents, that goes too far. The Department's policy violates the Free Exercise Clause. [Reversed.]

JUSTICE THOMAS, with whom JUSTICE GORSUCH joins, concurring in part.

The Court today reaffirms that "denying a generally available benefit solely on account of religious identity imposes a penalty on the free exercise of religion that can be justified," if at all, "only by a state interest 'of the highest order.' " * * * Despite this prohibition, the Court in *Locke* permitted a State to "disfavor . . . religion" by imposing what it deemed a "relatively minor" burden on religious exercise to advance the State's antiestablishment "interest in not funding the religious training of clergy." *Id.,* at 720, 722, n. 5. * * * This Court's endorsement in *Locke* of even a "mil[d] kind," *id.,* at 720, of discrimination against religion remains troubling. But because the Court today appropriately construes *Locke* narrowly, and because no party has asked us to reconsider it, I join nearly all of the Court's opinion. I do not, however, join footnote 3, for the reasons expressed by Justice GORSUCH.

JUSTICE GORSUCH, with whom JUSTICE THOMAS joins, concurring in part.

* * * I am pleased to join nearly all of the Court's opinion. I offer only two modest qualifications.

First, the Court leaves open the possibility a useful distinction might be drawn between laws that discriminate on the basis of religious *status* and religious *use.* Respectfully, I harbor doubts about the stability of such a line. * * * Is it a religious group that built the playground? Or did a group build the playground so it might be used to advance a religious mission? * * * Neither do I see why the First Amendment's Free Exercise Clause should care. After all, that Clause guarantees the free *exercise* of religion, not just the right to inward belief (or status). * * *

For these reasons, reliance on the status-use distinction does not suffice for me to distinguish *Locke v. Davey*, 540 U.S. 712 (2004). [C]an it really matter whether the restriction in *Locke* was phrased in terms of use instead of status (for was it a student who wanted a vocational degree in religion? or was it a religious student who wanted the necessary education for his chosen vocation?). If that case can be correct and distinguished, it seems it might be only because of the opinion's claim of a long tradition against the use of public funds for training of the clergy, a tradition the Court correctly explains has no analogue here.

Second and for similar reasons, I am unable to join the footnoted observation that "[t]his case involves express discrimination based on religious identity with respect to playground resurfacing." * * * I worry that some might mistakenly read it to suggest that only "playground resurfacing" cases, or only those with some association with children's safety or health, or perhaps some other social good we find sufficiently worthy, are governed by the legal rules recounted in and faithfully applied by the Court's opinion. Such a reading would be unreasonable for our cases are "governed by general principles, rather than ad hoc improvisations." *Elk Grove Unified School Dist. v. Newdow*, 542 U.S. 1, 25 (2004) (Rehnquist, C. J., concurring in judgment). And the general principles here do not permit discrimination against religious exercise—whether on the playground or anywhere else.

JUSTICE BREYER, concurring in the judgment.

I agree with much of what the Court says and with its result. But I find relevant, and would emphasize, the particular nature of the "public benefit" here at issue. * * * [T]he State would cut Trinity Lutheran off from participation in a general program designed to secure or to improve the health and safety of children. I see no significant difference. The fact that the program at issue ultimately funds only a limited number of projects cannot itself justify a religious distinction. Nor is there any administrative or other reason to treat church schools differently. The sole reason advanced that explains the difference is faith. And it is that last-mentioned fact that calls the Free Exercise Clause into play. We need not go further. Public benefits come in many shapes and sizes. I would leave the application of the Free Exercise Clause to other kinds of public benefits for another day.

JUSTICE SOTOMAYOR, with whom JUSTICE GINSBURG joins, dissenting.

To hear the Court tell it, this is a simple case about recycling tires to resurface a playground. The stakes are higher. This case is about nothing less than the relationship between religious institutions and the civil government—that is, between church and state. The Court today profoundly changes that relationship by holding, for the first time, that the Constitution requires the government to provide public funds directly to a church. Its decision slights both our precedents and our history, and its reasoning weakens this country's longstanding commitment to a separation of church and state beneficial to both.

Founded in 1922, Trinity Lutheran Church (Church) "operates . . . for the express purpose of carrying out the commission of . . . Jesus Christ as directed to His church on earth." * * * The Learning Center serves as "a ministry of the Church and incorporates daily religion and developmentally appropriate activities into . . . [its] program." * * * Properly understood then, this is a case about whether Missouri can decline to fund improvements to the facilities the Church

---

Food for Thought

Is it proper for the dissent to consider whether the law violates the Establishment Clause when both parties agreed that it does not? What alternatives might the dissent have had?

---

uses to practice and spread its religious views. This Court has repeatedly warned that funding of exactly this kind—payments from the government to a house of worship—would cross the line drawn by the Establishment Clause. See, *e.g., Walz v. Tax Comm'n of City of New York,* 397 U.S. 664, 675 (1970); *Rosenberger v. Rector and Visitors of Univ. of Va.,* 515 U.S. 819, 844 (1995); *Mitchell v. Helms,* 530 U.S. 793, 843–844 (2000) (O'Connor, J., concurring in judgment). * * * The Establishment Clause does not allow Missouri to grant the Church's funding request because the Church uses the Learning Center, including its playground, in conjunction with its religious mission. The Court's silence on this front signals either its misunderstanding of the facts of this case or a startling departure from our precedents.

The government may not directly fund religious exercise. See *Everson v. Board of Ed. of Ewing,* 330 U.S. 1, 16 (1947). Put in doctrinal terms, such funding violates the Establishment Clause because it impermissibly "advanc[es] . . . religion." *Agostini v. Felton,* 521 U.S. 203, 222–223 (1997). * * * Nowhere is this rule more clearly implicated than when funds flow directly from the public treasury to a house of worship.[2] * * *

The Church seeks state funds to improve the Learning Center's facilities, which, by the Church's own avowed description, are used to assist the spiritual growth of the children of its members and to spread the Church's faith to the

---

[2]   Because Missouri decides which Scrap Tire Program applicants receive state funding, this case does not implicate a line of decisions about indirect aid programs in which aid reaches religious institutions "only as a result of the genuine and independent choices of private individuals." *Zelman v. Simmons-Harris,* 536 U.S. 639, 649 (2002).

children of nonmembers. The Church's playground surface—like a Sunday School room's walls or the sanctuary's pews—are integrated with and integral to its religious mission. The conclusion that the funding the Church seeks would impermissibly advance religion is inescapable.

True, this Court has found some direct government funding of religious institutions to be consistent with the Establishment Clause. But the funding in those cases came with assurances that public funds would not be used for religious activity, despite the religious nature of the institution. See, *e.g., Rosenberger,* 515 U.S., at 875–876 (Souter, J., dissenting) (chronicling cases). The Church has not and cannot provide such assurances here. The Church has a religious mission, one that it pursues through the Learning Center. The playground surface cannot be confined to secular use any more than lumber used to frame the Church's walls, glass stained and used to form its windows, or nails used to build its altar.

Even assuming the absence of an Establishment Clause violation and proceeding on the Court's preferred front—the Free Exercise Clause—the Court errs. It claims that the government may not draw lines based on an entity's religious "status." But we have repeatedly said that it can. When confronted with government action that draws such a line, we have carefully considered whether the interests embodied in the Religion Clauses justify that line. The question here is thus whether those interests support the line drawn in Missouri's Article I, § 7, separating the State's treasury from those of houses of worship. They unquestionably do.

Even in the absence of a violation of one of the Religion Clauses, the interaction of government and religion can raise concerns that sound in both Clauses. For that reason, the government may sometimes act to accommodate those concerns, even when not required to do so by the Free Exercise Clause, without violating the Establishment Clause. And the government may sometimes act to accommodate those concerns, even when not required to do so by the Establishment Clause, without violating the Free Exercise Clause. * * * This space between the two Clauses gives government some room to recognize the unique status of religious entities and to single them out on that basis for exclusion from otherwise generally applicable laws.

Invoking this principle, this Court has held that the government may sometimes relieve religious entities from the requirements of government programs. A State need not, for example, require nonprofit houses of worship to pay property taxes. * * * Invoking this same principle, this Court has held that the government may sometimes close off certain government aid programs to religious entities. The State need not, for example, fund the training of a religious group's leaders * * *. It may instead avoid the historic "antiestablishment interests" raised by the use of "taxpayer funds to support church leaders." *Locke v. Davey,* 540 U.S. 712, 722 (2004). When reviewing a law that, like this one, singles out religious entities for exclusion from its reach, we thus have not myopically focused on the fact that a law singles out religious entities, but on the reasons that it does so.

Missouri has decided that the unique status of houses of worship requires a special rule when it comes to public funds. * * * Missouri's decision, which has deep roots in our Nation's history, reflects a reasonable and constitutional judgment.

This Nation's early experience with, and eventual rejection of, established religion—shorthand for "sponsorship, financial support, and active involvement of the sovereign in religious activity," *Walz,* 397 U.S., at 668—defies easy summary. [But the] use of public funds to support core religious institutions can safely be described as a hallmark of the States' early experiences with religious establishment. Every state establishment saw laws passed to raise public funds and direct them toward houses of worship and ministers. And as the States all disestablished, one by one, they all undid those laws.

Those who fought to end the public funding of religion based their opposition on a powerful set of arguments, all stemming from the basic premise that the practice harmed both civil government and religion. The civil government, they maintained, could claim no authority over religious belief. For them, support for religion compelled by the State marked an overstep of authority that would only lead to more. Equally troubling, it risked divisiveness by giving religions reason to compete for the State's beneficence. Faith, they believed, was a personal matter, entirely between an individual and his god. Religion was best served when sects reached out on the basis of their tenets alone, unsullied by outside forces, allowing adherents to come to their faith voluntarily. Over and over, these arguments gained acceptance and led to the end of state laws exacting payment for the support of religion.

As was true in *Locke,* a prophylactic rule against the use of public funds for houses of worship is a permissible accommodation of these weighty interests. The rule has a historical pedigree identical to that of the provision in *Locke.* Almost all of the States that ratified the Religion Clauses operated under this rule. Seven had placed this rule in their State Constitutions. Three enforced it by statute or in practice. Only one had not yet embraced the rule. Today, thirty-eight States have a counterpart to Missouri's Article I, § 7. The provisions, as a general matter, date back to or before these States' original Constitutions. That so many States have for so long drawn a line that prohibits public funding for houses of worship, based on principles rooted in this Nation's understanding of how best to foster religious liberty, supports the conclusion that public funding of houses of worship "is of a different ilk." *Locke,* 540 U.S., at 723.

Missouri has recognized the simple truth that, even absent an Establishment Clause violation, the transfer of public funds to houses of worship raises concerns that sit exactly between the Religion Clauses. To

> **Food for Thought**
>
> Although the Court describes this case as implicating the First Amendment, as a technical matter it involves the Religion Clauses of the First Amendment as incorporated by the Fourteenth Amendment. Is Justice Sotomayor arguing here that the states' approach to funding religion is relevant to determining the original meaning of the anti-establishment principle incorporated by the Fourteenth Amendment?

avoid those concerns, and only those concerns, it has prohibited such funding. In doing so, it made the same choice made by the earliest States centuries ago and many other States in the years since. The Constitution permits this choice.

The Court's desire to avoid what it views as discrimination is understandable. But in this context, the description is particularly inappropriate. A State's decision not to fund houses of worship does not disfavor religion; rather, it represents a valid choice to remain secular in the face of serious establishment and free exercise concerns. * * *

The Court today dismantles a core protection for religious freedom provided in [the Religion] Clauses. It holds not just that a government may support houses of worship with taxpayer funds, but that—at least in this case and perhaps in others, see *ante* at n. 3—it must do so whenever it decides to create a funding program. History shows that the Religion Clauses separate the public treasury from religious coffers as one measure to secure the kind of freedom of conscience that benefits both religion and government. If this separation means anything, it means that the government cannot, or at the very least need not, tax its citizens and turn that money over to houses of worship. The Court today blinds itself to the outcome this history requires and leads us instead to a place where separation of church and state is a constitutional slogan, not a constitutional commitment. I dissent.

POINTS FOR DISCUSSION

a. Free Exercise Clause or Establishment Clause?

Seven Justices treated this case as raising an issue under the Free Exercise Clause: they asked, can the state "discriminate" against churches in deciding to whom to grant money from a limited pot of funds? Two Justices treated this case as essentially raising an issue under the Establishment Clause: they asked, can a state provide funding directly to a church to advance its religious mission—or does the Establishment Clause at least permit the state to decline to do so?

Notice the relationship between the two Clauses in the case. If it would violate the Establishment Clause to grant the funds to a church under these circumstances, then surely it does not violate the Free Exercise Clause to refuse to grant the funds. But if it would not violate the Establishment Clause, and if the state lacks discretion about how to resolve tensions between the two clauses, then it might violate the Free Exercise Clause to decline to grant them. Which is a better way to think about the issues in the case?

b. Religious Identity and Religious Use

The Court reasoned that the denial of funds violated the Free Exercise Clause because churches were categorically excluded from eligibility for funds, solely on the basis of their religious "identity." But a plurality stated in footnote 3 that it was not addressing religious "uses" of funding. Suppose that a state has a grant program to refurbish historic buildings. Could the state deny funds to a church that wished to renovate its pews and altar?

Is there a difference between withholding funds from a church because of its "identity" and withholding funds that a church will use for religious activities? Which did *Locke* involve? Does the Court's opinion in *Trinity Lutheran Church* suggest that the Court will not continue to follow the approach it took in *Locke*?

ESPINOZA V. MONTANA DEPT. OF REVENUE
140 S.Ct. 2246 (2020)

CHIEF JUSTICE ROBERTS delivered the opinion of the Court.

In 2015, the Montana Legislature sought "to provide parental and student choice in education" by enacting a scholarship program for students attending private schools. 2015 Mont. Laws p. 2168, § 7. The program grants a tax credit of up to $150 to any taxpayer who donates to a participating "student scholarship organization." Mont. Code Ann. §§ 15–30–3103(1), –3111(1) (2019). The scholarship organizations then use the donations to award scholarships to children for tuition at a private school. §§ 15–30–3102(7)(a), –3103(1)(c). So far only one scholarship organization, Big Sky Scholarships, has participated in the program. Big Sky focuses on providing scholarships to families who face financial hardship or have children with disabilities. * * *

A family whose child is awarded a scholarship under the program may use it at [virtually any private school in Montana]. Upon receiving a scholarship, the family designates its school of choice, and the scholarship organization sends the scholarship funds directly to the school. § 15–30–3104(1). Neither the scholarship organization nor its donors can restrict awards to particular types of schools. See §§ 15–30–3103(1)(b), –3111(1).

The Montana Legislature also directed that the program be administered in accordance with Article X, section 6, of the Montana Constitution, which contains a "no-aid" provision barring government aid to sectarian schools. See Mont. Code Ann. § 15–30–3101. In full, that provision states:

> "Aid prohibited to sectarian schools. . . . The legislature, counties, cities, towns, school districts, and public corporations shall not make any direct or indirect appropriation or payment from any public fund or monies, or any grant of lands or other property for any sectarian purpose or to aid any church, school, academy, seminary, college, university, or other literary or scientific institution, controlled in whole or in part by any church, sect, or denomination." Mont. Const., Art. X, § 6(1).

Shortly after the scholarship program was created, the Montana Department of Revenue promulgated "Rule 1," [which] prohibited families from using scholarships at religious schools. Mont. Admin. Rule § 42.4.802(1)(a) (2015). * * * The Department explained that the Rule was needed to reconcile the scholarship program with the no-aid provision of the Montana Constitution.

This suit was brought by three mothers whose children attend Stillwater Christian School in northwestern Montana. Stillwater is a private Christian school that * * * serves students in prekindergarten through 12th grade, and petitioners chose the school in large part because it "teaches the same Christian values that [they] teach at home." The child of one petitioner has already received scholarships from Big Sky, and the other petitioners' children are eligible for scholarships and planned to apply. While in effect, however, Rule 1 blocked petitioners from using scholarship funds for tuition at Stillwater. [P]etitioners sued the Department of Revenue in Montana state court [challenging Rule 1]. * * *

The trial court enjoined Rule 1, [but] the Montana Supreme Court reversed * * *. 435 P.3d 603 (Mont. 2018). The Court first addressed the scholarship program unmodified by Rule 1, holding that the program aided religious schools in violation of the no-aid provision of the Montana Constitution. In the Court's view, the no-aid provision "broadly and strictly prohibits aid to sectarian schools." The scholarship program provided such aid by using tax credits to "subsidize tuition payments" at private schools that are "religiously affiliated" or "controlled in whole or in part by churches." * * * The Montana Supreme Court went on to hold that the violation of the no-aid provision required invalidating the entire scholarship program. The Court explained that the program provided "no mechanism" for preventing aid from flowing to religious schools, and therefore the scholarship program could not "under *any* circumstance" be construed as consistent with the no-aid provision. As a result, the tax credit is no longer available to support scholarships at either religious or secular private schools.

[T]he parties do not dispute that the scholarship program is permissible under the Establishment Clause. Nor could they. We have repeatedly held that the Establishment Clause is not offended when religious observers and organizations benefit from neutral government programs. See, *e.g.*, *Rosenberger v. Rector and Visitors of Univ. of Va.*, 515 U.S. 819, 839 (1995). Any Establishment Clause objection to the scholarship program here is particularly unavailing because the government support makes its way to religious schools only as a result of Montanans independently choosing to spend their scholarships at such schools. See *Zelman v. Simmons-Harris*, 536 U.S. 639, 649–653 (2002). The Montana Supreme Court, however, held as a matter of state law that even such indirect government support qualified as "aid" prohibited under the Montana Constitution.

The question for this Court is whether the Free Exercise Clause precluded the Montana Supreme Court from applying Montana's no-aid provision to bar religious schools from the scholarship program. * * * *Trinity Lutheran Church of Columbia, Inc. v. Comer*, 137 S.Ct. 2012, 2021–2022 (2017), [distilled prior Free Exercise decisions] into the "unremarkable" conclusion that disqualifying otherwise eligible recipients from a public benefit "solely because of their religious character" imposes "a penalty on the free exercise of religion that triggers the most exacting scrutiny." * * *

Montana's no-aid provision bars religious schools from public benefits solely because of the religious character of the schools. The provision also bars parents who wish to send their children to a religious school from those same benefits, again solely because of the religious character of the school. This is apparent from the plain text. * * * The provision's title—"Aid prohibited to sectarian schools"—confirms that the provision singles out schools based on their religious character. And the Montana Supreme Court explained that the provision forbids aid to any school that is "sectarian," "religiously affiliated," or "controlled in whole or in part by churches." 435 P.3d at 612–613. The provision plainly excludes schools from government aid solely because of religious status.

The Department counters that *Trinity Lutheran* does not govern here because the no-aid provision applies not because of the religious character of the recipients, but because of how the funds would be used—for "religious education." In *Trinity Lutheran*, [a] plurality declined to address discrimination with respect to "religious uses of funding or other forms of discrimination." 137 S.Ct., at 2024, n. 3. * * * The Department also contrasts what it characterizes as the "completely non-religious" benefit of playground resurfacing in *Trinity Lutheran* with the unrestricted tuition aid at issue here. General school aid, the Department stresses, could be used for religious ends by some recipients, particularly schools that believe faith should "*permeate*[ ]" everything they do. Regardless, those considerations were not the Montana Supreme Court's basis for applying the no-aid provision to exclude religious schools; that hinged solely on religious status. Status-based discrimination remains status based even if one of its goals or effects is preventing religious organizations from putting aid to religious uses.

Seeking to avoid *Trinity Lutheran*, the Department contends that this case is instead governed by *Locke v. Davey*, 540 U.S. 712 (2004). *Locke* also involved a scholarship program [but] differs from this case in two critical ways. First, *Locke* explained that Washington had "merely chosen not to fund a distinct category of instruction": the "essentially religious endeavor" of training a minister "to lead a congregation." Thus, Davey "was denied a scholarship because of what he proposed *to do*—use the funds to prepare for the ministry." *Trinity Lutheran*, 137 S.Ct., at 2023–2024. Apart from that narrow restriction, Washington's program allowed scholarships to be used at "pervasively religious schools" that incorporated religious instruction throughout their classes. By contrast, Montana's Constitution does not zero in on any particular "essentially religious" course of instruction at a religious school. Rather, as we have explained, the no-aid provision bars all aid to a religious school "simply because of what it is," putting the school to a choice between being religious or receiving government benefits. At the same time, the provision puts families to a choice between sending their children to a religious school or receiving such benefits.

Second, *Locke* invoked a "historic and substantial" state interest in not funding the training of clergy, 540 U.S. at 725, explaining that "opposition to . . . funding 'to support church leaders' lay at the historic core of the Religion Clauses." As evidence of that tradition, the Court in *Locke* emphasized that the propriety of state-supported clergy was a central subject of founding-era debates, and that most state constitutions from that era prohibited the expenditure of tax dollars to support the clergy. But no comparable "historic and substantial" tradition supports Montana's decision to disqualify religious schools from government aid. In the founding era and the early 19th century, governments provided financial support to private schools, including denominational ones. * * * Even States with bans on government-supported clergy, such as New Jersey,

Pennsylvania, and Georgia, provided various forms of aid to religious schools. See Kaestle, Pillars of the Republic: Common Schools and American Society, 1760–1860, pp. 166–167 (1983). Early federal aid (often land grants) went to religious schools. M. McConnell, et al., Religion and the Constitution 319 (4th ed. 2016). Congress provided support to denominational schools in the District of Columbia until 1848, *ibid.*, and [after] the Civil War, Congress spent large sums on education for emancipated freedmen, often by supporting denominational schools in the South through the Freedmen's Bureau. *Id.* at 323.

The Department argues that a tradition *against* state support for religious schools arose in the second half of the 19th century, as more than 30 States—including Montana—adopted no-aid provisions. Such a development, of course, cannot by itself establish an early American tradition. * * * In addition, many of the no-aid provisions belong to a more checkered tradition shared with the Blaine Amendment of the 1870s. That proposal—which Congress nearly passed—would have added to the Federal Constitution a provision similar to the state no-aid provisions, prohibiting States from aiding "sectarian" schools. See *Mitchell v. Helms*, 530 U.S. 793, 828 (2000) (plurality opinion). "[I]t was an open secret that 'sectarian' was code for 'Catholic.'" *Ibid.* The Blaine Amendment was "born of bigotry" and "arose at a time of pervasive hostility to the Catholic Church and to Catholics in general"; many of its state counterparts have a similarly "shameful pedigree." *Mitchell*, 530 U.S. at 828–829 (plurality opinion). The no-aid provisions of the 19th century hardly evince a tradition that should inform our understanding of the Free Exercise Clause. [I]t is clear that there is no "historic and substantial" tradition against aiding such schools comparable to the tradition against state-supported clergy invoked by *Locke*.

Because the Montana Supreme Court applied the no-aid provision to discriminate against schools and parents based on the religious character of the school, the "strictest scrutiny" is required. * * * To satisfy it, government action "must advance 'interests of the highest order' and must be narrowly tailored in pursuit of those interests." *Lukumi*, 508 U.S. at 546.

The Montana Supreme Court asserted that the no-aid provision serves Montana's interest in separating church and State "more fiercely" than the Federal Constitution. But "that interest cannot qualify as compelling" in the face of the infringement of free exercise here. *Trinity Lutheran*, 137 S.Ct., at 2024. A State's interest "in achieving greater separation of church and State than is already ensured under the Establishment Clause . . . is limited by the Free Exercise Clause." *Ibid.*

The Department, for its part, asserts that the no-aid provision actually *promotes* religious freedom. In the Department's view, the no-aid provision protects the religious liberty of taxpayers by ensuring that their taxes are not directed to religious organizations, and it safeguards the freedom of religious organizations by keeping the government out of their operations. An infringement of First Amendment rights, however, cannot be justified by a State's alternative view that the infringement advances religious liberty. * * * Furthermore, we do not see how the no-aid provision promotes religious freedom. [T]his Court has repeatedly upheld government programs that spend taxpayer funds on equal aid to religious observers and organizations, particularly when the link between government and religion is attenuated by private choices. A school, concerned about government involvement with its religious activities, might reasonably decide for itself not to participate in a government program. But we doubt that the school's liberty is enhanced by eliminating any option to participate in the first place.

And the prohibition before us today burdens not only religious schools but also the families whose children attend or hope to attend them. Drawing on "enduring American tradition," we have long recognized the rights of parents to direct "the religious upbringing" of their children. *Wisconsin v. Yoder*, 406 U.S. 205, 213–214, 232 (1972). Many parents exercise that right by sending their children to religious schools, a choice protected by the Constitution. See *Pierce v. Society of Sisters*, 268 U.S. 510, 534–535 (1925). But the no-aid provision penalizes that decision by cutting families off from otherwise available benefits if they choose a religious private school rather than a secular one, and for no other reason.

The Department also suggests that the no-aid provision advances Montana's interests in public education * * * by ensuring that government support is not diverted to private schools. But, under that framing, the no-aid provision is fatally underinclusive because its "proffered objectives are not pursued with respect to analogous nonreligious conduct." *Lukumi*, 508 U.S. at 546. On the Department's view, an interest in public education is undermined by diverting government support to *any* private school, yet the no-aid provision bars aid only to *religious* ones. * * * A State need not subsidize private education. But once a State decides to do so, it cannot disqualify some private schools solely because they are religious.

The Department argues that, at the end of the day, there is no free exercise violation here because the Montana Supreme Court ultimately eliminated the scholarship program altogether. According to the Department, now that there is no program, religious schools and adherents cannot complain that they are excluded from any generally available benefit. Two dissenters agree.

* * * The Montana Legislature created the scholarship program; the Legislature never chose to end it, for policy or other reasons. The program was eliminated by a court, and not based on some innocuous principle of state law. Rather, the Montana Supreme Court invalidated the program pursuant to a state law provision that expressly discriminates on the basis of religious status. The Court applied that provision to hold that religious schools were barred from participating in the program. Then, seeing no other "mechanism" to make absolutely sure that religious schools received no aid, the court chose to invalidate the entire program. 435 P.3d at 613–614.

> **Food for Thought**
>
> The Court holds that the no-aid provision of the Montana Constitution is unconstitutional as applied in this case. But the Court also declared that the provision "expressly discriminates on the basis of religious status." Did the Court implicitly invalidate the provision on its face, or are there applications of the provision that would survive scrutiny under the Free Exercise Clause?

The final step in this line of reasoning eliminated the program, to the detriment of religious and non-religious schools alike. But the Court's error of federal law occurred at the beginning. When the Court was called upon to apply a state law no-aid provision to exclude religious schools from the program, it was obligated by the Federal Constitution to reject the invitation. Had the Court [properly applied the Free Exercise Clause, it] would not have proceeded to find a violation of [the no-aid] provision. And, in the absence of such a state law violation, the Court would have had no basis for terminating the program. Because the elimination of the program flowed directly from the Montana Supreme Court's failure to follow the dictates of federal law, it cannot be defended as a neutral policy decision, or as resting on adequate and independent state law grounds.

The Supremacy Clause provides that "the Judges in every State shall be bound" by the Federal Constitution, "any Thing in the Constitution or Laws of any State to the Contrary notwithstanding." Art. VI, cl. 2. * * * Given the conflict between the Free Exercise Clause and the application of the no-aid provision here, the Montana Supreme Court should have "disregard[ed]" the no-aid provision and decided this case "conformably to the [C]onstitution" of the United States. Marbury v. Madison, 1 Cranch 137, 178 (1803). That "*supreme* law of the land" condemns discrimination against religious schools and the families whose children attend them. * * * [Reversed.]

JUSTICE THOMAS, with whom JUSTICE GORSUCH joins, concurring.

The Court correctly concludes that Montana's no-aid provision expressly discriminates against religion in violation of the Free Exercise Clause. * * * I write separately to explain how this Court's interpretation of the Establishment Clause continues to hamper free exercise rights. Until we correct course on that interpretation, individuals will continue to face needless obstacles in their attempts to vindicate their religious freedom.

* * * Under the modern, but erroneous, view of the Establishment Clause, the government must treat all religions equally and treat religion equally to nonreligion. * * * This "equality principle," the theory goes, prohibits the government from expressing any preference for religion—or even permitting any signs of religion in the governmental realm. Thus, when a plaintiff brings a free exercise claim, the government may defend its law, as Montana did here, on the ground that the law's restrictions are *required* to prevent it from "establishing" religion.

This understanding of the Establishment Clause is unmoored from the original meaning of the First Amendment. As I have explained in previous cases, at the founding, the Clause served only to "protec[t] States, and by extension their citizens, from the imposition of an established religion by the *Federal Government*." *Zelman v. Simmons-Harris*, 536 U.S. 639, 678 (2002) (THOMAS, J., concurring) (emphasis added). Under this view, the Clause resists incorporation against the States. Thus, the modern view * * * is fundamentally incorrect. Properly

> **Food for Thought**
>
> Under Justice Thomas's view of the Establishment Clause, could a state create an official church—such as the "Church of Alabama"—and fund its operations and ministers' salaries from general tax revenues?

understood, the Establishment Clause does not prohibit States from favoring religion. They can legislate as they wish, subject only to the limitations in the State and Federal Constitutions.

* * * The Court's current understanding of the Establishment Clause actually thwarts, rather than promotes, equal treatment of religion. * * * Historical evidence suggests that many advocates for this separationist view were originally motivated by hostility toward certain disfavored religions. See P. Hamburger, Separation of Church and State 391–454 (2002). * * * [M]anifestations of this "trendy disdain for deep religious conviction" assuredly live on. *Locke*, 540 U.S. at 733 (Scalia, J., dissenting). They * * * persist in the repeated denigration of those who continue to adhere to traditional moral standards, as well as laws even remotely influenced by such standards, as outmoded at best and bigoted at worst. See *Masterpiece Cakeshop, Ltd. v. Colorado Civil Rights Comm'n*, 138 S.Ct. 1719, 1747 (2018) (THOMAS, J., concurring in part and concurring in judgment); *Obergefell v. Hodges*, 576 U.S. 644, 712 (2015) (ROBERTS, C.J., dissenting). So long as this hostility remains, fostered by our distorted understanding of the Establishment Clause, free exercise rights will continue to suffer. * * * Returning the Establishment Clause to its proper scope * * * will go a long way toward allowing free exercise of religion to flourish as the Framers intended. I look forward to the day when the Court takes up this task in earnest.

[JUSTICE ALITO's concurring opinion has been omitted.]

JUSTICE GORSUCH, concurring.

[I] join [the Court's] opinion in full. I write separately only to address an additional point. The Court characterizes the Montana Constitution as discriminating against parents and schools based on "religious status and not religious use." * * * [W]hether the Montana Constitution is better described as discriminating against religious status or use makes no difference: It is a violation of the right to free exercise either way, unless the State can show its law serves some compelling and narrowly tailored governmental interest, conditions absent here for reasons the Court thoroughly explains.

JUSTICE GINSBURG, with whom JUSTICE KAGAN joins, dissenting.

[I]n *Trinity Lutheran Church of Columbia, Inc. v. Comer*, 137 S.Ct. 2012, 2019–2020 (2017), the Court observed that disqualifying an entity from a public benefit "solely because of [the entity's] religious character" can impose "a penalty on the free exercise of religion." * * * Petitioners argue that the Montana Supreme Court's decision fails when measured against *Trinity Lutheran*. I do not see how. Past decisions in this area have entailed *differential treatment* occasioning a burden on a plaintiff's religious exercise. This case is missing that essential component. [T]he Montana court remedied the state constitutional violation by striking the scholarship program in its entirety. Under that decree, secular and sectarian schools alike are ineligible for benefits, so the decision cannot be said to entail differential treatment based on petitioners' religion. Put somewhat differently, petitioners argue that the Free Exercise Clause requires a State to treat institutions and people neutrally when doling out a benefit—and neutrally is how Montana treats them in the wake of the state court's decision.

True, petitioners expected to be eligible for scholarships under the legislature's program, and to use those scholarships at a religious school. And true, the Montana court's decision disappointed those expectations along with those of parents who send their children to secular private schools. But * * * this Court has consistently refused to treat neutral government action as unconstitutional solely because it fails to benefit religious exercise. See *Sherbert v. Verner*, 374 U.S. 398, 412 (1963) (Douglas, J., concurring) ("[T]he Free Exercise Clause is written in terms of what the government cannot do to the individual, not in terms of what the individual can exact from the government.").

These considerations should be fatal to petitioners' free exercise claim, yet the Court does not confront them. Instead, the Court decides a question that, in my view, this case does not present: "[W]hether excluding religious schools and affected families from [the scholarship] program was consistent with the Federal Constitution." * * * In the Court's recounting, the Montana court first held that religious schools must be excluded from the scholarship program—necessarily determining that the Free Exercise Clause permitted that result—and only subsequently struck the entire program as a way of carrying out its holding. But the initial step described by this Court is imaginary. The Montana court determined that the scholarship program violated the no-aid provision because it resulted in aid to religious schools. Declining to rewrite the statute to exclude those schools, the state court struck the program in full. 435 P.3d 603, 612–614 (Mont. 2018). In doing so, the court never made religious schools ineligible for an otherwise available benefit, and it never decided that the Free Exercise Clause would allow that outcome.

* * * As this case demonstrates, [the] no-aid provision can be implemented in two ways. A State may distinguish within a benefit program between secular and sectarian schools, or it may decline to fund all private schools. The Court agrees that the First Amendment permits the latter course. Because that is the path the Montana Supreme Court took in this case, there was no reason for this Court to address the alternative. * * * Because Montana's Supreme Court did not [disqualify some private schools solely because they are religious]—its judgment put all private school parents in the same boat—this Court had no occasion to address the matter. On that sole ground, and reaching no other issue, I dissent from the Court's judgment.

JUSTICE BREYER, with whom JUSTICE KAGAN joins as to Part I, dissenting.

[I] * * * We all recognize that the First Amendment prohibits discrimination against religion. At the same time, our history and federal constitutional precedent reflect a deep concern that state funding for religious teaching, by stirring fears of preference or in other ways, might fuel religious discord and division and thereby threaten religious freedom itself. See, e.g., *Committee for Public Ed. & Religious Liberty v. Nyquist*, 413 U.S. 756, 794–796 (1973). * * * The inherent tension between the Establishment and Free Exercise Clauses * * *, in significant part, is why the Court has held that "there is room for play in the joints" between the Clauses' express prohibitions that is "productive of a benevolent neutrality," allowing "religious exercise to exist without sponsorship and without interference." *Walz v. Tax*

Comm'n of City of New York, 397 U.S. 664, 669 (1970) It has held that there "are some state actions permitted by the Establishment Clause but not required by the Free Exercise Clause." *Locke v. Davey*, 540 U.S. 712, 719 (2004). And that "play in the joints" should, in my view, play a determinative role here.

* * * In my view, the program at issue here is strikingly similar to the program we upheld in *Locke* and importantly different from the program we found unconstitutional in *Trinity Lutheran*. Like the State of Washington in *Locke*, Montana has chosen not to fund (at a distance) "an essentially religious endeavor"—an education designed to "induce religious faith." *Locke*, 540 U.S. at 716, 721. That kind of program simply cannot be likened to Missouri's decision to exclude a church school from applying for a grant to resurface its playground. * * * The majority's principal argument appears to be that, as in *Trinity Lutheran*, Montana has excluded religious schools from its program "solely because of the religious character of the schools." * * * It is true that Montana's no-aid provision broadly bars state aid to schools based on their religious affiliation. But this case does not involve a claim of status-based discrimination. The schools do not apply or compete for scholarships, they are not parties to this litigation, and no one here purports to represent their interests. We are instead faced with a suit by *parents* who assert that *their* free exercise rights are violated by the application of the no-aid provision to prevent them from *using* taxpayer-supported scholarships to attend the schools of their choosing. In other words, the problem, as in *Locke*, is what petitioners "propos[e] *to do*—use the funds to" obtain a religious education. *Trinity Lutheran*, 137 S.Ct., at 2022–2023.

Even if the schools' status were relevant, I do not see what bearing the majority's distinction could have here. There is no dispute that religious schools seek generally to inspire religious faith and values in their students. How else could petitioners claim that barring them from using state aid to attend these schools violates their free exercise rights? Thus, the question in this case—unlike in *Trinity Lutheran*—boils down to what the schools would *do* with state support. And the upshot is that here, as in *Locke*, we confront a State's decision not to fund the inculcation of religious truths.

* * * In his Memorial and Remonstrance against [a Virginia bill that would have levied a tax in support of "learned teachers" of "the Christian Religion,"] James Madison argued that compelling state sponsorship of religion in this way was "a signal of persecution" that "degrades from the equal rank of citizens all those whose opinions in religion do not bend to those of the Legislative authority." *Id.*, at 68–69. Even among those who might benefit from such a tax, Madison warned, the bill threatened to "destroy that moderation and harmony

which the forbearance of our laws to intermeddle with Religion, has produced among its several sects." *Id.*, at 69. The opposition galvanized by Madison's Remonstrance * * * spurred Virginia's Assembly to enact a very different law, the Bill for Religious Liberty drafted by Thomas Jefferson. *Everson*, 330 U.S. at 12. Like the Remonstrance, Jefferson's bill emphasized the risk to religious liberty that state-supported religious indoctrination threatened. "[T]o compel a man to furnish contributions of money for the propagation of opinions which he disbelieves," the preamble declared, "is sinful and tyrannical." A Bill for Establishing Religious Freedom (1779), in 2 The Papers of Thomas Jefferson 545 (J. Boyd ed. 1950). The statute accordingly provided "that no man shall be compelled to frequent or support any religious worship, place, or ministry whatsoever." *Id.*, at 546. Similar proscriptions were included in the early constitutions of many States. See *Locke*, 540 U.S. at 723 (collecting examples). * * * If, for 250 years, we have drawn a line at forcing taxpayers to pay the salaries of those who teach their faith from the pulpit, I do not see how we can today require Montana to adopt a different view respecting those who teach it in the classroom.

[II] * * * I think the majority is wrong to replace the flexible, context-specific approach of our precedents with a test of "strict" or "rigorous" scrutiny. * * * If the Court has found it possible to walk what we have called the "tight rope" between the two Religion Clauses, it is only by "preserving doctrinal flexibility and recognizing the need for a sensible and realistic application" of those provisions. *Yoder*, 406 U.S. at 221.

Montana's law does not punish religious exercise. It does not deny anyone, because of their faith, the right to participate in political affairs of the community. And it does not require students to choose between their religious beliefs and receiving secular government aid such as unemployment benefits. Cf. *Locke*, 540 U.S. at 720. The State has simply chosen not to fund programs that, in significant part, typically involve the teaching and practice of religious devotion. * * *

[The] majority's approach * * * burdens courts with the still more complex task of untangling disputes between religious organizations and state governments, instead of giving deference to state legislators' choices to avoid such issues altogether. At the same time, it puts States in a legislative dilemma, caught between the demands of the Free Exercise and Establishment Clauses, without "breathing room" to help ameliorate the problem. * * * [R]igid, bright-line rules like the one the Court adopts today too often work against the underlying purposes of the Religion Clauses. And a test that fails to advance the Clauses' purposes is, in my view, far worse than no test at all.

JUSTICE SOTOMAYOR, dissenting.

The Montana Supreme Court invalidated a state tax-credit program because it was inconsistent with the Montana Constitution's "no-aid provision," Art. X, § 6(1), which forbids government appropriations for sectarian purposes, including funding religious schools. 435 P.3d 603, 614 (Mont. 2018). In so doing, the court expressly declined to resolve federal constitutional issues. * * * The Court typically declines to read state-court decisions as impliedly resolving federal questions, especially ones not raised by the parties. See, *e.g.*, *Adams v. Robertson*, 520 U.S. 83, 88–89 (1997) (*per curiam*). * * * That rule respects not only federalism, but also the separation of powers. * * *

These principles exist to prevent this Court from issuing advisory opinions, sowing confusion, and muddying the law. This is case in point. Having held that petitioners may not be "exclu[ded] from the scholarship program" that no longer exists, the Court remands to the Montana Supreme Court for "further proceedings not inconsistent with this opinion." But it is hard to tell what this Court wishes the state court to do. There is no program from which petitioners are currently "exclu[ded]," so must the Montana Supreme Court order the State to recreate one? Has this Court just announced its authority to require a state court to order a state legislature to fund religious exercise, overruling centuries of contrary precedent and historical practice? Indeed, it appears that the Court has declared that once Montana created a tax subsidy, it forfeited the right to eliminate it if doing so would harm religion. This is a remarkable result, all the more so because the Court strains to reach it.

Even on its own terms, the Court's answer to its hypothetical question is incorrect. * * * The Court's analysis of Montana's defunct tax program reprises the error in *Trinity Lutheran*. * * * Until *Trinity Lutheran*, the right to exercise one's religion did not include a right to have the State pay for that religious practice. See *School Dist. of Abington Township v. Schempp*, 374 U.S. 203, 226 (1963). That is because a contrary rule risks reading the Establishment Clause out of the Constitution. Although the Establishment Clause "permit[s] some government funding of secular functions performed by sectarian organizations," the Court's decisions "provide[d] no precedent for the use of public funds to finance religious activities." *Rosenberger v. Rector and Visitors of Univ. of Va.*, 515 U.S. 819, 847 (1995) (O'Connor, J., concurring). * * * The relevant question had always been not whether a State singles out religious entities, but why it did so.

Here, a State may refuse to extend certain aid programs to religious entities when doing so avoids "historic and substantial" antiestablishment concerns. *Locke*, 540 U.S. at 725. * * * [A] State's decision not to fund religious activity does not "disfavor religion; rather, it represents a valid choice to remain secular in the face of serious establishment and free exercise concerns." [*Trinity Lutheran*, 137 S.Ct. at 2040 (SOTOMAYOR, J., dissenting).]

POINTS FOR DISCUSSION

a.   Free Exercise Clause

The Court concluded that the application of the Montana Constitution's "no-aid" provision to the scholarship program violated the Free Exercise Clause. What is the Court's test for determining whether a state has violated the Free Exercise Clause? Is the Court's focus on "religious status" or "identity" likely to be useful in the range of cases that might arise when the government declines to fund religious instruction, practice, or education?

b.   Establishment Clause

What does the Court's opinion, and the varying approaches of the Justices who wrote separately, suggest about the future of Establishment Clause jurisprudence? Two members of the Court indicated that the Court should overrule precedent that incorporated the Clause against the states. Conversely, Justice Sotomayor (and, to a lesser extent, Justice Breyer) urged the Court to reinvigorate the "no support" principle in particular and the principle of the separation of church and state more generally. Is it possible to maintain support for those principles while agreeing with the Court's approach to the Free Exercise Clause?

Executive Summary of This Chapter

Constitutional Provisions Addressing Freedom of Religion

The original Constitution addresses freedom of religion in Article VI, clause 3, which says "no religious Test shall ever be required as a Qualification to any Office or public Trust under the United States." The First Amendment augments the protection for the freedom of religion by saying: "Congress shall make no law respecting an establishment of religion, or prohibiting the free exercise thereof * * *." The two clauses in this phrase have become known, respectively, as the **Establishment Clause** and the **Free Exercise Clause**. Although the text of these clauses refers to Congress, the Supreme Court has held that the Due Process clause of the Fourteenth Amendment makes both of these clauses applicable to the states, as well. *Cantwell v. Connecticut*, 310 U.S. 296, 303 (1940).

The Establishment Clause: Aid to Religious Institutions

The Establishment Clause not only prevents the federal and state governments from establishing an official religion, but also restricts certain kinds of interactions between the government and religious groups. One important question is whether or when government aid to religious institutions violates the Establishment Clause. The Court has declared that, as a general principle, "[n]o tax in any amount, large or small, can be levied to support any religious activities or institutions * * *." This rule effectuates the principle of the **separation of church and state**. Because this principle, taken to its logical extreme, might forbid the government from providing a range of services to religious organizations, the Court has also held that the government may provide aid under certain circumstances to religious organizations if the government is "neutral in its relations with groups of religious believers and non-believers." *Everson v. Board of Education of Ewing Township*, 330 U.S. 1 (1947). This is generally known as the **neutrality principle**.

For many years, the Supreme Court sought to determine whether government actions complied with these principles by applying the *Lemon* **test**. In applying this test, courts consider (1) whether the challenged law has a secular purpose; (2) whether the principal or primary effect of the law is neither to advance nor inhibit religion; and (3) whether the law excessively entangles the government and religion. *Lemon v. Kurtzman*, 403 U.S. 602 (1971). The Supreme Court has not formally renounced the *Lemon* test, but it does not apply the test now as regularly as it did in the past.

The cases in this chapter provide various examples of the application of these principles. The government does not violate the Establishment Clause when it reimburses parents for costs incurred in transporting their children to parochial schools if the government also pays the costs of transporting children to public or other non-religious schools. *Everson v. Board of Education of Ewing Township*, 330 U.S. 1 (1947). The government does violate the Establishment Clause when it supplements teacher salaries at parochial schools or reimburses the schools for the cost of the salaries. *Lemon v. Kurtzman*, 403 U.S. 602 (1971). The government does not violate the Establishment Clause when it provides parents with vouchers to help cover the cost of educating their children if the vouchers can be redeemed at religious and non-religious schools alike. *Zelman v. Simmons-Harris*, 536 U.S. 639 (2002).

The Establishment Clause: Religion Within Government

Another important issue is the extent to which the Establishment Clause restricts religious activities and symbols within the government. The Establishment Clause bars **prayer in public schools** if the prayer is an official or approved part of school activities. Indeed, prayer is banned in schools whether the students say the prayer or merely hear the prayer, whether the prayer is denominational or non-denominational, whether the prayer is silent or spoken, and whether student participation in the prayer is voluntary or involuntary. *Engel v. Vitale*, 370 U.S. 421 (1962); *Wallace v. Jaffree*, 472 U.S. 38 (1985); *Lee v. Weisman*, 505 U.S. 577 (1992).

The Supreme Court has held that the Establishment Clause does not always bar activities like prayer in public institutions other than public schools, however, if they are **deeply embedded in the history and tradition** of the country. *Marsh v. Chambers*, 463 U.S. 783 (1983). In addition, the Establishment Clause does not prevent the display of **religious symbols on government property** if the symbols have a secular purpose and do not amount to an endorsement of a particular religion or religion in general. *Lynch v. Donnelly*, 465 U.S. 668 (1984), or if they have been displayed for many years in a secular context, *Van Orden v. Perry*, 545 U.S. 677 (2005); *American Legion v. American Humanist Association*, 139 S.Ct. 2067 (2019).

Free Exercise Clause: Burdens on Religious Practices

The Free Exercise Clause protects an individual freedom to engage in religious practices. The government may enforce a law that burdens a particular religious practice only if (1) the law is **both neutral and of general applicability**; or (2) the government has a **compelling interest for imposing the burden and the law is narrowly tailored** to advance that interest. A law is not neutral if the object of the law is to infringe upon or restrict practices because of their religious motivation. A law lacks general applicability if it is underinclusive, applying to religious practices but not to similar non-religious practices. *Employment Division, Dept. of Human Resources of Oregon v. Smith*, 494 U.S. 872 (1990); *Church of the Lukumi Babalu Aye, Inc. v. City of Hialeah*, 508 U.S. 520 (1993).

POINT-COUNTERPOINT

Has the Court properly answered the question, "Who does the First Amendment protect"?

POINT: PETER J. SMITH

The First Amendment is properly read to protect *dissenters*—those who choose not to accept the prevailing orthodoxy in matters of politics, religion, conscience, or opinion. This is not to say that the Amendment provides no protection to those who express popular views or adhere to the majority religion; but as a general matter, those people need no protection from majoritarian efforts to define what is orthodox. Although the Court has often construed the First

Amendment to advance this end, there are substantial areas of doctrine that are in tension with this view of the Amendment.

For example, although the Court has often properly interpreted the Free Speech Clause to extend protection to persons who express unpopular political or cultural views, see, e.g., *Texas v. Johnson,* 491 U.S. 397 (1989) (burning the flag as a form of protest); *Cohen v. California,* 403 U.S. 15 (1971) (protesting the Vietnam War with colorful language), the Court has also concluded that entire categories of expression are not entitled to any protection at all, solely because of the content of the expression. The Court's cases on obscenity, for example, effectively permit the censorship of expression—including books and films—of which the majority disapproves. That approach presumably would have permitted local majorities to ban D. H. Lawrence's *Lady Chatterley's Lover* and Vladimir Nabokov's *Lolita* at the time that they were first published. This cannot be reconciled with the view that the First Amendment protects the expression of unpopular ideas. Nor can the categorical approach to the Free Speech Clause itself, which permits the Court— as opposed to individuals exercising their judgment and consciences—to decide which ideas have value and which do not.

The Religion Clauses also protect dissenters—those, that is, who adhere to minority religions, or to no religion at all. The Free Exercise Clause directly protects adherents of minority religions in their beliefs and worship, and the Establishment Clause, properly understood, protects all dissenters by ensuring that they are not marginalized by official endorsements of, or support for, a particular religion or for religion in general. But the Court's interpretation of the Religion Clauses, like its interpretation of the Free Speech Clause, has also not always advanced the First Amendment's central goal. For example, the non-preferentialist view of the Establishment Clause, towards which the Court has increasingly drifted, see, e.g., *Zelman v. Simmons-Harris,* 536 U.S. 639, 677–680 (2002) (upholding the use of vouchers at parochial schools); cf. *Lynch v. Donnelly,* 465 U.S. 668 (1984) (upholding an official public display of a Christian crèche), inevitably will marginalize adherents of certain minority religions. This is because once some religion is permitted in the public square, or some religious institutions are permitted to receive government subsidies, it will be impossible to permit true equal treatment for all religions. Even holiday displays that include Christian, Jewish, and Muslim symbols generally exclude Buddhists, Sikhs, Hindus, Shintoists, Animists, and adherents of countless other faiths. And the non-preferentialist view *by design* fails to protect those who choose not to adhere to *any* religion, because the *whole point* of the non-preferentialist view is to permit government to prefer religion to non-religion, as long as it does not prefer one religion to another. In practice, this approach provides government sanction to displays of the majority religion, but provides little or no protection to religious (or non-religious) dissenters.

We would do well to recall Justice Jackson's eloquent statement more than a half-century ago in *West Virginia State Board of Education v. Barnette*, 319 U.S. 624 (1943): "If there is any fixed star in our constitutional constellation, it is that no official, high or petty, can prescribe what shall be orthodox in politics, nationalism, religion, or other matters of opinion or force citizens to confess by word or act their faith therein. If there are any circumstances which permit an exception, they do not now occur to us."

COUNTERPOINT: GREGORY E. MAGGS

In *Loving v. Virginia*, 388 U.S. 1 (1967), which we considered in Chapter 5, the Supreme Court emphasized an important general point about the Constitution: constitutional rights are individual rights, not group rights. Accordingly, Virginia could not justify its law prohibiting intermarriage by arguing that the law applied to every *race* equally. Instead, Virginia had to show that its law treated each *person* equally. The state could not make this showing. Although Virginia would have allowed a white person to be married to Mr. Loving, the state did not allow the woman who wanted to be married to him to do so because of her race.

Although *Loving v. Virginia* was an Equal Protection case, this fundamental principle applies—or should apply—to all of the rights secured by the First Amendment. The First Amendment protects individual rights of free speech, of free exercise of religion, and so forth. Accordingly, a person's inclusion or membership in a particular group should not affect his or her rights. The First Amendment does not differentiate between those holding majority opinions and dissenters, between the religiously orthodox and the unorthodox, between the rich and the poor, or between anything comparable.

The Supreme Court, unfortunately, does not have a consistent record of applying this principle. A good example where the Court followed the principle is *Davis v. Federal Election Commission*, 554 U.S. 724 (2008). In that case, the Supreme Court struck down the "millionaire's amendment," a statutory provision aimed at equalizing political candidates' campaign speech. The Court held that the government cannot burden the right of an individual candidate to spend however much of his own money he desires, even if this means that the wealthy as a group may have an advantage over the less affluent.

The Court, however, was not so faithful to the principle in *Buckley v. Valeo*, 424 U.S. 1 (1976). As discussed in the note following *NAACP v. Alabama ex rel. Patterson,* 357 U.S. 449 (1958), in Chapter 11, part of that case concerned a reporting requirement for donors to political campaigns. Although the court generally rejected the plaintiffs' claim that requiring donors to disclose their identities would substantially burden their freedom of association, it announced an exception for "minor parties" who can show "a reasonable probability that the compelled disclosure of a party's contributors' names will subject them to threats, harassment, or reprisals from either Government officials or private parties." *Buckley*, 424 U.S. at 74. This exception should not be limited to members of minor parties but should extend to any individual who can show a substantial burden on his or her freedom of association.

True, as a practical matter, legislatures are more likely to pass laws violating the First Amendment rights of minority groups—whether defined by political thought, religion, or some other characteristic—than of majority groups. Majority groups, in a democracy, usually can use their political power to prevent their own mistreatment. But this generalization does not change the fundamental nature of constitutional rights.

PART V

Protection of Economic Liberty

In Chapter 2, we considered the Court's efforts, in the late-nineteenth and early-twentieth centuries, to interpret the Due Process Clauses of the Fifth and Fourteenth Amendments to protect the "freedom of contract." As we saw, those efforts ultimately failed to produce enduring protections for economic rights.

But the original Constitution and the Bill of Rights also included at least two other explicit and direct protections for economic liberty. Article I, § 10, cl. 1 provides that "No State shall [pass] any * * * Law impairing the Obligation of Contracts," and the Fifth Amendment provides that "private property shall [not] be taken for public use, without just compensation." In this part, we consider these two provisions, known respectively as the "Contract Clause" and the "Takings Clause." As you read these materials, pay close attention to the tension between the government's interest in regulating private conduct and the economic interests of the persons regulated.

CHAPTER 12

Protection of Economic Liberty

A. IMPAIRMENT OF CONTRACTS BY STATE LAWS

The conventional view is that the Contract Clause was designed to prevent states from enacting laws to help debtors at the expense of creditors. See Laurence H. Tribe, *American Constitutional Law* 613 (2d ed. 1988). Such a prohibition was thought not only to protect individuals from majoritarian efforts at redistribution, but also to maintain an incentive for the provision of credit by removing one source of risk that creditors would not be repaid.

The Contract Clause was a frequent source of litigation during the years of the Marshall Court. In perhaps the most important case, *Ogden v. Saunders*, 25 U.S. (12 Wheat.) 213 (1827), the Court held that although the Contract Clause imposes limits on the power of the state to interfere with *existing* contracts, it does not limit the power of states to regulate the terms of *future* contracts. The Court reasoned that state laws that existed at the time a contract was entered effectively constituted terms of the contract, and thus could not be said to "impair" an obligation arising under a contract but in conflict with those existing laws. Chief Justice Marshall dissented—the only time in his 34-year tenure that he dissented in a case involving a constitutional question—asserting that contractual obligations were essentially a matter of natural law, and that states accordingly could not interfere with them.

> **Food for Thought**
>
> If *Ogden* had come out the other way, could states reform the common law of contracts by, for example, enacting the Uniform Commercial Code?

In the nineteenth century, the Court decided, in a series of cases, that a state could interfere even with *existing* contracts if it had a valid government interest in doing so. See, e.g., *Stone v. Mississippi*, 101 U.S. 814 (1880). In addition, the Court began to draw a distinction between substantial impairments of contracts and lesser interferences. For example, in *Penniman's Case*, 103 U.S. 714 (1880), the

Court held that the abolition of imprisonment for debt was not a change in the law that violated the Contract Clause, reasoning that modifying the remedy available for a breach of contract did not substantially impair the obligation of the contract. Although this approach tended to weaken substantially the importance of the Contract Clause as a limit on state authority, the ultimate effect was obscured by another doctrinal development. As we saw in Chapter 2, in the late-nineteenth and early-twentieth century the Court interpreted the Due Process Clauses to impose severe limits on the ability of the states (and, for that matter, the federal government) to interfere with private contractual relationships. Accordingly, during this period, the reach of the Contract Clause was not a particularly pressing question.

In the 1930s, however, the Court began to retreat from its aggressive protection of economic liberty through the Due Process Clauses. That made the question of the Contract Clause's protections ripe once again. The Court offered its most important interpretation of the Clause in the case that follows.

HOME BUILDING & LOAN ASS'N V. BLAISDELL
290 U.S. 398 (1934)

MR. CHIEF JUSTICE HUGHES delivered the opinion of the Court.

[In 1933, during the Great Depression, Minnesota enacted the Mortgage Moratorium Law, which authorized parties facing foreclosure to obtain from a court an extension of the time during which the mortgagee could not foreclose and an extension of the period of redemption after foreclosure. Extensions could be granted only until May 1, 1935, after which the statute would no longer be in effect. Extensions were conditioned upon the mortgagor's making continued payments, determined by the reasonable income or rental value of the property, to help to defray the cost of taxes, insurance, and the like. The Blaisdells obtained an order extending the contractual redemption period from May 2, 1932, to May 1, 1935, on the condition that they pay $40 per month to appellant, the mortgagee, during the extended period. Appellant challenged the constitutionality of the Act under the Contract Clause.]

> **Take Note**
>
> The Blaisdells borrowed money from the Home Building & Loan Association (HBLA). To help assure repayment of the loan, they gave the HBLA a property interest in their property called a "mortgage." If the Blaisdells defaulted on their loan (i.e., did not make the payments when they were due), HBLA had a right to "foreclose" on the property by selling it and applying the proceeds from the sale to their debt. The loan contract, however, gave the Blaisdells a limited period before the foreclosure sale to "redeem" the property by repaying HBLA the amount owed.

Emergency does not create power. Emergency does not increase granted power or remove or diminish the restrictions imposed upon power granted or reserved. [But while] emergency does not create power, emergency may furnish the occasion for the exercise of power. * * * [W]here constitutional grants and limitations of power are set forth in general clauses, which afford a broad outline, the process of construction is essential to fill in the details. That is true of the contract clause. [T]he reasons which led to the adoption of that clause, and of the other prohibitions of section 10 of article 1, are not left in doubt * * *. The

widespread distress following the revolutionary period and the plight of debtors had called forth in the States an ignoble array of legislative schemes for the defeat of creditors and the invasion of contractual obligations. Legislative interferences had been so numerous and extreme that the confidence essential to prosperous trade had been undermined and the utter destruction of credit was threatened. "The sober people of America" were convinced that some "thorough reform" was needed which would "inspire a general prudence and industry, and give a regular course to the business of society." The Federalist, No. 44.

But full recognition of the occasion and general purpose of the clause does not suffice to fix its precise scope. * * * [The state] continues to possess authority to safeguard the vital interests of its people. * * * Not only are existing laws read into contracts in order to fix obligations as between the parties, but the reservation of essential attributes of sovereign power is also read into contracts as a postulate of the legal order. The policy of protecting contracts against impairment presupposes the maintenance of a government by virtue of which contractual relations are worth while—a government which retains adequate authority to secure the peace and good order of society. This principle of harmonizing the constitutional prohibition with the necessary residuum of state power has had progressive recognition in the decisions of this Court.

Undoubtedly, [t]he reserved power cannot be construed so as to destroy the limitation, nor is the limitation to be construed to destroy the reserved power in its essential aspects. They must be construed in harmony with each other. This principle precludes a construction which would permit the state to adopt as its policy the repudiation of debts or the destruction of contracts or the denial of means to enforce them. But it does not follow that conditions may not arise in which a temporary restraint of enforcement may be consistent with the spirit and purpose of the constitutional provision and thus be found to be within the range of the reserved power of the state to protect the vital interests of the community.

[I]f state power exists to give temporary relief from the enforcement of contracts in the presence of disasters due to physical causes such as fire, flood, or earthquake, that power cannot be said to be nonexistent when the urgent public need demanding such relief is produced by other and economic causes. It is no answer to say that this public need was not apprehended a century ago, or to insist that what the provision of the Constitution meant to the vision of that day it must mean to the vision of our time. If by the statement that what the Constitution meant at the time of its adoption it means today, it is intended to say that the great clauses of the Constitution must be confined to the interpretation which the framers, with the conditions and outlook of their time, would have placed upon them, the statement carries its own refutation. It was to guard against such a narrow conception that Chief Justice Marshall uttered the memorable warning: "We must never forget, that it is a constitution we are expounding." *McCulloch v. Maryland*, 4 Wheat. 316, 407 (1819). * * * The vast body of law which has been developed was unknown to the fathers, but it is believed to have preserved the essential content and the spirit of the Constitution. With a growing recognition of public needs and the relation of individual right to public security, the court has sought to prevent the perversion of the clause through its use as an instrument to throttle the capacity of the states to protect their fundamental interests.

Applying the criteria established by our decisions, we conclude: An emergency existed in Minnesota which furnished a proper occasion for the exercise of the reserved power of the state to protect the vital interests of the community. The declarations of the existence of this emergency by the Legislature and by the Supreme Court of Minnesota cannot be regarded as a subterfuge or as lacking in adequate basis. * * * The legislation was addressed to a legitimate end; that is, the legislation was not for the mere advantage of particular individuals but for the protection of a basic interest of society. * * * The conditions upon which

> **Take Note**
>
> Is Chief Justice Hughes suggesting here that the original meaning of the Constitution is not (or need not be) the meaning of the Constitution today? If so, you will find no more explicit statement of this idea in any Supreme Court opinion. Or does he mean that when the Court applies the original meaning of the provisions of the Constitution to modern circumstances, results that the Framers did not anticipate might follow? If he means the latter, did he apply the Clause properly in this case?

the period of redemption is extended do not appear to be unreasonable. [T]he integrity of the mortgage indebtedness is not impaired; interest continues to run; the validity of the sale and the right of a mortgagee-purchaser to title or to obtain a deficiency judgment, if the mortgagor fails to redeem within the extended period, are maintained; and the conditions of redemption, if redemption there be, stand as they were under the prior law. * * * The mortgagee-purchaser during the time that he cannot obtain possession [is] not left without compensation for the withholding of possession. * * * The relief afforded by the statute has regard to the interest of mortgagees as well as to the interest of mortgagors. The legislation seeks to prevent the impending ruin of both by a considerate measure of relief. The legislation is temporary in operation [and] is limited to the exigency which called it forth.

We are of the opinion that the Minnesota statute as here applied does not violate the contract clause of the Federal Constitution. Whether the legislation is wise or unwise as a matter of policy is a question with which we are not concerned.

MR. JUSTICE SUTHERLAND, [joined by MR. JUSTICE VAN DEVANTER, MR. JUSTICE MCREYNOLDS, and MR. JUSTICE BUTLER,] dissenting.

If the contract impairment clause, when framed and adopted, meant that the terms of a contract for the payment of money could not be altered [by] a state statute enacted for the relief of hardly pressed debtors to the end and with the effect of postponing payment or enforcement during and because of an economic or financial emergency, it is but to state the obvious to say that it means the same now. * * * The provisions of the Federal Constitution, undoubtedly, are pliable in the sense that in appropriate cases they have the capacity of bringing within their grasp every new condition which falls within their meaning. But, their meaning is changeless; it is only their application which is extensible. Constitutional grants of power and restrictions upon the exercise of power are not flexible as the doctrines of the common law are flexible.

The whole aim of construction, as applied to a provision of the Constitution, is to discover the meaning, to ascertain and give effect to the intent of its framers and the people who adopted it. * * * A candid consideration of the history and circumstances which led up to and accompanied the framing and adoption of this clause will demonstrate conclusively that it was framed and adopted with the specific and studied purpose of preventing legislation designed to relieve debtors especially in time of financial distress.

[T]he question is not whether an emergency furnishes the occasion for the exercise of that state power, but whether an emergency furnishes an occasion for the relaxation of the restrictions upon the power imposed by the contract impairment clause; and the difficulty is that the contract impairment clause forbids state action under any circumstances, if it have the effect of impairing the obligation of contracts. That clause restricts every state power in the particular specified, no matter what may be the occasion. * * * The Minnesota statute either impairs the obligation of contracts or it does not. * * * If it does, the emergency no more furnishes a proper occasion for its exercise than if the emergency were nonexistent.

A statute which materially delays enforcement of the mortgagee's contractual right of ownership and possession does not modify the remedy merely; it destroys, for the period of delay, all remedy so far as the enforcement of that right is concerned. The phrase "obligation of a contract" in the constitutional sense imports a legal duty to perform the specified obligation of that contract, not to substitute and perform, against the will of one of the parties, a different, albeit equally valuable, obligation. And a state, under the contract impairment clause, has no more power to accomplish such a substitution than has one of the parties to the contract against the will of the other.

POINTS FOR DISCUSSION

a.   Emergencies and the Contract Clause

Did the Court uphold the regulation because the state was faced with an "emergency"? If so, would the Court have permitted this form of regulation if there had been no exigent circumstances? How did the Court decide if there was an emergency? In making such a determination, should it have deferred to the legislature that enacted the challenged regulation?

b.   What's Left?

If the state can interfere with contractual obligations—here, by effectively redefining the parties' respective rights under a pre-existing contract—to advance some legitimate state interest, then what limit does the Contract Clause impose? Does the Clause have any continuing vitality after the decision in *Blaisdell*? Consider the case that follows.

c.   Original Meaning?

What exactly is the disagreement between the majority and dissent with respect to the original meaning of the Contract Clause? Do they disagree about what the original meaning was, about whether the Supreme Court must follow the original meaning, or both? Although what *Blaisdell* says about the original meaning is famous, in no subsequent case has the Supreme Court relied on the statement in *Blaisdell* that courts must not be confined to interpretation of the framers. Can you think of an explanation for the Court's hesitation to cite and follow this language from *Blaisdell*?

ALLIED STRUCTURAL STEEL COMPANY V. SPANNAUS
438 U.S. 234 (1978)

MR. JUSTICE STEWART delivered the opinion of the Court.

[Appellant, an Illinois corporation with an office in Minnesota, maintained a pension plan that entitled employees who were at least 65 years old at retirement to receive benefits as long as the company was still in business and the plan was still in effect. In 1974, Minnesota enacted the Private Pension Benefits Protection Act, which required certain employers in Minnesota to pay a "pension funding charge" if they (1) terminated a pension plan or closed a Minnesota office and (2) at the time of termination or closure, existing pension funds were not sufficient to pay pensions to employees who had worked at least 10 years. When appellant closed its Minnesota office, at least nine of the newly discharged employees did not have vested pension rights under the company's plan but qualified for pension benefits under the Act because they had been employed by the company for more than 10 years. The State assessed appellant a pension funding charge of approximately $185,000, and appellant challenged the constitutionality of the Act under the Contract Clause.]

There can be no question of the impact of the Minnesota Private Pension Benefits Protection Act upon the company's contractual relationships with its employees. The Act substantially altered those relationships by superimposing pension obligations upon the company conspicuously beyond those that it had voluntarily agreed to undertake. But it does not inexorably follow that the Act, as applied to the company, violates the Contract Clause of the Constitution.

The language of the Contract Clause appears unambiguously absolute, [but] it is to be accepted as a commonplace that the Contract Clause does not operate to obliterate the police power of the States. * * * If the Contract Clause is to retain any meaning at all, however, it must be understood to impose *some* limits upon the power of a State to abridge existing contractual relationships, even in the exercise of its otherwise legitimate police power. [The Court in *Blaisdell*] implied that if the Minnesota moratorium legislation had not [been a reasonable response to an emergency,] it would have been invalid under the Contract Clause. * * * The most recent Contract Clause case in this Court was *United States Trust Co. v. New Jersey*, 431 U.S. 1 (1977). * * * Evaluating with particular scrutiny a modification of a contract to which the State itself was a party, the Court in that case held that legislative alteration of the rights and remedies of Port Authority bondholders violated the Contract Clause because the legislation was neither necessary nor reasonable.

In applying these principles to the present case, the first inquiry must be whether the state law has, in fact, operated as a substantial impairment of a contractual relationship.[16] The severity of the impairment measures the height of the hurdle the state legislation must clear. Minimal alteration of contractual obligations may end the inquiry at its first stage. Severe impairment, on the other hand, will push the inquiry to a careful examination of the nature and purpose of the state legislation.

The severity of an impairment of contractual obligations can be measured by the factors that reflect the high value the Framers placed on the protection of private contracts. Contracts enable individuals to order their personal and business affairs according to their particular needs and interests. Once arranged, those rights and obligations are binding under the law, and the parties are entitled to rely on them. * * * The company [had] no reason to anticipate that its employees' pension rights could become vested except in accordance with the terms of the plan. It relied heavily, and reasonably, on this legitimate contractual expectation in calculating its annual contributions to the pension fund. The effect of Minnesota's Private Pension Benefits Protection Act on this contractual obligation was severe. [A]lthough the company's past contributions were adequate when made, they were not adequate when computed under the 10-year statutory vesting requirement. The Act thus forced a current recalculation of the past 10 years' contributions based on the new, unanticipated 10-year vesting requirement. Not only did the state law thus retroactively modify the compensation that the company had agreed to pay its employees from 1963 to 1974, but also it did so by changing the company's obligations in an area where the element of reliance was vital—the funding of a pension plan.

[T]here is no showing in the record before us that this severe disruption of contractual expectations was necessary to meet an important general social problem. [And] because the Act applies only to private employers who have at least 100 employees, at least one of whom works in Minnesota, and who have established voluntary private pension plans, [it] can hardly be characterized, like the law at issue in the *Blaisdell* case, as one enacted to protect a broad societal

---

[16] The novel construction of the Contract Clause expressed in the dissenting opinion is wholly contrary to the decisions of this Court. The narrow view that the Clause forbids only state laws that diminish the duties of a contractual obligor and not laws that increase them [has] been expressly repudiated. *Detroit United R. Co. v. Michigan*, 242 U.S. 238 (1916). The even narrower view that the Clause is limited in its application to state laws relieving debtors of obligations to their creditors is, as the dissent recognizes, completely at odds with this Court's decisions. See *Dartmouth College v. Woodward*, 17 U.S. (4 Wheat.) 518 (1819).

interest rather than a narrow class. [Finally, the] legislation [was] not enacted to deal with a situation remotely approaching the broad and desperate emergency economic conditions of the early 1930's—conditions of which the Court in *Blaisdell* took judicial notice.

This Minnesota law simply does not possess the attributes of those state laws that in the past have survived challenge under the Contract Clause of the Constitution. The law was not even purportedly enacted to deal with a broad, generalized economic or social problem. It did not operate in an area already subject to state regulation at the time the company's contractual obligations were originally undertaken, but invaded an area never before subject to regulation by the State. It did not effect simply a temporary alteration of the contractual relationships of those within its coverage, but worked a severe, permanent, and immediate change in those relationships—irrevocably and retroactively. And its narrow aim was leveled, not at every Minnesota employer, not even at every Minnesota employer who left the State, but only at those who had in the past been sufficiently enlightened as voluntarily to agree to establish pension plans for their employees. * * * [I]f the Contract Clause means anything at all, it means that Minnesota could not constitutionally do what it tried to do to the company in this case.

> **Food for Thought**
>
> The "narrow class" to whom the challenged Act applies includes most employees who work at large employers in Minnesota. Do you agree with the Court's view that a statute designed to ensure the retirement security of workers in that class does not serve a "broad societal interest"? Or that retirement insecurity does not properly constitute an "emergency" that justifies state regulation? What was the Minnesota legislature's view of these questions?

MR. JUSTICE BRENNAN, with whom MR. JUSTICE WHITE and MR. JUSTICE MARSHALL join, dissenting.

Minnesota [adopted] the Act to remedy [what was viewed as a serious] social problem: the frustration of expectation interests that can occur when an employer closes a single plant and terminates the employees who work there. * * * The Minnesota Act addresses this problem by selecting a period [after] which this generally unforeseen contingency may not be the basis for depriving employees of their accumulated pension fund credits. [T]he Act will impose only minor economic burdens on employers whose pension plans have been adequately funded. * * * Indeed, without the Act, the closing of the plant would create a windfall for the employer, because, due to the resulting surplus in the fund, his future contributions would be reduced.

The Act does not relieve either the employer or his employees of any existing contract obligation. Rather, the Act simply creates an additional, supplemental duty of the employer, no different in kind from myriad duties created by a wide variety of legislative measures which defeat settled expectations but which have nonetheless been sustained by this Court. For this reason, the Minnesota Act, in my view, does not implicate the Contract Clause in any way. The basic fallacy of today's decision is its mistaken view that the Contract Clause protects all contract-based expectations, including that of an employer that his obligations to his employees will not be legislatively enlarged beyond those explicitly provided in his pension plan.

[T]he Framers never contemplated that the Clause would limit the legislative power of States to enact laws creating duties that might burden some individuals in order to benefit others * * * [T]he sole evil at which the Contract Clause was directed was the theretofore rampant state legislative interference with the ability of creditors to obtain the payment or security provided for by contract. The Framers regarded the Contract Clause as simply an adjunct to the currency provisions of Art. I, § 10, which operated primarily to bar legislation depriving creditors of the payment of the full value of their loans. The Clause was thus intended by the Framers to be applicable only to laws which altered the obligations of contracts by effectively relieving one party of the obligation to perform a contract duty. * * * This evil is identified with admirable precision: "Law[s] *impairing* the Obligation of Contracts." It is nothing less than an abuse of the English language to interpret, as does the Court, the term "impairing" as including laws which create new duties. While such laws may be conceptualized as "enlarging" the obligation of a contract when they add to the burdens that had previously been imposed by a private agreement, such laws cannot be prohibited by the Clause because they do not dilute or nullify a duty a person had previously obligated himself to perform.

Under the Court's opinion, any law that may be characterized as "superimposing" new obligations on those provided for by contract is to be regarded as creating "sudden, substantial, and unanticipated burdens" and then to be subjected to the most exacting scrutiny. The validity of such a law will turn upon whether judges see it as a law that deals with a generalized social problem, whether it is temporary (as few will be) or permanent, whether it operates in an area previously subject to regulation, and, finally, whether its duties apply to a broad class of persons. The necessary consequence of the extreme malleability of these rather vague criteria is to vest judges with broad subjective discretion to protect property interests that happen to appeal to them.

POINTS FOR DISCUSSION

a.   Scope of State Power

In concluding that the statute upset the contract-based expectations of the company, the Court emphasized that the challenged state law regulated in an "area never before subject to regulation by the State." But isn't this argument circular? If the Court had concluded that Minnesota had authority to regulate in this fashion, then wouldn't any company's expectations (after the decision) incorporate the possibility of state regulation? If the Court's point is that state regulation simply cannot *retroactively* change the terms of a contract, then why would it matter that the state regulation is in response to some form of emergency?

b.   Outlier or More Recent Trend?

Is *Allied Structural Steel* an outlier, or does it represent the Court's willingness to apply the Contract Clause more aggressively? It turns out that *Allied Structural Steel* is the only case since *Blaisdell* in which the Court invoked the Contract Clause to invalidate a state law that interfered with private contracts. In cases involving contracts between private parties since *Allied Structural Steel*, the Court has upheld the challenged state regulation, often expressly distinguishing the case. In *United States Trust Co. v. New Jersey*, 431 U.S. 1 (1977), however, the Court struck down a state law that effectively changed the terms of a contract to which the state itself was a party. There are reasons, however, to be particularly skeptical of such action. (Can you articulate what they are?)

Problem

In 1997, Mark and Kaye got married. In 1998, Mark bought a life insurance policy and designated Kaye as primary beneficiary and his two children as secondary beneficiaries. In 2007, Mark and Kaye divorced. Despite the divorce, Mark did not change the designation of his life insurance beneficiaries as would be permitted by his life insurance contract. In 2011, Mark died. When Kaye tried to claim the life insurance, the two children argued that she could not recover based on a law that Minnesota had passed in 2002. The law said "the dissolution or annulment of a marriage revokes any revocable . . . beneficiary designation . . . made by an individual to the individual's former spouse." Kaye responded that applying the 2002 law to the life insurance contract that Mark made in 1998 violated the Contract Clause. When the case reached the Supreme Court, the majority held that the 2002 law did not violate the Contract Clause because the law did "not substantially impair pre-existing contractual arrangements." *Sveen v. Melin*, 138 S.Ct. 1815 (2018). The dissent did not see how the majority could conclude that "a statute rewriting the most important term of a life insurance policy—who gets paid—somehow doesn't 'substantially impair' the contract." What reasoning, if any, might justify the majority's conclusion?

B. TAKINGS OF PRIVATE PROPERTY

Make the Connection

Recall that in *Barron v. Baltimore*, which we considered in Chapter 1, the Court held that the Takings Clause does not apply to the states. After the ratification of the Fourteenth Amendment, however, the Court held that the Takings Clause was "incorporated" and thus applied to limit state, as well as federal, action. See *Chicago, Burlington & Quincy Railroad v. Chicago*, 166 U.S. 226 (1897).

"**Eminent domain**"—the power of government to force a transfer of property—traces back at least as far as ancient Rome. The Constitution does not expressly authorize the federal government to exercise the power of eminent domain. Article I, § 8, which lists Congress's enumerated powers, does not include such a provision, but the Necessary and Proper Clause, along with Congress's other affirmative powers,

presumably permits the exercise of the power of eminent domain. And the Fifth Amendment has long been viewed as a "tacit recognition of [the] pre-existing power" of eminent domain. *United States v. Carmack*, 329 U.S. 230, 241–242 (1946). The Fifth Amendment, after listing the grand jury requirement, the double jeopardy rule, and the entitlement to due process, states: "nor shall private property be taken for public use, without just compensation." This is known as the "**Takings Clause**."

The Clause itself suggests several questions that must be resolved in any case arising under the Clause. First, in order to apply the Clause, the Court must have some way to determine what constitutes a taking. Second, the Clause, although inartfully drafted, seems to limit the government's power of eminent domain to instances in which the taking is for a "public use." Accordingly, courts are sometimes called upon to determine whether a

FYI

The Court has consistently held that, when the government takes property, "just compensation" is determined by assessing the loss to the owner, measured by the market value at the time of the taking. See, e.g., *Kirby Forest Industries, Inc. v. United States*, 467 U.S. 1 (1984).

taking satisfies this requirement. Third, when the government has taken property for a public use, the Takings Clause requires the government to pay "just compensation." In the materials that follow, we will focus on the first two questions.

1. Introduction

UNITED STATES V. CAUSBY

328 U.S. 256 (1946)

MR. JUSTICE DOUGLAS delivered the opinion of the Court.

[Respondents raised chickens on their land, which was less than one-half mile from an airport used by United States military aircraft. The planes passed over the property day and night at very low altitudes. The noise frightened the chickens, some of which died when they responded by flying into walls. Respondents eventually concluded that they could not use their property as a commercial chicken farm. The United States Court of Claims concluded that the United States had taken an easement over the property, and that the value of the property destroyed and the easement taken was $2,000. An "easement" is an "interest in land owned by another person, consisting in the right to use * * * the land, or an area above or below it, for a specific limited purpose (such as to cross it * * *)." *Black's Law Dictionary* (10th ed. 2014).]

If, by reason of the frequency and altitude of the flights, respondents could not use this land for any purpose, their loss would be complete. It would be as complete as if the United States had entered upon the surface of the land and taken exclusive possession of it. [In] those circumstances there would be a taking. * * * The fact that the planes never touched the surface would be [irrelevant]. The owner's right to possess and exploit the land—that is to say, his beneficial ownership of it—would be destroyed. It would not be a case of incidental damages arising from a legalized nuisance. * * * There is no material difference between the supposed case and the present one,

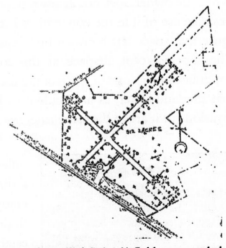

Greensboro-High Point Airfield, as expanded by the War Department. The Causby's farm was located 2000 feet from the end of the Northwest-Southeast runway, directly in the path of planes taking off or landing.
United States v. Causby, 328 U.S. 256 (1946)
(transcript of record at 228)

except that here enjoyment and use of the land are not completely destroyed. But that does not seem to us to be controlling. The path of glide for airplanes might reduce a valuable factory site to grazing land, an orchard to a vegetable patch, a residential section to a wheat field. Some value would remain. But the use of the airspace immediately above the land would limit the utility of the land and cause a diminution in its value.

[T]he airspace is a public highway. Yet it is obvious that if the landowner is to have full enjoyment of the land, he must have exclusive control of the immediate reaches of the enveloping atmosphere. Otherwise buildings could not be erected, trees could not be planted, and even fences could not be run. * * * The landowner owns at least as much of the space above the ground as he can occupy or use in connection with the land. The fact that he does not occupy it in a physical sense—by the erection of buildings and the like—is not material. [T]he flight of airplanes, which skim the surface but do not touch it, is as much an appropriation of the use of the land as a more conventional entry upon it. We would not doubt that if the United States erected an elevated railway over respondents' land at the precise altitude where its planes now fly, there would be a partial taking, even though none of the supports of the structure rested on the land. The reason is that there would be an intrusion so immediate and direct as to subtract from the owner's full enjoyment of the property and to limit his exploitation of it. * * * While the owner does not in any physical manner occupy that stratum of airspace or make use of it in the conventional sense, he does use it in somewhat the same sense that space left between buildings for the purpose of light and air is used. The superadjacent airspace at this low altitude is so close to the land that continuous invasions of it affect the use of the surface of the land itself. We think that the landowner, as an incident to his ownership, has a claim to it and that invasions of it are in the same category as invasions of the surface.

> **Food for Thought**
>
> If the government had built an airport ten miles away from respondents' property—far enough away that the chickens were not frightened by the sound, but close enough that a person on the property could clearly hear the sound of the jets overhead—isn't it likely that the value of the property would have gone down? Would that have constituted a taking, as well? If not, what is the difference?

Flights over private land are not a taking, unless they are so low and so frequent as to be a direct and immediate interference with the enjoyment and use of the land. * * * [T]he findings of the Court of Claims plainly establish that there was a diminution in value of the property and that the frequent, low-level flights were the direct and immediate cause. Since on this record it is not clear whether the easement taken is a permanent or a temporary one, it would be premature for us to consider whether the amount of the award made by the Court of Claims was proper. The judgment is reversed and the cause is remanded to the Court of Claims so that it may make the necessary findings in conformity with this opinion.

MR. JUSTICE BLACK, [with whom MR. JUSTICE BURTON joins,] dissenting.

The Court's opinion seems to indicate that the mere flying of planes through the column of air directly above respondents' land does not constitute a "taking." Consequently, it appears to be noise and glare, to the extent and under the circumstances shown here, which make the government a seizer of private property. But [the] concept of taking property as used in the Constitution has heretofore never been given so sweeping a meaning. The Court's opinion presents no case where a man who makes noise or shines light onto his neighbor's property has been ejected from that property for wrongfully taking possession of it. Nor would anyone take seriously a claim that noisy automobiles passing on a highway are taking wrongful possession of the homes located thereon, or that a city elevated train which greatly interferes with the sleep of those who live next to it wrongfully takes their property. * * *

Nor do I reach a different conclusion because of the fact that the particular circumstance which under the Court's opinion makes the tort here absolutely actionable, is the passing of planes through a column of air at an elevation of eighty-three feet directly over respondents' property. It is inconceivable to me that the Constitution guarantees that the airspace of this Nation needed for air navigation, is owned by the particular persons who happen to own the land beneath to the same degree as they own the surface below. No rigid Constitutional rule, in my judgment, commands that the air must be considered as marked off into separate compartments by imaginary metes and bounds in order to synchronize air ownership with land ownership. I think that the Constitution entrusts Congress with full power to control all navigable airspace * * * under the assumption that the Commerce Clause of the Constitution gave Congress the same plenary power to control navigable airspace as its plenary power over navigable waters. Today's opinion is, I fear, an opening wedge for an unwarranted judicial interference with the power of Congress to develop solutions for new and vital and national problems. In my opinion this case should be reversed on the ground that there has been no "taking" in the Constitutional sense.

> **Food for Thought**
>
> Does the fact that Congress has "plenary" power over the navigable airspace really answer the question in this case whether there was a taking in the first place? Isn't the Takings Clause a limitation on Congress's affirmative powers?

POINTS FOR DISCUSSION

a.   Types of Takings

The Court has identified two distinct types of takings. First, when the government actually takes title to property, or authorizes a "physical occupation" of it, the Court will find a "physical" or "possessory" taking, triggering the requirement of just compensation. Second, the Court has sometimes recognized "regulatory takings." As the Court has explained, when the government "merely regulates the *use* of property, compensation is required only if considerations such as the purpose of the regulation or the extent to which it deprives the owner of the economic use of the property suggest that the regulation has unfairly singled out the property owner to bear a burden that should be borne by the public as a whole." *Yee v. City of Escondido, infra* (emphasis added).

Which type of taking was at issue in *Causby*? Did the Court conclude that the government effectively physically occupied the respondents' land? Or that the government's interference with the respondents' use of their land was sufficiently great to amount to a regulatory taking?

b.   Definition of "Property"

In dissent, Justice Black suggested that because a common-law claim for ejectment would have failed, there could not have been any taking for constitutional purposes. (Ejectment is a "legal action by which a person wrongfully ejected from property seeks to recover possession, damages, and costs." *Black's Law Dictionary* (10th ed. 2014).) Justice Black, in other words, appeared to define the respondents' property rights by reference to existing—and presumably state—law. How did the Court determine the scope of the respondents' property interests? Does the Takings Clause require the Court to define property rights? Or does it leave that definition to other sources of positive law—such as state common or statutory law?

c.   Applying *Causby*

If the Environmental Protection Agency promulgated a regulation restricting the amount of methane—which is produced in large quantities by chickens on chicken farms—that can permissibly be emitted into the air, would owners of chicken farms be able to recover for a taking? In what way would such a takings claim be different from the claim in *Causby*?

d.   Nuisance, Sovereign Immunity, and Takings

State tort law in most states provides a cause of action for "nuisance," which consists of the intentional and unreasonable "invasion of another's interest in the private use and enjoyment of land." Restatement (Second) of the Law of Torts § 822 (1965). Courts in other cases have imposed liability for this tort on airports that have caused unreasonable noise for their neighbors. See, e.g., *Krueger v. Mitchell*, 332 N.W.2d 733, 742 (Wis. 1983).

Wouldn't it have been easier and less controversial for the Causbys to have sued the government under this traditional tort theory rather than to try to convince the Court that the government had invaded its property by flying planes overhead? The answer is that, even if the government appears to have caused a nuisance, the Causbys could not have prevailed under this tort theory. The federal government has not waived its sovereign immunity for the tort of nuisance. In contrast, the federal government does not assert sovereign immunity from takings claims. As a result, the Causbys, like many other plaintiffs with grievances against the government, were careful to couch their claim in terms of a taking. In light of the Fifth Amendment, *could* the federal government assert sovereign immunity to defeat a takings claim?

2. Physical Takings

The government effects a taking when it actually confiscates property, by taking title and possession. But the Court has made clear that the government also "takes" property within the meaning of the Takings Clause when it physically occupies property that is otherwise held privately. In *Loretto v. Teleprompter Manhattan CATV Corp.*, 458 U.S. 419 (1982), for example, the Court concluded that a city ordinance that required owners of apartment buildings to make space available for cable television providers to run wires constituted a compensable taking. The Court explained that the government takes property whenever a "physical intrusion reaches the extreme form of a permanent physical occupation," regardless of how small the amount of space occupied.

How far does the concept of the "physical intrusion" extend? Consider the following case.

YEE V. CITY OF ESCONDIDO
503 U.S. 519 (1992)

JUSTICE O'CONNOR delivered the opinion of the Court.

[Most mobile home owners rent the land on which their homes sit. The California Mobilehome Residency Law limits the bases upon which a mobile home park owner may terminate a mobile home owner's tenancy, and provides that while a rental agreement is in effect, the park owner generally may not require the removal of a mobile home when it is sold or disapprove of the purchaser, provided that the purchaser has the ability to pay the rent. In 1988, the voters of Escondido approved a rent control ordinance that set rents at their 1986 levels and prohibited rent increases without the approval of the City Council. Under the ordinance, park owners could apply for rent increases at any time, and the Council had to approve any increases it determined to be "just, fair and reasonable." Petitioners, John and Irene Yee, owners of a mobile home park in the city of Escondido, filed suit seeking damages and a declaration that, under those circumstances, the rent control ordinance was unconstitutional.]

Petitioners do not claim that the ordinary rent control statutes regulating housing throughout the country violate the Takings Clause. Cf. *Pennell v. City of San Jose*, 485 U.S. 1 (1988). Instead, their argument is predicated on the unusual economic relationship between park owners and mobile home owners. Park owners may no longer set rents or decide who their tenants will be. As a result,

> **Food for Thought**
>
> Why did California enact the statute at issue here? Why does it apply only to mobile home owners who are renting property, as opposed to all tenants?

according to petitioners, any reduction in the rent for a mobile home pad causes a corresponding increase in the value of a mobile home, because the mobile home owner now owns, in addition to a mobile home, the right to occupy a pad at a rent below the value that would be set by the free market. * * * And because the Mobilehome Residency Law permits the mobile home owner to sell the mobile home in place, the mobile home owner can receive a premium from the purchaser corresponding to this increase in value. * * * As a result, petitioners conclude, the rent control ordinance has transferred a discrete interest in land— the right to occupy the land indefinitely at a submarket rent—from the park owner to the mobile home owner. Petitioners contend that what has been transferred from park owner to mobile home owner is no less than a right of physical occupation of the park owner's land.

This argument, while perhaps within the scope of our regulatory taking cases, cannot be squared easily with our cases on physical takings. The government effects a physical taking only where it *requires* the landowner to submit to the physical occupation of his land. "This element of required acquiescence is at the heart of the concept of occupation." *FCC v. Florida Power Corp.*, 480 U.S. 245, 252 (1987). Thus whether the government floods a landowner's property, *Pumpelly v. Green Bay Co.*, 13 Wall. 166 (1872), or does no more than require the landowner to suffer the installation of a cable, *Loretto v. Teleprompter Manhattan CATV Corp.*, 458 U.S. 419 (1982), the Takings Clause requires compensation if the government authorizes a compelled physical invasion of property.

But the Escondido rent control ordinance, even when considered in conjunction with the California Mobilehome Residency Law, authorizes no such thing. Petitioners voluntarily rented their land to mobile home owners. At least on the face of the regulatory scheme, neither the city nor the State compels petitioners, once they have rented their property to tenants, to continue doing so. To the contrary, the Mobilehome Residency Law provides that a park owner who wishes to change the use of his land may evict his tenants, albeit with 6 or 12 months notice. Put bluntly, no government has required any physical invasion of petitioners' property. Petitioners' tenants were invited by petitioners, not forced upon them by the government. While the "right to exclude" is doubtless, as petitioners assert, "one of the most essential sticks in the bundle of rights that are commonly characterized as property," we do not find that right to have been taken from petitioners on the mere face of the Escondido ordinance. * * * A different case would be presented were the statute, on its face or as applied, to compel a landowner over objection to rent his property or to refrain in perpetuity from terminating a tenancy.

On their face, the state and local laws at issue here merely regulate petitioners' *use* of their land by regulating the relationship between landlord and tenant. "This Court has consistently affirmed that States have broad power to regulate housing conditions in general and the landlord-tenant relationship in particular without paying compensation for all economic injuries that such regulation entails." *Loretto*, 458 U.S. at 440. When a landowner decides to rent his land to tenants, the government may place ceilings on the rents the landowner can charge, see, *e.g.*, *Pennell*, 485 U.S. at 12, n. 6, or require the landowner to accept tenants he does not like, see, *e.g.*, *Heart of Atlanta Motel, Inc. v. United States*, 379 U.S. 241, 261 (1964), without automatically having to pay compensation. * * * In the words of Justice Holmes, "while property may be regulated to a certain extent, if regulation goes too far it will be recognized as a taking." *Pennsylvania Coal Co. v. Mahon*, 260 U.S. 393, 415 (1922).

Petitioners emphasize that the ordinance transfers wealth from park owners to incumbent mobile home owners. Other forms of land use regulation, however, can also be said to transfer wealth from the one who is regulated to another. Ordinary rent control often transfers wealth from landlords to tenants by reducing the landlords' income and the tenants' monthly payments * * *. Traditional zoning regulations can transfer wealth from those whose activities are prohibited to their neighbors. * * * The mobile home owner's ability to sell the mobile home at a premium may make this wealth transfer more *visible* than in the ordinary case, [but] the existence of the transfer in itself does not convert regulation into physical invasion.

[Petitioners also contend] that the ordinance amounts to compelled physical occupation because it deprives petitioners of the ability to choose their incoming tenants. Again, this effect may be relevant to a regulatory taking argument, [but] it does not convert regulation into the unwanted physical occupation of land. Because they voluntarily open their property to occupation by others, petitioners cannot assert a *per se* right to compensation based on their inability to exclude particular individuals.

In this Court, petitioners attempt to challenge the ordinance [as] a regulatory taking. [This claim was] not fairly included in the question on which we granted certiorari.

POINTS FOR DISCUSSION

a.   Physical Occupation

In *Loretto*, the Court found a taking when the government required landlords to accept the installation of cable wires on their property. In *Yee*, the Court found that there was not a taking when the government required landlords to accept tenants on their property. Why did the cases come out differently? Does it matter that the tenants in *Yee* would not occupy the land "permanently"? Should it matter?

b.   Rent Control

The Court declined to consider the petitioners' claim that the ordinance constituted a regulatory, as opposed to a physical, taking because it was not properly presented. Would that claim have been stronger? Several years before it decided *Yee*, the Court in *Pennell v. City of San Jose*, 485 U.S. 1 (1988), upheld a rent control ordinance that automatically permitted landlords to raise rents by up to 8 percent each year and provided for hearings to determine the validity of increases of more than that amount. In such hearings, the examiner was required to take into account seven factors, including whether the rent increase would produce "hardship" for the tenant. The Court stated that it was "premature" to decide whether the ordinance effected a transfer of the landlord's property to the tenant, because a hearing examiner had apparently never relied upon that factor. Justices Scalia and O'Connor, however, would have held that the tenant-hardship provision effected a taking of the landlord's property. Should rent control ordinances give rise to a government obligation to pay just compensation? If so, would it be as a physical taking or a regulatory taking?

3.   Regulatory Takings

A physical taking occurs, as we have seen, when the government actually confiscates or invades property. But the government can also impair a property owner's interests by regulating the property and thus reducing its value. Does regulation therefore constitute a taking for which the government must pay compensation? Justice Oliver Wendell Holmes famously addressed this question in *Pennsylvania Coal Co. v. Mahon*, 260 U.S. 393, 413 (1922), by saying: "The general rule at least is that while property may be regulated to a certain extent, if regulation goes too far it will be recognized as a taking."

The Supreme Court has repeated this principle in many cases, but has never defined the words "too far" in precise terms. Still, it is clear that most regulations of property do not go too far. Stop signs and speed limits restrict how you can drive your car, but the government does not have to pay you compensation for these restrictions. Similarly, local ordinances may restrict the hours at which you may operate your noisy lawn mower, but your city does not have to pay you for this imposition. State laws, moreover, may restrict your ability to sell home-made beer, but this is not a taking, either. Rather, only extreme laws that essentially deprive the property owner of the entire value of property or nearly all of the normal uses of property constitute regulatory takings. In reading the cases that follow, consider what arguments might justify this approach.

PENN CENTRAL TRANSPORTATION CO. V. CITY OF NEW YORK
438 U.S. 104 (1978)

MR. JUSTICE BRENNAN delivered the opinion of the Court.

[The New York City Landmarks Preservation Law authorizes the Landmarks Preservation Commission to designate as a landmark property that has "a special character or special historical or aesthetic interest or value as part of the development, heritage or cultural characteristics of the city, state or nation." Such a designation permits the property owner to alter the exterior architectural features of the landmark or to construct any exterior improvement on the landmark site only with the advance approval of the Commission. In 1967, the Commission designated Grand Central Terminal as a landmark. Shortly thereafter, Penn Central, which owned the Terminal, and UGP Properties, with whom it had entered into a lease agreement, applied to the Commission for permission to construct a new office building above the Terminal. The application included two proposed construction plans: the first provided for the office to be built above the existing façade of the terminal; and the second involved tearing down a portion of the Terminal. The Commission rejected the first proposal, stating that it would impair the dramatic view of the Terminal from the South, and rejected the second proposal on the ground that "[t]o protect a Landmark, one does not tear it down." Penn Central filed suit claiming that the denial of their application effected a taking of their property for which they had not received just compensation.]

"Government hardly could go on if to some extent values incident to property could not be diminished without paying for every such change in the general law," *Pennsylvania Coal Co. v. Mahon,* 260 U.S. 393, 413 (1922), and this Court has accordingly recognized, in a wide variety of contexts, that government may execute laws or programs that adversely affect recognized economic values. Exercises of the taxing power are one obvious example. A second are the decisions in which this Court has dismissed "taking" challenges on the ground that, while the challenged government action caused economic harm, it did not interfere with interests that were sufficiently bound up with the reasonable expectations of the claimant to constitute "property" for Fifth Amendment purposes.

More importantly for the present case, in instances in which a state tribunal reasonably concluded that "the health, safety, morals, or general welfare" would be promoted by prohibiting particular contemplated uses of land, this Court has upheld land-use regulations that destroyed or adversely affected recognized real property interests. See *Nectow v. Cambridge,* 277 U.S. 183, 188 (1928). Zoning laws are, of course, the classic example, which have been viewed as permissible governmental action even when prohibiting the most beneficial use of the property.

Zoning laws generally do not affect existing uses of real property, but "taking" challenges have also been held to be without merit in a wide variety of situations when the challenged governmental actions prohibited a beneficial use to which individual parcels had previously been devoted and thus caused substantial individualized harm. * * * *Goldblatt v. Hempstead,* 369 U.S. 590 (1962), is a recent example. There, a 1958 city safety ordinance banned any excavations below the water table and effectively prohibited the claimant from continuing a sand and gravel mining business that had been operated on the particular parcel since 1927. The Court upheld the ordinance against a "taking" challenge, although the ordinance prohibited the present and presumably most beneficial use of the property and [severely] affected a particular owner. The Court assumed that the ordinance did not prevent the owner's reasonable use of the property since the owner made no showing of an adverse effect on the value of the land. * * * It is, of course, implicit in *Goldblatt* that a use restriction on real property may constitute a "taking" if not reasonably necessary to the effectuation of a substantial public purpose, or perhaps if it has an unduly harsh impact upon the owner's use of the property.

Pennsylvania Coal Co. v. Mahon is the leading case for the proposition that a state statute that substantially furthers important public policies may so frustrate distinct investment-backed expectations as to amount to a "taking." There the claimant had sold the surface rights to particular parcels of property, but expressly reserved the right to remove the coal thereunder. A Pennsylvania statute, enacted

> **Take Note**
>
> Didn't the regulation in *Mahon* permit a "reasonable use" of the property and serve a substantial public purpose, as the Court held the regulation in *Goldblatt* did? Is there some way to distinguish the cases? Which is the regulation in *Penn Central* more like?

after the transactions, forbade any mining of coal that caused the subsidence of any house, unless the house was the property of the owner of the underlying coal and was more than 150 feet from the improved property of another. Because the statute made it commercially impracticable to mine the coal, *id.,* at 414, and thus had nearly the same effect as the complete destruction of rights claimant had reserved from the owners of the surface land, the Court held that the statute was invalid as effecting a "taking" without just compensation.

[Appellants observe] that the airspace above the Terminal is a valuable property interest, citing *United States v. Causby*, 328 U.S. 256 (1946). They urge that the Landmarks Law has deprived them of any gainful use of their "air rights" above the Terminal and that, irrespective of the value of the remainder of their parcel, the city has "taken" their right to this superadjacent airspace, thus entitling them to "just compensation" measured by the fair market value of these air rights. [But the] submission that appellants may establish a "taking" simply by showing that they have been denied the ability to exploit a property interest that they heretofore had believed was available for development is quite simply untenable. * * * "Taking" jurisprudence does not divide a single parcel into discrete segments and attempt to determine whether rights in a particular segment have been entirely abrogated. In deciding whether a particular governmental action has effected a taking, this Court focuses rather both on the character of the action and on the nature and extent of the interference with rights in the parcel as a whole—here, the city tax block designated as the "landmark site."

> **Make the Connection**
>
> Is the Court's conclusion here consistent with the Court's decision in *Causby*, which seemed to recognize a taking because of a regulation's effect on the airspace over an individual's property? Is there a way to distinguish *Causby*?

[T]he New York City law does not interfere in any way with the present uses of the Terminal. Its designation as a landmark not only permits but contemplates that appellants may continue to use the property precisely as it has been used for the past 65 years: as a railroad terminal containing office space and concessions. So the law does not interfere with what must be regarded as Penn Central's primary expectation concerning the use of the parcel. More importantly, on this record, we must regard the New York City law as permitting Penn Central not only to profit from the Terminal but also to obtain a "reasonable return" on its investment.

On this record, we conclude that the application of New York City's Landmarks Law has not effected a "taking" of appellants' property. The restrictions imposed are substantially related to the promotion of the general welfare and not only permit reasonable beneficial use of the landmark site but also afford appellants opportunities further to enhance not only the Terminal site proper but also other properties.

MR. JUSTICE REHNQUIST, with whom THE CHIEF JUSTICE and MR. JUSTICE STEVENS join, dissenting.

Only in the most superficial sense of the word can this case be said to involve "zoning." Typical zoning restrictions may, it is true, so limit the prospective uses of a piece of property as to diminish the value of that property in the abstract because it may not be used for the forbidden purposes. But any such abstract decrease in value will more than likely be at least partially offset by an increase in value which flows from similar restrictions as to use on neighboring properties. All property owners in a designated area are placed under the same restrictions, not only for the benefit of the municipality as a whole but also for the common benefit of one another. In the words of Mr. Justice Holmes, speaking for the Court in [*Mahon,*] there is "an average reciprocity of advantage." Where a relatively few individual buildings, all separated from one another, are singled out and treated differently from surrounding buildings, no such reciprocity exists.

[T]he Court has frequently emphasized that the term "property" as used in the Taking Clause includes the entire "group of rights inhering in the citizen's [ownership]." *United States v. General Motors Corp.*, 323 U.S. 373 (1945). * * * While neighboring landowners are free to use their land and "air rights" in any way consistent with the broad boundaries of New York zoning, Penn Central, absent the permission of appellees, must forever maintain its property in its present state. The property has been thus subjected to a nonconsensual servitude not borne by any neighboring or similar properties. * * * Appellees have thus destroyed—in a literal sense, "taken"—substantial property rights of Penn Central.

Unlike [permissible] land-use regulations, appellees' actions do not merely *prohibit* Penn Central from using its property in a narrow set of noxious ways. Instead, appellees have placed an *affirmative* duty on Penn Central to maintain the

Terminal in its present state and in "good repair." Appellants are not free to use their property as they see fit within broad outer boundaries but must strictly adhere to their past use except where appellees conclude that alternative uses would not detract from the landmark. While Penn Central may continue to use the Terminal as it is presently designed, appellees otherwise "exercise complete dominion and control over the surface of the land." [*Causby*.]

Appellees have imposed a substantial cost on less than one-tenth of one percent of the buildings in New York City for the general benefit of all its people. It is exactly this imposition of general costs on a few individuals at which the "taking" protection is directed. * * * Appellees in response would argue that a taking only occurs where a property owner is

> **Take Note**
>
> In what way does the Takings Clause prevent the government from imposing on the few the costs of actions that benefit the many? Should that principle apply in this case to require compensation to Penn Central?

denied *all* reasonable value of his property. The Court has frequently held that, even where a destruction of property rights would not *otherwise* constitute a taking, the inability of the owner to make a reasonable return on his property requires compensation under the Fifth Amendment. But the converse is not true. A taking does not become a noncompensable exercise of police power simply because the government in its grace allows the owner to make some "reasonable" use of his property.

ANDRUS V. ALLARD
444 U.S. 51 (1979)

MR. JUSTICE BRENNAN delivered the opinion of the Court.

[The Eagle Protection Act and the Migratory Bird Treaty Act are conservation statutes designed to prevent the destruction of certain species of birds. The Acts prohibit commercial transactions in parts of birds that are protected under the statutes, and regulations promulgated by the Secretary of the Interior apply the prohibition to birds killed before the statutes were in force. Appellees were engaged in the trade of Indian artifacts, a number of which are partly composed of feathers of birds protected by the statute, and some of them were prosecuted for selling artifacts in violation of the statute and regulations. They brought suit alleging that the regulations violated the Fifth Amendment.]

We [disagree] with the District Court's holding that, as construed to authorize the prohibition of commercial transactions in pre-existing avian artifacts, the Eagle Protection and Migratory Bird Treaty Acts violate appellees' Fifth Amendment property rights because the prohibition wholly deprives them of the opportunity to earn a profit from those relics. * * * Suffice it to say that government regulation—by definition—involves the adjustment of rights for the public good. Often this adjustment curtails some potential for the use or economic exploitation of private property. To require compensation in all such circumstances would effectively compel the government to regulate by *purchase*.

The regulations challenged here do not compel the surrender of the artifacts, and there is no physical invasion or restraint upon them. Rather, a significant restriction has been imposed on one means of disposing of the artifacts. But the denial of one traditional property right does not always amount to a taking. At least where an owner possesses a full "bundle" of property rights, the destruction of one "strand" of the bundle is not a taking, because the aggregate must be viewed in its entirety. In this case, it is crucial that appellees retain the rights to possess and transport their property, and to donate or devise the protected birds.

> **Take Note**
>
> The Court states that the loss of future profits is not sufficient to constitute a taking. If the government prohibited transactions involving stock certificates, would the loss of future profits be sufficient to constitute a taking? Why is this case (and cases involving Prohibition) different?

It is, to be sure, undeniable that the regulations here prevent the most profitable use of appellees' property. Again, however, that is not dispositive. When we review regulation, a reduction in the value of property is not necessarily equated with a taking. In the instant case, it is not clear that appellees will be unable to derive economic benefit from the artifacts; for example, they might exhibit the artifacts for an admissions charge. At any rate, loss of future profits—unaccompanied by any physical property restriction—provides a slender reed upon which to rest a takings claim. * * * For example, the Court has sustained regulations prohibiting the sale of alcoholic beverages despite the fact that individuals were left with previously acquired stocks. *Everard's Breweries v. Day*, 265 U.S. 545 (1924).

It is true that appellees must bear the costs of these regulations. But, within limits, that is a burden borne to secure "the advantage of living and doing business in a civilized community." *Pennsylvania Coal Co. v. Mahon*, 260 U.S. 393, 422 (1922) (Brandeis, J., dissenting). We hold that the simple prohibition of the sale of lawfully acquired property in this case does not effect a taking in violation of the Fifth Amendment.

POINTS FOR DISCUSSION

a.   Finding a Regulatory Taking

What is the test for determining whether government regulation of private property has effected a taking? Is it simply a multi-factored test that considers all of the circumstances? The Court in *Penn Central* suggested that a claim of a regulatory taking in most cases will fail if the regulation advances some valid government interest. But don't most exercises of the power of eminent domain—including classic physical takings—presumably advance some legitimate government interest? (Indeed, doesn't the Public Use Clause require at least that much?) Why should the context of regulatory takings be any different?

b.   History and Regulatory Takings

Before the Court's decision in *Pennsylvania Coal Co. v. Mahon*, 260 U.S. 393 (1922), to which the Court refers in *Penn Central*, the Court had typically found a compensable taking only when the government had confiscated property or physically occupied it. Since *Mahon*, however, the Court has recognized the possibility that government regulation of private property could amount to a taking if, in the words of Justice Holmes in *Mahon*, the regulation goes "too far." Does the fact that the Court did not recognize the possibility of a regulatory taking until 1922 suggest that the interpretation of the Takings Clause to embrace regulatory takings is inconsistent with the original meaning? Or does it simply reflect the fact that the government did not seek to regulate private property aggressively until more than 100 years after the founding?

c.   The Consequences of Requiring Compensation

What are the possible consequences of requiring the government to pay a property owner for a particular regulation? One, of course, is that the property owner will receive compensation for a loss of the property's value. But another, perhaps more likely, consequence is that the government will not impose the regulation in the first place, because paying compensation would be too expensive. Is it any wonder that some libertarian thinkers have urged a more generous view on what constitutes a regulatory taking for which compensation must be paid? See, e.g., Richard Epstein, *Takings* 57 (1985) (advancing the central thesis that the "protection afforded by the [takings] clause to each part of an endowment of private property is equal to the protection it affords the whole—no more and no less").

LUCAS V. SOUTH CAROLINA COASTAL COUNCIL
505 U.S. 1003 (1992)

JUSTICE SCALIA delivered the opinion of the Court.

[In 1986, Lucas purchased two lots on the Isle of Palms in South Carolina for over $1 million with the intention of building single-family homes on each, as had the owners of the immediately adjacent lots. In 1988, before Lucas began construction, the South Carolina legislature enacted the Beachfront Management Act, which prevented construction on land within a certain distance of the coastline, in order to stem beach erosion. The law did not require existing homes to be removed. Lucas's property fell within this restricted area. The state paid him nothing for the deprivation of the use of his land. He brought suit claiming that the regulation effected a taking without just compensation. The South Carolina Court of Common Pleas found that the permanent ban on construction deprived Lucas of any reasonable use of the lot and ordered the South Carolina Coastal Commission to pay just compensation. The Supreme Court of South Carolina reversed, holding that when a regulation respecting the use of property is designed "to prevent serious public harm," no compensation is required under the Takings Clause regardless of the regulation's effect on the property's value.]

[In *Pennsylvania Coal Co. v. Mahon*, 260 U.S. 393 (1922), Justice Holmes offered the] oft-cited maxim that, "while property may be regulated to a certain extent, if regulation goes too far it will be recognized as a taking." [But] our decision in *Mahon* offered little insight into when, and under what circumstances, a given regulation would be seen as going "too far" for purposes of the Fifth Amendment. In 70-odd years of succeeding "regulatory takings" jurisprudence, we have generally eschewed any "set formula" for determining how far is too far, preferring to "engage in essentially ad hoc, factual inquiries." *Penn Central Transportation Co. v. New York City*, 438 U.S. 104, 124 (1978). We have, however, described at least two discrete categories of regulatory action as compensable without case-specific inquiry into the public interest advanced in support of the restraint. The first encompasses regulations that compel the property owner to suffer a physical "invasion" of his property. In general (at least with regard to permanent invasions), no matter how minute the intrusion, and no matter how weighty the public purpose behind it, we have required compensation. [See, e.g. *United States v. Causby*, 328 U.S. 256 (1946) (physical invasions of airspace).] The second situation in which we have found categorical treatment appropriate is where regulation denies all economically beneficial or productive use of land.

[T]otal deprivation of beneficial use is, from the landowner's point of view, the equivalent of a physical appropriation. [And] regulations that leave the owner of land without economically beneficial or productive options for its use—typically, as here, by requiring land to be left substantially in its natural state—carry with them a heightened risk that private property is being pressed into some form of public service under the guise of mitigating serious public harm. [These reasons support] our frequently expressed belief that when the owner of real property has been called upon to sacrifice *all* economically beneficial uses in the name of the common good, that is, to leave his property economically idle, he has suffered a taking.

It is correct that many of our prior opinions have suggested that "harmful or noxious uses" of property may be proscribed by government regulation without the requirement of compensation. For a number of reasons, however, we think the South Carolina Supreme Court was too quick to conclude that that principle decides the present case. * * * "Harmful or noxious use" analysis was [simply] the progenitor of our more contemporary statements that "land-use regulation does not effect a taking if it 'substantially advances legitimate state interests.' " *Nollan v. California Coastal Comm'n,* 483 U.S. 825, 834 (1987). The transition from our early focus on control of "noxious" uses to our contemporary understanding of the broad realm within which government may regulate without compensation was an easy one, since the distinction between "harm-preventing" and "benefit-conferring" regulation is often in the eye of the beholder. It is quite possible, for example, to describe in *either* fashion the ecological, economic, and esthetic concerns that inspired the South Carolina Legislature in the present case. One could say that imposing a servitude on Lucas's land is necessary in order to prevent his use of it from "harming" South Carolina's ecological resources; or, instead, in order to achieve the "benefits" of an ecological preserve. * * * Whether Lucas's construction of single-family residences on his parcels should be described as bringing "harm" to South Carolina's adjacent ecological resources thus depends principally upon whether the describer believes that the State's use interest in nurturing those resources is so important that *any* competing adjacent use must yield.

When it is understood that "prevention of harmful use" was merely our early formulation of the police power justification necessary to sustain (without compensation) *any* regulatory diminution in value; and that the distinction

> **Food for Thought**
>
> In what way is the regulation here different from the regulation challenged in *Andrus*? Couldn't Lucas sit on the beach and watch the sunset, or charge people to use his beachfront property—say for picnics or parties—just as the appellees in *Andrus* could charge people to see their artifacts?

between regulation that "prevents harmful use" and that which "confers benefits" is difficult, if not impossible, to discern on an objective, value-free basis; it becomes self-evident that noxious-use logic cannot serve as a touchstone to distinguish regulatory "takings"—which require compensation—from regulatory deprivations that do not require compensation. *A fortiori* the legislature's recitation of a noxious-use justification cannot be the basis for departing from our categorical rule that total regulatory takings must be compensated. If it were, departure would virtually always be allowed, [essentially nullifying] *Mahon*'s affirmation of limits to the noncompensable exercise of the police power.

Where the State seeks to sustain regulation that deprives land of all economically beneficial use, we think it may resist compensation only if the logically antecedent inquiry into the nature of the owner's estate shows that the proscribed use interests were not part of his title to begin with. This accords, we think, with our "takings" jurisprudence, which has traditionally been guided by the understandings of our citizens regarding the content of, and the State's power over, the "bundle of rights" that they acquire when they obtain title to property. It seems to us that the property owner necessarily expects the uses of his property to be restricted, from time to time, by various measures newly enacted by the State in legitimate exercise of its police powers * * *. In the case of land, [however, we] think the notion pressed by the Council that title is somehow held subject to the "implied limitation" that the State may subsequently eliminate all economically valuable use is inconsistent with the historical compact recorded in the Takings Clause that has become part of our constitutional culture.

[C]onfiscatory regulations, *i.e.*, regulations that prohibit all economically beneficial use of land, [cannot] be newly legislated or decreed (without compensation), but must inhere in the title itself, in the restrictions that background principles of the State's law of property and nuisance already place upon land ownership. A law or decree with such an effect must, in other words, do no more than duplicate the result that could have been achieved in the courts—by adjacent landowners (or other uniquely affected persons) under the State's law of private nuisance, or by the State under its complementary power to abate nuisances that affect the public generally, or otherwise.

[As] it would be required to do if it sought to restrain Lucas in a common-law action for public nuisance, South Carolina must identify background principles of nuisance and property law that prohibit the uses he now intends in the circumstances in which the property is presently found. Only on this showing can the State fairly claim that, in proscribing all such beneficial uses, the

Beachfront Management Act is taking nothing. * * * The judgment is reversed, and the case is remanded for proceedings not inconsistent with this opinion.

JUSTICE KENNEDY, concurring in the judgment.

I agree with the Court that nuisance prevention accords with the most common expectations of property owners who face regulation, but I do not believe this can be the sole source of state authority to impose severe restrictions. Coastal property may present such unique concerns for a fragile land system that the State can go further in regulating its development and use than the common law of nuisance might otherwise permit.

JUSTICE BLACKMUN, dissenting.

The Court creates its new takings jurisprudence based on the trial court's finding that the property had lost all economic value. This finding is almost certainly erroneous. Petitioner still can enjoy other attributes of ownership, such as the right to exclude others, "one of the most essential sticks in the bundle of rights that are commonly characterized as property." *Kaiser Aetna v. United States,* 444 U.S. 164, 176 (1979). Petitioner can picnic, swim, camp in a tent, or live on the property in a movable trailer. Petitioner also retains the right to alienate the land, which would have value for neighbors and for those prepared to enjoy proximity to the ocean without a house.

If one fact about the Court's takings jurisprudence can be stated without contradiction, it is that "the particular circumstances of each case" determine whether a specific restriction will be rendered invalid by the government's failure to pay compensation. This is so because although we have articulated certain factors to be considered, including the economic impact on the property owner, the ultimate conclusion "necessarily requires a weighing of private and public interests." [Our cases show that] the State has full power to prohibit an owner's use of property if it is harmful to the public.

JUSTICE STEVENS, dissenting.

The Court's holding today effectively freezes the State's common law, denying the legislature much of its traditional power to revise the law governing the rights and uses of property. Until today, I had thought that we had long abandoned this approach to constitutional law. * * * Arresting the development of the common law is not only a departure from our prior decisions; it is also profoundly unwise. The human condition is one of constant learning and evolution—both moral and practical. Legislatures implement that new learning; in doing so they must often revise the definition of property and the rights of property owners. * * * Of course, some legislative redefinitions of property will effect a taking and must be compensated—but it certainly cannot be the case that every movement away from common law does so.

In addition to lacking support in past decisions, the Court's new rule is wholly arbitrary. A landowner whose property is diminished in value 95% recovers nothing, while an owner whose property is diminished 100% recovers the land's full value. * * * [E]ven assuming that petitioner's property was rendered valueless, the risk inherent in investments of the sort made by petitioner, the generality of the Act, and the compelling purpose motivating the South Carolina Legislature persuade me that the Act did not effect a taking of petitioner's property.

POINTS FOR DISCUSSION

a.   Rules v. Standards

Although the general test for finding a regulatory taking is a multi-factored standard, Justice Scalia sought in his opinion in *Lucas* to offer a categorical rule to address one potentially common set of circumstances. There is a long-standing debate over the relative virtues of rules and standards. See, e.g., Kathleen M. Sullivan, *The Justices of Rules and Standards*, 106 Harv. L. Rev. 22 (1992); Antonin Scalia, *The Rule of Law as a Law of Rules*, 56 U. Chi. L. Rev. 1175 (1989). Whatever the merits of rules in other contexts, is there any reason to think that they are particularly important in the context of regulatory takings?

b.   Background Principles of Property Law

Justice Stevens criticized the majority for "freez[ing]" state common law. After the Court's decision in *Lucas*, can a state modify its law of nuisance (or, for that matter, its laws defining property rights) to achieve the same result that the state sought in *Lucas*? After all, if a state decides to define more expansively the circumstances that constitute a nuisance, then arguably it would have broader power to regulate to abate those nuisances without incurring the obligation to pay just compensation. At bottom, the question is whether the Takings Clause provides a constitutional definition of property (or at least empowers judges to create one), or instead relies on positive state-law definitions of property.

Justice Scalia stated that to avoid the obligation to pay compensation after depriving private land of all economically beneficial use, the state must identify "background principles" of nuisance and property law that prohibit the uses in question. By "background," did he mean principles embodied in the Constitution, or that at least existed at the time of the framing of the Constitution? Or did he mean principles that are a function of state law, but that already existed at the time of the state's action (or the purchase of the property)? If the latter, *Lucas* effectively means that the state may not limit property rights retroactively, but may do so prospectively. But at common law, of course, principles of property law evolved over time, and were often applied retrospectively to the litigants in the cases that produced new rules. In any event, if states can—even if only prospectively—reduce the value of private property by redefining the law of nuisance or other property laws, is the Takings Clause really a strong protection for private ownership of property? Can a state alter property laws prospectively without affecting the current owner of existing property?

c. What Happened Next

The parties settled this case, with the state paying Lucas $850,000 for the property, plus additional sums in damages and costs. The state did not keep the property in an undeveloped state. Instead, it resold the property to a developer. What does this subsequent history suggest about the justice of the Supreme Court's decision?

4. Public Use

Most takings claims seek the payment of compensation as a remedy for the taking. But sometimes property owners would rather keep their property than be paid compensation for their loss of some or all of their rights in the property. One possible avenue for such property owners is to contend that the government lacks authority to take the property, because the taking is not for a "public use." The following case considers the meaning of that term.

KELO V. CITY OF NEW LONDON

545 U.S. 469 (2005)

JUSTICE STEVENS delivered the opinion of the Court.

[After years of economic decline in New London, Connecticut, state and local officials charged the New London Development Corporation (NLDC), a private nonprofit entity, with developing and implementing an economic revitalization project in the City's Fort Trumbull area. After the state authorized some initial funding for the project, the pharmaceutical company Pfizer, Inc. announced that it would build a $300 million research facility near Fort Trumbull. NLDC proposed a development plan to

> **FYI**
>
> The development project in this case was a complete failure. The city spent $80 million taking homes and clearing property, but no new construction ever took place. Pfizer left the area as soon as its tax breaks expired. Susette Kelo's house, slated for demolition, survived. Because of the public outcry over this case, the house was moved intact to a new location. For more about the case, see Jeff Benedict, *Little Pink House: A True Story of Defiance and Courage* (2009).

> **Take Note**
>
> The Court states that the "public use" requirement of the Fifth Amendment is satisfied if the taking serves a "public purpose." Why did the Court abandon the "use by the public" test? Can you think of a hypothetical situation in which the government could show that it was "necessary and proper" to take property in order to exercise its enumerated powers, but the government somehow could not also show the taking was for a "public purpose"? If not, does the Court's interpretation of the public purpose requirement constrain the government in any way? How is a public purpose to be determined? Wouldn't taking land from a wealthy person who owns significant acreage and giving it to a poor person who owns no land arguably serve a "public purpose," albeit one whose desirability would be hotly debated? Yet the Court also says that the state cannot take property from A simply to give it to B. Does the "public purpose" standard have any real content? Conversely, is taking land from A to give it to B really materially different from taking it from A to give it to a private railroad?

build residences, parkland, shops, a museum, and office space next to the proposed research facility. The city council approved the plan and gave NLDC authority to acquire property by purchase or through eminent domain. NLDC was able successfully to negotiate the purchase of most of the real estate in the 90-acre development area, but after negotiations with petitioners failed, NLDC initiated condemnation proceedings. Petitioner Susette Kelo had lived in the Fort Trumbull area since 1997 and had made extensive improvements to her home. Petitioner Wilhelmina Dery was born in her Fort Trumbull house in 1918 and had lived there her entire life, and her husband, also a petitioner, had lived in the house for 60 years. They and the other petitioners did not want to give up their homes even if they were paid just compensation. NLDC did not contend that petitioners' property was blighted, but rather sought to condemn it because it was in the development area. Petitioners brought suit claiming that the city's proposed disposition of the property did not qualify as a "public use" within the meaning of the Fifth Amendment.]

Two polar propositions are perfectly clear. On the one hand, it has long been accepted that the sovereign may not take the property of *A* for the sole purpose of transferring it to another private party *B*, even though *A* is paid just compensation. On the other hand, it is equally clear that a State may transfer property from one private party to another if future "use by the public" is the purpose of the taking; the condemnation of land for a railroad with common-carrier duties is a familiar example. Neither of these propositions, however, determines the disposition of this case.

[T]he City's development plan was not adopted "to benefit a particular class of identifiable individuals." On the other hand, this is not a case in which the City is planning to open the condemned land—at least not in its entirety—to use by the general public. [But] this "Court long ago rejected any literal requirement that condemned property be put into use for the general public." Indeed, while many state courts in the mid-19th century endorsed "use by the public" as the proper definition of public use, that narrow view steadily eroded over time. Not only was the "use by the public" test difficult to administer (*e.g.*, what proportion of the public need have access to the property? at what price?), but it proved to be impractical given the diverse and always evolving needs of society. Accordingly, when this Court began applying the Fifth Amendment to the States at the close of the 19th century, it embraced the broader and more natural interpretation of public use as "public purpose." See, *e.g., Fallbrook Irrigation Dist. v. Bradley,* 164 U.S. 112 (1896).

Without exception, our cases have defined ["public purpose"] broadly, reflecting our longstanding policy of deference to legislative judgments in this field. In *Berman v. Parker,* 348 U.S. 26 (1954), this Court upheld a redevelopment plan targeting a blighted area of Washington, D.C. The owner of a department store located in the area challenged the condemnation, pointing out that his store was not itself blighted and arguing that the creation of a "better balanced, more attractive community" was not a valid public use. Writing for a unanimous Court, Justice Douglas refused to evaluate this claim in isolation, deferring instead to the legislative and agency judgment that the area "must be planned as a whole" for the plan to be successful.

In *Hawaii Housing Authority v. Midkiff,* 467 U.S. 229 (1984), the Court considered a Hawaii statute whereby fee title was taken from lessors and transferred to lessees (for just compensation) in order to reduce the concentration of land ownership. * * * [W]e concluded that the State's purpose of eliminating the "social and economic evils of a land oligopoly" qualified as a valid public use. 467 U.S., at 241–242. Our opinion also rejected the contention that the mere fact that the State immediately transferred the properties to private individuals upon condemnation somehow diminished the public character of the taking. *Id.,* at 244.

Viewed as a whole, our jurisprudence has recognized that the needs of society have varied between different parts of the Nation, just as they have evolved over time in response to changed circumstances. * * * For more than a century, our public use jurisprudence has wisely eschewed rigid formulas and intrusive scrutiny in favor of affording legislatures broad latitude in determining what public needs justify the use of the takings power.

> **Take Note**
>
> Is the Court taking a non-originalist approach in considering society's evolving needs? Or is it simply applying the original meaning of the Takings Clause to changed circumstances?

Those who govern [New London] were not confronted with the need to remove blight in the Fort Trumbull area, but their determination that the area was sufficiently distressed to justify a program of economic rejuvenation is entitled to our deference. The City has carefully formulated an economic development plan that it believes will provide appreciable benefits to the community, including—but by no means limited to—new jobs and increased tax revenue. As with other exercises in urban planning and development, the City is endeavoring to coordinate a variety of commercial, residential, and recreational uses of land, with the hope that they will form a whole greater than the sum of its parts. * * * Given the comprehensive character of the plan, the thorough deliberation that preceded its adoption, and the limited scope of our review, it is appropriate for us, as it was in *Berman,* to resolve the challenges of the individual owners, not on a piecemeal basis, but rather in light of the entire plan. Because that plan unquestionably serves a public purpose, the takings challenged here satisfy the public use requirement of the Fifth Amendment.

To avoid this result, petitioners urge us to adopt a new bright-line rule that economic development does not qualify as a public use. [But promoting] economic development is a traditional and long-accepted function of government. There is, moreover, no principled way of distinguishing economic development from the other public purposes that we have recognized.

It is further argued that without a bright-line rule nothing would stop a city from transferring citizen *A*'s property to citizen *B* for the sole reason that citizen *B* will put the property to a more productive use and thus pay more taxes. Such a one-to-one transfer of property, executed outside the confines of an integrated development plan, is not presented in this case. While such an unusual exercise of government power would certainly raise a suspicion that a private purpose was afoot, the hypothetical cases posited by petitioners can be confronted if and when they arise. They do not warrant the crafting of an artificial restriction on the concept of public use.

In affirming the City's authority to take petitioners' properties, we do not minimize the hardship that condemnations may entail, notwithstanding the payment of just compensation. We emphasize that nothing in our opinion precludes any State from placing further restrictions on its exercise of the

---

Food for Thought

Once the Court has decided that a taking is for a public use as long as it serves a public purpose, and that legislative judgments are entitled to deference, doesn't it necessarily follow that the hypothetical cases suggested by petitioners would be a permissible exercise of the state's power of eminent domain? If so, what does that suggest about the Court's approach?

takings power. Indeed, many States already impose "public use" requirements that are stricter than the federal baseline. * * * As the submissions of the parties and their *amici* make clear, the necessity and wisdom of using eminent domain to promote economic development are certainly matters of legitimate public debate. This Court's authority, however, extends only to determining whether the City's proposed condemnations are for a "public use" within the meaning of the Fifth Amendment to the Federal Constitution. Because over a century of our case law interpreting that provision dictates an affirmative answer to that question, we may not grant petitioners the relief that they seek.

JUSTICE KENNEDY, concurring.

A court applying rational-basis review under the Public Use Clause should strike down a taking that, by a clear showing, is intended to favor a particular private party, with only incidental or pretextual public benefits. * * * A court confronted with a plausible accusation of impermissible favoritism to private parties should treat the objection as a serious one and review the record to see if it has merit, though with the presumption that the government's actions were reasonable and intended to serve a public purpose. Here, the trial court [concluded that] benefiting Pfizer was not "the primary motivation or effect of this development plan [and that respondents were not] motivated by a desire to aid [other] particular private entities." * * * [W]hile there may be categories of cases in which the transfers are so suspicious, or the procedures employed so prone to abuse, or the purported benefits are so trivial or implausible, that courts should presume an impermissible private purpose, no such circumstances are present in this case.

JUSTICE O'CONNOR, with whom THE CHIEF JUSTICE, JUSTICE SCALIA, and JUSTICE THOMAS join, dissenting.

In [*Berman* and *Midkiff*], the extraordinary, precondemnation use of the targeted property inflicted affirmative harm on society—in *Berman* through blight resulting from extreme poverty and in *Midkiff* through oligopoly resulting from extreme wealth. * * * Thus a public purpose was realized when the harmful use was eliminated. Because each taking *directly* achieved a public benefit, it did not matter that the property was turned over to private use. Here, in contrast, New London does not claim that Susette Kelo's and Wilhelmina Dery's well-maintained homes are the source of any social harm.

> **Take Note**
>
> Justice O'Connor wrote the Court's opinion in *Midkiff,* finding a public use. Is her distinction here convincing? Is the social harm of inequitable distribution of wealth meaningfully different from the social harm of community economic distress?

In moving away from our decisions sanctioning the condemnation of harmful property use, the Court today significantly expands the meaning of public use. It holds that the sovereign may take private property currently put to ordinary private use, and give it over for new, ordinary private use, so long as the new use is predicted to generate some secondary benefit for the public—such as increased tax revenue, more jobs, maybe even esthetic pleasure. But nearly any lawful use of real private property can be said to generate some incidental benefit to the public. Thus, if predicted (or even guaranteed) positive side effects are enough to render transfer from one private party to another constitutional, then the words "for public use" do not realistically exclude *any* takings, and thus do not exert any constraint on the eminent domain power.

Food for Thought

Is the parade of horribles that Justice O'Connor envisions likely to come to pass? Isn't the Just Compensation Clause—which requires the government to pay for the property that it takes—specifically designed to avoid such uses of the power of eminent domain, by internalizing the costs of the taking? Or does the government not internalize the cost of taking property, even though the government pays just compensation, in a situation where the government sells the taken property to a developer and thus recoups the amount paid?

The Court [suggests] two limitations on what can be taken after today's decision. First, it maintains a role for courts in ferreting out takings whose sole purpose is to bestow a benefit on the private transferee—without detailing how courts are to conduct that complicated inquiry. * * * The trouble with economic development takings is that private benefit and incidental public benefit are, by definition, merged and mutually reinforcing. [Moreover, if] it is true that incidental public benefits from new private use are enough to ensure the "public purpose" in a taking, why should it matter, as far as the Fifth Amendment is concerned, what inspired the taking in the first place?

A second proposed limitation is implicit in the Court's opinion. The logic of today's decision is that eminent domain may only be used to upgrade—not downgrade—property. [T]his constraint has no realistic import. For who among us can say she already makes the most productive or attractive possible use of her property? The specter of condemnation hangs over all property. Nothing is to prevent the State from replacing any Motel 6 with a Ritz-Carlton, any home with a shopping mall, or any farm with a factory.

Any property may now be taken for the benefit of another private party, but the fallout from this decision will not be random. The beneficiaries are likely to be those citizens with disproportionate influence and power in the political process, including large corporations and development firms. As for the victims, the government now has license to transfer property from those with fewer resources to those with more. The Founders cannot have intended this perverse result.

JUSTICE THOMAS, dissenting.

Today's decision is simply the latest in a string of our cases construing the Public Use Clause to be a virtual nullity, without the slightest nod to its original meaning. In my view, the Public Use Clause, originally understood, is a meaningful limit on the government's eminent domain power.

If the Public Use Clause served no function other than to state that the government may take property through its eminent domain power—for public or private uses—then it would be surplusage. * * * The most natural reading of the Clause is that it allows the government to take property only if the government owns, or the public has a legal right to use, the property, as opposed to taking it for any public purpose or necessity whatsoever. At the time of the founding, dictionaries primarily defined the noun "use" as "[t]he act of employing any thing to any purpose." 2 S. Johnson, A Dictionary of the English Language 2194 (4th ed. 1773). When the government takes property and gives it to a private individual, and the public has no right to use the property, it strains language to say that the public is "employing" the property, regardless of the incidental benefits that might accrue to the public from the private use. * * * The Constitution's text, in short, suggests that the Takings Clause authorizes the taking of property only if the public has a right to employ it, not if the public realizes any conceivable benefit from the taking.

The public purpose interpretation of the Public Use Clause also unnecessarily duplicates a similar inquiry required by the Necessary and Proper Clause. The Takings Clause is a prohibition, not a grant of power: The Constitution does not expressly grant the Federal Government the power to take property for any public purpose whatsoever. Instead, the Government may take property only when necessary and proper to the exercise of an expressly enumerated power. [A] taking is permissible under the Necessary and Proper Clause only if it serves a valid public purpose. Interpreting the Public Use Clause likewise to limit the government to take property only for sufficiently public purposes [renders the Public Use Clause] surplusage.

Our current Public Use Clause jurisprudence [has] rejected this natural reading of the Clause. * * * When faced with a clash of constitutional principle and a line of unreasoned cases wholly divorced from the text, history, and structure of our founding document, we should not hesitate to resolve the tension in favor of the Constitution's original meaning.

POINTS FOR DISCUSSION

a. Defining Public Use

It is virtually always possible to find some "public" purpose to the government's seizure of private property. Accordingly, the dissenting Justices criticized the Court for effectively reading the Public Use Clause out of the Fifth Amendment. But are the tests for public use proposed in the dissents any more manageable? Consider the following hypothetical exercises of the eminent domain power: (1) The government seizes private property to build a public park. (2) The government seizes private property to build a park open to members of the public willing to pay $50 per year as a usage fee. (3) The government seizes private property to build a park open to members of the public willing to pay $1,000 per year as a usage fee. (4) The government seizes private property to build a golf course open to members of the public willing to pay $1,000 per year in membership fees and $50 per round of golf. Presumably all of the Justices would agree that the first example satisfies the public use requirement. But as the price of access to the park goes up, the extent to which the benefit of the taking is shared goes down. At what point, under the dissent's approach, would the limitation on meaningful access violate the "public use" requirement?

b. Deference to State and Local Government

The Court concluded that deference is warranted to the judgment of state and local officials about what constitutes a public use. Does it make sense to defer to the government when what is at issue is the Constitution's protection for individual property rights? Would the Court defer to a police officer's view about whether the search of a private home was "reasonable" within the meaning of the Fourth Amendment? About whether a particular form of punishment is "cruel and unusual" within the meaning of the Eighth Amendment? If not, why is the Public Use Clause different?

c. The Takings Clause and Original Meaning

Justice Thomas sought the original meaning of the Takings Clause by consulting the understanding of the text of the Fifth Amendment in the late eighteenth century. But the Supreme Court has said that the Takings Clause applies to state action only by virtue of incorporation by the Fourteenth Amendment. Shouldn't Justice Thomas have sought the meaning of the public use requirement as it was understood in 1868, when the Fourteenth Amendment was ratified? Is it possible for the clause (or any other incorporated provisions of the Bill of Rights) to have one meaning with respect to action by the federal government and a different meaning with respect to action by state and local governments?

d.   Subsequent History

In the wake of *Kelo*, several states considered and adopted restrictions on their own power of eminent domain. Does this development tend to demonstrate that the Court was wrong, or does it instead vindicate it?

Executive Summary of This Chapter

The **Contract Clause** imposes some limits on the authority of the states to interfere with contractual relationships. It does not prevent states from regulating the terms of future contracts, *Ogden v. Saunders* (1827), but under some circumstances it prohibits the states from abridging the terms of existing contracts. Whether a state law that affects the terms of existing contracts violates the Contract Clause turns on the weight of the governmental interest advanced by the regulation, *Stone v. Mississippi* (1880), the exigency of the circumstances that produced the need for the regulation, *Home Building & Loan Ass'n v. Blaisdell* (1934), and the extent of the interference with the contract, *Allied Structural Steel Company v. Spannaus* (1978).

The **Takings Clause** of the Fifth Amendment limits the power of the government to take private property. Although the Clause originally applied only to the federal government, *Barron v. Baltimore* (1833), the Court has since held that it applies to the states by virtue of incorporation by the Due Process Clause of the Fourteenth Amendment, *Chicago, Burlington & Quincy Railroad v. Chicago* (1897). When analyzing a claim under the Takings Clause, the Court must address three principal questions: First, has there been a compensable taking? Second, if so, was the taking for a "public use"? Third, if so, has the government paid the person deprived of property "just compensation"?

The Court has recognized two types of takings. The government effects a **physical taking** (or **possessory taking**) when it actually confiscates property, by taking title and possession, or authorizes a compelled physical invasion of property that is otherwise held privately. *Loretto v. Teleprompter Manhattan CATV Corp.* (1982). Short of actual confiscation, the government effects a physical taking only where it *requires* the landowner to submit to the physical occupation of his land. *Yee v. City of Escondido* (1992).

Government regulation that reduces the value of private property can, under certain narrow circumstances, also amount to a taking. This type of taking is known as a **regulatory taking**. Regulatory takings occur only when government regulation goes "too far." *Pennsylvania Coal Co. v. Mahon* (1922). In determining whether a given regulation effects a regulatory taking, the Court considers the government's interest in the regulation and the extent to which the regulation interferes with the investment-backed expectations of the person alleging the deprivation. *Penn Central Transportation Co. v. City of New York* (1978); *Andrus v. Allard* (1979). Regulations that deprive an owner of land of all economically beneficial use effect a compensable taking unless background principles of nuisance and property law prohibit the uses to which the property owner seeks to put the land. *Lucas v. South Carolina Coastal Council* (1992).

The government may take private property only for a **public use**. Under this requirement, the government may not take the property of one private party for the sole purpose of transferring it to another private party, even if it pays just compensation to the person deprived of the property. But the "public use" requirement of the Fifth Amendment is satisfied as long as the taking serves a "public purpose." In determining whether a taking serves a public purpose, the Court defers to the governmental judgment supporting the taking. *Kelo v. City of New London* (2005). Applying this standard, the Court has found the public use requirement satisfied when the government has taken property to redevelop blighted areas, *Berman v. Parker* (1954); to reduce the concentration of land ownership, *Hawaii Housing Authority v. Midkiff* (1984); and to promote economic development in a depressed area, *Kelo v. City of New London* (2005).

If there has been a compensable taking, the government is obligated to pay **just compensation** for the deprivation. Just compensation is determined by assessing the loss to the owner, measured by the market value at the time of the taking. *Kirby Forest Industries, Inc. v. United States* (1984).

PART VI

Criminal Procedure

The rights that we have considered so far in this book limit many types of government conduct. The Equal Protection Clause, for example, limits the power of public universities to consider race in deciding which students to admit, see *Grutter v. Bollinger*, 539 U.S. 306 (2003), and the Free Speech Clause limits the power of a court to award damages in a civil suit for defamation, see *New York Times Co. v. Sullivan*, 376 U.S. 254 (1964). Sometimes a party asserts one of those rights as a defense to a criminal prosecution or as a means of escaping criminal punishment. For example, in *Yick Wo v. Hopkins*, 118 U.S. 356 (1886), Lee Yick relied on the Equal Protection Clause in seeking a writ of habeas corpus after his imprisonment for operating a laundry without a permit. And in *R.A.V. v. City of St. Paul, Minn.*, 505 U.S. 377 (1992), the petitioner relied on the Free Speech Clause of the First Amendment (as incorporated by the Fourteenth Amendment) to challenge his conviction under the city's Bias-Motivated Crime Ordinance. But those rights are not limited to the criminal context.

We turn now to rights that apply (virtually exclusively) in the context of criminal investigations and prosecutions. The Fourth Amendment prohibits unreasonable searches and seizures and requires police to obtain warrants before conducting certain searches. In addition to guaranteeing due process of law, which we have previously considered and which has special application in the criminal context, the Fifth Amendment requires a grand jury indictment before prosecution, protects a privilege against self-incrimination, and prohibits double jeopardy. The Sixth Amendment guarantees a right to counsel and a jury in criminal proceedings, and ensures the right of a criminal defendant to confront his accusers. And the Eighth Amendment prohibits cruel and unusual punishments.

The rights guaranteed by these Amendments are typically considered in a separate law school class called "Criminal Procedure" because understanding their application requires some knowledge about the operation of the criminal justice system. We include a part about these rights here, however, because—as crucial provisions in the Bill of Rights—their study is very much the study of constitutional law. Indeed, the broader methodological debates in the opinions that follow—about how to interpret the Constitution, the role of judges, and the force of precedent—are the same ones that we have considered throughout this book.

The Court has held that all of the rights that we consider in this part have been incorporated by the Fourteenth Amendment, and thus apply to actions by the state governments. Other rights, including the right to a grand jury indictment, do not apply against the states because the Supreme Court has decided that the Fourteenth Amendment does not incorporate them. At a few points in this part, the incorporation debate is front and center. See, e.g., *Mapp v. Ohio*, 367 U.S. 643 (1961); *Duncan v. Louisiana*, 391 U.S. 145 (1968). But even when it is not, do not lose sight of the fact that provisions of the Bill of Rights apply against the state governments only because of the force of the Fourteenth Amendment.

> **Make the Connection**
>
> We considered the incorporation doctrine in Chapter 1.

The Fourth Amendment

The Fourth Amendment states: "The right of the people to be secure in their persons, houses, papers, and effects, against unreasonable searches and seizures, shall not be violated, and no Warrants shall issue, but upon probable cause, supported by Oath or affirmation, and particularly describing the place to be searched, and the persons or things to be seized."

The Amendment thus prohibits "unreasonable searches and seizures" and requires that all warrants authorizing searches or seizures be justified by probable cause to believe that the target of the search or seizure has engaged in unlawful activity. These provisions raise several questions. First, what constitutes a search or a seizure, thus triggering the Amendment's requirements? Second, when, if ever, can the police conduct a search or seizure without first obtaining a warrant? Third, what happens when the police obtain evidence from a search or seizure that did not comply with the requirements of the Amendment? We address these questions in the sections that follow.

A. WHAT IS A SEARCH?

By its terms, the Fourth Amendment requires a warrant only when the government conducts a "search" or a "seizure." It thus matters a great deal how we define those terms. In this section, we consider the definition of the term "search," and in the section that follows we consider the definition of the term "seizure."

In *Olmstead v. United States*, 277 U.S. 438 (1928), the Supreme Court held that government wiretapping of a suspect's telephone over a period of five months did not constitute a search within the meaning of the Fourth Amendment. In his opinion for the Court, Chief Justice Taft stated:

> The well-known historical purpose of the Fourth Amendment, directed against general warrants and writs of assistance, was to prevent the use

of governmental force to search a man's house, his person, his papers, and his effects, and to prevent their seizure against his will. * * * The amendment itself shows that the search is to be of material things—the person, the house, his papers, or his effects. * * * It is plainly within the words of the amendment to say that the unlawful rifling by a government agent of a sealed letter is a search and seizure of the sender's papers of effects. * * * The United States takes no such care of telegraph or telephone messages as of mailed sealed letters. The amendment does not forbid what was done here. There was no searching. There was no seizure. The evidence was secured by the use of the sense of hearing and that only. There was no entry of the houses or offices of the defendants.

By the invention of the telephone 50 years ago, and its application for the purpose of extending communications, one can talk with another at a far distant place. The language of the amendment cannot be extended and expanded to include telephone wires, reaching to the whole world from the defendant's house or office. The intervening wires are not part of his house or office, any more than are the highways along which they are stretched. * * * The reasonable view is that one who installs in his house a telephone instrument with connecting wires intends to project his voice to those quite outside, and that the wires beyond his house, and messages while passing over them, are not within the protection of the Fourth Amendment. Here those who intercepted the projected voices were not in the house of either party to the conversation.

Justice Brandeis dissented. He declared:

In the application of a Constitution, [our] contemplation cannot be only of what has been but of what may be. * * * When the Fourth [Amendment was] adopted, "the form that evil had theretofore taken" had been necessarily simple. [The government] could secure possession of [an individual's] papers and other articles incident to his private life— a seizure effected, if need be, by breaking and entry. Protection against such invasion of "the sanctities of a man's home and the privacies of life" was provided in the Fourth [Amendment] by specific language. But "time works changes, brings into existence new conditions and purposes." Subtler and more far-reaching means of invading privacy have become available to the government. Discovery and invention have made it possible for the government, by means far more effective than stretching upon the rack, to obtain disclosure in court of what is whispered in the closet.

The progress of science in furnishing the government with means of espionage is not likely to stop with wire tapping. Ways may some day be developed by which the government, without removing papers from secret drawers, can reproduce them in court, and by which it will be enabled to expose to a jury the most intimate occurrences of the home. Advances in the psychic and related sciences may bring means of exploring unexpressed beliefs, thoughts and emotions. * * * Can it be that the Constitution affords no protection against such invasions of individual security?

The evil incident to invasion of the privacy of the telephone is far greater than that involved in tampering with the mails. Whenever a telephone line is tapped, the privacy of the persons at both ends of the line is invaded, and all conversations between them upon any subject, and although proper, confidential, and privileged, may be overheard. Moreover, the tapping of one man's telephone line involves the tapping of the telephone of every other person whom he may call, or who may call him. * * *

The makers of our Constitution undertook to secure conditions favorable to the pursuit of happiness. They recognized the significance of man's spiritual nature, of his feelings and of his intellect. They knew that only a part of the pain, pleasure and satisfactions of life are to be found in material things. They sought to protect Americans in their beliefs, their thoughts, their emotions and their sensations. They conferred, as against the government, the right to be let alone—the most comprehensive of rights and the right most valued by civilized men. To protect that right, every unjustifiable intrusion by the government upon the privacy of the individual, whatever the means employed, must be deemed a violation of the Fourth Amendment.

In these passages, Chief Justice Taft and Justice Brandeis disagreed about at least three significant points. First, they disagreed about the nature of the telephone, which at the time was a relatively recent invention, and whether conversations conducted by telephone are properly thought of as "private." Second, they disagreed about the nature of the protection afforded by the Fourth Amendment. Chief Justice Taft thought that the Amendment protected material things, while Justice Brandeis understood it to protect "privacy" more generally. Third, they disagreed about how to interpret the Constitution and in particular how to apply its text to circumstances that the Framers could not have contemplated. Which view do you find more convincing?

The Court departed from *Olmstead* in the case that follows. Did the Court adopt Justice Brandeis's approach, or something different?

KATZ V. UNITED STATES
389 U.S. 347 (1967)

MR. JUSTICE STEWART delivered the opinion of the Court.

> **FYI**
>
> Charles Katz had a reputation of being one of the best college basketball handicappers in the country. He routinely used public telephone booths near his home to transmit his predictions to wagerers. The FBI was able overhear and record what he said in his calls by placing a covert listening device on the top of one of these telephone booths. In a motion seeking to suppress this evidence of unlawfully transmitting wagering information, Katz's attorney made a most unfortunate typographical error in writing the word "be." The motion argued that the government had to respect Katz's privacy because "a man has as much right to *bet* alone in a public telephone booth as in his own home." The U.S. District Judge hearing the case reportedly howled with laughter before denying the motion. Harvey A. Schneider, *Katz v. United States: The Untold Story*, 40 McGeorge L. Rev. 13, 13–14 (2009).

The petitioner was convicted in the District Court for the Southern District of California under an eight-count indictment charging him with transmitting wagering information by telephone from Los Angeles to Miami and Boston in violation of [18 U.S.C. § 1084]. At trial the Government was permitted, over the petitioner's objection, to introduce evidence of the petitioner's end of the telephone conversation, overheard by FBI agents who had attached an electronic listening and recording device to the outside of the public telephone booth from which he had placed his calls. In affirming his conviction, the Court of Appeals rejected the contention that the recordings had been obtained in violation of the Fourth Amendment, because "(t)here was no physical entrance into the area occupied by (the petitioner)." We granted certiorari in order to consider the constitutional questions thus presented.

The petitioner had phrased those questions as follows:

"A. Whether a public telephone booth is a constitutionally protected area so that evidence obtained by attaching an electronic listening recording device to the top of such a booth is obtained in violation of the right to privacy of the user of the booth.

"B. Whether physical penetration of a constitutionally protected area is necessary before a search and seizure can be said to be violative of the Fourth Amendment to the United States Constitution."

We decline to adopt this formulation of the issues. In the first place the correct solution of Fourth Amendment problems is not necessarily promoted by incantation of the phrase "constitutionally protected area." Secondly, the Fourth Amendment cannot be translated into a general constitutional "right to privacy." That Amendment protects individual privacy against certain kinds of governmental intrusion, but its protections go further, and often have nothing to do with privacy at all. Other provisions of the Constitution protect personal privacy from other forms of governmental invasion. But the protection of a person's general right to privacy—his right to be let alone by other people—is, like the protection of his property and of his very life, left largely to the law of the individual States.

Because of the misleading way the issues have been formulated, the parties have attached great significance to the characterization of the telephone booth from which the petitioner placed his calls. The petitioner has strenuously argued that the booth was a "constitutionally protected area." The Government has maintained with equal vigor that it was not. But this effort to decide whether or not a given "area," viewed in the abstract, is "constitutionally protected" deflects attention from the problem presented by this case. For

> **Food for Thought**
>
> The Court declares that the Fourth Amendment protects "people, not places." Is this view consistent with the language of the Amendment?

the Fourth Amendment protects people, not places. What a person knowingly exposes to the public, even in his own home or office, is not a subject of Fourth Amendment protection. See *Lewis v. United States*, 385 U.S. 206, 210 (1966); *United States v. Lee*, 274 U.S. 559, 563 (1927). But what he seeks to preserve as private, even in an area accessible to the public, may be constitutionally protected. See *Rios v. United States*, 364 U.S. 253 (1960); *Ex parte Jackson*, 96 U.S. 727, 733 (1877).

The Government stresses the fact that the telephone booth from which the petitioner made his calls was constructed partly of glass, so that he was as visible after he entered it as he would have been if he had remained outside. But what he sought to exclude when he entered the booth was not the intruding eye—it was the uninvited ear. He did not shed his right to do so simply because he made his calls from a place where he might be seen. No less than an individual in a business office, in a friend's apartment, or in a taxicab, a person in a telephone booth may rely upon the protection of the Fourth Amendment. One who occupies it, shuts the door behind him, and pays the toll that permits him to place a call is surely entitled to assume that the words he utters into the mouthpiece will not be broadcast to the world. To read the Constitution more narrowly is to ignore the vital role that the public telephone has come to play in private communication.

The Government contends, however, that the activities of its agents in this case should not be tested by Fourth Amendment requirements, for the surveillance technique they employed involved no physical penetration of the telephone booth from which the petitioner placed his calls. It is true that the absence of such penetration was at one time thought to foreclose further Fourth Amendment inquiry, *Olmstead v. United States*, 277 U.S. 438, 457, 464, 466 (1928); *Goldman v. United States*, 316 U.S. 129, 134–136 (1942), for that Amendment was thought to limit only searches and seizures of tangible property. But [we] have since departed from the narrow view on which that decision rested. Indeed, we have expressly held that the Fourth Amendment governs not only the seizure of tangible items, but extends as well to the recording of oral statements overheard without any "technical trespass under . . . local property law." *Silverman v. United States*, 365 U.S. 505, 511 (1961). Once this much is acknowledged, and once it is recognized that the Fourth Amendment protects people—and not simply "areas"—against unreasonable searches and seizures it becomes clear that the reach of that Amendment cannot turn upon the presence or absence of a physical intrusion into any given enclosure.

> **Take Note**
>
> The Court here explains why the requirements of the Fourth Amendment apply to the government's actions in the case. How does a court know when a person "justifiably relied" on an expectation of "privacy"?

We conclude that the underpinnings of *Olmstead* and *Goldman* have been so eroded by our subsequent decisions that the "trespass" doctrine there enunciated can no longer be regarded as controlling. The Government's activities in electronically listening to and recording the petitioner's words violated the privacy upon which he justifiably relied while using the telephone booth and thus constituted a "search and seizure" within the meaning of the Fourth Amendment. The fact that the electronic device employed to achieve that end did not happen to penetrate the wall of the booth can have no constitutional significance.

The question remaining for decision, then, is whether the search and seizure conducted in this case complied with constitutional standards. In that regard, the Government's position is that its agents acted in an entirely defensible manner: They did not begin their electronic surveillance until investigation of the petitioner's activities had established a strong probability that he was using the telephone in question to transmit gambling information to persons in other States, in violation of federal law. Moreover, the surveillance was limited, both in scope and in duration, to the specific purpose of establishing the contents of the petitioner's unlawful telephonic communications. The agents confined their surveillance to the brief periods during which he used the telephone booth, and they took great care to overhear only the conversations of the petitioner himself.

Accepting this account of the Government's actions as accurate, it is clear that this surveillance was so narrowly circumscribed that a duly authorized magistrate, properly notified of the need for such investigation, specifically informed of the basis on which it was to proceed, and clearly apprised of the precise intrusion it would entail, could constitutionally have authorized, with appropriate safeguards, the very limited search and seizure that the Government asserts in fact took place.

The Government * * * argues that surveillance of a telephone booth should be exempted from the usual requirement of advance authorization by a magistrate upon a showing of probable cause. We cannot agree. Omission of such authorization "bypasses the safeguards provided by an objective predetermination of probable cause, and substitutes instead the far less reliable procedure of an after-the-event justification for the . . . search, too likely to be subtly influenced by the familiar shortcomings of hindsight judgment." *Beck v. State of Ohio*, 379 U.S. 89, 96 (1964). And bypassing a neutral predetermination of the scope of a search leaves individuals secure from Fourth Amendment violations "only in the discretion of the police." *Id.*, at 97.

These considerations do not vanish when the search in question is transferred from the setting of a home, an office, or a hotel room to that of a telephone booth. Wherever a man may be, he is entitled to know that he will remain free from unreasonable searches and seizures. The government agents here ignored "the procedure of antecedent justification . . . that is central to the Fourth Amendment," *Osborn v. United States*, 385 U.S. 323, 330 (1966), a procedure that we hold to be a constitutional precondition of the kind of electronic surveillance involved in this case. Because the surveillance here failed to meet that condition, and because it led to the petitioner's conviction, the judgment must be reversed.

MR. JUSTICE HARLAN, concurring.

As the Court's opinion states, "the Fourth Amendment protects people, not places." The question, however, is what protection it affords to those people. Generally, as here, the answer to that question requires reference to a "place." My understanding of the rule that has emerged from prior decisions is that there is a twofold requirement, first that a person have exhibited an actual (subjective) expectation of privacy and, second, that the expectation be one that society is prepared to recognize as "reasonable." Thus a man's home is, for most purposes, a place where he expects privacy, but objects, activities, or statements that he exposes to the "plain view" of outsiders are not "protected" because no intention to keep them to himself has been exhibited. On the other hand, conversations in the open would not be protected against being overheard, for the expectation of privacy under the circumstances would be unreasonable.

The critical fact in this case is that "[o]ne who occupies [a telephone booth] shuts the door behind him, and pays the toll that permits him to place a call is surely entitled to assume" that his conversation is not being intercepted. The point is not that the booth is "accessible to the public" at other times, but that it is a temporarily private place whose momentary occupants' expectations of freedom from intrusion are recognized as reasonable.

[JUSTICE DOUGLAS's and JUSTICE WHITE's concurring opinions are omitted.]

MR. JUSTICE BLACK, dissenting.

* * * The first clause [of the Fourth Amendment] protects "persons, houses, papers, and effects, against unreasonable searches and seizures . . . ." These words connote the idea of tangible things with size, form, and weight, things capable of being searched, seized, or both. The second clause of the Amendment still further establishes its Framers' purpose to limit its protection to tangible things by providing that no warrants shall issue but those "particularly describing the place to be searched, and the persons or things to be seized." A conversation overheard by eavesdropping, whether by plain snooping or wiretapping, is not tangible and, under the normally accepted meanings of the words, can neither be searched nor seized. In addition the language of the second clause indicates that the Amendment refers not only to something tangible so it can be seized but to something already in existence so it can be described. Yet the Court's interpretation would have the Amendment apply to overhearing future conversations which by their very nature are nonexistent until they take place. * * *

Tapping telephone wires, of course, was an unknown possibility at the time the Fourth Amendment was adopted. But eavesdropping (and wiretapping is nothing more than eavesdropping by telephone) was * * * "an ancient practice which at common law was condemned as a nuisance." IV Blackstone, Commentaries § 168. In those days the eavesdropper listened by naked ear under the eaves of houses or their windows, or beyond their walls seeking out private discourse." *Berger v. New York*, 388 U.S. 41, 45 (1967). There can be no doubt that the Framers were aware of this practice, and if they had desired to outlaw or restrict the use of evidence obtained by eavesdropping, I believe that they would have used the appropriate language to do so in the Fourth Amendment. They certainly would not have left such a task to the ingenuity of language-stretching judges. * * *

The Fourth Amendment was aimed directly at the abhorred practice of breaking in, ransacking and searching homes and other buildings and seizing people's personal belongings without warrants issued by magistrates. The Amendment deserves, and this Court has given it, a liberal construction in order to protect against warrantless searches of buildings and seizures of tangible personal effects. But until today this Court has refused to say that eavesdropping comes within the ambit of Fourth Amendment restrictions. * * *

With this decision the Court has completed, I hope, its rewriting of the Fourth Amendment, which started only recently when the Court began referring incessantly to the Fourth Amendment not so much as a law against unreasonable searches and seizures as one to protect an individual's privacy. * * * The Fourth Amendment protects privacy only to the extent that it prohibits unreasonable searches and seizures of "persons, houses, papers, and effects." No general right is created by the Amendment so as to give this Court the unlimited power to hold unconstitutional everything which affects privacy. Certainly the Framers, well acquainted as they were with the excesses of governmental power, did not intend to grant this Court such omnipotent lawmaking authority as that. The history of governments proves that it is dangerous to freedom to repose such powers in courts.

> **Make the Connection**
>
> Recall that Justice Black dissented in *Griswold v. Connecticut*, which relied in part on the Fourth Amendment in identifying a "zone of privacy" protected by the Constitution. We considered *Griswold* in Chapter 2.

For these reasons I respectfully dissent.

POINTS FOR DISCUSSION

a.   Persons or Places?

Is the Fourth Amendment properly read to protect persons from interference with their privacy, or instead to protect places and things from unreasonable searches? The text of the Amendment could plausibly be read to support the latter view; after all, it specifically guarantees the right of *persons* "to be secure in their persons, *houses, papers, and effects.*" In addition, cases decided before *Katz* had held that "searches and seizures inside a home without a warrant are presumptively unreasonable," *Brigham City v. Stuart*, 547 U.S. 398, 403 (2006), whereas searches of "open fields" do not require a warrant, even when the land belongs to the suspect, *Hester v. United States*, 265 U.S. 57 (1924). Do those cases suggest that the Fourth Amendment protects places rather than people? Or is the Court's point in *Katz* that it is impossible to separate the place from the person in determining the scope of the Fourth Amendment's protection?

b.   The Fourth Amendment in 1791 and Today

Justice Black advocated an originalist reading of the Fourth Amendment. He acknowledged that wiretapping (not to mention telephones) did not exist in 1791, when the states ratified the Fourth Amendment. How does an originalist apply the text of the Constitution—and the Fourth Amendment in particular—to technology that did not exist or to circumstances that could not have arisen in 1791? What would guide or constrain a non-originalist in deciding questions such as this? Consider the hypothetical below and the case that follows.

Problem

Indoor marijuana cultivation, which violates the Controlled Substances Act, typically requires high-intensity lamps. A police officer suspected that the residents of a home were growing marijuana indoors. In order to determine whether an amount of heat was emanating from a suspect's home consistent with the use of such lamps, the officer used a thermal imager to scan the home from outside. Thermal imagers detect infrared radiation, which virtually all objects emit but which is not visible to the naked eye. The imager converts radiation into images based on relative warmth, with different colors representing different temperatures. Thermal imagining does not show people or activity within the walls of the structure, and the device cannot reveal conversations or human activities.

The officer used the thermal imager to conduct a scan of the suspect's home at 3:00 a.m. from the passenger seat of his car across the street from the front of the house and also from the street behind the house; the entire scan took only a few minutes. The scan showed that the roof over the garage and a side wall of petitioner's home were relatively hot compared to the rest of the home and substantially warmer than neighboring homes. Based in large part on this information, the officer obtained a warrant authorizing a search of the suspect's home, where officers found more than 100 marijuana plants being cultivated under lamps. After he was indicted, the suspect moved to suppress the evidence seized from his home on the ground that it derived from an unlawful search.

Should the court conclude that the use of a thermal-imaging device aimed at a private home from a public street to detect relative amounts of heat within the home constitutes a "search" within the meaning of the Fourth Amendment (and thus presumptively requires a warrant)? (These facts are based on *Kyllo v. United States*, 533 U.S. 27 (2001), which held that such use of a thermal-imaging device was a search and thus was subject to the warrant requirement.) Can you explain why the officer's actions constitute a search under the *Katz* test?

UNITED STATES V. JONES
565 U.S. 400 (2012)

JUSTICE SCALIA delivered the opinion of the Court.

We decide whether the attachment of a Global-Positioning-System (GPS) tracking device to an individual's vehicle, and subsequent use of that device to monitor the vehicle's movements on public streets, constitutes a search or seizure within the meaning of the Fourth Amendment.

In 2004 respondent Antoine Jones, owner and operator of a nightclub in the District of Columbia, came under suspicion of trafficking in narcotics and was made the target of an investigation by a joint FBI and Metropolitan Police Department task force. Officers employed various investigative techniques, including visual surveillance of the nightclub, installation of a camera focused on the front door of the club, and a pen register and wiretap covering Jones's cellular phone.

Based in part on information gathered from these sources, in 2005 the Government applied to the United States District Court for the District of Columbia for a warrant authorizing the use of an electronic tracking device on the Jeep Grand Cherokee registered to Jones's wife. A warrant issued, authorizing installation of the device in the District of Columbia and within 10 days. On the 11th day, and not in the District of Columbia but in Maryland, agents installed a GPS tracking device on the undercarriage of the Jeep while it was parked in a public parking lot. Over the next 28 days, the Government used the device to track the vehicle's movements, and once had to replace the device's battery when the vehicle was parked in a different public lot in Maryland. By means of signals from multiple satellites, the device established the vehicle's location within 50 to 100 feet, and

> **Take Note**
>
> Even though a magistrate had issued a warrant to authorize the use of the tracking device, the officers exceeded the terms of the warrant in installing the device. Accordingly, it is as if the use of the device had not been authorized by a warrant at all.

communicated that location by cellular phone to a Government computer. It relayed more than 2,000 pages of data over the 4-week period.

[Relying in part on evidence obtained through the GPS device, which connected Jones to a house that contained $850,000 in cash, 97 kilograms of cocaine, and 1 kilogram of cocaine base, a jury convicted Jones of conspiracy to distribute and possess with intent to distribute cocaine base in violation of 21 U.S.C. §§ 841 and 846. The district court sentenced Jones to life imprisonment, but the court of appeals reversed, holding that the admission of the evidence obtained by warrantless use of the GPS device violated the Fourth Amendment.]

The Fourth Amendment provides in relevant part that "[t]he right of the people to be secure in their persons, houses, papers, and effects, against unreasonable searches and seizures, shall not be violated." It is beyond dispute that a vehicle is an "effect" as that term is used in the Amendment. *United States v. Chadwick*, 433 U.S. 1, 12 (1977). We hold that the Government's installation of a GPS device on a target's vehicle, and its use of that device to monitor the vehicle's movements, constitutes a "search."

It is important to be clear about what occurred in this case: The Government physically occupied private property for the purpose of obtaining information. We have no doubt that such a physical intrusion would have been considered a "search" within the meaning of the Fourth Amendment when it was adopted. * * * The text of the Fourth Amendment reflects its close connection to property, since otherwise it would have referred simply to "the right of the people to be secure against unreasonable searches and seizures"; the phrase "in their persons, houses, papers, and effects" would have been superfluous.

Consistent with this understanding, our Fourth Amendment jurisprudence was tied to common-law trespass, at least until the latter half of the 20th century. Thus, in *Olmstead v. United States*, 277 U.S. 438, 464 (1928), we held that wiretaps attached to telephone wires on the public streets did not constitute a Fourth Amendment search because "[t]here was no entry of the houses or offices of the defendants."

Our later cases, of course, have deviated from that exclusively property-based approach. In *Katz v. United States,* 389 U.S. 347, 351 (1967), we said that "the Fourth Amendment protects people, not places," and found a violation in attachment of an eavesdropping device to a public telephone booth. Our later cases have applied the analysis of Justice Harlan's concurrence in that case, which said that a violation occurs when government officers violate a person's "reasonable expectation of privacy," *id.,* at 360.

> **Take Note**
>
> In the years after the *Katz* decision, the Court tended to rely primarily on the understanding that Justice Harlan announced in his concurrence, rather than the approach that Justice Stewart announced for the Court. In what ways was Justice Harlan's approach different from the Court's in *Katz*?

The Government contends that the Harlan standard shows that no search occurred here, since Jones had no "reasonable expectation of privacy" in the area of the Jeep accessed by Government agents (its underbody) and in the locations of the Jeep on the public roads, which were visible to all. But we need not address the Government's contentions, because Jones's Fourth Amendment rights do not rise or fall with the *Katz* formulation. At bottom, we must "assur[e] preservation of that degree of privacy against government that existed when the Fourth Amendment was adopted." *Kyllo v. United States,* 533 U.S. 27, 34 (2001). [F]or most of our history the Fourth Amendment was understood to embody a particular concern for government trespass upon the areas ("persons, houses, papers, and effects") it enumerates.[3] *Katz* did not repudiate that understanding. Less than two years later the Court upheld defendants' contention that the Government could not introduce against them conversations between *other* people obtained by warrantless placement of electronic surveillance devices in their homes. The opinion rejected the dissent's contention that there was no Fourth Amendment violation "unless the conversational privacy of the homeowner himself is invaded." *Alderman v. United States,* 394 U.S. 165, 176 (1969). "[W]e [do not] believe that *Katz,* by holding that the Fourth Amendment protects persons and their private conversations, was intended to withdraw any of the protection which the

---

[3] Justice ALITO's concurrence (hereinafter concurrence) doubts the wisdom of our approach because "it is almost impossible to think of late-18th-century situations that are analogous to what took place in this case." But in fact it posits a situation that is not far afield—a constable's concealing himself in the target's coach in order to track its movements. There is no doubt that the information gained by that trespassory activity would be the product of an unlawful search—whether that information consisted of the conversations occurring in the coach, or of the destinations to which the coach traveled. In any case, it is quite irrelevant whether there was an 18th-century analog. Whatever new methods of investigation may be devised, our task, *at a minimum,* is to decide whether the action in question would have constituted a "search" within the original meaning of the Fourth Amendment. Where, as here, the Government obtains information by physically intruding on a constitutionally protected area, such a search has undoubtedly occurred.

Amendment extends to the home. . . ." *Id.*, at 180. * * * *Katz* did not narrow the Fourth Amendment's scope.[5]

The Government contends that several of our post-*Katz* cases foreclose the conclusion that what occurred here constituted a search. It relies principally on two cases in which we rejected Fourth Amendment challenges to "beepers," electronic tracking devices that represent another form of electronic monitoring. The first case, *United States v. Knotts*, 460 U.S. 276, 278 (1983), upheld against Fourth Amendment challenge the use of a "beeper" that had been placed in a container of chloroform, allowing law enforcement to monitor the location of the container. We said that there had been no infringement of Knotts' reasonable expectation of privacy since the information obtained—the location of the automobile carrying the container on public roads, and the location of the off-loaded container in open fields near Knotts' cabin—had been voluntarily conveyed to the public. *Id.*, at 281–282. But as we have discussed, the *Katz* reasonable-expectation-of-privacy test has been *added to*, not *substituted for*, the common-law trespassory test. The holding in *Knotts* addressed only the former, since the latter was not at issue. The beeper had been placed in the container before it came into Knotts' possession, with the consent of the then-owner. Knotts did not challenge that installation, and we specifically declined to consider its effect on the Fourth Amendment analysis. *Id.*, at 279, n. * *. * * *

The second "beeper" case, *United States v. Karo*, 468 U.S. 705 (1984), * * * addressed the question left open by *Knotts*, whether the installation of a beeper in a container amounted to a search or seizure. As in *Knotts*, at the time the beeper was installed the container belonged to a third party, and it did not come into possession of the defendant until later. Thus, the specific question we considered was whether the installation "*with the consent of the original owner* constitute[d] a search or seizure . . . when the container is delivered to a buyer having no

> **Food for Thought**
>
> Can you articulate the differences that the Court sees between the "beeper" cases and this one? Are you convinced that they are meaningfully different?

---

[5]   The concurrence notes that post-*Katz* we have explained that "an actual trespass is neither necessary *nor sufficient* to establish a constitutional violation." *Post* (quoting *United States v. Karo*, 468 U.S. 705, 713 (1984)). That is undoubtedly true, and undoubtedly irrelevant. *Karo* was considering whether a seizure occurred, and as the concurrence explains, a seizure of property occurs, not when there is a trespass, but "when there is some meaningful interference with an individual's possessory interests in that property." Likewise with a search. Trespass alone does not qualify, but there must be conjoined with that what was present here: an attempt to find something or to obtain information. Related to this, and similarly irrelevant, is the concurrence's point that, if analyzed separately, neither the installation of the device nor its use would constitute a Fourth Amendment search. Of course not. A trespass on "houses" or "effects," or a *Katz* invasion of privacy, is not alone a search unless it is done to obtain information; and the obtaining of information is not alone a search unless it is achieved by such a trespass or invasion of privacy.

knowledge of the presence of the beeper." *Id.,* at 707 (emphasis added). We held not. The Government, we said, came into physical contact with the container only before it belonged to the defendant Karo; and the transfer of the container with the unmonitored beeper inside did not convey any information and thus did not invade Karo's privacy. * * * Jones, who possessed the Jeep at the time the Government trespassorily inserted the information-gathering device, is on much different footing.

The concurrence begins by accusing us of applying "18th-century tort law." That is a distortion. What we apply is an 18th-century guarantee against unreasonable searches, which we believe must provide *at a minimum* the degree of protection it afforded when it was adopted. The concurrence does not share that belief. It would apply *exclusively Katz*'s reasonable-expectation-of-privacy test, even when that eliminates rights that previously existed.

The concurrence faults our approach for "present[ing] particularly vexing problems" in cases that do not involve physical contact, such as those that involve the transmission of electronic signals. We entirely fail to understand that point. For unlike the concurrence, which would make *Katz* the *exclusive* test, we do not make trespass the exclusive test. Situations involving merely the transmission of electronic signals without trespass would *remain* subject to *Katz* analysis.

In fact, it is the concurrence's insistence on the exclusivity of the *Katz* test that needlessly leads us into "particularly vexing problems" in the present case. * * * The concurrence posits that "relatively short-term monitoring of a person's movements on public streets" is okay, but that "the use of longer term GPS monitoring in investigations *of most offenses*" is no good. [But there] is no precedent for the proposition that whether a search has occurred depends on the nature of the crime being investigated. And even accepting that novelty, it remains unexplained why a 4-week investigation is "surely" too long and why a drug-trafficking conspiracy involving substantial amounts of cash and narcotics is not an "extraordinary offens[e]" which may permit longer observation. What of a 2-day monitoring of a suspected purveyor of stolen electronics? Or of a 6-month monitoring of a suspected terrorist? We may have to grapple with these "vexing problems" in some future case where a classic trespassory search is not involved and resort must be had to *Katz* analysis; but there is no reason for rushing forward to resolve them here.

The judgment of the Court of Appeals for the D.C. Circuit is affirmed.

JUSTICE SOTOMAYOR, concurring.

I join the Court's opinion because I agree that a search within the meaning of the Fourth Amendment occurs, at a minimum, "[w]here, as here, the Government obtains information by physically intruding on a constitutionally protected area." * * * [T]he trespassory test applied in the majority's opinion reflects an irreducible constitutional minimum: When the Government physically invades personal property to gather information, a search occurs. The reaffirmation of that principle suffices to decide this case.

Nonetheless, as Justice ALITO notes, physical intrusion is now unnecessary to many forms of surveillance. * * * In cases of electronic or other novel modes of surveillance that do not depend upon a physical invasion on property, the majority opinion's trespassory test may provide little guidance. * * * I agree with Justice ALITO that, at the very least, "longer term GPS monitoring in investigations of most offenses impinges on expectations of privacy."

In cases involving even short-term monitoring, some unique attributes of GPS surveillance relevant to the *Katz* analysis will require particular attention. GPS monitoring generates a precise, comprehensive record of a person's public movements that reflects a wealth of detail about her familial, political, professional, religious, and sexual associations. The Government can store such records and efficiently mine them for information years into the future. And because GPS monitoring is cheap in comparison to conventional surveillance techniques and, by design, proceeds surreptitiously, it evades the ordinary checks that constrain abusive law enforcement practices: "limited police resources and community hostility." *Illinois v. Lidster,* 540 U.S. 419, 426 (2004).

I would take these attributes of GPS monitoring into account when considering the existence of a reasonable societal expectation of privacy in the sum of one's public movements. * * * More fundamentally, it may be necessary to reconsider the premise that an individual has no reasonable expectation of privacy in information voluntarily disclosed to third parties. * * * Resolution of these difficult questions in this case is unnecessary, however, because the Government's physical intrusion on Jones' Jeep supplies a narrower basis for decision. I therefore join the majority's opinion.

JUSTICE ALITO, with whom JUSTICE GINSBURG, JUSTICE BREYER, and JUSTICE KAGAN join, concurring in the judgment.

This case requires us to apply the Fourth Amendment's prohibition of unreasonable searches and seizures to a 21st-century surveillance technique, the use of a Global Positioning System (GPS) device to monitor a vehicle's movements for an extended period of time. Ironically, the Court has chosen to decide this case based on 18th-century tort law. [This approach] strains the language of the Fourth Amendment; it has little if any support in current Fourth Amendment case law; and it is highly artificial. I would analyze the question presented in this case by asking whether respondent's reasonable expectations of privacy were violated by the long-term monitoring of the movements of the vehicle he drove.

The Fourth Amendment prohibits "unreasonable searches and seizures," and the Court makes very little effort to explain how the attachment or use of the GPS device fits within these terms. * * * The Court [claims] that the installation and use of the GPS constituted a search, but this conclusion is dependent on the questionable proposition that these two procedures cannot be separated for purposes of Fourth Amendment analysis. If these two procedures are analyzed separately, it is not at all clear from the Court's opinion why either should be regarded as a search. It is clear that the attachment of the GPS device was not itself a search; if the device had not functioned or if the officers had not used it, no information would have been obtained. And the Court does not contend that the use of the device constituted a search either. On the contrary, the Court accepts the holding in *United States v. Knotts,* 460 U.S. 276 (1983), that the use of a surreptitiously planted electronic device to monitor a vehicle's movements on public roads did not amount to a search.

The Court argues—and I agree—that "we must 'assur[e] preservation of that degree of privacy against government that existed when the Fourth Amendment was adopted.' " But it is almost impossible to think of late-18th-century situations that are analogous to what took place in this case. (Is it possible to imagine a case in which a constable secreted himself somewhere in a coach and remained there for a period of time in order to monitor the movements of the coach's owner?[3]) The Court's theory seems to be that the concept of a search, as originally understood, comprehended any technical trespass that led to the gathering of

> **Food for Thought**
>
> Is the constable hypothetical really so improbable? Charles Dickens tells the tale of a late 18th-century stowaway who traveled undetected—at least for a time—underneath a coach in a *Tale of Two Cities* bk. 2, ch. 8 (1859).

evidence, but we know that this is incorrect. At common law, any unauthorized intrusion on private property was actionable, but a trespass on open fields, as opposed to the "curtilage" of a home, does not fall within the scope of the Fourth Amendment because private property outside the curtilage is not part of a

---

[3]   The Court suggests that something like this might have occurred in 1791, but this would have required either a gigantic coach, a very tiny constable, or both—not to mention a constable with incredible fortitude and patience.

"hous[e]" within the meaning of the Fourth Amendment. See *Oliver v. United States*, 466 U.S. 170 (1984); *Hester v. United States*, 265 U.S. 57 (1924).

The Court's reasoning in this case is very similar to that in the Court's early decisions involving wiretapping and electronic eavesdropping, namely, that a technical trespass followed by the gathering of evidence constitutes a search. [See *Silverman v. United States*, 365 U.S. 505, 509 (1961).] By contrast, in cases in which there was no trespass, it was held that there was no search. Thus, in *Olmstead v. United States*, 277 U.S. 438 (1928), the Court found that the Fourth Amendment did not apply because "[t]he taps from house lines were made in the streets near the houses." *Id.*, at 457.

This trespass-based rule was repeatedly criticized. In *Olmstead*, Justice Brandeis wrote that it was "immaterial where the physical connection with the telephone wires was made." 277 U.S., at 479 (dissenting opinion). Although a private conversation transmitted by wire did not fall within the literal words of the Fourth Amendment, he argued, the Amendment should be understood as prohibiting "every unjustifiable intrusion by the government upon the privacy of the individual." *Id.*, at 478. See also, *e.g.*, *Silverman*, *supra*, at 513 (Douglas, J., concurring); *Goldman*, *supra*, at 139 (Murphy, J., dissenting).

Katz v. United States, 389 U.S. 347 (1967), finally did away with the old approach, holding that a trespass was not required for a Fourth Amendment violation. * * * What mattered, the Court now held, was whether the conduct at issue "violated the privacy upon which [the defendant] justifiably relied while using the telephone booth." *Katz*, *supra*, at 353. Under this approach, as the Court later put it when addressing the relevance of a technical trespass, "an actual trespass is neither necessary *nor sufficient* to establish a constitutional violation." *United States v. Karo*, 468 U.S. 705, 713 (1984) (emphasis added).

> **Take Note**
> The debate between Justice Scalia and Justice Alito is in part over what *Katz* held. Did the Court in *Katz* conclude that the existence of trespass was never relevant to determining whether there has been a search? Or did it conclude that sometimes there can be a search even absent trespass?

Disharmony with a substantial body of existing case law is only one of the problems with the Court's approach in this case. I will briefly note four others. First, the Court's reasoning largely disregards what is really important (the *use* of a GPS for the purpose of long-term tracking) and instead attaches great significance to something that most would view as relatively minor (attaching to the bottom of a car a small, light object that does not interfere in any way with the car's operation). Attaching such an object is generally regarded as so trivial that it does not provide a basis for recovery under modern tort law. See Prosser & Keeton § 14, at 87 (harmless or trivial contact with personal property not actionable). But under the Court's reasoning, this conduct may violate the Fourth Amendment. By contrast, if long-term monitoring can be accomplished without committing a technical trespass—suppose, for example, that the Federal Government required or persuaded auto manufacturers to include a GPS tracking device in every car—the Court's theory would provide no protection.

Second, the Court's approach leads to incongruous results. If the police attach a GPS device to a car and use the device to follow the car for even a brief time, under the Court's theory, the Fourth Amendment applies. But if the police follow the same car for a much longer period using unmarked cars and aerial assistance, this tracking is not subject to any Fourth Amendment constraints.

Third, under the Court's theory, the coverage of the Fourth Amendment may vary from State to State. If the events at issue here had occurred in a community property State or a State that has adopted the Uniform Marital Property Act, respondent would likely be an owner of the vehicle, and it would not matter whether the GPS was installed before or after his wife turned over the keys. In non-community-property States, on the other hand, the registration of the vehicle in the name of respondent's wife would generally be regarded as presumptive evidence that she was the sole owner. See 60 C.J.S., Motor Vehicles § 231, pp. 398–399 (2002).

Fourth, the Court's reliance on the law of trespass will present particularly vexing problems in cases involving surveillance that is carried out by making electronic, as opposed to physical, contact with the item to be tracked. For example, suppose that the officers in the present case had followed respondent by surreptitiously activating a stolen vehicle detection system that came with the car when it was purchased. Would the sending of a radio signal to activate this system constitute a trespass to chattels? Trespass to chattels has traditionally required a physical touching of the property. See Restatement (Second) of Torts § 217 and Comment *e* (1963 and 1964).

> **Take Note**
>
> Do you see why the *Katz* test, which asks whether the searched person had a "reasonable expectation of privacy," involves a "degree of circularity"? If the police have routinely been using GPS devices to track the movements of suspects, for example, can any suspect be said to have a reasonable expectation of privacy in his movements in his car?

The *Katz* expectation-of-privacy test avoids the problems and complications noted above, but it is not without its own difficulties. It involves a degree of circularity, and judges are apt to confuse their own expectations of privacy with those of the hypothetical reasonable person to which the *Katz* test looks. In addition, the *Katz* test rests on the assumption that this hypothetical reasonable person has a well-developed and stable set of privacy expectations. But technology can change those expectations.

In the pre-computer age, the greatest protections of privacy were neither constitutional nor statutory, but practical. Traditional surveillance for any extended period of time was difficult and costly and therefore rarely undertaken. The surveillance at issue in this case—constant monitoring of the location of a vehicle for four weeks—would have required a large team of agents, multiple vehicles, and perhaps aerial assistance. Only an investigation of unusual importance could have justified such an expenditure of law enforcement resources. Devices like the one used in the present case, however, make long-term monitoring relatively easy and cheap. In circumstances involving dramatic technological change, the best solution to privacy concerns may be legislative. A legislative body is well situated to gauge changing public attitudes, to draw detailed lines, and to balance privacy and public safety in a comprehensive way.

To date, however, Congress and most States have not enacted statutes regulating the use of GPS tracking technology for law enforcement purposes. The best that we can do in this case is to apply existing Fourth Amendment doctrine and to ask whether the use of GPS tracking in a particular case involved a degree of intrusion that a reasonable person would not have anticipated.

Under this approach, relatively short-term monitoring of a person's movements on public streets accords with expectations of privacy that our society has recognized as reasonable. See *Knotts*, 460 U.S., at 281–282. But the use of longer term GPS monitoring in investigations of most offenses impinges on expectations of privacy. For such offenses, society's expectation has been that law enforcement agents and others would not—and indeed, in the main, simply could not—secretly monitor and catalogue every single movement of an individual's car for a very long period. In this case, for four weeks, law enforcement agents tracked every movement that respondent made in the vehicle he was driving. We need not identify with precision the point at which the tracking of this vehicle became a search, for the line was surely crossed before the 4-week mark. Other cases may present more difficult questions. But where uncertainty exists with respect to whether a certain period of GPS surveil lance is long enough to constitute a Fourth Amendment search, the police may always seek a warrant. We also need not consider whether prolonged GPS monitoring in the context of investigations involving extraordinary offenses would similarly intrude on a constitutionally protected sphere of privacy. In such cases, long-term tracking might have been mounted using previously available techniques.

For these reasons, I conclude that the lengthy monitoring that occurred in this case constituted a search under the Fourth Amendment. I therefore agree with the majority that the decision of the Court of Appeals must be affirmed.

POINTS FOR DISCUSSION

a. People or Places?

The Court in *Katz* declared that "the Fourth Amendment protects people, not places," and that the " 'trespass' doctrine [enunciated in *Olmstead*] can no longer be regarded as controlling." The Court in *Katz* focused instead on whether the government's actions "violated the privacy upon which [the target of the action] justifiably relied"—or, as Justice Harlan put it, on whether the person "exhibited an actual (subjective) expectation of privacy" that "society is prepared to recognize as 'reasonable.' "

The concurring Justices in *Jones* followed this approach, concluding that "longer term GPS monitoring in investigations of most offenses impinges on expectations of privacy" and thus constitutes a search. Was Justice Scalia's approach for the Court different from this approach? He seemed to declare that the Fourth Amendment protects places, as long as those places were traditionally subject to such protection. On this view, anything that would traditionally have been considered a search is still considered a search today, regardless of reasonable expectations of privacy; but the *Katz* test can convert government action that was not traditionally a search (or that couldn't have occurred at all in the past) into a search today, if it interferes with reasonable expectations of privacy. Which approach affords greater protection for privacy?

b. Standards and Bright Line Rules

Under Justice Alito's (and the *Katz*) approach, judges must determine whether the government has interfered with reasonable expectations of privacy in order to determine whether the government's action constituted a search. Under Justice

Scalia's approach, in contrast, judges do not need to apply that test if the government's action would historically have been understood to constitute a search. Justice Alito's approach thus applies a "standard"—turning on reasonableness—in all cases, whereas Justice Scalia's approach at least sometimes applies a "rule"—turning on historical treatment. Is there an argument that bright-line rules are particularly desirable in this context? Or does the tremendous range of factual circumstances in this context suggest that having only a standard makes more sense?

B. WHAT IS A SEIZURE?

Searches often turn up evidence of wrongdoing, and officers are permitted to seize such evidence so long as the seizure satisfies the demands of the Fourth Amendment. Seizures of property, like the searches that lead to its discovery, can be authorized by warrant or justified by probable cause.

The arrest of a person—such as the arrest of a criminal suspect by the police—is also "seizure" within the meaning of the Fourth Amendment. The police may obtain a warrant to arrest a person if they can show probable cause to believe that the person has committed an offense. But an arrest warrant is not always necessary. The Court has made clear that the "usual rule is that a police officer may arrest without warrant one believed by the officer upon reasonable cause to have been guilty of a felony * * *." *Carroll v. United States*, 267 U.S. 132, 156 (1925). This rule reflects the "ancient common-law rule that a peace officer was permitted to arrest without a warrant for a misdemeanor or felony committed in his presence as well as for a felony not committed in his presence if there was reasonable ground for making the arrest." *United States v. Watson*, 423 U.S. 411 (1976). Although "[l]aw enforcement officers may find it wise to seek arrest warrants where practicable to do so, and their judgments about probable cause may be more readily accepted where backed by a warrant issued by a magistrate," the Court has declined "to transform this judicial preference into a constitutional rule when the judgment of the Nation and Congress has for so long been to authorize warrantless public arrests on probable cause rather than to encumber criminal prosecutions with endless litigation with respect to the existence of exigent circumstances, whether it was practicable to get a warrant, whether the suspect was about to flee, and the like." *Id.*

Are there actions short of actually arresting a suspect that constitute a seizure and therefore trigger the requirements of the Fourth Amendment? Consider the case that follows.

TERRY V. OHIO

392 U.S. 1 (1968)

MR. CHIEF JUSTICE WARREN delivered the opinion of the Court.

[While Police Detective Martin McFadden was] patrolling in plain clothes in downtown Cleveland at approximately 2:30 in the afternoon of October 31, 1963, his attention was attracted by two men, Chilton and Terry, standing on [a street corner]. He had never seen the two men before, and he was unable to say precisely what first drew his eye to them. However, he testified that he had been a policeman for 39 years and a detective for 35 and that he had been assigned to patrol this vicinity of downtown Cleveland for shoplifters and pickpockets for 30 years.

His interest aroused, Officer McFadden took up a post of observation in the entrance to a store 300 to 400 feet away from the two men. * * * He saw one of the men leave the other one and walk [past] some stores. The man paused for a moment and looked in a store window, then walked on a short distance, turned around and walked back toward the corner, pausing once again to look in the same store window. He rejoined his companion at the corner, and the two conferred briefly. Then the second man went through the same series of motions * * *. The two men repeated this ritual alternately between five and six times apiece—in all, roughly a dozen trips. At one point, while the two were standing together on the corner, a third man approached them and engaged them briefly in conversation. This man then left the two others [and] Chilton and Terry resumed their measured pacing, peering and conferring. After this had gone on for 10 to 12 minutes, the two men walked off together, [following] the path taken earlier by the third man.

By this time Officer McFadden had become thoroughly suspicious. He testified that [he] suspected the two men of "casing a job, a stick-up," [and] that he feared "they may have a gun." [After he observed them stop to talk to the same man who had conferred with them earlier on the street corner,] Officer McFadden approached the three men, identified himself as a police officer and asked for their names. * * * When the men "mumbled something" in response to his inquiries, Officer McFadden grabbed petitioner Terry, spun him around * * *, and patted down the outside of his clothing. In the left breast pocket of Terry's overcoat Officer McFadden felt a pistol. [He removed a .38-caliber revolver from the pocket and ordered all three men to face the wall with their hands raised.] Officer McFadden proceeded to pat down the outer clothing of Chilton and the third man, Katz. He discovered another revolver in the outer pocket of Chilton's overcoat, but no weapons were found on Katz. The officer testified that he only patted the men down to see whether they had weapons, and that he did not put his hands beneath the outer garments of either Terry or Chilton until he felt their guns. * * * Chilton and Terry were formally charged with carrying concealed weapons. [Chilton died before the Supreme Court's review.]

The question is whether in all the circumstances of this on-the-street encounter, [Terry's] right to personal security was violated by an unreasonable search and seizure. * * * The State has characterized the issue here as "the right of a police officer . . . to make an on-the-street stop, interrogate and pat down for weapons (known in street vernacular as 'stop and frisk')." But this is only partly accurate. For the issue is not the abstract propriety of the police conduct, but the admissibility against petitioner of the evidence uncovered by the search and seizure.

> **Take Note**
>
> We will consider the "exclusionary rule," which prohibits the introduction at trial of evidence seized in violation of the Fourth Amendment, later in this chapter.

The exclusionary rule has its limitations, however, as a tool of judicial control. * * * Street encounters between citizens and police officers are incredibly rich in diversity. They range from wholly friendly exchanges of pleasantries or mutually useful information to hostile confrontations of armed men involving arrests, or injuries, or loss of life. Moreover, hostile confrontations are not all of a piece. Some of them begin in a friendly enough manner, only to take a different turn upon the injection of some unexpected element into the conversation. Encounters are initiated by the police for a wide variety of purposes, some of which are wholly unrelated to a desire to prosecute for crime. * * * Regardless of how effective the [exclusionary] rule may be where obtaining convictions is an important objective of the police, it is powerless to deter invasions of constitutionally guaranteed rights where the police either have no interest in prosecuting or are willing to forgo successful prosecution in the interest of serving some other goal.

Proper adjudication of cases in which the exclusionary rule is invoked demands a constant awareness of these limitations. The wholesale harassment by certain elements of the police community, of which minority groups, particularly Negroes, frequently complain, will not be stopped by the exclusion of any evidence from any criminal trial. Yet a rigid and unthinking application of the exclusionary rule, in futile protest against practices which it can never be used effectively to control, may exact a high toll in human injury and frustration of efforts to prevent crime.

[We now] turn our attention to the quite narrow question posed by the facts before us: whether it is always unreasonable for a policeman to seize a person and subject him to a limited search for weapons unless there is probable cause for an arrest. * * * There is some suggestion in the use of such terms as "stop" and "frisk" that such police conduct is outside the purview of the Fourth Amendment because neither action rises to the level of a "search" or "seizure" within the meaning of the Constitution. We emphatically reject this notion. It is quite plain that the Fourth Amendment governs "seizures" of the person which do not eventuate in a trip to the station house and prosecution for crime—"arrests" in traditional terminology. It must be recognized that whenever a police officer accosts an individual and restrains his freedom to walk away, he has "seized" that person. And it is nothing less than sheer torture of the English language to suggest that a careful exploration of the outer surfaces of a person's clothing all over his or her body in an attempt to find weapons is not a "search." Moreover, it is simply fantastic to urge that such a procedure performed in public by a policeman while the citizen stands helpless, perhaps facing a wall with his hands raised, is a "petty indignity." It is a serious intrusion upon the sanctity of the person, which may inflict great indignity and arouse strong resentment, and it is not to be undertaken lightly. * * * We therefore reject the notions that the Fourth Amendment does not come into play at all as a limitation upon police conduct if the officers stop short of something called a "technical arrest" or a "full-blown search."

In this case there can be no question, then, that Officer McFadden "seized" petitioner and subjected him to a "search" when he took hold of him and patted down the outer surfaces of his clothing. * * * If this case involved police conduct subject to the Warrant Clause of the Fourth Amendment, we would have to ascertain whether "probable cause" existed to justify the search and seizure which took place. However, that is not the case. We do not retreat from our holdings that the police must, whenever practicable, obtain advance judicial approval of searches and seizures through the warrant procedure, or that in most instances failure to comply with the warrant requirement can only be excused by exigent circumstances. But we deal here with an entire rubric of police conduct—necessarily swift action predicated upon the on-the-spot observations of the officer on the beat—which historically has not

> **Take Note**
>
> In the paragraphs that follow, the Court explains why a warrantless "stop and frisk" can be consistent with the Fourth Amendment. Does the Court properly weigh the government and private interests?

been, and as a practical matter could not be, subjected to the warrant procedure. Instead, the conduct involved in this case must be tested by the Fourth Amendment's general proscription against unreasonable searches and seizures.

[In] order to assess the reasonableness of Officer McFadden's conduct as a general proposition, it is necessary "first to focus upon the governmental interest which allegedly justifies official intrusion upon the constitutionally protected interests of the private citizen," for there is "no ready test for determining reasonableness other than by balancing the need to search (or seize) against the invasion which the search (or seizure) entails." *Camara v. Municipal Court*, 387 U.S. 523, 534–535, 536–537 (1967). And in justifying the particular intrusion the police officer must be able to point to specific and articulable facts which, taken together with rational inferences from those facts, reasonably warrant that intrusion. The scheme of the Fourth Amendment becomes meaningful only when it is assured that at some point the conduct of those charged with enforcing the laws can be subjected to the more detached, neutral scrutiny of a judge who must evaluate the reasonableness of a particular search or seizure in light of the particular circumstances. And in making that assessment it is imperative that the facts be judged against an objective standard: would the facts available to the officer at the moment of the seizure or the search "warrant a man of reasonable caution in the belief" that the action taken was appropriate? Anything less would invite intrusions upon constitutionally guaranteed rights based on nothing more substantial than inarticulate hunches, a result this Court has consistently refused to sanction. See, e.g., *Beck v. State of Ohio*, 379 U.S. 89, 96–97 (1964).

Applying these principles to this case, we consider first the nature and extent of the governmental interests involved. One general interest is of course that of effective crime prevention and detection; it is this interest which underlies the recognition that a police officer may in appropriate circumstances and in an appropriate manner approach a person for purposes of investigating possibly criminal behavior even though there is no probable cause to make an arrest. It was this legitimate investigative function Officer McFadden was discharging when he decided to approach petitioner and his companions. He had observed [three men] go through a series of acts, each of them perhaps innocent in itself, but which taken together warranted further investigation. There is nothing unusual in two men standing together on a street corner, perhaps waiting for someone. Nor is there anything suspicious about people in such circumstances strolling up and down the street, singly or in pairs. Store windows, moreover, are made to be looked in. But the story is quite different where, as here, two men hover about a street corner for an extended period of time, at the end of which it becomes apparent that they are not waiting for anyone or anything; where these men pace alternately along an identical route, pausing to stare in the same store window roughly 24 times; where each completion of this route is followed immediately by a conference between the two men on the corner; where they are joined in one of these conferences by a third man who leaves swiftly; and where the two men finally follow the third and rejoin him a couple of blocks away. It would have been poor police work indeed for an officer of 30 years' experience in the detection of thievery from stores in this same neighborhood to have failed to investigate this behavior further.

The crux of this case, however, is not the propriety of Officer McFadden's taking steps to investigate petitioner's suspicious behavior, but rather, whether there was justification for McFadden's invasion of Terry's personal security by searching him for weapons in the course of that investigation. We are now concerned with more than the governmental interest in investigating crime; in addition, there is the more immediate interest of the police officer in taking steps to assure himself that the person with whom he is dealing is not armed with a weapon that could unexpectedly and fatally be used against him. Certainly it would be unreasonable to require that police officers take unnecessary risks in the performance of their duties. American criminals have a long tradition of armed violence, and every year in this country many law enforcement officers are killed in the line of duty, and thousands more are wounded. Virtually all of these deaths and a substantial portion of the injuries are inflicted with guns and knives.

In view of these facts, we cannot blind ourselves to the need for law enforcement officers to protect themselves and other prospective victims of violence in situations where they may lack probable cause for an arrest. When an officer is justified in believing that the individual whose suspicious behavior he is investigating at close range is armed and presently dangerous to the officer or to others, it would appear to be clearly unreasonable to deny the officer the power to take necessary measures to determine whether the person is in fact carrying a weapon and to neutralize the threat of physical harm.

We must still consider, however, the nature and quality of the intrusion on individual rights which must be accepted if police officers are to be conceded the right to search for weapons in situations where probable cause to arrest for crime is lacking. Even a limited search of the outer clothing for weapons constitutes a severe, though brief, intrusion upon cherished personal security, and it must surely be an annoying, frightening, and perhaps humiliating experience.

Petitioner does not argue that [an] officer is always unjustified in searching a suspect to discover weapons. Rather, he says it is unreasonable for the policeman to take that step until such time as the situation evolves to a point where there is probable cause to make an arrest.

There are two weaknesses in this line of reasoning however. First, it fails to take account of traditional limitations upon the scope of searches, and thus

recognizes no distinction in purpose, character, and extent between a search incident to an arrest and a limited search for weapons. The former, although justified in part by the acknowledged necessity to protect the arresting officer from assault with a concealed weapon, *Preston v. United States*, 376 U.S. 364, 367 (1964),

Make the Connection

We will consider "searches incident to arrest," and their validity even absent a warrant, later in this chapter.

is also justified on other grounds, and can therefore involve a relatively extensive exploration of the person. A search for weapons in the absence of probable cause to arrest, however, must, like any other search, be strictly circumscribed by the exigencies which justify its initiation. Thus it must be limited to that which is necessary for the discovery of weapons which might be used to harm the officer or others nearby, and may realistically be characterized as something less than a "full" search, even though it remains a serious intrusion.

A second, and related, objection to petitioner's argument is that it assumes that the law of arrest has already worked out the balance between the particular interests involved here—the neutralization of danger to the policeman in the investigative circumstance and the sanctity of the individual. But this is not so. An arrest is a wholly different kind of intrusion upon individual freedom from a limited search for weapons, and the interests each is designed to serve are likewise quite different. An arrest is the initial stage of a criminal prosecution. It is intended to vindicate society's interest in having its laws obeyed, and it is inevitably accompanied by future interference with the individual's freedom of movement, whether or not trial or conviction ultimately follows. The protective search for weapons, on the other hand, constitutes a brief, though far from inconsiderable, intrusion upon the sanctity of the person. It does not follow that because an officer may lawfully arrest a person only when he is apprised of facts sufficient to warrant a belief that the person has committed or is committing a crime, the officer is equally unjustified, absent that kind of evidence, in making any intrusions short of an arrest. Moreover, a perfectly reasonable apprehension of danger may arise long before the officer is possessed of adequate information to justify taking a person into custody for the purpose of prosecuting him for a crime.

Our evaluation of the proper balance that has to be struck in this type of case leads us to conclude that there must be a narrowly drawn authority to permit a reasonable search for weapons for the protection of the police officer, where he has reason to believe that he is dealing with an armed and dangerous individual, regardless of whether he has probable cause to arrest the individual for a crime.

> **Take Note**
>
> In this paragraph, the Court announces the standard for determining whether a "stop and frisk" satisfies the Fourth Amendment. Can you articulate the standard?

The officer need not be absolutely certain that the individual is armed; the issue is whether a reasonably prudent man in the circumstances would be warranted in the belief that his safety or that of others was in danger. And in determining whether the officer acted reasonably in such circumstances, due weight must be given, not to his inchoate and unparticularized suspicion or "hunch," but to the specific reasonable inferences which he is entitled to draw from the facts in light of his experience.

We think on the facts and circumstances Officer McFadden detailed before the trial judge a reasonably prudent man would have been warranted in believing petitioner was armed and thus presented a threat to the officer's safety while he was investigating his suspicious behavior. The actions of Terry and Chilton were consistent with McFadden's hypothesis that these men were contemplating a daylight robbery—which, it is reasonable to assume, would be likely to involve the use of weapons—and nothing in their conduct from the time he first noticed them until the time he confronted them and identified himself as a police officer gave him sufficient reason to negate that hypothesis. [W]hen Officer McFadden approached the three men gathered before the display window [he] had observed enough to make it quite reasonable to fear that they were armed; and nothing in their response to his hailing them, identifying himself as a police officer, and asking their names served to dispel that reasonable belief. We cannot say his decision at that point to seize Terry and pat his clothing for weapons was the product of a volatile or inventive imagination, or was undertaken simply as an act of harassment; the record evidences the tempered act of a policeman who in the course of an investigation had to make a quick decision as to how to protect himself and others from possible danger, and took limited steps to do so.

The manner in which the seizure and search were conducted is, of course, as vital a part of the inquiry as whether they were warranted at all. * * * The sole justification of the search in the present situation is the protection of the police officer and others nearby, and it must therefore be confined in scope to an intrusion reasonably designed to discover guns, knives, clubs, or other hidden instruments for the assault of the police officer.

The scope of the search in this case presents no serious problem in light of these standards. Officer McFadden patted down the outer clothing of petitioner and his two companions. He did not place his hands in their pockets or under the outer surface of their garments until he had felt weapons, and then he merely reached for and removed the guns. * * * Officer McFadden confined his search strictly to what was minimally necessary to learn whether the men were armed and to disarm them once he discovered the weapons. He did not conduct a general exploratory search for whatever evidence of criminal activity he might find.

[W]here a police officer observes unusual conduct which leads him reasonably to conclude in light of his experience that criminal activity may be afoot and that the persons with whom he is dealing may be armed and presently dangerous, where in the course of investigating this behavior he identifies himself as a policeman and makes reasonable inquiries, and where nothing in the initial stages of the encounter serves to dispel his reasonable fear for his own or others' safety, he is entitled for the protection of himself and others in the area to conduct a carefully limited search of the outer clothing of such persons in an attempt to discover weapons which might be used to assault him. Such a search is a reasonable search under the Fourth Amendment, and any weapons seized may properly be introduced in evidence against the person from whom they were taken.

Affirmed.

MR. JUSTICE HARLAN, concurring.

* * * The [Court's] holding has [two] logical corollaries that I do not think the Court has fully expressed. In the first place, if the frisk is justified in order to protect the officer during an encounter with a citizen, the officer must first have constitutional grounds to insist on an encounter, to make a forcible stop. Any person, including a policeman, is at liberty to avoid a person he considers dangerous. If and when a policeman has a right instead to disarm such a person for his own protection, he must first have a right not to avoid him but to be in his presence. That right must be more than the liberty (again, possessed by every citizen) to address questions to other persons, for ordinarily the person addressed has an equal right to ignore his interrogator and walk away; he certainly need not submit to a frisk for the questioner's protection. I would make it perfectly clear that the right to frisk in this case depends upon the reasonableness of a forcible stop to investigate a suspected crime.

Where such a stop is reasonable, however, the right to frisk must be immediate and automatic if the reason for the stop is, as here, an articulable suspicion of a crime of violence. Just as a full search incident to a lawful arrest requires no additional justification, a limited frisk incident to a lawful stop must often be rapid and routine. There is no reason why an officer, rightfully but forcibly confronting a person suspected of a serious crime, should have to ask one question and take the risk that the answer might be a bullet.

Officer McFadden's right to interrupt Terry's freedom of movement and invade his privacy arose only because circumstances warranted forcing an encounter with Terry in an effort to prevent or investigate a crime. Once that forced encounter was justified, however, the officer's right to take suitable measures for his own safety followed automatically.

MR. JUSTICE WHITE, concurring.

* * * There is nothing in the Constitution which prevents a policeman from addressing questions to anyone on the streets. Absent special circumstances, the person approached may not be detained or frisked but may refuse to cooperate and go on his way. However, given the proper circumstances, such as those in this case, it seems to me the person may be briefly detained against his will while pertinent questions are directed to him. Of course, the person stopped is not obliged to answer, answers may not be compelled, and refusal to answer furnishes no basis for an arrest, although it may alert the officer to the need for continued observation. In my view, it is temporary detention, warranted by the circumstances, which chiefly justifies the protective frisk for weapons.

MR. JUSTICE DOUGLAS, dissenting.

I agree that petitioner was "seized" within the meaning of the Fourth Amendment. I also agree that frisking petitioner and his companions for guns was a "search." But it is a mystery how that "search" and that "seizure" can be constitutional by Fourth Amendment standards, unless there was "probable cause" to believe that (1) a crime had been committed or (2) a crime was in the process of being committed or (3) a crime was about to be committed.

[T]he crime here is carrying concealed weapons; and there is no basis for concluding that the officer had "probable cause" for believing that that crime was being committed. Had a warrant been sought, a magistrate would, therefore, have been unauthorized to issue one, for he can act only if there is a showing of 'probable cause." We hold today that the police have greater authority to make a "seizure" and conduct a "search" than a judge has to authorize such action. We have said precisely the opposite over and over again.

POINTS FOR DISCUSSION

a.   Reasonable Suspicion and Probable Cause

The Court held in *Terry* that an officer may stop and frisk a suspect when the circumstances lead him "reasonably to conclude in light of his experience" that "criminal activity may be afoot and that the persons with whom he is dealing may be armed and presently dangerous." Although it is difficult to quantify exactly what evidence is required to satisfy this requirement of reasonable suspicion, it is clear from the Court's opinion that the standard is easier to satisfy than the standard of probable cause, which is the standard for an ordinary search or seizure under the Fourth Amendment. As we explain in greater detail below, the Court has held that probable cause "exists where the facts and circumstances within [the officers'] knowledge and of which they had reasonably trustworthy information [are] sufficient in themselves to warrant a man of reasonable caution in the belief that an offense has been or is being committed." *Brinegar v. United States*, 338 U.S. 160, 175–176 (1949).

In practice, what is the difference between "reasonable suspicion" and "probable cause"? If you were drafting a manual for police officers to educate them on when they are permitted to stop and frisk a suspect, what would you say?

b.   License to Discriminate?

In authorizing the police to stop persons based on something less than probable cause that a crime has been committed, does the *Terry* standard facilitate discrimination by police on the basis of race or national origin? See Tracey Maclin, Terry v. Ohio's *Fourth Amendment Legacy: Black Men and Police Discretion*, 72 St. John's L. Rev. 1271, 1287 (1998) (arguing that "the *Terry* Court succumbed to pressure to weaken constitutional principle when it was clear that many politicians, and a large segment of the public, had signaled their disapproval of the Court's effort to extend meaningful constitutional protection to those who needed it the most: Poor and minority persons suspected of criminal behavior").

C. THE WARRANT REQUIREMENT

In the previous two sections, we considered what constitutes a search or a seizure under the Fourth Amendment. These determinations are essential because they are the predicate for deciding whether the requirements of the Amendment are triggered. When the police perform a search or a seizure, the Fourth Amendment's requirement of a warrant generally applies.

Specifically, the Fourth Amendment prohibits "unreasonable searches and seizures," and it states that "no Warrants shall issue, but upon probable cause, supported by Oath or affirmation, and particularly describing the place to be searched, and the persons or things to be seized." This means at least three things. First, the government cannot conduct a search or seizure if it would be "unreasonable" to do so, regardless of whether the officers first obtain a warrant. Second, an officer is generally required to obtain a warrant before conducting a search or seizure, and the warrant cannot issue unless the officer can establish "probable cause" to believe that a search or seizure will yield evidence of a crime or "probable cause" to believe that a person to be arrested has committed a crime. Third, the warrant must describe in something more than general terms "the place to be searched, and the persons or things to be seized."

The Court has made clear that there is no mechanical inquiry that can readily determine the existence of probable cause. Instead, in "dealing with probable cause, [as] the very name implies, we deal with probabilities. These are not technical; they are the factual and practical considerations of everyday life on which reasonable and prudent men, not legal technicians, act." *Brinegar v. United States*, 338 U.S. 160, 175–176 (1949). Probable cause is thus "a fluid concept—turning on the assessment of probabilities in particular factual contexts—not readily, or even usefully, reduced to a neat set of legal rules." *Illinois v. Gates*, 462 U.S. 213 (1983). The "requirement of probable cause for the issuance of a warrant is to be applied, not according to a fixed and rigid formula, but rather in the light of the 'totality of the circumstances' made known to the magistrate." *Massachusetts v. Upton*, 466 U.S. 727 (1984).

The Court has, however, offered some guidance. The Court has explained that the term "has come to mean more than bare suspicion: Probable cause exists where 'the facts and circumstances within [the officers'] knowledge and of which they had reasonably trustworthy information [are] sufficient in themselves to warrant a man of reasonable caution in the belief that' an offense has been or is being committed." *Brinegar*, 338 U.S. at 175–76 (quoting *Carroll v. United States*, 267 U.S. 132, 162 (1925)). Although not easily quantifiable, probable cause clearly requires "less than evidence which would justify condemnation" or conviction. *Locke v. United States*, 11 U.S. (7 Cranch) 339, 348 (1813) (Marshall, C.J.).

The requirement that warrants shall particularly describe the place to be searched and the things or persons to be seized "makes general searches under them impossible and prevents the seizure of one thing under a warrant describing another. As to what is to be taken, nothing is left to the discretion of the officer executing the warrant." *Marron v. United States*, 275 U.S. 192, 196 (1927). Although police executing a warrant may seize evidence of crime that is in "plain view" even if that evidence is not described in the warrant, *Coolidge v. New Hampshire*, 403 U.S. 443 (1971), the particularity requirement prevents police from going on fishing expeditions based on something less than probable cause to believe that they will find specific evidence of a particular crime.

In the remainder of this section, we consider when officers can dispense with the requirement that they obtain a warrant from a neutral magistrate before conducting a search or seizure. As the Court has explained, "searches conducted outside the judicial process, without prior approval by judge or magistrate, are per se unreasonable under the Fourth Amendment—subject only to a few specifically established and well delineated exceptions." *Katz v. United States*, 389 U.S. 347, 357 (1967). The cases below explore those exceptions.

1. Exigent Circumstances

Police can usually obtain a warrant from a magistrate in fairly short order. But what if taking the time to obtain a warrant might frustrate the police's ability to catch a suspect, prevent the destruction of evidence, or stop a crime in progress? Consider the case that follows.

KENTUCKY V. KING
563 U.S. 452 (2011)

JUSTICE ALITO delivered the opinion of the Court.

It is well established that "exigent circumstances," including the need to prevent the destruction of evidence, permit police officers to conduct an otherwise permissible search without first obtaining a warrant. In this case, we consider whether this rule applies when police, by knocking on the door of a residence and announcing their presence, cause the occupants to attempt to destroy evidence. * * *

This case concerns the search of an apartment in Lexington, Kentucky. Police officers set up a controlled buy of crack cocaine outside an apartment complex. Undercover Officer Gibbons watched the deal take place from an unmarked car in a nearby parking lot. After the deal occurred, Gibbons radioed uniformed officers to move in on the suspect. He told the officers that the suspect was moving quickly toward the breezeway of an apartment building, and he urged them to "hurry up and get there" before the suspect entered an apartment.

In response to the radio alert, the uniformed officers drove into the nearby parking lot, left their vehicles, and ran to the breezeway. Just as they entered the breezeway, they heard a door shut and detected a very strong odor of burnt marijuana. At the end of the breezeway, the officers saw two apartments, one on the left and one on the right, and they did not know which apartment the suspect had entered. * * * Because they smelled marijuana smoke emanating from the apartment on the left, they approached the door of that apartment.

Officer Steven Cobb, one of the uniformed officers who approached the door, testified that the officers banged on the left apartment door "as loud as [they] could" and announced, "This is the police" or "Police, police, police." Cobb said that "[a]s soon as [the officers] started banging on the door," they "could hear people inside moving," and "[i]t sounded as [though] things were being moved inside the apartment." These noises, Cobb testified, led the officers to believe that drug-related evidence was about to be destroyed.

At that point, the officers announced that they "were going to make entry inside the apartment." Cobb then kicked in the door, the officers entered the apartment, and they found three people in the front room: respondent Hollis King, respondent's girlfriend, and a guest who was smoking marijuana. The officers performed a protective sweep of the apartment during which they saw marijuana and powder cocaine in plain view. In a subsequent search, they also discovered crack cocaine, cash, and drug paraphernalia. Police eventually entered the apartment on the right. Inside, they found the suspected drug dealer who was the initial target of their investigation.

[After respondent was charged with drug offenses he moved to suppress the evidence from the warrantless search, but the Circuit Court denied the motion. After entering a conditional guilty plea, the court sentenced respondent to 11 years' imprisonment. The Supreme Court of Kentucky reversed, concluding that the police may not rely on exigent circumstances if "it was reasonably foreseeable that the investigative tactics employed by the police would create the exigent circumstances."]

Although the text of the Fourth Amendment does not specify when a search warrant must be obtained, this Court has inferred that a warrant must generally be secured. "It is a 'basic principle of Fourth Amendment law,'" we have often said, "'that searches and seizures inside a home without a warrant are presumptively unreasonable.'" *Brigham City v. Stuart*, 547 U.S. 398, 403 (2006) (quoting *Groh v. Ramirez*, 540 U.S. 551, 559 (2004)). But we have also recognized that this presumption may be overcome in some circumstances because "[t]he ultimate touchstone of the Fourth Amendment is 'reasonableness.'" *Brigham City, supra,* at 403. Accordingly, the warrant requirement is subject to certain reasonable exceptions.

One well-recognized exception applies when "'the exigencies of the situation' make the needs of law enforcement so compelling that [a] warrantless search is objectively reasonable under the Fourth Amendment." *Mincey v. Arizona,* 437 U.S. 385, 394 (1978); see also *Payton v. New York,* 445 U.S. 573, 590 (1980) ("[T]he Fourth Amendment has drawn a firm line at the entrance to the house. Absent exigent circumstances, that threshold may not reasonably be crossed without a warrant").

This Court has identified several exigencies that may justify a warrantless search of a home. See *Brigham City,* 547 U.S., at 403. Under the "emergency aid" exception, for example, "officers may enter a home without a warrant to render emergency assistance to an injured occupant or to protect an occupant from imminent injury." *Ibid.* Police officers may enter premises without a warrant when they are in hot pursuit of a fleeing suspect. See *United States v. Santana,* 427 U.S. 38, 42–43 (1976). And—what is relevant here—the need "to prevent the imminent destruction of evidence" has long been recognized as a sufficient justification for a warrantless search. *Brigham City, supra,* at 403.

Over the years, lower courts have developed an exception to the exigent circumstances rule, the so-called "police-created exigency" doctrine. Under this doctrine, police may not rely on the need to prevent destruction of evidence when that exigency was "created" or "manufactured" by the conduct of the police. * * * In applying this exception for the "creation" or "manufacturing" of an exigency by the police, courts require something more than mere proof that fear of detection by the police caused the destruction of evidence. [I]n the vast majority of cases in which evidence is destroyed by persons who are engaged in illegal conduct, the reason for the destruction is fear that the evidence will fall into the hands of law enforcement. * * * Consequently, a rule that precludes the police from making a warrantless entry to prevent the destruction of evidence whenever their conduct causes the exigency would unreasonably shrink the reach of this well-established exception to the warrant requirement.

Presumably for the purpose of avoiding such a result, the lower courts have held that the police-created exigency doctrine requires more than simple causation, but the lower courts have not agreed on the test to be applied. * * * Despite the welter of tests devised by the lower courts, the answer to the question presented in this case follows directly and clearly from the principle that permits warrantless searches in the first place. As previously noted, warrantless searches are allowed when the circumstances make it reasonable, within the meaning of the Fourth Amendment, to dispense with the warrant requirement. Therefore, the answer to the question before us is that the exigent

> **Food for Thought**
>
> What would be an example of police conduct that "violates the Fourth Amendment" and that leads a person to destroy evidence?

circumstances rule justifies a warrantless search when the conduct of the police preceding the exigency is reasonable in the same sense. Where, as here, the police did not create the exigency by engaging or threatening to engage in conduct that violates the Fourth Amendment, warrantless entry to prevent the destruction of evidence is reasonable and thus allowed.

Some lower courts have adopted a rule that is similar to the one that we recognize today. But others, including the Kentucky Supreme Court, have imposed additional requirements that are unsound and that we now reject.

Bad faith. Some courts, including the Kentucky Supreme Court, ask whether law enforcement officers "deliberately created the exigent circumstances with the bad faith intent to avoid the warrant requirement." * * * This approach is fundamentally inconsistent with our Fourth Amendment jurisprudence. "Our cases have repeatedly rejected" a subjective approach, asking only whether "the circumstances, viewed *objectively,* justify the action." *Brigham City,* 547 U.S., at 404. [T]his Court has long taken the view that "evenhanded law enforcement is best achieved by the application of objective standards of conduct, rather than standards that depend upon the subjective state of mind of the officer." *Horton v. California,* 496 U.S. 128, 138 (1990).

Reasonable foreseeability. Some courts, again including the Kentucky Supreme Court, hold that police may not rely on an exigency if "it was reasonably foreseeable that the investigative tactics employed by the police would create the exigent circumstances." Courts applying this test have invalidated warrantless home searches on the ground that it was reasonably foreseeable that police officers, by knocking on the door and announcing their presence, would lead a drug suspect to destroy evidence.

Adoption of a reasonable foreseeability test would * * * introduce an unacceptable degree of unpredictability. * * * A simple example illustrates the difficulties that such an approach would produce. Suppose that the officers in the present case did not smell marijuana smoke and thus knew only that there was a 50% chance that the fleeing suspect had entered the apartment on the left rather than the apartment on the right. Under those circumstances, would it have been reasonably foreseeable that the occupants of the apartment on the left would seek to destroy evidence upon learning that the police were at the door? Or suppose that the officers knew only that the suspect had disappeared into one of the apartments on a floor with 3, 5, 10, or even 20 units? If the police chose a door at random and knocked for the purpose of asking the occupants if they knew a person who fit the description of the suspect, would it have been reasonably foreseeable that the occupants would seek to destroy evidence? * * * The reasonable foreseeability test would create unacceptable and unwarranted difficulties for law enforcement officers who must make quick decisions in the field, as well as for judges who would be required to determine after the fact whether the destruction of evidence in response to a knock on the door was reasonably foreseeable based on what the officers knew at the time.

Probable cause and time to secure a warrant. Some courts, in applying the police-created exigency doctrine, fault law enforcement officers if, after acquiring evidence that is sufficient to establish probable cause to search particular premises, the officers do not seek a warrant but instead knock on the door and seek either to speak with an occupant or to obtain consent to search.

This approach unjustifiably interferes with legitimate law enforcement strategies. There are many entirely proper reasons why police may not want to seek a search warrant as soon as the bare minimum of evidence needed to establish probable cause is acquired. * * * First, the police may * * * think that a short and simple conversation [with the occupants] may obviate the need to apply for and execute a warrant. See *Schneckloth v. Bustamonte,* 412 U.S. 218, 228 (1973). Second, the police may want to ask an occupant of the premises for consent to search because doing so is simpler, faster, and less burdensome than applying for a warrant. * * * Third, law enforcement officers may wish to obtain more evidence before submitting what might otherwise be considered a marginal warrant application. Fourth, prosecutors may wish to wait until they acquire evidence that can justify a search that is broader in scope than the search that a judicial officer is likely to authorize based on the evidence then available. And finally, in many cases, law enforcement may not want to execute a search that will disclose the existence of an investigation because doing so may interfere with the acquisition of additional evidence against those already under suspicion or evidence about additional but as yet unknown participants in a criminal scheme. * * * Faulting the police for failing to apply for a search warrant at the earliest possible time after obtaining probable cause imposes a duty that is nowhere to be found in the Constitution.

Standard or good investigative tactics. Finally, some lower court cases suggest that law enforcement officers may be found to have created or manufactured an exigency if the court concludes that the course of their investigation was "contrary to standard or good law enforcement practices (or to the policies or practices of their jurisdictions)." This approach fails to provide clear guidance for law enforcement officers and authorizes courts to make judgments on matters that are the province of those who are responsible for federal and state law enforcement agencies.

Respondent argues for a rule that differs from those discussed above, but his rule is also flawed. Respondent contends that law enforcement officers impermissibly create an exigency when they "engage in conduct that would cause a reasonable person to believe that entry is imminent and inevitable." In respondent's view, relevant factors include the officers' tone of voice in announcing their presence and the forcefulness of their knocks. But the ability of law enforcement officers to respond to an exigency cannot turn on such subtleties.

Police officers may have a very good reason to announce their presence loudly and to knock on the door with some force. A forceful knock may be necessary to alert the occupants that someone is at the door. Furthermore, unless police officers identify themselves loudly enough, occupants may not know who is at their doorstep. Officers are permitted—indeed, encouraged—to identify themselves to citizens, and "in many circumstances this is cause for assurance, not discomfort." *United States v. Drayton,* 536 U.S. 194, 204 (2002). Citizens who are startled by an unexpected knock on the door or by the sight of unknown persons in plain clothes on their doorstep may be relieved to learn that these persons are police officers. Others may appreciate the opportunity to make an informed decision about whether to answer the door to the police.

If respondent's test were adopted, it would be extremely difficult for police officers to know how loudly they may announce their presence or how forcefully they may knock on a door without running afoul of the police-created exigency rule. And in most cases, it would be nearly impossible for a court to determine whether that threshold had been passed. The Fourth Amendment does not require the nebulous and impractical test that respondent proposes.

For these reasons, we conclude that the exigent circumstances rule applies when the police do not gain entry to premises by means of an actual or threatened violation of the Fourth Amendment. This holding provides ample protection for the privacy rights that the Amendment protects.

When law enforcement officers who are not armed with a warrant knock on a door, they do no more than any private citizen might do. And whether the person who knocks on the door and requests the opportunity to speak is a police officer or a private citizen, the occupant has no obligation to open the door or to speak. When the police knock on a door but the occupants choose not to respond or to speak, "the investigation will have reached a conspicuously low point," and the occupants "will have the kind of warning that even the most elaborate

> **Food for Thought**
>
> If the police knocked on your door and loudly announced their presence, would you feel free to refuse to open the door or to deny them entry to your home?

security system cannot provide." *United States v. Chambers,* 395 F.3d 563, 577 (6th Cir. 2005) (Sutton, J., dissenting). And even if an occupant chooses to open the door and speak with the officers, the occupant need not allow the officers to enter the premises and may refuse to answer any questions at any time. Occupants who choose not to stand on their constitutional rights but instead elect to attempt to destroy evidence have only themselves to blame for the warrantless exigent-circumstances search that may ensue.

We need not decide whether exigent circumstances existed in this case. * * * The Kentucky Supreme Court "assum[ed] for the purpose of argument that exigent circumstances existed," and it held that the police had impermissibly manufactured the exigency. * * * Any question about whether an exigency actually existed is better addressed by the Kentucky Supreme Court on remand.

In this case, we see no evidence that the officers either violated the Fourth Amendment or threatened to do so prior to the point when they entered the apartment. Officer Cobb testified without contradiction that the officers "banged on the door as loud as [they] could" and announced either "Police, police, police" or "This is the police." This conduct was entirely consistent with the Fourth Amendment, and we are aware of no other evidence that might show that the officers either violated the Fourth Amendment or threatened to do so (for example, by announcing that they would break down the door if the occupants did not open the door voluntarily). * * * If there is contradictory evidence that has not been brought to our attention, the state court may elect to address that matter on remand.

JUSTICE GINSBURG, dissenting.

The Court today arms the police with a way routinely to dishonor the Fourth Amendment's warrant requirement in drug cases. In lieu of presenting their evidence to a neutral magistrate, police officers may now knock, listen, then break the door down, never mind that they had ample time to obtain a warrant.

There was little risk that drug-related evidence would have been destroyed had the police delayed the search pending a magistrate's authorization. As the Court recognizes, "[p]ersons in possession of valuable drugs are unlikely to destroy them unless they fear discovery by the police." Nothing in the record shows that, prior to the knock at the apartment door, the occupants were apprehensive about police proximity.

Under an appropriately reined-in "emergency" or "exigent circumstances" exception, the result in this case should not be in doubt. The target of the investigation's entry into the building, and the smell of marijuana seeping under the apartment door into the hallway, the Kentucky Supreme Court rightly determined, gave the police "probable cause . . . sufficient . . . to obtain a warrant to search the . . . apartment." 302 S.W.3d 649, 653 (2010). As that court observed, nothing made it impracticable for the police to post officers on the premises while proceeding to obtain a warrant authorizing their entry. * * * I [would] not allow an expedient knock to override the warrant requirement.

POINTS FOR DISCUSSION

a.   Exigent Circumstances

The Court explained in its opinion that "the need 'to prevent the imminent destruction of evidence' has long been recognized as a sufficient justification for a warrantless search." In your view, once the police had knocked on the door in question in *King*, was the destruction of evidence of a crime likely to occur inside? How do you know?

Suppose that the police walk through the halls of an apartment building, knocking on every door that they pass and announcing their presence. After knocking on each door, the police listen for activity inside. If the police then hear evidence of what they believe to be the imminent destruction of evidence, should they be permitted to enter without first obtaining a warrant? Under the Court's decision in *King*, are they?

b.   Exceptions to the Exigent Circumstances Exception

Are there any exceptions to the exigent-circumstances exception? Suppose the police believe that a suspect is likely to have drugs in his apartment, but the belief is based on a hunch that does not rise to the level of probable cause. One officer phones the suspect and, pretending to be a friend of the suspect's, tells the suspect that he heard that the police are on the way and that he "better do something about his stash quickly." The other officer stands outside the suspect's apartment and listens for evidence that there are drugs inside the apartment. If the second officer observes something that constitutes probable cause that there are illegal drugs inside the apartment, can he enter the apartment without first obtaining a warrant? If not, then what is the line between permissible and impermissible police conduct that creates exigent circumstances?

2.   Searches of Cars

The Court in *King* explained that "searches and seizures inside a home without a warrant are presumptively unreasonable." Most people have their highest expectation of privacy at home; as the British jurist Sir Edward Coke famously declared, "For a man's house is his castle, and each man's home is his safest refuge." In addition, if the police have probable cause to search a house, there is little risk that, in the time that it takes the police to obtain a warrant, the house will be whisked away or become otherwise unsearchable.

Arguably, the same cannot be said for cars. In *Carroll v. United States,* 267 U.S. 132 (1925), the Court announced an "automobile exception" to the warrant requirement. The Court has described the exception as follows: "If a car is readily mobile and probable cause exists to believe it contains contraband, the Fourth Amendment * * * permits police to search the vehicle without more." *Pennsylvania v. Labron,* 518 U.S. 938, 940 (1996) (per curiam). But what counts as an "automobile" for purposes of the automobile exception? Are there any circumstances under which the police must obtain a warrant before searching a car (or anything contained inside a car)? Consider the cases that follow.

CALIFORNIA V. CARNEY
471 U.S. 386 (1985)

CHIEF JUSTICE BURGER delivered the opinion of the Court.

We granted certiorari to decide whether law enforcement agents violated the Fourth Amendment when they conducted a warrantless search, based on probable cause, of a fully mobile "motor home" located in a public place.

On May 31, 1979, Drug Enforcement Agency Agent Robert Williams watched respondent, Charles Carney, approach a youth in downtown San Diego. The youth accompanied Carney to a Dodge Mini Motor Home parked in a nearby lot. Carney and the youth closed the window shades in the motor home, including one across the front window. Agent Williams had previously received uncorroborated information that the same motor home was used by another person who was exchanging marijuana for sex. Williams, with assistance from other agents, kept the motor home under surveillance for the entire one and one-quarter hours that Carney and the youth remained inside. When the youth left the motor home, the agents followed and stopped him. The youth told the agents that he had received marijuana in return for allowing Carney sexual contacts.

At the agents' request, the youth returned to the motor home and knocked on its door; Carney stepped out. The agents identified themselves as law enforcement officers. Without a warrant or consent, one agent entered the motor home and observed marijuana, plastic bags, and a scale of the kind used in weighing drugs on a table. Agent Williams took Carney into custody and took possession of the motor home. A subsequent search of the motor home at the police station revealed additional marijuana in the cupboards and refrigerator.

Respondent was charged with possession of marijuana for sale. [The trial court denied his motion to suppress the evidence discovered in the motor home, and respondent pleaded *nolo contendere* to the charges and was placed on probation for three years. On appeal, the California Supreme Court reversed the conviction, holding that the search was unreasonable because no warrant was obtained.]

> **Definition**
>
> *Nolo contendere* is a Latin phrase that means "I do not wish to contest." It is sometimes called "no contest," because the defendant does not contest the charges, but also does not admit guilt.

The Fourth Amendment [right] is preserved by a requirement that searches be conducted pursuant to a warrant issued by an independent judicial officer. There are, of course, exceptions to the general rule that a warrant must be secured before a search is undertaken; one is the so-called "automobile exception" at issue in this case. This exception to the warrant requirement was first set forth by the Court 60 years ago in *Carroll v. United States*, 267 U.S. 132 (1925). There, the Court recognized that the privacy interests in an automobile are constitutionally protected; however, it held that the ready mobility of the automobile justifies a lesser degree of protection of those interests. The Court rested this exception on a long-recognized distinction between stationary structures and vehicles:

> "[T]he guaranty of freedom from unreasonable searches and seizures by the Fourth Amendment has been construed, practically since the beginning of Government, as recognizing a necessary difference between a search of a store, dwelling house or other structure in respect of which a proper official warrant readily may be obtained, and a search of a ship, motor boat, wagon or automobile, for contraband goods, where it is not practicable to secure a warrant because the vehicle can be *quickly moved* out of the locality or jurisdiction in which the warrant must be sought." *Id.,* at 153 (emphasis added).

The capacity to be "quickly moved" was clearly the basis of the holding in *Carroll,* and our cases have consistently recognized ready mobility as one of the principal bases of the automobile exception. * * * In *Chambers v. Maroney,* 399 U.S. 42, 51 (1970), for example, commenting on the rationale for the vehicle exception, we noted that "the opportunity to search is fleeting since a car is readily movable."

However, although ready mobility alone was perhaps the original justification for the vehicle exception, our later cases have made clear that ready mobility is not the only basis for the exception. The reasons for the vehicle exception, we have said, are twofold. *South Dakota v. Opperman,* 428 U.S. 364, 367 (1976). "Besides the element of mobility, less rigorous warrant requirements govern because the expectation of privacy with respect to one's automobile is significantly less than that relating to one's home or office." *Ibid.*

Even in cases where an automobile was not immediately mobile, the lesser expectation of privacy resulting from its use as a readily mobile vehicle justified application of the vehicular exception. * * * In some cases, the configuration of the vehicle contributed to the lower expectations of privacy; for example, we held in *Cardwell v. Lewis,* 417 U.S. 583, 590 (1974), that, because the passenger compartment of a standard automobile is relatively open to plain view, there are lesser expectations of privacy. But even when enclosed "repository" areas have been involved, we have concluded that the lesser expectations of privacy warrant application of the exception. We have applied the exception in the context of a locked car trunk, *Cady v. Dombrowski,* 413 U.S. 433, 442 (1973), a sealed package in a car trunk, *United States v. Ross,* 456 U.S. 798, 806 (1982), a closed compartment under the dashboard, *Chambers v. Maroney,* the interior of a vehicle's upholstery, *Carroll,* or sealed packages inside a covered pickup truck, *United States v. Johns,* 469 U.S. 478 (1985).

These reduced expectations of privacy derive not from the fact that the area to be searched is in plain view, but from the pervasive regulation of vehicles capable of traveling on the public highways. As we explained in *Opperman* * * *:

> "Automobiles, unlike homes, are subjected to pervasive and continuing governmental regulation and controls, including periodic inspection and licensing requirements. As an everyday occurrence, police stop and examine vehicles when license plates or inspection stickers have expired, or if other violations, such as exhaust fumes or excessive noise, are noted, or if headlights or other safety equipment are not in proper working order." 428 U.S., at 368.

The public is fully aware that it is accorded less privacy in its automobiles because of this compelling governmental need for regulation. Historically, "individuals always [have] been on notice that movable vessels may be stopped and searched on facts giving rise to probable cause that the vehicle contains contraband, without the protection afforded by a magistrate's prior evaluation of those facts." *Ross,* 456 U.S., at 806, n. 8. In short, the

> **Food for Thought**
>
> Is the Court's reasoning here circular? The Court declares that people have a reduced expectation of privacy in their cars because of pervasive monitoring, including stops and inspections, of people driving. But if the police were required to obtain a warrant for such actions, wouldn't our expectation of privacy be greater?

pervasive schemes of regulation, which necessarily lead to reduced expectations of privacy, and the exigencies attendant to ready mobility justify searches without prior recourse to the authority of a magistrate so long as the overriding standard of probable cause is met.

When a vehicle is being used on the highways, or if it is readily capable of such use and is found stationary in a place not regularly used for residential purposes—temporary or otherwise—the two justifications for the vehicle exception come into play. First, the vehicle is obviously readily mobile by the turn of an ignition key, if not actually moving. Second, there is a reduced expectation of privacy stemming from its use as a licensed motor vehicle subject to a range of police regulation inapplicable to a fixed dwelling. At least in these circumstances, the overriding societal interests in effective law enforcement justify an immediate search before the vehicle and its occupants become unavailable.

While it is true that respondent's vehicle possessed some, if not many of the attributes of a home, it is equally clear that the vehicle falls clearly within the scope of the exception laid down in *Carroll* and applied in succeeding cases. Like the automobile in *Carroll,* respondent's motor home was readily mobile. Absent the prompt search and seizure, it could readily have been moved beyond the reach of the police. Furthermore, the vehicle was licensed to "operate on public streets; [was] serviced in public places; . . . and [was] subject to extensive regulation and inspection." *Rakas v. Illinois,* 439 U.S. 128, 154, n. 2 (1978) (POWELL, J., concurring). And the vehicle was so situated that an objective observer would conclude that it was being used not as a residence, but as a vehicle.

Respondent urges us to distinguish his vehicle from other vehicles within the exception because it was *capable of functioning as a home.* In our increasingly mobile society, many vehicles used for transportation can be and are being used not only for transportation but for shelter, *i.e.,* as a "home" or "residence." To distinguish between respondent's motor home and an ordinary sedan for purposes of the vehicle exception would require that we apply the exception depending upon the size of the vehicle and the quality of its appointments. Moreover, to fail to apply the exception to vehicles such as a motor home ignores the fact that a motor home lends itself easily to use as an instrument of illicit drug traffic and other illegal activity. * * *

Our application of the vehicle exception has never turned on the other uses to which a vehicle might be put. The exception has historically turned on the ready mobility of the vehicle, and on the presence of the vehicle in a setting that objectively indicates that the vehicle is being used for transportation.[3] These two requirements for application of the exception ensure that law enforcement officials are not unnecessarily hamstrung in their efforts to detect and prosecute criminal activity, and that the legitimate privacy interests of the public are protected. Applying the vehicle exception in these circumstances allows the essential purposes served by the exception to be fulfilled, while assuring that the exception will acknowledge legitimate privacy interests.

> **Take Note**
>
> The Court here explains why (and when) mobile homes should be treated as cars for purposes of the warrant requirement. Can you imagine circumstances under which the police would be required to obtain a warrant before searching a mobile home?

This search was not unreasonable; it was plainly one that the magistrate could authorize if presented with these facts. The DEA agents had fresh, direct, uncontradicted evidence that the respondent was distributing a controlled substance from the vehicle, apart from evidence of other possible offenses. The agents thus had abundant probable cause to enter and search the vehicle for evidence of a crime notwithstanding its possible use as a dwelling place. [Reversed.]

JUSTICE STEVENS, with whom JUSTICE BRENNAN and JUSTICE MARSHALL join, dissenting.

Our prior cases teach us that inherent mobility is not a sufficient justification for the fashioning of an exception to the warrant requirement, especially in the face of heightened expectations of privacy in the location searched. Motor homes, by their common use and construction, afford their owners a substantial and legitimate expectation of privacy when they dwell within. When a motor home is parked in a location that is removed from the public highway, I believe that society

---

[3] We need not pass on the application of the vehicle exception to a motor home that is situated in a way or place that objectively indicates that it is being used as a residence. Among the factors that might be relevant in determining whether a warrant would be required in such a circumstance is its location, whether the vehicle is readily mobile or instead, for instance, elevated on blocks, whether the vehicle is licensed, whether it is connected to utilities, and whether it has convenient access to a public road.

is prepared to recognize that the expectations of privacy within it are not unlike the expectations one has in a fixed dwelling. As a general rule, such places may only be searched with a warrant based upon probable cause. Warrantless searches of motor homes are only reasonable when the motor home is traveling on the public streets or highways, or when exigent circumstances otherwise require an immediate search without the expenditure of time necessary to obtain a warrant.

In this case, the motor home was parked in an off-the-street lot only a few blocks from the courthouse in downtown San Diego where dozens of magistrates were available to entertain a warrant application. The officers clearly had the element of surprise with them, and with curtains covering the windshield, the motor home offered no indication of any imminent departure. The officers plainly had probable cause to arrest the respondent and search the motor home, and on this record, it is inexplicable why they eschewed the safe harbor of a warrant.

In the absence of any evidence of exigency in the circumstances of this case, the Court relies on the inherent mobility of the motor home to create a conclusive presumption of exigency. This Court, however, has squarely held that mobility of the place to be searched is not a sufficient justification for abandoning the warrant requirement. In *United States v. Chadwick,* 433 U.S. 1 (1977), the Court held that a warrantless search of a footlocker violated the Fourth Amendment even though there was ample probable cause to believe it contained contraband. The Government had argued that the rationale of the automobile exception applied to movable containers in general, and that the warrant requirement should be limited to searches of homes and other "core" areas of privacy. We categorically rejected the Government's argument, observing that there are greater privacy interests associated with containers than with automobiles, and that there are less practical problems associated with the temporary detention of a container than with the detention of an automobile.

It is perfectly obvious that the citizen has a much greater expectation of privacy concerning the interior of a mobile home than of a piece of luggage such as a footlocker. If "inherent mobility" does not justify warrantless searches of containers, it cannot rationally provide a sufficient justification for the search of a person's dwelling place.

Unlike a brick bungalow or a frame Victorian, a motor home seldom serves as a permanent lifetime abode. The motor home in this case, however, was designed to accommodate a breadth of ordinary everyday living. Photographs in the record indicate that its height, length, and beam provided substantial living space inside: stuffed chairs surround a table; cupboards provide room for storage of personal effects; bunk beds provide sleeping space; and a refrigerator provides ample space for food and beverages. Moreover, curtains and large opaque walls inhibit viewing the activities inside from the exterior of the vehicle. The interior configuration of the motor home establishes that the vehicle's size, shape, and mode of construction should have indicated to the officers that it was a vehicle containing mobile living quarters.

The State contends that officers in the field will have an impossible task determining whether or not other vehicles contain mobile living quarters. It is not necessary for the Court to resolve every unanswered question in this area in a single case, but common English usage suggests that we already distinguish between a "motor home" which is "equipped as a self-contained traveling home," a "camper" which is only equipped for "casual travel and camping," and an automobile which is "designed for passenger transportation." Surely the exteriors of these vehicles contain clues about their different functions which could alert officers in the field to the necessity of a warrant.

In my opinion, searches of places that regularly accommodate a wide range of private human activity are fundamentally different from searches of automobiles which primarily serve a public transportation function. Although it may not be a castle, a motor home is usually the functional equivalent of a hotel room, a vacation and retirement home, or a hunting and fishing cabin. These places may be as spartan as a humble cottage when compared to the most majestic mansion, but the highest and most legitimate expectations of privacy associated with these temporary abodes should command the respect of this Court. In my opinion, a warrantless search of living quarters in a motor home is "presumptively unreasonable absent exigent circumstances."

POINT FOR DISCUSSION

In considering the automobile exception, think about the differences between houses, which presumptively require a warrant to search, and cars. Cars have windows on all sides, and our expectation of privacy is considerably lower in our cars than it is in our homes. In addition, if the police have to obtain a warrant before searching a car, there is a substantial risk that the car, which is mobile, simply will not be there when the police return. Accordingly, the Court has long recognized an automobile exception to the warrant requirement.

The rules, in other words, are different for houses and cars. As we saw above, the general rule is that police must obtain a warrant before searching a house, which is not mobile and in which the occupants have a substantial expectation of privacy. In contrast, the general rule is that police do not have to obtain a warrant before searching a car, which is mobile and in which we have a lesser expectation of privacy.

Is a mobile home more properly characterized, for purposes of the warrant requirement, as a home or a vehicle? The Court in *Carney* concluded that, ordinarily, it should be treated as the latter. According to the Court, are there any circumstances under which police must obtain a warrant before searching a mobile home? Conversely, under the dissent's approach, are there times, other than exigent circumstances, when the police would not need to obtain a warrant before searching a mobile home?

CALIFORNIA V. ACEVEDO

500 U.S. 565 (1991)

JUSTICE BLACKMUN delivered the opinion of the Court.

This case requires us [to] consider the so-called "automobile exception" to the warrant requirement of the Fourth Amendment and its application to the search of a closed container in the trunk of a car.

[Police observed Jamie Daza enter a Federal Express office in Santa Ana, California, and retrieve a package that they knew contained several wrapped packages of marijuana. They then observed him carry the package into his apartment. A few hours later, respondent Charles Steven Acevedo entered] Daza's apartment, stayed for about 10 minutes, and reappeared carrying a brown paper bag that looked full. The officers noticed that the bag was the size of one of the wrapped marijuana packages sent from Hawaii. Acevedo walked to a silver Honda in the parking lot. He placed the bag in the trunk of the car and started to drive away. Fearing the loss of evidence, officers in a marked police car stopped him. They opened the trunk and the bag, and found marijuana.

> **Food for Thought**
>
> From the Court's description of the facts, did the police have probable cause to search the entire car? Note that the suspected drugs were in a separate bag in the trunk of the car. Did the police at least have probable cause to search the trunk of the car? Or just the bag itself? We considered the probable cause standard earlier in this chapter.

Respondent was charged in state court with possession of marijuana for sale * * *. He moved to suppress the marijuana found in the car. The motion was denied. He then pleaded guilty but appealed the denial of the suppression motion. The California Court of Appeal, Fourth District, concluded that the marijuana found in the paper bag in the car's trunk should have been suppressed. [After the Supreme Court of California denied the State's petition for review, the Court granted certiorari] to reexamine the law applicable to a closed container in an automobile * * *.

[*Carroll v. United States*, 267 U.S. 132, 158–59 (1925)] held that a warrantless search of an automobile, based upon probable cause to believe that the vehicle contained evidence of crime in the light of an exigency arising out of the likely disappearance of the vehicle, did not contravene the Warrant Clause of the Fourth Amendment. * * *

In *United States v. Ross*, 456 U.S. 798 (1982), [we] held that a warrantless search of an automobile under the *Carroll* doctrine could include a search of a container or package found inside the car when such a search was supported by probable cause. The warrantless search of Ross' car occurred after an informant told the police that he had seen Ross complete a drug transaction using drugs stored in the trunk of his car. The police stopped the car, searched it, and discovered in the trunk a brown paper bag containing drugs. We decided that the search of Ross' car was not unreasonable under the Fourth Amendment: "The scope of a warrantless search based on probable cause is no narrower—and no broader—than the scope of a search authorized by a warrant supported by probable cause." *Id.*, at 823. Thus, "[i]f probable cause justifies the search of a lawfully stopped vehicle, it justifies the search of every part of the vehicle and its contents that may conceal the object of the search." *Id.*, at 825. In *Ross*, therefore, we clarified the scope of the *Carroll* doctrine as properly including a "probing search" of compartments and containers within the automobile so long as the search is supported by probable cause.

In addition to this clarification, *Ross* distinguished the *Carroll* doctrine from the separate rule that governed the search of closed containers. The Court had announced this separate rule, unique to luggage and other closed packages, bags, and containers, in *United States v. Chadwick*, 433 U.S. 1 (1977). In *Chadwick*, federal narcotics agents had probable cause to believe that a 200-pound double-locked footlocker contained marijuana. The agents tracked the locker as the defendants removed it from a train and carried it through the station to a waiting car. As soon as the defendants lifted the locker into the trunk of the car, the agents arrested them, seized the locker, and searched it. In this Court, the United States did not contend that the locker's brief contact with the automobile's trunk sufficed to make the *Carroll* doctrine applicable. Rather, the United States urged that the search of movable luggage could be considered analogous to the search of an automobile.

The Court rejected this argument because, it reasoned, a person expects more privacy in his luggage and personal effects than he does in his automobile. Moreover, it concluded that as "may often not be the case when automobiles are seized," secure storage facilities are usually available when the police seize luggage. *Id.*, at 13, n. 7.

In *Arkansas v. Sanders,* 442 U.S. 753 (1979), the Court extended *Chadwick*'s rule to apply to a suitcase actually being transported in the trunk of a car. In *Sanders,* the police had probable cause to believe a suitcase contained marijuana. They watched as the defendant placed the suitcase in the trunk of a taxi and was driven away. The police pursued the taxi for several blocks, stopped it, found the suitcase in the trunk, and searched it. Although the Court had applied the *Carroll* doctrine to searches of integral parts of the automobile itself, (indeed, in *Carroll,* contraband whiskey was in the upholstery of the seats), it did not extend the doctrine to the warrantless search of personal luggage "merely because it was located in an automobile lawfully stopped by the police." 442 U.S., at 765. Again, the *Sanders* majority stressed the heightened privacy expectation in personal luggage and concluded that the presence of luggage in an automobile did not diminish the owner's expectation of privacy in his personal items. Cf. *California v. Carney,* 471 U.S. 386 (1985).

In *Ross,* the Court endeavored to distinguish between *Carroll,* which governed the *Ross* automobile search, and *Chadwick,* which governed the *Sanders* automobile search. It held that the *Carroll* doctrine covered searches of automobiles when the police had probable cause to search an entire vehicle, but that the *Chadwick* doctrine governed searches of luggage when the officers had probable cause to search only a container within the vehicle. Thus, in a *Ross* situation, the police could conduct a reasonable search under the Fourth Amendment without obtaining a warrant, whereas in a *Sanders* situation, the police had to obtain a warrant before they searched.

* * * Thus, this Court in *Ross* took the critical step of saying that closed containers in cars could be searched without a warrant because of their presence within the automobile. Despite the protection that *Sanders* purported to extend to closed containers, the privacy interest in those closed containers yielded to the broad scope of an automobile search.

The facts in this case closely resemble the facts in *Ross.* In *Ross,* the police had probable cause to believe that drugs were stored in the trunk of a particular car. Here, the California Court of Appeal concluded that the police had probable cause to believe that respondent was carrying marijuana in a bag in his car's trunk. * * *

[The Court in *Ross*] concluded that the time and expense of the warrant process would be misdirected if the police could search every cubic inch of an automobile until they discovered a paper sack, at which point the Fourth Amendment required them to take the sack to a magistrate for permission to look inside. We now must decide the question deferred in *Ross:* whether the Fourth

Amendment requires the police to obtain a warrant to open the sack in a movable vehicle simply because they lack probable cause to search the entire car. We conclude that it does not.

[A] container found after a general search of [an] automobile and a container found in a car after a limited search for the container are equally easy for the police to store and for the suspect to hide or destroy. In fact, we see no principled distinction in terms of either the privacy expectation or the exigent circumstances between the paper bag found by the police in *Ross* and the paper bag found by the police here. Furthermore, by attempting to distinguish between a container for which the police are specifically searching and a container which they come across in a car, we have provided only minimal protection for privacy and have impeded effective law enforcement.

The line between probable cause to search a vehicle and probable cause to search a package in that vehicle is not always clear, and separate rules that govern the two objects to be searched may enable the police to broaden their power to make warrantless searches and disserve privacy interests. * * * At the moment when officers stop an automobile, it may be less than clear whether they suspect with a high degree of certainty that the vehicle contains drugs in a bag or simply contains drugs. If the police know that they may open a bag only if they are actually searching the entire car, they may search more extensively than they otherwise would in order to establish the general probable cause required by *Ross*. * * * We cannot see the benefit of a rule that requires law enforcement officers to conduct a more intrusive search in order to justify a less intrusive one.

To the extent that the *Chadwick-Sanders* rule protects privacy, its protection is minimal. Law enforcement officers may seize a container and hold it until they obtain a search warrant. *Chadwick,* 433 U.S., at 13. "Since the police, by hypothesis, have probable cause to seize the property, we can assume that a warrant will be routinely forthcoming in the overwhelming majority of cases." *Sanders,* 442 U.S., at 770 (dissenting opinion). And the police often will be able to search containers without a warrant, despite the *Chadwick-Sanders* rule, as a search incident to a lawful arrest.

Finally, the search of a paper bag intrudes far less on individual privacy than does the incursion sanctioned long ago in *Carroll*. In that case, prohibition agents slashed the upholstery of the automobile. This Court nonetheless found their search to be reasonable under the Fourth Amendment. If destroying the interior of an automobile is not unreasonable, we cannot conclude that looking inside a closed container is. In light of the minimal protection to privacy afforded by the *Chadwick-Sanders* rule, and our serious doubt whether that rule substantially serves privacy interests, we now hold that the Fourth Amendment does not compel separate treatment for an automobile search that extends only to a container within the vehicle. * * * We conclude that it is better to adopt one clear-cut rule to govern automobile searches and eliminate the warrant requirement for closed containers set forth in *Sanders*.

The interpretation of the *Carroll* doctrine set forth in *Ross* now applies to all searches of containers found in an automobile. In other words, the police may search without a warrant if their search is supported by probable cause. * * * In the case before us, the police had probable cause to believe that the paper bag in the automobile's trunk contained marijuana. That probable cause now allows a warrantless search of the paper bag. The facts in the record reveal that the police did not have probable cause to believe that contraband was hidden in any other part of the automobile and a search of the entire vehicle would have been without probable cause and unreasonable under the Fourth Amendment.

Until today, this Court has drawn a curious line between the search of an automobile that coincidentally turns up a container and the search of a container that coincidentally turns up in an automobile. The protections of the Fourth Amendment must not turn on such coincidences. We therefore interpret *Carroll* as providing one rule to govern all automobile searches. The police may search an automobile and the containers within it where they have probable cause to believe contraband or evidence is contained. [Reversed.]

JUSTICE SCALIA, concurring in the judgment.

I agree with the dissent that it is anomalous for a briefcase to be protected by the "general requirement" of a prior warrant when it is being carried along the street, but for that same briefcase to become unprotected as soon as it is carried into an automobile. On the other hand, I agree with the Court that it would be anomalous for a locked compartment in an automobile to be unprotected by the "general requirement" of a prior warrant, but for an unlocked briefcase within the automobile to be protected. I join in the judgment of the Court because I think its holding is more faithful to the text and tradition of the Fourth Amendment, and if these anomalies in our jurisprudence are ever to be eliminated that is the direction in which we should travel.

Food for Thought

Does the text of the Fourth Amendment indicate when a warrant is required?

In my view, the path out of this confusion should be sought by returning to the first principle that the "reasonableness" requirement of the Fourth Amendment affords the protection that the common law afforded. I have no difficulty with the proposition that that includes the requirement of a warrant, where the common law required a warrant * * *. But the supposed "general rule" that a warrant is always required does not appear to have any basis in the common law, and confuses rather than facilitates any attempt to develop rules of reasonableness in light of changed legal circumstances, as the anomaly eliminated and the anomaly created by today's holding both demonstrate.

I would reverse the judgment in the present case, not because a closed container carried inside a car becomes subject to the "automobile" exception to the general warrant requirement, but because the search of a closed container, outside a privately owned building, with probable cause to believe that the container contains contraband, and when it in fact does contain contraband, is not one of those searches whose Fourth Amendment reasonableness depends upon a warrant.

JUSTICE WHITE, dissenting.

Agreeing as I do with most of Justice STEVENS' opinion and with the result he reaches, I dissent and would affirm the judgment below.

JUSTICE STEVENS, with whom JUSTICE MARSHALL joins, dissenting.

In its opinion today, the Court recognizes that the police did not have probable cause to search respondent's vehicle and that a search of anything but the paper bag that respondent had carried from Daza's apartment and placed in the trunk of his car would have been unconstitutional. Moreover, as I read the opinion, the Court assumes that the police could not have made a warrantless inspection of the bag before it was placed in the car. Finally, the Court also does not question the fact that, under our prior cases, it would have been lawful for the police to seize the container and detain it (and respondent) until they obtained a search warrant. * * *

The Court does not attempt to identify any exigent circumstances that would justify its refusal to apply the general rule against warrantless searches. Instead, it advances these three arguments: First, the rules identified in the foregoing cases are confusing and anomalous. Second, the rules do not protect any significant interest in privacy. And, third, the rules impede effective law enforcement. None of these arguments withstands scrutiny.

The Court summarizes the alleged "anomaly" created by the coexistence of *Ross, Chadwick,* and *Sanders* with the statement that "the more likely the police are to discover drugs in a container, the less authority they have to search it." This juxtaposition is only anomalous, however, if one accepts the flawed premise that the degree to which the police are likely to discover contraband is correlated with their authority to search *without a warrant*. Yet, even proof beyond a reasonable doubt will not justify a warrantless search that is not supported by one of the exceptions to the warrant requirement. And, even when the police have a warrant or an exception applies, once the police possess probable cause, the extent to which they are more or less certain of the contents of a container has no bearing on their authority to search it.

To the extent there was any "anomaly" in our prior jurisprudence, the Court has "cured" it at the expense of creating a more serious paradox. For surely it is anomalous to prohibit a search of a briefcase while the owner is carrying it exposed on a public street yet to permit a search once the owner has placed the briefcase in the locked trunk of his car. One's privacy interest in one's luggage can certainly not be diminished by one's removing it from a public thoroughfare and placing it—out of sight—in a privately owned vehicle. Nor is the danger that evidence will escape increased if the luggage is in a car rather than on the street. In either location, if the police have probable cause, they are authorized to seize the luggage and to detain it until they obtain judicial approval for a search. Any line demarking an exception to the warrant requirement will appear blurred at the edges, but the Court has certainly erred if it believes that, by erasing one line and drawing another, it has drawn a clearer boundary.

The Court's statement that *Chadwick* and *Sanders* provide only "minimal protection to privacy" is also unpersuasive. Every citizen clearly has an interest in the privacy of the contents of his or her luggage, briefcase, handbag or any other container that conceals private papers and effects from public scrutiny. * * * Under the Court's holding today, the privacy interest that protects the contents of a suitcase or a briefcase from a warrantless search when it is in public view simply vanishes when its owner climbs into a taxicab. * * *

The Court's suggestion that *Chadwick* and *Sanders* have created a significant burden on effective law enforcement is unsupported, inaccurate, and, in any event, an insufficient reason for creating a new exception to the warrant requirement. * * * In the years since *Ross* was decided, the Court has heard argument in 30 Fourth Amendment cases involving narcotics. * * * All save two involved a search or seizure without a warrant or with a defective warrant. And, in all except three, the Court upheld the constitutionality of the search or seizure.

> **Food for Thought**
>
> Do the Supreme Court's decided cases provide a statistically sound basis for drawing conclusions about the effects of the Court's holdings on law enforcement practices? If not, why?

Even if the warrant requirement does inconvenience the police to some extent, that fact does not distinguish this constitutional requirement from any other procedural protection secured by the Bill of Rights. It is merely a part of the price that our society must pay in order to preserve its freedom.

POINTS FOR DISCUSSION

a. Containers and Cars

Before *Acevedo*, the Court had held in *Ross* that the police can search a container in a car without first obtaining a warrant if they have probable cause to search the entire car. (The search of the car, in turn, would be permissible without a warrant because of the automobile exception.) In *Acevedo*, the Court held that the automobile exception to the warrant requirement extends to cases in which the police have probable cause to believe that there is evidence in a specific movable container within the car, even if they do not have probable cause to search the vehicle itself. It remains the case, however, that the police generally cannot conduct a warrantless search of a movable container—such as a suitcase or a briefcase—if it is not in a car.

b. Warrants and Reasonable Searches

In concluding that the police were permitted to search the container in the car without first obtaining a warrant, the Court in *Acevedo* reasoned that the prior rule, announced in *Sanders*, "provided only minimal protection for privacy and [has] impeded effective law enforcement." How should the Court balance the interest in privacy against the need for effective law enforcement? Does the Fourth Amendment strike that balance by referring to the requirements for warrants? Or does it require courts to do so by referring to "unreasonable" searches?

3. Searches Based on Consent

The Fourth Amendment protects an individual right to be free from unreasonable searches and seizures. But that does not mean that an individual *must* insist that the police obtain a warrant before searching his house. If the police ask a person if he would be willing to let them enter his home and search it, the person, confident that he has nothing to hide, can consent to the search. In other words, a person may waive the protections that the Fourth Amendment otherwise would provide by voluntarily consenting to a search. In such circumstances, the police effectively can conduct a search without first obtaining a warrant (or without even having probable cause).

But what happens if more than one person lives in a place that the police want to search? Can any one of them consent to the search? What about others who are simply present there? Can the police ever rely on an expression of consent from a person who turns out not to have authority to give such consent? Consider the case that follows.

ILLINOIS V. RODRIGUEZ
497 U.S. 177 (1990)

JUSTICE SCALIA delivered the opinion of the Court.

On July 26, 1985, police were summoned to the residence of Dorothy Jackson on South Wolcott in Chicago. They were met by Ms. Jackson's daughter, Gail Fischer, who showed signs of a severe beating. She told the officers that she had been assaulted by respondent Edward Rodriguez earlier that day in an apartment on South California. Fischer stated that Rodriguez was then asleep in the apartment, and she consented to travel there with the police in order to unlock the door with her key so that the officers could enter and arrest him. During this conversation, Fischer several times referred to the apartment on South California as "our" apartment, and said that she had clothes and furniture there. It is unclear whether she indicated that she currently lived at the apartment, or only that she used to live there.

The police officers drove to the apartment on South California, accompanied by Fischer. They did not obtain an arrest warrant for Rodriguez, nor did they seek a search warrant for the apartment. At the apartment, Fischer unlocked the door with her key and gave the officers permission to enter. They moved through the door into the living room, where they observed in plain view drug paraphernalia and containers filled with white powder that they believed (correctly, as later analysis showed) to be cocaine. They proceeded to the bedroom, where they found Rodriguez asleep and discovered additional containers of white powder in two open attaché cases. The officers arrested Rodriguez and seized the drugs and related paraphernalia.

Rodriguez was charged with possession of a controlled substance with intent to deliver. He moved to suppress all evidence seized at the time of his arrest, claiming that Fischer had vacated the apartment several weeks earlier and had no authority to consent to the entry. The Cook County Circuit Court granted the motion, holding that at the time she consented to the entry Fischer did not have common authority over the apartment. The Court concluded that Fischer was not a "usual resident" but rather an "infrequent visitor" at the apartment on South California, based upon its findings that Fischer's name was not on the lease, that she did not contribute to the rent, that she was not allowed to invite others to the apartment on her own, that she did not have access to the apartment when respondent was away, and that she had moved some of her possessions from the apartment. [The appellate court affirmed and the state Supreme Court declined to review the decision.]

The Fourth Amendment generally prohibits the warrantless entry of a person's home, whether to make an arrest or to search for specific objects. *Payton v. New York,* 445 U.S. 573 (1980). The prohibition does not apply, however, to situations in which voluntary consent has been obtained, either from the individual whose property is searched, see *Schneckloth v. Bustamonte,* 412 U.S. 218 (1973), or from a third party who possesses common authority over the premises, see *United States v. Matlock,* 415 U.S. 164 (1974). The State of Illinois contends that that exception applies in the present case.

> **Take Note**
>
> The Court here explains the general rule that the police may search a dwelling if they obtain consent from the person who lives there or from others who possess "common authority" over the premises. The Court then explains that Fischer could not give valid consent to the search of the apartment in this case. Why wasn't that the end of the case?

As we stated in *Matlock, supra,* at 171, n. 7, "[c]ommon authority" rests "on mutual use of the property by persons generally having joint access or control for most purposes. . . ." The burden of establishing that common authority rests upon the State. On the basis of this record, it is clear that burden was not sustained. The evidence showed that although Fischer, with her two small children, had lived with Rodriguez beginning in December 1984, she had moved out on July 1, 1985, almost a month before the search at issue here, and had gone to live with her mother. She took her and her children's clothing with her, though leaving behind some furniture and household effects. During the period after July 1 she sometimes spent the night at Rodriguez's apartment, but never invited her friends there, and never went there herself when he was not home. Her name was not on the lease nor did she contribute to the rent. She had a key to the apartment, which she said at trial she had taken without Rodriguez's knowledge (though she testified at the preliminary hearing that Rodriguez had given her the key). On these facts the State has not established that, with respect to the South California apartment, Fischer had "joint access or control for most purposes." To the contrary, the Appellate

Court's determination of no common authority over the apartment was obviously correct.

The State contends that, even if Fischer did not in fact have authority to give consent, it suffices to validate the entry that the law enforcement officers reasonably believed she did. * * * [R]espondent asserts that permitting a reasonable belief of common authority to validate an entry would cause a defendant's Fourth Amendment rights to be "vicariously waived." We disagree.

What [Rodriguez] is assured by the Fourth Amendment itself [is] not that no government search of his house will occur unless he consents; but that no such search will occur that is "unreasonable." There are various elements, of course, that can make a search of a person's house "reasonable"—one of which is the consent of the person or his cotenant. The essence of respondent's argument is that we should impose upon this element a requirement that we have not imposed upon other elements that regularly compel government officers to exercise judgment regarding the facts: namely, the requirement that their judgment be not only responsible but correct.

The fundamental objective that alone validates all unconsented government searches is, of course, the seizure of persons who have committed or are about to commit crimes, or of evidence related to crimes. But "reasonableness," with respect to this necessary element, does not demand that the government be factually correct in its assessment that that is what a search will produce. Warrants need only be supported by "probable cause," which demands no more than a proper "assessment of probabilities in particular factual contexts. . . ." *Illinois v. Gates,* 462 U.S. 213, 232 (1983). If a magistrate, based upon seemingly reliable but factually inaccurate information, issues a warrant for the search of a house in which the sought-after felon is not present, has never been present, and was never likely to have been present, the owner of that house suffers one of the inconveniences we all expose ourselves to as the cost of living in a safe society; he does not suffer a violation of the Fourth Amendment.

[I]n order to satisfy the "reasonableness" requirement of the Fourth Amendment, what is generally demanded of the many factual determinations that must regularly be made by agents of the government—whether the magistrate issuing a warrant, the police officer executing a warrant, or the police officer conducting a search or seizure under one of the exceptions to the warrant requirement—is not that they always be correct, but that they always be reasonable. As we put it in *Brinegar v. United States,* 338 U.S. 160, 176 (1949): "Because many situations which confront officers in the course of executing their duties are more or less ambiguous, room must be allowed for some mistakes on their part. But the mistakes must be those of reasonable men, acting on facts leading sensibly to their conclusions of probability."

We see no reason to depart from this general rule with respect to facts bearing upon the authority to consent to a search. Whether the basis for such authority exists is the sort of recurring factual question to which law enforcement officials must be expected to apply their judgment; and all the Fourth Amendment requires is that they answer it reasonably. The Constitution is no more violated when officers enter without a warrant because they reasonably (though erroneously) believe that the person who has consented to their entry is a resident of the premises, than it is violated when they enter without a warrant because they reasonably (though erroneously) believe they are in pursuit of a violent felon who is about to escape.*

[W]hat we hold today does not suggest that law enforcement officers may always accept a person's invitation to enter premises. Even when the invitation is accompanied by an explicit assertion that the person lives there, the surrounding circumstances could conceivably be such that a reasonable person would doubt its truth and not act upon it without further inquiry. As with other factual determinations bearing upon search and seizure, determination of consent to enter must "be judged against an objective standard: would the facts available to the officer at the moment . . . 'warrant a man of reasonable caution in the belief' " that the consenting party had authority over the premises? *Terry v. Ohio,* 392 U.S. 1, 21–22 (1968). If not, then warrantless entry without further inquiry is unlawful unless authority actually exists. But if so, the search is valid.

In the present case, the Appellate Court found it unnecessary to determine whether the officers reasonably believed that Fischer had the authority to consent, because it ruled as a matter of law that a reasonable belief could not validate the entry. Since we find that ruling to be in error, we remand for consideration of that question.

JUSTICE MARSHALL, with whom JUSTICE BRENNAN and JUSTICE STEVENS join, dissenting.

---

* Justice MARSHALL's dissent rests upon a rejection of the proposition that searches pursuant to valid third-party consent are "generally reasonable." Only a warrant or exigent circumstances, he contends, can produce "reasonableness"; consent validates the search only because the object of the search thereby "limit [s] his expectation of privacy," so that the search becomes not really a search at all. We see no basis for making such an artificial distinction. To describe a consented search as a noninvasion of privacy and thus a non-search is strange in the extreme. And while it must be admitted that this ingenious device can explain why consented searches are lawful, it cannot explain why seemingly consented searches are "unreasonable," which is all that the Constitution forbids. The only basis for contending that the constitutional standard could not possibly have been met here is the argument that reasonableness must be judged by the facts as they were, rather than by the facts as they were known. As we have discussed in text, that argument has long since been rejected.

The majority agrees with the Illinois Appellate Court's determination that Fischer did not have authority to consent to the officers' entry of Rodriguez's apartment. The Court holds that the warrantless entry into Rodriguez's home was nonetheless valid if the officers reasonably believed that Fischer had authority to consent. The majority's defense of this position rests on a misconception of the basis for third-party consent searches. That such searches do not give rise to claims of constitutional violations rests not on the premise that they are "reasonable" under the Fourth Amendment, but on the premise that a person may voluntarily limit his expectation of privacy by allowing others to exercise authority over his possessions. Cf. *Katz v. United States,* 389 U.S. 347, 351 (1967) ("What a person knowingly exposes to the public, even in his own home or office, is not a subject of Fourth Amendment protection"). Thus, an individual's decision to permit another "joint access [to] or control [over the property] for most purposes," *United States v. Matlock,* 415 U.S. 164, 171, n. 7 (1974), limits that individual's reasonable expectation of privacy and to that extent limits his Fourth Amendment protections. If an individual has not so limited his expectation of privacy, the police may not dispense with the safeguards established by the Fourth Amendment.

The Court has tolerated departures from the warrant requirement only when an exigency makes a warrantless search imperative to the safety of the police and of the community. * * * Unlike searches conducted pursuant to the recognized exceptions to the warrant requirement, third-party consent searches are not based on an exigency and therefore serve no compelling social goal. Police officers, when faced with the choice of relying on consent by a third party or securing a warrant, should secure a warrant and must therefore accept the risk of error should they instead choose to rely on consent.

Our prior cases discussing searches based on third-party consent have never suggested that such searches are "reasonable." [T]hird-party consent limits a person's ability to challenge the reasonableness of the search only because that person voluntarily has relinquished some of his expectation of privacy by sharing access or control over his property with another person.

A search conducted pursuant to an officer's reasonable but mistaken belief that a third party had authority to consent is thus on an entirely different constitutional footing from one based on the consent of a third party who in fact has such authority. Even if the officers reasonably believed that Fischer had authority to consent, she did not, and Rodriguez's expectation of privacy was therefore undiminished. Rodriguez accordingly can challenge the warrantless intrusion into his home as a violation of the Fourth Amendment.

POINTS FOR DISCUSSION

a. The Test for Warrantless Searches Based on Consent

The Court in *Rodriguez* explained that police can search a home or apartment without first obtaining a warrant if they obtain voluntary consent from the "individual whose property is searched" or "from a third party who possesses common authority over the premises." The Court concluded that a warrantless search is also permissible under the Fourth Amendment when a person who does *not* have common authority over the premises consents, if the police reasonably believed that the person had authority to consent to the search.

Can the consent of a landlord who owns an apartment building justify a warrantless search of an apartment in the building if the tenant does not consent? In such a case, the person "whose property is searched," in one sense, has consented. But the Court has concluded that a landlord may not consent to a search of his tenant's apartment. See *Chapman v. United States*, 365 U.S. 610 (1961).

b. Reasonableness or Diminished Expectation of Privacy?

In the Court's view, consent—whether by the suspect or a co-tenant—renders a search reasonable, and thus consistent with the Fourth Amendment. In the dissent's view, consent takes the police's conduct outside of the scope of the Fourth Amendment entirely, by relinquishing the expectation of privacy that is the touchstone for determining if a search has occurred in the first place. Which view makes more sense? Which is more consistent with the text of the Fourth Amendment? Under the dissent's view, can the police ever rely on consent to a search from the suspect's co-tenant? Would it make more sense to conclude that searches preceded by consent are permissible because a person can *waive* a constitutional right, here the right to be free from unreasonable or warrantless searches?

4. Searches Incident to Arrest

If the police have probable cause to arrest a person, can they search him without first obtaining a warrant? The Supreme Court has answered this question affirmatively. The Court has said that a search incident to a lawful arrest is another exception to the usual warrant requirement of the Fourth Amendment. The police may search the person arrested and the area that is in the person's control. The Court in *Chimel v. California*, 395 U.S. 752 (1969), explained that such searches are exempt from the warrant requirement because they are necessary "to remove any weapons that the [arrestee] might seek to use in order to resist arrest or effect his escape" and to prevent the "concealment or destruction" of evidence. Accordingly, such searches, even without a warrant, are reasonable within the meaning of the Fourth Amendment. For an example, consider the case that follows.

UNITED STATES V. ROBINSON
414 U.S. 218 (1973)

MR. JUSTICE REHNQUIST delivered the opinion of the Court.

On April 23, 1968, at approximately 11 p.m., Officer Richard Jenks, a 15-year veteran of the District of Columbia Metropolitan Police Department, observed the respondent driving a 1965 Cadillac near the intersection of 8th and C Streets, N.E., in the District of Columbia. Jenks, as a result of previous investigation following a check of respondent's operator's permit four days earlier, determined there was reason to believe that respondent was operating a motor vehicle after the revocation of his operator's permit. This is an offense defined by statute in the District of Columbia * * *.

Jenks signaled respondent to stop the automobile, which respondent did, and all three of the occupants emerged from the car. At that point Jenks informed respondent that he was under arrest for "operating after revocation and obtaining a permit by misrepresentation." It was assumed by the Court of Appeals, and is conceded by the respondent here, that Jenks had probable cause to arrest respondent, and that he effected a full custody arrest.

In accordance with procedures prescribed in police department instructions, Jenks then began to search respondent. He explained at a subsequent hearing that he was "face-to-face" with the respondent, and "placed (his) hands on (the respondent), my right-hand to his left breast like this (demonstrating) and proceeded to pat him down thus (with the right hand)." During this patdown, Jenks felt an object in the left breast pocket of the heavy coat respondent was wearing, but testified that he "couldn't tell what it was" and also that he "couldn't actually tell the size of it." Jenks then reached into the pocket and pulled out the object, which turned out to be a "crumpled up cigarette package." Jenks testified that at this point he still did not know what was in the package, [but that] "I knew they weren't cigarettes."

The officer then opened the cigarette pack and found 14 gelatin capsules of white powder which he thought to be, and which later analysis proved to be, heroin. Jenks then continued his search of respondent to completion, feeling around his waist and trouser legs, and examining the remaining pockets. The heroin seized from the respondent was admitted into evidence at the trial which resulted in his conviction in the District Court [for possession and facilitation of concealment of heroin. The court of appeals reversed, concluding that the evidence against respondent had been obtained as a result of an unlawful search.]

We conclude that the search conducted by Jenks in this case did not offend the limits imposed by the Fourth Amendment, and we therefore reverse the judgment of the Court of Appeals.

It is well settled that a search incident to a lawful arrest is a traditional exception to the warrant requirement of the Fourth Amendment. This general exception has historically been formulated into two distinct propositions. The first is that a search may be made of the person of the arrestee by virtue of the lawful arrest. The second is that a search may be made of the area within the control of the arrestee.

> **Take Note**
>
> The Court explains here that when the police have authority to arrest a person—either because they obtained a warrant or had probable cause—they may search the person and the area within his control. This is known as a "search incident to arrest." What are the justifications for this exception to the warrant requirement?

Examination of this Court's decisions shows that these two propositions have been treated quite differently. The validity of the search of a person incident to a lawful arrest has been regarded as settled from its first enunciation, and has remained virtually unchallenged until the present case. The validity of the second proposition, while likewise conceded in principle, has been subject to differing interpretations as to the extent of the area which may be searched. * * * Throughout the series of cases in which the Court has addressed the second proposition relating to a search incident to a lawful arrest—the permissible area beyond the person of the arrestee which such a search may cover—no doubt has been expressed as to the unqualified authority of the arresting authority to search the person of the arrestee.

In its decision of this case, the Court of Appeals decided that even after a police officer lawfully places a suspect under arrest for the purpose of taking him into custody, he may not ordinarily proceed to fully search the prisoner. He must, instead, conduct a limited frisk of the outer clothing and remove such weapons that he may, as a result of that limited frisk, reasonably believe and ascertain that the suspect has in his possession. While recognizing that *Terry v. Ohio*, 392 U.S. 1 (1968), dealt with a permissible "frisk" incident to an investigative stop based on less than probable cause to arrest, the Court of Appeals felt that the principles of that case should be carried over to this probable-cause arrest for driving while one's license is revoked. Since there would be no further evidence of such a crime to be obtained in a search of the arrestee, the court held that only a search for weapons could be justified.

Terry v. Ohio did not involve an arrest for probable cause, and it made quite clear that the "protective frisk" for weapons which it approved might be conducted without probable cause. This Court's opinion explicitly recognized that there is a "distinction in purpose, character, and extent between a search incident to an arrest and a limited search for weapons." "The former, although justified in part by the acknowledged necessity to protect the arresting officer from assault with a concealed weapon, [is] also justified on other grounds, and can therefore involve a relatively extensive exploration of the person. A search for weapons in the absence of probable cause to arrest, however, must, like any other search, be strictly circumscribed by the exigencies which justify its initiation." *Id.*, at 25–26 (footnote omitted). *Terry*, therefore, affords no basis to carry over to a probable-cause arrest the limitations this Court placed on a stop-and-frisk search permissible without probable cause.

> **Make the Connection**
>
> We considered *Terry v. Ohio*, and the police's authority to "stop and frisk," earlier in this chapter.

The Court of Appeals in effect determined that the only reason supporting the authority for a full search incident to lawful arrest was the possibility of discovery of evidence or fruits. Concluding that there could be no evidence or fruits in the case of an offense such as that with which respondent was charged, it held that any protective search would have to be limited by the conditions laid down in *Terry* for a search upon less than probable cause to arrest. Quite apart from the fact that *Terry* clearly recognized the distinction between the two types of searches, and that a different rule governed one than governed the other, we find additional reason to disagree with the Court of Appeals.

The justification or reason for the authority to search incident to a lawful arrest rests quite as much on the need to disarm the suspect in order to take him into custody as it does on the need to preserve evidence on his person for later use at trial. *Agnello v. United States*, 269 U.S. 20 (1925); *Abel v. United States*, 362 U.S. 217 (1960). The standards traditionally governing a search incident to lawful arrest are not, therefore, commuted to the stricter *Terry* standards by the absence of probable fruits or further evidence of the particular crime for which the arrest is made.

Nor are we inclined, on the basis of what seems to us to be a rather speculative judgment, to qualify the breadth of the general authority to search incident to a lawful custodial arrest on an assumption that persons arrested for the offense of driving while their licenses have been revoked are less likely to possess dangerous weapons than are those arrested for other crimes. It is scarcely open to doubt that the danger to an officer is far greater in the case of the extended exposure which follows the taking of a suspect into custody and transporting him to the police station than in the case of the relatively fleeting contact resulting from the typical *Terry*-type stop. This is an adequate basis for treating all custodial arrests alike for purposes of search justification.

But quite apart from these distinctions, our more fundamental disagreement with the Court of Appeals arises from its suggestion that there must be litigated in each case the issue of whether or not there was present one of the reasons supporting the authority for a search of the person incident to a lawful arrest. We do not think the long line of authorities of this Court dating back to *Weeks v. United States*, 232 U.S. 383 (1914), or what we can glean from the history of practice in this country and in England, requires such a case-by-case adjudication. A police officer's determination as to how and where to search the person of a suspect whom he has arrested is necessarily a quick ad hoc judgment which the Fourth Amendment does not require to be broken down in each instance into an analysis of each step in the search. The authority to search the person incident to a lawful custodial arrest, while based upon the need to disarm and to discover evidence, does not depend on what a court may later decide was the probability in a particular arrest situation that weapons or evidence would in fact be found upon the person of the suspect. A custodial arrest of a suspect based on probable cause is a reasonable intrusion under the Fourth Amendment; that intrusion being lawful, a search incident to the arrest requires no additional justification. It is the fact of the lawful arrest which establishes the authority to search, and we hold that in the case of a lawful custodial arrest a full search of the person is not only an exception to the warrant requirement of the Fourth Amendment, but is also a "reasonable" search under that Amendment.

The search of respondent's person conducted by Officer Jenks in this case and the seizure from him of the heroin were permissible under established Fourth Amendment law. * * * Since it is the fact of custodial arrest which gives rise to the authority to search, it is of no moment that Jenks did not indicate any subjective fear of the respondent or that he did not himself suspect that respondent was armed. Having in the course of a lawful search come upon the crumpled package of cigarettes, he was entitled to inspect it; and when his inspection revealed the heroin capsules, he was entitled to seize them as "fruits, instrumentalities, or contraband" probative of criminal conduct. *Harris v. United States*, 331 U.S. 145, 154–155 (1947). The judgment of the Court of Appeals holding otherwise is reversed.

MR. JUSTICE MARSHALL, with whom MR. JUSTICE DOUGLAS and MR. JUSTICE BRENNAN join, dissenting.

[The Court holds] that "the fact of the lawful arrest" always establishes the authority to conduct a full search of the arrestee's person, regardless of whether in a particular case "there was present one of the reasons supporting the authority for a search of the person incident to a lawful arrest." The majority's approach represents a clear and marked departure from our long tradition of case-by-case adjudication of the reasonableness of searches and seizures under the Fourth Amendment. * * *

As I view the matter, the search in this case divides into three distinct phases: the patdown of respondent's coat pocket; the removal of the unknown object from the pocket; and the opening of the crumpled-up cigarette package.

No question is raised here concerning the lawfulness of the patdown of respondent's coat pocket. The Court of Appeals unanimously affirmed the right of a police officer to conduct a limited frisk for weapons when making an in-custody arrest, regardless of the nature of the crime for which the arrest was made. * * *

With respect to the removal of the unknown object from the coat pocket, the first issue presented is whether that aspect of the search can be sustained as part of the limited frisk for weapons. * * * It appears to have been conceded by the Government below that the removal of the object from respondent's coat pocket exceeded the scope of a *Terry* frisk for weapons, since, under *Terry*, an officer may not remove an object from the suspect's pockets unless he has reason to believe it to be a dangerous weapon. * * * In the present case, however, Officer Jenks had no reason to believe and did not in fact believe that the object in respondent's coat pocket was a weapon. * * * Since the removal of the object from the pocket cannot be justified as part of a limited *Terry* weapons frisk, the question arises whether it is reasonable for a police officer, when effecting an in-custody arrest of a traffic offender, to make a fuller search of the person than is permitted pursuant to *Terry*.

* * * A search incident to arrest, as the majority indicates, has two basic functions: the removal of weapons the arrestee might use to resist arrest or effect an escape, and the seizure of evidence or fruits of the crime for which the arrest is made, so as to prevent their concealment or destruction.

The Government does not now contend that the search of respondent's pocket can be justified by any need to find and seize evidence in order to prevent its concealment or destruction, for, as the Court of Appeals found, there is no evidence or fruits of the offense with which respondent was charged. The only rationale for a search in this case, then, is the removal of weapons which the arrestee might use to harm the officer and attempt an escape.

> **Food for Thought**
>
> Should it matter that the officer was not likely to find evidence of driving without a license? If the police execute a lawful search of an apartment in investigating a homicide and they find illegal drugs, the drugs can be seized and used as the basis for a prosecution for drug possession. Why, according to Justice Marshall, is this case different?

While the policeman who arrests a suspected rapist or robber may well have reason to believe he is dealing with an armed and dangerous person, certainly this does not hold true with equal force with respect to a person arrested for a motor vehicle violation of the sort involved in this case. * * * Nor was there any particular reason in this case to believe that respondent was dangerous. He had not attempted to evade arrest, but had quickly complied with the police both in bringing his car to a stop after being signaled to do so and in producing the documents Officer Jenks requested. * * *

The majority opinion fails to recognize that the search conducted by Officer Jenks did not merely involve a search of respondent's person. It also included a separate search of effects found on his person. And even were we to assume, arguendo, that it was reasonable for Jenks to remove the object he felt in respondent's pocket, clearly there was no justification consistent with the Fourth Amendment which would authorize his opening the package and looking inside.

To begin with, after Jenks had the cigarette package in his hands, there is no indication that he had reason to believe or did in fact believe that the package contained a weapon. More importantly, even if the crumpled-up cigarette package had in fact contained some sort of small weapon, it would have been impossible for respondent to have used it once the package was in the officer's hands. Opening the package, therefore, did not further the protective purpose of the search.

The search conducted by Officer Jenks in this case went far beyond what was reasonably necessary to protect him from harm or to ensure that respondent would not effect an escape from custody. In my view, it therefore fell outside the scope of a properly drawn "search incident to arrest" exception to the Fourth Amendment's warrant requirement. I would affirm the judgment of the Court of

Appeals holding that the fruits of the search should have been suppressed at respondent's trial.

POINTS FOR DISCUSSION

a. Search Incident to Arrest

When the police properly arrest a person, they may conduct a warrantless "search incident to arrest"—that is, a search of the person and the area within his immediate control. Searches incident to arrest need not be limited to mere patdowns or frisks, but can be full searches of the person in custody and things in his possession. The Court in *Robinson* held that such searches are permissible even when the police officer does not "indicate any subjective fear" of the suspect or does "not himself suspect that [the person] was armed."

b. Scope of Searches Incident to Arrest

What does it mean to say that the police may search the area within the arrestee's "immediate control" upon arresting him? Suppose that the police stop a vehicle because they have probable cause to believe that the driver has been driving with a suspended license. During the stop, the police discover that he has in fact been driving with a suspended license, and they arrest him, handcuff him, and place him in the patrol car. While the driver sits in the patrol car, the police search his car and find cocaine in the pocket of a jacket in the car. Is the search a permissible warrantless search incident to arrest?

In *Arizona v. Gant*, 556 U.S. 332 (2009), the Court held that such a search violated the Fourth Amendment. The Court reasoned that the police can search a car following an arrest as a search incident to arrest only if the person arrested "could have accessed his car at the time of the search." Because the suspect was confined to the patrol car, however, the police could not search the arrestee's car as a search incident to arrest. (If the police had had probable cause to believe that there were drugs in the car, however, they would have been permitted to search the car without a warrant pursuant to the automobile exception.) Is this conclusion consistent with the Court's reasoning in *Robinson*?

D. THE EXCLUSIONARY RULE

In some cases, the remedy for the government's violation of a constitutional right is clear. If a public university improperly considers race as a determinative factor in admissions, a person aggrieved by the policy can obtain an injunction ordering the school to change its admissions policy and to grant her admission to the school. Cf. *Regents of University of California v. Bakke*, 438 U.S. 265 (1978). If a public school places tributes to the Ten Commandments in classrooms, a person aggrieved can obtain an injunction to force the school to remove the display. Cf. *Stone v. Graham*, 449 U.S. 39 (1981). Sometimes compensatory damages are an appropriate remedy for the violation of a constitutional right. See *Bivens v. Six Unknown Named Agents of Federal Bureau of Narcotics*, 403 U.S. 388 (1971).

What is the remedy for a search that violates the Fourth Amendment? An injunction preventing future searches does not help the defendant on whose property or person the police have already found evidence of criminal activity. And the prospect of damages might chill lawful police conduct in close cases and thus impede the police's ability to investigate and solve crimes.

In *Weeks v. United States*, 232 U.S. 383 (1914), the Court reversed a conviction because it had been based on evidence seized in an unlawful search. The Court held that such evidence cannot be used at trial against the defendant. This approach soon became known as the "exclusionary rule," because it requires the exclusion from trial of evidence seized during unlawful searches.

In *Wolf v. Colorado*, 338 U.S. 25 (1949), the Court held that the Fourth Amendment incorporates the right against unreasonable searches and seizures, but that it does not incorporate the "exclusionary rule." After *Wolf*, accordingly, the exclusionary rule did not apply to searches by state and local police and to evidence offered during state prosecutions. The Court overruled that holding in the case that follows. The exclusionary rule now applies in both state and federal prosecutions.

> **Make the Connection**
>
> We considered the doctrine of "incorporation," by which the Court concluded that certain provisions of the Bill of Rights limit the power of the states, in Chapter 1.

MAPP V. OHIO
367 U.S. 643 (1961)

MR. JUSTICE CLARK delivered the opinion of the Court.

Appellant stands convicted of knowingly having had in her possession and under her control certain lewd and lascivious books, pictures, and photographs in violation of § 2905.34 of Ohio's Revised Code. [Police went to Mapp's residence after receiving a tip that there was a person "hiding out in the home" who was "wanted for questioning in connection with a recent bombing."] Upon their arrival at that house, the officers knocked on the door and demanded entrance but appellant, after telephoning her attorney, refused to admit them without a search warrant. They advised their headquarters of the situation and undertook a surveillance of the house.

The officers again sought entrance some three hours later when four or more additional officers arrived on the scene. When Miss Mapp did not come to the door immediately, at least one of the several doors to the house was forcibly opened and the policemen gained admittance. Meanwhile Miss Mapp's attorney arrived, but the officers, having secured their own entry, [would] permit him neither to see Miss Mapp nor to enter the house. * * * Mapp demanded to see the search warrant. A paper, claimed to be a warrant, was held up by one of the officers. She grabbed the "warrant" and placed it in her bosom. A struggle ensued in which the officers recovered the piece of paper and as a result of which they handcuffed appellant because she had been "belligerent" in resisting their official rescue of the "warrant" from her person. * * * Appellant, in handcuffs, was then forcibly taken upstairs to her bedroom where the officers searched a dresser, a chest of drawers, a closet and some suitcases. They also looked into a photo album and through personal papers belonging to the appellant. The search spread to the rest of the second floor including the child's bedroom, the living room, the kitchen and a dinette. The basement of the building and a trunk found therein were also searched. The obscene materials for possession of which she was ultimately convicted were discovered in the course of that widespread search.

> **Take Note**
>
> Can you explain why the search that produced the evidence in question in this case violated the Fourth Amendment? The search was of the defendant's home and it seems that the police did not obtain a proper warrant. Did any of the exceptions to the warrant requirement apply?

Specifically dealing with the use of the evidence unconstitutionally seized, the Court [in *Weeks v. United States*, 232 U.S. 383, 393 (1914),] concluded:

> "If letters and private documents can thus be seized and held and used in evidence against a citizen accused of an offense, the protection of the Fourth Amendment declaring his right to be secure against such searches and seizures is of no value, and, so far as those thus placed are concerned, might as well be stricken from the Constitution. The efforts of the courts and their officials to bring the guilty to punishment, praiseworthy as they are, are not to be aided by the sacrifice of those great principles established by years of endeavor and suffering which have resulted in their embodiment in the fundamental law of the land."

[T]he Court in that case clearly stated that use of the seized evidence involved "a denial of the constitutional rights of the accused." [*Id.* at 398.] Thus, in the year

1914, [this] Court "for the first time" held that "in a federal prosecution the Fourth Amendment barred the use of evidence secured through an illegal search and seizure." *Wolf v. People of State of Colorado*, 338 U.S. 25, 28 (1949). This Court has ever since required of federal law officers a strict adherence to that command which this Court has held to be a clear, specific, and constitutionally required—even if judicially implied—deterrent safeguard without insistence upon which the Fourth Amendment would have been reduced to "a form of words." *Silverthorne Lumber Co. v. United States*, 251 U.S. 385, 392 (1920) (Holmes, J.). * * *

There are in the cases of this Court some passing references to the *Weeks* rule as being one of evidence. But the plain and unequivocal language of *Weeks*—and its later paraphrase in *Wolf*—to the effect that the *Weeks* rule is of constitutional origin, remains entirely undisturbed. * * *

In 1949, 35 years after *Weeks* was announced, this Court, in *Wolf v. People of State of Colorado*, again for the first time, discussed the effect of the Fourth Amendment upon the States through the operation of the Due Process Clause of the Fourteenth Amendment. [A]fter declaring that the "security of one's privacy against arbitrary intrusion by the police" is "implicit in 'the concept of ordered liberty' and as such enforceable against the States through the Due Process Clause," cf. *Palko v. State of Connecticut*, 302 U.S. 319 (1937), and announcing that it "stoutly adhere[d]" to the *Weeks* decision, the Court decided that the *Weeks* exclusionary rule would not then be imposed upon the States as "an essential ingredient of the right." 338 U.S. at 27–29. The Court's reasons for not considering essential to the right to privacy, as a curb imposed upon the States by the Due Process Clause, that which decades before had been posited as part and parcel of the Fourth Amendment's limitations upon federal encroachment of individual privacy, were bottomed on factual considerations.

While they are not basically relevant to a decision that the exclusionary rule is an essential ingredient of the Fourth Amendment as the right it embodies is vouchsafed against the States by the Due Process Clause, we will consider the current validity of the factual grounds upon which *Wolf* was based.

The Court in *Wolf* [stated] that "[t]he contrariety of views of the States" on the adoption of the exclusionary rule of *Weeks* was "particularly impressive"; and, in this connection that it could not "brush aside the experience of States which deem the incidence of such conduct by the police too slight to call for a deterrent remedy . . . by overriding the [States'] relevant rules of evidence." While in 1949, prior to the *Wolf* case, almost two-thirds of the States were opposed to the use of the exclusionary rule, now, despite the *Wolf* case, more than half of those since passing upon it, by their own legislative or judicial decision, have wholly or partly adopted or adhered to the *Weeks* rule. Significantly, among those now following the rule is California, which, according to its highest court, was "compelled to reach that conclusion because other remedies have completely failed to secure compliance with the constitutional provisions . . . ." *People v. Cahan*, 44 Cal.2d 434, 445 (1955). * * * The experience of California that such other remedies have been worthless and futile is buttressed by the experience of other States. The obvious futility of relegating the Fourth Amendment of the protection of other remedies has, moreover, been recognized by this Court since *Wolf.* See *Irvine v. People of State of California*, 347 U.S. 128, 137 (1954).

Today we [re-examine] *Wolf*'s constitutional documentation of the right to privacy free from unreasonable state intrusion, and, after its dozen years on our books, are led by it to close the only courtroom door remaining open to evidence secured by official lawlessness in flagrant abuse of that basic right, reserved to all persons as a specific guarantee against that very same unlawful conduct. We hold that all evidence obtained by searches and seizures in violation of the Constitution is, by that same authority, inadmissible in a state court.

Since the Fourth Amendment's right of privacy has been declared enforceable against the States through the Due Process Clause of the Fourteenth, it is enforceable against them by the same sanction of exclusion as is used against the Federal Government. Were it otherwise, then just as without the *Weeks* rule the assurance against unreasonable federal searches and seizures would be "a form of words," valueless and undeserving of mention in a perpetual charter of inestimable human liberties, so too, without that rule the freedom from state invasions of privacy would be so ephemeral and so neatly severed from its conceptual nexus with the freedom from all brutish means of coercing evidence as not to merit this Court's high regard as a freedom "implicit in 'the concept of ordered liberty." At the time that the Court held in *Wolf* that the Amendment was applicable to the States through the Due Process Clause, the cases of this Court, as we have seen, had steadfastly held that as to federal officers the Fourth Amendment included the exclusion of the evidence seized in violation of its provisions. * * * Therefore, in extending the substantive protections of due process to all constitutionally unreasonable searches—state or federal—it was logically and constitutionally necessary that the exclusion doctrine—an essential part of the right to privacy—be also insisted upon as an essential ingredient of the right newly recognized by the *Wolf* case. In short, the admission of the new constitutional right by *Wolf* could not consistently tolerate denial of its most important constitutional privilege, namely, the exclusion of the evidence which an accused had been forced to give by reason of the unlawful seizure. To hold otherwise is to grant the right but in reality to withhold its privilege and enjoyment.

Indeed, we are aware of no restraint, similar to that rejected today, conditioning the enforcement of any other basic constitutional right. * * * This Court has not hesitated to enforce as strictly against the States as it does against the Federal Government the rights of free speech and of a free press, the rights to notice and to a fair, public trial, including, as it does, the right not to be convicted by use of a coerced confession, however logically relevant it be, and without regard to its reliability. *Rogers v. Richmond*, 365 U.S. 534 (1961). And nothing could be more certain that that when a coerced confession is involved, "the relevant rules of evidence" are overridden without regard to "the incidence of such conduct by the police," slight or frequent. Why should not the same rule apply to what is tantamount to coerced testimony by way of unconstitutional seizure of goods, papers, effect, documents, etc.? We find that, as to the Federal Government, the Fourth and Fifth Amendments and, as to the States, the freedom from unconscionable invasions of privacy and the freedom from convictions based upon coerced confessions do enjoy an "intimate relation" in their perpetuation of "principles of humanity and civil liberty (secured) . . . only after years of struggle." *Bram v. United States*, 168 U.S. 532, 543–544 (1897). * * * The philosophy of each Amendment and of each freedom is complementary to, although not dependent upon, that of the other in its sphere of influence—the very least that together they assure in either sphere is that no man is to be convicted on unconstitutional evidence. Cf. *Rochin v. People of State of California*, 342 U.S. 165, 173 (1952).

Moreover, our holding that the exclusionary rule is an essential part of both the Fourth and Fourteenth Amendments is not only the logical dictate of prior cases, but it also makes very good sense. * * * Presently, a federal prosecutor may make no use of evidence illegally seized, but a State's attorney across the street may, although he supposedly is operating under the enforceable prohibitions of the same Amendment. Thus the State, by admitting evidence unlawfully seized, serves to encourage disobedience to the Federal Constitution which it is bound to uphold. Moreover, * * * "(t)he very essence of a healthy federalism depends upon the avoidance of needless conflict between state and federal courts." * * * Yet the double standard recognized until today hardly put such a thesis into practice. In non-exclusionary States, federal officers, being human, were by it invited to and did, as our cases indicate, step across the street to the State's attorney with their unconstitutionally seized evidence. Prosecution on the basis of that evidence was then had in a state court in utter disregard of the enforceable Fourth Amendment. If the fruits of an unconstitutional search had been inadmissible in both state and federal courts, this inducement to evasion would have been sooner eliminated.

There are those who say, as did Justice (then Judge) Cardozo, that under our constitutional exclusionary doctrine "[t]he criminal is to go free because the constable has blundered." *People v. Defore*, 242 N.Y. 13, 21 (1926). In some cases this will undoubtedly

> **Food for Thought**
>
> In concluding that the Fourteenth Amendment requires the exclusion of evidence in state prosecutions, is the Court interpreting the language of the Fourteenth Amendment, attempting to discern what the drafters and ratifiers of the Amendment intended or understood the Amendment to mean, or instead creating a rule that the Court favors based on doctrinal logic and policy considerations?

be the result. [But] "there is another consideration—the imperative of judicial integrity." *Elkins v. United States*, 364 U.S. 206, 222 (1960). The criminal goes free, if he must, but it is the law that sets him free. Nothing can destroy a government more quickly than its failure to observe its own laws, or worse, its disregard of the charter of its own existence.

The ignoble shortcut to conviction left open to the State tends to destroy the entire system of constitutional restraints on which the liberties of the people rest. Having once recognized that the right to privacy embodied in the Fourth Amendment is enforceable against the States, and that the right to be secure against rude invasions of privacy by state officers is, therefore, constitutional in origin, we can no longer permit that right to remain an empty promise. Because it is enforceable in the same manner and to like effect as other basic rights secured by the Due Process Clause, we can no longer permit it to be revocable at the whim of any police officer who, in the name of law enforcement itself, chooses to suspend its enjoyment. Our decision, founded on reason and truth, gives to the individual no more than that which the Constitution guarantees him, to the police officer no less than that to which honest law enforcement is entitled, and, to the courts, that judicial integrity so necessary in the true administration of justice. [Reversed.]

MR. JUSTICE BLACK, concurring.

I am [not] persuaded that the Fourth Amendment, standing alone, would be enough to bar the introduction into evidence against an accused of papers and effects seized from him in violation of its commands. For the Fourth Amendment does not itself contain any provision expressly precluding the use of such evidence, and I am extremely doubtful that such a provision could properly be inferred from nothing more than the basic command against unreasonable searches and seizures. Reflection on the problem, however, in the light of cases coming before the Court since *Wolf*, has led me to conclude that when the Fourth Amendment's ban against unreasonable searches and seizures is considered together with the Fifth Amendment's ban against compelled self-incrimination, a constitutional basis emerges which not only justifies but actually requires the exclusionary rule.

The close interrelationship between the Fourth and Fifth Amendments, as they apply to this problem, [was] expressly made the ground for this Court's holding in *Boyd v. United States*, 116 U.S. 616 (1886). There the Court fully discussed this relationship and declared itself "unable to perceive that the seizure of a man's private books and papers to be used in evidence against him is substantially different from compelling him to be a witness against himself." * * * In the final analysis, it seems to me that the *Boyd* doctrine, though perhaps not required by the express language of the Constitution strictly construed, is amply justified from an historical standpoint, soundly based in reason, and entirely consistent with what I regard to be the proper approach to interpretation of our Bill of Rights * * *.

MR. JUSTICE DOUGLAS, concurring.

When we allowed States to give constitutional sanction to the "shabby business" of unlawful entry into a home * * *, we did indeed rob the Fourth Amendment of much meaningful force. There are, of course, other theoretical remedies. One is disciplinary action within the hierarchy of the police system, including prosecution of the police officer for a crime. Yet as Mr. Justice Murphy said in *Wolf*, 338 U.S. at 42, "Self-scrutiny is a lofty ideal, but its exaltation reaches new heights if we expect a District Attorney to prosecute himself or his associates for well-meaning violations of the search and seizure clause during a raid the District Attorney or his associates have ordered."

The only remaining remedy, if exclusion of the evidence is not required, is an action of trespass by the homeowner against the offending officer. Mr. Justice Murphy showed how onerous and difficult it would be for the citizen to maintain that action and how meagre the relief even if the citizen prevails. *Wolf*, 338 U.S. at 42–44. The truth is that trespass actions against officers who make unlawful searches and seizures are mainly illusory remedies. Without judicial action making the exclusionary rule applicable to the States, *Wolf* in practical effect reduced the guarantee against unreasonable searches and seizures to "a dead letter" * * *.

[JUSTICE STEWART's opinion, which did not address the exclusionary rule, has been omitted.]

MR. JUSTICE HARLAN, whom MR. JUSTICE FRANKFURTER and MR. JUSTICE WHITTAKER join, dissenting.

At the heart of the majority's opinion in this case is the following syllogism: (1) the rule excluding in federal criminal trials evidence which is the product of all illegal search and seizure is a "part and parcel" of the Fourth Amendment; (2) *Wolf* held that the "privacy" assured against federal action by the Fourth Amendment is also protected against state action by the Fourteenth Amendment; and (3) it is therefore "logically and constitutionally necessary" that the *Weeks* exclusionary rule should also be enforced against the States.

It cannot be too much emphasized that what was recognized in *Wolf* was not that the Fourth Amendment as such is enforceable against the States as a facet of due process, * * * but the principle of privacy "which is at the core of the Fourth Amendment." It would not be proper to expect or impose any precise equivalence, either as regards the scope of the right or the means of its implementation, between the requirements of the Fourth and Fourteenth Amendments. * * *

[W]hat the Court is now doing is to impose upon the States not only federal substantive standards of "search and seizure" but also the basic federal remedy for violation of those standards. For I think it entirely clear that the *Weeks* exclusionary rule is but a remedy which, by penalizing past official misconduct, is aimed at deterring such conduct in the future.

I would not impose upon the States this federal exclusionary remedy. The reasons given by the majority for now suddenly turning its back on *Wolf* seem to me notably unconvincing.

First, it is said that "the factual grounds upon which *Wolf* was based" have since changed, in that more States now follow the *Weeks* exclusionary rule than was so at the time *Wolf* was decided. While that is true, a recent survey indicates that at present one-half of the States still adhere to the common-law non-exclusionary rule, and one, Maryland, retains the rule as to felonies. But in any case surely all this is beside the point, as the majority itself indeed seems to recognize. Our concern here, as it was in *Wolf*, is not with the desirability of that rule but only with the question whether the States are Constitutionally free to follow it or not as they may themselves determine, and the relevance of the disparity of views among the States on this point lies simply in the fact that the judgment involved is a debatable one. Moreover, the very fact on which the majority relies, instead of lending support to what is now being done, points away from the need of replacing voluntary state action with federal compulsion.

The preservation of a proper balance between state and federal responsibility in the administration of criminal justice demands patience on the part of those who might like to see things move faster among the States in this respect. Problems of criminal law enforcement vary widely from State of State. One State, in considering the totality of its legal picture, may conclude that the need for embracing the *Weeks* rule is pressing because other remedies are unavailable or inadequate to secure compliance with the substantive Constitutional principle involved. Another, though equally solicitous of Constitutional rights, may choose to pursue one purpose at a time, allowing all evidence relevant to guilt to be brought into a criminal trial, and dealing with Constitutional infractions by other means. Still another may consider the exclusionary rule too rough-and-ready a remedy, in that it reaches only unconstitutional intrusions which eventuate in criminal prosecution of the victims. Further, a State after experimenting with the *Weeks* rule for a time may, because of unsatisfactory experience with it, decide to revert to a non-exclusionary rule. And so on. * * * For us the question remains, as it has always been, one of state power, not one of passing judgment on the wisdom of one state course or another. In my view this Court should continue to forbear from fettering the States with an adamant rule which may embarrass them in coping with their own peculiar problems in criminal law enforcement.

* * * Our role in promulgating the *Weeks* rule and its extensions * * * was quite a different one than it is here. There, in implementing the Fourth Amendment, we occupied the position of a tribunal having the ultimate responsibility for developing the standards and procedures of judicial administration within the judicial system over which it presides. Here we review state procedures whose measure is to be taken not against the specific substantive commands of the Fourth Amendment but under the flexible contours of the Due Process Clause. I do not believe that the Fourteenth Amendment empowers this Court to mould state remedies effectuating the right to freedom from "arbitrary intrusion by the police" to suit its own notions of how things should be done * * *.

I do not see how it can be said that a trial becomes unfair simply because a State determines that evidence may be considered by the trier of fact, regardless of how it was obtained, if it is relevant to the one issue with which the trial is concerned, the guilt or innocence of the accused. Of course, a court may use its procedures as an incidental means of pursuing other ends than the correct resolution of the controversies before it. Such indeed is the *Weeks* rule, but if a State does not choose to use its courts in this way, I do not believe that this Court is empowered to impose this much-debated procedure on local courts, however efficacious we may consider the *Weeks* rule to be as a means of securing Constitutional rights.

[I]n the last analysis I think this Court can increase respect for the Constitution only if it rigidly respects the limitations which the Constitution places upon it, and respects as well the principles inherent in its own processes. In the present case I think we exceed both, and that our voice becomes only a voice of power, not of reason.

POINTS FOR DISCUSSION

a. Incorporation

The Court's decision in *Mapp* came after several decades of controversy over which provisions in the Bill of Rights are applicable to the states under the Fourteenth Amendment. *Mapp* marked the beginning of an eleven-year period in which the Court overruled many prior decisions and concluded that around a dozen of the rights protected by the Bill of Rights are incorporated by the Fourteenth Amendment. Most of the decisions concerning the rights afforded to criminal defendants have reasoned that "due process" requires fair procedures and that criminal prosecutions can satisfy "due process" only if courts recognize these rights. Can the same logic apply to the incorporation of rights such as the freedom of speech or free exercise of religion?

b. Costs of and Alternatives to the Exclusionary Rule

By definition, the evidence at issue in cases implicating the exclusionary rule is probative of guilt. After all, the government seeks to introduce—and the defendant seeks to exclude—only evidence that reveals wrongdoing by the defendant. In other words, the exclusionary rule matters only when the police have discovered evidence that the defendant actually committed a crime. (In *Mapp*, for example, during their warrantless search the police discovered evidence that tended to show the violation of statutes prohibiting the possession of obscene materials.) Accordingly, the application of the exclusionary rule means that defendants who in fact have committed crimes are more likely to be acquitted.

On the other hand, if the government can rely at trial on evidence seized in the course of an unlawful search, then the limits imposed by the Fourth Amendment risk becoming illusory. Although criminal defendants in theory might seek damages from police officers who have violated their rights—as Justice Douglas suggested—various legal and practical obstacles may prevent them from recovering. The reality is that the exclusionary rule is what best deters such unlawful searches and prevents the government from benefiting from the unlawful actions of its officers. Do the benefits of the exclusionary rule outweigh its costs? Who should decide this question, judges or legislators? Or has the decision already been made in the Constitution?

The Court in *Mapp* made clear that the exclusionary rule applies in both state and federal prosecutions to evidence unlawfully seized by state or federal officers. Accordingly, if officers perform a warrantless search of a home, the search does not fall into any of the exceptions to the warrant requirement, and the officers during the search discover drugs, they generally cannot introduce the drugs into evidence during a prosecution of the target of the search.

The Court has also made clear that the government cannot subsequently seek to obtain through other means evidence found during an illegal search. In *Silverthorne Lumber Co. v. United States*, 251 U.S. 385 (1920), the Court held that the government could not evade the consequences of the exclusionary rule by seeking to subpoena from the defendants (and then use at trial) documents that it had discovered during an illegal search. Justice Holmes explained: "The essence of a provision forbidding the acquisition of evidence in a certain way is that not merely evidence so acquired shall not be used before the Court but that it shall not be used at all. Of course this does not mean that the facts thus obtained become sacred and inaccessible. If knowledge of them is gained from an independent source they may be proved like any others, but the knowledge gained by the Government's own wrong cannot be used by it in the way proposed."

But what if the evidence that the officers discovered during the illegal search leads them to *other* evidence of the crime? For example, what if, during the course of an illegal search, the defendant makes incriminating statements to the police? The Court held in *Wong Sun v. United States*, 371 U.S. 471 (1963), that the "exclusionary prohibition extends as well to the indirect as the direct products of such invasions," and thus that "verbal evidence which derives so immediately from an unlawful entry and an unauthorized arrest * * * is no less the 'fruit' of official illegality than the more common tangible fruits of the unwarranted intrusion." The Court in that case concluded that incriminating statements that the defendant made during an unlawful search should be excluded from trial.

This approach is known as the "fruit of the poisonous tree" doctrine. See *Nardone v. United States*, 308 U.S. 338 (1939). According to that metaphor, the illegal search is the "poisonous" (or tainted) "tree," and the incriminating statements are the "fruit." Under this doctrine, evidence obtained as a consequence of an illegal search, even if not during the search itself, is also subject to the exclusionary rule. (The converse is also true: if a suspect's responses during an unlawful interrogation lead the police to discover evidence of crime, both the responses and the seized evidence will be excluded.) The Court has held, however, that evidence will not be excluded as fruit of the poisonous tree if it was discovered from a source independent of the illegal activity, see *Silverthorne*; its discovery was "inevitable," see *Nix v. Williams*, 467 U.S. 431 (1984); or the connection between the evidence and the unlawful police conduct is sufficiently attenuated, see *Hudson v. Michigan*, 547 U.S. 586 (2006).

Are there exceptions to the exclusionary rule and its application to all of the "fruit" of the unlawful search? In the case that follows, the Court recognized the so-called "good-faith exception" to the exclusionary rule. The Court held that the exclusionary rule does not apply to evidence obtained when a police officer conducts a search pursuant to a search warrant, even if it turns out that the judge or magistrate erred in issuing the search warrant, so long as the police officer acted in "good faith."

UNITED STATES V. LEON
468 U.S. 897 (1984)

JUSTICE WHITE delivered the opinion of the Court.

This case presents the question whether the Fourth Amendment exclusionary rule should be modified so as not to bar the use in the prosecution's case in chief of evidence obtained by officers acting in reasonable reliance on a search warrant issued by a detached and neutral magistrate but ultimately found to be unsupported by probable cause. * * *

[Officers investigating possible drug crimes obtained a warrant to search respondents' residences, which resulted in the seizure of large quantities of drugs. To secure the warrant, Burbank Police Officer Rombach prepared an affidavit that relied in significant part on tips from an informant, but that information was "stale," and the affidavit did not seek to establish the informant's reliability or to corroborate the information. After respondents were indicted for conspiracy to possess and distribute cocaine and related offenses, they moved to suppress the evidence seized during the searches. The district court granted the motion, concluding that the officers had failed to establish probable cause and suppressed most of the evidence, and the court of appeals affirmed. In its petition for certiorari, the

> **Food for Thought**
>
> Consider how the Court phrases the question presented. Does the Supreme Court have the power to "modify" what the Constitution requires? Is the exclusionary rule simply a judicial creation that the Court can modify? Contrast what the majority says in this opinion with what Justice Brennan says in his dissent.

government did not challenge the court of appeals' determination that the search warrant was unsupported by probable cause.]

The Fourth Amendment contains no provision expressly precluding the use of evidence obtained in violation of its commands, and an examination of its origin and purposes makes clear that the use of fruits of a past unlawful search or seizure "work[s] no new Fourth Amendment wrong." *United States v. Calandra*, 414 U.S. 338, 354 (1974). The wrong condemned by the Amendment is "fully accomplished" by the unlawful search or seizure itself, and the exclusionary rule is neither intended nor able to "cure the invasion of the defendant's rights which he has already suffered." *Stone v. Powell*, 428 U.S. 465, 540 (1976) (WHITE, J., dissenting). The rule thus operates as "a judicially created remedy designed to safeguard Fourth Amendment rights generally through its deterrent effect, rather than a personal constitutional right of the party aggrieved." *Calandra*, 414 U.S., at 348.

> **Food for Thought**
>
> Is the Court's description of the exclusionary rule consistent with the Court's view of it in *Mapp*? If not, why not?

Whether the exclusionary sanction is appropriately imposed in a particular case, our decisions make clear, is "an issue separate from the question whether the Fourth Amendment rights of the party seeking to invoke the rule were violated by police conduct." *Illinois v. Gates*, 462 U.S. 213, 223 (1983). Only the former question is currently before us, and it must be resolved by weighing the costs and benefits of preventing the use in the prosecution's case in chief of inherently trustworthy tangible evidence obtained in reliance on a search warrant issued by a detached and neutral magistrate that ultimately is found to be defective.

The substantial social costs exacted by the exclusionary rule for the vindication of Fourth Amendment rights have long been a source of concern. "Our cases have consistently recognized that unbending application of the exclusionary sanction to enforce ideals of governmental rectitude would impede unacceptably the truth-finding functions of judge and jury." *United States v. Payner*, 447 U.S. 727, 734 (1980). An objectionable collateral consequence of this interference with the criminal justice system's truth-finding function is that some guilty defendants may go free or receive reduced sentences as a result of favorable plea bargains.[6] Particularly when law enforcement officers have acted in objective

---

[6] Researchers have only recently begun to study extensively the effects of the exclusionary rule on the disposition of felony arrests. One study suggests that the rule results in the nonprosecution or nonconviction of between 0.6% and 2.35% of individuals arrested for felonies. Davies, A Hard Look at What We Know (and Still Need to Learn) About the "Costs" of the Exclusionary Rule: The NIJ Study and Other Studies of "Lost" Arrests, 1983 A.B.F.Res.J. 611, 621. The estimates are higher for particular crimes the prosecution of which

good faith or their transgressions have been minor, the magnitude of the benefit conferred on such guilty defendants offends basic concepts of the criminal justice system. Indiscriminate application of the exclusionary rule, therefore, may well "generat[e] disrespect for the law and administration of justice." *Stone*, 428 U.S. at 491. Accordingly, "[a]s with any remedial device, the application of the rule has been restricted to those areas where its remedial objectives are thought most efficaciously served." *Calandra*, 414 U.S., at 348.

As cases considering the use of unlawfully obtained evidence in criminal trials [make] clear, it does not follow from the emphasis on the exclusionary rule's deterrent value that "anything which deters illegal searches is thereby commanded by the Fourth Amendment." *Alderman v. United States*, 394 U.S. 165, 174 (1969). * * * Standing to invoke the rule has [been] limited to cases in which the prosecution seeks to use the fruits of an illegal search or seizure against the victim of police misconduct. *Rakas v. Illinois*, 439 U.S. 128 (1978). * * * Even defendants with standing to challenge the introduction in their criminal trials of unlawfully obtained evidence cannot prevent every conceivable use of such evidence. Evidence obtained in violation of the Fourth Amendment and inadmissible in the prosecution's case in chief may be used to impeach a defendant's direct testimony. *Walder v. United States*, 347 U.S. 62 (1954). * * * We also have held that a witness' testimony may be admitted even when his identity was discovered in an unconstitutional search. *United States v. Ceccolini*, 435 U.S. 268 (1978). The perception underlying these decisions—that the connection between police misconduct and evidence of crime may be sufficiently attenuated to permit the use of that evidence at trial—is a product of considerations relating to the exclusionary rule and the constitutional principles it is designed to protect. * * *

As yet, we have not recognized any form of good-faith exception to the Fourth Amendment exclusionary rule. But the balancing approach that has evolved during the years of experience with the rule provides strong support for the modification currently urged upon us. * * *

---

depends heavily on physical evidence. Thus, the cumulative loss due to nonprosecution or nonconviction of individuals arrested on felony drug charges is probably in the range of 2.8% to 7.1%. *Id.*, at 680. * * *

Many of these researchers have concluded that the impact of the exclusionary rule is insubstantial, but the small percentages with which they deal mask a large absolute number of felons who are released because the cases against them were based in part on illegal searches or seizures. "[A]ny rule of evidence that denies the jury access to clearly probative and reliable evidence must bear a heavy burden of justification, and must be carefully limited to the circumstances in which it will pay its way by deterring official lawlessness." *Gates*, 462 U.S., at 257–258 (WHITE, J., concurring in judgment). Because we find that the rule can have no substantial deterrent effect in the sorts of situations under consideration in this case, we conclude that it cannot pay its way in those situations.

* * * To the extent that proponents of exclusion rely on its behavioral effects on judges and magistrates * * *, their reliance is misplaced. First, the exclusionary rule is designed to deter police misconduct rather than to punish the errors of judges and magistrates. Second, there exists no evidence suggesting that judges and magistrates are inclined to ignore or subvert the Fourth Amendment or that lawlessness among these actors requires application of the extreme sanction of exclusion.

Third, and most important, we discern no basis, and are offered none, for believing that exclusion of evidence seized pursuant to a warrant will have a significant deterrent effect on the issuing judge or magistrate. * * * Judges and magistrates are not adjuncts to the law enforcement team; as neutral judicial officers, they have no stake in the outcome of particular criminal prosecutions. The threat of exclusion thus cannot be expected significantly to deter them. Imposition of the exclusionary sanction is not necessary meaningfully to inform judicial officers of their errors, and we cannot conclude that admitting evidence obtained pursuant to a warrant while at the same time declaring that the warrant was somehow defective will in any way reduce judicial officers' professional incentives to comply with the Fourth Amendment, encourage them to repeat their mistakes, or lead to the granting of all colorable warrant requests.

If exclusion of evidence obtained pursuant to a subsequently invalidated warrant is to have any deterrent effect, therefore, it must alter the behavior of individual law enforcement officers or the policies of their departments. One could argue that applying the exclusionary rule in cases where the police failed to demonstrate probable cause in the warrant application deters future inadequate presentations or "magistrate shopping" and thus promotes the ends of the Fourth Amendment. Suppressing evidence obtained pursuant to a technically defective warrant supported by probable cause also might encourage officers to scrutinize more closely the form of the warrant and to point out suspected judicial errors. We find such arguments speculative and conclude that suppression of evidence obtained pursuant to a warrant should be ordered only on a case-by-case basis and only in those unusual cases in which exclusion will further the purposes of the exclusionary rule. * * * But even assuming that the [exclusionary] rule effectively deters some police misconduct and provides incentives for the law enforcement profession as a whole to conduct itself in accord with the Fourth Amendment, it cannot be expected, and should not be applied, to deter objectively reasonable law enforcement activity.

As we observed in *Michigan v. Tucker*, 417 U.S. 433, 447 (1974): "The deterrent purpose of the exclusionary rule necessarily assumes that the police have engaged in willful, or at the very least negligent, conduct which has deprived the defendant of some right. By refusing to admit evidence gained as a result of such conduct, the courts hope to instill in those particular investigating officers, or in their future counterparts, a greater degree of care toward the rights of an accused. Where the official action was pursued in complete good faith, however, the deterrence rationale loses much of its force."[20] * * *

This is particularly true, we believe, when an officer acting with objective good faith has obtained a search warrant from a judge or magistrate and acted within its scope. In most such cases, there is no police illegality and thus nothing to deter. It is the magistrate's responsibility to determine whether the officer's allegations establish probable cause and, if so, to issue a warrant comporting in form with the requirements of the Fourth Amendment. In the ordinary case, an officer cannot be expected to question the magistrate's probable-cause determination or his judgment that the form of the warrant is technically sufficient. * * * Penalizing the officer for the magistrate's error, rather than his own, cannot logically contribute to the deterrence of Fourth Amendment violations.

We conclude that the marginal or nonexistent benefits produced by suppressing evidence obtained in objectively reasonable reliance on a subsequently invalidated search warrant cannot justify the substantial costs of exclusion. We do not suggest, however, that exclusion is always inappropriate in cases where an officer has obtained a warrant and abided by its terms. [T]he officer's reliance on the magistrate's probable-cause determination and on the technical sufficiency of the warrant he issues must be objectively reasonable, and it is clear that in some circumstances the officer will have no reasonable grounds for believing that the warrant was properly issued.

Suppression therefore remains an appropriate remedy if the magistrate or judge in issuing a warrant was misled by information in an affidavit that the affiant knew was false or would have known was false except for his reckless disregard of the truth. *Franks v. Delaware*, 438 U.S. 154 (1978). The exception we recognize today will also not apply in cases where the issuing magistrate wholly abandoned his judicial role * * *; in such circumstances, no reasonably well trained officer should rely on the warrant. Nor would an officer manifest objective good faith in

---

[20] We emphasize that the standard of reasonableness we adopt is an objective one. Many objections to a good-faith exception assume that the exception will turn on the subjective good faith of individual officers. "Grounding the modification in objective reasonableness, however, retains the value of the exclusionary rule as an incentive for the law enforcement profession as a whole to conduct themselves in accord with the Fourth Amendment." *Gates*, 462 U.S., at 261, n. 15 (WHITE, J., concurring in judgment). The objective standard we adopt, moreover, requires officers to have a reasonable knowledge of what the law prohibits. * * *

relying on a warrant based on an affidavit "so lacking in indicia of probable cause as to render official belief in its existence entirely unreasonable." *Brown v. Illinois*, 422 U.S. 590, 610–611 (1975) (POWELL, J., concurring in part). Finally, depending on the circumstances of the particular case, a warrant may be so facially deficient—i.e., in failing to particularize the place to be searched or the things to be seized—that the executing officers cannot reasonably presume it to be valid.

The good-faith exception for searches conducted pursuant to warrants is not intended to signal our unwillingness strictly to enforce the requirements of the Fourth Amendment, and we do not believe that it will have this effect. As we have already suggested, the good-faith exception, turning as it does on objective reasonableness, should not be difficult to apply in practice. When officers have acted pursuant to a warrant, the prosecution should ordinarily be able to establish objective good faith without a substantial expenditure of judicial time.

Nor are we persuaded that application of a good-faith exception to searches conducted pursuant to warrants will preclude review of the constitutionality of the search or seizure, deny needed guidance from the courts, or freeze Fourth Amendment law in its present state. There is no need for courts to adopt the inflexible practice of always deciding whether the officers' conduct manifested objective good faith before turning to the question whether the Fourth Amendment has been violated. * * * If the resolution of a particular Fourth Amendment question is necessary to guide future action by law enforcement officers and magistrates, nothing will prevent reviewing courts from deciding that question before turning to the good-faith issue. Indeed, it frequently will be difficult to determine whether the officers acted reasonably without resolving the Fourth Amendment issue. Even if the Fourth Amendment question is not one of broad import, reviewing courts could decide in particular cases that magistrates under their supervision need to be informed of their errors and so evaluate the officers' good faith only after finding a violation. In other circumstances, those courts could reject suppression motions posing no important Fourth Amendment questions by turning immediately to a consideration of the officers' good faith. We have no reason to believe that our Fourth Amendment jurisprudence would suffer by allowing reviewing courts to exercise an informed discretion in making this choice.

When the principles we have enunciated today are applied to the facts of this case, it is apparent that the judgment of the Court of Appeals cannot stand. * * * In the absence of an allegation that the magistrate abandoned his detached and neutral role, suppression is appropriate only if the officers were dishonest or reckless in preparing their affidavit or could not have harbored an objectively reasonable belief in the existence of probable cause. * * * Officer Rombach's [affidavit] related the results of an extensive investigation and, as the opinions of the divided panel of the Court of Appeals make clear, provided evidence sufficient to create disagreement among thoughtful and competent judges as to the existence of probable cause. Under these circumstances, the officers' reliance on the magistrate's determination of probable cause was objectively reasonable, and application of the extreme sanction of exclusion is inappropriate. Accordingly, the judgment of the Court of Appeals is reversed.

JUSTICE BLACKMUN, concurring.

As the Court's opinion in this case makes clear, the Court has narrowed the scope of the exclusionary rule because of an empirical judgment that the rule has little appreciable effect in cases where officers act in objectively reasonable reliance on search warrants. Because I share the view that the exclusionary rule is not a constitutionally compelled corollary of the Fourth Amendment itself, I see no way to avoid making an empirical judgment of this sort, and I am satisfied that the Court has made the correct one on the information before it. * * *

What must be stressed, however, is that any empirical judgment about the effect of the exclusionary rule in a particular class of cases necessarily is a provisional one. * * * If it should emerge from experience that, contrary to our expectations, the good-faith exception to the exclusionary rule results in a material change in police compliance with the Fourth Amendment, we shall have to reconsider what we have undertaken here. The logic of a decision that rests on untested predictions about police conduct demands no less.

JUSTICE BRENNAN, with whom JUSTICE MARSHALL joins, dissenting.

At bottom, the Court's decision turns on the proposition that the exclusionary rule is merely a "judicially created remedy designed to safeguard Fourth Amendment rights generally through its deterrent effect, rather than a personal constitutional right." The germ of that idea is found in *Wolf v. Colorado*, 338 U.S. 25 (1949), and although I had thought that such a narrow conception of the rule had been forever put to rest by our decision in *Mapp v. Ohio*, 367 U.S. 643 (1961), it has been revived by the present Court and reaches full flower with today's decision. * * * This reading of the Amendment implies that its proscriptions are directed solely at those government agents who may actually invade an individual's constitutionally protected privacy. The courts are not subject to any direct constitutional duty to exclude illegally obtained evidence, because the question of the admissibility of such evidence is not addressed by the Amendment. This view of the scope of the Amendment relegates the judiciary to the periphery. Because the only constitutionally cognizable injury has already been "fully accomplished" by the police by the time a case comes before the courts, the Constitution is not itself violated if the judge decides to admit the tainted evidence. Indeed, the most the judge can do is wring his hands and hope that perhaps by excluding such evidence he can deter future transgressions by the police.

Such a reading appears plausible, because, as critics of the exclusionary rule never tire of repeating, the Fourth Amendment makes no express provision for the exclusion of evidence secured in violation of its commands. A short answer to this claim, of course, is that many of the Constitution's most vital imperatives are stated in general terms and the task of giving meaning to these precepts is therefore left to subsequent judicial decisionmaking in the context of concrete cases. * * * A more direct answer may be supplied by recognizing that the Amendment, like other provisions of the Bill of Rights, restrains the power of the government as a whole; it does not specify only a particular agency and exempt all others. The judiciary is responsible, no less than the executive, for ensuring that constitutional rights are respected.

When that fact is kept in mind, the role of the courts and their possible involvement in the concerns of the Fourth Amendment comes into sharper focus. Because seizures are executed principally to secure evidence, and because such evidence generally has utility in our legal system only in the context of a trial supervised by a judge, it is apparent that the admission of illegally obtained evidence implicates the same constitutional concerns as the initial seizure of that evidence. Indeed, by admitting unlawfully seized evidence, the judiciary becomes a part of what is in fact a single governmental action prohibited by the terms of the Amendment. * * * It is difficult to give any meaning at all to the limitations imposed by the Amendment if they are read to proscribe only certain conduct by the police but to allow other agents of the same government to take advantage of evidence secured by the police in violation of its requirements. The Amendment therefore must be read to condemn not only the initial unconstitutional invasion of privacy—which is done, after all, for the purpose of securing evidence—but also the subsequent use of any evidence so obtained.

[The Court nevertheless] has gradually pressed the deterrence rationale for the rule back to center stage. The various arguments advanced by the Court in this campaign have only strengthened my conviction that the deterrence theory is both misguided and unworkable. First, the Court has frequently bewailed the "cost" of excluding reliable evidence. In large part, this criticism rests upon a refusal to acknowledge the function of the Fourth Amendment itself. If nothing else, the Amendment plainly operates to disable the government from gathering information and securing evidence in certain ways. In practical terms, of course, this restriction of official power means that some incriminating evidence inevitably will go undetected if the government obeys these constitutional restraints. It is the loss of that evidence that is the "price" our society pays for enjoying the freedom and privacy safeguarded by the Fourth Amendment. Thus, some criminals will go free not, in Justice (then Judge) Cardozo's misleading epigram, "because the constable has blundered," *People v. Defore*, 242 N.Y. 13, 21 (1926), but rather because official compliance with Fourth Amendment requirements makes it more difficult to catch criminals. Understood in this way, the Amendment directly contemplates that some reliable and incriminating evidence will be lost to the government; therefore, it is not the exclusionary rule, but the Amendment itself that has imposed this cost.

In addition, the Court's decisions over the past decade have made plain that the entire enterprise of attempting to assess the benefits and costs of the exclusionary rule in various contexts is a virtually impossible task for the judiciary to perform honestly or accurately. Although the Court's language in those cases suggests that some specific empirical basis may support its analyses, the reality is that the Court's opinions represent inherently unstable compounds of intuition, hunches, and occasional pieces of partial and often inconclusive data. * * * The extent of this Court's fidelity to Fourth Amendment requirements, however, should not turn on such statistical uncertainties. * * *

[T]he Court suggests that society has been asked to pay a high price—in terms either of setting guilty persons free or of impeding the proper functioning of trials—as a result of excluding relevant physical evidence in cases where the police, in conducting searches and seizing evidence, have made only an "objectively reasonable" mistake concerning the constitutionality of their actions. [But recent] studies have demonstrated that federal and state prosecutors very rarely drop cases because of potential search and seizure problems. For example, a 1979 study prepared at the request of Congress by the General Accounting Office reported that only 0.4% of all cases actually declined for prosecution by federal prosecutors were declined primarily because of illegal search problems. Report of the Comptroller General of the United States, Impact of the Exclusionary Rule on Federal Criminal Prosecutions 14 (1979). If the GAO data are restated as a percentage of all arrests, the study shows that only 0.2% of all felony arrests are declined for prosecution because of potential exclusionary rule problems. Of course, these data describe only the costs attributable to the exclusion of evidence in all cases; the costs due to the exclusion of evidence in the narrower category of cases where police have made objectively reasonable mistakes must necessarily be even smaller. The Court, however, ignores this distinction and mistakenly weighs the aggregated costs of exclusion in all cases, irrespective of the circumstances that led to exclusion, against the potential benefits associated with only those cases in which evidence is excluded because police reasonably but mistakenly believe that their conduct does not violate the Fourth Amendment. When such faulty scales are used, it is little wonder that the balance tips in favor of restricting the application of the rule.

What then supports the Court's insistence that this evidence be admitted? Apparently, the Court's only answer is that even though the costs of exclusion are not very substantial, the potential deterrent effect in these circumstances is so marginal that exclusion cannot be justified. The key to the Court's conclusion in this respect is its belief that the prospective deterrent effect of the exclusionary rule operates only in those situations in which police officers, when deciding whether to go forward with some particular search, have reason to know that their planned conduct will violate the requirements of the Fourth Amendment. * * * The flaw in the Court's argument, however, is that its logic captures only one comparatively minor element of the generally acknowledged deterrent purposes of the exclusionary rule. [W]hat the Court overlooks is that the deterrence rationale for the rule is not designed to be, nor should it be thought of as, a form of "punishment" of individual police officers for their failures to obey the restraints imposed by the Fourth Amendment. Instead, the chief deterrent function of the rule is its tendency to promote institutional compliance with Fourth Amendment requirements on the part of law enforcement agencies generally. Thus, as the Court has previously recognized, "over the long term, [the] demonstration [provided by the exclusionary rule] that our society attaches serious consequences to violation of constitutional rights is thought to encourage those who formulate law enforcement policies, and the officers who implement them, to incorporate Fourth Amendment ideals into their value system." *Stone*, 428 U.S., at 492. It is only through such an institution-wide mechanism that information concerning Fourth Amendment standards can be effectively communicated to rank-and-file officers.

If the overall educational effect of the exclusionary rule is considered, application of the rule to even those situations in which individual police officers have acted on the basis of a reasonable but mistaken belief that their conduct was authorized can still be expected to have a considerable long-term deterrent effect. If evidence is consistently excluded in these circumstances, police departments will surely be prompted to instruct their officers to devote greater care and attention to providing sufficient information to establish probable cause when applying for a warrant, and to review with some attention the form of the warrant that they have been issued, rather than automatically assuming that whatever document the magistrate has signed will necessarily comport with Fourth Amendment requirements.

After today's decisions, however, that institutional incentive will be lost. Indeed, the Court's "reasonable mistake" exception to the exclusionary rule will tend to put a premium on police ignorance of the law. Armed with the assurance provided by today's decisions that evidence will always be admissible whenever an officer has "reasonably" relied upon a warrant, police departments will be encouraged to train officers that if a warrant has simply been signed, it is reasonable, without more, to rely on it. Since in close cases there will no longer be any incentive to err on the side of constitutional behavior, police would have every reason to adopt a "let's-wait-until-it's-decided" approach in situations in which there is a question about a warrant's validity or the basis for its issuance.

* * * Creation of this new exception for good-faith reliance upon a warrant [also] implicitly tells magistrates that they need not take much care in reviewing warrant applications, since their mistakes will from now on have virtually no consequence: If their decision to issue a warrant was correct, the evidence will be admitted; if their decision was incorrect but the police relied in good faith on the warrant, the evidence will also be admitted. Inevitably, the care and attention devoted to such an inconsequential chore will dwindle. Although the Court is correct to note that magistrates do not share the same stake in the outcome of a criminal case as the police, they nevertheless need to appreciate that their role is of some moment in order to continue performing the important task of carefully reviewing warrant applications. Today's [decision] effectively remove[s] that incentive.

JUSTICE STEVENS, [dissenting].

The majority's [conclusion] rests on the notion that it must be reasonable for a police officer to rely on a magistrate's finding. Until today that has plainly not been the law; it has been well settled that even when a magistrate issues a warrant there is no guarantee that the ensuing search and seizure is constitutionally reasonable. Law enforcement officers have long been on notice that despite the magistrate's decision a warrant will be invalidated if the officers did not provide sufficient facts to enable the magistrate to evaluate the existence of probable cause responsibly and independently. Reviewing courts have always inquired into whether the magistrate acted properly in issuing the warrant—not merely whether the officers acted properly in executing it. * * *

The notion that a police officer's reliance on a magistrate's warrant is automatically appropriate is one the Framers of the Fourth Amendment would have vehemently rejected. The precise problem that the Amendment was intended to address was the unreasonable issuance of warrants. As we have often observed, the Amendment was actually motivated by the practice of issuing general warrants—warrants which did not satisfy the particularity and probable-cause requirements. * * * Those who sought to amend the Constitution to include a Bill of Rights repeatedly voiced the view that the evil which had to be addressed was the issuance of warrants on insufficient evidence. * * * The Court's view that it is consistent with our Constitution to adopt a rule that it is presumptively reasonable to rely on a defective warrant is the product of constitutional amnesia.

The Court is of course correct that the exclusionary rule cannot deter when the authorities have no reason to know that their conduct is unconstitutional. But when probable cause is lacking, then by definition a reasonable person under the circumstances would not believe there is a fair likelihood that a search will produce evidence of a crime. Under such circumstances well-trained professionals must know that they are violating the Constitution. The Court's approach—which, in effect, encourages the police to seek a warrant even if they know the existence of probable cause is doubtful—can only lead to an increased number of constitutional violations.

POINTS FOR DISCUSSION

a.   Judicially Created Rule or Constitutional Right?

Is the exclusionary rule a prudential remedy designed to deter police misconduct, or is it a necessary and inevitable component of the right to be free from unreasonable searches and seizures? The Court in *Leon* treated it as the former, stating that the rule "operates as 'a judicially created remedy designed to safeguard Fourth Amendment rights generally through its deterrent effect, rather than a personal constitutional right of the party aggrieved.'" Justice Brennan, in contrast, viewed the exclusionary rule as a necessary component of the right protected by the Fourth Amendment. He reasoned: "Because seizures are executed principally to secure evidence, and because such evidence generally has utility in our legal system only in the context of a trial supervised by a judge, it is apparent that the admission of illegally obtained evidence implicates the same constitutional concerns as the initial seizure of that evidence. * * * The Amendment [must] be read to condemn not only the initial unconstitutional invasion of privacy—which is done, after all, for the purpose of securing evidence— but also the subsequent use of any evidence so obtained." Which position is more consistent with the Fourth Amendment?

Even if the exclusionary rule is properly viewed as an essential part of the constitutional right to be free from unreasonable searches and seizures, is there an argument that an officer's good-faith reliance on a warrant should render the exclusionary rule inapplicable? Conversely, even if the rule is correctly viewed as a means of deterring police misconduct, is there an argument that evidence seized after good-faith reliance on a warrant should be excluded from trial?

b.   Good Faith

Leon concerned good-faith reliance on a warrant issued by a neutral magistrate. Are there other contexts in which the exclusionary rule should not apply when the police seize evidence during an illegal search conducted in good faith? For example, suppose that the police conduct a warrantless search under circumstances that the Supreme Court has previously held are exempt from the Fourth Amendment's warrant requirement. Before the defendant's trial, however, the Supreme Court overrules the precedent authorizing this type of warrantless search. Should the police's good-faith reliance on Supreme Court precedent render the exclusionary rule inapplicable? In *Davis v. United States*, 564 U.S. 229 (2011), the Court held that the exclusionary rule should not apply in such circumstances.

Executive Summary of This Chapter

The Fourth Amendment prohibits "unreasonable searches and seizures" and requires that all warrants authorizing searches or seizures be justified by probable cause to believe that the target of the search or seizure has engaged in unlawful activity.

The requirements of the Amendment, including the warrant requirement, apply when the government has engaged in a search or a seizure. A **search** occurs when the government "physically occupie[s] private property for the purpose of obtaining information," *United States v. Jones* (2012), or the government "violate[s] the privacy upon which [the target of the action] justifiably relied," *Katz v. United States* (1967)—that is, the subject of the search "exhibited an actual (subjective) expectation of privacy" that "society is prepared to recognize as 'reasonable,' " *id.* (Justice Harlan, concurring).

Seizures of property can be authorized by warrant or justified by probable cause. The arrest of a person by the police is also "seizure" within the meaning of the Fourth Amendment. The police may obtain a warrant to arrest a person if they can show probable cause to believe that the person has committed an offense. But the "usual rule is that a police officer may arrest without warrant one believed by the officer upon reasonable cause to have been guilty of a felony * * *." *Carroll v. United States*, 267 U.S. 132, 156 (1925).

The Fourth Amendment also "governs 'seizures' of the person which do not eventuate in a trip to the station house and prosecution for crime—'arrests' in traditional terminology." *Terry v. Ohio* (1968). But an officer may **stop and frisk** a suspect without a warrant or probable cause when the circumstances lead him "reasonably to conclude in light of his experience" that "criminal activity may be afoot and that the persons with whom he is dealing may be armed and presently dangerous." *Id.* The standard for a "*Terry* stop" is easier to satisfy than the standard of probable cause, which is the standard for an ordinary search or seizure under the Fourth Amendment.

The general rule is that an officer must obtain a warrant before conducting a search or seizure, and the warrant cannot issue unless the officer can establish **probable cause** to believe that a search or seizure will yield evidence of a crime or probable cause to believe that a person to be arrested has committed a crime. Probable cause is "a fluid concept—turning on the assessment of probabilities in particular factual contexts—not readily, or even usefully, reduced to a neat set of legal rules." *Illinois v. Gates* (1983). The term "has come to mean more than bare suspicion: Probable cause exists where 'the facts and circumstances within [the officers'] knowledge and of which they had reasonably trustworthy information [are] sufficient in themselves to warrant a man of reasonable caution in the belief that' an offense has been or is being committed." *Brinegar v. United States* (1949).

The Fourth Amendment requires that warrants **particularly describe** the place to be searched and the things or persons to be seized. Although police executing a warrant may seize evidence of crime that is in "plain view" even if that evidence is not described in the warrant, *Coolidge v. New Hampshire* (1971), the particularity requirement prevents police from going on fishing expeditions based on something less than probable cause to believe that they will find specific evidence of a particular crime.

The Court has explained that "searches conducted outside the judicial process, without prior approval by judge or magistrate, are per se unreasonable under the Fourth Amendment—subject only to a few specifically established and well delineated exceptions." *Katz v. United States* (1967).

"**[E]xigent circumstances**, including the need to prevent the destruction of evidence, permit police officers to conduct an otherwise permissible search without first obtaining a warrant." *Kentucky v. King* (2011). This exception to the warrant requirement extends to cases in which the police, "by knocking on the door of a residence and announcing their presence, cause the occupants to attempt to destroy evidence." *Id.*

The Court has also recognized an **"automobile exception"** to the warrant requirement. *Carroll v. United States* (1925). "If a car is readily mobile and probable cause exists to believe it contains contraband, the Fourth Amendment * * * permits police to search the vehicle without more." *Pennsylvania v. Labron* (1996). Ordinarily, a mobile home is a car for purposes of the automobile exception. *California v. Carney* (1985). In addition, the automobile exception extends to cases in which the police have probable cause to believe that there is evidence in a specific movable container within a car, even if they do not have probable cause to search the vehicle itself. *California v. Acevedo* (1991).

The Fourth Amendment generally prohibits the warrantless entry of a person's home, either to make an arrest or to search for specific objects. *Payton v. New York* (1980). "The prohibition does not apply, however, to situations in which voluntary **consent** has been obtained, either from the individual whose property is searched, or from a third party who possesses common authority over the premises." *Illinois v. Rodriguez* (1990) (internal citations omitted). A warrantless search is also permissible when a person who does *not* have common authority over the premises consents, if the police reasonably believed that the person had authority to consent to the search. *Id.*

A **search incident to a lawful arrest** is another exception to the usual warrant requirement of the Fourth Amendment. The police may search the person arrested and the area that is in the person's immediate control. *Chimel v. California* (1969). Such searches are permissible even when the police officer does not "indicate any subjective fear" of the suspect or does "not himself suspect that [the person] was armed." *United States v. Robinson* (1973).

Under the **"exclusionary rule,"** evidence seized in an unlawful search cannot be used at trial against the defendant. *Weeks v. United States* (1914); *Mapp v. Ohio* (1961). The government cannot circumvent the rule by seeking to obtain through other means the evidence that it found during an illegal search. *Silverthorne Lumber Co. v. United States* (1920). Under the "fruit of the poisonous tree" doctrine, evidence obtained as a consequence of an illegal search, even if not during the search itself, is also subject to the exclusionary rule. *Wong Sun v. United States* (1963); *Nardone v. United States* (1939). The exclusionary rule does not, however, prevent the introduction of evidence seized in an unlawful search if the police relied in good faith on a warrant issued by a neutral magistrate, even if the warrant turns out to have been defective. *United States v. Leon* (1984).

The Fifth Amendment

The Fifth Amendment provides:

"No person shall be held to answer for a capital, or otherwise infamous crime, unless on a presentment or indictment of a grand jury, except in cases arising in the land or naval forces, or in the militia, when in actual service in time of war or public danger; nor shall any person be subject for the same offense to be twice put in jeopardy of life or limb; nor shall be compelled in any criminal case to be a witness against himself, nor be deprived of life, liberty, or property, without due process of law; nor shall private property be taken for public use, without just compensation."

The Amendment specifies five important rights: the right to indictment by a grand jury before the federal government can prosecute; the right not to be tried twice for the same crime, otherwise known as the protection against "double jeopardy"; the privilege against self-incrimination; the right to due process; and the right to compensation when the government takes private property—a right coupled with a limitation that the government can take property only for public use.

In this chapter, we address the requirement of due process of law; the privilege against self-incrimination, including the rights that arise during interrogation by the police; and the right against double jeopardy.

We do not address the Takings Clause in this chapter because it is covered in Chapter 12. For the right not to be tried for a serious crime unless indicted by a grand jury, a few words will suffice. This right was originally conceived as an important protection for criminal defendants. Suspects cannot face prosecution unless a panel of peers concludes that there is sufficient evidence for the state to proceed. The government therefore is limited in its ability to use criminal prosecutions to oppress political enemies and others. But the right to indictment by a grand jury in practice does not afford most criminal suspects much protection. The conventional wisdom today is that prosecutors usually have little difficulty obtaining indictments—an idea captured by the familiar quip that any prosecutor worth her salt could persuade a grand jury to indict a ham sandwich. One reason is that the defendant is not represented in grand jury proceedings. Indeed, because the proceedings are usually secret, the defendant often does not even know about them, and therefore the grand jury hears evidence only from one side. The right to indictment by grand jury also has less significance than other Fifth Amendment rights because the Supreme Court has held that the Fourteenth Amendment does not require state governments to obtain grand jury indictments before initiating prosecutions. *Hurtado v. California*, 110 U.S. 516 (1884). As a consequence, the right applies only in federal prosecutions, which constitute a small majority of prosecutions nationwide.

A. DUE PROCESS OF LAW

What limits does the Due Process Clause impose on the government when it seeks to prosecute a person for a crime? In thinking about this question, it is important to note at least three things about scope. First, as we have already seen, there are actually two Due Process Clauses in the Constitution, one in the Fifth Amendment and another in the Fourteenth Amendment. In this section, we focus on the Fifth Amendment, but the Court has made clear that the protection offered by the two Due Process Clauses is co-extensive. Accordingly, some of the cases that we consider below arose in the context of a state prosecution, and thus involved the Due Process Clause of the Fourteenth Amendment, and others arose in the federal context, and thus involved the Due Process Clause of the Fifth Amendment.

Second, as we have also seen, the Court has concluded that the Due Process Clauses are the source of a broad array of constitutional rights. We are not concerned in this chapter with the substantive component of the Due Process Clauses, which we considered in Chapter 2. We are also not directly concerned

> **Make the Connection**
>
> We considered the incorporation doctrine, and the role of the Due Process Clause of the Fourteenth Amendment, in Chapter 1.

here with the doctrine of incorporation, by which the Court concluded that most of the protections of the first eight amendments apply to the state governments, as well as to the federal governments. As you will see, however, the Court decided many of the cases that we consider in this section while the debate over incorporation was raging, and therefore incorporation is never far from the surface in some of the opinions.

Because of incorporation, the Due Process Clause of the Fourteenth Amendment imposes on the states several important requirements that are specified in the first eight amendments. For example, as we have seen, the Fourth Amendment imposes limits on when the police can conduct searches and seizures, and these limits apply to the states through the force of the Due Process Clause of the Fourteenth Amendment. Similarly, as we will see in Chapter 15, the Sixth Amendment right to counsel, right to a jury, and right to confront witnesses apply to the states through the Due Process Clause of the Fourteenth Amendment.

Third, the Court has developed a body of principles to govern the process that is due when the government seeks to deprive a person of something valuable outside of the criminal context. For example, the state is obligated to provide a hearing before terminating welfare benefits to which the recipient has a statutory entitlement. *Goldberg v. Kelly*, 397 U.S. 254 (1970). We considered this doctrine—known somewhat inartfully as "procedural due process"—in Chapter 3.

We are concerned here with whether there are other rights that are *not* specifically mentioned in the Bill of Rights that the Due Process Clauses nevertheless require the government to respect in the course of criminal prosecutions by the state and federal governments. In the cases that follow, we consider two examples. First, the Court concluded in *In re Winship*, 397 U.S. 358 (1970), that the requirement of due process means that the government must prove all of the elements of a criminal offense "beyond a reasonable doubt." A lower standard, like proof by a mere preponderance of the evidence, would violate the Due Process Clause. Second, the Court held in *Brady v. Maryland*, 373 U.S. 83 (1963), that the government must disclose exculpatory evidence to the defendant in a criminal case. For example, if someone who witnessed a crime tells the police that the perpetrator did not look like the defendant, the police must disclose this information to the defendant, who may wish to use it at trial. The results of these cases may not seem controversial today, but they both prompted substantial dissents when the Supreme Court decided them. The disagreement largely turned on the question of how the Supreme Court determines what the open-ended phrase "due process" requires.

IN RE WINSHIP
397 U.S. 358 (1970)

MR. JUSTICE BRENNAN delivered the opinion of the Court.

[New York law provided that a minor could be adjudicated to be a "juvenile delinquent" and subject to punishment if he or she committed an act that would have been a crime if committed by an adult. The state provided an "adjudicatory hearing" to determine whether a minor accused of such an act had in fact committed it. A judge on the New York Family Court concluded that the appellant, a twelve-year-old boy, had stolen $112 from a woman's pocketbook. The judge acknowledged that the evidence in the case might not have been sufficient to establish guilt beyond a reasonable doubt, but he applied a preponderance of the evidence standard under § 744(b) of the New York Family Court Act. The New York Court of Appeals affirmed.

In *In re Gault*, 387 U.S. 1, 13 (1967), the Court held that hearings to determine "whether a juvenile is a 'delinquent' as a result of alleged misconduct on his part, with the consequence that he may be committed to a state institution," must conform to "the essentials of due process and fair treatment."] This case presents the single, narrow question whether proof beyond a reasonable doubt is among the "essentials of due process and fair treatment" required during the adjudicatory stage when a juvenile is charged with an act which would constitute a crime if committed by an adult.

> **Take Note**
>
> In the four paragraphs that follow, the Court explains why the Due Process Clause requires that the government establish criminal charges by a reasonable doubt. How would you describe the Court's methodology? How does the Court decide what procedural protections are required by the Clause?

The requirement that guilt of a criminal charge be established by proof beyond a reasonable doubt dates at least from our early years as a Nation. The "demand for a higher degree of persuasion in criminal cases was recurrently expressed from ancient times, (though) its crystallization into the formula 'beyond a reasonable doubt' seems to have occurred as late as 1798. It is now accepted in common law jurisdictions as the measure of persuasion by which the prosecution must convince the trier of all the essential elements of guilt." C. McCormick, Evidence § 321, pp. 681–682 (1954); see also 9 J. Wigmore, Evidence, § 2497 (3d ed. 1940). Although virtually unanimous adherence to the reasonable-doubt standard in common-law jurisdictions may not conclusively establish it as a requirement of due process, such adherence does "reflect a profound judgment about the way in which law should be enforced and justice administered." *Duncan v. Louisiana*, 391 U.S. 145, 155 (1968).

Expressions in many opinions of this Court indicate that it has long been assumed that proof of a criminal charge beyond a reasonable doubt is constitutionally required. * * * The reasonable-doubt standard plays a vital role in the American scheme of criminal procedure. It is a prime instrument for reducing the risk of convictions resting on factual error. The standard provides concrete substance for the presumption of innocence—that bedrock "axiomatic and elementary" principle whose "enforcement lies at the foundation of the administration of our criminal law." *Coffin v. United States*, 156 U.S. 432, 453 (1895). As the dissenters in the New York Court of Appeals observed, and we agree, "a person accused of a crime . . . would be at a severe disadvantage, a disadvantage amounting to a lack of fundamental fairness, if he could be adjudged guilty and imprisoned for years on the strength of the same evidence as would suffice in a civil case." 24 N.Y.2d 196, 205 (1969).

The requirement of proof beyond a reasonable doubt has this vital role in our criminal procedure for cogent reasons. The accused during a criminal prosecution has at stake interest of immense importance, both because of the possibility that he may lose his liberty upon conviction and because of the certainty that he would be stigmatized by the conviction. Accordingly, a society that values the good name and freedom of every individual should not condemn a man for commission of a crime when there is reasonable doubt about his guilt. As we said in *Speiser v. Randall*, 357 U.S. 513, 525–526 (1958): "There is always in litigation a margin of error, representing error in factfinding, which both parties must take into account. Where one party has at stake an interest of transcending value—as a criminal defendant his liberty—this margin of error is reduced as to him by the process of placing on the other party the burden of . . . persuading the factfinder at the conclusion of the trial of his guilt beyond a reasonable doubt. Due process commands that no man shall lose his liberty unless the Government has borne the burden of . . . convincing the factfinder of his guilt." To this end, the reasonable-doubt standard is indispensable, for it "impresses on the trier of fact the necessity of reaching a subjective state of certitude of the facts in issue." Dorsen & Rezneck, *In Re Gault* and the Future of Juvenile Law, 1 Family Law Quarterly, No. 4, pp. 1, 26 (1967).

Moreover, use of the reasonable-doubt standard is indispensable to command the respect and confidence of the community in applications of the criminal law. It is critical that the moral force of the criminal law not be diluted by a standard of proof that leaves people in doubt whether innocent men are being condemned. It is also important in our free society that every individual going about his ordinary affairs have confidence that his government cannot adjudge him guilty of a criminal offense without convincing a proper factfinder of his guilt with utmost certainty.

Lest there remain any doubt about the constitutional stature of the reasonable-doubt standard, we explicitly hold that the Due Process Clause protects the accused against conviction except upon proof beyond a reasonable doubt of every fact necessary to constitute the crime with which he is charged.

[The Court concluded that "juveniles, like adults, are constitutionally entitled to proof beyond a reasonable doubt when they are charged with violation of a criminal law."] Reversed.

MR. JUSTICE HARLAN, concurring.

[W]e have before us a case where the choice of the standard of proof has made a difference: the juvenile court judge below forthrightly acknowledged that he believed by a preponderance of the evidence, but was not convinced beyond a reasonable doubt, that appellant stole $112 from the complainant's pocketbook. Moreover, even though the labels used for alternative standards of proof are vague and not a very sure guide to decisionmaking, the choice of the standard for a particular variety of adjudication does, I think, reflect a very fundamental assessment of the comparative social costs of erroneous factual determinations.

[A] standard of proof represents an attempt to instruct the fact-finder concerning the degree of confidence our society thinks he should have in the correctness of factual conclusions for a particular type of adjudication. Although the phrases "preponderance of the evidence" and "proof beyond a reasonable doubt" are quantitatively imprecise, they do communicate to the finder of fact different notions concerning the degree of confidence he is expected to have in the correctness of his factual conclusions. [A corollary] is that the trier of fact will sometimes, despite his best efforts, be wrong in his factual conclusions.

[If] the standard of proof for a criminal trial were a preponderance of the evidence rather than proof beyond a reasonable doubt, there would be a smaller risk of factual errors that result in freeing guilty persons, but a far greater risk of factual errors that result in convicting the innocent. Because the standard of proof affects the comparative frequency of these two types of erroneous outcomes, the choice of the standard to be applied in a particular kind of litigation should, in a rational world, reflect an assessment of the comparative social disutility of each.

When one makes such an assessment, the reason for different standards of proof in civil as opposed to criminal litigation becomes apparent. In a civil suit between two private parties for money damages, for example, we view it as no more serious in general for there to be an erroneous verdict in the defendant's favor than for there to be an erroneous verdict in the plaintiff's favor. A preponderance of the evidence standard therefore seems peculiarly appropriate * * *.

In a criminal case, on the other hand, we do not view the social disutility of convicting an innocent man as equivalent to the disutility of acquitting someone who is guilty. * * * I view the requirement of proof beyond a reasonable doubt in a criminal case as bottomed on a fundamental value determination of our society that it is far worse to convict an innocent man than to let a guilty man go free. It is only because of the nearly complete and long-standing acceptance of the reasonable-doubt standard by the States in criminal trials that the Court has not before today had to hold explicitly that due process, as an expression of fundamental procedural fairness, requires a more stringent standard for criminal trials than for ordinary civil litigation.

> **Food for Thought**
>
> Do you agree with Justice Harlan that it is "far worse to convict an innocent man than to let a guilty man go free"? How does Justice Harlan know that this view is so widely shared that it constitutes a "fundamental value determination of our society" such that it is required by the notion of Due Process? Was it a fundamental value determination in New York, where this case arose?

MR. CHIEF JUSTICE BURGER, with whom MR. JUSTICE STEWART joins, dissenting.

The Court's opinion today rests entirely on the assumption that all juvenile proceedings are "criminal prosecutions," hence subject to constitutional limitations. * * * The original concept of the juvenile court system was to provide a benevolent and less formal means than criminal courts could provide for dealing with the special and often sensitive problems of youthful offenders. Since I see no constitutional requirement of due process sufficient to overcome the legislative judgment of the States in this area, I dissent from further straitjacketing of an already overly restricted system.

MR. JUSTICE BLACK, dissenting.

The Bill of Rights, which in my view is made fully applicable to the States by the Fourteenth Amendment, see *Adamson v. California*, 332 U.S. 46, 71–75 (1947) (dissenting opinion), does by express language provide for, among other things, a right to counsel in criminal trials, a right to indictment, and the right of a defendant to be informed of the nature of the charges against him. And in two places the Constitution provides for trial by jury, but nowhere in that document is there any statement that conviction of crime requires proof of guilt beyond a reasonable doubt. The Constitution thus goes into some detail to spell out what kind of trial a defendant charged with crime should have, and I believe the Court has no power to add to or subtract from the procedures set forth by the Founders. I realize that it is far easier to substitute individual judges' ideas of "fairness" for the fairness prescribed by the Constitution, but I shall not at any time surrender my belief that that document itself should be our guide, not our own concept of what is fair, decent, and right. * * * As I have said time and time again, I prefer to put my faith in the words of the written Constitution itself rather than to rely on the shifting, day-to-day standards of fairness of individual judges.

* * * Some might think that the words [due process of law] are vague. But any possible ambiguity disappears when the phrase is viewed in the light of history and the accepted meaning of those words prior to and at the time our Constitution was written. "Due process of law" was originally used as a shorthand expression for governmental proceedings according to the "law of the land" as it existed at the time of those proceedings. Both phrases are derived from the laws of England [and Magna Carta] and have traditionally been regarded as meaning the same thing. * * *

For me the only correct meaning of that phrase is that our Government must proceed according to the "law of the land"—that is, according to written constitutional and statutory provisions as interpreted by court decisions. The Due Process Clause, in both the Fifth and Fourteenth Amendments, in and of itself does not add to those provisions, but in effect states that our governments are governments of law and constitutionally bound to act only according to law. To some that view may seem a degrading and niggardly view of what is undoubtedly a fundamental part of our basic freedoms. But that criticism fails to note the historical importance of our Constitution and the virtual revolution in the history of the government of nations that was achieved by forming a government that from the beginning had its limits of power set forth in one written document that also made it abundantly clear that all governmental actions affecting life, liberty, and property were to be according to law.

[T]he struggle had not been simply to put all the constitutional law in one document, it was also to make certain that men would be governed by law, not the arbitrary fiat of the man or men in power. * * * When this Court assumes for itself the power to declare any law—state or federal—unconstitutional because it offends the majority's own views of what is fundamental and decent in our society, our Nation ceases to be governed according to the "law of the land" and instead becomes one governed ultimately by the "law of the judges."

I admit a strong, persuasive argument can be made for a standard of proof beyond a reasonable doubt in criminal cases—and the majority has made that argument well—but it is not for me as a judge to say for that reason that Congress or the States are without constitutional power to establish another standard that the Constitution does not otherwise forbid. It is quite true that proof beyond a reasonable doubt has long been required in federal criminal trials. It is also true that this requirement is almost universally found in the governing laws of the

States. And as long as a particular jurisdiction requires proof beyond a reasonable doubt, then the Due Process Clause commands that every trial in that jurisdiction must adhere to that standard. See *Turner v. United States*, 396 U.S. 398, 430 (1970) (Black, J., dissenting). But when, as here, a State through its duly constituted legislative branch decides to apply a different standard, then that standard, unless it is otherwise unconstitutional, must be applied to insure that persons are treated according to the "law of the land." The State of New York has made such a decision, and in my view nothing in the Due Process Clause invalidates it.

POINTS FOR DISCUSSION

a. Standards of Proof

Courts in the United States apply three distinct standards of proof, depending on the type of case and the nature of the claims. First, in most civil suits, the plaintiff must establish her claims by a "preponderance of the evidence." Under this standard, the plaintiff must demonstrate that it is more likely than not that the facts are as she has alleged (and that the facts support the plaintiff's legal claims). This standard applies to most tort and contract claims. Under this standard, if the fact-finder believes that the evidence is in perfect equipoise between supporting the plaintiff's and defendant's claims, the plaintiff must lose.

Second, in a small number of civil suits, the plaintiff must establish her claims by "clear and convincing evidence." This standard requires the plaintiff to demonstrate by something more than merely a preponderance of the evidence that the facts are as she has alleged. Although difficult to quantify, the standard requires the plaintiff to demonstrate that it is substantially more likely than not that the facts are as she has alleged. (We considered the clear and convincing evidence standard in Chapter 8, when we addressed the rules that the First Amendment's Free Speech Clause requires for certain defamation claims.)

Third, in criminal prosecutions, the government historically has been required to establish the defendant's guilt "beyond a reasonable doubt." Although this standard also is difficult to quantify, it requires an even clearer showing than the clear and convincing evidence standard. In *In re Winship*, the Court concluded that the Due Process Clause requires this standard of proof in all criminal prosecutions.

b. Determining the Requirements of Due Process

How does the Court decide what procedures the government is required to follow under the Due Process Clause? A strong textual argument is that the Due Process Clause must require more than the specific procedural requirements enumerated in the Bill of Rights, such as the right to a jury trial and the right to counsel in a criminal case. Otherwise, the Due Process Clause of the Fifth Amendment would be superfluous. But how does the Court know whether a requirement beyond those specified in the Bill of Rights is required as a matter of Due Process? Is the Court's inquiry in *In re Winship* historical, limiting the protections of the Due Process Clause only to those procedural rights that were deemed fundamental in 1791 when the Fifth Amendment was added to the Constitution (or 1868, when the Fourteenth Amendment was ratified)? Or does the Court's approach suggest that the rules required by the Due Process Clause can evolve over time? If the latter, could the requirements under the Due Process Clause change if most states adopted an even higher standard of proof in criminal cases?

Justice Black believed that the Due Process clause of the Fourteenth Amendment protects a variety of individual rights, but he did not believe that the Supreme Court should identify those rights using natural law concepts like "fundamental principles of liberty and justice." *Adamson v. California*, 332 U.S. 46, 69 (1947) (Black, J., dissenting). That approach, according to Justice Black, "would convey to courts, at the expense of legislatures, ultimate power over public policies in fields where no specific provision of the Constitution limits legislative power." *Id.* at 75. Justice Black instead thought that the Due Process clause incorporates all of the rights listed in the Bill of Rights but no additional rights. *Id.* at 75. How did this view affect Justice Black's decision in *In re Winship*? Under his view, would a state violate the Due Process Clause if it decided that, henceforth, all trials (criminal and civil) would be resolved by a coin flip, and the state scrupulously adhered to that approach? What arguments might be made for the contrary view?

BRADY V. MARYLAND

373 U.S. 83 (1963)

Opinion of the Court by MR. JUSTICE DOUGLAS, announced by MR. JUSTICE BRENNAN.

Petitioner and a companion, Boblit, were found guilty of murder in the first degree and were sentenced to death, their convictions being affirmed by the Court of Appeals of Maryland. Their trials were separate, petitioner being tried first. At his trial Brady took the stand and admitted his participation in the crime, but he claimed that Boblit did the actual killing. And, in his summation to the jury, Brady's counsel conceded that Brady was guilty of murder in the first degree, asking only that the jury return that verdict "without capital punishment." Prior to the trial petitioner's counsel had requested the prosecution to allow him to examine Boblit's extrajudicial statements. Several of those statements were shown to him; but one dated July 9, 1958, in which Boblit admitted the actual homicide, was withheld by the prosecution and did not come to petitioner's notice until after he had been tried, convicted, and sentenced, and after his conviction had been affirmed.

Petitioner moved the trial court for a new trial based on the newly discovered evidence that had been suppressed by the prosecution. [The trial court denied the motion, and the Maryland Court of Appeals affirmed. Petitioner then sought post-conviction relief. The] Court of Appeals held that suppression of the evidence by the prosecution denied petitioner due process of law and remanded the case for a retrial of the question of punishment, not the question of guilt. * * * The question presented is whether petitioner was denied a federal right when the Court of Appeals restricted the new trial to the question of punishment.

> **Food for Thought**
>
> Why would it have been helpful to Brady in his criminal trial to have known about Boblit's statement admitting to the actual homicide?

We agree with the Court of Appeals that suppression of this confession was a violation of the Due Process Clause of the Fourteenth Amendment. [In] *Mooney v. Holohan*, 294 U.S. 103, 112 (1935), [the Court] ruled on what nondisclosure by a prosecutor violates due process:

> "It is a requirement that cannot be deemed to be satisfied by mere notice and hearing if a state has contrived a conviction through the pretense of a trial which in truth is but used as a means of depriving a defendant of liberty through a deliberate deception of court and jury by the presentation of testimony known to be perjured. Such a contrivance by a state to procure the conviction and imprisonment of a defendant is as inconsistent with the rudimentary demands of justice as is the obtaining of a like result by intimidation."

In *Pyle v. Kansas*, 317 U.S. 213, 215–216 (1942), we phrased the rule in broader terms:

> "Petitioner's papers are inexpertly drawn, but they do set forth allegations that his imprisonment resulted from perjured testimony, knowingly used by the State authorities to obtain his conviction, and from the deliberate suppression by those same authorities of evidence favorable to him. These allegations sufficiently charge a deprivation of rights guaranteed by the Federal Constitution, and, if proven, would entitle petitioner to release from his present custody."

* * * In *Napue v. Illinois*, 360 U.S. 264, 269 (1959), we extended the test formulated in *Mooney* when we said: "The same result obtains when the State,

although not soliciting false evidence, allows it to go uncorrected when it appears."

We now hold that the suppression by the prosecution of evidence favorable to an accused upon request violates due process where the evidence is material either to guilt or to punishment, irrespective of the good faith or bad faith of the prosecution.

> **Food for Thought**
>
> The decisions in *Mooney*, *Pyle*, and *Napue* involved the introduction of false or perjured evidence that became the basis of a conviction. This case, in contrast, involves the state's failure to share evidence with the defendant. Does the principle that the Court announces here follow logically or inevitably from the prior decisions? If so, why?

The principle of *Mooney* is not punishment of society for misdeeds of a prosecutor but avoidance of an unfair trial to the accused. Society wins not only when the guilty are convicted but when criminal trials are fair; our system of the administration of justice suffers when any accused is treated unfairly. An inscription on the walls of the Department of Justice states the proposition candidly for the federal domain: "The United States wins its point whenever justice is done its citizens in the courts." A prosecution that withholds evidence on demand of an accused which, if made available, would tend to exculpate him or reduce the penalty helps shape a trial that bears heavily on the defendant. That casts the prosecutor in the role of an architect of a proceeding that does not comport with standards of justice, even though, as in the present case, his action is not "the result of guile," to use the words of the Court of Appeals.

The question remains whether petitioner was denied a constitutional right when the Court of Appeals restricted his new trial to the question of punishment. [The Court concluded that, because as a matter of state law the suppressed confession would not have been admissible on the issue of innocence or guilt and thus could not have "reduced [the] offense below murder in the first degree," restricting the new trial to the question of punishment did not violate the Fourteenth Amendment.]

Affirmed.

[JUSTICE WHITE's separate opinion and JUSTICE HARLAN's dissenting opinion have been omitted.]

POINTS FOR DISCUSSION

a. The *Brady* Obligation

In civil litigation, the plaintiff and the defendant generally have equal rights to discover evidence before trial. For example, they can each depose witnesses or require the opposing party to answer interrogatories. In criminal cases, however, the government usually has an advantage in gathering evidence. The government can convene a grand jury and ask the grand jury to issues subpoenas to potential witnesses, forcing them to testify under oath. The defendant has no comparable right to make witnesses provide sworn statements before trial. Unlike in civil cases, the defendant typically cannot depose potential witnesses. As a result, in preparing for trial, the defendant usually can obtain only the information that witnesses voluntarily provide to the defendant or that the government turns over to the defendant.

Various federal and state statutes and court rules require the government to disclose certain kinds of information to the defendant. In *Brady*, the Court announced a constitutional rule about the prosecution's obligation to disclose certain material to the defendant. As the Court stated in its opinion, even if no statute or court rule requires disclosure, "suppression by the prosecution of evidence favorable to an accused upon request violates due process where the evidence is material either to guilt or to punishment." Because suppression of such material would violate the Due Process Clause, the prosecution has an obligation to disclose it. This disclosure requirement is known as the "*Brady* obligation."

b. Identifying "*Brady* Material"

What exactly is the scope of the *Brady* obligation? The Supreme Court has answered this question in a series of cases. For example, the Court has held that the prosecution must disclose evidence that demonstrates that the prosecution's case includes perjured testimony if the prosecution knew, or should have known, of the perjury. See, e.g., *Mooney v. Holohan*, 294 U.S. 103 (1935). In addition, the Court has held that exculpatory evidence that is clearly supportive of a claim of innocence counts as "material" under the *Brady* standard and thus must be disclosed to the defense. See, e.g., *United States v. Agurs*, 427 U.S. 97 (1976). But the Court has also stated that there is "no constitutional requirement that the prosecution make a complete and detailed accounting to the defense of all police investigatory work on a case." *Moore v. Illinois*, 408 U.S. 786, 795 (1972). "The mere possibility that an item of undisclosed information might have helped the defense, or might have affected the outcome of the trial, does not establish 'materiality' in the constitutional sense." *Agurs*. As a general matter, evidence is material and thus falls within the scope of the *Brady* obligation if there is a "reasonable probability" that its suppression would lead to a different outcome at trial. *United States v. Bagley*, 473 U.S. 667 (1985).

Problem

During the investigation of a robbery and murder, the police administered a polygraph test to the defendant's brother, who previously had told the police that he had no role in the crime. The polygraph examiner asked the defendant's brother whether he assisted the defendant in the robbery and the murder. The defendant's brother denied any such involvement, but the test indicated deception. The prosecution did not disclose the results of the polygraph test to the defendant. Under the rules of evidence, the results of polygraph tests are not admissible in evidence because no scientific consensus exists on whether polygraph tests are reliable.

The defendant's brother later testified at trial and gave testimony consistent with his pre-trial statements. In an effort to limit the impact of this testimony, the defendant sought to impeach his brother's credibility through cross-examination. The defendant also suggested that his brother participated in the commission of the crime. The jury convicted the defendant. Only after the conviction did the defendant learn about the polygraph test. He then challenged his conviction, arguing that the prosecution had an obligation to disclose the results of the polygraph test before trial. Did the prosecution have an obligation to disclose the results under *Brady*? Does it matter that under state law the polygraph results would not have been admissible as evidence at trial?

These facts are based on *Wood v. Bartholomew*, 516 U.S. 1 (1995), which held that the prosecution did not have an obligation to disclose the results of the polygraph test. Do you agree with the Court's conclusion?

B. THE PRIVILEGE AGAINST SELF-INCRIMINATION

The Fifth Amendment says that no person shall be "compelled in any criminal case to be a witness against himself." At a minimum, this right—known as the privilege against self-incrimination—prevents the government from forcing a defendant to testify at his trial. Accordingly, the government cannot call a criminal defendant to the witness stand to ask him whether he committed the crime of which he is accused.

The Supreme Court has explained that the privilege against self-incrimination "reflects many of our fundamental values and most noble aspirations," including:

"[O]ur unwillingness to subject those suspected of crime to the cruel trilemma of self-accusation, perjury or contempt; our preference for an accusatorial rather than an inquisitorial system of criminal justice; our fear that self-incriminating statements will be elicited by inhumane treatment and abuses; our sense of fair play which dictates 'a fair state-individual balance by requiring the government to leave the individual alone until good cause is shown for disturbing him and by requiring the government in its contest with the individual to shoulder the entire load'; our respect for the inviolability of the human personality and of the right of each individual 'to a private enclave where he may lead a private life'; our distrust of self-deprecatory statements; and our realization that the privilege, while sometimes 'a shelter to the guilty,' is often 'a protection to the innocent.' "

Murphy v. Waterfront Comm., 378 U.S. 52, 55 (1964) (internal citations omitted).

Despite these strong arguments for the privilege against self-incrimination, counter-arguments also exist. The general rule in criminal cases is that "the Government has the right to everyone's testimony." *Garner v. United States*, 424 U.S. 648, 658, n. 11 (1976). The privilege against self-incrimination is an exception to the rule, and this exception makes it more difficult for the government to prove in a criminal trial what actually happened. If the defendant in fact committed the crime of which he is accused, isn't his testimony relevant—indeed, crucial—in the case? Don't we want people to tell the truth and own up to their crimes? We are a nation, after all, that lionizes George Washington for allegedly having taken responsibility for cutting down a cherry tree with the declaration, "I cannot tell a lie." In addition, many other countries do not have a privilege against self-incrimination. In France, for example, a judge may start a criminal case by demanding that the defendant admit or deny the accusation that he committed the charged offense. See Renée Lettow Lerner, *The Intersection of Two Systems: An American on Trial for an American Murder in the French Cour D'assises*, 2001 U. Ill. L. Rev. 791, 793 (2001).

Regardless of whether the argument in favor of or against the privilege against self-incrimination is stronger, the privilege remains a fundamental aspect of criminal trials in the United States. In this part of the chapter, we consider four questions regarding the privilege. First, if a defendant exercises the privilege against self-incrimination and decides not to testify at trial, may a judge or jury draw an inference that the defendant is withholding incriminating facts? Second, if the police use physical force or mental pressure to coerce a suspect to confess to a crime, may the prosecution use the confession as evidence against the suspect in a subsequent criminal trial? Third, may the police obtain statements from the suspect without an attorney being present? Fourth, given that several rules regarding the privilege against self-incrimination depend on whether a suspect made statements during a "custodial interrogation," when is a suspect "in custody" and what constitutes an "interrogation"?

1. Drawing Inferences from a Defendant's Decision Not to Testify

Imagine that you are a juror in a robbery trial. The prosecution calls several witnesses who testify that they saw a man who looked like the defendant commit the robbery. The defendant's attorney calls to the stand a friend of the defendant who testifies that he and the defendant were at home watching television when the robbery occurred. The defendant himself chooses not to testify. Would you consider the defendant's silence to be a tacit admission of guilt? "After all," you might think, "if the defendant were innocent, surely he would take the stand and say so." While such reasoning is common and not without some logic, the Supreme Court has held that drawing an inference of guilt from silence would violate the privilege against self-incrimination. "The normal rule in a criminal case," the Court has said, "is that no negative inference from the defendant's failure to testify is permitted." *Mitchell v. United States*, 526 U.S. 314, 327 (1999). The government may not argue that the defendant's silence implies guilt, the court may not instruct the jury that it may infer guilt from the defendant's silence, and if the defendant so requests, the court must affirmatively instruct the jury not to make such an inference. *Carter v. Kentucky*, 450 U.S. 288 (1981). These rules do not appear in the text of the Fifth Amendment. Where did they come from? Consider the following case.

GRIFFIN V. CALIFORNIA
380 U.S. 609 (1965)

MR. JUSTICE DOUGLAS delivered the opinion of the Court.

Petitioner was convicted of murder in the first degree after a jury trial in a California court. He did not testify at the trial on the issue of guilt, though he did testify at the separate trial on the issue of penalty. The trial court instructed the jury on the issue of guilt, stating that a defendant has a constitutional right not to testify. But it told the jury:[2]

---

[2]   Article I, § 13, of the California Constitution provides in part: "[I]n any criminal case, whether the defendant testifies or not, his failure to explain or to deny by his testimony any evidence or facts in the case against him may be commented upon by the court and by counsel, and may be considered by the court or the jury."

"As to any evidence or facts against him which the defendant can reasonably be expected to deny or explain because of facts within his knowledge, if he does not testify or if, though he does testify, he fails to deny or explain such evidence, the jury may take that failure into consideration as tending to indicate the truth of such evidence and as indicating that among the inferences that may be reasonably drawn therefrom those unfavorable to the defendant are the more probable."

It added, however, that no such inference could be drawn as to evidence respecting which he had no knowledge. It stated that failure of a defendant to deny or explain the evidence of which he had knowledge does not create a presumption of guilt nor by itself warrant an inference of guilt nor relieve the prosecution of any of its burden of proof.

Petitioner had been seen with the deceased the evening of her death, the evidence placing him with her in the alley where her body was found. The prosecutor made much of the failure of petitioner to testify:

"The defendant certainly knows whether Essie Mae had this beat up appearance at the time he left her apartment and went down the alley with her."

"What kind of a man is it that would want to have sex with a woman that beat up [if] she was beat up at the time he left?"

"He would know that. He would know how she got down the alley. He would know how the blood got on the bottom of the concrete steps. He would know how long he was with her in that box. He would know how her wig got off. He would know whether he beat her or mistreated her. He would know whether he walked away from that place cool as a cucumber when he saw Mr. Villasenor because he was conscious of his own guilt and wanted to get away from that damaged or injured woman."

"These things he has not seen fit to take the stand and deny or explain. And in the whole world, if anybody would know, this defendant would know. Essie Mae is dead, she can't tell you her side of the story. The defendant won't."

The death penalty was imposed and the California Supreme Court affirmed. The case is here on a writ of certiorari which we granted [to] consider whether comment on the failure to testify violated the Self-Incrimination Clause of the Fifth Amendment which we made applicable to the States by the Fourteenth in

Malloy v. Hogan, 378 U.S. 1 (1964), decided after the Supreme Court of California had affirmed the present conviction.

[We think that California's "comment rule"] violates the Fifth Amendment. It is in substance a rule of evidence that allows the State the privilege of tendering to the jury for its consideration the failure of the accused to testify. No formal offer of proof is made as in other situations; but the prosecutor's comment and the court's acquiescence are the equivalent of an offer of evidence and its acceptance. The Court in *Wilson v. United States*, 149 U.S. 60 (1893), [which involved a federal statute that provides that a defendant's failure to request that he serve as a witness "shall not create any presumption against him,"] stated:

> "[T]he act was framed with a due regard also to those who might prefer to rely upon the presumption of innocence which the law gives to everyone, and not wish to be witnesses. It is not every one who can safely venture on the witness stand, though entirely innocent of the charge against him. Excessive timidity, nervousness when facing others and attempting to explain transactions of a suspicious character, and offenses charged against him, will often confuse and embarrass him to such a degree as to increase rather than remove prejudices against him. It is not every one, however, honest, who would therefore willingly be placed on the witness stand. The statute, in tenderness to the weakness of those who from the causes mentioned might refuse to ask to be witnesses, particularly when they may have been in some degree compromised by their association with others, declares that the failure of a defendant in a criminal action to request to be a witness shall not create any presumption against him." *Id.* at 66.

Food for Thought

The Court suggests here that even though the judge and the prosecutor may not comment on the defendant's failure to testify, the jury may nevertheless draw inferences about the defendant's guilt from the defendant's failure to testify. Is the Court's point that such inferences do not constitute a "penalty" for the exercise of a constitutional right? Or just that such inferences are inevitable and cannot be prevented?

If the words "[F]ifth Amendment" are substituted for "act" and for "statute" the spirit of the Self-Incrimination Clause is reflected. For comment on the refusal to testify is a remnant of the "inquisitorial system of criminal justice," *Murphy v. Waterfront Comm.*, 378 U.S. 52, 55 (1964), which the Fifth Amendment outlaws. It is a penalty imposed by courts for exercising a constitutional privilege. It cuts down on the privilege by making its assertion costly. It is said, however, that the inference of guilt for failure to testify as to facts peculiarly within the accused's knowledge is in any event

natural and irresistible, and that comment on the failure does not magnify that inference into a penalty for asserting a constitutional privilege. What the jury may infer, given no help from the court, is one thing. What it may infer when the court solemnizes the silence of the accused into evidence against him is quite another.
* * *

We [hold] that the Fifth Amendment, in its direct application to the Federal Government and in its bearing on the States by reason of the Fourteenth Amendment, forbids either comment by the prosecution on the accused's silence or instructions by the court that such silence is evidence of guilt. Reversed.

THE CHIEF JUSTICE took no part in the decision of this case.

[JUSTICE HARLAN's concurring opinion has been omitted.]

MR. JUSTICE STEWART, with whom MR. JUSTICE WHITE joins, dissenting.

[The question before us] has not arisen before, because until last year the self-incrimination provision of the Fifth Amendment had been held to apply only to federal proceedings, and in the federal judicial system the matter has been covered by a specific Act of Congress which has been in effect ever since defendants have been permitted to testify at all in federal criminal trials.

We must determine whether the petitioner has been "compelled . . . to be a witness against himself." Compulsion is the focus of the inquiry. Certainly, if any compulsion be detected in the California procedure, it is of a dramatically different and less palpable nature than that involved in the procedures which historically gave rise to the Fifth Amendment guarantee. When a suspect was brought before the Court of High Commission or the Star Chamber, he was commanded to answer whatever was asked of him, and subjected to a far-reaching and deeply probing inquiry in an effort to ferret out some unknown and frequently unsuspected crime. He declined to answer on pain of incarceration, banishment, or mutilation. And if he spoke falsely, he was subject to further punishment. Faced with this formidable array of alternatives, his decision to speak was unquestionably coerced.

> **FYI**
>
> The "Court of High Commission" was an English ecclesiastical court that became notorious as an instrument of repression against those who refused to acknowledge the authority of the Church of England. The "Star Chamber" was a British Court that was used to entertain actions against political opponents of the King, and it often meted out harsh and arbitrary justice. Defendants in the Star Chamber had to answer all questions asked, upon pain of contempt, which sometimes forced them to choose between incriminating themselves and committing perjury.

Those were the lurid realities which lay behind enactment of the Fifth Amendment, a far cry from the subject matter of the case before us. I think that the Court in this case stretches the concept of compulsion beyond all reasonable bounds, and that whatever compulsion may exist derives from the defendant's choice not to testify, not from any comment by court or counsel. In support of its conclusion that the California procedure does compel the accused to testify, the Court has only this to say: "It is a penalty imposed by courts for exercising a constitutional privilege. It cuts down on the privilege by making its assertion costly." Exactly what the penalty imposed consists of is not clear. It is not, as I understand the problem, that the jury becomes aware that the defendant has chosen not to testify in his own defense, for the jury will, of course, realize this quite evident fact, even though the choice goes unmentioned. Since comment by counsel and the court does not compel testimony by creating such an awareness, the Court must be saying that the California constitutional provision places some other compulsion upon the defendant to incriminate himself, some compulsion which the Court does not describe and which I cannot readily perceive.

It is not at all apparent to me, on any realistic view of the trial process, that a defendant will be at more of a disadvantage under the California practice than he would be in a court which permitted no comment at all on his failure to take the witness stand. How can it be said that the inferences drawn by a jury will be more detrimental to a defendant under the limiting and carefully controlling language of the instruction here involved than would result if the jury were left to roam at large with only its untutored instincts to guide it, to draw from the defendant's silence broad inferences of guilt? The instructions in this case expressly cautioned the jury that the defendant's failure to testify "does not create a presumption of guilt or by itself warrant an inference of guilt"; it was further admonished that such failure does not "relieve the prosecution of its burden of providing every essential element of the crime," and finally the trial judge warned that the prosecution's burden remained that of proof "beyond a reasonable doubt." Whether the same limitations would be observed by a jury without the benefit of protective instructions shielding the defendant is certainly open to real doubt.

Moreover, no one can say where the balance of advantage might lie as a result of the attorneys' discussion of the matter. No doubt the prosecution's argument will seek to encourage the drawing of inferences unfavorable to the defendant. However, the defendant's counsel equally has an opportunity to explain the various other reasons why a defendant may not wish to take the stand, and thus rebut the natural if uneducated assumption that it is because the defendant cannot truthfully deny the accusations made.

* * * California has honored the constitutional command that no person shall "be compelled in any criminal case to be a witness against himself." The petitioner was not compelled to testify, and he did not do so. But whenever in a jury trial a defendant exercises this constitutional right, the members of the jury are bound to draw inferences from his silence. No constitution can prevent the operation of the human mind. Without limiting instructions, the danger exists that the inferences drawn by the jury may be unfairly broad. Some States have permitted this danger to go unchecked, by forbidding any comment at all upon the defendant's failure to take the witness stand. * * * Some might differ, as a matter of policy, with the way California has chosen to deal with the problem, or even disapprove of the judge's specific instructions in this case. But, so long as the constitutional command is obeyed, such matters of state policy are not for this Court to decide.

POINTS FOR DISCUSSION

a. Compelled or Not Compelled

The Fifth Amendment says: "No person . . . *shall be compelled* in any criminal case to be a witness against himself" (emphasis added). In *Griffin*, the state of California did not compel Griffin to be a witness against himself. Instead, Griffin argued that the prosecutor's comments and the court's instructions about Griffin's failure to testify interfered with the privilege against self-incrimination. Should a violation of the privilege require a showing that the government *compelled* the defendant to incriminate himself (or to testify)? See *Mitchell v. United States*, 526 U.S. 314, 331 (1999) (Scalia, J., dissenting) ("As an original matter, it would seem to me that the threat of an adverse inference does not 'compel' anyone to testify. It is one of the natural (and not governmentally imposed) consequences of failing to testify—as is the factfinder's increased readiness to believe the incriminating testimony that the defendant chooses not to contradict.").

b. Jury Instructions About the Defendant's Decision Not to Testify

In *Griffin*, the Court held that the trial judge and the prosecutor are not permitted to suggest to the jury that the defendant's failure to testify is evidence of guilt. Should a court be required to instruct the jury that it should *disregard*, and thus not infer anything from, the defendant's decision not to testify? In *Carter v. Kentucky*, 450 U.S. 288 (1981), the Court held that the privilege against self-incrimination requires a trial court, upon request from the defendant, to instruct the jury that it should draw no adverse inference from the defendant's failure to testify. The Court reasoned that *Griffin* "stands for the proposition that a defendant must pay no court-imposed price for the exercise of his constitutional privilege not to testify. The penalty was exacted in *Griffin* by adverse comment on the defendant's silence; the penalty may be just as severe when there is no adverse comment, but when the jury is left to roam at large with only its untutored instincts to guide it, to draw from the defendant's silence broad inferences of guilt. Even without adverse comment, the members of a jury, unless instructed otherwise, may well draw adverse inferences from a defendant's silence."

Accordingly, although "[n]o judge can prevent jurors from speculating about why a defendant stands mute in the face of a criminal accusation," a judge "can, and must, if requested to do so, use the unique power of the jury instruction to reduce that speculation to a minimum." Should a trial judge instruct the jury not to draw any adverse inference from the defendant's failure to testify even if the defendant does *not* ask the judge for such an instruction? Or might that instruction backfire by unintentionally encouraging the jury to think about the reasons that the defendant might not have testified?

2. Exclusion of Confessions Obtained by Physical or Mental Coercion

The Constitution does not generally prohibit the police from obtaining confessions from suspects and does not generally prohibit prosecutors from using confessions as evidence against defendants in criminal trials. Indeed, confessions form the basis for a high percentage of guilty pleas and convictions in both state and federal courts. Confessions are important because a criminal suspect is often the only person who knows what really happened.

The Supreme Court, however, has held that the Constitution nevertheless makes some confessions inadmissible. We are concerned here with a constitutional rule, established by longstanding precedent, that the admission into evidence "of a defendant's confession obtained by coercion—whether physical or mental—is forbidden." *Payne v. Arkansas*, 356 U.S. 560, 561 (1958). For example, if the police beat and torture a suspect until he confesses to committing a crime, it would violate the Constitution to rely on the confession as a basis for a conviction.

What exactly is physical or mental coercion? The three cases that follow are well-known precedents that help to answer this question. The first case, *Brown v. Mississippi*, 297 U.S. 278 (1936), concerned a confession obtained with shocking violence and brutality, resulting in severe and painful injuries. The second case,

Watts v. Indiana, 338 U.S. 49 (1949), involved extremely long interrogation, solitary confinement, and deprivation of sleep but no physical injuries. The third case, *Spano v. New York*, 360 U.S. 315 (1959), considered a confession obtained by "official pressure" and "sympathy falsely aroused." In all three cases, the Supreme Court held that the confessions could not be used against the defendants at trial.

As a matter of policy, why should using coerced confessions to obtain a conviction be forbidden? Are coerced confessions excluded from evidence to make criminal trials more reliable because coerced confessions have dubious credibility? Or does the exclusion of coerced confessions remove the incentive of the police to engage in oppressive tactics? You will see both of these policy considerations in the cases that follow.

Which constitutional provision bars the government from using coerced confessions? In *Bram v. United States*, 168 U.S. 532 (1897), the Supreme Court held that the Fifth Amendment privilege against self-incrimination bars admission of involuntary confessions in *federal* criminal cases. But in state cases, the Supreme Court initially followed a different approach. In early decisions like *Brown*, *Watts*, and *Spano*, the Supreme Court held that using the coerced confessions violated due process because they rendered the trials fundamentally unfair. In subsequent state cases, however, the Supreme Court shifted the inquiry from due process to the privilege against self-incrimination. In *Malloy v. Hogan*, 378 U.S. 1 (1964), the Court held that the Fourteenth Amendment incorporates the privilege against self-incrimination, and that under the right as incorporated

> "the constitutional inquiry is not whether the conduct of state officers in obtaining the confession was shocking [and thus violates due process], but whether the confession was 'free and voluntary; that is, [it] must not be extracted by any sort of threats or violence, nor obtained by any direct or implied promises, however slight, nor by the exertion of any improper influence.' "

Id. at 7 (quoting *Bram*, 168 U.S. at 542–43). Modern federal and state cases now follow this approach and rely on the privilege against self-incrimination.

BROWN V. MISSISSIPPI
297 U.S. 278 (1936)

MR. CHIEF JUSTICE HUGHES delivered the opinion of the Court.

The question in this case is whether convictions, which rest solely upon confessions shown to have been extorted by officers of the state by brutality and violence, are consistent with the due process of law required by the Fourteenth Amendment of the Constitution of the United States.

Petitioners were indicted for the murder of one Raymond Stewart, whose death occurred on March 30, 1934. They were indicted on April 4, 1934, and were then arraigned and pleaded not guilty. Counsel were appointed by the court to defend them. Trial was begun the next morning and was concluded on the following day, when they were found guilty and sentenced to death.

Aside from the confessions, there was no evidence sufficient to warrant the submission of the case to the jury. After a preliminary inquiry, testimony as to the confessions was received over the objection of defendants' counsel. Defendants then testified that the confessions were false and had been procured by physical torture. * * *

The opinion of the state court did not set forth the evidence as to the circumstances in which the confessions were procured. That the evidence established that they were procured by coercion was not questioned. [As the facts] are clearly and adequately stated in the dissenting opinion of Judge Griffith (with whom Judge Anderson concurred), showing both the extreme brutality of the measures to extort the confessions and the participation of the state authorities, we quote this part of his opinion * * *:

> The crime with which these defendants, all ignorant negroes, are charged, was discovered about 1 o'clock p.m. on Friday, March 30, 1934. On that night one Dial, a deputy sheriff, accompanied by others, came to the home of Ellington, one of the defendants, and requested him to accompany them to the house of the deceased, and there a number of white men were gathered, who began to accuse the defendant of the crime. Upon his denial they seized him, and with the participation of the deputy they hanged him by a rope to the limb of a tree, and, having let him down, they hung him again, and when he was let down the second time, and he still protested his innocence, he was tied to a tree and whipped, and, still declining to accede to the demands that he confess, he was finally released, and he returned with some difficulty to his home, suffering intense pain and agony. The record of the testimony shows that the signs of the rope on his neck were plainly visible during the so-called trial. A day or two thereafter the said deputy, accompanied by another, returned to the home of the said defendant and arrested him, and departed with the prisoner towards the jail in an adjoining county, but went by a route which led into the state of Alabama; and while on the way, in that state, the deputy stopped and again severely whipped

the defendant, declaring that he would continue the whipping until he confessed, and the defendant then agreed to confess to such a statement as the deputy would dictate, and he did so, after which he was delivered to jail.

The other two defendants, Ed Brown and Henry Shields, were also arrested and taken to the same jail. On Sunday night, April 1, 1934, the same deputy, accompanied by a number of white men, one of whom was also an officer, and by the jailer, came to the jail, and the two last named defendants were made to strip and they were laid over chairs and their backs were cut to pieces with a leather strap with buckles on it, and they were likewise made by the said deputy definitely to understand that the whipping would be continued unless and until they confessed, and not only confessed, but confessed in every matter of detail as demanded by those present; and in this manner the defendants confessed the crime, and, as the whippings progressed and were repeated, they changed or adjusted their confession in all particulars of detail so as to conform to the demands of their torturers. When the confessions had been obtained in the exact form and contents as desired by the mob, they left with the parting admonition and warning that, if the defendants changed their story at any time in any respect from that last stated, the perpetrators of the outrage would administer the same or equally effective treatment.

* * * The evidence upon which the conviction was obtained was the so-called confessions. * * * The defendants were put on the stand, and by their testimony the facts and the details thereof as to the manner by which the confessions were extorted from them were fully developed, and it is further disclosed by the record that the same deputy, Dial, under whose guiding hand and active participation the tortures to coerce the confessions were administered, was actively in the performance of the supposed duties of a court deputy in the courthouse and in the presence of the prisoners during what is denominated, in complimentary terms, the trial of these defendants. This deputy was put on the stand by the state in rebuttal, and admitted the whippings. It is interesting to note that in his testimony with reference to the whipping of the defendant Ellington, and in response to the inquiry as to how severely he was whipped, the deputy stated, "Not too much for a negro; not as much as I would have done if it were left to me." Two others who had participated in these whippings were introduced and admitted it—not a single witness was introduced who denied it. The facts are not only

undisputed, they are admitted, and admitted to have been done by officers of the state, in conjunction with other participants, and all this was definitely well known to everybody connected with the trial, and during the trial, including the state's prosecuting attorney and the trial judge presiding.

[T]he question of the right of the state to withdraw the privilege against self-incrimination is not here involved. The compulsion * * * of the processes of justice by which the accused may be called as a witness and required to testify [is one thing]. Compulsion by torture to extort a confession is a different matter.

The state is free to regulate the procedure of its courts in accordance with its own conceptions of policy, unless in so doing it "offends some principle of justice so rooted in the traditions and conscience of our people as to be ranked as fundamental." *Snyder v. Massachusetts*, 291 U.S. 97, 105 (1934). * * * [T]he freedom of the state in establishing its policy is the freedom of constitutional government and is limited by the requirement of due process of law. Because a state may dispense with a jury trial, it does not follow that it may substitute trial by ordeal. The rack and torture chamber may not be substituted for the witness stand. The state may not permit an accused to be hurried to conviction under mob domination—where the whole proceeding is but a mask—without supplying corrective process. *Moore v. Dempsey*, 261 U.S. 86, 91 (1923). * * * And the trial equally is a mere pretense where the state authorities have contrived a conviction resting solely upon confessions obtained by violence. The due process clause requires "that state action, whether through one agency or another, shall be consistent with the fundamental principles of liberty and justice which lie at the base of all our civil and political institutions." *Hebert v. Louisiana*, 272 U.S. 312, 316 (1926). It would be difficult to conceive of methods more revolting to the sense of justice than those taken to procure the confessions of these petitioners, and the use of the confessions thus obtained as the basis for conviction and sentence was a clear denial of due process.

* * * The conviction and sentence were void for want of the essential elements of due process, and the proceeding thus vitiated could be challenged in any appropriate manner. It was challenged before the Supreme Court of the State by the express invocation of the Fourteenth Amendment. That court entertained the challenge, considered the federal question thus presented, but declined to enforce petitioners' constitutional right. The court thus denied a federal right fully established and specially set up and claimed, and the judgment must be reversed.

POINTS FOR DISCUSSION

a. Confessions Obtained by Torture

The Court held in *Brown* that a state violates the Due Process Clause when it convicts and sentences a defendant based on a confession obtained by torture. The facts of the case are shocking, and the conduct of the police was abhorrent. But how far does this principle extend? Must the police actually engage in conduct resulting in physical injuries before a confession becomes inadmissible? We consider this question below.

b. Incorporation and the Privilege Against Self-Incrimination

When the Court decided *Brown* in 1936, it had not yet held that the Fourteenth Amendment's Due Process Clause incorporates the Fifth Amendment privilege against self-incrimination. Instead, the Court relied on principles of justice implicit in the notion of due process. Post-incorporation, is the privilege against self-incrimination a more satisfying or sensible basis for the conclusion that confessions obtained by violence or torture cannot be the basis for conviction for a crime? Or is the privilege against self-incrimination a less satisfactory basis? (Were the defendants actually compelled to be witnesses against themselves?) As noted above, the Supreme Court subsequently held that using a coerced confession in a state trial may violate the Fifth Amendment's privilege against self-incrimination, as incorporated by the Fourteenth Amendment. See *Malloy v. Hogan*, 378 U.S. 1 (1964).

––––––––––––

The defendants' confessions in *Brown* clearly were not voluntary. The Court in *Brown* reversed the convictions because the police had used "compulsion by torture to extort [the] confession[s]." The Court confirmed in subsequent cases that it violates the Due Process Clause to compel a suspect to confess to a crime and that, accordingly, confessions must be voluntary if they are to serve as the basis for a conviction. In *Ashcraft v. Tennessee*, 322 U.S. 143 (1944), for example, the Court declared that the "Constitution of the United States stands as a bar against the conviction of any individual in an American court by means of a coerced confession." In that case, the Court concluded that the petitioner's confession, obtained after he had been questioned for thirty-six straight hours without sleep or rest while a bright light shone in his eyes, had not been voluntary. The Court reasoned that the interrogation was "so inherently coercive that its very existence is irreconcilable with the possession of mental freedom by a lone suspect against whom its full coercive force is brought to bear."

It is clear that a confession obtained by torture, as in *Brown*, is not voluntary in any meaningful sense. It is also not difficult to imagine circumstances, such as those in *Ashcraft*, that are so trying for a suspect that he feels that he has no choice but to confess if he wants the misery to end. But how far does the concept of involuntariness extend? After all, most confessions to police are not entirely voluntary; it is unusual for a person who committed a crime to show up uninvited at a police station and announce, without having been questioned, that he has committed a crime. Virtually all confessions come only after the police have questioned a suspect.

Suppose the police bring a suspect to the station for questioning about a murder. The police explain that, if he does not cooperate in the investigation now, he will face the death penalty if convicted—but that, if he does cooperate, the punishment likely will be less severe. If the suspect confesses, is the confession "voluntary"? It is in the sense that the suspect, after weighing the costs and benefits, made a choice to confess; the police did not torture him or subject him to emotional and mental abuse to coerce him to do so. But the suspect likely would not have confessed but for the fear of the consequences that the police described. In this sense, he confessed under a very real form of pressure.

Yet if a confession obtained under these circumstances is not genuinely voluntary, and thus would violate the Due Process Clause, then it is difficult to imagine how police could obtain confessions from suspects in most cases. The Court began to confront this tension in the case that follows.

WATTS V. INDIANA

338 U.S. 49 (1949)

MR. JUSTICE FRANKFURTER announced the judgment of the Court and an opinion in which MR. JUSTICE MURPHY and MR. JUSTICE RUTLEDGE join.

Take Note

Justice Frankfurter's opinion is for only a plurality of the Justices; a majority of the Justices could not agree on one rationale to decide the case.

* * * This case is here because the Supreme Court of Indiana rejected petitioner's claim that confessions elicited from him were procured under circumstances rendering their admission as evidence against him a denial of due process of law.

[O]nly those elements of the events and circumstances in which a confession was involved that are unquestioned in the State's version of what happened are relevant to the constitutional issue here. But if force has been applied, this Court does not leave to local determination whether or not the confession was voluntary. There is torture of mind as well as body; the will is as much affected by fear as by force. And there comes a point where this Court should not be ignorant as judges of what we know as men.

This brings us to the undisputed circumstances which must determine the issue of due process in this case. Thanks to the forthrightness of counsel for Indiana, these circumstances may be briefly stated. On November 12, 1947, a Wednesday, petitioner was arrested and held as the suspected perpetrator of an alleged criminal assault earlier in the day. Later the same day, in the vicinity of this occurrence, a woman was found dead under conditions suggesting murder in the course of an attempted criminal assault. Suspicion of murder quickly turned towards petitioner and the police began to question him. They took him from the county jail to State Police Headquarters, where he was questioned by officers in relays from about eleven thirty that night until sometime between 2:30 and 3 o'clock the following morning. The same procedure of persistent interrogation from about 5:30 in the afternoon until about 3 o'clock the following morning, by a relay of six to eight officers, was pursued on Thursday the 13th, Friday the 14th, Saturday the 15th, [and] Monday the 17th. Sunday was a day of rest from interrogation. About 3 o'clock on Tuesday morning, November 18, the petitioner made an incriminating statement after continuous questioning since 6 o'clock of the preceding evening. The statement did not satisfy the prosecutor who had been called in and he then took petitioner in hand. Petitioner, questioned by an interrogator of twenty years' experience as lawyer, judge and prosecutor, yielded a more incriminating document.

Until his inculpatory statements were secured, the petitioner was a prisoner in the exclusive control of the prosecuting authorities. He was kept for the first two days in solitary confinement in a cell aptly enough called "the hole" in view of its physical conditions as described by the State's witnesses. Apart from the five night sessions, the police intermittently interrogated Watts during the day and on three days drove him around town, hours at a time, with a view to eliciting identifications and other disclosures. Although the law of Indiana required that petitioner be given a prompt preliminary hearing before a magistrate, with all the protection a hearing was intended to give him, the petitioner was not only given no hearing during the entire period of interrogation but was without friendly or professional aid and without advice as to his constitutional rights. Disregard of rudimentary needs of life—opportunities for sleep and a decent allowance of food—are also relevant, not as aggravating elements of petitioner's treatment, but as part of the total situation out of which his confessions came and which stamped their character.

Take Note

In this paragraph, the plurality explains what it means for a confession to be "voluntary." Does the line that the plurality draws between voluntary and involuntary confessions make sense? Is it easy to administer?

A confession by which life becomes forfeit must be the expression of free choice. A statement to be voluntary of course need not be volunteered. But if it is the product of sustained pressure by the police it does not issue from a free choice. When a suspect speaks because he is overborne, it is immaterial whether he has been subjected to a physical or a mental ordeal. Eventual yielding to questioning under such circumstances is plainly the product of the suction process of interrogation and therefore the reverse of voluntary. We would have to shut our minds to the plain significance of what here transpired to deny that this was a calculated endeavor to secure a confession through the pressure of unrelenting interrogation. The very relentlessness of such interrogation implies that it is better for the prisoner to answer than to persist in the refusal of disclosure which is his constitutional right. To turn the detention of an accused into a process of wrenching from him evidence which could not be extorted in open court with all its safeguards, is so grave an abuse of the power of arrest as to offend the procedural standards of due process.

This is so because it violates the underlying principle in our enforcement of the criminal law. Ours is the accusatorial as opposed to the inquisitorial system. Such has been the characteristic of Anglo-American criminal justice since it freed itself from practices borrowed by the Star Chamber from the Continent whereby an accused was interrogated in secret for hours on end. Under our system society carries the burden of proving its charge against the accused not out of his own mouth. It must establish its case, not by interrogation of the accused even under judicial safeguards, but by evidence independently secured through skillful investigation. * * * The requirement of specific charges, their proof beyond a reasonable doubt, the protection of the accused from confessions extorted through whatever form of police pressures, the right to a prompt hearing before a magistrate, the right to assistance of counsel, to be supplied by government when circumstances make it necessary, the duty to advise an accused of his constitutional rights—these are all characteristics of the accusatorial system and manifestations of its demands. Protracted, systematic and uncontrolled subjection of an accused to interrogation by the police for the purpose of eliciting disclosures or confessions is subversive of the accusatorial system. It is the inquisitorial system without its safeguards. For while under that system the accused is subjected to judicial interrogation, he is protected by the disinterestedness of the judge in the presence of counsel.

In holding that the Due Process Clause bars police procedure which violates the basic notions of our accusatorial mode of prosecuting crime and vitiates a conviction based on the fruits of such procedure, we apply the Due Process Clause to its historic function of assuring appropriate procedure before liberty is curtailed or life is taken. We are deeply mindful of the anguishing problems which the incidence of crime presents to the States. But the history of the criminal law proves overwhelmingly that brutal methods of law enforcement are essentially self-defeating, whatever may be their effect in a particular case. Law triumphs when the natural impulses aroused by a shocking crime yield to the safeguards which our civilization has evolved for an administration of criminal justice at once rational and effective.

Reversed.

[The Court also reversed the judgments in two companion cases. In one, the police held and repeatedly questioned the suspect in a "stifling" hot cubicle for three days. After repeatedly denying that he had committed the murder under investigation, he confessed after the sheriff threatened to arrest his mother for handling stolen property. In the other, the police held and questioned the suspect repeatedly over five days; he finally confessed at 11:00 pm on the night of the fifth day in custody.]

MR. JUSTICE DOUGLAS, concurring.

It would be naive to think that this protective custody was less than the inquisition. The man was held until he broke. Then and only then was he arraigned and given the protection which the law provides all accused. Detention without arraignment is a time-honored method for keeping an accused under the exclusive control of the police. They can then operate at their leisure. The accused is wholly at their mercy. He is without the aid of counsel or friends; and he is denied the protection of the magistrate. We should unequivocally condemn the procedure and stand ready to outlaw * * * any confession obtained during the period of the unlawful detention. The

> **Take Note**
>
> Justice Douglas appears to assert that the Court should interpret the Constitution categorically to prohibit the police practice of custodial interrogation before the defendant has been charged, reasoning that such interrogations inevitably coerce suspects into confessing. Is such a prophylactic rule justified? If so, is the Court the right institution to require it?

procedure breeds coerced confessions. It is the root of the evil. It is the procedure without which the inquisition could not flourish in the country.

MR. JUSTICE JACKSON concurring in the result [and dissenting from the result in the two companion cases].

These three cases, from widely separated states, present essentially the same problem. Its recurrence suggests that it has roots in some condition fundamental and general to our criminal system.

In each case police were confronted with one or more brutal murders which the authorities were under the highest duty to solve. Each of these murders was unwitnessed, and the only positive knowledge on which a solution could be based was possessed by the killer. In each there was reasonable ground to *suspect* an individual but not enough legal evidence to *charge* him with guilt. In each the police attempted to meet the situation by taking the suspect into custody and interrogating him. This extended over varying periods. In each, confessions were made and received in evidence at the trial. Checked with external evidence, they are inherently believable, and were not shaken as to truth by anything that occurred at the trial. Each confessor was convicted by a jury and state courts affirmed. This Court sets all three convictions aside.

The seriousness of the Court's judgment is that no one suggests that any course held promise of solution of these murders other than to take the suspect into custody for questioning. The alternative was to close the books on the crime and forget it, with the suspect at large. This is a grave choice for a society in which two-thirds of the murders already are closed out as insoluble.

A concurring opinion, however, goes to the very limit and seems to declare for outlawing any confession, however freely given, if obtained during a period of custody between arrest and arraignment—which, in practice, means all of them.

Others would strike down these confessions because of conditions which they say make them "involuntary." In this, on only a printed record, they pit their judgment against that of the trial judge and the jury. Both, with the great advantage of hearing and seeing the confessor and also the officers whose conduct and bearing toward him is in question, have found that the confessions were voluntary. In addition, the majority overrule in each case one or more state appellate courts, which have the same limited opportunity to know the truth that we do.

Amid much that is irrelevant or trivial one serious situation seems to me to stand out in these cases. The suspect neither had nor was advised of his right to get counsel. This presents a real dilemma in a free society. To subject one without counsel to questioning which may and is intended to convict him, is a real peril to individual freedom. To bring in a lawyer means a real peril to solution of the crime because, under our adversary system, he deems that his sole duty is to protect his client—guilty or innocent—and that in such a capacity he owes no duty whatever to help society solve its crime problem. Under this conception of criminal procedure, any lawyer worth his salt will tell the suspect in no uncertain terms to make no statement to police under any circumstances.

If the State may arrest on suspicion and interrogate without counsel, there is no denying the fact that it largely negates the benefits of the constitutional guaranty of the right to assistance of counsel. Any lawyer who has ever been called into a case after his client has "told all" and turned any evidence he has over to the Government, knows how helpless he is to protect his client against the facts thus disclosed.

I suppose the view one takes will turn on what one thinks should be the right of an accused person against the State. Is it his right to have the judgment on the facts? Or is it his right to have a judgment based on only such evidence as he cannot conceal from the authorities, who cannot compel him to testify in court and also cannot question him before? Our system comes close to the latter by any interpretation, for the defendant is shielded by such safeguards as no system to law except the Anglo-American concedes to him.

Of course, no confession that has been obtained by any form of physical violence to the person is reliable and hence no conviction should rest upon one obtained in that manner. Such treatment not only breaks the will to conceal or lie, but may even break the will to stand by the truth. Nor is it questioned that the same result can sometimes be achieved by threats, promises, or inducements, which torture the mind but put no scar on the body. If the opinion of Mr. Justice Frankfurter [were] based solely on the State's admissions as to the treatment of Watts, I should not disagree. But if [the] ultimate quest in a criminal trial is the truth and if the circumstances indicate no violence or threats of it, should society be deprived of the suspect's help in solving a crime merely because he was confined and questioned when uncounseled?

We must not overlook that in these, as in some previous cases, once a confession is obtained it supplies ways of verifying its trustworthiness. In these cases before us the verification is sufficient to leave me in no doubt that the admissions of guilt were genuine and truthful. Such corroboration consists in one case of finding a weapon

> **Food for Thought**
>
> Is Justice Jackson suggesting here that even confessions that are not totally voluntary may be admitted against a defendant if they are reliable? Should reliability, rather than voluntariness, be the measure of validity for a confession?

where the accused has said he hid it, and in others that conditions which could only have been known to one who was implicated correspond with his story. It is possible, but it is rare, that a confession, if repudiated on the trial, standing alone will convict unless there is external proof of its verity.

In all such cases, along with other conditions criticized, the continuity and duration of the questioning is invoked and it is called an "inquiry," "inquest" or "inquisition," depending mainly on the emotional state of the writer. But as in some of the cases here, if interrogation is permissible at all, there are sound reasons for prolonging it—which the opinions here ignore. The suspect at first perhaps makes an effort to exculpate himself by alibis or other statements. These are verified, found false, and he is then confronted with his falsehood. Sometimes (though such cases do not reach us) verification proves them true or credible and the suspect is released. Sometimes, as here, more than one crime is involved. The duration of an interrogation may well depend on the temperament, shrewdness and cunning of the accused and the competence of the examiner. But assuming a right to examine at all, the right must include what is made reasonably necessary by the facts of the particular case.

If the right of interrogation be admitted, then it seems to me that we must leave it to trial judges and juries and state appellate courts to decide individual cases, unless they show some want of proper standards of decision. I find nothing to indicate that any of the courts below in these cases did not have a correct understanding of the Fourteenth Amendment, unless this Court thinks it means absolute prohibition of interrogation while in custody before arraignment.

I suppose no one would doubt that our Constitution and Bill of Rights, grounded in revolt against the arbitrary measures of George III and in the philosophy of the French Revolution, represent the maximum restrictions upon the power of organized society over the individual that are compatible with the maintenance of organized society itself. They were so intended and should be so interpreted. It cannot be denied that, even if construed as these provisions traditionally have been, they contain an aggregate of restrictions which seriously limit the power of society to solve such crimes as confront us in these cases. Those restrictions we should not for that reason cast aside, but that is good reason for indulging in no unnecessary expansion of them.

I doubt very much if they require us to hold that the State may not take into custody and question one suspected reasonably of an unwitnessed murder. If it does, the people of this country must discipline themselves to seeing their police stand by helplessly while those suspected of murder prowl about unmolested. Is it a necessary price to pay for the fairness which we know as "due process of law"? And if not a necessary one, should it be demanded by this Court? I do not know the ultimate answer to these questions; but, for the present, I should not increase the handicap on society.

[JUSTICE BLACK's separate concurring opinion has been omitted. THE CHIEF JUSTICE, joined by JUSTICE REED and JUSTICE BURTON, dissented without opinion.]

POINTS FOR DISCUSSION

a. Justice Frankfurter's Approach

Justice Frankfurter concluded that the interrogation of the petitioner was so relentless that the confession was essentially coerced, rather than voluntary. Justice Frankfurter noted that it is necessary to reject such methods in order to preserve the core attributes of the adversary system, which requires the state to prove its case "by evidence independently secured through skillful investigation." Under this approach, how much pressure during interrogation is too much? How much of the adversary system is required by the phrase "due process"?

b. Justice Douglas's Approach

Justice Douglas suggested that all confessions obtained during detention and interrogation without arraignment should be inadmissible. Under this approach, police would not be permitted to seek confessions from suspects who have not been charged. In addition, because the right to counsel would attach once the suspect has been charged, and good attorneys would advise their clients not to speak to the police, investigators likely would not be able to obtain confessions in most cases. Was Justice Douglas's concern that all confessions obtained during interrogations are inherently involuntary and thus an impermissible basis for a conviction? Even if that is so, what would it mean for the government's ability to solve crimes and punish criminals if the police could not elicit confessions from suspects?

c. Justice Jackson's Approach

Justice Jackson responded to Justice Douglas's approach by warning that, if police cannot interrogate a suspect before charging him, they effectively will not be able to obtain confessions—and many guilty people will escape punishment, as confessions serve as the basis for a large percentage of convictions and guilty pleas. But Justice Jackson also seemed to agree that confessions obtained from interrogations that "torture the mind" should be inadmissible at trial. Is there a middle ground between these two concerns?

SPANO V. NEW YORK

360 U.S. 315 (1959)

MR. CHIEF JUSTICE WARREN delivered the opinion of the Court.

This is another in the long line of cases presenting the question whether a confession was properly admitted into evidence under the Fourteenth Amendment. * * *

The State's evidence reveals the following: Petitioner Vincent Joseph Spano is a derivative citizen of this country, having been born in Messina, Italy. He was 25 years old at the time of the shooting in question and had graduated from junior high school. He had a record of regular employment. The shooting took place on January 22, 1957.

On that day, petitioner was drinking in a bar. The decedent, a former professional boxer weighing almost 200 pounds who had fought in Madison Square Garden, took some of petitioner's money from the bar. Petitioner followed him out of the bar to recover it. A fight ensued, with the decedent knocking petitioner down and then kicking him in the head three or four times. Shock from the force of these blow caused petitioner to vomit. After the bartender applied some ice to his head, petitioner left the bar, walked to his apartment, secured a gun, and walked eight or nine blocks to a candy store where the decedent was frequently to be found. He entered the store in which decedent, three friends of decedent, at least two of whom were ex-convicts, and a boy who was supervising the store were present. He fired five shots, two of which entered the decedent's body, causing his death. The boy was the only eyewitness; the three friends of decedent did not see the person who fired the shot. Petitioner then disappeared for the next week or so.

On February 1, 1957, the Bronx County Grand Jury returned an indictment for first-degree murder against petitioner. Accordingly, a bench warrant was issued for his arrest, commanding that he be forthwith brought before the court to answer the indictment, or, if the court had adjourned for the term, that he be delivered into the custody of the Sheriff of Bronx County.

On February 3, 1957, petitioner called one Gaspar Bruno, a close friend of 8 or 10 years' standing who had attended school with him. Bruno was a fledgling police officer, having at that time not yet finished attending police academy. According to Bruno's testimony, petitioner told him "that he took a terrific beating, that the deceased hurt him real bad and he dropped him a couple of times and he was dazed; he didn't know what he was doing and that he went and shot at him." Petitioner told Bruno that he intended to get a lawyer and give himself up. Bruno relayed this information to his superiors.

The following day, February 4, at 7:10 p.m., petitioner, accompanied by counsel, surrendered himself to the authorities in front of the Bronx County Building * * *. His attorney had cautioned him to answer no questions, and left him in the custody of the officers. He was promptly taken to the office of the Assistant District Attorney and at 7:15 p.m. the questioning began, being conducted by Assistant District Attorney Goldsmith, Lt. Gannon, Detectives Farrell, Lehrer and Motta, and Sgt. Clarke. The record reveals that the questioning was both persistent and continuous. Petitioner, in accordance with his attorney's instructions, steadfastly refused to answer. * * * He asked one officer, Detective Ciccone, if he could speak to his attorney, but that request was denied. Detective Ciccone testified that he could not find the attorney's name in the telephone book.[1] He was given two sandwiches, coffee and cake at 11 p.m.

At 12:15 a.m. on the morning of February 5, after five hours of questioning in which it became evident that petitioner was following his attorney's instructions, on the Assistant District Attorney's orders petitioner was transferred to the 46th Squad, Ryer Avenue Police Station. The Assistant District Attorney also went to the police station and to some extent continued to participate in the interrogation. Petitioner arrived at 12:30 and questioning was resumed at 12:40. * * * But petitioner persisted in his refusal to answer, and again requested permission to see his attorney, this time from Detective Lehrer. His request was again denied.

It was then that those in charge of the investigation decided that petitioner's close friend, Bruno, could be of use. He had been called out on the case around 10 or 11 p.m., although he was not connected with the 46th Squad or Precinct in any way. Although, in fact, his job was in no way threatened, Bruno was told to tell petitioner that petitioner's telephone call had gotten him "in a lot of trouble," and that he should seek to extract sympathy from petitioner for Bruno's pregnant wife and three children. Bruno developed this theme with petitioner without success, and petitioner, also without success, again sought to see his attorney, a request which Bruno relayed unavailingly to his superiors. After this first session with petitioner, Bruno was again directed by Lt. Gannon to play on petitioner's sympathies, but again no confession was forthcoming. But the Lieutenant a third time ordered Bruno falsely to importune his friend to confess but again petitioner

---

[1] How this could be so when the attorney's name, Tobias Russo, was concededly in the telephone book does not appear. The trial judge sustained objections by the Assistant District Attorney to questions designed to delve into this mystery.

clung to his attorney's advice. Inevitably, in the fourth such session directed by the Lieutenant, lasting a full hour, petitioner succumbed to his friend's prevarications and agreed to make a statement. Accordingly, at 3:25 a.m. the Assistant District Attorney, a stenographer, and several other law enforcement officials entered the room where petitioner was being questioned, and took his statement in question and answer form with the Assistant District Attorney asking the questions. The statement was completed at 4:05 a.m.

But this was not the end. At 4:30 a.m. three detectives took petitioner to Police Headquarters in Manhattan. On the way they attempted to find the bridge from which petitioner said he had thrown the murder weapon. They crossed the Triborough Bridge into Manhattan, arriving at Police Headquarters at 5 a.m., and left Manhattan for the Bronx at 5:40 a.m. via the Willis Avenue Bridge. When petitioner recognized neither bridge as the one from which he had thrown the weapon, they re-entered Manhattan via the Third Avenue Bridge, which petitioner stated was the right one, and then returned to the Bronx well after 6 a.m. During that trip the officers also elicited a statement from petitioner that the deceased was always "on [his] back," "always pushing" him and that he was "not sorry" he had shot the deceased. All three detectives testified to that statement at the trial.

Court opened at 10 a.m. that morning, and petitioner was arraigned at 10:15.

At the trial, the confession was introduced in evidence over appropriate objections. The jury was instructed that it could rely on it only if it was found to be voluntary. The jury returned a guilty verdict and petitioner was sentenced to death. The New York Court of Appeals affirmed the conviction over three dissents * * *.

Petitioner's first contention is that his absolute right to counsel in a capital case, *Powell v. State of Alabama*, 287 U.S. 45 (1932), became operative on the return of an indictment against him, for at that time he was in every sense a defendant in a criminal case, the grand jury having found sufficient cause to believe that he had committed the crime. He argues accordingly that following indictment no confession obtained in the absence of counsel can be used without violating the Fourteenth Amendment. * * * We find it unnecessary to reach that contention, for we find use of the confession obtained here inconsistent with the Fourteenth Amendment under traditional principles.

> **Make the Connection**
>
> The Sixth Amendment provides, in relevant part, "In all criminal prosecutions, the accused shall enjoy the right * * * to have the Assistance of Counsel for his defence." We will consider the right to counsel under the Sixth Amendment in some of the cases that follow, and more comprehensively in Chapter 15.

The abhorrence of society to the use of involuntary confessions does not turn alone on their inherent untrustworthiness. It also turns on the deep-rooted feeling that the police must obey the law while enforcing the law; that in the end life and liberty can be as much endangered from illegal methods used to convict those thought to be criminals as from the actual criminals themselves. Accordingly, the actions of police in obtaining confessions have come under scrutiny in a long series of cases. Those cases suggest that in recent years law enforcement officials have become increasingly aware of the burden which they share, along with our courts, in protecting fundamental rights of our citizenry, including that portion of our citizenry suspected of crime. The facts of no case recently in this Court have quite approached the brutal beatings in *Brown v. State of Mississippi*, 297 U.S. 278 (1936), or the 36 consecutive hours of questioning present in *Ashcraft v. State of Tennessee*, 322 U.S. 143 (1944). But as law enforcement officers become more responsible, and the methods used to extract confessions more sophisticated, our duty to enforce federal constitutional protections does not cease. It only becomes more difficult because of the more delicate judgments to be made. Our judgment here is that, on all the facts, this conviction cannot stand.

Petitioner was a foreign-born young man of 25 with no past history of law violation or of subjection to official interrogation, at least insofar as the record shows. He had progressed only one-half year into high school and the record indicates that he had a history of emotional instability.[3] He did not make a narrative statement, but was subject to the leading questions of a skillful prosecutor in a question and answer confession. He was subjected to questioning not by a few men, but by many. * * * Petitioner was questioned for virtually eight straight hours before he confessed, with his only respite being a transfer to an arena presumably considered more appropriate by the police for the task at hand. Nor was the questioning conducted during normal business hours, but began in early evening, continued into the night, and did not bear fruition until the not-too-early morning. The drama was not played out, with the final admissions obtained, until almost sunrise. In such circumstances slowly mounting fatigue does, and is calculated to, play its part. The questioners persisted in the face of his repeated refusals to answer on the advice of his attorney, and they ignored his reasonable requests to contact the local attorney whom he had already retained

---

[3]   Medical reports from New York City's Fordham Hospital introduced by defendant showed that he had suffered a cerebral concussion in 1955. He was described by a private physician in 1951 as "an extremely nervous tense individual who is emotionally unstable and maladjusted," and was found unacceptable for military service in 1951, primarily because of Psychiatric disorder. He failed the Army's AFQT-1 intelligence test. His mother had been in mental hospitals on three separate occasions.

and who had personally delivered him into the custody of these officers in obedience to the bench warrant.

Take Note

The Court states that its inquiry into the voluntariness of Spano's confession is based on the "totality of the situation." Can the standard that the Court applies for voluntariness be summarized with any more precision? If not, is that a problem for the Court's approach?

The use of Bruno, characterized in this Court by counsel for the State as a "childhood friend" of petitioner's, is another factor which deserves mention in the totality of the situation. Bruno's was the one face visible to petitioner in which he could put some trust. There was a bond of friendship between them going back a decade into adolescence. It was with this material that the officers felt that they could overcome petitioner's will. They instructed Bruno falsely to state that petitioner's telephone call had gotten him into trouble, that his job was in jeopardy, and that loss of his job would be disastrous to his three children, his wife and his unborn child. And Bruno played this part of a worried father, harried by his superiors, in not one, but four different acts, the final one lasting an hour. Petitioner was apparently unaware of John Gay's famous couplet—"An open foe may prove a curse, But a pretended friend is worse"—and he yielded to his false friend's entreaties.

We conclude that petitioner's will was overborne by official pressure, fatigue and sympathy falsely aroused after considering all the facts in their post-indictment setting. Here a grand jury had already found sufficient cause to require petitioner to face trial on a charge of first-degree murder, and the police had an eyewitness to the shooting. The police were not therefore merely trying to solve a crime, or even to absolve a suspect. They were rather concerned primarily with securing a statement from defendant on which they could convict him. The undeviating intent of the officers to extract a confession from petitioner is therefore patent. When such an intent is shown, this Court has held that the confession obtained must be examined with the most careful scrutiny, and has reversed a conviction on facts less compelling than these. Accordingly, we hold that petitioner's conviction cannot stand under the Fourteenth Amendment. * * * Reversed.

MR. JUSTICE DOUGLAS, with whom MR. JUSTICE BLACK and MR. JUSTICE BRENNAN join, concurring.

While I join the opinion of the Court, I add what for me is an even more important ground of decision. We have often divided on whether state authorities may question a suspect for hours on end when he has no lawyer present and when he has demanded that he have the benefit of legal advice. But here we deal not with a suspect but with a man who has been formally charged with a crime. The question is whether after the indictment and before the trial the Government can interrogate the accused in secret when he asked for his lawyer and when his request was denied. * * *

This is a case of an accused, who is scheduled to be tried by a judge and jury, being tried in a preliminary way by the police. This is a kangaroo court procedure whereby the police produce the vital evidence in the form of a confession which is useful or necessary to obtain a conviction. They in effect deny him effective representation by counsel. This seems to me to be a flagrant violation of the principle announced in *Powell v. State of Alabama*, 287 U.S. 45 (1932), that the right of counsel extends to the preparation for trial, as well as to the trial itself. * * * When he is deprived of that right after indictment and before trial, he may indeed be denied effective representation by counsel at the only stage when legal aid and advice would help him. * * *

> **Make the Connection**
>
> We will consider the Court's decision in *Powell* in Chapter 15.

[W]hat use is a defendant's right to effective counsel at every stage of a criminal case if, while he is held awaiting trial, he can be questioned in the absence of counsel until he confesses? In that event the secret trial in the police precincts effectively supplants the public trial guaranteed by the Bill of Rights.

MR. JUSTICE STEWART, whom MR. JUSTICE DOUGLAS and MR. JUSTICE BRENNAN join, concurring.

While I concur in the opinion of the Court, it is my view that the absence of counsel when this confession was elicited was alone enough to render it inadmissible under the Fourteenth Amendment.

* * * When the petitioner surrendered to the New York authorities he was under indictment for first degree murder. Under our system of justice an indictment is supposed to be followed by an arraignment and a trial. At every stage in those proceedings the accused has an absolute right to a lawyer's help if the case is one in which a death sentence may be imposed. Indeed the right to the assistance of counsel whom the accused has himself retained is absolute, whatever the offense for which he is on trial. *Chandler v. Fretag*, 348 U.S. 3 (1954).

What followed the petitioner's surrender in this case was not arraignment in a court of law, but an all-night inquisition in a prosecutor's office, a police station, and an automobile. Throughout the night the petitioner repeatedly asked to be allowed to send for his lawyer, and his requests were repeatedly denied. He finally was induced to make a confession. That confession was used to secure a verdict sending him to the electric chair.

Our Constitution guarantees the assistance of counsel to a man on trial for his life in an orderly courtroom, presided over by a judge, open to the public, and protected by all the procedural safeguards of the law. Surely a Constitution which promises that much can vouchsafe no less to the same man under midnight inquisition in the squad room of a police station.

POINTS FOR DISCUSSION

a. Voluntariness and the Due Process Clause

The Court in *Spano* focused on the voluntariness of the defendant's confession, concluding that the confession was inadmissible because "petitioner's will was overborne" by the police's conduct. Reasonable minds can disagree about where to draw the line between a voluntary confession and an involuntary confession. But is the Court's approach, which considers the totality of the circumstances, likely to produce clear rules about what the police may do in interrogating a suspect?

Or was the Court's ultimate concern in *Spano* more about the ethics of police interrogation tactics than it was about the voluntariness of the confession? In the case, the police appear to have lied about their ability to find contact information for the petitioner's lawyer, and they instructed Bruno to lie to the petitioner about the ways in which the petitioner's failure to cooperate might affect Bruno's job and family. And the Court stated that the "abhorrence" of involuntary confessions "does not turn alone on their inherent untrustworthiness," but also on "the deep-rooted feeling that the police must obey the law while enforcing the law." If this was the Court's concern, then where is the line between proper interrogation techniques and improper ones?

b. The Right to Counsel

Four Justices would have resolved this case based on the Sixth Amendment right to counsel, because the petitioner had already been indicted when the police interrogated him. Such an approach would be easier to apply. But police and prosecutors could evade the limits imposed by the Sixth Amendment simply by waiting to indict or arrest a suspect until after obtaining a confession. In addition, as Justice Jackson noted in *Watts*, because lawyers inevitably advise their clients not to speak with the police, a bright-line rule that prevents interrogation after arraignment or indictment would risk crippling investigations of crime. Is there a way to reconcile the societal interest in punishing those guilty of crimes and the interest in ensuring that those accused of crimes have the assistance of counsel?

3. Exclusions of Confessions by Suspects Who Do Not Have Counsel Present

In the preceding section, we considered cases in which the police had used mental or physical coercion to obtain a confession from a criminal suspect. Here we are concerned with another tactic that police sometimes have used in seeking confessions: Interrogating suspects when they do not have an attorney present to assist them. Suspects who do not have the advice of counsel often imprudently make statements against their interests, even if the police do not use mental or physical compulsion to obtain the statements. In the cases that follow, we will see several key principles that the Supreme Court has held follow from the Sixth Amendment's right to counsel and the Fifth Amendment's privilege against self-incrimination.

The Sixth Amendment says: "In all criminal prosecutions, the accused shall enjoy the right . . . to have the Assistance of Counsel for his defence." In *Massiah v. United States*, 377 U.S. 201 (1964), the Supreme Court held that this right to counsel prohibits the government from using a confession in court that the government elicited from a defendant who has been indicted (or against whom adversary judicial proceedings have otherwise begun), if the defendant was represented by counsel and counsel was not present. This rule greatly limits the ability of the police to obtain a confession from a defendant who has already been charged with a crime because counsel generally will advise the defendant not to make incriminating statements. But the Sixth Amendment does not provide protection to suspects before they are charged with a crime, such as a person whom the police have detained for questioning. By its terms, the Sixth Amendment applies only in "criminal prosecutions," not mere investigations.

But suspects who have not yet been indicted may find protection from three rules that the Supreme Court has held flow from the Fifth Amendment's privilege against self-incrimination. First, before the police interrogate a suspect who is in custody, the police must advise the suspect that he has the right to remain silent and the right to have an attorney present during the interrogation. *Miranda v. Arizona*, 384 U.S. 436, 479 (1966). Second, if a suspect who is in custody requests an attorney, the "interrogation must cease until an attorney is present." *Id.* at 474. Third, a confession obtained in violation of these rules cannot be introduced into evidence. *Edwards v. Arizona*, 451 U.S. 477, 480 (1981).

For example, in *Edwards v. Arizona*, the police arrested a man suspected of robbery, burglary, and first-degree murder. The police informed him of his rights. He told the police that he wanted to speak to an attorney. At that point, the initial interrogation ceased. But the next day the police came back to question the man further. The man was still in jail and still did not have an attorney. During the subsequent interrogation, he confessed to the crimes. The Supreme Court excluded the testimony. See *id.*

Notice that these three rules apply only when the police "interrogate" a suspect who is "in custody." Interrogation occurs when the police ask questions. If a suspect sitting alone in a jail cell voluntarily decides to write out a confession without his attorney present, the confession can be used in court because it is not the product of an interrogation. In *Edwards*, the Court explained: "an accused, such as Edwards, having expressed his desire to deal with the police only through counsel, is not subject to further interrogation by the authorities until counsel has been made available to him, *unless the accused himself initiates further communication, exchanges, or conversations with the police.*" *Id.* at 484–485 (emphasis added). We will see more about the definition of interrogation in *Rhode Island v. Innis*, 446 U.S. 291 (1980), below.

The test for whether someone is "in custody" is whether the person is free to go. The Court said in *Miranda* that a "custodial interrogation" takes place only if a suspect "has been taken into custody or otherwise deprived of his freedom of action in any significant way." *Id.* at 444. For example, suppose the police arrive at the scene of a fire and ask an onlooker what happened. The onlooker blurts out that he committed arson by starting the fire. The police could use the confession in court against the onlooker because the onlooker was not in custody when he made the statement. We will learn more about the meaning of "in custody" in *Oregon v. Mathiason*, 429 U.S. 492 (1977), below.

The following cases are presented in chronological order to show how the Supreme Court established the rules set forth above. In reading the majority and dissenting opinions in these cases, consider what factors influenced each decision. Were the Justices solely concerned with the text, original meaning, and logical implications of the constitutional amendments? Or were the Justices also seeking to balance fairness to criminal suspects against the needs of society to find and punish criminal suspects?

MASSIAH V. UNITED STATES

377 U.S. 201 (1964)

MR. JUSTICE STEWART delivered the opinion of the Court.

The petitioner, a merchant seaman, was in 1958 a member of the crew of the S. S. Santa Maria. In April of that year federal customs officials in New York received information that he was going to transport a quantity of narcotics aboard that ship from South America to the United States. As a result of this and other information, the agents searched the Santa Maria upon its arrival in New York and found in the afterpeak of the vessel five packages containing about three and a half pounds of cocaine. They also learned of circumstances, not here relevant, tending to connect the petitioner with the cocaine. He was arrested, promptly arraigned, and subsequently indicted for possession of narcotics aboard a United States vessel. In July a superseding indictment was returned, charging the petitioner and a man named Colson with the same substantive offense, and in separate counts charging the petitioner, Colson, and others with having conspired to possess narcotics aboard a United States vessel, and to import, conceal, and facilitate the sale of narcotics. The petitioner, who had retained a lawyer, pleaded not guilty and was released on bail, along with Colson.

A few days later, and quite without the petitioner's knowledge, Colson decided to cooperate with the government agents in their continuing investigation of the narcotics activities in which the petitioner, Colson, and others had allegedly been engaged. Colson permitted an agent named Murphy to install a Schmidt radio transmitter under the front seat of Colson's automobile, by means of which Murphy, equipped with an appropriate receiving device, could overhear from some distance away conversations carried on in Colson's car.

On the evening of November 19, 1959, Colson and the petitioner held a lengthy conversation while sitting in Colson's automobile, parked on a New York street. By prearrangement with Colson, and totally unbeknown to the petitioner, the agent Murphy sat in a car parked out of sight down the street and listened over the radio to the entire conversation. The petitioner made several incriminating statements during the course of this conversation. At the petitioner's trial these incriminating statements were brought before the jury through Murphy's testimony, despite the insistent objection of defense counsel. The jury convicted the petitioner of several related narcotics offenses, and the convictions were affirmed by the Court of Appeals.

The petitioner argues that it was an error of constitutional dimensions to permit the agent Murphy at the trial to testify to the petitioner's incriminating statements which Murphy had overheard under the circumstances disclosed by this record. This argument is based upon two distinct and independent grounds. First, we are told that Murphy's use of the radio equipment violated the petitioner's rights under the Fourth Amendment, and, consequently, that all evidence which Murphy thereby obtained was * * * inadmissible against the petitioner at the trial. Secondly, it is said that the petitioner's Fifth and Sixth Amendment rights were violated by the use in evidence against him of

> **Make the Connection**
>
> The police did not obtain a warrant to authorize the listening device in Colson's car because Colson consented to have it placed there. Did use of the device to obtain evidence from Massiah violate Massiah's rights under the Fourth Amendment? Should it? We considered the Fourth Amendment in Chapter 13.

incriminating statements which government agents had deliberately elicited from him after he had been indicted and in the absence of his retained counsel. Because of the way we dispose of the case, we do not reach the Fourth Amendment issue.

In *Spano v. New York*, 360 U.S. 315 (1959), this Court reversed a state criminal conviction because a confession had been wrongly admitted into evidence against the defendant at his trial. In that case the defendant had already been indicted for first-degree murder at the time he confessed. The Court held that the defendant's conviction could not stand under the Fourteenth Amendment. While the Court's opinion relied upon the totality of the circumstances under which the confession had been obtained, four concurring Justices pointed out that the Constitution required reversal of the conviction upon the sole and specific ground that the confession had been deliberately elicited by the police after the defendant had been indicted, and therefore at a time when he was clearly entitled to a lawyer's help. * * * It was said that a Constitution which guarantees a defendant the aid of counsel at such a trial could surely vouchsafe no less to an indicted defendant under interrogation by the police in a completely extrajudicial proceeding. Anything less, it was said, might deny a defendant "effective representation by counsel at the only stage when legal aid and advice would help him." 360 U.S., at 326 (DOUGLAS, J., concurring).

This view no more than reflects a constitutional principle established as long ago as *Powell v. Alabama*, 287 U.S. 45 (1932), where the Court noted that ". . . during perhaps the most critical period of the proceedings . . . that is to say, from the time of their arraignment until the beginning of their trial, when consultation, thorough-going investigation and preparation (are) vitally important, the defendants . . . (are) as much entitled to such aid (of counsel) during that period as at the trial itself." *Id.*, at 57. And since the *Spano* decision the same basic constitutional principle has been broadly reaffirmed by this Court. *Hamilton v. Alabama*, 368 U.S. 52 (1961); *White v. Maryland*, 373 U.S. 59 (1963). See *Gideon v. Wainwright*, 372 U.S. 335 (1963).

Here we deal not with a state court conviction, but with a federal case, where the specific guarantee of the Sixth Amendment directly applies.[6] We hold that the petitioner was denied the basic protections of that guarantee when there was used against him at his trial evidence of his own incriminating words, which federal agents had deliberately elicited from him after he had been indicted and in the absence of his counsel. It is true that in the *Spano* case the defendant was interrogated in a police station, while here the damaging testimony was elicited from the defendant without his knowledge while he was free on bail. But, as Judge Hays pointed out in his dissent in the Court of Appeals, "if such a rule is to have any efficacy it must apply to indirect and surreptitious interrogations as well as those conducted in the jailhouse. In this case, Massiah was more seriously imposed upon . . . because he did not even know that he was under interrogation by a government agent." 307 F.2d at 72–73.

> **Take Note**
>
> Observe carefully each of the factors that the Court mentions in stating its holding: (1) the government used Massiah's statements against him at trial; (2) government agents elicited the statements; (3) Massiah made the statement after he had been indicted; (4) Massiah had counsel at the time he made the statements; and (5) Massiah's counsel was absent when he made those statements. Is each factor essential to the Court's conclusion?

The Solicitor General, in his brief and oral argument, has strenuously contended that the federal law enforcement agents had the right, if not indeed the duty, to continue their investigation of the petitioner and his alleged criminal associates even though the petitioner had been indicted. * * *

---

[6]   "In all criminal prosecutions, the accused shall enjoy the right . . . to have the Assistance of Counsel for his defence."

> **Food for Thought**
>
> Suppose that the government had not sent Colson, the cooperating witness, to elicit the statements from Massiah, but had instead obtained a warrant from a judge to eavesdrop on Massiah's phone line. If the government had then heard and recorded Massiah making incriminating statements, would those statements have been admissible under the Court's approach in this case? If so, in what way would this example be different?

We do not question that in this case, as in many cases, it was entirely proper to continue an investigation of the suspected criminal activities of the defendant and his alleged confederates, even though the defendant had already been indicted. All that we hold is that the defendant's own incriminating statements, obtained by federal agents under the circumstances here disclosed, could not constitutionally be used by the prosecution as evidence against him at his trial.

Reversed.

MR. JUSTICE WHITE, with whom MR. JUSTICE CLARK and MR. JUSTICE HARLAN join, dissenting.

* * * In my view, a civilized society must maintain its capacity to discover transgressions of the law and to identify those who flout it. * * * It is therefore a rather portentous occasion when a constitutional rule is established barring the use of evidence which is relevant, reliable and highly probative of the issue which the trial court has before it—whether the accused committed the act with which he is charged. Without the evidence, the quest for truth may be seriously impeded and in many cases the trial court, although aware of proof showing defendant's guilt, must nevertheless release him because the crucial evidence is deemed inadmissible. * * * With all due deference, I am not at all convinced that the additional barriers to the pursuit of truth which the Court today erects rest on anything like the solid foundations which decisions of this gravity should require.

The importance of the matter should not be underestimated, for today's rule promises to have wide application well beyond the facts of this case. The reason given for the result here—the admissions were obtained in the absence of counsel—would seem equally pertinent to statements obtained at any time after the right to counsel attaches, whether there has been an indictment or not; to admissions made prior to arraignment, at least where the defendant has counsel or asks for it; to the fruits of admissions improperly obtained under the new rule; to criminal proceedings in state courts; and to defendants long since convicted upon evidence including such admissions. The new rule will immediately do service in a great many cases.

Whatever the content or scope of the rule may prove to be, I am unable to see how this case presents an unconstitutional interference with Massiah's right to counsel. Massiah was not prevented from consulting with counsel as often as he wished. No meetings with counsel were disturbed or spied upon. Preparation for trial was in no way obstructed. It is only a sterile syllogism—an unsound one, besides—to say that because Massiah had a right to counsel's aid before and during the trial, his out-of-court conversations and admissions must be excluded if obtained without counsel's consent or presence. * * *

Since the new rule would exclude all admissions made to the police, no matter how voluntary and reliable, the requirement of counsel's presence or approval would seem to rest upon the probability that counsel would foreclose any admissions at all. This is nothing more than a thinly disguised constitutional policy of minimizing or entirely prohibiting the use in evidence of voluntary out-of-court admissions and confessions made by the accused. Carried as far as blind logic may compel some to go, the notion that statements from the mouth of the defendant should not be used in evidence would have a severe and unfortunate impact upon the great bulk of criminal cases.

Viewed in this light, the Court's newly fashioned exclusionary principle goes far beyond the constitutional privilege against self-incrimination, which neither requires nor suggests the barring of voluntary pretrial admissions. The Fifth Amendment states that no person "shall be compelled in any criminal case to be a witness against himself . . . ." The defendant may thus not be compelled to testify at his trial, but he may if he wishes. Likewise he may not be compelled or coerced into saying anything before trial; but until today he could if he wished to, and if he did, it could be used against him. Whether as a matter of self-incrimination or of due process, the proscription is against compulsion—coerced incrimination. Under the prior law, announced in countless cases in this Court, the defendant's pretrial statements were admissible evidence if voluntarily made; inadmissible if not the product of his free will. Hardly any constitutional area has been more carefully patrolled by this Court, and until now the Court has expressly rejected the argument that admissions are to be deemed involuntary if made outside the presence of counsel. The Court presents no facts, no objective evidence, no reasons to warrant scrapping the voluntary-involuntary test for admissibility in this area. Without such evidence I would retain it in its present form.

> **Take Note**
>
> Justice White here discusses the Fifth Amendment privilege against self-incrimination. Did the Court rely on the privilege in its opinion? Should it have?

Applying the new exclusionary rule is peculiarly inappropriate in this case. At the time of the conversation in question, petitioner was not in custody but free on bail. He was not questioned in what anyone could call an atmosphere of official coercion. What he said was said to his partner in crime who had also been indicted. There was no suggestion or any possibility of coercion. What petitioner did not know was that Colson had decided to report the conversation to the police. Had there been no prior arrangements between Colson and the police, had Colson simply gone to the police after the conversation had occurred, his testimony relating Massiah's statements would be readily admissible at the trial, as would a recording which he might have made of the conversation. In such event, it would simply be said that Massiah risked talking to a friend who decided to disclose what he knew of Massiah's criminal activities. But, if, as occurred here, Colson had been cooperating with the police prior to his meeting with Massiah, both his evidence and the recorded conversation are somehow transformed into inadmissible evidence despite the fact that the hazard to Massiah remains precisely the same— the defection of a confederate in crime.

* * * Neither the ordinary citizen nor the confessed criminal should be discouraged from reporting what he knows to the authorities and from lending his aid to secure evidence of crime. Certainly after this case the Colsons will be few and far between; and the Massiahs can breathe much more easily, secure in the knowledge that the Constitution furnishes an important measure of protection against faithless compatriots and guarantees sporting treatment for sporting peddlers of narcotics.

* * * Massiah and those like him receive ample protection from the long line of precedents in this Court holding that confessions may not be introduced unless they are voluntary. In making these determinations the courts must consider the absence of counsel as one of several factors by which voluntariness is to be judged. This is a wiser rule than the automatic rule announced by the Court, which requires courts and juries to disregard voluntary admissions which they might well find to be the best possible evidence in discharging their responsibility for ascertaining truth.

POINTS FOR DISCUSSION

a.   Voluntariness and the Due Process Clause

Massiah voluntarily made incriminating statements to Colson; the government did not coerce him into confessing his crimes. Accordingly, the Court did not conclude that admission of the statements at trial violated the Due Process Clause.

Yet Massiah surely would not have made the incriminating statements if he had known that the government was listening. Is there an argument that the confession was involuntary, in the sense that Massiah did not voluntarily confess *to the police*?

b. The Sixth Amendment and the Right to Counsel

The Court reasoned that the statements were nevertheless inadmissible because they were obtained in violation of Massiah's right to counsel under the Sixth Amendment. The right to counsel applied in the case because the government had already indicted Massiah. Does the Court's conclusion mean that, once a suspect has been charged or indicted, the government can never obtain his confession?

In the case that follows, *Escobedo v. Illinois*, 378 U.S. 478 (1964), you will see how the Court continued to wrestle with the proper constitutional frame of reference for reviewing confessions made by suspects who did not have counsel present. Observe carefully the ways in which the facts in *Esobedo* are different from the facts in *Massiah* and the other cases that we have seen so far.

One aspect of the Court's decision in *Escobedo* is no longer good law. The Supreme Court said in *Escobedo* that the Sixth Amendment right to counsel may attach as soon as "the investigation is no longer a general inquiry into an unsolved crime but has begun to focus on a particular suspect, the suspect has been taken into police custody, [and] the police carry out a process of interrogations that lends itself to eliciting incriminating statements." The Supreme Court subsequently expressly disavowed this understanding of the Sixth Amendment. See *Moran v. Burbine*, 475 U.S. 412, 430 (1986). According to current Supreme Court precedent, the Sixth Amendment right to counsel does not arise until "the adversary judicial process has been initiated." *Montejo v. Louisiana*, 556 U.S. 778, 786 (2009).

ESCOBEDO V. ILLINOIS
378 U.S. 478 (1964)

MR. JUSTICE GOLDBERG delivered the opinion of the Court.

On the night of January 19, 1960, petitioner's brother-in-law was fatally shot. In the early hours of the next morning, at 2:30 a.m., petitioner was arrested without a warrant and interrogated. Petitioner made no statement to the police and was released at 5 that afternoon pursuant to a state court writ of habeas corpus obtained by Mr. Warren Wolfson, a lawyer who had been retained by petitioner.

On January 30, Benedict DiGerlando, who was then in police custody and who was later indicted for the murder along with petitioner, told the police that petitioner had fired the fatal shots. Between 8 and 9 that evening, petitioner and his sister, the widow of the deceased, were arrested and taken to police headquarters. En route to the police station, the police "had handcuffed the defendant behind his back," and "one of the arresting officers told defendant that DiGerlando had named him as the one who shot" the deceased. Petitioner testified, without contradiction, that the "detective said they had us pretty well, up pretty tight, and we might as well admit to this crime," and that he replied, "I am sorry but I would like to have advice from my lawyer." A police officer testified that although petitioner was not formally charged "he was in custody" and "couldn't walk out the door."

Shortly after petitioner reached police headquarters, his retained lawyer arrived. [Escobedo's lawyer stated that he learned from the mother of another defendant that Escobedo was at the police station. He went to the station and asked for permission to speak with his client. The officer on duty informed him that he could see Escobedo. The lawyer then went upstairs to the Homicide Bureau, identified himself, and asked to see his client. The officers told him that he could not see Escobedo. About an hour and a half after the lawyer first arrived at the station, the police chief informed the lawyer that he could not see Escobedo because "they hadn't completed questioning." The lawyer stated that at one point, for a "second or two," he spotted Escobedo in an office in the Homicide Bureau while the door was open. He "waved to him and he waved back" and then the door was closed by one of the officers. The lawyer stated that, for the next two hours, he "had a conversation with every police officer I could find," but none permitted him to meet with his client. He left the station at about 1:00 am. Testimony from police officers who were present confirmed this account.]

Petitioner testified that during the course of the interrogation he repeatedly asked to speak to his lawyer and that the police said that his lawyer "didn't want to see" him. The testimony of the police officers confirmed these accounts in substantial detail.

There is testimony by the police that during the interrogation, petitioner, a 22-year-old of Mexican extraction with no record of previous experience with the police, "was handcuffed" in a standing position and that he "was nervous, he had circles under his eyes and he was upset" and was "agitated" because "he had not slept well in over a week."

It is undisputed that during the course of the interrogation Officer Montejano, who "grew up" in petitioner's neighborhood, who knew his family, and who uses "Spanish language in [his] police work," conferred alone with petitioner "for about a quarter of an hour . . . ." Petitioner testified that the officer said to him "in Spanish that my sister and I could go home if I pinned it on

Benedict DiGerlando," that "he would see to it that we would go home and be held only as witnesses, if anything, if we had made a statement against DiGerlando . . ., that we would be able to go home that night." Petitioner testified that he made the statement in issue because of this assurance. Officer Montejano denied offering any such assurance.

> A police officer testified that during the interrogation the following occurred:

> "I informed him of what DiGerlando told me and when I did, he told me that DiGerlando was (lying) and I said, 'Would you care to tell DiGerlando that?' and he said, 'Yes, I will.' So, I brought . . . Escobedo in and he confronted DiGerlando and he told him that he was lying and said, 'I didn't shoot Manuel, you did it.' "

In this way, petitioner for the first time admitted to some knowledge of the crime. After that he made additional statements further implicating himself in the murder plot. At this point an Assistant State's Attorney, Theodore J. Cooper, was summoned "to take" a statement. Mr. Cooper, an experienced lawyer who was assigned to the Homicide Division to take "statements from some defendants and some prisoners that they had in custody," "took" petitioner's statement by asking carefully framed questions apparently designed to assure the admissibility into evidence of the resulting answers. Mr. Cooper testified that he did not advise petitioner of his constitutional rights, and it is undisputed that no one during the course of the interrogation so advised him.

Petitioner moved both before and during trial to suppress the incriminating statement, but the motions were denied. Petitioner was convicted of murder and he appealed the conviction. [The state Supreme Court affirmed.] We granted a writ of certiorari to consider whether the petitioner's statement was constitutionally admissible at his trial. We conclude, for the reasons stated below, that it was not and, accordingly, we reverse the judgment of conviction.

The interrogation here was conducted before petitioner was formally indicted. But in the context of this case, that fact should make no difference. When petitioner requested, and was denied, an opportunity to consult with his lawyer, the investigation had ceased to be a general investigation of "an unsolved crime." *Spano v. New York*, 360 U.S. 315, 327 (1959)

> **Take Note**
>
> The Court notes here that the facts in this case differed from those in *Massiah* in an important respect. Should that difference matter to the outcome based on the wording of the Sixth Amendment?

(STEWART, J., concurring). Petitioner had become the accused, and the purpose of the interrogation was to "get him" to confess his guilt despite his constitutional right not to do so. At the time of his arrest and throughout the course of the interrogation, the police told petitioner that they had convincing evidence that he had fired the fatal shots. Without informing him of his absolute right to remain silent in the face of this accusation, the police urged him to make a statement. * * *

Petitioner, a layman, was undoubtedly unaware that under Illinois law an admission of "mere" complicity in the murder plot was legally as damaging as an admission of firing of the fatal shots. The "guiding hand of counsel" was essential to advise petitioner of his rights in this delicate situation. *Powell v. Alabama*, 287 U.S. 45, 69 (1932). This was the "stage when legal aid and advice" were most critical to petitioner. *Massiah v. United States*, 377 U.S. 201, 204 (1964). It was a stage surely as critical as was the arraignment in *Hamilton v. Alabama*, 368 U.S. 52 (1961), and the preliminary hearing in *White v. Maryland*, 373 U.S. 59 (1963). What happened at this interrogation could certainly "affect the whole trial," *Hamilton*, 368 U.S. at 54, since rights "may be as irretrievably lost, if not then and there asserted, as they are when an accused represented by counsel waives a right for strategic purposes." It would exalt form over substance to make the right to counsel, under these circumstances, depend on whether at the time of the interrogation, the authorities had secured a formal indictment. Petitioner had, for all practical purposes, already been charged with murder.

In *Gideon v. Wainwright*, 372 U.S. 335 (1963), we held that every person accused of a crime, whether state or federal, is entitled to a lawyer at trial. The rule sought by the State here, however, would make the trial no more than an appeal from the interrogation; and the "right to use counsel at the formal trial (would be) a very hollow thing (if), for all practical purposes, the conviction is already assured by pretrial examination." *In re Groban*, 352 U.S. 330, 344 (1957) (BLACK, J., dissenting). * * *

> **Make the Connection**
>
> We consider *Gideon v. Wainwright*, and the right to counsel under the Sixth Amendment, in Chapter 15.

It is argued that if the right to counsel is afforded prior to indictment, the number of confessions obtained by the police will diminish significantly, because most confessions are obtained during the period between arrest and indictment, and "any lawyer worth his salt will tell the suspect in no uncertain terms to make no statement to police under any circumstances." *Watts v. Indiana*, 338 U.S. 49, 59 (1949) (Jackson, J., concurring in part and dissenting in part). This argument, of course, cuts two ways. The fact that many confessions are obtained during this period points up its critical nature as a "stage when legal aid and advice" are surely needed. *Massiah*, 377 U.S. at 204. The right to counsel would indeed be hollow if it began at a period when few confessions were obtained. There is necessarily a direct relationship between the importance of a stage to the police in their quest for a confession and the criticalness of that stage to the accused in his need for legal advice. Our Constitution, unlike some others, strikes the balance in favor of the right of the accused to be advised by his lawyer of his privilege against self-incrimination.

> **Take Note**
>
> The Court says here that the right to counsel is crucial even before the suspect is charged because the lawyer can advise the suspect that he enjoys a privilege against self-incrimination. Is the Court suggesting that confessions made during interrogation violate that privilege? What role does the privilege against self-incrimination play in the Court's analysis?

We have learned the lesson of history, ancient and modern, that a system of criminal law enforcement, which comes to depend on the "confession" will, in the long run, be less reliable and more subject to abuses than a system which depends on extrinsic evidence independently secured through skillful investigation. * * * This Court also has recognized that "history amply shows that confessions have often been extorted to save law enforcement officials the trouble and effort of obtaining valid and independent evidence . . . ." *Haynes v. Washington*, 373 U.S. 503, 519 (1963).

We have also learned the companion lesson of history that no system of criminal justice can, or should, survive if it comes to depend for its continued effectiveness on the citizens' abdication through unawareness of their constitutional rights. No system worth preserving should have to fear that if an accused is permitted to consult with a lawyer, he will become aware of, and exercise, these rights. If the exercise of constitutional rights will thwart the effectiveness of a system of law enforcement, then there is something very wrong with that system.[14]

We hold, therefore, that where, as here, the investigation is no longer a general inquiry into an unsolved crime but has begun to focus on a particular suspect, the suspect has been taken into police custody, the police carry out a process of interrogations that lends itself to eliciting incriminating statements, the suspect has requested and been denied an opportunity to consult with his lawyer, and the police have not effectively warned him of his absolute constitutional right to remain silent, the accused has been denied "The Assistance of Counsel" in violation of the Sixth Amendment to the Constitution as "made obligatory upon

---

[14] The accused may, of course, intelligently and knowingly waive his privilege against self-incrimination and his right to counsel either at a pretrial stage or at the trial. See *Johnson v. Zerbst*, 304 U.S. 458 (1938). But no knowing and intelligent waiver of any constitutional right can be said to have occurred under the circumstances of this case.

the States by the Fourteenth Amendment," *Gideon*, 372 U.S. at 342, and that no statement elicited by the police during the interrogation may be used against him at a criminal trial.

Nothing we have said today affects the powers of the police to investigate "an unsolved crime," *Spano*, 360 U.S. at 327 (STEWART, J., concurring), by gathering information from witnesses and by other "proper investigative efforts." *Haynes*, 373 U.S. at 519. We hold only that when the process shifts from investigatory to accusatory—when its focus is on the accused and its purpose is to elicit a confession—our adversary system begins to operate, and, under the circumstances here, the accused must be permitted to consult with his lawyer.

The judgment of the Illinois Supreme Court is reversed and the case remanded for proceedings not inconsistent with this opinion.

MR. JUSTICE STEWART, dissenting.

[T]he vital fact remains that this case does not involve the deliberate interrogation of a defendant after the initiation of judicial proceedings against him. The Court disregards this basic difference between the present case and [*Massiah v. United States*, 377 U.S. 201 (1964),] with the bland assertion that "that fact should make no difference."

It is "that fact," I submit, which makes all the difference. Under our system of criminal justice the institution of formal, meaningful judicial proceedings, by way of indictment, information, or arraignment, marks the point at which a criminal investigation has ended and adversary proceedings have commenced. It is at this point that the constitutional guarantees attach which pertain to a criminal trial. Among those guarantees are the right to a speedy trial, the right of confrontation, and the right to trial by jury. Another is the guarantee of the assistance of counsel.

The confession which the Court today holds inadmissible was a voluntary one. It was given during the course of a perfectly legitimate police investigation of an unsolved murder. The Court says that what happened during this investigation "affected" the trial. I had always supposed that the whole purpose of a police investigation of a murder was to "affect" the trial of the murderer, and that it would be only an incompetent, unsuccessful, or corrupt investigation which would not do so. The Court further says that the Illinois police officers did not advise the petitioner of his "constitutional rights" before he confessed to the murder. This Court has never held that the Constitution requires the police to give any "advice" under circumstances such as these.

Supported by no stronger authority than its own rhetoric, the Court today converts a routine police investigation of an unsolved murder into a distorted analogue of a judicial trial. It imports into this investigation constitutional concepts historically applicable only after the onset of formal prosecutorial proceedings. By doing so, I think the Court perverts those precious constitutional guarantees, and frustrates the vital interests of society in preserving the legitimate and proper function of honest and purposeful police investigation.

MR. JUSTICE WHITE, with whom MR. JUSTICE CLARK and MR. JUSTICE STEWART join, dissenting.

In *Massiah v. United States*, 377 U.S. 201 (1964), the Court held that as of the date of the indictment the prosecution is disentitled to secure admissions from the accused. The Court now moves that date back to the time when the prosecution begins to "focus" on the accused. Although the opinion purports to be limited to the facts of this case, it would be naive to think that the new constitutional right announced will depend upon whether the accused has retained his own counsel, or has asked to consult with counsel in the course of interrogation. At the very least the Court holds that once the accused becomes a suspect and, presumably, is arrested, any admission made to the police thereafter is inadmissible in evidence unless the accused has waived his right to counsel. The decision is thus another major step in the direction of the goal which the Court seemingly has in mind—to bar from evidence all admissions obtained from an individual suspected of crime, whether involuntarily made or not. * * * I reject this step and the invitation to go farther which the Court has now issued.

By abandoning the voluntary-involuntary test for admissibility of confessions, the Court seems driven by the notion that it is uncivilized law enforcement to use an accused's own admissions against him at his trial. It attempts to find a home for this new and nebulous rule of due process by attaching it to the right to counsel guaranteed in the federal system by the Sixth Amendment and binding upon the States by virtue of the due process guarantee of the Fourteenth Amendment. The right to counsel now not only entitles the accused to counsel's advice and aid in preparing for trial but stands as an impenetrable barrier to any interrogation once the accused has become a suspect. From that very moment apparently his right to counsel attaches, a rule wholly unworkable and impossible to administer unless police cars are equipped with public defenders and undercover agents and police informants have defense counsel at their side. I would not abandon the Court's prior cases defining with some care and analysis the circumstances requiring the presence or aid of counsel and substitute the amorphous and wholly unworkable principle that counsel is constitutionally required whenever he would or could be helpful. * * * Until now there simply has been no right guaranteed by the Federal Constitution to be free from the use at trial of a voluntary admission made prior to indictment.

It is incongruous to assume that the provision for counsel in the Sixth Amendment was meant to amend or supersede the self-incrimination provision of the Fifth Amendment, which is now applicable to the States. *Malloy v. Hogan*, 378 U.S. 1 (1964). That amendment addresses itself to the very issue of incriminating admissions of an accused and resolves it by proscribing only compelled statements. Neither the Framers, the constitutional language, [nor] a century of decisions of this Court [provides] an iota of support for the idea that an accused has an absolute constitutional right not to answer even in the absence of compulsion—the constitutional right not to incriminate himself by making voluntary disclosures. * * * The only "inquisitions" the Constitution forbids are those which compel incrimination. Escobedo's statements were not compelled and the Court does not hold that they were.

This new American judges' rule, which is to be applied in both federal and state courts, is perhaps thought to be a necessary safeguard against the possibility of extorted confessions. To this extent it reflects a deep-seated distrust of law enforcement officers everywhere, unsupported by relevant data or current material based upon our own experience. * * *

The Court may be concerned with a narrower matter: the unknowing defendant who responds to police questioning because he mistakenly believes that he must and that his admissions will not be used against him. But this worry hardly calls for the broadside the Court has now fired. The failure to inform an accused that he need not answer and that his answers may be used against him is very relevant indeed to whether the disclosures are compelled. * * * When the accused has not been informed of his rights at all the Court characteristically and properly looks very closely at the surrounding circumstances. I would continue to do so. But, in this case Danny Escobedo knew full well that he did not have to answer and knew full well that his lawyer had advised him not to answer.

I do not suggest for a moment that law enforcement will be destroyed by the rule announced today. The need for peace and order is too insistent for that. But it will be crippled and its task made a great deal more difficult, all in my opinion, for unsound, unstated reasons, which can find no home in any of the provisions of the Constitution.

[JUSTICE HARLAN's dissenting opinion has been omitted.]

POINTS FOR DISCUSSION

a. The Basis for the Holding in *Escobedo*

What was the basis of the Court's holding in *Escobedo*? Because Escobedo had not yet been charged with the crime to which he confessed, the *Massiah* case seemed to suggest that the Sixth Amendment right to counsel had not yet attached. And the confession did not appear to be involuntary, in the sense that it was obtained through means that were so oppressive or relentless that they essentially coerced Escobedo to confess. To be sure, the police lied to Escobedo about the whereabouts of his attorney, but they did not otherwise subject him to an interrogation that effectively tortured the mind. Accordingly, the Due Process Clause alone did not seem to provide a basis for invalidating the conviction. Yet the Court held that reliance on the confession violated Escobedo's right to counsel under the Sixth Amendment, as incorporated by the Fourteenth Amendment. Is there another plausible constitutional basis for the Court's conclusion? See *Moran v. Burbine*, 475 U.S. at 429–30 (explaining that "'[a]lthough *Escobedo* was originally decided as a Sixth Amendment case, 'the Court in retrospect perceived that the "prime purpose" of *Escobedo* was not to vindicate the constitutional right to counsel as such, but, like *Miranda*, "to guarantee full effectuation of the privilege against self-incrimination. . . ."'" (quoting *Kirby v. Illinois*, 406 U.S. 682, 689 (1972), and *Johnson v. New Jersey*, 384 U.S. 719, 729 (1966)).

b. Confessions and Criminal Justice

The Court declared that "a system of criminal law enforcement, which comes to depend on the 'confession' will, in the long run, be less reliable and more subject to abuses than a system which depends on extrinsic evidence independently secured through skillful investigation." Contrast this approach with the view that Justice Jackson expressed in *Watts*. He noted that the alternative to relying on a confession often is to "close the books on the crime and forget it, with the suspect at large * * *. But if [the] ultimate quest in a criminal trial is the truth and if the circumstances indicate no violence or threats of it, should society be deprived of the suspect's help in solving a crime merely because he was confined and questioned when uncounseled?"

Escobedo reveals this conundrum: We want to ensure that the state can convict and punish a person only after offering evidence obtained without undue pressure on the suspect, but we also recognize that voluntary (and truthful) confessions often are essential to proving the state's case. Do you agree with the *Escobedo* Court's resolution of the tension between these competing impulses?

Justice White asserted in his dissent in *Escobedo* that the Court's ultimate goal was "to bar from evidence all admissions obtained from an individual suspected of crime, whether involuntarily made or not." But there are clearly practical problems with the view that all confessions are suspect. As we just noted, we often need confessions to solve crimes and obtain convictions. And if the Sixth Amendment right to counsel extends to suspects who haven't yet been charged with a crime, then the police would almost never be able to interrogate suspects to gather critical information for solving crimes—and almost never be able to obtain confessions.

Although it relied on the Sixth Amendment right to counsel, the Court in *Escobedo* subtly suggested another potential ground for regulating the practice of obtaining confessions. The Court stated that the right to counsel applies even pre-indictment or pre-arraignment if the police "carry out a process of interrogations that lends itself to eliciting incriminating statements." The Court thus suggested that the privilege against self-incrimination is relevant in cases involving custodial interrogation.

Justice White also addressed the scope of the privilege against self-incrimination. Although he rejected the assertion that it required suppression of the confession in *Escobedo*, he noted that whether an accused has been informed of his rights should be relevant to whether a confession is admissible. And one week before the decision in *Escobedo*, the Court held for the first time that the Fifth Amendment privilege against self-incrimination applies to the states. *Malloy v. Hogan*, 378 U.S. 1 (1964). Does the privilege against self-incrimination supply a more satisfying basis for addressing the permissibility of confessions obtained through interrogation? Consider the famous case that follows.

MIRANDA V. ARIZONA

384 U.S. 436 (1966)

MR. CHIEF JUSTICE WARREN delivered the opinion of the Court.

> **Take Note**
>
> The Court's opinion addresses four cases, including Miranda's, that were consolidated on appeal.

The cases before us raise questions which go to the roots of our concepts of American criminal jurisprudence: the restraints society must observe consistent with the Federal Constitution in prosecuting individuals for crime. More specifically, we deal with the admissibility of statements obtained from an individual who is subjected to custodial police interrogation and the necessity for procedures which assure that the individual is accorded his privilege under the Fifth Amendment to the Constitution not to be compelled to incriminate himself.

We start here, as we did in *Escobedo v. State of Illinois,* 378 U.S. 478 (1964), with the premise that our holding is not an innovation in our jurisprudence, but is an application of principles long recognized and applied in other settings. We have undertaken a thorough re-examination of the *Escobedo* decision and the principles it announced, and we reaffirm it. That case was but an explication of basic rights that are enshrined in our Constitution—that "No person . . . shall be compelled in any criminal case to be a witness against himself," and that "the accused shall . . . have the Assistance of Counsel"—rights which were put in jeopardy in that case through official overbearing. These precious rights were fixed in our Constitution only after centuries of persecution and struggle. * * *

Our holding will be spelled out with some specificity in the pages which follow but briefly stated it is this: the prosecution may not use statements, whether exculpatory or inculpatory, stemming from custodial interrogation of the defendant unless it demonstrates the use of procedural safeguards effective to secure the privilege against self-incrimination. By custodial interrogation, we mean questioning initiated by law enforcement officers after a person has been taken into custody or otherwise deprived of his freedom of action in any significant way.[4] As for the procedural safeguards to be employed, unless other fully effective means are devised to inform accused persons of their right of silence and to assure a continuous opportunity to exercise it, the following measures are required. Prior to any questioning, the person must be warned that he has a right to remain silent, that any statement he does make may be used as evidence against him, and that he has a right to the presence of an attorney, either retained or appointed. The defendant may waive effectuation of these rights, provided the waiver is made voluntarily, knowingly and intelligently. If, however, he indicates in any manner and at any stage of the process that he wishes to consult with an attorney before speaking there can be no questioning. Likewise, if the individual is alone and indicates in any manner that he does not wish to be interrogated, the police may not question him. The mere fact that he may have answered some questions or volunteered some statements on his own does not deprive him of the right to refrain from answering any further inquiries until he has consulted with an attorney and thereafter consents to be questioned.

The constitutional issue we decide in each of these cases is the admissibility of statements obtained from a defendant questioned while in custody or otherwise deprived of his freedom of action in any significant way. In each, the defendant

---

4   This is what we meant in *Escobedo* when we spoke of an investigation which had focused on an accused.

was questioned by police officers, detectives, or a prosecuting attorney in a room in which he was cut off from the outside world. In none of these cases was the defendant given a full and effective warning of his rights at the outset of the interrogation process. In all the cases, the questioning elicited oral admissions, and in three of them, signed statements as well which were admitted at their trials. They all thus share salient features—incommunicado interrogation of individuals in a police-dominated atmosphere, resulting in self-incriminating statements without full warnings of constitutional rights.

An understanding of the nature and setting of this in-custody interrogation is essential to our decisions today. The difficulty in depicting what transpires at such interrogations stems from the fact that in this country they have largely taken place incommunicado. From extensive factual studies undertaken in the early 1930's, including the famous Wickersham Report to Congress by a Presidential Commission, it is clear that police violence and the "third degree" flourished at that time. In a series of cases decided by this Court long after these studies, the police resorted to physical brutality—beatings, hanging, whipping—and to sustained and protracted questioning incommunicado in order to extort confessions. The Commission on Civil Rights in 1961 found much evidence to indicate that "some policemen still resort to physical force to obtain confessions," 1961 Comm'n on Civil Rights Rep., Justice, pt. 5, 17. The use of physical brutality and violence is not, unfortunately, relegated to the past or to any part of the country.

> **FYI**
>
> President Hoover established the National Commission on Law Observance and Enforcement in 1929 to evaluate the criminal justice system in the era of Prohibition. The Commission became known as the Wickersham Commission, after former Attorney General George W. Wickersham, who served as the Commission's chair. The Commission's report documented extensive police misconduct in interrogations, including widespread use of the "third degree," the intentional infliction of pain and suffering on criminal suspects in order to induce confessions.

The examples given above are undoubtedly the exception now, but they are sufficiently widespread to be the object of concern. Unless a proper limitation upon custodial interrogation is achieved—such as these decisions will advance—there can be no assurance that practices of this nature will be eradicated in the foreseeable future. * * *

[W]e stress that the modern practice of in-custody interrogation is psychologically rather than physically oriented. * * * Interrogation still takes place in privacy. Privacy results in secrecy and this in turn results in a gap in our knowledge as to what in fact goes on in the interrogation rooms. A valuable source of information about present police practices, however, may be found in various police manuals and texts which document procedures employed with success in the past, and which recommend various other effective tactics. These texts are used by law enforcement agencies themselves as guides. * * * By considering these texts and other data, it is possible to describe procedures observed and noted around the country.

[T]he setting prescribed by the manuals and observed in practice [is] clear. In essence, it is this: To be alone with the subject is essential to prevent distraction and to deprive him of any outside support. The aura of confidence in his guilt undermines his will to resist. He merely confirms the preconceived story the police seek to have him describe. Patience and persistence, at times relentless questioning, are employed. To obtain a confession, the interrogator must "patiently maneuver himself or his quarry into a position from which the desired objective may be attained." When normal procedures fail to produce the needed result, the police may resort to deceptive stratagems such as giving false legal advice. It is important to keep the subject off balance, for example, by trading on his insecurity about himself or his surroundings. The police then persuade, trick, or cajole him out of exercising his constitutional rights.

Even without employing brutality, the "third degree" or the specific stratagems described above, the very fact of custodial interrogation exacts a heavy toll on individual liberty and trades on the weakness of individuals. * * *

In the cases before us today, given this background, we concern ourselves primarily with this interrogation atmosphere and the evils it can bring. In No. 759, *Miranda v. Arizona*, the police arrested the defendant and took him to a special interrogation room where they secured a confession. In No. 760, *Vignera v. New York*, the defendant made oral admissions to the police after interrogation in the afternoon, and then signed an inculpatory statement upon being questioned by an assistant district attorney later the same evening. In No. 761, *Westover v. United States*, the defendant was handed over to the Federal Bureau of Investigation by local authorities after they had detained and interrogated him for a lengthy period, both at night and the following morning. After some two hours of questioning, the federal officers had obtained signed statements from the defendant. Lastly, in No. 584, *California v. Stewart*, the local police held the defendant five days in the station and interrogated him on nine separate occasions before they secured his inculpatory statement.

In these cases, we might not find the defendants' statements to have been involuntary in traditional terms. Our concern for adequate safeguards to protect precious Fifth Amendment rights is, of course, not lessened in the slightest. In each of the cases, the defendant was thrust into an unfamiliar atmosphere and run through menacing police interrogation procedures. The potentiality for compulsion is forcefully apparent, for example, in *Miranda*, where the indigent Mexican defendant was a seriously disturbed individual with pronounced sexual fantasies, and in *Stewart*, in which the defendant was an indigent Los Angeles Negro who had dropped out of school in the sixth grade. To be sure, the records do not evince overt physical coercion or patent psychological ploys. The fact remains that in none of these cases did the officers undertake to afford appropriate safeguards at the outset of the interrogation to insure that the statements were truly the product of free choice.

It is obvious that such an interrogation environment is created for no purpose other than to subjugate the individual to the will of his examiner. This atmosphere carries its own badge of intimidation. To be sure, this is not physical intimidation, but it is equally destructive of human dignity. The current practice of incommunicado interrogation is at odds with one of our Nation's most cherished principles—that the individual may not be compelled to incriminate

> **Take Note**
>
> Is the Court suggesting here that *all* confessions made in the course of interrogation without a lawyer present are involuntary? If so, do you agree?

himself. Unless adequate protective devices are employed to dispel the compulsion inherent in custodial surroundings, no statement obtained from the defendant can truly be the product of his free choice.

From the foregoing, we can readily perceive an intimate connection between the privilege against self-incrimination and police custodial questioning. [W]e may view the historical development of the privilege as one which groped for the proper scope of governmental power over the citizen. * * * [T]he constitutional foundation underlying the privilege is the respect a government—state or federal—must accord to the dignity and integrity of its citizens. To maintain a "fair state-individual balance," to require the government "to shoulder the entire load," 8 Wigmore, Evidence 317 (McNaughton rev. 1961), to respect the inviolability of the human personality, our accusatory system of criminal justice demands that the government seeking to punish an individual produce the evidence against him by its own independent labors, rather than by the cruel, simple expedient of compelling it from his own mouth. *Chambers v. State of Florida*, 309 U.S. 227, 235–238 (1940). In sum, the privilege is fulfilled only when the person is guaranteed the right "to remain silent unless he chooses to speak in the unfettered exercise of his own will." *Malloy v. Hogan*, 378 U.S. 1, 8 (1964).

The question in these cases is whether the privilege is fully applicable during a period of custodial interrogation. * * * We are satisfied that all the principles embodied in the privilege apply to informal compulsion exerted by law-enforcement officers during in-custody questioning. An individual swept from familiar surroundings into police custody, surrounded by antagonistic forces, and subjected to the techniques of persuasion described above cannot be otherwise than under compulsion to speak. As a practical matter, the compulsion to speak in the isolated setting of the police station may well be greater than in courts or other official investigations, where there are often impartial observers to guard against intimidation or trickery.

Our holding [in *Escobedo*] stressed the fact that the police had not advised the defendant of his constitutional privilege to remain silent at the outset of the interrogation, and we drew attention to that fact at several points in the decision, 378 U.S., at 483, 485, 491. This was no isolated factor, but an essential ingredient in our decision. The entire thrust of police interrogation there, as in all the cases today, was to put the defendant in such an emotional state as to impair his capacity for rational judgment. * * *

A different phase of the *Escobedo* decision was significant in its attention to the absence of counsel during the questioning. There, as in the cases today, we sought a protective device to dispel the compelling atmosphere of the interrogation. In *Escobedo*, however, the police did not relieve the defendant of the anxieties which they had created in the interrogation rooms. Rather, they denied his request for the assistance of counsel. This heightened his dilemma, and made his later statements the product of this compulsion. The denial of the defendant's request for his attorney thus undermined his ability to exercise the privilege—to remain silent if he chose or to speak without any intimidation, blatant or subtle. The presence of counsel, in all the cases before us today, would be the adequate protective device necessary to make the process of police interrogation conform to the dictates of the privilege. His presence would insure that statements made in the government-established atmosphere are not the product of compulsion.

Today [there] can be no doubt that the Fifth Amendment privilege is available outside of criminal court proceedings and serves to protect persons in all settings in which their freedom of action is curtailed in any significant way from being compelled to incriminate themselves. We have concluded that without proper safeguards the process of in-custody interrogation of persons suspected or accused of crime contains inherently compelling pressures which work to undermine the individual's will to resist and to compel him to speak where he would not otherwise do so freely. In order to combat these pressures and to permit a full opportunity to exercise the privilege against self-incrimination, the accused must be adequately and effectively apprised of his rights and the exercise of those rights must be fully honored.

It is impossible for us to foresee the potential alternatives for protecting the privilege which might be devised by Congress or the States in the exercise of their creative rule-making capacities. Therefore we cannot say that the Constitution necessarily requires adherence to any particular solution for the inherent compulsions of the interrogation process as it is presently conducted. Our decision in no way creates a constitutional straitjacket which will handicap sound efforts at reform, nor is it intended to have this effect. We encourage Congress and the States to continue their laudable search for increasingly effective ways of protecting the rights of the individual while promoting efficient enforcement of our criminal laws. However, unless we are shown other procedures which are at least as effective in apprising accused persons of their right of silence and in assuring a continuous opportunity to exercise it, the following safeguards must be observed.

At the outset, if a person in custody is to be subjected to interrogation, he must first be informed in clear and unequivocal terms that he has the right to remain silent. For those unaware of the privilege, the warning is needed simply to make them aware of it—the threshold requirement for an intelligent decision as to its exercise. More important, such a warning is an absolute prerequisite in overcoming the inherent pressures of the interrogation atmosphere. It is not just the subnormal or woefully ignorant who succumb to an interrogator's imprecations, whether implied or expressly stated, that the interrogation will continue until a confession is obtained or that silence in the face of accusation is itself damning and will bode ill when presented to a jury. Further, the warning will show the individual that his interrogators are prepared to recognize his privilege should he choose to exercise it.

The Fifth Amendment privilege is so fundamental to our system of constitutional rule and the expedient of giving an adequate warning as to the availability of the privilege so simple, we will not pause to inquire in individual cases whether the defendant was aware of his rights without a warning being given. Assessments of the knowledge the defendant possessed, based on information as to his age, education, intelligence, or prior contact with authorities, can never be more than speculation; a warning is a clearcut fact. More important, whatever the background of the person interrogated, a warning at the time of the interrogation is indispensable to overcome its pressures and to insure that the individual knows he is free to exercise the privilege at that point in time.

The warning of the right to remain silent must be accompanied by the explanation that anything said can and will be used against the individual in court. This warning is needed in order to make him aware not only of the privilege, but also of the consequences of forgoing it. It is only through an awareness of these consequences that there can be any assurance of real understanding and intelligent exercise of the privilege. Moreover, this warning may serve to make the individual more acutely aware that he is faced with a phase of the adversary system—that he is not in the presence of persons acting solely in his interest.

The circumstances surrounding in-custody interrogation can operate very quickly to overbear the will of one merely made aware of his privilege by his interrogators. Therefore, the right to have counsel present at the interrogation is indispensable to the protection of the Fifth Amendment privilege under the system we delineate today. Our aim is to assure that the individual's right to choose between silence and speech remains unfettered throughout the interrogation process. A once-stated warning, delivered by those who will conduct the interrogation, cannot itself suffice to that end among those who most require knowledge of their rights. A mere warning given by the interrogators is not alone sufficient to accomplish that end. Prosecutors themselves claim that the admonishment of the right to remain silent without more "will benefit only the recidivist and the professional." Brief for the National District Attorneys Association as amicus curiae, p. 14. Even preliminary advice given to the accused by his own attorney can be swiftly overcome by the secret interrogation process. Thus, the need for counsel to protect the Fifth Amendment privilege comprehends not merely a right to consult with counsel prior to questioning, but also to have counsel present during any questioning if the defendant so desires.

The presence of counsel at the interrogation may serve several significant subsidiary functions as well. If the accused decides to talk to his interrogators, the assistance of counsel can mitigate the dangers of untrustworthiness. With a lawyer present the likelihood that the police will practice coercion is reduced, and if coercion is nevertheless exercised the lawyer can testify to it in court. The presence of a lawyer can also help to guarantee that the accused gives a fully accurate statement to the police and that the statement is rightly reported by the prosecution at trial.

An individual need not make a pre-interrogation request for a lawyer. While such request affirmatively secures his right to have one, his failure to ask for a lawyer does not constitute a waiver. No effective waiver of the right to counsel during interrogation can be recognized unless specifically made after the warnings we here delineate have been given. The accused who does not know his rights and therefore does not make a request may be the person who most needs counsel. * * *

Accordingly we hold that an individual held for interrogation must be clearly informed that he has the right to consult with a lawyer and to have the lawyer with him during interrogation under the system for protecting the privilege we delineate today. As with the warnings of the right to remain silent and that anything stated can be used in evidence against him, this warning is an absolute prerequisite to interrogation. No amount of circumstantial evidence that the person may have been aware of this right will suffice to stand in its stead. Only through such a warning is there ascertainable assurance that the accused was aware of this right.

* * * The need for counsel in order to protect the privilege exists for the indigent as well as the affluent. In fact, were we to limit these constitutional rights to those who can retain an attorney, our decisions today would be of little significance. The cases before us as well as the vast majority of confession cases with which we have dealt in the past involve those unable to retain counsel. While authorities are not required to relieve the accused of his poverty, they have the obligation not to take advantage of indigence in the administration of justice. Denial of counsel to the indigent at the time of interrogation while allowing an attorney to those who can afford one would be no more supportable by reason or logic than the similar situation at trial and on appeal struck down in *Gideon v. Wainwright*, 372 U.S. 335 (1963), and *Douglas v. People of State of California*, 372 U.S. 353 (1963).

In order fully to apprise a person interrogated of the extent of his rights under this system then, it is necessary to warn him not only that he has the right to consult with an attorney, but also that if he is indigent a lawyer will be appointed to represent him. Without this additional warning, the admonition of the right to consult with counsel would often be understood as meaning only that he can consult with a lawyer if he has one or has the funds to obtain one. * * * As with the warnings of the right to remain silent and of the general right to counsel, only by effective and express explanation to the indigent of this right can there be assurance that he was truly in a position to exercise it.

Once warnings have been given, the subsequent procedure is clear. If the individual indicates in any manner, at any time prior to or during questioning, that he wishes to remain silent, the interrogation must cease. At this point he has shown that he intends to exercise his Fifth Amendment privilege; any statement taken after the person invokes his privilege cannot be other than the product of compulsion, subtle or otherwise. * * * If the individual states that he wants an attorney, the interrogation must cease until an attorney is present. At that time, the individual must have an opportunity to confer with the attorney and to have him present during any subsequent questioning. If the individual cannot obtain an attorney and he indicates that he wants one before speaking to police, they must respect his decision to remain silent.

This does not mean, as some have suggested, that each police station must have a "station house lawyer" present at all times to advise prisoners. It does mean, however, that if police propose to interrogate a person they must make known to him that he is entitled to a lawyer and that if he cannot afford one, a lawyer will be provided for him prior to any interrogation. If authorities conclude that they will not provide counsel during a reasonable period of time in which investigation in the field is carried out, they may refrain from doing so without violating the person's Fifth Amendment privilege so long as they do not question him during that time.

If the interrogation continues without the presence of an attorney and a statement is taken, a heavy burden rests on the government to demonstrate that the defendant knowingly and intelligently waived his privilege against self-incrimination and his right to retained or appointed counsel. * * * Since the State is responsible for establishing the isolated circumstances under which the interrogation takes place and has the only means of making available corroborated evidence of warnings given during incommunicado interrogation, the burden is rightly on its shoulders.

An express statement that the individual is willing to make a statement and does not want an attorney followed closely by a statement could constitute a waiver. But a valid waiver will not be presumed simply from the silence of the accused after warnings are given or simply from the fact that a confession was in fact eventually obtained. * * * Moreover, where in-custody interrogation is involved, there is no room for the contention that the privilege is waived if the individual answers some questions or gives some information on his own prior to invoking his right to remain silent when interrogated.

The warnings required and the waiver necessary in accordance with our opinion today are, in the absence of a fully effective equivalent, prerequisites to the admissibility of any statement made by a defendant. No distinction can be drawn between statements which are direct confessions and statements which amount to "admissions" of part or all of an offense. The privilege against self-incrimination protects the individual from being compelled to incriminate himself in any manner; it does not distinguish degrees of incrimination. Similarly, for precisely the same reason, no distinction may be drawn between inculpatory statements and statements alleged to be merely "exculpatory." If a statement made were in fact truly exculpatory it would, of course, never be used by the prosecution. In fact, statements merely intended to be exculpatory by the defendant are often used to impeach his testimony at trial or to demonstrate untruths in the statement given under interrogation and thus to prove guilt by implication. These statements are incriminating in any meaningful sense of the word and may not be used without the full warnings and effective waiver required for any other statement. In *Escobedo* itself, the defendant fully intended his accusation of another as the slayer to be exculpatory as to himself.

The principles announced today deal with the protection which must be given to the privilege against self-incrimination when the individual is first subjected to police interrogation while in custody at the station or otherwise deprived of his freedom of action in any significant way. It is at this point that our adversary system of criminal proceedings commences, distinguishing itself at the outset from the inquisitorial system recognized in some countries. Under the system of warnings we delineate today or under any other system which may be devised and found effective, the safeguards to be erected about the privilege must come into play at this point.

> **Food for Thought**
>
> Why doesn't the obligation to provide warnings extend to "[g]eneral on-the-scene questioning"? If the police stopped you on the street to ask you some questions about a crime, would you feel free to remain silent or walk away?

Our decision is not intended to hamper the traditional function of police officers in investigating crime. When an individual is in custody on probable cause, the police may, of course, seek out evidence in the field to be used at trial against him. Such investigation may include inquiry of persons not under restraint. General on-the-scene questioning as to facts surrounding a crime or other general questioning of citizens in the fact-finding process is not affected by our holding. It is an act of responsible citizenship for individuals to give whatever information they may have to aid in law enforcement. In such situations the compelling atmosphere inherent in the process of in-custody interrogation is not necessarily present.

In dealing with statements obtained through interrogation, we do not purport to find all confessions inadmissible. Confessions remain a proper element in law enforcement. Any statement given freely and voluntarily without any compelling influences is, of course, admissible in evidence. The fundamental import of the privilege while an individual is in custody is not whether he is allowed to talk to the police without the benefit of warnings and counsel, but whether he can be interrogated. There is no requirement that police stop a person who enters a police station and states that he wishes to confess to a crime, or a person who calls the police to offer a confession or any other statement he desires to make. Volunteered statements of any kind are not barred by the Fifth Amendment and their admissibility is not affected by our holding today.

To summarize, we hold that when an individual is taken into custody or otherwise deprived of his freedom by the authorities in any significant way and is subjected to questioning, the privilege against self-incrimination is jeopardized. Procedural safeguards must be employed to protect the privilege and unless other fully effective means are adopted to notify the person of his right of silence and to assure that the exercise of the right will be scrupulously honored, the following measures are required. He must be warned prior to any questioning that he has the right to remain silent, that anything he says can be used against him in a court of law, that he has the right to the presence of an attorney, and that if he cannot afford an attorney one will be appointed for him prior to any questioning if he so desires. Opportunity to exercise these rights must be afforded to him throughout the interrogation. After such warnings have been given, and such opportunity afforded him, the individual may knowingly and intelligently waive these rights and agree to answer questions or make a statement. But unless and until such warnings and waiver are demonstrated by the prosecution at trial, no evidence obtained as a result of interrogation can be used against him.

> **Take Note**
>
> The Court here summarizes its holding and lists the required warnings.

A recurrent argument made in these cases is that society's need for interrogation outweighs the privilege. * * * In announcing these principles, we are not unmindful of the burdens which law enforcement officials must bear, often under trying circumstances. * * * The limits we have placed on the interrogation process should not constitute an undue interference with a proper system of law enforcement. As we have noted, our decision does not in any way preclude police from carrying out their traditional investigatory functions. Although confessions may play an important role in some convictions, the cases before us present graphic examples of the overstatement of the "need" for confessions. In each case authorities conducted interrogations ranging up to five days in duration despite the presence, through standard investigating practices, of considerable evidence against each defendant.[51]

---

[51] Miranda, Vignera, and Westover were identified by eyewitnesses. Marked bills from the bank robbed were found in Westover's car. Articles stolen from the victim as well as from several other robbery victims were found in Stewart's home at the outset of the investigation.

Over the years the Federal Bureau of Investigation has compiled an exemplary record of effective law enforcement while advising any suspect or arrested person, at the outset of an interview, that he is not required to make a statement, that any statement may be used against him in court, that the individual may obtain the services of an attorney of his own choice and, more recently, that he has a right to free counsel if he is unable to pay. * * * The practice of the FBI can readily be emulated by state and local enforcement agencies. * * *

It is also urged upon us that we withhold decision on this issue until state legislative bodies and advisory groups have had an opportunity to deal with these problems by rule making. We have already pointed out that the Constitution does not require any specific code of procedures for protecting the privilege against self-incrimination during custodial interrogation. Congress and the States are free to develop their own safeguards for the privilege, so long as they are fully as effective as those described above in informing accused persons of their right of silence and in affording a continuous opportunity to exercise it. In any event, however, the issues presented are of constitutional dimensions and must be determined by the courts. * * * Where rights secured by the Constitution are involved, there can be no rule making or legislation which would abrogate them.

* * * We turn now to these facts to consider the application to these cases of the constitutional principles discussed above. In each instance, we have concluded that statements were obtained from the defendant under circumstances that did not meet constitutional standards for protection of the privilege.

No. 759. *Miranda v. Arizona.*

On March 13, 1963, petitioner, Ernesto Miranda, was arrested at his home and taken in custody to a Phoenix police station. He was there identified by the complaining witness. The police then took him to "Interrogation Room No. 2" of the detective bureau. There he was questioned by two police officers. The officers admitted at trial that Miranda was not advised that he had a right to have an attorney present. Two hours later, the officers emerged from the interrogation room with a written confession signed by Miranda. At the top of the statement was a typed paragraph stating that the confession was made voluntarily, without threats or promises of immunity and "with full knowledge of my legal rights, understanding any statement I make may be used against me."

At his trial before a jury, the written confession was admitted into evidence over the objection of defense counsel, and the officers testified to the prior oral confession made by Miranda during the interrogation. Miranda was found guilty of kidnapping and rape. He was sentenced to 20 to 30 years' imprisonment on each count, the sentences to run concurrently. On appeal, the Supreme Court of Arizona held that Miranda's constitutional rights were not violated in obtaining the confession and affirmed the conviction. In reaching its decision, the court emphasized heavily the fact that Miranda did not specifically request counsel.

We reverse. From the testimony of the officers and by the admission of respondent, it is clear that Miranda was not in any way apprised of his right to consult with an attorney and to have one present during the interrogation, nor was his right not to be compelled to incriminate himself effectively protected in any other manner. Without these warnings the statements were inadmissible. The mere fact that he signed a statement which contained a typed-in clause stating that he had "full knowledge" of his "legal rights" does not approach the knowing and intelligent waiver required to relinquish constitutional rights.

[In the other three cases (*Vignera v. New York*, *Westover v. United States*, and *California v. Stewart*), the defendants similarly confessed after custodial interrogation that was not preceded by warnings about their rights. The Court reversed Vignera's and Westover's convictions and affirmed the decision of the California Supreme Court reversing Stewart's conviction.]

[JUSTICE CLARK's opinion dissenting in Nos. 759, 760, and 761, and concurring in the result in No. 584, has been omitted.]

MR. JUSTICE HARLAN, whom MR. JUSTICE STEWART and MR. JUSTICE WHITE join, dissenting.

I believe the decision of the Court represents poor constitutional law and entails harmful consequences for the country at large. How serious these consequences may prove to be only time can tell. But the basic flaws in the Court's justification seem to me readily apparent now once all sides of the problem are considered.

While the fine points of [the Court's new] scheme are far less clear than the Court admits, the tenor is quite apparent. The new rules are not designed to guard against police brutality or other unmistakably banned forms of coercion. Those who use third-degree tactics and deny them in court are equally able and destined to lie as skillfully about warnings and waivers. Rather, the thrust of the new rules is to negate all pressures, to reinforce the nervous or ignorant suspect, and ultimately to discourage any confession at all. The aim in short is toward "voluntariness" in a utopian sense, or to view it from a different angle, voluntariness with a vengeance.

[The Court's cases on the limits on confessions under the Due Process Clause of the Fourteenth Amendment] show that there exists a workable and effective means of dealing with confessions in a judicial manner * * *. It is "judicial" in its treatment of one case at a time, flexible in its ability to respond to the endless mutations of fact presented, and ever more familiar to the lower courts. Of course, strict certainty is not obtained in this developing process, but this is often so with constitutional principles, and disagreement is usually confined to that borderland of close cases where it matters least. * * *

Definition

"Trompe l'Oeil" is a French phrase meaning "deceives the eye" and is a genre of painting designed to create the illusion of a three-dimensional object.

I turn now to the Court's asserted reliance on the Fifth Amendment, an approach which I frankly regard as a trompe l'oeil. The Court's opinion in my view reveals no adequate basis for extending the Fifth Amendment's privilege against self-incrimination to the police station. Far more important, it fails to show that the Court's new rules are well supported, let alone compelled, by Fifth Amendment precedents. Instead, the new rules actually derive from quotation and analogy drawn from precedents under the Sixth Amendment, which should properly have no bearing on police interrogation.

The Court's opening contention, that the Fifth Amendment governs police station confessions, is perhaps not an impermissible extension of the law but it has little to commend itself in the present circumstances. * * * Certainly the privilege does represent a protective concern for the accused and an emphasis upon accusatorial rather than inquisitorial values in law enforcement * * *. Accusatorial values, however, have openly been absorbed into the due process standard governing confessions * * *. Since extension of the general principle has already occurred, to insist that the privilege applies as such serves only to carry over inapposite historical details and engaging rhetoric and to obscure the policy choices to be made in regulating confessions.

Having decided that the Fifth Amendment privilege does apply in the police station, the Court reveals that the privilege imposes more exacting restrictions than does the Fourteenth Amendment's voluntariness test. It then emerges from a discussion of *Escobedo* that the Fifth Amendment requires for an admissible confession that it be given by one distinctly aware of his right not to speak and shielded from "the compelling atmosphere" of interrogation. From these key premises, the Court finally develops the safeguards of warning, counsel, and so forth. * * * The [Court's] premise is that pressure on the suspect must be eliminated though it be only the subtle influence of the atmosphere and surroundings. The Fifth Amendment, however, has never been thought to forbid all pressure to incriminate one's self in the situations covered by it. * * *

Without at all subscribing to the generally black picture of police conduct painted by the Court, I think it must be frankly recognized at the outset that police questioning allowable under due process precedents may inherently entail some pressure on the suspect and may seek advantage in his ignorance or weaknesses. * * * Until today, the role of the Constitution has been only to sift out undue pressure, not to assure spontaneous confessions.

The Court's new rules aim to offset these minor pressures and disadvantages intrinsic to any kind of police interrogation. The rules do not serve due process interests in preventing blatant coercion since [they] do nothing to contain the policeman who is prepared to lie from the start. The rules work for reliability in confessions almost only in the Pickwickian sense that they can prevent some from being given at all. * * *

What the Court largely ignores is that its rules impair, if they will not eventually serve wholly to frustrate, an instrument of law enforcement that has long and quite reasonably been thought worth the price paid for it. There can be little doubt that the Court's new code would markedly decrease the number of confessions. To warn the suspect that he may remain silent and remind him that his confession may be used in court are minor obstructions. To require also an express waiver by the suspect and an end to questioning whenever he demurs must heavily handicap questioning. And to suggest or provide counsel for the suspect simply invites the end of the interrogation.

How much harm this decision will inflict on law enforcement cannot fairly be predicted with accuracy. * * * We do know that some crimes cannot be solved without confessions, that ample expert testimony attests to their importance in crime control, and that the Court is taking a real risk with society's welfare in imposing its new regime on the country. The social costs of crime are too great to call the new rules anything but a hazardous experimentation.

While passing over the costs and risks of its experiment, the Court portrays the evils of normal police questioning in terms which I think are exaggerated. Albeit stringently confined by the due process standards interrogation is no doubt often inconvenient and unpleasant for the suspect. However, it is no less so for a man to be arrested and jailed, to have his house searched, or to stand trial in court, yet all this may properly happen to the most innocent given probable cause, a warrant, or an indictment. Society has always paid a stiff price for law and order, and peaceful interrogation is not one of the dark moments of the law.

This brief statement of the competing considerations seems to me ample proof that the Court's preference is highly debatable at best and therefore not to be read into the Constitution. However, it may make the analysis more graphic to consider the actual facts of [*Miranda v. Arizona*].

On March 3, 1963, an 18-year-old girl was kidnapped and forcibly raped near Phoenix, Arizona. Ten days later, on the morning of March 13, petitioner Miranda was arrested and taken to the police station. At this time Miranda was 23 years old, indigent, and educated to the extent of completing half the ninth grade. He had "an emotional illness" of the schizophrenic type, according to the doctor who eventually examined him; the doctor's report also stated that Miranda was "alert and oriented as to time, place, and person," intelligent within normal limits, competent to stand trial, and sane within the legal definition. At the police station, the victim picked Miranda out of a lineup, and two officers then took him into a separate room to interrogate him, starting about 11:30 a.m. Though at first denying his guilt, within a short time Miranda gave a detailed oral confession and then wrote out in his own hand and signed a brief statement admitting and describing the crime. All this was accomplished in two hours or less without any force, threats or promises and—I will assume this though the record is uncertain—without any effective warnings at all.

Miranda's oral and written confessions are now held inadmissible under the Court's new rules. One is entitled to feel astonished that the Constitution can be read to produce this result. These confessions were obtained during brief, daytime questioning conducted by two officers and unmarked by any of the traditional indicia of coercion. They assured a conviction for a brutal and unsettling crime, for which the police had and quite possibly could obtain little evidence other than the victim's identifications, evidence which is frequently unreliable. There was, in sum, a legitimate purpose, no perceptible unfairness, and certainly little risk of injustice in the interrogation. Yet the resulting confessions, and the responsible course of police practice they represent, are to be sacrificed to the Court's own finespun conception of fairness which I seriously doubt is shared by many thinking citizens in this country.

In closing this necessarily truncated discussion of policy considerations attending the new confession rules, some reference must be made to their ironic untimeliness. There is now in progress in this country a massive re-examination of criminal law enforcement procedures on a scale never before witnessed. * * * Despite the Court's disclaimer, the practical effect of the decision made today must inevitably be to handicap seriously sound efforts at reform, not least by removing options necessary to a just compromise of competing interests. Of course legislative reform is rarely speedy or unanimous, though this Court has been more patient in the past. But the legislative reforms when they come would have the vast advantage of empirical data and comprehensive study, they would allow experimentation and use of solutions not open to the courts, and they would restore the initiative in criminal law reform to those forums where it truly belongs.

MR. JUSTICE WHITE, with whom MR. JUSTICE HARLAN and MR. JUSTICE STEWART join, dissenting.

[The Court's approach] makes very little sense in terms of the compulsion which the Fifth Amendment proscribes. That amendment deals with compelling the accused himself. It is his free will that is involved. Confessions and incriminating admissions, as such, are not forbidden evidence; only those which are compelled are banned. I doubt that the Court observes these distinctions today. By considering any answers to any interrogation to be compelled regardless of the content and course of examination and by escalating the requirements to prove waiver, the Court not only prevents the use of compelled confessions but for all practical purposes forbids interrogation except in the presence of counsel. That is, instead of confining itself to protection of the right against compelled self-incrimination the Court has created a limited Fifth Amendment right to counsel—or, as the Court expresses it, a "need for counsel to protect the Fifth Amendment privilege . . . ." The focus then is not on the will of the accused but on the will of counsel and how much influence he can have on the accused. Obviously there is no warrant in the Fifth Amendment for thus installing counsel as the arbiter of the privilege.

The obvious underpinning of the Court's decision is a deep-seated distrust of all confessions. As the Court declares that the accused may not be interrogated without counsel present, absent a waiver of the right to counsel, and as the Court all but admonishes the lawyer to advise the accused to remain silent, the result adds up to a judicial judgment that evidence from the accused should not be used against him in any way, whether compelled or not. This is the not so subtle overtone of the opinion—that it is inherently wrong for the police to gather evidence from the accused himself. And this is precisely the nub of this dissent. I see nothing wrong or immoral, and certainly nothing unconstitutional, in the police's asking a suspect whom they have reasonable cause to arrest whether or not he killed his wife or in confronting him with the evidence on which the arrest was based, at least where he has been plainly advised that he may remain completely silent. * * * Particularly when corroborated, as where the police have confirmed the accused's disclosure of the hiding place of implements or fruits of the crime, such confessions have the highest reliability and significantly contribute to the certitude with which we may believe the accused is guilty. * * *

The most basic function of any government is to provide for the security of the individual and of his property. These ends of society are served by the criminal laws which for the most part are aimed at the prevention of crime. Without the reasonably effective performance of the task of preventing private violence and retaliation, it is idle to talk about human dignity and civilized values. * * *

The rule announced today will measurably weaken the ability of the criminal law to perform these tasks. It is a deliberate calculus to prevent interrogations, to reduce the incidence of confessions and pleas of guilty and to increase the number of trials. Criminal trials, no matter how efficient the police are, are not sure bets for the prosecution, nor should they be if the evidence is not forthcoming. * * * There is, in my view, every reason to believe that a good many criminal defendants who otherwise would have been convicted on what this Court has previously thought to be the most satisfactory kind of evidence will now under this new version of the Fifth Amendment, either not be tried at all or will be acquitted if the State's evidence, minus the confession, is put to the test of litigation.

I have no desire whatsoever to share the responsibility for any such impact on the present criminal process. In some unknown number of cases the Court's rule will return a killer, a rapist or other criminal to the streets and to the environment which produced him, to repeat his crime whenever it pleases him. As a consequence, there will not be a gain, but a loss, in human dignity. The real concern is not the unfortunate consequences of this new decision on the criminal law as an abstract, disembodied series of authoritative proscriptions, but the impact on those who rely on the public authority for protection and who without it can only engage in violent self-help with guns, knives and the help of their neighbors similarly inclined. * * *

[T]he Court's per se approach may not be justified on the ground that it provides a "bright line" permitting the authorities to judge in advance whether interrogation may safely be pursued without jeopardizing the admissibility of any information obtained as a consequence. Nor can it be claimed that judicial time and effort, assuming that is a relevant consideration, will be conserved because of the ease of application of the new rule. Today's decision leaves open such questions as whether the accused was in custody, whether his statements were spontaneous or the product of interrogation, whether the accused has effectively waived his rights, and whether nontestimonial evidence introduced at trial is the fruit of statements made during a prohibited interrogation, all of which are certain to prove productive of uncertainty during investigation and litigation during prosecution. For all these reasons, if further restrictions on police interrogation are desirable at this time, a more flexible approach makes much more sense than the Court's constitutional straitjacket which forecloses more discriminating treatment by legislative or rule-making pronouncements.

POINTS FOR DISCUSSION

a.   The *Miranda* Warnings

The *Miranda* warnings are familiar to most Americans because of their frequent depiction in movies and television shows, and most Americans likely take them for granted as a part of police procedure. Now that you have read the Court's opinion in *Miranda*, do you think that the warnings are sensible and justified?

b.   The Privilege Against Self-Incrimination v. the Right to Counsel

The Court in *Miranda* appears to have decided that the approach in *Escobedo*—focusing on the Sixth Amendment right to counsel—was not the most promising approach for dealing with the problems of confessions obtained during interrogation. If the Sixth Amendment right applies even before a suspect had been charged, then the police effectively would never be able to obtain a confession. Instead, the Court focused on the Fifth Amendment privilege against self-incrimination, while retaining a focus on the importance of an attorney for suspects facing interrogation.

The Court relied on the privilege against self-incrimination because of the dynamics of custodial interrogation. In announcing the requirement that police provide warnings to suspects facing custodial interrogation, the Court declared that "the process of in-custody interrogation of persons suspected or accused of crime contains *inherently compelling pressures* which work to undermine the individual's will to resist, and to *compel* him to speak where he would not otherwise do so freely." Does this mean that, absent the warnings, any confession obtained during interrogation by the police is compelled and thereby violates the Fifth Amendment privilege against self-incrimination?

c.   The Nature of the Rule

At oral argument, a lawyer for one of the petitioners stated, in response to a question about the totality-of-the-circumstances test under the Due Process Clause: "[I]f we go back to the totality of the circumstances, that means that this Court will sit all by itself as it has so many years to overturn the few confessions it can take, necessarily, by the bulk of the work. The lower courts won't do their job. We need some specific guidelines as *Escobedo* to help them along the way." Can the *Miranda* warnings be justified as a prophylactic measure to avoid the difficult questions that arise under the Due Process test for voluntariness? On this view, courts do not have to decide, case by case, whether a particular confession was truly voluntary, or whether particular police conduct in interrogation was truly problematic. Instead, a court can usually just inquire whether the police properly gave the warnings.

Even assuming that the warnings function this way in practice, was the Court the right actor to formulate and announce them?

———————

Did the Court in *Miranda* conclude that all custodial police interrogations are inherently coercive, and thus will always violate the privilege against self-incrimination unless the police first give the warnings and obtain a waiver of rights before starting an interrogation? Or are the warnings a prophylactic device designed to ensure that custodial police interrogations do not stray so far as to violate the privilege against self-incrimination?

The question eventually reached the Court because of Congress's decision in 1968 to enact the Omnibus Crime Control and Safe Streets Act of 1968. Title II of that Act, codified at 18 U.S.C. § 3501, provided that in all federal prosecutions, confessions were admissible in evidence if "voluntarily given." The provision thus permitted the introduction into evidence of a confession obtained without *Miranda* warnings, as long as the confession was otherwise voluntary. In other words, the statute appeared to reinstate the pre-*Miranda* voluntariness test for the admissibility of confessions, and in so doing appeared effectively to reject or legislatively overrule *Miranda*.

For three decades, the United States Department of Justice did not rely on section 3501 in federal prosecutions, choosing instead to treat *Miranda* as applying the relevant rules for the admissibility of confessions. In 1999, however, the United States Court of Appeals for the Fourth Circuit, ignoring the approach of the Department of Justice, held that section 3501's voluntariness test, and not *Miranda*, applied in a federal prosecution. The court reasoned that the *Miranda* warnings were "prophylactic" and "not themselves rights protected by the Constitution."

The Supreme Court reversed in *Dickerson v. United States*, 530 U.S. 428 (2000), concluding that "*Miranda* announced a constitutional rule that Congress may not supersede legislatively." The Court noted that it does "not hold a supervisory power over" state courts, but instead has authority "limited to enforcing the commands of the United States Constitution." Because *Miranda* and two of the companion cases arose in state prosecutions, the Court reasoned that its decision must have announced a constitutional rule. The Court also noted that its *Miranda* opinion concluded that the confessions at issue had been obtained "under circumstances that did not meet constitutional standards for protection of the privilege" against self-incrimination. The Court acknowledged that the "requirement that *Miranda* warnings be given does not, of course, dispense with the voluntariness inquiry." But it explained that the *Miranda* rule ordinarily will be sufficient to resolve cases involving confessions, because cases "in which a defendant can make a colorable argument that a self-incriminating statement was 'compelled' despite the fact that the law enforcement authorities adhered to the dictates of *Miranda* are rare."

Justice Scalia, joined by Justice Thomas, dissented. Justice Scalia disagreed with the Court's conclusion that "failure to comply with *Miranda's* rules is itself a violation of the Constitution." He also asserted that "*Miranda,* if read as an explication of what the Constitution *requires,* is preposterous." He explained:

> There is, for example, simply no basis in reason for concluding that a response to the very first question asked, by a suspect who already *knows* all of the rights described in the *Miranda* warning, is anything other than a volitional act. And even if one assumes that the elimination of compulsion absolutely requires informing even the most knowledgeable suspect of his right to remain silent, it cannot conceivably require the right to have *counsel* present. There is a world of difference, which the Court recognized under the traditional voluntariness test but ignored in *Miranda,* between compelling a suspect to incriminate himself and preventing him from foolishly doing so of his own accord. Only the latter (which is *not* required by the Constitution) could explain the Court's inclusion of a right to counsel and the requirement that it, too, be knowingly and intelligently waived. Counsel's presence is not required to tell the suspect that he *need* not speak; the interrogators can do that. The only good reason for having counsel there is that he can be counted on to advise the suspect that he *should* not speak.

> Preventing foolish (rather than compelled) confessions is likewise the only conceivable basis for the rules [that] courts must exclude any confession elicited by questioning conducted, without interruption, after the suspect has indicated a desire to stand on his right to remain silent or initiated by police after the suspect has expressed a desire to have counsel present. Nonthreatening attempts to persuade the suspect to reconsider that initial decision are not, without more, enough to render a change of heart the product of anything other than the suspect's free will. Thus, what is most remarkable about the *Miranda* decision—and what made it unacceptable as a matter of straightforward constitutional interpretation in the *Marbury* tradition—is its palpable hostility toward

the act of confession *per se,* rather than toward what the Constitution abhors, *compelled* confession.

Id. at 448–450 (Scalia, J., dissenting). Do you agree that *Miranda*'s principal role in practice is to prevent "foolish (rather than compelled) confessions"?

4.   The Meaning of Custodial Interrogation

The Court in *Miranda* held that "the prosecution may not use statements, whether exculpatory or inculpatory, stemming from custodial interrogation of the defendant unless it demonstrates the use of procedural safeguards effective to secure the privilege against self-incrimination. By custodial interrogation, we mean questioning initiated by law enforcement officers after a person has been taken into custody or otherwise deprived of his freedom of action in any significant way." Accordingly, determining whether the police had an obligation to provide *Miranda* warnings requires consideration of at least two factors. First, was the suspect in "custody"? Second, was the suspect subject to "interrogation"? We consider these questions in turn.

OREGON V. MATHIASON
429 U.S. 492 (1977)

PER CURIAM.

Respondent Carl Mathiason was convicted of first-degree burglary after a bench trial in which his confession was critical to the State's case. At trial he moved to suppress the confession as the fruit of questioning by the police not preceded by the warnings required in *Miranda v. Arizona,* 384 U.S. 436 (1966). The trial court refused to exclude the confession because it found that Mathiason was not in custody at the time of the confession.

The Oregon Court of Appeals affirmed respondent's conviction, but on his petition for review in the Supreme Court of Oregon that court by a divided vote reversed the conviction. It found that although Mathiason had not been arrested or otherwise formally detained, "the interrogation took place in a 'coercive environment' " of the sort to which *Miranda* was intended to apply. * * * We think that court has read *Miranda* too broadly, and we therefore reverse its judgment.

The Supreme Court of Oregon described the factual situation surrounding the confession as follows:

"An officer of the State Police investigated a theft at a residence near Pendleton. He asked the lady of the house which had been burglarized if she suspected anyone. She replied that the defendant was the only one she could think of. The defendant was a parolee and a 'close associate' of her son. The officer tried to contact defendant on three or four occasions with no success. Finally, about 25 days after the burglary, the officer left his card at defendant's apartment with a note asking him to call because 'I'd like to discuss something with you.' The next afternoon the defendant did call. The officer asked where it would be convenient to meet. The defendant had no preference; so the officer asked if the defendant could meet him at the state patrol office in about an hour and a half, about 5:00 p.m. The patrol office was about two blocks from defendant's apartment. The building housed several state agencies.

The officer met defendant in the hallway, shook hands and took him into an office. The defendant was told he was not under arrest. The door was closed. The two sat across a desk. The police radio in another room could be heard. The officer told defendant he wanted to talk to him about a burglary and that his truthfulness would possibly be considered by the district attorney or judge. The officer further advised that the police believed defendant was involved in the burglary and (falsely stated that) defendant's fingerprints were found at the scene. The defendant sat for a few minutes and then said he had taken the property. This occurred within five minutes after defendant had come to the office. The officer then advised defendant of his *Miranda* rights and took a taped confession.

At the end of the taped conversation the officer told defendant he was not arresting him at this time; he was released to go about his job and return to his family. The officer said he was referring the case to the district attorney for him to determine whether criminal charges would be brought. It was 5:30 p.m. when the defendant left the office." * * *

Our decision in *Miranda* set forth rules of police procedure applicable to "custodial interrogation." "By custodial interrogation, we mean questioning initiated by law enforcement officers after a person has been taken into custody or otherwise deprived of his freedom of action in any significant way." 384 U.S., at 444. Subsequently we have found the *Miranda* principle applicable to questioning which takes place in a prison setting during a suspect's term of imprisonment on a separate offense, *Mathis v. United States*, 391 U.S. 1 (1968), and to questioning taking place in a suspect's home, after he has been arrested and is no longer free to go where he pleases, *Orozco v. Texas*, 394 U.S. 324 (1969).

In the present case, however, there is no indication that the questioning took place in a context where respondent's freedom to depart was restricted in any way.

He came voluntarily to the police station, where he was immediately informed that he was not under arrest. At the close of a ½-hour interview respondent did in fact leave the police station without hindrance. It is clear from these facts that Mathiason was not in custody "or otherwise deprived of his freedom of action in any significant way."

Such a noncustodial situation is not converted to one in which *Miranda* applies simply because a reviewing court concludes that, even in the absence of any formal arrest or restraint on freedom of movement, the questioning took place in a "coercive environment." Any interview of one suspected of a crime by a police officer will have coercive aspects to it, simply by virtue of the fact that the police officer is part of a law enforcement system which may ultimately cause the suspect to be charged with a crime. But police officers are not required to administer *Miranda* warnings to everyone whom they question. Nor is the requirement of warnings to be imposed simply because the questioning takes place in the station house, or because the questioned person is one whom the police suspect. *Miranda* warnings are required only where there has been such a restriction on a person's freedom as to render him "in custody." It was that sort of coercive environment to which *Miranda* by its terms was made applicable, and to which it is limited.

The officer's false statement about having discovered Mathiason's fingerprints at the scene was found by the Supreme Court of Oregon to be another circumstance contributing to the coercive environment which makes the *Miranda* rationale applicable. Whatever relevance this fact may have to other issues in the case, it has nothing to do with whether respondent was in custody for purposes of the *Miranda* rule.

The petition for certiorari is granted, the judgment of the Oregon Supreme Court is reversed, and the case is remanded for proceedings not inconsistent with this opinion.

MR. JUSTICE BRENNAN would grant the writ but dissents from the summary disposition and would set the case for oral argument.

MR. JUSTICE MARSHALL, dissenting.

The respondent in this case was interrogated behind closed doors at police headquarters in connection with a burglary investigation. He had been named by the victim of the burglary as a suspect, and was told by the police that they believed he was involved. He was falsely informed that his fingerprints had been found at the scene, and in effect was advised that by cooperating with the police he could help himself. Not until after he had confessed was he given the warnings set forth in *Miranda v. Arizona*, 384 U.S. 436 (1966).

The Court today holds that for constitutional purposes all this is irrelevant because respondent had not "been taken into custody or otherwise deprived of his freedom of action in any significant way." I do not believe that such a determination is possible on the record before us. It is true that respondent was not formally placed under arrest, but surely formalities alone cannot control. At the very least, if respondent entertained an objectively reasonable belief that he was not free to leave during the questioning, then he was "deprived of his freedom of action in a significant way." Plainly the respondent could have so believed, after being told by the police that they thought he was involved in a burglary and that his fingerprints had been found at the scene. Yet the majority is content to note that "there is no indication that . . . respondent's freedom to depart was restricted in any way," as if a silent record (and no state-court findings) means that the State has sustained its burden of demonstrating that respondent received his constitutional due.

More fundamentally, however, I cannot agree with the Court's conclusion that if respondent were not in custody no warnings were required. I recognize that *Miranda* is limited to custodial interrogations, but that is because, as we noted last Term, the facts in the Miranda cases raised only this "narrow issue." *Beckwith v. United States*, 425 U.S. 341, 345 (1976). The rationale of *Miranda*, however, is not so easily cabined.

Miranda requires warnings to "combat" a situation in which there are "inherently compelling pressures which work to undermine the individual's will to resist and to compel him to speak where he would not otherwise do so freely." It is of course true, as the Court notes, that "[a]ny interview of one suspected of a crime by a police officer will have coercive aspects to it." But it does not follow that because police "are not required to administer *Miranda* warnings to everyone whom they question" [they] need not administer warnings to anyone, unless the factual setting of the *Miranda* cases is replicated. Rather, faithfulness to *Miranda* requires us to distinguish situations that resemble the "coercive aspects" of custodial interrogation from those that more nearly resemble "[g]eneral on-the-scene questioning . . . or other general questioning of citizens in the fact-finding process" which *Miranda* states usually can take place without warnings.

In my view, even if respondent were not in custody, the coercive elements in the instant case were so pervasive as to require *Miranda*-type warnings. Respondent was interrogated in "privacy" and in "unfamiliar surroundings," factors on which *Miranda* places great stress. The investigation had focused on respondent. And respondent was subjected to some of the "deceptive stratagems," *Miranda*, supra, at 455, which called forth the *Miranda* decision. I therefore agree with the Oregon Supreme Court that to excuse the absence of warnings given these facts is "contrary to the rationale expressed in *Miranda*."

[JUSTICE STEVENS's dissenting opinion has been omitted.]

POINTS FOR DISCUSSION

a.   The Definition of Custody

The obligation under *Miranda* to provide warnings arises only in the context of custodial interrogation. In *Mathiason*, the Court concluded that a suspect is in custody only when he has been "deprived of his freedom of action"—and specifically his freedom to depart—"in any significant way." Although he dissented, Justice Marshall largely agreed with this test, and in fact the Court has tended to apply his formulation of the test: "[I]f respondent entertained an objectively reasonable belief that he was not free to leave during the questioning, then he was 'deprived of his freedom of action in a significant way.' " Under this test, can questioning at a suspect's home (when he is not being arrested) ever count as custodial interrogation?

b.   An Objective Test

The Court has explained that "whether a suspect is 'in custody' is an objective inquiry," which means that it does not focus on whether the suspect actually believed that he was free to terminate questioning and leave, but rather on whether a "reasonable person in the suspect's position" would believe that he can terminate the questioning and leave. *J.D.B. v. North Carolina*, 564 U.S. 261 (2011).

How does such a test apply when the police take a 13-year-old student out of his classroom at school, bring him to a conference room with two school administrators, and inform him that they want to ask him questions about two home break-ins, without first giving him the *Miranda* warnings? In *J.D.B.*, the Court concluded that "[s]o long as the child's age was known to the officer at the time of the interview, or would have been objectively apparent to any reasonable officer," the suspect's age is relevant to deciding whether the suspect would have felt free to terminate the questioning and leave. Does this test require police officers to be experts in developmental psychology? Or does the inquiry merely require common sense?

RHODE ISLAND V. INNIS

446 U.S. 291 (1980)

MR. JUSTICE STEWART delivered the opinion of the Court.

In *Miranda v. Arizona*, 384 U.S. 436, 474 (1966), the Court held that, once a defendant in custody asks to speak with a lawyer, all interrogation must cease until a lawyer is present. The issue in this case is whether the respondent was "interrogated" in violation of the standards promulgated in the *Miranda* opinion.

On the night of January 12, 1975, John Mulvaney, a Providence, R.I., taxicab driver, disappeared after being dispatched to pick up a customer. His body was discovered four days later buried in a shallow grave in Coventry, R.I. He had died from a shotgun blast aimed at the back of his head.

On January 17, 1975, shortly after midnight, the Providence police received a telephone call from Gerald Aubin, also a taxicab driver, who reported that he had just been robbed by a man wielding a sawed-off shotgun. Aubin further reported that he had dropped off his assailant near Rhode Island College in a section of Providence known as Mount Pleasant. While at the Providence police station waiting to give a statement, Aubin noticed a picture of his assailant on a bulletin board. Aubin so informed one of the police officers present. * * * Shortly thereafter, the Providence police began a search of the Mount Pleasant area.

At approximately 4:30 a.m. on the same date, Patrolman Lovell, while cruising the streets of Mount Pleasant in a patrol car, spotted the respondent standing in the street facing him. * * * Patrolman Lovell then arrested the respondent, who was unarmed, and advised him of his so-called *Miranda* rights. While the two men waited in the patrol car for other police officers to arrive, Patrolman Lovell did not converse with the respondent other than to respond to the latter's request for a cigarette.

Within minutes, Sergeant Sears arrived at the scene of the arrest, and he also gave the respondent the *Miranda* warnings. Immediately thereafter, Captain Leyden and other police officers arrived. Captain Leyden advised the respondent of his *Miranda* rights. The respondent stated that he understood those rights and wanted to speak with a lawyer. Captain Leyden then directed that the respondent be placed in a "caged wagon," a four-door police car with a wire screen mesh between the front and rear seats, and be driven to the central police station. Three officers, Patrolmen Gleckman, Williams, and McKenna, were assigned to accompany the respondent to the central station. They placed the respondent in the vehicle and shut the doors. Captain Leyden then instructed the officers not to question the respondent or intimidate or coerce him in any way. The three officers then entered the vehicle, and it departed.

While en route to the central station, Patrolman Gleckman initiated a conversation with Patrolman McKenna concerning the missing shotgun.[1] As Patrolman Gleckman later testified:

"A. At this point, I was talking back and forth with Patrolman McKenna stating that I frequent this area while on patrol and [that because a school for handicapped children is located nearby,] there's a lot of handicapped children running around in this area, and God forbid one of them might find a weapon with shells and they might hurt themselves."

Patrolman McKenna apparently shared his fellow officer's concern:

"A. I more or less concurred with him [Gleckman] that it was a safety factor and that we should, you know, continue to search for the weapon and try to find it."

While Patrolman Williams said nothing, he overheard the conversation between the two officers:

"A. He [Gleckman] said it would be too bad if the little—I believe he said a girl—would pick up the gun, maybe kill herself."

The respondent then interrupted the conversation, stating that the officers should turn the car around so he could show them where the gun was located. At this point, Patrolman McKenna radioed back to Captain Leyden that they were returning to the scene of the arrest and that the respondent would inform them of the location of the gun. At the time the respondent indicated that the officers should turn back, they had traveled no more than a mile, a trip encompassing only a few minutes.

The police vehicle then returned to the scene of the arrest where a search for the shotgun was in progress. There, Captain Leyden again advised the respondent of his *Miranda* rights. The respondent replied that he understood those rights but that he "wanted to get the gun out of the way because of the kids in the area in the school." The respondent then led the police to a nearby field, where he pointed out the shotgun under some rocks by the side of the road.

On March 20, 1975, a grand jury returned an indictment charging the respondent with the kidnaping, robbery, and murder of John Mulvaney. Before

---

[1] Although there was conflicting testimony about the exact seating arrangements, it is clear that everyone in the vehicle heard the conversation.

trial, the respondent moved to suppress the shotgun and the statements he had made to the police regarding it. [The trial judge concluded that the respondent had waived his right to remain silent and] sustained the admissibility of the shotgun and testimony related to its discovery. That evidence was later introduced at the respondent's trial, and the jury returned a verdict of guilty on all counts.

On appeal, the Rhode Island Supreme Court, in a 3–2 decision, set aside the respondent's conviction. [T]he court concluded that the respondent had invoked his *Miranda* right to counsel and that, contrary to *Miranda's* mandate that, in the absence of counsel, all custodial interrogation then cease, the police officers in the vehicle had "interrogated" the respondent without a valid waiver of his right to counsel. It was the view of the state appellate court that, even though the police officers may have been genuinely concerned about the public safety and even though the respondent had not been addressed personally by the police officers, the respondent nonetheless had been subjected to "subtle coercion" that was the equivalent of "interrogation" within the meaning of the *Miranda* opinion. Moreover, contrary to the holding of the trial court, the appellate court concluded that the evidence was insufficient to support a finding of waiver. * * *

In the present case, the parties are in agreement that the respondent was fully informed of his *Miranda* rights and that he invoked his *Miranda* right to counsel when he told Captain Leyden that he wished to consult with a lawyer. It is also uncontested that the respondent was "in custody" while being transported to the police station. The issue, therefore, is whether the respondent was "interrogated" by the police officers in violation of the respondent's undisputed right under *Miranda* to remain silent until he had consulted with a lawyer. In resolving this issue, we first define the term "interrogation" under *Miranda* before turning to a consideration of the facts of this case.

The starting point for defining "interrogation" in this context is, of course, the Court's *Miranda* opinion. There the Court observed that "[b]y custodial interrogation, we mean *questioning* initiated by law enforcement officers after a person has been taken into custody or otherwise deprived of his freedom of action in any significant way." *Id.*, 384 U.S. at 444 (emphasis added). This passage and other references throughout the opinion to "questioning" might suggest that the *Miranda* rules were to apply only to those police interrogation practices that involve express questioning of a defendant while in custody.

We do not, however, construe the *Miranda* opinion so narrowly. The concern of the Court in *Miranda* was that the "interrogation environment" created by the interplay of interrogation and custody would "subjugate the individual to the will of his examiner" and thereby undermine the privilege against compulsory self-incrimination. *Id.,* at 457–458. The police practices that evoked this concern included several that did not involve express questioning. For example, one of the practices discussed in *Miranda* was the use of line-ups in which a coached witness would pick the defendant as the perpetrator. This was designed to establish that the defendant was in fact guilty as a predicate for further interrogation. A variation on this theme discussed in *Miranda* was the so-called "reverse line-up" in which a defendant would be identified by coached witnesses as the perpetrator of a fictitious crime, with the object of inducing him to confess to the actual crime of which he was suspected in order to escape the false prosecution. * * * It is clear that these techniques of persuasion, no less than express questioning, were thought, in a custodial setting, to amount to interrogation.

This is not to say, however, that all statements obtained by the police after a person has been taken into custody are to be considered the product of interrogation. As the Court in *Miranda* noted:

> "Confessions remain a proper element in law enforcement. Any statement given freely and voluntarily without any compelling influences is, of course, admissible in evidence. *The fundamental import of the privilege while an individual is in custody is not whether he is allowed to talk to the police without the benefit of warnings and counsel, but whether he can be interrogated.* * * *" *Id.,* at 478 (emphasis added).

It is clear therefore that the special procedural safeguards outlined in *Miranda* are required not where a suspect is simply taken into custody, but rather where a suspect in custody is subjected to interrogation. "Interrogation," as conceptualized in the *Miranda* opinion, must reflect a measure of compulsion above and beyond that inherent in custody itself.

> **Take Note**
>
> The Court in this paragraph announces the test for interrogation. Is the test easy to administer?

We conclude that the *Miranda* safeguards come into play whenever a person in custody is subjected to either express questioning or its functional equivalent. That is to say, the term "interrogation" under *Miranda* refers not only to express questioning, but also to any words or actions on the part of the police (other than those normally attendant to arrest and custody) that the police should know are reasonably likely to elicit an incriminating response from the suspect. The latter portion of this definition focuses primarily upon the perceptions of the suspect, rather than the intent of the police. This focus reflects the fact that the *Miranda* safeguards were designed to vest a suspect in custody with an added measure of protection against coercive police practices, without regard to objective proof of the underlying intent of the police. A practice that the police should know is reasonably likely to evoke an incriminating response from a suspect thus amounts to interrogation.[7] But, since the police surely cannot be held accountable for the unforeseeable results of their words or actions, the definition of interrogation can extend only to words or actions on the part of police officers that they *should have known* were reasonably likely to elicit an incriminating response.[8]

Turning to the facts of the present case, we conclude that the respondent was not "interrogated" within the meaning of *Miranda.* It is undisputed that the first prong of the definition of "interrogation" was not satisfied, for the conversation between Patrolmen Gleckman and McKenna included no express questioning of the respondent. Rather, that conversation was, at least in form, nothing more than a dialogue between the two officers to which no response from the respondent was invited.

Moreover, it cannot be fairly concluded that the respondent was subjected to the "functional equivalent" of questioning. It cannot be said, in short, that Patrolmen Gleckman and McKenna should have known that their conversation was reasonably likely to elicit an incriminating response from the respondent. There is nothing in the record to suggest that the officers were aware that the respondent was peculiarly susceptible to an appeal to his conscience concerning the safety of handicapped children. Nor is there anything in the record to suggest that the police knew that the respondent was unusually disoriented or upset at the time of his arrest.

The case thus boils down to whether, in the context of a brief conversation, the officers should have known that the respondent would suddenly be moved to make a self-incriminating response. Given the fact that the entire conversation appears to have consisted of no more than a few off hand remarks, we cannot say that the officers should have known that it was reasonably likely that Innis would so respond. This is not a case where the police carried on a lengthy harangue in the presence of the suspect. Nor does the record support the respondent's contention that, under the circumstances, the officers' comments were particularly "evocative." It is our view, therefore, that the respondent was not subjected by

---

[7]   This is not to say that the intent of the police is irrelevant, for it may well have a bearing on whether the police should have known that their words or actions were reasonably likely to evoke an incriminating response. In particular, where a police practice is designed to elicit an incriminating response from the accused, it is unlikely that the practice will not also be one which the police should have known was reasonably likely to have that effect.

[8]   Any knowledge the police may have had concerning the unusual susceptibility of a defendant to a particular form of persuasion might be an important factor in determining whether the police should have known that their words or actions were reasonably likely to elicit an incriminating response from the suspect.

the police to words or actions that the police should have known were reasonably likely to elicit an incriminating response from him.

The Rhode Island Supreme Court erred, in short, in equating "subtle compulsion" with interrogation. That the officers' comments struck a responsive chord is readily apparent. Thus, it may be said, as the Rhode Island Supreme Court did say, that the respondent was subjected to "subtle compulsion." But that is not the end of the inquiry. It must also be established that a suspect's incriminating response was the product of words or actions on the part of the police that they should have known were reasonably likely to elicit an incriminating response.[10] This was not established in the present case.

[JUSTICE WHITE's concurring opinion has been omitted.]

MR. CHIEF JUSTICE BURGER, concurring in the judgment.

Since the result is not inconsistent with *Miranda v. Arizona*, 384 U.S. 436 (1966), I concur in the judgment. * * * I fear, however, that [the Court's opinion] may introduce new elements of uncertainty; under the Court's test, a police officer, in the brief time available, apparently must evaluate the suggestibility and susceptibility of an accused. Few, if any, police officers are competent to make the kind of evaluation seemingly contemplated; even a psychiatrist asked to express an expert opinion on these aspects of a suspect in custody would very likely employ extensive questioning and observation to make the judgment now charged to police officers. Trial judges have enough difficulty discerning the boundaries and nuances flowing from post-*Miranda* opinions, and we do not clarify that situation today.

MR. JUSTICE MARSHALL, with whom MR. JUSTICE BRENNAN joins, dissenting.

I am substantially in agreement with the Court's definition of "interrogation" within the meaning of *Miranda v. Arizona*, 384 U.S. 436 (1966). In my view, the *Miranda* safeguards apply whenever police conduct is intended or likely to produce a response from a suspect in custody. As I read the Court's opinion, its definition of "interrogation" for *Miranda* purposes is equivalent, for practical purposes, to my formulation * * *. [T]he Court requires an objective inquiry into the likely effect of police conduct on a typical individual, taking into account any special

---

[10]   By way of example, if the police had done no more than to drive past the site of the concealed weapon while taking the most direct route to the police station, and if the respondent, upon noticing for the first time the proximity of the school for handicapped children, had blurted out that he would show the officers where the gun was located, it could not seriously be argued that this "subtle compulsion" would have constituted "interrogation" within the meaning of the *Miranda* opinion.

susceptibility of the suspect to certain kinds of pressure of which the police know or have reason to know.

I am utterly at a loss, however, to understand how this objective standard as applied to the facts before us can rationally lead to the conclusion that there was no interrogation. * * * One can scarcely imagine a stronger appeal to the conscience of a suspect—*any* suspect—than the assertion that if the weapon is not found an innocent person will be hurt or killed. And not just any innocent person, but an innocent child—a little girl—a helpless, handicapped little girl on her way to school. The notion that such an appeal could not be expected to have any effect unless the suspect were known to have some special interest in handicapped children verges on the ludicrous. As a matter of fact, the appeal to a suspect to confess for the sake of others, to "display some evidence of decency and honor," is a classic interrogation technique.

Gleckman's remarks would obviously have constituted interrogation if they had been explicitly directed to respondent, and the result should not be different because they were nominally addressed to McKenna. This is not a case where police officers speaking among themselves are accidentally overheard by a suspect. These officers were "talking back and forth" in close quarters with the handcuffed suspect, traveling past the very place where they believed the weapon was located. They knew respondent would hear and attend to their conversation, and they are chargeable with knowledge of and responsibility for the pressures to speak which they created.

MR. JUSTICE STEVENS, dissenting.

In my view any statement that would normally be understood by the average listener as calling for a response is the functional equivalent of a direct question, whether or not it is punctuated by a question mark. The Court, however, takes a much narrower view. It holds that police conduct is not the "functional equivalent" of direct questioning unless the police should have known that what they were saying or doing was likely to elicit an incriminating response from the suspect. This holding represents a plain departure from the principles set forth in *Miranda*.

[I]n order to give full protection to a suspect's right to be free from any interrogation at all, the definition of "interrogation" must include any police statement or conduct that has the same purpose or effect as a direct question. Statements that appear to call for a response from the suspect, as well as those that are designed to do so, should be considered interrogation. By prohibiting only those relatively few statements or actions that a police officer should know are likely to elicit an incriminating response, the Court today accords a suspect considerably less protection. Indeed, since I suppose most suspects are unlikely to incriminate themselves even when questioned directly, this new definition will almost certainly exclude every statement that is not punctuated with a question mark from the concept of "interrogation."

The difference between the approach required by a faithful adherence to *Miranda* and the stinted test applied by the Court today can be illustrated by comparing three different ways in which Officer Gleckman could have communicated his fears about the possible dangers posed by the shotgun to handicapped children. He could have:

(1)   directly asked Innis: Will you please tell me where the shotgun is so we can protect handicapped school children from danger?

(2)   announced to the other officers in the wagon: If the man sitting in the back seat with me should decide to tell us where the gun is, we can protect handicapped children from danger.

or (3) stated to the other officers: It would be too bad if a little handicapped girl would pick up the gun that this man left in the area and maybe kill herself.

In my opinion, all three of these statements should be considered interrogation because all three appear to be designed to elicit a response from anyone who in fact knew where the gun was located. Under the Court's test, on the other hand, the form of the statements would be critical. The third statement would not be interrogation because in the Court's view there was no reason for Officer Gleckman to believe that Innis was susceptible to this type of an implied appeal; therefore, the statement would not be reasonably likely to elicit an incriminating response. Assuming that this is true, then it seems to me that the first two statements, which would be just as unlikely to elicit such a response, should also not be considered interrogation. But, because the first statement is clearly an express question, it *would* be considered interrogation under the Court's test. The second statement, although just as clearly a deliberate appeal to Innis to reveal the location of the gun, would presumably not be interrogation because (a) it was not in form a direct question and (b) it does not fit within the "reasonably likely to elicit an incriminating response" category that applies to indirect interrogation.

As this example illustrates, the Court's test creates an incentive for police to ignore a suspect's invocation of his rights in order to make continued attempts to extract information from him. If a suspect does not appear to be susceptible to a particular type of psychological pressure, the police are apparently free to exert that pressure on him despite his request for counsel, so long as they are careful not to punctuate their statements with question marks. And if, contrary to all reasonable expectations, the suspect makes an incriminating statement, that statement can be used against him at trial. The Court thus turns *Miranda*'s unequivocal rule against any interrogation at all into a trap in which unwary suspects may be caught by police deception.

Under my view of the correct standard, the judgment of the Rhode Island Supreme Court should be affirmed because the statements made within Innis' hearing were as likely to elicit a response as a direct question. * * *

POINTS FOR DISCUSSION

a. The Test for Interrogation

The Court in *Innis* held that "interrogation" means "either express questioning or its functional equivalent." The Court explained that the latter includes "any words or actions on the part of the police (other than those normally attendant to arrest and custody) that the police should know are reasonably likely to elicit an incriminating response from the suspect." Should it have been clear to the police that discussing a serious risk to disabled children would prompt a reasonable suspect to offer an incriminating response?

b. The Functional Equivalent of Express Questioning

How broad is the test for interrogation? Consider *Arizona v. Mauro*, 481 U.S. 520 (1987). Mr. Mauro was a suspect in the murder of his son. He was at the police station, the police had already given him the *Miranda* warnings, and he had invoked his right to counsel. His wife, who the police were questioning in another room, asked to speak with him. The police informed Mr. and Mrs. Mauro that they could speak together if an officer were present in the room. An officer then brought Mrs. Mauro into the room where Mr. Mauro was waiting, seated himself at a desk, and placed a tape recorder in plain sight on the desk. The officer recorded the couple's brief conversation, in which Mrs. Mauro expressed despair about their situation.

Mauro's defense at trial was that he had been insane at the time of the crime. In rebuttal, the prosecution played the tape of the meeting between Mauro and his wife, arguing that it demonstrated that Mauro was sane on the day of the murder. Mauro sought to suppress the recording on the ground that it was a product of police interrogation in violation of his *Miranda* rights. Mauro had indicated that he did not wish to be questioned further without a lawyer present, and he never waived his right to have a lawyer present. Accordingly, the police could not interrogate Mauro further unless his counsel was present or Mauro decided to initiate a conversation. The issue was whether the officers' subsequent actions in permitting Mrs. Mauro to speak with her husband and recording the conversation constituted impermissible "interrogation" within the meaning of *Miranda*. The Court concluded that because (1) the officer did not ask Mr. Mauro any questions during his conversation with his wife; (2) there was "no evidence that the officers sent Mrs. Mauro in to see her husband for the purpose of eliciting incriminating statements"; and (3) there was no evidence that the police's decision to allow Mrs. Mauro to see the defendant was "the kind of psychological ploy that properly could be treated as the functional equivalent of interrogation," the police had not interrogated Mauro within the meaning of *Miranda*.

C. DOUBLE JEOPARDY

The Fifth Amendment provides that no person shall "be subject for the same offence to be twice put in jeopardy of life or limb * * *." This is known as the protection against "double jeopardy." For example, the Double Jeopardy Clause would prohibit the United States from prosecuting a person for a crime for which he had previously been acquitted by a jury in a federal court. Likewise, the Clause would also prohibit the United States from prosecuting a person for a crime, obtaining a conviction and a sentence, and then prosecuting him again for the same crime.

The Supreme Court has explained the purpose of the Double Jeopardy Clause as follows: "[T]he framers of the Bill of Rights were concerned to protect defendants from oppression and from efforts to secure, through the callousness of repeated prosecutions, convictions for whose justice no man could vouch." *Green v. United States*, 355 U.S. 184, 218–19 (1957). Allowing the government to retry a defendant after an acquittal would be inequitable because a defendant who has been convicted does not have a right to insist on a retrial to seek a different result. Allowing multiple trials would also be oppressive because the government has almost unlimited resources. If the government adamantly wanted to secure a conviction, the government typically could afford to litigate a criminal charge two, three, four, or more times until a jury returned a guilty verdict. In contrast, criminal defendants rarely have the money and certainly never want to spend their time in multiple trials, even if each one results in an acquittal.

Some features of the protection afforded by the Double Jeopardy Clause are complex. Consider the following challenging examples:

1.   The defendant was tried in the United States District Court for the Northern District of Illinois on December 18, 1953, for robbery of the General Savings and Loan Association of Cicero, Illinois, a federally insured savings and

loan association, in violation of 18 U.S.C. § 2113. After a trial, the jury returned a verdict of acquittal. On January 8, 1954, an Illinois grand jury indicted the defendant. The facts recited in the Illinois indictment were substantially identical to those contained in the prior federal indictment. The Illinois indictment charged that these facts constituted a violation of Illinois's robbery statute. After a trial in the Criminal Court of Cook County, the defendant was convicted and sentenced to life imprisonment under the Illinois Habitual Criminal Statute. The defendant challenged the conviction, relying on the Double Jeopardy Clause as incorporated by the Fourteenth Amendment. Should the appellate court have reversed the conviction?

In *Bartkus v. Illinois*, 359 U.S. 121 (1959), the Supreme Court upheld the conviction. The Court noted that "state and federal courts have for years refused to bar a second trial even though there had been a prior trial by another government for a similar offense," and it refused to "disregard [a] long, unbroken, unquestioned course of impressive adjudication" of the question. The Court also noted a "practical justification" for this conclusion. The Court observed that in *Screws v. United States*, 325 U.S. 91 (1945), the federal government prosecuted the defendants, who were police officers, for violation of the federal Civil Rights Act for beating a prisoner to death. They were convicted under the act, which authorized maximum sentences of two years. The Court explained, however, that "the state crime there involved was a capital offense. Were the federal prosecution of a comparatively minor offense to prevent state prosecution of so grave an infraction of state law, the result would be a shocking and untoward deprivation of the historic right and obligation of the States to maintain peace and order within their confines. It would be in derogation of our federal system to displace the reserved power of States over state offenses by reason of prosecution of minor federal offenses by federal authorities beyond the control of the States." Do you agree that successive prosecutions, first by the federal government and then by a state government, should not violate the Double Jeopardy Clause? If the Double Jeopardy Clause did prohibit successive prosecutions, couldn't the federal government and the state government address the practical concerns expressed by the Court in *Bartkus* simply by discussing the matter and then deciding whether a state or federal prosecution was more important?

The rule that successive prosecutions by different sovereigns does not violate the Double Jeopardy Clause also allows separate prosecutions by different states. See *Heath v. Alabama*, 474 U.S. 82 (1985) (holding that Alabama could try a criminal suspect for murder even after he had been tried and convicted in Georgia of murdering the same victim). Is the permissibility of successive prosecutions by different sovereigns a problem with our federal system of government or a desirable feature?

The Supreme Court affirmed the rule that different sovereigns can prosecute the same person for the same criminal conduct in *Gamble v. United States*, 139 S.Ct. 1960 (2019).

2. The defendant pleaded guilty to burglary, a felony under Arkansas law. He was then sentenced under Arkansas's habitual offender statute, which provides that a defendant who is convicted of a felony and has previously been convicted of four or more felonies may be sentenced to an enhanced term of between 20 and 40 years. The habitual offender statute provides that the state must prove beyond a reasonable doubt, at a separate sentencing hearing, that the defendant has the requisite number of felony convictions. At the hearing, the prosecutor introduced certified copies of four prior felony convictions. Unbeknownst to the prosecutor and defense counsel, however, one of those four convictions had been pardoned by the Governor several years after its entry. The defendant indicated on cross-examination that he believed that the conviction had been pardoned, but under questioning from the court, the defendant agreed (erroneously) that the conviction had been commuted rather than pardoned. The parties did not pursue the matter any further, and the judge imposed an enhanced sentence. The appellate courts upheld the sentence, despite the defendant's argument that one of the convictions had in fact been pardoned.

Several years later, the defendant sought a writ of habeas corpus, again contending that the enhanced sentence was invalid because one of the prior convictions upon which it was based had been pardoned. At the district court's request, the state conducted an investigation of the prior conviction and concluded that it had in fact been pardoned. The court then held that the enhanced sentence was invalid. The state announced its intention to resentence the defendant as a habitual offender, relying on another prior conviction that had not been offered into evidence in the original sentencing hearing. The defendant has argued that to do so would violate the Double Jeopardy Clause. How should the court rule?

In *Lockhart v. Nelson*, 488 U.S. 33 (1988), the Court concluded that the Double Jeopardy Clause did not prevent the state from seeking to resentence the defendant under the habitual offender statute using the newly discovered evidence. The Court noted that the Clause's "general prohibition against successive prosecutions does not prevent the government from retrying a defendant who succeeds in getting his first conviction set aside, through direct appeal or collateral attack, because of some error in the proceedings leading to conviction." The Court acknowledged an exception to this rule: when a "conviction is reversed by an appellate court on the sole ground that the evidence was insufficient to sustain the jury's verdict, the Double Jeopardy Clause bars a retrial on the same charge." The Court reasoned, however, that "a reversal based solely on evidentiary insufficiency has fundamentally different implications, for double jeopardy purposes, than a reversal based on such ordinary 'trial errors' as the 'incorrect receipt or rejection of evidence.' While the former is in effect a finding 'that the government has failed to prove its case' against the defendant, the latter 'implies nothing with respect to the guilt or innocence of the defendant,' but is simply 'a determination that [he] has been convicted through a judicial *process* which is defective in some fundamental respect.' " Do you agree that the state should be permitted to resentence the defendant under the habitual offender statute under these circumstances?

3.   The defendant was indicted on five counts of violating the federal drug laws. The jury returned a verdict against the defendant on the second, third, and fifth counts only. Each of these counts charged a sale of morphine hydrochloride, a controlled substance, to the same purchaser. The second count charged a sale on a specified day of ten grams of the drug not in or from the original stamped package; the third count charged a sale on the following day of eight grams of the drug not in or from the original stamped package; and the fifth count charged the latter sale also as having been made not in pursuance of a written order of the purchaser as required by the statute. The court sentenced the defendant to five years' imprisonment on each count, with the terms of imprisonment to run consecutively.

The defendant appealed his convictions. He argued: (1) that the two sales charged in the second and third counts constitute a "single offense" within the meaning of the Double Jeopardy Clause, and thus could give rise to only one punishment, because they were close in time and made to the same person; and (2) that the sale charged in the third count as having been made not from the original stamped package, and the same sale charged in the fifth count as having been made not in pursuance of a written order of the purchaser, constitute the same offense, for which only a single penalty may be imposed consistently with the Double Jeopardy Clause. How should the court rule?

The Court has made clear that the protection of the Double Jeopardy Clause applies "both to successive punishments and to successive prosecutions for the same criminal offense." *United States v. Dixon*, 509 U.S. 688 (1993). But how does a court decide whether two different charges in an indictment constitute the "same criminal offense"? In *Blockburger v. United States*, 284 U.S. 299 (1932), the Court held that the convictions and separate sentences described above did not violate the Double Jeopardy Clause. The Court concluded that the second and third counts did not constitute the same offense because the federal drug law at issue "does not create the offense of engaging in the business of selling the forbidden drugs, but penalizes any sale made in the absence of either of the qualifying requirements set forth." Accordingly, "[e]ach of several successive sales constitutes a distinct offense, however closely they may follow each other."

The relationship between the third and fifth counts was different. The Court acknowledged that "there was but one sale" that constituted the basis for both charges. But the federal law at issue created "two distinct offenses": section 1 created the offense of selling any of the forbidden drugs except in or from the original stamped package; and section 2 created the offense of selling such drugs not in pursuance of a written order of the person to whom the drug is sold. The question was "whether, [two] sections [of the statute] being violated by the same act, the accused committed two offenses or only one." The Court concluded that the defendant had been properly charged for two separate offenses, and thus could be punished separately under the two sections of the Act, because "[e]ach of the offenses created requires proof of a different element." The Court declared that the "applicable rule is that, where the same act or transaction constitutes a violation of two distinct statutory provisions, the test to be applied to determine whether there are two offenses or only one, is whether each provision requires proof of a fact which the other does not." This test has come to be known as the "same-elements" test: it "inquires whether each offense contains an element not contained in the other; if not, they are the 'same offence' and the Double Jeopardy Clause bars additional punishment and successive prosecution." *Dixon*, 509 U.S. at 696. Do you agree that the government should have authority to punish a person for two crimes arising out of the same conduct?

Executive Summary of This Chapter

The **Fifth Amendment** specifies five important rights: the right to indictment by a grand jury before the federal government can prosecute; the right not to be tried twice for the same crime, otherwise known as the protection against "double jeopardy"; the privilege against self-incrimination; the right to due process; and the right to compensation when the government takes private property—a right coupled with a limitation that the government can take property only for public use (or at least only for a public purpose).

The **grand jury** right requires the federal government to convince a panel of the defendant's peers that there is sufficient evidence of a crime before proceeding with a prosecution. We considered the Takings Clause in Chapter 12.

The **Due Process Clause** of the Fifth Amendment requires the government to prove all of the elements of a criminal offense "beyond a reasonable doubt." *In re Winship* (1970). A lower **standard of proof,** such as proof by a mere preponderance of the evidence, would violate the Due Process Clause. In addition, the Clause requires the government to **disclose exculpatory evidence** to the defendant in a criminal case. *Brady v. Maryland* (1963).

The provision in the Fifth Amendment that states that no person shall be "compelled in any criminal case to be a witness against himself"—known as the **privilege against self-incrimination**—prevents the government from forcing a defendant to testify at his trial. The provision also "forbids either comment by the prosecution on the accused's silence or instructions by the court that such silence is evidence of guilt." *Griffin v. California* (1965). In addition, a trial court is required to instruct the jury that it should not infer anything from the defendant's decision not to testify if the defendant requests such an instruction. *Carter v. Kentucky* (1981).

The Fifth Amendment bars the admission into evidence at trial of **involuntary confessions**. *Bram v. United States* (1897); *Malloy v. Hogan* (1964). Accordingly, convictions that "rest solely upon confessions shown to have been extorted by officers of the state by brutality and violence" are unconstitutional, *Brown v. Mississippi* (1936), as are convictions based on confessions obtained during an interrogation that was "so inherently coercive that its very existence is irreconcilable with the possession of mental freedom by a lone suspect against whom its full coercive force is brought to bear." *Ashcraft v. Tennessee* (1944); *Watts v. Indiana* (1949); *Spano v. New York* (1959).

The Court has held that the privilege against self-incrimination imposes other limits on the power of the police to interrogate suspects. Before the police may interrogate a suspect who is in custody, the police must advise the suspect that he has the **right to remain silent** and the **right to have an attorney present** during the interrogation. *Miranda v. Arizona* (1966). These statements from the police are known as the "*Miranda* **warnings**." If a suspect who is in custody requests an attorney, the "interrogation must cease until an attorney is present." *Id.* A confession obtained in violation of these rules cannot be introduced into evidence. *Edwards v. Arizona* (1981). Although there originally was some question, the Court has clarified that "*Miranda* announced a constitutional rule that Congress may not supersede legislatively." *Dickerson v. United States* (2000).

A suspect is in "custody" within the meaning of *Miranda* only when he has been "deprived of his freedom of action"—and specifically his freedom to depart—"in any significant way." *Oregon v. Mathiason* (1977). "[W]hether a suspect is 'in custody' is an objective inquiry," which means that it does not focus on whether the suspect actually believed that he was free to terminate questioning and leave, but rather on whether a "reasonable person in the suspect's position" would believe that he can terminate the questioning and leave. *J.D.B. v. North Carolina* (2011).

For purposes of the *Miranda* requirement, "interrogation" means "either express questioning or its functional equivalent." The latter includes "any words or actions on the part of the police (other than those normally attendant to arrest and custody) that the police should know are reasonably likely to elicit an incriminating response from the suspect." *Rhode Island v. Innis* (1980).

Relatedly, the Sixth Amendment's right to counsel prohibits the government from using a confession in court that the government elicited from a defendant who has been indicted (or against whom adversary judicial proceedings have otherwise begun), if the defendant was represented by counsel and counsel was not present. *Massiah v. United States* (1964); *Escobedo v. Illinois* (1964).

The **Double Jeopardy Clause** of the Fifth Amendment prohibits the government from prosecuting a person for the same crime for which he had previously been tried in the same jurisdiction. *Green v. United States* (1957). The Clause does not, however, protect a person who has been prosecuted for a crime by one sovereign, such as the federal government, from prosecution by another sovereign, such as one of the states, for the same conduct. *Bartkus v. Illinois* (1959); *Gamble v. United States* (2019). Although the Clause prohibits the government from retrying a defendant after his conviction has been reversed by an appellate court "on the sole ground that the evidence was insufficient to sustain the jury's verdict," it does not prohibit retrial after "a reversal based on such ordinary 'trial errors' as the 'incorrect receipt or rejection of evidence.'" *Lockhart v. Nelson* (1988).

The Sixth Amendment

The Sixth Amendment provides:

"In all criminal prosecutions, the accused shall enjoy the right to a speedy and public trial, by an impartial jury of the State and district wherein the crime shall have been committed, which district shall have been previously ascertained by law, and to be informed of the nature and cause of the accusation; to be confronted with the witnesses against him; to have compulsory process for obtaining witnesses in his favor, and to have the Assistance of Counsel for his defence."

The Amendment thus explicitly guarantees seven rights in criminal prosecutions: the right to a speedy trial (i.e., a trial that takes place without undue delay after indictment); the right to a trial that members of the public may observe; the right to an impartial jury whose members come from the place where the charged offense or offenses were committed; the right to notice of the charges; the right to confront adverse witnesses (i.e., witnesses who testify for the prosecution, such as the alleged victim); the right to compulsory process (i.e., a summons or subpoena issued by the court) to ensure the attendance at trial of witnesses whom the defendant wishes to testify or to obtain other evidence necessary for putting on a defense; and the right to counsel (i.e., an attorney).

We focus in this chapter on the three rights about which the Court has had the most to say: the right to counsel, the right to a jury trial, and the right to confront adverse witnesses. We address them in turn in the sections that follow.

For the other four rights in the Sixth Amendment, a few words must suffice. The speedy trial right ensures that a person accused of a crime does not have to endure long periods of uncertainty about his fate and the societal opprobrium that might follow from the accusation of wrongdoing. Given the size of the country today and the volume of criminal prosecutions, however, it is not always possible for trials to take place immediately after charging or indictment. The Court has explained that a speedy trial claim is colorable only if the delay passes the "threshold dividing ordinary from 'presumptively prejudicial' delay, since, by definition, [a defendant] cannot complain that the government has denied him a 'speedy' trial if it has, in fact, prosecuted his case with customary promptness." *Doggett v. United States*, 505 U.S. 647, 652 (1992) (quoting *Barker v. Wingo,* 407 U.S. 514, 530–31 (1972)). The Court applies a four-part test in deciding whether there has been undue delay, considering the length of the delay, the reason for the delay, the defendant's promptness in asserting the right, and prejudice to the defendant. It takes a substantial, unreasonable delay to violate the speedy trial right. See, e.g., *Doggett* (holding that eight-and-a-half-year delay between indictment and trial violated the right).

The Sixth Amendment public trial right ensures that the government cannot seek to prosecute and punish a person in secret. The Court has explained that the "requirement of a public trial is for the benefit of the accused; that the public may see he is fairly dealt with and not unjustly condemned, and that the presence of interested spectators may keep his triers keenly alive to a sense of their responsibility and to the importance of their functions * * *." *Gannett Co. v. DePasquale*, 443 U.S. 368, 380 (1979). The Court has held, however, that the "right to an open trial may give way in certain cases to other rights or interests, such as the defendant's right to a fair trial or the government's interest in inhibiting disclosure of sensitive information." *Waller v. Georgia*, 467 U.S. 39, 45 (1984). The Court has made clear that "[s]uch circumstances will be rare," and that "the balance of interests must be struck with special care." *Id.* Only the defendant may assert a Sixth Amendment right to a public trial, but members of the public—including the press—have a qualified First Amendment right to attend some parts of a criminal trial. See *Press-Enterprise Co. v. Superior Court of California for Riverside Cty.*, 478 U.S. 1, 7 (1986).

The right to notice of the charges "compel[s] the Government to state and define specifically what it must prove in order to convict the defendant so that he can intelligently prepare to defend himself on each of the essential elements of the charge." *Turner v. United States*, 396 U.S. 398, 427–28 (1970). A criminal prosecution in which the government did not provide the accused with notice of the charges would be "Kafkaesque," meaning it would resemble Franz Kafka's dystopian novel, *The Trial*, in which the protagonist, an unassuming bank clerk called Joseph K., suffers the uncertainty of facing a trial without ever knowing the offenses he is accused of committing.

The right of compulsory process for securing the attendance of witnesses and the production of evidence ensures that a defendant can present an adequate defense. The right ensures that the defendant can present the testimony of reluctant witnesses, who might prefer not to be involved in a criminal trial. Justice Joseph Story explained that the Framers of the Bill of Rights wanted this right to be included in the Constitution in reaction to a "tyrannical and unjust" Act of Parliament that deprived defendants accused of treason and other capital crimes of the right to summon witnesses. See 3 Joseph Story, *Commentaries on the Constitution* § 1786 (1835) (cited in *Washington v. Texas*, 388 U.S. 14, 20 n.12 (1967)). Chief Justice Marshall decided in the treason trial of Aaron Burr that the right of compulsory process guarantees not only that a court will summon witnesses needed by the defendant, but also that the court will issues subpoenas for the production of physical evidence. In that case, Chief Justice Marshall granted Burr's motion for a subpoena requiring President Thomas Jefferson to produce a letter that allegedly incriminated Burr. See *United States v. Hubbell*, 530 U.S. 27, 54 (2000) (Thomas, J., dissenting) (citing *United States v. Burr*, 25 F. Cas. 30 (No. 14,692d) (CC Va. 1807)).

A. RIGHT TO COUNSEL

In the early eighteenth century, the common law allowed a defendant to hire an attorney to represent him at a criminal trial if the defendant was charged with a misdemeanor or treason, but not a felony other than treason. See *Betts v. Brady*, 316 U.S. 455, 466 (1942). But by the time the Bill of Rights was added to the Constitution in 1791, many states by statute or through a state constitutional provision allowed defendants to hire counsel to represent them in state misdemeanor and felony cases. See *id.* The Sixth Amendment guaranteed the right to counsel in federal criminal cases.

The right to counsel is very important. Criminal trials are complex. Government prosecutors are trained lawyers who know the applicable law and procedure and generally have experience with trial strategy. In contrast, most criminal defendants are not lawyers and would have little chance of presenting the best possible defense to criminal charges unless they could have an attorney represent them. Indeed, even lawyers hire attorneys with expertise in criminal law if they are charged with a crime.

Today, the right to counsel is an intricate subject. Before turning to some cases, a summary of some basic principles may be helpful. To begin, the Sixth Amendment right to counsel applies only in criminal prosecutions, not in civil lawsuits. See *Turner v. Rogers*, 564 U.S. 431 (2011). For example, suppose that a person does not pay required federal income taxes. If the IRS brings a civil lawsuit to obtain the money owed, the Sixth Amendment does not apply to the case. But if the United States brings criminal charges for federal tax evasion, the person has a right to counsel under the Sixth Amendment.

Although the Sixth Amendment—like all provisions of the Bill of Rights—originally applied only to federal prosecutions, the Supreme Court in a series of twentieth-century cases held that the Due Process Clause of the Fourteenth Amendment guarantees a right to counsel in state criminal prosecutions. See, e.g., *Powell v. Alabama*, 287 U.S. 45 (1932) (state capital cases); *Gideon v. Wainwright*, 372 U.S. 335 (1963) (state felony cases); *Argersinger v. Hamlin*, 407 U.S. 25 (1972) (misdemeanors). More about the incorporation of the right to counsel by the Fourteenth Amendment appears in the opinions included below.

As we saw in Chapter 14, the Fifth Amendment may provide a right to representation by an attorney at an early stage of a criminal investigation, such as custodial interrogation. See *Miranda v. Arizona*, 384 U.S. 436 (1966). In contrast, the Sixth Amendment right to counsel attaches only after criminal adversarial proceedings have begun. See *Moran v. Burbine*, 475 U.S. 412 (1986). Once the right to counsel has attached, the Sixth Amendment guarantees the defendant a right to hire an attorney, to consult with an attorney, and to have an attorney speak for the defendant. It further guarantees that the attorney must provide "effective assistance." *Strickland v. Washington*, 466 U.S. 668 (1984). The right to effective assistance of counsel extends not only through trial but also to a criminal defendant's first appeal as of right. See *Evitts v. Lucey*, 469 U.S. 387 (1985).

What if a criminal defendant cannot afford to hire an attorney? Must the government provide one to represent the defendant? The Supreme Court has said that "[t]here is considerable doubt that the Sixth Amendment itself, as originally drafted by the Framers of the Bill of Rights, contemplated any guarantee other than the right of an accused in a criminal prosecution in a federal court to employ a lawyer to assist in his defense." *Scott v. Illinois*, 440 U.S. 367, 370 (1979). Modern cases, however, say that the Sixth and Fourteenth Amendments require that "no indigent criminal defendant be sentenced to a term of imprisonment unless the State has afforded him the right to assistance of appointed counsel in his defense." See *id.* at 373–74. Sometimes government attorneys, who are independent from the prosecution and called "public defenders," represent indigent defendants. In other cases, the government pays private lawyers to represent the accused. In still other cases, private lawyers are appointed to represent indigent clients without compensation with the understanding that such service is a professional obligation incurred by being a member of the bar.

In the following cases, we look at how the Supreme Court adopted the positions that the right to counsel applies in state criminal prosecutions and that the right to counsel requires a state to provide an attorney to a defendant who cannot afford to hire one.

POWELL V. ALABAMA
287 U.S. 45 (1932)

MR. JUSTICE SUTHERLAND delivered the opinion of the Court.

The petitioners, hereinafter referred to as defendants, are negroes charged with the crime of rape, committed upon the persons of two white girls. The crime is said to have been committed on March 25, 1931. The indictment was returned in a state court [on] March 31, and the record recites that on the same day the defendants were arraigned and entered pleas of not guilty. * * * There was a severance upon the request of the state, and the defendants were tried in three several groups * * *. Each of the three trials was completed within a single day. * * * The juries found defendants guilty and imposed the death penalty upon all. * * * The judgments were affirmed by the state supreme court. * * *

The record shows that on the day when the offense is said to have been committed, these defendants, together with a number of other negroes, were upon a freight train on its way through Alabama. On the same train were seven white boys and the two white girls. A fight took place between the negroes and the white boys, in the course of which the white boys, with the exception of one named Gilley, were thrown off the train. A message was sent ahead, reporting the fight and asking that every negro be gotten off the train. The participants in the fight, and the two girls, were in an open gondola car. The two girls testified that each of them was assaulted by six different negroes in turn, and they identified the seven defendants as having been among the number. None of the white boys was called to testify, with the exception of Gilley, who was called in rebuttal.

Before the train reached Scottsboro, Ala., a sheriff's posse seized the defendants and two other negroes. Both girls and the negroes then were taken to Scottsboro, the county seat. Word of their coming and of the alleged assault had preceded them, and they were met at Scottsboro by a large crowd. [T]he attitude of the community was one of great hostility. The sheriff thought it necessary to call for the militia to assist in safeguarding the prisoners. * * * It is perfectly apparent that the proceedings, from beginning to end, took place in an atmosphere of tense, hostile, and excited public sentiment. During the entire time, the defendants were closely confined or were under military guard. The record does not disclose their ages, except that one of them was nineteen; but the record clearly indicates that most, if not all, of them were youthful, and they are constantly referred to as "the boys." They were ignorant and illiterate. All of them were residents of other states, where alone members of their families or friends resided.

The record shows that immediately upon the return of the indictment defendants were arraigned and pleaded not guilty. Apparently they were not asked whether they had, or were able to employ, counsel, or wished to have counsel appointed; or whether they had friends or relatives who might assist in that regard if communicated with. That it would not have been an idle ceremony to have given the defendants reasonable opportunity to communicate with their families and endeavor to obtain counsel is demonstrated by the fact that very soon after conviction, able counsel appeared in their behalf. * * *

It is hardly necessary to say that the right to counsel being conceded, a defendant should be afforded a fair opportunity to secure counsel of his own choice. Not only was that not done here, but such designation of counsel as was attempted was either so indefinite or so close upon the trial as to amount to a denial of effective and substantial aid in that regard. This will be amply demonstrated by a brief review of the record.

April 6, six days after indictment, the trials began. When the first case was called, the court inquired whether the parties were ready for trial. The state's attorney replied that he was ready to proceed. No one answered for the defendants or appeared to represent or defend them. Mr. Roddy, a Tennessee lawyer not a member of the local bar, addressed the court, saying that he had not been employed, but that people who were interested had spoken to him about the case. [Roddy explained that he had not been retained or paid to represent the defendants; he stated, "I have not prepared this case for trial and have only been called into it by people who are interested in these boys from Chattanooga. Now, they have not given me an opportunity to prepare the case and I am not familiar with the procedure in Alabama, but I merely came down here as a friend of the people who are interested and not as paid counsel." The trial judge stated, "I appointed all the members of the bar for the purpose of arraigning the defendants and then of course I anticipated them to continue to help them if no counsel appears." Mr. Moody, a local member of the bar, then stated, "I am willing to go ahead and help Mr. Roddy in anything I can do about it, under the circumstances."] And in this casual fashion the matter of counsel in a capital case was disposed of.

It thus will be seen that until the very morning of the trial no lawyer had been named or definitely designated to represent the defendants. Prior to that time, the trial judge had "appointed all the members of the bar" for the limited "purpose of arraigning the defendants." Whether they would represent the defendants thereafter, if no counsel appeared in their behalf, was a matter of speculation only, or, as the judge indicated, of mere anticipation on the part of the court. Such a designation, even if made for all purposes, would, in our opinion, have fallen far short of meeting, in any proper sense, a requirement for the appointment of counsel. How many lawyers were members of the bar does not appear; but, in the very nature of things, whether many or few, they would not, thus collectively named, have been given that clear appreciation of responsibility or impressed with that individual sense of duty which should and naturally would accompany the appointment of a selected member of the bar, specifically named and assigned.

That this action of the trial judge in respect of appointment of counsel was little more than an expansive gesture, imposing no substantial or definite obligation upon any one, is borne out by the fact that prior to the calling of the case for trial on April 6, a leading member of the local bar accepted employment on the side of the prosecution and actively participated in the trial. It is true that he said that before doing so he had understood Mr. Roddy would be employed as counsel for the defendants. [T]he circumstance lends emphasis to the conclusion that during perhaps the most critical period of the proceedings against these defendants, that is to say, from the time of their arraignment until the beginning of their trial, when consultation, thorough-going investigation and preparation were vitally important, the defendants did not have the aid of counsel in any real sense, although they were as much entitled to such aid during that period as at the trial itself.

Nor do we think the situation was helped by what occurred on the morning of the trial. * * * With [the] dubious understanding [about who would represent the defendants], the trials immediately proceeded. The defendants, young, ignorant, illiterate, surrounded by hostile sentiment, haled back and forth under guard of soldiers, charged with an atrocious crime regarded with especial horror in the community where they were to be tried, were thus put in peril of their lives within a few moments after counsel for the first time charged with any degree of responsibility began to represent them.

> **Make the Connection**
>
> When does the right to counsel arise? Upon arrest? During interrogation? After indictment? We considered these questions in Chapter 14, in our discussion of the privilege against self-incrimination.

* * * No attempt was made to investigate. No opportunity to do so was given. Under the circumstances disclosed, we hold that defendants were not accorded the right of counsel in any substantial sense. To decide otherwise, would simply be to ignore actualities. * * *

It is true that great and inexcusable delay in the enforcement of our criminal law is one of the grave evils of our time. * * * The prompt disposition of criminal cases is to be commended and encouraged. But in reaching that result a defendant, charged with a serious crime, must not be stripped of his right to have sufficient time to advise with counsel and prepare his defense. To do that is not to proceed promptly in the calm spirit of regulated justice but to go forward with the haste of the mob.

The question [which] it is our duty, and within our power, to decide, is whether the denial of the assistance of counsel contravenes the due process clause of the Fourteenth Amendment to the Federal Constitution.

If recognition of the right of a defendant charged with a felony to have the aid of counsel depended upon the existence of a similar right at common law as it existed in England when our Constitution was adopted, there would be great difficulty in maintaining it as necessary to due process. Originally, in England, a person charged with treason or felony was denied the aid of counsel, except in respect of legal questions which the accused himself might suggest. At the same time parties in civil cases and persons accused of misdemeanors were entitled to the full assistance of counsel. * * *

An affirmation of the right to the aid of counsel in petty offenses, and its denial in the case of crimes of the gravest character, where such aid is most needed, is so outrageous and so obviously a perversion of all sense of proportion that the rule was constantly, vigorously and sometimes passionately assailed by English statesmen and lawyers. * * * The [English] rule was rejected by the colonies [in the constitutions that they adopted before the ratification of the United States Constitution]. [I]n at least twelve of the thirteen colonies the rule of the English common law, in the respect now under consideration, had been definitely rejected and the right to counsel fully recognized in all criminal prosecutions, save that in one or two instances the right was limited to capital offenses or to the more serious crimes * * *.

Make the Connection

When the Court decided *Powell*, it had not yet settled on a consistent approach to deciding which rights are protected by the Due Process Clause of the Fourteenth Amendment. We considered the various approaches, and the process of incorporation, in Chapter 1.

The Sixth Amendment, in terms, provides that in all criminal prosecutions the accused shall enjoy the right "to have the Assistance of Counsel for his defence." * * * The fact that the right involved is of such a character that it cannot be denied without violating those "fundamental principles of liberty and justice which lie at the base of all our civil and political institutions" (*Hebert v. State of Louisiana*, 272

U.S. 312, 316 (1926)) is obviously one of those compelling considerations which must prevail in determining whether it is embraced within the due process clause of the Fourteenth Amendment ***. While the question has never been categorically determined by this court, a consideration of the nature of the right and a review of the expressions of this and other courts makes it clear that the right to the aid of counsel is of this fundamental character.

It never has been doubted by this court, or any other so far as we know, that notice and hearing are preliminary steps essential to the passing of an enforceable judgment, and that they, together with a legally competent tribunal having jurisdiction of the case, constitute basic elements of the constitutional requirement of due process of law. * * * What, then, does a hearing include? Historically and in practice, in our own country at least, it has always included the right to the aid of counsel when desired and provided by the party asserting the right. The right to be heard would be, in many cases, of little avail if it did not comprehend the right to be heard by counsel. Even the intelligent and educated layman has small and sometimes no skill in the science of law. If charged with crime, he is incapable, generally, of determining for himself whether the indictment is good or bad. He is

> **Take Note**
>
> In this paragraph and the ones that follow, the Court explains why a right to counsel is protected by the Due Process Clause. Is the Court's reasoning limited to cases involving serious criminal charges? To criminal (rather than civil) cases?

unfamiliar with the rules of evidence. Left without the aid of counsel he may be put on trial without a proper charge, and convicted upon incompetent evidence, or evidence irrelevant to the issue or otherwise inadmissible. He lacks both the skill and knowledge adequately to prepare his defense, even though he have a perfect one. He requires the guiding hand of counsel at every step in the proceedings against him. Without it, though he be not guilty, he faces the danger of conviction because he does not know how to establish his innocence. If that be true of men of intelligence, how much more true is it of the ignorant and illiterate, or those of feeble intellect. If in any case, civil or criminal, a state or federal court were arbitrarily to refuse to hear a party by counsel, employed by and appearing for him, it reasonably may not be doubted that such a refusal would be a denial of a hearing, and, therefore, of due process in the constitutional sense.

In the light of the facts outlined in the forepart of this opinion—the ignorance and illiteracy of the defendants, their youth, the circumstances of public hostility, the imprisonment and the close surveillance of the defendants by the military forces, the fact that their friends and families were all in other states and communication with them necessarily difficult, and above all that they stood in deadly peril of their lives—we think the failure of the trial court to give them reasonable time and opportunity to secure counsel was a clear denial of due process.

But passing that, and assuming their inability, even if opportunity had been given, to employ counsel, as the trial court evidently did assume, we are of opinion that, under the circumstances just stated, the necessity of counsel was so vital and imperative that the failure of the trial court to make an effective appointment of counsel was likewise a denial of due process within the meaning of the Fourteenth Amendment. Whether this would be so in other criminal prosecutions, or under other circumstances, we need not determine. All that it is necessary now to decide, as we do decide, is that in a capital case, where the defendant is unable to employ counsel, and is incapable adequately of making his own defense because of ignorance, feeble-mindedness, illiteracy, or the like, it is the duty of the court, whether requested or not, to assign counsel for him as a necessary requisite of due process of law; and that duty is not discharged by an assignment at such a time or under such circumstances as to preclude the giving of effective aid in the preparation and trial of the case. To hold otherwise would be to ignore the fundamental postulate, already adverted to, "that there are certain immutable principles of justice which inhere in the very idea of free government which no member of the Union may disregard." *Holden v. Hardy*, 169 U.S. 366 (1898). * * *

The judgments must be reversed and the causes remanded for further proceedings not inconsistent with this opinion.

[JUSTICE BUTLER's dissenting opinion, which JUSTICE MCREYNOLDS joined, has been omitted.]

POINTS FOR DISCUSSION

a.   The Facts of the Case

The Alabama prosecution of the defendants in *Powell* is a notorious example of racist enforcement of the criminal laws in the South in the first half of the twentieth century. The defendants—who became known as the "Scottsboro Boys"—were young black men who were accused of raping two young white women. Their arrest and trial were surrounded by the constant threat of mob violence. The defendants were not permitted to contact their families and, as the Court explains, were not permitted the time or opportunity to secure representation by a lawyer. The facts of the case undoubtedly help to explain why the Court was willing to reverse the conviction and declare a federal constitutional right to counsel in state capital cases.

b.   Due Process and the Right to Counsel

The Court in *Powell* held that the trial court violated the Due Process Clause of the Fourteenth Amendment by failing to give the defendants "reasonable time and opportunity to secure counsel." The Court reasoned that the assistance of counsel is vital to an effective defense to criminal charges. The need for counsel is most clear in cases—perhaps including *Powell*, though it is not clear from the Court's opinion—in which the defendant did not in fact commit the crime of which he has been accused. But is the presence of counsel also important in cases in which the defendant is in fact guilty? Would it be possible to assign counsel only to defendants who are innocent?

c.   The Appointment of Counsel

The Court in *Powell* also held that, under the circumstances, the trial court's failure "to make an effective appointment of counsel" violated the Due Process Clause. In reaching this conclusion, did it matter that the defendants were charged with a capital crime? That they were, in the Court's description, "young, ignorant, [and] illiterate"? That the trial appears to have been conducted in the midst of mob-like pressure, accompanied by threats of violence, from the community?

Who would bear the cost of appointment of counsel for an indigent defendant? The court? Or should lawyers be required to take such cases as a condition of membership in the bar?

What is the scope of the right to counsel that the Court announced in *Powell*? Six years after the Court's decision, it held in *Johnson v. Zerbst*, 304 U.S. 458 (1938), that the "Sixth Amendment withholds from federal courts, in all criminal proceedings, the power and authority to deprive an accused of his life or liberty unless he has or waives the assistance of counsel." The Court explained:

> "Since the Sixth Amendment constitutionally entitles one charged with crime to the assistance of counsel, compliance with this constitutional mandate is an essential jurisdictional prerequisite to a federal court's authority to deprive an accused of his life or liberty. When this right is properly waived, the assistance of counsel is no longer a necessary element of the court's jurisdiction to proceed to conviction and sentence. If the accused, however, is not represented by counsel and has not competently and intelligently waived his constitutional right, the Sixth Amendment stands as a jurisdictional bar to a valid conviction and sentence depriving him of his life or his liberty."

The consequence of this approach is that if a defendant in a federal criminal prosecution cannot afford a lawyer and has not waived the right to the assistance of counsel, he has a right under the Sixth Amendment to have a lawyer provided for him.

The Court in *Johnson* did not address whether the federal government has a constitutional obligation to compensate lawyers appointed to represent indigent defendants. In the years after the decision, courts typically did not do so, and lawyers accepted such cases as part of their professional obligation.

Johnson concerned the Sixth Amendment right to counsel in federal prosecutions. But what about the right to counsel under the Due Process Clause of the Fourteenth Amendment, which the Court recognized in *Powell*? Does it require states to provide lawyers for indigent criminal defendants who cannot afford representation?

In *Betts v. Brady*, 316 U.S. 455 (1942), the Court held that a person indicted for robbery in Maryland did not have a right under the Due Process Clause of the Fourteenth Amendment to have counsel appointed to represent him. The Court concluded that the Fourteenth Amendment does not incorporate the Sixth Amendment right to counsel and thus does not require the same set of rights afforded by the Sixth Amendment, as interpreted in *Johnson*. The Court considered the "common understanding of those who have lived under the Anglo-American system of law," as evidenced by state constitutional provisions and statutes, and concluded that "the considered judgment of the people, their representatives and their courts [was that] appointment of counsel is not a fundamental right, essential to a fair trial. On the contrary, the matter has generally been deemed one of legislative policy." Accordingly, the Court concluded that although "[e]very court has power, if it deems proper, to appoint counsel where that course seems to be required in the interest of fairness," the Due Process Clause does not "obligate[ ] the states * * * to furnish counsel in every such case."

The Court revisited and overruled *Betts* in the case that follows.

GIDEON V. WAINWRIGHT
372 U.S. 335 (1963)

MR. JUSTICE BLACK delivered the opinion of the Court.

Petitioner was charged in a Florida state court with having broken and entered a poolroom with intent to commit a misdemeanor. This offense is a felony under Florida law. Appearing in court without funds and without a lawyer, petitioner asked the court to appoint counsel for him, [but the court explained that Florida law permitted appointment of counsel only for defendants charged with capital offenses].

Put to trial before a jury, Gideon conducted his defense about as well as could be expected from a layman. He made an opening statement to the jury, cross-examined the State's witnesses, presented witnesses in his own defense, declined to testify himself, and made a short argument "emphasizing his innocence to the charge contained in the Information filed in this case." The jury returned a verdict of guilty, and petitioner was sentenced to serve five years in the state prison. Later, petitioner filed in the Florida Supreme Court this habeas corpus petition attacking his conviction and sentence on the ground that the trial court's refusal to appoint counsel for him denied him rights "guaranteed by the Constitution and the Bill of Rights by the United States Government." [The state court denied all relief.] Since 1942, when *Betts v. Brady*, 316 U.S. 455 (1942), was decided by a divided Court, the problem of a defendant's federal constitutional right to counsel in a state court has been a continuing source of controversy and litigation in both state and federal courts. To give this problem another review here, we granted certiorari. Since Gideon was proceeding *in forma pauperis*, we appointed counsel to represent him and requested both sides to discuss in their briefs and oral arguments the following: "Should this Court's holding in *Betts* be reconsidered?"

> **Definition**
>
> *In forma pauperis* means "in the form of a pauper." Courts usually waive filing costs for litigants proceeding *in forma pauperis* and before the Court's decision in *Gideon* sometimes appointed counsel to represent them.

The facts upon which Betts claimed that he had been unconstitutionally denied the right to have counsel appointed to assist him are strikingly like the facts upon which Gideon here bases his federal constitutional claim. * * * Since the facts and circumstances of the two cases are so nearly indistinguishable, we think the *Betts v. Brady* holding if left standing would require us to reject Gideon's claim that the Constitution guarantees him the assistance of counsel. Upon full reconsideration we conclude that *Betts v. Brady* should be overruled.

We have construed [the Sixth Amendment] to mean that in federal courts counsel must be provided for defendants unable to employ counsel unless the right is competently and intelligently waived. [*Johnson v. Zerbst*, 304 U.S. 458 (1938).] Betts argued that this right is extended to indigent defendants in state courts by the Fourteenth Amendment. * * * In order to decide whether the Sixth Amendment's guarantee of counsel is of this fundamental nature, the Court in *Betts* set out and considered "[r]elevant data on the subject . . . afforded by constitutional and statutory provisions subsisting in the colonies and the states prior to the inclusion of the Bill of Rights in the national Constitution, and in the constitutional, legislative, and judicial history of the states to the present date." 316 U.S., at 465. On the basis of this historical data the Court concluded that "appointment of counsel is not a fundamental right, essential to a fair trial." *Id.* at 471. * * * Plainly, had the Court concluded that appointment of counsel for an indigent criminal defendant was "a fundamental right, essential to a fair trial," it would have held that the Fourteenth Amendment requires appointment of counsel in a state court, just as the Sixth Amendment requires in a federal court.

We accept *Betts v. Brady*'s assumption, based as it was on our prior cases, that a provision of the Bill of Rights which is "fundamental and essential to a fair trial"

> **Make the Connection**
>
> We considered the doctrine of incorporation, and the application of provisions in the Bill of Rights to the states, in Chapter 1.

is made obligatory upon the States by the Fourteenth Amendment. We think the Court in *Betts* was wrong, however, in concluding that the Sixth Amendment's guarantee of counsel is not one of these fundamental rights. Ten years before *Betts v. Brady*, this Court, after full consideration of all the historical data examined in *Betts*, had unequivocally declared that "the right to the aid of counsel is of this fundamental character." *Powell v. Alabama*, 287 U.S. 45, 68 (1932). While the Court at the close of its *Powell* opinion did by its language, as this Court frequently does, limit its holding to the particular facts and circumstances of that case, its conclusions about the fundamental nature of the right to counsel are unmistakable. Several years later, in 1936, the Court reemphasized what it had said about the fundamental nature of the right to counsel in this language:

> "We concluded that certain fundamental rights, safeguarded by the first eight amendments against federal action, were also safeguarded against state action by the due process of law clause of the Fourteenth Amendment, and among them the fundamental right of the accused to the aid of counsel in a criminal prosecution." *Grosjean v. American Press Co.*, 297 U.S. 233, 243–244 (1936).

* * * The fact is that in deciding as it did—that "appointment of counsel is not a fundamental right, essential to a fair trial"—the Court in *Betts v. Brady* made an abrupt break with its own well-considered precedents. In returning to these old precedents, sounder we believe than the new, we but restore constitutional principles established to achieve a fair system of justice. Not only these precedents but also reason and reflection require us to recognize that in our adversary system of criminal justice, any person haled into court, who is too poor to hire a lawyer, cannot be assured a fair trial unless counsel is provided for him. This seems to us to be an obvious truth. Governments, both state and federal, quite properly spend vast sums of money to establish machinery to try defendants accused of crime. Lawyers to prosecute are everywhere deemed essential to protect the public's interest in an orderly society. Similarly, there are few defendants charged with crime, few indeed, who fail to hire the best lawyers they can get to prepare and present their defenses. That government hires lawyers to prosecute and defendants who have the money hire lawyers to defend are the strongest indications of the wide-spread belief that lawyers in criminal courts are necessities, not luxuries. The right of one charged with crime to counsel may not be deemed fundamental and essential to fair trials in some countries, but it is in ours. From the very beginning, our state and national constitutions and laws have laid great emphasis on procedural and substantive safeguards designed to assure fair trials before impartial tribunals in which every defendant stands equal before the law. This noble ideal cannot be realized if the poor man charged with crime has to face his accusers without a lawyer to assist him. A defendant's need for a lawyer is nowhere better stated than in the moving words of Mr. Justice Sutherland in *Powell v. Alabama*:

> "The right to be heard would be, in many cases, of little avail if it did not comprehend the right to be heard by counsel. Even the intelligent and educated layman has small and sometimes no skill in the science of law. If charged with crime, he is incapable, generally, of determining for himself whether the indictment is good or bad. He is unfamiliar with the rules of evidence. Left without the aid of counsel he may be put on trial without a proper charge, and convicted upon incompetent evidence, or evidence irrelevant to the issue or otherwise inadmissible. He lacks both the skill and knowledge adequately to prepare his defense, even though he have a perfect one. He requires the guiding hand of counsel at every step in the proceedings against him. Without it, though he be not guilty, he faces the danger of conviction because he does not know how to establish his innocence." 287 U.S., at 68–69.

The Court in *Betts v. Brady* departed from the sound wisdom upon which the Court's holding in *Powell v. Alabama* rested. Florida, supported by two other States, has asked that *Betts v. Brady* be left intact. Twenty-two States, as friends of the Court, argue that *Betts* was "an anachronism when handed down" and that it should now be overruled. We agree.

The judgment is reversed and the cause is remanded to the Supreme Court of Florida for further action not inconsistent with this opinion.

Mr. Justice Clark, concurring in the result.

In *Bute v. Illinois*, 333 U.S. 640 (1948), this Court found no special circumstances requiring the appointment of counsel but stated that "if these charges had been capital charges, the court would have been required, both by the state statute and the decisions of this Court interpreting the Fourteenth Amendment, to take some such steps." *Id.*, at 674. * * * At the next Term of the Court Mr. Justice Reed revealed that the Court was divided as to noncapital cases but that "the due process clause . . . requires counsel for all persons charged with serious crimes . . . ." *Uveges v. Pennsylvania*, 335 U.S. 437, 441 (1948). Finally, in *Hamilton v. Alabama*, 368 U.S. 52, 55 (1961), we said that "(w)hen one pleads to a capital charge without benefit of counsel, we do not stop to determine whether prejudice resulted." * * * It is [clear] from [these] cases, all decided after *Betts v. Brady*, 316 U.S. 455 (1942), that the Fourteenth Amendment requires [appointment of counsel] in all prosecutions for capital crimes. * * *

I must conclude here [that] the Constitution makes no distinction between capital and noncapital cases. The Fourteenth Amendment requires due process of law for the deprival of "liberty" just as for deprival of "life," and there cannot constitutionally be a difference in the quality of the process based merely upon a supposed difference in the sanction involved. How can the Fourteenth Amendment tolerate a procedure which it condemns in capital cases on the ground that deprival of liberty may be less onerous than deprival of life—a value judgment not universally accepted—or that only the latter deprival is irrevocable? I can find no acceptable rationalization for such a result, and I therefore concur in the judgment of the Court.

MR. JUSTICE HARLAN, concurring.

I agree that *Betts v. Brady* should be overruled, but consider it entitled to a more respectful burial than has been accorded, at least on the part of those of us who were not on the Court when that case was decided. I cannot subscribe to the view that *Betts v. Brady* represented "an abrupt break with its own well-considered precedents." In 1932, in *Powell v. Alabama*, 287 U.S. 45 (1932), a capital case, this Court declared that under the particular facts there presented—"the ignorance and illiteracy of the defendants, their youth, the circumstances of public hostility . . . and above all that they stood in deadly peril of their lives" (287 U.S., at 71)—the state court had a duty to assign counsel for the trial as a necessary requisite of due process of law. It is evident that these limiting facts were not added to the opinion as an after-thought; they were repeatedly emphasized, and were clearly regarded as important to the result.

Thus when this Court, a decade later, decided *Betts v. Brady*, it did no more than to admit of the possible existence of special circumstances in noncapital as well as capital trials, while at the same time insisting that such circumstances be shown in order to establish a denial of due process. * * *

The principles declared in *Powell* and in *Betts*, however, have had a troubled journey throughout the years that have followed first the one case and then the other. * * * In noncapital cases, the "special circumstances" rule has continued to exist in form while its substance has been substantially and steadily eroded. In the first decade after *Betts*, there were cases in which the Court found special circumstances to be lacking, but usually by a sharply divided vote. However, no such decision has been cited to us, and I have found none, after *Quicksall v. Michigan*, 339 U.S. 660 (1950) * * *. At the same time, there have been not a few cases in which special circumstances were found in little or nothing more than the "complexity" of the legal questions presented, although those questions were often of only routine difficulty. The Court has come to recognize, in other words, that the mere existence of a serious criminal charge constituted in itself special circumstances requiring the services of counsel at trial. In truth the *Betts v. Brady* rule is no longer a reality.

This evolution, however, appears not to have been fully recognized by many state courts, in this instance charged with the front-line responsibility for the enforcement of constitutional rights. To continue a rule which is honored by this Court only with lip service is not a healthy thing and in the long run will do disservice to the federal system. The special circumstances rule has been formally abandoned in capital cases, and the time has now come when it should be similarly abandoned in noncapital cases, at least as to offenses which, as the one involved here, carry the possibility of a substantial prison sentence. (Whether the rule should extend to all criminal cases need not now be decided.) This indeed does no more than to make explicit something that has long since been foreshadowed in our decisions.

[JUSTICE DOUGLAS's concurring opinion has been omitted.]

POINTS FOR DISCUSSION

a.   Right to Counsel and Right to Appointed Counsel

The Sixth Amendment provides that "the accused shall enjoy the right * * * to have the Assistance of Counsel for his defence." In *Betts v. Brady*, the Court acknowledged that our common-law tradition, dating to the colonial era, was "intended to do away with the rules which denied representation, in whole or in part, by counsel in criminal prosecutions," but the Court concluded that the prevailing rules "were not aimed to compel the state to provide counsel for a defendant." In *Gideon*, in contrast, the Court concluded that the Fourteenth Amendment not only requires the states to permit criminal defendants to use a lawyer, but also requires the states to appoint one when those defendants cannot afford one. Which approach would have been a more natural reading of the text of the Sixth Amendment in 1791? Do you think the that system would function effectively (and could be trusted to reach just and reliable results) if defendants who cannot afford a lawyer were not entitled to have one appointed for them? If the Constitution does not require the government to appoint lawyers, would that mean that the government cannot appoint them?

b.   When Does the Sixth Amendment Right to Counsel Apply?

The defendant in *Gideon* was prosecuted for committing a felony, and after his conviction he was sentenced to five years in prison. Would the case have been any different if he had been charged with a misdemeanor and faced the prospect of a much less severe sentence? In *Argersinger v. Hamlin*, 407 U.S. 25 (1972), the Court considered a claim by an indigent man who had been convicted in Florida of carrying a concealed weapon, a misdemeanor subject to a maximum penalty of six months in jail and a $1,000 fine. The trial court declined to appoint counsel, and the defendant was convicted and sentenced to serve ninety days in jail. The Supreme Court reversed the conviction, unanimously holding that "no person may be imprisoned for any offense, whether classified as petty, misdemeanor, or felony, unless he was represented by counsel at his trial." Accordingly, the right identified in *Gideon* extends to all defendants who face the possibility of a jail sentence. Do you agree that the state should have to provide representation even in prosecutions for minor or petty offenses?

c.   The Sixth Amendment Right to Counsel and the Fifth Amendment

In Chapter 14, we saw that the Court has construed the Fifth Amendment's privilege against self-incrimination to require the police to provide warnings to suspects in custody before interrogating them. See *Miranda v. Arizona*, 384 U.S. 436 (1966). Those warnings must inform the suspect that he has the right to attorney. Once informed of his rights, the suspect can waive them and speak with the police. How does the Fifth Amendment privilege against self-incrimination—and the important role that the right to counsel plays in making the privilege effective—interact with the Sixth Amendment right to counsel?

Imagine that the police suspect an indigent person of murder. They bring him to the police station and read him his *Miranda* warnings. He waives his rights and makes several incriminating statements. The police then arrest him, and at his arraignment the court appoints counsel to represent him. Before he meets with his appointed attorney, the police visit the defendant in prison, read him the *Miranda* warnings again, and then ask him to accompany him to the crime scene to locate the murder weapon. He agrees to go and leads the police to the murder weapon.

Have the police violated the defendant's right to counsel? After all, counsel had already been appointed to represent the defendant when the police interrogated him the second time, but the defendant had not had an opportunity to meet the lawyer, and the lawyer was not present to advise the defendant. In *Michigan v. Jackson,* 475 U.S. 625 (1986), the Court held that "a defendant who has been formally charged with a crime and who has requested appointment of counsel at his arraignment" cannot be subject to uncounseled interrogation unless he initiates "exchanges or conversations with the police." But the Court overruled *Jackson* in *Montejo v. Louisiana,* 556 U.S. 778 (2009), reasoning that a represented defendant can knowingly and voluntarily waive the right to have an attorney present during interrogation and thus waive his Sixth Amendment rights; the Court saw "no reason categorically to distinguish an unrepresented defendant from a represented one."

d. Effective Assistance of Counsel

The Court in *Gideon* required the appointment of counsel for defendants who cannot afford one. Is there a constitutional right to the appointment of a *good* lawyer? The Court has grappled for years with this question. The Court has made clear that the proper standard for attorney performance is that of "reasonably effective assistance." *Strickland v. Washington,* 466 U.S. 668 (1984). In applying this standard, the Court begins with "a strong presumption that counsel's conduct falls within the wide range of reasonable professional assistance," and grants relief only if the defendant can overcome this presumption and prove that any deficiency in representation was not harmless. This standard is difficult for defendants. Although defendants frequently raise ineffective assistance of counsel as a ground for reversing their convictions, they seldom prevail. One study found: "A claim of ineffective assistance of counsel in trial or appellate proceedings was raised in about half of the 2,384 noncapital cases [studied]. Only one of those claims was granted; that grant was later reversed." Joseph L. Hoffmann & Nancy J. King, *Rethinking the Federal Role in State Criminal Justice,* 84 N.Y.U. L. Rev. 791, 811 (2009). Does this finding suggest that the *Strickland* standard is unrealistic? Or does it indicate that most defendants actually receive effective assistance of counsel? Can you come up with objective ways to measure whether an attorney's representation of a criminal defendant was "effective"?

B. RIGHT TO A JURY

The Sixth Amendment guarantees a right to an impartial jury. In this section, we consider three questions that arise in the interpretation of that right. First, when does the right apply? Second, what limits does the Constitution impose on the selection of jurors to serve on juries? Third, what matters must juries resolve in the course of a criminal prosecution?

The text of the Sixth Amendment suggests that a defendant should have a right to a jury "[i]n *all* criminal prosecutions" (emphasis added). But the Supreme Court has held that criminal defendants do not have a Sixth Amendment right to a jury in all cases. Specifically, they do not have a right to a jury trial when charged only with "petty offenses." *Duncan v. Louisiana*, 391 U.S. 145 (1968). What is a "petty offense"? The Supreme Court has explained:

> "[T]o determine whether an offense is petty, we consider the maximum penalty attached to the offense. This criterion is considered the most relevant with which to assess the character of an offense, because it reveals the legislature's judgment about the offense's severity. * * * While penalties such as probation or a fine may infringe on a defendant's freedom, the deprivation of liberty imposed by imprisonment makes that penalty the best indicator of whether the legislature considered an offense to be "petty" or "serious." An offense carrying a maximum prison term of six months or less is presumed petty, unless the legislature has authorized additional statutory penalties so severe as to indicate that the legislature considered the offense serious.

Lewis v. United States, 518 U.S. 322, 325 (1996). Consider in reading the following cases why the Supreme Court has determined that the Sixth Amendment does not apply to petty offenses.

DUNCAN V. STATE OF LOUISIANA

391 U.S. 145 (1968)

MR. JUSTICE WHITE delivered the opinion of the Court.

Appellant, Gary Duncan, was convicted of simple battery in the Twenty-fifth Judicial District Court of Louisiana. Under Louisiana law simple battery is a misdemeanor, punishable by a maximum of two years' imprisonment and a $300 fine. Appellant sought trial by jury, but because the Louisiana Constitution grants jury trials only in cases in which capital punishment or imprisonment at hard labor may be imposed, the trial judge denied the request. Appellant was convicted and sentenced to serve 60 days in the parish prison and pay a fine of $150. Appellant sought review in the Supreme Court of Louisiana, asserting that the denial of jury trial violated rights guaranteed to him by the United States Constitution. The [state] Supreme Court * * * denied appellant a writ of certiorari. [A]ppellant sought review in this Court, alleging that the Sixth and Fourteenth Amendments to the United States Constitution secure the right to jury trial in state criminal prosecutions where a sentence as long as two years may be imposed.

Appellant was 19 years of age when tried. While driving on Highway 23 in Plaquemines Parish on October 18, 1966, he saw two younger cousins engaged in a conversation by the side of the road with four white boys. Knowing his cousins, Negroes who had recently transferred to a formerly all-white high school, had reported the occurrence of racial incidents at the school, Duncan stopped the car, got out, and approached the six boys. At trial the white boys and a white onlooker testified, as did appellant and his cousins. The testimony was in dispute on many points, but the witnesses agreed that appellant and the white boys spoke to each other, that appellant encouraged his cousins to break off the encounter and enter his car, and that appellant was about to enter the car himself for the purpose of driving away with his cousins. The whites testified that just before getting in the car appellant slapped Herman Landry, one of the white boys, on the elbow. The Negroes testified that appellant had not slapped Landry, but had merely touched him. The trial judge concluded that the State had proved beyond a reasonable doubt that Duncan had committed simple battery, and found him guilty.

* * * Because we believe that trial by jury in criminal cases is fundamental to the American scheme of justice, we hold that the Fourteenth Amendment guarantees a right of jury trial in all criminal cases which—were they to be tried in a federal court—would come within the Sixth Amendment's guarantee.[14] Since we consider the appeal

> **Make the Connection**
>
> The Court explains here and in the footnote the standard for concluding that a right mentioned in the Bill of Rights is "incorporated" by the Due Process Clause of the Fourteenth Amendment. We considered this doctrine in Chapter 1.

---

[14] In one sense recent cases applying provisions of the first eight Amendments to the States represent a new approach to the "incorporation" debate. Earlier the Court can be seen as having asked, when inquiring into whether some particular procedural safeguard was required of a State, if a civilized system could be imagined that would not accord the particular protection. [See, e.g., *Palko v. State of Connecticut*, 302 U.S. 319, 325 (1937).] The recent cases, on the other hand, have proceeded upon the valid assumption that state criminal processes are not imaginary and theoretical schemes but actual systems bearing virtually every characteristic of the common-law system that has been developing contemporaneously in England and in this country. The question thus is whether given this kind of system a particular procedure is fundamental—whether, that is, a procedure is necessary to an Anglo-American regime of ordered liberty. It is this sort of inquiry that can justify the conclusions that state courts must exclude evidence seized in violation of the Fourth Amendment, *Mapp v. State of Ohio*, 367 U.S. 643 (1961); that state prosecutors may not comment on a defendant's failure to testify, *Griffin v. State of California*, 380 U.S. 609 (1965); and that criminal punishment may not be imposed for the status of narcotics addiction, *Robinson v. State of California*, 370 U.S. 660 (1962). Of immediate relevance for this case are the Court's holdings that the States must comply with certain provisions of the Sixth Amendment, specifically that the States may not refuse a speedy trial, confrontation of witnesses, and the assistance, at state expense if necessary, of counsel. Of each of these determinations that a constitutional provision originally written to bind the Federal Government should bind the States as well it might be said that the limitation in question is not necessarily fundamental to fairness in every criminal system that might be imagined but is fundamental in the context of the criminal processes maintained by the American States.

When the inquiry is approached in this way the question whether the States can impose criminal punishment without granting a jury trial appears quite different from the way it appeared in the older cases opining that States might abolish jury trial. See, e.g., *Maxwell v. Dow*, 176 U.S. 581 (1900). A criminal process before us to be such a case, we hold that the Constitution was violated when appellant's demand for jury trial was refused.

The history of trial by jury in criminal cases has been frequently told. It is sufficient for present purposes to say that by the time our Constitution was written, jury trial in criminal cases had been in existence in England for several centuries and carried impressive credentials traced by many to Magna Carta. Its preservation and proper operation as a protection against arbitrary rule were among the major objectives of the revolutionary settlement which was expressed in the Declaration and Bill of Rights of 1689. * * *

Jury trial came to America with English colonists, and received strong support from them. Royal interference with the jury trial was deeply resented. Among the resolutions adopted by the First Congress of the American Colonies (the Stamp Act Congress) on October 19, 1765—resolutions deemed by their authors to state "the most essential rights and liberties of the colonists"—was the declaration: "That trial by jury is the inherent and invaluable right of every British subject in these colonies."

The First Continental Congress, in the resolve of October 14, 1774, objected to trials before judges dependent upon the Crown alone for their salaries and to trials in England for alleged crimes committed in the colonies; the Congress therefore declared: "That the respective colonies are entitled to the common law of England, and more especially to the great and inestimable privilege of being tried by their peers of the vicinage, according to the course of that law."

The Declaration of Independence stated solemn objections to the King's making "judges dependent on his will alone, for the tenure of their offices, and the amount and payment of their salaries," to his "depriving us in many cases, of the benefits of Trial by Jury," and to his "transporting us beyond Seas to be tried for pretended offenses." The Constitution itself, in Art. III, § 2, commanded: "The Trial of all Crimes, except in Cases of Impeachment, shall be by Jury; and such Trial shall be held in the State where the said Crimes shall have been committed."

Objections to the Constitution because of the absence of a bill of rights were met by the immediate submission and adoption of the Bill of Rights. Included was

---

which was fair and equitable but used no juries is easy to imagine. It would make use of alternative guarantees and protections which would serve the purposes that the jury serves in the English and American systems. Yet no American State has undertaken to construct such a system. Instead, every American State, including Louisiana, uses the jury extensively, and imposes very serious punishments only after a trial at which the defendant has a right to a jury's verdict. In every State, including Louisiana, the structure and style of the criminal process—the supporting framework and the subsidiary procedures—are of the sort that naturally complement jury trial, and have developed in connection with and in reliance upon jury trial.

the Sixth Amendment which, among other things, provided: "In all criminal prosecutions, the accused shall enjoy the right to a speedy and public trial, by an impartial jury of the State and district wherein the crime shall have been committed." The constitutions adopted by the original States guaranteed jury trial. Also, the constitution of every State entering the Union thereafter in one form or another protected the right to jury trial in criminal cases.

Even such skeletal history is impressive support for considering the right to jury trial in criminal cases to be fundamental to our system of justice, an importance frequently recognized in the opinions of this Court. * * * Jury trial continues to receive strong support. The laws of every State guarantee a right to jury trial in serious criminal cases; no State has dispensed with it; nor are there significant movements underway to do so. * * *

We are aware of prior cases in this Court in which the prevailing opinion contains statements contrary to our holding today that the right to jury trial in serious criminal cases is a fundamental right and hence must be recognized by the States as part of their obligation to extend due process of law to all persons within their jurisdiction. Louisiana relies especially on *Maxwell v. Dow*, 176 U.S. 581 (1900); *Palko v. State of Connecticut*, 302 U.S. 319 (1937); and *Snyder v. Commonwealth of Massachusetts*, 291 U.S. 97 (1934). None of these cases, however, dealt with a State which had purported to dispense entirely with a jury trial in serious criminal cases. *Maxwell* held that no provision of the Bill of Rights applied to the States— a position long since repudiated—and that the Due Process Clause of the Fourteenth Amendment did not prevent a State from trying a defendant for a noncapital offense with fewer than 12 men on the jury. It did not deal with a case in which no jury at all had been provided. In neither *Palko* nor *Snyder* was jury trial actually at issue, although both cases contain important dicta asserting that the right to jury trial is not essential to ordered liberty and may be dispensed with by the States regardless of the Sixth and Fourteenth Amendments. These observations, though weighty and respectable, are nevertheless dicta, unsupported by holdings in this Court that a State may refuse a defendant's demand for a jury trial when he is charged with a serious crime. Perhaps because the right to jury trial was not directly at stake, the Court's remarks about the jury in *Palko* and *Snyder* took no note of past or current developments regarding jury trials, did not consider its purposes and functions, attempted no inquiry into how well it was performing its job, and did not discuss possible distinctions between civil and criminal cases. * * * Respectfully, we reject the prior dicta regarding jury trial in criminal cases.

> **Take Note**
>
> The Court explains in this paragraph why the right to trial by jury is an important protection for criminal defendants. Do you find the arguments convincing? Can you think of ways in which juries might make convictions of defendants even more likely?

The guarantees of jury trial in the Federal and State Constitutions reflect a profound judgment about the way in which law should be enforced and justice administered. A right to jury trial is granted to criminal defendants in order to prevent oppression by the Government. Those who wrote our constitutions knew from history and experience that it was necessary to protect against unfounded criminal charges brought to eliminate enemies and against judges too responsive to the voice of higher authority. The framers of the constitutions strove to create an independent judiciary but insisted upon further protection against arbitrary action. Providing an accused with the right to be tried by a jury of his peers gave him an inestimable safeguard against the corrupt or overzealous prosecutor and against the compliant, biased, or eccentric judge. If the defendant preferred the common-sense judgment of a jury to the more tutored but perhaps less sympathetic reaction of the single judge, he was to have it. Beyond this, the jury trial provisions in the Federal and State Constitutions reflect a fundamental decision about the exercise of official power—a reluctance to entrust plenary powers over the life and liberty of the citizen to one judge or to a group of judges. Fear of unchecked power, so typical of our State and Federal Governments in other respects, found expression in the criminal law in this insistence upon community participation in the determination of guilt or innocence. The deep commitment of the Nation to the right of jury trial in serious criminal cases as a defense against arbitrary law enforcement qualifies for protection under the Due Process Clause of the Fourteenth Amendment, and must therefore be respected by the States.

Of course jury trial has "its weaknesses and the potential for misuse," *Singer v. United States*, 380 U.S. 24, 35 (1965). We are aware of the long debate, especially in this century, among those who write about the administration of justice, as to the wisdom of permitting untrained laymen to determine the facts in civil and criminal proceedings. Although the debate has been intense, with powerful voices on either side, most of the controversy has centered on the jury in civil cases. * * * In addition, at the heart of the dispute have been express or implicit assertions that juries are incapable of adequately understanding evidence or determining issues of fact, and that they are unpredictable, quixotic, and little better than a roll of dice. Yet, the most recent and exhaustive study of the jury in criminal cases concluded that juries do understand the evidence and come to sound conclusions in most of the cases presented to them and that when juries differ with the result at which the judge would have arrived, it is usually because they are serving some of the very purposes for which they were created and for which they are now employed.

The State of Louisiana urges that holding that the Fourteenth Amendment assures a right to jury trial will cast doubt on the integrity of every trial conducted without a jury. Plainly, this is not the import of our holding. Our conclusion is that in the American States, as in the federal judicial system, a general grant of jury trial for serious offenses is a fundamental right, essential for preventing miscarriages of justice and for assuring that fair trials are provided for all defendants. We would not assert, however, that every criminal trial—or any particular trial—held before a judge alone is unfair or that a defendant may never be as fairly treated by a judge as he would be by a jury. Thus we hold no constitutional doubts about the practices, common in both federal and state courts, of accepting waivers of jury trial and prosecuting petty crimes without extending a right to jury trial. * * *

Louisiana's final contention is that even if it must grant jury trials in serious criminal cases, the conviction before us is valid and constitutional because here the petitioner was tried for simple battery and was sentenced to only 60 days in the parish prison. We are not persuaded. It is doubtless true that there is a category of petty crimes or offenses which is not subject to the Sixth Amendment jury trial provision and should not be subject to the Fourteenth Amendment jury trial requirement here applied to the States. * * * In the case before us the Legislature of Louisiana has made simple battery a criminal offense punishable by imprisonment for up to two years and a fine.

> **Take Note**
>
> The Court declares here that certain petty crimes do not give rise to a right to a jury trial. How does the Court distinguish between petty crimes and serious offenses?

The question, then, is whether a crime carrying such a penalty is an offense which Louisiana may insist on trying without a jury.

We think not. So-called petty offenses were tried without juries both in England and in the Colonies and have always been held to be exempt from the otherwise comprehensive language of the Sixth Amendment's jury trial provisions. There is no substantial evidence that the Framers intended to depart from this established common-law practice, and the possible consequences to defendants from convictions for petty offenses have been thought insufficient to outweigh the benefits to efficient law enforcement and simplified judicial administration resulting from the availability of speedy and inexpensive nonjury adjudications. These same considerations compel the same result under the

Fourteenth Amendment. Of course the boundaries of the petty offense category have always been ill-defined, if not ambulatory. In the absence of an explicit constitutional provision, the definitional task necessarily falls on the courts, which must either pass upon the validity of legislative attempts to identify those petty offenses which are exempt from jury trial or, where the legislature has not addressed itself to the problem, themselves face the question in the first instance. In either case it is necessary to draw a line in the spectrum of crime, separating petty from serious infractions. This process, although essential, cannot be wholly satisfactory, for it requires attaching different consequences to events which, when they lie near the line, actually differ very little.

In determining whether the length of the authorized prison term or the seriousness of other punishment is enough in itself to require a jury trial, we * * * refer to objective criteria, chiefly the existing laws and practices in the Nation. In the federal system, petty offenses are defined as those punishable by no more than six months in prison and a $500 fine. In 49 of the 50 States crimes subject to trial without a jury, which occasionally include simple battery, are punishable by no more than one year in jail. Moreover, in the late 18th century in America crimes triable without a jury were for the most part punishable by no more than a six-month prison term, although there appear to have been exceptions to this rule. We need not, however, settle in this case the exact location of the line between petty offenses and serious crimes. It is sufficient for our purposes to hold that a crime punishable by two years in prison is, based on past and contemporary standards in this country, a serious crime and not a petty offense. Consequently, appellant was entitled to a jury trial and it was error to deny it.

The judgment below is reversed and the case is remanded for proceedings not inconsistent with this opinion.

MR. JUSTICE HARLAN, whom MR. JUSTICE STEWART joins, dissenting.

Every American jurisdiction provides for trial by jury in criminal cases. The question before us is not whether jury trial is an ancient institution, which it is; nor whether it plays a significant role in the administration of criminal justice, which it does; nor whether it will endure, which it shall. The question in this case is whether the State of Louisiana, which provides trial by jury for all felonies, is prohibited by the Constitution from trying charges of simple battery to the court alone. In my view, the answer to that question, mandated alike by our constitutional history and by the longer history of trial by jury, is clearly "no."

* * * If the problem is to discover and articulate the rules of fundamental fairness in criminal proceedings, there is no reason to assume that the whole body

of rules developed in this Court constituting Sixth Amendment jury trial must be regarded as a unit. The requirement of trial by jury in federal criminal cases has given rise to numerous subsidiary questions respecting the exact scope and content of the right. It surely cannot be that every answer the Court has given, or will give, to such a question is attributable to the Founders; or even that every rule announced carries equal conviction of this Court; still less can it be that every such subprinciple is equally fundamental to ordered liberty.

Examples abound. I should suppose it obviously fundamental to fairness that a "jury" means an "impartial jury." I should think it equally obvious that the rule, imposed long ago in the federal courts, that "jury" means "jury of exactly twelve," is not fundamental to anything: there is no significance except to mystics in the number 12. Again, trial by jury has been held to require a unanimous verdict of jurors in the federal courts, although unanimity has not been found essential to liberty in Britain, where the requirement has been abandoned.

> **Food for Thought**
>
> Do you agree that it is not fundamentally unfair to convict a person with a non-unanimous jury verdict? We consider this question in the points for discussion that follow.

One further example is directly relevant here. The co-existence of a requirement of jury trial in federal criminal cases and a historic and universally recognized exception for "petty crimes" has compelled this Court, on occasion, to decide whether a particular crime is petty, or is included within the guarantee. Individual cases have been decided without great conviction and without reference to a guiding principle. The Court today holds, for no discernible reason, that if and when the line is drawn its exact location will be a matter of such fundamental importance that it will be uniformly imposed on the States. This Court is compelled to decide such obscure borderline questions in the course of administering federal law. This does not mean that its decisions are demonstrably sounder than those that would be reached by state courts and legislatures, let alone that they are of such importance that fairness demands their imposition throughout the Nation.

* * * The Court has held, properly I think, that in an adversary process it is a requisite of fairness, for which there is no adequate substitute, that a criminal defendant be afforded a right to counsel and to cross-examine opposing witnesses. But it simply has not been demonstrated, nor, I think, can it be demonstrated, that trial by jury is the only fair means of resolving issues of fact.

The jury is of course not without virtues. It affords ordinary citizens a valuable opportunity to participate in a process of government, an experience fostering, one hopes, a respect for law. It eases the burden on judges by enabling them to share a part of their sometimes awesome responsibility. A jury may, at times, afford a higher justice by refusing to enforce harsh laws (although it necessarily does so haphazardly, raising the questions whether arbitrary enforcement of harsh laws is better than total enforcement, and whether the jury system is to be defended on the ground that jurors sometimes disobey their oaths). And the jury may, or may not, contribute desirably to the willingness of the general public to accept criminal judgments as just.

It can hardly be gainsaid, however, that the principal original virtue of the jury trial—the limitations a jury imposes on a tyrannous judiciary—has largely disappeared. We no longer live in a medieval or colonial society. Judges enforce laws enacted by democratic decision, not by regal fiat. They are elected by the people or appointed by the people's elected officials, and are responsible not to a distant monarch alone but to reviewing courts, including this one.

The jury system can also be said to have some inherent defects, which are multiplied by the emergence of the criminal law from the relative simplicity that existed when the jury system was devised. It is a cumbersome process, not only imposing great cost in time and money on both the State and the jurors themselves, but also contributing to delay in the machinery of justice. Untrained jurors are presumably less adept at reaching accurate conclusions of fact than judges, particularly if the issues are many or complex. And it is argued by some that trial by jury, far from increasing public respect for law, impairs it: the average man, it is said, reacts favorably neither to the notion that matters he knows to be complex are being decided by other average men, nor to the way the jury system distorts the process of adjudication.

That trial by jury is not the only fair way of adjudicating criminal guilt is well attested by the fact that it is not the prevailing way [of resolving criminal cases.] Two experts have estimated that, of all prosecutions for crimes triable to a jury, 75% are settled by guilty plea and 40% of the remainder are tried to the court. * * * I therefore see no reason why this Court should reverse the conviction of appellant, absent any suggestion that his particular trial was in fact unfair, or compel the State of Louisiana to afford jury trial in an as yet unbounded category of cases that can, without unfairness, be tried to a court.

Indeed, even if I were persuaded that trial by jury is a fundamental right in some criminal cases, I could see nothing fundamental in the rule, not yet formulated by the Court, that places the prosecution of appellant for simple battery within the category of "jury crimes" rather than "petty crimes." * * * [T]hrough the long course of British and American history, summary procedures have been used in a varying category of lesser crimes as a flexible response to the burden jury trial would otherwise impose. * * * The reason for the historic exception for relatively minor crimes is the obvious one: the burden of jury trial was thought to outweigh its marginal advantages. Exactly why the States should not be allowed to make continuing adjustments, based on the state of their criminal dockets and the difficulty of summoning jurors, simply escapes me.

[JUSTICE BLACK's and JUSTICE FORTAS's concurring opinions have been omitted.]

BLANTON V. CITY OF NORTH LAS VEGAS
489 U.S. 538 (1989)

JUSTICE MARSHALL delivered the opinion of the Court.

The issue in this case is whether there is a constitutional right to a trial by jury for persons charged under Nevada law with driving under the influence of alcohol (DUI). Nev.Rev.Stat. § 484.379(1) (1987). We hold that there is not.

DUI is punishable by a minimum term of two days' imprisonment and a maximum term of six months' imprisonment. § 484.3792(1)(a)(2). Alternatively, a trial court may order the defendant "to perform 48 hours of work for the community while dressed in distinctive garb which identifies him as [a DUI offender]." *Ibid.* The defendant also must pay a fine ranging from $200 to $1,000. § 484.3792(1)(a)(3). In addition, the defendant automatically loses his driver's license for 90 days, § 483.460(1)(c), and he must attend, at his own expense, an alcohol abuse education course. § 484.3792(1)(a)(1). Repeat DUI offenders are subject to increased penalties.[2]

Petitioners Melvin R. Blanton and Mark D. Fraley were charged with DUI in separate incidents. Neither petitioner had a prior DUI conviction. The North Las Vegas, Nevada, Municipal Court denied their respective pretrial demands for a jury trial. * * * After consolidating the two cases along with several others raising the same issue, the Supreme Court [of Nevada] concluded, *inter alia,* that the Federal Constitution does not guarantee a right to a jury trial for a DUI offense because the maximum term of incarceration is only six months and the maximum possible fine is $1,000. We granted certiorari to consider whether petitioners were entitled to a jury trial and now affirm.

It has long been settled that "there is a category of petty crimes or offenses which is not subject to the Sixth Amendment jury trial provision." *Duncan v. Louisiana*, 391 U.S. 145, 159 (1968). In determining whether a particular offense

---

2   * * * A prosecutor may not dismiss a DUI charge "in exchange for a plea of guilty or *nolo contendere* to a lesser charge or for any other reason unless he knows or it is obvious" that there is insufficient evidence to prove the offense. § 484.3792(3). Trial courts may not suspend sentences or impose probation for DUI convictions. *Ibid.*

should be categorized as "petty," our early decisions focused on the nature of the offense and on whether it was triable by a jury at common law. See, *e.g., District of Columbia v. Colts,* 282 U.S. 63, 73 (1930); *Callan v. Wilson,* 127 U.S. 540, 555–57 (1888). In recent years, however, we have sought more "objective indications of the seriousness with which society regards the offense." *Frank v. United States,* 395 U.S. 147, 148 (1969). "[W]e have found the most relevant such criteria in the severity of the maximum authorized penalty." *Baldwin v. New York,* 399 U.S. 66, 68 (1970) (plurality opinion); see also *Duncan,* 391 U.S., at 159. In fixing the maximum penalty for a crime, a legislature "include[s] within the definition of the crime itself a judgment about the seriousness of the offense." *Frank,* 395 U.S., at 149. The judiciary should not substitute its judgment as to seriousness for that of a legislature, which is "far better equipped to perform the task, and [is] likewise more responsive to changes in attitude and more amenable to the recognition and correction of their misperceptions in this respect." *Landry v. Hoepfner,* 840 F.2d 1201, 1209 (5th Cir. 1988) (en banc), cert. pending, No. 88–5043.

In using the word "penalty," we do not refer solely to the maximum prison term authorized for a particular offense. A legislature's view of the seriousness of an offense also is reflected in the other penalties that it attaches to the offense. We thus examine "whether the length of the authorized prison term *or the seriousness of other punishment* is enough in itself to require a jury trial." *Duncan,* 391 U.S., at 161 (emphasis added); see also *Frank,* 395 U.S., at 152 (three years' probation is not "onerous enough to make an otherwise petty offense 'serious' "). Primary emphasis, however, must be placed on the maximum authorized period of incarceration. Penalties such as probation or a fine may engender "a significant infringement of personal freedom," *id.,* at 151, but they cannot approximate in severity the loss of liberty that a prison term entails. Indeed, because incarceration is an "intrinsically different" form of punishment, *Muniz v. Hoffman,* 422 U.S. 454, 477 (1975), it is the most powerful indication whether an offense is "serious."

Following this approach, our decision in *Baldwin* established that a defendant is entitled to a jury trial whenever the offense for which he is charged carries a maximum authorized prison term of greater than six months. 399 U.S., at 69. The possibility of a sentence exceeding six months, we determined, is "sufficiently severe by itself" to require the opportunity for a jury trial. *Id.,* at 69, n. 6. As for a prison term of six months or less, we recognized that it will seldom be viewed by the defendant as "trivial or 'petty.' " *Id.,* at 73. But we found that the disadvantages of such a sentence, "onerous though they may be, may be outweighed by the benefits that result from speedy and inexpensive nonjury adjudications." *Ibid.*

Although we did not hold in *Baldwin* that an offense carrying a maximum prison term of six months or less automatically qualifies as a "petty" offense, and decline to do so today, we do find it appropriate to presume for purposes of the Sixth Amendment that society views such an offense as "petty." A defendant is entitled to a jury trial in such circumstances only if he can demonstrate that any additional statutory penalties, viewed in conjunction with the maximum authorized period of incarceration, are so severe that they clearly reflect a legislative determination that the offense in question is a "serious" one. This standard, albeit somewhat imprecise, should ensure the availability of a jury trial in the rare situation where a legislature packs an offense it deems "serious" with onerous penalties that nonetheless "do not puncture the 6-month incarceration line." Brief for Petitioners 16.

> **Take Note**
>
> The Court here announces the test for when an offense is "serious" and thus triggers a right to a trial by jury. Can you imagine a set of official consequences for an offense with a maximum penalty of less than six months that would make the offense count as serious under the Court's test?

Applying these principles here, it is apparent that petitioners are not entitled to a jury trial. The maximum authorized prison sentence for first-time DUI offenders does not exceed six months. A presumption therefore exists that the Nevada Legislature views DUI as a "petty" offense for purposes of the Sixth Amendment. Considering the additional statutory penalties as well, we do not believe that the Nevada Legislature has clearly indicated that DUI is a "serious" offense.

In the first place, it is immaterial that a first-time DUI offender may face a minimum term of imprisonment. In settling on six months' imprisonment as the constitutional demarcation point, we have assumed that a defendant convicted of the offense in question would receive the *maximum* authorized prison sentence. It is not constitutionally determinative, therefore, that a particular defendant may be required to serve some amount of jail time *less* than six months. Likewise, it is of little moment that a defendant may receive the maximum prison term because of the prohibitions on plea bargaining and probation. As for the 90-day license suspension, it, too, will be irrelevant if it runs concurrently with the prison sentence, which we assume for present purposes to be the maximum of six months.[9]

---

[9] It is unclear whether the license suspension and prison sentence in fact run concurrently. See Nev.Rev.Stat. § 483.460(1) (1987). But even if they do not, we cannot say that a 90-day license suspension is that significant as a Sixth Amendment matter, particularly when a restricted license may be obtained after only 45 days. Furthermore, the requirement that an offender attend an alcohol abuse education course can only be described as *de minimis*.

We are also unpersuaded by the fact that, instead of a prison sentence, a DUI offender may be ordered to perform 48 hours of community service dressed in clothing identifying him as a DUI offender. Even assuming the outfit is the source of some embarrassment during the 48-hour period, such a penalty will be less embarrassing and less onerous than six months in jail. As for the possible $1,000 fine, it is well below the $5,000 level set by Congress in its most recent definition of a "petty" offense, 18 U.S.C. § 1 (1982 ed., Supp. IV), and petitioners do not suggest that this congressional figure is out of step with state practice for offenses carrying prison sentences of six months or less.[11] Finally, we ascribe little significance to the fact that a DUI offender faces increased penalties for repeat offenses. Recidivist penalties of the magnitude imposed for DUI are commonplace and, in any event, petitioners do not face such penalties here.

Viewed together, the statutory penalties are not so severe that DUI must be deemed a "serious" offense for purposes of the Sixth Amendment. It was not error, therefore, to deny petitioners jury trials. Accordingly, the judgment of the Supreme Court of Nevada is affirmed.

POINTS FOR DISCUSSION

a.   When Does the Sixth Amendment Right to a Jury Apply?

In *Duncan* and *Blanton*, the Court held that the Sixth Amendment guarantees a right to a jury in trials for "serious" offenses, but does not for "petty" offenses. The Court explained that petty offenses are defined principally by the maximum punishment that a defendant charged with the offense faces.

In contrast, as we saw above, the Court has held that the Sixth Amendment right to *counsel* applies even for misdemeanors, or "petty" offenses," as long as there is a prospect of *any* jail time for the defendant. See *Argersinger v. Hamlin*, 407 U.S. 25 (1972). Why does the right to counsel apply even when the right to a jury trial does not? Is the right to counsel more important than the right to a jury trial?

---

[11] We have frequently looked to the federal classification scheme in determining when a jury trial must be provided. See, *e.g., Muniz v. Hoffman*, 422 U.S. 454, 476–477 (1975). Although Congress no longer characterizes offenses as "petty," 98 Stat. 2027, 2031, 99 Stat. 1728 (repealing 18 U.S.C. § 1), under the current scheme, 18 U.S.C. § 3559 (1982 ed., Supp. V), an individual facing a maximum prison sentence of six months or less remains subject to a maximum fine of no more than $5,000. 18 U.S.C. § 3571(b)(6) (1982 ed., Supp. V).

We decline petitioners' invitation to survey the statutory penalties for drunken driving in other States. The question is not whether other States consider drunken driving a "serious" offense, but whether Nevada does. Although we looked to state practice in our past decisions, we did so chiefly to determine whether there was a nationwide consensus on the potential term of imprisonment or amount of fine that triggered a jury trial regardless of the particular offense involved. See, *e.g., Baldwin*, 399 U.S., at 70–73; *Duncan*, 391 U.S., at 161.

b.   The Jury as a Protection for the Defendant

The Court in *Duncan* (and the defendants in *Blanton*) clearly envisioned the right to a jury trial in a criminal case as an important protection for people accused of crimes. This view builds on the founding-era belief that juries are an important bulwark against the power of the government to impose punishment for arbitrary reasons or under unjust laws.

But is it always obvious that juries are an important protection for defendants? The rules of evidence limit the admissibility of all sorts of relevant evidence because of concern that jurors will be unduly influenced by prejudice or emotion. (Prosecutors, for example, generally want to introduce photos of the victim in murder cases based on a belief that the photos will inflame the jury, whereas defendants generally object to the introduction of such evidence as unduly prejudicial.) In addition, other forms of jury bias can make juries ineffective guardians of the defendant's rights. For example, in *Powell v. Alabama*, 287 U.S. 45 (1932), which we considered earlier in this chapter, African-American defendants were convicted and sentenced to death by a jury in a community clearly infected by racism and mob violence.

On the other hand, when members of racial minority groups serve on juries, some writers believe that they might refuse to convict a defendant if they believe that the system is unfairly biased against minority defendants. See Paul Butler, *Racially Based Jury Nullification: Black Power in the Criminal Justice System*, 105 Yale L.J. 677 (1995). But see *Batson v. Kentucky*, 476 U.S. 79, 97 (1986) (rejecting a presumption that racial minorities "would be partial to the defendant because of their shared race").

If you were accused of a crime, would you want a trial by jury, or instead a bench trial? What factors might influence your decision?

c.   Jury Size and Unanimity

Does the Constitution regulate the permissible size of a jury? The Sixth Amendment merely refers to an "impartial jury," but it does not say whether a jury must be of a particular size. In *Williams v. Florida*, 399 U.S. 78 (1970), the Court held that the state did not violate the defendant's right to an impartial jury under the Sixth Amendment, as incorporated by the Fourteenth Amendment, when it empaneled a six-member jury. In *Ballew v. Georgia*, 435 U.S. 223 (1978), however, the Court held that a trial by a five-member jury violated the defendant's rights under the Sixth and Fourteenth Amendment. Why does it matter how many members are on a jury? If small juries are constitutionally deficient, what about large juries? Could a state empanel a jury of 40 people? 50? If the size of the jury is a matter of constitutional importance, how does the Court decide how small is too small (or how big is too big)?

Must a jury decision in a criminal case be unanimous? In *Apodaca v. Oregon*, 406 U.S. 404 (1972), the Court held that a state law that permitted a jury verdict based on a 10–2 vote of the jurors in a felony case did not violate the defendant's right to an impartial jury. But the Court held in *Burch v. Louisiana*, 441 U.S. 130 (1979), that a jury verdict based on a 5–1 vote on a six-member jury in a case involving a non-petty offense violated the defendant's rights under the Sixth and Fourteenth Amendments. Should juries have to reach unanimous opinions? For a fascinating and provocative view of how juries operate, and why unanimity might matter, consider watching *Ten Angry Men*, a classic film from 1957.

In Chapter 5, we considered *Strauder v. West Virginia*, 100 U.S. 303 (1879), in which the Court invalidated a Louisiana law that excluded African Americans from service on juries. The Court reasoned that the law violated the Equal Protection Clause of the Fourteenth Amendment. When the Court decided *Strauder*, it had not yet held that the Fourteenth Amendment incorporates the provisions of the Sixth Amendment. But the case arguably implicated the Sixth Amendment right to an "impartial jury," as well.

The law at issue in *Strauder* categorically excluded all African Americans from the pool of persons who could be selected as jurors. But what if a state summons African Americans to the "venire"—the pool of persons from whom jurors will be selected—but then devises means to exclude them from service on juries in cases involving African-American defendants? Consider the case that follows.

BATSON V. KENTUCKY
476 U.S. 79 (1986)

JUSTICE POWELL delivered the opinion of the Court.

Petitioner, a black man, was indicted in Kentucky on charges of second-degree burglary and receipt of stolen goods. On the first day of trial in Jefferson Circuit Court, the judge conducted *voir dire* examination of the venire, excused certain jurors for cause, and permitted the parties to exercise peremptory challenges. The prosecutor used his peremptory challenges to strike all four black persons on the venire, and a jury composed only of white persons was selected. Defense counsel moved to discharge the jury before it was sworn on the ground that the prosecutor's removal of the black veniremen violated petitioner's rights under the Sixth and Fourteenth Amendments to a jury drawn from a cross section of the community, and under the Fourteenth Amendment to equal protection of the laws. Counsel requested a hearing on his motion. Without expressly ruling on the request for a hearing, the trial judge observed that the parties were entitled to use their peremptory challenges to "strike anybody they want to." The judge then denied petitioner's motion, reasoning that the cross-section requirement applies only to selection of the venire and not to selection of the petit jury itself.

The jury convicted petitioner on both counts. * * * The Supreme Court of Kentucky affirmed. * * *

More than a century ago, the Court decided that the State denies a black defendant equal protection of the laws when it puts him on trial before a jury from which members of his race have been purposefully excluded. *Strauder v. West Virginia*, 100 U.S. 303 (1880). That decision laid the foundation for the Court's unceasing efforts to eradicate racial discrimination in the procedures used to select the venire from which individual jurors are drawn. * * *

> **FYI**
>
> Jurors are usually selected from the venire after a process known as "voir dire," which is French for "to see to say." During this process, the parties (and sometimes the judge) question the potential jurors to determine whether they might suffer from bias or are otherwise unsuitable as jurors. The parties can generally use an unlimited number of challenges for cause to exclude jurors who demonstrate bias. In addition, in most jurisdictions, each party has a limited number of "peremptory challenges." Traditionally, when a party exercised a peremptory challenge, he could dismiss a juror without the need to demonstrate cause; indeed, the party traditionally had no obligation to provide any reason for the dismissal at all.

Purposeful racial discrimination in selection of the venire violates a defendant's right to equal protection because it denies him the protection that a trial by jury is intended to secure. * * * The petit jury has occupied a central position in our system of justice by safeguarding a person accused of crime against the arbitrary exercise of power by prosecutor or judge. *Duncan v. Louisiana*, 391 U.S. 145, 156 (1968). Those on the venire must be "indifferently chosen," to secure the defendant's right under the Fourteenth Amendment to "protection of life and liberty against race or color prejudice." *Strauder*, 100 U.S., at 309.

Racial discrimination in selection of jurors harms not only the accused whose life or liberty they are summoned to try. Competence to serve as a juror ultimately depends on an assessment of individual qualifications and ability impartially to consider evidence presented at a trial. See *Thiel v. Southern Pacific Co.*, 328 U.S. 217, 223–224 (1946). A person's race simply "is unrelated to his fitness as a juror." *Id.*, at 227 (Frankfurter, J., dissenting). As long ago as *Strauder*, therefore, the Court recognized that by denying a person participation in jury service on account of his race, the State unconstitutionally discriminated against the excluded juror. 100 U.S., at 308.

> **Definition**
>
> A "venire" is the panel of person from which a jury is drawn. A "petit jury" is the term for the jury that decides after a trial whether the defendant is guilty; the term is used in contrast to a "grand jury," which is the body that decides whether to issue an indictment and thus commence a criminal prosecution.

While decisions of this Court have been concerned largely with discrimination during selection of the venire, the principles announced there also forbid discrimination on account of race in selection of the petit jury. Since the Fourteenth Amendment protects an accused throughout the proceedings bringing him to justice, *Hill v. Texas,* 316 U.S. 400, 406 (1942), the State may not draw up its jury lists pursuant to neutral procedures but then resort to discrimination at "other stages in the selection process," *Avery v. Georgia,* 345 U.S. 559, 562 (1953).

Accordingly, the component of the jury selection process at issue here, the State's privilege to strike individual jurors through peremptory challenges, is subject to the commands of the Equal Protection Clause. Although a prosecutor ordinarily is entitled to exercise permitted peremptory challenges "for any reason at all, as long as that reason is related to his view concerning the outcome" of the case to be tried, the Equal Protection Clause forbids the prosecutor to challenge potential jurors solely on account of their race or on the assumption that black jurors as a group will be unable impartially to consider the State's case against a black defendant.

[In *Swain v. Alabama,* 380 U.S. 202 (1965), the Court rejected a claim by a black defendant that the state had violated the Equal Protection Clause when the prosecutor exercised peremptory challenges to strike all six black persons on the venire.] To preserve the peremptory nature of the prosecutor's challenge, the Court in *Swain* declined to scrutinize his actions in a particular case by relying on a presumption that he properly exercised the State's challenges. *Id.,* at 221–222.

The Court went on to observe, however, that a State may not exercise its challenges in contravention of the Equal Protection Clause. * * * A number of lower courts following the teaching of *Swain* reasoned that proof of repeated striking of blacks over a number of cases was necessary to establish a violation of the Equal Protection Clause. Since this interpretation of *Swain* has placed on defendants a crippling burden of proof, prosecutors' peremptory challenges are now largely immune from constitutional scrutiny. For reasons that follow, we reject this evidentiary formulation as inconsistent with standards that have been developed since *Swain* for assessing a prima facie case under the Equal Protection Clause.

[S]ince *Swain,* we have recognized that a black defendant alleging that members of his race have been impermissibly excluded from the venire may make out a prima facie case of purposeful discrimination by showing that the totality of the relevant facts gives rise to an inference of discriminatory purpose. *Washington v. Davis,* 426 U.S. 229, 239–242 (1976). Once the defendant makes the requisite showing, the burden shifts to the State to explain adequately the racial exclusion. *Alexander v. Louisiana,* 405 U.S. 625, 632(1972). The State cannot meet this burden on mere general assertions that its officials did not discriminate or that they properly performed their official duties. Rather, the State must demonstrate that "permissible racially neutral selection criteria and procedures have produced the monochromatic result." *Alexander, supra,* at 632. * * * These decisions are in accordance with the proposition, articulated in *Arlington Heights v. Metropolitan Housing Development Corp.,* 429 U.S. 252, 266 (1977), that "a consistent pattern of official racial discrimination" is not "a necessary predicate to a violation of the Equal Protection Clause. A single invidiously discriminatory governmental act" is not "immunized by the absence of such discrimination in the making of other comparable decisions." 429 U.S., at 266, n. 14. * * *

These principles support our conclusion that a defendant may establish a prima facie case of purposeful discrimination in selection of the petit jury solely on evidence concerning the prosecutor's exercise of peremptory challenges at the defendant's trial. To establish such a case, the defendant first must show that he is a member of a cognizable racial group, and that the prosecutor has exercised peremptory challenges to remove from the venire members of the defendant's race. Second, the defendant is entitled to rely on the fact, as to which there can be no dispute, that peremptory challenges constitute a jury selection practice that permits "those to discriminate who are of a mind to discriminate." *Avery v. Georgia,* 345 U.S., at 562. Finally, the defendant must show that these facts and any other relevant circumstances raise an inference that the prosecutor used that practice to exclude the veniremen from the petit jury on account of their race. This combination of factors in the empaneling of the petit jury, as in the selection of the venire, raises the necessary inference of purposeful discrimination.

In deciding whether the defendant has made the requisite showing, the trial court should consider all relevant circumstances. For example, a "pattern" of strikes against black jurors included in the particular venire might give rise to an inference of discrimination. Similarly, the prosecutor's questions and statements during *voir dire* examination and in exercising his challenges may support or refute an inference of discriminatory purpose. These examples are merely illustrative. We have confidence that trial judges, experienced in supervising *voir dire,* will be able

> **Make the Connection**
>
> We considered the Court's cases on how to prove that the government acted with a racially discriminatory purpose, and the general burden-shifting regime that the Court describes here, in Chapter 5.

to decide if the circumstances concerning the prosecutor's use of peremptory challenges creates a prima facie case of discrimination against black jurors.

Once the defendant makes a prima facie showing, the burden shifts to the State to come forward with a neutral explanation for challenging black jurors. Though this requirement imposes a limitation in some cases on the full peremptory character of the historic challenge, we emphasize that the prosecutor's explanation need not rise to the level justifying exercise of a challenge for cause. But the prosecutor may not rebut the defendant's prima facie case of discrimination by stating merely that he challenged jurors of the defendant's race on the assumption—or his intuitive judgment—that they would be partial to the defendant because of their shared race. Just as the Equal Protection Clause forbids the States to exclude black persons from the venire on the assumption that blacks as a group are unqualified to serve as jurors, so it forbids the States to strike black veniremen on the assumption that they will be biased in a particular case simply because the defendant is black. The core guarantee of equal protection, ensuring citizens that their State will not discriminate on account of race, would be meaningless were we to approve the exclusion of jurors on the basis of such assumptions, which arise solely from the jurors' race. Nor may the prosecutor rebut the defendant's case merely by denying that he had a discriminatory motive or "affirm[ing] [his] good faith in making individual selections." *Alexander v. Louisiana,* 405 U.S., at 632. * * * The prosecutor [must] articulate a neutral explanation related to the particular case to be tried. The trial court then will have the duty to determine if the defendant has established purposeful discrimination.

The State contends that our holding will eviscerate the fair trial values served by the peremptory challenge. * * * While we recognize, of course, that the peremptory challenge occupies an important position in our trial procedures, we do not agree that our decision today will undermine the contribution the challenge generally makes to the administration of justice. The reality of practice, amply reflected in many state- and federal-court opinions, shows that the challenge may be, and unfortunately at times has been, used to discriminate against black jurors. By requiring trial courts to be sensitive to the racially discriminatory use of peremptory challenges, our decision enforces the mandate of equal protection and furthers the ends of justice. In view of the heterogeneous population of our Nation, public respect for our criminal justice system and the rule of law will be strengthened if we ensure that no citizen is disqualified from jury service because of his race.

In this case, petitioner made a timely objection to the prosecutor's removal of all black persons on the venire. Because the trial court flatly rejected the objection without requiring the prosecutor to give an explanation for his action, we remand this case for further proceedings. If the trial court decides that the facts establish, prima facie, purposeful discrimination and the prosecutor does not come forward with a neutral explanation for his action, our precedents require that petitioner's conviction be reversed.[25]

JUSTICE MARSHALL, concurring.

I join Justice POWELL's eloquent opinion for the Court, which takes a historic step toward eliminating the shameful practice of racial discrimination in the selection of juries. * * * [But the] decision today will not end the racial discrimination that peremptories inject into the jury-selection process. That goal can be accomplished only by eliminating peremptory challenges entirely.

Evidentiary analysis similar to that set out by the Court has been adopted as a matter of state law in States including Massachusetts and California. Cases from those jurisdictions illustrate the limitations of the approach. First, defendants cannot attack the discriminatory use of peremptory challenges at all unless the challenges are so flagrant as to establish a prima facie case. This means, in those States, that where only one or two black jurors survive the challenges for cause, the prosecutor need have no compunction about striking them from the jury because of their race. See *Commonwealth v. Robinson,* 415 N.E.2d 805, 809–810 (1981) (no prima facie case of discrimination where defendant is black, prospective jurors include three blacks and one Puerto Rican, and prosecutor excludes one for cause and strikes the remainder peremptorily, producing all-white jury); *People v. Rousseau,* 179 Cal.Rptr. 892, 897–898 (1982) (no prima facie case where prosecutor peremptorily strikes only two blacks on jury panel). Prosecutors are left free to discriminate against blacks in jury selection provided that they hold that discrimination to an "acceptable" level.

Second, when a defendant can establish a prima facie case, trial courts face the difficult burden of assessing prosecutors' motives. Any prosecutor can easily assert facially neutral reasons for striking a juror, and trial courts are ill equipped to second-guess those reasons. * * * Nor is outright prevarication by prosecutors the only danger here. * * * A prosecutor's own conscious or unconscious racism

---

[25] To the extent that anything in *Swain v. Alabama,* 380 U.S. 202 (1965), is contrary to the principles we articulate today, that decision is overruled.

may lead him easily to the conclusion that a prospective black juror is "sullen," or "distant," a characterization that would not have come to his mind if a white juror had acted identically. A judge's own conscious or unconscious racism may lead him to accept such an explanation as well supported. * * *

I applaud the Court's holding that the racially discriminatory use of peremptory challenges violates the Equal Protection Clause, and I join the Court's opinion. However, only by banning peremptories entirely can such discrimination be ended.

CHIEF JUSTICE BURGER, joined by JUSTICE REHNQUIST, dissenting.

Today the Court sets aside the peremptory challenge, a procedure which has been part of the common law for many centuries and part of our jury system for nearly 200 years. * * * Instead of even considering the history or function of the peremptory challenge, the bulk of the Court's opinion is spent recounting the well-established principle that intentional exclusion of racial groups from jury venires is a violation of the Equal Protection Clause. I too reaffirm that principle, which has been a part of our constitutional tradition since at least *Strauder v. West Virginia,* 100 U.S. 303 (1880). But if today's decision is nothing more than mere "application" of the "principles announced in *Strauder,*" as the Court maintains, some will consider it curious that the application went unrecognized for over a century.

A moment's reflection quickly reveals the vast differences between the racial exclusions involved in *Strauder* and the allegations before us today:

> "Exclusion from the venire summons process implies that the government (usually the legislative or judicial branch) . . . has made the general determination that those excluded are unfit to try *any* case. Exercise of the peremptory challenge, by contrast, represents the discrete decision, made by one of two or more opposed *litigants* in the trial phase of our adversary system of justice, that the challenged venireperson will likely be more unfavorable to that litigant in that *particular case* than others on the same venire. Thus, excluding a particular cognizable group from all venire pools is stigmatizing and discriminatory in several interrelated ways that the peremptory challenge is not. * * *" *United States v. Leslie,* 783 F.2d 541, 554 (CA5 1986) (en banc).

Unwilling to rest solely on jury venire cases such as *Strauder,* the Court also invokes general equal protection principles in support of its holding. But [in] making peremptory challenges, both the prosecutor and defense attorney necessarily act on only limited information or hunch. * * * As a result, unadulterated equal protection analysis is simply inapplicable to peremptory challenges exercised in any particular case. [A] constitutional principle that may invalidate state action on the basis of "stereotypic notions," *Mississippi University for Women v. Hogan,* 458 U.S. 718, 725 (1982), does not explain the breadth of a procedure exercised on the "sudden impressions and unaccountable prejudices we are apt to conceive upon the bare looks and gestures of another." *Lewis,* 146 U.S., at 376 (quoting 4 W. Blackstone, Commentaries * 353).

That the Court is not applying conventional equal protection analysis is shown by its limitation of its new rule to allegations of impermissible challenge *on the basis of race* * * *. But if conventional equal protection principles apply, then presumably defendants could object to exclusions on the basis of not only race, but also sex, *Craig v. Boren,* 429 U.S. 190 (1976); age, *Massachusetts Bd. of Retirement v. Murgia,* 427 U.S. 307 (1976); religious or political affiliation, *Karcher v. Daggett,* 462 U.S. 725, 748 (1983) (STEVENS, J., concurring); mental capacity, *Cleburne v. Cleburne Living Center, Inc.,* 473 U.S. 432 (1985); number of children, *Dandridge v. Williams,* 397 U.S. 471 (1970); living arrangements, *Department of Agriculture v. Moreno,* 413 U.S. 528 (1973); and employment in a particular industry, *Minnesota v. Clover Leaf Creamery Co.,* 449 U.S. 456 (1981), or profession, *Williamson v. Lee Optical Co.,* 348 U.S. 483 (1955).

In short, it is quite probable that every peremptory challenge could be objected to on the basis that, because it excluded a venireman who had some characteristic not shared by the remaining members of the venire, it constituted a "classification" subject to equal protection scrutiny. Compounding the difficulties, under conventional equal protection principles some uses of peremptories would be reviewed under "strict scrutiny and . . . sustained only if . . . suitably tailored to serve a compelling state interest," *Cleburne,* 473 U.S., at 440; others would be reviewed to determine if they were "substantially related to a sufficiently important government interest," *id.,* at 441; and still others would be reviewed to determine whether they were "a rational means to serve a legitimate end." *Id.,* at 442.

Make the Connection

If peremptory challenges based on race violate the Equal Protection Clause, does it necessarily follow that challenges based on sex and the other grounds that Chief Justice Burger suggests here do, as well? Does it matter whether the basis for classification triggers heightened scrutiny under the Equal Protection Clause? We considered these bases for discrimination in Chapters 4–6, and we consider the use of peremptory challenges to excuse jurors based on sex in the notes that follow.

The Court never applies this conventional equal protection framework to the claims at hand, perhaps to avoid acknowledging that the state interest involved here has historically been regarded by this Court as substantial, if not compelling. Peremptory challenges have long been viewed as a means to achieve an impartial jury that will be sympathetic toward neither an accused nor witnesses for the State on the basis of some shared factor of race, religion, occupation, or other characteristic. Nearly a century ago the Court stated that the peremptory challenge is "essential to the fairness of trial by jury." *Lewis,* 146 U.S., at 376. Under conventional equal protection principles, a state interest of this magnitude and ancient lineage might well overcome an equal protection objection to the application of peremptory challenges. However, the Court is silent on the strength of the State's interest * * *.

Rather than applying straightforward equal protection analysis, the Court [announces] a curious hybrid. The defendant must first establish a "prima facie case" of invidious discrimination, then the "burden shifts to the State to come forward with a neutral explanation for challenging black jurors." * * * The Court then adds [that] "the prosecutor must give a 'clear and reasonably specific' explanation of his 'legitimate reasons' for exercising the challenges."

While undoubtedly these rules are well suited to other contexts, [they] seem curiously out of place when applied to peremptory challenges in criminal cases. Our system permits two types of challenges: challenges for cause and peremptory challenges. Challenges for cause obviously have to be explained; by definition, peremptory challenges do not. "It is called a peremptory challenge, because the prisoner may challenge peremptorily, on his own dislike, *without showing of any cause.*" H. Joy, On Peremptory Challenge of Jurors 1 (1844) (emphasis added). Analytically, there is no middle ground: A challenge either has to be explained or it does not. It is readily apparent, then, that to permit inquiry into the basis for a peremptory challenge would force "the peremptory challenge [to] collapse into the challenge for cause." *United States v. Clark,* 737 F.2d 679, 682 (7th Cir. 1984).

Confronted with the dilemma it created, the Court today attempts to decree a middle ground. To rebut a prima facie case, the Court requires a "neutral explanation" for the challenge, but is at pains to "emphasize" that the "explanation need not rise to the level justifying exercise of a challenge for cause." I am at a loss to discern the governing principles here. A "clear and reasonably specific" explanation of "legitimate reasons" for exercising the challenge will be difficult to distinguish from a challenge for cause. Anything short of a challenge for cause may well be seen as an "arbitrary and capricious" challenge, to use Blackstone's characterization of the peremptory. See 4 W. Blackstone,

Commentaries *353. Apparently the Court envisions permissible challenges short of a challenge for cause that are just a little bit arbitrary—but not too much. While our trial judges are "experienced in supervising *voir dire*," they have no experience in administering rules like this.

JUSTICE REHNQUIST, with whom THE CHIEF JUSTICE joins, dissenting.

* * * In my view, there is simply nothing "unequal" about the State's using its peremptory challenges to strike blacks from the jury in cases involving black defendants, so long as such challenges are also used to exclude whites in cases involving white defendants, Hispanics in cases involving hispanic defendants, Asians in cases involving Asian defendants, and so on. This case-specific use of peremptory challenges by the State does not single out blacks, or members of any other race for that matter, for discriminatory treatment. Such use of peremptories is at best based upon seat-of-the-pants instincts, which are undoubtedly crudely stereotypical and may in many cases be hopelessly mistaken. But as long as they are applied across-the-board to jurors of all races and nationalities, I do not see— and the Court most certainly has not explained—how their use violates the Equal Protection Clause.

Nor does such use of peremptory challenges by the State infringe upon any other constitutional interests. The Court does not suggest that exclusion of blacks from the jury through the State's use of peremptory challenges results in a violation of either the fair-cross-section or impartiality component of the Sixth Amendment. And because the case-specific use of peremptory challenges by the State does not deny blacks the right to serve as jurors in cases involving nonblack defendants, it harms neither the excluded jurors nor the remainder of the community.

The use of group affiliations, such as age, race, or occupation, as a "proxy" for potential juror partiality, based on the assumption or belief that members of one group are more likely to favor defendants who belong to the same group, has long been accepted as a legitimate basis for the State's exercise of peremptory challenges. Indeed, given the need for reasonable limitations on the time devoted to *voir dire,* the use of such "proxies" by both the State and the defendant may be extremely useful in eliminating from the jury persons who might be biased in one way or another. The Court today holds that the State may not use its peremptory challenges to strike black prospective jurors on this basis without violating the Constitution. But I do not believe there is anything in the Equal Protection Clause, or any other constitutional provision, that justifies [the Court's conclusion].

[JUSTICE WHITE's concurring opinion, JUSTICE STEVENS concurring opinion, which JUSTICE BRENNAN joined, and JUSTICE O'CONNOR's concurring opinion have been omitted.]

POINTS FOR DISCUSSION

a.   Peremptory Challenges, the Sixth Amendment, and the Equal Protection Clause

The Court concluded that it violates the Constitution when the prosecution exercises peremptory challenges with the purpose of excluding potential jurors of a particular race. Did the Court hold that such use of peremptory challenges violates the Sixth Amendment right to an impartial jury (as incorporated by the Fourteenth Amendment)? Or did it hold that it violates the Equal Protection Clause? The Court borrowed the method of proving a case of discriminatory use of peremptory challenges from its Equal Protection cases, but a jury from which all jurors of the same race as the defendant have been excluded might not be an "impartial jury" within the meaning of the Sixth Amendment.

Should the Court have gone farther and banned the use of peremptory challenges altogether, as Justice Marshall urged in his concurring opinion? Or are there important and defensible grounds for preserving the tradition of challenges without cause? In *Miller-El v. Dretke*, 545 U.S. 231 (2005), the Court granted federal habeas relief to the petitioner after concluding that the prosecutor's challenge of 10 of the 11 African-American members of the venire was motivated by a racially discriminatory purpose. In his concurring opinion, Justice Breyer echoed Justice Marshall's call to abolish the practice altogether. He asserted that cases involving claims of racially discriminatory use of peremptory challenges inevitably involved "practical problems of proof," and that "peremptory challenges seem increasingly anomalous in our judicial system." What might be examples of "the practical problems of proof"?

b.   Other Grounds for Peremptory Challenges

If it violates the Sixth Amendment and the Equal Protection Clause to dismiss jurors on the basis of race, then does it also violate those provisions to dismiss them on the basis of gender? In *J.E.B. v. Alabama ex rel. T.B.*, 511 U.S. 127 (1994), the Court held that such uses of peremptory challenges are unconstitutional, as well. Should it be impermissible to challenge jurors based on age? Disability? Profession? Political views? How should the Court decide which grounds for peremptory challenges—which, after all, are supposed to be challenges that do not require a reason—are constitutionally impermissible?

c. Use by Defense Counsel

In a portion of Justice Marshall's concurring opinion that was omitted above, Justice Marshall noted that some scholars had argued that the courts should prohibit prosecutors from using peremptory challenges but that they should "zealously guard" defendants' peremptory challenges as "one of the most important of the rights secured to the accused." Justice Marshall rejected that argument, asserting that "[o]ur criminal justice system 'requires not only freedom from any bias against the accused, but also from any prejudice against his prosecution.' " He would have banned the use of peremptory challenges by prosecutors and "allowed the States to eliminate the defendant's peremptories as well."

Notice that Justice Marshall did not expressly assert that the Constitution should be read to forbid the use of peremptory challenges by defendants. This presumably was because the Constitution, generally speaking, regulates only government, rather than private, conduct. Are a defendant's peremptory challenges "state action" subject to the requirements of the Fourteenth Amendment?

When the prosecution exercises peremptory challenges based on some impermissible basis, it is not difficult to see how the state is affecting the composition of the jury—and thus potentially is affecting the defendant's right to an impartial jury. In *Georgia v. McCollum*, 505 U.S. 42 (1992), the Court concluded that racially discriminatory use of peremptory challenges by criminal defendants constituted state action for purposes of the Fourteenth Amendment, and that such use of the challenges violates the Constitution. Can you come up with an argument about how such actions by defendants being prosecuted by the government constitute "state action"?

> **Make the Connection**
>
> We considered the state action doctrine in Volume 1.

In *McCollum*, the NAACP Legal Defense and Educational Fund, Inc., filed an amicus brief asserting that "whether white defendants can use peremptory challenges to purge minority jurors presents quite different issues from whether a minority defendant can strike majority group jurors." Why might the issues be different? Should the rules on peremptory challenges differ depending on the defendant's race?

d. Jury Deliberations

Jury decision-making has often been viewed as a "black box" into which courts cannot pry. The courts have long applied a "no-impeachment rule" to jury decision-making: once a verdict has been entered, it will not later be called into question based on the comments or conclusions that the jurors expressed during deliberations. The Court's decisions in *Batson* and its progeny, however, suggested a willingness of the Court to supervise the jury selection process to purge the taint of racial discrimination.

What should a court do when confronted with evidence that the taint of racial discrimination affected a jury's verdict?

In *Peña-Rodriguez v. Colorado*, 137 S. Ct. 855 (2017), the Court held that where a juror makes a clear statement that indicates that he relied on racial stereotypes or animus to convict a criminal defendant, the Sixth Amendment requires courts to depart from the no-impeachment rule and to consider the evidence of the juror's statement and any resulting denial of the jury trial guarantee. In *Peña-Rodriguez*, the defendant, who was Hispanic, was prosecuted for sexual assault and related charges. After he was convicted, several jurors submitted sworn statements asserting that another juror had stated that he "believed the defendant was guilty because, in [his] experience as an ex-law enforcement officer, Mexican men had a bravado that caused them to believe they could do whatever they wanted with women."

Why do the courts apply a presumptive no-impeachment rule for jury verdicts? Do you agree that evidence of racial bias in the jury's decision-making should be sufficient grounds to depart from the rule? If so, how strong should the evidence be?

In Chapter 14, we considered the requirements that the Due Process Clause imposes on criminal proceedings. We noted that the Court has held that the Due Process Clause requires the state to prove all criminal charges beyond a reasonable doubt. See *In re Winship*, 397 U.S. 358 (1970).

Once a jury convicts a defendant of a crime according to that standard, the court imposes a sentence on the defendant. In many jurisdictions, the judge determines and imposes the sentence. Does that practice interfere with the Sixth Amendment right to a jury trial? What if the judge bases the sentence on facts that the jury did not resolve? Consider the case that follows.

APPRENDI V. NEW JERSEY
530 U.S. 466 (2000)

JUSTICE STEVENS delivered the opinion of the Court.

A New Jersey statute classifies the possession of a firearm for an unlawful purpose as a "second-degree" offense. N.J. Stat. Ann. § 2C:39–4(a). Such an offense is punishable by imprisonment for "between five years and 10 years." § 2C:43–6(a)(2). A separate statute, described by that State's Supreme Court as a "hate crime" law, provides for an "extended term" of imprisonment if the trial judge finds, by a preponderance of the evidence, that "[t]he defendant in committing the crime acted with a purpose to intimidate an individual or group of individuals because of race, color, gender, handicap, religion, sexual orientation or ethnicity." N.J. Stat. Ann. § 2C:44–3(e). The extended term authorized by the hate crime law for second-degree offenses is imprisonment for "between 10 and 20 years." § 2C:43–7(a)(3).

The question presented is whether the Due Process Clause of the Fourteenth Amendment requires that a factual determination authorizing an increase in the maximum prison sentence for an offense from 10 to 20 years be made by a jury on the basis of proof beyond a reasonable doubt.

At 2:04 a.m. on December 22, 1994, petitioner Charles C. Apprendi, Jr., fired several .22-caliber bullets into the home of an African-American family that had recently moved into a previously all-white neighborhood in Vineland, New Jersey. Apprendi was promptly arrested and, at 3:05 a.m., admitted that he was the shooter. After further questioning, at 6:04 a.m., he made a statement—which he later retracted—that even though he did not know the occupants of the house personally, "because they are black in color he does not want them in the neighborhood." 731 A.2d 485, 486 (1999).

A New Jersey grand jury returned a 23-count indictment charging Apprendi with * * * shootings on four different dates, as well as the unlawful possession of various weapons. None of the counts referred to the hate crime statute, and none alleged that Apprendi acted with a racially biased purpose.

The parties entered into a plea agreement, pursuant to which Apprendi pleaded guilty to two counts (3 and 18) of second-degree possession of a firearm for an unlawful purpose, N.J. Stat. Ann. § 2C:39–4a, and one count (22) of the third-degree offense of unlawful possession of an antipersonnel bomb, § 2C:39–3a; the prosecutor dismissed the other 20 counts. Under state law, a second-degree offense carries a penalty range of 5 to 10 years, § 2C:43–6(a)(2); a third-degree offense carries a penalty range of between 3 and 5 years, § 2C:43–6(a)(3). As part of the plea agreement, however, the State reserved the right to request the court to impose a higher "enhanced" sentence on count 18 (which was based on the December 22 shooting) on the ground that that offense was committed with a biased purpose, as described in § 2C:44–3(e). Apprendi, correspondingly, reserved the right to challenge the hate crime sentence enhancement on the ground that it violates the United States Constitution.

At the plea hearing, the trial judge heard sufficient evidence to establish Apprendi's guilt on [the three counts]. * * * After the trial judge accepted the three guilty pleas, the prosecutor filed a formal motion for an extended term. The trial judge thereafter held an evidentiary hearing on the issue of Apprendi's "purpose" for the shooting on December 22. Apprendi adduced evidence from a psychologist and from seven character witnesses who testified that he did not have a reputation for racial bias. He also took the stand himself, explaining that the incident was an unintended consequence of overindulgence in alcohol, denying that he was in any way biased against African-Americans, and denying that his statement to the police had been accurately described. The judge, however, found the police officer's testimony credible, and concluded that the evidence supported a finding "that the crime was motivated by racial bias." Having found "by a preponderance of the evidence" that Apprendi's actions were taken "with a purpose to intimidate" as provided by the statute, the trial judge held that the hate crime enhancement applied. Rejecting Apprendi's constitutional challenge to the

> **Take Note**
>
> Without the sentencing enhancement, the statutory maximum penalty for count 18 was ten years. The judge, relying on the hate crime law, imposed a longer sentence based on his findings about the defendant's motives.

statute, the judge sentenced him to a 12-year term of imprisonment on count 18, and to shorter concurrent sentences on the other two counts.

Apprendi appealed, arguing, *inter alia*, that the Due Process Clause of the United States Constitution requires that the finding of bias upon which his hate crime sentence was based must be proved to a jury beyond a reasonable doubt, *In re Winship*, 397 U.S. 358 (1970). Over dissent, the Appellate Division of the Superior Court of New Jersey upheld the enhanced sentence. * * * A divided New Jersey Supreme Court affirmed. 159 N.J. 7, 731 A.2d 485 (1999). * * * We granted certiorari, and now reverse.

At stake in this case are constitutional protections of surpassing importance: the proscription of any deprivation of liberty without "due process of law," Amdt. 14, and the guarantee that "[i]n all criminal prosecutions, the accused shall enjoy the right to a speedy and public trial, by an impartial jury," Amdt. 6. Taken together, these rights indisputably entitle a criminal defendant to "a jury determination that [he] is guilty of every element of the crime with which he is charged, beyond a reasonable doubt." *United States v. Gaudin,* 515 U.S. 506, 510 (1995).

Any possible distinction between an "element" of a felony offense and a "sentencing factor" was unknown to the practice of criminal indictment, trial by jury, and judgment by court as it existed during the years surrounding our Nation's founding. As a general rule, criminal proceedings were submitted to a jury after being initiated by an indictment containing "all the facts and circumstances which constitute the offence, . . . stated with such certainty and precision, that the defendant . . . may be enabled to determine the species of offence they constitute, in order that he may prepare his defence accordingly . . . and *that there may be no doubt as to the judgment which should be given,* if the defendant be convicted." J. Archbold, Pleading and Evidence in Criminal Cases 44 (15th ed. 1862) (emphasis added). The defendant's ability to predict with certainty the judgment from the face of the felony indictment flowed from the invariable linkage of punishment with crime. See 4 Blackstone 369–370.

Thus, with respect to the criminal law of felonious conduct, "the English trial judge of the later eighteenth century had very little explicit discretion in sentencing. The substantive criminal law tended to be sanction-specific; it prescribed a particular sentence for each offense. The judge was meant simply to impose that sentence (unless he thought in the circumstances that the sentence was so inappropriate that he should invoke the pardon process to commute it)." Langbein, The English Criminal Trial Jury on the Eve of the French Revolution, in The Trial Jury in England, France, Germany 1700–1900, pp. 36–37 (A. Schioppa ed.1987). * * *

We should be clear that nothing in this history suggests that it is impermissible for judges to exercise discretion—taking into consideration various factors relating both to offense and offender—in imposing a judgment *within the range* prescribed by statute. We have often noted that judges in this country have long exercised discretion of this nature in imposing sentence *within statutory limits* in the individual case. See, *e.g., Williams v. New York,* 337 U.S. 241, 246 (1949). * * * The historic link between verdict and judgment and the consistent limitation on judges' discretion to operate within the limits of the legal penalties provided highlight the novelty of a legislative scheme that removes the jury from the determination of a fact that, if found, exposes the criminal defendant to a penalty *exceeding* the maximum he would receive if punished according to the facts reflected in the jury verdict alone.

We do not suggest that trial practices cannot change in the course of centuries and still remain true to the principles that emerged from the Framers' fears "that the jury right could be lost not only by gross denial, but by erosion." *Jones v. United States,* 526 U.S. 227, 247–248 (1999). But practice must at least adhere to the basic principles undergirding the requirements of trying to a jury all facts necessary to constitute a statutory offense, and proving those facts beyond reasonable doubt. As we made clear in *Winship,* the "reasonable doubt" requirement "has [a] vital role in our criminal procedure for cogent reasons." 397 U.S., at 363. Prosecution subjects the criminal defendant both to "the possibility that he may lose his liberty upon conviction and . . . the certainty that he would be stigmatized by the conviction." *Ibid.* We thus require this, among other, procedural protections in order to "provid[e] concrete substance for the presumption of innocence," and to reduce the risk of imposing such deprivations erroneously. *Ibid.* If a defendant faces punishment beyond that provided by statute when an offense is committed under certain circumstances but not others, it is obvious that both the loss of liberty and the stigma attaching to the offense are heightened; it necessarily follows that the defendant should not—at the moment the State is put to proof of those circumstances—be deprived of protections that have, until that point, unquestionably attached.

Other than the fact of a prior conviction, any fact that increases the penalty for a crime beyond the prescribed statutory maximum must be submitted to a jury, and proved beyond a reasonable doubt. * * * The New Jersey statutory scheme that Apprendi asks us to invalidate allows a jury to convict a defendant of a second-degree offense based on its finding beyond a reasonable doubt that he unlawfully possessed a prohibited weapon; after a subsequent and separate proceeding, it then allows a judge to impose punishment identical to that New Jersey provides for crimes of the first degree, N.J. Stat. Ann. § 2C:43–6(a)(1), based upon the judge's finding, by a preponderance of the evidence, that the defendant's "purpose" for unlawfully possessing the weapon was "to intimidate" his victim on the basis of a particular characteristic the victim possessed. In light of the constitutional rule explained above, and all of the cases supporting it, this practice cannot stand.

New Jersey [defends its hate crime enhancement statute by arguing that the] required finding of biased purpose is not an "element" of a distinct hate crime offense, but rather the traditional "sentencing factor" of motive * * *. [This argument] is nothing more than a disagreement with the rule we apply today. Beyond this, we do not see how the argument can succeed on its own terms. * * * The text of the [hate crime] statute requires the factfinder to determine whether the defendant possessed, at the time he committed the subject act, a "purpose to intimidate" on account of, *inter alia,* race. By its very terms, this statute mandates an examination of the defendant's state of mind— a concept known well to the criminal law as the defendant's *mens rea.* It makes no difference in identifying the nature of this finding that Apprendi was also required, in order to receive

> **Definition**
>
> *Mens rea* is a Latin term that means "guilty mind." It refers to the mental state—usually intention or knowledge of wrongdoing—that constitutes part of a crime, as opposed to the action or conduct of the accused. For example, first-degree murder usually requires proof that the homicide was both willful and premeditated. Here, the hate crime law authorized an enhanced sentence when the judge found, by a preponderance of the evidence, that the defendant had acted with a purpose to intimidate on the basis of race.

the sentence he did for weapons possession, to have possessed the weapon with a "purpose to use [the weapon] unlawfully against the person or property of another," § 2C:39–4(a). A second *mens rea* requirement hardly defeats the reality that the enhancement statute imposes of its own force an intent requirement necessary for the imposition of sentence. On the contrary, the fact that the language and structure of the "purpose to use" criminal offense is identical in relevant respects to the language and structure of the "purpose to intimidate" provision demonstrates to us that it is precisely a particular criminal *mens rea* that the hate crime enhancement statute seeks to target. The defendant's intent in committing a crime is perhaps as close as one might hope to come to a core criminal offense "element."

[T]he New Jersey Supreme Court correctly recognized that it does not matter whether the required finding is characterized as one of intent or of motive, because "[l]abels do not afford an acceptable answer." 731 A.2d, at 492. That point applies as well to the constitutionally novel and elusive distinction between "elements" and "sentencing factors." *McMillan v. Pennsylvania,* 477 U.S. 79, 86 (1986). Despite what appears to us the clear "elemental" nature of the factor here, the relevant inquiry is one not of form, but of effect—does the required finding expose the defendant to a greater punishment than that authorized by the jury's guilty verdict? [T]he effect of New Jersey's sentencing "enhancement" here is unquestionably to turn a second-degree offense into a first degree offense, under the State's own criminal code. * * *

The New Jersey procedure challenged in this case is an unacceptable departure from the jury tradition that is an indispensable part of our criminal justice system. Accordingly, the judgment of the Supreme Court of New Jersey is reversed, and the case is remanded for further proceedings not inconsistent with this opinion.

JUSTICE SCALIA, concurring.

I feel the need to say a few words in response to Justice BREYER's dissent. It sketches an admirably fair and efficient scheme of criminal justice designed for a society that is prepared to leave criminal justice to the State. (Judges, it is sometimes necessary to remind ourselves, are part of the State—and an increasingly bureaucratic part of it, at that.) The founders of the American Republic were not prepared to leave it to the State, which is why the jury-trial guarantee was one of the least controversial provisions of the Bill of Rights. It has never been efficient; but it has always been free.

As for fairness, which Justice BREYER believes "[i]n modern times" the jury cannot provide: I think it not unfair to tell a prospective felon that if he commits his contemplated crime he is exposing himself to a jail sentence of 30 years—and that if, upon conviction, he gets anything less than that he may thank the mercy of a tenderhearted judge (just as he may thank the mercy of a tenderhearted parole commission if he is let out inordinately early, or the mercy of a tenderhearted governor if his sentence is commuted). Will there be disparities? Of course. But the criminal will never get *more* punishment than he bargained for when he did the crime, and his guilt of the crime (and hence the length of the sentence to which he is exposed) will be determined *beyond a reasonable doubt by the unanimous vote of 12 of his fellow citizens.*

In Justice BREYER's bureaucratic realm of perfect equity, by contrast, the facts that determine the length of sentence to which the defendant is exposed will be determined to exist (on a more-likely-than-not basis) by a single employee of the State. It is certainly arguable (Justice BREYER argues it) that this sacrifice of prior protections is worth it. But it is not arguable that, just because one thinks it is a better system, it must be, or is even more likely to be, the system envisioned by a Constitution that guarantees trial by jury. What ultimately demolishes the case for the dissenters is that they are unable to say what the right to trial by jury *does* guarantee if, as they assert, it does not guarantee—what it has been assumed to guarantee throughout our history—the right to have a jury determine those facts that determine the maximum sentence the law allows. They provide no coherent alternative.

Justice BREYER proceeds on the erroneous and all-too-common assumption that the Constitution means what we think it ought to mean. It does not; it means what it says. And the guarantee that "[i]n all criminal prosecutions, the accused shall enjoy the right to . . . trial, by an impartial jury," has no intelligible content unless it means that all the facts which must exist in order to subject the defendant to a legally prescribed punishment *must* be found by the jury.

JUSTICE THOMAS, with whom JUSTICE SCALIA joins [in relevant part], concurring.

I join the opinion of the Court in full. I write separately to explain my view that the Constitution requires a broader rule than the Court adopts.

This case turns on the seemingly simple question of what constitutes a "crime." * * * [The protections afforded by the grand jury clause in the Fifth Amendment and the jury trial right in the Sixth Amendment] turn on determining which facts constitute the "crime"—that is, which facts are the "elements" or "ingredients" of a crime. In order for an accusation of a crime (whether by indictment or some other form) to be proper under the common law, and thus proper under the codification of the common-law rights in the Fifth and Sixth Amendments, it must allege all elements of that crime; likewise, in order for a jury trial of a crime to be proper, all elements of the crime must be proved to the jury (and, under *Winship,* proved beyond a reasonable doubt).

Thus, it is critical to know which facts are elements. * * * Sentencing enhancements may be new creatures, but the question that they create for courts is not. Courts have long had to consider which facts are elements in order to determine the sufficiency of an accusation (usually an indictment). * * * A long line of essentially uniform authority addressing accusations, and stretching from the earliest reported cases after the founding until well into the 20th century, establishes that the original understanding of which facts are elements was even broader than the rule that the Court adopts today.

This authority establishes that a "crime" includes every fact that is by law a basis for imposing or increasing punishment (in contrast with a fact that mitigates punishment). Thus, if the legislature defines some core crime and then provides for increasing the punishment of that crime upon a finding of some aggravating fact—of whatever sort, including the fact of a prior conviction—the core crime and the aggravating fact together constitute an aggravated crime, just as much as grand larceny is an aggravated form of petit larceny. The aggravating fact is an element of the aggravated crime. Similarly, if the legislature, rather than creating grades of crimes, has provided for setting the punishment of a crime based on some fact—such as a fine that is proportional to the value of stolen goods—that fact is also an element. No multifactor parsing of statutes [is] necessary. One need only look to the kind, degree, or range of punishment to which the prosecution is by law entitled for a given set of facts. Each fact necessary for that entitlement is an element.

Cases from the founding to roughly the end of the Civil War establish the rule that I have described, applying it to all sorts of facts, including recidivism. As legislatures varied common-law crimes and created new crimes, American courts, particularly from the 1840's on, readily applied to these new laws the common-law understanding that a fact that is by law the basis for imposing or increasing punishment is an element. * * * Today's decision, far from being a sharp break with the past, marks nothing more than a return to the *status quo ante*—the status quo that reflected the original meaning of the Fifth and Sixth Amendments.

JUSTICE O'CONNOR, with whom THE CHIEF JUSTICE, JUSTICE KENNEDY, and JUSTICE BREYER join, dissenting.

[T]he Court [fails] to explain adequately why the Due Process Clauses of the Fifth and Fourteenth Amendments and the jury trial guarantee of the Sixth Amendment require application of its rule. Upon closer examination, it is possible that the Court's "increase in the maximum penalty" rule rests on a meaningless formalism that accords, at best, marginal protection for the constitutional rights that it seeks to effectuate.

As the Court acknowledges, we have never doubted that the Constitution permits Congress and the state legislatures to define criminal offenses, to prescribe broad ranges of punishment for those offenses, and to give judges discretion to decide where within those ranges a particular defendant's punishment should be set. * * * Under discretionary-sentencing schemes, a judge bases the defendant's sentence on any number of facts neither presented at trial nor found by a jury beyond a reasonable doubt.

> **Take Note**
>
> In a "discretionary sentencing scheme," the legislature provides that a judge has broad discretion to decide a sentence within broad ranges—say, 0 to 20 years—based on the judge's assessment of all the equities. In a "determinate sentencing scheme," in contrast, the legislature provides that a judge must choose a particular sentence, based on weight accorded to certain identified factors. What are the virtues of the competing approaches? What are the consequences of the Court's decision for those two types of sentencing schemes?

Under our precedent, [a] State may leave the determination of a defendant's sentence to a judge's discretionary decision within a prescribed range of penalties. When a judge, pursuant to that sentencing scheme, decides to increase a defendant's sentence on the basis of certain contested facts, those facts need not be proved to a jury beyond a reasonable doubt. The judge's findings, whether by proof beyond a reasonable doubt or less, suffice for purposes of the Constitution. Under the Court's decision today, however, it appears that once a legislature constrains judges' sentencing discretion by prescribing certain sentences that may only be imposed (or must be imposed) in connection with the same determinations of the same contested facts, the Constitution requires that the facts instead be proved to a jury beyond a reasonable doubt. I see no reason to treat the two schemes differently. * * * Although the Court acknowledges the legitimacy of discretionary sentencing by judges, it never provides a sound reason for treating judicial factfinding under determinate-sentencing schemes differently under the Constitution.

Consideration of the purposes underlying the Sixth Amendment's jury trial guarantee further demonstrates why our acceptance of judge-made findings in the context of discretionary sentencing suggests the approval of the same judge-made findings in the context of determinate sentencing as well. One important purpose of the Sixth Amendment's jury trial guarantee is to protect the criminal defendant against potentially arbitrary judges. It effectuates this promise by preserving, as a constitutional matter, certain fundamental decisions for a jury of one's peers, as opposed to a judge. * * * Clearly, the concerns animating the Sixth Amendment's jury trial guarantee, if they were to extend to the sentencing context at all, would apply with greater strength to a discretionary-sentencing scheme than to determinate sentencing. In the former scheme, the potential for mischief by an arbitrary judge is much greater, given that the judge's decision of where to set the defendant's sentence within the prescribed statutory range is left almost entirely to discretion. In contrast, under a determinate-sentencing system, the discretion the judge wields within the statutory range is tightly constrained. Accordingly, our approval of discretionary-sentencing schemes, in which a defendant is not entitled to have a jury make factual findings relevant to sentencing despite the effect those findings have on the severity of the defendant's sentence, demonstrates that the defendant should have no right to demand that a jury make the equivalent factual determinations under a determinate-sentencing scheme.

The Court appears to hold today, however, that a defendant is entitled to have a jury decide, by proof beyond a reasonable doubt, every fact relevant to the determination of sentence under a determinate-sentencing scheme. If this is an accurate description of the constitutional principle underlying the Court's opinion, its decision will have the effect of invalidating significant sentencing reform accomplished at the federal and state levels over the past three decades. * * *

Prior to the most recent wave of sentencing reform, the Federal Government and the States employed indeterminate-sentencing schemes in which judges and executive branch officials (*e.g.,* parole board officials) had substantial discretion to determine the actual length of a defendant's sentence. Studies of indeterminate-sentencing schemes found that similarly situated defendants often received widely disparate sentences. Although indeterminate sentencing was intended to soften the harsh and uniform sentences formerly imposed under mandatory-sentencing systems, some studies revealed that indeterminate sentencing actually had the opposite effect.

In response, Congress and the state legislatures shifted to determinate-sentencing schemes that aimed to limit judges' sentencing discretion and, thereby, afford similarly situated offenders equivalent treatment. The most well known of these reforms was the federal Sentencing Reform Act of 1984, 18 U.S.C. § 3551 *et seq.* In the Act, Congress created the United States Sentencing Commission, which in turn promulgated the Sentencing Guidelines that now govern sentencing by federal judges. Whether one believes the determinate-sentencing reforms have proved successful or not—and the subject is one of extensive debate among commentators—the apparent effect of the Court's opinion today is to halt the current debate on sentencing reform in its tracks and to invalidate with the stroke of a pen three decades' worth of nationwide reform, all in the name of a principle with a questionable constitutional pedigree. Indeed, it is ironic that the Court, in the name of constitutional rights meant to protect criminal defendants from the potentially arbitrary exercise of power by prosecutors and judges, appears to rest its decision on a principle that would render unconstitutional efforts by Congress and the state legislatures to place constraints on that very power in the sentencing context.

Finally, perhaps the most significant impact of the Court's decision will be a practical one—its unsettling effect on sentencing conducted under current federal and state determinate-sentencing schemes. [T]he Court does not say whether these schemes are constitutional, but its reasoning strongly suggests that they are not. Thus, with respect to past sentences handed down by judges under determinate-sentencing schemes, the Court's decision threatens to unleash a flood of petitions by convicted defendants seeking to invalidate their sentences in whole or in part on the authority of the Court's decision today. * * *

JUSTICE BREYER, with whom THE CHIEF JUSTICE joins, dissenting.

[The majority's] rule would seem to promote a procedural ideal—that of juries, not judges, determining the existence of those facts upon which increased punishment turns. But the real world of criminal justice cannot hope to meet any such ideal. It can function only with the help of procedural compromises, particularly in respect to sentencing. And those compromises, which are themselves necessary for the fair functioning of the criminal justice system, preclude implementation of the procedural model that today's decision reflects. At the very least, the impractical nature of the requirement that the majority now recognizes supports the proposition that the Constitution was not intended to embody it.

In modern times, the law has left it to the sentencing judge to find those facts which (within broad sentencing limits set by the legislature) determine the sentence of a convicted offender. The judge's factfinding role is not inevitable. One could imagine, for example, a pure "charge offense" sentencing system in which the degree of punishment depended only upon the crime charged (*e.g.*, eight mandatory years for robbery, six for arson, three for assault). But such a system would ignore many harms and risks of harm that the offender caused or created, and it would ignore many relevant offender characteristics. Hence, that imaginary "charge offense" system would not be a fair system, for it would lack proportionality, *i.e.,* it would treat different offenders similarly despite major differences in the manner in which each committed the same crime.

There are many such manner-related differences in respect to criminal behavior. Empirical data collected by the Sentencing Commission make clear that, before the Guidelines, judges who exercised discretion within broad legislatively determined sentencing limits (say, a range of 0 to 20 years) would impose very different sentences upon offenders engaged in the same basic criminal conduct, depending, for example, upon the amount of drugs distributed (in respect to drug crimes), the amount of money taken (in respect to robbery, theft, or fraud), the presence or use of a weapon, injury to a victim, the vulnerability of a victim, the offender's role in the offense, recidivism, and many other offense-related or offender-related factors. The majority does not deny that judges have exercised, and, constitutionally speaking, *may* exercise sentencing discretion in this way.

Nonetheless, it is important for present purposes to understand why *judges,* rather than *juries,* traditionally have determined the presence or absence of such sentence-affecting facts in any given case. And it is important to realize that the reason is not a theoretical one, but a practical one. It does not reflect (Justice SCALIA's opinion to the contrary notwithstanding) an ideal of procedural "fairness," but rather an administrative need for procedural *compromise.* There are, to put it simply, far too many potentially relevant sentencing factors to permit submission of all (or even many) of them to a jury. * * *

At the same time, to require jury consideration of all such factors—say, during trial where the issue is guilt or innocence—could easily place the defendant in the awkward (and conceivably unfair) position of having to deny he committed the crime yet offer proof about how he committed it, *e.g.,* "I did not sell drugs, but I sold no more than 500 grams." And while special postverdict sentencing juries could cure this problem, they have seemed (but for capital cases) not worth their administrative costs. * * *

By placing today's constitutional question in a broader context, this brief survey may help to clarify the nature of today's decision. It also may explain why, in respect to sentencing systems, proportionality, uniformity, and administrability are all aspects of that basic "fairness" that the Constitution demands. And it suggests my basic problem with the Court's rule: A sentencing system in which judges have discretion to find sentencing-related factors is a workable system and one that has long been thought consistent with the Constitution; why, then, would the Constitution treat sentencing *statutes* any differently?

[U]ntil fairly recent times many legislatures rarely focused upon sentencing factors. Rather, it appears they simply identified typical forms of antisocial conduct, defined basic "crimes," and attached a broad sentencing range to each definition—leaving judges free to decide how to sentence within those ranges in light of such factors as they found relevant. But the Constitution does not freeze 19th-century sentencing practices into permanent law. And dissatisfaction with the traditional sentencing system (reflecting its tendency to treat similar cases differently) has led modern legislatures to write new laws that refer specifically to sentencing factors.

Legislatures have tended to address the problem of too much judicial sentencing discretion in two ways. First, legislatures sometimes have created sentencing commissions armed with delegated authority to make more uniform judicial exercise of that discretion. * * * Second, legislatures sometimes have directly limited the use [of] particular factors in sentencing, either by specifying statutorily how a particular factor will affect the sentence imposed * * *. Such a statute might state explicitly, for example, that a particular factor, say, use of a weapon, recidivism, injury to a victim, or bad motive, "shall" increase, or "may" increase, a particular sentence in a particular way.

The issue the Court decides today involves this second kind of legislation. The Court holds that a legislature cannot enact such legislation (where an increase in the maximum is involved) unless the factor at issue has been charged, tried to a jury, and found to exist beyond a reasonable doubt. My question in respect to this holding is, simply, "*why* would the Constitution contain such a requirement"?

* * * The majority raises no objection to traditional pre-Guidelines sentencing procedures under which judges, not juries, made the factual findings that would lead to an increase in an individual offender's sentence. How does a legislative determination differ in any significant way? For example, if a judge may on his or her own decide that victim injury or bad motive should increase a bank robber's sentence from 5 years to 10, why does it matter that a legislature instead enacts a statute that increases a bank robber's sentence from 5 years to 10 based on this same judicial finding?

The majority appears to offer two responses. First, it argues for a limiting principle that would prevent a legislature with broad authority from transforming (jury-determined) facts that constitute elements of a crime into (judge-determined) sentencing factors, thereby removing procedural protections that the Constitution would otherwise require. The majority's cure, however, is not aimed at the disease.

The same "transformational" problem exists under traditional sentencing law, where legislation, silent as to sentencing factors, grants the judge virtually unchecked discretion to sentence within a broad range. Under such a system, judges or prosecutors can similarly "transform" crimes, punishing an offender convicted of one crime as if he had committed another. A prosecutor, for example, might charge an offender with five counts of embezzlement (each subject to a 10-year maximum penalty), while asking the judge to impose maximum and consecutive sentences because the embezzler murdered his employer. And, as part of the traditional sentencing discretion that the majority concedes judges retain, the judge, not a jury, would determine the last-mentioned relevant fact, *i.e.,* that the murder actually occurred.

This egregious example shows the problem's complexity. The source of the problem lies not in a legislature's power to enact sentencing factors, but in the traditional legislative power to select elements defining a crime, the traditional legislative power to set broad sentencing ranges, and the traditional judicial power to choose a sentence within that range on the basis of relevant offender conduct. Conversely, the solution to the problem lies, not in prohibiting legislatures from enacting sentencing factors, but in sentencing rules that determine punishments on the basis of properly defined relevant conduct * * *

Second, the majority, in support of its constitutional rule, emphasizes the concept of a statutory "maximum." The Court points out that a sentencing judge (or a commission) traditionally has determined, and now still determines, sentences *within* a legislated range capped by a maximum (a range that the legislature itself sets). I concede the truth of the majority's statement, but I do not understand its relevance.

From a defendant's perspective, the legislature's decision to cap the possible range of punishment at a statutorily prescribed "maximum" would affect the actual sentence imposed no differently than a sentencing commission's (or a sentencing judge's) similar determination. Indeed, as a practical matter, a legislated mandatory "minimum" is far more important to an actual defendant. A judge and a commission, after all, are legally free to select any sentence below a statute's maximum, but they are not free to subvert a statutory minimum. And, as Justice THOMAS indicates, all the considerations of fairness that might support submission to a jury of a factual matter that increases a statutory maximum apply *a fortiori* to any matter that would increase a statutory minimum. To repeat, I do not understand why, when a legislature *authorizes* a judge to impose a higher penalty for bank robbery (based, say, on the court's finding that a victim was injured or the defendant's motive was bad), a new crime is born; but where a legislature *requires* a judge to impose a higher penalty than he otherwise would (within a pre-existing statutory range) based on similar criteria, it is not.

I certainly do not believe that the present sentencing system is one of "perfect equity," *ante* (SCALIA, J., concurring), and I am willing, consequently, to assume that the majority's rule would provide a degree of increased procedural protection in respect to those particular sentencing factors currently embodied in statutes. I nonetheless believe that any such increased protection provides little practical help and comes at too high a price. [B]y leaving mandatory minimum sentences untouched, the majority's rule simply encourages any legislature interested in asserting control over the sentencing process to do so by creating those minimums. That result would mean significantly less procedural fairness, not more.

POINTS FOR DISCUSSION

a. The Due Process Clause and the Sixth Amendment Right to an Impartial Jury

The Court in *Apprendi* concluded that, "[o]ther than the fact of a prior conviction, any fact that increases the penalty for a crime beyond the prescribed statutory maximum must be submitted to a jury, and proved beyond a reasonable doubt." Did the Court view this rule as a general requirement of Due Process, as a corollary of the *Winship* reasonable doubt requirement? Or did it view it as a specific requirement of the Sixth Amendment right to a jury trial (as incorporated by the Fourteenth Amendment)?

b. The Scope of the Court's Holding

Imagine that a state statute provides that the punishment for a crime shall be no less than 10 years and no more than 20 years. The statute gives the judge complete discretion about which sentence within the range to choose. After *Apprendi*, can the judge impose a 20-year sentence based on her finding that the defendant acted with racist intent, even if the jury has not found such a fact beyond a reasonable doubt? If such a decision would not violate the rule announced in *Apprendi*, then is the rule significant?

c. Sentencing Guidelines

Since the mid-1980s, the federal courts have followed sentencing guidelines issued by the United States Sentencing Commission. The object of the system of guidelines was to create more consistency in sentences and to reduce the disparities that were common in sentencing in the pre-guidelines system. Many provisions in the guidelines authorized trial judges to impose enhanced sentences based on findings that the judge made during the sentencing phase of a trial by something less than a reasonable doubt standard. In *Blakely v. Washington*, 542 U.S. 296 (2004), the Court held that a state trial court's sentencing of a defendant to more than the statutory maximum of the standard range for his offense, on the basis of the judge's finding that the defendant acted with deliberate cruelty, violated defendant's Sixth Amendment right to trial by jury. One year later, the Court held in *United States v. Booker*, 543 U.S. 220 (2005), that the Sixth Amendment requirements announced in *Apprendi* apply to the federal sentencing guidelines, as well. (At the time of the *Booker* decision, the federal sentencing guidelines were binding on the courts. Because of the *Apprendi* issues raised in *Booker*, the guidelines now are no longer binding. See *Peugh v. United States*, 569 U.S. 530 (2013).)

C. THE RIGHT TO CONFRONTATION

The Sixth Amendment provides: "In all criminal prosecutions, the accused shall enjoy the right * * * to be confronted with the witnesses against him * * *." This provision is usually known as the "Confrontation Clause."

Rules of evidence typically allow a defendant to "confront" the witnesses against him by cross-examining them. For example, in a hypothetical bank robbery case, suppose that the prosecution calls Smith, a bystander, as a witness. The prosecutor asks Smith what he saw on the night of the robbery. Smith answers that he saw Maggs break into the bank. After the prosecutor has finished asking Smith questions, Maggs has the opportunity to cross-examine Smith. Maggs's attorney might ask Smith questions like: "Isn't it true that it was dark outside that night? And isn't it true you were more than 100 feet away? You weren't wearing your eyeglasses, were you?"

Why does the Constitution afford defendants a right to confront the witnesses against them? Part of the answer, in the words of the great evidence scholar Professor John H. Wigmore, is that "[c]ross-examination is the greatest legal engine ever invented for the discovery of truth." By cross-examining Smith, Maggs can expose the limits of Smith's observation, and perhaps catch him if he tries to exaggerate or prevaricate. Another part of the answer is that the Framers knew that tyrants throughout history had unfairly treated defendants in criminal trials by denying them the opportunity to question their accusers. The cases below discuss some of this history.

The federal and state governments have never sought to eliminate all opportunity for cross-examination of witnesses in criminal cases. But occasionally they have created exceptions to the ordinary right of confrontation to address special cases where cross-examination might be oppressive to victims or burdensome to the government. In reviewing these actions, the Supreme Court has held that cross-examination does not have to involve an actual face-to-face confrontation to satisfy the Confrontation Clause. But the Sixth Amendment prohibits the government from introducing testimonial evidence against a defendant unless the defendant can cross-examine the witness or unless the witness is unavailable and the defendant previously had an opportunity to cross-examine the witness. We consider these rules in the cases that follow.

MARYLAND V. CRAIG
497 U.S. 836 (1990)

JUSTICE O'CONNOR delivered the opinion of the Court.

This case requires us to decide whether the Confrontation Clause of the Sixth Amendment categorically prohibits a child witness in a child abuse case from testifying against a defendant at trial, outside the defendant's physical presence, by one-way closed circuit television.

In October 1986, a Howard County grand jury charged respondent, Sandra Ann Craig, with child abuse, first and second degree sexual offenses, perverted sexual practice, assault, and battery. The named victim in each count was a 6-year-old girl who, from August 1984 to June 1986, had attended a kindergarten and prekindergarten center owned and operated by Craig.

In March 1987, before the case went to trial, the State sought to invoke a Maryland statutory procedure that permits a judge to receive, by one-way closed circuit television, the testimony of a child witness who is alleged to be a victim of child abuse. To invoke the procedure, the trial judge must first "determin[e] that testimony by the child victim in the courtroom will result in the child suffering serious emotional distress such that the child cannot reasonably communicate." Md. Cts. & Jud. Proc. Code Ann. § 9–102(a)(1)(ii) (1989). Once the procedure is invoked, the child witness, prosecutor, and defense counsel withdraw to a separate room; the judge, jury, and defendant remain in the courtroom. The child witness is then examined and cross-examined in the separate room, while a video monitor records and displays the witness' testimony to those in the courtroom. During this time the witness cannot see the defendant. The defendant remains in electronic communication with defense counsel, and objections may be made and ruled on as if the witness were testifying in the courtroom.

Craig objected to the use of the procedure on Confrontation Clause grounds, but the trial court rejected that contention, concluding that although the statute "take[s] away the right of the defendant to be face to face with his or her accuser," the defendant retains the "essence of the right of confrontation," including the right to observe, cross-examine, and have the jury view the demeanor of the witness. The trial court further found that, "based upon the evidence presented . . . the testimony of each of these children in a courtroom will result in each child suffering serious emotional distress . . . such that each of these children cannot reasonably communicate." The trial court then found the named victim and three other children competent to testify and accordingly permitted them to testify against Craig via the one-way closed circuit television procedure. The jury convicted Craig on all counts, and the Maryland Court of Special Appeals affirmed the convictions.

The Court of Appeals of Maryland reversed and remanded for a new trial. The Court of Appeals rejected Craig's argument that the Confrontation Clause requires in all cases a face-to-face courtroom encounter between the accused and his accusers, but concluded [that the Sixth Amendment requires the witness to testify in the presence of the defendant "[u]nless prevention of 'eyeball-to-eyeball' confrontation is necessary to obtain the trial testimony of the child * * *." The Court of Appeals concluded that the state had not made such a showing.]

The central concern of the Confrontation Clause is to ensure the reliability of the evidence against a criminal defendant by subjecting it to rigorous testing in the context of an adversary proceeding before the trier of fact. The word "confront," after all, also means a clashing of forces or ideas, thus carrying with it the notion of adversariness. As we noted in our earliest case interpreting the Clause:

> "The primary object of the constitutional provision in question was to prevent depositions or *ex parte* affidavits, such as were sometimes admitted in civil cases, being used against the prisoner in lieu of a personal examination and cross-examination of the witness in which the accused has an opportunity, not only of testing the recollection and sifting the conscience of the witness, but of compelling him to stand face to face with the jury in order that they may look at him, and judge by his demeanor upon the stand and the manner in which he gives his testimony whether he is worthy of belief." *Mattox v. United States*, 156 U.S. 237, 242 (1895).

As this description indicates, the right guaranteed by the Confrontation Clause includes not only a "personal examination," but also "(1) insures that the witness will give his statements under oath—thus impressing him with the seriousness of the matter and guarding against the lie by the possibility of a penalty for perjury; (2) forces the witness to submit to cross-examination, the 'greatest legal engine ever invented for the discovery of truth'; [and] (3) permits the jury that is to decide the defendant's fate to observe the demeanor of the witness in making his statement, thus aiding the jury in assessing his credibility." *California v. Green,* 399 U.S. 149, 158 (1970).

The combined effect of these elements of confrontation—physical presence, oath, cross-examination, and observation of demeanor by the trier of fact—serves the purposes of the Confrontation Clause by ensuring that evidence admitted against an accused is reliable and subject to the rigorous adversarial testing that is the norm of Anglo-American criminal proceedings. See *Kentucky v. Stincer,* 482 U.S. 730, 739 (1987) ("[T]he right to confrontation is a functional one for the purpose of promoting reliability in a criminal trial").

We have recognized, for example, that face-to-face confrontation enhances the accuracy of factfinding by reducing the risk that a witness will wrongfully implicate an innocent person. See *Coy v. Iowa,* 487 U.S. 1012, 1019–20 (1988) ("It is always more difficult to tell a lie about a person 'to his face' than 'behind his back.' . . . That face-to-face presence may, unfortunately, upset the truthful rape victim or abused child; but by the same token it may confound and undo the false accuser, or reveal the child coached by a malevolent adult"). We have also noted the strong symbolic purpose served by requiring adverse witnesses at trial to testify in the accused's presence. See *Coy,* 487 U.S., at 1017 ("[T]here is something deep in human nature that regards face-to-face confrontation between accused and accuser as 'essential to a fair trial in a criminal prosecution' ").

Although face-to-face confrontation forms "the core of the values furthered by the Confrontation Clause," *Green,* 399 U.S., at 157, we have nevertheless recognized that it is not the *sine qua non* of the confrontation right. See *Delaware v. Fensterer,* 474 U.S. 15, 22 (1985) (*per curiam*) ("[T]he Confrontation Clause is generally satisfied when the defense is given a full and fair opportunity to probe and expose [testimonial] infirmities [such as forgetfulness, confusion, or evasion] through cross-examination, thereby calling to the attention of the factfinder the reasons for giving scant weight to the witness' testimony").

For this reason, we have never insisted on an actual face-to-face encounter at trial in *every* instance in which testimony is admitted against a defendant. Instead, we have repeatedly held that the Clause permits, where necessary, the admission of certain hearsay statements against a defendant despite the defendant's inability to confront the declarant at trial. In *Mattox,* for example, we held that the testimony of a Government witness at a former trial against the defendant, where the witness was fully cross-examined but had died after the first trial, was admissible in evidence against the defendant at his second trial. See 156 U.S., at 240–244. * * *

Make the Connection

Is the admission into evidence of a statement by an accuser, without calling the accuser to testify, consistent with the Confrontation Clause? We consider this question later in this chapter.

We have accordingly stated that a literal reading of the Confrontation Clause would "abrogate virtually every hearsay exception, a result long rejected as unintended and too extreme." *Ohio v. Roberts,* 448 U.S. 56, 63 (1980). Thus, in certain narrow circumstances, "competing interests, if 'closely examined,' may warrant dispensing with confrontation at trial." *Id.,* at 64. * * * Given our hearsay cases, the word "confronted," as used in the Confrontation Clause, cannot simply mean face-to-face confrontation, for the Clause would then, contrary to our cases, prohibit the admission of any accusatory hearsay statement made by an absent declarant—a declarant who is undoubtedly as much a "witness against" a defendant as one who actually testifies at trial.

In sum, our precedents establish that "the Confrontation Clause reflects a *preference* for face-to-face confrontation at trial," *Roberts,* 448 U.S., at 63, a preference that "must occasionally give way to considerations of public policy and the necessities of the case," *Mattox,* 156 U.S., at 243. * * * We have accordingly interpreted the Confrontation Clause in a manner sensitive to its purposes and sensitive to the necessities of trial and the adversary process. Thus, though we reaffirm the importance of face-to-face confrontation with witnesses appearing at trial, we cannot say that such confrontation is an indispensable element of the Sixth Amendment's guarantee of the right to confront one's accusers. * * *

That the face-to-face confrontation requirement is not absolute does not, of course, mean that it may easily be dispensed with. As we suggested in *Coy,* our precedents confirm that a defendant's right to confront accusatory witnesses may be satisfied absent a physical, face-to-face confrontation at trial only where denial of such confrontation is necessary to further an important public policy and only where the reliability of the testimony is otherwise assured. See 487 U.S., at 1021.

Maryland's statutory procedure, when invoked, prevents a child witness from seeing the defendant as he or she testifies against the defendant at trial. We find it significant, however, that Maryland's procedure preserves all of the other elements of the confrontation right: The child witness must be competent to testify and must testify under oath; the defendant retains full opportunity for contemporaneous cross-examination; and the judge, jury, and defendant are able to view (albeit by video monitor) the demeanor (and body) of the witness as he or she testifies. Although we are mindful of the many subtle effects face-to-face confrontation may have on an adversary criminal proceeding, the presence of these other elements of confrontation—oath, cross-examination, and observation of the witness' demeanor—adequately ensures that the testimony is both reliable and subject to rigorous adversarial testing in a manner functionally equivalent to that accorded live, in-person testimony. These safeguards of reliability and adversariness render the use of such a procedure a far cry from the undisputed prohibition of the Confrontation Clause: trial by *ex parte* affidavit or inquisition * * *. Rather, we think these elements of effective confrontation not only permit a defendant to "confound and undo the false accuser, or reveal the child coached by a malevolent adult," *Coy,* 487 U.S., at 1020, but may well aid a defendant in eliciting favorable testimony from the child witness. Indeed, to the extent the child witness' testimony may be said to be technically given out of court (though we do not so hold), these assurances of reliability and adversariness are far greater than those required for admission of hearsay testimony under the Confrontation Clause. We are therefore confident that use of the one-way closed circuit television procedure, where necessary to further an important state interest, does not impinge upon the truth-seeking or symbolic purposes of the Confrontation Clause.

The critical inquiry in this case, therefore, is whether use of the procedure is necessary to further an important state interest. The State contends that it has a substantial interest in protecting children who are allegedly victims of child abuse from the trauma of testifying against the alleged perpetrator and that its statutory procedure for receiving testimony from such witnesses is necessary to further that interest.

We have of course recognized that a State's interest in "the protection of minor victims of sex crimes from further trauma and embarrassment" is a "compelling" one. *Globe Newspaper Co. v. Superior Court of Norfolk County,* 457 U.S. 596, 607 (1982). "[W]e have sustained legislation aimed at protecting the physical and emotional well-being of youth even when the laws have operated in the sensitive area of constitutionally protected rights." *New York v. Ferber,* 458 U.S. 747, 756–757 (1982).

> **Make the Connection**
>
> The Court held in *Ferber* that child pornography is outside of the protection of the free speech clause of the First Amendment. We considered the Court's decision in *Ferber* in Chapter 8.

We likewise conclude today that a State's interest in the physical and psychological well-being of child abuse victims may be sufficiently important to outweigh, at least in some cases, a defendant's right to face his or her accusers in court. That a significant majority of States have enacted statutes to protect child witnesses from the trauma of giving testimony in child abuse cases attests to the widespread belief in the importance of such a public policy. Thirty-seven States, for example, permit the use of videotaped testimony of sexually abused children; 24 States have authorized the use of one-way closed circuit television testimony in child abuse cases; and 8 States authorize the use of a two-way system in which the child witness is permitted to see the courtroom and the defendant on a video monitor and in which the jury and judge are permitted to view the child during the testimony.

* * * Given the State's traditional and "transcendent interest in protecting the welfare of children," *Ginsberg v. New York,* 390 U.S. 629, 640 (1968), and buttressed by the growing body of academic literature documenting the psychological trauma suffered by child abuse victims who must testify in court, see Brief for American Psychological Association as *Amicus Curiae* 7–13; G. Goodman et al., Emotional Effects of Criminal Court Testimony on Child Sexual Assault Victims, Final Report to the National Institute of Justice (presented as conference paper at annual convention of American Psychological Assn., Aug.1989), we will not second-guess the considered judgment of the Maryland Legislature regarding the importance of its interest in protecting child abuse victims from the emotional trauma of testifying. Accordingly, we hold that, if the State makes an adequate showing of necessity, the state interest in protecting child witnesses from the trauma of testifying in a child abuse case is sufficiently important to justify the use of a special procedure that permits a child witness in such cases to testify at trial against a defendant in the absence of face-to-face confrontation with the defendant.

The requisite finding of necessity must of course be a case-specific one: The trial court must hear evidence and determine whether use of the one-way closed circuit television procedure is necessary to protect the welfare of the particular child witness who seeks to testify. The trial court must also find that the child witness would be traumatized, not by the courtroom generally, but by the presence of the defendant. Denial of face-to-face confrontation is not needed to further the state interest in protecting the child witness from trauma unless it is the presence of the defendant that causes the trauma. In other words, if the state interest were merely the interest in protecting child witnesses from courtroom trauma generally, denial of face-to-face confrontation would be unnecessary because the child could be permitted to testify in less intimidating surroundings, albeit with the defendant present. Finally, the trial court must find that the emotional distress suffered by the child witness in the presence of the defendant is more than *de minimis, i.e.,* more than "mere nervousness or excitement or some reluctance to testify," *Wildermuth v. State,* 530 A.2d 275, 289 (1987). We need not decide the minimum showing of emotional trauma required for use of the special procedure, however, because the Maryland statute, which requires a determination that the child witness will suffer "serious emotional distress such that the child cannot reasonably communicate," § 9–102(a)(1)(ii), clearly suffices to meet constitutional standards.

To be sure, face-to-face confrontation may be said to cause trauma for the very purpose of eliciting truth, but we think that the use of Maryland's special procedure, where necessary to further the important state interest in preventing trauma to child witnesses in child abuse cases, adequately ensures the accuracy of the testimony and preserves the adversary nature of the trial. Indeed, where face-to-face confrontation causes significant emotional distress in a child witness, there is evidence that such confrontation would in fact *disserve* the Confrontation Clause's truth-seeking goal. See, *e.g., Coy,* 487 U.S., at 1032 (BLACKMUN, J., dissenting) (face-to-face confrontation "may so overwhelm the child as to prevent the possibility of effective testimony, thereby undermining the truth-finding function of the trial itself"); Brief for American Psychological Association as *Amicus Curiae* 18–24.

Food for Thought

How would you describe the Court's approach to constitutional interpretation? Note that the Court ascertains the purpose of the Confrontation Clause, and then asks whether the challenged procedure is consistent with that purpose. Would it make more sense to consider whether the challenged procedure is consistent with the text of the Confrontation Clause? Would that approach obviously lead to a different conclusion?

In sum, we conclude that where necessary to protect a child witness from trauma that would be caused by testifying in the physical presence of the defendant, at least where such trauma would impair the child's ability to communicate, the Confrontation Clause does not prohibit use of a procedure that, despite the absence of face-to-face confrontation, ensures the reliability of the evidence by subjecting it to rigorous adversarial testing and thereby preserves the essence of effective confrontation. Because there is no dispute that the child witnesses in this case testified under oath, were subject to full cross-examination, and were able to be observed by the judge, jury, and defendant as they testified, we conclude that, to the extent that a proper finding of necessity has been made, the admission of such testimony would be consonant with the Confrontation Clause.

[W]e cannot be certain whether the Court of Appeals would reach the same conclusion in light of the legal standard we establish today. We therefore vacate the judgment of the Court of Appeals of Maryland and remand the case for further proceedings not inconsistent with this opinion.

JUSTICE SCALIA, with whom JUSTICE BRENNAN, JUSTICE MARSHALL, and JUSTICE STEVENS join, dissenting.

Seldom has this Court failed so conspicuously to sustain a categorical guarantee of the Constitution against the tide of prevailing current opinion. The Sixth Amendment provides, with unmistakable clarity, that "[i]n all criminal prosecutions, the accused shall enjoy the right . . . to be confronted with the witnesses against him." The purpose of enshrining this protection in the Constitution was to assure that none of the many policy interests from time to time pursued by statutory law could overcome a defendant's right to face his or her accusers in court. The Court, however, [concludes that] "a State's interest in the physical and psychological well-being of child abuse victims may be sufficiently important to outweigh, at least in some cases, a defendant's right to face his or her accusers in court. * * *"

Because of this subordination of explicit constitutional text to currently favored public policy, the following scene can be played out in an American courtroom for the first time in two centuries: A father whose young daughter has been given over to the exclusive custody of his estranged wife, or a mother whose young son has been taken into custody by the State's child welfare department, is sentenced to prison for sexual abuse on the basis of testimony by a child the parent has not seen or spoken to for many months; and the guilty verdict is rendered without giving the parent so much as the opportunity to sit in the presence of the child, and to ask, personally or through counsel, "it is really not true, is it, that I—your father (or mother) whom you see before you—did these terrible things?" Perhaps that is a procedure today's society desires; perhaps (though I doubt it) it is even a fair procedure; but it is assuredly not a procedure permitted by the Constitution.

According to the Court, "we cannot say that [face-to-face] confrontation [with witnesses appearing at trial] is an indispensable element of the Sixth Amendment's guarantee of the right to confront one's accusers." That is rather like saying "we cannot say that being tried before a jury is an indispensable element of the Sixth Amendment's guarantee of the right to jury trial." The Court makes the impossible plausible by recharacterizing the Confrontation Clause, so that confrontation (redesignated "face-to-face confrontation") becomes only one of many "elements of confrontation." The reasoning is as follows: The Confrontation Clause guarantees not only what it explicitly provides for—"face-to-face" confrontation—but also implied and collateral rights such as cross-examination, oath, and observation of demeanor (TRUE); the purpose of this entire cluster of rights is to ensure the reliability of evidence (TRUE); the Maryland procedure preserves the implied and collateral rights (TRUE), which adequately ensure the reliability of evidence (perhaps TRUE); therefore the Confrontation Clause is not violated by denying what it explicitly provides for—"face-to-face" confrontation (unquestionably FALSE). This reasoning abstracts from the right to its purposes, and then eliminates the right. It is wrong because the Confrontation Clause does not guarantee reliable evidence; it guarantees specific trial procedures that were thought to *assure* reliable evidence, undeniably among which was "face-to-face" confrontation. Whatever else it may mean in addition, the defendant's constitutional right "to be confronted with the witnesses against him" means, always and everywhere, at least what it explicitly says: the "right to meet face to face all those who appear and give evidence at trial." *Coy v. Iowa,* 487 U.S. 1012, 1016 (1988), quoting *California v. Green,* 399 U.S. 149, 175 (1970) (Harlan, J., concurring).

Much of the Court's opinion consists of applying to this case the mode of analysis we have used in the admission of hearsay evidence. * * * [But we] have [found] implicit in the Confrontation Clause some limitation upon hearsay evidence, since otherwise the government could subvert the confrontation right by putting on witnesses who know nothing except what an absent declarant said. And in determining the scope of that implicit limitation, we have focused upon whether the reliability of the hearsay statements (which are not *expressly* excluded by the Confrontation Clause) "is otherwise assured." The same test cannot be applied, however, to permit what is explicitly forbidden by the constitutional text; there is simply no room for interpretation with regard to "the irreducible literal meaning of the Clause." *Coy,* 487 U.S., at 1020–1021.

The Court characterizes the State's interest which "outweigh[s]" the explicit text of the Constitution as an "interest in the physical and psychological well-being of child abuse victims," an "interest in protecting" such victims "from the emotional trauma of testifying." That is not so. A child who meets the Maryland statute's requirement of suffering such "serious emotional distress" from confrontation that he "cannot reasonably communicate" would seem entirely safe. Why would a prosecutor want to call a witness who cannot reasonably communicate? * * * Protection of the child's interest—as far as the Confrontation Clause is concerned[2]—is entirely within Maryland's control. The State's interest

---

[2] A different situation would be presented if the defendant sought to call the child. In that event, the State's refusal to compel the child to appear, or its insistence upon a procedure such as that set forth in the Maryland statute as a condition of its compelling him to do so, would call into question—initially, at least, and

here is in fact no more and no less than what the State's interest always is when it seeks to get a class of evidence admitted in criminal proceedings: more convictions of guilty defendants. That is not an unworthy interest, but it should not be dressed up as a humanitarian one.

And the interest on the other side is also what it usually is when the State seeks to get a new class of evidence admitted: fewer convictions of innocent defendants—specifically, in the present context, innocent defendants accused of particularly heinous crimes. The "special" reasons that exist for suspending one of the usual guarantees of reliability in the case of children's testimony are perhaps matched by "special" reasons for being particularly insistent upon it in the case of children's testimony. Some studies show that children are substantially more vulnerable to suggestion than adults, and often unable to separate recollected fantasy (or suggestion) from reality. * * *

In the last analysis, however, this debate is not an appropriate one. I have no need to defend the value of confrontation, because the Court has no authority to question it. * * * For good or bad, the Sixth Amendment requires confrontation, and we are not at liberty to ignore it. To quote the document one last time (for it plainly says all that need be said): "In *all* criminal prosecutions, the accused shall enjoy the right . . . to be confronted with the witnesses against him" (emphasis added).

The Court today has applied "interest-balancing" analysis where the text of the Constitution simply does not permit it. We are not free to conduct a cost-benefit analysis of clear and explicit constitutional guarantees, and then to adjust their meaning to comport with our findings. The Court has convincingly proved that the Maryland procedure serves a valid interest, and gives the defendant virtually everything the Confrontation Clause guarantees (everything, that is, except confrontation). I am persuaded, therefore, that the Maryland procedure is virtually constitutional. Since it is not, however, actually constitutional I would affirm the judgment of the Maryland Court of Appeals reversing the judgment of conviction.

POINTS FOR DISCUSSION

a.   The Confrontation Clause and Victims of Child Abuse

The Court concluded in *Craig* that "use of the one-way closed circuit television procedure, where necessary to further an important state interest, does not impinge

---

perhaps exclusively—the scope of the defendant's Sixth Amendment right "to have compulsory process for obtaining witnesses in his favor."

upon the truth-seeking or symbolic purposes of the Confrontation Clause," and that "a State's interest in the physical and psychological well-being of child abuse victims may be sufficiently important to outweigh, at least in some cases, a defendant's right to face his or her accusers in court." Does this mean that anytime an alternative procedure advances the truth-seeking functions of confrontation, the state can dispense with face-to-face confrontation in the courtroom if it can articulate an important interest advanced by the alternative procedure? Or is there something unique about child abuse and child testimony?

b.   Approach to Constitutional Interpretation

The Court sought to interpret the Confrontation Clause to accommodate competing interests: the interest in truth-seeking advanced by the procedure of confrontation, on the one hand, and the interest in protecting children from psychological trauma, on the other. Is it appropriate for the Court to limit the right of confrontation in order to advance other interests? Justice Scalia accused the Court effectively of dispensing with a clear constitutional requirement. Which approach is more defensible? Which approach makes more sense in this context?

In *Craig*, the Court asserted, "we have repeatedly held that the [Confrontation] Clause permits, where necessary, the admission of certain hearsay statements against a defendant despite the defendant's inability to confront the declarant at trial." Hearsay is an out-of-court statement offered to prove the truth of the matter asserted in the statement. When should the admission of such out-of-court statements implicate the Confrontation Clause? Consider the case that follows.

CRAWFORD V. WASHINGTON
541 U.S. 36 (2004)

JUSTICE SCALIA delivered the opinion of the Court.

Petitioner Michael Crawford stabbed a man who allegedly tried to rape his wife, Sylvia. At his trial, the State played for the jury Sylvia's tape-recorded statement to the police describing the stabbing, even though he had no opportunity for cross-examination. The Washington Supreme Court upheld petitioner's conviction after determining that Sylvia's statement was reliable. The question presented is whether this procedure complied with the Sixth Amendment's guarantee that, "[i]n all criminal prosecutions, the accused shall enjoy the right . . . to be confronted with the witnesses against him."

On August 5, 1999, Kenneth Lee was stabbed at his apartment. Police arrested petitioner later that night. After giving petitioner and his wife *Miranda* warnings, detectives interrogated each of them twice. Petitioner eventually confessed that he and Sylvia had gone in search of Lee because he was upset over an earlier incident in which Lee had tried to rape her. The two had found Lee at his apartment, and a fight ensued in which Lee was stabbed in the torso and petitioner's hand was cut.

[Petitioner's account of the fight stated that Lee had reached for something, possibly a weapon, and pulled it out.] Sylvia generally corroborated petitioner's story about the events leading up to the fight, but her account of the fight itself was arguably different—particularly with respect to whether Lee had drawn a weapon before petitioner assaulted him * * *. [She stated that she didn't see anything in Lee's hands at the moment when the petitioner stabbed him.]

The State charged petitioner with assault and attempted murder. At trial, he claimed self-defense. Sylvia did not testify because of the state marital privilege, which generally bars a spouse from testifying without the other spouse's consent. See Wash. Rev.Code § 5.60.060(1) (1994). In Washington, this privilege does not extend to a spouse's out-of-court statements admissible under a hearsay exception, see *State v. Burden,* 841 P.2d 758, 761 (1992), so the State sought to introduce Sylvia's tape-recorded statements to the police as evidence that the stabbing was not in self-defense. Noting that Sylvia had admitted she led petitioner to Lee's apartment and thus had facilitated the assault, the State invoked the hearsay exception for statements against penal interest, Wash. Rule Evid. 804(b)(3) (2003).

> **Take Note**
>
> Although all court systems in the United States generally exclude the introduction into evidence of hearsay—preferring instead the in-court testimony of the declarant, subject to cross-examination—every jurisdiction has a series of exceptions that permit the introduction of hearsay under certain circumstances.

Petitioner countered that, state law notwithstanding, admitting the evidence would violate his federal constitutional right to be "confronted with the witnesses against him." Amdt. 6. According to our description of that right in *Ohio v. Roberts,* 448 U.S. 56, 66 (1980), it does not bar admission of an unavailable witness's statement against a criminal defendant if the statement bears "adequate 'indicia of reliability.'" To meet that test, evidence must either fall within a "firmly rooted hearsay exception" or bear "particularized guarantees of trustworthiness." *Ibid.* The trial court here admitted the statement on the latter ground, offering several reasons why it was trustworthy: Sylvia was not shifting blame but rather corroborating her husband's story that he acted in self-defense or "justified reprisal"; she had direct knowledge as an eyewitness; she was describing recent events; and she was being questioned by a "neutral" law enforcement officer. The prosecution played the tape for the jury and relied on it in closing, arguing that it was "damning evidence" that "completely refutes [petitioner's] claim of self-defense." The jury convicted petitioner of assault.

The Washington Court of Appeals reversed. It applied a nine-factor test to determine whether Sylvia's statement bore particularized guarantees of trustworthiness, and [concluded that it did not]. The Washington Supreme Court reinstated the conviction, unanimously concluding that, although Sylvia's statement did not fall under a firmly rooted hearsay exception, it bore guarantees of trustworthiness: "[W]hen a codefendant's confession is virtually identical [to, *i.e.,* interlocks with,] that of a defendant, it may be deemed reliable." 54 P.3d 656, 663 (2002).

The Sixth Amendment's Confrontation Clause provides that, "[i]n all criminal prosecutions, the accused shall enjoy the right . . . to be confronted with the witnesses against him." * * * The Constitution's text does not alone resolve this case. One could plausibly read "witnesses against" a defendant to mean those who actually testify at trial, those whose statements are offered at trial, or something in-between. We must therefore turn to the historical background of the Clause to understand its meaning.

The right to confront one's accusers is a concept that dates back to Roman times. The founding generation's immediate source of the concept, however, was the common law. English common law has long differed from continental civil law in regard to the manner in which witnesses give testimony in criminal trials. The common-law tradition is one of live testimony in court subject to adversarial testing, while the civil law condones examination in private by judicial officers. See 3 W. Blackstone, Commentaries on the Laws of England 373–374 (1768).

Nonetheless, England at times adopted elements of the civil-law practice. Justices of the peace or other officials examined suspects and witnesses before trial. These examinations were sometimes read in court in lieu of live testimony, a practice that "occasioned frequent demands by the prisoner to have his 'accusers,' *i.e.* the witnesses against him, brought before him face to face." 1 J. Stephen, History of the Criminal Law of England 326 (1883). In some cases, these demands were refused. See 9 W. Holdsworth, History of English Law 216–217, 228 (3d ed.1944); *e.g., Raleigh's Case,* 2 How. St. Tr. 1, 15–16, 24 (1603).

Pretrial examinations became routine under two statutes passed during the reign of Queen Mary in the 16th century, 1 & 2 Phil. & M., c. 13 (1554), and 2 &

3 *id.,* c. 10 (1555). These Marian bail and committal statutes required justices of the peace to examine suspects and witnesses in felony cases and to certify the results to the court. Whatever the original purpose, [these examinations] came to be used as evidence in some cases, resulting in an adoption of continental procedure.

The most notorious instances of civil-law examination occurred in the great political trials of the 16th and 17th centuries. One such was the 1603 trial of Sir Walter Raleigh for treason. Lord Cobham, Raleigh's alleged accomplice, had implicated him in an examination before the Privy Council and in a letter. At Raleigh's trial, these were read to the jury. Raleigh argued that Cobham had lied to save himself * * *. 1 D. Jardine, Criminal Trials 435 (1832). Suspecting that Cobham would recant, Raleigh demanded that the judges call him to appear * * *. The judges refused, How. St. Tr., at 24, and, despite Raleigh's protestations that he was being tried "by the Spanish Inquisition," *id.,* at 15, the jury convicted, and Raleigh was sentenced to death.

One of Raleigh's trial judges later lamented that "the justice of England has never been so degraded and injured as by the condemnation of Sir Walter Raleigh." 1 Jardine, *supra,* at 520. Through a series of statutory and judicial reforms, English law developed a right of confrontation that limited these abuses. For example, treason statutes required witnesses to confront the accused "face to face" at his arraignment. Courts, meanwhile, developed relatively strict rules of unavailability, admitting examinations only if the witness was demonstrably unable to testify in person. * * *

One recurring question was whether the admissibility of an unavailable witness's pretrial examination depended on whether the defendant had had an opportunity to cross-examine him. In 1696, the Court of King's Bench answered this question in the affirmative, in the widely reported misdemeanor libel case of *King v. Paine,* 5 Mod. 163, 87 Eng. Rep. 584. The court ruled that, even though a witness was dead, his examination was not admissible where "the defendant not being present when [it was] taken before the mayor . . . had lost the benefit of a cross-examination." *Id.,* at 165, 87 Eng. Rep., at 585. * * *

Controversial examination practices were also used in the Colonies. Early in the 18th century, for example, the Virginia Council protested against the Governor for having "privately issued several commissions to examine witnesses against particular men *ex parte,*" complaining that "the person accused is

> **Definition**
>
> *Ex parte* means "for one party." An *ex parte* examination of a witness means an examination when only one party (and here, not the defendant) is present.

not admitted to be confronted with, or defend himself against his defamers." A Memorial Concerning the Maladministrations of His Excellency Francis Nicholson, reprinted in 9 English Historical Documents 253, 257 (D. Douglas ed.1955). * * *

Many declarations of rights adopted [by the states] around the time of the Revolution guaranteed a right of confrontation. * * * The proposed Federal Constitution, however, did not. At the Massachusetts ratifying convention, Abraham Holmes objected to this omission precisely on the ground that it would lead to civil-law practices * * *. [After this and other criticisms,] the First Congress responded by including the Confrontation Clause in the proposal that became the Sixth Amendment.

Early state decisions shed light upon the original understanding of the common-law right. *State v. Webb,* 2 N.C. 103 (Super. L. & Eq. 1794) *(per curiam),* decided a mere three years after the adoption of the Sixth Amendment, held that depositions could be read against an accused only if they were taken in his presence. * * * Many other decisions are to the same effect. * * *

This history supports two inferences about the meaning of the Sixth Amendment. First, the principal evil at which the Confrontation Clause was directed was the civil-law mode of criminal procedure, and particularly its use of *ex parte* examinations as evidence against the accused. * * * The Sixth Amendment must be interpreted with this focus in mind.

Accordingly, we once again reject the view that the Confrontation Clause applies of its own force only to in-court testimony, and that its application to out-of-court statements introduced at trial depends upon "the law of Evidence for the time being." 3 Wigmore § 1397, at 101; accord, *Dutton v. Evans,* 400 U.S. 74, 94 (1970) (Harlan, J., concurring in result). Leaving the regulation of out-of-court statements to the law of evidence would render the Confrontation Clause powerless to prevent even the most flagrant inquisitorial practices. * * *

This focus also suggests that not all hearsay implicates the Sixth Amendment's core concerns. An off-hand, overheard remark might be unreliable evidence and thus a good candidate for exclusion under hearsay rules, but it bears little resemblance to the civil-law abuses the Confrontation Clause targeted. On the other hand, *ex parte* examinations might sometimes be admissible under modern hearsay rules, but the Framers certainly would not have condoned them.

The text of the Confrontation Clause reflects this focus. It applies to "witnesses" against the accused—in other words, those who "bear testimony." 2 N. Webster, An American Dictionary of the English Language (1828).

"Testimony," in turn, is typically "[a] solemn declaration or affirmation made for the purpose of establishing or proving some fact." *Ibid.* An accuser who makes a formal statement to government officers bears testimony in a sense that a person who makes a casual remark to an acquaintance does not. The constitutional text, like the history underlying the common-law right of confrontation, thus reflects an especially acute concern with a specific type of out-of-court statement.

Various formulations of this core class of "testimonial" statements exist: "*ex parte* in-court testimony or its functional equivalent—that is, material such as affidavits, custodial examinations, prior testimony that the defendant was unable to cross-examine, or similar pretrial statements that declarants would reasonably expect to be used prosecutorially," Brief for Petitioner 23; "extrajudicial statements . . . contained in formalized testimonial materials, such as affidavits, depositions, prior testimony, or confessions," *White v. Illinois,* 502 U.S. 346, 365 (1992) (THOMAS, J., joined by SCALIA, J., concurring in part and concurring in judgment); "statements that were made under circumstances which would lead an objective witness reasonably to believe that the statement would be available for use at a later trial," Brief for National Association of Criminal Defense Lawyers et al. as *Amici Curiae* 3. These formulations all share a common nucleus and then define the Clause's coverage at various levels of abstraction around it. Regardless of the precise articulation, some statements qualify under any definition—for example, *ex parte* testimony at a preliminary hearing.

Statements taken by police officers in the course of interrogations are also testimonial under even a narrow standard. Police interrogations bear a striking resemblance to examinations by justices of the peace in England. The statements are not *sworn* testimony, but the absence of oath was not dispositive. * * *

That interrogators are police officers rather than magistrates does not change the picture either. * * * England did not have a professional police force until the 19th century, so it is not surprising that other government officers performed the investigative functions now associated primarily with the police. The involvement of government officers in the production of testimonial evidence presents the same risk, whether the officers are police or justices of the peace.

In sum, even if the Sixth Amendment is not solely concerned with testimonial hearsay, that is its primary object, and interrogations by law enforcement officers fall squarely within that class.

The historical record also supports a second proposition: that the Framers would not have allowed admission of testimonial statements of a witness who did not appear at trial unless he was unavailable to testify, and the defendant had had a prior opportunity for cross-examination. The text of the Sixth Amendment does not suggest any open-ended exceptions from the confrontation requirement to be developed by the courts. Rather, the "right . . . to be confronted with the witnesses against him," Amdt. 6, is most naturally read as a reference to the right of confrontation at common law, admitting only those exceptions established at the time of the founding. [T]he common law in 1791 conditioned admissibility of an absent witness's examination on unavailability and a prior opportunity to cross-examine. The Sixth Amendment therefore incorporates those limitations. The numerous early state decisions applying the same test confirm that these principles were received as part of the common law in this country.

> **Take Note**
>
> The Court here announces two principles: first, the Confrontation Clause applies to all "testimonial" out-of-court statements offered at trial; and second, such statements can be admitted at trial consistent with the Confrontation Clause only if the person who made the statement is unavailable to testify at trial and the defendant previously had an opportunity to cross-examine the person.

Our case law has been largely consistent with these two principles. Our leading early decision, for example, involved a deceased witness's prior trial testimony. *Mattox v. United States,* 156 U.S. 237 (1895). In allowing the statement to be admitted, we relied on the fact that the defendant had had, at the first trial, an adequate opportunity to confront the witness * * *. Our later cases conform to *Mattox's* holding that prior trial or preliminary hearing testimony is admissible only if the defendant had an adequate opportunity to cross-examine. See *Mancusi v. Stubbs,* 408 U.S. 204, 213–216 (1972); *California v. Green,* 399 U.S. 149, 165–168 (1970). Even where the defendant had such an opportunity, we excluded the testimony where the government had not established unavailability of the witness. See *Barber v. Page,* 390 U.S. 719, 722–725 (1968). * * *

Even our recent cases, in their outcomes, hew closely to the traditional line. *Ohio v. Roberts,* 448 U.S., at 67–70, admitted testimony from a preliminary hearing at which the defendant had examined the witness. * * * Our cases have thus remained faithful to the Framers' understanding: Testimonial statements of witnesses absent from trial have been admitted only where the declarant is unavailable, and only where the defendant has had a prior opportunity to cross-examine.

Although the results of our decisions have generally been faithful to the original meaning of the Confrontation Clause, the same cannot be said of our rationales. *Roberts* conditions the admissibility of all hearsay evidence on whether it falls under a "firmly rooted hearsay exception" or bears "particularized guarantees of trustworthiness." 448 U.S., at 66. This test departs from the historical principles identified above in two respects. First, it is too broad: It applies the same mode of analysis whether or not the hearsay consists of *ex parte* testimony. This often results in close constitutional scrutiny in cases that are far removed from the core concerns of the Clause. At the same time, however, the test is too narrow: It admits statements that *do* consist of *ex parte* testimony upon a mere finding of reliability. This malleable standard often fails to protect against paradigmatic confrontation violations.

* * * Sylvia Crawford's statement is testimonial under any definition. * * * Where testimonial statements are involved, we do not think the Framers meant to leave the Sixth Amendment's protection to the vagaries of the rules of evidence, much less to amorphous notions of "reliability." * * * Admitting statements deemed reliable by a judge is fundamentally at odds with the right of confrontation. To be sure, the Clause's ultimate goal is to ensure reliability of evidence, but it is a procedural rather than a substantive guarantee. It commands, not that evidence be reliable, but that reliability be assessed in a particular manner: by testing in the crucible of cross-examination. The Clause thus reflects a judgment, not only about the desirability of reliable evidence (a point on which there could be little dissent), but about how reliability can best be determined.

The *Roberts* test allows a jury to hear evidence, untested by the adversary process, based on a mere judicial determination of reliability. It thus replaces the constitutionally prescribed method of assessing reliability with a wholly foreign one. * * * Dispensing with confrontation because testimony is obviously reliable is akin to dispensing with jury trial because a defendant is obviously guilty. This is not what the Sixth Amendment prescribes.

Roberts' failings were on full display in the proceedings below. Sylvia Crawford made her statement while in police custody, herself a potential suspect in the case. Indeed, she had been told that whether she would be released "depend[ed] on how the investigation continues." In response to often leading questions from police detectives, she implicated her husband in Lee's stabbing and at least arguably undermined his self-defense claim. Despite all this, the trial court admitted her statement, listing several reasons why it was reliable. In its opinion reversing, the Court of Appeals listed several *other* reasons why the statement was *not* reliable. Finally, the State Supreme Court relied exclusively on the interlocking character of the statement and disregarded every other factor the lower courts had considered. The case is thus a self-contained demonstration of *Roberts'* unpredictable and inconsistent application.

Each of the courts also made assumptions that cross-examination might well have undermined. The trial court, for example, stated that Sylvia Crawford's statement was reliable because she was an eyewitness with direct knowledge of the events. But Sylvia at one point told the police that she had "shut [her] eyes and . . . didn't really watch" part of the fight, and that she was "in shock." The trial court also buttressed its reliability finding by claiming that Sylvia was "being questioned by law enforcement, and, thus, the [questioner] is . . . neutral to her and not someone who would be inclined to advance her interests and shade her version of the truth unfavorably toward the defendant." The Framers would be astounded to learn that *ex parte* testimony could be admitted against a criminal defendant because it was elicited by "neutral" government officers. But even if the court's assessment of the officer's motives was accurate, it says nothing about Sylvia's perception of her situation. Only cross-examination could reveal that.

We have no doubt that the courts below were acting in utmost good faith when they found reliability. The Framers, however, would not have been content to indulge this assumption. They knew that judges, like other government officers, could not always be trusted to safeguard the rights of the people * * *. They were loath to leave too much discretion in judicial hands. Cf. U.S. Const., Amdt. 6 (criminal jury trial); Amdt. 7 (civil jury trial). By replacing categorical constitutional guarantees with open-ended balancing tests, we do violence to their design. Vague standards are manipulable, and, while that might be a small concern in run-of-the-mill assault prosecutions like this one, the Framers had an eye toward politically charged cases * * *—great state trials where the impartiality of even those at the highest levels of the judiciary might not be so clear. It is difficult to imagine *Roberts'* providing any meaningful protection in those circumstances.

Where nontestimonial hearsay is at issue, it is wholly consistent with the Framers' design to afford the States flexibility in their development of hearsay law * * *. Where testimonial evidence is at issue, however, the Sixth Amendment demands what the common law required: unavailability and a prior opportunity for cross-examination. We leave for another day any effort to spell out a comprehensive definition of "testimonial." Whatever else the term covers, it applies at a minimum to prior testimony at a preliminary hearing, before a grand jury, or at a former trial; and to police interrogations. These are the modern practices with closest kinship to the abuses at which the Confrontation Clause was directed.

In this case, the State admitted Sylvia's testimonial statement against petitioner, despite the fact that he had no opportunity to cross-examine her. That alone is sufficient to make out a violation of the Sixth Amendment. [W]e decline to mine the record in search of indicia of reliability. Where testimonial statements are at issue, the only indicium of reliability sufficient to satisfy constitutional demands is the one the Constitution actually prescribes: confrontation.

The judgment of the Washington Supreme Court is reversed, and the case is remanded for further proceedings not inconsistent with this opinion.

CHIEF JUSTICE REHNQUIST, with whom JUSTICE O'CONNOR joins, concurring in the judgment.

I dissent from the Court's decision to overrule *Ohio v. Roberts,* 448 U.S. 56 (1980). I believe that the Court's adoption of a new interpretation of the Confrontation Clause is not backed by sufficiently persuasive reasoning to overrule long-established precedent. Its decision casts a mantle of uncertainty over future criminal trials in both federal and state courts, and is by no means necessary to decide the present case.

[W]hile I agree that the Framers were mainly concerned about sworn affidavits and depositions, it does not follow that they were similarly concerned about the Court's broader category of testimonial statements. See 2 N. Webster, An American Dictionary of the English Language (1828) (defining "Testimony" as "[a] solemn declaration or affirmation made for the purpose of establishing or proving some fact. *Such affirmation in judicial proceedings, may be verbal or written, but must be under oath*" (emphasis added)). As far as I can tell, unsworn testimonial statements were treated no differently at common law than were nontestimonial statements, and it seems to me any classification of statements as testimonial beyond that of sworn affidavits and depositions will be somewhat arbitrary, merely a proxy for what the Framers might have intended had such evidence been liberally admitted as substantive evidence like it is today. I therefore see no reason why the distinction the Court draws is preferable to our precedent.

I am also not convinced that the Confrontation Clause categorically requires the exclusion of testimonial statements. Although many States had their own Confrontation Clauses, they were of recent vintage and were not interpreted with any regularity before 1791. * * * Nor was the English law at the time of the framing entirely consistent in its treatment of testimonial evidence. Generally *ex parte* affidavits and depositions were excluded as the Court notes, but even that proposition was not universal. See *King v. Eriswell,* 3 T.R. 707, 100 Eng. Rep. 815 (K.B.1790) (affirming by an equally divided court the admission of an *ex parte* examination because the declarant was unavailable to testify). With respect to unsworn testimonial statements, there is no indication that once the hearsay rule was developed courts ever excluded these statements if they otherwise fell within a firmly rooted exception. * * *

Between 1700 and 1800 the rules regarding the admissibility of out-of-court statements were still being developed. There were always exceptions to the general rule of exclusion, and it is not clear to me that the Framers categorically wanted to eliminate further ones. It is one thing to trace the right of confrontation back to the Roman Empire; it is quite another to conclude that such a right absolutely excludes a large category of evidence. It is an odd conclusion indeed to think that the Framers created a cut-and-dried rule with respect to the admissibility of testimonial statements when the law during their own time was not fully settled.

To find exceptions to exclusion under the Clause is not to denigrate it as the Court suggests. * * * Exceptions to confrontation have always been derived from the experience that some out-of-court statements are just as reliable as cross-examined in-court testimony due to the circumstances under which they were made. We have recognized, for example, that co-conspirator statements simply "cannot be replicated, even if the declarant testifies to the same matters in court." *United States v. Inadi,* 475 U.S. 387, 395 (1986). Because the statements are made while the declarant and the accused are partners in an illegal enterprise, the statements are unlikely to be false and their admission "actually furthers the 'Confrontation Clause's very mission' which is to 'advance the accuracy of the truth-determining process in criminal trials.' " *Id.,* at 396 (quoting *Tennessee v. Street,* 471 U.S. 409, 415 (1985)). Similar reasons justify the introduction of spontaneous declarations, see *White v. Illinois,* 502 U.S. 346, 356 (1992), statements made in the course of procuring medical services, see *ibid.,* dying declarations, see *Kirby v. United States,* 174 U.S. 47, 61 (1899), and countless other hearsay exceptions. That a statement might be testimonial does nothing to undermine the wisdom of one of these exceptions.

To its credit, the Court's analysis of "testimony" excludes at least some hearsay exceptions, such as business records and official records. To hold otherwise would require numerous additional witnesses without any apparent gain in the truth-seeking process. * * * But these are palliatives to what I believe is a mistaken change of course. It is a change of course not in the least necessary to reverse the judgment of the Supreme Court of Washington in this case. The result the Court reaches follows inexorably from *Roberts* and its progeny without any need for overruling that line of cases. In *Idaho v. Wright,* 497 U.S. 805, 820–824 (1990), we held that an out-of-court statement was not admissible simply because the truthfulness of that statement was corroborated by other evidence at trial. As the Court notes, the Supreme Court of Washington gave decisive weight to the "interlocking nature of the two statements." No re-weighing of the "reliability factors," which is hypothesized by the Court, is required to reverse the judgment here. A citation to *Idaho v. Wright* would suffice. For the reasons stated, I believe that this would be a far preferable course for the Court to take here.

POINTS FOR DISCUSSION

a.   The Rule of *Crawford*

The Court in *Crawford* concluded that out-of-court statements may not be offered against a criminal defendant if they are testimonial in nature and the witness is available for trial or has not previously been subject to cross-examination. In other words, the ordinary requirements of confrontation—that the defendant have the opportunity to confront his accusers and subject their testimony to cross-examination—applies any time the state seeks to introduce evidence that is testimonial in nature.

Is the Court's approach in *Crawford* consistent with the Court's approach in *Craig*? In *Craig*, the Court permitted the state to dispense with face-to-face confrontation (though not cross-examination) where the procedure provided sufficient guarantees that the testimony would be reliable. Should testimonial statements like the one at issue *Crawford*—hearsay that is subject to one of the exceptions to the general rule of admissibility for such statements—be deemed admissible if they too have sufficient indicia of reliability?

b.   Defining "Testimonial" Statements

The Court explained that not all out-of-court statements are "testimonial" in nature, and thus that not all out-of-court statements must satisfy the requirements of confrontation and cross-examination. What was the Court's definition of "testimonial" statements?

Suppose that a woman calls 911 to report an intruder in her house. She describes him to the dispatcher, who records the call. Before the police arrive, the suspect assaults the woman. The state prosecutes the suspect, but the woman is afraid to testify because she was traumatized by the attack. At trial, the prosecution seeks to play the recording of the 911 call. Is it admissible after *Crawford* if the woman is otherwise available to testify and hasn't been subjected to cross-examination by the defendant?

Executive Summary of This Chapter

The **Sixth Amendment** explicitly guarantees the right to a speedy trial; the right to a trial that members of the public may observe; the right to an impartial jury whose members come from the place where the charged offense or offenses were committed; the right to notice of the charges; the right to confront adverse witnesses; the right to compulsory process to ensure the attendance of witnesses at trial whom the defendant wishes to testify or to obtain other evidence necessary for putting on a defense; and the right to counsel.

The **speedy trial right** is violated only if the delay passes the "threshold dividing ordinary from presumptively prejudicial delay, since, by definition, [a defendant] cannot complain that the government has denied him a speedy trial if it has, in fact, prosecuted his case with customary promptness." *Doggett v. United States* (1992) (internal quotations omitted). It takes a substantial, unreasonable delay to violate the speedy trial right. *Id.*

The **right to a public trial** "may give way in certain cases to other rights or interests, such as the defendant's right to a fair trial or the government's interest in inhibiting disclosure of sensitive information." *Waller v. Georgia* (1984). But "[s]uch circumstances will be rare," and "the balance of interests must be struck with special care." *Id.* Only the defendant may assert a Sixth Amendment right to a public trial, but members of the public—including the press—have a qualified First Amendment right to attend some parts of a criminal trial. *Press-Enterprise Co. v. Superior Court of California for Riverside Cty.* (1986).

The **right to notice of the charges** "compel[s] the Government to state and define specifically what it must prove in order to convict the defendant so that he can intelligently prepare to defend himself on each of the essential elements of the charge." *Turner v. United States* (1970). The **right of compulsory process** ensures that the defendant can present the testimony of reluctant witnesses, who might prefer not to be involved in a criminal trial.

The **right to counsel** applies only in criminal prosecutions, not in civil lawsuits, *Turner v. Rogers* (2011), but it applies in both federal and state prosecutions, *Powell v. Alabama* (1932) (state capital cases); *Gideon v. Wainwright* (1963) (state felony cases); *Argersinger v. Hamlin* (1972) (misdemeanors).

The right to counsel attaches only after criminal adversarial proceedings have begun. *Moran v. Burbine* (1986). Once the right to counsel has attached, the Sixth Amendment guarantees the defendant a right to hire an attorney, to consult with an attorney, and to have an attorney speak for the defendant. It further guarantees that the attorney must provide "effective assistance." *Strickland v. Washington* (1984). The right to effective assistance of counsel extends not only through trial but also to a criminal defendant's first appeal as of right. *Evitts v. Lucey* (1985). The Sixth Amendment also requires that "no indigent criminal defendant be sentenced to a term of imprisonment unless the State has afforded him the right to assistance of appointed counsel in his defense," *Scott v. Illinois* (1979), which means that if the defendant cannot afford counsel, the government must provide one for him, *Johnson v. Zerbst* (1938); *Gideon v. Wainwright* (1963).

The **right to a jury trial** guarantees criminal defendants a jury in most, but not all, criminal prosecutions. Although the right applies in both federal and state court, *Duncan v. Louisiana* (1968), there is no right to a jury trial for "petty offenses." To determine whether an offense is petty, the Court focuses primarily on "the maximum penalty attached to the offense." *Lewis v. United States* (1996). The Court has held that the crime of driving under the influence can be a petty offense when it carries a maximum penalty of only six months' imprisonment. *Blanton v. City of North Las Vegas* (1989). In contrast, the Court has held that offenses that carry a possible prison term of two years are not petty, and thus give rise to the right to a jury trial. *Duncan v. Louisiana* (1968).

Most juries in criminal cases have twelve members. The Court has held, however, that a state need not use juries with that many members. The Court has concluded that a six-member jury does not violate the jury trial right, *Williams v. Florida* (1970), but that a five-member jury does, *Ballew v. Georgia* (1978). The Court has also held that a jury decision does not have to be unanimous, *Apodaca v. Oregon* (1972), but that a jury verdict based on a 5–1 vote on a six-member jury in a case involving a non-petty offense violated the defendant's rights under the Sixth and Fourteenth Amendments, *Burch v. Louisiana* (1979).

It is unconstitutional for the prosecution to exercise **peremptory challenges** with the purpose of excluding potential jurors of a particular race. *Batson v. Kentucky* (1986). The Court has extended this rule to peremptory challenges exercised by counsel for the defendant, *Georgia v. McCollum* (1992), and to peremptory challenges with the purpose of excluding potential jurors of a particular gender, *J.E.B. v. Alabama ex rel. T.B.* (1994).

"Other than the fact of a prior conviction, any fact that increases the penalty for a crime beyond the prescribed statutory maximum must be submitted to a jury, and proved beyond a reasonable doubt." *Apprendi v. New Jersey* (2000). As a consequence, the government cannot permit a trial judge to increase a defendant's **sentence** based upon the judge's findings, by a preponderance of the evidence, that some statutory sentencing element has been satisfied.

The Sixth Amendment guarantees a right of the accused "to be confronted with the witnesses against him * * *." This provision is known as the **"Confrontation Clause"** and generally guarantees the defendant the right to confront and cross-examine adverse witnesses. The Court has held, however, that the state can dispense with face-to-face confrontation "where necessary to protect a child witness from trauma that would be caused by testifying in the physical presence of the defendant, at least where such trauma would impair the child's ability to communicate," so long as the state uses a procedure that "ensures the reliability of the evidence by subjecting it to rigorous adversarial testing and thereby preserves the essence of effective confrontation." *Maryland v. Craig* (1990).

However, out-of-court statements may not be offered against a criminal defendant if they are testimonial in nature and the witness is available for trial or has not previously been subject to cross-examination. In other words, the ordinary requirements of confrontation—that the defendant have the opportunity to confront his accusers and subject their testimony to cross-examination—applies any time the state seeks to introduce evidence that is testimonial in nature. *Crawford v. Washington* (2004).

The Eighth Amendment

The Eighth Amendment contains three prohibitions relating to the criminal justice system: "Excessive bail shall not be required, nor excessive fines imposed, nor cruel and unusual punishments inflicted."

The prohibition on requiring excessive bail protects criminal suspects. To explain the prohibition, we first must describe the function of "bail." Consider this example. The police arrest a suspect because they have probable cause to believe that the suspect committed a theft. The next day, the suspect is arraigned. At the arraignment, a magistrate informs the suspect of the pending criminal charge, and the magistrate also sets bail. Bail is "security required by a court for the release of a criminal defendant who must appear in court at a future time." *Black's Law Dictionary* (10th ed. 2014). The magistrate sets bail at $10,000. If the suspect does not provide the court with $10,000 (either in cash or through a bond issued by a bail bondsman), the police can confine the suspect pending trial. The Eighth Amendment prohibits the magistrate from requiring excessive bail. For instance, in one case, a lower court held that bail set at $1 million was excessive for a suspect charged with selling cannabis. The court saw no justification for so large an amount, observing that the defendant had "strong family and business ties to the community," that he was "financially stable," and that there was "absolutely no evidence that [he] was dangerous to the community." *Alvarez v. Crowder*, 645 So. 2d 63, 64 (Fla. Dist. Ct. App. 1994). While criminal defendants often challenge bail as being excessive, the lower courts routinely resolve their claims; accordingly, there are very few modern Supreme Court cases that address excessive bail. The Supreme Court has never squarely held that the Fourteenth Amendment incorporates the prohibition on excessive bail, but it has "assumed" that it does. *Schilb v. Kuebel*, 404 U.S. 357, 365 (1971).

The prohibition against excessive fines protects criminal defendants who have been found guilty of an offense. In sentencing the defendant for the offense, the court may impose a "fine." A fine is a payment imposed as punishment for an offense. *Austin v. United States*, 509 U.S. 602 (1993). The Eighth Amendment, however, limits the size of the fine. For example, in *United States v. Bajakajian*, 524 U.S. 321 (1998), the defendants violated a statute requiring anyone who takes more than $10,000 of currency out of the country to report the amount to customs officials. They were caught at the airport with $357,144 of unreported currency in their luggage. The Supreme Court held that requiring them to forfeit the entire amount would violate the prohibition against excessive fines because the amount was "grossly disproportional to the gravity" of the offense. The Court has held, however, that the Excessive Fines clause does not apply to punitive damages in civil cases. *Browning-Ferris Indus. of Vermont, Inc. v. Kelco Disposal, Inc.*, 492 U.S. 257 (1989).

The Supreme Court has held that the Eighth Amendment's prohibition on excessive fines applies to the states by incorporation through the Fourteenth Amendment. *Timbs v. Indiana*, 139 S.Ct. 682 (2019). The Court has not decided "whether the Eighth Amendment protects corporations as well as individuals." *Browning-Ferris Indus.*, 492 U.S. at 276 n.22.

The prohibition against "cruel and unusual punishments" is farther reaching. Among its other effects, the prohibition prevents courts from sentencing defendants to certain modes of punishment (such as the lash), restricts the circumstances in which courts may sentence defendants to certain punishments (such as the death penalty), bars excessively disproportionate sentences, regulates prison conditions, and limits methods of carrying out the death penalty. The Supreme Court has considered the prohibition against cruel and unusual punishment in numerous cases, and has held that the prohibition applies to the states under the Fourteenth Amendment. *Robinson v. California*, 370 U.S. 660 (1962).

The phrase "cruel and unusual punishments" derives from the English Declaration of Rights, which Parliament adopted in 1689, and was included in the Virginia Declaration of Rights, which the state convention adopted in 1776, shortly before the issuance of the Declaration of Independence. Indeed, the language of the Eighth Amendment is drawn verbatim from the Virginia Declaration.

At the Virginia ratifying convention for the federal Constitution, Patrick Henry expressed concern about the lack of a provision prohibiting cruel and unusual punishments. He declared that, absent such a provision, Congress "may introduce the practice of France, Spain, and Germany of torturing, to extort a confession of the crime. They will * * * tell you that there is such a necessity of strengthening the arm of government, that they must have a criminal equity, and extort confession by torture, in order to punish with still more relentless severity. We are then lost and undone." As we have seen, the first Congress responded to such fears by adopting a Bill of Rights, including the Eighth Amendment.

In light of this background, it seems clear that the Amendment prohibits the use of genuinely barbaric forms of punishment, such as torture, drawing and quartering, and the rack, that were known to the framing generation. But what else does the Amendment's prohibition on cruel and unusual punishment prohibit?

One possibility is that it prohibits only punishments that the framers would have deemed cruel and unusual. At the time of the framing, the death penalty was commonplace as a punishment for felonies, and forms of punishment that many likely would view as barbaric today likewise were tolerated. On this view, all such punishments would be permissible under the Eighth Amendment today. But Justice Scalia, a leading proponent of originalism, was reluctant to accept the full consequences of that approach. He called himself a "faint-hearted originalist," confessing that he could not "imagine [himself], any more than any other federal judge, upholding a statute that imposes the punishment of flogging." Antonin Scalia, *Originalism: The Lesser Evil*, 57 U. Cin. L. Rev. 849, 864 (1989). But if the Supreme Court untethers itself from the framers' understanding of the Eighth Amendment, how should the Court decide which forms of punishment are properly considered cruel and unusual today?

In the sections that follow, we address two important questions about the scope of the Eighth Amendment. First, does it prohibit punishments that are not barbaric but that are disproportionate to the offenses for which they are imposed? Second, does the Eighth Amendment prohibit capital punishment, either for specific crimes or more generally?

A. DISPROPORTIONATE PUNISHMENTS

The text of the Eighth Amendment appears to establish a proportionality test for bail and fines. In prohibiting "excessive" bail and "excessive" fines, the Eighth Amendment apparently requires courts to determine whether the amount of bail or the amount of a fine exceeds what is needed to ensure that a suspect appears for trial or that a defendant is sufficiently punished. But does the Eighth Amendment also establish a proportionality test for determining whether a punishment is "cruel or unusual"? The Supreme Court has struggled with this question.

A simple example illustrates the issue. A court might conclude that life imprisonment is not a cruel or unusual punishment for premeditated murder. But the fact that life imprisonment is permissible for homicide does not mean that it is necessarily permissible for any offense. What if a state sought to impose the penalty of life in prison for a person who shoplifted a 50¢ package of chewing gum? Surely all would agree that life imprisonment would be a disproportionate sentence for that minor offense. But does this disproportionality make the offense cruel and unusual? In the following, closely divided case, the plurality opinion asserts that the Eighth Amendment forbids "extreme sentences" that are "grossly disproportionate" to the offense committed. Why did some Justices disagree?

EWING V. CALIFORNIA
538 U.S. 11 (2003)

JUSTICE O'CONNOR announced the judgment of the Court and delivered an opinion, in which THE CHIEF JUSTICE and JUSTICE KENNEDY join.

In this case, we decide whether the Eighth Amendment prohibits the State of California from sentencing a repeat felon to a prison term of 25 years to life under the State's "Three Strikes and You're Out" law.

California's current three strikes law consists of two virtually identical statutory schemes "designed to increase the prison terms of repeat felons." *People v. Superior Court of San Diego Cty. ex rel. Romero,* 917 P.2d 628, 630 (1996). When a defendant is convicted of a felony, and he has previously been convicted of one or more prior felonies defined as "serious" or "violent" in Cal. Penal Code Ann. §§ 667.5 and 1192.7 (West Supp.2002), sentencing is conducted pursuant to the three strikes law. Prior convictions must be alleged in the charging document, and the defendant has a right to a jury determination that the prosecution has proved the prior convictions beyond a reasonable doubt. § 1025; § 1158 (West 1985).

If the defendant has one prior "serious" or "violent" felony conviction, he must be sentenced to "twice the term otherwise provided as punishment for the current felony conviction." § 667(e)(1) (West 1999); § 1170.12(c)(1) (West Supp.2002). If the defendant has two or more prior "serious" or "violent" felony convictions, he must receive "an indeterminate term of life imprisonment." § 667(e)(2)(A) (West 1999); § 1170.12(c)(2)(A) (West Supp.2002). Defendants sentenced to life under the three strikes law become eligible for parole on a date calculated by reference to a "minimum term," which is the greater of (a) three times the term otherwise provided for the current conviction, (b) 25 years, or (c) the term determined by the court pursuant to § 1170 for the underlying conviction, including any enhancements. §§ 667(e)(2)(A)(i)–(iii) (West 1999); §§ 1170.12(c)(2)(A)(i)–(iii) (West Supp.2002).

On parole from a 9-year prison term, petitioner Gary Ewing walked into the pro shop of the El Segundo Golf Course in Los Angeles County on March 12, 2000. He walked out with three golf clubs, priced at $399 apiece, concealed in his pants leg. A shop employee, whose suspicions were aroused when he observed Ewing limp out of the pro shop, telephoned the police. The police apprehended Ewing in the parking lot.

Ewing is no stranger to the criminal justice system. [Between 1984, when he was 22 years old, and September 1993, Ewing plead guilty to or was convicted of crimes, including theft, burglary, and battery, on nine separate occasions, and sentenced to jail terms ranging from 10 days to one year.]

In October and November 1993, Ewing committed three burglaries and one robbery at a Long Beach, California, apartment complex over a 5-week period. He awakened one of his victims, asleep on her living room sofa, as he tried to disconnect her video cassette recorder from the television in that room. When she screamed, Ewing ran out the front door. On another occasion, Ewing accosted a victim in the mailroom of the apartment complex. Ewing claimed to have a gun and ordered the victim to hand over his wallet. When the victim resisted, Ewing produced a knife and forced the victim back to the apartment itself. While Ewing rifled through the bedroom, the victim fled the apartment screaming for help. Ewing absconded with the victim's money and credit cards.

On December 9, 1993, Ewing was arrested on the premises of the apartment complex for trespassing and lying to a police officer. The knife used in the robbery and a glass cocaine pipe were later found in the back seat of the patrol car used to transport Ewing to the police station. A jury convicted Ewing of first-degree robbery and three counts of residential burglary. Sentenced to nine years and eight months in prison, Ewing was paroled in 1999.

Only 10 months later, Ewing stole the golf clubs at issue in this case. He was charged with, and ultimately convicted of, one count of felony grand theft of personal property in excess of $400. See Cal. Penal Code Ann. § 484 (West Supp.2002); § 489 (West 1999). As required by the three strikes law, the prosecutor formally alleged, and the trial court later found, that Ewing had been convicted previously of four serious or violent felonies for the three burglaries and the robbery in the Long Beach apartment complex. See § 667(g) (West 1999); § 1170.12(e) (West Supp.2002).

As a newly convicted felon with two or more "serious" or "violent" felony convictions in his past, Ewing was sentenced under the three strikes law to 25 years to life. The California Court of Appeal affirmed [and the] Supreme Court of California denied Ewing's petition for review * * *.

The Eighth Amendment, which forbids cruel and unusual punishments, contains a "narrow proportionality principle" that "applies to noncapital sentences." *Harmelin v. Michigan,* 501 U.S. 957, 996–997 (1991) (KENNEDY, J., concurring in part and concurring in judgment); cf. *Weems v. United States,* 217 U.S. 349, 371 (1910); *Robinson v. California,* 370 U.S. 660, 667 (1962) (applying the Eighth Amendment to the States via the Fourteenth Amendment). We have most recently addressed the proportionality principle as applied to terms of years in a series of cases beginning with *Rummel v. Estelle,* 445 U.S. 263 (1980).

In *Rummel,* we held that it did not violate the Eighth Amendment for a State to sentence a three-time offender to life in prison with the possibility of parole. *Id.,* at 284–285. Like Ewing, Rummel was sentenced to a lengthy prison term under a recidivism statute. Rummel's two prior offenses were a 1964 felony for "fraudulent use of a credit card to obtain $80 worth of goods or services," and a 1969 felony conviction for "passing a forged check in the amount of $28.36." *Id.,* at 265. His triggering offense was a conviction for felony theft—"obtaining $120.75 by false pretenses." *Id.,* at 266.

This Court ruled that "[h]aving twice imprisoned him for felonies, Texas was entitled to place upon Rummel the onus of one who is simply unable to bring his conduct within the social norms prescribed by the criminal law of the State." *Id.,* at 284. * * * We noted that this Court "has on occasion stated that the Eighth Amendment prohibits imposition of a sentence that is grossly disproportionate to the severity of the crime." *Id.,* at 271. But "[o]utside the context of capital punishment, successful challenges to the proportionality of particular sentences have been exceedingly rare." *Id.,* at 272. Although we stated that the proportionality principle "would . . . come into play in the extreme example . . . if a legislature made overtime parking a felony punishable by life imprisonment," *id.,* at 274, n. 11, we held that "the mandatory life sentence imposed upon this petitioner does not constitute cruel and unusual punishment under the Eighth and Fourteenth Amendments," *id.,* at 285.

Three years after *Rummel,* in *Solem v. Helm,* 463 U.S. 277, 279 (1983), we held that the Eighth Amendment prohibited "a life sentence without possibility of parole for a seventh nonviolent felony." The triggering offense in *Solem* was "uttering a 'no account' check for $100." *Id.,* at 281. We specifically stated that the Eighth Amendment's ban on cruel and unusual punishments "prohibits . . .

sentences that are disproportionate to the crime committed," and that the "constitutional principle of proportionality has been recognized explicitly in this Court for almost a century." *Id.,* at 284, 286. * * * [We] struck down the defendant's sentence of life without parole, [specifically noting] the contrast between that sentence and the sentence in *Rummel,* pursuant to which the defendant was eligible for parole. * * *

Eight years after *Solem,* we grappled with the proportionality issue again in *Harmelin. Harmelin* was not a recidivism case, but rather involved a first-time offender convicted of possessing 672 grams of cocaine. He was sentenced to life in prison without possibility of parole. A majority of the Court rejected Harmelin's claim that his sentence was so grossly disproportionate that it violated the Eighth Amendment. The Court, however, could not agree on why his proportionality argument failed. * * * Justice KENNEDY, joined by two other Members of the Court, [identified] four principles of proportionality review—"the primacy of the legislature, the variety of legitimate penological schemes, the nature of our federal system, and the requirement that proportionality review be guided by objective factors"—that "inform the final one: The Eighth Amendment does not require strict proportionality between crime and sentence. Rather, it forbids only extreme sentences that are 'grossly disproportionate' to the crime." *Id.,* at 1001. * * *

> **Take Note**
>
> The Court declares here that the Eighth Amendment prohibits punishments that are "grossly disproportionate" to the crime. How does the Court determine whether a punishment is grossly disproportionate?

The proportionality principles in our cases distilled in Justice KENNEDY's concurrence guide our application of the Eighth Amendment in the new context that we are called upon to consider.

For many years, most States have had laws providing for enhanced sentencing of repeat offenders. See, *e.g.,* U.S. Dept. of Justice, Bureau of Justice Assistance, National Assessment of Structured Sentencing (1996). Yet between 1993 and 1995, three strikes laws effected a sea change in criminal sentencing throughout the Nation. [In that period, 24 States and the Federal Government enacted three strikes laws.] These laws responded to widespread public concerns about crime by targeting the class of offenders who pose the greatest threat to public safety: career criminals. * * *

Throughout the States, legislatures enacting three strikes laws made a deliberate policy choice that individuals who have repeatedly engaged in serious or violent criminal behavior, and whose conduct has not been deterred by more conventional approaches to punishment, must be isolated from society in order to protect the public safety. Though three strikes laws may be relatively new, our tradition of deferring to state legislatures in making and implementing such important policy decisions is longstanding.

Our traditional deference to legislative policy choices finds a corollary in the principle that the Constitution "does not mandate adoption of any one penological theory." *Harmelin*, 463 U.S. at 999 (KENNEDY, J., concurring in part and concurring in judgment). A sentence can have a variety of justifications, such as incapacitation, deterrence, retribution, or rehabilitation. See 1 W. LaFave & A. Scott, Substantive Criminal Law § 1.5, pp. 30–36 (1986) (explaining theories of punishment). Some or all of these justifications may play a role in a State's sentencing scheme. Selecting the sentencing rationales is generally a policy choice to be made by state legislatures, not federal courts.

When the California Legislature enacted the three strikes law, it made a judgment that protecting the public safety requires incapacitating criminals who have already been convicted of at least one serious or violent crime. Nothing in the Eighth Amendment prohibits California from making that choice. To the contrary, our cases establish that "States have a valid interest in deterring and segregating habitual criminals." *Parke v. Raley*, 506 U.S. 20, 27 (1992). Recidivism has long been recognized as a legitimate basis for increased punishment. See *Almendarez-Torres v. United States*, 523 U.S. 224, 230 (1998) (recidivism "is as typical a sentencing factor as one might imagine").

California's justification is no pretext. Recidivism is a serious public safety concern in California and throughout the Nation. According to a recent report, approximately 67 percent of former inmates released from state prisons were charged with at least one "serious" new crime within three years of their release. See U.S. Dept. of Justice, Bureau of Justice Statistics, P. Langan & D. Levin, Special Report: Recidivism of Prisoners Released in 1994, p. 1 (June 2002). In particular, released property offenders like Ewing had higher recidivism rates than those released after committing violent, drug, or public-order offenses. *Id.,* at 8. * * *

The State's interest in deterring crime also lends some support to the three strikes law. * * * Four years after the passage of California's three strikes law, the recidivism rate of parolees returned to prison for the commission of a new crime dropped by nearly 25 percent. California Dept. of Justice, Office of the Attorney General, "Three Strikes and You're Out"—Its Impact on the California Criminal Justice System After Four Years, p. 10 (1998). * * *

To be sure, California's three strikes law has sparked controversy. Critics have doubted the law's wisdom, cost-efficiency, and effectiveness in reaching its goals. See, *e.g.,* Zimring, Hawkins, & Kamin, Punishment and Democracy: Three Strikes and You're Out in California (2001); Vitiello, Three Strikes: Can We Return to Rationality? 87 J.Crim. L. & C. 395, 423 (1997). This criticism is appropriately directed at the legislature, which has primary responsibility for making the difficult policy

> **Food for Thought**
>
> Doesn't the Court's articulation, earlier in the opinion, of a proportionality standard under the Eighth Amendment require it to second-guess at least some legislative policy choices about sentencing? Is the Court suggesting here that all enhanced penalties for recidivism are consistent with the proportionality standard?

choices that underlie any criminal sentencing scheme. We do not sit as a "superlegislature" to second-guess these policy choices. It is enough that the State of California has a reasonable basis for believing that dramatically enhanced sentences for habitual felons "advance[s] the goals of [its] criminal justice system in any substantial way." See *Solem,* 463 U.S., at 297, n. 22.

Against this backdrop, we consider Ewing's claim that his three strikes sentence of 25 years to life is unconstitutionally disproportionate to his offense of "shoplifting three golf clubs." We first address the gravity of the offense compared to the harshness of the penalty. At the threshold, we note that Ewing incorrectly frames the issue. The gravity of his offense was not merely "shoplifting three golf clubs." Rather, Ewing was convicted of felony grand theft for stealing nearly $1,200 worth of merchandise after previously having been convicted of at least two "violent" or "serious" felonies. * * *

In weighing the gravity of Ewing's offense, we must place on the scales not only his current felony, but also his long history of felony recidivism. Any other approach would fail to accord proper deference to the policy judgments that find expression in the legislature's choice of sanctions. In imposing a three strikes sentence, the State's interest is not merely punishing the offense of conviction, or the "triggering" offense: "[I]t is in addition the interest . . . in dealing in a harsher manner with those who by repeated criminal acts have shown that they are simply incapable of conforming to the norms of society as established by its criminal law." *Rummel,* 445 U.S., at 276. * * *

Ewing's sentence is justified by the State's public-safety interest in incapacitating and deterring recidivist felons, and amply supported by his own long, serious criminal record. Ewing has been convicted of numerous misdemeanor and felony offenses, served nine separate terms of incarceration, and committed most of his crimes while on probation or parole. His prior "strikes" were serious felonies including robbery and three residential burglaries. To be sure, Ewing's sentence is a long one. But it reflects a rational legislative judgment, entitled to deference, that offenders who have committed serious or violent felonies and who continue to commit felonies must be incapacitated. * * * Ewing's is not "the rare case in which a threshold comparison of the crime committed and the sentence imposed leads to an inference of gross disproportionality." *Harmelin,* 501 U.S., at 1005 (KENNEDY, J., concurring in part and concurring in judgment).

> **Take Note**
>
> Justice O'Connor wrote only for a plurality. What is the precedential value of her opinion? Does her opinion state the most "narrow" ground that could command a majority of the Court?

We hold that Ewing's sentence of 25 years to life in prison, imposed for the offense of felony grand theft under the three strikes law, is not grossly disproportionate and therefore does not violate the Eighth Amendment's prohibition on cruel and unusual punishments. The judgment of the California Court of Appeal is affirmed.

JUSTICE SCALIA, concurring in the judgment.

In my opinion in *Harmelin v. Michigan,* 501 U.S. 957, 984, 985 (1991), I concluded that the Eighth Amendment's prohibition of "cruel and unusual punishments" was aimed at excluding only certain *modes* of punishment, and was not a "guarantee against disproportionate sentences." Out of respect for the principle of *stare decisis,* I might nonetheless accept the contrary holding of *Solem v. Helm,* 463 U.S. 277 (1983)—that the Eighth Amendment contains a narrow proportionality principle—if I felt I could intelligently apply it. This case demonstrates why I cannot.

Proportionality—the notion that the punishment should fit the crime—is inherently a concept tied to the penological goal of retribution. "[I]t becomes difficult even to speak intelligently of 'proportionality,' once deterrence and rehabilitation are given significant weight," *Harmelin, supra,* at 989—not to mention giving weight to the purpose of California's three strikes law: incapacitation. In the present case, the game is up once the plurality has acknowledged that "the Constitution does not mandate adoption of any one penological theory," and that a "sentence can have a variety of justifications, such as incapacitation, deterrence, retribution, or rehabilitation." That acknowledgment having been made, it no longer suffices merely to assess "the gravity of the offense compared to the harshness of the penalty"; that classic description of the proportionality principle (alone and in itself quite resistant to policy-free, legal analysis) now becomes merely the "first" step of the inquiry. Having completed that step (by a discussion which, in all fairness, does not convincingly establish that 25-years-to-life is a "proportionate" punishment for stealing three golf clubs), the plurality must then *add* an analysis to show that "Ewing's sentence is justified by the State's public-safety interest in incapacitating and deterring recidivist felons."

Which indeed it is—though why that has anything to do with the principle of proportionality is a mystery. Perhaps the plurality should revise its terminology, so that what it reads into the Eighth Amendment is not the unstated proposition that all punishment should be reasonably proportionate to the gravity of the offense, but rather the unstated proposition that all punishment should reasonably pursue the multiple purposes of the criminal law. That formulation would make it clearer than ever, of course, that the plurality is not applying law but evaluating policy.

> **Food for Thought**
>
> Justice Scalia rejected the proportionality principle as indeterminate and impossible for a court to administer in a principled fashion. Under Justice Scalia's approach, could a state sentence a person to life imprisonment for overtime parking? If so, does that suggest a problem with his approach?

Because I agree that petitioner's sentence does not violate the Eighth Amendment's prohibition against cruel and unusual punishments, I concur in the judgment.

JUSTICE THOMAS, concurring in the judgment.

I agree with Justice SCALIA's view that the proportionality test [is] incapable of judicial application. Even were [the] test perfectly clear, however, I would not feel compelled by *stare decisis* to apply it. In my view, the Cruel and Unusual Punishments Clause of the Eighth Amendment contains no proportionality principle. Because the plurality concludes that petitioner's sentence does not violate the Eighth Amendment's prohibition on cruel and unusual punishments, I concur in the judgment.

JUSTICE STEVENS, with whom JUSTICE SOUTER, JUSTICE GINSBURG, and JUSTICE BREYER join, dissenting.

Justice BREYER has cogently explained why the sentence imposed in this case is both cruel and unusual. The concurrences prompt this separate writing to emphasize that proportionality review is not only capable of judicial application but also required by the Eighth Amendment.

"The Eighth Amendment succinctly prohibits 'excessive' sanctions." *Atkins v. Virginia*, 536 U.S. 304, 311 (2002); see also U.S. Const., Amdt. 8 ("Excessive bail shall not be required, nor excessive fines imposed, nor cruel and unusual punishments inflicted"). Faithful to the Amendment's text, this Court has held that the Constitution directs judges to apply their best judgment in determining the proportionality of fines, see, *e.g., United States v. Bajakajian*, 524 U.S. 321, 334–336 (1998), bail, see, *e.g., Stack v. Boyle*, 342 U.S. 1, 5 (1951), and other forms of punishment, including the imposition of a death sentence, see, *e.g., Coker v. Georgia*, 433 U.S. 584, 592 (1977). It "would be anomalous indeed" to suggest that the Eighth Amendment makes proportionality review applicable in the context of bail and fines but not in the context of other forms of punishment, such as imprisonment. *Solem v. Helm*, 463 U.S. 277, 289 (1983). Rather, by broadly prohibiting excessive sanctions, the Eighth Amendment directs judges to exercise their wise judgment in assessing the proportionality of all forms of punishment.

The absence of a black-letter rule does not disable judges from exercising their discretion in construing the outer limits on sentencing authority that the Eighth Amendment imposes. After all, judges are "constantly called upon to draw . . . lines in a variety of contexts," *id.*, at 294, and to exercise their judgment to give meaning to the Constitution's broadly phrased protections. For example, the Due Process Clause directs judges to employ proportionality review in assessing the constitutionality of punitive damages awards on a case-by-case basis. See, *e.g., BMW of North America, Inc. v. Gore*, 517 U.S. 559, 562 (1996). Also, although the Sixth Amendment guarantees criminal defendants the right to a speedy trial, the courts often are asked to determine on a case-by-case basis whether a particular delay is constitutionally permissible or not. See, *e.g., Doggett v. United States*, 505 U.S. 647 (1992).

Throughout most of the Nation's history—before guideline sentencing became so prevalent—federal and state trial judges imposed specific sentences pursuant to grants of authority that gave them uncabined discretion within broad ranges. * * * In exercising their discretion, sentencing judges wisely employed a proportionality principle that took into account all of the justifications for punishment—namely, deterrence, incapacitation, retribution, and rehabilitation. Likewise, I think it clear that the Eighth Amendment's prohibition of "cruel and unusual punishments" expresses a broad and basic proportionality principle that takes into account all of the justifications for penal sanctions. It is this broad proportionality principle that would preclude reliance on any of the justifications for punishment to support, for example, a life sentence for overtime parking. See *Rummel v. Estelle*, 445 U.S. 263, 274, n. 11 (1980).

JUSTICE BREYER, with whom JUSTICE STEVENS, JUSTICE SOUTER, and JUSTICE GINSBURG join, dissenting.

First, precedent makes clear that Ewing's sentence raises a serious disproportionality question. * * * The one critical factor that explains the difference in the outcome[s in *Rummel* and *Solem*] is the length of the likely prison term measured in real time. In *Rummel,* where the Court upheld the sentence, the state sentencing statute authorized parole for the offender after 10 or 12 years. In *Solem,* where the Court struck down the sentence, the sentence required the offender, Helm, to spend the rest of his life in prison.

* * * Ewing's sentence here amounts, in real terms, to at least 25 years without parole or good-time credits. That sentence is considerably shorter than Helm's sentence in *Solem,* which amounted, in real terms, to life in prison. Nonetheless Ewing's real prison term is more than twice as long as the term at issue in *Rummel,* which amounted, in real terms, to at least 10 or 12 years. And, Ewing's sentence, unlike Rummel's (but like Helm's sentence in *Solem*), is long enough to consume the productive remainder of almost any offender's life. (It means that Ewing himself, seriously ill when sentenced at age 38, will likely die in prison.) * * * Overall, the comparison places Ewing's sentence well within the twilight zone between *Solem* and *Rummel*—a zone where the argument for unconstitutionality is substantial, where the cases themselves cannot determine the constitutional outcome.

Second, Ewing's sentence on its face imposes one of the most severe punishments available upon a recidivist who subsequently engaged in one of the less serious forms of criminal conduct. I do not deny the seriousness of shoplifting, which an *amicus curiae* tells us costs retailers in the range of $30 billion annually. But consider that conduct in terms of the factors that this Court mentioned in *Solem*—the "harm caused or threatened to the victim or society," the "absolute magnitude of the crime," and the offender's "culpability." In respect to all three criteria, the sentence-triggering behavior here ranks well toward the bottom of the criminal conduct scale.

Third, some objective evidence suggests that many experienced judges would consider Ewing's sentence disproportionately harsh. The United States Sentencing Commission (having based the federal Sentencing Guidelines primarily upon its review of how judges had actually sentenced offenders) does not include shoplifting (or similar theft-related offenses) among the crimes that might trigger especially long sentences for recidivists, see USSG § 4B1.1 (Nov.2002) (Guideline for sentencing "career offenders"). * * *

Believing Ewing's argument a strong one, sufficient to pass the threshold, I turn to the comparative analysis. A comparison of Ewing's sentence with other sentences requires answers to two questions. First, how would other jurisdictions (or California at other times, *i.e.,* without the three strikes penalty) punish the *same offense conduct?* Second, upon what other conduct would other jurisdictions (or California) impose the *same prison term?* * * *

As to California itself, we know the following: First, between the end of World War II and 1994 (when California enacted the three strikes law), no one like Ewing could have served more than *10* years in prison. * * * We also know that the time that any offender actually served was likely far less than 10 years. This is because statistical data show that the median time actually served for grand theft (other than auto theft) was about two years, and 90 percent of all those convicted of that crime served less than three or four years.

Second, statistics suggest that recidivists *of all sorts* convicted during that same time period in California served a small fraction of Ewing's real-time sentence. * * * Third, we know that California has reserved, and still reserves, Ewing-type prison time, *i.e.,* at least 25 real years in prison, for criminals convicted of crimes far worse than was Ewing's. Statistics for the years 1945 to 1981, for example, indicate that typical (nonrecidivist) male first-degree murderers served between 10 and 15 real years in prison, with 90 percent of all such murderers serving less than 20 real years. * * *

As to other jurisdictions, we know the following: The United States, bound by the federal Sentencing Guidelines, would impose upon a recidivist, such as Ewing, a sentence that, in any ordinary case, would not exceed 18 months in prison. USSG § 2B1.1(a) (Nov.1999)

With [also know] that the law would make it legally impossible for a Ewing-type offender to serve more than 10 years in prison in 33 jurisdictions, as well as the federal courts, more than 15 years in 4 other States, and more than 20 years in 4 additional States. In nine other States, the law *might* make it legally possible to impose a sentence of 25 years or more—though that fact by itself, of course, does not mean that judges have actually done so. * * * Outside the California three strikes context, Ewing's recidivist sentence is virtually unique in its harshness for his offense of conviction, and by a considerable degree.

Justice SCALIA and Justice THOMAS argue that we should not review for gross disproportionality a sentence to a term of years. * * * I concede that a bright-line rule would give legislators and sentencing judges more guidance. But application of the Eighth Amendment to a sentence of a term of years requires a case-by-case approach. And, in my view, like that of the plurality, meaningful enforcement of the Eighth Amendment demands that application—even if only at sentencing's outer bounds.

A case-by-case approach can nonetheless offer guidance through example. Ewing's sentence is, at a minimum, 2 to 3 times the length of sentences that other jurisdictions would impose in similar circumstances. That sentence itself is sufficiently long to require a typical offender to spend virtually all the remainder of his active life in prison. These and the other factors that I have discussed, along with the questions that I have asked along the way, should help to identify "gross disproportionality" in a fairly objective way—at the outer bounds of sentencing.

In sum, * * * Ewing's sentence (life imprisonment with a minimum term of 25 years) is grossly disproportionate to the triggering offense conduct—stealing three golf clubs—Ewing's recidivism notwithstanding.

POINTS FOR DISCUSSION

a. The Proportionality Principle

The plurality concluded that the Eighth Amendment includes a "proportionality principle," but it reasoned that the principle "forbids only extreme sentences that are 'grossly disproportionate' to the crime." According to the plurality, what factors are relevant in deciding whether a particular sentence is grossly disproportionate? Would requiring strict proportionality create any practical difficulties?

Did the dissenters agree with the plurality that the Eighth Amendment prohibits only *grossly* disproportionate punishments? Or did they conclude that it requires a more searching proportionality standard? If the latter, could you articulate the factors that a court should consider in determining whether a sentence is disproportionate to the crime?

b. Rules and Standards

Justices Scalia and Thomas would have abandoned the proportionality principle, reasoning that such a standard is not subject to principled judicial application. Justice Breyer, in contrast, sought to exercise judgment about the length of Ewing's sentence in relation to his crimes. In your view, did Justice Breyer's approach demonstrate that judges can apply such a test in a principled fashion? Or does his nuanced, multi-factored analysis tend to prove Justice Scalia's point that there is no objective way to apply a proportionality standard? If so, are you comfortable with an interpretation of the Eighth Amendment that would permit a state to sentence a person who steals a pack of gum to life in prison?

B. CAPITAL PUNISHMENT

The Fifth Amendment begins by stating, "No person shall be held to answer for a capital, or otherwise infamous crime, unless on a presentment or indictment of a Grand Jury * * *." This provision contemplates that some crimes will be "capital" crimes, meaning that persons convicted of such crimes will be subject to the death penalty. Indeed, capital punishment was commonplace for felonies at the time of the ratification of the Constitution. Does this mean that the death penalty can never violate the Eighth Amendment's prohibition on cruel and unusual punishments?

It is possible that the proportionality principle, which we considered above, could prohibit the death penalty for petty offenses. For example, it almost certainly would violate the proportionality principle to sentence a person convicted of jaywalking to the death penalty. In addition, it is possible to imagine a means of execution that would be so cruel and barbaric that it would violate the Amendment, even if the death penalty more generally were not constitutionally suspect. Cf. *Glossip v. Gross*, 576 U.S. 863 (2015) (rejecting challenge to three-drug protocol for lethal injection because it did not create an unacceptable risk of severe pain). But is there an argument that the death penalty, even if administered in ways that are largely painless and for crimes that historically were subject to capital punishment, should categorically be considered cruel and unusual today?

For the first two centuries of the nation's history, the Court did not seriously consider the argument that the death penalty is cruel and unusual. In *In re Kemmler*, 136 U.S. 436, 447 (1890), for example, the Court rejected a constitutional challenge to a New York law that provided that capital punishment would be carried out by electrocution. The Court reasoned, "Punishments are cruel when they involve torture or a lingering death; but the punishment of death is not cruel within the meaning of that word as used in the constitution. It implies there something inhuman and barbarous—something more than the mere extinguishment of life." *Kemmler* involved a defendant convicted of first-degree murder, which means that the Court did not have occasion to consider the constitutionality of the death penalty as applied to a person who was convicted of a less serious offense. But under the Court's view of the Eighth Amendment, unless the death penalty is administered in an unusually cruel or painful fashion, its imposition does not violate the Amendment (as incorporated by the Fourteenth Amendment). This was the (relatively) consistent assumption of the Court for almost two centuries, a time during which the death penalty was rarely challenged under the Eighth Amendment.

But in *Furman v. Georgia*, 408 U.S. 238 (1972), the Court held that the imposition of the death penalty in a murder case and in two rape cases violated the Eighth and Fourteenth Amendments. The Justices in the majority could not agree on one rationale for the Court's decision. But three of the five Justices who agreed with the disposition in the case refrained from asserting that the death penalty is categorically unconstitutional, instead pointing out the problems in the way the punishment had been administered. Justice Douglas, for example, asserted that the death penalty had often been applied in a discriminatory fashion, imposed more often on "minorities or members of lower castes." Justice Stewart similarly reasoned that the death penalty had been applied capriciously, with nothing to explain why it had been "so wantonly and freakishly imposed." In his view, such use of the death penalty is "cruel and unusual in the same way that being struck by lightning is cruel and unusual." These Justices (and Justice White, who also concurred) reasoned that the death penalty was unconstitutional *as it had been applied*, but held open the possibility that the punishment could be applied in a sufficiently even-handed and non-arbitrary fashion to render it constitutional.

Justice Brennan, in contrast, asserted that the death penalty categorically constitutes cruel and unusual punishment in violation of the Eighth Amendment. He began by rejecting an originalist approach to the Eighth Amendment, noting that the Court had previously held that the Clause "must draw its meaning from the evolving standards of decency that mark the progress of a maturing society." *Id.* at 269–70 (quoting *Trop v. Dulles*, 356 U.S. 86, 100–101 (1958)). He reasoned that the "uncivilized and inhuman" punishments that the Clause prohibits are those that do "not comport with human dignity." He then concluded:

> "Death is an unusually severe and degrading punishment; there is a strong probability that it is inflicted arbitrarily; its rejection by contemporary society is virtually total; and there is no reason to believe that it serves any penal purpose more effectively than the less severe punishment of imprisonment. The function of these principles is to enable a court to determine whether a punishment comports with human dignity. Death, quite simply, does not."

Justice Marshall also wrote separately to explain his view that the death penalty is cruel and unusual punishment under any circumstances. In his view, death is always an excessive punishment for crime. But he reasoned that, "even if capital punishment is not excessive, it nonetheless violates the Eighth Amendment because it is morally unacceptable to the people of the United States at this time in their history." He acknowledged that many Americans express support for capital punishment, but he thought that they likely would find it to be "barbarously cruel" if they were aware of "all information presently available." He then noted that the following "supporting evidence would be critical to an informed judgment on the morality of the death penalty":

"[T]he death penalty is no more effective a deterrent than life imprisonment[;] convicted murderers are rarely executed, but are usually sentenced to a term in prison; [convicted] murderers usually are model prisoners, and [they] almost always become law-abiding citizens upon their release from prison; [the] costs of executing a capital offender exceed the costs of imprisoning him for life; [while] in prison, a convict under sentence of death performs none of the useful functions that life prisoners perform; [no] attempt is made in the sentencing process to ferret out likely recidivists for execution; and [the] death penalty may actually stimulate criminal activity."

Justice Marshall conceded that, although this "information would almost surely convince the average citizen that the death penalty was unwise," it might not "convince him that the penalty was morally reprehensible." In his view, the "problem arises from the fact that the public's desire for retribution * * * might influence the citizenry's view of the morality of capital punishment." But, he asserted, the

"solution to the problem lies in the fact that no one has ever seriously advanced retribution as a legitimate goal of our society. Defenses of capital punishment are always mounted on deterrent or other similar theories. This should not be surprising. It is the people of this country who have urged in the past that prisons rehabilitate as well as isolate offenders, and it is the people who have injected a sense of purpose into our penology. I cannot believe that at this stage in our history, the American people would ever knowingly support purposeless vengeance. Thus, I believe that the great mass of citizens would conclude on the basis of the material already considered that the death penalty is immoral and therefore unconstitutional."

Chief Justice Burger and Justices Blackmun, Powell, and Rehnquist dissented. They primarily objected to the Court's conclusion on the ground that it impermissibly substituted the judgment of the Justices for the policy judgments of the state legislatures that had approved the use of the death penalty.

The decision in *Furman* prompted a flurry of new legislation in the states, which sought to regulate the availability of capital punishment in order to make it more acceptable to the Court. Four years after the decision in *Furman*, the Court held that the death penalty is not categorically unconstitutional. In *Gregg v. Georgia*, 428 U.S. 153 (1976), the Court upheld Georgia's new capital sentencing procedures. Those procedures specified aggravating and mitigating circumstances that juries were required to consider before deciding whether to impose the death penalty. The procedures also provided for bifurcated trials, separating the punishment phase of the prosecution from the phase designed to determine the defendant's guilt. This approach lessened the risk that the death penalty would be applied arbitrarily.

On the same day, however, the Court invalidated state laws *requiring* the death penalty for persons convicted of crimes identified in the statute. See *Woodson v. North Carolina*, 428 U.S. 280 (1976); *Roberts v. Louisiana*, 428 U.S. 325 (1976). Although there was no opinion for a majority of the Court, a plurality reasoned that because capital punishment is different from other forms of punishment, it cannot be imposed without a sentencing process that attends to the particular circumstances of the case and the mitigating and aggravating factors relevant in the case of the particular defendant.

The Court has also made clear that the proportionality principle applies to the death penalty. In *Coker v. Georgia*, 433 U.S. 584 (1977), for example, the Supreme Court held that a state cannot apply the death penalty to the crime of rape of an adult woman. The Court reasoned:

"We do not discount the seriousness of rape as a crime. It is highly reprehensible, both in a moral sense and in its almost total contempt for the personal integrity and autonomy of the female victim and for the latter's privilege of choosing those with whom intimate relationships are to be established. Short of homicide, it is the 'ultimate violation of self.' It is also a violent crime because it normally involves force, or the threat of force or intimidation, to overcome the will and the capacity of the victim to resist. Rape is very often accompanied by physical injury to the female and can also inflict mental and psychological damage. Because it undermines the community's sense of security, there is public injury as well.

Rape is without doubt deserving of serious punishment; but in terms of moral depravity and of the injury to the person and to the public, it does not compare with murder, which does involve the unjustified taking of human life. Although it may be accompanied by another crime, rape by definition does not include the death of or even the serious injury to another person. The murderer kills; the rapist, if no more than that, does not. Life is over for the victim of the murderer; for the rape victim, life may not be nearly so happy as it was, but it is not over and normally is not beyond repair. We have the abiding conviction that the death penalty, which 'is unique in its severity and irrevocability,' *Gregg*, 428

U.S., at 187, is an excessive penalty for the rapist who, as such, does not take human life."

Are there crimes other than murder for which the death penalty, on this view, would not be "grossly disproportionate"? Consider the following hypothetical and the case that follows.

Problem

The defendant was convicted in a Louisiana court of aggravated rape of his eight-year-old stepdaughter and was sentenced to death. He challenged his sentence by arguing that the death penalty for the crime of child rape constitutes cruel and unusual punishment under the Eighth Amendment as incorporated by the Fourteenth Amendment. A survey of the law of other jurisdictions revealed that although 36 states and the federal government authorized the imposition of capital punishment, only six states authorized it for child rape. (The federal government permitted capital punishment for child rape only for crimes committed within the jurisdiction of the military courts.) In the other 44 states, the defendant could not be executed for child rape of any kind. The state of Louisiana argued that child rape has a devastating impact on the child and that the death penalty serves the state's interests in retribution and deterrence. How should the Court rule on the defendant's Eighth Amendment claim?

These facts are based on *Kennedy v. Louisiana*, 554 U.S. 407 (2008), which held that a sentence of death for the crime of child rape violates the Eighth Amendment, as incorporated by the Fourteenth Amendment.

ROPER V. SIMMONS
543 U.S. 551 (2005)

JUSTICE KENNEDY delivered the opinion of the Court.

This case requires us to address, for the second time in a decade and a half, whether it is permissible under the Eighth and Fourteenth Amendments to the Constitution of the United States to execute a juvenile offender who was older than 15 but younger than 18 when he committed a capital crime. In *Stanford v. Kentucky*, 492 U.S. 361 (1989), a divided Court rejected the proposition that the Constitution bars capital punishment for juvenile offenders in this age group. We reconsider the question.

At the age of 17, when he was still a junior in high school, Christopher Simmons, the respondent here, committed murder. About nine months later, after he had turned 18, he was tried and sentenced to death. There is little doubt that Simmons was the instigator of the crime. Before its commission Simmons said he wanted to murder someone. In chilling, callous terms he talked about his plan, discussing it for the most part with two friends, Charles Benjamin and John Tessmer, then aged 15 and 16 respectively. Simmons proposed to commit burglary and murder by breaking and entering, tying up a victim, and throwing the victim off a bridge. Simmons assured his friends they could "get away with it" because they were minors.

[Simmons and Benjamin entered the home of the victim, Shirley Crook, after reaching through an open window and unlocking the back door. They used duct tape to cover her eyes and mouth and bind her hands, and then drove her to a state park.] They reinforced the bindings, covered her head with a towel, and walked her to a railroad trestle spanning the Meramec River. There they tied her hands and feet together with electrical wire, wrapped her whole face in duct tape and threw her from the bridge, drowning her in the waters below. Simmons later bragged to friends that] he had killed a woman "because the bitch seen my face."

The next day, after receiving information of Simmons' involvement, police arrested him at his high school and took him to the police station in Fenton, Missouri. * * * After less than two hours of interrogation, Simmons confessed to the murder and agreed to perform a videotaped reenactment at the crime scene.

The State charged Simmons with burglary, kidnaping, stealing, and murder in the first degree. As Simmons was 17 at the time of the crime, he was outside the criminal jurisdiction of Missouri's juvenile court system. See Mo.Rev.Stat. §§ 211.021 (2000) and 211.031 (Supp.2003). He was tried as an adult. At trial the State introduced Simmons' confession and the videotaped reenactment of the crime, along with testimony that Simmons discussed the crime in advance and bragged about it later. The defense called no witnesses in the guilt phase. The jury having returned a verdict of murder, the trial proceeded to the penalty phase.

The State sought the death penalty. [The jury heard evidence of aggravating factors from the State—including that the murder involved depravity of mind and was outrageously and wantonly vile, horrible, and inhuman—and mitigating evidence from the defense—including that Simmons had demonstrated responsibility in taking care of his two younger half-brothers and his grandmother.] During closing arguments, both the prosecutor and defense counsel addressed Simmons' age, which the trial judge had instructed the jurors they could consider as a mitigating factor. * * *

The jury recommended the death penalty after finding the State had proved each of the three aggravating factors submitted to it. Accepting the jury's recommendation, the trial judge imposed the death penalty.

> **Food for Thought**
>
> The Court held in the *Atkins* case that it violates the Eighth Amendment to impose the death penalty on a mentally retarded person convicted of a crime. What do you think was the defendant's argument that the punishment under those circumstances constitutes cruel and unusual punishment?

[After the appeals and a habeas proceeding in Simmons' case] had run their course, this Court held that the Eighth and Fourteenth Amendments prohibit the execution of a mentally retarded person. *Atkins v. Virginia,* 536 U.S. 304 (2002). Simmons filed a new petition for state postconviction relief, arguing that the reasoning of *Atkins* established that the Constitution prohibits the execution of a juvenile who was under 18 when the crime was committed. The Missouri Supreme Court agreed. *State ex rel. Simmons v. Roper,* 112 S.W.3d 397 (2003) (en banc). [I]t set aside Simmons' death sentence and resentenced him to "life imprisonment without eligibility for probation, parole, or release except by act of the Governor." *Id.,* at 413. We granted certiorari and now affirm.

* * * As the Court explained in *Atkins,* the Eighth Amendment guarantees individuals the right not to be subjected to excessive sanctions. The right flows from the basic "precept of justice that punishment for crime should be graduated and proportioned to [the] offense." 536 U.S., at 311 (quoting *Weems v. United States,* 217 U.S. 349, 367 (1910)). By protecting even those convicted of heinous crimes, the Eighth Amendment reaffirms the duty of the government to respect the dignity of all persons.

The prohibition against "cruel and unusual punishments," like other expansive language in the Constitution, must be interpreted according to its text, by considering history, tradition, and precedent, and with due regard for its purpose and function in the constitutional design. To implement this framework we have established the propriety and affirmed the necessity of referring to "the evolving standards of decency that mark the progress of a maturing society" to determine which punishments are so disproportionate as to be cruel and unusual. *Trop v. Dulles,* 356 U.S. 86, 100–101 (1958) (plurality opinion).

In *Thompson v. Oklahoma,* 487 U.S. 815 (1988), a plurality of the Court determined that our standards of decency do not permit the execution of any offender under the age of 16 at the time of the crime. The plurality opinion explained that no death penalty State that had given express consideration to a minimum age for the death penalty had set the age lower than 16. The plurality also observed that "[t]he conclusion that it would offend civilized standards of decency to execute a person who was less than 16 years old at the time of his or her offense is consistent with the views that have been expressed by respected professional organizations, by other nations that share our Anglo-American heritage, and by the leading members of the Western European community." *Id.,* at 830. * * *

Bringing its independent judgment to bear on the permissibility of the death penalty for a 15-year-old offender, the *Thompson* plurality stressed that "[t]he reasons why juveniles are not trusted with the privileges and responsibilities of an adult also explain why their irresponsible conduct is not as morally reprehensible as that of an adult." *Id.,* at 835. According to the plurality, the lesser culpability of offenders under 16 made the death penalty inappropriate as a form of retribution, while the low likelihood that offenders under 16 engaged in "the kind of cost-benefit analysis that attaches any weight to the possibility of execution" made the death penalty ineffective as a means of deterrence. *Id.,* at 836–838. With Justice O'CONNOR concurring in the judgment on narrower grounds, the Court set aside the death sentence that had been imposed on the 15-year-old offender.

The next year, in *Stanford v. Kentucky,* 492 U.S. 361 (1989), the Court, over a dissenting opinion joined by four Justices, referred to contemporary standards of decency in this country and concluded the Eighth and Fourteenth Amendments did not proscribe the execution of juvenile offenders over 15 but under 18. The Court noted that 22 of the 37 death penalty States permitted the death penalty for 16-year-old offenders, and, among these 37 States, 25 permitted it for 17-year-old offenders. These numbers, in the Court's view, indicated there was no national consensus "sufficient to label a particular punishment cruel and unusual." *Id.,* at 370–371. * * *

The same day the Court decided *Stanford,* it held that the Eighth Amendment did not mandate a categorical exemption from the death penalty for the mentally retarded. *Penry v. Lynaugh,* 492 U.S. 302 (1989). In reaching this conclusion it stressed that only two States had enacted laws banning the imposition of the death penalty on a mentally retarded person convicted of a capital offense. According to the Court, "the two state statutes prohibiting execution of the mentally retarded, even when added to the 14 States that have rejected capital punishment completely, [did] not provide sufficient evidence at present of a national consensus." *Id.,* at 334.

Three Terms ago the subject was reconsidered in *Atkins.* We held that standards of decency have evolved since *Penry* and now demonstrate that the execution of the mentally retarded is cruel and unusual punishment. The Court noted objective indicia of society's standards, as expressed in legislative enactments and state practice with respect to executions of the mentally retarded. When *Atkins* was decided only a minority of States permitted the practice, and even in those States it was rare. * * *

The inquiry into our society's evolving standards of decency did not end there. * * * Mental retardation, the [*Atkins*] Court said, diminishes personal culpability even if the offender can distinguish right from wrong. The impairments of mentally retarded offenders make it less defensible to impose the death penalty as retribution for past crimes and less likely that the death penalty will have a real deterrent effect. *Id.,* at 319–320. Based on these considerations and on the finding of national consensus against executing the mentally retarded, the Court ruled that the death penalty constitutes an excessive sanction for the entire category of mentally retarded offenders, and that the Eighth Amendment " 'places a substantive restriction on the State's power to take the life' of a mentally retarded offender." *Id.,* at 321 (quoting *Ford v. Wainwright,* 477 U.S. 399, 405 (1986)).

Just as the *Atkins* Court reconsidered the issue decided in *Penry,* we now reconsider the issue decided in *Stanford.* * * *

The evidence of national consensus against the death penalty for juveniles is similar, and in some respects parallel, to the evidence *Atkins* held sufficient to demonstrate a national consensus against the death penalty for the mentally retarded. When *Atkins* was decided, 30 States prohibited the death penalty for the mentally retarded. This number comprised 12 that had abandoned the death penalty altogether, and 18 that maintained it but excluded the mentally retarded from its reach. By a similar calculation in this case, 30 States prohibit the juvenile death penalty, comprising 12 that have rejected the death penalty altogether and 18 that maintain it but, by express provision or judicial interpretation, exclude juveniles from its reach. [E]ven in the 20 States without a formal prohibition on executing juveniles, the practice is infrequent. Since *Stanford,* six States have executed prisoners for crimes committed as juveniles. In the past 10 years, only three have done so: Oklahoma, Texas, and Virginia. * * *

As noted in *Atkins,* with respect to the States that had abandoned the death penalty for the mentally retarded since *Penry,* "[i]t is not so much the number of these States that is significant, but the consistency of the direction of change." 536 U.S., at 315. * * * Since *Stanford,* no State that previously prohibited capital punishment for juveniles has reinstated it. This fact, coupled with the trend toward abolition of the juvenile death penalty, carries special force in light of the general popularity of anticrime legislation, and in light of the particular trend in recent years toward cracking down on juvenile crime in other respects, see H. Snyder &

M. Sickmund, National Center for Juvenile Justice, Juvenile Offenders and Victims: 1999 National Report 89, 133 (Sept.1999). * * *

As in *Atkins,* the objective indicia of consensus in this case—the rejection of the juvenile death penalty in the majority of States; the infrequency of its use even where it remains on the books; and the consistency in the trend toward abolition of the practice—provide sufficient evidence that today our society views juveniles, in the words *Atkins* used respecting the mentally retarded, as "categorically less culpable than the average criminal." 536 U.S., at 316.

A majority of States have rejected the imposition of the death penalty on juvenile offenders under 18, and we now hold this is required by the Eighth Amendment. Because the death penalty is the most severe punishment, the Eighth Amendment applies to it with special force. *Thompson,* 487 U.S., at 856 (O'CONNOR, J., concurring in judgment). Capital punishment must be limited to those offenders who commit "a narrow category of the most serious crimes" and whose extreme culpability makes them "the most deserving of execution." *Atkins, supra,* at 319. This principle is implemented throughout the capital sentencing process. States must give narrow and precise definition to the aggravating factors that can result in a capital sentence. *Godfrey v. Georgia,* 446 U.S. 420, 428–429 (1980) (plurality opinion). In any capital case a defendant has wide latitude to raise as a mitigating factor "any aspect of [his or her] character or record and any of the circumstances of the offense that the defendant proffers as a basis for a sentence less than death." *Lockett v. Ohio,* 438 U.S. 586, 604 (1978) (plurality opinion). There are a number of crimes that beyond question are severe in absolute terms, yet the death penalty may not be imposed for their commission. *Coker v. Georgia,* 433 U.S. 584 (1977) (rape of an adult woman); *Enmund v. Florida,* 458 U.S. 782 (1982) (felony murder where defendant did not kill, attempt to kill, or intend to kill). The death penalty may not be imposed on certain classes of offenders, such as juveniles under 16, the insane, and the mentally retarded, no matter how heinous the crime. *Thompson; Ford v. Wainwright,* 477 U.S. 399 (1986); *Atkins.* These rules vindicate the underlying principle that the death penalty is reserved for a narrow category of crimes and offenders.

Three general differences between juveniles under 18 and adults demonstrate that juvenile offenders cannot with reliability be classified among the worst offenders. First, as any parent knows and as the scientific and sociological studies respondent and his *amici* cite tend to confirm, "[a] lack of maturity and an underdeveloped sense of responsibility are found in youth more often than in adults and are more understandable among the young. These qualities often result in impetuous and ill-considered actions and decisions." *Johnson, supra,* at 367. It has been noted that "adolescents are overrepresented statistically in virtually every category of reckless behavior." Arnett, Reckless Behavior in Adolescence: A Developmental Perspective, 12 Developmental Rev. 339 (1992). In recognition of the comparative immaturity and irresponsibility of juveniles, almost every State prohibits those under 18 years of age from voting, serving on juries, or marrying without parental consent.

The second area of difference is that juveniles are more vulnerable or susceptible to negative influences and outside pressures, including peer pressure. This is explained in part by the prevailing circumstance that juveniles have less control, or less experience with control, over their own environment. See Steinberg & Scott, Less Guilty by Reason of Adolescence: Developmental Immaturity, Diminished Responsibility, and the Juvenile Death Penalty, 58 Am. Psychologist 1009, 1014 (2003).

The third broad difference is that the character of a juvenile is not as well formed as that of an adult. The personality traits of juveniles are more transitory, less fixed. See generally E. Erikson, Identity: Youth and Crisis (1968).

These differences render suspect any conclusion that a juvenile falls among the worst offenders. The susceptibility of juveniles to immature and irresponsible behavior means "their irresponsible conduct is not as morally reprehensible as that of an adult." *Thompson, supra,* at 835 (plurality opinion). Their own vulnerability and comparative lack of control over their immediate surroundings mean juveniles have a greater claim than adults to be forgiven for failing to escape negative influences in their whole environment. See *Stanford,* 492 U.S., at 395 (Brennan, J., dissenting). The reality that juveniles still struggle to define their identity means it is less supportable to conclude that even a heinous crime committed by a juvenile is evidence of irretrievably depraved character. From a moral standpoint it would be misguided to equate the failings of a minor with those of an adult, for a greater possibility exists that a minor's character deficiencies will be reformed. * * *

In *Thompson,* a plurality of the Court recognized the import of these characteristics with respect to juveniles under 16, and relied on them to hold that the Eighth Amendment prohibited the imposition of the death penalty on juveniles below that age. We conclude the same reasoning applies to all juvenile offenders under 18.

Once the diminished culpability of juveniles is recognized, it is evident that the penological justifications for the death penalty apply to them with lesser force than to adults. We have held there are two distinct social purposes served by the death penalty: "retribution and deterrence of capital crimes by prospective offenders." *Atkins*, 536 U.S., at 319. * * * Retribution is not proportional if the law's most severe penalty is imposed on one whose culpability or blameworthiness is diminished, to a substantial degree, by reason of youth and immaturity.

As for deterrence, it is unclear whether the death penalty has a significant or even measurable deterrent effect on juveniles, as counsel for petitioner acknowledged at oral argument. In general we leave to legislatures the assessment of the efficacy of various criminal penalty schemes, see *Harmelin v. Michigan*, 501 U.S. 957, 998–999 (1991) (KENNEDY, J., concurring in part and concurring in judgment). Here, however, the absence of evidence of deterrent effect is of special concern because the same characteristics that render juveniles less culpable than adults suggest as well that juveniles will be less susceptible to deterrence. In particular, as the plurality observed in *Thompson*, "[t]he likelihood that the teenage offender has made the kind of cost-benefit analysis that attaches any weight to the possibility of execution is so remote as to be virtually nonexistent." 487 U.S., at 837. To the extent the juvenile death penalty might have residual deterrent effect, it is worth noting that the punishment of life imprisonment without the possibility of parole is itself a severe sanction, in particular for a young person.

In concluding that neither retribution nor deterrence provides adequate justification for imposing the death penalty on juvenile offenders, we cannot deny or overlook the brutal crimes too many juvenile offenders have committed. Certainly it can be argued, although we by no means concede the point, that a rare case might arise in which a juvenile offender has sufficient psychological maturity, and at the same time demonstrates sufficient depravity, to merit a sentence of death. [P]etitioner and his *amici* [assert] that even assuming the truth of the observations we have made about juveniles' diminished culpability in general, jurors nonetheless should be allowed to consider mitigating arguments related to youth on a case-by-case basis, and in some cases to impose the death penalty if justified. * * * Given this Court's own insistence on individualized consideration, petitioner maintains that it is both arbitrary and unnecessary to adopt a categorical rule barring imposition of the death penalty on any offender under 18 years of age.

We disagree. The differences between juvenile and adult offenders are too marked and well understood to risk allowing a youthful person to receive the death penalty despite insufficient culpability. An unacceptable likelihood exists that the brutality or cold-blooded nature of any particular crime would overpower mitigating arguments based on youth as a matter of course, even where the juvenile offender's objective immaturity, vulnerability, and lack of true depravity should require a sentence less severe than death. * * * When a juvenile offender commits a heinous crime, the State can exact forfeiture of some of the most basic liberties, but the State cannot extinguish his life and his potential to attain a mature understanding of his own humanity.

Drawing the line at 18 years of age is subject, of course, to the objections always raised against categorical rules. The qualities that distinguish juveniles from adults do not disappear when an individual turns 18. * * * For the reasons we have discussed, however, a line must be drawn. * * * The age of 18 is the point where society draws the line for many purposes between childhood and adulthood. It is, we conclude, the age at which the line for death eligibility ought to rest.

Our determination that the death penalty is disproportionate punishment for offenders under 18 finds confirmation in the stark reality that the United States is the only country in the world that continues to give official sanction to the juvenile death penalty. This reality does not become controlling, for the task of interpreting the Eighth Amendment remains our responsibility. Yet at least from the time of the Court's decision in *Trop,* the Court has referred to the laws of other countries and to international authorities as instructive for its interpretation of the Eighth Amendment's prohibition of "cruel and unusual punishments." * * *

Make the Connection

We consider the practice of citing foreign authorities in determining the meaning of the United States Constitution in Volume 1, when we consider the judicial power, and in Chapter 2 of this Volume, in our discussion of the Court's decision in *Lawrence v. Texas.*

As respondent and a number of *amici* emphasize, Article 37 of the United Nations Convention on the Rights of the Child, which every country in the world has ratified save for the United States and Somalia, contains an express prohibition on capital punishment for crimes committed by juveniles under 18. United Nations Convention on the Rights of the Child, Art. 37, Nov. 20, 1989, 1577 U.N.T.S. 3, 28 I.L.M. 1448, 1468–1470 (entered into force Sept. 2, 1990). Parallel prohibitions are contained in other significant international covenants. * * * Respondent and his *amici* have submitted, and petitioner does not contest, that only seven countries other than the United States have executed juvenile offenders since 1990: Iran, Pakistan, Saudi Arabia, Yemen, Nigeria, the Democratic Republic of Congo, and China. Since then each of these countries has either abolished capital punishment for juveniles or made public disavowal of the practice. In sum, it is fair to say that the United States now stands alone in a world that has turned its face against the juvenile death penalty.

It is proper that we acknowledge the overwhelming weight of international opinion against the juvenile death penalty, resting in large part on the understanding that the instability and emotional imbalance of young people may often be a factor in the crime. The opinion of the world community, while not controlling our outcome, does provide respected and significant confirmation for our own conclusions. * * * It does not lessen our fidelity to the Constitution or our pride in its origins to acknowledge that the express affirmation of certain fundamental rights by other nations and peoples simply underscores the centrality of those same rights within our own heritage of freedom.

The Eighth and Fourteenth Amendments forbid imposition of the death penalty on offenders who were under the age of 18 when their crimes were committed. The judgment of the Missouri Supreme Court setting aside the sentence of death imposed upon Christopher Simmons is affirmed.

JUSTICE STEVENS, with whom JUSTICE GINSBURG joins, concurring.

Perhaps even more important than our specific holding today is our reaffirmation of the basic principle that informs the Court's interpretation of the Eighth Amendment. If the meaning of that Amendment had been frozen when it was originally drafted, it would impose no impediment to the execution of 7-year-old children today. See *Stanford v. Kentucky,* 492 U.S. 361, 368 (1989) (describing the common law at the time of the Amendment's adoption). The evolving standards of decency that have driven our construction of this critically important part of the Bill of Rights foreclose any such reading of the Amendment. In the best tradition of the common law, the pace of that evolution is a matter for continuing debate; but that our understanding of the Constitution does change from time to time has been settled since John Marshall breathed life into its text. If great lawyers of his day—Alexander Hamilton, for example—were sitting with us today, I would expect them to join Justice KENNEDY's opinion for the Court. In all events, I do so without hesitation.

JUSTICE O'CONNOR, dissenting.

The Court's decision today establishes a categorical rule forbidding the execution of any offender for any crime committed before his 18th birthday, no matter how deliberate, wanton, or cruel the offense. Neither the objective

> **Food for Thought**
>
> What would count as a "genuine national consensus" about the inappropriateness of the death penalty under particular circumstances? If it would mean that all states prohibit the punishment, then there would be no need for judicial intervention. Should the Court find a "consensus," for these purposes, when two-thirds of the states take a particular approach? Three-quarters? How does the Court know?

evidence of contemporary societal values, nor the Court's moral proportionality analysis, nor the two in tandem suffice to justify this ruling.

Although the Court finds support for its decision in the fact that a majority of the States now disallow capital punishment of 17-year-old offenders, it refrains from asserting that its holding is compelled by a genuine national consensus. Indeed, the evidence before us fails to demonstrate conclusively that any such consensus has emerged in the brief period since we upheld the constitutionality of this practice in *Stanford v. Kentucky,* 492 U.S. 361 (1989).

Instead, the rule decreed by the Court rests, ultimately, on its independent moral judgment that death is a disproportionately severe punishment for any 17-year-old offender. I do not subscribe to this judgment. Adolescents *as a class* are undoubtedly less mature, and therefore less culpable for their misconduct, than adults. But the Court has adduced no evidence impeaching the seemingly reasonable conclusion reached by many state legislatures: that at least *some* 17-year-old murderers are sufficiently mature to deserve the death penalty in an appropriate case. Nor has it been shown that capital sentencing juries are incapable of accurately assessing a youthful defendant's maturity or of giving due weight to the mitigating characteristics associated with youth.

[I] agree [that in] determining whether the Eighth Amendment permits capital punishment of a particular offense or class of offenders, we must look to whether such punishment is consistent with contemporary standards of decency. We are obligated to weigh both the objective evidence of societal values and our own judgment as to whether death is an excessive sanction in the context at hand. In the instant case, the objective evidence is inconclusive; standing alone, it does not demonstrate that our society has repudiated capital punishment of 17-year-old offenders in all cases. Rather, the actions of the Nation's legislatures suggest that, although a clear and durable national consensus against this practice may in time emerge, that day has yet to arrive. By acting so soon after our decision in *Stanford,* the Court both pre-empts the democratic debate through which genuine consensus might develop and simultaneously runs a considerable risk of inviting lower court reassessments of our Eighth Amendment precedents.

JUSTICE SCALIA, with whom THE CHIEF JUSTICE and JUSTICE THOMAS join, dissenting.

In urging approval of a constitution that gave life-tenured judges the power to nullify laws enacted by the people's representatives, Alexander Hamilton assured the citizens of New York that there was little risk in this, since "[t]he judiciary . . . ha[s] neither FORCE nor WILL but merely judgment." The Federalist No. 78, p. 465 (C. Rossiter ed.1961). But Hamilton had in mind a traditional judiciary, "bound down by strict rules and precedents which serve to define and point out their duty in every particular case that comes before them." *Id.,* at 471. Bound down, indeed. What a mockery today's opinion makes of Hamilton's expectation, announcing the Court's conclusion that the meaning of our Constitution has changed over the past 15 years—not, mind you, that this Court's decision 15 years ago was *wrong,* but that the Constitution *has changed.* The Court reaches this implausible result by purporting to advert, not to the original meaning of the Eighth Amendment, but to "the evolving standards of decency" of our national society. It then finds, on the flimsiest of grounds, that a national consensus which could not be perceived in our people's laws barely 15 years ago now solidly exists. Worse still, the Court says in so many words that what our people's laws say about the issue does not, in the last analysis, matter: "[I]n the end our own judgment will be brought to bear on the question of the acceptability of the death penalty under the Eighth Amendment." The Court thus proclaims itself sole arbiter of our Nation's moral standards—and in the course of discharging that awesome responsibility purports to take guidance from the views of foreign courts and legislatures. Because I do not believe that the meaning of our Eighth Amendment, any more than the meaning of other provisions of our Constitution, should be determined by the subjective views of five Members of this Court and like-minded foreigners, I dissent.

Of course, the real force driving today's decision is [the] Court's "own judgment" that murderers younger than 18 can never be as morally culpable as older counterparts. * * * If the Eighth Amendment set forth an ordinary rule of law, it would indeed be the role of this Court to say what the law is. But the Court having pronounced that the Eighth Amendment is an ever-changing reflection of "the evolving standards of decency" of our society, it makes no sense for the Justices then to *prescribe* those standards rather than discern them from the practices of our people. On the evolving-standards hypothesis, the only legitimate function of this Court is to identify a moral consensus of the American people. By what conceivable warrant can nine lawyers presume to be the authoritative conscience of the Nation?

Nor does the Court suggest a stopping point for its reasoning. If juries cannot make appropriate determinations in cases involving murderers under 18, in what other kinds of cases will the Court find jurors deficient? We have already held that no jury may consider whether a mentally deficient defendant can receive the death penalty, irrespective of his crime. Why not take other mitigating factors, such as considerations of childhood abuse or poverty, away from juries as well? Surely jurors "overpower[ed]" by "the brutality or cold-blooded nature" of a crime could not adequately weigh these mitigating factors either.

Though the views of our own citizens are essentially irrelevant to the Court's decision today, the views of other countries and the so-called international community take center stage. * * * [T]he basic premise of the Court's argument—that American law should conform to the laws of the rest of the world—ought to be rejected out of hand. In fact the Court itself does not believe it. In many significant respects the laws of most other countries differ from our law—including not only such explicit provisions of our Constitution as the right to jury trial and grand jury indictment, but even many interpretations of the Constitution prescribed by this Court itself. The Court-pronounced exclusionary rule, for example, is distinctively American. * * *

The Court has been oblivious to the views of other countries when deciding how to interpret our Constitution's requirement that "Congress shall make no law respecting an establishment of religion. . . ." Amdt. 1. Most other countries—including those committed to religious neutrality—do not insist on the degree of separation between church and state that this Court requires. * * * And let us not

> **Make the Connection**
>
> Is there a plausible distinction between cases involving the Eighth Amendment, on the one hand, and the Establishment Clause of the First Amendment and the Due Process Clause of the Fourteenth Amendment, on the other, that might justify the Court's reliance on foreign sources of law here? We considered the Establishment Clause of the First Amendment in Chapter 11 and the right to an abortion in Chapter 2.

forget the Court's abortion jurisprudence, which makes us one of only six countries that allow abortion on demand until the point of viability. * * * The Court should either profess its willingness to reconsider all these matters in light of the views of foreigners, or else it should cease putting forth foreigners' views as part of the *reasoned basis* of its decisions. To invoke alien law when it agrees with one's own thinking, and ignore it otherwise, is not reasoned decisionmaking, but sophistry.

Foreign sources are cited today, *not* to underscore our "fidelity" to the Constitution, our "pride in its origins," and "our own [American] heritage." To the contrary, they are cited *to set aside* the centuries-old American practice—a practice still engaged in by a large majority of the relevant States—of letting a jury of 12 citizens decide whether, in the particular case, youth should be the basis for withholding the death penalty. What these foreign sources "affirm," rather than repudiate, is the Justices' own notion of how the world ought to be, and their diktat that it shall be so henceforth in America. * * *

In a system based upon constitutional and statutory text democratically adopted, the concept of "law" ordinarily signifies that particular words have a fixed meaning. Such law does not change, and this Court's pronouncement of it therefore remains authoritative until (confessing our prior error) we overrule. The Court has purported to make of the Eighth Amendment, however, a mirror of the passing and changing sentiment of American society regarding penology. * * * The result will be to crown arbitrariness with chaos.

POINTS FOR DISCUSSION

a. The Rule of *Roper*

The Court held in *Roper* that it violates the Eighth Amendment to impose the death penalty on a person who committed a crime before he was 18 years old. The Court reasoned that the offender's youth and immaturity make the punishment categorically impermissible and not simply factors to be considered by a jury in deciding whether to impose the punishment. Do you agree that the death penalty is always effectively barbaric when applied to teenagers under the age of 18? Consider the facts of *Roper* itself, which involved a cold, calculated crime of exceeding cruelty and violence. Even if the death penalty ordinarily is inappropriate for defendants who committed their crimes before the age of 18, are there at least some cases where it is warranted? Does it depend on why we impose criminal punishment in the first place?

b. Evolving Meaning or Fixed Meaning?

In concluding that the death penalty violates the Eighth Amendment when it is applied to defendants who committed their crimes before the age of 18, the Court applied "evolving standards of decency." The Court reasoned that penalties that were once not considered cruel and unusual, within the meaning of the Amendment, can become so as societal values change.

Justice Scalia, in contrast, asserted that the Constitution's meaning does not evolve without formal amendment, and therefore that punishments that were not considered cruel and unusual in 1791 (or 1868, when the Fourteenth Amendment was ratified) cannot, for constitutional purposes, suddenly become cruel and unusual. On his view, because the death penalty historically would not have been considered cruel and unusual punishment under the circumstances of this case, it *a fortiori* is not cruel and unusual now.

Under the Court's approach, the Justices must have some way of determining when in fact society's views have evolved sufficiently to warrant a new constitutional rule. What sort of evidence is relevant in that inquiry? If society's views have genuinely evolved, then wouldn't the punishment at issue be prohibited in all (or most) states?

Under Justice Scalia's view, the death penalty presumably would be permissible not only for someone like Christopher Simmons, who committed a murder when he was 17, but also a younger child—say, a 12-year-old boy—who intentionally shot someone. Indeed, under Justice Scalia's view the death penalty presumably would be available for all felonies, not just murder, if a state legislature were to authorize the death penalty for all felonies. Is that too high a price to pay for fidelity to the original meaning? If the Supreme Court does not limit the Eighth Amendment to its original meaning, how heavily should the Court's interpretation of the Amendment depend on highly unlikely hypothetical cases such as a court imposing the death penalty on someone who is 12 years old or a state legislature authorizing the death penalty for all felonies?

c.   **Determining a "National Consensus"**

In seeking to ascertain the content of our "evolving standards of decency," the Court attempted to determine whether there is now a "national consensus" against the use of capital punishment for offenders who committed crimes before they were 18 years old. In conducting that inquiry, the Court looked at the number of states where the death penalty is unavailable for offenders who were younger than 18 when they committed their crimes. That group of states included all the states that have abolished the death penalty in all cases and all of the death penalty states that prohibit the penalty for juvenile offenders.

In a section of the opinion that was omitted above, Justice Scalia objected to this approach. He reasoned:

> "Consulting States that bar the death penalty concerning the necessity of making an exception to the penalty for offenders under 18 is rather like including old-order Amishmen in a consumer-preference poll on the electric car. Of *course* they don't like it, but that sheds no light whatever on the point at issue. That 12 States favor *no* executions says something about consensus against the death penalty, but nothing—absolutely nothing— about consensus that offenders under 18 deserve special immunity from such a penalty."

Justice Scalia then noted that fewer than half of the states that permit the death penalty under at least some circumstances prohibited it for offenders who were under the age of 18 when they committed their crimes. He declared, "Words have no meaning if the views of less than 50% of death penalty States can constitute a national consensus."

If evolving standards of decency is the right standard for determining what punishment is cruel and unusual, what is the correct denominator for determining a national consensus? Whose view do you find more persuasive?

d. The Battle over the Death Penalty, Reprised

In *Glossip v. Gross*, 576 U.S. 863 (2015), the Court held that the three-drug lethal injection protocol that Oklahoma used to execute inmates sentenced to death did not create an unacceptable risk of severe pain in violation of Eighth Amendment. In dissent, Justice Breyer asserted that the Court should have asked "for full briefing on a more basic question: whether the death penalty violates the Constitution." He reasoned:

> "In 1976, [in *Gregg v. Georgia*, 428 U.S. 153, 187 (1976),] the Court thought that the constitutional infirmities in the death penalty could be healed; the Court in effect delegated significant responsibility to the States to develop procedures that would protect against those constitutional problems. Almost 40 years of studies, surveys, and experience strongly indicate, however, that this effort has failed. Today's administration of the death penalty involves three fundamental constitutional defects: (1) serious unreliability, (2) arbitrariness in application, and (3) unconscionably long delays that undermine the death penalty's penological purpose. Perhaps as a result, (4) most places within the United States have abandoned its use."

Do you agree that the Court should revisit the question whether the death penalty categorically constitutes cruel and unusual punishment under the Eighth Amendment? Notice that Justice Breyer's argument turned on defects in the way that the punishment is administered, not on the barbarism of the punishment itself. Does a finding that a particular punishment is cruel and unusual ultimately require a moral judgment that the punishment is simply too barbaric to be used? Or can the punishment be cruel and unusual simply because it is applied capriciously or because it fails to deter crime?

Executive Summary of This Chapter

The Eighth Amendment prohibits excessive bail, excessive fines, and cruel and unusual punishments. The prohibition on **excessive bail** prevents the government from setting bail at a level dramatically higher than what would be required to ensure the defendant's attendance at trial. The prohibition on **excessive fines** limits the size of financial penalties that the government may impose as a punishment for crime; fines cannot be "grossly disproportional to the gravity" of the offense. *United States v. Bajakajian* (1998).

The Eighth Amendment prohibits **cruel and unusual punishments**. At a minimum, this provision prohibits truly barbaric forms of punishment, such as torture on the rack. The provision also "contains a narrow **proportionality principle** that applies to noncapital sentences." *Ewing v. California* (2003) (internal quotations omitted). The Court has held that a sentence of 25 years to life in prison, imposed for the offense of felony grand theft under a state's "three strikes law," "is not grossly disproportionate and therefore does not violate the Eighth Amendment's prohibition on cruel and unusual punishments." *Ewing v. California* (2003).

Although the Court has held that **capital punishment** does not automatically violate the Eighth Amendment's prohibition on cruel and unusual punishments, it has said that the proportionality principle applies to the death penalty. Applying that principle, the Court has held that a state cannot apply the death penalty to the crime of rape of an adult woman, *Coker v. Georgia* (1977); to mentally retarded defendants, *Atkins v. Virginia* (2002); or to defendants who committed crimes when they were younger than 18, *Thompson v. Oklahoma* (1988); *Roper v. Simmons* (2005).

The Constitution of the United States of America

We the People of the United States, in Order to form a more perfect Union, establish Justice, insure domestic Tranquility, provide for the common defence, promote the general Welfare, and secure the Blessings of Liberty to ourselves and our Posterity, do ordain and establish this Constitution for the United States of America.

ARTICLE I

SECTION 1.   All legislative Powers herein granted shall be vested in a Congress of the United States, which shall consist of a Senate and House of Representatives.

SECTION 2.   [1] The House of Representatives shall be composed of Members chosen every second Year by the People of the several States, and the Electors in each State shall have the Qualifications requisite for Electors of the most numerous Branch of the State Legislature.

[2] No Person shall be a Representative who shall not have attained to the Age of twenty five Years, and been seven Years a Citizen of the United States, and who shall not, when elected, be an Inhabitant of that State in which he shall be chosen.

[3] [Representatives and direct Taxes shall be apportioned among the several States which may be included within this Union, according to their respective Numbers, which shall be determined by adding to the whole Number of free Persons, including those bound to Service for a Term of Years, and excluding Indians not taxed, three fifths of all other Persons.] The actual Enumeration shall be made within three Years after the first Meeting of the Congress of the United States, and

> **Take Note**
>
> The bracketed text has been modified by Section 2 of the Fourteenth Amendment.

1385

within every subsequent Term of ten Years, in such Manner as they shall by Law direct. The Number of Representatives shall not exceed one for every thirty Thousand, but each State shall have at Least one Representative; and until such enumeration shall be made, the State of New Hampshire shall be entitled to chuse three, Massachusetts eight, Rhode-Island and Providence Plantations one, Connecticut five, New-York six, New Jersey four, Pennsylvania eight, Delaware one, Maryland six, Virginia ten, North Carolina five, South Carolina five, and Georgia three.

[4] When vacancies happen in the Representation from any State, the Executive Authority thereof shall issue Writs of Election to fill such Vacancies.

[5] The House of Representatives shall chuse their Speaker and other Officers; and shall have the sole Power of Impeachment.

SECTION 3. [1] The Senate of the United States shall be composed of two Senators from each State, [chosen by the Legislature thereof for six Years]; and each Senator shall have one Vote.

> **Take Note**
> The bracketed text in the first two clauses of Section 3 has been modified by the Seventeenth Amendment.

[2] Immediately after they shall be assembled in Consequence of the first Election, they shall be divided as equally as may be into three Classes. The Seats of the Senators of the first Class shall be vacated at the Expiration of the second Year, of the second Class at the Expiration of the fourth Year, and of the third Class at the Expiration of the sixth Year, so that one third may be chosen every second Year; [and if Vacancies happen by Resignation, or otherwise, during the Recess of the Legislature of any State, the Executive thereof may make temporary Appointments until the next Meeting of the Legislature, which shall then fill such Vacancies.]

[3] No Person shall be a Senator who shall not have attained to the Age of thirty Years, and been nine Years a Citizen of the United States, and who shall not, when elected, be an Inhabitant of that State for which he shall be chosen.

[4] The Vice President of the United States shall be President of the Senate, but shall have no Vote, unless they be equally divided.

[5] The Senate shall chuse their other Officers, and also a President pro tempore, in the Absence of the Vice President, or when he shall exercise the Office of President of the United States.

[6]   The Senate shall have the sole Power to try all Impeachments. When sitting for that Purpose, they shall be on Oath or Affirmation. When the President of the United States is tried, the Chief Justice shall preside: And no Person shall be convicted without the Concurrence of two thirds of the Members present.

[7]   Judgment in Cases of Impeachment shall not extend further than to removal from Office, and disqualification to hold and enjoy any Office of honor, Trust or Profit under the United States: but the Party convicted shall nevertheless be liable and subject to Indictment, Trial, Judgment and Punishment, according to Law.

SECTION 4.   [1]   The Times, Places and Manner of holding Elections for Senators and Representatives, shall be prescribed in each State by the Legislature thereof; but the Congress may at any time by Law make or alter such Regulations, except as to the Places of chusing Senators.

[2]   The Congress shall assemble at least once in every Year, and such Meeting shall be [on the first Monday in December], unless they shall by Law appoint a different Day.

> **Take Note**
>
> The bracketed text has been modified by Section 2 of the Twentieth Amendment.

SECTION 5.   [1]   Each House shall be the Judge of the Elections, Returns and Qualifications of its own Members, and a Majority of each shall constitute a Quorum to do Business; but a smaller Number may adjourn from day to day, and may be authorized to compel the Attendance of absent Members, in such Manner, and under such Penalties as each House may provide.

[2]   Each House may determine the Rules of its Proceedings, punish its Members for disorderly Behaviour, and, with the Concurrence of two thirds, expel a Member.

[3]   Each House shall keep a Journal of its Proceedings, and from time to time publish the same, excepting such Parts as may in their Judgment require Secrecy; and the Yeas and Nays of the Members of either House on any question shall, at the Desire of one fifth of those Present, be entered on the Journal.

[4]   Neither House, during the Session of Congress, shall, without the Consent of the other, adjourn for more than three days, nor to any other Place than that in which the two Houses shall be sitting.

SECTION 6.   [1]   The Senators and Representatives shall receive a Compensation for their Services, to be ascertained by Law, and paid out of the Treasury of the United States. They shall in all Cases, except Treason, Felony and Breach of the Peace, be privileged from Arrest during their Attendance at the

Session of their respective Houses, and in going to and returning from the same; and for any Speech or Debate in either House, they shall not be questioned in any other Place.

[2]   No Senator or Representative shall, during the Time for which he was elected, be appointed to any civil Office under the Authority of the United States, which shall have been created, or the Emoluments whereof shall have been encreased during such time; and no Person holding any Office under the United States, shall be a Member of either House during his Continuance in Office.

Section 7.   [1]   All Bills for raising Revenue shall originate in the House of Representatives; but the Senate may propose or concur with Amendments as on other Bills.

[2]   Every Bill which shall have passed the House of Representatives and the Senate, shall, before it become a Law, be presented to the President of the United States: If he approve he shall sign it, but if not he shall return it, with his Objections to that House in which it shall have originated, who shall enter the Objections at large on their Journal, and proceed to reconsider it. If after such Reconsideration two thirds of that House shall agree to pass the Bill, it shall be sent, together with the Objections, to the other House, by which it shall likewise be reconsidered, and if approved by two thirds of that House, it shall become a Law. But in all such Cases the Votes of both Houses shall be determined by yeas and Nays, and the Names of the Persons voting for and against the Bill shall be entered on the Journal of each House respectively. If any Bill shall not be returned by the President within ten Days (Sundays excepted) after it shall have been presented to him, the Same shall be a Law, in like Manner as if he had signed it, unless the Congress by their Adjournment prevent its Return, in which Case it shall not be a Law.

[3]   Every Order, Resolution, or Vote to which the Concurrence of the Senate and House of Representatives may be necessary (except on a question of Adjournment) shall be presented to the President of the United States; and before the Same shall take Effect, shall be approved by him, or being disapproved by him, shall be repassed by two thirds of the Senate and House of Representatives, according to the Rules and Limitations prescribed in the Case of a Bill.

Section 8.   [1]   The Congress shall have Power To lay and collect Taxes, Duties, Imposts and Excises, to pay the Debts and provide for the common Defence and general Welfare of the United States; but all Duties, Imposts and Excises shall be uniform throughout the United States;

[2]   To borrow Money on the credit of the United States;

[3] To regulate Commerce with foreign Nations, and among the several States, and with the Indian Tribes;

[4] To establish an uniform Rule of Naturalization, and uniform Laws on the subject of Bankruptcies throughout the United States;

[5] To coin Money, regulate the Value thereof, and of foreign Coin, and fix the Standard of Weights and Measures;

[6] To provide for the Punishment of counterfeiting the Securities and current Coin of the United States;

[7] To establish Post Offices and post Roads;

[8] To promote the Progress of Science and useful Arts, by securing for limited Times to Authors and Inventors the exclusive Right to their respective Writings and Discoveries;

[9] To constitute Tribunals inferior to the supreme Court;

[10] To define and punish Piracies and Felonies committed on the high Seas, and Offences against the Law of Nations;

[11] To declare War, grant Letters of Marque and Reprisal, and make Rules concerning Captures on Land and Water;

[12] To raise and support Armies, but no Appropriation of Money to that Use shall be for a longer Term than two Years;

[13] To provide and maintain a Navy;

[14] To make Rules for the Government and Regulation of the land and naval Forces;

[15] To provide for calling forth the Militia to execute the Laws of the Union, suppress Insurrections and repel Invasions;

[16] To provide for organizing, arming, and disciplining, the Militia, and for governing such Part of them as may be employed in the Service of the United States, reserving to the States respectively, the Appointment of the Officers, and the Authority of training the Militia according to the discipline prescribed by Congress;

[17] To exercise exclusive Legislation in all Cases whatsoever, over such District (not exceeding ten Miles square) as may, by Cession of particular States, and the Acceptance of Congress, become the Seat of the Government of the United States, and to exercise like Authority over all Places purchased by the

Consent of the Legislature of the State in which the Same shall be, for the Erection of Forts, Magazines, Arsenals, dock-Yards, and other needful Buildings;—And

[18] To make all Laws which shall be necessary and proper for carrying into Execution the foregoing Powers, and all other Powers vested by this Constitution in the Government of the United States, or in any Department or Officer thereof.

SECTION 9. [1] The Migration or Importation of such Persons as any of the States now existing shall think proper to admit, shall not be prohibited by the Congress prior to the Year one thousand eight hundred and eight, but a Tax or duty may be imposed on such Importation, not exceeding ten dollars for each Person.

[2] The Privilege of the Writ of Habeas Corpus shall not be suspended, unless when in Cases of Rebellion or Invasion the public Safety may require it.

[3] No Bill of Attainder or ex post facto Law shall be passed.

> **Take Note**
>
> The bracketed text has been modified by the Sixteenth Amendment.

[4] No Capitation, or other direct, Tax shall be laid, [unless in Proportion to the Census or enumeration herein before directed to be taken.]

[5] No Tax or Duty shall be laid on Articles exported from any State.

[6] No Preference shall be given by any Regulation of Commerce or Revenue to the Ports of one State over those of another; nor shall Vessels bound to, or from, one State, be obliged to enter, clear, or pay Duties in another.

[7] No Money shall be drawn from the Treasury, but in Consequence of Appropriations made by Law; and a regular Statement and Account of the Receipts and Expenditures of all public Money shall be published from time to time.

[8] No Title of Nobility shall be granted by the United States: And no Person holding any Office of Profit or Trust under them, shall, without the Consent of the Congress, accept of any present, Emolument, Office, or Title, of any kind whatever, from any King, Prince, or foreign State.

SECTION 10. [1] No State shall enter into any Treaty, Alliance, or Confederation; grant Letters of Marque and Reprisal; coin Money; emit Bills of Credit; make any Thing but gold and silver Coin a Tender in Payment of Debts; pass any Bill of Attainder, ex post facto Law, or Law impairing the Obligation of Contracts, or grant any Title of Nobility.

[2]   No State shall, without the Consent of the Congress, lay any Imposts or Duties on Imports or Exports, except what may be absolutely necessary for executing [its] inspection Laws: and the net Produce of all Duties and Imposts, laid by any State on Imports or Exports, shall be for the Use of the Treasury of the United States; and all such Laws shall be subject to the Revision and Controul of the Congress.

[3]   No State shall, without the Consent of Congress, lay any Duty of Tonnage, keep Troops, or Ships of War in time of Peace, enter into any Agreement or Compact with another State, or with a foreign Power, or engage in War, unless actually invaded, or in such imminent Danger as will not admit of delay.

ARTICLE II

SECTION 1.   [1]   The executive Power shall be vested in a President of the United States of America. He shall hold his Office during the Term of four Years, and, together with the Vice President, chosen for the same Term, be elected, as follows:

[2]   Each State shall appoint, in such Manner as the Legislature thereof may direct, a Number of Electors, equal to the whole Number of Senators and Representatives to which the State may be entitled in the Congress: but no Senator or Representative, or Person holding an Office of Trust or Profit under the United States, shall be appointed an Elector.

[3]   [The Electors shall meet in their respective States, and vote by Ballot for two Persons, of whom one at least shall not be an Inhabitant of the same State with themselves. And they shall make a List of all the Persons voted for, and of the Number of Votes for each; which List they shall sign and certify, and

> **Take Note**
>
> The bracketed text has been superseded by the Twelfth Amendment, part of which in turn was modified by Section 3 of the Twentieth Amendment.

transmit sealed to the Seat of the Government of the United States, directed to the President of the Senate. The President of the Senate shall, in the Presence of the Senate and House of Representatives, open all the Certificates, and the Votes shall then be counted. The Person having the greatest Number of Votes shall be the President, if such Number be a Majority of the whole Number of Electors appointed; and if there be more than one who have such Majority, and have an equal Number of Votes, then the House of Representatives shall immediately chuse by Ballot one of them for President; and if no Person have a Majority, then from the five highest on the List the said House shall in like Manner chuse the

President. But in chusing the President, the Votes shall be taken by States, the Representation from each State having one Vote; A quorum for this purpose shall consist of a Member or Members from two thirds of the States, and a Majority of all the States shall be necessary to a Choice. In every Case, after the Choice of the President, the Person having the greatest Number of Votes of the Electors shall be the Vice President. But if there should remain two or more who have equal Votes, the Senate shall chuse from them by Ballot the Vice President.]

[4]   The Congress may determine the Time of chusing the Electors, and the Day on which they shall give their Votes; which Day shall be the same throughout the United States.

[5]   No Person except a natural born Citizen, or a Citizen of the United States, at the time of the Adoption of this Constitution, shall be eligible to the Office of President; neither shall any Person be eligible to that Office who shall not have attained to the Age of thirty five Years, and been fourteen Years a Resident within the United States.

> **Take Note**
>
> The bracketed text has been modified by the Twenty-Fifth Amendment.

[6]   [In Case of the Removal of the President from Office, or of his Death, Resignation, or Inability to discharge the Powers and Duties of the said Office, the Same shall devolve on the Vice President, and the Congress may by Law provide for the Case of Removal, Death, Resignation or Inability, both of the President and Vice President, declaring what Officer shall then act as President, and such Officer shall act accordingly, until the Disability be removed, or a President shall be elected.]

[7]   The President shall, at stated Times, receive for his Services, a Compensation, which shall neither be increased nor diminished during the Period for which he shall have been elected, and he shall not receive within that Period any other Emolument from the United States, or any of them.

[8]   Before he enter on the Execution of his Office, he shall take the following Oath or Affirmation:—"I do solemnly swear (or affirm) that I will faithfully execute the Office of President of the United States, and will to the best of my Ability, preserve, protect and defend the Constitution of the United States."

SECTION 2.   [1]   The President shall be Commander in Chief of the Army and Navy of the United States, and of the Militia of the several States, when called into the actual Service of the United States; he may require the Opinion, in writing, of the principal Officer in each of the executive Departments, upon any Subject relating to the Duties of their respective Offices, and he shall have Power to grant

Reprieves and Pardons for Offences against the United States, except in Cases of Impeachment.

[2] He shall have Power, by and with the Advice and Consent of the Senate, to make Treaties, provided two thirds of the Senators present concur; and he shall nominate, and by and with the Advice and Consent of the Senate, shall appoint Ambassadors, other public Ministers and Consuls, Judges of the supreme Court, and all other Officers of the United States, whose Appointments are not herein otherwise provided for, and which shall be established by Law: but the Congress may by Law vest the Appointment of such inferior Officers, as they think proper, in the President alone, in the Courts of Law, or in the Heads of Departments.

[3] The President shall have Power to fill up all Vacancies that may happen during the Recess of the Senate, by granting Commissions which shall expire at the End of their next Session.

SECTION 3. He shall from time to time give to the Congress Information of the State of the Union, and recommend to their Consideration such Measures as he shall judge necessary and expedient; he may, on extraordinary Occasions, convene both Houses, or either of them, and in Case of Disagreement between them, with Respect to the Time of Adjournment, he may adjourn them to such Time as he shall think proper; he shall receive Ambassadors and other public Ministers; he shall take Care that the Laws be faithfully executed, and shall Commission all the Officers of the United States.

SECTION 4. The President, Vice President and all civil Officers of the United States, shall be removed from Office on Impeachment for, and Conviction of, Treason, Bribery, or other high Crimes and Misdemeanors.

ARTICLE III

SECTION 1. The judicial Power of the United States shall be vested in one supreme Court, and in such inferior Courts as the Congress may from time to time ordain and establish. The Judges, both of the supreme and inferior Courts, shall hold their Offices during good Behaviour, and shall, at stated Times, receive for their Services a Compensation, which shall not be diminished during their Continuance in Office.

SECTION 2. [1] The judicial Power shall extend to all Cases, in Law and Equity, arising under this Constitution, the Laws of the United States, and Treaties made, or which shall be made, under their Authority;—to all Cases affecting Ambassadors, other public Ministers and Consuls;—to all Cases of admiralty and maritime Jurisdiction;—to Controversies to which the United States shall be a Party;—to Controversies between two or more States;[—between a State and

Take Note

The bracketed text has been modified by the Eleventh Amendment.

Citizens of another State;]—between Citizens of different States;—between Citizens of the same State claiming Lands under Grants of different States, [and between a State, or the Citizens thereof, and foreign States, Citizens or Subjects.]

[2] In all Cases affecting Ambassadors, other public Ministers and Consuls, and those in which a State shall be Party, the supreme Court shall have original Jurisdiction. In all the other Cases before mentioned, the supreme Court shall have appellate Jurisdiction, both as to Law and Fact, with such Exceptions, and under such Regulations as the Congress shall make.

[3] The Trial of all Crimes, except in Cases of Impeachment, shall be by Jury; and such Trial shall be held in the State where the said Crimes shall have been committed; but when not committed within any State, the Trial shall be at such Place or Places as the Congress may by Law have directed.

SECTION 3. [1] Treason against the United States, shall consist only in levying War against them, or in adhering to their Enemies, giving them Aid and Comfort. No Person shall be convicted of Treason unless on the Testimony of two Witnesses to the same overt Act, or on Confession in open Court.

[2] The Congress shall have Power to declare the Punishment of Treason, but no Attainder of Treason shall work Corruption of Blood, or Forfeiture except during the Life of the Person attainted.

ARTICLE IV

SECTION 1. Full Faith and Credit shall be given in each State to the public Acts, Records, and judicial Proceedings of every other State. And the Congress may by general Laws prescribe the Manner in which such Acts, Records and Proceedings shall be proved, and the Effect thereof.

SECTION 2. [1] The Citizens of each State shall be entitled to all Privileges and Immunities of Citizens in the several States.

[2] A Person charged in any State with Treason, Felony, or other Crime, who shall flee from Justice, and be found in another State, shall on Demand of the executive Authority of the State from which he fled, be delivered up, to be removed to the State having Jurisdiction of the Crime.

[3] [No Person held to Service or Labour in one State, under the Laws thereof, escaping into another, shall, in Consequence of any Law or Regulation

therein, be discharged from such Service or Labour, but shall be delivered up on Claim of the Party to whom such Service or Labour may be due.]

Take Note

The bracketed text has been superseded by the Thirteenth Amendment.

SECTION 3. [1] New States may be admitted by the Congress into this Union; but no new State shall be formed or erected within the Jurisdiction of any other State; nor any State be formed by the Junction of two or more States, or Parts of States, without the Consent of the Legislatures of the States concerned as well as of the Congress.

[2] The Congress shall have Power to dispose of and make all needful Rules and Regulations respecting the Territory or other Property belonging to the United States; and nothing in this Constitution shall be so construed as to Prejudice any Claims of the United States, or of any particular State.

SECTION 4. The United States shall guarantee to every State in this Union a Republican Form of Government, and shall protect each of them against Invasion; and on Application of the Legislature, or of the Executive (when the Legislature cannot be convened), against domestic Violence.

ARTICLE V

The Congress, whenever two thirds of both Houses shall deem it necessary, shall propose Amendments to this Constitution, or, on the Application of the Legislatures of two thirds of the several States, shall call a Convention for proposing Amendments, which, in either Case, shall be valid to all Intents and Purposes, as Part of this Constitution, when ratified by the Legislatures of three fourths of the several States, or by Conventions in three fourths thereof, as the one or the other Mode of Ratification may be proposed by the Congress; Provided that no Amendment which may be made prior to the Year One thousand eight hundred and eight shall in any Manner affect the first and fourth Clauses in the Ninth Section of the first Article; and that no State, without its Consent, shall be deprived of its equal Suffrage in the Senate.

ARTICLE VI

[1] All Debts contracted and Engagements entered into, before the Adoption of this Constitution, shall be as valid against the United States under this Constitution, as under the Confederation.

[2] This Constitution, and the Laws of the United States which shall be made in Pursuance thereof; and all Treaties made, or which shall be made, under the Authority of the United States, shall be the supreme Law of the Land; and the

Judges in every State shall be bound thereby, any Thing in the Constitution or Laws of any State to the Contrary notwithstanding.

[3]   The Senators and Representatives before mentioned, and the Members of the several State Legislatures, and all executive and judicial Officers, both of the United States and of the several States, shall be bound by Oath or Affirmation, to support this Constitution; but no religious Test shall ever be required as a Qualification to any Office or public Trust under the United States.

ARTICLE VII

The Ratification of the Conventions of nine States, shall be sufficient for the Establishment of this Constitution between the States so ratifying the Same.

ARTICLES IN ADDITION TO, AND AMENDMENT OF THE CONSTITUTION OF THE UNITED STATES OF AMERICA, PROPOSED BY CONGRESS, AND RATIFIED BY THE LEGISLATURES OF THE SEVERAL STATES, PURSUANT TO THE FIFTH ARTICLE OF THE ORIGINAL CONSTITUTION:

Food for Thought

The Amendments are listed at the end of the text of the original document. Would it matter, for purposes of interpreting the Constitution, if instead the text of the Amendments was integrated with the language of the original document, in the relevant provisions? For example, would it matter if the text of the Eleventh Amendment were incorporated into Section 2 of Article 3, rather than simply included here at the end?

AMENDMENT I [1791]

Congress shall make no law respecting an establishment of religion, or prohibiting the free exercise thereof; or abridging the freedom of speech, or of the press; or the right of the people peaceably to assemble, and to petition the Government for a redress of grievances.

AMENDMENT II [1791]

A well regulated Militia, being necessary to the security of a free State, the right of the people to keep and bear Arms, shall not be infringed.

AMENDMENT III [1791]

No Soldier shall, in time of peace be quartered in any house, without the consent of the Owner, nor in time of war, but in a manner to be prescribed by law.

AMENDMENT IV [1791]

The right of the people to be secure in their persons, houses, papers, and effects, against unreasonable searches and seizures, shall not be violated, and no Warrants shall issue, but upon probable cause, supported by Oath or affirmation, and particularly describing the place to be searched, and the persons or things to be seized.

AMENDMENT V [1791]

No person shall be held to answer for a capital, or otherwise infamous crime, unless on a presentment or indictment of a Grand Jury, except in cases arising in the land or naval forces, or in the Militia, when in actual service in time of War or public danger; nor shall any person be subject for the same offence to be twice put in jeopardy of life or limb; nor shall be compelled in any criminal case to be a witness against himself, nor be deprived of life, liberty, or property, without due process of law; nor shall private property be taken for public use, without just compensation.

AMENDMENT VI [1791]

In all criminal prosecutions, the accused shall enjoy the right to a speedy and public trial, by an impartial jury of the State and district wherein the crime shall have been committed, which district shall have been previously ascertained by law, and to be informed of the nature and cause of the accusation; to be confronted with the witnesses against him; to have compulsory process for obtaining witnesses in his favor, and to have the Assistance of Counsel for his defence.

AMENDMENT VII [1791]

In Suits at common law, where the value in controversy shall exceed twenty dollars, the right of trial by jury shall be preserved, and no fact tried by a jury, shall be otherwise re-examined in any Court of the United States, than according to the rules of the common law.

AMENDMENT VIII [1791]

Excessive bail shall not be required, nor excessive fines imposed, nor cruel and unusual punishments inflicted.

AMENDMENT IX [1791]

The enumeration in the Constitution, of certain rights, shall not be construed to deny or disparage others retained by the people.

AMENDMENT X [1791]

The powers not delegated to the United States by the Constitution, nor prohibited by it to the States, are reserved to the States respectively, or to the people.

AMENDMENT XI [1798]

The Judicial power of the United States shall not be construed to extend to any suit in law or equity, commenced or prosecuted against one of the United States by Citizens of another State, or by Citizens or Subjects of any Foreign State.

AMENDMENT XII [1804]

The Electors shall meet in their respective states and vote by ballot for President and Vice-President, one of whom, at least, shall not be an inhabitant of the same state with themselves; they shall name in their ballots the person voted for as President, and in distinct ballots the person voted for as Vice-President, and they shall make distinct lists of all persons voted for as President, and of all persons voted for as Vice-President, and of the number of votes for each, which lists they shall sign and certify, and transmit sealed to the seat of the government of the United States, directed to the President of the Senate;—the President of the Senate shall, in the presence of the Senate and House of Representatives, open all the certificates and the votes shall then be counted;—The person having the greatest number of votes for President, shall be the President, if such number be a majority of the whole number of Electors appointed; and if no person have such majority, then from the persons having the highest numbers not exceeding three on the list of those voted for as President, the House of Representatives shall choose immediately, by ballot, the President. But in choosing the President, the votes shall be taken by states, the representation from each state having one vote; a quorum for this purpose shall consist of a member or members from two-thirds of the states, and a majority of all the states shall be necessary to a choice. [And if

> **Take Note**
>
> The bracketed text has been superseded by the Twentieth Amendment.

the House of Representatives shall not choose a President whenever the right of choice shall devolve upon them, before the fourth day of March next following, then the Vice-President shall act as President, as in case of the death or other constitutional disability of the President.] The person having the greatest number of votes as Vice-President, shall be the Vice-President, if such number be a majority of the whole number of Electors appointed, and if no person have a majority, then from the two highest numbers on the list, the Senate shall choose the Vice-President; a quorum for the purpose shall consist of two-thirds of the whole number of Senators, and a majority of the whole number shall be necessary to a choice. But no person constitutionally ineligible to the office of President shall be eligible to that of Vice-President of the United States.

Amendment XIII [1865]

Section 1.   Neither slavery nor involuntary servitude, except as a punishment for crime whereof the party shall have been duly convicted, shall exist within the United States, or any place subject to their jurisdiction.

Section 2.   Congress shall have power to enforce this article by appropriate legislation.

Amendment XIV [1868]

Section 1.   All persons born or naturalized in the United States, and subject to the jurisdiction thereof, are citizens of the United States and of the State wherein they reside. No State shall make or enforce any law which shall abridge the privileges or immunities of citizens of the United States; nor shall any State deprive any person of life, liberty, or property, without due process of law; nor deny to any person within its jurisdiction the equal protection of the laws.

[handwritten annotation: → DP]
[handwritten annotation: → equal protection]

Section 2.   Representatives shall be apportioned among the several States according to their respective numbers, counting the whole number of persons in each State, excluding Indians not taxed. [But when the right to vote at any election for the choice of electors for President and Vice-President of the United States, Representatives in Congress, the Executive and Judicial officers of a State, or the members of the Legislature thereof, is denied to any of the male inhabitants of such State, being twenty-one years of age, and citizens of the United States, or in any way abridged, except for participation in rebellion, or other crime, the basis of representation therein shall be reduced in the proportion which the number of such male citizens shall bear to the whole number of male citizens twenty-one years of age in such State.]

> **Take Note**
> The bracketed text has been modified by the Twenty-Sixth Amendment.

Section 3.   No person shall be a Senator or Representative in Congress, or elector of President and Vice-President, or hold any office, civil or military, under the United States, or under any State, who, having previously taken an oath, as a member of Congress, or as an officer of the United States, or as a member of any State legislature, or as an executive or judicial officer of any State, to support the Constitution of the United States, shall have engaged in insurrection or rebellion against the same, or given aid or comfort to the enemies thereof. But Congress may by a vote of two-thirds of each House, remove such disability.

Section 4.   The validity of the public debt of the United States, authorized by law, including debts incurred for payment of pensions and bounties for services in suppressing insurrection or rebellion, shall not be questioned. But neither the

United States nor any State shall assume or pay any debt or obligation incurred in aid of insurrection or rebellion against the United States, or any claim for the loss or emancipation of any slave; but all such debts, obligations and claims shall be held illegal and void.

SECTION 5.   The Congress shall have the power to enforce, by appropriate legislation, the provisions of this article.

AMENDMENT XV [1870]

SECTION 1.   The right of citizens of the United States to vote shall not be denied or abridged by the United States or by any State on account of race, color, or previous condition of servitude.

SECTION 2.   The Congress shall have the power to enforce this article by appropriate legislation.

AMENDMENT XVI [1913]

The Congress shall have power to lay and collect taxes on incomes, from whatever source derived, without apportionment among the several States, and without regard to any census or enumeration.

AMENDMENT XVII [1913]

[1]   The Senate of the United States shall be composed of two Senators from each State, elected by the people thereof, for six years; and each Senator shall have one vote. The electors in each State shall have the qualifications requisite for electors of the most numerous branch of the State legislatures.

[2]   When vacancies happen in the representation of any State in the Senate, the executive authority of such State shall issue writs of election to fill such vacancies: Provided, That the legislature of any State may empower the executive thereof to make temporary appointments until the people fill the vacancies by election as the legislature may direct.

[3]   This amendment shall not be so construed as to affect the election or term of any Senator chosen before it becomes valid as part of the Constitution.

AMENDMENT XVIII [1919]

Take Note

The Eighteenth Amendment was repealed by the Twenty-First Amendment.

SECTION 1.   After one year from the ratification of this article the manufacture, sale, or transportation of intoxicating liquors within, the importation thereof into, or the exportation thereof from the United States and all territory subject to the jurisdiction thereof for beverage purposes is hereby prohibited.

SECTION 2.   The Congress and the several States shall have concurrent power to enforce this article by appropriate legislation.

SECTION 3.   This article shall be inoperative unless it shall have been ratified as an amendment to the Constitution by the legislatures of the several States, as provided in the Constitution, within seven years from the date of the submission hereof to the States by the Congress.

AMENDMENT XIX [1920]

[1]   The right of citizens of the United States to vote shall not be denied or abridged by the United States or by any State on account of sex.

[2]   Congress shall have power to enforce this article by appropriate legislation.

AMENDMENT XX [1933]

SECTION 1.   The terms of the President and the Vice President shall end at noon on the 20th day of January, and the terms of Senators and Representatives at noon on the 3d day of January, of the years in which such terms would have ended if this article had not been ratified; and the terms of their successors shall then begin.

SECTION 2.   The Congress shall assemble at least once in every year, and such meeting shall begin at noon on the 3d day of January, unless they shall by law appoint a different day.

SECTION 3.   If, at the time fixed for the beginning of the term of the President, the President elect shall have died, the Vice President elect shall become President. If a President shall not have been chosen before the time fixed for the beginning of his term, or if the President elect shall have failed to qualify, then the Vice President elect shall act as President until a President shall have qualified; and the Congress may by law provide for the case wherein neither a President elect nor a Vice President shall have qualified, declaring who shall then act as President, or the manner in which one who is to act shall be selected, and such person shall act accordingly until a President or Vice President shall have qualified.

SECTION 4.   The Congress may by law provide for the case of the death of any of the persons from whom the House of Representatives may choose a President whenever the right of choice shall have devolved upon them, and for the case of the death of any of the persons from whom the Senate may choose a Vice President whenever the right of choice shall have devolved upon them.

SECTION 5.   Sections 1 and 2 shall take effect on the 15th day of October following the ratification of this article.

SECTION 6.   This article shall be inoperative unless it shall have been ratified as an amendment to the Constitution by the legislatures of three-fourths of the several States within seven years from the date of its submission.

AMENDMENT XXI [1933]

SECTION 1.   The eighteenth article of amendment to the Constitution of the United States is hereby repealed.

SECTION 2.   The transportation or importation into any State, Territory, or Possession of the United States for delivery or use therein of intoxicating liquors, in violation of the laws thereof, is hereby prohibited.

SECTION 3.   This article shall be inoperative unless it shall have been ratified as an amendment to the Constitution by conventions in the several States, as provided in the Constitution, within seven years from the date of the submission hereof to the States by the Congress.

AMENDMENT XXII [1951]

SECTION 1.   No person shall be elected to the office of the President more than twice, and no person who has held the office of President, or acted as President, for more than two years of a term to which some other person was elected President shall be elected to the office of President more than once. But this Article shall not apply to any person holding the office of President when this Article was proposed by Congress, and shall not prevent any person who may be holding the office of President, or acting as President, during the term within which this Article becomes operative from holding the office of President or acting as President during the remainder of such term.

SECTION 2.   This article shall be inoperative unless it shall have been ratified as an amendment to the Constitution by the legislatures of three-fourths of the several States within seven years from the date of its submission to the States by the Congress.

AMENDMENT XXIII [1961]

SECTION 1.   The District constituting the seat of Government of the United States shall appoint in such manner as Congress may direct:

A number of electors of President and Vice President equal to the whole number of Senators and Representatives in Congress to which the District would be entitled if it were a State, but in no event more than the least populous State;

they shall be in addition to those appointed by the States, but they shall be considered, for the purposes of the election of President and Vice President, to be electors appointed by a State; and they shall meet in the District and perform such duties as provided by the twelfth article of amendment.

SECTION 2. The Congress shall have power to enforce this article by appropriate legislation.

AMENDMENT XXIV [1964]

SECTION 1. The right of citizens of the United States to vote in any primary or other election for President or Vice President, for electors for President or Vice President, or for Senator or Representative in Congress, shall not be denied or abridged by the United States or any State by reason of failure to pay poll tax or other tax.

SECTION 2. The Congress shall have power to enforce this article by appropriate legislation.

AMENDMENT XXV [1967]

SECTION 1. In case of the removal of the President from office or of his death or resignation, the Vice President shall become President.

SECTION 2. Whenever there is a vacancy in the office of the Vice President, the President shall nominate a Vice President who shall take office upon confirmation by a majority vote of both Houses of Congress.

SECTION 3. Whenever the President transmits to the President pro tempore of the Senate and the Speaker of the House of Representatives his written declaration that he is unable to discharge the powers and duties of his office, and until he transmits to them a written declaration to the contrary, such powers and duties shall be discharged by the Vice President as Acting President.

SECTION 4. [1] Whenever the Vice President and a majority of either the principal officers of the executive departments or of such other body as Congress may by law provide, transmit to the President pro tempore of the Senate and the Speaker of the House of Representatives their written declaration that the President is unable to discharge the powers and duties of his office, the Vice President shall immediately assume the powers and duties of the office as Acting President.

[2] Thereafter, when the President transmits to the President pro tempore of the Senate and the Speaker of the House of Representatives his written declaration that no inability exists, he shall resume the powers and duties of his office unless the Vice President and a majority of either the principal officers of

the executive department or of such other body as Congress may by law provide, transmit within four days to the President pro tempore of the Senate and the Speaker of the House of Representatives their written declaration that the President is unable to discharge the powers and duties of his office. Thereupon Congress shall decide the issue, assembling within forty-eight hours for that purpose if not in session. If the Congress, within twenty-one days after receipt of the latter written declaration, or, if Congress is not in session, within twenty-one days after Congress is required to assemble, determines by two-thirds vote of both Houses that the President is unable to discharge the powers and duties of his office, the Vice President shall continue to discharge the same as Acting President; otherwise, the President shall resume the powers and duties of his office.

AMENDMENT XXVI [1971]

SECTION 1.   The right of citizens of the United States, who are eighteen years of age or older, to vote shall not be denied or abridged by the United States or by any State on account of age.

SECTION 2.   The Congress shall have power to enforce this article by appropriate legislation.

AMENDMENT XXVII [1992]

No law, varying the compensation for the services of the Senators and Representatives, shall take effect, until an election of representatives shall have intervened.

FYI

The Twenty-Seventh Amendment was proposed on September 25, 1789, along with the Amendments that became the Bill of Rights. The amendment was ratified quickly by six states, but not by the rest of the states. The amendment had no "sunset provision," however, and over time it was ratified by other states until, in 1992, Michigan became the 38th state to ratify it, satisfying the three-fourths requirement.

Index